Cases and Commentary on Tort

Fifth edition

Barbara Harvey LLB, LLM
Principal Lecturer, School of Law, De Montfort University, Leicester

John Marston LLB, Solicitor
Principal Lecturer, School of Law, De Montfort University, Leicester

LexisNexis™ UK

Members of the LexisNexis Group worldwide

United Kingdom	LexisNexis UK, a Division of Reed Elsevier (UK) Ltd, Halsbury House, 35 Chancery Lane, LONDON, WC2A 1EL, and 4 Hill Street, EDINBURGH EH2 3JZ
Argentina	LexisNexis Argentina, BUENOS AIRES
Australia	LexisNexis Butterworths, CHATSWOOD, New South Wales
Austria	LexisNexis Verlag ARD Orac GmbH & Co KG, VIENNA
Canada	LexisNexis Butterworths, MARKHAM, Ontario
Chile	LexisNexis Chile Ltda, SANTIAGO DE CHILE
Czech Republic	Nakladatelství Orac sro, PRAGUE
France	Editions du Juris-Classeur SA, PARIS
Germany	LexisNexis Deutschland GmbH, FRANKFURT and MUNSTER
Hong Kong	LexisNexis Butterworths, HONG KONG
Hungary	HVG-Orac, BUDAPEST
India	LexisNexis Butterworths, NEW DELHI
Ireland	LexisNexis, DUBLIN
Italy	Giuffrè Editore, MILAN
Malaysia	Malayan Law Journal Sdn Bhd, KUALA LUMPUR
New Zealand	LexisNexis Butterworths, WELLINGTON
Poland	Wydawnictwo Prawnicze LexisNexis, WARSAW
Singapore	LexisNexis Butterworths, SINGAPORE
South Africa	LexisNexis Butterworths, DURBAN
Switzerland	Stämpfli Verlag AG, BERNE
USA	LexisNexis, DAYTON, Ohio

A CIP Catalogue record for this book is available from the British Library.

Fourth edition 2000

ISBN 0 406 97138 2

Typeset by Columns Design Ltd, Reading, UK
Printed and bound in Great Britain by CPI Bath

Visit LexisNexis UK at www.lexisnexis.co.uk

Preface

Once again we have aimed to provide an appropriate selection of edited cases together with a commentary comprising a brief analysis and cross-references. These are intended to encourage students to widen their quest for further relevant sources. The vast range of easily accessible electronic sources of both case and statute law may sometimes prove confusing, and this book provides a firm platform from which the reader may embark upon an exploration of both paper and electronic sources.

The intervening years between this and the previous edition have seen the expected crop of new cases (many decided by the House of Lords) in those areas within the scope of this book. These include: the operation of policy in relation to the existence of a duty of care in negligence; negligently induced psychiatric damage; private nuisance; defamation; vicarious liability; the law relating to animals; and occupiers' liability. Some newly included cases are useful in illustrating basic principles, while others develop or extend such principles. The Human Rights Act 1998 has proved to be influential and will continue to be relevant to the development of the law of Tort.

Such omissions as there may be are inevitable, given the need to provide as wide a coverage as possible of extracts of useful length within the overall constraint of the length of the book.

We should like once again to thank David, Patrick and Jemima, and Virginia, Katie and Sophie for their continued support and forbearance during the preparation of the text.

We should particularly like to thank our publishers for their help, guidance and patience throughout.

We have stated the law as understood by us at 21 March 2004.

Barbara Harvey

John Marston

Acknowledgements

We would like to express our thanks to the following copyright owners who willingly gave permission to publish extracts.

Extracts from the *Law Reports* and *Weekly Law Reports* are published with kind permission of the Incorporated Council of Law Reporting for England & Wales, Stone Buildings, Lincoln's Inn, London.

Extracts from *Anchor Brewhouse Developments Ltd v Berkley House (Docklands Development) Ltd* are reproduced by kind permission of Barnet Lenton.

Contents

Chapter 3

Chapter 4

Chapter 5

Chapter 6

Chapter 7

Chapter 13

Private nuisance   **603**

Chapter 14

Public nuisance   **679**

Chapter 15

Rylands v Fletcher   **691**

Chapter 16

Chapter 17

Table of statutes

Where a statute is substantially extracted or discussed, the page number is shown in **bold**.

Table of cases

Where a case is substantially extracted, the name and page reference are shown in **bold** type.

A

B

C

D

F

H

I

J

K

G

M

N

O

P

S

T

X

CHAPTER 1

Duty 1 – General principles

Liability in negligence arises when the breach of a duty owed by the defendant to the claimant results in damage to the claimant. It follows that the first step in establishing such liability is to show that such a duty exists. Naturally enough, the emergence of negligence as a tort in its own right has led to a desire for a single test or set of principles of universal application for determining the existence of a duty. As the case law on negligence has developed, at times it has appeared that the courts had identified such a formula: however, it now seems that a more realistic view is that, while a number of specific factors may commonly be taken into account, the process may vary considerably according to the type of damage involved. So, for example, where personal injury or property damage are concerned the test may be quite simple; where the damage consists of pure economic loss or nervous shock a more complex appraisal of the situation is required. This should be borne in mind when the cases are read since the reasoning in negligence cases cannot generally be separated from the individual facts of the case.

A recurring theme in the search for a formula has been the notion of 'proximity', and it is quite common for the court's finding that there is no duty of care to be based, apparently quite simply, on the lack of proximity. The concept of proximity is one which has evolved from the relatively straightforward test identified by Lord Atkin in *Donoghue v Stevenson* to the point where it now seems to be used by a court, after the existence of a duty of care has been determined, to denote the whole of the circumstances taken into account. Such a view is reflected in Lord Oliver's comment in *Caparo Industries plc v Dickman*, p 16, that the term is 'no more than a label' and by Goff LJ's statement in *The Aliakmon* that proximity could not be used as a test for liability 'once [it] is no longer treated as expressing a relationship founded simply on foreseeability of damage'.

Most recently – for example in *Marc Rich & Co AG v Bishop Rock Marine Co Ltd*, p 17, *Spring v Guardian Assurance plc*, p 25 and in *Arthur J S Hall v Simons*, p 41 – the House of Lords has shown a tendency to emphasise the importance of the 'fair, just and reasonable' factor when deciding whether to impose liability, linking this increasingly closely with matters of public, judicial or legal policy. In *Arthur J S Hall*, however, Lord Hobhouse of Woodborough observed that: '… the question of public policy is based not upon some higher moral imperative but upon a pragmatic assessment of what is justifiable in our society' – which as a final test seems no more capable of definition than is proximity and, if anything, more likely to be applied subjectively.

Donoghue (or M'Alister) v Stevenson
[1932] All ER Rep 1 House of Lords

Mrs D went to a Paisley cafe with a friend who bought her a tumbler with ice-cream over which the shopkeeper poured a quantity of ginger beer from an opaque bottle. She drank from the tumbler and when her friend topped up the drink the remains of a decomposed snail floated out of the bottle. Mrs D became rather ill. In the absence of any contractual relationship between Mrs D and the shopkeeper, the question referred to the House of Lords was whether, in the circumstances, the manufacturer of the ginger beer owed a duty of care to the ultimate consumer.

Lord Atkin: '… We are solely concerned with the question whether as a matter of law in the circumstances alleged the defender owed any duty to the pursuer to take care.

It is remarkable how difficult it is to find in the English authorities statements of general application defining the relations between parties that give rise to the duty. The courts are concerned with the particular relations which come before them in actual litigation, and it is sufficient to say whether the duty exists in those circumstances. The result is that the courts have been engaged upon an elaborate classification of duties as they exist in respect of property, whether real or personal, with further divisions as to ownership, occupation or control, and distinctions based on the particular relations of the one side or the other, whether manufacturer, salesperson or landlord, customer, tenant, stranger, and so on. In this way it can be ascertained at any time whether the law recognises a duty, but only where the case can be referred to some particular species which has been examined and classified. And yet the duty which is common to all the cases where liability is established must logically be based upon some element common to the cases where it is found to exist. To seek a complete logical definition of the general principle is probably to go beyond the function of the judge, for, the more general the definition, the more likely it is to omit essentials or introduce non-essentials.

The attempt was made by Lord Esher in *Heaven v Pender* in a definition to which I will later refer. As framed it was demonstrably too wide, though it appears to me, if properly limited, to be capable of affording a valuable practical guide.

At present I content myself with pointing out that in English law there must be and is some general conception of relations giving rise to a duty of care, of which the particular cases found in the books are but instances. The liability for negligence, whether you style it such or treat it as in other systems as a species of "culpa", is no doubt based upon a general public sentiment of moral wrongdoing for which the offender must pay. But acts or omissions which any moral code would censure cannot in a practical world be treated so as to give a right to every person injured by them to demand relief. In this way rules of law arise which limit the range of complainants and the extent of their remedy. The rule that you are to love your neighbour becomes in law: You must not injure your neighbour, and the lawyers' question: Who is my neighbour? receives a restricted reply. You must take reasonable care to avoid acts or omissions which you can reasonably foresee would be likely to injure your neighbour. Who then, in law, is my neighbour? The answer seems to be persons who are so closely and directly affected by my act that I ought reasonably to have them in contemplation as being so affected when I am directing my mind to the acts or omissions which are called in question. This appears to me to be the doctrine of *Heaven v Pender* as laid down by Lord Esher when it is limited by the notion of proximity introduced by Lord Esher himself and A L Smith LJ in *Le Lievre and another v Gould*. Lord Esher MR says:

> "That case established that, under certain circumstances, one man may owe a duty to another, even though there is no contract between them. If one man is near to another, or is near to the property of another, a duty lies upon him not to do that which may cause a personal injury to that other, or may injure his property."

So A L Smith LJ says:

> "The decision of *Heaven v Pender* was founded upon the principle that a duty to take due care did arise when the person or property of one was in such proximity to the person or property of another that, if due care was not taken damage might be done by the one to the other."

I think that this sufficiently states the truth if proximity be not confined to mere physical proximity, but be used, as I think it was intended, to extend to such close and direct relations that the act complained of directly affects a person whom the person alleged to be bound to take care would know would be directly affected by his careless act. That this is the sense in which nearness or "proximity" was intended by Lord Esher is obvious from his own illustration in *Heaven v Pender* of the application of his doctrine to the sale of goods.

> "This [i.e. the rule he has just formulated] includes the case of goods, &c supplied to be used immediately by a particular person or persons, or one of

a class of persons, where it would be obvious to the person supplying, if he thought, that the goods would in all probability be used at once by such persons before a reasonable opportunity for discovering any defect which might exist, and where the thing supplied would be of such a nature that a neglect of ordinary care or skill as to its condition or the manner of supplying it would probably cause danger to the person or property of the person for whose use it was supplied, and who was about to use it. It would exclude a case in which the goods are supplied under circumstances in which it would be a chance by whom they would be used, or whether they would be used or not, or whether they would be used before there would probably be means of observing any defect, or where the goods would be of such a nature that a want of care or skill as to their condition or the manner of supplying them would not probably produce danger of injury to person or property."

I draw particular attention to the fact that Lord Esher emphasises the necessity of goods having to be "used immediately" and "used at once before a reasonable opportunity of inspection". This is obviously to exclude the possibility of goods having their condition altered by lapse of time, and to call attention to the proximate relationship, which may be too remote where inspection even by the person using, certainly by an intermediate person, may reasonably be interposed. With this necessary qualification of proximate relationship, as explained in *Le Lievre and another v Gould*, I think the judgment of Lord Esher expresses the law of England. Without the qualification, I think that the majority of the court in *Heaven v Pender*, was justified in thinking that the principle was expressed in too general terms. There will, no doubt, arise cases where it will be difficult to determine whether the contemplated relationship is so close that the duty arises. But in the class of case now before the court I cannot conceive any difficulty to arise. A manufacturer puts up an article of food in a container which he knows will be opened by the actual consumer. There can be no inspection by any purchaser and no reasonable preliminary inspection by the consumer. Negligently in the course of preparation he allows the contents to be mixed with poison. It is said that the law of England and Scotland is that the poisoned consumer has no remedy against the negligent manufacturer. If this were the result of the authorities, I should consider the result a grave defect in the law and so contrary to principle that I should hesitate long before following any decision to that effect which had not the authority of this House. I would point out that in the assumed state of the authorities not only would the consumer have no remedy against the manufacturer, he would have none against anyone else, for in the circumstances alleged there would be no evidence of negligence against anyone other than the manufacturer, and except in the case of a consumer who was also a purchaser no contract and no warranty of fitness, and in the cases of the purchase of a specific article under its patent or trade name, which might well be the case in the purchase of some articles of food or drink, no warranty protecting even the purchaser-consumer. There are other instances than of articles of food and drink where goods are sold intended to be used immediately by the consumer, such as many forms of goods sold for cleaning purposes, when the same liability must exist. The doctrine supported by the decision below would not only deny a remedy to the consumer who was injured by consuming bottled beer or chocolates poisoned by the negligence of the manufacturer, but also to the user of what should be a harmless proprietary medicine, an ointment, a soap, a cleaning fluid or cleaning powder. I confine myself to articles of common household use, where everyone, including the manufacturer, knows that the articles will be used by persons other than the actual ultimate purchaser – namely, by members of his family and his servants, and, in some cases, his guests. I do not think so ill of our jurisprudence as to suppose that its principles are so remote from the ordinary needs of civilised society and the ordinary claims which it makes upon its members as to deny a legal remedy where there is so obviously a social wrong.'

Comment

(1)   Note how Lord Atkin's formula, the 'neighbour' test, arises from a close analysis of previous case law interpreted in the light of his perception that society would expect a remedy to exist in like circumstances. His view of the role of judicial policy is echoed in the judgment of Lord Pearce in *Hedley Byrne & Co Ltd v Heller & Partners*:

'The law of negligence has been deliberately limited in its range by the courts' insistence that there can be no actionable negligence *in vacuo* without the existence of some duty to the plaintiff. For it would be impracticable to grant relief to everybody who suffers damage through the carelessness of another ... How wide the sphere of the duty of care in negligence is to be laid depends ultimately on the demands of society for protection from the carelessness of others. Economic protection has lagged behind ... It may be that the size and possible width of claims has acted as a deterrent to extension of economic protection.'

(2)   Lord Macmillan also acknowledges the ability of a general principle of negligence to meet the changing needs of society. He said:

'In the daily contacts of social and business life human beings are thrown into, or place themselves in, an infinite variety of relations with their fellows; and the law can refer only to the standards of the reasonable man in order to determine whether any particular relation gives rise to a duty to take care as between those who stand in that relation to each other. The grounds of action may be as various and manifold as human errancy; and the conception of legal responsibility may develop in adaptation to altering social conditions and standards. The criterion of judgment must adjust and adapt itself to the changing circumstances of life. The categories of negligence are never closed.

The cardinal principle is that the party complained of should owe to the party complaining a duty to take care, and that the party complaining should be able to prove that he has suffered damage in consequence of a breach of that duty. Where there is room for diversity of view, it is in determining what circumstances will establish such a relationship between the parties as to give rise, on the one side, to a duty to take care, and on the other side to a right to have care taken.'

(3)   For the liability of manufacturers see p 418.

Home Office v Dorset Yacht Co Ltd
[1970] 2 All ER 294 House of Lords

A number of borstal trainees from a working party on Brownsea Island in Poole harbour escaped during the night while, it was alleged, the officers had all gone to sleep. In the course of their escape the boys took a yacht which subsequently collided with the respondent's yacht, damaging it. The House of Lords concluded that a duty of care was owed by the appellants to the respondent.

Lord Reid: '... The case for the Home Office is that under no circumstances can borstal officers owe any duty to any member of the public to take care to prevent trainees under their control or supervision from injuring him or his property. If that is the law then enquiry into the facts of this case would be a waste of time and money because whatever the facts may be the respondents must lose. That case is based on three main arguments. First, it is said that there is virtually no authority for imposing a duty of this kind. Secondly, it is said that no person can be liable for a wrong done by another who is of full age and capacity and who is not the servant or acting on behalf of that person. And thirdly, it is said that public policy (or the policy of the relevant legislation) requires that these officers should be immune from any such liability.

The first would at one time have been a strong argument. About the beginning of this century most eminent lawyers thought that there were a number of separate torts involving negligence each with its own rules, and they were most unwilling to add more. They were of course aware from a number of leading cases that in the past the courts had from time to time recognised new duties and new grounds of action. But the heroic age was over, it was time to cultivate certainty and security in the law; the categories of negligence were virtually closed. The learned Attorney-General invited us to return to those halcyon days, but, attractive though it may be, I cannot accede to his invitation.

In later years there has been a steady trend towards regarding the law of negligence as depending on principle so that, when a new point emerges, one should ask not whether it is covered by authority but whether recognised principles apply to it. *Donoghue v Stevenson* may be regarded as a milestone, and the well-known passage in Lord Atkin's speech should I think be regarded as a statement of principle. It is not to be treated as if it were a statutory definition. It will require qualification in new circumstances. But I think that the time has come when we can and should say that it ought to apply unless there is some justification or valid explanation for its exclusion. For example, causing economic loss is a different matter; for one thing it is often caused by deliberate action. Competition involves traders being entitled to damage their rivals' interests by promoting their own, and there is a long chapter of the law determining in what circumstances owners of land can, and in what circumstances they may not, use their proprietary rights so as to injure their neighbours. But where negligence is involved the tendency has been to apply principles analogous to those stated by Lord Atkin (cf. *Hedley Byrne & Co Ltd v Heller & Partners Ltd*). And when a person has done nothing to put himself in any relationship with another person in distress or with his property mere accidental propinquity does not require him to go to that person's assistance. There may be a moral duty to do so, but it is not practicable to make it a legal duty. And then there are cases, e.g. with regard to landlord and tenant, where the law was settled long ago and neither Parliament nor this House sitting judicially has made any move to alter it. But I can see nothing to prevent our approaching the present case with Lord Atkin's principles in mind …

It was suggested that a decision against the Home Office would have very far reaching effects; it was indeed suggested in the Court of Appeal that it would make the Home Office liable for the loss occasioned by a burglary committed by a trainee on parole or a prisoner permitted to go out to attend a funeral. But there are two reasons why in the vast majority of cases that would not be so. In the first place it would have to be shown that the decision to allow any such release was so unreasonable that it could not be regarded as a real exercise of discretion by the responsible officer who authorised the release. And secondly it would have to be shown that the commission of the offence was the natural and probable, as distinct from merely a foreseeable, result of the release – that there was no *novus actus interveniens*… I think the fears of the Home Office are unfounded; I cannot believe that negligence or dereliction of duty is widespread among prison or borstal officers.

Finally, I must deal with public policy. It is argued that it would be contrary to public policy to hold the Home Office or its officers liable to a member of the public for this carelessness – or indeed any failure of duty on their part. The basic question is who shall bear the loss caused by that carelessness – the innocent respondents or the Home Office who are vicariously liable for the conduct of their careless officers? I do not think that the argument for the Home Office can be put better than it was put by the Court of Appeals of New York in *Williams v New York State*:

"… public policy also requires that the State be not held liable. To hold otherwise would impose a heavy responsibility upon the State, or dissuade the wardens and principal keepers of our prison system from continued experimentation with 'minimum security' work details – which provide a means for encouraging better-risk prisoners to exercise their senses of responsibility and honor and so prepare themselves for their eventual return to society. Since 1917, the Legislature has expressly provided for out-of-prison work ... and its intention should be respected without fostering the reluctance of prison officials to assign eligible men to minimum security work, lest they thereby give rise to costly claims against the State, or indeed inducing the State itself to terminate this 'salutary procedure' looking toward rehabilitation."

It may be that public servants of the State of New York are so apprehensive, easily dissuaded from doing their duty, and intent on preserving public funds from costly claims, that they could be influenced in this way. But my experience leads me to believe that Her Majesty's servants are made of sterner stuff. So I have no hesitation in rejecting this argument. I can see no good ground in public policy for giving this immunity to a government department. I would dismiss this appeal.'

Comment

(1)   For a further extract from Lord Diplock's speech, see *Hill v Chief Constable of West Yorkshire*, p 30.

(2)   Although this case marks a clear acceptance of Lord Atkin's neighbour test as the basis of a general principle of negligence, it should be noted that Lord Reid does not claim that the principle is capable of universal application. In particular, he excepts those cases where the damage complained of can be classified as economic loss. This reservation should be borne in mind when reviewing the cases which followed as, for a while, the courts' enthusiasm for the 'Atkinian formula' pushed the consideration of other factors into the shade. This approach reached its peak in *Anns v Merton London Borough Council*, in which Lord Wilberforce formulated a two-stage test:

'Through the trilogy of cases in this House, *Donoghue v Stevenson, Hedley Byrne & Co Ltd v Heller & Partners Ltd*, and *Home Office v Dorset Yacht Co Ltd*, the position has now been reached that in order to establish that a duty of care arises in a particular situation, it is not necessary to bring the facts of that situation within those of previous situations in which a duty of care has been held to exist. Rather the question has to be approached in two stages. First one has to ask whether, as between the alleged wrongdoer and the person who has suffered damage there is a sufficient relationship of proximity or neighbourhood such that, in the reasonable contemplation of the former, carelessness on his part may be likely to cause damage to the latter, in which case a *prima facie* duty of care arises. Secondly, if the first question is answered affirmatively, it is necessary to consider whether there are any considerations which ought to negative, or to reduce or limit the scope of the duty or the class of person to whom it is owed or the damages to which a breach of it may give rise (see the *Dorset Yacht* case per Lord Reid).'

Criticism of this test and the courts' retreat from it can be charted through the cases which follow.

(3) In *Dorset Yacht* the public policy argument failed, but for cases where the existence of a duty has been denied by the court on the ground of public policy see e.g. *Hill v Chief Constable of West Yorkshire, Elguzouili-Daf v Metropolitan Police Comr* and *Rondel v Worsley*, though note that it is in the very nature of policy to change over time, and that the advocates' immunity in *Rondel* has now been abolished (see *Arthur J S Hall v Simons*, p 41).

Governors of the Peabody Donation Fund v Sir Lindsay Parkinson & Co Ltd and others
[1984] 3 All ER 529 House of Lords

The plaintiffs, in the course of developing a housing estate, were obliged by the London Government Act 1963 to install a drainage system which conformed with the specifications of the local authority. It was agreed that a system with flexible joints was needed because of the terrain but subsequently the architects, with the agreement of the drainage inspector, and to the knowledge of his successor in office, changed the system to include rigid joints. As a result, a substantial portion of the system failed and the plaintiffs incurred considerable financial losses from the necessary reconstruction of the site. They sued, *inter alios*, the local authority alleging that it was in breach of its duty to enforce compliance with the Act. The House of Lords, affirming the Court of Appeal decision, held that no such duty existed for the protection of the plaintiffs.

Lord Keith: '... Lord Atkin's famous enunciation of the general principles on which the law of negligence is founded, in *Donoghue v Stevenson*, has long been recognised as not intended to afford a comprehensive definition, to the effect that every situation which is capable of falling within the terms of the utterance and which results in loss automatically affords a remedy in damages. Lord Reid said in *Home Office v Dorset Yacht Co Ltd*:

"It is not to be treated as if it were a statutory definition. It will require qualification in new circumstances. But I think that the time has come when we can and should say that it ought to apply unless there is some justification or valid explanation for its exclusion. For example, causing economic loss is a different matter; for one thing it is often caused by deliberate action. Competition involves traders being entitled to damage their rivals' interests by promoting their own, and there is a long chapter of the law determining in what circumstances owners of land can, and in what circumstances they may not, use their proprietary rights so as to injure their neighbours. But where negligence is involved the tendency has been to apply principles analogous to those stated by Lord Atkin (cf. *Hedley Byrne & Co Ltd v Heller & Partners Ltd*). And when a person has done nothing to put himself in any relationship with another person in distress or with his property mere accidental propinquity does not require him to go to that person's assistance. There may be a moral duty to do so, but it is not practicable to make it a legal duty."

Lord Wilberforce spoke on similar lines in *Anns v Merton London Borough* [Lord Keith quoted the passage cited on p 8 above and continued]. There has been a tendency in some recent cases to treat these passages as being themselves of a definitive character. This is a temptation which should be resisted. The true question in each case is whether the particular defendant owed to the particular plaintiff a duty of care having the scope which is contended for, and whether he was in breach of that duty with consequent loss to the plaintiff. A relationship of proximity in Lord Atkin's sense must exist before any duty of care can arise, but the scope of the duty must depend on all the circumstances of the case.

In *Home Office v Dorset Yacht Co Ltd* Lord Morris, after observing that at the conclusion of his speech in *Donoghue v Stevenson*, Lord Atkin said that it was advantageous if the law "is in accordance with sound common sense" and expressing the view that a special relation existed between the prison officers and the yacht company which gave rise to a duty on the former to control their charges so as to prevent them doing damage, continued:

"Apart from this I would conclude that in the situation stipulated in the present case it would not only be fair and reasonable that a duty of care should exist but that it would be contrary to the fitness of things were it not so. I doubt whether it is necessary to say, in cases where the court is asked whether in a particular situation a duty existed, that the court is called on to make a decision as to policy. Policy need not be invoked where reason and good sense will at once point the way. If the test whether in some particular situation a duty of care arises may in some cases have to be whether it is fair and reasonable that it should so arise the court must not shrink from being the arbiter. As Lord Radcliffe said in his speech in *Davis Contractors Ltd v Fareham Urban District Council*, the court is the 'spokesman of the fair and reasonable man'."

So in determining whether or not a duty of care of particular scope was incumbent on a defendant it is material to take into consideration whether it is just and reasonable that it should be so.'

Yuen Kun-yeu and others v Attorney-General of Hong Kong
[1987] 2 All ER 705 Privy Council

The appellants lost money when a registered deposit-taking company went into liquidation. They brought an action against the Attorney-General as representative of the Commissioner of Deposit-taking Companies who was charged, under the Deposit-taking Ordinance 1976, with various regulatory functions, claiming that he knew or ought to have known that the company was not a fit and proper body and that he owed potential depositors a duty not to register, or to revoke the registration of, the company. The Privy Council concluded that the relationship between the Commissioner and the depositors was not such as to give rise to a duty of care.

Lord Keith: '... The foremost question of principle is whether in the present case the commissioner owed to members of the public who might be minded to deposit their money with deposit-taking companies in Hong Kong a duty, in the discharge of his supervisory powers under the ordinance, to exercise reasonable care to see that such members of the public did not suffer loss through the affairs of such companies being carried on by their managers in a fraudulent or improvident fashion. That question is one of law, which is capable of being answered on the averments, assumed to be true, contained in the appellants' pleadings. If it is answered in the negative, the appellants have no reasonable cause of action, and their statement of claim was rightly struck out.

The argument for the appellants in favour of an affirmative answer to the question started from the familiar passage in the speech of Lord Wilberforce in *Anns v Merton London Borough* [Lord Keith quoted the passage cited on p 8 above and continued:] This passage has been treated with some reservation in subsequent cases in the House of Lords, in particular by Lord Keith in *Governors of the Peabody Donation Fund v Sir Lindsay Parkinson & Co Ltd*, by Lord Brandon in *Leigh & Sillavan Ltd v Aliakmon Shipping Co Ltd* and by Lord Bridge in *Curran v Northern Ireland Co-ownership Housing Association Ltd*. The speeches containing these reservations were concurred in by all the other members of the House who were party to the decisions. In *Sutherland Shire Council v Heyman* Brennan J in the High Court of Australia indicated his disagreement with the nature of the approach indicated by Lord Wilberforce, saying:

"Of course, if foreseeability of injury to another were the exhaustive criterion of a *prima facie* duty to act to prevent the occurrence of that injury, it would be essential to introduce some kind of restrictive qualification – perhaps a qualification of the kind stated in the second stage of the general proposition in *Anns*. I am unable to accept that approach. It is preferable, in my view, that the law should develop novel categories of negligence incrementally and by analogy with established categories, rather than by a massive extension of a *prima facie* duty of care restrained only by indefinable 'considerations which ought to negative, or to reduce or limit the scope of the duty or the class of person to whom it is owed'. The proper role of the 'second stage', as I attempted to explain in *Jaensch v Coffey*, embraces no more than 'those further elements [in addition to the neighbour principle] which are appropriate to the particular category of negligence and *which confine the duty of care within narrower limits* than those which would be defined by an unqualified application of the neighbour principle'." (My emphasis.)

Their Lordships venture to think that the two-stage test formulated by Lord Wilberforce for determining the existence of a duty of care in negligence has been elevated to a degree of importance greater than it merits, and greater perhaps than its author intended. Further, the expression of the first stage of the test carries with it a risk of misinterpretation. As Gibbs CJ pointed out in *Sutherland Shire Council v Heyman* there are two possible views of what Lord Wilberforce meant. The first view, favoured in a number of cases mentioned by Gibbs CJ, is that he meant to test the sufficiency of proximity simply by the reasonable contemplation of likely harm. The second view, favoured by Gibbs CJ himself, is that Lord Wilberforce meant the expression "proximity or neighbourhood" to be a composite one, importing the whole concept of necessary relationship between plaintiff and defendant described by Lord Atkin in *Donoghue v Stevenson*. In their Lordships' opinion the second view is the correct one. As Lord Wilberforce himself observed in *McLoughlin v O'Brian*, it is clear that foreseeability does not of itself, and automatically, lead to a duty of care. There are many other statements to the same effect. The truth is that the trilogy of cases referred to by Lord Wilberforce each demonstrate particular sets of circumstances, differing in character, which were adjudged to have the effect of bringing into being a relationship apt to give rise to a duty of care. Foreseeability of harm is a necessary ingredient of such a relationship, but it is not the only one. Otherwise there would be liability in negligence on the part of one who sees another about to walk over a cliff with his head in the air, and forbears to shout a warning.

Donoghue v Stevenson established that the manufacturer of a consumable product who carried on business in such a way that the product reached the consumer in the shape in which it left the manufacturer, without any prospect of intermediate examination, owed the consumer a duty to take reasonable care that the product was free from defect likely to cause injury to health. The speech of Lord Atkin stressed not only the requirement of foreseeability of harm but also that of a close and direct relationship of proximity. The relevant passages are:

> "Who, then, in law is my neighbour? The answer seems to be – persons who are so closely and directly affected by my act that I ought reasonably to have them in contemplation as being so affected when I am directing my mind to the acts or omissions which are called in question."

"I think that this sufficiently states the truth if proximity be not confined to mere physical proximity, but be used, as I think it was intended, to extend to such close and direct relations that the act complained of directly affects a person whom the person alleged to be bound to take care would know would be directly affected by his careless act."

"There will no doubt arise cases where it will be difficult to determine whether the contemplated relationship is so close that the duty arises."

Lord Atkin clearly had in contemplation that all the circumstances of the case, not only the foreseeability of harm, were appropriate to be taken into account in determining whether a duty of care arose. *Hedley Byrne & Co Ltd v Heller & Partners Ltd* was concerned with the assumption of responsibility. On the facts of the case no liability was held to exist because responsibility for the advice given had been disclaimed, but there was established the principle that a duty of care arises where a party is asked for and gives gratuitous advice on a matter within his particular skill or knowledge and knows or ought to have known that the person asking for the advice will rely on it and act accordingly. In such a case the directness and closeness of the relationship between the parties are very apparent. *Dorset Yacht Co Ltd v Home Office* was an example of the kind of situation where a special relationship between a defendant and a third party gives rise to a duty on the part of the defendant to take reasonable care to control the third party so as to prevent him causing damage to the plaintiff ... The relationship of the officers to the boys was analogous to that between parents and children, a relationship described by Dixon J in *Smith v Leurs* as capable of giving rise to a duty of control, saying:

"... apart from vicarious responsibility, one man may be responsible to another for the harm done to the latter by a third person; he may be responsible on the ground that the act of the third person could not have taken place but for his own fault or breach of duty. There is more than one description of duty the breach of which may produce this consequence. For instance, it may be a duty of care in reference to things involving special danger. It may even be a duty of care with reference to the control of actions or conduct of the third person. It is, however, exceptional to find in the law a duty to control another's actions to prevent harm to strangers. The general rule is that one man is under no duty of controlling another man to prevent his doing damage to a third. There are, however, special relations which are the source of a duty of this nature. It appears now to be recognised that it is incumbent upon a parent who maintains control over a young child to take reasonable care so to exercise that control as to avoid conduct on his part exposing the person or property of others to unreasonable danger. Parental control, where it exists, must be exercised with due care to prevent the child inflicting intentional damage on others or causing damage by conduct involving unreasonable risk of injury to others."

It is true that in the *Dorset Yacht* case a question arose whether the decision of the Home Office to give borstal boys a measure of freedom in order to assist in their rehabilitation fell within the ambit of a discretionary power the exercise of which was not capable of being called in question. But that question did not reach into the conduct of the officers who were in charge of the boys in the circumstances prevailing on the island. Having regard to these circumstances, it was not difficult to arrive, as a matter of judgment, at the conclusion that a close and direct relationship of proximity existed between the officers and the owners of the yachts, sufficient to require the former, as a matter of law, to take reasonable care to prevent the boys from interfering with the yachts and damaging them.

The second stage of Lord Wilberforce's test is one which will rarely have to be applied. It can arise in a limited category of cases where, notwithstanding that a case of negligence is made out on the proximity basis, public policy requires that there should be no liability ...

In view of the direction in which the law has since been developing, their Lordships consider that for the future it should be recognised that the two-stage test in *Anns* is not to be regarded as in all circumstances a suitable guide to the existence of a duty of care.

The primary and all-important matter for consideration, then, is whether in all the circumstances of this case there existed between the commissioner and would-be depositors with the company such close and direct relations as to place the commissioner, in the exercise of his functions under the ordinance, under a duty of care towards would-be depositors ... That raises the question whether there existed between the commissioner and company and its managers a special relationship of the nature described by Dixon J in *Smith v Leurs*, and such as was held to exist between the prison officers and the borstal boys in the *Dorset Yacht* case, so as to give rise to a duty on the commissioner to take reasonable care to prevent the company and its managers from causing financial loss to persons who might subsequently deposit with it.

In contradistinction to the position in the *Dorset Yacht* case, the commissioner had no power to control the day-to-day activities of those who caused the loss and damage. As has been mentioned, the commissioner had power only to stop the company carrying on business, and the decision whether or not to do so was clearly well within the discretionary sphere of his functions. In their Lordships' opinion the circumstance that the commissioner had, on the appellants' averments, cogent reason to suspect that the company's business was being carried on fraudulently and improvidently did not create a special relationship between the commissioner and the company of the nature described in the authorities. They are also of opinion that no special relationship existed between the commissioner and those unascertained members of the public who might in future become exposed to the risk of financial loss through depositing money with the company. Accordingly, their Lordships do not consider that the commissioner owed to the appellants any duty of care on the principle which formed the *ratio* of the *Dorset Yacht* case. To hark back to Lord Atkin's words, there were not such close and direct relations between the commissioner and appellants as to give rise to the duty of care desiderated ...

The final matter for consideration is the argument for the Attorney-General that it would be contrary to public policy to admit the appellants' claim ... It was maintained that, if the commissioner were to be held to owe actual or potential depositors a duty of care in negligence, there would be reason to apprehend that the prospect of claims would have a seriously inhibiting effect on the work of his department. A sound judgment would be less likely to be exercised if the commissioner were to be constantly looking over his shoulder at the prospect of claims against him, and his activities would be likely to be conducted in a detrimentally defensive frame of mind. In the result, the effectiveness of his functions would be at risk of diminution.

Consciousness of potential liability could lead to distortions of judgment. In addition, the principles leading to his liability would surely be equally applicable to a wide range of regulatory agencies, not only in the financial field, but also, for example, to the factory inspectorate and social workers, to name only a few. If such liability were to be desirable on any policy grounds, it would be much better that the liability were to be introduced by the legislature, which is better suited than the judiciary to weigh up competing policy considerations.

Their Lordships are of opinion that there is much force in these arguments, but as they are satisfied that the appellants' statement of claim does not disclose a cause of action against the commissioner in negligence they prefer to rest their decision on that rather than on the public policy argument.'

Comment

(1) *Sutherland Shire Council v Heyman* concerned facts similar to those in *Anns*. The High Court of Australia rejected the two-stage test, and held that the existence of a duty was to be determined from a wider notion of 'proximity' which embraces all of the circumstances of the parties' relationship.

(2) It would seem that there is unlikely to be a duty of care owed by such a regulatory body unless it has the power to exercise a very high degree of control over those whom it is to regulate.

(3) Although 'proximity', in its modern usage, had the appearance of being a single test for the existence of a duty (subject always to considerations of pure policy), it was acknowledged that it could prove problematic in practice, as Lord Oliver commented in *Caparo Industries plc v Dickman*:

'... It is now clear from a series of decisions in this House that, at least so far as concerns the law of the United Kingdom, the duty of care in tort depends not solely on the existence of the essential ingredient of the foreseeability of damage to the plaintiff but on its coincidence with a further ingredient to which has been attached the label "proximity" and which was described by Lord Atkin in the course of his speech in *Donoghue v Stevenson* as "such close and direct relations that the act complained of directly affects a person whom the person alleged to be bound to take care would know would be directly affected by his careless act".

It must be remembered, however, that Lord Atkin was using these words in the context of loss caused by physical damage where the existence of the nexus between the careless defendant and the injured plaintiff can rarely give rise to any difficulty. To adopt the words of Bingham LJ in the instant case: "It is enough that the plaintiff chances to be (out of the whole world) the person with whom the defendant collided or who purchased the offending ginger beer."

The extension of the concept of negligence since the decision of this House in *Hedley Byrne & Co Ltd v Heller & Partners Ltd* to cover cases of pure economic loss not resulting from physical damage has given rise to a considerable and as yet unsolved difficulty of definition. The opportunities for the infliction of pecuniary loss from the imperfect performance of everyday tasks on the proper performance of which people rely for regulating their affairs are illimitable and the effects are far reaching. A defective bottle of ginger beer may injure a single consumer but the damage stops there. A single statement may be repeated endlessly with or without the permission of its author and may be relied on in a different way by many different people. Thus the postulate of a simple duty to avoid any harm that is, with hindsight, reasonably capable of being foreseen becomes untenable without the imposition of some intelligible limits to keep the law of negligence within the bounds of common sense and practicality. Those limits have been found by the requirement of what has been called a "relationship of proximity" between plaintiff and defendant and by the imposition of a further requirement that the attachment of liability for harm which has occurred be "just and reasonable". But, although the cases in which the courts have imposed or withheld liability are capable of an approximate categorisation, one looks in vain for some common denominator by which the existence of the essential relationship can be tested. Indeed, it is difficult to resist a conclusion that what have been treated as three separate requirements are, at least in most cases, in fact merely facets of the same thing, for in some cases the degree of foreseeability is such that it is from that alone that the requisite proximity can be deduced, whilst in others the absence of that essential relationship can most rationally be attributed simply to the court's view that it would not be fair and reasonable to hold the defendant responsible. "Proximity" is, no doubt, a convenient expression so long as it is realised that it is no more than a label which embraces not a definable concept but merely a description of circumstances from which, pragmatically, the courts conclude that a duty of care exists.

There are, of course, cases where, in any ordinary meaning of the words, a relationship of proximity (in the literal sense of "closeness") exists but where the law, whilst recognising the fact of the relationship, nevertheless denies a remedy to the injured party on the ground of public policy. *Rondel v Worsley* was such a case, as was *Hill v Chief Constable of West Yorkshire*, so far as concerns the alternative ground of that decision. But such cases do nothing to assist in the identification of those features from which the law will deduce the essential relationship on which liability depends and, for my part, I think that it has to be recognised that to search for any single formula which will serve as a general test of liability is to pursue a will-o'-the-wisp. The fact is that once one discards, as it is now clear that one must, the concept of foreseeability of harm as the single exclusive test, even a *prima facie* test, of the existence of the duty of care, the attempt to state some general principle which will determine liability in an infinite variety of circumstances serves not to clarify the law but merely to bedevil its development in a way which corresponds with practicality and common sense.'

For the facts of *Caparo* and Lord Bridge's speech see p 183.

Marc Rich & Co AG and others v Bishop Rock Marine Co Ltd and others, The Nicholas H
[1995] 3 All ER 307 House of Lords

The question for the court was whether a classification society, NKK, owed a duty of care to the owners of cargo lost when a damaged vessel sank after having been allowed to sail as the result of a survey negligently performed by a surveyor acting for the society. At first instance it was held that there was a duty of care, but a majority in the House of Lords upheld the Court of Appeal decision that no such duty arose.

Lord Steyn: '... [Counsel for] the cargo owners ... submitted that, since the claim involved foreseeable physical damage to the cargo owners' property, the additional requirements of proximity and that it is fair, just and reasonable to impose a duty of care are inapplicable. Secondly, and assuming that those requirements are applicable, he submitted that those requirements are fulfilled. He described this way of putting the case as being squarely based on the principles laid down in *Donoghue v Stevenson*. ...

THE REQUIREMENTS IN PHYSICAL DAMAGE CASES

Counsel for the cargo owners submitted that in cases of physical damage to property ... the only requirement is proof of reasonable foreseeability. For this proposition he relied on observations of Lord Oliver of Aylmerton in *Caparo Industries plc v Dickman*. Those observations, seen in context, do not support his argument. They merely underline the qualitative difference between cases of direct physical damage and indirect economic loss. The materiality of that distinction is plain. But, since the decision in *Home Office v Dorset Yacht Co Ltd*, it has been settled law that the elements of foreseeability and proximity as well as considerations of fairness, justice and reasonableness are relevant to all cases whatever the nature of the harm sustained by the plaintiff. Saville LJ explained:

> "... whatever the nature of the harm sustained by the plaintiff, it is necessary to consider the matter not only by inquiring about foreseeability but also by considering the nature of the relationship between the parties; and to be satisfied that in all the circumstances it is fair, just and reasonable to impose a duty of care. Of course ... these three matters overlap with each other and are really facets of the same thing. For example, the relationship between the parties may be such that it is obvious that a lack of care will create a risk of harm and that as a matter of common sense and justice a duty should be imposed ... Again in most cases of the direct infliction of physical loss or injury through carelessness, it is self-evident that a civilised system of law should hold that a duty of care has been broken, whereas the infliction of financial harm may well pose a more difficult problem. Thus the three so-called requirements for a duty of care are not to be treated as wholly separate and distinct requirements but rather as convenient and helpful approaches to the pragmatic question whether a duty should be imposed in any given case. In the end whether the law does impose a duty in any particular circumstances depends upon those circumstances ..."

That seems to me a correct summary of the law as it now stands. It follows that I would reject the first argument of counsel for the cargo owners.

THE DUTY OF CARE DERIVING FROM *DONOGHUE V STEVENSON*

In the course of their submissions counsel took your Lordships on a tour of many of the landmark cases on negligence from *Donoghue v Stevenson* to *White v Jones*. In this area the common law develops incrementally on the basis of a consideration of analogous cases where a duty has been recognised or desired. But none of the cases cited provided any realistic analogy to be used as a springboard for a decision one way or the other in this case. The present case can only be decided on the basis of an intense and particular focus on all its distinctive features, and then applying established legal principles to it. No doubt those principles are capable of further development but, for present purposes, the applicable principles can readily be identified and require no re-examination.

THE FACTORS POINTING TOWARDS THE EXISTENCE OF A DUTY OF CARE

Not surprisingly, there are substantial factors pointing in favour and against the recognition of a duty of care. Counsel for the cargo owners emphasised that except for the legal question whether a duty of care exists every element of the cargo owners' cause of action must be assumed to be satisfied. Specifically, he emphasised that it is assumed that it was foreseeable that carelessness of the surveyor in conducting the survey of the damaged vessel, or in the making of recommendations, was likely to expose the cargo actually on board the vessel to the danger of physical damage. The surveyor was brought in because there was concern for the safety of the vessel on the intended voyage. But exactly the same dangers would affect the hull and cargo on that voyage. Counsel for the cargo owners argued that in the circumstances, and particularly in the light of the fact that the cargo was on board when the surveyor carelessly performed his professional services, the element of proximity was satisfied. Turning to the question whether it is fair, just and reasonable to impose a duty of care on the classification society against the cargo owners, he said that neither the contract of carriage between owners of the vessel and the cargo owners nor the contract between the owners and the classification society militated against the recognition of a legal duty of care. Given that third parties, such as cargo owners, are known in practice to rely on the recommendations of classification societies, he submitted that it is fair, just and reasonable to recognise a legal duty of care in this case. Alternatively, he argued that the reliance placed on recommendations of classification societies by third parties in maritime trade warranted an inference of an assumption of responsibility by classification societies as against owners of cargo in cases when the survey work is performed while the cargo is on board. Lastly, he said that a recognition of a duty of care in such cases would promote the safety of life, ships and cargo at sea. All these factors and arguments are relevant and must be taken into account in the eventual decision.

OTHER MATERIAL FACTORS

It is now necessary to examine a number of other factors in order to put the case in its right perspective, and to consider whether some of those factors militate against the recognition of a duty of care. For convenience these factors can be considered under six headings, namely: (a) did the surveyor's carelessness cause direct physical loss; (b) did the cargo owners rely on the surveyor's recommendations; (c) the impact of the contract between the shipowners and the owners of the cargo; (d) the impact of the contract between the classification society and the shipowners; (e) the position and role of NKK; and (f) policy factors arguably tending to militate against the recognition of a duty of care.

Only after an examination of these features will it be possible to address directly the element of proximity and the question whether it is fair, just and reasonable to impose a duty of care.

(a) Direct physical loss?

Counsel for the cargo owners argued that the present case involved the infliction of *direct* physical loss. At first glance the issue of directness may seem a matter of terminology rather than substance. In truth it is a material factor. The law more readily attaches the consequences of actionable negligence to directly inflicted physical loss than to indirectly inflicted physical loss. For example, if the NKK surveyor had carelessly dropped a lighted cigarette into a cargo hold known to contain a combustible cargo, thereby causing an explosion and the loss of the vessel and cargo, the assertion that the classification society was in breach of a duty of care might have been a strong one. That would be a paradigm case of directly inflicted physical loss. Counsel for the cargo owners referred your Lordships to *Clay v A J Crump & Sons Ltd* by way of support for the proposition that, in this case, there was a direct infliction of loss in the relevant sense. In that case an architect assured a demolition contractor that he could safely leave a wall standing. The demolition contractor acted on this advice. The wall collapsed on a workman. The workman sued the architect in tort. It was held that the architect owed a duty of care to the workman. The architect was primarily responsible for leaving the wall in a dangerous condition. In the present case the shipowner was primarily responsible for the vessel sailing in a seaworthy condition. The role of the NKK was a subsidiary one. In my view the carelessness of the NKK surveyor did not involve the direct infliction of physical damage in the relevant sense. That by no means concludes the answer to the general question. But it does introduce the right perspective on one aspect of this case.

(b) Reliance

It is possible to visualise direct exchanges between cargo owners and a classification society, in the context of a survey on behalf of owners of a vessel laden with cargo, which might give rise to an assumption of responsibility in the sense explained by Lord Goff in *Henderson v Merrett Syndicates Ltd* ... In the present case there was no contact whatever between the cargo owners and the classification society. Moreover, as Saville LJ pointed out, in this case it is not even suggested that the cargo owners were aware that NKK had been brought in to survey the vessel. The cargo owners simply relied on the owners of the vessel to keep the vessel seaworthy and to look after the cargo. Saville LJ and Balcombe LJ regarded this feature as sufficient to demonstrate that the necessary element of proximity was absent. I would approach the matter differently. In my view this feature is not necessarily decisive but it also contributes to placing the claim in the correct perspective.

(c) The bill of lading contracts

... The dealings between shipowners and cargo owners are based on a contractual structure, the Hague Rules, and tonnage limitation, on which the insurance of international trade depends: see Dr Malcolm Clarke, "Misdelivery and Time Bars" [1990] LMCLQ 314. Underlying it is the system of double or overlapping insurance of cargo. Cargo owners take out direct insurance in respect of the cargo. Shipowners take out liability risks insurance in respect of breaches of their duties of care in respect of the cargo. The insurance system is structured on the basis that the potential liability of shipowners to cargo owners is limited under the Hague Rules and by virtue of tonnage limitation provisions. And insurance premiums payable by owners obviously reflect such limitations on the shipowners' exposure.

If a duty of care by classification societies to cargo owners is recognised in this case, it must have a substantial impact on international trade. In his article Mr Cane described the likely effect of imposing such duty of care as follows:

> "Societies would be forced to buy appropriate liability insurance unless they could bargain with shipowners for an indemnity. To the extent that societies were successful in securing indemnities from shipowners in respect of loss suffered by cargo owners, the limitation of the liability of shipowners to cargo owners under the Hague(–Visby) Rules would effectively be destroyed. Shipowners would need to increase their insurance cover in respect of losses suffered by cargo owners; but at the same time, cargo owners would still need to insure against losses above the Hague–Visby recovery limit which did not result from actionable negligence on the part of a classification society. At least if classification societies are immune from non-contractual liability, they can confidently go without insurance in respect of third-party losses, leaving third parties to insure themselves in respect of losses for which they could not recover from shipowners."

Counsel for the cargo owners challenged this analysis. On instructions he said that classification societies already carry liability risks insurance. That is no doubt right since classification societies do not have a blanket immunity from all tortious liability. On the other hand, if a duty of care is held to exist in this case, the potential exposure of classification societies to claims by cargo owners will be large. That greater exposure is likely to lead to an increase in the cost to classification societies of obtaining appropriate liability risks insurance. Given their role in maritime trade classification societies are likely to seek to pass on the higher cost to owners. Moreover, it is readily predictable that classification societies will require owners to give appropriate indemnities. Ultimately, shipowners will pay.

The result of a recognition of a duty of care in this case will be to enable cargo owners, or rather their insurers, to disturb the balance created by the Hague Rules and Hague–Visby Rules as well as by tonnage limitation provisions, by enabling cargo owners to recover in tort against a peripheral party to the prejudice of the protection of shipowners under the existing system. For these reasons I would hold that the international trade system tends to militate against the recognition of the claim in tort put forward by the cargo owners against the classification society.

(d) The contract between the classification society and shipowners

[Counsel] for NKK argued that the contract between the shipowners and the classification society must be a factor against the recognition of the suggested duty of care. He referred to *Pacific Associates Inc v Baxter*. That was a case where the Court of Appeal held that the network of contracts between a building owner, the head contractor, subcontractors and even suppliers militated against imposing duties in tort on peripheral parties. In the present case the classification society was not involved in such a web of contracts.

(e) The position and role of NKK

The fact that a defendant acts for the collective welfare is a matter to be taken into consideration when considering whether it is fair, just and reasonable to impose a duty of care: see *Hill v Chief Constable of West Yorkshire* and *Elguzouli-Daf v Comr of Police of the Metropolis*. Even if such a body has no general immunity from liability in tort, the question may arise whether it owes a duty of care to aggrieved persons, and, if so, in what classes of case, e.g. only in cases involving the direct infliction of physical harm or on a wider basis ... [Classification societies] act in the public interest. The reality is simply that NKK ... is an independent and non-profit-making entity, created and operating for the sole purpose of promoting the collective welfare, namely the safety of lives and ships at sea. In common with other classification societies NKK fulfils a role which in its absence would have to be fulfilled by states. And the question is whether NKK, and other classification societies, would be able to carry out their functions as efficiently if they become the ready alternative target of cargo owners, who already have contractual claims against shipowners. In my judgment there must be some apprehension that the classification societies would adopt, to the detriment of their traditional role, a more defensive position.

(f) Policy factors

Counsel for the cargo owners argued that a decision that a duty of care existed in this case would not involve wide ranging exposure for NKK and other classification societies to claims in tort. That is an unrealistic position. If a duty is recognised in this case there is no reason why it should not extend to annual surveys, docking surveys, intermediate surveys, special surveys, boiler surveys, and so forth. And the scale of NKK's potential liability is shown by the fact that NKK conducted an average of 14,500 surveys per year over the last five years.

At present the system of settling cargo claims against shipowners is a relatively simple one. The claims are settled between the two sets of insurers. If the claims are not settled, they are resolved in arbitration or court proceedings. If a duty is held to exist in this case as between the classification society and cargo owners, classification societies would become potential defendants in many cases. An extra layer of insurance would become involved. The settlement process would inevitably become more complicated and expensive. Arbitration proceedings and court proceedings would often involve an additional party. And often similar issues would have to be canvassed in separate proceedings since the classification societies would not be bound by arbitration clauses in the contracts of carriage. If such a duty is recognised, there is a risk that classification societies might be unwilling from time to time to survey the very vessels which most urgently require independent examination. It will also divert men and resources from the prime function of classification societies, namely to save life and ships at sea. These factors are, by themselves, far from decisive. But in an overall assessment of the case they merit consideration.

IS THE IMPOSITION OF A DUTY OF CARE FAIR, JUST AND REASONABLE?

Like Mann LJ in the Court of Appeal, I am willing to assume (without deciding) that there was a sufficient degree of proximity in this case to fulfil that requirement for the existence of a duty of care. The critical question is therefore whether it would be fair, just and reasonable to impose such a duty. For my part I am satisfied that the factors and arguments advanced on behalf of cargo owners are decisively outweighed by the cumulative effect, if a duty is recognised, of the matters discussed in paras (c), (e) and (f), i.e. the outflanking of the bargain between shipowners and cargo owners; the negative effect on the public role of NKK and the other considerations of policy. By way of summary, I look at the matter from the point of view of the three parties concerned. I conclude that the recognition of a duty would be unfair, unjust and unreasonable as against the shipowners who would ultimately have to bear the cost of holding classification societies liable, such consequence being at variance with the bargain between shipowners and cargo owners based on an internationally agreed contractual structure. It would also be unfair, unjust and unreasonable towards classification societies, notably because they act for the collective welfare and unlike shipowners they would not have the benefit of any limitation provisions. Looking at the matter from the point of view of cargo owners, the existing system provides them with the protection of the Hague Rules or Hague–Visby Rules. But that protection is limited under such Rules and by tonnage limitation provisions. Under the existing system any shortfall is readily insurable. In my judgment the lesser injustice is done by not recognising a duty of care.'

Comment

(1)   At first instance Hirst J had held that the close relationship between NKK and the cargo owners was sufficient to give rise to a duty of care in negligence. The Court of Appeal reversed this decision: although each member of the court gave a separate judgment, they were broadly in agreement that it would not be

fair, just and reasonable to impose such a duty. In addition, Saville and Balcombe LJJ felt that, in the absence of any direct dealings between the parties, their relationship was not such as would support the existence of a duty.

(2)   Lord Steyn commented that the fact that this was 'a novel question' despite classification societies having operated for over a century and a half 'may not be entirely without significance', although this should not create 'any *a priori* disposition for or against the legal sustainability of such a claim'.

(3)   One of the complicating features of this case was the assortment of different contractual relationships amongst the parties, and whether these might be used to determine the existence or otherwise of a duty of care in negligence. In both *Norwich City Council v Harvey* and *Pacific Associates Inc v Baxter* it was held that an examination of the structure of the contractual framework might reveal an understanding on the part of the plaintiff of the defendant's legitimate expectation of non-liability. In *Marc Rich* this was held not to be the case: furthermore, the lack of any knowledge by either party of the other defeated any suggestion that a duty might arise on the basis of assumption of responsibility.

(4)   Note the observation, in relation to policy factors, that the existence of a duty of care would 'divert men and resources from the [societies'] prime function ... namely to save life and ships at sea'. This paraphrases Lord Keith's justification, in *Hill v Chief Constable of West Yorkshire*, for the immunity from liability enjoyed by the police (see p 28): however, here it is used in a different way – not as the decisive factor, but as one of several factors leading to the conclusion that the imposition of a duty would not be fair, just and reasonable. In *Elguzouli-Daf v Commissioner of Police of the Metropolis* Steyn LJ (as he was then) had applied the two approaches in the alternative – either that the policy factor negatived the existence of a duty of care or, if not, that it created an 'immunity from liability in negligence'.

(5)   Lord Lloyd of Berwick gave the only dissenting speech. He said:

'... The concept of proximity, and the requirement that it should be fair, just and reasonable to impose a duty of care on the defendant in the particular circumstances of the case, have been developed as a means of containing liability for pure economic loss under the principles stated in *Donoghue v Stevenson*. At the same time, and by a parallel movement in the opposite direction, the House has in two recent decisions reaffirmed liability for economic loss based on the principle of assumption of responsibility as expounded by the House in *Hedley Byrne & Co Ltd v Heller & Partners Ltd*, and going back beyond that decision to *Nocton v Lord Ashburton*. None of these difficulties arise in the present case. We are not here asked to extend the law of negligence into a new field. We are not even asked to make an incremental advance. All that is required is a straightforward application of *Donoghue v Stevenson* ... Where the facts cry out for the imposition of a duty of care between the parties, as they do here, it would require an exceptional case to refuse to impose a duty on the ground that it would not be fair, just and reasonable. Otherwise there is a risk that the law of negligence will disintegrate into a series of isolated decisions without any coherent principles at all, and the retreat from *Anns* will turn into a rout.'

(6) In *Mulcahy v Ministry of Defence* the Court of Appeal had to decide whether a duty of care was owed by one soldier to another while engaging the enemy in the course of hostilities. The court, following the approach in *Marc Rich*, concluded that it would not be fair, just or reasonable to impose a duty if one considered 'all the circumstances including the position of the alleged tortfeasor and any relevant policy considerations'. Likewise, there was no duty on the Ministry of Defence to maintain a safe system of work in such circumstances. See also *Barrett v Ministry of Defence*.

(7) In *Perrett v Collins*, the plaintiff, P, suffered personal injury when the plane in which he was a passenger crashed. The plane had been assembled from a kit by the first defendant – the pilot, C. It had been inspected several times during its construction and, when finished, issued with a certificate of airworthiness by the second defendant, an inspector for the third defendant, the PFA. The case concerns the question, as a preliminary issue, whether, in the light of the decision in *Marc Rich*, the PFA owed a duty of care to the plaintiff. The presumed facts were that C had been supplied with, and had fitted, parts whose incompatibility should have been noticed on inspection. The Court of Appeal upheld the finding of the trial judge that the Association and its inspectors did owe a duty of care in these circumstances. Hobhouse LJ said, '*Marc Rich* should not be regarded as an authority which has a relevance to cases of personal injuries or as adding any requirement that an injured plaintiff do more than bring his case within established principles'. When deciding whether a duty existed it was relevant to take into account the fact that persons entering aircraft are entitled to believe that it is airworthy, and that the defendants assumed a degree of responsibility in that regard. With reference to Lord Steyn's closing observation in *Marc Rich* that 'the lesser injustice is done by not recognising a duty of care', Swinton Thomas LJ felt that, on the facts of *Perrett*, the scales tipped the other way.

Spring v Guardian Assurance plc and others
[1994] 3 All ER 129 House of Lords

The plaintiff, who had been employed under a contract for services, sued in respect of a negligently prepared reference given by a former employer. The plaintiff had been employed in the life insurance industry where the rules of the self-regulatory supervising body LAUTRO obliged new employers to obtain a reference from previous employers who in turn were required to make full and frank disclosure of relevant matters. The reference provided was highly critical and the plaintiff was unable to find employment. The plaintiff sued for breach of contract, negligence and malicious falsehood. The claim for malicious falsehood failed because the plaintiff was unable to establish malice. The case before the House of Lords turned on whether the existence of a duty of care would undermine the protection in defamation offered to the giver of a reference by the defence of qualified privilege and should therefore be rejected. The House of Lords held by a majority of four to one that the plaintiff was owed a duty of care.

Lord Woolf: '... There would be no purpose in extending the tort of negligence to protect the subject of an inaccurate reference if he was already adequately protected by the law of defamation. However, because of the defence of qualified privilege, before an action for defamation can succeed (or, for that matter, an action for injurious falsehood) it is necessary to establish malice. In my judgment the result of this requirement is that an action for defamation provides a wholly inadequate remedy for an employee who is caused damage by a reference which due to negligence is inaccurate. This is because it places a wholly disproportionate burden on the employee. Malice is extremely difficult to establish. This is demonstrated by the facts of this case. The plaintiff ... was able to establish that one of his colleagues, who played a part in compiling the information on which the reference was based, had lied about interviewing him, but this was still insufficient to prove malice. Without an action for negligence the employee may, therefore, be left with no practical prospect of redress, even though the reference may have permanently prevented him from obtaining employment in his chosen vocation.

If the law provides a remedy for references which are inaccurate due to carelessness this would be beneficial. It would encourage the adoption of appropriate standards when preparing references. This would be an important advantage as frequently an employee will be ignorant that it is because of the terms of an inaccurate reference, of the contents of which he is unaware, that he is not offered fresh employment.

The availability of a remedy without having to prove malice will not open the floodgates. In cases where the employee discovers the existence of the inaccurate reference, he will have a remedy if, but only if, he can establish, instead of malice, that the reason for the inaccuracy is the default of the employer, in the sense that he has been careless. To make an employer liable for an inaccurate reference, but only if he is careless, is, I would suggest, wholly fair. It would balance the respective interests of the employer and employee. It would amount to a development of the law of negligence which accords with the principles which should control its development. It would, in addition, avoid a rather unattractive situation continuing of a recipient of a reference, but not the subject of a reference, being able to bring an action for negligence. It would also recognise that while both in negligence and defamation it is the untrue statement which causes the damage, there is a fundamental difference between the torts. An action for defamation is founded upon the inaccurate terms of the reference itself. An action for negligence is based on the lack of care of the author of the reference.

Notwithstanding the distinction between the two causes of action, it was the different principles which govern an action for damages for defamation which the Court of Appeal found to be fatal to the attempt of the plaintiff to establish that the defendants owed him a duty of care in respect of the accuracy of the contents of a reference ...

The principal point which the plaintiff has to overcome ... is the fact that to allow an action for negligence would be to introduce a "distorting element" into the law of defamation, that is, into the area of law which deals with unjustified injury to reputation, which is an area of the law which up to now defamation has had to itself ...

This appeal is not concerned with a claim for mere loss of reputation. What concerns the plaintiff is his loss of an opportunity to obtain employment due to the negligence, as the judge found, in the preparation of the reference. I am afraid I do not accept the logic of the argument that to have an action for negligence will undermine the law of defamation. If this appeal is allowed, this will leave the law of defamation in exactly the same state as it was previously. The plaintiff would not have succeeded in an action for defamation. Negligence has always been an irrelevant consideration (I am not referring to quantum of damages) and it will remain irrelevant in an action for defamation. In the present context the two causes of action are not primarily directed at the same mischief although they, admittedly, overlap. I have already indicated that an action for negligence is concerned with the care exercised in ascertaining the facts and defamation with the truth of the contents of what is published.

This is also demonstrated by what would be the respective approaches to damages in an action based on defamation and negligence. In the case of defamation the primary head, but not the only head, of damages is as to the loss of reputation. In an action for negligence, on the other hand, the subject of the reference will be primarily interested in and largely limited to his economic loss. To prevent the law of negligence applying to the present situation, when it is otherwise fair and just that it should apply, by the imposition of a requirement to prove malice in effect amounts to transferring a defence which has been developed for one tort to another tort to which it has never been previously applied when it is inappropriate to do so.

The historic development of the two actions has been quite separate. Just as it has never been a requirement of an action for defamation to show that the defamatory statement was made negligently, so, if the circumstances establish that it is fair and just that a duty of care should exist, the person who suffers harm in consequence of a breach of that duty should not have to establish malice, merely because that would be a requirement in an action for defamation. I can see no justification for erecting a fence around the whole of the field to which defamation can apply and treating any other tort, which can beneficially from the point of view of justice enter into part of that field, as a trespasser if it does so. The conclusive answer in the present context to applying the approach of Cooke P [in *Bell-Booth Group Ltd v A-G*] is that it will, here, result in real injustice. It would mean that a plaintiff who would otherwise be entitled to succeed in an action for negligence would go away empty-handed because he could not succeed in an action for defamation. This cannot be a desirable result ...'

Comment

For a further extract from Lord Woolf's speech see p 46.

Hill v Chief Constable of West Yorkshire
[1988] 2 All ER 238 House of Lords

The appellant, whose daughter was the last victim of the 'Yorkshire Ripper', brought an action claiming that the existence of sufficient information for the police to have supposed that one person had committed the preceding murders, and that they would continue, placed them under a duty of care towards potential victims. This, she alleged, was breached by their failure to apprehend the murderer. The House of Lords, on the grounds both of lack of proximity and as a matter of policy, affirmed the decisions of the lower courts that no such duty was owed to individual members of the public.

Lord Keith of Kinkel: '... The question of law which is opened up by the case is whether the individual members of a police force, in the course of carrying out their functions of controlling and keeping down the incidence of crime, owe a duty of care to individual members of the public who may suffer injury to person or property through the activities of criminals, such as to result in liability in damages, on the ground of negligence, to anyone who suffers such injury by reason of breach of that duty.

There is no question that a police officer, like anyone else, may be liable in tort to a person who is injured as a direct result of his acts or omissions. So he may be liable in damages for assault, unlawful arrest, wrongful imprisonment and malicious prosecution, and also for negligence. Instances where liability for negligence has been established are *Knightley v Johns* and *Rigby v Chief Constable of Northamptonshire* ...

By common law police officers owe to the general public a duty to enforce the criminal law: see *R v Metropolitan Police Comr, ex parte Blackburn* ... [But] the common law ... makes no specific requirements as to the manner in which the obligation is to be discharged. That is not a situation where there can readily be inferred an intention of the common law to create a duty towards individual members of the public.

Counsel for the appellant, however, sought to equiparate the situation to that which resulted in liability on the ground of negligence in *Anns v Merton London Borough*. There the borough were under a duty, imposed by legislation, to supervise compliance with building byelaws, in particular as regards the construction of foundations. It was held that though the borough had a discretion whether or not to carry out an inspection of foundations in any particular case, in order to check compliance, once a decision had been made to carry out an inspection the borough owed to future owners and occupiers of the building in question a common law duty to exercise reasonable care in the inspection. In the present case, so it was maintained, the respondent, having decided to investigate the Sutcliffe murders, owed to his potential future victims a duty to do with reasonable care.

The foundation of the duty of care was said to be reasonable foreseeability of harm to potential future victims if Sutcliffe were not promptly apprehended. Lord Atkin's classic propositions in *M'Alister (or Donoghue) v Stevenson* were prayed in aid, as was Lord Wilberforce's well-known two-stage test of liability in negligence in *Anns v Merton London Borough*.

It has been said almost too frequently to require repetition that foreseeability of likely harm is not in itself a sufficient test of liability in negligence. Some further ingredient is invariably needed to establish the requisite proximity of relationship between the plaintiff and defendant, and all the circumstances of the case must be carefully considered and analysed in order to ascertain whether such an ingredient is present. The nature of the ingredient will be found to vary in a number of different categories of decided cases. In the *Anns* case there was held to be sufficient proximity of relationship between the borough and future owners and occupiers of a particular building the foundations of which it was decided to inspect, and there was also a close relationship between the borough and the builder who had constructed the foundations.

In *Home Office v Dorset Yacht Co* Lord Diplock said of Lord Atkin's proposition:

> "Used as a guide to characteristics which will be found to exist in conduct and relationships which give rise to a legal duty of care this aphorism marks a milestone in the modern development of the law of negligence. But misused as a universal it is manifestly false."

Earlier, he had said:

> "... the judicial development of the law of negligence rightly proceeds by seeking first to identify the relevant characteristics that are common to the kinds of conduct and relationship between the parties which are involved in

the case for decision and the kinds of conduct and relationship which have been held in previous decisions of the courts to give rise to a duty of care."

... However, the class of persons to whom a duty of care might be owed to prevent the escape of detainees was held to be limited. Lord Diplock said:

"The risk of sustaining damage from the tortious acts of criminals is shared by the public at large. It has never been recognised at common law as giving rise to any cause of action against anyone but the criminal himself. It would seem arbitrary and therefore unjust to single out for the special privilege of being able to recover compensation from the authorities responsible for the prevention of crime a person whose property was damaged by the tortious act of a criminal, merely because the damage to him happened to be caused by a criminal who had escaped from custody before completion of his sentence instead of by one who had been lawfully released or who had been put on probation or given a suspended sentence or who had never been previously apprehended at all. To give rise to a duty on the part of the custodian owed to a member of the public to take reasonable care to prevent a borstal trainee from escaping from his custody before completion of the trainee's sentence there should be some relationship between the custodian and the person to whom the duty is owed which exposes that person to a particular risk of damage in consequence of that escape which is different in its incidence from the general risk of damage from criminal acts of others which he shares with all members of the public. What distinguishes a borstal trainee who has escaped from one who has been duly released from custody, is his liability to recapture, and the distinctive added risk which is a reasonably foreseeable consequence of a failure to exercise due care in preventing him from escaping is the likelihood that in order to elude pursuit immediately on the discovery of his absence the escaping trainee may steal or appropriate and damage property which is situated in the vicinity of the place of detention from which he has escaped. So long as Parliament is content to leave the general risk of damage from criminal acts to lie where it falls without any remedy except against the criminal himself, the courts would be exceeding their limited function in developing the common law to meet changing conditions if they were to recognise a duty of care to prevent criminals escaping from penal custody owed to a wider category of members of the public than those whose property was exposed to an exceptional added risk by the adoption of a custodial system for young offenders which increased the likelihood of their escape unless due care was taken by those responsible for their custody. I should therefore hold that any duty of a borstal officer to use reasonable care to prevent a borstal trainee from escaping from his custody was owed only to persons whom he could reasonably foresee had property situate in the vicinity of the place of detention of the detainee which the detainee was likely to steal or to appropriate and damage in the course of eluding immediate pursuit and recapture. Whether or not any person fell within this category would depend on the facts of the particular case including the previous criminal and escaping record of the individual trainee concerned and the nature of the place from which he escaped."

The *Dorset Yacht* case was concerned with the special characteristics or ingredients beyond reasonable foreseeability of likely harm which may result in civil liability for failure to control another man to prevent his doing harm to a third. The present case falls broadly into the same category. It is plain that vital characteristics which were present in the *Dorset Yacht* case and which led to the imposition of liability are here lacking. Sutcliffe was never in the custody of the police force. Miss H was one of a vast number of the female general public who might be at risk from his activities but was at no special distinctive risk in relation to them, unlike the owners of yachts moored off Brownsea Island in relation to the foreseeable conduct of borstal boys. It appears from the passage quoted from the speech of Lord Diplock in the *Dorset Yacht* case that in his view no liability would rest on a prison authority, which carelessly allowed the escape of an habitual criminal, for damage which he subsequently caused, not in the course of attempting to make good his getaway to persons at special risk, but in further pursuance of his general criminal career to the person or property of members of the general public. The same rule must apply as regards failure to recapture the criminal before he had time to resume his career. In the case of an escaped criminal his identity and description are known. In the instant case the identity of the wanted criminal was at the material time unknown and it is not averred that any full or clear description of him was ever available. The alleged negligence of the police consists in a failure to discover his identity. But, if there is no general duty of care owed to individual members of the public by the responsible authorities to prevent the escape of a known criminal or to recapture him, there cannot reasonably be imposed on any police force a duty of care similarly owed to identify and apprehend an unknown one. Miss H cannot for this purpose be regarded as a person at special risk simply because she was young and female. Where the class of potential victims of a particular habitual criminal is a large one the precise size of it cannot in principle affect the issue. All householders are potential victims of a habitual burglar, and all females those of an habitual rapist. The conclusion must be that although there existed reasonable foreseeability of likely harm to such as Miss H if Sutcliffe were not identified and apprehended, there is absent from the case any such ingredient or characteristic as led to the liability of the Home Office in the *Dorset Yacht* case. Nor is there present any additional characteristic such as might make up the deficiency. The circumstances of the case are therefore not capable of establishing a duty of care owed towards Miss H by the West Yorkshire police.

That is sufficient for the disposal of the appeal. But in my opinion there is another reason why an action for damages in negligence should not lie against the police in circumstances such as those of the present case, and that is public policy. In *Yuen Kun-yeu v A-G of Hong Kong*, I expressed the view that the category of cases where the second stage of Lord Wilberforce's two-stage test in *Anns v Merton London Borough* might fall to be applied was a limited one, one example of that category being *Rondel v Worsley*. Application of that second stage is, however, capable of constituting a separate and independent ground for holding that the existence of liability in negligence should not be entertained. Potential existence of such liability may in many instances be in the general public interest, as tending towards the observance of a higher standard of care in the carrying on of various different types of activity. I do not, however, consider that this can be said of police activities. The general sense of public duty which motivates police forces is unlikely to be appreciably reinforced by the imposition of such liability so far as concerns their function in the investigation and suppression of crime. From time to time they make mistakes in the exercise of that function, but it is not to be doubted that they apply their best endeavours to the performance of it. In some instances the imposition of liability may lead to the exercise of a function being carried on in a detrimentally defensive frame of mind. The possibility of this happening in relation to the investigative operations of the police cannot be excluded. Further, it would be reasonable to expect that if potential liability were to be imposed it would be not uncommon for actions to be raised against police forces on the ground that they had failed to catch some criminal as soon as they might have done, with the result that he went on to commit further crimes. While some such actions might involve allegations of a simple and straightforward type of failure, for example that a police officer negligently tripped and fell while pursuing a burglar, others would be likely to enter deeply into the general nature of a police investigation, as indeed the present action would seek to do. The manner of conduct of such an investigation must necessarily involve a variety of decisions to be made on matters of policy and discretion, for example as to which particular line of inquiry is most advantageously to be pursued and what is the most advantageous way to deploy the available resources. Many such decisions would not be regarded by the courts as appropriate to be called in question, yet elaborate investigation of the facts might be necessary to ascertain whether or not this was so. A great deal of police time, trouble and expense might be expected to have to be put into the preparation of the defence to the action and the attendance of witnesses at the trial. The result would be a significant diversion of police manpower and attention from their most important function, that of the suppression of crime. Closed investigations would require to be reopened and retraversed, not with the object of bringing any criminal to justice but to ascertain whether or not they had been competently conducted.'

Comment

(1)   In *Rigby v Chief Constable of Northamptonshire* (see also p 585) the court drew a distinction between the decision not to replace an older type of CS gas canister with a newer version which carried a reduced fire risk, which it

regarded as a policy matter, and the operational decision to use such a canister in the absence of adequate fire precautions, which was held to give rise to liability in negligence.

(2)   *Hill* has since been applied in a number of police cases, e.g. *Alexandrou v Oxford, Osman v Ferguson* and *Ancell v McDermott* in the Court of Appeal. The effect of policy considerations is particularly marked in *Osman*, in which the continued activities of the plaintiff's attacker had been known to the police for almost a year and the court conceded that a relationship of sufficient proximity could probably be made out on the facts. Nevertheless, in each case the court held that the existence of a duty of care owed by the police would 'not promote the observance of a higher standard of care ... and would result in a significant diversion of police resources from the investigation and suppression of crime'.

In *Swinney and another v Chief Constable of the Northumbria Police* the plaintiff and her husband suffered psychiatric damage as a result of threats of violence received after the defendant negligently allowed their names as police informants to fall into the wrong hands. The chief constable argued that their claim should be struck out because, *inter alia*, the police were immune from claims arising out of their activities in relation to the suppression or investigation of crime. Ward LJ, in rejecting the chief constable's argument, summarised the competing public policy considerations:

> '... On the one hand there is, as more fully set out in *Hill v Chief Constable of West Yorkshire*, an important public interest that the police should carry out their difficult duties to the best of their endeavours without being fettered by, or even influenced by, the spectre of litigation looming over every judgment they make, every discretion they exercise, every act they undertake or omit to perform, in their ceaseless battle to investigate and suppress crime. The greater public good rightly outweighs any individual hardship. On the other hand, it is incontrovertible that the fight against crime is daily dependent upon information fed to the police by members of the public, often at real risk of villainous retribution from the criminals and their associates. The public interest will not accept that good citizens should be expected to entrust information to the police, without also expecting that they are entrusting their safety to the police. The public interest would be affronted were it to be the law that members of the public should be expected, in the execution of public service, to undertake the risk of harm to themselves without the police, in return, being expected to take no more than reasonable care to ensure that the confidential information imparted to them is protected. The welfare of the community at large demands the encouragement of the free flow of information without inhibition. Accordingly, it is arguable that there is a

duty of care, and that no consideration of public policy precludes the prosecution of the plaintiffs' claim, which will be judged on its merits later.'

For a similar approach to the balancing of policy factors, see *Costello v Chief Constable of the Northumbria Police* and *Leach v Chief Constable of Gloucestershire Constabulary* below.

(3)   The expanding influence of the *Hill* (so-called) immunity may be seen in *Skinner v Secretary of State for Transport*, in which Judge Gareth Edwards QC, sitting as a judge of the Queen's Bench Division, held that the same public policy considerations applied 'even more so' in the case of a coastguard who failed to respond to a distress signal from a sinking vessel. In *OLL Ltd v Secretary of State for Transport* the plaintiffs, whose negligent organisation of a canoeing trip had resulted in a number of injuries and deaths, sought indemnity from the Secretary of State on the basis of the coastguard's alleged negligence in the conduct of a rescue operation. May J, observing that any 'distinctions between the fire services and the coastguard are illusory and immaterial', applied the decision in *Capital & Counties plc v Hampshire County Council* (see below) and concluded that no duty would be owed except where intervention resulted in 'positive injury', which it had not in this case:

> '[No] duty of care arises if the coastguard misdirect their own rescuing people or equipment, just as there would be no liability if a fire brigade misdirected its own fire engine. In my view, a distinction which would render the coastguard potentially liable if they gave misdirections to other people (which do not result in positive injury directly inflicted) is quite artificial. If there were two helicopters, one belonging to the coastguard and the other to the Royal Navy, it would be quite nonsensical if the coastguard were liable for misdirections given to one but not the other.'

See also *Marc Rich & Co AG and others v Bishop Rock Marine Co Ltd*, p 17.

(4)   *Capital & Counties plc v Hampshire County Council and others; and other appeals* concerned a number of claims arising out of fires which, it was alleged, had been negligently dealt with by the fire services. In the first case, the fire officer at the scene ordered the sprinkler system to be turned off before the seat of the fire had been located, with the result that the fire, which had previously been contained, spread causing considerable damage. In the second case, the fire brigade left the scene of an explosion believing all fires to have been extinguished but without having checked the plaintiff's adjoining premises; and in the third, the fire brigade attended a fire but failed to locate in time a sufficient number of water hydrants which worked. The Court of Appeal held the defendants liable in the first case but not in the others.

On the issue of proximity, Stuart-Smith LJ said:

'The peculiarity of fire brigades, together with other rescue services, such as ambulance or coastal rescue and protective services such as the police, is that they do not as a rule create the danger which causes injury to the plaintiff or loss to his property. For the most part they act in the context of a danger already created and damage already caused, whether by the forces of nature, or the acts of some third party or even of the plaintiff himself, and whether those acts are criminal, negligent or non-culpable.

But where the rescue/protective service itself by negligence creates the danger which caused the plaintiff's injury there is no doubt in our judgment the plaintiff can recover. There are many examples of this. In *Rigby v Chief Constable of Northamptonshire* the plaintiff's gun shop was at risk from a lunatic. The police came to deal with the situation; they fired a CS canister of gas into the shop, though it caused a high risk of fire, without ensuring that the fire engine which had previously been available was there to put out any fire that resulted. In *Knightley v Johns*, in the course of traffic control following an accident two police constables were instructed to take a course which involved them riding against the traffic flow round a blind bend causing a collision in which the plaintiff was injured. In *Home Office v Dorset Yacht Co Ltd* the defendant's prison officers had brought the borstal boys who had a known propensity to escape into the locality where the yachts were moored and so had created a potential situation of danger for the owners of those yachts, in which they failed to exercise proper supervision over the boys (see *Hill v Chief Constable of West Yorkshire* per Lord Keith of Kinkel). Similarly in *Alcock v Chief Constable of South Yorkshire* where the question in issue was the liability of the police to those suffering shock as a result of the Hillsborough disaster. There was never any dispute that the police were liable to the primary victims because they had created the danger by incompetent crowd control.

These are all cases, however, where a new or different danger has been created from that which the police were seeking to guard against, except perhaps in *Alcock*. A comparable situation would be if, on arrival at the scene of a fire, the fire engine was negligently driven into the owner's car parked in the street. But it seems to us that there is no difference in principle if, by some positive negligent act, the rescuer/protective service substantially increases the risk; he is thereby creating a fresh danger, albeit of the same kind or of the same nature, namely fire.'

Considering the question whether the fire service enjoys a similar 'immunity' to that found in cases involving the police, Stuart-Smith LJ said:

'Rougier J in the *London Fire Brigade* case, after citing from the speeches of Lord Keith and Lord Templeman in *Hill*'s case, set out a number of reasons why in his judgment it was not appropriate to impose a common law duty to take care on fire brigades. He said:

"I think that as regards the fire brigade, many of these considerations are applicable and militate on grounds of public policy against the imposition of any common law duty. In particular, I would single out the following. (1) I do not think that any extra standard of care would be achieved. (2) Rather the reverse; if a common law duty of care can lead to defensive policing, by the same token it can lead to defensive fire-fighting. Fearful of being accused of leaving the scene too early, the officer in charge might well commit his resources when they would have been better employed elsewhere. He would be open to criticism every time there was a balance to be struck or that sort of operational choice to be made. (3) If the efficiency of the emergency services is to be tested, it should be done not in private litigation but by an inquiry instituted by national or local authorities who are responsible to the electorate. This follows the reasoning of Lord Templeman in *Hill's* case. (4) The case of *Marc Rich & Co AG v Bishop Rock Marine Co Ltd, The Nicholas H* suggests that the fact that a defendant in the position of the fire brigade acts for the collective welfare is one that should be taken into account. (5) Last, and to my mind by far the most important consideration is what is sometimes referred to as the 'floodgates' argument."

Judge Crawford in the *West Yorkshire* case added a number of others, namely (we continue the numbering from that set out in the passage above): (6) The distraction that court cases would involve from the proper task of fire-fighting. (7) It might create massive claims which would be an unreasonable burden on the taxpayer. (8) It is for the individual to insure against fire risks.

These reasons have been subjected to considerable criticism by counsel for the plaintiffs ... In our judgment there is considerable force in the criticisms made. If we had found a sufficient relationship of proximity in the *London Fire Brigade* and *West Yorkshire* cases, we do not think that we would have found the arguments for excluding a duty of care on the grounds that it would not be just fair and reasonably convincing. The analogy with the police exercising their functions of investigating and suppressing crime is not close. The floodgates argument is not persuasive; nor is that based on insurance. Many of the other arguments are equally applicable to other public services, for example the National Health Service. We do not think that the principles which underlie those decisions where immunity has been granted can be sufficiently identified in the case of fire brigades.'

Costello v Chief Constable of the Northumbria Police
[1999] I All ER 550 Court of Appeal

The claimant, a police officer, was attacked by a prisoner in a police cell in the presence of B, a police inspector, who made no attempt to assist. The Court of Appeal held the defendant vicariously liable for B's negligence which arose from a breach of his police duty. In the circumstances B had assumed responsibility for his fellow officer.

May LJ: '... There is, in my judgment, only one point of difficulty in the present appeal ... whether, in a novel situation, it is just and reasonable to impose incrementally the duties contended for or whether as a matter of public policy no such duty should be imposed. In my view, this last difficult point must be addressed by reference to a range of decided cases relating to police officers and other public services.

[After an extensive review of the police and other rescue cases, May LJ continued.]

I now summarise relevant strands drawn from the cases. For public policy reasons, the police are under no general duty of care to members of the public for their activities in the investigation and suppression of crime (*Hill's* case). But this is not an absolute blanket immunity and circumstances may exceptionally arise when the police assume a responsibility, giving rise to a duty of care to a particular member of the public (*Hill's* case and *Swinney's* case). The public policy considerations which prevailed in *Hill's* case may not always be the only relevant public policy considerations (*Swinney's* case).

Neither the police nor other public rescue services are under any general obligation, giving rise to a duty of care, to respond to emergency calls (*Alexandrou's* case), nor, if they do respond, are they to be held liable for want of care in any attempt to prevent crime or effect a rescue. But if their own positive negligent intervention directly causes injury which would not otherwise have occurred or if it exacerbates injury or damage, there may be liability (the *Capital and Counties plc* case).

For public policy reasons, a senior police officer is not generally to be held liable to a subordinate for operational decisions taken in the heat of the moment and when resources may be inadequate to cover all possibilities (*Hughes's* case). But a senior police officer may be liable to a subordinate for positive negligent intervention which causes injury to the subordinate and for particular failure or particular instructions given in breach of specific regulations which result in injury (*Knightley v Johns*). Just as circumstances may occur in which a police officer assumes responsibility in particular circumstances to a particular member of the public not to expose the member of the public to a specific risk of injury (*Swinney's* case), so in my judgment a police officer may in particular circumstances assume a similar responsibility to another police officer. The latter part of the last sentence is, I think, the only increment in this summary which goes beyond matters decided in the authorities to which I have referred. It is not in my view in any sense a difficult incremental step to take, since for obvious reasons the relationship between individual police officers working together is likely to be closer than any relationship between the police and particular members of the public.

If a police officer tries to protect a member of the public from attack but fails to prevent injury to the member of the public, there should in my view generally be no liability in tort on the police officer for public policy reasons. This is analogous to the law relating to the fire services and quite close factually to *Alexandrou v Oxford*. If a police officer tries to protect a fellow officer from attack but fails to prevent injury to the fellow officer, there should in my view generally be no liability in tort. The relationship between the two police officers is arguably closer than the relationship between the police officer and the member of the public, but the public policy considerations are essentially the same and are compelling. One such consideration is that in the circumstances liability should not turn on, and the court should not have to inquire into, shades of personal judgment and courage in the heat of the potentially dangerous moment.

But in this case, B acknowledged his police duty to help the plaintiff. Yet he did not, on the extraordinary facts found by the judge, even try to do so. In my judgment, his acknowledged breach of police duty should also incrementally be seen as a breach of a legal duty of care. The duty is a duty to comply with a specific or acknowledged police duty where failure to do so will expose a fellow officer to unnecessary risk of injury. Although I have expressed the duty so formulated as an increment, it is the same as, or very close to, the duty which founded liability in *Knightley v Johns*. There is also a sense in which B (and perhaps the chief constable) assumed a responsibility, not absolute, for the plaintiff's safety. There is in my view in this case a strong public policy consideration to balance with those identified in *Hill's* case, that is that the law should accord with common sense and public perception. I am sure that Astill J was correct to say that the public would be greatly disturbed if the law held that there was no duty of care in this case. The particular circumstances of this case should not be left solely to internal police discipline. In addition, the public interest would be ill-served if the common law did not oblige police officers to do their personal best in situations such as these. The possibility of other sources of compensation is a relevant consideration, but not in my view more than that.

[Counsel for the defendant's] floodgates submission is no more persuasive in this case than in others where there should be a duty.

An ingredient of my conclusion is the close relationship between B and the plaintiff. They were police colleagues and he was in close attendance for the specific purpose of coming to her help if she needed help. It would not therefore follow from this analysis that I would also have found a duty of care owed by a police officer to a member of the public in otherwise similar circumstances. The balance of public policy could, depending on the circumstances, then be different.

CONCLUSION

For these reasons, I consider that, on the extraordinary facts found by the judge, B was in breach of duty in law in not trying to help the plaintiff. The chief constable is vicariously responsible for that breach, but was not personally in breach. I would dismiss the appeal.'

Comment

(1)   May LJ made reference, while considering the proposition that *Hill* gives rise to blanket immunity, to the case of *R v Dytham* in which similar facts had given rise to criminal liability for wilful neglect of duty when a police officer, present at the scene of a violent assault, had taken no steps to intervene. In the context of vicarious liability, on which the decision in *Costello* was based, a criminal act generally takes the employee outside the scope of his or her employment, see *Lister and others v Hesley Hall Ltd*, p 793. Insofar as *Costello* appears to be an exception to the general rule, it may be that a distinction is to be made between acts (which may fall inside or outside the scope of employment) and omissions which, by definition, can never amount to more than non-performance.

(2)   In *Leach v Chief Constable of Gloucestershire Constabulary*, the claimant was a woman who had, at the request of the police, acted as appropriate adult for the purposes of their interviews with the notorious Frederick West, whom they considered to be mentally disordered. Mrs L was not told anything about the suspect, nor assessed as to her suitability for such a harrowing role, nor offered support or counselling during or after the investigation. Her claim against the defendant was for psychiatric damage induced by her experiences and which had led, she alleged, to her suffering a stroke. The defendant sought to have her claims struck out, arguing that the *Hill* immunity precluded the possibility of a successful claim. The Court of Appeal, by a majority, held that the balance of public policy issues was against the claimant, except in respect of the last category. As in the case of *Swinney*, there was an overriding public interest in encouraging a pool of potential appropriate adults who might be deterred from this role were they to be wholly unprotected: however, the duty could relate only to the matter of support and counselling, since any wider scope could foreseeably hinder the police in the efficient conduct of investigations.

(3)   The application of the *Hill* and similar 'immunities' fell into question in the light of the decision of the European Court of Human Rights in *Osman v UK* (see the passage in Lord Browne-Wilkinson's speech in *Barrett v Enfield London Borough Council* on p 55) in which the ECHR had held the operation of the immunity resulted in a breach of article 6 of the European Convention for the Protection of Human Rights and Fundamental Freedoms. The Court's

analysis was much criticised and has been modified by the more recent decision of the ECHR in *Z v United Kingdom*, though in *Matthews v Ministry of Defence*, a case concerning Crown immunity, Lord Walker of Gestingthorpe observed that confusion still existed: 'The uncertain shadow of *Osman v UK* still lies over this area.'

(4)   In *Waters v Metropolitan Police Comr* the House of Lords unanimously upheld an appeal against striking out of a claim by a female police officer who alleged that the defendant had negligently failed to investigate her complaint of serious sexual assault by a colleague, and that he had allowed to continue a campaign of harassment against her. On the issue of the *Hill* policy argument, Lord Hutton said:

'If the present case goes to trial the preparation of the defence will take up much time and effort on the part of police officers, but this is a consequence faced by defendants in many actions and I do not consider that it is a consideration of sufficient potency to counterbalance the plaintiff's claim that she is entitled to have a remedy for a serious wrong. Moreover if the plaintiff succeeds at the trial in proving in whole or in substantial part the truth of her allegation that she was subjected to serious and prolonged victimisation and harassment which caused her psychiatric harm because she had made an allegation of a serious offence against a fellow officer and that the commissioner through his senior officers was guilty of negligence in failing to take adequate steps to protect her against such treatment, such proof would reveal a serious state of affairs in the Metropolitan Police. If such a state of affairs exists I consider that it is in the public interest that it should be brought to light so that steps can be taken to seek to ensure that it does not continue, because if officers (and particularly women officers who complain of a sexual offence committed against them by a male colleague) are treated as the plaintiff alleges, citizens will be discouraged from joining the police, or from continuing to serve in the police after they have joined, with consequent harm to the interests of the community. In my opinion this is a consideration which carries significant weight when placed in the scales against the argument that the continuance of the action will place unreasonable and disproportionate burdens on the police and distract them from their primary task of combating crime.'

(5)   The position of emergency services was again considered in *Kent v Griffiths*, in which the claimant, an asthmatic, suffered a respiratory arrest when the ambulance that had been called was unjustifiably delayed. The Court of Appeal upheld the judge's decision that a duty of care was owed by the ambulance service to the claimant on the facts of this particular case. While acknowledging the line of previous authority, Lord Woolf MR held that proximity was made out by the fact that the defendants had accepted the call,

thereby causing all alternative plans for transporting the claimant to hospital to be set aside. He echoed the reasoning of May LJ in *Costello* and concluded that: 'The reaction of the judge to the facts of this case accords with the likely reaction of any well-informed member of the public. In such a situation it would be regrettable indeed if there were not to be a right to compensation.'

Arthur J S Hall & Co (a firm) v Simons and other appeals
[2000] All ER (D) 1027 House of Lords

The appeals concerned three claims of negligence against solicitors. In each case the solicitors sought to rely on the immunity of advocates from suits in negligence. In all three cases it was held at first instance that the claims were unsustainable and should be struck out. On appeal the Court of Appeal reversed those decisions. The solicitors appealed, raising two fundamental general questions: (i) whether the current immunity of an advocate in respect of and relating to the conduct of legal proceedings should be maintained; and (ii) what was or should be the proper scope of the general principle barring a collateral attack in a civil action on the decision of a criminal court.

The House of Lords held unanimously that advocates should no longer enjoy immunity in respect of their conduct of civil cases, and by a four-to-three majority (Lords Hope, Hutton and Hobhouse dissenting) that the immunity should be lost in criminal cases.

Lord Steyn: '... For more than two centuries barristers have enjoyed an immunity from actions in negligence. The reasons for this immunity were various. It included the dignity of the Bar, the "cab rank" principle, the assumption that barristers may not sue for their fees, the undesirability of relitigating cases decided or settled, and the duty of a barrister to the court: Roxburgh, "*Rondel v Worsley*: The Historical Background" (1968) 84 LQR 178; and Roxburgh, "*Rondel v Worsley*: Immunity of the Bar" (1968) 84 LQR 513. In 1967 when the House decided *Rondel v Worsley* the dignity of the Bar was no longer regarded as a reason which justified conferring an immunity on advocates whilst withholding it from all other professional men. In *Hedley Byrne & Co. Ltd. v Heller & Partners Ltd* the rule was established that irrespective of contract, if someone possessed of a special skill undertakes to apply that skill for the assistance of another person who relies upon such skill, a duty of care will arise. The fact that the barrister did not enter into a contract with his solicitor or client ceased to be a ground of justification for the immunity. Nevertheless, in a unanimous decision the House in *Rondel v Worsley* upheld the ancient immunity on considerations of "public policy [which are] not immutable:" per Lord Reid. [Lord Steyn considered *Ali (Saif) v Sydney Mitchell & Co* and continued.]

It is now possible to take stock of the arguments for and against the immunity. I will examine the relevant matters in turn. First, there is the ethical "cab rank" principle.

It provides that barristers may not pick and choose their clients. It binds barristers but not solicitor advocates. It cannot therefore account for the immunity of solicitor advocates. It is a matter of judgment what weight should be placed on the "cab rank" rule as a justification for the immunity. It is a valuable professional rule. But its impact on the administration of justice in England is not great. In real life a barrister has a clerk whose enthusiasm for the unwanted brief may not be great, and he is free to raise the fee within limits. It is not likely that the rule often obliges barristers to undertake work which they would not otherwise accept. When it does occur, and vexatious claims result, it will usually be possible to dispose of such claims summarily. In any event, the "cab rank" rule cannot justify depriving all clients of a remedy for negligence causing them grievous financial loss. It is "a very high price to pay for protection from what must, in practice, be the very small risk of being subjected to vexations litigation (which is, anyway, unlikely to get very far):" Cane, [in *Tort Law and Economic Interests*, 2nd ed (1996)] at p 236. Secondly, there is the analogy of the immunities enjoyed by those who participate in court proceedings: compare however Cane's observation about the strength of the case for removing the immunity from paid expert witnesses: at p 237. Those immunities are founded on the public policy which seeks to encourage freedom of speech in court so that the court will have full information about the issues in the case. For these reasons they prevent legal actions based on what is said in court. As Pannick [*Advocates*, 1992] has pointed out this has little, if anything, to do with the alleged legal policy which requires immunity from actions for negligent acts: ibid, at p 202. If the latter immunity has merit it must rest on other grounds. Whilst this factor seemed at first to have some attractiveness, it has on analysis no or virtually no weight at all.

The third factor is the public policy against re-litigating a decision of a court of competent jurisdiction. This factor cannot support an immunity extending to cases where there was no verdict by the jury or decision by the court. It cannot arguably justify the immunity in its present width. The major question arises in regard to criminal trials which have resulted in a verdict by a jury or a decision by the court. Prosecuting counsel owes no duty of care to a defendant: *Elguzouli-Daf v Commissioner of Police of the Metropolis*. The position of defence counsel must however be considered. Unless debarred from doing so, defendants convicted after a full and fair trial who failed to appeal successfully, will from time to time attempt to challenge their convictions by suing advocates who appeared for them. This is the paradigm of an abusive challenge. It is a principal focus of the principle in *Hunter v Chief Constable of the West Midlands Police*. Public policy requires a defendant, who seeks to challenge his conviction, to do so directly by seeking to appeal his conviction. ... I have no doubt that the principle underlying the *Hunter* case must be maintained as a matter of high public policy. In the *Hunter* case the House did not, however, "lay down an inflexible rule to be applied willy-nilly to all cases which might arguably be said to be within it:" *Smith v Linskills* per Sir Thomas Bingham, M.R. (now Lord Bingham of Cornhill). It is, however, prima facie an abuse to initiate a collateral civil challenge to a criminal conviction. Ordinarily therefore a collateral civil challenge to a criminal conviction will be struck out as an abuse of process. On the other hand, if the convicted person has succeeded in having his conviction set aside on any ground, an action against a barrister in negligence will no longer be barred by the particular public policy identified in the *Hunter* case. But, in such a case the civil action in negligence against the barrister may nevertheless be struck out as unsustainable under the new flexible Civil Procedure rules, 1999; rules 3.4(2)(a) and 24.2. If the *Hunter* case is interpreted and applied in this way, the principal force of the fear of oblique challenges to criminal convictions disappears. Relying on my experience of the criminal justice system as a presiding judge on the Northern Circuit and as a member of the Court of Appeal (Criminal Division), I do not share intuitive judgments that the public policy against re-litigation still requires the immunity to be maintained in criminal cases. That leaves collateral challenges to civil decisions. The principles of *res judicata*, issue estoppel and abuse of process as understood in private law should be adequate to cope with this risk. It would not ordinarily be necessary to rely on the *Hunter* principle in the civil context but I would accept that the policy underlying it should still stand guard against unforeseen gaps. In my judgment a barrister's immunity is not needed to deal with collateral attacks on criminal and civil decisions. The public interest is satisfactorily protected by independent principles and powers of the court.

The critical factor is, however, the duty of a barrister to the court. It also applies to every person who exercises rights of audience before any court, or who exercises rights to conduct litigation before a court: see ss 27(2A) and 28(2A) of the Courts and Legal Services Act 1990 as inserted by section 42 of the Access to Justice Act 1999. It is essential that nothing should be done which might undermine the overriding duty of an advocate to the court. The question is however whether the immunity is needed to ensure that barristers will respect their duty to the court. The view of the House in 1967 was that assertions of negligence would tend to erode this duty. In the world of today there are substantial grounds for questioning this ground of public policy. In 1967 the House considered that for reasons of public policy barristers must be accorded a special status. Nowadays a comparison with other professionals is important. Thus doctors have duties not only to their patients but also to an ethical code. Doctors are sometimes faced with a tension between these duties. ... Such decisions may easily be as difficult as those facing barristers. And nobody argues that doctors should have an immunity from suits in negligence.

Comparative experience may throw some light on the question whether in the public interest such an immunity of advocates is truly necessary. In 1967 no comparative material was placed before the House. Lord Reid did, however, mention other countries where public policy points in a different direction. In the present case we have had the benefit of a substantial comparative review. ... It is a matter of significance that the High Court of Australia and the Court of Appeal of New Zealand came to the conclusion that a barristers immunity from actions in negligence is required by public policy considerations in those countries. On the other hand, in countries in the European Union advocates have no immunity. ... In the United States prosecutors have an immunity. In a few states the immunity is extended to public defenders. But otherwise lawyers have no immunity from suits of negligence by their clients. ... In Canada trial lawyers owe a duty to the court. After a detailed and careful review the court found there was no evidence that the work of Canadian courts was hampered in any way by counsel's fear of civil liability. ... I regard the Canadian empirically tested experience as the most relevant. It tends to demonstrate that the fears that the possibility of actions in negligence against barristers would tend to undermine the public interest are unnecessarily pessimistic.

There would be benefits to be gained from the ending of immunity. First, and most importantly, it will bring to an end an anomalous exception to the basic premise that there should be a remedy for a wrong. There is no reason to fear a flood of negligence suits against barristers. The mere doing of his duty to the court by the advocate to the detriment of his client could never be called negligent. Indeed if the advocate's conduct was bona fide dictated by his perception of his duty to the court there would be no possibility of the court holding him to be negligent. Moreover, when such claims are made courts will take into account the difficult decisions faced daily by barristers working in demanding situations to tight timetables. In this context the observations of Sir Thomas Bingham MR (now Lord Bingham of Cornhill) in *Ridehalgh v Horsefield* are instructive. Dealing with the circumstances in which a wasted costs order against a barrister might be appropriate he observed:

> "Any judge who is invited to make or contemplates making an order arising out of an advocate's conduct of court proceedings must make full allowance for the fact that an advocate in court, like a commander in battle, often has to make decisions quickly and under pressure, in the fog of war and ignorant of developments on the other side of the hill. Mistakes will inevitably be made, things done which the outcome shows to have been unwise. But advocacy is more an art than a science. It cannot be conducted according to formulae. Individuals differ in their style and approach. It is only when, with all allowances made, an advocate's conduct of court proceedings is quite plainly unjustifiable that it can be appropriate to make a wasted costs order against him."

For broadly similar reasons it will not be easy to establish negligence against a barrister. The courts can be trusted to differentiate between errors of judgment and true negligence. In any event, a plaintiff who claims that poor advocacy resulted in an unfavourable outcome will face the very great obstacle of showing that a better standard of advocacy would have resulted in a more favourable outcome. Unmeritorious claims against barristers will be struck out. The new Civil Procedure Rules, 1999, have made it easier to dispose summarily of such claims: rules 3.4(2)(a) and 24.2. The only argument that remains is that the fear of unfounded actions might have a negative effect on the conduct of advocates. This is a most flimsy foundation, unsupported by empirical evidence, for the immunity. Secondly, it must be borne in mind that one of the functions of tort law is to set external standards of behaviour for the benefit of the public. And it would be right to say that while standards at the Bar are generally high, in some respects there is room for improvement. An exposure of isolated acts of incompetence at the Bar will strengthen rather than weaken the legal system. Thirdly, and most importantly, public confidence in the legal system is not enhanced by the existence of the immunity. The appearance is created that the law singles out its own for protection no matter how flagrant the breach of the barrister. The world has changed since 1967. The practice of law has become more commercialised: barristers may now advertise. They may now enter into contracts for legal services with their professional clients. They are now obliged to carry insurance. On the other hand, today we live in a consumerist society in which people have a much greater awareness of their rights. If they have suffered a wrong as a result of the provision of negligent professional services, they expect to have the right to claim redress. It tends to erode confidence in the legal system if advocates, alone among professional men, are immune from liability for negligence. ...

My Lords, one is intensely aware that *Rondel v Worsley* was a carefully reasoned and unanimous decision of the House. On the other hand, it is now clear that when the balance is struck between competing factors it is no longer in the public interest that the immunity in favour of barristers should remain. I am far from saying that *Rondel v Worsley* was wrongly decided. But on the information now available and developments since *Rondel v Worsley* I am satisfied that in today's world that decision no longer correctly reflects public policy. The basis of the immunity of barristers has gone. And exactly the same reasoning applies to solicitor advocates. There are differences between the two branches of the profession but not of a character to differentiate materially between them in respect of the issue before the House. I would treat them in the same way.

That brings me to the argument that the ending of the immunity, if it is to be undertaken, is a matter for Parliament. This argument is founded on section 62 of the Courts and Legal Services Act 1990. ... The background to this provision is, of course, the judicially created immunity of barristers, which in 1967 was held by the House to be founded on public policy. And it will be recollected that Lord Reid observed that public policy is not immutable. Against this background the meaning of section 62 is clear. It provides that solicitor advocates will have the same immunity as barristers have. In other words, the immunity of solicitors will follow the fortunes of the immunity of barristers, or track it. Section 62 did not either expressly or by implication give Parliamentary endorsement to the immunity of barristers. In these circumstances the argument that it is beyond the power of the House of Lords, which created the immunity spelt out in *Rondel v Worsley*, to reverse that decision in changed circumstances involving a different balance of policy considerations is not right. Should the House as a matter of discretion leave it to Parliament? This issue is more finely balanced. It would certainly be the easy route for the House to say "let us leave it to Parliament." On balance my view is that it would be an abdication of our responsibilities with the unfortunate consequence of plunging both branches of the legal profession in England into a state of uncertainty over a prolonged period. That would be a disservice to the public interest. On the other hand, if the decision is made to end the immunity now, both branches of the profession will know where they stand. They ought to find it relatively easy to amend their rules where necessary and to adjust their already existing insurance arrangements insofar as that may be necessary.

My Lords, the cards are now heavily stacked against maintaining the immunity of advocates. I would rule that there is no longer any such immunity in criminal and civil cases. In doing so I am quite confident that the legal profession does not need the immunity.'

Comment

(1)   Prior to this decision, the effect of pure policy considerations was to deprive a claimant of a remedy even though all of the other factors required for the existence of a duty are present.

(2)   In *Welsh v Chief Constable of Merseyside* the court held that the same policy considerations might apply to the Crown Prosecution Service in relation to its conduct of a case in court but not in relation to its 'general administrative responsibility or practice as prosecutor to keep the court informed as to the state of an adjourned criminal case'. In that case the plaintiff succeeded in a claim for damages against the Service when he was held in custody after failing to answer to his bail in the magistrates' court in relation to certain offences which had already been taken into account by the Crown Court in another case against him. More recently, in *Elguzouili-Daf v Metropolitan Police Comr*, the Court of Appeal held that the CPS is immune from liability in negligence. In that case the CPS had failed to ensure the prompt release from custody of a prisoner once it was clear that evidence existed which exonerated him. The court distinguished *Welsh* on the basis that its facts involved the assumption of responsibility by the CPS, a factor which was not present in *Elguzouili-Daf*. It is to be anticipated that these immunities, too, will be reviewed in light of the *Arthur J S Hall* decision, and of the general current trend for the boundaries of immunity to be receding.

(3)   A useful review of a number of different aspects of public policy is to be found in *Spring v Guardian Assurance plc* (see p 25) in which Lord Woolf, deciding whether a duty is owed by an employer to an employee in relation to the provision of a reference, stated:

'... It would alter the situation, if it would be contrary to some identifiable principle of public policy for there to be a liability for negligence imposed on the giver of a negligent reference. If there were to be such a principle it would be an unusual one since, unless *Hedley Byrne & Co Ltd v Heller & Partners Ltd* was wrongly decided, it would apparently apply to the negligent provider of a bad but not a good reference ...

It is obviously in accord with public policy that references should be full and frank. It is also in accord with public policy that they should not be based upon careless investigations. In the case of references for positions of responsibility this is particularly important ... It has also to be accepted that some referees may be more timid in giving full and frank references if they feel there is a risk of their being found liable for negligence. However, there is already such a possible liability in respect of a negligently favourable reference, so all that needs to be considered is the possible adverse consequences of a negligently unfavourable reference. For reasons to which I have already referred I consider there is little practical likelihood of no reference at all being given nowadays ...

However, the real issue is not whether there would be any adverse effect on the giving of references. Rather the issue is whether the adverse effects, when balanced against the benefits which would flow from giving the subject a right of action, sufficiently outweigh the benefits to justify depriving the subject of a remedy unless he can establish malice. In considering this issue it is necessary to take into account contemporary practices in the field of employment: the fact that nowadays most employment is conditional upon a reference being provided. There are also the restrictions on unfair dismissal which mean that an employee is ordinarily not capable of being dismissed except after being told of what is alleged against him and after he has been given an opportunity of giving an explanation. There is also the widespread practice, especially in the Civil Service, of having annual reports which the subject is entitled to see – which practice, apparently even in an ongoing employment situation, is not defeated by any lack of candour. There is now an openness in employment relationships which did not exist even a few years ago. There is also the advantage, already referred to, of it being appreciated that you cannot give a reference which could cause immense harm to its subject without exercising reasonable care.

A further consideration mentioned by Cooke P in *Bell-Booth Group Ltd v A-G* is the undesirability of infringing freedom of speech. This is a consideration as least as important to the common law as it is under the international conventions by which it is also protected. Here it is necessary to bear in mind that, as is the case with all fundamental freedoms, the protection is qualified and not absolute. Freedom of speech does not necessarily entitle the speaker to make a statement without exercising reasonable care. Freedom of speech has to be balanced against the equally well recognised freedom both at common law and under the conventions that an individual should not be deprived of the opportunity of earning his livelihood in his chosen occupation. A development of the law which does no more than protect an employee from being deprived of employment as a result of a negligent reference would fully justify any limited intrusion on freedom of speech.

When I weigh these considerations I find that public policy comes down firmly in favour of not depriving an employee of a remedy to recover the damages to which he would otherwise be entitled as a result of being a victim of a negligent reference.

Under this head there remains to be considered whether it is preferable for the law in this area to be developed by Parliament or by the courts. It is an area of law where previous decisions of the courts have already clearly identified the tests which should be applied in deciding whether the law should be developed. It is also an area where a case-by-case approach is particularly appropriate and so as happened in *Hedley Byrne & Co Ltd v Heller & Partners Ltd* it appears to me desirable for the courts to provide the remedy which I believe is clearly required.'

In the same case, a cautionary note was sounded by Lord Lowry who believed that:

'... the courts in general and [the House of Lords] in particular ought to think very carefully before resorting to public policy considerations which will defeat a claim which ex hypothesi is a perfectly good cause of action ... public policy should be invoked only in the clear cases in which the potential harm to the public is incontestable ... public policy ought not to be invoked if the arguments are evenly balanced: in such a situation the ordinary rule of law, once established, should prevail'.

See also Lord Denning, quoting, in *Enderby Town Football Club v Football Association*, Hobart CJ's comment that 'Public policy is an unruly horse'.

Rowling and another v Takaro Properties Ltd
[1988] 1 All ER 163 Privy Council

The respondent company needed additional finance and entered negotiations with a Japanese company. The Minister of Finance, acting in accordance with his own construction of certain regulations under a banking Act, refused the necessary consent and the deal eventually fell through. The respondents claimed that the minister's erroneous construction of the statute and his failure to seek legal advice amounted to negligence. The Privy Council held that even if a duty was owed by the minister he was not in breach of it.

Lord Keith of Kinkel:'... For reasons which will appear, their Lordships do not find it necessary to reach any final conclusion on the question of the existence, or (if it exists) the scope, of the duty of care resting on a minister in a case such as the present; and they have come to the conclusion that it would not be right for them to do so, because the matter was not fully exposed before them in argument. In particular, no reference was made in argument to the extensive academic literature on the subject of the liability of public authorities in negligence, study of which can be of such great assistance to the courts in considering areas of the law which, as in the case of negligence, are in a continuing state of development. Even so, such is the importance of the present case, especially in New Zealand, that their Lordships feel that it would be inappropriate, and perhaps be felt to be discourteous, if they were to make no reference to the relevant considerations affecting the decision whether a duty of care should arise in a case such as the present.

Quilliam J considered the question with particular reference to the distinction between policy (or planning) decisions and operational decisions. His conclusion was expressed as follows:

> "The distinction between the policy and the operational areas can be both fine and confusing. Various expressions have been used instead of operational, e.g. 'administrative' or 'business powers'. It may not be easy to attach any of these labels to the decision of the Minister in this case, but what appears to me to emerge clearly enough is that for the reasons I have indicated his decision was the antithesis of policy or discretion. I therefore equate it with having been operational. The result of that conclusion is that I consider the *prima facie* existence of a duty of care has been established."

Their Lordships feel considerable sympathy with Quilliam J's difficulty in solving the problem by simple reference to this distinction. They are well aware of the references in the literature to this distinction (which appears to have originated in the United States of America) and of the critical analysis to which it has been subjected. They incline to the opinion, expressed in the literature, that this distinction does not provide a touchstone of liability, but rather is expressive of the need to exclude altogether those cases in which the decision under attack is of such a kind that a question whether it has been made negligently is unsuitable for judicial resolution, of which notable examples are discretionary decisions on the allocation of scarce resources or the distribution of risks (see especially the discussion in Craig, *Administrative Law* (1983)). If this is right, classification of the relevant decision as a policy or planning decision in this sense may exclude liability; but a conclusion that it does not fall within that category does not, in their Lordships' opinion, mean that a duty of care will necessarily exist.

It is at this stage that it is necessary, before concluding that a duty of care should be imposed, to consider all the relevant circumstances. One of the considerations underlying certain recent decisions of the House of Lords (*Governors of the Peabody Donation Fund v Sir Lindsay Parkinson & Co Ltd*) and of the Privy Council (*Yuen*

Kun-yeu v A-G of Hong Kong) is the fear that a too literal application of the well-known observation of Lord Wilberforce in *Anns v Merton London Borough* may be productive of a failure to have regard to, and to analyse and weigh, all the relevant considerations in considering whether it is appropriate that a duty of care should be imposed. Their Lordships consider that question to be of an intensely pragmatic character, well suited for gradual development but requiring most careful analysis. It is one on which all common law jurisdictions can learn much from each other, because, apart from exceptional cases, no sensible distinction can be drawn in this respect between the various countries and the social conditions existing in them. It is incumbent on the courts in different jurisdictions to be sensitive to each other's reactions; but what they are all searching for in others, and each of them is striving to achieve, is a careful analysis and weighing of the relevant competing considerations.

It is in this spirit that a case such as the present has, in their Lordships' opinion, to be approached. They recognise that the decision of the minister is capable of being described as having been of a policy rather than an operational character; but, if the function of the policy/operational dichotomy is as they have already described it, the allegation of negligence in the present case is not, they consider, of itself of such a character as to render the case unsuitable for judicial decision. Be that as it may, there are certain considerations which militate against imposition of liability in a case such as the present.

Their Lordships wish to refer in particular to certain matters which they consider to be of importance. The first is that the only effect of a negligent decision, such as is here alleged to have been made, is delay. This is because the processes of judicial review are available to the aggrieved party; and, assuming that the alleged error of law is so serious that it can properly be described as negligent, the decision will assuredly be quashed by a process which, in New Zealand as in the United Kingdom, will normally be carried out with promptitude.

The second is that, in the nature of things, it is likely to be very rare indeed that an error of law of this kind by a minister or other public authority can properly be categorised as negligent. As is well known, anybody, even a judge, can be capable of misconstruing a statute; and such misconstruction, when it occurs, can be severely criticised without attracting the epithet "negligent". Obviously, this simple fact points rather to the extreme unlikelihood of a breach of duty being established in these cases, a point to which their Lordships will return; but it is nevertheless a relevant factor to be taken into account when considering whether liability in negligence should properly be imposed.

The third is the danger of overkill. It is to be hoped that, as a general rule, imposition of liability in negligence will lead to a higher standard of care in the performance of the relevant type of act; but sometimes not only may this not be so, but the imposition of liability may even lead to harmful consequences. In other words, the cure may be worse than the disease. There are reasons for believing that this may be so in cases where liability is imposed on local authorities whose building inspectors have been negligent in relation to the inspection of foundations, as in the *Anns* case itself, because there is a danger that the building inspectors of some local authorities may react to that decision by simply increasing, unnecessarily, the requisite depth of foundations, thereby imposing a very substantial and unnecessary financial burden on members of the community. A comparable danger may exist in cases such as the present, because, once it became known that liability in negligence may be imposed on the ground that a minister has misconstrued a statute and so acted ultra vires, the cautious civil servant may go to extreme lengths in ensuring that legal advice, or even the opinion of the court, is obtained before decisions are taken, thereby leading to unnecessary delay in a considerable number of cases.

Fourth, it is very difficult to identify any particular case in which it can properly be said that a minister is under a duty to seek legal advice. It cannot, their Lordships consider, reasonably be said that a minister is under a duty to seek legal advice in every case in which he is called on to exercise a discretionary power conferred on him by legislation; and their Lordships find it difficult to see how cases in which a duty to seek legal advice should be imposed should be segregated from those in which it should not ... Again, it is not to be forgotten that the minister, in exercising his statutory discretion, is acting essentially as a guardian of the public interest ... for the protection of the community as a whole. Furthermore, he is, so far as their Lordships are aware, normally under no duty to exercise his discretion within any particular time ...

No doubt there may be possible answers to some of these points, taken individually. But, if the matter is looked at as a whole, it cannot be said to be free from difficulty. Indeed their Lordships share the opinion expressed by Richmond P in *Rowling v Takaro Properties Ltd* that the whole subject is of the greatest importance and difficulty ... Doubtless it was considerations such as those to which their Lordships have already referred that led Lord Diplock in *Dunlop v Woollahra Municipal Council* to express doubts whether a duty of care can exist in such circumstances. In particular, it is being suggested that liability in negligence should be imposed in cases such as the present, when the effect of any such imposition of liability will on the one hand lead to recovery only in very rare cases and then only for the consequences of delay, which should not be long, and may, on the other hand, lead to considerable delay occurring in a greater number of cases, for which there can be no redress. In all the circumstances, it must be a serious question for consideration whether it would be appropriate to impose liability in negligence in these cases, or whether it would not rather be in the public interest that citizens should be confined to their remedy, as at present, in those cases where the minister or public authority has acted in bad faith.'

Comment

The Privy Council did not reject entirely the distinction between operational and policy decisions although commented that such a classification is not always clear. It seems that the distinction may be of use in eliminating the existence of a duty in relation to policy decisions while the existence of a duty in relation to other activities remains to be determined from all the circumstances. This approach was followed by Browne-Wilkinson V-C in *Lonrho plc v Tebbit*.

X and others (minors) v Bedfordshire County Council; and other appeals
[1995] 3 All ER 353 House of Lords

The court was asked to decide, *inter alia*, whether children who had suffered harm as a result of the careless performance (or non-performance) by a local authority of statutory duties in respect of children's welfare or education were owed a duty of care in negligence.

Lord Browne-Wilkinson: '...

(2) DISCRETION, JUSTICIABILITY AND THE POLICY/OPERATIONAL TEST

(a) Discretion

... [I]n seeking to establish that a local authority is liable at common law for negligence in the exercise of a discretion conferred by statute, the first requirement is to show that the decision was outside the ambit of the discretion altogether: if it was not, a local authority cannot itself be in breach of any duty of care owed to the plaintiff.

In deciding whether or not this requirement is satisfied, the court has to assess the relevant factors taken into account by the authority in exercising the discretion. Since what are under consideration are discretionary powers conferred on public bodies for public purposes the relevant factors will often include policy matters, for example social policy, the allocation of finite financial resources between the different calls made upon them or (as in the *Dorset Yacht* case) the balance between pursuing desirable social aims as against the risk to the public inherent in so doing. It is established that the courts cannot enter upon the assessment of such "policy" matters. The difficulty is to identify in any particular case whether or not the decision in question is a "policy" decision.

(b) Justiciability and the policy/operational dichotomy

In English law the first attempt to lay down the principles applicable in deciding whether or not a decision was one of policy was made by Lord Wilberforce in *Anns v Merton London Borough*:

> "Most, indeed probably all, statutes relating to public authorities or public bodies, contain in them a large area of policy. The courts call this 'discretion', meaning that the decision is one for the authority or body to make, and not for the courts. Many statutes, also, prescribe or at least pre-suppose the practical execution of policy decisions: a convenient description of this is to say that in addition to the area of policy or discretion, there is an operational area. Although this distinction between the policy area and the operational area is convenient, and illuminating, it is probably a distinction of degree; many 'operational' powers or duties have in them some element of 'discretion'. It can safely be said that the more 'operational' a power or duty may be, the easier it is to superimpose on it a common law duty of care."

As Lord Wilberforce appreciated, this approach did not provide a hard and fast test as to those matters which were open to the court's decision. In *Rowling v Takaro Properties Ltd* the Privy Council reverted to the problem. In that case the trial judge had found difficulty in applying the policy/operational test, but having classified the decision in question as being operational, took the view that as a result there was a common law duty of care. Commenting on the judge's view, Lord Keith of Kinkel said:

> "Their Lordships feel considerable sympathy with Quilliam J's difficulty in solving the problem by reference to this distinction. They are well aware of the references in the literature to this distinction (which appears to have originated in the United States of America) and of the critical analysis to which it has been subjected. They incline to the opinion, expressed in the literature, that this distinction does not provide a touchstone of liability, but rather is expressive of the need to exclude altogether those cases in which the decision under attack is of such a kind that a question whether it has been made negligently is unsuitable for judicial resolution, of which notable examples are discretionary decisions on the allocation of scarce resources or the distribution of risks (see especially the discussion in Craig *Administrative Law* (1983) pp. 534–538). If this is right, classification of the relevant decision as a policy or planning decision in this sense may exclude liability; but a conclusion that it does not fall within that category does not, in their Lordships' opinion, mean that a duty of care will *necessarily* exist." (My emphasis.)

From these authorities I understand the applicable principles to be as follows. Where Parliament has conferred a statutory discretion on a public authority, it is for that authority, not for the courts, to exercise the discretion: nothing which the authority does within the ambit of the discretion can be actionable at common law. If the decision complained of falls outside the statutory discretion, it *can* (but not necessarily will) give rise to common law liability. However, if the factors relevant to the exercise of the discretion include matters of policy, the court cannot adjudicate on such policy matters and therefore cannot reach the conclusion that the decision was outside the ambit of the statutory discretion. Therefore a common law duty of care in relation to the taking of decisions involving policy matters cannot exist.

(3) IF JUSTICIABLE, THE ORDINARY PRINCIPLES OF NEGLIGENCE APPLY

If the plaintiff's complaint alleges carelessness, not in the taking of a discretionary decision to do some act, but in the practical manner in which that act has been performed (e.g. the running of a school) the question whether or not there is a common law duty of care falls to be decided by applying the usual principles, i.e. those laid down in *Caparo Industries plc v Dickman*. Was the damage to the plaintiff reasonably foreseeable? Was the relationship between the plaintiff and the defendant sufficiently proximate? Is it just and reasonable to impose a duty of care? See *Rowling v Takaro Properties Ltd* and *Hill v Chief Constable of West Yorkshire*.

However, the question whether there is such a common law duty and if so its ambit, must be profoundly influenced by the statutory framework within which the acts complained of were done. The position is directly analogous to that in which a tortious duty of care owed by A to C can arise out of the performance by A of a contract between A and B. In *Henderson v Merrett Syndicates Ltd* your Lordships held that A (the managing agent) who had contracted with B (the members' agent) to render certain services for C (the names) came under a duty of care to C in the performance of those services. It is clear that any tortious duty of care owed to C in those circumstances could not be inconsistent with the duty owed in contract by A to B. Similarly, in my judgment, a common law duty of care cannot be imposed on a statutory duty if the observance of such common law duty of care would be inconsistent with, or have a tendency to discourage, the due performance by the local authority of its statutory duties.'

Comment

(1) For further extracts of these cases, in relation to claims for breach of statutory duty, see p 449.

(2) In *Stovin v Wise*, the defendant W emerged from a junction in her car and, owing to her view being obscured by a large earth bank, struck S's motor cycle and injured him. W joined the highway authority as third party claiming that it was in breach of its duty to highway users to remove dangers which impaired visibility. The Court of Appeal had dismissed the authority's appeal, on the ground that it knew of the danger and had taken a decision to carry out

remedial work, so its failure – unreasonable delay – was an operational matter. The House of Lords, by a majority of three to two, held that the authority's common law duty should be read in the light of the policy behind the statute which conferred a power to carry out such works, and would only arise, if at all, when an authority acted irrationally. Moreover, where the policy behind the Act created no right to compensation (as in this case) it would not be appropriate for the court to create such a right at common law.

Lord Hoffmann felt that the imposition of a duty on local authorities could only be detrimental to the overall role they perform, without any justification in terms of benefit to individuals:

'In my view the creation of a duty of care upon a highway authority, even on grounds of irrationality in failing to exercise a power, would inevitably expose the authority's budgetary decisions to judicial inquiry. This would distort the priorities of local authorities, which would be bound to try to play safe by increasing their spending on road improvements rather than risk enormous liabilities for personal injury accidents. They will spend less on education or social services. I think that it is important, before extending the duty of care owed by public authorities, to consider the cost to the community of the defensive measures which they are likely to take in order to avoid liability ... On the other hand, denial of liability does not leave the road user unprotected. Drivers of vehicles must take the highway network as they find it. Everyone knows that there are hazardous bends, intersections and junctions. It is primarily the duty of drivers of vehicles to take due care. And if, as in the case of W, they do not, there is compulsory insurance to provide compensation to the victims.'

Stovin was distinguished in *Kane v New Forest District Council*, in which the Court of Appeal held (a) that it was far from clear that a planning authority enjoyed immunity in relation to a foreseeably dangerous footpath; and (b) the authority was not free to stand idly by while a hazard it had created remained unremedied.

Barrett v Enfield London Borough Council
[1999] 3 All ER 193 House of Lords

The claimant, B, had been in the care of the defendant local authority from the age of ten months until he was 17 years old. He claimed damages for personal injury, alleging that the authority had negligently failed to make adequate arrangements to provide him with a stable family environment, or to provide adequate psychiatric support, or to make proper arrangements for reuniting him with his mother. As a result of these failures, he alleged, he was left with various psychiatric problems, including a propensity for self-harm. The House of Lords reversed the Court of Appeal's decision to uphold the defendant's application to strike out the plaintiff's claim.

Lord Browne-Wilkinson: '... I find it impossible to say that all careless acts or omissions of a local authority in relation to a child in its care are not actionable: indeed I do not read the Court of Appeal so to have held. If certain careless conduct (operational) of a local authority is actionable and certain conduct (policy) is not, it becomes necessary to divide the decisions of the local authority between those which are "policy" and those which are "operational". It is far from clear what the expressions "operational" and "policy" connote. Therefore unless it can be said (as did the Court of Appeal) that operational carelessness could not have caused the damage alleged in the present case it would be impossible to strike out any part of the claim. But causation is quintessentially a matter of fact and one would have thought that where there is a substantial doubt as to what is an operational decision there must equally be doubt as to the extent or nature of the damage capable of being caused by negligence in making such an operational decision.

Moreover, there have been two developments since the conclusion of the argument in the present case, both of which have been drawn to our attention by the parties. For reasons which I will seek to demonstrate, they both emphasise the extreme care which must be taken in striking out claims in this confused and developing area of the law, and clearly reinforce the conclusion that the case cannot be struck out.

Striking out

In my speech in *X and others (minors) v Bedfordshire CC*, with which the other members of the House agreed, I pointed out that unless it was possible to give a *certain* answer to the question whether the plaintiff's claim would succeed, the case was inappropriate for striking out. I further said that in an area of the law which was uncertain and developing (such as the circumstances in which a person can be held liable in negligence for the exercise of a statutory duty or power) it is not normally appropriate to strike out. In my judgment it is of great importance that such development should be on the basis of actual facts found at trial not on hypothetical facts assumed (possibly wrongly) to be true for the purpose of the strike out.

This latter point is graphically illustrated by the decision of the Court of Appeal in *Phelps v Hillingdon London BC*. In that case, the plaintiff was claiming damages for the negligent failure of an educational psychologist employed by a local authority to identify that the plaintiff was dyslexic. The case went to trial and all relevant findings of fact made. The judge had held for the plaintiff, relying to a substantial extent on *dicta* of mine in *X and others (minors) v Bedfordshire CC* to the effect that where a local authority provides a psychology service such authority could be liable in damages for failure of the service to diagnose dyslexia. As the Court of Appeal rightly held in *Phelps's* case those remarks were based on the mistaken assumption that such psychology service would be a service open to the public in the same way as a hospital is open for the purpose of treating the child as the patient of the service. In fact the evidence at the trial had demonstrated that the arrangements in that case were of a different nature: the psychology service was established to advise the local authority as to the performance of its functions as educational authority: the child was no more the patient of the psychology service in that case than was the psychiatrist in the abuse cases who is advising the local authority as to its duties not the child: see *X and others (minors) v Bedfordshire CC.*

This erroneous *dictum* of mine made in the course of seeking to determine a striking out application on hypothetical facts has apparently given rise to "a proliferation of claims" against psychology services provided by local authorities in dealing with those suffering from reading disability. It vividly illustrates how important it is to decide these cases on actual facts and not on mistaken hypotheticals.

EUROPEAN CONVENTION ON HUMAN RIGHTS, ART 6

In *Osman v UK* the European Court of Human Rights upheld a claim by the Osmans that their rights under art 6 of the European Convention for the Protection of Human Rights and Fundamental Freedoms (Rome, 4 November 1950; TS 71 (1953); Cmd 8969) (the convention) had been infringed. They had sought to bring proceedings in the United Kingdom against the police alleging negligence in the prevention and pursuit of crime. Those proceedings were struck out by the Court of Appeal applying the decision of this House in *Hill v Chief Constable of West Yorkshire*: see *Osman v Ferguson.*

I confess that I find the decision of the Strasbourg court extremely difficult to understand. Article 6(1) of the convention provides: "In the determination of his civil rights and obligations ... everyone is entitled to a fair and public hearing ..." At first sight this would seem to require that the applicant has, under the local law, a right (right A) enforceable in the local court. Under art 6 he is given as a separate right (right B) a right of access to the local courts to assert right A being a separate, free standing right. Thus one would assume that right A would consist of, for example, a contractual right or a tortious right not to be negligently injured. If a person is prevented from enforcing those rights that is not an infringement of right A but an infringement of right B, i.e. the right of access to the court. However, that is apparently not how the European Court of Human Rights construes art 6. In their judgment the court said:

"139.   On that understanding the court considers that the applicants must be taken to have had a right, derived from the law of negligence, to seek an adjudication on the admissibility and merits of an arguable claim that they were in a relationship of proximity to the police, that the harm caused was foreseeable and that in the circumstances it was fair, just and reasonable not to apply the exclusionary rule outlined in *Hill v Chief Constable of West Yorkshire*. In the view of the court the assertion of that right by the applicants is in itself sufficient to ensure the applicability of art 6(1) of the convention.

140.   For the above reasons, the court concludes that art 6(1) is applicable. It remains to be determined whether the restriction which was imposed on the exercise of the applicants' right under that provision was lawful."

This passage seems to treat the Osmans as having a right under English law to go to court for a declaration that, apart from the public policy preventing suits against the police, they would have had a claim in negligence against the police and further, that it was not fair, just and reasonable in the circumstances of that case to apply the "exclusionary rule", i.e. the rule excluding negligence actions against the police.

Having so defined the ambit of art 6, the Strasbourg court held that there was in *Osman's* case a breach of such right of access to the English court, such breach lying in the application of a blanket exclusionary rule which excludes all claims against the police for negligent failure to investigate or protect from crime. In the view of the Strasbourg court, apparently, the applicability of such exclusionary rule has to be decided afresh in each individual case. If this is not done then it is impossible to determine whether the public interest in an efficient police force is or is not proportionate to the seriousness of the harm suffered by the plaintiff in the individual case. On these grounds, the Strasbourg court held that the English court had breached art 6 by striking out the claim made by the Osmans against the police without hearing any evidence by reference to which the proportionality of the rule in that particular case could be judged. The court said that the police had been granted a "blanket immunity" which was disproportionate and therefore an unjustifiable restriction on the Osmans' right of access to the court. The Osmans were entitled to have their case against the police determined in deserving cases. The problems in applying this reasoning to the English law of negligence are many and various. For example, the correct answer to the following points is not immediately apparent. (1) Although the word "immunity" is sometimes incorrectly used, a holding that it is not fair, just and reasonable to hold liable a particular class of defendants whether generally or in relation to a particular type of activity is not to give immunity from a liability to which the rest of the world is subject. It is a prerequisite to there being any liability in negligence at all that as a matter of policy it is fair, just and reasonable in those circumstances to impose liability in negligence. (2) In a wide range of cases public policy has led to the decision that the imposition of liability would not be fair and reasonable in the circumstances, e.g. some activities of financial regulators, building inspectors, ship surveyors, social workers dealing with sex abuse cases. In all these cases and many others the view has been taken that the proper performance of the defendant's primary functions for the benefit of society as a whole will be inhibited if they are required to look over their shoulder to avoid liability in negligence. In English law the decision as to whether it is fair, just and reasonable to impose a liability in negligence on a particular class of would-be defendants depends on weighing in the balance the total detriment to the public interest in all cases from holding such class liable in negligence as against the total loss to all would-be plaintiffs if they are not to have a cause of action in respect of the loss they have individually suffered. (3) In English law, questions of public policy and the question whether it is fair and reasonable to impose liability in negligence are decided as questions of law. Once the decision is taken that, say, company auditors though liable to shareholders for negligent auditing are not liable to those proposing to invest in the company (see *Caparo Industries plc v Dickman*), that decision will apply to all future cases of the same kind. The decision does not depend on weighing the balance between the extent of the damage to the plaintiff and the damage to the public in each particular case.

In view of the decision in *Osman's* case it is now difficult to foretell what would be the result in the present case if we were to uphold the striking out order. It seems to me that it is at least probable that the matter would then be taken to Strasbourg. That court, applying its decision in *Osman's* case if it considers it to be correct, would say that we had deprived the plaintiff of his right to have the balance struck between the hardship suffered by him and the damage to be done to the public interest in the present case if an order were to be made against the defendant council. In the present very unsatisfactory state of affairs, and bearing in mind that under the Human Rights Act 1998 art 6 will shortly become part of English law, in such cases as these it is difficult to say that it is a clear and obvious case calling for striking out. (See also *Markesinis and Deakin on Torts* (4th edn, 1999) p 145ff.)

For these reasons in my judgment this action should proceed to trial and when all the facts are known the difficult issues of law which arise may be confronted in the light of the real, as opposed to hypothetical, facts. In the meantime one can only hope that the law applicable under art 6 is further interpreted.'

Lord Hutton:' ... The Court of Appeal also held that the plaintiff's action should be struck out on the separate and distinct ground that it would not be just and reasonable to impose a duty of care on the defendant. Lord Woolf MR observed that in the present case the defendant was regarded as being in the position of a parent to the plaintiff. He said:

> "The very fact that the defendant is stated to have been in the position of a parent to the plaintiff at the material time brings home the public policy aspects of the situation. Decisions of this nature often require a difficult and delicate balancing of conflicting interests. If a parent when driving a car injures his child who is a passenger, then of course, as is the case with any other driver, there is no reason why he should not be liable for damages. However, parents are daily making decisions with regard to their children's future and it seems to me that it would be wholly inappropriate that those

decisions, even if they could be shown to be wrong should be ones which give rise to a liability for damages. (This point was not argued in *S v W* (*child abuse: damages*) and this court in that case was solely concerned with the limitation point.) If the decisions are taken by the local authority in place of the parents the position should be the same. The relationship of the parent and the local authority to the child in their care is different from that which exists between a school's staff and its pupils where the staff are providing educational services for the pupils."

My Lords, I agree that it would be wholly inappropriate that a child should be permitted to sue his parents for decisions made by them in respect of his upbringing which could be shown to be wrong, and I also agree with the observation of Browne-Wilkinson V-C in *Surtees v Kingston-upon-Thames BC*:

"I further agree with Stocker LJ that the court should be wary in its approach to holding parents in breach of a duty of care owed to their children. It is accepted that the duty owed by Mr and Mrs H, as foster-parents, to the plaintiff was exactly the same as that owed by the ordinary parent to his or her own children. There are very real public policy considerations to be taken into account if the conflicts inherent in legal proceedings are to be brought into family relationships."

But I do not agree, with great respect, that because the law should not permit a child to sue his parents, the law should not permit a child to sue a local authority which is under a duty by statute to take him into care and to make arrangements for his future. I consider that the comparison between a parent and a local authority is not an apt one in the present case because the local authority has to make decisions of a nature which a parent with whom a child is living in a normal family relationship does not have to make, viz whether the child should be placed for adoption or placed with foster parents, or whether a child should remain with foster parents or be placed in a residential home. I think that it is erroneous to hold that because a child should not be permitted to sue his parents he should not be permitted to sue a local authority in respect of decisions which a parent never has to take. Moreover, a local authority employs trained staff to make decisions and to advise it in respect of the future of a child in its care, and if it can be shown that decisions taken in respect of the child constitute, in the circumstances, a failure to take reasonable care, I do not think that the local authority should be held to be free from liability on the ground that it is in the position of a parent to the child. In *A v Liverpool City Council* Lord Wilberforce stated:

"It was suggested that, as the local authority is put effectively in the position of the natural parent (see s 24(2) of the [Children and Young Persons Act 1969]), the High Court must have the same power in the interest of the infant, to review and control its actions, as it undoubtedly has over those of the natural parent. But I can see no parallel between the responsibilities of a natural parent and those entrusted by Parliament by statute to a public authority possessed of the necessary administrative apparatus to form and carry out, if necessary against the wishes of the natural parent, its discretionary decisions. In my opinion Parliament has marked out an area in which, subject to the enacted limitations and safeguards, decisions for the child's welfare are removed from the parents and from supervision by the courts."

Lord Wilberforce made this statement in rejecting the argument that the High Court could overrule the decision of the local authority as to the nature of the access which the mother should have, but that context does not, in my opinion, alter the weight of the observation that there is no parallel between the responsibilities of a natural parent and the responsibilities of a local authority who assumes the care of a child under a statutory provision.

In *X and others (minors) v Bedfordshire CC* Lord Browne-Wilkinson said that "the public policy consideration which has first claim on the loyalty of the law is that wrongs should be remedied", but he held that in that case there were very potent counter-considerations to override that consideration. In the present case the circumstances are different in a number of important respects. Unlike *X and others (minors) v Bedfordshire CC* this is not a case where the child was in the care of his natural parent or parents when the negligence by the local authority is alleged to have occurred. And this is not a case, unlike *X and others (minors) v Bedfordshire CC*, where the local authority is alleged to have been negligent in respect of investigating or acting upon an allegation or suspicion of sexual abuse. Whilst I recognise that the arguments are closely balanced I have come to the view that the arguments on behalf of the local authority are not sufficiently powerful to outweigh the argument that if the plaintiff has suffered personal injury by reason of its negligence he should be compensated by the courts.

In *X and others (minors) v Bedfordshire CC* the counter-considerations which this House considered should prevail are those enumerated by Lord Browne-Wilkinson. In my opinion, by reason of the differences in the circumstances to which I have referred, these considerations become less powerful and are of insufficient weight to prevail. The first consideration was that a common law duty of care would cut across the whole inter-disciplinary system set up by statute for the protection of children at risk, which involved the participation of the police, educational bodies, doctors and others. But in the present case it appears that other disciplines were not involved, or were not closely involved. The second consideration was that the task of a local authority and its servants in deciding whether to remove a child from his parents because of the fear of sexual abuse was an extraordinarily delicate one. But in the present case, where the plaintiff was already removed from his natural mother, the duties of the defendant were not so delicate, although questions did arise as to whether the plaintiff should remain with particular foster parents. The third consideration was that if liability and damages were to be imposed it might well be that local authorities would adopt a more cautious and defensive approach to their duties. In the circumstances of this case I would not give this consideration great weight and I am in agreement with the opinion of Evans LJ in this case that:

"If the conduct in question is of a kind which can be measured against the standards of the reasonable man, placed as the defendant was, then I do not see why the law in the public interest should not require those standards to be observed."

The next consideration was that the relationship between a social worker and a child's parents is frequently one of conflict, particularly in a case of child abuse, and a fertile ground in which to breed hopeless and costly litigation. But again, in the circumstances of the present case, this consideration is of less weight.

A further consideration was that there was a statutory procedure for complaint and for the investigation of grievances, and that the local authority ombudsman would have power to investigate the cases. Again this consideration applies here, but if the plaintiff suffered psychiatric injury by reason of carelessness amounting to negligence at common law, I consider that the jurisdiction of the court should not be excluded because of the existence of other avenues of complaint. The final consideration in *X and others (minors) v Bedfordshire CC* was that there was no analogous category of cases to justify the imposition of liability on the local authority, and that the nearest analogy was cases where the courts had declined to impose common law liability on bodies, such as the police or statutory regulators of financial dealings, seeking to protect members of society from injury by criminals or from financial loss by the dishonesty of others. But in the present case the plaintiff was not a member of a wide class of society which the defendant was obliged to seek to protect, but was an individual person who had been placed in the care of the defendant by statute, and I consider that it would not constitute a novel category of negligence to hold that the defendant owed him a common law duty of care.

In support of his decision that the plaintiff's cause of action should be struck out Lord Woolf MR cited the judgment of Simon Brown LJ (with which Waite LJ agreed) in *H v Norfolk CC*. In that case the plaintiff, who had been taken into care at the age of four and placed with foster parents until he was 14, alleged that he had been physically and sexually abused by his foster father and that the council had been negligent in failing to supervise his placement, to investigate reports of abuse and to remove him from foster care. The High Court struck out the action on the ground that the public policy considerations referred to by Lord Browne-Wilkinson in *X and others (minors) v Bedfordshire CC* were also applicable in that case, and that accordingly the council owed no duty of care. The circumstances of that case, involving allegations of sexual abuse by the foster father, were very different from the circumstances in the present case and, unlike the present defendant, the council was able to rely strongly on the point that the system for the protection of children at risk was an interdisciplinary one and that there would be difficulty in disentangling the respective roles of the various agencies concerned if there was to be liability. Therefore as, in my opinion, the case is clearly distinguishable I consider it unnecessary to express an opinion upon the correctness of the decision.

As I have reached the conclusion that under the common law principles applicable to a claim alleging negligence in the exercise of a statutory discretion the plaintiff's action should not have been struck out I consider it unnecessary to discuss the implications of the judgment of the European Court of Human Rights in *Osman v UK* in relation to the present appeal.'

Comment

(1)   Lord Slynn's speech contains an exhaustive review of the development of common law negligence in relation to local authorities and other public bodies. In particular, he examines the issues surrounding the discretion exercised by such bodies and the policy/operational divide:

> 'Where a statutory power is given to a local authority and damage is caused by what it does pursuant to that power, the ultimate question is whether the particular issue is justiciable or whether the court should accept that it has no role to play. The two tests (discretion and policy/operational) ... are guides in deciding that question. The greater the element of policy involved, the wider the area of discretion accorded, the more likely it is that the matter is not justiciable so that no action in negligence can be brought. It is true that Lord Reid and Lord Diplock in *Home Office v Dorset Yacht Co Ltd* accepted that before a claim can be brought in negligence, the plaintiffs must show that the authority is behaving so unreasonably that it is not in truth exercising the real discretion given to it. But [this] was, as I read it, *obiter*, since Lord Reid made it clear that the case did not concern such a claim, but rather was a claim that Borstal officers had been negligent when they had disobeyed orders given to them.
>
> Moreover, I share Lord Browne-Wilkinson's reluctance to introduce the concepts of administrative law into the law of negligence, as Lord Diplock appears to have done. But in any case I do not read what either Lord Reid or Lord Wilberforce in *Anns'* case (and in particular Lord Reid) said as to the need to show that there has been an abuse of power before a claim can be brought in negligence in the exercise of a statutory discretion as meaning that an action can never be brought in negligence where an act has been done pursuant to the exercise of the discretion. A claim of negligence in the taking of a decision to exercise a statutory discretion is likely to be barred, unless it is wholly unreasonable so as not to be a real exercise of the discretion, or if it involves the making

of a policy decision involving the balancing of different public interests; acts done pursuant to the lawful exercise of the discretion can, however, in my view be subject to a duty of care, even if some element of discretion is involved. Thus accepting that a decision to take a child into care pursuant to a statutory power is not justiciable, it does not in my view follow that, having taken a child into care, an authority cannot be liable for what it or its employees do in relation to the child without it being shown that they have acted in excess of power. It may amount to an excess of power, but that is not in my opinion the test to be adopted: the test is whether the conditions in *Caparo Industries plc v Dickman* have been satisfied ...

Both in deciding whether particular issues are justiciable and whether if a duty of care is owed, it has been broken, the court must have regard to the statutory context and to the nature of the tasks involved.'

(2)   On the issue of causation, both Lord Slynn and Lord Hutton noted that such factual matters should be established at trial and should not therefore form the basis of a claim being struck out.

Phelps v Hillingdon London Borough Council; and other appeals [2000] 4 All ER 504 House of Lords

Each of four appeals concerned failure by professionals, employed by local authorities, to diagnose specific educational needs, and by the authorities to provide adequate special educational support. The Court of Appeal in P's case held that the authority could not be liable for damages in negligence; further, that the psychologist in the case was acting for the authority and owed no duty to individual children. Similar arguments were raised in the other appeals.

The House of Lords unanimously held both that, in appropriate cases, a duty was owed to individuals who might reasonably be expected to rely on the professionals' skill and care, and that direct liability on the part of an authority could not be ruled out.

Lord Slynn of Hadley: '... It does not follow that the local authority can never be liable in common law negligence for damage resulting from acts done in the course of the performance of a statutory duty by the authority or by its servants or agents. This House decided in *Barrett v Enfield London BC* that the fact that acts which are claimed to be negligent are carried out within the ambit of a statutory discretion is not in itself a reason why it should be held that no claim for negligence can be brought in respect of them. It is only where what is done has involved the weighing of competing public interests or has been dictated by considerations on which Parliament could not have intended that the courts would substitute their views for the views of ministers or officials that the courts will hold that the issue is non-justiciable on the ground that the decision was made in the exercise of a statutory discretion. In P's case there is no such ground for holding that her claim is non-justiciable and therefore the question to be determined is whether the damage relied on is foreseeable and proximate and whether it is just and reasonable to recognise a duty of care (*Caparo Industries plc v Dickman*). If a duty of care would exist where advice was given other than pursuant to the exercise of statutory powers, such duty of care is not excluded because the advice is given pursuant to the exercise of statutory powers. This is particularly important where other remedies laid down by the statute (e.g. an appeals review procedure) do not in themselves provide sufficient redress for loss which has already been caused.

Where, as in P's case, a person is employed by a local education authority to carry out professional services as part of the fulfilment of the authority's statutory duty, it has to be asked whether there is any overriding reason in principle why (a) that person should not owe a duty of care (the first question) and (b) why, if the duty of care is broken by that person, the authority as employer or principal should not be vicariously liable (the second question).

I accept that, as was said in *X (minors) v Bedfordshire CC*, there may be cases where to recognise such a vicarious liability on the part of the authority may so interfere with the performance of the local education authority's duties that it would be wrong to recognise any liability on the part of the authority. It must, however, be for the local authority to establish that: it is not to be presumed and I anticipate that the circumstances where it could be established would be exceptional.

As to the first question, it is long and well-established, now elementary, that persons exercising a particular skill or profession may owe a duty of care in the performance to people who it can be foreseen will be injured if due skill and care are not exercised, and if injury or damage can be shown to have been caused by the lack of care. Such duty does not depend on the existence of any contractual relationship between the person causing and the person suffering the damage. A doctor, an accountant and an engineer are plainly such a person. So in my view is an educational psychologist or psychiatrist or a teacher including a teacher in a specialised area, such as a teacher concerned with children having special educational needs. So may be an education officer performing the functions of a local education authority in regard to children with special educational needs. There is no more justification for a blanket immunity in their cases than there was in *Capital and Counties plc v Hampshire CC, Digital Equipment Co Ltd v Hampshire CC, John Munroe (Acrylics) Ltd v London Fire and Civil Defence Authority, Church of Jesus Christ of Latter Day Saints (Great Britain) v West Yorkshire Fire and Civil Defence Authority*.

I fully agree with what was said by Lord Browne-Wilkinson in *X (minors) v Bedfordshire CC* that a head teacher owes "a duty of care to exercise the reasonable skills of a headmaster in relation to such [sc a child's] educational needs" and a special advisory teacher brought in to advise on the educational needs of a specific pupil, particularly if he knows that his advice will be communicated to the pupil's parents, "owes a duty to the child to exercise the skill and care of a reasonable advisory teacher". A similar duty on specific facts may arise for others engaged in the educational process, e.g. an educational psychologist being part of the local authority's team to provide the necessary services. The fact that the educational psychologist owes a duty to the authority to exercise skill and care in the performance of his contract of employment does not mean that no duty of care can be or is owed to the child. Nor does the fact that the educational psychologist is called in pursuance of the performance of the local authority's statutory duties mean that no duty of care is owed by him, if in exercising his profession he would otherwise have a duty of care.

That, however, is only the beginning of the enquiry. It must still be shown that the educational psychologist is acting in relation to a particular child in a situation where the law recognises a duty of care. A casual remark, an isolated act may occur in a situation where there is no sufficient nexus between the two persons for a duty of care to exist. But where an educational psychologist is specifically called in to advise in relation to the assessment and future provision for a specific child, and it is clear that the parents acting for the child and the teachers will follow that advice, prima facie a duty of care arises. It is sometimes said that there has to be an assumption of responsibility by the person concerned. That phrase can be misleading in that it can suggest that the professional person must knowingly and deliberately accept responsibility. It is, however, clear that the test is an objective one (*Henderson v Merrett Syndicates Ltd*). The phrase means simply that the law recognises that there is a duty of care. It is not so much that responsibility is assumed as that it is recognised or imposed by the law.

The question is thus whether in the particular circumstances the necessary nexus has been shown.

The result of a failure by an educational psychologist to take care may be that the child suffers emotional or psychological harm, perhaps even physical harm. There can be no doubt that if foreseeability and causation are established, psychological injury may constitute damage for the purpose of the common law. But so in my view can a failure to diagnose a congenital condition and to take appropriate action as a result of which failure a child's level of achievement is reduced, which leads to loss of employment and wages. Questions as to causation and as to the quantum of damage, particularly if actions are brought long after the event, may be very difficult, but there is no reason in principle to rule out such claims.

As to the second question, if a breach of the duty of care to the child by such an employee is established, *prima facie* a local or education authority is vicariously liable for the negligence of its employee. If the educational psychologist does have a duty of care on the facts is it to be held that it is not just and reasonable that the local education authority should be vicariously liable if there is a breach of that duty? Are there reasons of public policy why the courts should not recognise such a liability? I am very conscious of the need to be cautious in recognising such a duty of care where so much is discretionary in these as in other areas of social policy. As has been said, it is obviously important that those engaged in the provision of educational services under the statutes should not be hampered by the imposition of such a vicarious liability. I do not, however, see that to recognise the existence of the duties necessarily leads or is likely to lead to that result. The recognition of the duty of care does not of itself impose unreasonably high standards. The courts have long recognised that there is no negligence if a doctor "exercises the ordinary skill of an ordinary competent man exercising that particular art".

"A doctor is not guilty of negligence if he has acted in accordance with a practice accepted as proper by a responsible body of medical men skilled in that particular art. Putting it the other way round, a doctor is not negligent, if he is acting in accordance with such a practice, merely because there is a body of opinion that takes a contrary view." (See *Bolam v Friern Hospital Management Committee* per McNair J.)

The difficulties of the tasks involved and of the circumstances under which people have to work in this area must also be borne fully in mind. The professionalism, dedication and standards of those engaged in the provision of educational services are such that cases of liability for negligence will be exceptional. Claims should not be encouraged and the courts should not find negligence too readily: but the fact that some claims may be without foundation or exaggerated does not mean that valid claims should necessarily be excluded.

The House has been referred to a number of decisions of the United States courts in some of which it has been held that a local education authority did not owe an actionable duty of care. But the legislative and administrative provisions and the approach of the courts in those cases are different and there is not complete unanimity. I do not consider that these cases assist in the determination of the present problem.

The duty in this case, on the basis, therefore, that an educational psychologist may owe a duty of care in performing duties on behalf of the local education authority. Was the judge justified in finding that there was a duty here and that there was a breach?

As to the duty, [the psychologist] had a degree in Developmental Psychology and a diploma in Education Psychology in addition to her certificate in Education. She had over four years' teaching experience and six months' or so experience as an educational psychologist. It has not been suggested that the authority was negligent in appointing her in the first place or that she was not competent to hold the post.

She was specifically asked on a number of occasions to assess and advise as to P, whose learning difficulties were very plain, whatever their cause. Finding the cause was a major task. She was called in to and did advise not only Hillingdon, but the staff. She had a number of interviews with the parents, who were clearly anxious about their daughter and Mrs P certainly had her own views about sending P to a special school. She knew, or ought to have known, of the fact that her advice would be followed and of the importance of her assessment and advice to P's future.

I do not think that in this case it is any answer to the claim that a duty of care existed that others had been involved in psychological advice at an earlier stage, or that she was said to be part of the multi-disciplinary team, including the teaching staff. At Mellow Lane, she was the professional person brought in to this case and her role, difficult though it was, was pivotal. I see no reason why in this situation she did not have a duty of care to P. Her relationship with the child and what she was doing created the necessary nexus and duty. The learned judge was both entitled and right to find that she owed a duty of care. He was equally entitled and might hold that, if she was in breach of her duty, Hillingdon was vicariously liable. ...

I am very conscious of the great experience of the members of the Court of Appeal in this area, but on my conclusions as to the issues of principle it follows that the Court of Appeal was not justified in holding that the educational psychologist did not assume responsibility and therefore that Hillingdon could not be liable. On my conclusions, Garland J adopted the correct approach and was entitled on the evidence to find liability and on that approach he was entitled, in my view, to accept that "the adverse consequences of the plaintiff's dyslexia could have been mitigated by early diagnosis and appropriate treatment or educational provision". He was right to have regard to the judgments of Bingham MR and Evans LJ in *E (a minor) v Dorset CC*. ...

DIRECT LIABILITY

In *X (minors) v Bedfordshire CC* Lord Browne-Wilkinson said:

> "For these reasons I reach the conclusion that an educational authority owe no common law duty of care in the exercise of the powers and discretions relating to children with special educational needs specifically conferred on them by the 1981 Act."

It seems to me that if he had not thought that the service of psychological advice was offered to the public (which in fact in the present case it was not), but was "merely part and parcel of the system established by the defendant authority for the discharge of its statutory duties under the 1981 Act", he would have accepted that there was no duty of care in respect of an educational psychologist in the present case.

I do not rule out the possibility of a direct claim in all situations where the local authority is exercising its powers. If it exercises its discretion by deciding to set up a particular scheme pursuant to a policy which it has lawfully adopted, there is no, or at least there is unlikely to be any, common law duty of care. If, however, it then, for example, appoints to carry out the duties in regard to children with special educational needs a psychologist or other professionals who at the outset transparently are neither qualified nor competent to carry out the duties, the position is different. That may be an unlikely scenario, but if it happens, I do not see why as a matter of principle a claim at common law in negligence should never be possible. Over-use of the distinction between policy and operational matters so as respectively to limit or create liability has been criticised, but there is some validity in the distinction. Just as the individual social worker in *Barrett v Enfield London BC* could be "negligent in an operational manner", so it seems to me that the local education authority could in some circumstances owe a duty of care and be negligent in the performance of it. The fact that the parents have their own duties under s 36 of the 1944 Act and that consultation and appeal procedures exist (of which the parents may or may not be informed) does not seem to me to lead to the conclusion that a duty of care does not or should not exist.

Since the authority can only act through its employees or agents, and if they are negligent vicarious liability will arise, it may rarely be necessary to invoke a claim for direct liability. After the argument in these cases, I do not, however, accept the absolute statement that an education authority "owe[s] no common law duty of care in the exercise of the powers … relating to children with special educational needs" under the 1981 Act.'

Comment

(1) Note under Lord Slynn's second question his reference to the 'fair, just and reasonable' test, and his asking, 'Are there reasons of public policy why the courts should not recognise such a liability?'. This reads rather oddly in the context of a traditional view of vicarious liability, in which those questions would be relevant only to the issue of duty on the part of the employee. For vicarious liability generally, see Chapter 17.

(2) Lord Nicholls of Birkenhead considered the position of teachers:

'… I can see no escape from the conclusion that teachers do, indeed, owe such duties. The principal objection raised to this conclusion is the spectre of a rash of "gold digging" actions brought on behalf of under-achieving children by discontented parents, perhaps years after the events complained of. If teachers are liable, education authorities will be vicariously liable, since the negligent acts or omissions were committed in the course of the teachers' employment. So, it is said, the limited resources of education authorities and the time of teaching staff will be diverted away from teaching and into defending unmeritorious legal claims. Further, schools will have to prepare and keep full records, lest they be unable to rebut negligence allegations, brought out of the blue years later. For one or more of these reasons, the overall standard of education given to children is likely to suffer if a legal duty of care were held to exist.

I am not persuaded by these fears. I do not think they provide sufficient reason for treating work in the classroom as territory which the courts must never enter. "Never" is an unattractive absolute in this context. This would bar a claim, however obvious it was that something had gone badly wrong, and however serious the consequences for the particular child. If a teacher carelessly teaches the wrong syllabus for an external examination, and provable financial loss follows, why should there be no liability? Denial of the existence of a cause of action is seldom, if ever, the appropriate response to fear of its abuse. Rather, the courts, with their enhanced powers of case management, must seek to evolve means of weeding out obviously hopeless claims as expeditiously as is consistent with the court having a sufficiently full factual picture of all the circumstances of the case.

This is not to open the door to claims based on poor quality of teaching. It is one thing for the law to provide a remedy in damages when there is manifest incompetence or negligence comprising specific, identifiable mistakes. It would be an altogether different matter to countenance claims of a more general nature, to the effect that the child did not receive an adequate education at the school, or that a particular teacher failed to teach properly. Proof of under-performance by a child is not by itself evidence of negligent teaching. There are many, many reasons for under-performance. ... Suffice to say, the existence of a duty of care owed by teachers to their pupils should not be regarded as furnishing a basis on which generalised "educational malpractice" claims can be mounted.'

(3) In *W and others v Essex County Council and another* an action was brought by children who had been sexually abused by a 15-year-old boy placed in their family for fostering. The parents had made it clear that they would not accept any suspected or known sexual abuser. The defendants assured them that nothing was known or suspected about the boy despite, to their knowledge, his having previously been cautioned for a sexual assault on his sister. The Court of Appeal upheld the judge's refusal to strike out the claims. The majority held that it was arguable that the policy considerations which militate against it being fair, just and reasonable to impose a duty of care on local authorities in matters concerning the welfare of children did not, on the facts of this case, apply because the claimants were not in the care of the authority, and were therefore outside the scope of any statutory duty. On appeal, the House of Lords reinstated a claim by the parents for negligently inflicted psychiatric harm.

(4) In *A & B v Essex County Council* it was held, applying *Phelps*, that an authority could be vicariously liable to prospective adopters for the negligence of social workers and a doctor in their assessment of the suitability for adoption of a particular child.

(5) In *Welton v North Cornwall District Council* an environmental health officer, after inspecting the plaintiff's premises, told her (wrongly) that substantial improvements were required in order to comply with the relevant legislation. The plaintiff sought to recover the cost of the alterations she had made in reliance on the officer's advice. The Court of Appeal held that in similar cases where the advisory service operated in the private sector damages would be recoverable under the *Hedley Byrne* principle; here, there was no public policy reason for denying a remedy since the activity in question fell 'outwith the legislation'. Reviewing this reasoning, Ward LJ said:

'Looking at the matter from the point of view of the plaintiff, she has no other remedy than this action. She has undoubtedly suffered damage which would be recoverable on *Hedley Byrne* principles and an important element of public policy is that such damage should be compensated. From the point of view of the local authority, the court is not intruding upon the manner in which the local authority exercises its discretionary powers. The burden of performing the advisory service carefully, which is the burden cast upon those in the private sector, is not so onerous or demanding upon a fair allocation of finite resources as to make it unreasonable that care be taken. Finally, from the point of view of the public at large, public safety is important but in the special circumstances of this case it does not seem to me that it would be imperilled if the need for justice to [the plaintiff] was given its proper place.'

(6) In *Harris v Evans and another* the claimant sought damages for economic loss caused to him when his bungee jumping business had to cease operating. He had started up the business and acquired equipment after having checked the safety requirements, but E, an inspector with the Health and Safety Executive, subsequently advised certain local authorities that the telescopic crane used should first be certified as safe for the purpose. The defendant denied any duty of care in negligence. Sir Richard Evans Scott V-C in the Court of Appeal considered the effect of the *Welton* decision:

'There are ... two notable differences between the facts of *Welton*'s case and the facts of the present case. First, in *Welton*'s case negligent advice was given to and acted on by the plaintiffs. In the present case the advice was given to and acted on not by the plaintiff but by the local authorities in purported exercise of their statutory functions. Second, the actions of the local authorities which caused the economic damage sought to be recovered could in the present case have been challenged under the statutory procedures provided for in the 1974 Act. In *Welton*'s case, nothing had been done by the officer that could be challenged under the comparable statutory procedures.

So *Welton*'s case is, in my judgment, distinguishable ...

I must confess ... that I find some difficulty with the decision. I do not understand how it was possible to come to the conclusion that the plaintiffs' claim based on the principles in the *Hedley Byrne* case was "incontrovertible" without considering whether the duty of care contended for was consistent with the statutory framework of the 1984 and 1990 Acts ... If the imposition of the duty was not consistent with the statutory scheme, there should have been no liability under the *Hedley Byrne* principle or under any other common law duty of care principle ...

It could be that a particular requirement imposed by an inspector ... might introduce a new risk or danger not present in the business activity as previously conducted. The new risk or danger might materialise and result in economic damage to the business itself as well as physical damage to person or to property. We do not need to decide the point but I would not be prepared to rule out the possibility that damage thus caused could be recovered by means of a negligence action. *Capital and Counties plc v Hampshire CC, Digital Equipment Co Ltd v Hampshire CC, John Munroe (Acrylics) Ltd v London Fire and Civil Defence Authority, Church of Jesus Christ of Latter Day Saints (GB) v West Yorkshire Fire and Civil Defence Authority* seems to me to provide support to such an action.'

CHAPTER 2

Duty II – Particular claimants

It is not enough for the claimant to establish in general terms that the defendant was under a duty to take care. It must also be shown that the defendant owed a duty of care specifically to the claimant. Lord Porter in *Hay (or Bourhill) v Young* said:

'... In the case of a civil action there is no such thing as negligence in the abstract: there must be neglect of the use of care towards a person towards whom the defendant owes the duty of observing care. And I am content to take the statement of Lord Atkin in *Donoghue v Stevenson*, as indicating the extent of the duty: "You must take reasonable care to avoid acts and omissions which you can reasonably foresee would be likely to injure your neighbour. Who, then, in law is my neighbour? The answer seems to be – persons who are so closely and directly affected by my act that I ought reasonably to have them in contemplation as being so affected when I am directing my mind to the acts or omissions which are called in question." Is the result of this view that all persons in or near the street down which the negligent driver is progressing are potential victims of his negligence? Though from their position it is quite impossible that any injury should happen to them and though they have no relatives or even friends who might be endangered, is a duty of care to them owed and broken because they might have been but were not in a spot exposed to the errant driving of the peccant car? I cannot think so. The duty is not to the world at large. It must be tested by asking with reference to each several complainant was a duty owed to him or her. If no one of them was in such a position that direct physical injury could reasonably be anticipated to them or their relations or friends, normally I think no duty would be owed: and if, in addition, no shock was reasonably anticipated to them as a result of the defender's negligence, the defender might, indeed, be guilty of actionable negligence to others but not of negligence towards them.'

So, in order to claim, the claimant must be foreseeable in terms of his or her presence at the scene, and of the type of person he or she is, for example, as regards age or ability to take care of him or herself; and of the nature of the damage he or she sustains.

Haley v London Electricity Board
[1964] 3 All ER 185 House of Lords

The appellant, who had been blind for many years, was used to walking unaccompanied, and with the aid of his white stick he had learned to avoid all ordinary obstacles. On the day in question he tripped over a large hammer which the respondents' workmen had placed as a warning to pedestrians of the trench they were digging in the pavement. He fell heavily and, as a result of his head striking the pavement, became deaf. The House of Lords held that the passage of a reasonably prudent blind pedestrian was foreseeable and that a duty of care was owed to such a person.

Lord Reid: '... The trial judge held that what the respondents' men did gave adequate warning to ordinary people with good sight, and I am not disposed to disagree with that ... On the other hand, if it was the duty of the respondents to have in mind the needs of blind or infirm pedestrians, I think that what they did was quite insufficient. Indeed the evidence shows that an obstacle attached to a heavy weight and only nine inches above the ground may well escape detection by a blind man's stick and is for him a trap rather than a warning. So the question for your lordships' decision is the nature and extent of the duty owed to pedestrians by persons who carry out operations on a city pavement. The respondents argue that they were only bound to have in mind or to safeguard ordinary able-bodied people and were under no obligation to give particular consideration to the blind or infirm. If that is right, it means that a blind or infirm person who goes out alone goes at his peril. He may meet obstacles which are a danger to him, but not to those with good sight, because no one is under any obligation to remove or protect them; and if such an obstacle causes him injury he must suffer the damage in silence.

I could understand the respondents' contention if it was based on an argument that it was not reasonably foreseeable that a blind person might pass along that pavement on that day; or that, although foreseeable, the chance of a blind man coming there was so small and the difficulty of affording protection to him so great that it would have been in the circumstances unreasonable to afford that protection. Those are well-recognised grounds of defence; but in my judgment neither is open to the respondents in this case.

In deciding what is reasonably foreseeable one must have regard to common knowledge. We are all accustomed to meeting blind people walking alone with their white sticks on city pavements. No doubt there are many places open to the public where for one reason or another one would be surprised to see a blind person walking alone, but a city pavement is not one of them; and a residential street cannot be different from any other. The blind people whom we meet must live somewhere, and most of them probably left their homes unaccompanied. It may seem surprising that blind people can avoid ordinary obstacles so well as they do, but we must take account of the facts. There is evidence in this case about the number of blind people in London and it appears from government publications that the proportion in the whole country is near one in five hundred. By no means all are sufficiently skilled or confident to venture out alone, but the number who habitually do so must be very large. I find it quite impossible to say that it is not reasonably foreseeable that a blind person may pass along a particular pavement on a particular day.

No question can arise in this case of any great difficulty in affording adequate protection for the blind. In considering what is adequate protection again one must have regard to common knowledge. One is entitled to expect of a blind person a high degree of skill and care because none but the most foolhardy would venture to go out alone without having that skill and exercising that care. We know that in fact blind people do safely avoid all ordinary obstacles on pavements; there can be no question of padding lamp posts as was suggested in one case. A moment's reflection, however, shows that a low obstacle in an unusual place is a grave danger: on the other hand it is clear from the evidence in this case and also I think from common knowledge that quite a light fence some two feet high is an adequate warning. There would have been no difficulty in providing such a fence here. The evidence is that the Post Office always provide one, and that the respondents have similar fences which are often used. Indeed the evidence suggests that the only reason why there was no fence here was that the accident occurred before the necessary fences had arrived. So, if the respondents are to succeed, it can only be on the ground that there was no duty to do more than safeguard ordinary able-bodied people ...

I can see no justification for laying down any hard and fast rule limiting the classes of persons for whom those interfering with a pavement must make provision ... It appears to me that the ordinary principles of the common law must apply in streets as well as elsewhere, and that fundamentally they depend on what a reasonable man, careful of his neighbour's safety, would do having the knowledge which a reasonable man in the position of the defendant must be deemed to have.'

Comment

(1) This case is a good illustration of how difficult it can be to separate the question of the existence of a duty from that of the standard to be expected.

(2) Applying the general principle in this case, it can be seen that particular care is to be taken wherever children are to be expected, although in many

circumstances a defendant may be entitled to expect that young children will be under the control of a responsible adult: see *Phipps v Rochester Corporation*, p 391.

Videan and another v British Transport Commission
[1963] 2 All ER 860 Court of Appeal

The plaintiff's husband, a stationmaster, was killed in the act of saving his young son from a heavy trolley which was proceeding towards him on the railway track on to which he had wandered. The Court of Appeal rejected the defendants' argument that no duty could be owed to the father since the presence of his (trespasser) son on the line could not have been foreseen.

Lord Denning MR: '... I turn now to the widow's claim in respect of the death of her husband. In order to establish it, the widow must prove that [the driver] owed a duty of care to the stationmaster, that he broke that duty, and that, in consequence of the breach, the stationmaster was killed. Counsel for the defendants says that the widow can prove none of these things. All depends, he says, on the test of foreseeability; and, applying that test, he puts the following dilemma: If [the driver] could not reasonably be expected to foresee the presence of the child, he could not reasonably be expected to foresee the presence of the father. He could not foresee that a trespasser would be on the line. So how could he be expected to foresee that anyone would be attempting to rescue him? Counsel for the defendants points out that, in all the rescue cases that have hitherto come before the courts, such as *Haynes v G Harwood & Son* and *Baker v T E Hopkins & Sons Ltd*, the conduct of the defendant was a wrong to the victim or the potential victim. How can he be liable to the rescuer when he is not liable to the rescued?

I cannot accept this view. The right of the rescuer is an independent right, and is not derived from that of the victim. The victim may have been guilty of contributory negligence – or his right may be excluded by contractual stipulation – but still the rescuer can sue. So, also, the victim may, as here, be a trespasser and excluded on that ground, but still the rescuer can sue. Foreseeability is necessary, but not foreseeability of the particular emergency that arose. Suffice it that he ought reasonably to foresee that, if he did not take care, some emergency or other might arise, and that someone or other might be impelled to expose himself to danger in order to effect a rescue. Such is the case here. [The driver] ought to have anticipated that some emergency or other might arise. His trolley was not like an express train which is heralded by signals and whistles and shouts of "Keep clear". His trolley came silently and swiftly on the unsuspecting quietude of a country station. He should have realised that someone or other might be put in peril if he came too fast or did not keep a proper look-out; and that, if anyone was put in peril, then someone would come to the rescue. As it happened, it was the stationmaster trying to rescue his child; but it would be the same if it had been a passer-by. Whoever comes to the rescue, the law should see that he does not suffer for it. It seems to me that, if a person by his fault creates a situation of peril, he must answer for it to any person who attempts to rescue the person who is in danger. He owes a duty to such a person above all others. The rescuer may act instinctively out of humanity or deliberately out of courage. But whichever it is, so long as it is not wanton interference, if the rescuer is killed or injured in the attempt, he can recover damages from the one whose fault has been the cause of it.'

Comment

(1) For the duty owed by occupiers to trespassers see p 400. Note that under the Occupiers' Liability Act 1984, s 1(3) such a duty arises only when the presence of a trespasser is reasonably foreseeable.

(2) Rescuers enjoy, up to a point, a protected status in law. This case establishes that the duty owed to them is not derived from any duty owed to a third party; they have in the past been recognised as a special category in nervous shock cases, see *Chadwick v British Railways Board*, although this issue was reviewed in *White and others v Chief Constable of the South Yorkshire Police and others*. In addition, rescuers, generally, are immune from the causation argument that their injury stems from a wilful act of their own, and from the defences of *volenti* and contributory negligence.

McKay and another v Essex Area Health Authority and another
[1982] 2 All ER 771 Court of Appeal

The infant plaintiff had been born with serious disabilities as a result of her mother's rubella infection during pregnancy. In an action against the defendants it was argued that they were negligent in failing to advise the mother of the desirability of an abortion. The Court of Appeal held that the duty owed to an unborn child, which is not to cause it injury, cannot, as a matter of policy, encompass a duty to terminate its life.

Stephenson LJ: '... Here the court is considering not "ancient law" but a novel cause of action, for or against which there is no authority in any reported case in the courts of the United Kingdom or the Commonwealth. It is tempting to say that the question whether it exists is so difficult and so important that it should be argued out at a trial and on appeal up to the House of Lords. But it may become just as plain and obvious, after argument on the defendants' application to strike it out, that the novel cause of action is unarguable or unsustainable or has no chance of succeeding ...

The importance of this cause of action to this child is somewhat reduced by the existence of her other claim and the mother's claims, which, if successful, will give her some compensation in money or in care. However, this is the first occasion on which the courts of this country or the Commonwealth have had to consider this cause of action, and I shall give my reasons for holding that it should be struck out.

If, as is conceded, any duty is owed to an unborn child, the authority's hospital laboratory and the doctor looking after the mother during her pregnancy undoubtedly owed the child a duty not to injure it, and, if she had been injured as a result of lack of reasonable care and skill on their part after birth, she could have sued them (as she is suing the doctor) for damages to compensate her for the injury they had caused her in the womb. (Cf. the thalidomide cases, where it was assumed that such an action might lie: e.g. *Distillers Co (Biochemicals) Ltd v Thompson.*) But this child has not been injured by either defendant, but by the rubella which has infected the mother without fault on anybody's part. Her right not to be injured before birth by the carelessness of others has not been infringed by either defendant, any more than it would have been if she had been disabled by disease after birth. Neither defendant has broken any duty to take reasonable care not to injure her. The only right on which she can rely as having been infringed is a right not to be born deformed or disabled, which means, for a child deformed or disabled before birth by nature or disease, a right to be aborted or killed; or, if that last plain word is thought dangerously emotive, deprived of the opportunity to live after being delivered from the body of her mother. The only duty which either defendant can owe to the unborn child infected with disabling rubella is a duty to abort or kill her or deprive her of that opportunity.

It is said that the duty does not go as far as that, but only as far as a duty to give the mother an opportunity to choose her abortion and death. That is true as far as it goes. The doctor's alleged negligence is in misleading the mother as to the advisability of an abortion, failing to inform or advise her of its advisability or desirability; the laboratory's alleged negligence is not so pleaded in terms but the negligence pleaded against them in failing to make or interpret the tests of the mother's blood samples or to inform the doctor of their results must, like the doctor's negligence, be a breach of their duty to give the doctor an opportunity to advise the mother of the risks in continuing to let the fetus live in the womb and be born alive. But the complaint of the child, as of the mother, against [the defendants], is that their negligence burdened her (and her mother) with her injuries. That is another way of saying that the defendants' breaches of their duties resulted not just in the child's being born but in her being born injured or, as the judge put it, with deformities. But, as the injuries or deformities were not the result of any act or omission of the defendants, the only result for which they were responsible was her being born. For that they were responsible because if they had exercised due care the mother would have known that the child might be born injured or deformed, and the plaintiffs' pleaded case is that, if the mother had known that she would have been willing to undergo an abortion, which must mean she would have undergone one or she could not claim that the defendants were responsible for burdening her with an injured child. If she would not have undergone an abortion had she known the risk of the child being born injured, any negligence on the defendants' part could not give either plaintiff a cause of action in respect of the child being born injured.

I am accordingly of opinion that, though the judge was right in saying that the child's complaint is that she was born with deformities without which she would have suffered no damage and have no complaint, her claim against the defendants is a claim that they were negligent in allowing her, injured as she was in the womb, to be born at all, a claim for "wrongful entry into life" or "wrongful life".

This analysis leads inexorably on to the question: how can there be a duty to take away life? How indeed can it be lawful? It is still the law that it is unlawful to take away the life of a born child or of any living person after birth. But the Abortion Act 1967 has given mothers a right to terminate the lives of their unborn children and made it lawful for doctors to help to abort them ...

There is no doubt that this child could legally have been deprived of life by the mother's undergoing an abortion with the doctor's advice and help. So the law recognises a difference between the life of a fetus and the life of those who have been born. But, because a doctor can lawfully by statute do to a fetus what he cannot lawfully do to a person who has been born, it does not follow that he is under a legal obligation to a fetus to do it and terminate its life, or that the fetus has a legal right to die.

Like this court when it had to consider the interests of a child born with Down's syndrome in *Re B (a minor) (wardship: medical treatment)*, I would not answer until it is necessary to do so the question whether the life of a child could be so certainly "awful" and "intolerable" that it would be in its best interests to end it and it might be considered that it had a right to be put to death. But that is not this case. We have no exact information about the extent of this child's serious and highly debilitating congenital injuries; the judge was told that she is partly blind and deaf, but it is not and could not be suggested that the quality of her life is such that she is certainly better dead, or would herself wish that she had not been born or should now die.

I am therefore compelled to hold that neither defendant was under any duty to the child to give the child's mother an opportunity to terminate the child's life. That duty may be owed to the mother, but it cannot be owed to the child.

To impose such a duty towards the child would, in my opinion, make a further inroad on the sanctity of human life which would be contrary to public policy. It would mean regarding the life of a handicapped child as not only less valuable than the life of a normal child, but so much less valuable that it was not worth preserving, and it would even mean that a doctor would be obliged to pay damages to a child infected with rubella before birth who was in fact born with some mercifully trivial abnormality. These are the consequences of the necessary basic assumption that a child has a right to be born whole or not at all, not to be born unless it can be born perfect or "normal", whatever that may mean.

Added to that objection must be the opening of the courts to claims by children born handicapped against their mothers for not having an abortion. For the reasons given by the Royal Commission on Civil Liability and Compensation for Personal Injury (Report, vol. 1; Cmnd 7054–1), cited by Ackner LJ, that is, to my mind, a graver objection than the extra burden on doctors already open to actions for negligent treatment of a fetus, which weighed with the Law Commission.

Finally, there is the nature of the injury and damage which the court is being asked to ascertain and evaluate.

The only duty of care which courts of law can recognise and enforce are duties owed to those who can be compensated for loss by those who owe the duties, in most cases, including cases of personal injury, by money damages which will as far as possible put the injured party in the condition in which he or she was before being injured. The only way in which a child injured in the womb can be compensated in damages is by measuring what it has lost, which is the difference between the value of its life as a whole and healthy normal child and the value of its life as an injured child. But to make those who have not injured the child pay for that difference is to treat them as if they injured the child, when all they have done is not taken steps to prevent its being born injured by another cause.

The only loss for which those who have not injured the child can be held liable to compensate the child is the difference between its condition as a result of their allowing it to be born alive and injured and its condition if its embryonic life had been ended before its life in the world had begun. But how can a court of law evaluate that second condition and so measure the loss to the child? Even if a court were competent to decide between the conflicting views of theologians and philosophers and to assume an "afterlife" or non-existence as the basis for the comparison, how can a judge put a value on the one or the other, compare either alternative with the injured child's life in this world and determine that the child has lost anything, without the means of knowing what, if anything, it has gained?'

Comment

(1)   It should be noted that this is, as Lord Ackner says in his judgment, 'for all practical purposes … a "one-off" case', because in relation to the duty owed to an unborn child it has been superseded by the Congenital Disabilities (Civil Liability) Act 1976 which covers all births after 22 July 1976. Nevertheless, in its unequivocal rejection of 'wrongful life' claims, the court draws on principles of general importance. The two main policy considerations which influenced the court were: (a) the undesirability of undermining the 'sanctity of life'; and (b)

an unwillingness to find that a duty exists in circumstances where the required standard is impossible to determine. The second of these is echoed in *ex turpi causa* cases, e.g. *Jackson v Harrison, Pitts v Hunt*.

(2)   The courts do recognise 'wrongful birth' claims by parents in relation to the upkeep of an unexpected child, for example where a sterilisation operation fails as in *Emeh v Kensington and Chelsea and Westminster Area Health Authority* and *Thake v Maurice*. In *Thake*, the plaintiff had not been warned of the slight risk that her husband's vasectomy might reverse itself and therefore never considered the possibility that she might be pregnant until it was too late for an abortion. In *Emeh* the court rejected an argument that the plaintiff's decision not to have an abortion on finding herself 20 weeks pregnant was so unreasonable 'as to eclipse the defendants' wrongdoing'. If the courts maintain their attitude to the 'sanctity of life', then presumably a plaintiff's refusal to abort a child will never undermine her claim.

(3)   In relation to a claim by the mother in *McKay*, the conduct complained of consisted of an *omission* to advise her of the desirability of an abortion. It has been argued, as in *Kirkham v Chief Constable of the Greater Manchester Police*, that 'there is as yet no generalised duty to act positively so as to prevent harm to others' or that 'the common law does not impose liability for pure omissions'. In that case, in which the police had failed to pass on to the remand authorities information concerning a prisoner's suicidal tendencies, Lloyd LJ said that 'the question depends in each case on whether, having regard to the particular relationship between the parties, the defendant has assumed a responsibility towards the plaintiff, and whether the plaintiff has relied on that assumption of responsibility'. (See also *Welsh v Chief Constable of Merseyside* in which it was held that a duty was owed by the Crown Prosecution Service to an accused person to keep the court informed as to the state of an adjourned case.) In *Kirkham* the court had no difficulty in concluding that a duty did exist, but the issues become particularly complicated in relation to medical patients where a doctor who acts may run the risk of an action in battery, while if the doctor fails to act he or she may be in breach of a duty: see Chapter 11.

McLoughlin v O'Brian and others
[1982] 2 All ER 298 House of Lords

As a result of the defendants' negligence, the plaintiff's husband and three children were involved in a road accident some two miles from where she was at home. About an hour later a motorist came to the house, told her of the accident, and drove her to the hospital where she learned of her daughter's death and found the rest of her family variously in pain, screaming and covered in mud, oil and blood. The plaintiff suffered severe and persistent psychiatric symptoms and succeeded in her claim against the defendants despite not having been at the scene of the accident. The House of Lords extended the previous requirement that the plaintiff be present at the scene of the injury to include those who came upon the 'immediate aftermath'.

Lord Wilberforce: '... Although we continue to use the hallowed expression "nervous shock", English law, and common understanding, have moved some distance since recognition was given to this symptom as a basis for liability. Whatever is unknown about the mind–body relationship (and the area of ignorance seems to expand with that of knowledge), it is now accepted by medical science that recognisable and severe physical damage to the human body and system may be caused by the impact, through the senses, of external events on the mind. There may thus be produced what is as identifiable an illness as any that may be caused by direct physical impact. It is safe to say that this, in general terms, is understood by the ordinary man or woman who is hypothesised by the courts in situations where claims for negligence are made. Although in the only case which has reached this House (*Hay (or Bourhill) v Young*) a claim for damages in respect of "nervous shock" was rejected on its facts, the House gave clear recognition to the legitimacy, in principle, of claims of that character. As the result of that and other cases, assuming that they are accepted as correct, the following position has been reached:

(1)   While damages cannot, at common law, be awarded for grief and sorrow, a claim for damages for "nervous shock" caused by negligence can be made without the necessity of showing direct impact or fear of immediate personal injuries for oneself. The reservation made by Kennedy J in *Dulieu v White & Sons*, though taken up by Sargant LJ in *Hambrook v Stokes Bros*, has not gained acceptance, and although the respondents, in the courts below, reserved their right to revive it, they did not do so in argument. I think that it is now too late to do so. The arguments on this issue were fully and admirably stated by the Supreme Court of California in *Dillon v Legg*.

(2)   A plaintiff may recover damages for "nervous shock" brought on by injury caused not to him or herself but to a near relative, or by the fear of such injury. So far (subject to (5) below), the cases do not extend beyond the spouse or children of the plaintiff (*Hambrook v Stokes Bros, Boardman v Sanderson, Hinz v Berry* including foster children (where liability was assumed), and see *King v Phillips*).

(3)   Subject to the next paragraph, there is no English case in which a plaintiff has been able to recover nervous shock damages where the injury to the near relative occurred out of sight and earshot of the plaintiff. In *Hambrook v Stokes Bros* an express distinction was made between shock caused by what the mother saw with her own eyes and what she might have been told by bystanders, liability being excluded in the latter case.

(4)   An exception from, or I would prefer to call it an extension of, the latter case has been made where the plaintiff does not see or hear the incident but comes on

its immediate aftermath. In *Boardman v Sanderson* the father was within earshot of the accident to his child and likely to come on the scene; he did so and suffered damage from what he then saw. In *Marshall v Lionel Enterprises* the wife came immediately on the badly injured body of her husband. And in *Benson v Lee* a situation existed with some similarity to the present case. The mother was in her home 100 yards away, and, on communication by a third party, ran out to the scene of the accident and there suffered shock. Your Lordships have to decide whether or not to validate these extensions.

(5)   A remedy on account of nervous shock has been given to a man who came on a serious accident involving people immediately thereafter and acted as a rescuer of those involved (*Chadwick v British Railways Board*). "Shock" was caused neither by fear for himself nor by fear or horror on account of a near relative. The principle of "rescuer" cases was not challenged by the respondents and ought, in my opinion, to be accepted. But we have to consider whether, and how far, it can be applied to such cases as the present.

Throughout these developments, as can be seen, the courts have proceeded in the traditional manner of the common law from case to case, on a basis of logical necessity. If a mother, with or without accompanying children, could recover on account of fear for herself, how can she be denied recovery on account of fear for her accompanying children? If a father could recover had he seen his child run over by a backing car, how can he be denied recovery if he is in the immediate vicinity and runs to the child's assistance? If a wife and mother could recover if she had witnessed a serious accident to her husband and children, does she fail because she was a short distance away and immediately rushes to the scene? (Cf. *Benson v Lee*.) I think that, unless the law is to draw an arbitrary line at the point of direct sight and sound, these arguments require acceptance of the extension mentioned above under principle (4) in the interests of justice.

If one continues to follow the process of logical progression, it is hard to see why the present plaintiff also should not succeed. She was not present at the accident, but she came very soon after on its aftermath. If, from a distance of some 100 yards (Cf. *Benson v Lee*), she had found her family by the roadside, she would have come within principle (4) above. Can it make any difference that she comes on them in an ambulance, or, as here, in a nearby hospital, when, as the evidence shows, they were in the same condition, covered with oil and mud, and distraught with pain? If Mr Chadwick can recover when, acting in accordance with normal and irresistible human instinct, and indeed moral compulsion, he goes to the scene of an accident, may not a mother recover if, acting under the same motives, she goes to where her family can be found?

I could agree that a line can be drawn above her case with less hardship than would have been apparent in *Boardman's* and *Hinz's* cases, but so to draw it would not appeal to most people's sense of justice. To allow her claim may be, I think it is, on the margin of what the process of logical progression would allow. But where the facts are strong and exceptional, and, as I think, fairly analogous, her case ought, *prima facie*, to be assimilated to those which have passed the test.

To argue from one factual situation to another and to decide by analogy is a natural tendency of the human and legal mind. But the lawyer still has to inquire whether, in so doing, he has crossed some critical line behind which he ought to stop. That is said to be the present case. The reasoning by which the Lords Justices decided not to grant relief to the plaintiff is instructive. Both Stephenson and Griffiths LJJ accepted that the "shock" to the plaintiff was foreseeable, but from this, at least in presentation, they diverge. Stephenson LJ considered that the defendants owed a duty of care to the plaintiff, but that for reasons of policy the law should stop short of giving her damages: it should limit relief to those on or near the highway at or near the time of the accident caused by the defendant's negligence. He was influenced by the fact that the courts of this country, and of other common law jurisdictions, had stopped at this point: it was indicated by the barrier of commercial sense and practical convenience. Griffiths LJ took the view that, although the injury to the plaintiff was foreseeable, there was no duty of care. The duty of care of drivers of motor vehicles was, according to decided cases, limited to persons and owners of property on the road or near to it who might be directly affected. The line should be drawn at this point. It was not even in the interest of those suffering from shock as a class to extend the scope of the defendant's liability: to do so would quite likely delay their recovery by immersing them in the anxiety of litigation.

I am deeply impressed by both of these arguments, which I have only briefly summarised. Though differing in expression, in the end, in my opinion, the two presentations rest on a common principle, namely that, at the margin, the boundaries of a man's responsibility for acts of negligence have to be fixed as a matter of policy. Whatever is the correct jurisprudential analysis, it does not make any essential difference whether one says, with Stephenson LJ, that there is a duty but, as a matter of policy, the consequences of breach of it ought to be limited at a certain point, or whether, with Griffiths LJ, one says that the fact that consequences may be foreseeable does not automatically impose a duty of care, does not do so in fact where policy indicates the contrary. This is an approach which one can see very clearly from the way in which Lord Atkin stated the neighbour principle in *Donoghue v Stevenson* "... persons who are so closely and directly affected by my act that I ought reasonably to have them in contemplation as being so affected ..."

This is saying that foreseeability must be accompanied and limited by the law's judgment as to persons who ought, according to its standards of value or justice, to have been in contemplation. Foreseeability, which involves a hypothetical person, looking with hindsight at an event which has occurred, is a formula adopted by English Law, not merely for defining, but also for limiting the persons to whom duty may be owed, and the consequences for which an actor may be held responsible. It is not merely an issue of fact to be left to be found as such. When it is said to result in a duty of care being owed to a person or a class, the statement that there is a "duty of care" denotes a conclusion into the forming of which considerations of policy have entered. That foreseeability does not of itself, and automatically, lead to a duty of care is, I think, clear. I gave some examples in *Anns v Merton London Borough, Anns* itself being one. I may add what Lord Reid said in *McKew v Holland & Hannen & Cubitts*: "A defender is not liable for a consequence of a kind which is not foreseeable. But it does not follow that he is liable for every consequence which a reasonable man could foresee."

We must then consider the policy arguments. In doing so we must bear in mind that cases of "nervous shock" and the possibility of claiming damages for it are not necessarily confined to those arising out of accidents in public roads. To state, therefore, a rule that recoverable damages must be confined to persons on or near the highway is to state not a principle in itself but only an example of a more general rule that recoverable damages must be confined to those within sight and sound of an event caused by negligence or, at least, to those in close, or very close, proximity to such a situation.

The policy arguments against a wider extension can be stated under four heads. First, it may be said that such extension may lead to a proliferation of claims, and possibly fraudulent claims, to the establishment of an industry of lawyers and psychiatrists who will formulate a claim for nervous shock damages, including what in America is called the customary miscarriage, for all, or many, road accidents and industrial accidents. Second, it may be claimed that an extension of liability would be unfair to defendants, as imposing damages out of proportion to the negligent conduct complained of. In so far as such defendants are insured, a large additional burden will be placed on insurers, and ultimately on the class of persons insured: road users or employers. Third, to extend liability beyond the most direct and plain cases would greatly increase evidentiary difficulties and tend to lengthen litigation. Fourth, it may be said (and the Court of Appeal agreed with this) that an extension of the scope of liability ought only to be made by the legislature, after careful research. This is the course which has been taken in New South Wales and the Australian Capital Territory.

The whole argument has been well summed up by Dean Prosser in *The Law of Torts* (4th edn, 1971):

> "The reluctance of courts to enter this zone even where the mental injury is clearly foreseeable, and the frequent mention of the difficulties of proof, the facility of fraud and the problem of finding a place to stop and draw the line, suggests that here it is the nature of the interest invaded and the type of damages which is the real obstacle."

Since he wrote, the type of damage has, in this country at least, become more familiar and less deterrent to recovery. And some of the arguments are susceptible of answer. Fraudulent claims can be contained by the courts, which also can cope with evidentiary difficulties. The scarcity of cases which have occurred in the past, and the modest sums recovered, give some indication that fears of a flood of litigation may be exaggerated: experience in other fields suggests that such fears usually are. If some increase does occur, that may only reveal the existence of a genuine social need; that legislation has been found necessary in Australia may indicate the same thing.

But, these discounts accepted, there remains, in my opinion, just because "shock" in its nature is capable of affecting so wide a range of people, a real need for the law to place some limitation on the extent of admissible claims. It is necessary to consider three elements inherent in any claim: the class of persons whose claims should be recognised; the proximity of such persons to the accident; and the means by which the shock is caused. As regards the class of persons, the possible range is between the closest of family ties, of parent and child, or husband and wife, and the ordinary bystander. Existing law recognises the claims of the first; it denies that of the second, either on the basis that such persons must be assumed to be possessed of fortitude sufficient to enable them to endure the calamities of modern life or that defendants cannot be expected to compensate the world at large. In my opinion, these positions are justifiable, and since the present case falls within the first class it is strictly unnecessary to say more. I think, however, that it should follow that other cases involving less close relationships must be very carefully scrutinised. I cannot say that they should never be admitted. The closer the tie (not merely in relationship, but in care) the greater the claim for consideration. The claim, in any case, has to be judged in the light of the other factors, such as proximity to the scene in time and place, and the nature of the accident.

As regards proximity to the accident, it is obvious that this must be close in both time and space. It is after all, the fact and consequence of the defendant's negligence that must be proved to have caused the "nervous shock". Experience has shown that to insist on direct and immediate sight or hearing would be impractical and unjust and that under what may be called the "aftermath" doctrine, one who, from close proximity comes very soon on the scene, should not be excluded.

In my opinion, the result in *Benson v Lee* was correct and indeed inescapable. It was based, soundly, on "direct perception of some of the events which go to make up the accident as an entire event, and this includes … the immediate aftermath". The High Court of Australia's majority decision in *Chester v Waverley Municipal Council*, where a child's body was found floating in a trench after a prolonged search, may perhaps be placed on the other side of a recognisable line (Evatt J in a powerful dissent placed it on the same side), but in addition, I find the conclusion of Lush J in *Benson v Lee* to reflect developments in the law.

Finally, and by way of reinforcement of "aftermath" cases, I would accept, by analogy with "rescue" situations, that a person of whom it could be said that one could expect nothing else than that he or she would come immediately to the scene (normally a parent or a spouse) could be regarded as being within the scope of foresight and duty. Where there is not immediate presence, account must be taken of the possibility of alterations in the circumstances, for which the defendant should not be responsible.

Subject only to these qualifications, I think that a strict test of proximity by sight or hearing should be applied by the courts.

Lastly, as regards communication, there is no case in which the law has compensated shock brought about by communication by a third party. In *Hambrook v Stokes Bros*, indeed, it was said that liability would not arise in such a case, and this is surely right. It was so decided in *Abramzik v Brenner*. The shock must come through sight or hearing of the event or of its immediate aftermath. Whether some equivalent of sight or hearing, e.g. through simultaneous television, would suffice may have to be considered.

My Lords, I believe that these indications, imperfectly sketched, and certainly to be applied with common sense to individual situations in their entirety, represent either the existing law, or the existing law with only such circumstantial extension as the common law process may legitimately make. They do not introduce a new principle. Nor do I see any reason why the law should retreat behind the lines already drawn.'

Comment

(1)   In many of the nervous shock cases it can be hard to distinguish the arguments relating to remoteness of damage from those concerned with the existence of a duty, since both are described in terms of reasonable foreseeability. In *Hay (or Bourhill) v Young* the two issues are very closely entwined; note the closing sentence of the passage of Lord Porter's judgment quoted at the start of this chapter (see p 73). In that case the appellant, who had just alighted from a tram, suffered a severe shock and other injuries when a motorcyclist negligently turned into the path of an oncoming car and was killed. Her view of the accident had been obscured by the tram but she heard the sound of the collision and saw blood on the road after the body had been removed. The House of Lords held that the motorcyclist did not owe her a duty of care since he could not reasonably have foreseen that she would suffer such injuries in the circumstances.

Lord Porter went on to say that:

'The driver of a car or vehicle even though careless is entitled to assume that the ordinary frequenter of the streets has sufficient fortitude to endure such incidents as may from time to time be expected to occur in them, including the noise of a collision and the sight of injury to others, and is not to be considered negligent towards one who does not possess the customary phlegm.'

This is not quite the whole story since a form of the 'eggshell skull' principle applies to nervous shock cases. In *Brice v Brown* a mother suffered psychiatric damage as a result of seeing her daughter injured when the taxi in which they were travelling was in collision with a bus. There was evidence that a pre-existing instability had caused her condition to be worse than it might otherwise have been. The court held that a duty was owed in circumstances where a person of ordinary phlegm would foreseeably have suffered *some* damage of the same sort.

(2)   Lord Scarman, with whom Lord Bridge agreed, said:

'... common law principle requires the judges to follow the logic of the "reasonably foreseeable test" so as, in circumstances where it is appropriate, to apply it untrammelled by spatial, physical or temporal limits. Space, time, distance, the nature of the injuries sustained and the relationship of the plaintiff to the immediate victim of the accident are factors to be weighed, but not legal limitations, when the test of reasonable foreseeability is to be applied.

But I am by no means sure that the result is socially desirable. The "floodgates" argument may be exaggerated. Time alone will tell; but I foresee social and financial problems if damages for "nervous shock" should be made available to persons other than parents and children who without seeing or hearing the accident, or being present in the immediate aftermath, suffer nervous shock in consequence of it ...'

This view, that foreseeability of harm was a sufficient test for the existence of a duty in nervous shock, was followed in several subsequent cases, notwithstanding Lord Scarman's cautionary note. In both *Hevican v Ruane* and *Ravenscroft v Rederiaktiebolaget Transatlantic* at first instance parents were able to claim damages for nervous shock. Despite the news of the son's death in each case having been relayed by a third party, it was held to be reasonably foreseeable that a parent in like circumstances would suffer psychiatric damage. The House of Lords in *Alcock* (see below) preferred Lord Wilberforce's approach and seriously doubted these two decisions. *Ravenscroft* has since been reversed in the Court of Appeal.

(3)   In *Attia v British Gas* the plaintiff claimed to have suffered nervous shock as a result of returning home to find her house burning down because of the defendants' negligence. The Court of Appeal held that there was no reason in principle why a nervous shock claim could not stem from property damage, provided that it was reasonably foreseeable that an ordinary householder (or for that matter, owner of other property) would suffer such harm as a result of

seeing their property so damaged. It would appear, at least at first sight, that foreseeability that witnessing the destruction of one's home, with its connected emotional attachment, could result in psychiatric damage was the sole basis for a duty of care in such circumstances. An alternative analysis, and one more consistent with the restrictive approach adopted in subsequent cases, would be to suggest that a duty to the plaintiff existed by virtue of the work the defendants were carrying out at her home. Her claim for psychiatric harm, added as it was to a claim for property damage, becomes a question only of remoteness for which foreseeability is the legitimate test.

Alcock and others v Chief Constable of the South Yorkshire Police [1991] 4 All ER 907 House of Lords

This case arose out of the well-known Hillsborough football stadium disaster. The 16 appellants were, with the exception of one fiancée, all relatives of persons who were in the section of the ground in which 95 spectators died and over 400 were injured. In the case of 13 of the appellants their relative died; for two the relative was injured; and one escaped unhurt. Amongst the appellants were parents who were not present at the ground, siblings both at the ground and at home, a brother-in-law who was present, and a fiancée and a grandparent who were not. The House of Lords held that none of the appellants satisfied all of the criteria necessary for them to fall within the class of persons to whom a duty of care was owed by the respondent.

Lord Keith of Kinkel: '... The question of liability in negligence for what is commonly, if inaccurately, described as "nervous shock" has only twice been considered by this House, in *Hay (or Bourhill) v Young* and in *McLoughlin v O'Brian*. In the latter case ... the leading speech was delivered by Lord Wilberforce. Having set out the position so far reached in the decided cases on nervous shock, he expressed the opinion that foreseeability did not of itself and automatically give rise to a duty of care owed to a person or class of persons and that considerations of policy entered into the conclusion that such a duty existed ...

It was argued for the appellants in the present case that reasonable foreseeability of the risk of injury to them in the particular form of psychiatric illness was all that was required to bring home liability to the respondent. In the ordinary case of direct physical injury suffered in an accident at work or elsewhere, reasonable foreseeability of the risk is indeed the only test that need be applied to determine liability. But injury by psychiatric illness is more subtle, as Lord Macmillan observed in *Bourhill v Young*. In the present type of case it is a secondary sort of injury brought about by the infliction of physical injury, or the risk of physical injury, upon another person.

That can affect those closely connected with that person in various ways. One way is by subjecting a close relative to the stress and strain of caring for the injured person over a prolonged period, but psychiatric illness due to such stress and strain has not so far been treated as founding a claim in damages. So I am of the opinion that in addition to reasonable foreseeability liability for injury in the particular form of psychiatric illness must depend in addition upon a requisite relationship of proximity between the claimant and the party said to owe the duty. Lord Atkin in *M'Alister (or Donoghue) v Stevenson* described those to whom a duty of care is owed as being:

> "persons who are so closely and directly affected by my act that I ought reasonably to have them in contemplation as being so affected when I am directing my mind to the acts or omissions which are called in question".

The concept of a person being closely and directly affected has been conveniently labelled "proximity", and this concept has been applied in certain categories of cases, particularly those concerned with pure economic loss, to limit and control the consequences as regards liability which would follow if reasonable foreseeability were the sole criterion.

As regards the class of persons to whom a duty may be owed to take reasonable care to avoid inflicting psychiatric illness through nervous shock sustained by reason of physical injury or peril to another, I think it sufficient that reasonable foreseeability should be the guide. I would not seek to limit the class by reference to particular relationships such as husband and wife or parent and child. The kinds of relationship which may involve close ties of love and affection are numerous, and it is the existence of such ties which leads to mental disturbance when the loved one suffers a catastrophe. They may be present in family relationships or those of close friendship, and may be stronger in the case of engaged couples than in that of persons who have been married to each other for many years. It is common knowledge that such ties exist, and reasonably foreseeable that those bound by them may in certain circumstances be at real risk of psychiatric illness if the loved one is injured or put in peril. The closeness of the tie would, however, require to be proved by a plaintiff, though no doubt being capable of being presumed in appropriate cases. The case of the bystander unconnected with the victims of an accident is difficult. Psychiatric injury to him would not ordinarily, in my view, be within the range of reasonable foreseeability, but could not perhaps be entirely excluded from it if the circumstances of a catastrophe occurring very close to him were particularly horrific.

In the case of those within the sphere of reasonable foreseeability the proximity factors mentioned by Lord Wilberforce in *McLoughlin v O'Brian* must, however, be taken into account in judging whether a duty of care exists. The first of these is proximity of the plaintiff to the accident in time and space. For this purpose the accident is to be taken to include its immediate aftermath, which in *McLoughlin's* case was held to cover the scene at the hospital which was experienced by the plaintiff some two hours after the accident. In *Jaensch v Coffey* the plaintiff saw her injured husband at the hospital to which he had been taken in severe pain before and between his undergoing a series of emergency operations, and the next day stayed with him in the intensive care unit and thought he was going to die. She was held entitled to recover damages for the psychiatric illness she suffered as a result. Deane J said:

> "... the aftermath of the accident extended to the hospital to which the injured person was taken and persisted for so long as he remained in the state produced by the accident up to and including immediate post-accident treatment ... Her psychiatric injuries were the result of the impact upon her of the facts of the accident itself and its aftermath while she was present at the aftermath of the accident at the hospital."

As regards the means by which the shock is suffered, Lord Wilberforce said in *McLoughlin's* case that it must come through sight or hearing of the event or of its immediate aftermath. He also said that it was surely right that the law should not compensate shock brought about by communication by a third party. On that basis it is open to serious doubt whether *Hevican v Ruane* and *Ravenscroft v Rederiaktie-bolaget Transatlantic* were correctly decided, since in both of these cases the effective cause of the psychiatric illness would appear to have been the fact of a son's death and the news of it.

Of the present appellants two, Brian Harrison and Robert Alcock, were present at the ground, both of them in the West Stand, from which they witnessed the scenes in pens 3 and 4. Brian Harrison lost two brothers, while Robert Alcock lost a brother-in-law and identified the body at the mortuary at midnight. In neither of these cases was there any evidence of particularly close ties of love or affection with the brothers or brother-in-law. In my opinion the mere fact of the particular relationship was insufficient to place the plaintiff within the class of persons to whom a duty of care could be owed by the defendant as being foreseeably at risk of psychiatric illness by reason of injury or peril to the individuals concerned. The same is true of other plaintiffs who were not present at the ground and who lost brothers, or in one case a grandson. I would, however, place in the category of members to which risk of psychiatric illness was reasonably foreseeable Mr and Mrs Copoc, whose son was killed, and Alexandra Penk, who lost her fiancé. In each of these cases the closest ties of love and affection fall to be presumed from the fact of the particular relationship, and there is no suggestion of anything which might tend to rebut that presumption. These three all watched scenes from Hillsborough on television, but none of these depicted suffering of recognisable individuals, such being excluded by the broadcasting code of ethics, a position known to the defendant. In my opinion the viewing of these scenes cannot be equiparated with the viewer being within "sight or hearing of the event or of its immediate aftermath", to use the words of Lord Wilberforce in *McLoughlin v O'Brian*, nor can the scenes reasonably be regarded as giving rise to shock, in the sense of a sudden assault on the nervous system. They were capable of giving rise to anxiety for the safety of relatives known or believed to be present in the area affected by the crush, and undoubtedly did so, but that is very different from seeing the fate of the relative or his condition shortly after the event. The viewing of the television scenes did not create the necessary degree of proximity.'

Comment

(1)   Lord Ackner quoted Deane J in *Jaensch v Coffey*:

'Reasonable foreseeability on its own indicates no more than that such a duty of care will exist if, and to the extent that, it is not precluded or modified by some applicable overriding requirement or limitation. It is to do little more than to state a truism to say that the essential function of such requirements or limitations is to confine the existence of a duty to take reasonable care to avoid reasonably foreseeable injury to the circumstances or classes of case in which it is the policy of the law to admit it. Such overriding requirements or limitations shape the frontiers of the common law of negligence.'

He went on to say that such a limitation, in the case of nervous shock, comprised three elements: '(1) the class of persons whose claims should be recognised; (2) the proximity of such persons to the accident – in time and space; and (3) the means by which the shock has been caused.' Lord Ackner agreed that the plaintiff's relationship with the victim should be assessed on a case-by-case basis, and that even a claim by a bystander should not be ruled out if they had witnessed a particularly gruesome accident such as 'a petrol tanker careering out of control into a school in session and bursting into flames'. He considered that the eight-hour interval between the incident and the earliest identification of a body in the mortuary was far too long to be 'immediate' even if the circumstances could properly be described as the 'aftermath'. He also considered whether the simultaneous broadcasts were the equivalent of sight and hearing, on the basis that the respondent could reasonably have foreseen that such transmissions would occur. He concluded, however, that it was equally foreseeable that the broadcasters' code of ethics would prevent the transmission of identifiable individuals suffering so that, were such shots to be shown, the breach of the code would constitute a *novus actus*, breaking the chain of causation and relieving the respondent of liability. This was not to rule out the possibility of a duty in such cases where there could be no doubt as to the identity of the victims, for example shots of 'a special event of children travelling in a balloon, in which there was media interest, particularly amongst the parents, [showing] the balloon suddenly bursting into flames'.

(2)   Although there was broad agreement as to the outcome of this case, the different emphasis on the various factors by each judge led to a different analysis of the facts. Lord Ackner eliminated all but the plaintiffs, one a brother and one a brother-in-law, who were present at the ground and then discounted

these on the basis that there was no evidence of a close tie of love and affection: 'the quality of brotherly love is well known to differ widely – from Cain and Abel to David and Jonathan'. Lord Oliver agreed but added that in any case, 'their perception of the actual consequences of the disaster to those to whom they were related was ... gradual'. Lord Jauncey narrowed the claimants down to the two parents of a victim, but eliminated them on the basis that the identification, next day, of the body could not qualify as coming on the immediate aftermath not only because of the time delay but also because the purpose of the visit did not equate to the situation 'in which a relative goes ... to rescue or comfort a victim'. Lord Lowry had nothing to add.

(3)   There appears to be no clear principle for identifying the dividing line between the event itself and the aftermath, nor for distinguishing with certainty between sudden and gradual realisation. In *North Glamorgan NHS Trust v Walters* the Court of Appeal had to consider these questions in relation to the claim of a mother who suffered psychiatric injury after a series of negligent errors caused the death of her baby. Ward LJ said:

'35   In my judgment the law as presently formulated does permit a realistic view being taken from case to case of what constitutes the necessary "event". Our task is not to construe the word as if it had appeared in legislation but to gather the sense of the word in order to inform the principle to be drawn from the various authorities. As a word, it has a wide meaning as shown by its definition in the Concise Oxford Dictionary as: "An item in a sports programme, or the programme as a whole". It is a useful metaphor or at least a convenient description for the "fact and consequence of the defendant's negligence", per Lord Wilber-force, or the series of events which make up the entire event beginning with the negligent infliction of damage through to the conclusion of the immediate aftermath whenever that may be. It is a matter of judgment from case to case depending on the facts and circumstance of each case. In my judgment on the facts of this case there was an inexorable progression from the moment when the fit occurred as a result of the failure of the hospital properly to diagnose and then to treat the baby, the fit causing the brain damage which shortly thereafter made termination of this child's life inevitable and the dreadful climax when the child died in her arms. It is a seamless tale with an obvious beginning and an equally obvious end. It was played out over a period of 36 hours, which for her both at the time and as subsequently recollected was undoubtedly one drawn-out experience.'

(4)   It was common ground in *Alcock* that rescuers should fall within the class of persons to whom a duty is owed. In *Chadwick v British Railways Board* the plaintiff, whose home was near to the site of the Lewisham train disaster of 1957, volunteered to help in the rescue operations. He was sent crawling under

the wreckage to administer injections and spent some time trying to comfort a victim who subsequently proved to have died. The court, in allowing his claim for damages for nervous shock, rejected an argument that the risk run by a rescuer was sufficiently different from that of a passenger as to place him outside the duty of care. This decision was again approved by the House of Lords in *White and others v Chief Constable of the South Yorkshire Police and others*, albeit on a narrow view of the basis for recovery: see p 105.

(5)   Another category of 'stranger' recognised in *Alcock* as having a legitimate claim can be described as the 'unwilling participant'. Such a situation may arise, per Lord Oliver:

> 'where the negligent act of the defendant has put the plaintiff in the position of being, or thinking that he is about to be or has been, the involuntary cause of another's death or injury and the illness complained of stems from the shock to the plaintiff of the consciousness of this supposed fact. The fact that the defendant's negligent conduct has foreseeably put the plaintiff in a position of being an unwilling participant in the event establishes of itself a sufficiently proximate relationship between them and the principal question is whether, in the circumstances, injury of that type to that plaintiff was ... reasonably foreseeable.'

Such a claim succeeded in *Dooley v Cammell Laird & Co Ltd* in which the plaintiff was a crane operator who suffered nervous shock when, owing to the negligence of a third party, the load in the sling of his crane slipped and fell into the hold of a ship where his fellows were working. See also *Galt v BRB* and *Wigg v BRB*.

It appears that such a claimant must be able to show sufficient physical and temporal proximity to the death or injury that he or she believes they have caused. In *Hunter v British Coal Corporation and another* the plaintiff's vehicle struck a hydrant, due entirely to the defendants' negligence in failing to provide the minimum required safety clearance, causing it to leak. While the plaintiff was away from the scene looking for a hose, the hydrant exploded killing one of the plaintiff's work colleagues. The Court of Appeal, by a two-to-one majority, held that, in the absence of any cases in which a plaintiff succeeded despite not being present at the scene of the accident, it would be 'quite wrong for the court to push forward the frontiers of liability when the Law Commission, whose report had not yet been published, had just completed a major review of that area of law'.

McFarlane v EE Caledonia Ltd
[1994] 2 All ER 1 Court of Appeal

The plaintiff, a painter on the Piper Alpha oil rig, was off duty and resting on a nearby support vessel when the rig exploded and caught fire, resulting in the deaths of 164 men. For almost two hours, before being evacuated, the plaintiff watched the violent destruction of the rig from a distance of never less than 100 metres. The Court of Appeal rejected his claim for damages for nervous shock.

Stuart-Smith LJ: '... [Smith J] posed the question of law that she had to answer in these terms:

> "... The question to be determined is whether the defendant owed the plaintiff a duty to exercise reasonable care to avoid causing the plaintiff psychiatric injury. The existence of a duty of care depends upon the tests of foreseeability of harm and a proximity of relationship between the plaintiff and the defendant."

Although this formulation is correct so far as it goes, the judge does not specifically remind herself that it is the foreseeability of the reasonable man in the position of the defendant that is material. The question is an objective one. What ought the reasonable owner and operator of a drilling rig and platform in the position of the defendants to have foreseen in the light of the facts which were known or ought to have been known to the defendants? Specifically should he have foreseen that a person of ordinary fortitude in the position of the plaintiff would reasonably be in such fear of his life and safety as to suffer psychiatric shock? ... Although the plaintiff, in order to succeed, had to establish that he in fact had such a fear ... it was irrelevant to the foresight of the reasonable man in the defendant's position ...

In *Alcock v Chief Constable of the South Yorkshire Police*, Lord Oliver of Aylmerton identified two categories of those who suffered nervous shock through fear of injury. First, those involved mediately or immediately as a participant in the event who feared injury to themselves and secondly, those who are no more than passive and unwilling witnesses of injury caused to others ... There are I think basically three situations in which a plaintiff may be a participant when he sustains psychiatric injury through fear of physical injury to himself. First, where he is in the actual area of danger created by the event, but escapes physical injury by chance or good fortune. Such a person would be one who while actually on the Piper Alpha rig at the time of the fire, escaped physical injury, but might well be in fear for his life or safety. Secondly, where the plaintiff is not actually in danger, but because of the sudden and unexpected nature of the event he reasonably thinks that he is ... Thirdly, the situation may arise where the plaintiff who is not originally within the area of danger comes into it later. In the ordinary way, such a person, who is a volunteer, cannot recover if he has freely and voluntarily entered the area of danger. This is not something that the tortfeasor can reasonably foresee, and the plaintiff may also be met with a defence of *volenti non fit injuria*. However if he comes as a rescuer, he can recover ...

A rescuer is entitled to put his own safety at risk, but not that of others, unless they too consent to be part of the rescue ... But what is the position if the captain of a rescue vessel takes what seems to be a justified risk, and in doing so his vessel comes into actual danger with the result that it is damaged and personal injury sustained by those on board? In such circumstances the owners of the rig would be liable to an injured plaintiff on the rescue vessel in respect of both physical injury and psychiatric injury resulting from a reasonable fear of personal injury. But in these circumstances the captain, although with hindsight it will be seen that he committed an error of judgment, is not negligent. A reasonable man in the position of the defendant should foresee that if his negligence caused such a catastrophic emergency, those in charge of rescue vessels may not be able to judge to a nicety exactly how near it is safe to bring their vessels. The plaintiff does not come into either of the first two categories, and [counsel for the defendants] submits that he does not come into the third ... I agree ... there is no reason to doubt that he would have given more help if he could. But since the defendant's liability to a rescuer depends upon his reasonable foreseeability, I do not think that a defendant could reasonably foresee that this very limited degree of involvement could possibly give rise to psychiatric injury ...

[I]t is submitted that the plaintiff was obliged to witness the catastrophe at close range and that it was of such a horrendous nature that even as a bystander the defendants owed him a duty of care. [Counsel for the plaintiff] relies on *dicta* from three of their Lordships in *Alcock v Chief Constable of the South Yorkshire Police*... [He] submits that it is hardly possible to imagine anything more horrific than the holocaust on the Piper Alpha, especially to the plaintiff who knew that some of his mates were on board. I share Lord Keith's difficulty [in *Alcock*, that "psychiatric injury to [a bystander] would not ordinarily ... be within the range of reasonable foreseeability"]. The whole basis of the decision in *Alcock's* case is that where the shock is caused by fear of injury to others as opposed to fear of injury to the participant, the test of proximity is not simply reasonable foreseeability. There must be a sufficiently close tie of love and affection between the plaintiff and the victim. To extend the duty to those who have no such connection, is to base the test purely on foreseeability.

It seems to me that there are great practical problems as well. Reactions to horrific events are entirely subjective; who is to say that it is more horrific to see a petrol tanker advancing out of control on a school, when perhaps unknown to the plaintiff none of the children are in the building but are somewhere safe, than to see a child or group of children run over on a pedestrian crossing? There must be few scenes more harrowing than seeing women and children trapped at the window of a blazing building, yet many people gather to witness these calamities.

In my judgment both as a matter of principle and policy the court should not extend the duty to those who are mere bystanders or witnesses of horrific events unless there is a sufficient degree of proximity, which requires both nearness in time and place and a close relationship of love and affection between plaintiff and victim. Even if I am wrong in this view, I think the plaintiff faces insuperable difficulty in this case. Not only is there no finding that it was reasonably foreseeable that a man of ordinary fortitude and phlegm would be so affected by what he saw, a finding which I would certainly decline to make on the evidence, but there is the finding that the plaintiff was probably not such a person. I think this is fatal to this submission.'

Comment

This approach has been approved in a number of subsequent cases, but in *Alcock* Lord Keith commented that in most cases it is the closeness of the tie of love and affection with the victim that makes it foreseeable that an individual will suffer psychiatric damage, although in some cases it may be the sheer gruesomeness of the incident that makes it foreseeable that a mere bystander will suffer. Arguably, then, the requirement of proximity in time and space is the factor that establishes the proximate relationship between plaintiff and defendant, in which case a bystander in such circumstances should not be denied a remedy. After all, leaving aside the subjectiveness of gruesomeness, there is unlikely to be a floodgates problem since very few potential plaintiffs would ever be sufficiently close to a sufficiently awful incident.

Page v Smith
[1995] 2 All ER 736 House of Lords

The plaintiff, P, suffered no physical injury as a result of a very minor collision at 30 mph between his vehicle and that of the defendant, but the accident triggered a recurrence of his pre-existing condition of myalgic encephalomyelitis (ME). The House of Lords, by a majority of three to two, restored the first instance decision (reversed in the Court of Appeal) that the defendant owed the plaintiff a duty of care.

Lord Lloyd of Berwick: '... In the present case, by contrast [with *Bourhill* and *Alcock*], the plaintiff was a participant. He was himself directly involved in the accident, and well within the range of foreseeable physical injury. He was the primary victim. This is thus the first occasion on which your Lordships have had to decide whether, in such a case, the foreseeability of physical injury is enough to enable the plaintiff to recover damages for nervous shock. ...

Though the distinction between primary and secondary victims is a factual one, it has, as will be seen, important legal consequences. So the classification of all nervous shock cases under the same head may be misleading. In *Alcock's* case Lord Oliver said:

"It is customary to classify cases in which damages are claimed for injury occasioned in this way under a single generic label as cases of 'liability for nervous shock'. This may be convenient but in fact the label is misleading if and to the extent that it is assumed to lead to a conclusion that they have more in common than the factual similarity of the medium through which the injury is sustained – that of an assault upon the nervous system of the plaintiff through witnessing or taking part in an event – and that they will, on account of this factor, provide a single common test for the circumstances which give rise to a duty of care."

It is of cardinal importance in the present case to bear that warning in mind.

Although the plaintiff was, as I have said, the primary victim, the peculiarity of the present case is that, by good fortune, he suffered no broken bones and no bruising; indeed he had no external physical injury of any kind. But as a direct result of the accident he suffered a recrudescence of an illness or condition known variously as ME, CFS or PVFS, from which he had previously suffered in a mild form on sporadic occasions, but which, since the accident, has become an illness of "chronic intensity and permanency" ...

THE CORRECT APPROACH

Against that factual background, [Otton J] dealt with the law quite shortly. He referred to *Malcolm v Broadhurst*, a decision of Geoffrey Lane J. In that case, a woman suffered head injuries in a car accident, as a result of which a pre-existing nervous disturbance was exacerbated. Geoffrey Lane J said:

"The defendant must take the wife as he finds her and there is no difference in principle between an egg-shell skull and an egg-shell personality, *Love v Port of London Authority*. Exacerbation of her nervous depression was a readily foreseeable consequence of injuring her ... I do not derive any assistance from the 'nervous shock' cases; they are concerned with the effect of the sudden traumatic effect of witnessing or hearing of an accident and their somewhat special rules do not seem to me to be applicable to the present circumstances."

Otton J adopted the same line of reasoning ...

Since physical injury to the plaintiff was clearly foreseeable, although it did not in the event occur, the judge did not consider, as a separate question, whether the defendant should have foreseen injury by nervous shock.

When the case got to the Court of Appeal, the approach became more complicated. [Counsel for the defendant's] argument, as summarised by Ralph Gibson LJ, was as follows:

"If a plaintiff establishes that he has suffered some physical injury, he may advance a claim in respect of a recognised psychiatric illness which has resulted from that physical injury. If a plaintiff has suffered no physical injury, and his only injuries are a recognised form of psychiatric illness, he may succeed if the court decides that psychiatric illness was foreseeable in the case of a person of reasonable fortitude. There is no difference in this respect, it was submitted, between a bystander and a person directly involved in an event, except that the consequences are more likely to be foreseeable in the case of the latter than in the case of the former."

The Court of Appeal accepted [counsel's] argument. ...

If, as in *Malcolm v Broadhurst*, the plaintiff had suffered a head injury or a broken leg, or significant bruising, with consequential psychiatric illness, it is very doubtful whether the case would ever have reached the Court of Appeal at all. It would be like many other personal injury cases which are tried or settled every day in the High Court and the county courts. Of course, it would have been necessary to prove that the psychiatric illness was genuine, and that it was caused by the accident. But nobody would have stopped to consider the foreseeability of nervous shock. Nobody would have referred to *Bourhill v Young*. We now know that the plaintiff escaped without external injury. Can it be the law that this makes all the difference? Can it be the law that the fortuitous absence of foreseeable physical injury means that a different test has to be applied? Is it to become necessary, in ordinary personal injury claims, where the plaintiff is the primary victim, for the court to concern itself with different "kinds" of injury?

Suppose, in the present case, the plaintiff had been accompanied by his wife, just recovering from a depressive illness, and that she had suffered a cracked rib, followed by an onset of psychiatric illness. Clearly, she would have recovered damages, including damages for her illness, since it is conceded that the defendant owed the occupants of the car a duty not to cause physical harm. Why should it be necessary to ask a different question, or apply a different test, in the case of the plaintiff? Why should it make any difference that the physical illness that the plaintiff undoubtedly suffered as a result of the accident operated through the medium of the mind, or of the nervous system, without physical injury? If he had suffered a heart attack, it cannot be doubted that he would have recovered damages for pain and suffering, even though he suffered no broken bones. It would have been no answer that he had a weak heart.

I must say at once that I prefer the simplicity of the judge's approach to what, with respect, seems to be an unnecessary complication introduced by the Court of Appeal. Foreseeability of psychiatric injury remains a crucial ingredient when the plaintiff is the secondary victim, for the very reason that the secondary victim is almost always outside the area of physical impact, and therefore outside the range of foreseeable physical injury. But where the plaintiff is the primary victim of the defendant's negligence, the nervous shock cases, by which I mean the cases following on from *Bourhill v Young*, are not in point. Since the defendant was admittedly under a duty of care not to cause the plaintiff foreseeable physical injury, it was unnecessary to ask whether he was under a separate duty of care not to cause foreseeable psychiatric injury.

Apart from its simplicity, Otton J's approach has other attractions. As medical science advances, it is important that the law should not be seen to limp too far behind: see *Mount Isa Mines Ltd v Pusey* per Windeyer J. ...

In an age when medical knowledge is expanding fast, and psychiatric knowledge with it, it would not be sensible to commit the law to a distinction between physical and psychiatric injury, which may already seem somewhat artificial, and may soon be altogether outmoded. Nothing will be gained by treating them as different "kinds" of personal injury, so as to require the application of different tests in law.

My noble and learned friend, Lord Keith of Kinkel, has drawn attention to an observation of Lord Wright in *Bourhill v Young* that in nervous shock cases the circumstances of the accident or event must be viewed *ex post facto*. There are similar observations by Lord Wilberforce and Lord Bridge in *McLoughlin v O'Brian*. This makes sense, as Lord Keith points out, where the plaintiff is a secondary victim. For if you do not know the outcome of the accident or event, it is impossible to say whether the defendant should have foreseen injury by shock. It is necessary to take account of what happened in order to apply the test of reasonable foreseeability at all. But it makes no sense in the case of a primary victim. Liability for physical injury depends on what was reasonably foreseeable by the defendant before the event. It could not be right that a negligent defendant should escape liability for psychiatric injury just because, though serious physical injury was foreseeable, it did not in fact transpire. Such a result in the case of a primary victim is neither necessary, logical nor just. To introduce hindsight into the trial of an ordinary running-down action would do the law no service.

Are there any disadvantages in taking the simple approach adopted by Otton J? It may be said that it would open the door too wide, and encourage bogus claims. As for opening the door, this is a very important consideration in claims by secondary victims. It is for this reason that the courts have, as a matter of policy, rightly insisted on a number of control mechanisms. Otherwise, a negligent defendant might find himself being made liable to all the world. Thus in the case of secondary victims, foreseeability of injury by shock is not enough. The law also requires a degree of proximity: see *Alcock* per Lord Keith, and the illuminating judgment of Stuart-Smith LJ in *McFarlane v EE Caledonia Ltd*. This means not only proximity to the event in time and space, but also proximity of relationship between the primary victim and the secondary victim. A further control mechanism is that the secondary victim will only recover damages for nervous shock if the defendant should have foreseen injury by shock to a person of normal fortitude or "ordinary phlegm".

None of these mechanisms are required in the case of a primary victim. Since liability depends on foreseeability of physical injury, there could be no question of the defendant finding himself liable to all the world. Proximity of relationship cannot arise, and proximity in time and space goes without saying. Nor in the case of a primary victim is it appropriate to ask whether he is a person of "ordinary phlegm". In the case of physical injury there is no such requirement. The negligent defendant, or more usually his insurer, takes his victim as he finds him. The same should apply in the case of psychiatric injury. There is no difference in principle, as Geoffrey Lane J pointed out in *Malcolm v Broadhurst*, between an eggshell skull and an eggshell personality. Since the number of potential claimants is limited by the nature of the case, there is no need to impose any further limit by reference to a person of ordinary phlegm. Nor can I see any justification for doing so.

As for bogus claims, it is sometimes said that if the law were such as I believe it to be, the plaintiff would be able to recover damages for a fright. This is not so. Shock by itself is not the subject of compensation, any more than fear or grief or any other human emotion occasioned by the defendant's negligent conduct. It is only when shock is followed by recognisable psychiatric illness that the defendant may be held liable.

There is another limiting factor. Before a defendant can be held liable for psychiatric injury suffered by a primary victim, he must at least have foreseen the risk of physical injury. So that if, to take the example given by my noble and learned friend, Lord Jauncey of Tullichettle, the defendant bumped his neighbour's car while parking in the street, in circumstances in which he could not reasonably foresee that the occupant would suffer any physical injury at all, or suffer injury so trivial as not to found an action in tort, there could be no question of his being held liable for the onset of hysteria. Since he could not reasonably foresee any injury, physical or psychiatric, he would owe the plaintiff no duty of care. That example is, however, very far removed from the present. So I do not foresee any great increase in unmeritorious claims. The court will, as ever, have to be vigilant to discern genuine shock resulting in recognised psychiatric illness. But there is nothing new in that. The floodgates argument has made regular appearances in this field, ever since it first appeared in *Victorian Railways Comrs v Coultas*. I do not regard it as a serious obstacle here.

My provisional conclusion, therefore, is that Otton J's approach was correct. The test in every case ought to be whether the defendant can reasonably foresee that his conduct will expose the plaintiff to risk of personal injury. If so, then he comes under a duty of care to that plaintiff. If a working definition of "personal injury" is needed, it can be found in s 38(1) of the Limitation Act 1980: "'Personal injuries' includes any disease and any impairment of a person's physical or mental condition …" There are numerous other statutory definitions to the same effect. In the case of a secondary victim, the question will usually turn on whether the foreseeable injury is psychiatric, for the reasons already explained.

In the case of a primary victim the question will almost always turn on whether the foreseeable injury is physical. But it is the same test in both cases, with different applications. There is no justification for regarding physical and psychiatric injury as different "kinds" of injury. Once it is established that the defendant is under a duty of care to avoid causing personal injury to the plaintiff, it matters not whether the injury in fact sustained is physical, psychiatric or both. The utility of a single test is most apparent in those cases such as *Schneider v Eisovitch*, *Malcolm v Broadhurst* and *Brice v Brown*, where the plaintiff is both primary and secondary victim of the same accident.

Applying that test in the present case, it was enough to ask whether the defendant should have reasonably foreseen that the plaintiff might suffer physical injury as a result of the defendant's negligence, so as to bring him within the range of the defendant's duty of care. It was unnecessary to ask, as a separate question, whether the defendant should reasonably have foreseen injury by shock; and it is irrelevant that the plaintiff did not, in fact, suffer any external physical injury.

THE AUTHORITIES

[Lord Lloyd found nothing in the authorities to support any other conclusion, and continued.]

I return to the facts of the present case to mention a fall-back argument on which [counsel for the plaintiff] relied. Assuming, contrary to his primary argument, that it was necessary to establish foreseeability of injury by nervous shock in a person of normal fortitude, then the Court of Appeal were wrong to hold that such injury was not foreseeable. The judge held, as I have said, that the collision was one of moderate severity. He had no doubt that the plaintiff suffered nervous shock in the broad sense of that word. He concluded that since the plaintiff was actually involved in the accident, it became a foreseeable consequence.

I have some difficulty in understanding how the Court of Appeal was justified in disturbing the judge's primary findings, or the inference which he drew from those findings. Ralph Gibson LJ was impressed by the fact that the plaintiff suffered no physical injury. If he was using this piece of hindsight in order to qualify the judge's finding that the accident was one of moderate severity, then, with respect, he was wrong. If he was saying that a person of normal fortitude involved in an accident does not suffer shock, with recognised psychiatric consequences, unless he receives some physical injury, then I would disagree. As Lord Bridge said in *McLoughlin v O'Brian*:

> "... an acute emotional trauma, like a physical trauma, can well cause a psychiatric illness in a wide range of circumstances and in a wide range of individuals whom it would be wrong to regard as having any abnormal psychological make-up."

When cars collide at 30 miles per hour, the possibility that those involved will suffer nervous shock, resulting in some form of psychiatric illness, is not something to be brushed aside. In my opinion, the Court of Appeal were wrong to find that psychiatric illness, in some form, was not a foreseeable consequence of the accident in a person of normal fortitude. But for reasons already mentioned, I do not regard that as the relevant test.

In conclusion, the following propositions can be supported.

(1) In cases involving nervous shock, it is essential to distinguish between the primary victim and secondary victims.

(2) In claims by secondary victims the law insists on certain control mechanisms, in order as a matter of policy to limit the number of potential claimants. Thus, the defendant will not be liable unless psychiatric injury is foreseeable in a person of normal fortitude. These control mechanisms have no place where the plaintiff is the primary victim.

(3) In claims by secondary victims, it may be legitimate to use hindsight in order to be able to apply the test of reasonable foreseeability at all. Hindsight, however, has no part to play where the plaintiff is the primary victim.

(4) Subject to the above qualifications, the approach in all cases should be the same, namely, whether the defendant can reasonably foresee that his conduct will expose the plaintiff to the risk of personal injury, whether physical or psychiatric. If the answer is yes, then the duty of care is established, even though physical injury does not, in fact, occur. There is no justification for regarding physical and psychiatric injury as different "kinds of damage".

(5) A defendant who is under a duty of care to the plaintiff, whether as primary or secondary victim, is not liable for damages for nervous shock unless the shock results in some recognised psychiatric illness. It is no answer that the plaintiff was predisposed to psychiatric illness. Nor is it relevant that the illness takes a rare form or is of unusual severity. The defendant must take his victim as he finds him.

These propositions do not, I think, involve any radical departure from the law as it was left by Kennedy J in *Dulieu v White & Sons* and by the Court of Appeal in *Hambrook v Stokes Bros* and *King v Phillips*, although the decision in the latter case can no longer be supported on its facts. In *McLoughlin v O'Brian* your Lordships had the opportunity to take the law forward by holding that the plaintiff could recover damages for nervous shock, even though she was two miles away at the time of the accident. No such opportunity offers in the present case. But it is at least as important that the law should not take a step backwards. This would, I fear, be the result if the decision of the Court of Appeal were allowed to stand.'

Comment

(1) Lord Lloyd considered the application of his approach to the facts in the case of *Brice v Brown*, saying:

> 'There can be no doubt that the case was correctly decided on the facts. It would have been a reproach to the law if the plaintiff had not been able to recover damages for the severe mental illness which she suffered as a result of the accident, partly out of fear for herself, and partly out of fear for

her daughter. But as she was herself involved in the accident, and as the accident was quite severe (her daughter suffered quite serious injuries), she was plainly owed a duty of care by the defendant. In these circumstances it was, in my opinion, unnecessary to ask as a separate question whether the defendant should have foreseen injury by shock to a person of normally robust constitution. It sufficed that she was a primary victim of the defendant's negligence.'

(2)   Although the appeal was allowed, there remained the question of causation which had not been settled in the Court of Appeal. Two members of that court had left the question open but Ralph Gibson LJ had concluded that, since ME is what is known as a syndrome – a consistent set of symptoms for which no medically accepted cause has yet been established – it must follow that the plaintiff cannot prove that the defendant's negligence has caused the condition.

In *Page v Smith* (*No 2*) the Court of Appeal, approving the reasoning of Ralph Gibson LJ in *Page v Smith*, unanimously upheld the trial judge's finding that:

'... the test is: did the accident, on the balance of probabilities, cause or materially contribute or materially increase the risk of the development or prolongation of the symptoms of CFS which he currently suffers? ... The vital element is that it should be a material contribution, i.e. it should not be merely a minimal or trivial or insignificant contribution. I have come to the conclusion that although [other factors] undoubtedly play their part in the make up of the plaintiff before and after the accident, none can be promoted to the sole cause or the "joint sole cause" of the relapse, so as to exclude any significant contribution of the effects of the accident.'

(3)   The class which Lord Lloyd terms 'bystanders' should not be confused with those so described in *Alcock*. In *Page* the term includes all secondary victims, whether possessing a close tie of love and affection with the primary victim or merely unconnected spectators. For the sake of clarity, such unconnected spectators may conveniently be termed '*mere* bystanders'.

(4)   Contrast Lord Lloyd's statements that 'it would not be sensible to commit the law to a distinction between physical and psychiatric injury' and that there is 'no justification for regarding physical and psychiatric injury as different kinds of injury' with Lord Ackner's view in *Alcock* that 'Shock is no longer a variant of physical injury but a separate kind of damage'. The distinction between physical and psychiatric causes of injury continues to trouble the courts as, for example, in *Pickford v Imperial Chemical Industries plc*, where the House of Lords held that the claimant had failed to establish that her repetitive strain injury was organic rather than psychogenic in origin. The criminal law adopts a similar approach to that of Lord Lloyd, see *R v Ireland, R v Burstow*.

(5)   Note the explicit references to the need 'as a matter of policy' to introduce a number of mechanisms to control the number of claims in relation to secondary victims.

(6)   Before the decision in *Page*, a plaintiff might base a claim on having feared for his or her safety. For these purposes 'fear' meant a reasonable belief that personal injuries were about to be suffered, rather than terror at the prospect. After *Page* a person who reasonably fears for his or her own safety must presumably be a primary victim, although such fear is clearly not an essential requirement, but what of a person in the position, for example, of the plaintiff in *McFarlane*? Arguably, were the situation to be judged without the benefit of hindsight, the defendants ought reasonably to have foreseen some personal injury to him. In *Hegarty v EE Caledonia*, the plaintiff's genuine fear for his own safety was deemed to be unreasonable since the fireball that he saw approaching the ship, causing him to run and hide, never in fact reached it and, with the benefit of hindsight, the ship was judged never to have been in danger. Perhaps the answer is that, where the victim is physically less proximate to the danger than in *Page*'s case, such fear may be taken as evidence that he or she should be regarded as a primary victim, though the argument seems a circular one. The decision in *White* has done nothing to clarify the position, since Lord Steyn's threshold requirement for a rescuer 'that he objectively exposed himself to danger or reasonably believed that he was doing so' still begs the question when such belief might be reasonable although erroneous.

(7)   Page was applied in *Donachie v Chief Constable of the Greater Manchester Police*. The Court of Appeal allowed a claim by an officer who suffered psychiatric illness leading to a stroke after being negligently exposed to foreseeable physical injury during a police surveillance operation.

White and others v Chief Constable of the South Yorkshire Police and others
[1999] I All ER I House of Lords

The claimants were police officers whose claims against their 'employer' arose out of the Hillsborough football stadium disaster. One officer's claim had been rejected by the Court of Appeal on the basis that the role she had played was not that of rescuer, nor was she within the 'zone of danger'. The other officers' claims were allowed by a majority of the Court of Appeal on the basis that they were rescuers and in a primary relationship with the tortfeasor, so the control mechanisms used by the courts for secondary claimants had no application to them. The House of Lords considered arguments based on the employer/employee duty, and on the proposition that the officers were rescuers and, by a majority of three to two, held that there was no liability.

Lord Steyn: '... My Lords, in my view the claims of the four police officers were rightly dismissed by Waller J (now Waller LJ) and the majority in the Court of Appeal erred in reversing him: *Frost v Chief Constable of South Yorkshire Police.*

DIFFERENT KINDS OF HARM

The horrific events of 15 April 1989 at the Hillsborough Football Stadium in Sheffield resulted in the death of 96 spectators and physical injuries to more than 400. It also scarred many others for life by emotional harm. It is admitted by the chief constable that the events were caused by the negligence of the police in allowing the overcrowding of two spectator pens. In an ideal world all those who have suffered as a result of the negligence ought to be compensated. But we do not live in Utopia: we live in a practical world where the tort system imposes limits to the classes of claims that rank for consideration as well as to the heads of recoverable damages. This results, of course, in imperfect justice but it is by and large the best that the common law can do. The application of the requirement of reasonable foreseeability was sufficient for the disposal of the resulting claims for death and physical injury. But the common law regards reasonable foreseeability as an inadequate tool for the disposal of claims in respect of emotional injury.

The law divides those who were mentally scarred by the events of Hillsborough in different categories. There are those whose mental suffering was a concomitant of physical injury. This type of mental suffering is routinely recovered as "pain and suffering". Next, there are those who did not suffer any physical injuries but sustained mental suffering. For present purposes this category must be subdivided into two groups. First, there are those who suffered from extreme grief. This category may include cases where the condition of the sufferer is debilitating. Secondly, there are those whose suffering amounts to a recognisable psychiatric illness. Diagnosing a case as falling within the first or second category is often difficult. The symptoms can be substantially similar and equally severe. The difference is a matter of aetiology: see the explanation in Munkman, *Damages for Personal Injuries and Death* (10th edn, 1996) p. 118, note 6. Yet the law denies redress in the former case: see *Hinz v Berry* but compare the observations of Thorpe LJ in *Vernon v Bosley (No 1)*, that grief constituting pathological grief disorder is a recognisable psychiatric illness and is recoverable. Only recognisable psychiatric harm ranks for consideration. Where the line is to be drawn is a matter for expert psychiatric evidence. This distinction serves to demonstrate how the law cannot compensate for all emotional suffering even if it is acute and truly debilitating.

The four police officers were actively helping to deal with the human consequences of the tragedy and as a result suffered from post traumatic stress disorder. The police officers put in the forefront of their case that they suffered harm as a result of a tort and that justice demands that they should be compensated. A constant theme of the argument of counsel for the police officers was that there is no justification for regarding physical and psychiatric injury as different kinds of damage, and in so arguing he was repeating an observation of Lord Lloyd of Berwick in *Page v Smith*. It is of some importance to examine this proposition. Courts of law must act on the best medical insight of the day. Nowadays courts accept that there is no rigid distinction between body and mind. Courts accept that a recognisable psychiatric illness results from an impact on the central nervous system. In this sense, therefore, there is no qualitative difference between physical harm and psychiatric harm. And psychiatric harm may be far more debilitating than physical harm.

It would, however, be an altogether different proposition to say that no distinction is made or ought to be made between principles governing the recovery of damages in tort for physical injury and psychiatric harm. The contours of tort law are profoundly affected by distinctions between different kinds of damage or harm: see *Caparo Industries plc v Dickman* per Lord Bridge of Harwich. The analogy of the relatively liberal approach to recovery of compensation for physical damage and the more restrictive approach to the recovery for economic loss springs to mind. Policy considerations encapsulated by Cardozo J's spectre of liability for economic loss "in an indeterminate amount for an indeterminate time to an indeterminate class" played a role in the emergence of a judicial scepticism since *Murphy v Brentwood DC* about an overarching principle in respect of the recovery of economic loss: see Steele "Scepticism and the Law of Negligence" [1993] CLJ 437. The differences between the two kinds of damage have led to the adoption of incremental methods in respect of the boundaries of liability for economic loss.

Similarly, in regard to the distinction between physical injury and psychiatric harm it is clear that there are policy considerations at work. That can be illustrated by reference to the Criminal Injuries Compensation Scheme. Section 109(2) of the Criminal Justice Act 1988 contains this restrictive rule:

> "Harm to a person's mental condition is only a criminal injury if it is attributable – (a) to his having been put in fear of immediate physical injury to himself or another; or (b) to his being present when another sustained a criminal injury other than harm to his mental condition."

The reason for the restriction is that Parliament was fearful that a more liberal rule would impose an intolerable burden on the public purse. Parliament has also decided that the only persons who can claim bereavement damages are parents and spouses: s 1(A)(7) of the Fatal Accidents Act 1976. The spectre of wide a class of claimants in respect of bereavement led to an arbitrary but not necessarily irrational rule.

POLICY CONSIDERATIONS AND PSYCHIATRIC HARM

Policy considerations have undoubtedly played a role in shaping the law governing recovery for pure psychiatric harm. The common law imposes different rules for the recovery of compensation for physical injury and psychiatric harm. Thus it is settled law that bystanders at tragic events, even if they suffer foreseeable psychiatric harm, are not entitled to recover damages: *Alcock v Chief Constable of the South Yorkshire Police*. The courts have regarded the policy reasons against admitting such claims as compelling.

It seems to me useful to ask why such different rules have been created for the recovery of the two kinds of damage. In his *Casebook on Tort* (7th edn, 1992) p. 88, Weir gives the following account:

> "... there is equally no doubt that the public ... draws a distinction between the neurotic and the cripple, between the man who loses his concentration and the man who loses his leg. It is widely felt that being frightened is less than being struck, that trauma to the mind is less than lesion to the body. Many people would consequently say that the duty to avoid injuring strangers is greater than the duty not to upset them. The law has reflected this distinction as one would expect, not only by refusing damages for grief altogether, but by granting recovery for other physical harm only late and grudgingly, and then only in very clear cases. In tort, clear means close – close to the victim, close to the accident, close to the defendant."

I do not doubt that public perception has played a substantial role in the development of this branch of the law. But nowadays we must accept the medical reality that psychiatric harm may be more serious than physical harm. It is therefore necessary to consider whether there are other objective policy considerations which may justify different rules for the recovery of compensation for physical injury and psychiatric harm. And in my view it would be insufficient to proceed on the basis that there are unspecified policy considerations at stake. If, as I believe, there are such policy considerations it is necessary to explain what the policy considerations are so that the validity of my assumptions can be critically examined by others.

My impression is that there are at least four distinctive features of claims for psychiatric harm which in combination may account for the differential treatment. Firstly, there is the complexity of drawing the line between acute grief and psychiatric harm: see Hedley, "Nervous shock: wider still and wider" (1997) CLJ 254. The symptoms may be the same. But there is greater diagnostic uncertainty in psychiatric injury cases than in physical injury cases. The classification of emotional injury is often controversial. In order to establish psychiatric harm expert evidence is required. That involves the calling of consultant psychiatrists on both sides. It is a costly and time-consuming exercise. If claims for psychiatric harm were to be treated as generally on a par with physical injury it would have implications for the administration of justice. On its own this factor may not be entitled to great weight and may not outweigh the considerations of justice supporting genuine claims in respect of pure psychiatric injury. Secondly, there is the effect of the expansion of the availability of compensation on potential claimants who have witnessed gruesome events. I do not have in mind fraudulent or bogus claims. In general it ought to be possible for the administration of justice to expose such claims. But I do have in mind the *unconscious* effect of the prospect of compensation on potential claimants. Where there is generally no prospect of recovery, such as in the case of injuries sustained in sport, psychiatric harm appears not to obtrude often. On the other hand, in the case of industrial accidents, where there is often a prospect of recovery of compensation, psychiatric harm is repeatedly encountered and often endures until the process of claiming compensation comes to an end: see *James v Woodall Duckham Construction Co Ltd*. The litigation is sometimes an unconscious disincentive to rehabilitation. It is true that this factor is already present in cases of physical injuries with concomitant mental suffering. But it may play a larger role in cases of pure psychiatric harm, particularly if the categories of potential recovery are enlarged. For my part this factor cannot be dismissed.

The third factor is important. The abolition or a relaxation of the special rules governing the recovery of damages for psychiatric harm would greatly increase the class of persons who can recover damages in tort. It is true that compensation is routinely awarded for psychiatric harm where the plaintiff has suffered some physical harm. It is also well established that psychiatric harm resulting from the apprehension of physical harm is enough: *Page v Smith*. These two principles are not surprising. Inbuilt in such situations are restrictions on the classes of plaintiff who can sue: the requirement of the infliction of some physical injury or apprehension of it introduces an element of immediacy which restricts the category of potential plaintiffs. But in cases of pure psychiatric harm there is potentially a wide class of plaintiffs involved. Fourthly, the imposition of liability for pure psychiatric harm in a wide range of situations may result in a burden of liability on defendants which may be disproportionate to tortious conduct involving perhaps momentary lapses of concentration, e.g. in a motor car accident.

The wide scope of potential liability for pure psychiatric harm is not only illustrated by the rather unique events of Hillsborough but also by accidents involving trains, coaches and buses, and the everyday occurrence of serious collisions of vehicles all of which may result in gruesome scenes. In such cases there may be many claims for psychiatric harm by those who have witnessed and in some ways assisted at the scenes of the tragic events. Moreover, protagonists of very wide theories of liability for pure psychiatric loss have suggested that "workplace claims loom large as the next growth area of psychiatric injury law", the paradigm case being no doubt a workman who has witnessed a tragic accident to an employee: Mullany and Handford "Hillsborough replayed" (1998) 113 LQR 410 at 415.

THE POLICE OFFICERS' CLAIMS

In the present case, the police officers were more than mere bystanders. They were all on duty at the stadium. They were all involved in assisting in the course of their duties in the aftermath of the terrible events. And they have suffered debilitating psychiatric harm. The police officers therefore argue, and are entitled to argue, that the law ought to provide compensation for the wrong which caused them harm. This argument cannot be lightly dismissed. But I am persuaded that a recognition of their claims would substantially expand the existing categories in which compensation can be recovered for pure psychiatric harm. Moreover, as the majority in the Court of Appeal was uncomfortably aware, the awarding of damages to these police officers sits uneasily with the denial of the claims of bereaved relatives by the decision of the House of Lords in *Alcock v Chief Constable of the South Yorkshire Police*. The decision of the Court of Appeal has introduced an imbalance in the law of tort which might perplex the man on the Underground. Since the answer may be that there should be compensation in all these categories I must pursue the matter further.

THE CASE LAW

In order to understand the law as it stands it is necessary to trace in outline its development. [Lord Steyn briefly considered *Dulieu v White & Sons*, *Hambrook v Stokes Bros*, *Bourhill v Young* and *McLoughlin v O'Brian*, and continued.]

The leading decision of the House of Lords is *Alcock v Chief Constable of the South Yorkshire Police*. Before this case the general rule was that only parents and spouses could recover for psychiatric harm suffered as a result of witnessing a traumatic event. In *Alcock's* case the group of plaintiffs who sued for psychiatric injury resulting from the events at Hillsborough included relatives who were in the stadium. The House dismissed all the claims, including the claim of a plaintiff who himself witnessed the scenes at the football ground where two of his brothers died: see Lord Ackner's comment that "the quality of brotherly love is well known to differ widely ..." This decision established that a person who suffers reasonably foreseeable psychiatric illness as a result of another person's death or injury cannot recover damages unless he can satisfy three requirements, viz: (i) that he had a close tie of love and affection with the person killed, injured or imperilled; (ii) that he was close to the incident in time and space; (iii) that he directly perceived the incident rather than, for example, hearing about it from a third person.

Lord Oliver observed that the law was not entirely satisfactory or logically defensible but he thought that considerations of policy made it explicable. Professor Jane Stapleton has described the law as stated in *Alcock's* case as difficult to justify: see "In restraint of tort", an essay in *Frontiers of Liability*, ed Birks (1994). She remarked (p. 95):

"That at present claims can turn on the requirement of 'close ties of love and affection' is guaranteed to produce outrage. Is it not a disreputable sight to see brothers of Hillsborough victims turned away because they had *no more* than brotherly love towards the victim? In future cases will it not be a grotesque sight to see relatives scrabbling to prove their especial love for the deceased in order to win money damages and for the defendant to have to attack that argument?"

But *Alcock's* case is the controlling decision.

The decision of the House of Lords in *Page v Smith* was the next important development in this branch of the law. The plaintiff was directly involved in a motor car accident. He was within the range of potential physical injury. As a result of the accident he suffered from chronic fatigue syndrome. In this context Lord Lloyd of Berwick adopted a distinction between primary and secondary victims: Lord Ackner and Lord Browne-Wilkinson agreed. Lord Lloyd said that a plaintiff who had been within the range of foreseeable injury was a primary victim. Mr Page fulfilled this requirement and could in principle recover compensation for psychiatric loss. In my view it follows that all other victims, who suffer pure psychiatric harm, are secondary victims and must satisfy the control mechanisms laid down in *Alcock's* case. There has been criticism of this classification: see Teff, "Liability for negligently inflicted psychiatric harm: justifications and boundaries" (1998) CLJ 91 at 93. But, if the narrow formulation by Lord Lloyd of Berwick of who may be a primary victim is kept in mind, this classification ought not to produce inconsistent results. In any event, the decision of the House of Lords in *Page v Smith* was plainly intended, in the context of pure psychiatric harm, to narrow the range of potential secondary victims. The reasoning of Lord Lloyd and the Law Lords who agreed with him was based on concerns about an ever-widening circle of plaintiffs.

THE PROCEEDINGS BELOW

Waller J rejected the claims of the police officers. The majority in the Court of Appeal upheld their claims. The first route followed by the majority was to allow some claims because the police officers were on duty in the stadium when they witnessed the gruesome events. The second route was to allow some claims because the police officers were said to be rescuers.

THE EMPLOYMENT ARGUMENT

The majority in the Court of Appeal upheld the argument of counsel for two police officers that they fall into a special category. That argument was again deployed on appeal to the House. The argument was that the present case can be decided on conventional employer's liability principles. And counsel relies on the undoubted duty of an employer to protect employees from harm through work. It is true that there is no contract between police officers and a chief constable. But it would be artificial to rest a judgment on this point: the relationship between the police officers and the chief constable is closely analogous to a contract of employment. And I am content to approach the problem as if there was an ordinary contract of employment between the parties. Approaching the matter in this way it became obvious that there were two separate themes to the argument. The first rested on the duty of an employer to care for the safety of his employees and to take reasonable steps to safeguard them from harm. When analysed this argument breaks down. It is a non sequitur to say that because an employer is under a duty to an employee not to cause him physical injury, the employer should as a necessary consequence of that duty (of which there is no breach) be under a duty not to cause the employee psychiatric injury: see Hilson "Nervous shock and categorisation of victims" (1998) Tort L Rev 37 at 42. The rules to be applied when an employee brings an action against his employer for harm suffered at his workplace are the rules of tort. One is therefore thrown back to the ordinary rules of the law of tort which contain restrictions on the recovery of compensation for psychiatric harm. This way of putting the case does not therefore advance the case of the police officers. The duty of an employer to safeguard his employees from harm could also be formulated in contract. In that event, and absent relevant express provisions, a term is implied by law into the contract as an incident of a standardised contract: see *Scally v Southern Health and Social Services Board*. But such a term could not be wider in scope than the duty imposed by the law of tort. Again one is thrown back to the ordinary rules of the law of tort.

The first way of formulating the argument based on the duty of an employer does not therefore assist the police officers.

The second theme is, on analysis, an argument as to where the justice lay on this occasion. One is considering the claims of police officers who sustained serious psychiatric harm in the course of performing their duties and assisting in harrowing circumstances. That is, a weighty moral argument: the police perform their duties for the benefit of us all. The difficulty is, however, twofold. First, the pragmatic rules governing the recovery of damages for pure psychiatric harm do not at present include police officers who sustain such injuries while on duty. If such a category were to be created by judicial decision, the new principle would be available in many different situations, e.g. doctors and hospital workers who are exposed to the sight of grievous injuries and suffering. Secondly, it is common ground that police officers who are traumatised by something they encounter in their work have the benefit of statutory schemes which permit them to retire on pension. In this sense they are already better off than bereaved relatives who were not allowed to recover in *Alcock's* case. The claim of the police officers on our sympathy, and the justice of the case, is great but not as great as that of others to whom the law denies redress.

THE RESCUE ARGUMENT

The majority in the Court of Appeal held that three of the police officers could be classed as rescuers because they actively gave assistance in the aftermath of the tragedy: the majority used the concept of rescuer in an undefined but very wide sense: see Rose LJ; Henry LJ expressly agreed with this passage. This reasoning was supported by counsel for the respondents on the appeal.

The law has long recognised the moral imperative of encouraging citizens to rescue persons in peril. Those who altruistically expose themselves to danger in an emergency to save others are favoured by the law. A rescue attempt to save someone from danger will be regarded as foreseeable. A duty of care to a rescuer may arise even if the defendant owed no duty to the primary victim, for example, because the latter was a trespasser. If a rescuer is injured in a rescue attempt, a plea of *volenti non fit injuria* will not avail a wrongdoer. A plea of contributory negligence will usually receive short shrift. A rescuer's act in endangering himself will not be treated as a *novus actus interveniens*. The meaning given to the concept of a rescuer in these situations is of no assistance in solving the concrete case before the House. Here the question is: who may recover in respect of pure psychiatric harm sustained as a rescuer?

Counsel for the respondent is invoking the concept of a rescuer as an exception to the limitations recognised by the House of Lords in *Alcock's* case and *Page v Smith*. The restrictive rules, and the underlying policy considerations, of the decisions of the House are germane. The specific difficulty counsel faces is that it is common ground that none of the four police officers were at any time exposed to personal danger and none thought that they were so exposed. Counsel submitted that this is not a requirement. He sought comfort in the general observations in *Alcock's* case of Lord Oliver about the category of "participants". None of the other Law Lords in *Alcock's* case discussed this category. Moreover, the issue of rescuers' entitlement to recover for psychiatric harm was not before the House on that occasion and Lord Oliver was not considering the competing arguments presently before the House. The explanation of Lord Oliver's observations has been the subject of much debate. It was also vigorously contested at the bar. In my view counsel for the respondent has tried to extract too much from general observations not directed to the issue now before the House: see also the careful analysis of the Lord President in *Robertson v Forth Road Bridge Joint Board, Rough v Forth Road Bridge Joint Board*. Counsel was only able to cite one English decision in support of his argument namely the first instance judgment in *Chadwick v British Transport Commission*. Mr Chadwick had entered a wrecked railway carriage to help and work among the injured. There was clearly a risk that the carriage might collapse. Waller J (later Waller LJ) said: "although there was clearly an element of personal danger in what Mr Chadwick was doing, I think I must deal with this case on the basis that it was the horror of the whole experience which caused his reaction."

On the judge's findings the rescuer had passed the threshold of being in personal danger but his psychiatric injury was caused by "the full horror of his experience" when he was presumably not always in personal danger. This decision has been cited with approval: see *McLoughlin v O'Brian* per Lord Wilberforce, Lord Edmund Davies and Lord Bridge of Harwich; and in *Alcock v Chief Constable of the South Yorkshire Police* per Lord Oliver. I too would accept that *Chadwick's* case was correctly decided. But it is not authority for the proposition that a person who never exposed himself to any personal danger and never thought that he was in personal danger can recover pure psychiatric injury as a rescuer. In order to recover compensation for pure psychiatric harm as rescuer it is not necessary to establish that his psychiatric condition was *caused* by the perception of personal danger. And Waller J rightly so held. But in order to contain the concept of rescuer in reasonable bounds for the purposes of the recovery of compensation for pure psychiatric harm the plaintiff must at least satisfy the threshold requirement that he objectively exposed himself to danger or reasonably believed that he was doing so. Without such limitation one would have the unedifying spectacle that, while bereaved relatives are not allowed to recover as in *Alcock's* case, ghoulishly curious spectators, who assisted in some peripheral way in the aftermath of a disaster, might recover. For my part the limitation of actual or apprehended dangers is what proximity in this special situation means. In my judgment it would be an unwarranted extension of the law to uphold the claims of the police officers. I would dismiss the argument under this heading.

THUS FAR AND NO FURTHER

My Lords, the law on the recovery of compensation for pure psychiatric harm is a patchwork quilt of distinctions which are difficult to justify. There are two theoretical solutions. The first is to wipe out recovery in tort for pure psychiatric injury. The case for such a course has been argued by Professor Stapleton. But that would be contrary to precedent and, in any event, highly controversial. Only Parliament could take such a step. The second solution is to abolish all the special limiting rules applicable to psychiatric harm. That appears to be the course advocated by Mullany and Handford, *Tort Liability for Psychiatric Damage: The Law of Nervous Shock* (1993). They would allow claims for pure psychiatric damage by mere bystanders: see "Hillsborough replayed" (1998) 113 LQR 410 at 415. Precedent rules out this course and, in any event, there are cogent policy considerations against such a bold innovation. In my view the only sensible general strategy for the courts is to say thus far and no further. The only prudent course is to treat the pragmatic categories as reflected in authoritative decisions such as *Alcock's* case and *Page v Smith* as settled for the time being but by and large to leave any expansion or development in this corner of the law to Parliament. In reality there are no refined analytical tools which will enable the courts to draw lines by way of compromise solution in a way which is coherent and morally defensible. It must be left to Parliament to undertake the task of radical law reform.'

Lord Hoffmann: '... The second way in which the plaintiffs put their case is that they were not "bystanders or spectators" but participants in the sense that they actually did things to help. They submit that there is an analogy between their position and that of a "rescuer", who, on the basis of the decision of Waller J in *Chadwick v British Transport Commission* is said to be treated as a primary victim, exempt from the control mechanisms ...

References in the authorities to rescuers sometimes give the impression that they are a category of persons who would not qualify for compensation under the strict rules of the law of negligence but receive special treatment on grounds of humanity and as a reward for altruism. A florid passage by Cardozo J in *Wagner v International Rly Co* is frequently quoted. If rescuers formed a specially privileged category of plaintiff, one would expect that the rule would give rise to a definitional problem about who counted as a rescuer and so qualified for special treatment. In fact, as one can see from the absence of any such problem in the cases, rescuers can be accommodated without difficulty in the general principles of the law of negligence. There are two questions which may arise. The first is whether injury to the rescuer was foreseeable. There is usually no difficulty in holding that if it was foreseeable that someone would be put in danger, it was also foreseeable that someone would go to look for him or try to rescue him or otherwise help him in his distress. The second question is whether the voluntary act of the rescuer, searcher or helper in putting himself in peril negatives the causal connection between the original negligent conduct and his injury. Again, the courts have had equally little difficulty in holding that such a person, acting out of a sense of moral obligation, does not make the free choice which would be necessary to eliminate the causal effect of the defendant's conduct. In the same way, its causal effect is not negatived by an unsuccessful attempt of the person in peril, whose freedom of choice has been limited by the position into which the defendant has put him, to extricate himself from danger: see *Lord v Pacific Steam Navigation Co Ltd, The Oropesa*.

The cases on rescuers are therefore quite simple illustrations of the application of general principles of foreseeability and causation to particular facts. There is no authority which decides that a rescuer is in any special position in relation to liability for psychiatric injury. And it is no criticism of the excellent judgment of Waller J in *Chadwick's* case to say that such a question obviously never entered his head. Questions of such nicety did not arise until the *Alcock* control mechanisms had been enunciated.

There does not seem to me to be any logical reason why the normal treatment of rescuers on the issues of foreseeability and causation should lead to the conclusion that, for the purpose of liability for psychiatric injury, they should be given special treatment as primary victims when they were not within the range of foreseeable physical injury and their psychiatric injury was caused by witnessing or participating in the aftermath of accidents which caused death or injury to others. It would of course be possible to create such a rule by an *ex post facto* rationalisation of *Chadwick's* case ... If one is looking for an *ex post facto* rationalisation of *Chadwick's* case, I think that the most satisfactory is that offered in the Court of Appeal in *McLoughlin v O'Brian* by my noble and learned friend Lord Griffiths, who had been the successful counsel for Mr Chadwick. He said: "Mr Chadwick might have been injured by a wrecked carriage collapsing on him as he worked among the injured. A duty of care is owed to a rescuer in such circumstances ..." If Mr Chadwick was, as Lord Griffiths said, within the range of foreseeable physical injury, then the case is no more than an illustration of the principle applied by the House in *Page v Smith*, namely that such a person can recover even if the injury he actually suffers is not physical but psychiatric. And in addition (unlike *Page v Smith*) Waller J made a finding that psychiatric injury was also foreseeable.

Should then your Lordships take the incremental step of extending liability for psychiatric injury to "rescuers" (a class which would now require definition) who give assistance at or after some disaster without coming within the range of foreseeable physical injury? It may be said that this would encourage people to offer assistance. The category of secondary victims would be confined to "spectators and bystanders" who take no part in dealing with the incident or its aftermath. On the authorities, as it seems to me, your Lordships are free to take such a step.

In my opinion there are two reasons why your Lordships should not do so. The less important reason is the definitional problem to which I have alluded. The concept of a rescuer as someone who puts himself in danger of physical injury is easy to understand. But once this notion is extended to include others who give assistance, the line between them and bystanders becomes difficult to draw with any precision. For example, one of the plaintiffs in *Alcock's* case ... went to look for his nephew. "He searched among the bodies ... and assisted those who staggered out from the terraces". He did not contend that his case was different from those of the other relatives and it was also dismissed. Should he have put himself forward as a rescuer?

But the more important reason for not extending the law is that in my opinion the result would be quite unacceptable ... I think that such an extension would be unacceptable to the ordinary person because (though he might not put it this way) it would offend against his notions of distributive justice. He would think it unfair between one class of claimants and another, at best not treating like cases alike and, at worst, favouring the less deserving against the more deserving. He would think it wrong that policemen, even as part of a general class of persons who rendered assistance, should have the right to compensation for psychiatric injury out of public funds while the bereaved relatives are sent away with nothing ...

It may be said that the common law should not pay attention to these feelings about the relative merits of different classes of claimants. It should stick to principle and not concern itself with distributive justice. An extension of liability to rescuers and helpers would be a modest incremental development in the common law tradition and, as between these plaintiffs and these defendants, produce a just result. My Lords, I disagree. It seems to me that in this area of the law, the search for principle was called off in *Alcock v Chief Constable of the South Yorkshire Police*. No one can pretend that the existing law, which your Lordships have to accept, is founded upon principle. I agree with Professor Jane Stapleton's remark (see *The Frontiers of Liability*, ed Birks (1994) vol 2, p. 87) that "once the law has taken a wrong turning or otherwise fallen into an unsatisfactory internal state in relation to a particular cause of action, incrementalism cannot provide the answer". Consequently your Lordships are now engaged, not in the bold development of principle, but in a practical attempt, under adverse conditions, to preserve the general perception of the law as a system of rules which is fair between one citizen and another.

I should say in passing that I do not suggest that someone should be unable to recover for injury caused by negligence, in circumstances in which he would normally be entitled to sue, merely because his occupation required him to run the risk of such injury. Such a rule, called "the fireman's rule" obtains in some of the United States but was rejected by your Lordships' House in *Ogwo v Taylor*. This would be too great an affront to the idealised model of the law of torts as a system of corrective justice between equals. But the question here is rather different. It is not whether a policeman should be disqualified in circumstances in which he would ordinarily have a right of action, but whether there should be liability to rescuers and helpers as a class. And in considering whether liability for psychiatric injury should be extended to such a class, I think it is legitimate to take into account the fact that, in the nature of things, many of its members will be from occupations in which they are trained and required to run such risks and which provide for appropriate benefits if they should suffer such injuries.

Naturally I feel great sympathy for the plaintiffs' claims, as I do for all those whose lives were blighted by that day at Hillsborough. But I think that fairness demands that your Lordships should reject them.'

Comment

(1)   Lord Hoffmann, while acknowledging that the 'fire-fighters' rule', as such, plays no part in English law, appears to adopt a variant of it by suggesting that professional rescuers are required to possess more than the customary phlegm and fortitude which is to be expected of claimants generally.

(2)   Lord Griffiths (in the minority) rejected the claim based solely on an employment relationship with the defendant, but would have allowed the claims of officers as rescuers. He considered the horrific events at Hillsborough to be comparable with those experienced by Mr Chadwick, and rejected the need for further control mechanisms for rescuers, although he acknowledged that a line should be drawn between 'rescue in the sense of immediate help at the scene of the disaster, and treatment of the victims after they are safe'. He also said that he did not 'share the view that the public would find it in some way offensive that those who suffered disabling psychiatric illness as a result of their efforts to rescue the victims should receive compensation, but that those who suffered the grief of bereavement should not ... I think better of my fellow men than to believe that they would, although bereaved, look like dogs in the manger upon those who went to the rescue at Hillsborough.'

(3)   Lord Goff (also in the minority) felt that it was wrong to impose control mechanisms on claimants who, but for the fact that they had not been exposed

to risk of physical injury, had participated in events to such an extent as to be properly regarded as primary victims. He argued that the undesirability of imposing such controls could be tested by imagining a train crash at which two Chadwick brothers assisted in identical ways, save that one of them (unknown to himself) was working in an area where existed a physical danger, whereas the other was at all times safe. It would, he contended, be absurd that one claim would succeed while the other must fail. He regarded the majority view as being unduly driven by a misconceived desire to avoid a decision whereby the police officers would be 'better off' than the relatives in *Alcock* – misconceived because the circumstances of the two classes of claimant were so different that they could not sensibly be compared.

(4)   Immediately after the decision in *Alcock*, it appeared there were several categories of claimant who fell outside the usual control mechanisms for secondary claimants: unwilling participants (as in *Dooley v Cammell Laird & Co Ltd*), rescuers, and bystanders who witnessed events of a particularly horrifying nature. The position of the last two groups has since been clarified and restricted, and it remains to be seen whether future claims by unwilling participants will succeed.

(5)   It is not always clear what should be understood by the term 'participant'. In *Young v Charles Church (Southern) Ltd* the plaintiff, a scaffolder, suffered psychiatric damage when the workmate alongside him was electrocuted and killed when a scaffold pole touched an overhead power line. Two of the judges in the Court of Appeal had no difficulty in holding that the plaintiff was a primary victim in the *Page v Smith* sense, since he was 'at risk of physical injury, which he was fortunate to avoid, from an accident which could be foreseen'. The third judge, Hobhouse LJ, regarded the plaintiff as a secondary victim but within Lord Oliver's category of participants, being more than 'the passive and unwilling witness of injury caused to others'. He felt bound to follow Rose LJ's approach in *Frost*, and held that the plaintiff, although strictly self-employed, was owed a duty of care analogous to that owed by an employer which includes a duty 'not to expose the employee to avoidable traumatic experiences'.

(6)   In *Hegarty v EE Caledonia*, which concerned a second claim arising out of the Piper Alpha disaster, the Court of Appeal noted the difficulties that might be caused if the same plaintiff were to be regarded as both a primary and secondary victim in relation to the same occasion. Hegarty's circumstances were very similar to those of McFarlane, except that at one point he feared that a fireball from an explosion on the rig was going to engulf the *Tharos*. He ran for his life and hid, praying, in a hangar. The court concluded that, although he had genuinely feared for his own safety, his fear was irrational as the fireball fizzled out some 50 metres from the ship. Had the fear been reasonable, however, problems might have been encountered in separating the psychiatric damage caused by that experience from the irrecoverable damage caused to him as a mere bystander.

(7)   In *Re The Creutzfeld Jakob Disease Litigation – Group B* (*Human Growth Hormone*) the plaintiffs were a group of people who had been injected with a human growth hormone, Hartree HGH, some of which may have been infected with CJD. It was impossible to say whether any, or all, of the plaintiffs had been infected but it was accepted that the defendants were in breach of a duty owed to the plaintiffs at the time they were injected. The trial was to establish certain preliminary issues: whether there was a duty to avoid the risk of psychiatric as well as physical injury; whether psychiatric injury can, as a matter of law, be held to be caused by the defendant's negligence; and whether damages for such psychiatric injury are recoverable as a matter of law. Morland J considered Lord Lloyd's five propositions in *Page v Smith* and concluded that, although in some respects the plaintiffs could be likened to primary victims since the breach of duty consisted of an impact – namely the injection – such an approach would have the undesirable effect of opening the floodgates to vast numbers of claims from people worrying about possible exposure to asbestos, radiation and so on. Because of this, there might be difficulties in obtaining insurance; also, companies might be deterred from publicising, for example, the fact that a batch of canned food had been contaminated because it might result in liability to people who had already eaten the food and feared that they may be poisoned. In the light of these concerns, Morland J held that the plaintiffs should not be treated as primary victims, free from the control mechanisms, although he could see 'no logical reason why foreseeability of and responsibility for shock and psychiatric injury should be limited to an area of time contemporaneous or almost contemporaneous to the negligent physical event'. Since it was, in his view, reasonably foreseeable that persons of normal phlegm and reasonable fortitude might well suffer psychiatric injury on learning of the risk to them, the plaintiffs should recover provided they could establish causation.

(8)   The Law Commission Report on Liability for Psychiatric Illness concluded that the control mechanisms are 'drawn unnecessarily tightly' and recommends that the requirements relating to a plaintiff's physical and temporal proximity to the accident, and the means by which he or she learned of it, be abolished. The report recommends the retention of the need for a close tie of love and affection and for a recognisable psychiatric illness, but would remove the need for the illness to be caused by shock, and any barrier preventing a claim based on the defendant's negligent imperilment of him or herself.

A case whose facts amply illustrate the effect of the present control mechanisms and the need for reform is *Tranmore v TE Scudder Ltd*, in which the claimant's son was killed when a building in which he was working collapsed due to the defendants' negligence. The claimant arrived at the scene approximately two hours after the collapse and was taken to see the pile of rubble under which his son was trapped. He remained there for some time, but the body was not recovered until the following day. Clearly, since *Alcock*, identifying a body could not be equated with coming upon 'the immediate aftermath', but the

Court of Appeal went further, holding that the claimant's attendance at the scene also fell outside the immediate aftermath. Brooke LJ noted Lord Jauncey's observation in *Alcock* that: 'What constitutes the immediate aftermath of an accident must necessarily depend upon the surrounding circumstances. To essay any comprehensive definition would be a fruitless exercise.' On the facts of the case, the combined effect of the time delay together with the fact (perhaps crucially) that the claimant did not see his son took him 'just beyond the lines drawn by the decided cases'.

Greatorex v Greatorex and another
[2000] 4 All ER 769 QBD

The claimant was a fire officer who was one of a team who attended the scene of a road traffic accident caused by the negligence of his son, the defendant. The defendant was seriously injured and had to be released from wreckage. The claimant subsequently suffered severe long-term post traumatic stress disorder. The court held that no duty was owed to third parties by a primary victim in respect of self-inflicted injuries.

Cazalet J: '... There is no reported English decision on the question whether a victim of self-inflicted injuries owes a duty of care to a third party not to cause him psychiatric injury. Lord Ackner referred to the issue in *Alcock v Chief Constable of the South Yorkshire Police*:

> "As yet there is no authority establishing that there is liability on the part of the injured person, his or her estate, for mere psychiatric injury which was sustained by another by reason of shock, as a result of a self-inflicted death, injury or peril of the negligent person, in circumstances where the risk of such psychiatric injury was reasonably foreseeable. On the basis that there must be a limit at some reasonable point to the extent of the duty of care owed to third parties which rests upon everyone in all his actions, Lord Robertson, the Lord Ordinary, in his judgment in *Bourhill*'s case, did not view with favour the suggestion that a negligent window-cleaner who loses his grip and falls from a height, impaling himself on spiked railings, would be liable for the shock-induced psychiatric illness occasioned to a pregnant woman looking out of the window of a house situated on the opposite side of the street."

Lord Oliver also considered the question. He said as follows:

> "Whilst not dissenting from the case-by-case approach advocated by Lord Bridge in *McLoughlin*'s case, the ultimate boundaries within which claims for damages in such cases can be entertained must I think depend in the end upon considerations of policy. For example, in his illuminating judgment in *Jaensch v Coffey* Deane J expressed the view that no claim could be

entertained as a matter of law in a case where the primary victim is the negligent defendant himself and the shock to the plaintiff arises from witnessing the victim's self-inflicted injury. The question does not, fortunately, fall to be determined in the instant case, but I suspect that an English court would be likely to take a similar view. But if that be so, the limitation must be based upon policy rather than upon logic for the suffering and shock of a wife or mother at witnessing the death of her husband or son is just as immediate, just as great and just as foreseeable whether the accident be due to the victim's own or to another's negligence and if the claim is based, as it must be, on the combination of proximity and foreseeability, there is certainly no logical reason why a remedy should be denied in such a case ..."

Jaensch v Coffey, referred to by Lord Oliver, was a decision of the High Court of Australia. It has been considered in other decisions in that jurisdiction. It is right that I should take into account further Commonwealth authorities bearing upon the issue which I have to decide.

I can do no better than refer to the words of Lord Goff in *White v Chief Constable of the South Yorkshire Police*:

"In this, as in other areas of tortious liability in which the law is in a state of development, the courts proceed cautiously from one category of case to another. We should be wise to heed the words of Windeyer J spoken nearly 30 years ago in *Mount Isa Mines Ltd v Pusey*: 'The field is one in which the common law is still in course of development. Courts must therefore act in company and not alone. Analogies in other courts, and persuasive precedents as well as authoritative pronouncements, must be regarded.'"

In *Jaensch's* case a motor cyclist suffered severe injuries in a collision with a vehicle which was driven negligently. The motor cyclist's wife, who was not at the scene of the accident but who saw him in hospital and was told that he was "pretty bad", suffered nervous shock as a result of what she had seen and been told. The wife succeeded in her claim for damages on the basis of her relationship with her husband and the fact that the events which had caused the nervous shock to her were part of the aftermath of the accident resulting from the defendant's negligence.

Deane J, in referring to the duty of care to avoid psychiatric injury unassociated with physical injury, said:

"[It] will not exist unless the reasonably foreseeable psychiatric injury was sustained as a result of the death, injury or peril of someone other than a person whose carelessness is alleged to have caused the injury".

Dawson J appears to have inclined towards the same view. He said:

"On the other hand, there appear to be strictures upon liability for the infliction of nervous shock which are not readily explicable in terms of foreseeability and which may be seen to be the result of the application of policy considerations. For example, if no action will lie in negligence against a defendant who carelessly injures himself and thereby inflicts nervous shock upon the plaintiff, there would seem to be a limit imposed which is outside the test of foreseeability."

These observations were not necessary for the decision in the case and thus were plainly *obiter*.

[Counsel for the defendant] has referred me to a number of other Australian authorities in which the issue in question has received consideration. In *Harrison v State Government Insurance Office*, a decision of the Supreme Court of Queensland, the claimant was a passenger in a car driven by her husband which was involved in a collision through his negligence. Her husband was seriously injured and later died from his injuries. The claimant suffered minor physical injuries but suffered psychiatric illness as a result of the trauma of the accident and of concern for her husband's injuries.

Vasta J held that the claimant's psychiatric illness was reasonably foreseeable but that this was not the sole test for determining liability for negligence. He distinguished between the claimant's claim for damages for nervous shock which came from the major emotional trauma which she had experienced as a primary victim of the collision on the one hand, and that which flowed from her concern for her husband and her realisation that he had sustained shocking injuries on the other. Following Deane J's observations in *Jaensch's* case, he held that the claim in respect of the latter, if launched separately, would have been doomed to failure. I note in passing that it was not considered possible to separate the nervous shock suffered by the claimant as a result of her concern for her husband from the emotional trauma arising from the accident itself, but in my view that fact does not detract from the force of Vasta J's observations.

In the course of his judgment Vasta J referred to *obiter dicta* in two earlier Australian authorities which, he suggested, bore out Deane J's statement of principle in *Jaensch's* case. Since the reports of those cases have not been made available to me, I shall draw upon Vasta J's reference to them.

As to the first of these two authorities, *Dwyer v Dwyer*, Vasta J recorded that Wallace P, giving the judgment of the Court of Appeal of New South Wales, in effect stated that a wife owes no duty to her husband not to injure herself.

In the second case, *Kohn v State Government Insurance Commission*, Vasta J cited Bray CJ as having observed: "a man or his representatives can hardly be legally responsible for the injurious effect of his own death." [Counsel] also referred me to the judgment of Zeeman J in *Klug v Motor Accidents Insurance Board* (Supreme Court of Tasmania). In that case the claimant was a passenger in a car which was being driven by his wife and which was involved in a collision as a result of her negligence. The wife was killed. The claimant claimed damages for psychiatric injury arising not from the accident itself but from the death of his wife. Zeeman J dismissed the claim, saying:

> "As a matter of principle it might be thought that the plaintiff ought not to be denied damages for his psychiatric injury merely because of the fact that it is the product of the death of the tortfeasor. A possible basis for denying relief is that there existed no duty of care on the part of the tortfeasor not to injure herself and that the damages are the product of such injury (cf *Dwyer v Dwyer*). I do not find that persuasive. There appears to be no reported case where a plaintiff was permitted to recover or denied damages for psychiatric injuries solely resulting from the death of or injury to the tortfeasor. Certainly I was not referred to any such case. Uninstructed by authority I would have thought such a claim to be maintainable if otherwise it satisfied the legal pre-requisites for liability to exist. However I must accept that this area of the law is governed by policy considerations which limit the availability of a remedy. The dictum of Deane J in *Jaensch v Coffey* to which I have referred, whilst acknowledging that the common law in Australia may change to recognise liability in a case such as the present, ought to be followed by me, sitting at first instance. It requires the plaintiff's claim for damages for his psychiatric injury to be denied upon the basis that it falls into a category which is not compensatable by reason of policy considerations."

This passage is part of the *ratio decidendi* of the judgment.

[Counsel] further pointed out that the same conclusion was reached in an unreported decision of the Supreme Court of British Columbia, *Cady v Anderson*. In that case the plaintiff was prevented from recovering for psychiatric injury caused by witnessing the death of her fiancé in a car accident caused by his negligence. One of the two grounds given for this decision was the fact that the fiancé was the tortfeasor.

The weight of the Commonwealth authorities to which I have been referred clearly tends to support [counsel's] submission that there is no duty of care in the situation presently under consideration.

[Cazalet J considered and dismissed an argument for the claimant based on *A v B's Trustees* which he said was decided in contract, and continued.]

[Counsel for the claimant] went on to submit that Deane J's approach in *Jaensch's* case, that as a matter of law no claim can be entertained where the primary victim is the negligent defendant himself and the shock to the claimant arises from witnessing the victim's self-inflicted injury, is not only unworkable but also unjust in that, for example, it would preclude claims such as those of train drivers who suffer nervous shock when a person throws himself in front of their train in order to commit suicide. Although I shall be referring to potentially relevant policy considerations later in this judgment, it seems convenient to deal with this submission at this stage, because [counsel] relies upon authority in support of it.

The authority relied upon is an *obiter dictum* in the judgment of Watkins LJ in *R v Criminal Injuries Commission Board, ex p Warner*, where he said, referring to this type of case, that the person attempting to commit suicide "may well be in breach of a duty of care owed to the driver of and the passengers on the train". He expressed no final conclusion on the point.

It is clear, however, that the case of the train driver falls into a particular category of cases, including *Dooley v Cammell Laird & Co Ltd*, in which a duty of care has been held to exist, and which was described by Lord Oliver in *Alcock v Chief Constable of the South Yorkshire Police*:

"... where the negligent act of the defendant has put the plaintiff in the position of being, or of thinking that he is about to be or has been, the involuntary cause of another's death or injury and the illness complained of stems from the shock to the plaintiff of the consciousness of this supposed fact."

Whether this category of cases has survived *White v Chief Constable of the South Yorkshire Police* has not yet been authoritatively decided. In *White's* case Lord Hoffmann made the following comment upon Lord Oliver's analysis:

"This is an elegant, not to say ingenious, explanation, which owes nothing to the actual reasoning (so far as we have it) in any of the cases. And there may be grounds for treating such a rare category of case as exceptional and exempt from the *Alcock* control mechanisms. I do not need to express a view because none of the plaintiffs in this case come within it."

A degree of further support for Lord Oliver's observations can be drawn from Lord Slynn's speech in *W v Essex CC*, where he indicated that he did not regard as unarguable a claim for psychiatric injury to the parents suffered as a result of their sense of responsibility for having caused or failed to prevent the sexual abuse suffered by their children.

Whether claimants in this category are to be treated as primary victims, as Lord Oliver treated them, or as secondary victims, as Lord Hoffmann appears to have viewed them, does not seem to me to be a matter of critical importance. There is room for the law to make provision for them on either basis.

My conclusion on this issue is that cases which fall into this particular category raise materially different considerations from those which arise in the instant case, and that the authorities would not necessarily preclude such cases from receiving separate treatment were I to rule against the claimant on the preliminary issue which I have to decide. I therefore do not find myself assisted by the submission based on the case of Watkins LJ's engine driver.

DUTY OWED BY VICTIM OF SELF-INFLICTED INJURIES: POLICY CONSIDERATIONS

Although it appears from the body of authority referred to above that the preponderance of opinion is unfavourable to the concept of a victim of self-inflicted injuries owing a duty of care to a third party not to cause him psychiatric harm in consequence of his injuries, there is no decision on the point which is binding upon this court. Accordingly the court, in the light of such guidance as has been given, including such assistance as may be gleaned from the Commonwealth decisions, must reach its own conclusion. It is at this stage that policy considerations come into play.

I observe, first, that since a claim for psychiatric illness suffered by a secondary victim in consequence of injury to a primary victim is not admitted by our law unless the three elements of the control mechanism are present, it follows that it will normally only be in cases where close family ties exist between the primary and secondary victim that the particular issue with which this case is concerned will arise. For reasons which will shortly appear, I regard that as a matter of significance.

In the second place, the issue which I have to resolve raises, as it seems to me, a question which impinges upon a person's right of self-determination. ...

Both counsel maintain that self-harming, whether by negligence or deliberately, would not be expected to give rise to any criminal liability. [Counsel for the defendant], relying upon the opinion of the Bundesgerichtshof [which appears in *The German Law of Torts* (3rd edn, 1994) p 109 by Professor Basil Markesinis], argues that to impose the proposed liability for psychiatric harm caused to another through such acts would be to curtail the right of self-determination and the liberty of the individual. There is, of course, a duty not to cause foreseeable physical injury to another in such circumstances, but in my judgment to extend that duty so as to bring within its compass purely psychiatric injury would indeed be to create a significant further limitation upon an individual's freedom of action. That seems to me to be a powerful objection to the imposition of such a duty.

[Counsel] maintains that there are strong policy reasons for holding that the victim of self-inflicted injury, whether caused negligently or deliberately, should not owe a duty of care to someone who suffers psychiatric injury as a result of seeing him in an injured state. He postulates certain examples, in each of which A causes himself harm and B, who fulfils all the preconditions for classification as a secondary victim, suffers psychiatric injury as a result of seeing A in his injured state: (1) A commits suicide and the body is found by B, his son; (2) A negligently wounds himself with a kitchen knife in front of B, his wife; or (3) A suffers extensive loss of blood as a result of a fall caused by his own negligence and is found by B, his mother. In all these circumstances, he submits, public policy ought to prevent B from suing A or A's estate if he or she suffers psychiatric injury in consequence of what he or she has seen.

His argument is as follows. The first *Alcock* control mechanism means that such claims must of necessity be between close relatives. Regrettably, the suffering of close relatives for self-induced or natural reasons is an inherent part of family life. It is only when someone else inflicts the injuries that the incident is taken out of the category of everyday family life and into the law of tort. There seems to me to be force in this argument. Tragedy and misfortune may befall any family. Where the cause arises within the family there would, in my view, have to be good reason for further extending the law to provide a remedy in such a case.

That takes me to a related point, which in my view is of some importance. Home life may involve many instances of a family member causing himself injury through his own fault. Should the law allow one family member B to sue another family member A or his estate in respect of psychiatric illness suffered as a result of B either having been present when the injury was sustained or having come upon A in his injured state? [Counsel for the claimant] argues that such claims will be rare, because such events will not normally cause psychiatric illness, and because the courts may be expected strictly to enforce the requirement that a secondary victim must show that the circumstances were such that a person of normal fortitude might foreseeably suffer psychiatric harm. That may be so, but experience shows that it is not only successful claimants who sue. To allow a cause of action in this type of situation is to open up the possibility of a particularly undesirable type of litigation within the family, involving questions of relative fault as between its members. Issues of contributory negligence might be raised, not only where the self-inflicted harm is caused negligently, but also where it is caused intentionally. To take an example, A, while drunk, seriously injures himself. B, his wife, suffers nervous shock. What if A raises, by way of defence the fact that he had drunk too much because B had unjustifiably threatened to leave him for another man or had fabricated an allegation of child sexual abuse against him? Should the law of tort concern itself with this kind of issue? In a case where A's self-harm is deliberate, the possibility that B's claim may be met by a defence of contributory negligence, alleging that B's behaviour caused A to harm himself, is an alarming one. And that is without allowing for the further impact of possible Pt 20 claims being brought against other members of the family.

I appreciate, of course, that one member of the family may already sue another family member in respect of physical injury caused by that other, so that in cases of physical injury there is already the potential for personal injury litigation within the family; but the fact that family members have the same right as others to make a claim for physical injury does not necessarily mean that they should have the right to make a claim for a different kind of harm in respect of which, because of the first *Alcock* control mechanism, others have no such right. Further, where a family member suffers psychiatric harm as a result of the self-inflicted injuries of another family member, the psychiatric illness in itself may well have an adverse effect upon family relationships which the law should be astute not to exacerbate by allowing litigation between those family members. In my judgment, to permit a cause of action for purely psychiatric injury in these circumstances would be potentially productive of acute family strife.

[Counsel for the claimant's] best point in answer to these policy considerations, as it seems to me, derives from the passage in Lord Oliver's speech in *Alcock v Chief Constable of the South Yorkshire Police* to which I have already referred, where Lord Oliver referred to the anomaly that might arise where an accident, though not solely caused by the primary victim, has been materially contributed to by his negligence. Lord Oliver pointed to the unfair situation which would arise if a claimant were to recover damages in full for his or her traumatic injuries from a person who had in fact been responsible in only a minor degree whilst he in turn remained unable to recover any contribution from the person primarily responsible, since the latter's negligence vis-à-vis the claimant would not even have been tortious.

I fully recognise the force of this objection to a denial of a duty of care in the type of situation under consideration in this judgment, but it does not seem to me to outweigh the policy considerations to which I have referred above. There is no easy answer to the point, save to observe that, as has often been pointed out, the area of law relating to so-called nervous shock cases is bedevilled by inconsistencies.'

CHAPTER 3

Duty III – Economic loss

Where the loss to the claimant consists of personal injury or some other physical damage, it would seem that the courts' approach to the question of proximity is a fairly straightforward one; however, where the damage complained of consists of a financial or economic loss the courts are particularly wary. There is little problem where the economic loss is consequential on some form of physical damage, but in cases of 'pure' economic loss the courts are most unwilling to find that liability exists in the absence of a very close relationship between claimant and defendant.

Although economic losses may arise in a variety of ways, two groups of situation, in particular, are developed below: (i) defective products and buildings and (ii) negligent misstatements. In the latter, the nature of the loss is generally easy to identify, but in many situations there may be considerable scope for disagreement as to whether the loss is purely economic or not: as, for example, in *McFarlane v Tayside Health Board*, see p 190.

Spartan Steel & Alloys Ltd v Martin & Co (Contractors) Ltd
[1972] 3 All ER 557 Court of Appeal

The defendants' employees, who were engaged in digging up the road outside the plaintiffs' plant, negligently damaged the cable which supplied electricity to the plant direct from the power station. The power-cut necessitated the removal of the melt which was in the furnace at the time, at a cost of £368 reduction in value plus £400 lost profit. Also, while the cable was being repaired the electricity board shut off the power for some 14 hours during which time the plaintiffs lost £1767 in profit on a further four melts which could have been processed in the time. The Court of Appeal allowed the claim for the first two sums as being for physical damage and consequential losses. The lost profits on the remaining four melts were held to be irrecoverable as pure economic loss.

Lord Denning MR:'... At bottom I think the question of recovering economic loss is one of policy. Whenever the courts draw a line to mark out the bounds of *duty*, they do it as a matter of policy so as to limit the responsibility of the defendant. Whenever the courts set bounds to the *damages* recoverable – saying that they are, or are not, too remote – they do it as matter of policy so as to limit the liability of the defendant.

In many of the cases where economic loss has been held not to be recoverable, it has been put on the ground that the defendant was under no *duty* to the plaintiff. Thus where a person is injured in a road accident by the negligence of another, the negligent driver owes a duty to the injured man himself, but he owes no duty to the servant of the injured man: see *Best v Samuel Fox & Co Ltd*; nor to the master of the injured man: *Inland Revenue Comrs v Hambrook*; nor to anyone else who suffers loss because he had a contract with the injured man: see *Simpson & Co v Thomson*; nor indeed to anyone who only suffers economic loss on account of the accident: see *Kirkham v Boughey*. Likewise, when property is damaged by the negligence of another, the negligent tortfeasor owes a duty to the owner or possessor of the chattel, but not to one who suffers loss only because he had a contract entitling him to use the chattel or giving him a right to receive it at some later date: see *Elliott Steam Tug Co v Shipping Controller* and *Margarine Union GmbH v Cambay Prince Steamship Co Ltd*.

In other cases, however, the defendant seems clearly to have been under a duty to the plaintiff, but the economic loss has not been recovered because it is too remote. Take the illustration given by Blackburn J in *Cattle v Stockton Waterworks Co*: when water escapes from a reservoir and floods a coalmine where many men are working; those who had their tools or clothes destroyed could recover, but those who only lost their wages could not. Similarly, when the defendants' ship negligently sank a ship which was being towed by a tug, the owner of the tug lost his remuneration, but he could not recover it from the negligent ship although the same duty (of navigation with reasonable care) was owed to both tug and tow: see *Société Remorquage à Hélice v Bennetts*. In such cases if the plaintiff or his property had been physically injured, he would have recovered; but, as he only suffered economic loss, he is held not entitled to recover. This is, I should think, because the loss is regarded by the law as too remote: see *King v Phillips*.

On the other hand, in the cases where economic loss by itself has been held to be recoverable, it is plain that there was a duty to the plaintiff and the loss was not too remote. Such as when one ship negligently runs down another ship, and damages it, with the result that the cargo has to be discharged and reloaded. The negligent ship was already under a duty to the cargo-owners; and they can recover the cost of discharging and reloading it, as it is not too remote: see *Morrison Steamship Co Ltd v Steamship Greystoke Castle (owners of cargo lately laden on)*. Likewise, when a banker negligently gives a reference to one who acts on it, the duty is plain and the damage is not too remote: see *Hedley Byrne & Co Ltd v Heller & Partners Ltd*.

The more I think about these cases, the more difficult I find it to put each into its proper pigeon-hole. Sometimes I say: "There was no duty." In others I say: "The damage was too remote." So much so that I think the time has come to discard those tests which have proved so elusive. It seems to me better to consider the particular relationship in hand, and see whether or not, as a matter of policy, economic loss should be recoverable. Thus in *Weller & Co v Foot and Mouth Disease Research Institute* it was plain that the loss suffered by the auctioneers was not recoverable, no matter whether it is put on the ground that there was no duty or that the damage was too remote. Again, in *Electrochrome Ltd v Welsh Plastics Ltd*, it is plain that the economic loss suffered by the plaintiffs' factory (due to the damage to the fire hydrant) was not recoverable, whether because there was no duty or that it was too remote.

So I turn to the relationship in the present case. It is of common occurrence. The parties concerned are the electricity board who are under a statutory duty to maintain supplies of electricity in their district; the inhabitants of the district, including this factory, who are entitled by statute to a continuous supply of electricity for their use; and the contractors who dig up the road. Similar relationships occur with other statutory bodies, such as gas and water undertakings. The cable may be damaged by the negligence of the statutory undertaker, or by the negligence of the contractor, or by accident without any negligence by anyone; and the power may have to be cut off while the cable is repaired. Or the power may be cut off owing to a short-circuit in the powerhouse; and so forth. If the cutting off of the supply causes economic loss to the consumers, should it as matter of policy be recoverable? And against whom?

The first consideration is the position of the statutory undertakers. If the board do not keep up the voltage or pressure of electricity, gas or water – or likewise, if they shut it off for repairs – and thereby cause economic loss to their consumers, they are not liable in damages, not even if the cause of it is due to their own negligence. The only remedy (which is hardly ever pursued) is to prosecute the board before the justices ... There is [a] group of cases which go to show that, if the board, by their negligence in the conduct of their supply cause direct physical damage to person or property ... they are liable ... But one thing is clear, the board have never been held liable for economic loss only. If such be the policy of the legislature in regard to electricity boards, it would seem right for the common law to adopt a similar policy in regard to contractors. If the electricity boards are not liable for economic loss due to negligence which results in the cutting off of the supply, nor should a contractor be liable.

The second consideration is the nature of the hazard, namely, the cutting of the supply of electricity. This is a hazard which we all run. It may be due to a short circuit, to a flash of lightning, to a tree falling on the wires, to an accidental cutting of the cable, or even to the negligence of someone or other. And when it does happen, it affects a multitude of persons; not as a rule by way of physical damage to them or their property, but by putting them to inconvenience, and sometimes to economic loss. The supply is usually restored in a few hours, so the economic loss is not very large. Such a hazard is regarded by most people as a thing they must put up with – without seeking compensation from anyone. Some there are who install a stand-by system. Others seek refuge by taking out an insurance policy against breakdown in the supply. But most people are content to take the risk on themselves. When the supply is cut off, they do not go running round to their solicitor. They do not try to find out whether it was anyone's fault. They just put up with it. They try to make up the economic loss by doing more work next day. This is a healthy attitude which the law should encourage.

The third consideration is this. If claims for economic loss were permitted for this particular hazard, there would be no end of claims. Some might be genuine, but many might be inflated, or even false. A machine might not have been in use anyway, but it would be easy to put it down to the cut in supply. It would be well-nigh impossible to check the claims. If there was economic loss on one day, did the applicant do his best to mitigate it by working harder next day? And so forth. Rather than expose claimants to such temptation and defendants to such hard labour – on comparatively small claims – it is better to disallow economic loss altogether, at any rate when it stands alone, independent of any physical damage.

The fourth consideration is that, in such a hazard as this, the risk of economic loss should be suffered by the whole community who suffer the losses – usually many but comparatively small losses – rather than on the one pair of shoulders, that is, on the contractor on whom the total of them, all added together, might be very heavy.

The fifth consideration is that the law provides for deserving cases. If the defendant is guilty of negligence which cuts off the electricity supply and causes actual physical damage to person or property, that physical damage can be recovered: see *Baker v Crow Carrying Co Ltd*, referred to by Buckley LJ in *SCM v Whittall*, and also any economic loss truly consequential on the material damage: see *British Celanese Ltd v AH Hunt (Capacitors) Ltd* and *SCM v Whittall*. Such cases will be comparatively few. They will be readily capable of proof and will be easily checked. They should be and are admitted.'

Comment

(1)   Distinguishing between different types of losses is by no means a straight-forward task in every case, see for example *Anns v Merton* and *Murphy v Brentwood*. Lawton LJ in *Spartan Steel* commented:

> 'The differences which undoubtedly exist between what damage can be recovered in one type of case and what in another cannot be reconciled on any logical basis. I agree with Lord Denning MR that such differences

have arisen because of the policy of the law. Maybe there should be one policy for all cases; the enunciation of such a policy is not, in my judgment, a task for this court.'

(2)   Lord Denning's justification based on concerns about the evidential problems of substantiating claims for economic loss could just as logically be applied to many cases of physical damage, e.g. back injuries.

Muirhead v Industrial Tank Specialities Ltd
[1985] 3 All ER 705 Court of Appeal

The plaintiffs, who were fish merchants, employed the defendants to install tanks for the storage of live lobsters. The units included pumps manufactured by the second defendants and powered by motors manufactured by the third defendants. The motors, which were unsuitable for use with UK voltages, failed to operate the pumps properly and the stock of lobsters died from lack of oxygen. The Court of Appeal held that the plaintiffs' reliance upon the third defendants to supply adequate motors was sufficient to give rise to liability for the physical damage to the lobsters and any consequential losses, but that future profits fell into the class of economic loss and were not recoverable.

Robert Goff LJ: '... In order to decide whether the judge was right to approach the case before him on the basis of the principle in the *Junior Books* case, it is necessary first of all to seek to identify the principle. Both Lord Fraser of Tullybelton and Lord Roskill appear to have been influenced in particular by what Lord Fraser of Tullybelton described as "the very close proximity between the parties". In seeking to understand what they had in mind it is perhaps important to bear in mind what is usually meant by the word "proximity" when used in this context. It does not bear its normal meaning in ordinary speech; as is plain from Lord Atkin's speech in *Donoghue v Stevenson*, it is used as a convenient label to describe a relationship between the parties by virtue of which the defendant can reasonably foresee that his act or omission is liable to cause damage to the plaintiff of the relevant type. In this context, the word "relationship" refers to no more than the relative situations of the parties, as a consequence of which such foreseeability of damage may exist. As I see it, Lord Fraser of Tullybelton cannot have been referring to proximity in the sense I have described; and Lord Roskill, when he spoke of the very close "relationship" between the parties must, I think, have had in mind the dealings between the parties which led to the pursuers nominating the defenders, who were specialists in flooring, as sub-contractors to lay the flooring in their factory.

A particular problem arises, however, with reference to reliance. Lord Roskill ... appears to have regarded reliance by the plaintiff on the defendants as significant, as does Lord Fraser of Tullybelton. But neither explains why he regarded such reliance as important. Lord Roskill referred to *Hedley Byrne & Co Ltd v Heller & Partners Ltd*, in which reliance by the plaintiff was relevant because, without it, the defendant's negligent misstatement would have caused the plaintiff no damage: he also referred to s 14(1) of the Sale of Goods Act 1893, which was concerned with a manifestation of reliance by the plaintiff on the defendant's skill and judgment which supports the implication of a term in a contract of sale (cf. now s 14(3) of the Sale of Goods Act 1979). *Junior Books Ltd v Veitchi Co Ltd* was concerned with neither such case, but with reliance by the pursuers on the defenders to install a floor which was not defective. It is not, however, clear why reliance should distinguish a case such as *Junior Books Ltd v Veitchi Co Ltd* from other cases in which a defendant may not be held liable. There is, of course, a sense in which it can be said that every successful plaintiff in an action of negligence has relied on the defendant not to be negligent, as every motorist relies on every other motorist in the vicinity to drive carefully; but presumably neither Lord Fraser of Tullybelton nor Lord Roskill had that kind of reliance in mind. There is also a sense in which a purchaser of goods relies on the manufacturer to have manufactured goods which are not defective, and so decides to order goods, made by the particular manufacturer, from his immediate supplier. Lord Fraser of Tullybelton and Lord Roskill were, however, at pains to distinguish such a case from the case before them. But they did not identify the ground of distinction; and we can see the difficulty which the judge in the present case faced in grappling with the notion of reliance on the facts of the case before him.

Yet another problem arises from the fact that Lord Fraser of Tullybelton considered that the building owner in the *Junior Books* case, who had full knowledge of the sub-contractors' contractual duties to the main contractor, could be in no better position than the main contractor; and that Lord Roskill, although expressing no concluded opinion, appears to have inclined to the same view. But the question then arises: on what principle are contractual terms, not arising under a contract between the parties, to be relevant to a claim in negligence? For only if that principle is identified can we discern in what cases they are to be held applicable in future.

Having studied the speeches of Lord Fraser of Tullybelton and Lord Roskill in the *Junior Books* case the only principle I feel able to formulate which is consistent with (1) the relevance of "the very close proximity between the parties"; (2) the relevance of reliance by the plaintiff on the defendant; and (3) the fact that the defendant may be able to rely on contractual terms with a third party in order to defeat the plaintiff's claim against him, is that, on the facts in the *Junior Books* case, it was considered by the majority of the House of Lords that the nominated sub-contractor had assumed a direct responsibility to the building owner. Voluntary assumption of responsibility, in circumstances akin to contract, was the basis of liability in *Hedley Byrne & Co Ltd v Heller & Partners Ltd* which Lord Roskill regarded as relevant in *Junior Books Ltd v Veitchi Co Ltd* both to the invocation by the defendant of contractual terms with a third party, and to reliance. However, I feel very diffident in so analysing the *Junior Books* case, because that analysis appears to me to be difficult to reconcile with the factual situation in that case, in which the parties had deliberately structured their contractual relationship in order to achieve the result that (apart from any special arrangements) there should be no direct liability *inter se*.

Faced with these difficulties it is, I think, safest for this court to treat *Junior Books* as a case in which, on its particular facts, there was considered to be such a very close relationship between the parties that the defenders could, if the facts as pleaded were proved, be held liable to the pursuers. I feel fortified in adopting that approach by three matters. First, Lord Fraser of Tullybelton stressed that he was deciding the appeal before him "strictly on its own facts".

Second, in the advice of the Privy Council in *Candlewood Navigation Corporation Ltd v Mitsui OSK Lines Ltd*, Lord Fraser of Tullybelton, who delivered the advice, appears to have treated *Junior Books Ltd v Veitchi Co Ltd* as a decision of limited application. Third, both Lord Fraser of Tullybelton and Lord Roskill in the *Junior Books* case gave examples which assist us in approaching the present case on a pragmatic basis. For Lord Fraser of Tullybelton considered that the very close proximity between the parties in his view distinguished the case before him from "the case of producers of goods to be offered for sale to the public"; and Lord Roskill contrasted cases in which (as in *Hedley Byrne & Co Ltd v Heller & Partners Ltd* and s 14(1) of the Sale of Goods Act 1893) there was reliance by the plaintiff on the defendant, with cases of claims by ultimate purchasers against manufacturers in respect of goods purchased under ordinary everyday transactions where "it is obvious that in truth the real reliance was upon the immediate vendor and not upon the manufacturer".

It was with these passages in mind, no doubt, that ... counsel for the plaintiff sought before the judge, and again before this court, to identify the present as a case where the plaintiff's "real reliance" was upon the manufacturer, the third defendant. In this I do not think that, despite his admirable argument before this court, he came anywhere near to success. I have already quoted the passage from the judgment of the judge, in which he held that there was the requisite reliance by the plaintiff on the third defendant as manufacturer, and that the third defendant must reasonably have foreseen that any user in the United Kingdom would rely upon them to ensure the adequacy of their motors at least in the fundamental respect that they would be suitable for use on United Kingdom voltages. Certainly this was a matter of fundamental importance, and would affect every user of the motors in the United Kingdom. But I find it impossible to differentiate this case from any other case of manufactured goods which, through a fundamental defect, result in financial loss being suffered by an ultimate purchaser who buys them for use in his business and, by reason of the defect, suffers a loss of profits. Furthermore, there was no "very close proximity" between the plaintiff and the third defendant, in the sense that there was no very close relationship between the parties; so that factor, too, is missing from the case.

[Counsel], in his argument before this court, relied in particular on the fact that the motors were plated with plates stating that they were suitable for use with electricity of 220/240 volts. But the case was not run on the basis of negligent misstatement, which is understandable in that there was no evidence that the plaintiff relied on the statement on the plates as such, rather than on the simple fact that the motors had been bought for use in this country. For that reason, the plates could be relevant only to defeat any argument founded on the proposition that the plaintiff, in seeking to rectify the particular motors rather than having them replaced by others, had failed to act reasonably in mitigation of his damage.

As I see the present case it must fall within those cases, described by Lord Fraser of Tullybelton and Lord Roskill, of ordinary purchase of chattels, in which the buyer, if he seeks to recover damages for purely economic loss arising from defects in the goods, must on the law as it stands look to his immediate vendor and not to the ultimate manufacturer for his remedy.

For these reasons I am unable to accept the conclusion of the judge that the third defendant is liable to the plaintiff in a claim for pure economic loss.'

Comment

(1)   In *Junior Books v Veitchi* the pursuers had engaged contractors to build them a factory. The defenders were specialist subcontractors nominated by the pursuers' architect to lay flooring and their contract was with the builders. As a result of their negligence the flooring proved to be defective and had to be replaced, during which time further expense was incurred by the pursuers who had to remove their business operations elsewhere. The House of Lords, by a majority of four to one, held that all of the losses – the cost of replacement flooring and the operational losses – were recoverable. The decision rested on the closeness of the relationship and the degree of reliance on the skill of the subcontractors which led, according to the majority, to there being no difference in principle between economic losses arising from physical damage and 'pure' economic loss.

(2)   Subsequent case law has shown that the decision in *Junior Books* is, at best, of very limited application. It was the dissenting judgment of Lord Brandon which found favour with Lord Bridge in *D & F Estates* (below).

(3)   In relation to recovery for defective products see p 418.

D & F Estates Ltd and others v Church Commissioners for England and others
[1988] 2 All ER 992 House of Lords

The plaintiffs were lessees and occupiers of a flat in a block which had been built by the third defendants. Subcontractors, employed by the builders in the reasonable belief that they were competent, had negligently carried out plastering work which necessitated remedial work for which the plaintiffs were seeking compensation. The House of Lords held that the only duty owed by the builders was to employ a competent plasterer and, in any case, the cost of repairing the defective plaster was economic loss and irrecoverable.

Lord Bridge of Harwich: '... The decision of your Lordships' House in *Junior Books Ltd v Veitchi Co Ltd* has been analysed in many subsequent decisions of the Court of Appeal. I do not intend to embark on a further such analysis. The consensus of judicial opinion, with which I concur, seems to be that the decision of the majority is so far dependent on the unique, albeit non-contractual, relationship between the pursuer and the defender in that case and the unique scope of the duty of care owed by the defender to the pursuer arising from that relationship that the decision cannot be regarded as laying down any principle of general application in the law of tort or delict. The dissenting speech of Lord Brandon on the other hand enunciates with cogency and clarity principles of fundamental importance which are clearly applicable to determine the scope of the duty of care owed by one party to another in the absence, as in the instant case, of either any contractual relationship or any such uniquely proximate relationship as that on which the decision of the majority in *Junior Books* was founded. Lord Brandon said:

> "My Lords, it appears to me clear beyond doubt that, there being no contractual relationship between the pursuers and the defenders in the present case, the foundation, and the only foundation, for the existence of a duty of care owed by the defenders to the pursuers, is the principle laid down in the decision of your Lordships' House in *Donoghue v Stevenson*. The actual decision in that case related only to the duty owed by a manufacturer of goods to their ultimate user or consumer, and can be summarised in this way: a person who manufactures goods which he intends to be used or consumed by others is under a duty to exercise such reasonable care in their manufacture as to ensure that they can be used or consumed in the manner intended without causing physical damage to persons or their property. While that was the actual decision in *Donoghue v Stevenson*, it was based on a much wider principle embodied in passages in the speech of Lord Atkin, which have been quoted so often that I do not find it necessary to quote them again here. Put shortly, that wider principle is that, when a person can or ought to appreciate that a careless act or omission on his part may result in physical injury to other persons or their property, he owes a duty to all such persons to exercise reasonable care to avoid such careless act or omission. It is, however, of fundamental importance to observe that the duty of care laid down in *Donoghue v Stevenson* was based on the existence of a danger of physical injury to persons or their property. That this is so is clear from the observations made by Lord Atkin with regard to the statements of law of Brett MR in *Heaven v Pender*. It has further, until the present case, never been doubted, so far as I know, that the relevant property for the

purpose of the wider principle on which the decision in *Donoghue v Stevenson* was based was property other than the very property which gave rise to the danger of physical damage concerned."

Later Lord Brandon, having referred to the well-known two-stage test of the existence of a duty of care propounded by Lord Wilberforce in *Anns'* case, asked himself, at the second stage, the question "whether there are any considerations which ought, *inter alia*, to limit the scope of the duty which exists". He continued:

"To that second question I would answer that there are two important considerations which ought to limit the scope of the duty of care which it is common ground was owed by the defenders to the pursuers on the assumed facts of the present case. The first consideration is that in *Donoghue v Stevenson* itself and in all the numerous cases in which the principle of that decision has been applied to different but analogous factual situations, it has always been either stated expressly, or taken for granted, that an essential ingredient in the cause of action relied on was the existence of danger, or the threat of danger, of physical damage to persons or their property, excluding for this purpose the very piece of property from the defective condition of which such danger or threat of danger, arises. To dispense with that essential ingredient in a cause of action of the kind concerned in the present case would, in my view, involve a radical departure from long-established authority. The second consideration is that there is no sound policy reason for substituting the wider scope of the duty of care put forward for the pursuers for the more restricted scope of such duty put forward by the defenders. The effect of accepting the pursuers' contention with regard to the scope of the duty of care involved would be, in substance, to create, as between two persons who are not in any contractual relationship with each other, obligations of one of those two persons to the other which are only really appropriate as between persons who do have such a relationship between them. In the case of a manufacturer or distributor of goods, the position would be that he warranted to the ultimate user or consumer of such goods that they were as well designed, as merchantable and as fit for their contemplated purpose as the exercise of reasonable care could make them. In the case of sub-contractors such as those concerned in the present case, the position would be that they warranted to the building owner that the flooring, when laid, would be well designed, as free from defects of any kind and as fit for its contemplated purpose as the exercise of reasonable care could make it. In my view, the imposition of warranties of this kind on one person in favour of another, when there is no contractual relationship between them, is contrary to any sound policy requirement. It is, I think, just worthwhile to consider the difficulties which would arise if the wider scope of the duty of care put forward by the pursuers were accepted. In any case where complaint was made by an ultimate consumer that a product made by some persons with whom he himself had no contract was defective, by what standard or standards of quality would the question of defectiveness fall to be decided? In the case of goods bought from a retailer, it could hardly be the standard prescribed by the contract between the retailer and the wholesaler, or between the wholesaler and the distributor, or between the distributor and the manufacturer, for the terms of such contracts would not even be known to the ultimate buyer. In the case of sub-contractors such as the defenders in the present case, it could hardly be the standard prescribed by the contract between the sub-contractors and the main contractors, for, although the building owner would probably be aware of those terms, he could not, since he was not a party to such contract, rely on any standard or standards prescribed in it. It follows that the question by what standard or standards alleged defects in a product complained of by its ultimate user or consumer are to be judged remains entirely at large and cannot be given any just or satisfactory answer."

... The opinion of Lord Brandon in *Junior Books Ltd v Veitchi Co Ltd* and that expressed by the Supreme Court of the United States of America are entirely in line with the majority decision of the Supreme Court of Canada in *Rivtow Marine Ltd v Washington Iron Works* that the damages recoverable from the manufacturer by the hirers of a crane which was found to have a defect which made it unsafe to use did not include the cost of repairing the defect.

These principles are easy enough to comprehend and probably not difficult to apply when the defect complained of is in a chattel supplied complete by a single manufacturer. If the hidden defect in the chattel is the cause of personal injury or of damage to property other than the chattel itself, the manufacturer is liable. But if the hidden defect is discovered before any such damage is caused, there is no longer any room for the application of the *Donoghue v Stevenson* principle. The chattel is now defective in quality, but is no longer dangerous. It may be valueless or it may be capable of economic repair. In either case the economic loss is recoverable in contract by a buyer or hirer of the chattel entitled to the benefit of a relevant warranty of quality, but is not recoverable in tort by a remote buyer or hirer of the chattel.

If the same principle applies in the field of real property to the liability of the builder of a permanent structure which is dangerously defective, that liability can only arise if the defect remains hidden until the defective structure causes personal injury or damage to property other than the structure itself. If the defect is discovered before any damage is done, the loss sustained by the owner of the structure, who has to repair or demolish it to avoid a potential source of danger to third parties, would seem to be purely economic. Thus, if I acquire a property with a dangerously defective garden wall which is attributable to the bad workmanship of the original builder, it is difficult to see any basis in principle on which I can sustain an action in tort against the builder for the cost of either repairing or demolishing the wall. No physical damage has been caused. All that has happened is that the defect in the wall has been discovered in time to prevent damage occurring ...'

Comment

Lord Bridge acknowledged that there might be room, in the case of a complex structure, to distinguish the separate elements of the structure and thus identify recoverable physical damage caused to one element by the defective part. This is developed further in *Murphy* (below). See also similar comments in *Aswan v Lupdine*, p 426.

Murphy v Brentwood District Council
[1990] 2 All ER 908 House of Lords

The plaintiff bought one of a pair of semi-detached houses from a construction company. Some years later serious cracks developed in the house and it transpired that the foundations were defective despite the plans having been approved by the local authority who had had them checked by consulting engineers. The plaintiff did not have sufficient funds to pay for the foundations to be repaired and was obliged to sell the house for some £35,000 less than its market value if in a sound condition. The House of Lords held that a dangerous defect, once known, became a defect in quality and that such economic loss was not recoverable in negligence.

Lord Bridge of Harwich: '...

THE PRESENT POSITION IN OUR OWN JURISDICTION

[W]e have shown a marked inclination to confine the *Anns* doctrine within narrow limits, as in *Governors of the Peabody Donation Fund v Sir Lindsay Parkinson & Co Ltd* and *Curran v Northern Ireland Co-ownership Housing Association Ltd* and ... the reasoning of the speeches in *D & F Estates Ltd v Church Comrs for England* has gone far to question the principles on which the doctrine rests. Meanwhile, uncertainty in the law has inevitably been a fertile breeding ground for litigation and the Court of Appeal has grappled as best it could with the problem of seeking to determine where the limits of the doctrine are to be drawn ... Sooner or later, in this unhappy situation, a direct challenge to the authority of Anns was inevitable. Perhaps it is unfortunate that it did not come sooner, but the House could not, I think, have contemplated departing from the decision of an Appellate Committee so eminently constituted unless directly invited to do so. Now that the challenge has to be faced, I believe, for reasons which I hope will become apparent, that the choice before the House lies between following Australia and rejecting Anns altogether or following Canada and New Zealand in carrying the *Anns* doctrine a large, legislative step forward to its logical conclusion and holding that the scope of the duty of care, imposed by the law on local authorities for the negligent performance of their functions under the relevant statutes, embraces all economic loss sustained by the owner or occupier of a building by reason of defects in it arising from construction in breach of building byelaws or regulations.

DANGEROUS DEFECTS AND DEFECTS OF QUALITY

If a manufacturer negligently puts into circulation a chattel containing a latent defect which renders it dangerous to persons or property, the manufacturer, on the well-known principles established by *Donoghue v Stevenson*, will be liable in tort for injury to persons or damage to property which the chattel causes. But if a manufacturer produces and sells a chattel which is merely defective in quality, even to the extent that it is valueless for the purpose for which it is intended, the manufacturer's liability at common law arises only under and by reference to the terms of any contract to which he is a party in relation to the chattel; the common law does not impose on him any liability in tort to persons to whom he owes no duty in contract but who, having acquired the chattel, suffer economic loss because the chattel is defective in quality. If a dangerous defect in a chattel is discovered before it causes any personal injury or damage to property, because the danger is now known and the chattel cannot be safely used unless the defect is repaired, the defect becomes merely a defect in quality. The chattel is either capable of repair at economic cost or it is worthless and must be scrapped. In either case the loss sustained by the owner or hirer of the chattel is purely economic. It is recoverable against any party who owes the loser a relevant contractual duty. But it is not recoverable in tort in the absence of a special relationship of proximity imposing on the tortfeasor a duty of care to safeguard the plaintiff from economic loss. There is no such special relationship between the manufacturer of a chattel and a remote owner or hirer.

I believe that these principles are equally applicable to buildings. If a builder erects a structure containing a latent defect which renders it dangerous to persons or property, he will be liable in tort for injury to persons or damage to property resulting from that dangerous defect. But, if the defect becomes apparent before any injury or damage has been caused, the loss sustained by the building owner is purely economic. If the defect can be repaired at economic cost, that is the measure of the loss. If the building cannot be repaired, it may have to be abandoned as unfit for occupation and therefore valueless. These economic losses are recoverable if they flow from breach of a relevant contractual duty, but, here again, in the absence of a special relationship of proximity they are not recoverable in tort. The only qualification I would make to this is that, if a building stands so close to the boundary of the building owner's land that after discovery of the dangerous defect it remains a potential source of injury to persons or property on neighbouring land or on the highway, the building owner ought, in principle, to be entitled to recover in tort from the negligent builder the cost of obviating the danger, whether by repair or by demolition, so far as that cost is necessarily incurred in order to protect himself from potential liability to third parties.

The fallacy which, in my opinion, vitiates the judgments of Lord Denning MR and Sachs LJ in *Dutton* is that they brush these distinctions aside as of no consequence. Stamp LJ, on the other hand, fully understood and appreciated them and his statement of the applicable principles as between the building owner and the builder seems to me unexceptionable. He rested his decision in favour of the plaintiff against the local authority on a wholly distinct principle which will require separate examination.

THE COMPLEX STRUCTURE THEORY

In my speech in the *D & F Estates* case I mooted the possibility that in complex structures or complex chattels one part of a structure or chattel might, when it caused damage to another part of the same structure or chattel, be regarded in the law of tort as having caused damage to "other property" for the purpose of the application of *Donoghue v Stevenson* principles ... [I]t is, so far as I can see, only if and to the extent that this theory can be affirmed and applied that there can be any escape from the conclusions I have indicated above under the rubric "Dangerous defects and defects of quality".

The complex structure theory has, so far as I know, never been subjected to express and detailed examination in any English authority. I shall not attempt a review of the numerous authorities which bear on it in the different state jurisdictions in the United States of America. However, some significant landmarks must be mentioned. In *Quackenbush v Ford Motor Co*, a decision of the Appellate Division of the Supreme Court of New York, the plaintiff recovered damages in tort from the manufacturer for damage to her Ford motor car caused by an accident attributable to faulty manufacture of the brakes. It is at least highly doubtful if the reasoning of this decision can now be supported consistently with the unanimous opinion of the United States Supreme Court in *East River Steamship Corp v Transamerica Delaval Inc* that a manufacturer incurs no liability in tort for damage occasioned by a defect in a product which injures itself. Blackmun J, delivering the opinion of the court, said:

> "We realise that the damage may be qualitative, occurring through gradual deterioration or internal breakage. Or it may be calamitous ... But either way, since by definition no person or other property is damaged, the resulting loss is purely economic. Even when the harm to the product itself occurs through an abrupt, accident-like event, the resulting loss due to repair costs, decreased value, and lost profits is essentially the failure of the purchaser to receive the benefit of its bargain – traditionally the core concern of contract law."

Quackenbush is, in any event, no authority for the proposition that, once a defect in a complex chattel is discovered, there is a remedy in tort against the manufacturer on the ground that the cost of repairing the defect was necessarily incurred in order to prevent further damage to other parts of the chattel. A striking illustration of this is *Trans World Airline Inc v Curtiss-Wright Corp*, in which the airline, having discovered defects in the engines fitted to some of their planes, fortunately before any accident occurred, chose not to sue the plane manufacturer in contract, but sued the engine manufacturer in tort. The manufacturer was held not liable. This and other relevant American authorities are extensively reviewed in the illuminating judgment of the British Columbia Court of Appeal delivered by Tysoe JA in *Rivtow Marine Ltd v Washington Iron Works*. The court held that the manufacturers were not liable in tort to the hirers of a crane for the cost of repair rendered necessary when the crane was found to be dangerously defective in use. This decision was affirmed by the Supreme Court of Canada by a majority of seven to two. Since Lord Wilberforce in *Anns* referred with approval to the dissenting judgment of Laskin J in that case, which he described as "of strong persuasive force", I have read and reread that judgment with the closest attention. I have to say, with all respect, that I find it wholly unconvincing. It depends on the same fallacy as that which vitiates the judgments of Lord Denning MR and Sachs LJ in *Dutton*. In particular, in equating the damage sustained in repairing the chattel to make it safe with the damage which would have been suffered if the latent defect had never been discovered and the chattel had injured somebody in use, the judgment ignores the circumstance that once a chattel is known to be dangerous it is simply unusable. If I buy a second hand car and find it to be faulty, it can make no difference to the manufacturer's liability in tort whether the fault is in the brakes or in the engine, i.e. whether the car will not stop or will not start. In either case the car is useless until repaired. The manufacturer is no more liable in tort for the cost of the repairs in the one case than in the other.

Bowen v Paramount Builders (Hamilton) Ltd was a case where the plaintiff building owner sued the builder in tort for the cost of making good damage caused by subsidence caused by inadequate foundations. The trial judge dismissed the claim on the ground that the principle of *Donoghue v Stevenson* did not apply to entitle the plaintiff to recover in tort for a defect in the quality of the building. The judgments of the New Zealand Court of Appeal to the opposite effect were referred to with approval by Lord Wilberforce in *Anns*. The critical paragraph from the judgment of Richmond P reads:

> "Does damage to the house itself give rise to a cause of action? As I have already said, I agree with Speight J that the principles laid down in *Donoghue v Stevenson* apply to a builder erecting a house under a contract with the owner. He is under a duty of care not to create latent sources of physical danger to the person or property of third persons whom he ought reasonably to foresee as likely to be affected thereby. If the latent defect causes actual physical damage to the structure of the house then I can see no

reason in principle why such damage should not give rise to a cause of action, at any rate if that damage occurs after the house has been purchased from the original owner. This was clearly the view of Lord Denning MR and of Sachs LJ in *Dutton v Bognor Regis Urban District Council*. In the field of product liability this has long been the law in the United States: see *Prosser's Law of Torts* and *Quackenbush v Ford Motor Co*. For the purposes of the present case it is not necessary to deal with the question of 'pure' economic loss, that is to say economic loss which is not associated with a latent defect which causes or threatens physical harm to the structure itself."

Richmond P goes on to hold that the measure of damages would include the whole cost of remedial works plus any diminution in value of the house in so far as it was impossible to effect a complete remedy.

I cannot see any way in which the reasoning in the paragraph quoted and the consequences in relation to the measure of damages can in principle be supported except by an extreme application of the complex structure theory treating each part of the entire structure as a separate item of property. But such an application of the theory seems to me quite unrealistic. The reality is that the structural elements in any building form a single indivisible unit of which the different parts are essentially interdependent. To the extent that there is any defect in one part of the structure it must to a greater or lesser degree necessarily affect all other parts of the structure. Therefore any defect in the structure is a defect in the quality of the whole and it is quite artificial, in order to impose a legal liability which the law would not otherwise impose, to treat a defect in an integral structure, so far as it weakens the structure, as a dangerous defect liable to cause damage to "other property".

A critical distinction must be drawn here between some part of a complex structure which is said to be a "danger" only because it does not perform its proper function in sustaining the other parts and some distinct item incorporated in the structure which positively malfunctions so as to inflict positive damage on the structure in which it is incorporated. Thus, if a defective central heating boiler explodes and damages a house or a defective electrical installation malfunctions and sets the house on fire, I see no reason to doubt that the owner of the house, if he can prove that the damage was due to the negligence of the boiler manufacturer in the one case or the electrical contractor in the other, can recover damages in tort on *Donoghue v Stevenson* principles. But the position in law is entirely different where, by reason of the inadequacy of the foundations of the building to support the weight of the superstructure, differential settlement and consequent cracking occurs. Here, once the first cracks appear, the structure as a whole is seen to be defective and the nature of the defect is known. Even if, contrary to my view, the initial damage could be regarded as damage to other property caused by a latent defect, once the defect is known the situation of the building owner is analogous to that of the car owner who discovers that the car has faulty brakes. He may have a house which, until repairs are effected, is unfit for habitation, but, subject to the reservation I have expressed with respect to ruinous buildings at or near the boundary of the owner's property, the building no longer represents a source of danger and as it deteriorates will only damage itself.

For these reasons the complex structure theory offers no escape from the conclusion that damage to a house itself which is attributable to a defect in the structure of the house is not recoverable in tort on *Donoghue v Stevenson* principles, but represents purely economic loss which is only recoverable in contract or in tort by reason of some special relationship of proximity which imposes on the tortfeasor a duty of care to protect against economic loss.

THE RELATIVE POSITIONS OF THE BUILDER AND THE LOCAL AUTHORITY

I have so far been considering the potential liability of a builder for negligent defects in the structure of a building to persons to whom he owes no contractual duty. Since the relevant statutory function of the local authority is directed to no other purpose than securing compliance with building by-laws or regulations by the builder, I agree with the view expressed in *Anns* and by the majority of the Court of Appeal in *Dutton* that a negligent performance of that function can attract no greater liability than attaches to the negligence of the builder whose fault was the primary tort giving rise to any relevant damage. I am content for present purposes to assume, though I am by no means satisfied that the assumption is correct, that where the local authority, as in this case or in *Dutton*, has in fact approved the defective plans or inspected the defective foundations and negligently failed to discover the defect, its potential liability in tort is coextensive with that of the builder.

Only Stamp LJ in *Dutton* was prepared to hold that the law imposed on the local authority a duty of care going beyond that imposed on the builder and extending to protection of the building owner from purely economic loss. I must return later to consider the question of liability for economic loss more generally, but here I need only say that I cannot find in *Hedley Byrne & Co Ltd v Heller & Partners Ltd* or *Home Office v Dorset Yacht Co Ltd* any principle applicable to the circumstances of *Dutton* or the present case that provides support for the conclusion which Stamp LJ sought to derive from those authorities.

IMMINENT DANGER TO HEALTH OR SAFETY

A necessary element in the building owner's cause of action against the negligent local authority, which does not appear to have been contemplated in *Dutton* but which, it is said in *Anns*, must be present before the cause of action accrues, is that the state of the building is such that there is present or imminent danger to the health or safety of persons occupying it. Correspondingly the damages recoverable are said to include the amount of expenditure necessary to restore the building to a condition in which it is no longer such a danger, but presumably not any further expenditure incurred in any merely qualitative restoration. I find these features of the *Anns* doctrine very difficult to understand. The theoretical difficulty of reconciling this aspect of the doctrine with previously accepted legal principle was pointed out by Lord Oliver in *D & F Estates*. But apart from this there are, as it appears to me, two insuperable difficulties arising from the requirement of imminent danger to health or safety as an ingredient of the cause of action which led to quite irrational and capricious consequences in the application of the *Anns* doctrine. The first difficulty will arise where the relevant defect in the building, when it is first discovered, is not a present or imminent danger to health or safety. What is the owner to do if he is advised that the building will gradually deteriorate, if not repaired, and will in due course become a danger to health and safety, but that the longer he waits to effect repairs the greater the cost will be? Must he spend £1000 now on the necessary repairs with no redress against the local authority? Or is he entitled to wait until the building has so far deteriorated that he has a cause of action and then to recover from the local authority the £5000 which the necessary repairs are now going to cost? I can find no answer to this conundrum. A second difficulty will arise where the latent defect is not discovered until it causes the sudden and total collapse of the building, which occurs when the building is temporarily unoccupied and causes no damage to property except to the building itself. The building is now no longer capable of occupation and hence cannot be a danger to health or safety. It seems a very strange result that the building owner should be without remedy in this situation if he would have been able to recover from the local authority the full cost of repairing the building if only the defect had been discovered before the building fell down.

LIABILITY FOR ECONOMIC LOSS

All these considerations lead inevitably to the conclusion that a building owner can only recover the cost of repairing a defective building on the ground of the authority's negligence in performing its statutory function of approving plans or inspecting buildings in the course of construction if the scope of the authority's duty of care is wide enough to embrace purely economic loss. The House has already held in *D & F Estates* that a builder, in the absence of any contractual duty or of a special relationship of proximity introducing the *Hedley Byrne* principle of reliance, owes no duty of care in tort in respect of the quality of his work. As I pointed out in *D & F Estates*, to hold that the builder owed such a duty of care to any person acquiring an interest in the product of a builder's work would be to impose on him the obligations of an indefinitely transmissible warranty of quality ...

As I have already said, since the function of a local authority in approving plans or inspecting buildings in the course of construction is directed to ensuring that the builder complies with building by-laws or regulations, I cannot see how, in principle, the scope of the liability of the authority for a negligent failure to ensure compliance can exceed that of the liability of the builder for his negligent failure to comply.

There may, of course, be situations where, even in the absence of contract, there is a special relationship of proximity between builder and building owner which is sufficiently akin to contract to introduce the element of reliance so that the scope of the duty of care owed by the builder to the owner is wide enough to embrace purely economic loss. The decision in *Junior Books Ltd v Veitchi Co Ltd* can, I believe, only be understood on this basis.

In *Sutherland Shire Council v Heyman* the critical role of the reliance principle as an element in the cause of action which the plaintiff sought to establish is the subject of close examination, particularly in the judgment of Mason J. The central theme of his judgment, and a subordinate theme in the judgments of Brennan and Deane JJ, who together with Mason J formed the majority rejecting the *Anns* doctrine, is that a duty of care of a scope sufficient to make the authority liable for damage of the kind suffered can only be based on the principle of reliance and that there is nothing in the ordinary relationship of a local authority, as statutory supervisor of building operations, and the purchaser of a defective building capable of giving rise to such a duty. I agree with these judgments. It cannot, I think, be suggested, nor do I understand *Anns* or the cases which have followed *Anns* in Canada and New Zealand to be in fact suggesting, that the approval of plans or the inspection of a building in the course of construction by the local authority in performance of their statutory function and a subsequent purchase of the building by the plaintiff are circumstances in themselves sufficient to introduce the principle of reliance which is the foundation of a duty of care of the kind identified in *Hedley Byrne*.

In *Dutton* Lord Denning MR said:

" ... Mrs Dutton has suffered a grievous loss. The house fell down without any fault of hers. She is in no position herself to bear the loss. Who ought in justice to bear it? I should think those who were responsible. Who are they? In the first place, the builder was responsible. It was he who laid the foundations so badly that the house fell down. In the second place, the council's inspector was responsible. It was his job to examine the foundations to see if they would take the load of the house. He failed to do it properly. In the third place, the council should answer for his failure. They were entrusted by Parliament with the task of seeing that houses were properly built. They received public funds for the purpose. The very object was to protect purchasers and occupiers of houses. Yet, they failed to protect them. Their shoulders are broad enough to bear the loss."

These may be cogent reasons of social policy for imposing liability on the authority. But the shoulders of a public authority are only "broad enough to bear the loss" because they are financed by the public at large. It is pre-eminently for the legislature to decide whether these policy reasons should be accepted as sufficient for imposing on the public the burden of providing compensation for private financial losses. If they do so decide, it is not difficult for them to say so.'

Comment

(1)   In relation to breach of statutory duty see p 449.

(2)   In *Bellefield Computers Ltd and others v E Turner Ltd,* the claimant had purchased from the original owner a dairy which had been built by the defendants. The defendants had not followed good building practice in that an internal wall dividing the building was too short to prevent a fire, which started in a storage area, from spreading to the rest of the building. Despite the claimant's argument that the building should be regarded as divisible, and the claim therefore not one for pure economic loss, the Court of Appeal held that the judge had been correct in applying the guidance in *Murphy* and treating the fire damage as damage to the building itself and irrecoverable. By contrast, it was said, a claim for damage to chattels within the building would be successful.

(3)   Note the court's policy concerns both about the 'floodgates' risk of a proliferation of claims if the principle of liability were to be extended to cover chattels as well as buildings; and about the fact that to uphold the existence of a duty in such cases would effectively introduce product liability and destroy the doctrine of privity of contract.

(4)   In New Zealand the law relating to local authorities' liability for economic loss in such circumstances has developed rather differently. In *Invercargill City Council v Hamlin* the Privy Council, holding the defendant council liable, commented that: '[This] particular branch of the law of negligence … is especially unsuited for the imposition of a single monolithic solution … The decision whether to hold a local authority liable for the negligence of a building inspector is bound to be based at least in part on policy considerations …'. Although this decision was inconsistent with *Murphy*, it was entirely appropriate for the law in different common law jurisdictions to reflect 'community standards and expectations'.

Hedley Byrne & Co Ltd v Heller & Partners Ltd
[1963] 2 All ER 575 House of Lords

The appellants, an advertising company, became concerned about the financial stability of a client, E Ltd. They asked their own bank to make enquiries of the respondents, E Ltd's bankers. This they did, first by telephone and, three months later, by letter. The respondents gave their opinion 'without responsibility' that E Ltd was a respectable company 'considered good for its ordinary business engagements'. This proved to be untrue and the appellants duly suffered losses when E Ltd went into liquidation. The House of Lords held, *obiter*, that a duty of care was owed in such circumstances by the supplier of information although, in this case, the respondents were protected by their exclusion clause.

Lord Morris: '... My Lords, I consider that it follows and that it should now be regarded as settled that if someone possessed of a special skill undertakes, quite irrespective of contract, to apply that skill for the assistance of another person who relies on such skill, a duty of care will arise. The fact that the service is to be given by means of, or by the instrumentality of, words can make no difference. Furthermore if, in a sphere in which a person is so placed that others could reasonably rely on his judgment or his skill or on his ability to make careful inquiry, a person takes it on himself to give information or advice to, or allows his information or advice to be passed on to, another person who, as he knows or should know, will place reliance on it, then a duty of care will arise.'

Lord Devlin: '... The respondents in this case cannot deny that they were performing a service. Their sheet anchor is that they were performing it gratuitously and therefore no liability for its performance can arise. My lords, in my opinion this is not the law. A promise given without consideration to perform a service cannot be enforced as a contract by the promisee; but if the service is in fact performed and done negligently, the promisee can recover in an action in tort.

[Lord Devlin cited a number of authorities and continued.]

I think, therefore, that there is ample authority to justify your lordships in saying now that the categories of special relationships, which may give rise to a duty to take care in word as well as in deed, are not limited to contractual relationships or to relationships of fiduciary duty, but include also relationships which in the words of Lord Shaw in *Nocton v Lord Ashburton* are "equivalent to contract", that is, where there is an assumption of responsibility in circumstances in which, but for the absence of consideration, there would be a contract. Where there is an express undertaking, an express warranty as distinct from mere representation, there can be little difficulty. The difficulty arises in discerning those cases in which the undertaking is to be implied. In this respect the absence of consideration is not irrelevant. Payment for information or advice is very good evidence that it is being relied on and that the informer or adviser knows that it is. Where there is no consideration, it will be necessary to exercise greater care in distinguishing between social and professional relationships and between those which are of a contractual character and those which are not. It may often be material to consider whether the adviser is acting purely out of good nature or whether he is getting his reward in some indirect form.

The service that a bank performs in giving a reference is not done simply out of a desire to assist commerce. It would discourage the customers of the bank if their deals fell through because the bank had refused to testify to their credit when it was good. I have had the advantage of reading all the opinions prepared by your lordships and of studying the terms which your lordships have framed by way of definition of the sort of relationship which gives rise to a responsibility towards those who act on information or advice and so creates a duty of care towards them. I do not understand any of your lordships to hold that it is a responsibility imposed by law on certain types of persons or in certain sorts of situations. It is a responsibility that is voluntarily accepted or undertaken either generally where a general relationship, such as that of solicitor and client or banker and customer, is created, or specifically in relation to a particular transaction ...

Since the essence of the matter in the present case and in others of the same type is the acceptance of responsibility, I should like to guard against the imposition of restrictive terms notwithstanding that the essential condition is fulfilled. If a defendant says to a plaintiff – "Let me do this for you, do not waste your money in employing a professional, I will do it for nothing and you can rely on me" – I do not think he could escape liability simply because he belonged to no profession or calling, had no qualifications or special skill and did not hold himself out as having any. The relevance of these factors is to show the unlikelihood of a defendant in such circumstances assuming a legal responsibility and as such they may often be decisive. But they are not theoretically conclusive, and so cannot be the subject of definition. It would be unfortunate if they were. For it would mean that plaintiffs would seek to avoid the rigidity of the definition by bringing the action in contract as in *De La Bere v Pearson Ltd* and setting up something that would do for consideration. That to my mind would be an undesirable development in the law; and the best way of avoiding it is to settle the law so that the presence or absence of consideration makes no difference.'

Ministry of Housing and Local Government v Sharp and another [1970] I All ER 1009 Court of Appeal

In 1960 the Ministry paid compensation in relation to land for which planning permission had been refused. They then served a compensation notice on the local council which registered it in the local land charges register pursuant to the Town and Country Planning Act 1954. Two years later, when planning permission was granted and the land sold, the compensation was due to be repaid but the council employee who made a search of the register failed to notice the charge and issued a clear certificate to the prospective purchaser. The Court of Appeal held that the council were in breach of a duty owed to the Ministry.

Salmon LJ: '... The only real question on this part of the case is, did the council or their servant owe the Minister any duty of care. I entirely agree with the learned judge that the answer to this question is "Yes" ...

The servant and certainly the council must or should have known that unless the search was conducted and the certificate prepared with reasonable care, any chargee or incumbrancer whose registered charge or quasi-charge was carelessly omitted from the certificate would lose it and be likely to suffer damage. In my view, this factor certainly creates as close a degree of proximity between the council and the incumbrancer as existed between the appellant and respondent in *Donoghue v Stevenson*. It matters not that the primary duty under the statute may have been on the local registrar. It would, in my view, be altogether too pedantic and unrealistic to hold that the council's servant who searched the register must be deemed to have ceased to be in their employment and to have been transferred for this purpose to another master, namely the council clerk.

It is true that in *Donoghue v Stevenson* it was physical injury that was to be foreseen as a result of the failure to take reasonable care whereas in the present case it is financial loss. But this no longer matters, and it is now well established that, quite apart from any contractual or fiduciary relationship, a man may owe a duty of care in what he writes or says just as much as in what he does: see *Hedley Byrne & Co Ltd v Heller & Partners Ltd*. No doubt in our criminal law, injury to the person is or should be regarded as more serious than damage to property and punished accordingly. So far, however, as the law of negligence relating to civil actions is concerned, the existence of a duty to take reasonable care no longer depends on whether it is physical injury or financial loss which can reasonably be foreseen as a result of a failure to take such care.

The present case does not precisely fit into any category of negligence yet considered by the courts. The Ministry has not been misled by any careless statement made to it by the defendants or made by the defendants to someone else who the defendants knew would be likely to pass it on to a third party such as the Ministry, in circumstances in which the third party might reasonably be expected to rely on it, see for example, Denning LJ's dissenting judgment in *Candler v Crane, Christmas & Co* which was adopted and approved by the House of Lords in *Hedley Byrne & Co Ltd v Heller & Partners Ltd*. I am not, however, troubled by the fact that the present case is, in many respects, unique. I rely on the celebrated *dictum* of Lord Macmillan that "The categories of negligence are never closed", *Donoghue v Stevenson*, and the words of Lord Devlin in *Hedley Byrne & Co Ltd v Heller & Partners Ltd* ... Lord Devlin thought that responsibility could attach only to giving the reference "... and only if the doing of that act implied a voluntary undertaking to assume responsibility" ...

It has been argued, in the present case, that since the council did not voluntarily make the search or prepare the certificate for their clerk's signature they did not voluntarily assume responsibility for the accuracy of the certificate and, accordingly, owed no duty of care to the Minister. I do not accept that, in all cases, the obligation to take reasonable care necessarily depends on a voluntary assumption of responsibility. Even if it did, I am far from satisfied that the council did not voluntarily assume responsibility in the present case. On the contrary, it seems to me that they certainly chose to undertake the duty of searching the register and preparing the certificate. There was nothing to compel them to discharge this duty through their servant. It obviously suited them better that this somewhat pedestrian task should be performed by one of their comparatively minor servants than by their clerk so that he might be left free to carry out other far more difficult and important functions on their behalf.

I do not think that it matters that the search was made at the request of the purchasers and that the certificate issued to him. It would be absurd if a duty of care were owed to a purchaser but not to an incumbrancer ... If, in such cases, a clear certificate is carelessly given, it will be the purchaser and not the incumbrancer who will suffer. Clearly land may be worth much more unincumbered than if it is subject to a charge. The purchaser who buys on the faith of a clear certificate might suffer very heavy financial loss if the certificate turns out to be incorrect. Such a loss is reasonably to be foreseen as a result of any carelessness in the search of the register or the preparation of the certificate. The proximity between the council and the purchaser is even closer than that between the plaintiff and the defendants in *Candler v Crane, Christmas & Co.* The council even receive a fee, although a small one, for the certificate. Clearly a duty to take care must exist in such a case. Our law would be grievously defective if the council did owe a duty of care to the purchaser in the one case but no duty to the incumbrancer in the other. The damage in each case is equally foreseeable. It is in my view irrelevant that in the one case the certificate is issued to the person it injures and in the other case it is not. The purchaser is deceived by the certificate about his legal rights when s 17(3) of the Land Charges Act 1925 does not apply while the incumbrancer's legal rights are taken away by the certificate when s 17(3) does apply. In my view the proximity is as close in one case as in the other and certainly sufficient to impose on the council through their servant a duty to take reasonable care.'

Comment

A slightly curious feature of this case is that the loss suffered by the Ministry arose not from any misstatement to them but to a third party. Similarly, in *Spring v Guardian Assurance plc* (see p 25) the House of Lords held that an employer owed a duty of care to an ex-employee in respect of a negligently prepared reference supplied to third parties. In *White v Jones* (see p 168) the plaintiffs recovered damages for a financial loss arising not from a misstatement but from an omission in relation to a third party.

Mutual Life and Citizens' Assurance Co Ltd and another v Clive Raleigh Evatt
[1971] I All ER 150 Privy Council

The plaintiff, who was a policyholder with the defendants, sought from them information about the financial stability of an associated company in which he was considering investing. The plaintiff knew that the defendants were in a position to acquire accurate information and on the strength of their opinion he made his investment. The opinion proved to have been negligently given and inaccurate and the plaintiff lost his money. A majority of three to two of the Judicial Committee held that the company owed no duty of care to the plaintiff since it was not in the business of giving such advice.

Lord Diplock: '... The several speeches in *Hedley Byrne & Co Ltd v Heller and Partners Ltd* have lain at the heart of the argument in the courts of Australia and before their Lordships' Board. That case broadened the category of relationships between one man and another which give rise to a duty at common law to use reasonable skill and care in making statements of fact or of opinion. Prior to *Hedley Byrne* it was accepted law in England that in the absence of contract the maker of a statement of fact or of opinion owed to a person whom he could reasonably foresee would rely upon it in a matter affecting his economic interest, a duty to be honest in making the statement. But he did not owe any duty to be careful, unless the relationship between him and the person who acted upon it to his economic detriment fell within the category of relationships which the law classified as fiduciary.

Hedley Byrne decided that the class of relationships between the maker of the statement and the person who acted upon it to his economic detriment which attracted the duty to be careful was not so limited, but could extend to relationships which though not fiduciary in character possessed other characteristics.

In *Hedley Byrne* itself and in the previous English cases on negligent statements which were analysed in the speeches, with the notable exceptions of *Fish v Kelly, Derry v Peek* and *Low v Bouverie*, the relationship possessed the characteristics (1) that the maker of the statement had made it in the ordinary course of his business or profession and (2) that the subject-matter of the statement called for the exercise of some qualification, skill or competence not possessed by the ordinary reasonable man, to which the maker of the statement was known by the recipient to lay claim by reason of his engaging in that business or profession.

In the United States of America, where the development of this branch of the common law of negligence had anticipated the English decision in *Hedley Byrne* the American *Restatement of the Law of Torts*, which was referred to by Lord Devlin, and by Lord Pearce, specifies as a necessary characteristic of a relationship which gives rise to a duty of care on the part of the maker of the statement that he should be a person who makes it a part of his business or profession to supply for the guidance of others in their business transactions information of the kind contained in the statement and that the statement should be made by him in the course of that business or profession.

A requirement that the existence of a similar characteristic is necessary in order to attract a duty of care is not stated unequivocally in any of the speeches in *Hedley*

Byrne. But those speeches like all judgments under the common law system must be understood *secundum subjectam materiam*. The fact that the characteristics were present in the relationship between the maker and the recipient of the statement under consideration in *Hedley Byrne* made it unnecessary for those who expressed the reasons for their decision of the case to direct their minds to the question whether the terms in which the reasons were expressed would have called for some qualification in their application to cases where those characteristics were absent – as they are in the instant appeal. The speeches in *Hedley Byrne* cannot thus be determinative in themselves of whether or not the presence of these characteristics in the relationship between the maker and the recipient is necessary in order to give rise to a duty of care at common law.

Their Lordships accordingly conceive it to be their task in the instant appeal to examine that question as one of principle in the light of the earlier development of this branch of the law of negligence in the cases which preceded, and were for the most part referred to, in *Hedley Byrne*, as well as in the light of the speeches in *Hedley Byrne* themselves.

The instant appeal is concerned with a statement consisting of "information and advice concerning the financial stability of a certain company ... and as to the safety of investments therein". In regard to this subject-matter, viz. financial stability and safety of investment, no distinction need be drawn between "information" and "advice" and it is convenient to use the latter word. Such advice to be reliable (i.e. to be of a quality upon which it would be reasonable for the advisee to rely in determining his course of action in a matter which affected his economic interests) calls for the exercise on the part of the adviser of special skill and competence to form a judgment in the subject-matter of the advice, which the advisee does not possess himself. The problem to be solved arises in that field of human activity which calls for the services of a skilled man.

The proposition stated in the maxim *spondet peritiam artis et imperitia culpae adnumeratur* is one of the oldest principles in English law. The duty imposed by law upon those who followed a calling which required skill and competence to exercise in their calling such reasonable skill and competence as was appropriate to it lies at the origin of the action of assumpsit itself ... The duty to conform to the standard was attracted by engaging in that particular calling, business or profession because by doing so a man holds himself out as possessing the necessary skill and competence for it. To undertake to do an act requiring special skill and competence for reward was also a sufficient holding out by the obligor to the obligee. But the doing of the act gratuitously by a person who did not engage in the calling, business or profession did not attract the duty to exercise skill and competence: *Shiells v Blackburne*; see also the references to the relevant cases in the speeches in *Hedley Byrne* of Lord Hodson and Lord Pearce.

Where advice which calls for the exercise of special skill and competence by the adviser is not to be based exclusively upon facts communicated to him by the advisee no relevant distinction can be drawn between the ascertaining by the adviser of the facts upon which to base his judgment as to the advice to be given, and the forming of that judgment itself. The need for special skill and competence extends to the selection of the particular facts which need to be ascertained in order to form a reliable judgment and to the identification of the sources from which such facts can be obtained.

As in the case of a person who gratuitously does an act which calls for the exercise of some special skill and competence, a duty of care which lies upon an adviser must be a duty to conform to an ascertainable standard of skill and competence in relation to the subject-matter of the advice. Otherwise there can be no way of determining whether the adviser was in breach of his duty of care. The problem cannot be solved by saying that the adviser must do his honest best according to the skill and competence which he in fact possesses, for in the law of negligence standards of care are always objective. The passages in the judgment of Cozens-Hardy MR in *Parsons v Barclay & Co Ltd and Goddard* and of Pearson LJ in the Court of Appeal in *Hedley Byrne* itself, which were quoted with approval in the House of Lords, make it clear that a banker giving a gratuitous reference is not required to do his best by, for instance, making inquiries from outside sources which are available to him, though this would make his reference more reliable. All that he is required to do is to conform to that standard of skill and competence and diligence which is generally shown by persons who carry on the business of providing references of that kind. Equally it is no excuse to him to say that he has done his honest best, if what he does falls below that standard because in fact he lacks the necessary skill and competence to attain it.

The reason why the law requires him to conform to this standard of skill and competence and diligence is that by carrying on a business which includes the giving of references of this kind he has let it be known to the recipient of the reference that he claims to possess that degree of skill and competence and is willing to apply that degree of diligence to the provision of any reference which he supplies in the course of that business, whether gratuitously so far as the recipient is concerned or not. If he supplies the reference the law requires him to make good his claim.

It would not in their Lordships' view be consonant with the principles hitherto accepted in the common law that the duty to comply with that objective standard should be extended to an adviser who, at the time at which the advice is sought, has not let it be known to the advisee that he claims to possess the standard of skill and competence and is prepared to exercise diligence which is generally shown by persons who carry on the business of giving advice of the kind sought. He has given the advisee no reason to suppose that he is acquainted with the standard or capable of complying with it or that he has such appreciation of the nature and magnitude of the loss which the advisee may sustain by reason of any failure by that adviser to attain that standard as a reasonable man would require before assuming a liability to answer for the loss.

But if it would not be just or reasonable to require him to conform to this objective standard of care which would be incumbent upon a person who carried on the business of giving advice of the kind sought, there is in their Lordships' view no half-way house between that and the common law duty which each man owes his neighbour irrespective of his skill – the duty of honesty. No half-way house has been suggested in the argument in the instant appeal or in any of the decided cases ...

The carrying on of a business or profession which involves the giving of advice of a kind which calls for special skill and competence is the normal way in which a person lets it be known to the recipient of the advice that he claims to possess that degree of skill and competence and is willing to exercise that degree of diligence which is generally possessed and exercised by persons who carry on the business or profession of giving advice of the kind sought. The *American Restatement of the Law of Torts* (2nd) confines the duty of care in giving advice to persons who make it part of their business to supply advice; though later tentative redrafts suggest that the duty also attaches where the adviser has a financial interest in the transaction – a situation which is not relevant to the instant appeal. Denning LJ also so confined it in his dissenting judgment in *Candler*'s case where after stating that the persons subject to a duty of care in giving advice are:

> "those persons such as accountants, surveyors, valuers and analysts *whose profession and occupation it is* to examine books, accounts and other things, and to make reports on which other people – other than their clients – rely in the ordinary course of business," added "Herein lies the difference between these professional men and other persons who have been held to be under no duty to use care in their statements, such as promoters who issue a prospectus: *Derry v Peek* (now altered by statute) and trustees who answer inquiries about the trust funds: *Low v Bouverie*. Those persons do not bring, and are not expected to bring, any professional knowledge or skill into the preparation of their statements: they can only be made responsible by the law affecting persons generally, such as contract, estoppel, innocent misrepresentation or fraud."

This dissenting judgment was referred to with approval in *Hedley Byrne* in the speeches of Lord Hodson, Lord Devlin and Lord Pearce.

While accepting this as the common case giving rise to the duty of care their Lordships would not wish to exclude the case where the adviser, although not carrying on the business or profession generally, has, at or before the time at which his advice is sought, let it be known in some other way that he claims to possess skill and competence in the subject-matter of the particular inquiry comparable to those who do carry on the business or profession of advising on that subject-matter and is prepared to exercise a comparable skill and competence in giving the advice. Here too, by parity of reasoning, the law should require him to make good his claim. But the mere giving of advice with knowledge, as in *Low v Bouverie*, that the inquirer intends to rely upon it does not, of itself, in their Lordships' view, amount to such a claim.

The converse of this is the case where a person who does carry on a business or profession which involves the giving of advice of the kind sought by the inquirer, does so in circumstances which should let it be known to a reasonable inquirer that he was not prepared to exercise in relation to the particular advice sought that degree of diligence which he would exercise in giving such advice for reward in the course of his business or profession. Casual advice given by a professional man upon a social or informal occasion is the typical example, of which *Fish v Kelly* provides an illustration among the decided cases.

There are two passages in the speeches in *Hedley Byrne* which have been particularly relied upon, in the argument before their Lordships and in the majority judgments in each of the courts below, as amounting to a decision that the law imposes a "duty of care" upon a person who gives advice to another on a subject-matter requiring skill and competence and diligence, so long as he knows or ought to have known that the other intends to rely upon it in a matter affecting his economic interests, notwithstanding that the adviser neither carries on the business of giving advice of that kind nor has let it be known in some other way to the advisee at or before the time his advice is sought that *he claims* to possess a comparable skill and competence and is prepared to exercise a comparable diligence.

The passage in Lord Reid's speech is that in which he poses the courses of action open to a reasonable man upon being asked for advice on a matter requiring skill and competence and diligence. It reads as follows:

> "A reasonable man, knowing that he was being trusted or that his skill and judgment were being relied on, would, I think, have three courses open to him. He could keep silent or decline to give the information or advice sought: or he could give an answer with a clear qualification that he accepted no responsibility for it or that it was given without that reflection or inquiry which a careful answer would require; or he could simply answer without any such qualification. If he chooses to adopt the last course he must, I think, be held to have accepted some responsibility for his answer being given carefully, or to have accepted a relationship with the inquirer which requires him to exercise such care as the circumstances require."

This is not the language of statutory codification of the law of tort but of judicial exposition of the reasons for reaching a particular decision upon the facts of the case. Read out of the context in which the whole argument in *Hedley Byrne* proceeded, viz. advice given in the course of a business or profession which involved the giving of skilled, competent and diligent advice, these words are wide enough to sustain Mr Evatt's case in the instant appeal. But in their Lordships' view the reference to "such care as the circumstances require" presupposes an ascertainable standard of skill, competence and diligence with which the adviser is acquainted or has represented that he is. Unless he carries on the business or profession of giving advice of that kind he cannot be reasonably expected to know whether any and if so what degree of skill, competence or diligence is called for, and *a fortiori*, in their Lordships' view, he cannot be reasonably held to have accepted the responsibility of conforming to a standard of skill, competence and diligence of which he is unaware, simply because he answers the inquiry with knowledge that the advisee intends to rely on his answer. This passage should in their Lordships' view be understood as restricted to advisers who carry on the business or profession of giving advice of the kind sought and to advice given by them in the course of that business.'

Comment

(1) In their dissenting judgment Lord Reid and Lord Morris of Borth-y-Gest rejected the restriction set out in the final sentence above. They considered that such a rule would be unworkable except in the clearest cases: 'Even a man with a professional qualification is seldom an expert on all matters dealt with by members of his profession. Must the adviser be an expert or specialist in the matter on which his advice is sought?' Their conclusion was as follows:

'... when an inquirer consults a business man in the course of his business and makes it plain to him that he is seeking considered advice and intends to act on it in a particular way, any reasonable business man would realise that, if he chooses to give advice without any warning or qualification, he is putting himself under a moral obligation to take some care. It appears to us to be well within the principles established by the *Hedley Byrne* case to regard his action in giving such advice as creating a special relationship between him and the inquirer and to translate his moral obligation into a legal obligation to take such care as is reasonable in the whole circumstances.'

Both the majority and the minority judgments have found supporters in subsequent cases. See *Esso v Mardon* and *Meates v A-G for New Zealand*.

(2) Normally, a duty of care will not arise when advice is given at a social or informal occasion but there may be exceptions to this when all the circumstances are taken into account: see *Chaudry v Prabhaker* in which the defendant had recommended to his friend a car which subsequently proved to be unroadworthy. The Court of Appeal held that the relationship between the parties for this purpose was somewhat akin to that of principal and agent and was sufficient for a duty of care to arise.

(3)   In *Williams and another v Natural Life Health Foods Ltd and another* the House of Lords held that the director of a company would not be personally liable for negligent advice given by that company unless he had assumed personal responsibility for the negligent advice and the claimant had reasonably relied on that assumption of personal responsibility. Speaking of the application of the extended *Hedley Byrne* principle to the case, Lord Steyn said:

> 'It will be recalled that Waite LJ [in the Court of Appeal] took the view that in the context of directors of companies the general principle must not "set at naught" the protection of limited liability. In *Trevor Ivory Ltd v Anderson* Cooke P (now Lord Cooke of Thorndon) expressed a very similar view. It is clear what they meant. What matters is not that the liability of the shareholders of a company is limited but that a company is a separate entity, distinct from its directors, servants or other agents. The trader who incorporates a company to which he transfers his business creates a legal person on whose behalf he may afterwards act as director. For present purposes, his position is the same as if he had sold his business to another individual and agreed to act on his behalf. Thus the issue in this case is not peculiar to companies. Whether the principal is a company or a natural person, someone acting on his behalf may incur personal liability in tort as well as imposing vicarious or attributed liability upon his principal. But in order to establish personal liability under the principle of *Hedley Byrne*, which requires the existence of a special relationship between plaintiff and tortfeasor, it is not sufficient that there should have been a special relationship with the principal. There must have been an assumption of responsibility such as to create a special relationship with the director or employee himself.'

Henderson and others v Merrett Syndicates Ltd and others; and other appeal
[1994] 3 All ER 506 House of Lords

The plaintiffs were Lloyd's names who had suffered disastrous financial losses as a result of negligent management of the syndicates of which they were members. It was vital for limitation purposes for the plaintiffs to establish that the defendant managers owed the members a duty of care in tort in addition to any contractual duty which may have arisen. The House of Lords upheld the lower courts' decisions that the defendants owed the plaintiffs a duty of care in negligence.

Lord Goff of Chieveley: '... The main argument advanced by the managing agents against the existence of a duty of care in tort was that the imposition of such a duty upon them was inconsistent with the contractual relationship between the parties. In the case of direct names, where there was a direct contract between the names and the managing agents, the argument was that the contract legislated exclusively for the relationship between the parties, and that a parallel duty of care in tort was therefore excluded by the contract. In the case of indirect names, reliance was placed on the fact that there had been brought into existence a contractual chain, between name and members' agent, and between members' agent and managing agent; and it was said that, by structuring their contractual relationship in this way, the indirect names and the managing agents had deliberately excluded any direct responsibility, including any tortious duty of care, to the indirect names by the managing agents. In particular, the argument ran, it was as a result not permissible for the names to pray in aid, for limitation purposes, the more favourable time for accrual of a cause of action in tort. To do so, submitted the managing agents, would deprive them of their contractual expectations, and would avoid the policy of Parliament that there are different limitation regimes for contract and tort ...

I think it desirable first to consider the principle upon which a duty of care in tort may in the present context be imposed upon the managing agents, assuming that to impose such a duty would not be inconsistent with the relevant contractual relationship. In considering this principle, I bear in mind in particular the separate submission of the managing agents that no such duty should be imposed, because the loss claimed by the names is purely economic loss. However the identification of the principle is, in my opinion, relevant to the broader question of the impact of the relevant contract or contracts.

(3) THE GOVERNING PRINCIPLE

... [*Hedley Byrne*] has always been regarded as important in that it established that, in certain circumstances, a duty of care may exist in respect of words as well as deeds, and further that liability may arise in negligence in respect of pure economic loss which is not parasitic upon physical damage. But, perhaps more important for the future development of the law, and certainly more relevant for the purposes of the present case, is the principle upon which the decision was founded. The governing principles are perhaps now perceived to be most clearly stated in the speeches of Lord Morris of Borth-y-Gest (with whom Lord Hodson agreed) and of Lord Devlin. [Lord Goff quoted the passages cited on p 148 and continued.]

From these statements, and from their application in *Hedley Byrne*, we can derive some understanding of the breadth of the principle underlying the case. We can see that it rests upon a relationship between the parties, which may be general or specific to the particular transaction, and which may or may not be contractual in nature. All of their Lordships spoke in terms of one party having assumed or undertaken a responsibility towards the other. On this point, Lord Devlin spoke in particularly clear terms in both passages from his speech which I have quoted above. Further, Lord Morris spoke of that party being possessed of a "special skill" which he undertakes to "apply for the assistance of another who relies upon such skill". But the facts of *Hedley Byrne* itself, which was concerned with the liability of a banker to the recipient for negligence in the provision of a reference gratuitously supplied, show that the concept of a "special skill" must be understood broadly, certainly broadly enough to include special knowledge. Again, though *Hedley Byrne* was concerned with the provision of information and advice, the example given by Lord Devlin of the relationship between solicitor and client, and his and Lord Morris's statements of principle, show that the principle extends beyond the provision of information and advice to include the performance of other services. It follows, of course, that although, in the case of the provision of information and advice, reliance upon it by the other party will be necessary to establish a cause of action (because otherwise the negligence will have no causative effect), nevertheless there may be other circumstances in which there will be the necessary reliance to give rise to the application of the principle. In particular, as cases concerned with solicitor and client demonstrate, where the plaintiff entrusts the defendant with the conduct of his affairs, in general or in particular, he may be held to have relied on the defendant to exercise due skill and care in such conduct.

In subsequent cases concerned with liability under the *Hedley Byrne* principle in respect of negligent mis-statements, the question has frequently arisen whether the plaintiff falls within the category of persons to whom the maker of the statement owes a duty of care. In seeking to contain that category of persons within reasonable bounds, there has been some tendency on the part of the courts to criticise the concept of "assumption of responsibility" as being "unlikely to be a helpful or realistic test in most cases" (see *Smith v Eric S Bush (a firm)*, *Harris v Wyre Forest DC* per Lord Griffiths; and see also *Caparo Industries plc v Dickman* per Lord Roskill). However, at least in cases such as the present, in which the same problem does not arise, there seems to be no reason why recourse should not be had to the concept, which appears after all to have been adopted, in one form or another, by all of their Lordships in *Hedley Byrne & Co Ltd v Heller & Partners Ltd* … Furthermore, especially in a context concerned with a liability which may arise under a contract or in a situation "equivalent to contract", it must be expected that an objective test will be applied when asking the question whether, in a particular case, responsibility should be held to have been assumed by the defendant to the plaintiff: see *Caparo Industries plc v Dickman* per Lord Oliver of Aylmerton. In addition, the concept provides its own explanation why there is no problem in cases of this kind about liability for pure economic loss; for if a person assumes responsibility to another in respect of certain services, there is no reason why he should not be liable in damages for that other in respect of economic loss which flows from the negligent performance of those services. It follows that, once the case is identified as falling within the *Hedley Byrne* principle, there should be no need to embark upon any further inquiry whether it is "fair, just and reasonable" to impose liability for economic loss – a point which is, I consider, of some importance in the present case. The concept indicates too that in some circumstances, for example where the undertaking to furnish the relevant service is given on an informal occasion, there may be no assumption of responsibility; and likewise that an assumption of responsibility may be negatived by an appropriate disclaimer. I wish to add in parenthesis that ... an assumption of responsibility by, for example, a professional man may give rise to liability in respect of negligent omissions as much as negligent acts of commission, as for example when a solicitor assumes responsibility for business on behalf of his client and omits to take a certain step, such as the service of a document, which falls within the responsibility so assumed by him.

(4) THE APPLICATION OF THE PRINCIPLE TO MANAGING AGENTS AT LLOYD'S

Since it has been submitted on behalf of the managing agents that no liability should attach to them in negligence in the present case because the only damage suffered by the names consists of pure economic loss, the question arises whether the principle in *Hedley Byrne* is capable of applying in the case of underwriting agents at Lloyd's who are managing agents. Like Saville J and the Court of Appeal, I have no difficulty in concluding that the principle is indeed capable of such application. The principle has been expressly applied to a number of different categories of person who perform services of a professional or quasi-professional nature, such as bankers (in *Hedley Byrne* itself); solicitors (as foreshadowed by Lord Devlin in *Hedley Byrne*, and as held in the leading case of *Midland Bank Trust Co Ltd v Hett Stubbs & Kemp (a firm)*, and other cases in which that authority has been followed); surveyors and valuers (as in *Smith v Eric S Bush (a firm)*, *Harris v Wyre Forest DC*); and accountants (as in *Caparo Industries plc v Dickman*). Another category of persons to whom the principle has been applied, and on which particular reliance was placed by the names in the courts below and in argument before your Lordships, is insurance brokers. As Phillips J pointed out in *Youell v Bland Welch & Co Ltd (The 'Superhulls Cover' Case) (No 2)*, it has been accepted, since before 1964, that an insurance broker owes a duty of care in negligence towards his client, whether the broker is bound by contract or not. Furthermore, in *Punjab National Bank v de Boinville* it was held by the Court of Appeal, affirming the decision of Hobhouse J, that a duty of care was owed by an insurance broker not only to his client but also to a specific person whom he knew was to become an assignee of the policy. For my part I can see no reason why a duty of care should not likewise be owed by managing agents at Lloyd's to a name who is a member of a syndicate under the management of the agents. Indeed, as Saville J and the Court of Appeal both thought, the relationship between name and managing agent appears to provide a classic example of the type of relationship to which the principle in *Hedley Byrne* applies. In so saying, I put on one side the question of the impact, if any, upon the relationship of the contractual context in which it is set. But, that apart, there is in my opinion plainly an assumption of responsibility in the relevant sense by the managing agents towards the names in their syndicates. The managing agents have accepted the names as members of a syndicate under their management. They obviously hold themselves out as possessing a special expertise to advise the names on the suitability of risks to be underwritten; and on the circumstances in which, and the extent to which, reinsurance should be taken out and claims should be settled. The names, as the managing agents well knew, placed implicit reliance on that expertise, in that they gave authority to the managing agents to bind them to contracts of insurance and reinsurance and to the settlement of claims. I can see no escape from the conclusion that, in these circumstances, *prima facie* a duty of care is owed in tort by the managing agents to such names. To me, it does not matter if one proceeds by way of analogy from the categories of relationship already recognised as falling within the principle in *Hedley Byrne* or by a straight application of the principle stated in the *Hedley Byrne* case itself. On either basis the conclusion is, in my opinion, clear. Furthermore, since the duty rests on the principle in *Hedley Byrne*, no problem arises from the fact that the loss suffered by the names is pure economic loss.

This conclusion is, however, subject to the impact, if any, of the contractual context. In argument before your Lordships this was regarded as constituting the main basis for the managing agents' challenge to the conclusion on this point of the courts below. To this point I must therefore turn; but before I do so I propose to consider briefly, if only to put it on one side, the question whether ... a duty of care on the part of the managing agents was excluded by the absolute discretion vested in them under their contract with the direct names, or with the members' agents in cases involving indirect names.

(5) ABSOLUTE DISCRETION

... [I]t appears to me ... that in the present context the words used cannot have the effect of excluding a duty of care, contractual or otherwise. Clear words are required to exclude liability in negligence; and in the present case the words can, and in my opinion should, be directed towards the scope of the agents' authority. No doubt the result is that very wide authority has been vested in the agents; but the suggestion that the agent should as a result be under no duty to exercise due skill and care in the exercise of his function under the agreement is, in the present context, most surprising ...

(6) THE IMPACT OF THE CONTRACTUAL CONTEXT

All systems of law which recognise a law of contract and a law of tort (or delict) have to solve the problem of the possibility of concurrent claims arising from breach of duty under the two rubrics of the law. Although there are variants, broadly speaking two possible solutions present themselves: either to insist that the claimant should pursue his remedy in contract alone, or to allow him to choose which remedy he prefers. [Lord Goff reviewed the approach in other jurisdictions and continued.]

At first, as is shown in particular by cases concerned with liability for solicitors' negligence, the courts adopted something very like the French solution, holding that a claim against a solicitor for negligence must be pursued in contract, and not in tort ...; and in *Groom v Crocker* this approach was firmly adopted. It has to be said, however, that decisions such as these, though based on prior authority, were supported by only a slender citation of cases, none of great weight; and the jurisprudential basis of the doctrine so adopted cannot be said to have been explored in any depth ... I must confess to finding it startling that, in the second half of the twentieth century, a problem of considerable practical importance should fall to be solved by reference to such an outmoded form of categorisation as this ...

The decision in *Hedley Byrne*, and the statement of general principle in that case, provided the opportunity to reconsider the question of concurrent liability in contract and tort afresh ... The requisite analysis is ... to be found in the judgment of Oliver J in *Midland Bank Trust Co Ltd v Hett Stubbs & Kemp (a firm)*, in which he held that a solicitor could be liable to his client for negligence either in contract or in tort, with the effect that in the case before him it was open to the client to take advantage of the more favourable date of accrual of the cause of action for the purposes of limitation ... It is evident that the early authorities did not play a very significant part in Oliver J's decision ... His main concern was with the impact of the decision of this House in *Hedley Byrne & Co Ltd v Heller & Partners Ltd*, and of subsequent cases in the Court of Appeal in which *Hedley Byrne* had been applied. As he read the speeches in *Hedley Byrne*, the principle there stated was not limited to circumstances in which the responsibility of the defendant had been gratuitously assumed ...

He expressed his conclusion concerning the impact of *Hedley Byrne* on the case before him in the following words:

"The case of a layman consulting a solicitor for advice seems to me to be as typical a case as one could find of the sort of relationship in which the duty of care described in the *Hedley Byrne* case exists; and if I am free to do so in the instant case, I would, therefore, hold that the relationship of solicitor and client gave rise to a duty on the defendants under the general law to exercise that care and skill upon which they must have known perfectly well that their client relied. To put it another way, their common law duty was not to injure their client by failing to do that which they had undertaken to do and which, at their invitation, he relied on them to do. That duty was broken, but no cause of action in tort arose until the damage occurred; and none did until 17 August 1967. I would regard it as wholly immaterial that their duty arose because they accepted a retainer which entitled them, if they chose to do so, to send a bill to their client."

I wish to express my respectful agreement with these passages in Oliver J's judgment.

Thereafter, Oliver J proceeded to consider the authorities since *Hedley Byrne* ... [I]n the course of considering [which], he rejected the idea that there is some general principle of law that a plaintiff who has claims against a defendant for breach of duty both in contract and in tort is bound to rely upon his contractual rights alone. He said:

> "There is not and never has been any rule of law that a person having alternative claims must frame his action in one or the other. If I have a contract with my dentist to extract a tooth, I am not thereby precluded from suing him in tort if he negligently shatters my jaw."

The origin of concurrent remedies in this type of case may lie in history; but in a modern context the point is a telling one. Indeed it is consistent with the decision in *Donoghue v Stevenson* itself, and the rejection in that case of the view, powerfully expressed in the speech of Lord Buckmaster, that the manufacturer or repairer of an article owes no duty of care apart from that implied from contract or imposed by statute. That there might be co-existent remedies for negligence in contract and in tort was expressly recognised by Lord Macmillan in *Donoghue v Stevenson* and by Lord Wright in *Grant v Australian Knitting Mills Ltd*. Attempts have been made to explain how doctors and dentists may be concurrently liable in tort while other professional men may not be so liable, on the basis that the former cause physical damage whereas the latter cause pure economic loss (see the discussion by Christine French "The Contract/Tort Dilemma" (1981–84) 5 Otago LR 236 at 280–281). But this explanation is not acceptable, if only because some professional men, such as architects, may also be responsible for physical damage. As a matter of principle, it is difficult to see why concurrent remedies in tort and contract, if available against the medical profession, should not also be available against members of other professions, whatever form the relevant damage may take.

The judgment of Oliver J in *Midland Bank Trust Co Ltd v Hett Stubbs & Kemp (a firm)* provided the first analysis in depth of the question of concurrent liability in tort and contract. Following upon *Esso Petroleum Co Ltd v Mardon*, it also broke the mould, in the sense that it undermined the view which was becoming settled that, where there is an alternative liability in tort, the claimant must pursue his remedy in contract alone. The development of the case law in other common law countries is very striking. [Lord Goff noted the acceptance of the "concurrent approach" in Ireland, Canada, Australia, New Zealand and the United States, and continued.]

I have dealt with the matter at some length because, before your Lordships, [counsel] for the managing agents boldly challenged the decision of Oliver J in the *Midland Bank Trust* case, seeking to persuade your Lordships that this House should now hold that case to have been wrongly decided ... [He] adopted as part of his argument the reasoning of Mr J M Kaye in an article "The Liability of Solicitors in Tort" (1984) 100 LQR 680. In his article Mr Kaye strongly criticised the reasoning of Oliver J both on historical grounds and with regard to his interpretation of the speeches in *Hedley Byrne*. However, powerful though Mr Kaye's article is, I am not persuaded by it to treat the *Midland Bank Trust* case as wrongly decided. First, so far as the historical approach is concerned, this is no longer of direct relevance in a case such as the present, having regard to the development of the general principle in *Hedley Byrne* ...

So far as *Hedley Byrne* itself is concerned, Mr Kaye reads the speeches as restricting the principle of assumption of responsibility there established to cases where there is no contract ... I must confess however that ... I remain of the opinion that Oliver J's reading of them is justified. It is, I suspect, a matter of the angle of vision with which they are read. For here, I consider, Oliver J was influenced not only by what he read in the speeches themselves, notably the passage from Lord Devlin's speech quoted above, but also by the internal logic reflected in that passage, which led inexorably to the conclusion which he drew. Mr Kaye's approach involves regarding the law of tort as supplementary to the law of contract, i.e. as providing for a tortious liability in cases where there is no contract. Yet the law of tort is the general law, out of which the parties can, if they wish, contract; and, as Oliver J demonstrated, the same assumption of responsibility may, and frequently does, occur in a contractual context. Approached as a matter of principle, therefore, it is right to attribute to that assumption of responsibility, together with its concomitant reliance, a tortious liability, and then to inquire whether or not that liability is excluded by the contract because the latter is inconsistent with it. This is the reasoning which Oliver J, as I understand it, found implicit, where not explicit, in the speeches in *Hedley Byrne*. With his conclusion I respectfully agree. But even if I am wrong in this, I am of the opinion that this House should now, if necessary, develop the principle of assumption of responsibility as stated in *Hedley Byrne* to its logical conclusion so as to make it clear that a tortious duty of care may arise not only in cases where the relevant services are rendered gratuitously, but also where they are rendered under a contract. This indeed is the view expressed by Lord Keith of Kinkel in *Murphy v Brentwood DC*, in a speech with which all the other members of the Appellate Committee agreed ...

[I]n the present case liability can, and in my opinion should, be founded squarely on the principle established in *Hedley Byrne* itself, from which it follows that an assumption of responsibility coupled with the concomitant reliance may give rise to a tortious duty of care irrespective of whether there is a contractual relationship between the parties, and in consequence, unless his contract precludes him from doing so, the plaintiff, who has available to him concurrent remedies in contract and tort, may choose that remedy which appears to him to be the most advantageous.

(7) APPLICATION OF THE ABOVE PRINCIPLES IN THE PRESENT CASE

I have already concluded that *prima facie* a duty of care was owed in tort on the *Hedley Byrne* principle by managing agents both to direct names and indirect names. So far as the direct names are concerned, there is plainly a contract between them and the managing agents ... in which a term falls to be implied that the agents will exercise due care and skill in the exercise of their functions as managing agents under the agreement. That duty of care is no different from the duty of care owed by them to the relevant names in tort; and, having regard to the principles already stated, the contract does not operate to exclude the tortious duty, leaving it open to the names to pursue either remedy against the agents.

I turn to the indirect names ... [It is] submitted on behalf of the managing agents that the indirect names and the managing agents, as parties to the chain of contracts contained in the relevant agency and sub-agency agreements, must be taken to have thereby structured their relationship so as to exclude any duty of care owed directly by the managing agents to the indirect names in tort.

In essence the argument must be that, because the managing agents have, with the consent of the indirect names, assumed responsibility in respect of the relevant activities to another party, i.e. the members' agents, under a sub-agency agreement, it would be inconsistent to hold that they have also assumed responsibility in respect of the same activities to the indirect names. I for my part cannot see why in principle a party should not assume responsibility to more than one person in respect of the same activity. Let it be assumed (unlikely though it may be) that, in the present case, the managing agents were in a contractual relationship not only with the members' agents under a sub-agency agreement but also directly with the relevant names, under both of which they assumed responsibility for the same activities. I can see no reason in principle why the two duties of care so arising should not be capable of co-existing.

Of course I recognise that the present case presents the unusual feature that claims against the managing agents, whether by the members' agents under the sub-agency agreement or by the indirect names in tort, will in both cases have the purpose, immediate or ultimate, of obtaining compensation for the indirect names. In these circumstances, concurrent duties of care could, in theory at least, give rise to problems, for example in the event of the insolvency of the managing agents or the members' agents. Furthermore, as [counsel] suggested in the course of his submissions on behalf of the managing agents, questions of contribution might, at least in theory, arise. But your Lordships' task, like that of the courts below, is to answer the questions of principle raised by the issues presented for decision; and in these circumstances it would be quite wrong to embark upon the examination of questions which do not arise on those issues, and indeed may never arise in practice. For myself, I am all the more reluctant to do so since, because the liability (if any) of the managing agents will in each case flow from claims by the indirect names, it may well be that practical problems such as these will, if they arise, find a practical solution.

I wish, however, to add that I strongly suspect that the situation which arises in the present case is most unusual; and that in many cases in which a contractual chain comparable to that in the present case is constructed it may well prove to be inconsistent with an assumption of responsibility which has the effect of, so to speak, short-circuiting the contractual structure so put in place by the parties. It cannot therefore be inferred from the present case that other sub-agents will be held directly liable to the agent's principal in tort. Let me take the analogy of the common case of an ordinary building contract, under which main contractors contract with the building owner for the construction of the relevant building, and the main contractor sub-contracts with sub-contractors or suppliers (often nominated by the building owner) for the performance of work or the supply of materials in accordance with standards and subject to terms established in the sub-contract. I put on one side cases in which the sub-contractor causes physical damage to property of the building owner, where the claim does not depend on an assumption of responsibility by the sub-contractor to the building owner; though the sub-contractor may be protected from liability by a contractual exemption clause authorised by the building owner. But if the sub-contracted work or materials do not in the result conform to the required standard, it will not ordinarily be open to the building owner to sue the sub-contractor or supplier direct under the *Hedley Byrne* principle, claiming damages from him on the basis that he has been negligent in relation to the performance of his functions. For there is generally no assumption of responsibility by the sub-contractor or supplier direct to the building owner, the parties having so structured their relationship that it is inconsistent with any such assumption of responsibility. This was the conclusion of the Court of Appeal in *Simaan General Contracting Co v Pilkington Glass Ltd (No 2)*. As Bingham LJ put it:

> "I do not, however, see any basis on which [the nominated suppliers] could be said to have assumed a direct responsibility for the quality of the goods to [the building owners]; such a responsibility is, I think, inconsistent with the structure of the contract the parties have chosen to make."

It is true that, in this connection, some difficulty has been created by the decision of your Lordships' House in *Junior Books Ltd v Veitchi Co Ltd*. In my opinion, however, it is unnecessary for your Lordships to reconsider that decision for the purposes of the present appeal. Here however I can see no inconsistency between the assumption of responsibility by the managing agents to the indirect names, and that which arises under the sub-agency agreement between the managing agents and the members' agents, whether viewed in isolation or as part of the contractual chain stretching back to and so including the indirect names. For these reasons, I can see no reason why the indirect names should not be free to pursue their remedy against the managing agents in tort under the *Hedley Byrne* principle.'

Comment

(1) It would have been strange if the principle of assumption of responsibility in *Hedley Byrne*, which requires a relationship between the parties approaching that of a contract, should not apply when a contract actually existed. On the other hand, both Lord Browne-Wilkinson and Lord Goff recognised that there

may be situations where 'the tortious duty is so inconsistent with the applicable contract that, in accordance with ordinary principle, the parties must be taken to have agreed that the tortious remedy is to be limited or excluded'.

(2)   In *Aiken and others v Stewart Wrightson Members' Agency and others* the duty of care was extended to include not only existing names but also those who joined the syndicate at a later date provided that the threefold test of (i) foreseeability, (ii) proximity and (iii) that it would be fair, just and reasonable to impose liability was satisfied.

White and another v Jones and others
[1995] I All ER 691 House of Lords

Some four months after executing a will cutting the plaintiffs, his daughters, out of his will, the testator was reconciled with them and wrote instructing the defendant solicitors to prepare a new will which was to include gifts to each plaintiff. Two months after receiving the letter the defendants arranged to visit the testator but he died three days before the appointment, and before the new dispositions were put into effect. The House of Lords by a majority of three to two held that a duty was owed to an intended beneficiary in such circumstances.

Lord Goff of Chieveley: '... I turn to the principal issue which arises on the appeal, which is whether in the circumstances of cases such as *Ross v Caunters* and the present case the testator's solicitors are liable to the disappointed beneficiary. As I have already stated, the question is one which has been much discussed, not only in this country and other common law countries, but also in some civil law countries, notably Germany. There can be no doubt that *Ross v Caunters* has been generally welcomed by academic writers. Furthermore it does not appear to have been the subject of adverse comment in the higher courts in this country, though it has not been approved except by the Court of Appeal in the present case. Indeed, as far as I am aware, *Ross v Caunters* has created no serious problems in practice since it was decided nearly 15 years ago.

[Lord Goff referred to a number of countries in which a similar approach is adopted, and continued.]

Even so, it has been recognised on all hands that *Ross v Caunters* raises difficulties of a conceptual nature, and that as a result it is not altogether easy to accommodate the decision within the ordinary principles of our law of obligations ... It is right ... that I should immediately summarise these conceptual difficulties. They are as follows.

(1)   First, the general rule is well established that a solicitor acting on behalf of a client owes a duty of care only to his client. The relationship between a solicitor and his client is nearly always contractual, and the scope of the solicitor's duties will be set by the terms of his retainer; but a duty of care owed by a solicitor to his

client will arise concurrently in contract and in tort (see *Midland Bank Trust Co Ltd v Hett, Stubbs & Kemp (a firm)* recently approved by your Lordships' House in *Henderson v Merrett Syndicates Ltd*). But, when a solicitor is performing his duties to his client, he will generally owe no duty of care to third parties ... In these circumstances, it is said, there can be no liability of the solicitor to a beneficiary under a will who has been disappointed by reason of negligent failure by the solicitor to give effect to the testator's intention. There can be no liability in contract, because there is no contract between the solicitor and the disappointed beneficiary ... Nor could there be liability in tort, because in the performance of his duties to his client a solicitor owes no duty of care in tort to a third party such as a disappointed beneficiary under his client's will.

(2)　A further reason is given which is said to reinforce the conclusion that no duty of care is owed by the solicitor to the beneficiary in tort. Here, it is suggested, is one of those situations in which a plaintiff is entitled to damages if, and only if, he can establish a breach of contract by the defendant. First, the plaintiff's claim is one for purely financial loss; and as a general rule, apart from cases of assumption of responsibility arising under the principle in *Hedley Byrne & Co Ltd v Heller & Partners Ltd*, no action will lie in respect of such loss in the tort of negligence. Furthermore, in particular, no claim will lie in tort for damages in respect of a mere loss of an expectation, as opposed to damages in respect of damage to an existing right or interest of the plaintiff. Such a claim falls within the exclusive zone of contractual liability; and it is contrary to principle that the law of tort should be allowed to invade that zone. Of course, Parliament can create exceptions to that principle by extending contractual rights to persons who are not parties to a contract, as was done, for example, in the Bills of Lading Act 1855 and the Carriage of Goods by Sea Act 1992. But as a matter of principle a step of this kind cannot be taken by the courts, though they can redefine the boundaries of the exclusive zone, as they did in *Donoghue v Stevenson*.

The present case, it is suggested, falls within that exclusive zone. Here, it is impossible to frame the suggested duty except by reference to the contract between the solicitor and the testator – a contract to which the disappointed beneficiary is not a party, and from which, therefore, he can derive no rights. Second, the loss suffered by the disappointed beneficiary is not in reality a loss at all; it is, more accurately, a failure to obtain a benefit. All that has happened is that what is sometimes called a *spes succesionis* has failed to come to fruition. As a result, he has not become better off; but he is not made worse off. A claim in respect of such a loss of expectation falls, it is said, clearly within the exclusive zone of contractual liability.

(3)　A third, and distinct, objection is that, if liability in tort was recognised in cases such as *Ross v Caunters*, it would be impossible to place any sensible bounds to cases in which such recovery was allowed. In particular, the same liability should logically be imposed in cases where an *inter vivos* transaction was ineffective, and the defect was not discovered until the donor was no longer able to repair it. Furthermore, liability could not logically be restricted to cases where a specific named beneficiary was disappointed, but would inevitably have to be extended to cases in which wide, even indeterminate, classes of persons could be said to have been adversely affected.

(4)   Other miscellaneous objections were taken, though in my opinion they were without substance. In particular – (a) Since the testator himself owes no duty to the beneficiary, it would be illogical to impose any such duty on his solicitor. I myself cannot however see any force in this objection. (b) To enable the disappointed beneficiary to recover from the solicitor would have the undesirable, and indeed fortuitous, effect of substantially increasing the size of the testator's estate – even of doubling it in size; because it would not be possible to recover any part of the estate which had lawfully devolved upon others by an unrevoked will or on an intestacy, even though that was not in fact the testator's intention. I cannot however see what impact this has on the disappointed beneficiary's remedy. It simply reflects the fact that those who received the testator's estate, either under an unrevoked will or on an intestacy, were lucky enough to receive a windfall; and in consequence the estate is, so far as the testator and the disappointed beneficiary are concerned, irretrievably lost.

(5)   There is however another objection of a conceptual nature, which was not adumbrated in argument before the Appellate Committee. In the present case, unlike *Ross v Caunters* itself, there was no act of the defendant solicitor which could be characterised as negligent. All that happened was that the solicitor did nothing at all for a period of time, with the result that the testator died before his new testamentary intentions could be implemented in place of the old. As a general rule, however, there is no liability in tortious negligence for an omission, unless the defendant is under some pre-existing duty. Once again, therefore, the question arises how liability can arise in the present case in the absence of a contract.

Point (5) apart, such were the principal arguments addressed to the Appellate Committee by [Counsel for] the appellants in the present case ...

THE IMPULSE TO DO PRACTICAL JUSTICE

Before addressing the legal questions which lie at the heart of the present case, it is, I consider, desirable to identify the reasons of justice which prompt judges and academic writers to conclude, like Megarry V-C in *Ross v Caunters*, that a duty should be owed by the testator's solicitor to a disappointed beneficiary. The principal reasons are, I believe, as follows.

(1)   In the forefront stands the extraordinary fact that, if such a duty is not recognised, the only persons who might have a valid claim (i.e. the testator and his estate) have suffered no loss, and the only person who has suffered a loss (i.e. the disappointed beneficiary) has no claim: see *Ross v Caunters*. It can therefore be said

that, if the solicitor owes no duty to the intended beneficiaries, there is a lacuna in the law which needs to be filled. This I regard as being a point of cardinal importance in the present case.

(2) The injustice of denying such a remedy is reinforced if one considers the importance of legacies in a society which recognises ... the right of citizens to leave their assets to whom they please, and in which, as a result, legacies can be of great importance to individual citizens, providing very often the only opportunity for a citizen to acquire a significant capital sum; or to inherit a house, so providing a secure roof over the heads of himself and his family; or to make special provision for his or her old age ...

(3) There is a sense in which the solicitors' profession cannot complain if such a liability may be imposed upon their members. If one of them has been negligent in such a way as to defeat his client's testamentary intentions, he must regard himself as very lucky indeed if the effect of the law is that he is not liable to pay damages in the ordinary way. It can involve no injustice to render him subject to such a liability, even if the damages are payable not to his client's estate for distribution to the disappointed beneficiary (which might have been the preferred solution) but direct to the disappointed beneficiary.

(4) That such a conclusion is required as a matter of justice is reinforced by consideration of the role played by solicitors in society. The point was well made by Cooke J in *Gartside v Sheffield, Young & Ellis* when he observed:

"To deny an effective remedy in a plain case would seem to imply a refusal to acknowledge the solicitor's professional role in the community. In practice the public relies on solicitors (or statutory officers with similar functions) to prepare effective wills."

The question therefore arises whether it is possible to give effect in law to the strong impulse for practical justice which is the fruit of the foregoing considerations ...

Ross v Caunters AND THE CONCEPTUAL PROBLEMS

In *Ross v Caunters*, Megarry V-C approached the problem as one arising under the ordinary principles of the tort of negligence. He found himself faced with two principal objections to the plaintiff's claim. The first, founded mainly upon the decision of the Court of Appeal in *Groom v Crocker*, was that a solicitor could not be liable in negligence in respect of his professional work to anyone except his client, his liability to his client arising only in contract and not in tort. This proposition Megarry V-C rejected without difficulty, relying primarily upon the judgment of Oliver J in *Midland Bank Trust Co Ltd v Hett, Stubbs & Kemp* (recently approved by this House in *Henderson v Merrett Syndicates Ltd*). The second, and more fundamental, argument was that, apart from cases falling within the principle established in *Hedley Byrne*, no action lay in the tort of negligence for pure economic loss. This argument Megarry V-C approached following the path traced by Lord Wilberforce in *Anns v Merton London Borough*; and on that basis, relying in particular on *Ministry of Housing and Local Government v Sharp* (which he regarded as conclusive of the point before him), he held that here liability could properly be imposed in negligence for pure economic loss, his preferred basis being by direct application of *Donoghue v Stevenson* itself.

It will at once be seen that some of the conceptual problems raised by the appellants in argument before the Appellate Committee were not raised in *Ross v Caunters*. Others which were raised plainly did not loom so large in argument as they have done in the present case. Thus the point founded on the fact that in cases of this kind the plaintiff is claiming damages for the loss of an expectation was briefly touched upon by Megarry V-C and as briefly dismissed by him, but ... there is no further analysis of the point. It is however my opinion that, these conceptual arguments having been squarely raised in argument in the present case, they cannot lightly be dismissed. They have to be faced; and it is immediately apparent that they raise the question whether the claim properly falls within the law of contract or the law of tort ... Here I refer not only to the fact that the claim is one for damages for pure economic loss, but also to the need for the defendant solicitor to be entitled to invoke as against the disappointed beneficiary any terms of the contract with his client which may limit or exclude his liability; to the fact that the damages claimed are for the loss of an expectation; and also to the fact (not adverted to below) that the claim in the present case can be said to arise from a pure omission, and as such will not (apart from special circumstances) give rise to a claim in tortious negligence. Faced with points such as these, the strict lawyer may well react by saying that the present claim can lie only in contract, and is not therefore open to a disappointed beneficiary as against the testator's solicitor. This was indeed the reaction of Lush and Murphy JJ in *Seale v Perry*, and is one which is entitled to great respect.

It must not be forgotten however that a solicitor who undertakes to perform services for his client may be liable to his client for failure to exercise due care and skill in relation to the performance of those services not only in contract, but also in negligence under the principle in *Hedley Byrne v Heller* (see *Midland Bank Trust Co Ltd v Hett Stubbs & Kemp*) on the basis of assumption of responsibility by the solicitor towards his client. Even so there is great difficulty in holding, on ordinary principles, that the solicitor has assumed any responsibility towards an intended beneficiary under a will which he has undertaken to prepare on behalf of his client but which, through his negligence, has failed to take effect in accordance with his client's instructions. The relevant work is plainly performed by the solicitor for his client; but, in the absence of special circumstances, it cannot be said to have been undertaken for the intended beneficiary. Certainly, again in the absence of special circumstances, there will have been no reliance by the intended beneficiary on the exercise by the solicitor of due care and skill; indeed, the intended beneficiary may not even have been aware that the solicitor was engaged on such a task, or that his position might be affected ...

[Lord Goff considered and rejected a number of non-tortious approaches from both German and English law, and continued.]

I therefore return to the law of tort for a solution to the problem. For the reasons I already given, an ordinary action in tortious negligence on the lines proposed by Megarry V-C in *Ross v Caunters* must, with the greatest respect, be regarded as inappropriate, because it does not meet any of the conceptual problems which have been raised. Furthermore, for the reasons I have previously given, the *Hedley Byrne* principle cannot, in the absence of special circumstances, give rise on ordinary principles to an assumption of responsibility by the testator's solicitor towards an intended beneficiary. Even so, it seems to me that it is open to your Lordships' House, as in *Linden Gardens Trust Ltd v Lenesta Sludge Disposals Ltd*, to fashion a remedy to fill a lacuna in the law and so prevent the injustice which would otherwise occur on the facts of cases such as the present. In the *Lenesta Sludge* case, as I have said, the House made available a remedy as a matter of law to solve the problem of transferred loss in the case before them. The present case is, if anything, *a fortiori*, since the nature of the transaction was such that, if the solicitors were negligent and their negligence did not come to light until after the death of the testator, there would be no remedy for the ensuing loss unless the intended beneficiary could claim. In my opinion, therefore, your Lordships' House should in cases such as these extend to the intended beneficiary a remedy under the *Hedley Byrne* principle by holding that the assumption of responsibility by the solicitor towards his client should be held in law to extend to the intended beneficiary who (as the solicitor can reasonably foresee) may, as a result of the solicitor's negligence, be deprived of his intended legacy in circumstances in which neither the testator nor his estate will have a remedy against the solicitor. Such liability will not of course arise in cases in which the defect in the will comes to light before the death of the testator, and the testator either leaves the will as it is or otherwise continues to exclude the previously intended beneficiary from the relevant benefit. I only wish to add that, with the benefit of experience during the fifteen years in which *Ross v Caunters* has been regularly applied, we can say with some confidence that a direct remedy by the intended beneficiary against the solicitor appears to create no problems in practice. That is therefore the solution which I would recommend to your Lordships.

As I see it, not only does this conclusion produce practical justice as far as all parties are concerned, but it also has the following beneficial consequences.

(1) There is no unacceptable circumvention of established principles of the law of contract.

(2) No problem arises by reason of the loss being of a purely economic character.

(3)   Such assumption of responsibility will of course be subject to any term of the contract between the solicitor and the testator which may exclude or restrict the solicitor's liability to the testator under the principle in *Hedley Byrne*. It is true that such a term would be most unlikely to exist in practice; but as a matter of principle it is right that this largely theoretical question should be addressed.

(4)   Since the *Hedley Byrne* principle is founded upon an assumption of responsibility, the solicitor may be liable for negligent omissions as well as negligent acts of commission: see *Midland Bank Trust Co Ltd v Hett Stubbs & Kent*, per Oliver J, and my own speech in *Henderson v Merrett Syndicates Ltd*. This conclusion provides justification for the decision of the Court of Appeal to reverse the decision of Turner J in the present case, although this point was not in fact raised below or before your Lordships.

(5)   I do not consider that damages for loss of an expectation are excluded in cases of negligence arising under the principle in *Hedley Byrne*, simply because the cause of action is classified as tortious. Such damages may in principle be recoverable in cases of contractual negligence; and I cannot see that, for present purposes, any relevant distinction can be drawn between the two forms of action. In particular, an expectation loss may well occur in cases where a professional man, such as a solicitor, has assumed responsibility for the affairs of another; and I for my part can see no reason in principle why the professional man should not, in an appropriate case, be liable for such loss under the *Hedley Byrne* principle.

In the result, all the conceptual problems … can be seen to fade innocuously away. Let me emphasise that I can see no injustice in imposing liability upon a negligent solicitor in a case such as the present where, in the absence of a remedy in this form, neither the testator's estate nor the disappointed beneficiary will have a claim for the loss caused by his negligence. This is the injustice which, in my opinion, the judges of this country should address by recognising that cases such as these call for an appropriate remedy, and that the common law is not so sterile as to be incapable of supplying that remedy when it is required.

UNLIMITED CLAIMS

I come finally to the objection that, if liability is recognised in a case such as the present, it will be impossible to place any sensible limits to cases in which recovery is allowed. Before your Lordships, as before the Court of Appeal, [counsel] conjured up the spectre of solicitors being liable to an indeterminate class, including persons unborn at the date of the testator's death. I must confess that my reaction to this kind of argument was very similar to that of Cooke J in *Gartside v Sheffield, Young & Ellis*, when he said that he was not "persuaded that we should decide a fairly straightforward case against the dictates of justice because of foreseeable troubles in more difficult cases". We are concerned here with a liability which is imposed by law to do practical justice in a particular type of case. There must be boundaries to the availability of a remedy in such cases; but these will have to be worked out in the future, as practical problems come before the courts. In the present case Nicholls V-C observed that, in cases of this kind, liability is not to an indeterminate class, but to the particular beneficiary or beneficiaries whom the client intended to benefit through the particular will. I respectfully agree, and I also agree with him that the ordinary case is one in which the intended beneficiaries are a small number of identified people. If by any chance a more complicated case should arise to test the precise boundaries of the principle in cases of this kind, that problem can await solution when such a case comes forward for decision.'

Comment

(1)   In *Ross v Caunters* the defendant solicitors had, at the testator's request, drawn up a will which included gifts to the plaintiff, his sister-in-law, with whom he was staying. The will was sent to the testator with instructions on executing it but with no indication that under the Wills Act 1837, s 15 attestation by the spouse of a beneficiary would invalidate the gift; nor did the defendants notice when the will was returned to them attested by the plaintiff's husband. Sir Robert Megarry V-C, in finding for the plaintiff, was much influenced by the fact that, if the defendant's argument were to succeed, 'However grave the negligence, and however great the loss, the solicitors would be under no liability to pay substantial damages to anyone'.

(2)   The unique features of negligence in relation to the preparation and execution of wills were highlighted by Lord Browne-Wilkinson in *White v Jones*:

'... in transactions *inter vivos* the transaction takes immediate effect and the consequences of solicitors' negligence are immediately apparent. When discovered, they can either be rectified (by the parties) or damages recovered by the client. But in the case of a negligently drawn will ... In the majority of cases the negligence will lie hidden until it takes effect on the death of the testator, i.e. at the very point in time when normally the error will become incapable of remedy.'

(3)   Lord Goff referred to something akin to a public policy interest in ensuring that solicitors perform their duties properly, especially given the importance accorded to legacies: however, Lord Mustill, dissenting, doubted the propriety of punishing a delinquent solicitor by awarding damages to the disappointed beneficiaries:

'... it is tempting to say that the solicitor failed to do his job properly; that it was all his fault that the plaintiffs are less well off than they should have been; and that the law ought to do something about it. This temptation should in my opinion be resisted ... The purpose of the courts when recognising tortious acts and their consequences is to compensate those plaintiffs who suffer actionable breaches of duty, not to act as second-line disciplinary tribunals imposing punishment in the shape of damages.'

(4)   In Lord Mustill's view the problem in such cases arises from 'the rule of law which ... prescribes that a disposition of property designed to take effect after death is ineffectual unless embodied in a valid will'. Such a defect should not, he thought, be compensated by stretching the law of negligence, and he was not convinced that *Ross v Caunters*, which had been decided while the *Anns* two-stage test was in its heyday, would have the same outcome today.

Lord Mustill acknowledged that the tort of negligence can develop so as to embrace new claims but concluded that 'it does not conduce to the orderly development of the law, or to the certainty which practical convenience demands, if duties are simply conjured up as a matter of positive law, to answer the apparent justice of an individual case'. Although the present case concerned, at first sight, a fairly limited situation, he feared that a finding for the plaintiffs might result in a more general principle which went 'far beyond anything so far contemplated by the law of negligence'.

(5)   In *Smith v Claremont Haynes & Co* it was held that a duty to draw up the will with appropriate speed was owed to the intended legatees of a testator who was unwell. By contrast, in *Clarke v Bruce, Lance*, the court held that a solicitor, in subsequent transactions concerning a living testator's property, owed no duty to a probable residual legatee in relation to any effect that such transactions might have on the value of his future inheritance.

(6)   In *Carr-Glynn v Frearsons (a firm)* the Court of Appeal held that the defendant solicitors owed a duty of care to an intended beneficiary in respect of an intended gift of the testatrix's share in a property. The gift could not take effect because the defendants had failed to ensure that a joint tenancy in respect of the property was severed, so on the testatrix's death, the property vested in the surviving joint tenant. Chadwick LJ said:

'At first sight the facts in the present case take it outside the principle as stated by Lord Goff. This is a case in which the estate, itself, would have a remedy. The question, therefore, is whether the remedy which the House of Lords was prepared to extend to a disappointed beneficiary in *White v Jones* is confined to those cases, of which *White v Jones* was an example, in which the estate itself has no remedy – so that, absent a remedy at the suit of the beneficiary, there is no remedy at all; or is to be further extended to cases in which the estate does have a remedy but where the estate's remedy will be of no advantage to the disappointed beneficiary.

The judge answered that question in the negative. He said: "It seems to me unacceptable that solicitors should be at risk of two separate claims for identical loss at the suit both of the personal representatives and a beneficiary, when recovery by one would not bar recovery by the other."

I agree. If that were the result which the law required it would properly be regarded as unacceptable and unjust. But, as it seems to me, it ought properly be regarded as equally unacceptable and unjust if the result which the law requires is that, because of the solicitors' negligence, the loss which the personal representatives are able to recover on behalf of the estate passes to someone who was not the beneficiary intended by the testatrix; leaving the intended beneficiary without recompense ... If the law in this field is to reflect what would generally be recognised as acceptable and just, the application of the relevant principles should lead to the result that the estate and its beneficiaries are restored to the position in which they would have been if the solicitors had not failed in their duty to the testatrix ...

It is essential ... to have in mind that this is a case in which, *prima facie*, the appellant would receive no benefit from a successful claim by the estate against the solicitors. The proceeds would form part of the residuary estate in which she has no beneficial interest. They would pass to another. Lord Goff identified as "the real cause for concern" in cases such as *White v Jones* what he described as – "the extraordinary fact that, if a duty owed by the testator's solicitor to the disappointed beneficiary is not recognised, the only person who may have a valid claim has suffered no loss, and the only person who has suffered a loss has no claim."

That was the lacuna which had to be filled in cases of that nature. Lord Goff held that the courts were entitled – indeed, bound – to fashion a remedy to meet the need. For my part, I would find it equally extraordinary and as much a real cause for concern if the only person for whose benefit a valid claim could be pursued (the residuary legatee) was a person who had suffered no loss – because, absent the respondents' negligence, the property would not have formed any part of the residue – and the only person who has suffered a loss (the appellant) has no claim. I am satisfied that it would be consistent with the approach of the majority of the House of Lords in *White v Jones* to fashion a remedy in cases of this nature also, if that can be done without imposing a double liability on the solicitors, in order to avoid what would otherwise be an injustice ... I am not persuaded that the powers of the court are so limited that it cannot do justice to each of the three interests concerned – the specific legatee, the estate and the solicitors.'

It follows that the principle in *White v Jones* will not avail a claimant in circumstances where there exists an adequate alternative remedy. See *Worby v Rosser*, in which the Court of Appeal rejected a claim for costs incurred by the beneficiary of an earlier will in resisting probate of a later will which, it was argued, had been subject to the malign influence of a third party. Chadwick LJ found 'no need to fashion an independent remedy for a beneficiary who had been engaged in the probate proceedings'. In *Walker v Geo H Medlicott & Son (a firm)* the Court of Appeal held that the principle would have no application where rectification of the will had not been sought.

(7) In *Gorham and others v British Telecommunications and others*, the Court of Appeal extended the principle in *White v Jones* to other professional advisers, here an insurance company. In that case the claimant's husband, who was employed by BT, was given negligent advice concerning provision for his family under the company pension scheme in the event of his death. The court held that the insurance company owed a duty of care to the claimant dependants, whose interests were 'fundamental to the transaction, to the knowledge of the insurance company representative giving advice as well as to his customer'. By contrast, in *Chappell v Somers & Blake (a firm)* the judge held that an executrix owed no duty of care in respect of losses accruing to an estate or its beneficiaries due to an inordinate delay in the administration of an estate. Neuberger J related this to the fact that there is no duty to take on the role of executor and that it is not uncommon for such a person to be unaware he has been nominated for the task until some time after a testator has died. The executrix did enjoy rights, however, against the negligent solicitor in order to protect the interests of the estate on behalf of the beneficiaries.

(8) In *Al-kandari v Brown* the defendants were solicitors acting for the husband in matrimonial proceedings. They had undertaken to take custody of their client's passport but released it to him, upon which he left the country with the children of the marriage. The court held that the defendants' clear assumption of responsibility took them outside their role as their client's representative and imposed on them a duty of care towards the plaintiff despite the fact that she was the adversary of their own client.

Smith v Eric S Bush
Harris and another v Wyre Forest District Council and another
[1989] 2 All ER 514 House of Lords

In the first case, the respondent had applied to a building society for a mortgage. She paid the standard fee to the society who engaged the appellants, an independent firm of surveyors, to prepare a report and valuation of the property in order to ensure that it would provide adequate security for the proposed loan. The respondent bought the house on the strength of the report but it proved to have been prepared negligently when a serious structural defect which had not been noticed by the surveyor resulted in the collapse of part of the house. The House of Lords, affirming the decision of the lower courts, held the appellants liable despite the existence of disclaimers both in the agreement and in the report.

In the second case, the appellants had applied to their local council for a mortgage. A survey was carried out by a council employee and a report prepared 'solely for the information of the council'. The appellants were not shown the report but assumed, because the council advanced 90 per cent of the cost of the property, that the valuation showed it to be worth the price. A survey three years later, when they tried to sell the house, showed it to be virtually unsaleable on account of structural defects which would have cost more to repair than the market value of the house in sound condition. The House of Lords, reversing the Court of Appeal decision that the council were protected by a disclaimer, awarded damages.

Lord Griffiths: '... I do not think that voluntary assumption of responsibility is a helpful or realistic test for liability. It is true that reference is made in a number of the speeches in the *Hedley Byrne* case to the assumption of responsibility as a test of liability but it must be remembered that those speeches were made in the context of a case in which the central issue was whether a duty of care could arise when there had been an express disclaimer of responsibility for the accuracy of the advice. Obviously, if an adviser expressly assumes responsibility for his advice, a duty of care will arise, but is extremely unlikely in the ordinary course of events. The House of Lords approved a duty of care being imposed on the facts in *Cann v Willson* and in *Candler v Crane, Christmas & Co*. But, if the surveyor in *Cann v Willson* or the accountant in *Candler v Crane, Christmas & Co* had actually been asked if he was voluntarily assuming responsibility for his advice to the mortgagee or the purchaser of the shares, I have little doubt he would have replied: "Certainly not. My responsibility is limited to the person who employs me." The phrase "assumption of responsibility" can only have any real meaning if it is understood as referring to the circumstances in which the law will deem the maker of the statement to have assumed responsibility to the person who acts on the advice.

In *Ministry of Housing and Local Government v Sharp* both Lord Denning MR and Salmon LJ rejected the argument that a voluntary assumption of responsibility was the sole criterion for imposing a duty of care for the negligent preparation of a search certificate in the local land charges register.

The essential distinction between the present case and the situation being considered in the *Hedley Byrne* case and in the two earlier cases is that in those cases the advice was being given with the intention of persuading the recipient to act on it. In the present case the purpose of providing the report is to advise the mortgagee but it is given in circumstances in which it is highly probable that the purchaser will in fact act on its contents, although that was not the primary purpose of the report. I have had considerable doubts whether it is wise to increase the scope of the duty for negligent advice beyond the person directly intended by the giver of the advice to act on it to those whom he knows may do so. Certainly in the field of the law of mortgagor and mortgagee there is authority that points in the other direction. In *Odder v Westbourne Park Building Society*

Harman J held that a building society owed no duty of care to purchasers in respect of the valuation report for mortgage purposes prepared by the chairman of the society. From the tenor of the short report it appears that Harman J regarded it as unthinkable that a mortgagee could owe a duty of care to the mortgagor in respect of any action taken by the mortgagee for the purpose of appraising the value of the property. In *Curran v Northern Ireland Co-ownership Housing Association Ltd* the Court of Appeal in Northern Ireland held that the Northern Ireland Housing Executive, which had lent money on mortgage pursuant to powers contained in the Housing Act (Northern Ireland) 1971, owed no duty of care to their mortgagor in respect of the valuation of the property. The claim against the executive had been struck out by the judge on the ground that the pleadings disclosed no cause of action. For the purpose of the appeal, the following facts were assumed: (1) that the executive had instructed an independent valuer to prepare a valuation of the property; (2) that the valuation had been negligently prepared; (3) that the executive had negligently instructed an incompetent valuer; (4) that the valuer's report would not be shown to the purchaser; (5) that the purchaser knew that the executive would not lend money without a valuation to justify the loan; (6) that the executive knew that the purchaser would assume that the valuation showed that the property was worth at least as much as the figure which the executive was willing to advance on mortgage, and that the purchaser would rely on the valuation to that extent. Gibson LJ based his judgment on the absence of any acceptance of responsibility on the part of the executive. In the course of his judgment he said:

> "Responsibility can only attach if the defendant's act implied a voluntary undertaking to assume responsibility. Were it otherwise a person who offered to an expert any object for sale, making it clear that he was unaware of its value and that he was relying on the other to pay a proper price, could sue the other should he later discover that he has not received the full value even though the purchaser had made no representation that he was doing any more than look after his own interests. Nor can any class of persons who to the knowledge of another habitually fail to take precautions for their own protection in a business relationship cast upon another without his consent an obligation to exercise care for their protection in such transaction so as to protect them from their own lack of ordinary business prudence. Generally, a mortgage contract in itself imports no obligation on the part of a mortgagee to use care in protecting the interests of a mortgagor ..."

Gibson LJ said:

> "But in so far as the facts of this case are clearly within the area of contemplation in the *Hedley Byrne* case, I have no doubt that the condition precedent to liability is that the executive should have indicated to the plaintiffs, or so acted as to mislead them into believing, that the executive was accepting responsibility for its opinion."

Commenting on *Yianni v Edwin Evans & Sons (a firm)* Kerr LJ in his judgment in the Court of Appeal in the present case said:

"But its inherent jurisprudential weakness in any ordinary situation is clear. Suppose that A approaches B with a request for a loan to be secured on a property or chattel, such as a painting, which A is proposing to acquire. A knows that for the purpose of considering whether or not to make the requested loan, and of its amount, B is bound to make some assessment of the value of the security which is offered, possibly on the basis of some expert inspection and formal valuation. Then assume that B knows that in all probability A will not have had any independent advice or valuation and is also unlikely to commission anything of the kind as a check on B's valuation. B also knows, of course, that any figure which he may then put forward to A by way of a proposed loan on the basis of the offered security will necessarily be seen to reflect B's estimate of the minimum value of the offered security. Suppose that A then accepts B's offer and acquires the property or chattel with the assistance of B's loan and in reliance, at least in part, on B's willingness to advance the amount of the loan as an indication of the value of the property or chattel. Given those facts and no more, I do not think that B can properly be regarded as having assumed, or as being subjected to, any duty of care towards A in his valuation of the security. Even in the absence of any disclaimer of responsibility I do not think that the principles stated in *Hedley Byrne & Co Ltd v Heller & Partners Ltd* support the contrary conclusion. B has not been asked for advice or information but merely for a loan. His valuation was carried out for his own commercial purposes. If it was done carelessly, with the result that the valuation and loan were excessive, I do not think that A can have any ground for complaint. And if B made a small service charge for investigating A's request for a loan, I doubt whether the position would be different; certainly not if he were also to add a disclaimer of responsibility and a warning that A should carry out his own valuation."

Kerr LJ, however, added:

"It may be, but I agree that we should not decide this general question on the present appeal, that the particular circumstances of purchasers of houses with the assistance of loans from building societies or local authorities are capable of leading to a different analysis and conclusion."

I have come to the conclusion that *Yianni's* case was correctly decided. I have already given my view that the voluntary assumption of responsibility is unlikely to be a helpful or realistic test in most cases. I therefore return to the question ... in what circumstances should a duty of care be owed by the adviser to those who act on his advice? I would answer: only if it is foreseeable that if the advice is negligent the recipient is likely to suffer damage, that there is a sufficiently proximate relationship between the parties and that it is just and reasonable to impose the liability. In the case of a surveyor valuing a small house for a building society or local authority, the application of these three criteria leads to the conclusion that he owes a duty of care to the purchaser. If the valuation is negligent and is relied on damage in the form of economic loss to the purchaser is obviously foreseeable. The necessary proximity arises from the surveyor's knowledge that the overwhelming probability is that the purchaser will rely on his valuation, the evidence was that surveyors knew that approximately 90 per cent of purchasers did so, and the fact that the surveyor only obtains the work because the purchaser is willing to pay his fee. It is just and reasonable that the duty should be imposed for the advice is given in a professional as opposed to a social context and liability for breach of the duty will be limited both as to its extent and amount. The extent of the liability is limited to the purchaser of the house: I would not extend it to subsequent purchasers. The amount of the liability cannot be very great because it relates to a modest house. There is no question here of creating a liability of indeterminate amount to an indeterminate class. I would certainly wish to stress that, in cases where the advice has not been given for the specific purpose of the recipient acting on it, it should only be in cases when the adviser knows that there is a high degree of probability that some other identifiable person will act on the advice that a duty of care should be imposed. It would impose an intolerable burden on those who give advice in a professional or commercial context if they were to owe a duty not only to those to whom they give the advice but to any other person who might choose to act on it.

I accept that the mere fact of a contract between mortgagor and mortgagee will not of itself in all cases be sufficient to found a duty of care. But I do not accept the view of the Court of Appeal in *Curran v Northern Ireland Co-ownership Housing Association Ltd* that a mortgagee who accepts a fee to obtain a valuation of a small house owes no duty of care to the mortgagor in the selection of the valuer to whom he entrusts the work. In my opinion, the mortgagee in such a case, knowing that the mortgagor will rely on the valuation, owes a duty to the mortgagor to take reasonable care to employ a reasonably competent valuer. Provided he does this the mortgagee will not be held liable for the negligence of the independent valuer who acts as an independent contractor.

I have already pointed out that the only real distinction between the present case and *Yianni's* case is that the valuation was carried out by an in-house valuer. In my opinion this can make no difference. The valuer is discharging the duties of a professional man whether he is employed by the mortgagee or acting on his own account or is employed by a firm of independent surveyors. The essence of the case against him is that he as a professional man realised that the purchaser was relying on him to exercise proper skill and judgment in his profession and that it was reasonable and fair that the purchaser should do so. Mr L was in breach of his duty of care to the H's and the local authority, as his employers, are vicariously liable for that negligence.'

Comment

(1)   In *Yianni v Edwin Evans & Sons* the plaintiffs borrowed money for the purchase of a house after it was valued by the defendants. It subsequently proved to be in need of repairs costing half as much again as the house. The court, accepting evidence which showed that fewer than 15 per cent of house buyers commission an independent survey together with the fact that the survey fee is, in reality, paid by the purchaser and that an independent survey would merely duplicate the work, concluded that the relationship between the parties was such as to give rise to a duty of care.

(2)   It has been suggested that such a relationship would not necessarily exist between a surveyor and the purchaser of a more complex or valuable building since the surveyor would be entitled to expect a higher degree of care from the purchaser. Of such a case, Lord Griffiths in *Smith* said, '... it may well be that the general expectation of the behaviour of the purchaser is quite different. With large sums of money at stake prudence would seem to demand that the purchaser obtain his own structural survey.'

(3)   A similar situation occurred in *Merrett v Babb*, in which the building society had engaged the services of a firm of surveyors and valuers. A copy of the resulting report was passed to the claimants, but with no reference to the name of the firm or of the defendant. By the time the survey was found to have been negligent, the firm had gone into liquidation. The Court of Appeal held by a two-to-one majority that the defendant knew the use the claimants would make of his report and that he assumed responsibility in a personal capacity when he signed it. Aldous LJ, dissenting, was troubled by the prospect of individual employees finding themselves in need of professional indemnity insurance in a wide range of circumstances such as these. His analysis of the facts, in light of the principles in *Williams v Natural Life Health Foods Ltd* (see p 158), led him to a conclusion that no special relationship existed between the parties as individuals.

Caparo Industries plc v Dickman and others
[1990] 1 All ER 568 House of Lords

The respondents, who owned shares in a public company, took advantage of a dramatic drop in share prices following the publication of the company's audited accounts which showed a lower profit than predicted, to make a takeover bid. When it transpired that the accounts were inaccurate the respondents brought an action against the auditors alleging that they ought to have known that the figures as published made the company vulnerable to a takeover bid and that they therefore owed a duty of care to potential investors. The House of Lords held that no such duty was owed to the respondents, either as members of the public at large or as individual shareholders.

Lord Bridge of Harwich: '... In determining the existence and scope of the duty of care which one person may owe to another in the infinitely varied circumstances of human relationships there has for long been a tension between two different approaches. Traditionally the law finds the existence of the duty in different specific situations each exhibiting its own particular characteristics. In this way the law has identified a wide variety of duty situations, all falling within the ambit of the tort of negligence, but sufficiently distinct to require separate definition of the essential ingredients by which the existence of the duty is to be recognised. Commenting on the outcome of this traditional approach, Lord Atkin, in his seminal speech in *Donoghue v Stevenson* observed:

> "The result is that the Courts have been engaged upon an elaborate classification of duties as they exist in respect of property, whether real or personal, with further divisions as to ownership, occupation or control, and distinctions based on the particular relations of the one side or the other, whether manufacturer, salesman or landlord, customer, tenant, stranger, and so on. In this way it can be ascertained at any time whether the law recognises a duty, but only where the case can be referred to some particular species which has been examined and classified. And yet the duty which is common to all the cases where liability is established must logically be based upon some element common to the cases where it is found to exist."

It is this last sentence which signifies the introduction of the more modern approach of seeking a single general principle which may be applied in all circumstances to determine the existence of a duty of care. Yet Lord Atkin himself sounds the appropriate note of caution by adding:

> "To seek a complete logical definition of the general principle is probably to go beyond the function of the judge, for the more general the definition the more likely it is to omit essentials or to introduce non-essentials."

Lord Reid gave a large impetus to the modern approach in *Home Office v Dorset Yacht Co Ltd* [Lord Bridge quoted the passage cited at p 6 above and went on]...

The most comprehensive attempt to articulate a single general principle is reached in the well-known passage from the speech of Lord Wilberforce in *Anns v Merton London Borough* [he quoted the passage at p 8 above and continued] ... But since *Anns'* case a series of decisions of the Privy Council and of your Lordships' House, notably in judgments and speeches delivered by Lord Keith, have emphasised the inability of any single general principle to provide a practical test which can be applied to every situation to determine whether a duty of care is owed and, if so, what is its scope. What emerges is that, in addition to the foreseeability of damage, necessary ingredients in any situation giving rise to a duty of care are that there should exist between the party owing the duty and the party to whom it is owed a relationship characterised by the law as one of "proximity" or "neighbourhood" and that the situation should be one in which the court considers it fair, just and reasonable that the law should impose a duty of a given scope on the one party for the benefit of the other. But it is implicit in the passages referred to that the concepts of proximity and fairness embodied in these additional ingredients are not susceptible of any such precise definition as would be necessary to give them utility as practical tests, but amount in effect to little more than convenient labels to attach to the features of different specific situations which, on a detailed examination of all the circumstances, the law recognises pragmatically as giving rise to a duty of care of a given scope. Whilst recognising, of course, the importance of the underlying general principles common to the whole field of negligence, I think the law has now moved in the direction of attaching greater significance to the more traditional categorisation of distinct and recognisable situations as guides to the existence, the scope and the limits of the varied duties of care which the law imposes. We must now, I think, recognise the wisdom of the words of Brennan J in the High Court of Australia in *Sutherland Shire Council v Heyman* where he said:

> "It is preferable in my view, that the law should develop novel categories of negligence incrementally and by analogy with established categories, rather than by a massive extension of a *prima facie* duty of care restrained only by indefinable 'considerations which ought to negative, or to reduce or limit the scope of the duty or the class of person to whom it is owed'."

One of the most important distinctions always to be observed lies in the law's essentially different approach to the different kinds of damage which one party may have suffered in consequence of the acts or omissions of another. It is one thing to owe a duty of care to avoid causing injury to the person or property of others. It is quite another to avoid causing others to suffer purely economic loss ...

The damage which may be caused by the negligently spoken or written word will normally be confined to economic loss sustained by those who rely on the accuracy of the information or advice they receive as a basis for action. The question what, if any, duty is owed by the maker of a statement to exercise due care to ensure its accuracy arises typically in relation to statements made by a person in the exercise of his calling or profession. In advising the client who employs him the professional man owes a duty to exercise that standard of skill and care appropriate to his professional status and will be liable both in contract and in tort for all losses which his client may suffer by reason of any breach of that duty. But the possibility of any duty of care being owed to third parties with whom the professional man was in no contractual relationship was for long denied because of the wrong turning taken by the law in *Le Lievre v Gould* in over-ruling *Cann v Willson*. In *Candler v Crane, Christmas & Co* Denning LJ, in his dissenting judgment, made a valiant attempt to correct the error. But it was not until the decision of this House in *Hedley Byrne & Co Ltd v Heller & Partners Ltd* that the law was once more set on the right path.

Consistently with the traditional approach it is to these authorities and to subsequent decisions directly relevant to this relatively narrow corner of the field that we should look to determine the essential characteristics of a situation giving rise, independently of any contractual or fiduciary relationship, to a duty of care owed by one party to another to ensure that the accuracy of any statement which the one party makes and on which the other party may foreseeably rely to his economic detriment.

[Lord Bridge referred to *Cann v Willson, Candler v Crane, Christmas & Co Ltd* and *Hedley Byrne v Heller* and continued.] ... The most recent decision of the House, which is very much in point, is that of the two appeals heard together of *Smith v Eric S Bush (a firm), Harris v Wyre Forest DC* ... The House held that in both cases the surveyor making the inspection and valuation owed a duty of care to the plaintiff house purchaser and that the contractual clauses purporting to exclude liability were struck down by ss 2(2) and 11(3) of the Unfair Contract Terms Act 1977.

The salient feature of all these cases is that the defendant giving advice or information was fully aware of the nature of the transaction which the plaintiff had in contemplation, knew that the advice or information would be communicated to him directly or indirectly and knew that it was very likely that the plaintiff would rely on that advice or information in deciding whether or not to engage in the transaction in contemplation. In these circumstances the defendant could clearly be expected, subject always to the effect of any disclaimer of responsibility, specifically to anticipate that the plaintiff would rely on the advice or information given by the defendant for the very purpose for which he did in the event rely on it. So also the plaintiff, subject again to the effect of any disclaimer, would in that situation reasonably suppose that he was entitled to rely on the advice or information communicated to him for the very purpose for which he required it. The situation is entirely different where a statement is put into more or less general circulation and may foreseeably be relied on by strangers to the maker of the statement for any one of a variety of different purposes which the maker of the statement has no specific reason to anticipate. To hold the maker of the statement to be under a duty of care in respect of the accuracy of the statement to all and sundry for any purpose for which they may choose to rely on it is not only to subject him, in the classic words of Cardozo CJ, to "liability in an indeterminate amount for an indeterminate time to an indeterminate class" (see *Ultramares Corp v Touche*), it is also to confer on the world at large a quite unwarranted entitlement to appropriate for their own purposes the benefit of the expert knowledge or professional expertise attributed to the maker of the statement. Hence, looking only at the circumstances of these decided cases where a duty of care in respect of negligent statements has been held to exist, I should expect to find that the "limit or control mechanism ... imposed on the liability of a wrongdoer towards those who have suffered economic damage in consequence of his negligence" (see the *Candlewood* case) rested on the necessity to prove, in this category of the tort of negligence, as an essential ingredient of the "proximity" between the plaintiff and the defendant, that the defendant knew that his statement would be communicated to the plaintiff, either as an individual or as a member of an identifiable class, specifically in connection with a particular transaction or transactions of a particular kind (e.g. in a prospectus inviting investment) and that the plaintiff would be very likely to rely on it for the purpose of deciding whether or not to enter on that transaction or on a transaction of that kind ...

These considerations amply justify the conclusion that auditors of a public company's accounts owe no duty of care to members of the public at large who rely on the accounts in deciding to buy shares in the company. If a duty of care were owed so widely, it is difficult to see any reason why it should not equally extend to all who rely on the accounts in relation to other dealings with a company as lenders or merchants extending credit to the company. A claim that such a duty was owed by auditors to a bank lending to a company was emphatically and convincingly rejected by Millett J in *Al Saudi Banque v Clark Pixley (a firm)*. The only support for an unlimited duty of care owed by auditors for the accuracy of their accounts to all who may foreseeably rely on them is to be found in some jurisdictions in the United States of America, where there are striking differences in the law in different states. In this jurisdiction I have no doubt that the creation of such an unlimited duty would be a legislative step which it would be for Parliament, not the courts, to take ...

The crucial question concerns the extent of the shareholder's interest which the auditor has a duty to protect. The shareholders of a company have a collective interest in the company's proper management and in so far as a negligent failure of the auditor to report accurately on the state of the company's finances deprives the shareholders of the opportunity to exercise their powers in general meeting to call the directors to book and to ensure that errors in management are corrected, the shareholders ought to be entitled to a remedy. But in practice no problem arises in this regard since the interest of the shareholders in the proper management of the company's affairs is indistinguishable from the interest of the company itself and any loss suffered by the shareholders, e.g. by the negligent failure of the auditor to discover and expose a misappropriation of funds by a director of the company, will be recouped by a claim against the auditor in the name of the company, not by individual shareholders.

I find it difficult to visualise a situation arising in the real world in which the individual shareholder could claim to have sustained a loss in respect of his existing shareholding referable to the negligence of the auditor which could not be recouped by the company. But on this part of the case your Lordships were much pressed with the argument that such a loss might occur by a negligent undervaluation of the company's assets in the auditor's report relied on by the individual shareholder in deciding to sell his shares at an undervalue. The argument then runs thus. The shareholder, qua shareholder, is entitled to rely on the auditor's report as the basis of his investment decision to sell his existing shareholding. If he sells at an undervalue he is entitled to recover the loss from the auditor. There can be no distinction in law between the shareholder's investment decision to sell the shares he has or to buy additional shares. It follows, therefore, that the scope of the duty of care owed to him by the auditor extends to cover any loss sustained consequent on the purchase of additional shares in reliance on the auditor's negligent report.

I believe this argument to be fallacious. Assuming without deciding that a claim by a shareholder to recover a loss suffered by selling his shares at an undervalue attributable to an undervaluation of the company's assets in the auditor's report could be sustained at all, it would not be by reason of any reliance by the shareholder on the auditor's report in deciding to sell: the loss would be referable to the depreciatory effect of the report on the market value of the shares before ever the decision of the shareholder to sell was taken. A claim to recoup a loss alleged to flow from the purchase of overvalued shares, on the other hand, can only be sustained on the basis of the purchaser's reliance on the report. The specious equation of "investment decisions" to sell or to buy as giving rise to parallel claims thus appears to me to be untenable. Moreover, the loss in the case of the sale would be of a loss of part of the value of the shareholder's existing holding, which, assuming a duty of care owed to individual shareholders, it might sensibly lie within the scope of the auditor's duty to protect. A loss, on the other hand, resulting from the purchase of additional shares would result from a wholly independent transaction having no connection with the existing shareholding.

I believe it is this last distinction which is of critical importance and which demonstrates the unsoundness of the conclusion reached by the majority of the Court of Appeal. It is never sufficient to ask simply whether A owes B a duty of care. It is always necessary to determine the scope of the duty by reference to the kind of damage from which A must take care to save B harmless:

> "The question is always whether the defendant was under a duty to avoid or prevent that damage, but the actual nature of the damage suffered is relevant to the existence and extent of any duty to avoid or prevent it."

(See *Sutherland Shire Council v Heyman* per Brennan J.)

Assuming for the purpose of the argument that the relationship between the auditor of a company and individual shareholders is of sufficient proximity to give rise to a duty of care, I do not understand how the scope of that duty can possibly extend beyond the protection of any individual shareholder from losses in the value of the shares which he holds. As a purchaser of additional shares in reliance on the auditor's report, he stands in no different position from any other investing member of the public to whom the auditor owes no duty.'

Comment

(1)   Lord Oliver formulated a list of criteria, based on an analysis of the *Hedley Byrne* case, from which a sufficient relationship of proximity might be established:

'(1) the advice is required for a purpose, whether particularly specified or generally described, which is made known, either actually or inferentially, to the adviser at the time when the advice is given, (2) the adviser knows, either actually or inferentially, that his advice will be communicated to the advisee, either specifically or as a member of an ascertainable class, in order that it should be used by the advisee for that purpose, (3) it is known, either actually or inferentially, that the advice so communicated is likely to be acted on by the advisee for that purpose without independent inquiry, and (4) it is so acted on by the advisee to his detriment.'

Lord Oliver went on to say that this list should not be regarded as 'either conclusive or exclusive' and that 'in [such] a swiftly developing field of law, there can be no necessary assumption that those features which have served in one case to create the relationship ... on which liability depends will necessarily be determinative ... in the different circumstances of another case'. An extended list of relevant features was set out by Neill LJ in *James McNaughton Papers Group Ltd v Hicks Anderson & Co.*

(2)   The multitude of uses to which a company's financial statements might be put makes the position of auditors and accountants particularly vulnerable to 'liability of an indeterminate amount to an indeterminate class'. The application of the decision in *Caparo* to various aspects of a company's statements has been considered in a number of subsequent cases. Of particular relevance in these cases is the purpose for which a statement has been made. In *Al-Nakib Investments v Longcroft* it was held that a duty in relation to a prospectus issued to existing shareholders in relation to a rights issue could cover only the rights issue itself and not losses arising from additional shares bought by existing shareholders on the open market. In *Possfund Custodian Trustee Ltd and another v Diamond and others (McGrigor Donald (a firm), third party)* Lightman J held that a duty might be owed not only to plaintiffs who were subscribers at the time of issue of a company's shares, but also to subsequent purchasers provided they could show that the prospectus had been intended to inform and encourage after-market purchasers. Such circumstances might well establish a relationship of proximity between representor and purchaser such that the imposition of liability would be fair, just and reasonable, not least because the defendants could scarcely claim that the plaintiffs were unforeseeable since they had intended them to rely on the prospectus.

In *Andrew and others v Kounnis Freeman (a firm)*, the Court of Appeal upheld the claimants' appeal against a decision to strike out their claim for damages against the auditors of a company which had traded as air travel organisers. The company's licence had been renewed on the strength of accounts produced specifically to assure the licensing body of the company's financial health. When the company collapsed, the claimants had to meet the costs of repatriating stranded clients and of fulfilling future bookings. In *The Law Society v*

KPMG Peat Marwick and others the Court of Appeal held that a duty of care is owed by reporting accountants to the Law Society in preparing solicitors' accounts. In each of the examples above, the *Caparo* criteria were satisfied.

(3)   In the *McNaughton* case it was held that no duty was owed in relation to draft accounts drawn up in order to facilitate negotiations during a proposed takeover. By contrast, in *Morgan Crucible v Hill Samuel* it was held that statements made during negotiations for a takeover and with the aim of inducing the potential investors to increase their bid might give rise to a duty of care. See also *Galoo Ltd v Bright Grahame Murray*.

McFarlane v Tayside Health Board
[1999] 4 All ER 961 House of Lords

The claimants were informed by the defendants that M's vasectomy had been successful and that he had no further need of contraception. Nonetheless, Mrs M became pregnant and gave birth to a healthy daughter, C. The claimants brought an action for 'wrongful birth' and sought damages under the *Hedley Byrne* principle, not only for matters relating to the pregnancy and childbirth, but also for the cost of C's upbringing. The House of Lords reversed the decision of the Scottish Inner House that the costs of upbringing were recoverable, but held that damages were recoverable by Mrs M in relation to the pregnancy.

Lord Steyn:' ...

THE COST OF BRINGING UP C

It will be convenient to examine first the line of English cases on which the Inner House founded its decision that the cost of bringing up C is a sustainable claim. In *Udale v Bloomsbury Area Health Authority* Jupp J rejected a claim for the cost of bringing up an unwanted child. The judge observed that the birth of a child is "a blessing and an occasion for rejoicing". In *Thake v Maurice* Peter Pain J refused to follow *Udale's* case and allowed such a claim. He observed that social policy, which permitted abortion and sterilisation, implied that it was generally recognised that the birth of a healthy child was not always a blessing. In *Emeh v Kensington and Chelsea and Westminster Area Health Authority* the Court of Appeal had to consider divergent approaches in *Udale's* case and *Thake's* case. But the unwanted child in *Emeh's* case had been born with congenital disabilities. The defendants' contention was that the cost of upbringing should be limited to the extra costs attributable to the child's disabilities. Full costs were allowed but in a modest sum of the order of £6000. Angus Stewart QC in "Damages for the Birth of a Child" (1995) 40 JLSS 298 at 300 pointed out:

"The issue [in *Emeh's* case] possibly presented as one of deceptive simplicity given that the claim was by the mother alone: it was held that the compensable loss extended to any reasonably foreseeable financial loss directly caused by the unexpected pregnancy. The formulation equates pregnancy with personal injury giving rise to *consequential* (as opposed to *pure*) economic loss which includes upbringing costs."

That I regard as a perceptive explanation of the context of the judgment. In unreserved judgments the Court of Appeal chose to follow the judgment of Peter Pain J rather than the judgment of Jupp J. This decision has been considered binding on lower courts and on the Court of Appeal in regard to claims by parents for wrongful birth of a healthy child. It is the critical decision in the line of authority in England. It is unnecessary to discuss the subsequent English decisions which followed *Emeh's* case but I list them in chronological order: see *Thake v Maurice, Gold v Haringey Health Authority, Benarr v Kettering Health Authority, Allen v Bloomsbury Health Authority, Salih v Enfield Health Authority, Robinson v Salford Health Authority, Fish v Wilcox, Walkin v South Manchester Health Authority* and *Goodwill v British Pregnancy Advisory Service.* It is only necessary to mention one specific matter about those decisions. In *Benarr's* case the court held that health authorities were liable to pay for private education of the unwanted child.

It is right to point out that the Court of Appeal decision in *Emeh's* case predates the full retreat from *Anns v Merton London Borough* which was announced by the decision of the House in *Murphy v Brentwood DC.* Since then a judicial scepticism has prevailed about an overarching principle for the recovery of new categories of economic loss. Here the father's part of the claim for the cost of bringing up the unwanted child is undoubtedly a claim for pure economic loss. Realistically, despite the pregnancy and childbirth, the mother's part of the claim is also for pure economic loss. In any event, in respect of the claim for the costs of bringing up the unwanted child, it would be absurd to distinguish between the claims of the father and mother. This feature of the claim is important. The common law has a great capacity for growth but the development of a new ground of liability, or a new head of such liability, for the recovery of economic loss must be justified by cogent reasons.

Even before *Murphy's* case there was unease among judges about the decision in *Emeh's* case. This was memorably articulated in *Jones v Berkshire Area Health Authority*, another unwanted pregnancy case. Ognall J said:

"I pause only to observe that, speaking purely personally, it remains a matter of surprise to me that the law acknowledges an entitlement in a mother to claim damages for the blessing of a healthy child. Certain it is that those who are afflicted with a handicapped child or who long desperately to have a child at all and are denied that good fortune would regard an award for this sort of contingency with a measure of astonishment. But there it is: that is the law."

In *Gold v Haringey Health Authority* Lloyd LJ (with the agreement of the other members of the court) cited this observation and said: "Many would no doubt agree with this observation."

In the present case your Lordships have had the advantage of considering this issue in the light of far more analytical and comprehensive arguments from both counsel than were put before the Court of Appeal in *Emeh's* case. Counsel took your Lordships on a valuable *tour d'horizon* of comparative jurisprudence. Claims by parents for the cost of bringing up an unwanted but healthy child as opposed to more limited claims by the mother in respect of pain, suffering and distress associated with the pregnancy have proved controversial in foreign jurisdictions: compare the valuable comparative article by Angus Stewart QC. In the United States the overwhelming majority of state courts do not allow recovery of the costs of bringing up a healthy child: see the review in *Johnson v University Hospitals of Cleveland*. In Canada the trend is against such claims: see *Kealey v Berezowski*. By a majority the New South Wales Court of Appeal in *CES v Superclinics (Australia) Pty Ltd* held that the plaintiff had, through the negligence of the defendants, lost the opportunity to have an abortion which would not necessarily have been unlawful. The court ordered a retrial on the issue as to whether an abortion would have been unlawful. Kirby P considered that damages could be awarded for the cost of bringing up the child. Priestley JA was prepared to allow a limited recovery for "wrong birth" but not for child-rearing expenses.

Meagher JA agreed with Priestly JA on this point, though, in a dissenting opinion, he concluded that public policy was an absolute bar to the award of damages in "wrongful birth" cases. In New Zealand there is a no-fault compensation scheme. It is, however, instructive to note that the Accident and Compensation Authority held that there was no causal connection between the medical error and the cost of raising the child: *Re Z and XY v Accident Compensation Corp*. In Germany the Constitutional Court has ruled that such a claim is unconstitutional inasmuch as it is subversive of the dignity of the child. But the Bundesgerichtshof has rejected this view and permits recovery of the costs of bringing up the child. The Federal Court observed that "compensation not only has no detrimental effect on this child, but can be beneficial to it": see B S Markesinis, *The German Law of Obligations, vol 2, The Law of Torts: A Comparative Introduction* (3rd edn, 1997) pp.155–156. In France the Cour de Cassation has ruled that "Whereas the existence of the child she has conceived cannot *in itself* constitute for the mother a loss legally justifying compensation, even if the birth occurred after an unsuccessful intervention intended to terminate the pregnancy:" see *Mlle X c Picard*. Such claims are not allowed. From this comparative survey I deduce that claims by parents for full compensation for the financial consequences of the birth of the healthy child have sometimes been allowed. It may be that the major theme in such cases is that one is simply dealing with an ordinary tort case in which there are no factors negativing liability in delict. Considerations of corrective justice as between the negligent surgeon and the parents were dominant in such decisions. In an overview one would have to say that more often such claims are not allowed. The grounds for decision are diverse. Sometimes it is said that there was no personal injury, a lack of foreseeability of the costs of bringing up the child, no causative link between the breach of duty and the birth of a healthy child, or no loss since the joys of having a healthy child always outweigh the financial losses. Sometimes the idea that the couple could have avoided the financial cost of bringing up the unwanted child by abortion or adoption influenced decisions. Policy considerations undoubtedly played a role in decisions denying a remedy for the cost of bringing up an unwanted child. My Lords, the discipline of comparative law does not aim at a poll of the solutions adopted in different countries. It has the different and inestimable value of sharpening our focus on the weight of competing considerations. And it reminds us that the law is part of the world of competing ideas markedly influenced by cultural differences. Thus Fleming has demonstrated that it may be of relevance, depending on the context, to know whether the particular state has an effective social security safety net: see Fleming, *The American Tort Process* (1988) pp. 26–27.

I will now eliminate the grounds upon which I would not decide against the parents claim for compensation for financial loss arising from the child's birth. Counsel for the health authority rightly did not argue that it is a factor against the claim that the parents should have resorted to abortion or adoption. I cannot conceive of any circumstances in which the autonomous decision of the parents not to resort to even a lawful abortion could be questioned. For similar reasons the parents' decision not to have the child adopted was plainly natural and commendable. It is difficult to envisage any circumstances in which it would be right to challenge such a decision of the parents. The starting point is the right of parents to make decisions on family planning and, if those plans fail, their right to care for an initially unwanted child. The law does and must respect these decisions of parents which are so closely tied to their basic freedoms and rights of personal autonomy.

Counsel for the health authority argued as his primary submission that the whole claim should fail because the natural processes of conception and childbirth cannot in law amount to personal injury. This is a view taken in some jurisdictions. On the other hand, it is inconsistent with many other decisions, notably where limited recovery of compensation for pain, suffering and distress is allowed. I would not follow this path. After all, the hypothesis is that the negligence of the surgeon caused the physical consequences of pain and suffering associated with pregnancy and childbirth. And every pregnancy involves substantial discomfort and pain. I would therefore reject the argument of the health authority on this point. In the alternative counsel argued that, if money spent on C is regarded as a detriment to her parents, it is outweighed by the many and undisputed benefits which they have derived and will derive from C. While this factor is relevant in an assessment of the justice of the parents' claim I do not regard such a "set off" as the correct legal analysis of the position.

It is possible to view the case simply from the perspective of corrective justice. It requires somebody who has harmed another without justification to indemnify the other. On this approach the parents' claim for the cost of bringing up C must succeed. But one may also approach the case from the vantage point of distributive justice. It requires a focus on the just distribution of burdens and losses among members of a society. If the matter is approached in this way, it may become relevant to ask of the commuters on the Underground the following question: Should the parents of an unwanted but healthy child be able to sue the doctor or hospital for compensation equivalent to the cost of bringing up the child for the years of his or her minority, i.e. until about 18 years? My Lords, I have not consulted my fellow travellers on the London Underground but I am firmly of the view that an overwhelming number of ordinary men and women would answer the question with an emphatic No. And the reason for such a response would be an inarticulate premise as to what is morally acceptable and what is not. Like Ognall J in *Jones v Berkshire Area Health Authority* they will have in mind that many couples cannot have children and others have the sorrow and burden of looking after a disabled child. The realisation that compensation for financial loss in respect of the upbringing of a child would necessarily have to discriminate between rich and poor would surely appear unseemly to them. It would also worry them that parents may be put in a position of arguing in court that the unwanted child, which they accepted and care for, is more trouble than it is worth. Instinctively, the traveller on the Underground would consider that the law of tort has no business to provide legal remedies consequent upon the birth of a healthy child, which all of us regard as a valuable and good thing.

My Lords, to explain decisions denying a remedy for the cost of bringing up an unwanted child by saying that there is no loss, no foreseeable loss, no causative link or no ground for reasonable restitution is to resort to unrealistic and formalistic propositions which mask the real reasons for the decisions. And judges ought to strive to give the real reasons for their decision. It is my firm conviction that where courts of law have denied a remedy for the cost of bringing up an unwanted child the real reasons have been grounds of distributive justice. That is, of course, a moral theory. It may be objected that the House must act like a court of law and not like a court of morals. That would only be partly right. The court must apply positive law. But judges' sense of the moral answer to a question, or the justice of the case, has been one of the great shaping forces of the common law. What may count in a situation of difficulty and uncertainty is not the subjective view of the judge but what he reasonably believes that the ordinary citizen would regard as right. Two recent illustrations of the relevance of the moral dimension in the development of the law illustrate the point. In *Smith New Court Securities Ltd v Scrimgeour Vickers (Asset Management) Ltd* the House differentiated between the measure of damages for fraudulent and negligent misrepresentation. Pointing out that tort law and morality are inextricably interwoven, I said (with the agreement of Lord Keith of Kinkel and Lord Jauncey of Tullichettle) that as between the fraudster and the innocent party, moral considerations militate in favour of requiring the fraudster to bear the risk of misfortunes directly caused by the fraud. In *White v Chief Constable of the South Yorkshire Police* the police officers claimed compensation for psychiatric loss they sustained as a result of the Hillsborough disaster. By a majority the House ruled against the claim. The principal theme of the judgments of the majority was based on considerations of distributive justice. In separate judgments Lord Hoffmann and I reasoned that it would be morally unacceptable if the law denied a remedy to bereaved relatives, as happened in *Alcock v Chief Constable of the South Yorkshire Police*, but granted it to police officers who were on duty. Lord Hoffmann expressly invoked considerations of distributive justice. Lord Browne-Wilkinson and I expressed agreement with this reasoning. In my judgment I observed: "The claim of the police officers on our sympathy, and the justice of their case, is great but not as great as that of others to whom the law denies redress." That is the language of distributive justice. The truth is that tort law is a mosaic in which the principles of corrective justice and distributive justice are interwoven. And in situations of uncertainty and difficulty a choice sometimes has to be made between the two approaches.

In my view it is legitimate in the present case to take into account considerations of distributive justice. That does not mean that I would decide the case on grounds of public policy. On the contrary, I would avoid those quick sands. Relying on principles of distributive justice I am persuaded that our tort law does not permit parents of a healthy unwanted child to claim the costs of bringing up the child from a health authority or a doctor. If it were necessary to do so, I would say that the claim does not satisfy the requirement of being fair, just and reasonable. This conclusion is reinforced by an argument of coherence. There is no support in Scotland and England for a claim by a disadvantaged child for damage to him arising from his birth: see *McKay v Essex Area Health Authority*. Given this position, which also prevails in Australia, Trindade and Cane, *The Law of Torts in Australia* (2nd edn, 1993) p. 434 observe:"... it might seem inconsistent to allow a claim by the parents while that of the child, whether healthy or disabled, is rejected. Surely the parents' claim is equally repugnant to ideas of the sanctity and value of human life and rests, like that of the child, on a comparison between a situation where a human being exists and one where it does not." In my view this reasoning is sound. Coherence and rationality demand that the claim by the parents should also be rejected.

Two supplementary points remain to be mentioned. First, I have taken into account that the claim in the present case is based on an assumption of responsibility by the doctor who gave negligent advice. But in regard to the sustainability of a claim for the cost of bringing up the child it ought not to make any difference whether the claim is based on negligence *simpliciter* or on the extended *Hedley Byrne* principle. After all, the latter is simply the rationalisation adopted by the common law to provide a remedy for the recovery of economic loss for a species of negligently-performed services: see *Williams v Natural Life Health Foods Ltd*. Secondly, counsel for the health authority was inclined to concede that in the case of an unwanted child, who was born seriously disabled, the rule may have to be different. There may be force in this concession but it does not arise in the present appeal and it ought to await decision where the focus is on such cases.

I would hold that the Inner House erred in ruling that Mr and Mrs M are entitled in principle to recover the costs of bringing up C.

THE CLAIM FOR PAIN, SUFFERING AND DISTRESS

The claim for a *solatium* simply alleges that Mrs M became pregnant and had to undergo a pregnancy and confinement and the pain and distress of giving birth to the child. It will be recalled that I have already rejected the argument that Mrs M suffered no personal injury. The constituent elements of a claim in delict are present. The considerations of distributive justice, which militated against the claim for the cost of bringing up C, do not apply to the claim for a *solatium*. There is nothing objectionable to allowing such a claim. And such limited recovery is supported by a great deal of authority worldwide. I would uphold it.'

Comment

(1)   For a more detailed review of the English, Scottish, American, Commonwealth and other European cases, see Lord Slynn's speech.

(2)   Lord Millett accepted the reasoning that led the court to hold the costs of C's upbringing were irrecoverable, but continued:

'Unlike your Lordships, I consider that the same reasoning leads to the rejection of Mrs M's claim in respect of the pain and distress of pregnancy and delivery. The only difference between the two heads of damage claimed is temporal. Normal pregnancy and delivery were as much an inescapable precondition of C's birth as the expense of maintaining her afterwards was its inevitable consequence. They are the price of parenthood. The fact that it is paid by the mother alone does not alter this. It does not, however, follow that Mr and Mrs M should be sent away empty-handed. The rejection of their claim to measure their loss by the consequences of C's conception and birth does not lead to the conclusion that they have suffered none. They have suffered both injury and loss. They have lost the freedom to limit the size of their family. They have been denied an important aspect of their personal autonomy. Their decision to have no more children is one the law should respect and protect. They are entitled to general damages to reflect the true nature of the wrong done to them. This should be a conventional sum which should be left to the trial judge to assess, but which I would not expect to exceed £5000 in a straightforward case like the present.'

(3)   The special costs associated with bringing up a child born with congenital abnormalities were held by the Court of Appeal to be recoverable in *Parkinson v St James and Seacroft University Hospital NHS Trust*. After analysing the

speeches in the House of Lords in *McFarlane* and the approach to policy issues in similar cases in the United States in which the 'special' upbringing costs were recoverable, Brooke LJ said:

'50. Unless we are bound by authority to the contrary, I find this argument persuasive. On this side of the Atlantic I would apply the battery of tests which the House of Lords has taught us to use, and arrive at the same answer. My route would be as follows:

i) For the reasons given by Waller LJ in *Emeh*, the birth of a child with congenital abnormalities was a foreseeable consequence of the surgeon's careless failure to clip a Fallopian tube effectively;

ii) There was a very limited group of people who might be affected by this negligence: viz Mrs P and her husband (and, in theory, any other man with whom she had sexual intercourse before she realised that she had not been effectively sterilised);

iii) There is no difficulty in principle in accepting the proposition that the surgeon should be deemed to have assumed responsibility for the foreseeable and disastrous economic consequences of performing his services negligently;

iv) The purpose of the operation was to prevent Mrs P from conceiving any more children, including children with congenital abnormalities, and the surgeon's duty of care is strictly related to the proper fulfilment of that purpose;

v) Parents in Mrs P's position were entitled to recover damages in these circumstances for 15 years between the decisions in *Emeh* and *McFarlane*, so that this is not a radical step forward into the unknown;

vi) For the reasons set out in (i) and (ii) above, Lord Bridge's tests of foreseeability and proximity are satisfied, and for the reasons given by the Supreme Court of Florida in *Fassoulas*, an award of compensation which is limited to the special upbringing costs associated with rearing a child with a serious disability would be fair, just and reasonable.

vii) If principles of distributive justice are called in aid, I believe that ordinary people would consider that it would be fair for the law to make an award in such a case, provided that it is limited to the extra expenses associated with the child's disability.

51. I can see nothing in any majority reasoning in *McFarlane* to deflect this court from adopting this course, which in my judgment both logic and justice demands. ...

52. What constitutes a significant disability for this purpose will have to be decided by judges, if necessary, on a case by case basis.'

(4)   See also *Greenfield v Flather and others* and *Enwright and another v Kwun and another*. For a case in which the mother was disabled, rather than the child, see *Rees v Darlington Memorial Hospital NHS Trust* (below).

Rees v Darlington Memorial Hospital NHS Trust
[2003] 4 All ER 987 House of Lords

The claimant, Ms R, suffered from a severe and degenerative eye condition, and concluded she should not attempt to raise children. Her reason for requesting sterilisation was known to the surgeon undertaking (negligently, as it proved) the operation. Ms R later gave birth to a normal healthy child. A majority in the Court of Appeal held that she should recover such additional child-rearing costs as were attributable to her disability. The House of Lords, by a four-to-three majority, reversed the decision, though adding that claimants in such cases should receive a conventional award of £15,000 to 'mark the injury and loss'.

Lord Millett: '...

112.   *McFarlane* decides that the costs of bringing up a normal, healthy child must be taken to be outweighed by the incalculable blessings which such a child brings to his or her parents and do not sound in damages. *Parkinson* decides that the additional costs of bringing up a disabled child are recoverable in damages. It may be that strict logic demands a different answer. A disabled child is not "worth" less than a healthy one. The blessings of his or her birth are no less incalculable. Society must equally "regard the balance as beneficial". But the law does not develop by strict logic; and most people would instinctively feel that there was a difference, even if they had difficulty in articulating it. Told that a friend has given birth to a normal, healthy baby, we would express relief as well as joy. Told that she had given birth to a seriously disabled child, most of us would feel (though not express) sympathy for the parents. Our joy at the birth would not be unalloyed; it would be tinged with sorrow for the child's disability. Speaking for myself, I would not find it morally offensive to reflect this difference in an award of compensation. But it is not necessary for the disposal of the present appeal to reach any conclusion whether *Parkinson* was rightly decided, and I would wish to keep the point open. It would in any case be necessary to limit the compensation to the additional costs attributable to the child's disability; and this may prove difficult to achieve without introducing nice distinctions and unacceptable refinements of a kind which tend to bring the law into disrepute. For the reasons I gave in my speech in *McFarlane* I would not for my part wish to distinguish between the various motives which the parties might have for desiring to avoid a pregnancy.

113.   However that may be, the decision of the Court of Appeal in the present case is not a legitimate extension of *Parkinson*, but an illegitimate gloss on *McFarlane*. The conventional approach to damages would allow the costs of bringing

up a healthy child, but only so far as they were reasonable. Costs which are incurred unreasonably are not recoverable. So what *McFarlane* decides is that the costs of bringing up a healthy child, even though reasonably incurred, are not recoverable.

114. Such costs are infinitely variable. They will differ as between one family and another. They will vary, not only according to the needs of the individual child, but according to the circumstances of the parents and other members of the family. They may be greater in the case of a single parent, and less where there are grandparents or siblings to fetch and carry and help with the care of the child. They may be greater where the mother chooses or has to go out to work and so must employ a child minder or home help. They may be very great if the mother is a highly paid professional woman or works at a job which takes her frequently away from home; or if the family is accustomed to private health care or education. All these factors, which are referable to the personal circumstances of the child's family and not to those of the child, go to increase the costs which are reasonably incurred in bringing up the child. But *McFarlane* teaches that none of these costs are recoverable in the case of a healthy child, however reasonably they may be incurred. In principle, the same must be true of the disabled parent. To the extent that her disability has any effect, it increases the amount of the costs which she reasonably incurs in bringing up the child, costs which are nevertheless not recoverable.

115. It is, with respect, no answer to say that the disabled parent has no choice in the matter; and that if a mother's disability makes it impossible for her to look after the child, she must perforce employ someone to do it for her. The normal, healthy parent may also have no real choice in the matter. A single mother with no disability allowance may have no choice but to go out to work. A mother who, like the old woman who lived in a shoe, has "so many children she doesn't know what to do" may have no choice but to employ someone to look after them. A family which has already resorted to private health care and private education for the existing children cannot realistically choose to do less for their latest child. By contrast, a disabled mother may have a husband, parents and other members of the family to give support and look after the child. There is no relevant difference between costs which are "necessary" and those which are "reasonable", even if it were practicable to attempt to draw it; but it cannot be drawn on the line which distinguishes the disabled parent from the normal, healthy one.

116. There is another consideration. A child who is born disabled is disabled throughout his or her childhood. Likewise a disabled parent is disabled throughout his or her child's childhood. But there is a significant difference. The factors which make it appropriate to award compensation for the birth of a disabled child are present throughout; those which appear to make it appropriate to award damages for the birth of a healthy child to a disabled parent gradually disappear to be overtaken by the advantages. Once the child is able to go to school alone and be of

some help around the house, his or her presence will to a greater or lesser extent help to alleviate the disadvantages of the parent's disability. And once the child has grown to adulthood, he or she can provide immeasurable help to an ageing and disabled parent.

117.   It is a mistake to assume that, because the costs attributable to the disability are "extras" whether the disabled party is the child or the parent, there is any symmetry. It is true that *McFarlane* was concerned with a normal, healthy baby born to normal, healthy parents, though this group includes parents who for one reason or another could ill afford to have to look after another child. We expressly confined our decision to the case of a healthy child because we recognised that the case of a disabled child might be distinguishable. But, speaking for myself, I made no assumptions about the health or other characteristics of the parents. I considered their circumstances to be irrelevant. It was enough that they did not want or could not properly look after another child. I expressly said that their motives for not wanting another child were irrelevant. I still regard this to be the case.

118.   Disability is a misfortune, and it is the mark of a civilised society that it should provide financial assistance to the disabled. The United Kingdom discharges this responsibility by payment of disability allowance. But this is the responsibility of the state and is properly funded by general taxation. It is not the responsibility of the private citizen whose conduct has neither caused nor contributed to the disability. *McFarlane* teaches that the costs of bringing up a healthy child by an unimpaired parent do not sound in damages. Whatever we may say to the contrary, an award of the "extra" costs which are attributable to the fact that the parent is disabled is an award of damages for the disability.

119.   It is accepted that care must be taken not to award damages for the parent's disability. An immediate difficulty is that the costs which are attributable to the parent's disability cannot be disentangled from those which are attributable to the birth of the child. If the parent is unable through disability to look after her healthy child, she must employ someone to do so. How are those costs to be characterised? They must be due at least in part to the birth of the child, and in part to the parent's disability. It is impossible to separate the two elements. They are not different components of the cost, but a single cost with composite causes.

120.   But even if they could be separately identified it would not help, for in principle no part of the costs is recoverable. This is what marks the difference between the present case and *Parkinson*. Where it is the child who is disabled the costs are attributable either to the birth of the child or to the fact that the child is disabled. The former are not recoverable; the latter are. Where it is the mother who is disabled they are attributable either to the birth of the child or to the fact that the mother is disabled. There is no third possibility. To the extent that they are due to the birth of the child *McFarlane* precludes recovery and to the extent that they are not due to the birth of the child, the causal link with the wrong is broken and the defendants are not liable for them in any case. The fact that the mother is

disabled aggravates the financial consequences of the birth of a healthy child, and the birth of a healthy child aggravates the financial consequences of the mother's disability. The former is the defendants' responsibility but does not sound in damages and the latter is not the responsibility of the defendants at all.

121. In my opinion, principle mandates the rejection of the parent's claim. But in this case principle also marches with justice. The decision of the majority of the Court of Appeal is destructive of the concept of distributive justice. It renders the law incoherent and is bound to lead to artificial and indefensible distinctions being drawn as the courts struggle to draw a principled line between costs which are recoverable and those which are not. …

122. … In my opinion, principle, common justice and the coherence of the law alike demand that the line be drawn between those costs which are referable to the characteristics of the child and those which are referable to the characteristics of the parent. I agree with Waller LJ that ordinary people would think it unfair that a disabled person should recover the costs of looking after a healthy child when a person not suffering from disability who through no fault of her own was no better able to look after such a child could not. I can identify no legal principle by which such a distinction could be defended.

123. I still regard the proper outcome in all these cases is to award the parents a modest conventional sum by way of general damages, not for the birth of the child, but for the denial of an important aspect of their personal autonomy, viz the right to limit the size of their family. This is an important aspect of human dignity, which is increasingly being regarded as an important human right which should be protected by law. The loss of this right is not an abstract or theoretical one. As my noble and learned friend Lord Bingham of Cornhill has pointed out, the parents have lost the opportunity to live their lives in the way that they wished and planned to do. The loss of this opportunity, whether characterised as a right or a freedom, is a proper subject for compensation by way of damages.'

Comment

(1) As to the propriety of departing from or distinguishing *McFarlane*, Lord Bingham said:

'7. I am of the clear opinion, for reasons more fully given by my noble and learned friends, that it would be wholly contrary to the practice of the House to disturb its unanimous decision in *McFarlane* given as recently as 4 years ago, even if a differently constituted committee were to conclude that a different solution should have been adopted. It would reflect no credit on the administration of the law if a line of English authority were to be disapproved in 1999 and reinstated in 2003 with no reason for the change beyond a change in the balance of judicial opinion. I am not in any event persuaded that the arguments which the House rejected in 1999 should now be accepted, or that the policy considerations which (as I think) drove the decision have lost their potency.'

(2)   Lord Steyn, in the minority, was against the notion of a conventional award, saying:

'46.   Like Lord Hope I regard the idea of a conventional award in the present case as contrary to principle. It is a novel procedure for judges to create such a remedy. There are limits to permissible creativity for judges. In my view the majority have strayed into forbidden territory. It is also a backdoor evasion of the legal policy enunciated in *McFarlane*. If such a rule is to be created it must be done by Parliament. The fact is, however, that it would be a hugely controversial legislative measure. It may well be that the Law Commissions and Parliament ought in any event, to consider the impact of the creation of a power to make a conventional award in the cases under consideration for the coherence of the tort system.'

(3)   In *Goodwill v British Pregnancy Advisory Service* the plaintiff had given birth to a child after having been informed by her partner that he had had a vasectomy. She argued, by analogy with *White v Jones*, that she had relied on advice given by the defendants to her partner that he need not use contraception in future. In the Court of Appeal Peter Gibson LJ said:

'I am wholly unpersuaded by the analogy. It must be recognised that *White v Jones* belonged to an unusual class of cases. A remedy in tort was fashioned to overcome the rank injustice [in that case] ... I do not see any comparable injustice in the present case ... The doctor who performs a vasectomy ... cannot realistically be described as employed to confer a benefit on the man's sexual partners in the form of avoiding pregnancy.'

CHAPTER 4

Breach of duty

Having established the existence of a duty of care owed by the defendant to the claimant, it must be decided whether that duty has been breached. For this, attention is focused on the conduct of the defendant and the test is an objective one – has the defendant behaved reasonably in all the circumstances? There are two stages in the process: first, the court must decide on the appropriate standard against which the defendant is to be judged; and second, it must be proved on the balance of probabilities that the defendant's conduct has failed to meet the required standard.

The basic standard is that which is to be expected of the 'reasonable man', although in certain circumstances – for example where the defendant is either a particularly highly-skilled, or under-skilled, individual – it seems that the test may change to that which the reasonable man is entitled to expect of that individual.

Where the damage complained of arises from a decision by the defendant either to engage in or to continue with a particular activity, the courts approach the question of liability as one of risk assessment. In other words, would the reasonable person in the defendant's position have been justified in taking such a risk? The courts, in answering this question, have taken a number of factors into account. When assessing the magnitude of the risk, the courts look at a combination of two factors in particular: (i) the likelihood of harm occurring; and (ii) the likely severity if harm should occur. Another relevant factor is the utility of the conduct in which the claimant is engaged. Furthermore, the defendant is required only to take all reasonable precautions, so it follows that inconvenience and expense, the 'burden of the adequate precautions', are to be taken into account. Where the burden outweighs the risk, it would not be reasonable to expect the precautions to be taken.

Ordinarily, it is for the claimant to prove that the defendant was negligent. The main exception is when circumstances are such that the damage *prima facie* could not have occurred if the defendant had been taking proper care. In this situation the defendant will be liable unless he or she can give some reasonable explanation of how the damage occurred. This principle is contained in the maxim *res ipsa loquitur* – 'the thing speaks for itself'.

Blyth v The Company of Proprietors of the Birmingham Waterworks (1856) 11 Ex 781 Exchequer Division

The defendants were responsible for the laying and maintenance of a system of water pipes. The plaintiff's house was damaged one winter when a large quantity of water was forced up into it from the main when a safety device failed to operate due to a heavy encrustation of ice. The court held that the reasonable water company was not obliged to take extraordinary precautions in order to avoid being negligent.

Alderson B: '... Negligence is the omission to do something which a reasonable man, guided upon those considerations which ordinarily regulate the conduct of human affairs, would do, or doing something which a prudent and reasonable man would not do. The defendants might have been liable for negligence, if, unintentionally, they omitted to do that which a reasonable person would have done, or did that which a person taking reasonable precautions would not have done. A reasonable man would act with reference to the average circumstances of the temperature in ordinary years. The defendants had provided against such frosts as experience would have led men, acting prudently, to provide against; and they are not guilty of negligence, because their precautions proved insufficient against the effects of the extreme severity of the frost of 1855, which penetrated to a greater depth than any which ordinarily occurs south of the polar regions. Such a state of circumstances constitutes a contingency against which no reasonable man can provide. The result was an accident, for which the defendants cannot be held liable.'

Corporation of Glasgow v Muir [1943] 2 All ER 44 House of Lords

The appellants owned tea rooms in a Glasgow park. Their manageress had allowed, for a small fee, members of a church picnic party to take their tea indoors because of bad weather. While two of the party were carrying their tea urn past some children who were queuing in a passage, the urn tipped up, scalding the respondents with hot tea. It was argued for the respondents that the manageress ought to have foreseen the risk from spillage and was therefore negligent in failing to remove the children from the passage while the urn was being moved. The House of Lords allowed the appeal.

Lord Macmillan: 'My Lords, the degree of care for the safety of others which the law requires human beings to observe in the conduct of their affairs varies according to the circumstances. There is no absolute standard, but it may be said generally that the degree of care required varies directly with the risk involved. Those who engage in operations inherently dangerous must take precautions which are not required of persons engaged in the ordinary routine of daily life. It is no doubt true that in every act which an individual performs there is present a potentiality of injury to others. All things are possible and, indeed, it has become proverbial that the unexpected always happens. But while the precept *alterum non laedere* requires us to abstain from intentionally injuring others, it does not impose liability for every injury which our conduct may occasion. In Scotland, at any rate, it has never been a maxim of the law that a man acts at his peril. Legal liability is limited to those consequences of our acts which a reasonable man of ordinary intelligence and experience so acting would have in contemplation. As I essayed to formulate it in *Bourhill v Young*:

> "The duty to take care is the duty to avoid doing or omitting to do anything the doing or omitting to do which may have as its reasonable and probable consequence injury to others, and the duty is owed to those to whom injury may reasonably and probably be anticipated if the duty is not observed."

This, in my opinion, expresses the law of Scotland and I apprehend that it is also the law of England.

The standard of foresight of the reasonable man is in one sense an impersonal test. It eliminates the personal equation and is independent of the idiosyncrasies of the particular person whose conduct is in question. Some persons are by nature unduly timorous and imagine every path beset with lions; others, of more robust temperament, fail to foresee or nonchalantly disregard even the most obvious dangers. The reasonable man is presumed to be free both from over-apprehension and from over-confidence. But there is a sense in which the standard of care of the reasonable man involves in its application a subjective element. It is still left to the judge to decide what in the circumstances of the particular case the reasonable man would have in contemplation and what accordingly the party sought to be made liable ought to have foreseen. Here there is room for diversity of view ... What to one judge may seem far-fetched may seem to another both natural and probable.'

Comment

(1) The mythical 'reasonable man' is often described as 'the man on the Clapham omnibus', or, in *Hall v Brooklands Auto Racing Club*, as 'the man who takes the magazines at home and in the evening pushes the lawn-mower in his shirt sleeves'. He is presumed to be reasonably prudent but he is not required to possess superhuman foresight or caution.

(2) In theory, at least, the reasonable man's response to any particular set of circumstances is determinable by reference to a set pattern. Nevertheless,

despite the apparent objectivity of the test, it is evident that the standard may vary according to the perceptions of individual judges. Also, it must be recognised that in many situations the reasonable man test is inappropriate and must give way to a standard which might reasonably be expected of this defendant, either because he or she professes to possess a particular skill or, perhaps because of his or her youth, because he or she cannot reasonably be expected to reach the standard.

Bolam v Friern Hospital Management Committee [1957] 2 All ER 118 Queen's Bench Division

The plaintiff consented to and underwent electroconvulsive therapy as treatment for his mental illness. As a result of the procedure he suffered severe injuries and sued the defendants in negligence claiming: (a) that he should have been warned of the risk of fracture; and (b) that relaxant drugs should have been administered to eliminate the risk. At the time, medical opinion on each of these issues was divided. The court held that medical treatment is not negligent provided that the practice adopted is one which is considered proper by a responsible body of medical men skilled in that particular field. On the facts this test was satisfied.

McNair J: '... In the ordinary case which does not involve any special skill, negligence in law means this: Some failure to do some act which a reasonable man in the circumstances would do, or doing some act which a reasonable man in the circumstances would not do; and if that failure or doing of that act results in injury, then there is a cause of action. How do you test whether this act or failure is negligent? In an ordinary case it is generally said, that you judge that by the action of the man in the street. He is the ordinary man. In one case it has been said that you judge it by the conduct of the man on the top of a Clapham omnibus. He is the ordinary man. But where you get a situation which involves the use of some special skill or competence, then the test whether there has been negligence or not is not the test of the man on the top of a Clapham omnibus, because he has not got this special skill. The test is the standard of the ordinary skilled man exercising and professing to have that special skill. A man need not possess the highest expert skill at the risk of being found negligent. It is well-established law that it is sufficient if he exercises the ordinary skill of an ordinary competent man exercising that particular art. I do not think that I quarrel much with any of the submissions in law which have been put before you by counsel. Counsel for the plaintiff put it in this way, that in the case of a medical man negligence means failure to act in accordance with the standards of reasonably competent medical men at the time. That is a perfectly accurate statement, as long as it is remembered that there may be one or more perfectly proper standards; and if a medical man conforms with one of those proper standards then he is not negligent. Counsel for the plaintiff was also right, in my judgment, in saying that a mere personal belief that a particular technique is best is no defence unless that belief is based on reasonable grounds. That again is unexceptional. But the emphasis which is laid by counsel for the defendants is on this aspect of negligence: He submitted to you that the real question on which you have to make up your mind on each of the three major points to be considered is whether the defendants, in acting in the way in which they did, were acting in accordance with a practice of competent respected professional opinion. Counsel for the defendants submitted that if you are satisfied that they were acting in accordance with a practice of a competent body of professional opinion, then it would be wrong for you to hold that negligence was established ... I myself would prefer to put it this way: A doctor is not guilty of negligence if he has acted in accordance with a practice accepted as proper by a responsible body of medical men skilled in that particular art ... Putting it the other way round, a doctor is not negligent, if he is acting in accordance with such a practice, merely because there is a body of opinion that takes a contrary view. At the same time, that does not mean that a medical man can obstinately and pig-headedly carry on with some old technique if it has been proved to be contrary to what is really substantially the whole of informed medical opinion.'

Comment

(1) Note the general statement about the standard to be expected of any skilled individual.

(2) The closing statements set out what has become known as 'the *Bolam* test' which is of particular application to doctors; see also *F v West Berkshire HA*, although it has subsequently been adopted in relation to other professions, e.g. accountants: *Mutual Life Assurance Co Ltd v Evatt*; and lawyers: *Saif Ali v Sydney Mitchell & Co.*

(3) In *Bolitho v City and Hackney HA* the House of Lords reviewed the *Bolam* test. Both the trial judge and the Court of Appeal had held that a doctor would not have been negligent in failing to intubate a sick child, despite a conflict of expert evidence and the fact that the child in question had suffered two previous episodes of respiratory failure during the night in question. Lord Browne-Wilkinson said:

'[Counsel for the appellant] submitted that the judge had wrongly treated the *Bolam* test as requiring him to accept the views of one truthful body of expert professional advice even though he was unpersuaded of its logical force. He submitted that the judge was wrong in law in adopting that approach and that ultimately it was for the court, not for medical opinion, to decide what was the standard of care required of a professional in the circumstances of each particular case.

My Lords, I agree with these submissions to the extent that, in my view, the court is not bound to hold that a defendant doctor escapes liability for negligent treatment or diagnosis just because he leads evidence from a number of medical experts who are genuinely of opinion that the defendant's treatment or diagnosis accorded with sound medical practice. In the *Bolam* case itself, McNair J stated that the defendant had to have acted in accordance with the practice accepted as proper by a *"responsible* body of medical men" [my emphasis]. Later he referred to "a standard of practice recognised as proper by a competent *reasonable* body of opinion"[my emphasis].

Again, [in *Maynard's* case], Lord Scarman refers to a "respectable" body of professional opinion. The use of these adjectives – responsible, reasonable and respectable – all show that the court has to be satisfied that the exponents of the body of opinion relied on can demonstrate that such opinion has a logical basis. In particular in cases involving, as they so often do, the weighing of risks against benefits, the judge before accepting a body of opinion as being responsible, reasonable or respectable, will need to be satisfied that, in forming their views, the experts have directed their minds to the question of comparative risks and benefits and have reached a defensible conclusion on the matter ...

[*Hucks v Cole* and *Edward Wong Finance Co Ltd v Johnson Stokes & Master*] demonstrate that in cases of diagnosis and treatment there are cases where, despite a body of professional opinion sanctioning the defendant's conduct, the defendant can properly be held liable for negligence (I am not here considering questions of disclosure of risk). In my judgment that is because, in some cases, it cannot be demonstrated to the judge's satisfaction that the body of opinion relied on is reasonable or responsible. In the vast majority of cases the fact that distinguished experts in the field are of a particular opinion will demonstrate the reasonableness of that opinion. In particular, where there are questions of assessment of the relative risks and benefits of adopting a particular medical practice, a reasonable view necessarily presupposes that the relative risks and benefits have been weighed by the experts in forming their opinions. But if, in a rare case, it can be demonstrated that the professional opinion is not capable of withstanding logical analysis, the judge is entitled to hold that the body of opinion is not reasonable or responsible.

I emphasise that, in my view, it will very seldom be right for a judge to reach the conclusion that views genuinely held by a competent medical expert are unreasonable. The assessment of medical risks and benefits is a matter of clinical judgment which a judge would not normally be able to make without expert evidence. As ... Lord Scarman makes clear, it would be wrong to allow such assessment to deteriorate into seeking to persuade the judge to prefer one of two views both of which are capable of being logically supported. It is only where a judge can be satisfied that the body of expert opinion cannot be logically supported at all that such opinion will not provide the bench mark by reference to which the defendant's conduct falls to be assessed.'

Sidaway v Bethlem Royal Hospital Governors and others [1985] I All ER 643 House of Lords

Mrs S consented to an operation on her spinal column to relieve persistent pain in her neck and shoulders. She was advised by the surgeon of some of the risks inherent in the operation but not of the small (less than one per cent) risk of damage to the spinal cord which she in fact suffered, resulting in her being severely disabled. Mrs S brought an action against the hospital governors in negligence, alleging that the surgeon had failed in his duty to inform her of all the risks. The House of Lords upheld the decisions of the lower courts that the surgeon had acted as a reasonable doctor.

Lord Diplock: '... For the last quarter of a century the test applied in English law whether a doctor has fulfilled his duty of care owed to his patient has been that set out in the summing up to the jury by McNair J in *Bolam v Friern Hospital Management Committee.* I will call this the *Bolam* test. At any rate, so far as diagnosis and treatment are concerned, the *Bolam* test has twice received the express approval of this House.

The *Bolam* test is far from new; its value is that it brings up to date and re-expresses in the light of modern conditions in which the art of medicine is now practised an ancient rule of common law ... The standard of skill and judgment in the particular area of the art of medicine in which the doctor practised that was called for by the expression peritia was the standard of ordinary skill and care that could be expected to be shown by a doctor who had successfully completed the training to qualify as a doctor, whether as general practitioner or as consultant in a speciality if he held himself out as practising as such, as the case might be. But, unless the art in which the artificer claims to have acquired skill and judgment is stagnant so that no improvement in methods or knowledge is sought (and of few is this less true than medicine and surgery over the last half-century), advances in the ability to heal resulting from the volume of research, clinical as well as technological, will present doctors with alternative treatments to adopt and a choice to select that treatment (it may be one of several) that is in their judgment likely at the time to prove most efficacious or ameliorating to the health of each particular patient committed to their care.

Those members of the public who seek medical or surgical aid would be badly served by the adoption of any legal principle that would confine the doctor to some long-established, well-tried method of treatment only, although its past record of success might be small, if he wanted to be confident that he would not run the risk of being held liable in negligence simply because he tried some more modern treatment, and by some unavoidable mischance it failed to heal but did some harm to the patient. This would encourage "defensive medicine" with a vengeance. The merit of the *Bolam* test is that the criterion of the duty of care owed by a doctor to his patient is whether he has acted in accordance with a practice accepted as proper by a body of responsible and skilled medical opinion. There may be a number of different practices which satisfy this criterion at any particular time. These practices are likely to alter with advances in medical knowledge. Experience shows that, to the great benefit of humankind, they have done so, particularly in the recent past. That is why fatal diseases such as smallpox and tuberculosis have within living memory become virtually extinct in countries where modern medical care is generally available.

In English jurisprudence the doctor's relationship with his patient which gives rise to the normal duty of care to exercise his skill and judgment to improve the patient's health in any particular respect in which the patient has sought his aid has hitherto been treated as a single comprehensive duty covering all the ways in which a doctor is called on to exercise his skill and judgment in the improvement of the physical or mental condition of the patient for which his services either as a general practitioner or as a specialist have been engaged. This general duty is not subject to dissection into a number of component parts to which different criteria of what satisfy the duty of care apply, such as diagnosis, treatment and advice (including warning of any risks of something going wrong however skilfully the treatment advised is carried out). The *Bolam* case itself embraced failure to advise the patient of the risk involved in the electric shock treatment as one of the allegations of negligence against the surgeon as well as negligence in the actual carrying out of treatment in which that risk did result in injury to the patient. The same criteria were applied to both these aspects of the surgeon's duty of care. In modern medicine and surgery such dissection of the various things a doctor has to do in the exercise of his whole duty of care owed to his patient is neither legally meaningful nor medically practicable. Diagnosis itself may involve exploratory surgery, the insertion of drugs by injection (or vaccination) involves intrusion on the body of the patient and oral treatment by drugs, although it involves no physical intrusion by the doctor on the patient's body, may in the case of particular patients involve serious and unforeseen risks.

My Lords, no convincing reason has in my view been advanced before your Lordships that would justify treating the *Bolam* test as doing anything less than laying down a principle of English law that is comprehensive and applicable to every aspect of the duty of care owed by a doctor to his patient in the exercise of his healing functions as respects that patient. What your Lordships have been asked to do, and it is within your power to do so, is to substitute a new and different rule for that part only of the well-established *Bolam* test as comprises a doctor's duty to advise and warn the patient of risks of something going wrong in the surgical or other treatment that he is recommending.

The juristic basis of the proposed substitution, which originates in certain state court jurisdictions of the United States of America and has found some favour in modified form by the Supreme Court of Canada, appears to me, with great respect, to be contrary to English law. Its foundation is the doctrine of "informed consent" which was originally based on the assumption made in the United States Court of Appeals, District of Columbia Circuit, in *Canterbury v Spence* where the cynic might be forgiven for remarking that it enabled a defence under the state statute of limitations to be outmanoeuvred, that *prima facie* the cause of action in a case of surgery was trespass to the person unless "informed consent" to the particular battery involved in the surgical operation could be proved. From a period long before American independence this, as I have pointed out, has never been so in English law. The relevant form of action has been based in negligence ... alone.

The Supreme Court of Canada, after some initial vacillation, rejected trespass to the person, i.e. battery, as the cause of action in cases of surgery but endeavoured to transfer the concept of "informed consent" to a patient's cause of action in negligence, into which, in my opinion, it simply cannot be made to fit. Consent to battery is a state of mind personal to the victim of the battery and any information required to make his consent qualify as informed must be relevant information either actually possessed by him or which he is estopped from denying he possessed, because he so acted towards the defendant as to lead the latter reasonably to assume the relevant information was known to him. There is no room in the concept of informed consent for the "objective" patient (as he is referred to at one point by the Supreme Court of Canada) to whom the doctor is entitled, without making any inquiry whether it is the fact or not, to attribute knowledge of some risks but not of others. It may be that most patients, though not necessarily all, have a vague knowledge that there may be some risk in any form of medical treatment; but it is flying in the face of reality to assume that all patients from the highest to the lowest standard of education or intelligence are aware of the extent and nature of the risks which, notwithstanding the exercise of skill and care in carrying out the treatment, are inevitably involved in medical treatment of whatever kind it be but particularly surgical. Yet it is not merely conceded but specifically asserted in the Canadian cases that it is no part of the duty of care on the part of the doctor to go out of his way to draw the attention of his patient to these. On what logical or juristic basis can the need for informed consent be confined to some risks and not extended to others that are also real, and who decides which risk falls into which class?

My Lords, I venture to think that in making this separation between that part of the doctor's duty of care that he owes to each individual patient, which can be described as a duty to advise on treatment and warn of its risks, the courts have misconceived their functions as the finders of fact in cases depending on the negligent exercise of professional skill and judgment. In matters of diagnosis and the carrying out of treatment the court is not tempted to put itself in the surgeon's shoes; it has to rely on and evaluate expert evidence, remembering that it is no part of its task of evaluation to give effect to any preference it may have for one responsible body of professional opinion over another, provided it is satisfied by the expert evidence that both qualify as responsible bodies of medical opinion. But, when it comes to warning about risks, the kind of training and experience that a judge will have undergone at the Bar makes it natural for him to say (correctly) it is my right to decide whether any particular thing is done to my body, and I want to be fully informed of any risks there may be involved of which I am not already aware from my general knowledge as a highly educated man of experience, so that I may form my own judgment whether to refuse the advised treatment or not.

No doubt, if the patient in fact manifested this attitude by means of questioning, the doctor would tell him whatever it was the patient wanted to know; but we are concerned here with volunteering unsought information about risks of the proposed treatment failing to achieve the result sought or making the patient's physical or mental condition worse rather than better. The only effect that mention of risks can have on the patient's mind, if it has any at all, can be in the direction of deterring the patient from undergoing the treatment which in the expert opinion of the doctor it is in the patient's interest to undergo. To decide what risks the existence of which a patient should be voluntarily warned and the terms in which such warning, if any, should be given, having regard to the effect that the warning may have, is as much an exercise of professional skill and judgment as any other part of the doctor's comprehensive duty of care to the individual patient, and expert medical evidence on this matter should be treated in just the same way. The *Bolam* test should be applied.'

Comment

(1)   Note the role of policy in Lord Diplock's judgment: he considered that it would not be in the public interest if the legitimate development of new forms of medical treatment were to be hindered by the fear of liability in negligence.

(2)   It is clear that the *Bolam* 'reasonable doctor' test applies not only to diagnosis and treatment but also to decisions as to whether to inform patients of risks inherent in proposed treatment. For informed consent and trespass to the person see p 561.

(3)   Lord Bridge favoured, to some extent, a reasonable patient test and said: 'When questioned specifically by a patient of apparently sound mind about risks involved in a particular treatment proposed, the doctor's duty must ... be to answer both truthfully and as fully as the questioner requires.'

(4)   In *Brooks v Home Office* the question arose whether a prisoner should receive the same standard of medical treatment as people generally are entitled to expect. The claimant was 36 weeks pregnant with twins when an ultrasound scan carried out by medical staff at the prison revealed that one of the foetuses

had not grown as much as would have been expected since the last scan. The prison arranged an appointment for the claimant with the local clinic, but in several days' time rather than as an emergency. Two days later, when only one foetal heartbeat could be found, the claimant was transferred to hospital where one twin was stillborn and the survivor developed complications leading to severe disability. The High Court rejected the Home Office's argument that the relevant standard of care was to be determined by reference to the fact that the claimant was in custody, saying that she should be entitled to 'the same level of antenatal care, both for herself and her unborn infants, as if she were at liberty, subject ... to the constraints of having to be escorted and, to some extent, movement being retarded by those requirements'. Applying the approach from *Bolitho v City & Hackney HA* (see p 207), the court accepted medical evidence that a 48-hour delay would not have been a breach of duty, and therefore the claimant failed to establish the necessary causation.

This decision may be contrasted with *Knight v Home Office*. In that case, a mentally ill prisoner was detained in a prison hospital where there were insufficient staff to provide the regular monitoring needed to prevent him from harming himself. The court held that psychiatric and prison hospitals performed different functions which might properly be reflected in differing standards of medical care. Pill J said:

'In making the decision as to the standard to be demanded the court must ... bear in mind as one factor that resources available for the public service are limited and that the allocation of resources is a matter for Parliament. I am unable to accept the submission that the law requires the standard of care in a prison hospital to be as high as the standard of care for all purposes in a psychiatric hospital outside prison. I am unable to accept that the practices in a prison hospital are to be judged in all respects by the standard appropriate to a psychiatric hospital outside prison.'

(5)   In the context of alternative medicine, the High Court held in *Shakoor v Situ (t/a Eternal Health Co)*, that an alternative medical practitioner (in this case of Chinese herbal medicine) should not be judged by the standard of the orthodox medical man, since he was not holding himself out as such and the claimant had chosen to reject orthodox treatment. Instead, he should be expected to exercise the skill and care appropriate to his 'art', unless the prevailing standard in that 'art' was deficient in the UK. The judge reached the second limb of this test on the basis that an uncritical application of the *Bolam* test might otherwise allow practitioners to dictate their own standard to the court. He considered that an equivalent standard in this context would be that of an 'ordinary careful general practitioner', a standard which the defendant had met.

Nettleship v Weston
[1971] 3 All ER 581 Court of Appeal

The plaintiff, Mr N, was teaching a friend, Mrs W, to drive using her husband's car. She steered and controlled the pedals while Mr N used the gear lever and handbrake and sometimes helped with the steering. During her third lesson Mrs W turned a corner and, despite help and instruction from Mr N, mounted the kerb and hit a lamp-post, injuring Mr N's knee. The court concluded that, when assessing the standard of care to be expected, no allowance should be made for the fact that Mrs W was a learner-driver.

Lord Denning MR: '...

THE RESPONSIBILITY OF THE LEARNER-DRIVER TOWARDS PERSONS ON OR NEAR THE HIGHWAY

Mrs W is clearly liable for the damage to the lamp-post. In the civil law if a driver goes off the road on to the pavement and injures a pedestrian, or damages property, he is *prima facie* liable. Likewise if he goes on to the wrong side of the road. It is no answer for him to say: "I was a learner-driver under instruction. I was doing my best and could not help it." The civil law permits no such excuse. It requires of him the same standard of care as any other driver. "It eliminates the personal equation and is independent of the idiosyncrasies of the particular person whose conduct is in question": see *Glasgow Corporation v Muir* per Lord Macmillan. The learner-driver may be doing his best, but his incompetent best is not good enough. He must drive in as good a manner as a driver of skill, experience and care, who is sound in wind and limb, who makes no errors of judgment, has good eyesight and hearing, and is free from any infirmity: see *Richley v Faull* and *Watson v Thomas S Whitney & Co Ltd*.

The high standard thus imposed by the judges is, I believe, largely the result of the policy of the Road Traffic Acts. Parliament requires every driver to be insured against third-party risks. The reason is so that a person injured by a motor car should not be left to bear the loss on his own, but should be compensated out of the insurance fund. The fund is better able to bear it than he can. But the injured person is only able to recover if the driver is liable in law. So the judges see to it that he is liable, unless he can prove care and skill of high standard: see *The Merchant Prince* and *Henderson v Henry E Jenkins & Sons Ltd*. Thus we are, in this branch of the law, moving away from the concept: "No liability without fault". We are beginning to apply the test: "On whom should the risk fall?" Morally the learner-driver is not at fault; but legally she is liable to be because she is insured and the risk should fall on her ...

THE RESPONSIBILITY OF A LEARNER-DRIVER TOWARDS HIS INSTRUCTOR

The special factor in this case is that Mr N was not a mere passenger in the car. He was an instructor teaching Mrs W to drive. Seeing that the law lays down, for all drivers of motor cars, a standard of care to which all must conform, I think that even a learner-driver, so long as he is the sole driver, must attain the same standard towards all passengers in the car, including an instructor. But the instructor may be debarred from claiming for a reason peculiar to himself. He may be debarred because he has voluntarily agreed to waive any claim for any injury that may befall him. Otherwise he is not debarred. He may, of course, be guilty of contributory negligence and have his damages reduced on that account. He may, for instance, have let the learner take control too soon, he may not have been quick enough to correct his errors, or he may have participated in the negligent act himself: see *Stapley v Gipsum Mines Ltd*. But, apart from contributory negligence, he is not excluded unless it be that he had voluntarily agreed to incur the risk.

This brings me to the defence of *volenti non fit injuria*. Does it apply to the instructor? In former times this defence was used almost as an alternative defence to contributory negligence. Either defence defeated the action. Now that contributory negligence is not a complete defence, but only a ground for reducing the damages, the defence of *volenti non fit injuria* has been closely considered, and, in consequence, it has been severely limited. Knowledge of the risk of injury is not enough. Nor is a willingness to take the risk of injury. Nothing will suffice short of an agreement to waive any claim for negligence. The plaintiff must agree, expressly or impliedly, to waive any claim for any injury that may befall him due to the lack of reasonable care by the defendant: or more accurately, due to the failure of the defendant to measure up to the standard of care that the law requires of him. That is shown in *England by Dann v Hamilton* and *Slater v Clay Cross Co Ltd*; and in Canada by *Lehnert v Stein*; and in New Zealand by *Morrison v Union Steamship Co of New Zealand Ltd*. The doctrine has been so severely curtailed that in the view of Diplock LJ: "... the maxim, in the absence of express contract, has no application to negligence *simpliciter* where the duty of care is based solely on proximity or 'neighbourship' in the Atkinian sense": see *Wooldridge v Summer*.

Applying the doctrine in this case, it is clear that Mr N did not agree to waive any claim for injury that might befall him. Quite the contrary. He enquired about the insurance policy so as to make sure that he was covered. If and in so far as Mrs W fell short of the standard of care which the law required of her, he has a cause of action. But his claim may be reduced in so far as he was at fault himself – as in letting her take control too soon or in not being quick enough to correct her error. I do not say that the professional instructor – who agrees to teach for reward – can likewise sue. There may well be implied in the contract an agreement by him to waive any claim for injury. He ought to insure himself, and may do so, for aught I know. But the instructor who is just a friend helping to teach never does insure himself. He should, therefore, be allowed to sue.

CONCLUSION THUS FAR

In all that I have said, I have treated Mrs W as the driver who was herself in control of the car. On that footing, she is plainly liable for the damage done to the lamp-post. She is equally liable for the injury done to Mr N. She owed a duty of care to each. The standard of care is the same in either case. It is measured objectively by the care to be expected of an experienced, skilled and careful driver. Mr N is not defeated by the maxim *volenti non fit injuria*. He did not agree, expressly or impliedly, to waive any claim for damages owing to her failure to measure up to the standard. But his damages may fall to be reduced owing to his failure to correct her error quickly enough. Although the judge dismissed the claim, he did (in case he was wrong) apportion responsibility. He thought it would be just and equitable to regard them equally to blame. I would accept this apportionment.'

Comment

(1)   Although it might be thought that the ability to drive is a skill which would ordinarily attract the same test as for other 'experts', with unqualified drivers being placed in a separate category, this is clearly not the position in law. All drivers are to be judged by the same standard although, perhaps oddly, in *McComiskey v McDermott* it was held that a particularly skilled rally driver should meet a higher standard in relation to his passenger.

(2)   At least where pedestrians are concerned the decision seems to be based on the notion that they are entitled to expect a single objective standard from drivers, perhaps because they have no choice as to the quality of drivers to whom they are exposed, and no way of protecting themselves better from the less able. The same duty was held to be owed to passengers, although their damages may be reduced for contributory negligence if they knowingly travel with a driver of impaired ability: see p 339.

(3)   The same high standard applies even to drivers who are old or ill, as in *Roberts v Ramsbottom* where the defendant continued on a journey after having, unbeknown to him, suffered a mild stroke. He collided with several other vehicles, but despite the fact that the illness had impaired his judgment the court concluded that a reasonably prudent driver would have stopped driving after the first accident. Any such condition short of automatism would not affect the standard required by law.

(4)   Note Lord Denning's remarks on the role of policy where he comments that the courts' approach has been influenced by the availability of funds, in the form of compulsory insurance, to compensate the victims of road accidents provided that the driver is found to be liable.

(5)   The Australian courts have held that it is possible for a lower standard to be applied to less experienced drivers, see *Cook v Cook*, but this approach has not been followed in English law.

Mullin v Richards and another
[1998] I All ER 920 Court of Appeal

The plaintiff, a girl of 15, suffered serious injury while she and the defendant (also aged 15) were fencing with plastic rulers and a piece snapped off and entered her eye. The Court of Appeal, taking into account the fact that the defendant was not an adult, reversed the decision at first instance and held that she was not negligent.

Hutchison LJ: '... So far as negligence is concerned, the relevant principles are well settled ... In order to succeed the plaintiff must show that the defendant did an act which it was reasonably foreseeable would cause injury to the plaintiff, that the relationship between the plaintiff and the defendant was such as to give rise to a duty of care, and that the act was one which caused injury to the plaintiff. In the present case ... no difficulty arose as to the second and third requirements ... The argument centres on foreseeability. The test of foreseeability is an objective one; but the fact that the first defendant was at the time a 15-year-old schoolgirl is not irrelevant. The question for the Judge is not whether the actions of the defendant were such as an ordinarily prudent and reasonable adult in the defendant's situation would have realised gave rise to a risk of injury, it is whether an ordinarily prudent and reasonable 15-year-old schoolgirl in the defendant's situation would have realised as much. In that connection both counsel referred us to, and relied upon, the Australian decision in *McHale v Watson* [and, in particular, a passage] in the judgment of Kitto J. I cite a portion of the passage I have referred to, all of which was cited to us by [counsel for the defendant], and which [counsel for the plaintiff] has adopted as epitomising the correct approach:

> "The standard of care being objective, it is no answer for him, [that is a child] any more than it is for an adult, to say that the harm he caused was due to his being abnormally slow-witted, quick-tempered, absent-minded or inexperienced. But it does not follow that he cannot rely in his defence upon a limitation upon the capacity for foresight or prudence, not as being personal to himself, but as being characteristic of humanity at his stage of development and in that sense normal. By doing so he appeals to a standard of ordinariness, to an objective and not a subjective standard."

[Counsel for the plaintiff] also cited to us a passage in the judgment of Owen J:

> "... the standard by which his conduct is to be measured is not that to be expected of a reasonable adult but that reasonably to be expected of a child of the same age, intelligence and experience."

I venture to question the word "intelligence" in that sentence, but I understand Owen J to be making the same point essentially as was made by Kitto J. It is perhaps also material to have in mind the words of Salmon LJ in the case of *Gough v Thorne*, which is cited also by [counsel for the plaintiff], where he said:

"The question as to whether the Plaintiff can be said to have been guilty of contributory negligence depends on whether any ordinary child of 13½ can be expected to have done any more than this child did. I say 'any ordinary child'. I do not mean a paragon of prudence; nor do I mean a scatter-brained child; but the ordinary girl of 13½."

I need say no more about that principle as to the way in which age affects the assessment of negligence because counsel are agreed upon it and, despite the fact that we have been told that there has been a good deal of controversy in other jurisdictions and that there is no direct authority in this jurisdiction, the approach in *McHale* seems to me to have the advantage of obvious, indeed irrefutable, logic. Then, even if the requirements that I have so far summarised are satisfied with the consequence that negligence has been proved, the defendant will not be liable if the injury actually sustained is not foreseeable, that is to say is of a different kind from that which the defendant ought to have foreseen as the likely outcome of his want of care (see in that regard *Hughes v The Lord Advocate*).

Applying those principles to the facts of the present case the central question to which this appeal gives rise is whether on the facts found by the judge and in the light of the evidence before him he was entitled to conclude that an ordinary, reasonable 15-year-old schoolgirl in the first defendant's position would have appreciated that by participating to the extent that she did in a play fight, involving the use of plastic rulers as though they were swords, gave rise to a risk of injury to the plaintiff of the same general kind as she sustained. In that connection I emphasise that a mere possibility is not enough as passages in the well-known case of *Bolton v Stone* ... make clear ...

The judge, it seems to me, found negligence without there being material on which he could properly do so. He seems indeed from the language he used to have regarded it as axiomatic that if there was a fight going on, such as he found there was, a play fight, that imported that injury was reasonably foreseeable and from his finding that the ruler broke that there was necessarily dangerous or excessive violence. For my part, I would say that in the absence of evidence one simply does not know why the ruler broke, whether because it was unusually weak, unlike other rulers; whether because it had been damaged in some way; or whether because rulers of this sort are particularly prone to break; one does not know. What certainly one cannot infer, and the Judge was, I consider, not entitled to infer, was that there was here excessive violence or inappropriate violence over and above that which was inherent in the play fencing in which these two girls were indulging. This was in truth nothing more than a schoolgirls' game such as on the evidence was commonplace in this school and there was, I would hold, no justification for attributing to the participants the foresight of any significant risk of the likelihood of injury. They had seen it done elsewhere with some frequency. They had not heard it prohibited or received any warning about it. They had not been told of any injuries occasioned by it. They were not in any sense behaving culpably.

So far as foresight goes, had they paused to think they might, I suppose, have said: "It is conceivable that some unlucky injury might happen", but if asked if there was any likelihood of it or any real possibility of it, they would, I am sure, have said that they did not foresee any such possibility. Taking the view therefore that the learned Judge – who, as I have said, readily and almost without question accepted that on his findings of fact there was negligence on the part of both these young ladies – was wrong in his view and there was no evidence on which he could come to it, I would allow the appeal and direct that judgment be entered for the first defendant. I have to say that I appreciate that this result will be disappointing to the plaintiff for whom one can have nothing but sympathy, because she has suffered a grave injury through no fault of her own. But unfortunately she has failed to establish in my view that anyone was legally responsible for that injury and, accordingly, her claim should have failed.'

Comment

(1) In *Walmsley v Humenick*, a Canadian case, the British Columbia Supreme Court held that a five-year-old child was incapable of negligence because a child of such tender years had not sufficient mental capacity. In contributory negligence, the courts have recognised that a lower standard of care is to be expected of children, see *Gough v Thorne*; see also Occupiers' Liability Act 1957, s 2(3)(a). For another case concerning horseplay between schoolchildren, see *Wilson v Pringle* (p 504).

(2) It is possible that the defendant may be relieved of liability if the defendant's mental condition is such as to render the act involuntary: see the Canadian case *Buckley v Smith Transport*.

Wells v Cooper
[1958] 2 All ER 527 Court of Appeal

The plaintiff was injured when a door handle fitted by the defendant – a householder with some experience in do-it-yourself work – using three-quarter-inch screws came off in his hand, causing him to lose his balance. The Court of Appeal decided that the defendant had discharged his duty of care by meeting the standard of a reasonably competent carpenter.

Jenkins LJ: '... The duty owed by the defendant to the plaintiff was a duty to take reasonable care for his safety, and the question is whether on the facts of this case the defendant did take reasonable care to that end.

Counsel for the plaintiff formulates the issues (in effect) in this way: First, ought the defendant to have foreseen that if the handle came away when a person pulled it to shut the door as the plaintiff did that person might suffer injury; and secondly, if so, ought the defendant to have known that the screws which he used were not adequate to fix the handle to the door firmly enough to prevent any likelihood of such an occurrence?

We think that if the defendant had envisaged the possibility of the handle coming off in the hand of a person pulling on it he could hardly have failed to appreciate the likelihood of untoward consequences such as did in fact occur; and accordingly counsel for the plaintiff's second issue appears to us to be the substantial issue in the case. It involves consideration of the standard of care to be demanded of the defendant in relation to the fixing of the handle. As above related, the defendant did the work himself. We do not think the mere fact that he did it himself instead of employing a professional carpenter to do it constituted a breach of his duty of care. No doubt some kinds of work involve such highly specialised skill and knowledge, and create such serious dangers if not properly done, that an ordinary occupier owing a duty of care to others in regard to the safety of premises would fail in that duty if he undertook such work himself instead of employing experts to do it for him (see *Haseldine v Daw & Son Ltd* per Scott LJ). But the work here in question was not of that order. It was a trifling domestic replacement well within the competence of a householder accustomed to doing small carpentering jobs about his home, and of a kind which must be done every day by hundreds of householders up and down the country.

Accordingly, we think that the defendant did nothing unreasonable in undertaking the work himself. It behoved him, however, if he was to discharge his duty of care to persons such as the plaintiff, to do the work with reasonable care and skill, and we think that the degree of care and skill required of him must be measured not by reference to the degree of competence in such matters which he personally happened to possess, but by reference to the degree of care and skill which a reasonably competent carpenter might be expected to apply to the work in question. Otherwise, the extent of the protection that an invitee could claim in relation to work done by the invitor himself would vary according to the capacity of the invitor, who could free himself from liability merely by showing that he had done the best of which he was capable, however good, bad or indifferent that best might be.

Accordingly, we think that the standard of care and skill to be demanded of the defendant in order to discharge his duty of care to the plaintiff in the fixing of the new handle in the present case must be the degree of care and skill to be expected of a reasonably competent carpenter doing the work in question. This does not mean that the degree of care and skill required is to be measured by reference to the contractual obligations as to the quality of his work assumed by a professional carpenter working for reward, which would in our view set the standard too high. The question is simply what steps would a reasonably competent carpenter wishing to fix a handle such as this securely to a door such as this have taken with a view to achieving that object ...

In relation to a trifling and perfectly simple operation such as the fixing of the new handle we think that the defendant's experience of domestic carpentry is sufficient to justify his inclusion in the category of reasonably competent carpenters. The matter then stands thus. The defendant, a reasonably competent carpenter, used three-quarter inch screws, believing them to be adequate for the purpose of fixing the handle. There is no doubt that he was doing his best to make the handle secure and believed he had done so. Accordingly, he must be taken to have discharged his duty of reasonable care, unless the belief that three-quarter inch screws would be adequate was one which no reasonably competent carpenter could reasonably entertain, or in other words an obvious blunder which should at once have been apparent to him as a reasonably competent carpenter.'

Comment

(1)   So a person practising a skilled activity, despite having no formal qualifications in that field, is required to meet the standard of a reasonably competent person with that skill. In *The Lady Gwendolen*, for example, brewers who transported stout from Ireland in a negligently operated ship were held liable when it was involved in a collision. 'The law must apply a standard which is not relaxed to cater for their factual ignorance of all activities outside brewing: having become owners of ships, they must behave as reasonable ship-owners.'

(2)   While children fall at one end of the spectrum of standards imposed in negligence cases and experts fall at the other, in reality, the vast bulk of cases fall somewhere in between. It is for the court to decide exactly where on the scale each defendant fits. For example, in *Phillips v William Whitely Ltd* the plaintiff, who had had her ears pierced by a jeweller, suffered an infection. The court held that, even if the infection had been caused by the earpiercing, the defendants were not liable since their hygiene precautions met the standard of a reasonably competent earpiercing jeweller, and they were not required to achieve the standard of a surgeon.

Bolton v Stone and others
[1951] 1 All ER 1078 House of Lords

The respondent was standing on the highway beside the appellants' cricket ground when she was struck and injured by a cricket ball hit by a visiting batsman. The ball had travelled some 75 yards, cleared a 17-foot fence and continued a further 25 yards before hitting the respondent. The cricket ground had been used for 90 years and evidence from the last 30 revealed only six incidents of escaped balls with no damage having been caused by any. The House of Lords allowed the appeal on the basis that the likelihood of injury occurring was so slight that a reasonable man would be justified in ignoring it.

Lord Reid: '... This case, therefore, raises sharply the question what is the nature and extent of the duty of a person who promotes on his land operations which may cause damage to persons on an adjoining highway. Is it that he must not carry out or permit an operation which he knows or ought to know clearly can cause such damage, however improbable that result may be, or is it that he is only bound to take into account the possibility of such damage if such damage is a likely or probable consequence of what he does or permits, or if the risk of damage is such that a reasonable man, careful of the safety of his neighbour, would regard that risk as material? I do not know of any case where this question has had to be decided or even where it has been fully discussed. Of course there are many cases in which somewhat similar questions have arisen, but, generally speaking, if injury to another person from the defendants' acts is reasonably foreseeable the chance that injury will result is substantial and it does not matter in which way the duty is stated. In such cases I do not think that much assistance is to be got from analysing the language which a judge has used. More assistance is to be got from cases where judges have clearly chosen their language with care in setting out a principle, but even so, statements of the law must be read in light of the facts of the particular case. Nevertheless, making all allowances for this, I do find at least a tendency to base duty rather on the likelihood of damage to others than on its foreseeability alone.

The definition of negligence which has, perhaps, been most often quoted is that of Alderson B, in *Blyth v Birmingham Waterworks Co* ... I think that reasonable men do, in fact, take into account the degree of risk and do not act on a bare possibility as they would if the risk were more substantial. A more recent attempt to find a basis for man's legal duty to his neighbour is that of Lord Atkin in *Donoghue v Stevenson*: "You must take reasonable care to avoid acts or omissions which you can reasonably foresee would be likely to injure your neighbour." Parts of Lord Atkin's statement have been criticised as being too wide, but I am not aware that it has been stated that any part of it is too narrow. Lord Atkin does not say "Which you can reasonably foresee could injure your neighbour": he introduces the limitation "would be likely to injure your neighbour". Lord Macmillan said in *Bourhill v Young*:

> "The duty to take care is the duty to avoid doing or omitting to do anything the doing or omitting to do which may have as its reasonable and probable consequence injury to others and the duty is owed to those to whom injury may reasonably and probably be anticipated if the duty is not observed."

Lord Thankerton in *Glasgow Corpn v Muir*, after quoting this statement, said:

> "In my opinion, it has long been held in Scotland that all that a person can be held bound to foresee are the reasonable and probable consequences of the failure to take care, judged by the standard of the ordinary reasonable man ... The court must be careful to place itself in the position of the person charged with the duty and to consider what he or she should have

reasonably anticipated as a natural and probable consequence of neglect, and not to give undue weight to the fact that a distressing accident has happened ..."

The law of Scotland does not differ in this matter from the law of England.

There are other statements which may seem to differ but which I do not think are really inconsistent with this. For example, in *Fardon v Harcourt-Rivington*, Lord Dunedin said:

"This is such an extremely unlikely event that I do not think any reasonable man could be convicted of negligence if he did not take into account the possibility of such an occurrence and provide against it ... people must guard against reasonable probabilities, but they are not bound to guard against fantastic possibilities."

I doubt whether Lord Dunedin meant the division into reasonable probabilities and fantastic possibilities to be exhaustive so that anything more than a fantastic possibility must be regarded as a reasonable probability. What happened in that case was that a dog left in a car broke the window and a splinter from the glass entered the plaintiff's eye. Before that had happened it might well have been described as a fantastic possibility and Lord Dunedin did not have to consider a case nearer the border-line. I do not think it necessary to discuss other statements which may seem to be at variance with the trend of authority which I have quoted because I have not found any which is plainly inconsistent with it, and I have left out of account cases where the defendant clearly owed a duty to the plaintiff and by his negligence caused damage to the plaintiff. In such cases questions have arisen whether damages can only be recovered in respect of consequences which were foreseeable or were natural and probable, or whether damages can be recovered in respect of all consequences, whether foreseeable or probable or not, but remoteness of damage in this sense appears to me to be a different question from that which arises in the present case.

Counsel for the respondent in the present case had to put his case so high as to say that, at least as soon as one ball had been driven into the road in the ordinary course of a match, the appellants could and should have realised that that might happen again, and that, if it did, someone might be injured, and that that was enough to put on the appellants a duty to take steps to prevent such an occurrence. If the true test is foreseeability alone I think that must be so. Once a ball has been driven on to a road without there being anything extraordinary to account for the fact, there is clearly a risk that another will follow and if it does there is clearly a chance, small though it may be, that somebody may be injured. On the theory that it is foreseeability alone that matters it would be irrelevant to consider how often a ball might be expected to land in the road and it would not matter whether the road was the busiest street or the quietest country lane. The only difference between these cases is in the degree of risk. It would take a good deal to make me believe that the law has departed so far from the standards which guide ordinary careful people in ordinary life. In the crowded conditions of modern life even the most careful person cannot avoid creating some risks and accepting others. What a man must not do, and what I think a careful man tries not to do, is to create a risk which is substantial. Of course, there are numerous cases where special circumstances require that a higher standard shall be observed and where that is recognised by the law, but I do not think that this case comes within any such special category.'

Lord Radcliffe: '... I can see nothing unfair in the appellants being required to compensate the respondent for the serious injury that she has received as a result of the sport that they have organised on their cricket ground at Cheetham Hill, but the law of negligence is concerned less with what is fair than with what is culpable, and I cannot persuade myself that the appellants have been guilty of any culpable act or omission in this case ...

If the test whether there has been a breach of duty were to depend merely on the answer to the question whether this accident was a reasonably foreseeable risk, I think that there would have been a breach of duty, for that such an accident might take place some time or other might very reasonably have been present to the minds of the appellants. It was quite foreseeable, and there would have been nothing unreasonable in allowing the imagination to dwell on the possibility of its occurring. There was, however, only a remote, perhaps I ought to say only a very remote, chance of the accident taking place at any particular time, for, if it was to happen, not only had a ball to carry the fence round the ground, but it had also to coincide in its arrival with the presence of some person on what does not look like a crowded thoroughfare and actually to strike that person in some way that would cause sensible injury.

Those being the facts, a breach of duty has taken place if they show the appellants guilty of a failure to take reasonable care to prevent the accident. One may phrase it as "reasonable care" or "ordinary care" or "proper care" – all these phrases are to be found in decisions of authority – but the fact remains that, unless there here has been something which a reasonable man would blame as falling beneath the standard of conduct that he would set for himself and require of his neighbour, there has been no breach of legal duty, and here, I think, the respondent's case breaks down. It seems to me that a reasonable man, taking account of the chances against an accident happening, would not have felt himself called on either to abandon the use of the ground for cricket or to increase the height of his surrounding fences. He would have done what the appellants did. In other words, he would have done nothing. Whether, if the unlikely event of an accident did occur and his play turn to another's hurt, he would have thought it equally proper to offer no more consolation to his victim than the reflection that a social being is not immune from social risks, I do not say, for I do not think that that is a consideration which is relevant to legal liability.'

Comment

(1) Note that it is *likelihood* and not mere *foreseeability* which matters. Likelihood was calculated here on a statistical basis, taking into account not only the chances of a ball escaping but also the likelihood of its causing damage if it did. This was based on past evidence over a considerable length of time. Clearly the calculation might not have been so straightforward were a ball to have escaped on the very first day of play at the ground.

(2) It must be remembered that likelihood is only one factor to be weighed, and that even a very small risk is not to be ignored without justification: see *The Wagon Mound (No 2)*.

(3) For another case illustrating judicial attitudes towards the playing of cricket see *Miller v Jackson*.

(4) The likelihood of injury may be increased by some aspect of the plaintiff him or herself, as in *Haley v London Electricity Board* where a blind pedestrian was injured when a barrier which would have protected a sighted person from a hole in the pavement proved insufficient to save him from harm. Similarly, the increased risk to children may dictate that special precautions be taken, even, as in *Black v Kent County Council*, that the activity be refrained from altogether.

Watson v British Boxing Board of Control Ltd and another [2001] QB 1134 Court of Appeal

W, a professional boxer, suffered head injuries during a fight. He was treated at the scene by doctors, present in accordance with the regulations of the defendant Board. He was then taken to hospital and, some 30 minutes later, resuscitated. He later underwent surgery but had by then suffered permanent brain damage. He brought an action in negligence against the Board claiming that they were under a duty to ensure that all reasonable steps were taken to ensure that he received immediate and effective medical treatment should he sustain injury in the fight, including immediate resuscitation at the ringside.

Lord Phillips of Worth Matravers MR: '...

BREACH OF DUTY

The relevant allegations of negligence can be summarised as follows. The board failed to inform itself adequately about the risks inherent in a blow to the head. The board failed to require the provision of resuscitation equipment at the venue, together with the presence of persons capable of operating such equipment. The board failed to require a medical examination of W immediately following the conclusion of the contest. The board failed to ensure that those running the contest knew which hospitals in the vicinity had a neurosurgical capability.

In order to explain these allegations, I propose to summarise the evidence on: the nature of injuries such as those suffered by W; ... the manner in which such injuries should have been treated at the ringside; and the treatment actually provided to W.

BOXER'S BRAIN DAMAGE

Where a blow to the head results in immediate impairment or loss of consciousness, this is normally the result of temporary deformation of the brain caused by acceleration or deceleration of movement of the head. Effects are usually short-lived and do not produce lasting damage. W suffered such an injury when he was knocked down in the eleventh round. Any loss of consciousness was short lived – he regained his feet and walked to his corner.

A primary injury such as that described can have secondary consequences which are much more serious. ... [which] can result in cumulative damage to the brain, leading sooner or later to death. W suffered some, at least, of these secondary effects, which were the cause of his permanent brain damage. ...

TREATMENT THAT SHOULD HAVE BEEN PROVIDED AT THE RINGSIDE

It was the evidence of W's experts that, while brain damage of the type I have described is cumulative, what happens in the first ten minutes is particularly critical. In view of this, they said that there should have been available at the ringside resuscitation equipment and doctors who knew how to use this. W should have been resuscitated on losing consciousness and then taken directly to the nearest hospital with a neurosurgical capability, which should have been standing by to operate without delay. ...

THE MEDICAL FACILITIES PROVIDED TO W AT THE RINGSIDE

The facilities provided accorded with the advice to medical officers issued by the board's medical committee ... The material passages of this advice were:

> "The role of medical officer at a professional boxing tournament is a very important one and requires an adequate working knowledge of sports medicine, the diagnosis and treatment of acute medical conditions and a working knowledge of the training and dietary requirements of a professional boxer and athlete ...
>
> Each doctor is expected to attend a tournament fully equipped to cover all emergencies. He should certainly carry ... a Brooks airway and a padded spatula in case of a rare occurrence of fitting and the need to establish an airway ...

As already stated, no tournament is allowed to commence or continue without one doctor sitting ringside. It is not sufficient for the doctor to be in the vicinity of the ring as in the case of an emergency the speed of the doctor's reactions in treating this are all-important ... Throughout these contests the boxers' performance should be noted and any untoward medical problems arising should be reported to the area council or board. ... If any doubt arises concerning a boxer's condition then referral to a local hospital for emergency treatment or advice should be undertaken and a report sent to the board ...

As already mentioned the referee is in sole charge of the contest, but if a boxer is counted out and fails to rise it is the doctor's duty to get into the ring as quickly as possible and institute emergency treatment should this be required.

Most boxers recover very quickly having been knocked down and counted out and most, in fact, are fully conscious, if somewhat dazed, by the time the count reaches ten. However, ... If the boxer remains unconscious, then full emergency procedures should be undertaken, ... and, if needs be, the other doctor should by then have rung ambulance control and have contacted the local hospital to inform them of the problem. It is always better to err on the side of caution ..."

In addition to the two doctors required by the rules, there was, on the direction of the board, a third medical officer present. There was also an ambulance standing by which had resuscitation equipment and a paramedic who knew how to use this. His evidence was that it was his practice to use it where a patient was experiencing breathing difficulties.

THE JUDGE'S FINDINGS

The judge's findings in relation to breach of duty appear from the following passages in his judgment:

"The standard response where the presence of subdural bleeding is known or suspected has been agreed since at least 1980, which is to intubate, ventilate, sedate, paralyse, and, in Britain at least, to administer mannitol. The patient can then be taken straight to the nearest neurosurgical unit. ... I have not heard evidence to the effect that the board or its medical advisers had before this incident considered, and for some reason decided not to follow, what may not unfairly be called this protocol. I can only conclude that for some reason no thought was given to the practicality of introducing this standard response ...

Nothing that I have heard persuades me that there was any impracticality, whether in terms of manpower or in cost to the promoters, in the board having included such a requirement in their rules. I have had no evidence to suggest that a doctor of suitable grade and with the necessary skills would command a fee substantially in excess of that payable to the board's doctors under its system, nor that there would be any significant cost in having the necessary equipment to hand ...

I am left with the clear impression that the board's medical advisers have not looked outside their personal expertise. The board has argued that until this accident no one had suggested that they should institute this protocol. That is true as a fact. The duty of the board and of those advising it on medical matters was to be prospective in their thinking and seek competent advice as to how a recognised danger could be combated. In some circumstances it can be very relevant to show that no criticism had been received about this or that practice but I have seen nothing to suggest that that is a point in this context ...

Accordingly, I am left in no doubt that the board was in breach of its duty in that it did not institute some such system or protocol as Mr H [the consultant neurosurgeon who had operated on W] was to propose. There is no question but that anyone with the appropriate expertise would have advised such a system whatever reservations they may have had, as had Professor Teasdale, about its ultimate utility."

Later in the judgment the judge suggested, by implication, that the board's rules should have included a requirement that a boxer who was knocked out, or seemed unfit to defend himself, should be immediately seen by a doctor. ...

THE BOARD'S CHALLENGE TO THE JUDGMENT

The first challenge to the judge's finding on breach of duty was that he applied the wrong test. The board's grounds of appeal argued that in making policy decisions, the board ought not to be held to be negligent unless such decisions were found to be wholly irrational. This appears to be an attempt to import into the law of negligence concepts of public law. If so, it is misguided. The issue in this action is not whether the right policy was adopted but simply whether proper care was used in making provision for medical treatment of W. The ordinary test of reasonable skill and care is the correct one to apply.

The board next drew attention to evidence that a member of the public having sustained brain damage in a road accident would not expect to receive from the ambulance attending the scene the resuscitation service which the judge held should have been available at the ringside. The board argued that this demonstrated that the standard applied by the judge was too high. This point was put to the judge. He rejected it, holding that the standard to be expected of an ambulance dealing with every kind of medical emergency was not the same as the standard to be expected from those making provision for a particular and serious risk which was one of a limited number likely to arise. I think that the judge was right. Serious brain damage such as that suffered by W, though happily an uncommon consequence of a boxing injury, represented the most serious risk posed by the sport and one that required to be addressed.

The next ground advanced by the board in support of the contention that the judge applied too high a standard was that there was no evidence that any other boxing authority in the world imposed more rigorous requirements than those of the board's rules. The judge accepted that this was the case but ruled that in the final analysis it was for the court to determine whether even the most widely followed practice was acceptable. In this the judge was correct.

Next the board argued that the presence of an ambulance, with resuscitation equipment, should have satisfied the judge that this aspect of medical care was adequately provided. There are a number of problems with this submission. In the first place the paramedic in the ambulance was not trained to use resuscitation equipment as a matter of course where a head injury was involved. He would only use it to overcome breathing difficulties. In the second place it was not practical to use this equipment while the ambulance was on the move. In these circumstances, it is no cause for surprise that the equipment was not in fact used. The essence of W's case is that there should have been a system under which such equipment would not merely be available, but used immediately in the event of a brain injury.

The board also argued that the nearest hospital with an accident and emergency department was so close that a system which delayed the possibility of resuscitation for the few minutes that would be necessary to get to the hospital was satisfactory. In fact, it took very much longer than a few minutes to get to the hospital, for reasons that were not identified at the trial. In my judgment the judge was entitled to conclude that the standard of reasonable care required that there should be a resuscitation facility at the ringside. Had the ambulance been, in fact, just as satisfactory, this would have meant that the absence of a rule requiring such a facility would have had no causative effect. That, however, did not prove to be the position.

Next the board attacked the implicit finding of the judge that the rules should have required the doctor to enter the ring as soon as a boxer was counted out or deemed unfit to defend himself. The board contended that this was unjustifiable, since it would require rules which in effect instructed doctors as to how to perform their duties. I find this distinction between instructions as to duties and instructions as to how to perform duties elusive and over-subtle. I see no reason why the rules should not have contained the provision suggested by the judge. In any event I believe that this point vanishes when causation is considered.

The final point taken by the board was that it did not receive advice in relation to the desirability of ringside resuscitation until after W's injuries. The board argued that, until it received such advice, it could not reasonably be expected to alter its recommendations and rules in relation to ringside treatment. ...

W's injuries were not, however, without precedent. There had been a number of similar cases in the 1980s. The issue is whether the standard of reasonable care required the board to change its practice in order to address the risks of such injuries before [this] fight.

There was evidence that the board's medical committee met regularly to consider medical precautions. [But] the judge concluded that for some reason no thought was given to the practicality of introducing at the ringside what he found had been a standard response, where the presence of subdural bleeding was known or suspected, since at least 1980. The judge went on to review such statistical evidence as there was in relation to the frequency of occurrence of head injuries in boxing and observed that there had been no evidence to suggest that the board considered and balanced the difficulty of providing the adequate response to the risks of head injury against their frequency of occurrence and severity of outcome.

...

The judge held that it was the duty of the board, and of those advising it on medical matters, to be prospective in their thinking and to seek competent advice as to how a recognised danger could best be combated. He held that he was left in no doubt that the board was in breach of its duty in that it did not institute some such system or protocol as that which Mr H was later to propose. He held that anyone with the appropriate expertise would have advised the adoption of such a system. I consider that these were proper findings on the evidence and that W's case on breach of duty was made out.'

Comment

(1) In *Gillon v Chief Constable, Strathclyde Police* a police officer on crowd control duty at a football match was injured when one of the players accidentally ran into her as she patrolled the edge of the pitch. She sued both the football club for failing to provide a barrier around the pitch, and the chief constable for failing to warn her to keep a lookout for her own safety. The court applied the approach in *Bolton v Stone*, and concluded from 'the lack of any previous incidents ... across the whole spectrum of football, given the literally thousands of hours police officers must spend in [similar] positions' that the risk was so minimal that a reasonable man might be justified in ignoring it, particularly in the light of the impracticability of providing precautions in terms of expense, the fact that a barrier would interfere with the spectators' view and that it might, in any event, constitute a hazard for the players. Her claim against the chief constable failed as she could not show that a warning would have prevented the accident from happening.

(2) In *Smoldon v Whitworth and another* a 17-year-old rugby player was seriously injured when a scrum collapsed. He sued the referee alleging that he had failed to reach the appropriate standard of care for a referee of Colts

matches, i.e. for players aged under 19. The Court of Appeal noted that certain new rules had been introduced specifically to 'protect young players against spinal injuries caused by excessive impact on engagement and by collapsed scrums' and that 'the physical differences between teenagers and grown men' which had prompted the introduction of these rules indicated the need for a higher standard of care from a referee in such matches.

(3) The standard to be expected from participants in competitive sports *vis-à-vis* one another was analysed by the Court of Appeal in *Caldwell v Maguire and Fitzgerald*, in which the claimant, C, had been seriously injured during a horse race and the defendants had been found guilty by a stewards' enquiry of careless riding. The claimant lost at first instance and appealed, arguing that the judge, in setting a high threshold for liability, had set a standard of recklessness rather than negligence. The Court of Appeal, dismissing the appeal, held that the high threshold reflected the realities of a highly competitive sport in which momentary carelessness could not be equated with negligence. Applying principles derived from earlier sporting authorities such as *Condon v Basi* and *Wooldridge v Sumner* (see p 336), Judge LJ said:

'30 ... In an action for damages by one participant in a sporting contest against another participant in the same game or event, the issue of negligence cannot be resolved in a vacuum. It is fact specific.

31 We are here concerned with a split-second, virtually instantaneous, decision made by professional sportsmen entrusted with powerful animals, paid and required by the rules of their sport to ride them, at speed, to victory or, failing victory, to the best possible placing: in other words, to beat all the other horses in the race, or endeavour to do so. The course has no lanes; nor is it straight. The horse, as this case demonstrated, has a will of its own. The demands on professional jockeys to ride at all are very heavy. They require skill and physical and mental courage. To win, beyond skill and courage, they need determination and concentration, the ability rapidly to assess and re-assess the constantly changing racing conditions, and to adjust their own riding and tactics accordingly – a quality that must depend in part on experience and in part on intuition or instinct.

32 Accidents and the risk of injury, sometimes catastrophic, both to horses and to riders, are an inevitable concomitant of every horse race – certainly over hurdles. All National Hunt jockeys know the risks. The rules of racing which bind them all, and the jockeys' own responsibilities to each other during the race, properly fulfilled, are intended to reduce the inevitable risks. But they cannot extinguish them. And, as a final ingredient, what is actually taking place on the real racecourse is not nearly as sanitised as it can appear to be even to spectators in the stand or, more particularly, to those watching at home on television. Jockeys and horses

are often in close proximity to the other runners. There is a good deal of noise and inevitable tension. Mistakes by riders and horses are inevitable; and fortune, good or bad, plays its part in each race, as it does in any other sporting event.'

Tuckey LJ, agreeing, also commented:

'The Jockey Club's rules and its findings are of course relevant matters to be taken into account, but, as the authorities make clear, the finding that the respondents were guilty of careless riding is not determinative of negligence. As the judge said, there is a difference between response by the regulatory authority and response by the courts in the shape of a finding of legal liability.'

Paris v Stepney Borough Council
[1951] 1 All ER 42 House of Lords

The appellant was employed as a fitter in the garage of the respondent borough council. To the knowledge of the respondents he had only one eye. While he was using a hammer to remove a bolt, a chip of metal flew off and entered his good eye so injuring it that he became totally blind. The respondent did not provide goggles for the appellant to wear and there was evidence that it was not the ordinary practice for employers to supply goggles to men employed in garages on the repair and maintenance of vehicles. The House of Lords found the respondents liable, taking into account the likelihood of injury and its serious effect on this appellant.

Lord Normand:'... My Lords, this appeal involves a question of general importance affecting the common law duty which an employer owes to his employee. It is this. A workman is suffering, to the employer's knowledge, from a disability which, though it does not increase the risk of an accident's occurring while he is at work, does increase the risk of serious injury if an accident should befall him. Is the special risk of injury a relevant consideration in determining the precautions which the employer should take in fulfilment of the duty of care which he owes to the workman? ...

It is not disputed that the respondents' duty of care is a duty owed to their employees as individuals. The respondents contend, however, that, though it is not a duty owed to the employees collectively, they must take account in fulfilling the duty only of any disability that increases the risk of an accident's occurring. For that proposition no authority was cited, and, in my opinion, it is contrary to principle. The test is what precautions would the ordinary, reasonable and prudent man take? The relevant considerations include all those facts which could affect the conduct of a reasonable and prudent man and his decision the precautions to be taken. Would a reasonable and prudent man be influenced, not only by the greater or less probability of an accident occurring but also by the gravity of the consequences if an accident does occur? In *Mackintosh v Mackintosh* Lord Neaves, considering a case of alleged negligence in muir burning, said:

" ... it must be observed that in all cases the amount of care which a prudent man will take must vary infinitely according to circumstances. No prudent man in carrying a lighted candle through a powder magazine would fail to take more care than if he was going through a damp cellar. The amount of care will be proportionate to the degree of risk run, and to the magnitude of the mischief that may be occasioned."

In *Northwestern Utilities Ltd v London Guarantee & Accident Co Ltd* Lord Wright, dealing with the risk of grave damage which may be caused by gas escaping from a main, said:

"The degree of care which that duty involves must be proportioned to the degree of risk involved if the duty should not be fulfilled."

The learned editor of *Salmond on the Law of Torts* (10th edn.) similarly says: "There are two factors in determining the magnitude of a risk – the seriousness of the injury risked, and the likelihood of the injury being in fact caused." These are, in my opinion, accurate statements both of the law and of the ordinary man's conduct in taking precautions for his own safety. "No reasonable man handles a stick of dynamite and a walking-stick in the same way." See *Winfield's Textbook of the Law of Tort* (4th edn.).

The court's task of deciding what precautions a reasonable and prudent man would take in the circumstances of a particular case may not be easy. Nevertheless, the judgment of the reasonable and prudent man should be allowed its common everyday scope, and it should not be restrained from considering the foreseeable consequences of an accident and their seriousness for the person to whom the duty of care is owed. Such a restriction, if it might sometimes simplify the task of the judge or jury, would be an undue and artificial simplification of the problem to be solved. If the courts were now to take the narrow view proposed by the respondents the cleavage between the legal conception of the precautions which a reasonable and prudent man would take and the precautions which reasonable and prudent men do in fact take would lessen the respect which the administration of justice ought to command. To guard against possible misunderstanding it may be well to add here that the seriousness of the injury or damage risked and the likelihood of its being in fact caused may not be the only relevant factors. For example, Asquith LJ, in *Daborn v Bath Tramways Motor Co Ltd & Trevor Smithey*, pointed out that it is sometimes necessary to take account of the consequence of not assuming a risk.'

Comment

The duty of an employer is owed to each employee as an individual, and so a reasonable employer will take into account any factor which increases the risk of particular harm. This does not mean, however, that the employer must guarantee the safety of an individual merely because of knowledge that he or she is particularly vulnerable in some way. In *Withers v Perry Chain Co Ltd* the plaintiff, to her employers' knowledge, suffered from dermatitis which was aggravated by her job. The court held that, by allocating her tasks in the cleanest process available, the defendants had taken all reasonable steps and were not therefore negligent.

Hatton v Sutherland, Barber v Somerset County Council, Jones v Sandwell Metropolitan Borough Council, Bishop v Baker Refractories Ltd
[2002] 2 All ER 1 Court of Appeal

The defendant employers appealed against findings of liability in respect of four claimants awarded damages for psychiatric illness caused by stress at work. Two were teachers in comprehensive schools, one was an administrative assistant at a local authority training centre, and the other was a raw material operative in a factory. J had twice formally complained to her employer that her health was being harmed by problems at work, but the other claimants had not informed their employers that they were suffering from work-related stress. The Court of Appeal allowed three of the appeals, but upheld the decision in J's case. It held that no special control mechanisms applied in such cases, and outlined the factors to be taken into account by the court in determining whether the harm was reasonably foreseeable. It also held that no occupation was to be regarded as so inherently stressful as to render resulting psychological illness always foreseeable, emphasising instead the need to assess the foreseeable effect on each employee as an individual.

Hale LJ: '...

[13] When imposing duties and setting standards, the law tries to strike a balance which is reasonable to both sides. Here there are weighty considerations on each side. It is in everyone's interests that management should be encouraged to recognise the existence and causes of occupational stress and take sensible steps to minimise it within their organisation. It is in the interest of the individual employees who may suffer harm if their employers do not. It is in the interest of the particular enterprise which may lose efficiency and workers if it does not. It is in the public interest that public services should not suffer or public money be wasted. ...

[14] The law of tort has an important function in setting standards for employers as well as for drivers, manufacturers, health care professionals and many others whose carelessness may cause harm. But if the standard of care expected of employers is set too high, or the threshold of liability too low, there may also be unforeseen and unwelcome effects upon the employment market. In particular,

employers may be even more reluctant than they already are to take on people with a significant psychiatric history or an acknowledged vulnerability to stress-related disorders. If employers are expected to make searching inquiries of employees who have been off sick, then more employees may be vulnerable to dismissal or demotion on ill-health grounds. If particular employments are singled out as ones in which special care is needed, then other benefits which are available to everyone in those employments, such as longer holidays, better pensions or earlier retirement, may be under threat.

[15]   Some things are no one's fault. No one can blame an employee who tries to soldier on despite his own desperate fears that he cannot cope, perhaps especially where those fears are groundless. No one can blame an employee for being reluctant to give clear warnings to his employer of the stress he is feeling. His very job, let alone his credibility or hopes of promotion, may be at risk. Few would blame an employee for continuing or returning to work despite the warnings of his doctor that he should give it up. There are many reasons why the job may be precious to him. On the other hand it may be difficult in those circumstances to blame the employer for failing to recognise the problem and what might be done to solve it.

[16]   There is an argument that stress is so prevalent in some employments, of which teaching is one, and employees so reluctant to disclose it, that all employers should have in place systems to detect it and prevent its developing into actual harm. As the above discussion shows, this raises some difficult issues of policy and practice which are unsuitable for resolution in individual cases before the courts. If knowledge advances to such an extent as to justify the imposition of obligations upon some or all employers to take particular steps to protect their employees from stress-related harm, this is better done by way of regulations imposing specific statutory duties. In the meantime the ordinary law of negligence governs the matter.

[17]   However, we do know of schemes now being developed and encouraged which recognise and respond to the peculiar problems presented both to employees and employers. ... Obviously, not all employers have the resources to put such systems in place, but an employer who does have a system along those lines is unlikely to be found in breach of his duty of care towards his employees.

3. THE LAW

[18]   Several times while hearing these appeals we were invited to go back to first principles. Liability in negligence depends upon three interrelated requirements: the existence of a duty to take care; a failure to take the care which can reasonably be expected in the circumstances; and damage suffered as a result of that failure. These elements do not exist in separate compartments: the existence of the duty, for example, depends upon the type of harm suffered. Foreseeability of what might

happen if care is not taken is relevant at each stage of the inquiry. Nevertheless, the traditional elements are always a useful tool of analysis, both in general and in particular cases.

Duty

[19]   The existence of a duty of care can be taken for granted. All employers have a duty to take reasonable care for the safety of their employees: to see that reasonable care is taken to provide them with a safe place of work, safe tools and equipment, and a safe system of working (see *Wilsons and Clyde Coal Co Ltd v English*). However, where psychiatric harm is suffered, the law distinguishes between "primary" and "secondary" victims. [Hale LJ referred to the analysis in *Page v Smith*, *Alcock v Chief Constable of South Yorkshire Police* and *White v Chief Constable of the South Yorkshire Police*, and continued.] Taken to its logical conclusion this would apply the same distinction between those inside and those outside the zone of foreseeable risk of physical harm to the employer's general duty of care to his employees.

[20]   We have not been invited to go down that road, no doubt because it is not open to us. In *Petch v Comrs of Customs and Excise* it was accepted that the ordinary principles of employers' liability applied to a claim for psychiatric illness arising from employment, although the claim failed. In the landmark case of *Walker v Northumberland CC*, Colman J applied those same principles in upholding the claim. Both have recently been cited with approval in this court in *Garrett v Camden London BC*. Also in *White's* case, Lord Hoffmann stated:

> "The control mechanisms were plainly never intended to apply to all cases of psychiatric injury. They contemplate that the injury has been caused in consequence of death or injury suffered (or apprehended to have been suffered or as likely to be suffered) by someone else."

As to *Walker's* case, he commented: "The employee ... was in no sense a secondary victim. His mental breakdown was caused by the strain of doing the work which his employer had required him to do." ...

[22]   There are, therefore, no special control mechanisms applying to claims for psychiatric (or physical) injury or illness arising from the stress of doing the work which the employee is required to do. But these claims do require particular care in determination, because they give rise to some difficult issues of foreseeability and causation and, we would add, identifying a relevant breach of duty. As Simon Brown LJ pithily put it in *Garrett's* case:

> "Many, alas, suffer breakdowns and depressive illnesses and a significant proportion could doubtless ascribe some at least of their problems to the strains and stresses of their work situation: be it simply overworking, the tensions of difficult relationships, career prospect worries, fears or feelings of

discrimination or harassment, to take just some examples. *Unless, however, there was a real risk of breakdown which the claimant's employers ought reasonably to have foreseen and which they ought properly to have averted, there can be no liability.*" (My emphasis.)

Foreseeability

[23]   To say that the employer has a duty of care to his employee does not tell us what he has to do (or refrain from doing) in any particular case. The issue in most if not all of these cases is whether the employer should have taken positive steps to safeguard the employee from harm: his sins are those of omission rather than commission. [Counsel] for the appellant defendant in *Bishop's* case, saw this as a question of defining the duty; [Counsel] for the appellant defendant in *Jones'* case, saw it as a question of setting the standard of care in order to decide whether it had been broken. Whichever is the correct analysis, the threshold question is whether this kind of harm to this particular employee was reasonably foreseeable. The question is not whether psychiatric injury is foreseeable in a person of "ordinary fortitude". The employer's duty is owed to each individual employee, not to some as yet unidentified outsider (see *Paris v Stepney BC*). The employer knows who his employee is. It may be that he knows, as in *Paris'* case, or ought to know, of a particular vulnerability; but he may not. Because of the very nature of psychiatric disorder, as a sufficiently serious departure from normal or average psychological functioning to be labelled a disorder, it is bound to be harder to foresee than is physical injury. ...

[24]   However, are there some occupations which are so intrinsically stressful that resulting physical or psychological harm is always foreseeable? ... The notion that some occupations are in themselves dangerous to mental health is not borne out by the literature to which we have already referred: it is not the job but the interaction between the individual and the job which causes the harm. Stress is a subjective concept: the individual's perception that the pressures placed upon him are greater than he may be able to meet. Adverse reactions to stress are equally individual, ranging from minor physical symptoms to major mental illness.

[25]   All of this points to there being a single test: whether a harmful reaction to the pressures of the workplace is reasonably foreseeable in the individual employee concerned. Such a reaction will have two components: (1) an injury to health; which (2) is attributable to stress at work. The answer to the foreseeability question will therefore depend upon the interrelationship between the particular characteristics of the employee concerned and the particular demands which the employer casts upon him. As was said in *McLoughlin v Grovers*, expert evidence may be helpful although it can never be determinative of what a reasonable employer should have foreseen. A number of factors are likely to be relevant.

[26]   These include the nature and extent of the work being done by the employee. Employers should be more alert to picking up signs from an employee

who is being overworked in an intellectually or emotionally demanding job than from an employee whose workload is no more than normal for the job or whose job is not particularly demanding for him or her. It will be easier to conclude that harm is foreseeable if the employer is putting pressure upon the individual employee which is in all the circumstances of the case unreasonable. Also relevant is whether there are signs that others doing the same work are under harmful levels of stress. There may be others who have already suffered injury to their health arising from their work. Or there may be an abnormal level of sickness and absence amongst others at the same grade or in the same department. But if there is no evidence of this, then the focus must turn to the individual, as Colman J put it in *Walker's* case:

> "Accordingly, the question is whether it ought to have been foreseen that Mr Walker was exposed to a risk of mental illness materially higher than that which would ordinarily affect a social services middle manager in his position with a really heavy workload."

[27]   More important are the signs from the employee himself. Here again, it is important to distinguish between signs of stress and signs of impending harm to health. Stress is merely the mechanism which may but usually does not lead to damage to health. *Walker's* case is an obvious illustration: Mr Walker was a highly conscientious and seriously overworked manager of a social work area office with a heavy and emotionally demanding case load of child abuse cases. Yet although he complained and asked for help and for extra leave, the judge held that his first mental breakdown was not foreseeable. There was, however, liability when he returned to work with a promise of extra help which did not materialise and experienced a second breakdown only a few months later. If the employee or his doctor makes it plain that unless something is done to help there is a clear risk of a breakdown in mental or physical health, then the employer will have to think what can be done about it.

[28]   Harm to health may sometimes be foreseeable without such an express warning. Factors to take into account would be frequent or prolonged absences from work which are uncharacteristic for the person concerned; these could be for physical or psychological complaints; but there must also be good reason to think that the underlying cause is occupational stress rather than other factors; this could arise from the nature of the employee's work or from complaints made about it by the employee or from warnings given by the employee or others around him.

[29]   But when considering what the reasonable employer should make of the information which is available to him, from whatever source, what assumptions is he entitled to make about his employee and to what extent he is bound to probe further into what he is told? Unless he knows of some particular problem or vulnerability, an employer is usually entitled to assume that his employee is up to the normal pressures of the job. It is only if there is something specific about the

job or the employee or the combination of the two that he has to think harder. But thinking harder does not necessarily mean that he has to make searching or intrusive inquiries. Generally he is entitled to take what he is told by or on behalf of the employee at face value. If he is concerned he may suggest that the employee consults his own doctor or an occupational health service. But he should not without a very good reason seek the employee's permission to obtain further information from his medical advisors. Otherwise he would risk unacceptable invasions of his employee's privacy.

[30] It was argued that the employer is entitled to take the expiry of a GP's certificate as implicitly suggesting that the employee is now fit to return to work and even that he is no longer at risk of suffering the same sort of problem again. This cannot be right. A GP's certificate is limited in time but many disorders are not self-limiting and may linger on for some considerable time. Yet an employee who is anxious to return to work, for whatever reason, may not go back to his GP for a further certificate when the current one runs out. Even if the employee is currently fit for work, the earlier time-limited certificate carries no implication that the same or a similar condition will not recur. The point is a rather different one: an employee who returns to work after a period of sickness without making further disclosure or explanation to his employer is usually implying that he believes himself fit to return to the work which he was doing before. The employer is usually entitled to take that at face value unless he has other good reasons to think to the contrary (see *McIntyre v Filtrona Ltd*).

[31] These then are the questions and the possible indications that harm was foreseeable in a particular case. But how strong should those indications be before the employer has a duty to act? Mr Hogarth argued that only "clear and unequivocal" signs of an impending breakdown should suffice. That may be putting it too high. But in view of the many difficulties of knowing when and why a particular person will go over the edge from pressure to stress and from stress to injury to health, the indications must be plain enough for any reasonable employer to realise that he should do something about it.

Breach of duty

[32] What then is it reasonable to expect the employer to do? His duty is to take reasonable care. What is reasonable depends, as we all know, upon the foreseeability of harm, the magnitude of the risk of that harm occurring, the gravity of the harm which may take place, the cost and practicability of preventing it, and the justifications for running the risk (see the oft-quoted summary of Swanwick J in *Stokes v Guest, Keen and Nettlefold (Bolts and Nuts) Ltd*).

[33] It is essential, therefore, once the risk of harm to health from stresses in the workplace is foreseeable, to consider whether and in what respect the employer has broken that duty. There may be a temptation, having concluded that some harm

was foreseeable and that harm of that kind has taken place, to go on to conclude that the employer was in breach of his duty of care in failing to prevent that harm (and that that breach of duty caused the harm). But in every case it is necessary to consider what the employer not only could but should have done. We are not here concerned with such comparatively simple things as gloves, goggles, earmuffs or non-slip flooring. Many steps might be suggested: giving the employee a sabbatical; transferring him to other work; redistributing the work; giving him some extra help for a while; arranging treatment or counselling; providing buddying or mentoring schemes to encourage confidence; and much more. But in all of these suggestions it will be necessary to consider how reasonable it is to expect the employer to do this, either in general or in particular: the size and scope of its operation will be relevant to this, as will its resources, whether in the public or private sector, and the other demands placed upon it. Among those other demands are the interests of other employees in the workplace. It may not be reasonable to expect the employer to rearrange the work for the sake of one employee in a way which prejudices the others. As we have already said, an employer who tries to balance all these interests by offering confidential help to employees who fear that they may be suffering harmful levels of stress is unlikely to be found in breach of duty: except where he has been placing totally unreasonable demands upon an individual in circumstances where the risk of harm was clear.

[34]   Moreover, the employer can only reasonably be expected to take steps which are likely to do some good. This is a matter on which the court is likely to require expert evidence. In many of these cases it will be very hard to know what would have done some let alone enough good. In some cases the only effective way of safeguarding the employee would be to dismiss or demote him. There may be no other work at the same level of pay which it is reasonable to expect the employer to offer him. In principle the law should not be saying to an employer that it is his duty to sack an employee who wants to go on working for him for the employer's own good. As Devlin LJ put it in *Withers v Perry Chain Co Ltd*:

> "The relationship between employer and employee is not that of schoolmaster and pupil ... The employee is free to decide for herself what risks she will run ... if the common law were to be otherwise it would be oppressive to the employee by limiting his ability to find work, rather than beneficial to him."

Taken to its logical conclusion, of course, this would justify employers in perpetuating the most unsafe practices (not alleged in that case) on the basis that the employee can always leave. But we are not here concerned with physical dangers: we have already rejected the concept of an unsafe occupation for this purpose. If there is no alternative solution, it has to be for the employee to decide whether or not to carry on in the same employment and take the risk of a breakdown in his health or whether to leave that employment and look for work elsewhere before he becomes unemployable.

Causation

[35] Having shown a breach of duty, it is still necessary to show that the particular breach of duty found caused the harm. It is not enough to show that occupational stress caused the harm. Where there are several different possible causes, as will often be the case with stress related illness of any kind, the claimant may have difficulty proving that the employer's fault was one of them (see *Wilsher v Essex Area Health Authority*). This will be a particular problem if, as in *Garrett v Camden London BC*, the main cause was a vulnerable personality which the employer knew nothing about. However, the employee does not have to show that the breach of duty was the whole cause of his ill-health: it is enough to show that it made a material contribution (see *Bonnington Castings Ltd v Wardlaw*).

Apportionment and quantification

[36] Many stress-related illnesses are likely to have a complex aetiology with several different causes. In principle a wrongdoer should pay only for that proportion of the harm suffered for which he by his wrongdoing is responsible (see eg *Thompson v Smiths Shiprepairers (North Shields) Ltd, Holtby v Brigham & Cowan (Hull) Ltd* and *Rahman v Arearose Ltd*). ... This may raise some difficult factual questions. *Calascione v Dixon* is an example of apportionment between different causes, one the fault of the defendant, the other not: the claimant suffered post traumatic stress disorder as a result of seeing the aftermath of the accident in which her son was killed, but her normal grief reaction had become abnormal as a result of later events. ...

[41] Hence if it is established that the constellation of symptoms suffered by the claimant stems from a number of different extrinsic causes then in our view a sensible attempt should be made to apportion liability accordingly. There is no reason to distinguish these conditions from the chronological development of industrial diseases or disabilities. The analogy with the polluted stream is closer than the analogy with the single fire. Nor is there anything in the *Bonnington* case or *McGhee's* case requiring a different approach.

[42] Where the tortfeasor's breach of duty has exacerbated a pre-existing disorder or accelerated the effect of pre-existing vulnerability, the award of general damages for pain, suffering and loss of amenity will reflect only the exacerbation or acceleration. Further, the quantification of damages for financial losses must take some account of contingencies. In this context, one of those contingencies may well be the chance that the claimant would have succumbed to a stress-related disorder in any event. As it happens, all of these principles are exemplified by the decision of Otton J at first instance in *Page v Smith* (and not appealed by the claimant: see *Page v Smith (No 2)*). He reduced the multiplier for future loss of earnings (as it happens as a teacher) from ten to six to reflect the many factors making it probable that the claimant would not have had a full and unbroken period

of employment in any event and the real possibility that his employers would have terminated his employment because of his absences from work.'

Comment

(1) Hale LJ went on to summarise the position as a number of practical propositions:

'(1) There are no special control mechanisms applying to claims for psychiatric (or physical) illness or injury arising from the stress of doing the work the employee is required to do ... The ordinary principles of employer's liability apply ... (2) The threshold question is whether this kind of harm to this particular employee was reasonably foreseeable ...: this has two components (a) an injury to health (as distinct from occupational stress) which (b) is attributable to stress at work (as distinct from other factors) ... (3) Foreseeability depends upon what the employer knows (or ought reasonably to know) about the individual employee. Because of the nature of mental disorder, it is harder to foresee than physical injury, but may be easier to foresee in a known individual than in the population at large ... An employer is usually entitled to assume that the employee can withstand the normal pressures of the job unless he knows of some particular problem or vulnerability ... (4) The test is the same whatever the employment: there are no occupations which should be regarded as intrinsically dangerous to mental health ... (5) Factors likely to be relevant in answering the threshold question include: (a) The nature and extent of the work done by the employee ... Is the workload much more than is normal for the particular job? Is the work particularly intellectually or emotionally demanding for this employee? Are demands being made of this employee unreasonable when compared with the demands made of others in the same or comparable jobs? Or are there signs that others doing this job are suffering harmful levels of stress? Is there an abnormal level of sickness or absenteeism in the same job or the same department? (b) Signs from the employee of impending harm to health ... Has he a particular problem or vulnerability? Has he already suffered from illness attributable to stress at work? Have there recently been frequent or prolonged absences which are uncharacteristic of him? Is there reason to think that these are attributable to stress at work, for example because of complaints or warnings from him or others? (6) The employer is generally entitled to take what he is told by his employee at face value, unless he has good reason to think to the contrary. He does not generally have to make searching inquiries of the employee or seek permission to make further inquiries of his medical advisers ... (7) To trigger a duty to take steps, the indications of impending harm to health arising from stress at work must be plain enough for any reasonable employer to realise that he should do something about it ... (8) The employer is only in breach of duty if he has failed to take the steps which are reasonable in the circumstances, bearing in mind the magnitude of the risk of harm occurring, the gravity of the harm which may occur, the costs and practicability of preventing it, and the justifications for running the risk ... (9) The size and scope of the employer's operation, its resources and the demands it faces are relevant in deciding what is reasonable; these include the interests of other employees and the need to treat them fairly, for example, in any redistribution of duties ... (10) An employer can only reasonably be expected to take steps which are likely to do some good: the court is likely to need expert evidence on this ... (11) An employer who offers a confidential advice service, with referral to appropriate counselling or treatment services, is unlikely to be found in breach of duty ... (12) If the only reasonable and effective step would have been to dismiss or demote the employee, the employer will not be in breach of duty in allowing a willing employee to continue in the job ... (13) In all cases, therefore, it is necessary to identify the steps which the employer both could and should have taken before finding him in breach of his duty of care ... (14) The claimant must show that that breach of duty has caused or materially contributed to the harm suffered. It is not enough to show that occupational stress has caused the harm ... (15) Where the harm suffered has more than one cause, the employer should only pay for that proportion of the harm suffered which is attributable to his wrongdoing, unless the harm is truly indivisible. It is for the defendant to raise the question of apportionment ... (16) The assessment of damages will take account of any pre-existing disorder or vulnerability and of the chance that the claimant would have succumbed to a stress-related disorder in any event.'

(2) The decision in *Barber v Somerset County Council* was reversed in the House of Lords, though without challenging the principles set out in Hale LJ's judgment. The issue for the House was 'whether the Court of Appeal was entitled to conclude, as it did, that the evidence before the judge did not, even taken at its highest, sustain a finding that the County Council were in breach of the duty of care which they owed, as employer, to Mr Barber'. By a majority of four-to-one the House of Lords held that it was not.

(3) In *Walker Northumberland County Council* the claimant had been employed by the defendant council as an area social services officer responsible for a number of teams in a particularly difficult region. He suffered a nervous breakdown as a consequence of the considerable work pressures he was subjected to, both as a result of the nature of the cases with which he was involved, and because of the structure and manning of the management of the service. On his return to work, the defendants took no effective steps to relieve the pressure, and he suffered a second and permanent breakdown. The court

held the defendants in breach of their duty of care, at least in respect of the second breakdown. In response to the Council's argument that its role in providing social services took the matter into the field of public law, Colman J said:

'I therefore conclude that the council could only have provided W with substantial assistance in March 1987 at the expense of some disruption of other social work ... such as to preclude the council from providing at least some services which it would otherwise have been able to provide. In deciding whether the council was acting reasonably in failing to provide additional staffing to W, it is clearly right to take into account and to attach some weight to the fact and extent of that disruption. However, [counsel for] the council contends that because the extent to which the council provided social services to the public in particular areas was a discretionary or policy decision in respect of the exercise of statutory powers, as distinct from an operational one, if the secondment of additional staff to assist W involved withdrawal of services, the council's policy decision not to disrupt its services merely to enable it to support W could not amount to a breach of duty of care to W. [Counsel] relies in particular on the developing distinction between policy decisions and operational decisions enunciated by Lord Wilberforce in *Anns v Merton London Borough* and further explored by the Court of Appeal in *Lavis v Kent CC*. In other words ... the court is shut out from characterising as unreasonable conduct on the part of a public body which is the consequence of a decision by that body in a policy-making area to carry out its statutory powers in a particular way or to a particular extent ...

In my judgment, the policy decision/operational decision dichotomy has no more part to play in the context of the duty of care to an employee with whom a statutory body has a contract of employment than it would have in the context of any other contract made by such a body. Just as it would be no defence to a claim for non-performance of a contract for the sale of goods that the local authority had resolved as a matter of policy that the use of its scarce resources for the performance of the contract was inexpedient, so it would be no defence to a claim for breach of the implied term in a contract of employment that the employer would exercise reasonable care for the safety of his employee, that its failure to do so was the result of a policy decision on the exercise of its statutory powers. Since the scope of the duty of care owed to an employee to take reasonable steps to provide a safe system of work is co-extensive with the scope of the implied term as to the employee's safety in the contract of employment (*Johnstone v Bloomsbury Health Authority*) to introduce a ring fence round policy decisions giving rise to unsafe systems of work for the purposes of claims in tort which was not available to the defendant statutory body in defence to claims in contract would be to implant into employment law a disparity which, in my judgment, would be wholly wrong in principle. Whereas the mutual intention to be imputed to the parties to a contract of employment with a public body could be expected to qualify the employer's duty of safety by requiring the employer to do no more than take reasonable steps to procure the employee's safety at work, it is inconceivable that such mutual intention would require the employer to take only such steps for the employee's safety as political expediency from time to time permitted if the exercise of statutory powers were involved. In the absence of authority to the contrary or of compelling common law principle, there can be no sustainable basis for subjecting the duty of care in tort to such a qualification.

That said, the duty of an employer public body, whether in contract or tort, to provide a safe system of work is, as I have said, a duty only to do what is reasonable, and in many cases it may be necessary to take into account decisions which are within the policy-making area and the reasons for those decisions in order to test whether the body's conduct has been reasonable. In that exercise there can be no basis for treating the public body differently in principle from any other commercial employer, although there would have to be taken into account considerations such as budgetary constraints and perhaps lack of flexibility of decision-taking which might not arise with a commercial employer. Having regard to the reasonably foreseeable size of the risk of repetition of W's illness if his duties were not alleviated by effective additional assistance and to the reasonably foreseeable gravity of the mental breakdown which might result if nothing were done, I have come to the conclusion that the standard of care to be expected of a reasonable local authority required that in March 1987 such additional assistance should be provided, if not on a permanent basis, at least until restructuring of the social services had been effected and the workload on W thereby permanently reduced. That measure of additional assistance ought to have been provided, notwithstanding that it could be expected to have some disruptive effect on the council's provision of services to the public.'

(4) For more on the policy/operational dichotomy, see also *Rowling v Takaro Properties Ltd, X v Bedfordshire County Council*, pp 48 and 52.

(5) In an employer/employee situation, the existence of a duty is often, as here, easily established. In some circumstances, however, issues of standard of care become merged with the question whether a duty exists. In *Barrett v Ministry of Defence*, for example, the Court of Appeal held that the duty owed to a serviceman by the defendants did not extend to preventing him from becoming so drunk (on their premises) that he subsequently died. By contrast, in *Jebson v Ministry of Defence* an off-duty Grenadier Guard was injured when he fell from the tailgate of an army lorry. The occasion for this incident was a

social night out organised by his commanding officer. The Court of Appeal held that the duty owed to the claimant encompassed an obligation to provide a 'transport "package" that was reasonably safe to avoid the possibility of injury from rowdy behaviour in the back of the lorry'. As in the case of *Barrett*, the assumption of responsibility for someone already drunk, or as in *Jebson*, for someone 'expressly anticipated' to become drunk calls for reasonable steps to be taken. On the facts of *Jebson*, no provision was made, for example by way of active supervision, and the Court of Appeal found for the claimant, though reducing his damages by 75 per cent for contributory negligence.

(6)   See also *White and others v Chief Constable of the South Yorkshire Police and others* (p 105), in which the majority in the House of Lords held that the employer's duty did not extend to protecting employees from psychiatric injury in the circumstances of that case; and *Donachie v Chief Constable of the Greater Manchester Police*.

Watt v Hertfordshire County Council
[1954] 2 All ER 368 Court of Appeal

The defendants' fire station had on loan a heavy jack. One day, while the only vehicle equipped to carry the jack was out on other service, the brigade was called to free a woman who was trapped under a heavy vehicle several hundred yards away. It was decided to load the jack, which stood on four wheels, onto a lorry and that three firefighters, including the plaintiff, should hold the jack steady while in transit. During the short journey the driver was obliged to brake suddenly and the jack moved, injuring the plaintiff's leg. He brought an action against the defendants in negligence. The Court of Appeal, in affirming the first instance decision, balanced the nature of the risk against the importance of the end to be achieved.

Denning LJ: '... It is well settled that in measuring due care one must balance the risk against the measures necessary to eliminate the risk. To that proposition there ought to be added this. One must balance the risk against the end to be achieved. If this accident had occurred in a commercial enterprise without any emergency, there could be no doubt that the servant would succeed. But the commercial end to make profit is very different from the human end to save life or limb. The saving of life or limb justifies taking considerable risk, and I am glad to say there have never been wanting in this country men of courage ready to take those risks, notably in the fire service.

In this case the risk involved in sending out the lorry was not so great as to prohibit the attempt to save life. I quite agree that fire engines, ambulances and doctors' cars should not shoot past the traffic lights when they show a red light. That is because the risk is too great to warrant the incurring of the danger. It is always a question of balancing the risk against the end.'

Comment

(1)   In *Daborn v Bath Tramways Motor Co Ltd & Trevor Smithey*, Asquith LJ observed that:

'In determining whether a party is negligent, the standard of reasonable care is that which is reasonably to be demanded in the circumstances. A relevant circumstance to take into account may be the importance of the end to be served by behaving in this way or in that. As has often been pointed out, if all the trains in this country were restricted to a speed of five miles an hour, there would be fewer accidents, but our national life would be intolerably slowed down. The purpose to be served, if sufficiently important, justifies the assumption of abnormal risks.'

(2)   Although when the balance to be struck is between one person's life and another's leg the decision seems fairly straightforward, it is hard to envisage the application of this principle to less urgent situations.

Latimer v AEC Ltd
[1952] 1 All ER 1302 Court of Appeal

Through no lack of care on the part of the defendants, their factory was flooded during an exceptionally heavy rainstorm and the factory floor was coated with oil from the cooling mixture normally pumped to the machines through channels in the floor. A quantity of sawdust was distributed but there was insufficient sawdust for the whole floor and the plaintiff slipped on an untreated patch, seriously damaging his ankle. The Court of Appeal (and subsequently the House of Lords) considered that the defendants had taken all reasonable steps for the safety of their employees.

Denning LJ: '... It seems to me that the learned judge has fallen into error by assuming that it was sufficient to constitute negligence that there was a foreseeable risk which the defendants could have avoided by some measure or other, however extreme. That is not the law. It is always necessary to consider what measures the defendants could have taken and to say whether they could reasonably be expected of them. Let me give a converse case. A man tries to stop a runaway horse. It is a known and serious risk, but no one would suggest that he could reasonably be expected to stand idly by. It is not negligence on his part to run the risk. So here the employers knew that the floor was slippery and that there was some risk in letting the men work on it, but, still, they could not reasonably be expected to shut down the whole works and send all the men home. In every case of foreseeable risk it is a matter of balancing the risk against the measures necessary to eliminate it. It is only negligence if, on balance, the defendants did something which they ought not to have done or omitted to do something which they ought to have done. In the circumstances of this case it is clear that the defendants did everything they could reasonably be expected to do. It would be quite unreasonable to expect them to send all the men home.'

Comment

In the House of Lords, Lord Oaksey concluded that this incident arose from 'an error of judgment in circumstances of difficulty and such an error of judgment does not ... amount to negligence'. His view was approved by Lord Denning in *Miller v Jackson*.

The Wagon Mound (No 2)
Overseas Tankship (UK) Ltd v Miller Steamship Co Pty Ltd and another
[1966] 2 All ER 709 Privy Council

The appellants' engineer carelessly allowed a large quantity of furnace oil to spill from their vessel, the *Wagon Mound*, into Sydney Harbour. It drifted on the surface of the water to a nearby wharf where it ignited, causing extensive damage to two of the respondent's vessels which were undergoing repairs. The Privy Council held the appellants liable on the ground that the risk of fire, although slight, was not such as a reasonable man in the position of the engineer would ignore, particularly since the trouble involved in stopping the discharge was negligible.

Lord Reid: '... It does not follow that, no matter what the circumstances may be, it is justifiable to neglect a risk of such a small magnitude. A reasonable man would only neglect such a risk if he had some valid reason for doing so: e.g., that it would involve considerable expense to eliminate the risk. He would weigh the risk against the difficulty of eliminating it. If the activity which caused the injury to Miss Stone had been an unlawful activity there can be little doubt but that *Bolton v Stone* would have been decided differently. In their Lordships' judgment *Bolton v Stone* did not alter the general principle that a person must be regarded as negligent if he does not take steps to eliminate a risk which he knows or ought to know is a real risk and not a mere possibility which would never influence the mind of a reasonable man. What that decision did was to recognise and give effect to the qualification that it is justifiable not to take steps to eliminate a real risk if it is small and if the circumstances are such that a reasonable man, careful of the safety of his neighbour, would think it right to neglect it.

In the present case there was no justification whatever for discharging the oil into Sydney Harbour. Not only was it an offence to do so, but also it involved considerable loss financially. If the ship's engineer had thought about the matter there could have been no question of balancing the advantages and disadvantages. From every point of view it was both his duty and his interest to stop the discharge immediately.

It follows that in their Lordships' view the only question is whether a reasonable man having the knowledge and experience to be expected of the chief engineer of the *Wagon Mound* would have known that there was a real risk of the oil on the water catching fire in some way: if it did, serious damage to ships or other property was not only foreseeable but very likely ...

In their Lordships' view a properly qualified and alert chief engineer would have realised there was a real risk here, and they do not understand Walsh J to deny that; but he appears to have held that, if a real risk can properly be described as remote, it must then be held to be not reasonably foreseeable. That is a possible interpretation of some of the authorities; but this is still an open question and on principle their Lordships cannot accept this view. If a real risk is one which would occur to the mind of a reasonable man in the position of the defendant's servant and which he would not brush aside as far-fetched, and if the criterion is to be what that reasonable man would have done in the circumstances, then surely he would not neglect such a risk if action to eliminate it presented no difficulty, involved no disadvantage and required no expense.

In the present case the evidence shows that the discharge of so much oil on to the water must have taken a considerable time, and a vigilant ship's engineer would have noticed the discharge at an early stage. The findings show that he ought to have known that it is possible to ignite this kind of oil on water, and that the ship's engineer probably ought to have known that this had in fact happened before. The most that can be said to justify inaction is that he would have known that this could only happen in very exceptional circumstances; but that does not mean that a reasonable man would dismiss such risk from his mind and do nothing when it was so easy to prevent it. If it is clear that the reasonable man would have realised or foreseen and prevented the risk, then it must follow that the appellants are liable in damages.'

Comment

(1)   Taking the formula approach to the question of adequate precautions, it is clear that even the smallest genuine risk cannot reasonably be ignored when the burden is so light.

(2)   For the standard of care and breach in relation to occupiers, see Chapter 7 and in particular *Tomlinson v Congleton Borough Council and another*, p 403.

Ward v Tesco Stores Ltd
[1976] I All ER 219 Court of Appeal

The plaintiff was injured when she slipped on some yoghurt which had been spilled on the floor of the defendants' supermarket. The defendants argued that the plaintiff had failed to prove that they had been negligent but the Court of Appeal held that, since such an accident would not have occurred if the floor had been kept clean, it was for the defendants to show that the injury had not been caused by any lack of care on their part. This they had failed to do.

Lawton LJ:'... The manager in cross-examination said that spillages did occur from time to time; he thought there were about ten breakages a week, but most of them came from the breaking of squash bottles.

It follows that those in charge of the store knew that during the course of a working week there was a likelihood of spillages occurring from time to time. It was accepted at the trial that shoppers, intent on looking to see what is on offer, cannot be expected to look where they are putting their feet. The management should have appreciated that if there are patches of slippery substances on the floor people are liable to step into them and that, if they do, they may slip. It follows too that if those are the conditions to be expected in the store there must be some reasonable, effective system for getting rid of the dangers which may from time to time exist. The only precautions which were taken were, first, the system of having the floor brushed five or six times during the working day and, secondly, giving instructions to the staff that if they saw any spillage on the floor they were to stay where the spill had taken place and call somebody to clean it up.

The main complaint of the defendants in this case has been that the trial judge should never have taken the view that the plaintiff had proved a *prima facie* case. It was submitted before this court that it was for the plaintiff to show that the spillage had been on the floor an unduly long time and that there had been opportunities for the management to clean it up which they had not taken. In support of that proposition, counsel for the defendants invited our attention to *Richards v W F White & Co.* It is necessary to say something about the facts of that case because, as in all cases of negligence, the facts are important. A dock labourer who was working on a ship in dock which was being unloaded slipped on a patch of oil and injured himself. At the material time between 300 and 400 men in various trades were working on the ship. In the course of his judgment Devlin J said:

> "If there had been evidence which showed that there was some danger, not perhaps of oil but some other danger, which was being left on the ship for two or three days, or anything of that sort, which the shipowners were doing nothing about, a *prima facie* case of negligence would be made out; but to make out a *prima facie* case of negligence in a case of this sort, there must, I think, be some evidence to show how long the oil had been there, some evidence from which it can be inferred that a prudent shipowner, who had a reasonable system of inspection for the purpose of seeing that dangers of this sort were not created, ought to have noticed it."

That case was decided on its own facts. I doubt whether Devlin J intended to make any general statement of principle. If he did, I would not agree with what he said.

This case, too, has to be decided on its own facts, to which established principles must be applied. The relevant principles were enunciated in the classical judgment of Erle CJ in *Scott v The London and St Katherine Docks Co*:

> "But where the thing is shewn to be under the management of the defendant or his servants, and the accident is such as in the ordinary course of things does not happen if those who have the management use proper care, it affords reasonable evidence, in the absence of explanation by the defendants that the accident arose from want of care."

In this case the floor of this supermarket was under the management of the defendants and their servants. The accident was such as in the ordinary course of things does not happen if floors are kept clean and spillages are dealt with as soon as they occur. If an accident does happen because the floors are covered with spillage, then in my judgment some explanation should be forthcoming from the defendants to show that the accident did not arise from any want of care on their part; and in the absence of any explanation the judge may give judgment for the plaintiff. Such burden of proof as there is on defendants in such circumstances is evidential, not probative. The trial judge thought that *prima facie* this accident would not have happened had the defendants taken reasonable care. In my judgment he was justified in taking that view because the probabilities were that the spillage had been on the floor long enough for it to have been cleaned up by a member of the staff.

The next question is whether the defendants by their evidence gave any explanation to show that they had taken all reasonable care. The only explanation which they gave was that to which I have already referred. The judge weighed the evidence and decided as a matter of fact from which in this case there can be no appeal that the precautions taken were not enough, and that the plaintiff in consequence had proved her case. In coming to that conclusion he followed the judgment of Lord Goddard CJ in *Turner v Arding & Hobbs Ltd*:

> "The duty of the shopkeeper in this class of case is well established. It may be said to be a duty to use reasonable care to see that the shop floor, on which people are invited, is kept reasonably safe, and if an unusual danger is present of which the injured person is unaware, and the danger is one which would not be expected and ought not to be present, the onus of proof is on the defendants to explain how it was that the accident happened."

It is clear from a later passage in his judgment that Lord Goddard CJ, in referring to the burden of proof, was not saying that the defendant had to disprove negligence. What he had intended to say is apparent from what he said later:

> "Here, however, I think that there is a burden thrown on the defendants either of explaining how this thing got on the floor or giving me far more evidence than they have as to the state of the floor and the watch that was kept on it immediately before the accident."

The learned judge had that passage in mind when he decided as he did. In my judgment he was right; and accordingly I would dismiss this appeal.'

Megaw LJ: '... It seems to me that the essence of the argument put forward on behalf of the defendants in this appeal is this. Never mind whether the defendants had any system of any sort to protect their customers against the risk of slipping on the floor of the supermarket as a result of breakages or spillages, which on their own evidence happened about ten times a week. Even if they had no system of any sort to guard against such a risk to their customers, nevertheless, when an accident happens such as the accident in this case, a lady customer who undoubtedly slips, through no fault of her own, on such a spillage on the floor, she cannot recover against the defendants. And why can she not recover? Because she is unable to prove that the spillage did not take place within a matter of a few seconds before she slipped and fell on it: so that, however perfect a system the defendants had had, it would not have enabled them to prevent this particular accident.

With great respect to those who support that proposition, it appears to me to be contrary to the law as I understand it to be. It is for the plaintiff to show that there has occurred an event which is unusual and which, in the absence of explanation, is more consistent with fault on the part of the defendants than the absence of fault; and to my mind the learned judge was wholly right in taking that view of the presence of this slippery liquid on the floor of the supermarket in the circumstances of this case: that is that the defendants knew or should have known that it was a not uncommon occurrence; and that if it should happen, and should not be promptly attended to, it created a serious risk that customers would fall and injure themselves. When the plaintiff has established that, the defendants can still escape from liability. They could escape from liability if they could show that the accident must have happened, or even on balance of probability would have been likely to have happened, irrespective of the existence of a proper and adequate system, in relation to the circumstances, to provide for the safety of customers. But, if the defendants wish to put forward such a case, it is for them to show that, on balance of probability, either by evidence or by inference from the evidence that is given or is not given, this accident would have been at least equally likely to have happened despite a proper system designed to give reasonable protection to customers. That, in this case, they wholly failed to do. Really the essence of counsel for the defendants' argument — and he did not shrink from it— was: "Never mind whether we had no system at all: still, as the plaintiff has failed to show that the yoghurt was spilt within a few seconds before the accident, she must fail." As I have said, in the circumstances of this case, I do not think that the plaintiff, to succeed, had to prove how long it was since the defendants' floor had become slippery.'

Comment

(1) Note the two requirements from *Scott v London and St Katherine Docks Co*: the element of control by the defendant and that the accident is

'such as in the ordinary course of events does not happen' without negligence. In that particular case, several bags of sugar fell from a warehouse on to a person below. If the element of control is weakened by the participation or the possibility of intervention by a third party the principle will not apply, see *Easson v London & North Eastern Railway.*

(2) The defendant is not required to prove the absence of negligence, or that the innocent explanation offered is the correct one – it is sufficient to dislodge the assertion that the facts speak for themselves and it will then be for the plaintiff to prove negligence in the usual way.

(3) In *Carroll and others v Fearon and others* the internal structure of a car tyre was defective so that, after some years of use, it failed, causing a serious accident. Counsel for the defendants had argued that the judge had proceeded on an impermissible process of reasoning. Counsel relied on Lord Macmillan's comment in *Donoghue v Stevenson:* 'There is no presumption of negligence in such a case as the present, nor is there any justification for applying the maxim *res ipsa loquitur.* Negligence must be both averred and proved.' Since Lord Macmillan proceeded to treat the presence of the snail in the bottle as *prima facie* evidence of negligence, Judge LJ (with whom the rest of the Court of Appeal agreed) interpreted his words more as a caution against creating the appearance of strict liability in what was at the time a new field of negligence. In Judge LJ's view, '*Res ipsa loquitur* is not a principle of substantive law. These three words are used to encapsulate a common sense reasoning process which is no more or less profound for being expressed in Latin. In any given case either the thing, the facts, speak for themselves, or they do not.' He considered the passage from *Scott v London & Saint Katherine Docks* (quoted on p 251) and noted Steyn LJ's observation in *Bergin v David Wickes Television Ltd* that *res ipsa loquitur* 'is simply a convenient label for a group of situations in which an unexplained accident is, as a matter of common sense, the basis for an inference of negligence'. Judge LJ agreed with this approach, saying that:

> 'Provided the principle is understood the citation of decisions where the court on particular facts decided that *res ipsa loquitur* did or did not apply, or expressed the same concept using different language, is not helpful. Indeed, I very much doubt whether *res ipsa loquitur* is ever susceptible to refined argument and detailed analysis of authority.'

On the facts of *Carroll* itself, he concluded that the principle could not apply since the passage of time and regular use of the tyre meant that there might be many possible explanations for its failure. Once the defect had been traced back to the manufacturing process, however, as it had been in this case, it was not necessary for the plaintiff to identify the precise act of negligence: it was enough that 'something had gone wrong with the [manufacturing] process for which the manufacturer could not apparently provide any explanation'. See also Chapter 8 on product liability.

(4)   In *Jenney v North Lincolnshire County Council* the claimant, a nine-year-old who suffered from global development delay, was injured when he strayed outside the defendants' primary school and onto a major road. The Court of Appeal held that the principle of *res ipsa loquitur* applied – the facts called for an explanation from the defendants. Referring to *Carmarthanshire County Council v Lewis*, the court concluded that the effect of the principle went beyond establishing only breach of duty, it also satisfied the requirement of causation. Henry LJ said:

> 'The school failed to discharge the evidential burden on it to show that the accident was not due to negligence on its part. Accordingly, the plaintiff is entitled to judgment. As the evidential burden does not shift back to him, he need not prove causation. By definition the plaintiff cannot prove how the accident happened, and so cannot put forward any set of facts as causing the accident. And the law does not require him to.'

CHAPTER 5

Causation and remoteness

Once it has been established that the defendant owes a duty of care to the claimant and was in breach of that duty, nevertheless there will be no liability if the claimant fails to show that there is a causal link between the breach and the damage suffered, or if the court decides that the damage is too remote to be compensated. Strictly, causation is a question of fact while remoteness is a question of law. In practice the issues are very closely related and judges often describe damage with which there is no causal link as being too remote.

There is no simple test for causation. Often the events leading to a negligence action are quite complex and the cases tend to ask whether the defendant's conduct was a 'substantial' or 'material' contribution to the claimant's damage. Lord Reid in *McGhee v National Coal Board* remarked that 'the legal concept of causation is not based on logic or philosophy' but on 'the practical way in which the ordinary man's mind works in the every-day affairs of life'. Generally, the common-sense starting point is what is known as the 'but for' test – if one cannot say that, but for the negligence of the defendant, the claimant would not have suffered damage, then there is no causal link between the two. In exceptional cases, however, such as in *Fairchild v Glenhaven Funeral Services* (see p 268) it has proven necessary to adopt a less rigid approach in order to achieve a just outcome.

Having established between the defendant's act and the claimant's damage a chain of causation which will survive the 'but for' test, it is then necessary to consider whether the connection is compromised by any external factor, or *novus actus interveniens*, which may be said to break the chain, ending the defendant's liability. Such events fall into three categories: natural events, third-party acts and unreasonable acts by the claimant.

An example of a natural event occurred in *Carslogie Steamship Co v Royal Norwegian Government* in which the plaintiff's ship was damaged by a collision caused by the defendants' negligence. Temporary repairs were effected and the ship set out for the United States in order to be fully repaired. In the course of its transatlantic voyage there was a severe storm and the ship suffered further extensive damage. Despite the fact that this voyage had been necessitated by the original collision the court held that the storm, being one of the ordinary natural hazards of shipping, broke the chain of causation between the defendants and the eventual damage. Furthermore, since the original damage was permanently repaired at the same time as the storm damage the plaintiff was unable to claim damages for the fact that the ship was out of action.

On the basis that the defendant should be liable only for his own fault, the general rule is that the act of a third party will break the chain of causation. However, some third-party acts follow almost inevitably from certain acts of negligence, for example, where a person is negligently injured he or she will probably require some kind of medical treatment. The question is, how likely does the third-party act have to be if it is not to break the chain?

For the claimant's own conduct to break the chain of causation, the courts require a high degree of unreasonableness, although a lesser degree may result in a reduction of damages on the basis of contributory negligence.

Even when a direct causal link has been established between the defendant's conduct and the claimant's loss there may be no remedy if the damage can be said to be legally too remote. This limit on the defendant's liability is imposed, according to Lord Denning, as a matter of judicial policy. In *Compania Financiera Soleada SA v Hamoor Tanker Corpn Inc, The Borag* he said that '... it is not every consequence of a wrongful act which is the subject of compensation. The law has to draw a line somewhere'. The question in relation to remoteness is where that line should be drawn and on what grounds.

Barnett v Chelsea and Kensington Hospital Management Committee [1968] I All ER 1068 Queen's Bench Division

The plaintiff's husband visited the casualty department of the defendants' hospital suffering from what subsequently proved to be arsenical poisoning. The casualty officer, without examining him, told the man to go away and see his own doctor. Some hours later the man died and his widow brought an action against the hospital in negligence. Her claim failed because the casualty officer's negligence was not shown to have caused the man's death.

Nield J: '... It remains to consider whether it is shown that the deceased's death was caused by this negligence or whether, as the defendants have said, the deceased must have died in any event. In his concluding submission counsel for the plaintiff submitted that [the casualty officer] should have examined the deceased and, had he done so, he would have caused tests to be made which would have indicated the treatment required and that, since the defendants were at fault in these respects, therefore the onus of proof passed to the defendants to show that the appropriate treatment would have failed, and authorities were cited to me. I find myself unable to accept this argument and I am of the view that the onus of proof remains on the plaintiff, and I have in mind (without quoting it) the decision quoted by counsel for the defendants in *Bonnington Castings Ltd v Wardlaw*. However, were it otherwise and the onus did pass to the defendants, then I would find that they have discharged it, as I would proceed to show.

There has been put before me a timetable which, I think, is of much importance. The deceased attended at the casualty department at 8.05 or 8.10 a.m. If [the casualty officer] had got up and dressed and come to see the three men and examined them and decided to admit them, the deceased (and Dr L agreed with this) could not have been in bed in a ward before 11 a.m. I accept Dr G's evidence that an intravenous drip would not have been set up before 12 noon, and if potassium loss was suspected it could not have been discovered until 12.30. Dr L, dealing with this, said

"If [the deceased] had not been treated until after 12 noon the chances of survival were not good".

Without going in detail into the considerable volume of technical evidence which has been put before me, it seems to me to be the case that when death results from arsenical poisoning it is brought about by two conditions; on the one hand dehydration and on the other disturbance of the enzyme processes. If the principal condition is one of enzyme disturbance – as I am of the view that it was here – then the only method of treatment which is likely to succeed is the use of the specific or antidote which is commonly called BAL. Dr G said this in the course of his evidence: "The only way to deal with this is to use the specific BAL. I see no reasonable prospect of the deceased being given BAL before the time at which he died," and at a later point in his evidence: "I feel that even if fluid loss had been discovered death would have been caused by the enzyme disturbance. Death might have occurred later." I regard that evidence as very moderate, and that it might be a true assessment of the situation to say that there was no chance of BAL being administered before the death of the deceased. For these reasons, I find that the plaintiff has failed to establish, on the grounds of probability, that the defendants' negligence caused the death of the deceased.'

Comment

While the 'but for' test can be very useful as a means of demonstrating the absence of a causal link, very few cases will be so straightforward that this on its own will establish the existence of a sufficiently strong link as to justify liability on the part of the defendant.

Cummings (or McWilliams) v Sir William Arrol & Co Ltd and another [1962] 1 All ER 623 House of Lords

The plaintiff's husband was a steel erector who fell to his death from a tower which he was building. His widow claimed damages in negligence on the basis that the defendant employers had failed to ensure that the deceased was supplied with a safety belt. The House of Lords held that in the absence of any evidence to prove that the deceased would have worn a safety belt, the lack of one had not been shown to be the cause of his death.

Lord Devlin:'... The courts below have held that the employers were in breach of their duty in failing to provide a safety belt, but that that was not the cause of the deceased's death since he would not have worn it if it had been provided.

On [this] matter three points have been taken. First, whether the employers can be heard to say that the deceased would not have worn what they in breach of their duty failed to provide. Secondly, as to the burden of proof: whether it is for the appellant to prove that the deceased would have worn a safety belt if provided or for the employers to prove that he would not. Thirdly, whether, in order to establish as a matter of probability that the deceased either would or would not have worn a safety belt if provided, inferences can be drawn from the deceased's habits and past conduct and from the habits of his fellow employees.

On the first of these matters counsel for the appellant based his case on the proposition that the failure to provide the safety belt was the cause of the defendant's death. In my opinion this proposition is incomplete. There is a missing link. The immediate cause of the deceased's death was the fact that at the time of the fall he was not wearing a safety belt. The cause or reason he was not wearing a safety belt may have been the fact that one was not provided, but the failure to provide operates only through the failure to wear. The correct way of stating the appellant's case is, I think, as follows. The immediate cause of the deceased's death was that at the time of the fall he was not wearing a safety belt: but for the fault of his employers, he would have been wearing a safety belt: therefore the fault of his employers was an effective cause of his death. So stated, it is plain that the reason why the deceased was not wearing a safety belt must be a proper subject for inquiry.

Counsel for the appellant relied on the decision of the Court of Appeal in *Roberts v Dorman Long & Co Ltd*. This also was a case in which the death of a steel erector was caused by his not wearing a safety belt and his employers were in breach of duty in not making one available. The duty relied on was created by reg 97 of the Building (Safety, Health and Welfare) Regulations 1948, which provided that: " ... there shall be available safety belts ... which will so far as practicable enable such persons who elect to use them to carry out the work without risk of serious injury." The court held that it was no answer for the employers in such circumstances to say that if they had made safety belts available, the deceased would not have used them; the fact that they were not available gave him no opportunity of exercising his election. It is clear that this reasoning was based on the words of the regulation: the court held the employers to be guilty of a breach of the regulation but not a breach of their duty at common law. The case does not therefore, in my opinion, assist counsel in his argument against the first respondents; though I shall consider it again when I consider the case against the second respondents which is based on the breach of statutory duty.

The second point raises the question of the burden of proof. The proposition, as I have stated it above, appears to put on the appellant the burden of showing why the deceased was not wearing a safety belt; she must prove her case and it is part of her case that he was not wearing a belt because of the fault of his employers. But since *ex hypothesi* a prudent employer would provide a belt, it must follow that a prudent employee would wear it when provided. Any inquiry of this sort starts from the presumption that the pursuer or the defendant, as the case may be, has done what is reasonable and prudent; and it is for the opposite party to displace that presumption by pleading and proving negligence or contributory negligence, as the case may be. So if there were no evidence at all to show why the deceased was not wearing a safety belt, it would be proper to conclude that the reason was because the employers had failed to provide one. The question of the burden of proof is frequently important when what is in issue is what a dead workman in fact did. Without his evidence it may be difficult to prove that negligence by the employers was an effective cause of the death: once negligence is proved, the fact that the workman cannot be called to account for his actions often defeats the proof of contributory negligence. But in the present case the question is not what the deceased actually did but what he would have done in circumstances that never arose. Whether the workman is alive or dead, this cannot be proved positively as a matter of fact but can only be inferred as a matter of likelihood or probability. Even when the workman himself is perforce silent, there may be plenty of material, as there is in this case, from which an inference can be drawn one way or the other; and then the question of burden of proof is unimportant.

That brings me to the third of counsel for the appellant's submissions. He submits that what the deceased would have done cannot be proved by inference. It must be proved, he says, by direct evidence, such as a statement by him that he never in any circumstances wore a safety belt. The fact that in the past the deceased never wore a safety belt is not admissible to show that he would not have worn one on the material occasion: such is the argument. There is here, I think with respect, a confusion of thought. The fact that a man under certain conditions on Monday, Tuesday and Wednesday (I take this example from counsel's argument) drove carelessly may be inadmissible to prove the fact that he drove carelessly under the same conditions on Thursday ... But here the question is not what the deceased did but what he would have done. That is a matter that is incapable of direct proof; it must be a matter of inference. His statement about what he would have done, if he were alive to make it, is only one of the factors which the court would have to take into consideration in its task of arriving at the correct inference. A man's actions in the past may well be a safer guide than his own forecast of his actions in the future.

In my judgment the courts below were right to receive and consider the evidence that the deceased had never used a safety belt in the past when it was available. That is material from which it is permissible to draw the inference that he probably would not have used one if it had been provided on the day of his death. I think also, though with more hesitation, that the courts below were right in considering for what it was worth the evidence of the general practice of steel erectors, though without some evidence of the deceased's own attitude towards safety belts I do not think it would have been worth much.

Undoubtedly a court should be very careful about finding what one may call hypothetical contributory negligence. A defendant, whose negligence has prevented the matter in issue from being put directly to the proof, must expect that a court will be very careful to make sure that it is acting on legitimate inference and not on speculation. But in the present case the evidence, even if it were confined to the deceased's own past acts, is in my opinion conclusive. If he had been injured only by the fall and could have gone into the witness-box, and if he had there sworn that he would have been wearing a safety belt if one had been available that morning, I do not see how he could have been believed.'

Comment

(1)   It is for the plaintiff to prove that his or her damage was factually caused by the defendant's act. The court demonstrated its practical common-sense approach to the hypothetical question of how the deceased might have acted if provided with a safety belt in the willingness to draw inferences from his past conduct in the matter.

(2)   Although in this case the plaintiff was required to prove that the defendants' conduct was the decisive cause of her husband's death, the standard, at least in relation to industrial accidents, has apparently subsequently been relaxed. In *McGhee v National Coal Board* it was held to be enough that the defendants, on the balance of probabilities, had materially increased the risk of injury to the plaintiff.

(3)   See also liability for breach of statutory duty, e.g. *Ginty v Belmont Building Supplies Ltd, Boyle v Kodak*, p 464.

Wilsher v Essex Area Health Authority
[1988] I All ER 871 House of Lords

The plaintiff, M, was a baby born prematurely with a number of illnesses including oxygen deficiency. When he was later found to be suffering from an incurable retinal condition causing blindness it was argued on his behalf that the defendants had caused the damage by their negligence in administering oxygen to him in excess. The House of Lords (reversing the Court of Appeal decision) held that excess oxygen was only one of five known causes of the blindness, each of which was present in the baby, and it had not been proved on the balance of probabilities that this was the effective cause.

Lord Bridge of Harwich: '... The starting point for any consideration of the relevant law of causation is the decision of this House in *Bonnington Castings Ltd v Wardlaw*. This was the case of a pursuer who, in the course of his employment by the defenders, contracted pneumoconiosis over a period of years by the inhalation of invisible particles of silica dust from two sources. One of these (pneumatic hammers) was an "innocent" source, in the sense that the pursuer could not complain that his exposure to it involved any breach of duty on the part of his employers. The other source (swing grinders), however, arose from a breach of statutory duty by the employer. Delivering the leading speech in the House Lord Reid said:

> "The Lord Ordinary and the majority of the First Division have dealt with this case on the footing that there was an onus on the defenders, the appellants, to prove that the dust from the swing grinders did not cause the respondent's disease. This view was based on a passage in the judgment of the Court of Appeal in *Vyner v Waldenberg Bros Ltd* per Scott LJ: 'If there is a definite breach of a safety provision imposed on the occupier of a factory, and a workman is injured in a way which could result from the breach, the onus of proof shifts on to the employer to show that the breach was not the cause. We think that that principle lies at the very basis of statutory rules of absolute duty.'

> ... Of course the onus was on the defendants to prove delegation (if that was an answer) and to prove contributory negligence, and it may be that that is what the Court of Appeal has in mind. But the passage which I have cited appears to go beyond that and, in so far as it does so, I am of opinion that it is erroneous. It would seem obvious in principle that a pursuer or plaintiff must prove not only negligence or breach of duty but also that such fault caused, or materially contributed to, his injury, and there is ample authority for that proposition both in Scotland and in England. I can find neither reason nor authority for the rule being different where there is breach of a statutory duty. The fact that Parliament imposes a duty for the protection of employees has been held to entitle an employee to sue if he is injured as a result of a breach of that duty, but it would be going a great deal further to hold that it can be inferred from the enactment of a duty that Parliament intended that any employee suffering injury can sue his employer merely because there was a breach of duty and it is shown to be possible that his injury may have been caused by it. In my judgment, the employee must, in all cases, prove his case

by the ordinary standard of proof in civil actions; he must make it appear at least that, on a balance of probabilities, the breach of duty caused, or materially contributed to, his injury."

Lord Tucker said of Scott LJ's dictum in *Vyner v Waldenberg Bros Ltd*:

"... I think it is desirable that your Lordships should take this opportunity to state in plain terms that no such onus exists unless the statute or statutory regulation expressly or impliedly so provides, as in several instances it does. No distinction can be drawn between actions for common law negligence and actions for breach of statutory duty in this respect. In both, the plaintiff or pursuer must prove (a) breach of duty, and (b) that such breach caused the injury complained of (see *Wakelin v London & South Western Ry Co* and *Caswell v Powell Duffryn Associated Collieries Ltd*). In each case, it will depend on the particular facts proved, and the proper inferences to be drawn therefrom, whether the respondent has sufficiently discharged the onus that lies on him."

Lord Keith said:

"The onus is on the respondent [the pursuer] to prove his case, and I see no reason to depart from this elementary principle by invoking certain rules of onus said to be based on a correspondence between the injury suffered and the evil guarded against by some statutory regulation. I think most, if not all, of the cases which professed to lay down or to recognise some such rule could have been decided as they were on simple rules of evidence, and I agree that *Vyner v Waldenberg Bros Ltd*, in so far as it professed to enunciate a principle of law inverting the onus of proof, cannot be supported."

Viscount Simonds and Lord Somervell agreed.

Their Lordships concluded, however, from the evidence that the inhalation of dust to which the pursuer was exposed by the defender's breach of statutory duty had made a material contribution to his pneumoconiosis which was sufficient to discharge the onus on the pursuer of proving that his damage was caused by the defenders' tort.

A year later the decision in *Nicholson v Atlas Steel Foundry and Engineering Co Ltd* followed the decision in *Bonnington Castings Ltd v Wardlaw* and held, in another case of pneumoconiosis, that the employers were liable for the employee's disease arising from the inhalation of dust from two sources, one "innocent" the other "guilty", on facts virtually indistinguishable from those in *Bonnington Castings Ltd v Wardlaw*.

In *McGhee v National Coal Board* the pursuer worked in a brick kiln in hot and dusty conditions in which brick dust adhered to his sweaty skin. No breach of duty by his employers, the defenders, was established in respect of his working conditions. However, the employers were held to be at fault in failing to provide adequate washing facilities which resulted in the pursuer having to bicycle home after work with his body still caked in brick dust. The pursuer contracted dermatitis and the evidence that this was caused by the brick dust was accepted. Brick dust adhering to the skin was a recognised cause of industrial dermatitis and the provision of showers to remove it after work was a usual precaution to minimise the risk of the disease. The precise mechanism of causation of the disease, however, was not known and the furthest the doctors called for the pursuer were able to go was to say that the provision of showers would have materially reduced the risk of dermatitis. They were unable to say that it would probably have prevented the disease.

The pursuer failed before the Lord Ordinary and the First Division of the Court of Session on the ground that he had not discharged the burden of proof of causation. He succeeded on appeal to the House of Lords. Much of the academic discussion to which this decision has given rise has focused on the speech of Lord Wilberforce, particularly on two paragraphs. He said:

"But the question remains whether a pursuer must necessarily fail if, after he has shown a breach of duty, involving an increase of risk of disease, he cannot positively prove that this increase of risk caused or materially contributed to the disease while his employers cannot positively prove the contrary. In this intermediate case there is an appearance of logic in the view that the pursuer, on whom the onus lies, should fail – a logic which dictated the judgments below. The question is whether we should be satisfied in factual situations like the present, with this logical approach. In my opinion, there are further considerations of importance. First, it is a sound principle that where a person has, by breach of duty of care, created a risk, and injury occurs within the area of that risk, the loss should be borne by him *unless he shows that it had some other cause.* Secondly, from the evidential point of view, one may ask, why should a man who is able to show that his employer should have taken certain precautions, because without them there is a risk, or an added risk, of injury or disease, and who in fact sustains exactly that injury or disease, have to assume the burden of proving more: namely, that it was the addition to the risk, caused by the breach of duty, which caused or materially contributed to the injury? In many cases of which the present is typical, this is impossible to prove, just because honest medical opinion cannot segregate the causes of an illness between compound causes. And if one asks which of the parties, the workman or the employers, should suffer from this inherent evidential difficulty, the answer as a matter in policy or justice should be that it is the creator of the risk who, *ex hyphothesi,* must be taken to have foreseen the possibility of damage, who should bear its consequences." (My emphasis.)

He then referred to *Bonnington Castings Ltd v Wardlaw* and *Nicholson v Atlas Steel Foundry and Engineering Co Ltd* and added:

"The present factual situation has its differences: the default here consisted not in adding a material quantity to the accumulation of injurious particles but by failure to take a step which materially increased the risk that the dust already present would cause injury. And I must say that, at least in the present case, to bridge the evidential gap by inference seems to me something of a fiction, since it was precisely this inference which the medical expert declined to make. But I find in the cases quoted an analogy which suggests the conclusion that, *in the absence of proof that the culpable condition had, in the results, no effect,* the employers should be liable for an injury, squarely within the risk which they created and that they, not the pursuer, should suffer the consequence of the impossibility, foreseeably inherent in the nature of his injury, of segregating the precise consequence of their default." (My emphasis.)

My Lords, it seems to me that both these paragraphs, particularly in the words I have emphasised, amount to saying that, in the circumstances, the burden of proof of causation is reversed and thereby to run counter to the unanimous and emphatic opinions expressed in *Bonnington Castings Ltd v Wardlaw* to the contrary effect. I find no support in any of the other speeches for the view that the burden of proof is reversed and, in this respect, I think Lord Wilberforce's reasoning must be regarded as expressing a minority opinion.

A distinction is, of course, apparent between the facts of *Bonnington Castings Ltd v Wardlaw,* where the "innocent" and "guilty" silica dust particles which together caused the pursuer's lung disease were inhaled concurrently and the facts of *McGhee v National Coal Board* where the "innocent" and "guilty" brick dust was present on the pursuer's body for consecutive periods. In the one case the concurrent inhalation of "innocent" and "guilty" dust must both have contributed to the cause of the disease. In the other case the consecutive periods when "innocent" and "guilty" brick dust was present on the pursuer's body may both have contributed to the cause of the disease or, theoretically at least, one or other may have been the sole cause. But where the layman is told by the doctors that the longer the brick dust remains on the body, the greater the risk of dermatitis, although the doctors cannot identify the process of causation scientifically, there seems to be nothing irrational in drawing the inference, as a matter of common sense, that the consecutive periods when brick dust remained on the body probably contributed cumulatively to the causation of the dermatitis. I believe that a process of inferential reasoning on these general lines underlies the decision of the majority in *McGhee's* case.

In support of this view, I refer to the following passages ... Lord Simon said:

"But *Bonnington Castings Ltd v Wardlaw* and *Nicholson v Atlas Steel Foundry and Engineering Co Ltd* establish, in my view, that where an injury is caused by two (or more) factors operating cumulatively, one (or more) of which factors is a breach of duty and one (or more) is not so, in such a way that it is impossible to ascertain the proportion in which the factors were effective in producing the injury or which factor was decisive, the law does not require a pursuer or plaintiff to prove the impossible, but holds that he is entitled to damages for the injury if he proves on a balance of probabilities that the breach of duty contributed substantially to causing the injury. If such factors so operate cumulatively, it is, in my judgment, immaterial whether they do so concurrently or successively."

Lord Kilbrandon said:

"In the present case, the appellant's body was vulnerable, while he was bicycling home, to the dirt which had been deposited on it during his working hours. It would not have been if he had had a shower. If showers had been provided he would have used them. It is admittedly more probable that disease will be contracted if a shower is not taken. In these circumstances I cannot accept the argument that nevertheless it is not more probable than not that, if the duty to provide a shower had been neglected, he would not have contracted the disease. The appellant has, after all, only to satisfy the court of a probability, not to demonstrate an irrefragable chain of causation, which in a case of dermatitis, in the present state of medical knowledge, he could probably never do."

Lord Salmon said:

"I, of course, accept that the burden rests on the appellant, to prove, on a balance of probabilities, a causal connection between his injury and the respondents' negligence. It is not necessary, however, to prove, that the respondents' negligence was the only cause of injury. A factor, by itself, may not be sufficient to cause injury but if, with other factors, it materially contributes to causing injury, it is clearly a cause of injury ... In the circumstances of the present case it seems to me unrealistic and contrary to ordinary common sense to hold that the negligence which materially increased the risk of injury did not materially contribute to causing the injury."

Then, after referring to *Bonnington Castings Ltd v Wardlaw* and *Nicholson v Atlas Steel Foundry and Engineering Co Ltd*, he added:

"I do not find the attempts to distinguish those authorities from the present case at all convincing. In the circumstances of the present case, the possibility of a distinction existing between (a) having materially increased the risk of contracting the disease, and (b) having materially contributed to causing the disease may no doubt be a fruitful source of interesting academic discussions between students of philosophy. Such a distinction is, however, far too unreal to be recognised by the common law."

The conclusion I draw from these passages is that *McGhee v National Coal Board* laid down no new principle of law whatever. On the contrary, it affirmed the principle that the onus of proving causation lies on the pursuer or plaintiff. Adopting a robust and pragmatic approach to the undisputed primary facts of the case, the majority concluded that it was a legitimate inference of fact that the defenders' negligence had materially contributed to the pursuer's injury. The decision, in my opinion, is of no greater significance than that and the attempt to extract from it some esoteric principle which in some way modifies, as a matter of law, the nature of the burden of proof of causation which a plaintiff or pursuer must discharge once he has established a relevant breach of duty is a fruitless one.

In the Court of Appeal in the instant case Sir Nicolas Browne-Wilkinson V-C, being in a minority, expressed his view on causation with understandable caution. But I am quite unable to find any fault with the following passage in his dissenting judgment:

> "To apply the principle in *McGhee v National Coal Board* to the present case would constitute an extension of that principle. In *McGhee* there was no doubt that the pursuer's dermatitis was physically caused by brick dust; the only question was whether the continued presence of such brick dust on the pursuer's skin after the time when he should have been provided with a shower caused or materially contributed to the dermatitis which he contracted. There was only one possible agent which could have caused the dermatitis, viz. brick dust, and there was no doubt that the dermatitis from which he suffered was caused by that brick dust. In the present case the question is different. There are a number of different agents which could have caused the RLF. Excess oxygen was one of them ... [But] there is no satisfactory evidence that excess oxygen is more likely than any of those other four candidates to have caused RLF in this baby. To my mind, the occurrence of RLF following a failure to take a necessary precaution to prevent excess oxygen causing RLF provides no evidence and raises no presumption that it was excess oxygen rather than one or more of the four other possible agents which caused or contributed to RLF in this case. The position, to my mind, is wholly different from that in *McGhee*, where there was only one candidate (brick dust) which could have caused the dermatitis, and the failure to take a precaution against brick dust causing dermatitis was followed by dermatitis caused by brick dust ..."

So here, in the absence of relevant findings of fact by the judge, there was really no alternative to a retrial ... To have to order a retrial is a highly unsatisfactory result and one cannot help feeling the profoundest sympathy for M and his family that the outcome is once again in doubt and that this litigation may have to drag on. Many may feel that such a result serves only to highlight the shortcomings of a system in which the victim of some grievous misfortune will recover substantial compensation or none at all according to the unpredictable hazards of the forensic process. But, whether we like it or not, the law, which only Parliament can change, requires proof of fault causing damage as the basis of liability in tort. We should do society

nothing but disservice if we made the forensic process still more unpredictable and hazardous by distorting the law to accommodate the exigencies of what may seem hard cases.'

Comment

(1) Since the plaintiff must prove that the defendant caused the injury, where there are a number of potential causes the plaintiff must show that the defendant's conduct is more likely to be to blame, on the balance of probabilities, than all of the other causes. In *Wilsher*, the existence of five possible causes, without further clear evidence, reduced the statistical likelihood of its being the defendants' fault that caused the damage to well below the required threshold.

(2) Even where expert medical evidence suggests that one factor has probably caused the claimant's condition, the presence of other potential factors and contradictory expert evidence may defeat a claim. In *Temple v South Manchester HA* the claimant suffered from cerebral oedema after receiving negligent medical treatment. Two expert witnesses considered that the defendant's negligence was the probable cause of his condition, but the Court of Appeal held that the judge had been entitled to prefer the evidence of one expert witness who cited a range of possible causes, thus leaving the case indistinguishable from *Wilsher*.

(3) It may be particularly difficult for sufferers from medical syndromes to establish causation. In *Page v Smith* (see p 97) the plaintiff suffered from Chronic Fatigue Syndrome which he claimed had been made worse by a motor accident carelessly caused by the defendant. Ralph Gibson LJ, in the Court of Appeal, considered that the test for causation had not been satisfied since, by its nature, a syndrome 'means a collection of symptoms which tend to occur together and form a characteristic pattern but which may not always be due to the same cause'. In the absence of any further evidence linking the type of event which had occurred with the condition suffered by the plaintiff, he could not be said to have proved causation.

(4) Similar difficulties may occur in the context of natural nuisances, where liability depends in large part on a finding of negligence. For example, in *Loftus-Brigham v Ealing LBC* there were two competing causes of desiccation leading to property damage – trees, the responsibility of the defendant, and a creeper belonging to the claimant. The Court of Appeal held that the claimant had failed to prove 'which vegetation was the dominant cause'.

Fairchild v Glenhaven Funeral Services Ltd and others
Fox v Spousal (Midlands) Ltd
Matthews v Associated Portland Cement Manufacturers (1978) Ltd and others
[2002] 3 All ER 305 House of Lords

Each of the appeals concerned an employee who had successively been exposed to asbestos dust by more than one negligent employer. Each employee had contracted mesothelioma which, it was agreed, must have been caused by inhalation of asbestos dust. The Court of Appeal had held that the claims must necessarily fail since the manner in which asbestos triggers the disease made it impossible to satisfy the 'but for' test against any individual employer and the question for the House of Lords was whether any modification of this approach was called for in the special circumstances. It was held, unanimously, that a modified approach was justified in these circumstances on grounds of principle, authority and policy.

Lord Hoffmann: '...

[48]   I shall first consider the question in principle. It is axiomatic that the law will not impose liability to pay compensation for damage unless there is a relevant causal connection between the damage and the defendant's tort, breach of contract or statutory duty. But what amounts to a relevant causal connection?

[49]   Everyone agrees that there is no scientific or philosophical touchstone for determining the relevant causal connection in any particular case. The relevance of a causal connection depends upon the purpose of the inquiry. In the present case, the House is required to say what should be the relevant causal connection for breach of a duty to protect an employee against the risk of contracting (among other things) mesothelioma by exposure to asbestos.

[50]   It is frequently said that causation is a question of fact or a matter of common sense. Both of these propositions are true but they need to be analysed with some care in order to avoid confusion.

[51]   First, in what sense is causation a question of fact? In order to describe something as a question of fact, it is necessary to be able to identify the question. For example, whether someone was negligent or not is a question of fact. What is the question? It is whether he failed to take reasonable care to avoid such damage as a reasonable man would have foreseen might result from his conduct. That question is formulated by the law. It is the law which says that failure to take reasonable care gives rise to liability. And the question is then answered by applying the standard of conduct prescribed by the law to the facts.

[52]   The same is true of causation. The question of fact is whether the causal requirements which the law lays down for that particular liability have been satisfied. But those requirements exist by virtue of rules of law. Before one can

answer the question of fact, one must first formulate the question. This involves deciding what, in the circumstances of the particular case, the law's requirements are. Unless one pays attention to the need to determine this preliminary question, the proposition that causation is a question of fact may be misleading. It may suggest that one somehow knows instinctively what the question is or that the question is always the same. As we shall see, this is not the case. The causal requirements for liability often vary, sometimes quite subtly, from case to case. And since the causal requirements for liability are always a matter of law, these variations represent legal differences, driven by the recognition that the just solution to different kinds of case may require different causal requirement rules.

[53] Then there is the role of common sense. Of course the causal requirements for liability are normally framed in accordance with common sense. But there is sometimes a tendency to appeal to common sense in order to avoid having to explain one's reasons. It suggests that causal requirements are a matter of incommunicable judicial instinct. I do not think that this is right. It should be possible to give reasons why one form of causal relationship will do in one situation but not in another.

[54] In my opinion, the essential point is that the causal requirements are just as much part of the legal conditions for liability as the rules which prescribe the kind of conduct which attracts liability or the rules which limit the scope of that liability. If I may repeat what I have said on another occasion, one is never simply liable, one is always liable for something – to make compensation for damage, the nature and extent of which is delimited by the law. The rules which delimit what one is liable for may consist of causal requirements or may be rules unrelated to causation, such as the foreseebility requirements in the rule in *Hadley v Baxendale*. But in either case they are rules of law, part and parcel of the conditions of liability. Once it is appreciated that the rules laying down causal requirements are not autonomous expressions of some form of logic or judicial instinct but creatures of the law, part of the conditions of liability, it is possible to explain their content on the grounds of fairness and justice in exactly the same way as the other conditions of liability.

[55] In the law of negligence, for example, it has long been recognised that the imposition of a duty of care in respect of particular conduct depends upon whether it is just and reasonable to impose it. Over vast areas of conduct one can generalise about the circumstances in which it will be considered just and reasonable to impose a duty of care: that is a consequence of *Donoghue* (or *M'Alister*) *v Stevenson*. But there are still situations in which Lord Atkin's generalisation cannot fairly be applied and in which it is necessary to return to the underlying principle and inquire whether it would be just and reasonable to impose liability and what its nature and extent should be: see *Caparo Industries plc v Dickman*.

[56] The same is true of causation. The concepts of fairness, justice and reason underlie the rules which state the causal requirements of liability for a particular form of conduct (or non-causal limits on that liability) just as much as they underlie

the rules which determine that conduct to be tortious. And the two are inextricably linked together: the purpose of the causal requirement rules is to produce a just result by delimiting the scope of liability in a way which relates to the reasons why liability for the conduct in question exists in the first place.

[57]   Across most grounds of liability, whether in tort, contract or by statute, it is possible to generalise about causal requirements. These generalisations are explored in detail by Hart and Honoré *Causation in the Law* (2nd edn, 1985). They represent what in ordinary life would normally be regarded as the reasonable limits for attributing blame or responsibility for harm: for example, that the defendant's conduct was a necessary condition for the occurrence of the harm (the 'but for' test), that it was not caused by the informed and voluntary act of another responsible human being and so on. To that extent, these causal requirements are based upon common sense. But, as Hart and Honoré also point out, there are situations in which these generalisations would fail to give effect to the reasons why it was thought just and reasonable to impose liability. For example, if it is thought just and reasonable to impose a duty to take care to protect someone against harm caused by the informed and voluntary act of another responsible human being, it would be absurd to retain a causal requirement that the harm should not have been so caused. An extreme case of this kind was *Reeves v Metropolitan Police Comr*, in which the defendant accepted that in the circumstances of the case, he owed a duty to take reasonable care to prevent a responsible human being from causing injury to himself. Your Lordships decided that in those circumstances it would be contradictory to hold that the causal requirements of the tort excluded liability for harm so caused. Thus the causal requirements are always adapted to conform to the grounds upon which liability is imposed. Again, it may be said that this is no more than common sense. But it is capable of rational explanation.

[58]   The same link between the grounds of liability and the causal requirements can be seen in cases of statutory liability. Sometimes the causal requirements are expressly stated; if not, the courts will construe the statute as requiring the causal connection which best gives effect to its policy. In *Empress Car Co (Abertillery) Ltd v National Rivers Authority* this House decided that the causal requirements of a statutory duty not to "cause 'polluting matter' to enter any controlled waters" did not exclude liability in cases in which the immediate cause of the pollution was the deliberate act of a responsible third party. It based this conclusion on the policy of the statute to impose a strict liability for the protection of the environment.

[59]   My Lords, even the much derided "last opportunity rule" which was applied in cases of contributory negligence before the Law Reform (Contributory Negligence) Act 1945 was in my opinion a perfectly rational attempt by the courts to fashion the causal requirements of the tort of negligence so as best to achieve a just and fair result in a situation in which the law insisted that any contributory negligence was a complete bar to recovery. To say that it was illogical or inelegant

seems to me neither here nor there. If it is recognised that the causal requirements are a matter of law and that the last opportunity rule was a development of the common law to mitigate the rigour of the contributory negligence rule, there was nothing illogical about it. As for inelegance, it was the best which could be done in the circumstances.

[60] The problem in this appeal is to formulate a just and fair rule. Clearly the rule must be based upon principle. However deserving the claimants may be, your Lordships are not exercising a discretion to adapt causal requirements to the individual case. That does not mean, however, that it must be a principle so broad that it takes no account of significant differences which affect whether it is fair and just to impose liability.

[61] What are the significant features of the present case? First, we are dealing with a duty specifically intended to protect employees against being unnecessarily exposed to the risk of (among other things) a particular disease. Secondly, the duty is one intended to create a civil right to compensation for injury relevantly connected with its breach. Thirdly, it is established that the greater the exposure to asbestos, the greater the risk of contracting that disease. Fourthly, except in the case in which there has been only one significant exposure to asbestos, medical science cannot prove whose asbestos is more likely than not to have produced the cell mutation which caused the disease. Fifthly, the employee has contracted the disease against which he should have been protected.

[62] In these circumstances, a rule requiring proof of a link between the defendant's asbestos and the claimant's disease would, with the arbitrary exception of single-employer cases, empty the duty of content. If liability depends upon proof that the conduct of the defendant was a necessary condition of the injury, it cannot effectively exist. It is however open to your Lordships to formulate a different causal requirement in this class of case. The Court of Appeal was in my opinion wrong to say that in the absence of a proven link between the defendant's asbestos and the disease, there was no "causative relationship" whatever between the defendant's conduct and the disease. It depends entirely upon the level at which the causal relationship is described. To say, for example, that the cause of Mr Matthews' cancer was his significant exposure to asbestos during two employments over a period of eight years, without being able to identify the day upon which he inhaled the fatal fibre, is a meaningful causal statement. The medical evidence shows that it is the only kind of causal statement about the disease which, in the present state of knowledge, a scientist would regard as possible. There is no *a priori* reason, no rule of logic, which prevents the law from treating it as sufficient to satisfy the causal requirements of the law of negligence. The question is whether your Lordships think such a rule would be just and reasonable and whether the class of cases to which it applies can be sufficiently clearly defined.

[63] So the question of principle is this: in cases which exhibit the five features I have mentioned, which rule would be more in accordance with justice and the

policy of common law and statute to protect employees against the risk of contracting asbestos-related diseases? One which makes an employer in breach of his duty liable for the claimant's injury because he created a significant risk to his health, despite the fact that the physical cause of the injury may have been created by someone else? Or a rule which means that unless he was subjected to risk by the breach of duty of a single employer, the employee can never have a remedy? My Lords, as between the employer in breach of duty and the employee who has lost his life in consequence of a period of exposure to risk to which that employer has contributed, I think it would be both inconsistent with the policy of the law imposing the duty and morally wrong for your Lordships to impose causal requirements which exclude liability.

[64] My Lords, I turn from principle to authority. The case which most closely resembles the present is *McGhee v National Coal Board*, which my noble and learned friend Lord Bingham of Cornhill has analysed in some detail. There too, the employer was under a duty (to provide washing facilities) specifically intended to protect employees against being unnecessarily exposed to the risk of (among other things) a particular disease, namely dermatitis. Secondly, the duty was one intended to create a civil right to compensation for injury relevantly connected with its breach. Thirdly, it was established that the longer the workman exerted himself while particles of dust adhered to his skin, the greater was the risk of his contracting dermatitis. Fourthly, the mechanism by which dust caused the disease was unknown, so that medical science was unable to prove whether the particular dust abrasions which caused the dermatitis were more likely than not to have occurred before or after the dust would have been removed if washing facilities had been provided. All that could be said was that the absence of facilities added materially to the risk that he would contract the disease. Fifthly, the employee contracted the disease against which he should have been protected.

[65] My Lords, in these circumstances, which in my opinion reproduce the essential features of the present case, the House decided that materially increasing the risk that the disease would occur was sufficient to satisfy the causal requirements for liability. It is true that Lord Wilberforce spoke of reversing the burden of proof and imposing liability unless the employer could prove that washing would have made no difference. But I respectfully think that it is artificial to treat the employer as having a burden of proof in a case in which *ex hypothesi* the state of medical knowledge is such that the burden cannot be discharged. There are also passages in the speeches which suggest that materially increasing the risk of disease is being treated as equivalent to materially contributing to the injury – making the illness worse than it would otherwise have been. But this, as Lord Wilberforce pointed out, is precisely what the doctors did not say. They refused to say that it was more likely than not that the absence of washing facilities had had any effect at all. So when some members of the House said that in the circumstances there was no distinction between materially increasing the risk of disease and materially contributing to the disease, what I think they meant was

that, in the particular circumstances, a breach of duty which materially increased the risk should be treated as if it had materially contributed to the disease. I would respectfully prefer not resort to legal fictions and to say that the House treated a material increase in risk as sufficient in the circumstances to satisfy the causal requirements for liability. That this was the effect of the decision seems to me inescapable.

[66] The grounds upon which the House was willing to formulate a special causal requirements rule in *McGhee's* case seem to me equally applicable in this case. So Lord Wilberforce said:

"if one asks which of the parties, the workman or the employers, should suffer from this inherent evidential difficulty [i.e. the absence of knowledge of the mechanism by which dust caused the disease], the answer as a matter of policy or justice should be that it is the creator of the risk who, *ex hypothesi*, must be taken to have foreseen the possibility of damage, who should bear its consequences."

Lord Simon of Glaisdale said:

"To hold otherwise would mean that the respondents were under a legal duty which they could, in the present state of medical knowledge, with impunity ignore."

Lord Salmon said:

"it would mean that in the present state of medical knowledge and in circumstances such as these (which are by no means uncommon) an employer would be permitted by the law to disregard with impunity his duty to take reasonable care for the safety of his employees."

[67] I therefore regard *McGhee's* case as a powerful support for saying that when the five factors I have mentioned are present, the law should treat a material increase in risk as sufficient to satisfy the causal requirements for liability. The only difficulty lies in the way *McGhee's* case was explained in *Wilsher v Essex Area Health Authority*. The latter was not a case in which the five factors were present. It was an action for clinical negligence in which it was alleged that giving a premature baby excessive oxygen had caused retrolental fibroplasia, resulting in blindness. The evidence was that the fibroplasia could have been caused in a number of different ways including excessive oxygen but the judge had made no finding that the oxygen was more likely than not to have been the cause. The Court of Appeal held that the health authority was nevertheless liable because even if the excessive oxygen could not be shown to have caused the injury, it materially increased the risk of the injury happening.

[68] The Court of Appeal reached this conclusion by treating the causal requirement rule applied in *McGhee's* case as being of general application. Mustill LJ said:

"If it is an established fact that conduct of a particular kind creates a risk that injury will be caused to another or increases an existing risk that injury will ensue, and if the two parties stand in such a relationship that the one party owes a duty not to conduct himself in that way, and if the other party does suffer injury of the kind to which the risk related, then the first party is taken to have caused the injury by his breach of duty, even though the existence and extent of the contribution made by the breach cannot be ascertained."

[69]   The House of Lords, in a speech by Lord Bridge of Harwich with which all other noble Lords concurred, rejected this broad principle. I would respectfully agree. The principle in *McGhee's* case is far narrower and I have tried to indicate what its limits are likely to be. It is true that actions for clinical negligence notoriously give rise to difficult questions of causation. But it cannot possibly be said that the duty to take reasonable care in treating patients would be virtually drained of content unless the creation of a material risk of injury were accepted as sufficient to satisfy the causal requirements for liability. And the political and economic arguments involved in the massive increase in the liability of the National Health Service which would have been a consequence of the broad rule favoured by the Court of Appeal in *Wilsher's* case are far more complicated than the reasons given by Lord Wilberforce for imposing liability upon an employer who has failed to take simple precautions.

[70]   I therefore think that *Wilsher's* case was correctly decided. The appellants have not made any submission to the contrary. But the grounds upon which *McGhee's* case was distinguished are unsatisfactory. Lord Bridge said that it represented a "robust and pragmatic approach" to the facts which had enabled the House to draw a "legitimate inference of fact" that the "defenders' negligence had materially contributed to the pursuer's injury". My Lords, however robust or pragmatic the tribunal may be, it cannot draw inferences of fact in the teeth of the undisputed medical evidence. My noble and learned friend Lord Bingham has demonstrated that such an analysis of *McGhee's* case is untenable.

[71]   An alternative ground of distinction is to be found in a passage in the dissenting judgment of Browne-Wilkinson V-C in the Court of Appeal, which was approved by the House. He said that the difference was that in *McGhee's* case the agent of injury was the same – brick dust – and the only question was whether it happened before or after it should have been washed off. In *Wilsher's* case, the fibroplasia could have been caused by a number of different agencies.

[72]   That distinction would leave the present case on the right side of the line because the agent of injury was the same – asbestos dust. But I do not think it is a principled distinction. What if Mr Matthews had been exposed to two different agents – asbestos dust and some other dust – both of which created a material risk of the same cancer and it was equally impossible to say which had caused the fatal cell mutation? I cannot see why this should make a difference.

[73]   The question is how narrowly the principle developed in *McGhee's* case and applied in this case should be confined. In my opinion, caution is advisable. *Wilsher's* case shows the dangers of over-generalisation. In *Rutherford v Owens-Illinois Inc* the Supreme Court of California, in a valuable and lucid judgment, said that in cases of asbestos-related cancer, the causal requirements of the tort were satisfied by proving that exposure to a particular product was a substantial factor contributing to the "plaintiff's or decedent's risk of developing cancer". That is precisely the rule your Lordships are being invited to apply in this case. The Californian Supreme Court stated the principle specifically in relation to asbestos-related cancer cases. No doubt it could also apply in other cases which were thought to have sufficient common features, but that was left for decision on a case-by-case basis. Likewise I would suggest that the rule now laid down by the House should be limited to cases which have the five features I have described.

[74]   That does not mean that the principle is not capable of development and application in new situations. As my noble and learned friend Lord Rodger of Earlsferry has demonstrated, problems of uncertainty as to which of a number of possible agents caused an injury have required special treatment of one kind or another since the time of the Romans. But the problems differ quite widely and the fair and just answer will not always be the same. For example, in the famous case of *Sindell v Abbott Laboratories* the plaintiff had suffered pre-natal injuries from exposure to a drug which had been manufactured by any one of a potentially large number of defendants. The case bears some resemblance to the present but the problem is not the same. For one thing, the existence of the additional manufacturers did not materially increase the risk of injury. The risk from consuming a drug bought in one shop is not increased by the fact that it can also be bought in another shop. So the case would not fall within the *McGhee's* case principle. But the Supreme Court of California laid down the imaginative rule that each manufacturer should be liable in proportion to his market share. Cases like this are not before the House and should in my view be left for consideration when they arise. For present purposes, the *McGhee* principle is sufficient. I would therefore allow the appeals.'

Comment

(1)   Each of their Lordships, while expressing general approval of the standard 'but for' approach, recognised that such rigidity might sometimes result in an unacceptable injustice. Lord Bingham said:

'[8]   ... In the generality of personal injury actions, it is of course true that the claimant is required to discharge the burden of showing that the breach of which he complains caused the damage for which he claims and to do so by showing that but for the breach he would not have suffered the damage.

[9]   The issue in these appeals does not concern the general validity and applicability of that requirement, which is not in question, but is whether in special circumstances such as those in these cases there should be any variation or relaxation of it. The overall object of tort law is to define cases in which the law may justly hold one party liable to compensate another.'

And Lord Nicholls, agreeing, said:

'[36]   ... Any other outcome would be deeply offensive to instinctive notions of what justice requires and fairness demands. The real difficulty lies is elucidating in sufficiently specific terms the principle being applied in reaching this conclusion. To be acceptable the law must be coherent. It must be principled. The basis on which one case, or one type of case, is distinguished from another should be transparent and capable of identification. When a decision departs from principles normally applied, the basis for doing so must be rational and justifiable if the decision is to avoid the reproach that hard cases make bad law. ...

[37]   In the normal way, in order to recover damages for negligence, a plaintiff must prove that but for the defendant's wrongful conduct he would not have sustained the harm or loss in question. He must establish at least this degree of causal connection between his damage and the defendant's conduct before the defendant will be held responsible for the damage.

[38]   Exceptionally this is not so. In some circumstances a lesser degree of causal connection may suffice. This sometimes occurs where the damage flowed from one or other of two alternative causes. Take the well-known example where two hunters, acting independently of each other, fire their guns carelessly in a wood, and a pellet from one of the guns injures an innocent passer-by. No one knows, and the plaintiff is unable to prove, from which gun the pellet came. Should the law of negligence leave the plaintiff remediless, and allow both hunters to go away scot-free, even though one of them must have fired the injurious pellet?'

(2)   After an extensive review of a wide range of European, American and Commonwealth cases, all of which supported the principle of a modified approach, Lord Bingham observed:

'Development of the law in this country cannot of course depend on a head-count of decisions and codes adopted in other countries around the world, often against a background of different rules and traditions. The law must be developed coherently, in accordance with principle, so as to serve, even-handedly, the ends of justice. If, however, a decision is given in this country which offends one's basic sense of justice, and if consideration of international sources suggests that a different and more acceptable decision would be given in most other jurisdictions, whatever their legal tradition, this must prompt anxious review of the decision in question. In a shrinking world (in which the employees of asbestos companies may work for those companies in any one or more of several countries) there must be some virtue in uniformity of outcome whatever the diversity of approach in reaching that outcome.'

(3)   A different analysis was adopted by the Court of Appeal in *Holtby v Brigham & Cowan (Hull) Ltd*, in which the claimant suffered asbestosis rather than mesothelioma. The claimant had been exposed to asbestos by more than one employer, but had spent half of the overall period of exposure working for the defendant. The Court of Appeal approved the judge's approach, since asbestosis is a condition that worsens with prolonged exposure, which was to calculate the defendant's liability 'on a time exposure basis'. By contrast, in *Barker v Saint Gobain Pipelines plc*, another mesothelioma claim, the Court of Appeal rejected the notion of apportionment in respect of a claimant whose exposure had been partly during periods of self-employment.

(4)   The *Fairchild* approach was applied by the Court of Appeal in *Griggs v Transco plc* in which the claimant had worked for some 24 years using a variety of vibratory tools such as road-breakers and whackers. The defendants disputed the causal link between their negligence and the precise form of injury suffered by the claimant. Hale LJ said:

'33.   Bearing in mind the length and magnitude of this claimant's exposure to vibration, as demonstrated by the engineering experts, and the extensive breaches of duty admitted by the defendant, it is possible to conclude that the but for test is indeed satisfied in this case. If the breach of duty was sufficient to cause one type of vibration induced injury why should it not also be sufficient to cause another? ...

35.   In any event even if the but for test could not be satisfied, there can be little doubt that the employer's failure to have a proper system for detecting and preventing vibration induced diseases materially increased the risk of an employee sustaining such a disease. Once the degree of exposure, the breaches of duty and the medical causation had been established, it would be an unjust legal system which did not hold the employer responsible for what had happened.'

(5)   Similarly, in *Watson v British Boxing Board of Control Ltd* (see also p 225), the Court of Appeal considered the causative effect of a negligent delay in providing appropriate treatment to an unconscious boxer. Lord Phillips of Worth Matravers MR quoted the trial judge's statement:

'On the evidence earlier treatment would have made a significant differ-ence to the outcome ... The final question is: to what extent? I do not believe that the evidence admits of any accurate answer to this question but that is by no means an uncommon situation in cases of this sort. Medical knowledge does not enable one to say what, on the balance of probabilities, would have been the outcome if the protocol had been in place and followed ... Here all that is clear is that on the balance of probabilities the claimant's present state would have been materially better than it actually is. It is not possible to measure even on the balance of probabilities where the damage would have stopped if the protocol had been followed.'

He approved the judge's application of the *McGhee* approach, and the finding that the defendants should be liable in full.

(6)   In *Hotson v East Berks AHA* the 13-year-old plaintiff fell from a tree and injured his hip. He was taken to the defendants' hospital where the injury was incorrectly diagnosed. After five days of severe pain the plaintiff returned to the hospital but despite correct diagnosis and treatment developed a major permanent disability of his leg by the age of 20. He claimed damages alleging that the delay resulting from the defendants' admitted negligence was the cause of his final condition. The trial judge had awarded 25 per cent of the total damages to reflect his finding that the plaintiff had had a 75 per cent chance of developing the condition even in the absence of any delay. The House of Lords allowed the appeal on the basis that the 25 per cent chance that the damage was due to the defendants' negligence did not satisfy the balance of probabilities which is the test for causation. Lord Ackner said:

'... To my mind, the first issue which the judge had to determine was an issue of causation: did the breach of duty cause the damage alleged? If it did not, as the judge so held, then no question of quantifying damage arises. The debate on the loss of a chance cannot arise where there has been a positive finding that before the duty arose the damage complained of had already been sustained or had become inevitable ... In a sentence, the plaintiff was not entitled to any damages in respect of the deformed hip because the judge had decided that this was not caused by the admitted breach by the authority of their duty of care but was caused by the separation of the left femoral epiphysis when he fell some 12 feet from a rope on which he had been swinging.

On this simple basis I would allow this appeal. I have sought to stress that this case was a relatively simple case concerned with the proof of causation, on which the plaintiff failed, because he was unable to prove, on the balance of probabilities, that his deformed hip was caused by the authority's breach of duty in delaying over a period of five days a proper diagnosis and treatment. Where *causation* is in issue, the judge decides that issue on the balance of the probabilities. Unless there is some special situation, e.g. joint defendants where the apportionment of liability between them is required, there is no point or purpose in expressing in percentage terms the certainty or near certainty which the plaintiff has achieved in establishing his cause of action.

Once liability is established, on the balance of probabilities, the loss which the plaintiff has sustained is payable in full. It is not discounted by reducing his claim by the extent to which he has failed to prove his case with 100 per cent certainty. The decision by Simon Brown J in the subsequent case of *Bagley v North Herts Health Authority*, in which he discounted an award for a still birth because there was a 5 per cent risk that the plaintiff would have had a stillborn child even if the hospital had not been negligent, was clearly wrong. In that case, the plaintiff had established on a balance of probabilities, indeed with near certainty, that the hospital's negligence had caused the still birth. Causation was thus fully established. Such a finding does not permit any discounting: to do so would be to propound a wholly new doctrine which has no support in principle or authority and would give rise to many complications in the search for mathematical or statistical exactitude.

Of course, where the cause of action has been established, the assessment of that part of the plaintiff's loss where the future is uncertain, involves the evaluation of that uncertainty. In *Bagley*, if the child had, by reason of the hospital's breach of duty, been born with brain injury, which could lead in later life to epilepsy, then it would have been a classic case for the evaluation, *inter alia*, of the chance of epilepsy occurring and discounting, to the extent that the chance of that happening fell below 100 per cent, what would have been the sum of damages appropriate if epilepsy was a certain consequence.'

Hotson demonstrates very clearly the courts' 'all or nothing' approach to the question of causation. The principle of treating anything which is more probable than not as a certainty means that, subject to the possibility of multiple causation, the defendant is either liable or the defendant is not. The defendant will not be held partially liable for damage which he or she might possibly have caused. The question of damages for the lost chance, as in *Chaplin v Hicks*, is based on the proposition that before the negligent delay the plaintiff had a 25 per cent probability of escaping disability whereas afterwards he had none. Lord Ackner's rejection of this argument follows logically from the conclusion in law that, having failed the balance of probabilities test, the plaintiff's disability is to be regarded as an inevitability from the time of his original fall.

(7) In *Bolitho v City and Hackney HA* (see also p 207) a doctor negligently failed to attend a sick baby who subsequently died. Expert medical evidence

suggested that the death could have been avoided had a particular form of intervention (intubation to avoid respiratory failure followed by cardiac arrest) been adopted. On the issue of causation Lord Browne-Wilkinson, speaking for the House of Lords, observed that:

> 'In all cases, the primary question is one of fact: did the wrongful act cause the injury? But in cases where the breach of duty consists of an omission to do an act which ought to be done (e.g. the failure by a doctor to attend) that factual inquiry is, by definition, in the realms of hypothesis. The question is what would have happened if an event which by definition did not occur, had occurred.'

The doctor in the case argued that, since she would not have intubated even if she had attended, her admitted negligence had not factually caused the baby's death. The House of Lords held that this in itself was not enough:

> 'In the present case, the answer to the question "what would have happened" is not determinative of the issue of causation ... A defendant cannot escape liability by saying that the damage would have occurred in any event because he would have committed some other breach of duty thereafter.'

It was therefore necessary for the doctor to prove that her hypothetical decision as to treatment would not have been negligent. Applying the *Bolam* test, the court concluded that there was evidence that a reasonable body of medical opinion supported the doctor's decision and that her negligence had not therefore caused the baby's death.

(8)   In *Allied Maples Group Ltd v Simmons & Simmons (a firm)* the Court of Appeal held that damages should be awarded for the loss of a 'substantial chance'. In this case the plaintiffs had been negligently advised by the defendant solicitors in relation to documents in a company takeover, and had failed to negotiate steps to protect themselves from potential future liability. The defendants argued that they could not be proved to have caused the resulting losses since the plaintiffs' conduct in the light of different advice could be no more than hypothetical. The Court of Appeal held that, properly advised, the plaintiffs would, on the balance of probabilities, have sought some protection. It would then be necessary, in order to calculate the quantum of damages, to consider the level of protection which might have been negotiated, and the probability of such terms being accepted – an issue quite separate from that of causation.

(9)   In *Gregg v Scott* the claimant's tumour was repeatedly mis-diagnosed with the result that, by the time it was properly identified, he was beyond hope of a cure. At first instance, the judge held that the claimant had failed to prove that the negligent delay affected the outcome of the disease but the claimant appealed on the ground that his case should more properly be regarded as a

'lost chance' claim, inviting the Court of Appeal to follow *Fairchild* in applying policy to achieve a just outcome. The Court of Appeal, while expressing great sympathy for the claimant, held by a two-to-one majority that the facts fell outwith the narrow circumstances justifying a modified approach to causation. As to the lost chance, Mance LJ said:

'I do not think that English law can or should contemplate what would be essentially speculative actions for loss of life expectancy, based on no more than general statistical evidence. ... Further, if it was open to an English claimant to claim for loss of a chance in a case such as the present, then a claimant in the position of the claimant in *Wilsher* ought to be able to recover damages apportioned to reflect the percentage prospect that the negligence played a part, rather than nothing at all. There is no suggestion of this, even in argument, in any prior authority put before us, and it would represent a considerable increase in exposure.'

(10)   A differently constituted Court of Appeal has since, in *Normans Bay Ltd (formerly Illingworth Morris Ltd) v Coudert Brothers*, unanimously expressed 'disquiet' at the outcome in *Gregg*. Laws LJ said:

'68.   I understand and respect the reasons why the majority in *Gregg v Scott* held as they did, not least given the impact of the earlier decision of their Lordships' House in *Hotson*. But I am driven to an unhappy sense that the common law has lost its way. If a man's chance of a cure from a potentially fatal cancer has been reduced by another's negligence from 42% to 25%, would not a reasonable jury say that he had been grievously hurt by the negligence? The correctness of *Gregg v Scott* is, of course, for the House of Lords, or possibly the legislature, and not for us. But there is in my judgment no good reason to extend its application.'

The court went on to uphold the finding that a lost chance was established, here in a commercial context, but reduced the level of damages.

Jobling v Associated Dairies Ltd
[1981] 2 All ER 752 House of Lords

The appellant suffered a back injury caused by the respondent employers' breach of duty. As a result his earning capacity was reduced by 50 per cent. Before the case came to trial the appellant was found to be suffering from an entirely unrelated spinal condition which rendered him completely unfit for work. The House of Lords held that no damages were payable for loss of earnings after the onset of his illness.

Lord Keith of Kinkel: '... The facts in *Baker v Willoughby* were that the plaintiff suffered an injury to his left leg through the defendant's negligence, resulting in a continuing disability which reduced his earning capacity. Before his case came to trial he was shot by a robber in the same leg, which in consequence had to be amputated. As a result the plaintiff's disability was rather greater than it had been before. This House, reversing the Court of Appeal, held that the award of damages for loss of earnings did not fall to be diminished by reason of the later injuries on the view that they represented no more than a concurrent cause, along with the original injury, of the plaintiff's disability.

It was argued for the respondent, defendant in the action, that the second injury removed the very limb from which the earlier disability had stemmed, and that therefore no loss suffered thereafter could be attributed to the respondent's negligence. In rejecting this argument Lord Reid, whose speech was concurred in by Lord Guest, Viscount Dilhorne and Lord Donovan, said:

> "If it were the case that in the eye of the law an effect could only have one cause then the respondent might be right. It is always necessary to prove that any loss for which damages can be given was caused by the defendant's negligent act. But it is commonplace that the law regards many events as having two causes; that happens whenever there is a contributory negligence, for then the law says that the injury was caused both by the negligence of the defendant and by the negligence of the plaintiff. And generally it does not matter which negligence occurred first in point of time."

Lord Reid took the view that the appellant's disability could be regarded as having two causes ... [He] later went on to distinguish the case where damages might properly fall to be diminished by reason of the death of the plaintiff before trial, on the basis that in such a case the supervening event had reduced the plaintiff's loss. He said:

> "If the later injury suffered before the date of the trial either reduces the disabilities from the injury for which the defendant is liable, or shortens the period during which they will be suffered by the plaintiff then the defendant will have to pay less damages. But if the later injuries merely become a concurrent cause of the disabilities caused by the injury inflicted by the defendant, then in my view they cannot diminish the damages. Suppose that the plaintiff has to spend a month in bed before the trial because of some illness unconnected with the original injury, the defendant cannot say that he does not have to pay anything in respect of that month; during that month the original injuries and the new illness are concurrent causes of his inability to work and that does not reduce the damages."

It seems clear from this passage that the principle of concurrent causes which Lord Reid selected as the *ratio decidendi* of the case would, if sound, apply with the same force where the supervening event is natural disease, as in the present case, as it does where the supervening event is a tortious act.

Lord Pearson's main reason for rejecting the respondent's argument was that it would produce manifest injustice. He said:

"The supervening event has not made the plaintiff less lame nor less disabled nor less deprived of amenities. It has not shortened the period over which he will be suffering. It has made him more lame, more disabled, more deprived of amenities. He should not have less damages through being worse off than might have been expected."

Lord Pearson went on to illustrate the nature of the injustice by pointing out that, where the supervening event was a tortious act, the later tortfeasor, on the principle that he takes his victim as he finds him, would be liable for damages in respect of loss of earnings only to the extent that the act had caused an additional diminution of earning capacity. If the earlier incapacity were treated, in a question with the first tortfeasor, as submerged by the later, the plaintiff would be left in the position of being unable to recover from anyone a substantial part of the loss suffered after the date of the second tort. So he would not be fully compensated in respect of the combined effects of both torts. It is to be observed that this was the consideration which had been principally urged in the argument for the appellant.

A notable feature of the speeches in *Baker v Willoughby* is the absence of any consideration of the possible implications of what may be termed the "vicissitudes" principle. The leading exposition of this principle is to be found in the judgment of Brett LJ in *Phillips v London and South Western Railway Co:*

" … if no accident had happened, nevertheless many circumstances might have happened to prevent the plaintiff from earning his previous income; he may be disabled by illness, he is subject to the ordinary accidents and vicissitudes of life; and if all these circumstances of which no evidence can be given are looked at, it will be impossible to exactly estimate them; yet if the jury wholly pass them over they will go wrong, because these accidents and vicissitudes ought to be taken in account. It is true that the chances of life cannot be accurately calculated, but the judge must tell the jury to consider them in order that they may give a fair and reasonable compensation."

This principle is to be applied in conjunction with the rule that the court will not speculate when it knows, so that when an event within its scope has actually happened prior to the trial date, that event will fall to be taken into account in the assessment of damages …

It is implicit in [*Baker v Willoughby*] that the scope of the "vicissitudes" principle is limited to supervening events of such a nature as either to reduce the disabilities resulting from the accident or else to shorten the period during which they will be suffered. I am of opinion that failure to consider or even advert to this implication weakens the authority of the *ratio decidendi* of the case, and must lead to the conclusion that in its full breadth it is not acceptable. The assessment of damages for personal injuries involves a process of *restitutio in integrum*. The object is to place the injured plaintiff in as good a position as he would have been in but for the accident. He is not to be placed in a better position. The process involves a comparison between the plaintiff's circumstances as regards capacity to enjoy the amenities of life and to earn a living as they would have been if the accident had not occurred and his actual circumstances in those respects following the accident. In considering how matters might have been expected to turn out if there had been no accident, the "vicissitudes" principle says that it is right to take into account events, such as illness, which not uncommonly occur in the ordinary course of human life. If such events are not taken into account, the damages may be greater than are required to compensate the plaintiff for the effects of the accident, and that result would be unfair to the defendant ...

I am therefore of opinion that the majority in *Baker v Willoughby* were mistaken in approaching the problems common to the case of a supervening tortious act and to that of supervening illness wholly from the point of view of causation. While it is logically correct to say that in both cases the original tort and the supervening event may be concurrent causes of incapacity, that does not necessarily, in my view, provide the correct solution. In the case of supervening illness, it is appropriate to keep in view that this is one of the ordinary vicissitudes of life, and when one is comparing the situation resulting from the accident with the situation, had there been no accident, to recognise that the illness would have overtaken the plaintiff in any event, so that it cannot be disregarded in arriving at proper compensation, and no more than proper compensation.

Additional considerations come into play when dealing with the problems arising where the plaintiff has suffered injuries from two or more successive and independent tortious acts. In that situation it is necessary to secure that the plaintiff is fully compensated for the aggregate effects of all his injuries. As Lord Pearson noted in *Baker v Willoughby* it would clearly be unjust to reduce the damages awarded for the first tort because of the occurrence of the second tort, damages for which are to be assessed on the basis that the plaintiff is already partially incapacitated. I do not consider it necessary to formulate any precise juristic basis for dealing with this situation differently from the case of supervening illness. It might be said that a supervening tort is not one of the ordinary vicissitudes of life, or that it is too remote a possibility to be taken into account, or that it can properly be disregarded because it carries its own remedy. None of these formulations, however, is entirely satisfactory. The fact remains that the principle of full compensation requires that a just and practical solution should be found. In the event that damages against two successive tortfeasors fall to be assessed at the same time, it would be highly unreasonable if the aggregate of both awards were less than the total loss suffered by the plaintiff. The computation should start from an assessment of that total loss. The award against the second tortfeasor cannot in fairness to him fail to recognise that the plaintiff whom he injured was already to some extent incapacitated. In order that the plaintiff may be fully compensated, it becomes necessary to deduct the award so calculated from the assessment of the plaintiff's total loss and award the balance against the first tortfeasor. If that be a correct approach, it follows that, in proceedings against the first tortfeasor alone, the occurrence of the second tort cannot be successfully relied on by the defendant as reducing the damages which he must pay. That, in substance, was the result of the decision in *Baker v Willoughby*, where the supervening event was a tortious act, and to that extent the decision was, in my view, correct.

Before leaving the case, it is right to face up to the fact that, if a non-tortious supervening event is to have the effect of reducing damages but a subsequent tortious act is not, there may in some cases be difficulty in ascertaining whether the event in question is or is not of a tortious character, particularly in the absence of the alleged tortfeasor. Possible questions of contributory negligence may cause additional complications. Such difficulties are real, but are not sufficient, in my view, to warrant the conclusion that the distinction between tortious and non-tortious supervening events should not be accepted. The court must simply do its best to arrive at a just assessment of damages in a pragmatical way in the light of the whole circumstances of the case.'

Comment

The division of supervening events into two categories according to whether they are tortious or not may, at first sight, seem somewhat artificial although the principles to be applied to each class are logical enough. It stems from the courts' anxiety that a plaintiff should be neither over- nor under-compensated.

Lamb and another v London Borough of Camden and another [1981] 2 All ER 408 Court of Appeal

In 1972 the plaintiff let her house while she was abroad. A year later some council contractors breached the water main outside the plaintiff's house making it unsafe so that the tenants left and the plaintiff's furniture was moved into storage. While the house was empty awaiting repair, some squatters moved in but were evicted and the house boarded up. In 1975 squatters again moved in and caused extensive damage to the house. The Court of Appeal rejected the plaintiff's claim for damages saying that the invasion of the squatters amounted to a *novus actus*.

Oliver LJ: '... I am not able to accept the submission of counsel for the council in the form in which he put it, namely that reasonable foreseeability is but one ingredient in a composite test of remoteness, which involves a further ingredient which he has described as "nexus". This seems to me to be restoring that very fallacy which was exemplified in *Re Polemis* and was so decisively rejected in *The Wagon Mound (No 2)*. That case established that the test of causation is reasonable foreseeability, and I can find no room for the suggestion that, even though a particular result may be reasonably foreseen as the consequence of an act, yet the result may be too remote a consequence because of a lack of "nexus". Nexus, after all, means only "connection" and it must be comprehended in the very concept of foreseeability itself. If there is, as a matter of fact, no connection between the act and the result, it is difficult to see how the result could be foreseen by any reasonable man *as a consequence* of the act.

Counsel for the council advances his submission as the groundwork for the further submission that, where one of the links in the chain between act and result is the act of an independent third person, the nexus is broken, unless that act is not merely foreseen but is either "likely" or "very likely". This concept is … based on the analysis in the speech of Lord Reid in *Home Office v Dorset Yacht Co Ltd* …

> "These cases show that, where human action forms one of the links between the original wrongdoing of the defendant and the loss suffered by the plaintiff, that action must at least have been something very likely to happen if it is not to be regarded as *novus actus interveniens* breaking the chain of causation. I do not think that a mere foreseeable possibility is or should be sufficient, for then the intervening human action can more properly be regarded as a new cause than as a consequence of the original wrongdoing. But if the intervening action was likely to happen I do not think it can matter whether that action was innocent or tortious or criminal. Unfortunately tortious or criminal action by a third party is often the 'very kind of thing' which is likely to happen as a result of the wrongful or careless act of the defendant."

The views which Lord Reid there expressed are not reflected in the speeches of the others of their Lordships in the case, and were, I think, *obiter*, since there was no scope for argument on the assumed facts that the damage which occurred was not the very thing that was likely to happen. But, *obiter* or no, Lord Reid's opinion must be at least of the very highest persuasive authority. For my part, however, I very much doubt whether he was, in what he said regarding the likelihood of the act of a third party, intending to bring back into the test of remoteness some further philosophical consideration of nexus or direct or indirect causation. As it seems to me, all that Lord Reid was saying was this, that, where as a matter of fact the consequence which the court is considering is one which results from, or would not have occurred but for, the intervention of some independent human agency over which the tortfeasor has no control it has to approach the problem of what could be reasonably foreseen by the tortfeasor, and thus of the damage for which he is responsible, with particular care. The immediate cause is known: it is the independent human agency; and one has therefore to ask: on what basis can the act of that person be attributed back to the tortfeasor? It may be because the tortfeasor is responsible for his actions or because the third party act which has precipitated the damage is the very thing that the tortfeasor is employed to prevent. But what is the position in the absence of some such consideration? Few things are less certainly predictable than human behaviour, and if one is asked whether in any given situation a human being may behave idiotically, irrationally or even criminally the answer must always be that that is a possibility, for every society has its proportion of idiots and criminals. It cannot be said that you cannot foresee the possibility that people will do stupid or criminal acts, because people are constantly doing stupid or criminal acts.

But the question is not what is foreseeable merely as a possibility but what would the reasonable man actually foresee if he thought about it, and all that Lord Reid seems to me to be saying is that the hypothetical reasonable man in the position of the tortfeasor cannot be said to foresee the behaviour of another person unless that behaviour is such as would, viewed objectively, be very likely to occur. Thus, for instance, if by my negligent driving I damage another motorist's car, I suppose that theoretically I *could* foresee that, whilst he leaves it by the roadside to go and telephone his garage, some ill-intentioned passer-by may jack it up and remove the wheels. But I cannot think that it could be said that, merely because I have created the circumstances in which such a theft might become possible, I ought reasonably to foresee that it would happen.

Now if this is right, it does raise a difficulty over the official referee's finding. If the likelihood of human behaviour is an element in reasonable foreseeability the official referee's disposition to say that the invasion of squatters was reasonably foreseeable is inconsistent with his actual finding of fact that squatting was unlikely, and that is the only actual finding. What I think, with respect, he was doing in this passage of his judgment was confusing "foreseeable" with "reasonably foreseeable". That indeed would be consistent with the passage from Lord Reid's speech on which he was relying as stating the principle. Lord Reid said in terms that foreseeability "as a possibility" was not sufficient and I think that what the official referee has done is to treat that as meaning, in the context, "*reasonable* foreseeability as a possibility". In the context in which, as I think, Lord Reid was using the expression "as a possibility" (that is to say, as meaning "*only* a bare possibility and no more") that seems to me to be a contradiction in terms, and for the reasons which I have endeavoured to explain it was not what Lord Reid intended and it was not what he said. The critical finding here is, to my mind, that the incursion of squatters was in fact unlikely.

Given this finding, it seems to me that, accepting Lord Reid's test as correct (which counsel for the plaintiff challenges), it must be fatal to the plaintiff's contentions on this appeal, because it constitutes in effect a finding that the damage claimed is not such as could be reasonably foreseen. And that, indeed, seems to me to accord with the common sense of the matter.

The test of remoteness is said to be the same as the test of duty in negligence (see *The Wagon Mound (No 1)*). If the instant case is approached as a case of negligence and one asks the question, did the defendants owe a duty not to break a water pipe so as to cause the plaintiff's house to be invaded by squatters a year later, the tenuousness of the linkage between act and result becomes apparent. I confess that I find it inconceivable that the reasonable man, wielding his pick in the road in 1973, could be said reasonably to foresee that his puncturing of a water main would fill the plaintiff's house with uninvited guests in 1974. Whilst, therefore, I am not altogether in accord with the official referee's reasoning, I think that he came to the right conclusion in the light of his finding of fact, which has not been challenged.

Accordingly, the appeal should, in my judgment, be dismissed.

I should perhaps add that I do not dissent from the view of Lord Denning MR that the test expressed by Lord Reid (with, as I think, the intention of restricting the ambit of the duty in tort) was incorrect, in that it was not exhaustive and did not go far enough in that direction. To apply a straight test of foreseeability or likelihood to hypothetical circumstances which could arise in relation to the acts of independent third parties in the case of, for instance, carelessness on the part of servants of the Home Office does, as Lord Denning MR points out, produce some astonishing results. Suppose that as a result of the carelessness of a prison officer a prisoner escapes and commits a crime of the same type as that for which he is in custody a fortnight later and 400 miles away from the place at which escaped. Is it any less foreseeable that he will do so than that he will steal his rail fare from a house adjoining the prison? And is the Home Office to be liable without limit until the prisoner is apprehended? Does it make any difference if he is, at the date of his escape, on remand or due for parole? Happily, such hypothetical questions do not, on the view that I take, have to be answered in the instant case, but whether or not it is right to regard questions of remoteness according to some flexible test of the policy of the law from time to time (on which I prefer at the moment to express no view) I concur with Lord Denning MR in regarding the straight test of foreseeability, at least in cases where the acts of independent third parties are concerned, as one which can, unless subjected to some further limitation, produce results which extend the ambit of liability beyond all reason. Speaking for myself, I would respectfully regard Lord Reid's test as a workable and sensible one, subject only to this, that I think that he may perhaps have understated the *degree* of likelihood required before the law can or should attribute the free act of a responsible third person to the tortfeasor. Such attribution cannot, as I think, rationally be made simply on the basis of some geographical or temporal proximity, and even "likelihood" is a somewhat uncertain touchstone. It may be that some more stringent standard is required. There may, for instance, be circumstances in which the court would require a degree of likelihood amounting almost to inevitability before it fixes a defendant with responsibility for the act of a third party over whom he has and can have no control. On the official referee's finding, however, that does not arise here, and the problem can be left for a case in which it directly arises.'

Comment

(1)   All three judges in the case arrived at the same decision although for a variety of reasons. Lord Denning MR considered that the scope of liability was

a question of policy and that the notion of causation was merely a device by which judges might justify their conclusions. In his view, responsibility for the house lay entirely with the plaintiff who ought to have taken better steps to protect it and who was, in any case, probably insured. Watkins LJ, commenting on the 'obscurity and difficulty' of questions of causation, stated that a 'robust and sensible approach ... will more often than not produce ... an instinctive feeling' that the event is too remote.

(2)   In *Stansbie v Troman* a painter and decorator was held liable when thieves entered and stole jewellery from a house which he had negligently left unlocked while he went to fetch materials. Although it could not strictly be said that a theft was 'very likely', the connection between the nature of the duty owed (i.e. to leave the house secure) and the damage suffered was a direct one. A similar approach is to be found in *Reeves v Commissioner of Police for the Metropolis* (see p 296) in which the Court of Appeal held that the act of suicide by a prisoner could not constitute a *novus actus* when the duty in question was precisely to prevent suicide.

(3)   In *Hogan v Bentinck West Hartley Collieries (Owners) Ltd* the plaintiff suffered an injury at work to his thumb. The poor medical advice and treatment received by the plaintiff resulted in the amputation of his thumb. The court reviewed the circumstances in which negligent medical treatment ought to break the chain of causation. Lord Reid said:

'... Let me, however, now assume that it is too late to review the rule that wrong medical treatment may break the chain of causation so that its effect cannot be held to result from the original injury. I do not think that it has ever been decided what degree of error or inattention is necessary to bring this rule into operation. It is clear that there are many cases of wrong treatment which cannot have this effect. A medical man may have to act in an emergency or in circumstances where there are no facilities for full diagnosis, or he may be given wrong or inadequate information by the patient or those looking after him. Moreover, there must be a permissible margin of error even for the doctor or surgeon who is highly efficient: the highest degree of skill on every occasion cannot be expected of any man. It could not, I think, be maintained that the chain of causation is broken by a mistake which is not in any degree blameworthy. Treatment by a doctor whose skill had never been of the highest order, whose methods were rather out of date and who had no access to elaborate equipment, might well be much less efficient than the treatment which would have been given by a first-class specialist equipped with every modern discovery and invention, and the difference might easily lead to the prolongation of an incapacity which would otherwise have been completely cured. I do not think that such a degree of inefficiency has ever been held to be *novus actus interveniens.* I do not find in any of the cases any warrant for applying the doctrine of *novus actus interveniens* unless there has been grave lack of skill or care on the part of the doctor. Indeed, I think that the dividing line between that degree of lack of skill or care which may break the chain of causation and that degree which will not ought to be the dividing line between that degree of lack of skill or care which may make the doctor liable in damages and that which will not.'

It would seem from *Webb v Barclays Bank plc and Portsmouth Hospitals NHS Trust* that even negligence of a degree that would make the doctor liable in damages may not break the chain. The case concerned a female employee whose knee, already damaged by polio, was severely damaged due to her employer's negligence. As a result of negligent medical advice, she consented to the amputation of her injured leg and suffered further complications. Henry LJ, giving the judgment of the Court, said:

'55   Finally, we agree with the editors of Clerk & Lindsell on Torts, when they say:

"Moreover, it is submitted that only medical treatment so grossly negligent as to be a completely inappropriate response to the injury inflicted by the defendant should operate to break the chain of causation" (18th ed., 2–55).

56   We are of clear opinion that where the chain of causation was not broken. We have in mind that:

(a)   the original wrong-doing remained a causative force, as it had increased the vulnerability of the claimant and reduced the mobility of the claimant over and above the effect of the amputation;

(b)   the medical intervention was plainly foreseeable, and it was also foreseeable that the claimant's pre-existing vulnerability would impose its own risks;

(c)   given the doctor's conduct was negligent, but was not grossly negligent, and given the findings expressed at (a) and (b) it would not be just and equitable, nor in keeping with the expansive philosophy of the [Civil Liability (Contribution) Act, 1978] for the wrongdoer to be given, in these circumstances, a shield against (i) being liable to the claimant for any part of the amputation damages; and (ii) being liable to make such contribution to the Trust's amputation damages as was just and equitable.

57   In short, the negligence in advising amputation did not eclipse the original wrong-doing. The [employer] remained responsible for their share of the amputation damages. The negligence of [the surgeon] was not an intervening act breaking the chain of causation.'

(4)   For liability for third parties in nuisance see p 627.

Knightley v Johns and others
[1982] I All ER 851 Court of Appeal

The defendant, J, had negligently overturned his car part-way through a road tunnel. When the police reached the scene the senior officer realised that he had not closed the tunnel and sent the plaintiff to do so. The plaintiff was riding his motorcycle cautiously up the tunnel in the direction of the oncoming traffic when he was struck by another car. The Court of Appeal held that the catalogue of errors after the original accident, and in particular the negligence of the senior officers, was sufficient to break the chain of causation.

Stephenson LJ: '... Having assessed the character of the acts and omissions of the plaintiff and the inspector, I accordingly reach the conclusion that they were causes of the plaintiff's accident and injuries ... Now comes the question the judge decided first: were they causes concurrent with the negligence of J or were they new causes which broke the chain of causation? ...

After reviewing some of the relevant authorities he came to his conclusion "that the injury to the plaintiff was the natural and probable result of the original negligence of J" and that consequently "his negligence was an operative cause of the plaintiff's injury".

[Stephenson LJ considered *Brandon v Osborne Garrett & Co, Haynes v Harwood, Hyett v GWR Co, Baker v Hopkins, Videan v BTC* and *Chadwick v BRB* and continued:] ... I conclude from these rescue cases that the original tortfeasor, whose negligence created the danger which invites rescuers, will be responsible for injury and damage which are the natural and probable results of the wrongful act, and that those results include injury and damage from accidents of a kind or class which might normally be foreseen or contemplated, though the particular accidents could not be expected. There is no difference between what is natural and probable and what is reasonably foreseeable either in the act of rescue or in the steps taken to accomplish it. If it is natural and probable that someone will come to the rescue it is also foreseeable; if it is foreseeable that in doing so he may take a particular kind of risk or cope with the emergency in ways not precisely foreseeable, his acts will be natural and probable consequences of the wrongful act which created the emergency.

Those alternative formulations of the jury question which has to be decided when an emergency is followed by intervention may seem to draw little distinction between damage resulting from a tort and damage resulting from a breach of contract, or between the first and second limbs of the well-known rule in *Hadley v Baxendale*. For this purpose, the purpose of discovering whether the intervention is a new cause which breaks the chain of causation, and is not a cause concurrent with the act which preceded it, there may not be much difference. In *The Oropesa* Lord Wright, sitting in this court, said:

"To break the chain of causation it must be shown that there is something which I will call ultroneous, something unwarrantable, a new cause which disturbs the sequence of events, something which can be described as either unreasonable or extraneous or extrinsic. I doubt whether the law can be stated more precisely than that."

He went on to quote from the speech of Lord Haldane in *Canadian Pacific Rly Co v Kelvin Shipping Co*, including this passage:

"... what those in charge of the injured ship do to save it, may be mistaken, but if they do whatever they do reasonably, although unsuccessfully, their mistaken judgment may be a natural consequence for which the offending ship is responsible, just as much as is any physical occurrence. Reasonable human conduct is part of the ordinary course of things which extends to the reasonable conduct of those who have sustained the damage and who are seeking to save further loss."

... The question to be asked is accordingly whether that whole sequence of events is a natural and probable consequence of J's negligence and a reasonably foreseeable result of it. In answering the question it is helpful but not decisive to consider which of these events were deliberate choices to do positive acts and which were mere omissions or failures to act; which acts and omissions were innocent mistakes or miscalculations and which were negligent having regard to the pressures and the gravity of the emergency and the need to act quickly. Negligent conduct is more likely to break the chain of causation than conduct which is not; positive acts will more easily constitute new causes than inaction. Mistakes and mischances are to be expected when human beings, however well trained, have to cope with a crisis; what exactly they will be cannot be predicted, but if those which occur are natural the wrongdoer cannot, I think, escape responsibility for them and their consequences simply by calling them improbable or unforeseeable. He must accept the risk of some unexpected mischances: see *Ward v T E Hopkins & Son Ltd*, per Willmer LJ and *Chadwick's* case, per Waller J. But what mischances?

The answer to this difficult question must be dictated by common sense rather than logic on the facts and circumstances of each case ...

In the long run the question is, as Lord Reid said in the *Dorset Yacht Co* case, one of remoteness of damage, to be answered, as has so often been stated, not by the logic of philosophers but by the common sense of plain men: cf. the very recent decision of this court in *Compania Financiera Soleada SA v Hamoor Tanker Corp Inc, The Borag*, disallowing an item of damage indifferently as too unreasonable or too unforeseeable or too remote to be included in damages for breach of contract. In my judgment, too much happened here, too much went wrong, the chapter of accidents and mistakes was too long and varied, to impose on J liability for what happened to the plaintiff in discharging his duty as a police officer, although it would not have happened had not J negligently overturned his car. The ordinary course of things took an extraordinary course. The length and the irregularities of the line leading from the first accident to the second have no parallel in the reported rescue cases, in all of which the plaintiff succeeded in establishing the original wrongdoer's liability. It was natural, it was probable, it was foreseeable, it was indeed certain, that the police would come to the overturned car and control the tunnel traffic. It was also natural and probable and foreseeable that some steps would be taken in controlling the traffic and clearing the tunnel and some things be done that might be more courageous than sensible. The reasonable hypothetical observer would anticipate some human errors, some forms of what might be called folly, perhaps even from trained police officers, and some unusual and unexpected accidents in the course of their rescue duties. But would he anticipate such a result as this from so many errors as these, so many departures from the common-sense procedure prescribed by the standing orders for just such an emergency as this? I can see that it is a question on which the opinions of plain men and women in the jury box and judges who have now to perform their function may reasonably differ. I can only say that, in my opinion, the judge's decision carries J's responsibility too far: in trying to be fair to the inspector the judge was unfair to J and gave the wrong answer to the first jury question put by Swift J in *Brandon's* case.'

Comment

(1)   In *Brandon v Osborne Garrett & Co* in which a woman was injured in trying to rescue her husband from glass which fell from a skylight due to the defendants' negligence, Swift J said:

'where a person sustains injury through a combination of acts, some done by the defendants and some by himself, it is for the jury to say, having regard to the whole of the circumstances, whether (1) the injury is the natural and probable consequence of the defendants' act, and (2) whether the plaintiff has been guilty of contributory negligence.'

At the time, contributory negligence was a complete defence.

(2)   An important factor in relation to the plaintiff's own actions was the fact that he was, in a sense, a rescuer. There is no doubt that an unreasonable act by the plaintiff can amount to a *novus actus* (see *McKew* below), but in the case of rescuers the courts are unwilling to reach such a conclusion except in the most extreme cases. In *Haynes v Harwood* a police officer was injured in stopping a runaway horse negligently left unattended on the highway. The Court of Appeal approved Swift J's approach. Greer LJ:

'If what is relied upon as *novus actus interveniens* is the very kind of thing which is likely to happen if the want of care which is alleged takes place, the principle embodied in the maxim is no defence ... If [the accident] is the very thing which ought to be anticipated by a man leaving his horses, or one of the things likely to arise as a consequence of his wrongful act, it is no defence; it is only a step in the way of providing that the damage is the result of the wrongful act.'

Contrast *Cutler v United Dairies* in which a bolting horse had gone into a field and the danger passed before the plaintiff approached the animal in order to restrain it and was injured. In his case, since the rescue was not reasonably necessary, his intervention amounted to a *novus actus*.

A rescuer who acts with reckless disregard for his or her own safety may break the chain of causation, but this is to be judged by the circumstances of the rescue. In *Hyett v Great Western Rly Co* Tucker LJ said:

'... if a man is going to act at all, in a case of fire he must act swiftly, and, applying the tests laid down in the two cases to which I have referred, the conclusion I have reached is that the act of the plaintiff was not *novus actus interveniens* breaking the chain of causation, but was the kind of act which the defendants might reasonably have anticipated as likely to follow from their act of negligence in leaving the leaking paraffin on this siding.'

The courts' approach was summarised by Lord Denning in *Videan v British Transport Commission* (see p 76):

'... Whoever comes to the rescue, the law should see that he does not suffer for it ... The rescuer may act instinctively out of humanity or deliberately out of courage. But whichever it is, so long as it is not wanton interference, if the rescuer is killed or injured in the attempt, he can recover damages from the one whose fault has been the cause of it.'

McKew v Holland & Hannen & Cubitts (Scotland) Ltd
[1969] 3 All ER 1621 House of Lords

For some time after an injury caused by the negligence of the respondents, the appellant suffered from a temporary condition which meant that his leg occasionally gave way. During this period the appellant was carrying his young daughter down a steep flight of stairs with no handrail when his leg failed. Apparently in the hope of saving himself, he jumped down the remaining ten steps and seriously injured his ankle. The House of Lords held that his act of attempting the descent in his condition and without any of the help available was so unreasonable as to amount to a *novus actus*.

Lord Reid:'... In my view the law is clear. If a man is injured in such a way that his leg may give way at any moment he must act reasonably and carefully. It is quite possible that in spite of all reasonable care his leg may give way in circumstances such that as a result he sustains further injury. Then that second injury was caused by his disability which in turn was caused by the defender's fault. But if the injured man acts unreasonably he cannot hold the defender liable for injury caused by his own unreasonable conduct. His unreasonable conduct is *novus actus interveniens*. The chain of causation has been broken and what follows must be regarded as caused by his own conduct and not by the defender's fault or the disability caused by it. Or one may say that unreasonable conduct of the pursuer and what follows from it is not the natural and probable result of the original fault of the defender or of the ensuing disability. I do not think that foreseeability comes into this. A defender is not liable for a consequence of a kind which is not foreseeable. But it does not follow that he is liable for every consequence which a reasonable man could foresee. What can be foreseen depends almost entirely on the facts of the case, and it is often easy to foresee unreasonable conduct or some other *novus actus interveniens* as being quite likely. But that does not mean that the defender must pay for damage caused by the *novus actus*. It only leads to trouble that if one tries to graft on to the concept of foreseeability some rule of law to the effect that a wrongdoer is not bound to foresee something which in fact he could readily foresee as quite likely to happen. For it is not at all unlikely or unforeseeable that an active man who has suffered such a disability will take some quite unreasonable risk. But if he does he cannot hold the defender liable for the consequences.

So in my view the question here is whether the second accident was caused by the appellant doing something unreasonable. It was argued that the wrongdoer must take his victim as he finds him and that that applies not only to a thin skull but also to his intelligence. But I shall not deal with that argument because there is nothing in the evidence to suggest that the appellant is abnormally stupid. This case can be dealt with equally well by asking whether the appellant did something which a moment's reflection would have shown him was an unreasonable thing to do.

He knew that his left leg was liable to give way suddenly and without warning. He knew that this stair was steep and that there was no handrail. He must have realised, if he had given the matter a moment's thought, that he could only safely descend the stair if he either went extremely slowly and carefully so that he could sit down if his leg gave way, or waited for the assistance of his wife and brother-in-law. But he chose to descend in such a way that when his leg gave way he could not stop himself ... I think it right to say a word about the argument that the fact that the appellant made to jump when he felt himself falling is conclusive against him. When his leg gave way the appellant was in a very difficult situation. He had to decide what to do in a fraction of a second. He may have come to a wrong decision; he probably did. But if the chain of causation had not been broken before this by his putting himself in a position where he might be confronted with an emergency, I do not think that he would put himself out of court by acting wrongly in the emergency unless his action was so utterly unreasonable that even on the spur of the moment no ordinary man would have been so foolish as to do what he did. In an emergency it is natural to try to do something to save oneself and I do not think that his trying to jump in this emergency was so wrong that it could be said to be no more than an error of judgment.'

Comment

(1)   In order for the plaintiff's conduct to operate as a *novus actus* it must be so unreasonable as to sever any connection between the defendant and the injury. This is to be distinguished from contributory negligence which does not absolve the defendant from liability but merely apportions the damages according to responsibility (see p 323).

(2)   As with third party acts, the defendant must bear the responsibility for subsequent acts by the plaintiff which follow naturally from the negligence. In *Wieland v Cyril Lord Carpets Ltd* the plaintiff had suffered a neck injury as a result of the defendant's negligence and was obliged to wear a support collar. This meant that she was unable to see properly through her bifocal spectacles so, feeling that she was unsafe to use public transport, she went to her son's place of work so that he could take her home. She fell down a flight of stairs and was further injured. The court held that her actions were entirely reasonable and that the fresh injuries flowed directly from the defendant's negligence.

Reeves v Commissioner of Police of the Metropolis
[1999] 3 All ER 897 House of Lords

The plaintiff's partner, L, hanged himself when the door hatch of the police cell in which he was being kept was negligently left open by an officer responsible for him. L had previously made two suicide attempts while in police custody, and the defendant admitted a duty of care was owed to L, but denied liability on the ground that, having been assessed as of sound mind, his suicide was a voluntary act which either broke the chain of causation or supported the defence of *volenti*. The majority in the House of Lords upheld the Court of Appeal's decision for the plaintiff, but reduced damages by 50 per cent for contributory negligence.

Lord Hoffmann: '... [Counsel for the defendant] argued two points on his behalf. The first was the question of causation: was the breach of duty by the police a cause of L's death? The way he put the answer was to say that the deliberate act of suicide, while of sound mind, was a *novus actus interveniens* which negatived the causal connection between the breach of duty and the death. He said at first that he was going to argue the application of the maxim *volenti non fit injuria* as a separate point. But when it came down to it, he accepted that if the breach of duty was a cause of the death, he could not succeed on *volenti non fit injuria*. I think that is right. In the present case, *volenti non fit injuria* can only mean that L voluntarily caused his own death to the exclusion of any causal effect on the part of what was done by the police. So I think it all comes to the same thing: was the breach of duty by the police a cause of the death?

The other point argued by [counsel for the defendant] was contributory negligence. The question of public policy or *ex turpi causa non oritur actio*, which had not found favour with any member of the Court of Appeal, was not pursued.

On the first question, [counsel for the defendant] relied upon the general principle stated in Hart and Honoré, *Causation in the Law* (2nd edn, 1985) p. 136: "... *the free, deliberate and informed act or omission of a human being, intended to exploit the situation created by defendant, negatives causal connection.*" (Authors' emphasis.) However, as Hart and Honoré pp. 194–204 also point out there is an exception to this undoubted rule in the case in which the law imposes a duty to guard against loss caused by the free, deliberate and informed act of a human being. It would make nonsense of the existence of such a duty if the law were to hold that the occurrence of the very act which ought to have been prevented negatived causal connection between the breach of duty and the loss. This principle has been recently considered by your Lordships' House in *Empress Car Co (Abertillery) Ltd v National Rivers Authority*. In that case, examples are given of cases in which liability has been imposed for causing events which were the immediate consequence of the deliberate acts of third parties but which the defendant had a duty to prevent or take reasonable care to prevent.

[Counsel for the defendant] accepted this principle when the deliberate act was that of a third party. But he said that it was different when it was the act of the plaintiff himself. Deliberately inflicting damage on oneself had to be an act which negatived causal connection with anything which had gone before.

This argument is based upon the sound intuition that there is a difference between protecting people against harm caused to them by third parties and protecting them against harm which they inflict upon themselves. It reflects the individualist philosophy of the common law. People of full age and sound understanding must look after themselves and take responsibility for their actions. This philosophy expresses itself in the fact that duties to safeguard from harm deliberately caused by others are unusual and a duty to protect a person of full understanding from causing harm to himself is very rare indeed. But, once it is admitted that this is the rare case in which such a duty is owed, it seems to me self-contradictory to say that the breach could not have been a cause of the harm because the victim caused it to himself.

Morritt LJ drew a distinction between a prisoner who was of sound mind and one who was not. He said that when a prisoner was of sound mind, "I find it hard to see how there is any material increase in the risk in any causative sense". In *Kirkham v Chief Constable of the Greater Manchester Police* Lloyd LJ said much the same. It seems to me, however, they were really saying that the police should not owe a person of sound mind a duty to take reasonable care to prevent him from committing suicide. If he wants to take his life, that is his business. He is a responsible human being and should accept the intended consequences of his acts without blaming anyone else. *Volenti non fit injuria.* The police might owe a general moral duty not to provide any prisoner with the means of committing suicide, whether he is of sound mind or not. Such a duty might even be enforceable by disciplinary measures. But the police did not owe L, a person of sound mind, a duty of care so as to enable him or his widow to bring an action in damages for its breach.

My Lords, I can understand this argument, although I do not agree with it. It is not, however, the position taken by the commissioner. He accepts that he owed a duty of care to L to take reasonable care to prevent him from committing suicide. L could not rely on a duty owed to some other hypothetical prisoner who was of unsound mind. The commissioner does not seek to withdraw this concession on the ground that L has been found to have been of sound mind. For my part, I think that the commissioner is right not to make this distinction. The difference between being of sound and unsound mind, while appealing to lawyers who like clear-cut rules, seems to me inadequate to deal with the complexities of human psychology in the context of the stresses caused by imprisonment. The duty, as I have said, is a very unusual one, arising from the complete control which the police or prison authorities have over the prisoner, combined with the special danger of people in prison taking their own lives.

[Counsel for the defendant] also suggested that the principle of human autonomy might be infringed by holding the commissioner liable. Autonomy means that every individual is sovereign over himself and cannot be denied the right to certain kinds of behaviour, even if intended to cause his own death. On this principle, if L had decided to go on hunger strike, the police would not have been entitled to administer forcible feeding. But autonomy does not mean that he would have been entitled to demand to be given poison, or that the police would not have been entitled to control his environment in non-invasive ways calculated to make suicide more difficult. If this would not infringe the principle of autonomy, it cannot be infringed by the police being under a duty to take such steps. In any case, this argument really goes to the existence of the duty which the commissioner admits rather than to the question of causation.

The decision of the majority of the Court of Appeal is supported by the Commonwealth and United States authority to which we were referred ... This brings me to the question of contributory negligence. [Lord Hoffmann cited the Law Reform (Contributory Negligence) Act 1945, ss 1(1) and 4 (see p 323) and continued.] Plainly L's act in committing suicide would not have given rise to liability in tort. That part of the definition is concerned with fault on the part of the defendant. The question is whether, apart from the Act, it would have given rise to a defence of contributory negligence. I recognise, of course, that it is odd to describe L as having been negligent. He acted intentionally and intention is a different state of mind from negligence. On the other hand, the "defence of contributory negligence" at common law was based upon the view that a plaintiff whose failure to take care for his own safety was a cause of his injury could not sue. One would therefore have thought that the defence applied *a fortiori* to a plaintiff who intended to injure himself. The late Professor Glanville Williams, in his book *Joint Torts and Contributory Negligence* (1951) p. 199 expressed the view that "contributory *intention* should be a defence". It is not surprising that there is little authority on the point, because the plaintiff's act in deliberately causing injury to himself is almost invariably regarded as negativing causal connection between any prior breach of duty by the defendant and the damage suffered by the plaintiff. The question can arise only in the rare case, such as the present, in which someone owes a duty to prevent, or take reasonable care to prevent, the plaintiff from deliberately causing injury to himself. Logically, it seems to me that Professor Glanville Williams is right.

Buxton LJ took a different view and I must examine the reasons which he gave. First, he said that there was no authority that the intentional act of the plaintiff could be "fault' within the meaning of s 4 of the 1945 Act. This, as I have said, is true but, logically, I think it can be.

Secondly, he said that the conclusion that L's act did not prevent the negligence of the police from being a cause of his death meant that his death could not have been partly as a result of his own fault and partly as a result of the fault of the police. The way he put it was as follows:

" ... on the assumption that L's alleged 'fault' is to have killed himself, did L suffer death partly as a result of his killing himself and partly as a result of the defendants giving him an opportunity to kill himself, to adapt the terms of s 1 of the 1945 Act to this case? The commonsense answer to a question posed in those terms is that given by the judge: that L suffered death *entirely* as a result of his killing himself. That conclusion would however entail, and be the same as saying, that L's act of self-destruction *was in law a novus actus: which, as I have sought to demonstrate, is not the case.*" (Buxton LJ's emphasis.)

This reasoning seems to me fallacious. It is saying that because L's own act did not negative the causal connection between the negligence of the police and his death, it would be inconsistent to say that he caused his own death at all. Neither logic nor common sense requires such a conclusion. L's suicide did not prevent the breach of duty by the police from being a cause of his death but that does not mean that his suicide was not also a cause of his death. As I said in *Empress Car Co (Abertillery) Ltd v National Rivers Authority*:

" ... one cannot give a commonsense answer to a question of causation for the purpose of attributing responsibility under some rule without knowing the purpose and scope of the rule."

Because the police were under a duty to take reasonable care not to give L the opportunity to kill himself, the commonsense answer to the question whether their carelessness caused his death is Yes. Because L also had responsibility for his own life, the commonsense answer to the question whether he caused his own death is Yes. Therefore both causes contributed to his death and the 1945 Act provides the means of reflecting this division of responsibility in the award of damages.

Thirdly, Buxton LJ referred to cases under the Factories Acts, in which appellate judges have warned against allowing the legislative policy in imposing an absolute duty on the employer to be undermined by too readily allowing a defence of contributory negligence. He quoted Goddard LJ's remarks in *Hutchinson v London and North Eastern Rly Co*:

> "It is only too common to find in cases where the plaintiff alleges that a defendant employer has been guilty of breach of a statutory duty, that a plea of contributory negligence has been set up. In such a case I always directed myself to be exceedingly chary of finding contributory negligence where the contributory negligence alleged was the very thing which the statutory duty of the employer was designed to prevent."

It is important to notice that these remarks were made before the 1945 Act was passed. It is not surprising that judges, faced with an all or nothing decision between the policy of the Factories Acts and the common law rule which made contributory negligence a complete defence, should have given priority to the legislative policy even if in practice it often meant overriding the common law rule. But Goddard LJ did not say that contributory negligence could not in principle be a defence and it has always been recognised as such. Buxton LJ also quoted an observation of Lord Tucker in *Staveley Iron and Chemical Co Ltd v Jones*:

> " ... in cases under the Factories Act the purpose of imposing the absolute obligation is to protect the workmen against those very acts of inattention which are sometimes relied on as constituting contributory negligence, so that too strict a standard would defeat the object of the statute."

This citation performs the valuable function of reminding us that what s 1 requires the court to apportion is not merely degrees of carelessness but "responsibility", and that an assessment of responsibility must take into account the policy of the rule, such as the Factories Acts, by which liability is imposed. A person may be responsible although he has not been careless at all, as in the case of breach of an absolute statutory duty. And he may have been careless without being responsible, as in the case of "acts of inattention" by workmen. I shall return to this point when I consider the proper apportionment of responsibility in this case. But the two citations do not support the view that contributory negligence can in principle have no application when the plaintiff's carelessness is something which the defendant had a duty to guard against. It is commonly the case that people are held liable in negligence for not taking precautions against the possibility that someone may do something careless and hurt themselves, like diving into a shallow swimming pool, but I do not think it has been suggested that in such cases damages can never be reduced on account of the plaintiff's contributory negligence.

Fourthly, Buxton LJ referred to cases in which a defence of contributory negligence failed against child plaintiffs who had injured themselves by taking opportunities to play with dangerous things which the defendant had carelessly given them or left unguarded. He treated these as cases in which the defence failed because the child had done the very thing which it was the defendant's duty to take reasonable care to prevent. In my opinion, however, they have a different explanation. It is because the plaintiffs were children, without full understanding of the dangers they were running, that it would not have been just and equitable to attribute responsibility to them. This may be equally true in the case of a prisoner of unsound mind who commits suicide.

In *Kirkham v Chief Constable of the Greater Manchester Police*, where a prisoner suffering from clinical depression committed suicide in his cell, Tudor Evans J decided that no share of responsibility for his death should be attributed to him under the 1945 Act. There appears to have been no appeal against this finding. But it does not follow that no prisoner committing suicide in consequence of a breach of duty by the police or prison officers can ever be treated as sharing the responsibility for his own death.

In my view it would therefore have been right to apportion responsibility between the commissioner and L in accordance with the 1945 Act. The judge and Morritt LJ would have apportioned 100 per cent to L. But I think that this conclusion was heavily influenced by their view, expressed in connection with the question of causation, that L, as a person of sound mind, bore full responsibility for taking his own life. This is of course a tenable moral view, which was powerfully advocated by the late Lord Denning MR in 1981 in *Hyde v Thameside Area Health Authority*. But whatever views one may have about suicide in general, a 100 per cent apportionment of responsibility to L gives no weight at all to the policy of the law in imposing a duty of care upon the police. It is another different way of saying that the police should not have owed L a duty of care. The law of torts is not just a matter of simple morality but contains many strands of policy, not all of them consistent with each other, which reflect the complexity of life. An apportionment of responsibility "as the court thinks just and equitable" will sometimes require a balancing of different goals. It is at this point that I think that Buxton LJ's reference to the cases on the Factories Acts is very pertinent. The apportionment must recognise that a purpose of the duty accepted by the commissioner in this case is to demonstrate publicly that the police do have a responsibility for taking reasonable care to prevent prisoners from committing suicide. On the other hand, respect must be paid to the finding of fact that L was "of sound mind". I confess to my unease about this finding, based on a seven minute interview with a doctor of unstated qualifications, but there was no other evidence and the judge was entitled to come to the conclusion which he did. I therefore think it would be wrong to attribute no responsibility to L and compensate the plaintiff as if the police had simply killed him. In these circumstances, I think that the right answer is that which was favoured by the Lord Bingham CJ, namely to apportion responsibility equally.'

Comment

(1)   Lord Hobhouse, in his dissenting speech, placed greater emphasis on L's autonomy. He said:

'The simplest way in which to express the relevant principles, both the basic principle of autonomy and the qualification, is in terms of causation. Both as a matter of the ordinary use of language and as a matter of law it is correct to say that the plaintiff's voluntary choice was *the* cause of his loss ... If L, knowing that the police officers had put him in a cell with a defective door and had failed to close the hatch, then voluntarily and deliberately, in full possession of his faculties, made the rational choice to commit suicide, principle and language say that it was his choice which was the cause of his subsequent death. He was not, on the judge's findings, acting under any disability or compulsion. He made a free choice: he is responsible for the consequence of that choice.'

(2)   In *Orange v Chief Constable of West Yorkshire Police*, in which the claimant's husband hanged himself while in police custody having been left with his belt in his possession, the Court of Appeal distinguished *Reeves* and *Kirkham* on the grounds that it should not be assumed, in the absence of evidence to the contrary in the individual case, that every prisoner is a potential suicide risk.

(3)   In *Barrett v Ministry of Defence*, the Court of Appeal held that the deceased serviceman should take full responsibility for having drunk himself into such a state of intoxication that he died. In that instance, the principle of autonomy led to the conclusion that the defendants were under no duty to prevent such an action.

(4)   For the role of autonomy in relation to medical treatment and trespass to the person see pp 551–570.

Fitzgerald v Lane and another
[1988] 2 All ER 961 House of Lords

The plaintiff set off across a pelican crossing while the lights were against him. He was struck by two different cars and suffered serious injury. The House of Lords, agreeing that all three parties were at fault, set out the correct approach to apportionment of damages.

Lord Ackner: '... It is axiomatic that, whether the plaintiff is suing one or more defendants for damages for personal injuries, the first question which the judge has to determine is whether the plaintiff has established liability against one or other or all the defendants, i.e. that they, or one or more of them, were negligent (or in breach of statutory duty) and that that negligence (or breach of statutory duty) caused or materially contributed to his injuries. The next step, of course, once liability has been established, is to assess what is the total of the damage that the plaintiff has sustained as a result of the established negligence. It is only after these two decisions have been made that the next question arises, namely whether the defendant or defendants have established (for the onus is on them) that the plaintiff, by his own negligence, contributed to the damage which he suffered. If, and only if, contributory negligence is established does the court then have to decide, pursuant to s 1 of the Law Reform (Contributory Negligence) Act 1945, to what extent it is just and equitable to reduce the damages which would otherwise be recoverable by the plaintiff, having regard to his "share in the responsibility for the damage".

All the decisions referred to above are made in the main action. Apportionment of liability in a case of contributory negligence between plaintiff and defendants must be kept separate from apportionment of *contribution between the defendants inter se.* Although the defendants are each liable to the plaintiff for the whole amount for which he has obtained judgment, the proportions in which, as between themselves, the defendants must meet the plaintiff's claim do not have any direct relationship to the extent to which the total damages have been reduced by the contributory negligence, although the facts of any given case may justify the proportions being the same.

Once the questions referred to above in the main action have been determined in favour of the plaintiff to the extent that he has obtained a judgment against two or more defendants, then and only then should the court focus its attention on the claims which may be made between those defendants for contribution pursuant to the Civil Liability (Contribution) Act 1978, re-enacting and extending the court's powers under s 6 of the Law Reform (Married Women and Tortfeasors) Act 1935. In the contribution proceedings, whether or not they are heard during the trial of the main action or by separate proceedings, the court is concerned to discover what contribution is just and equitable, having regard to the responsibility between the tortfeasors *inter se,* for the damage which the plaintiff has been adjudged entitled to recover. That damage may, of course, have been subject to a reduction as a result of the decision in the main action that the plaintiff, by his own negligence, contributed to the damage which he sustained.

Thus, where the plaintiff successfully sues more than one defendant for damages for personal injuries and there is a claim between co-defendants for contribution, there are two distinct and different stages in the decision-making process, the one in the main action and the other in the contribution proceedings.

THE TRIAL JUDGE'S ERROR

Counsel for the plaintiff accepted that the judge telescoped or elided the two separate stages referred to above into one when he said: "I find that it is impossible to say that one of the parties is more or less to blame than the other and hold that the responsibility should be borne equally by all three." The judge, in my judgment, misdirected himself by thinking in tripartite terms, instead of pursuing separately the two stages: phase 1, was the plaintiff guilty of contributory negligence and, if so, to what extent should the recoverable damages be reduced, issues which concerned the plaintiff on the one hand and the defendants jointly on the other hand; and phase 2, the amount of the contribution recoverable between the two defendants having regard to the extent of their responsibility for the damage recovered by the plaintiff, an issue which affected only the defendants *inter se* and in no way involved the plaintiff.

The vice of this misdirection is that it can, and, in my judgment, for reasons which I shall explain, in this case it did, result in the judge taking into account the proportions in which the defendants between themselves were liable for the plaintiff's recoverable damages, in deciding on the degree of contributory negligence of which the plaintiff was guilty. He allowed his judgment on the issue of contributory negligence to be coloured by his decision as to the proper apportionment of blame between the defendants. While stating in the substance on the one hand that the plaintiff's responsibility was no more and no less than that of either of the defendants, his ultimate conclusion, as mirrored in his order, was that each of the defendants was twice as much to blame as the plaintiff. This could not be right on the facts ...

In my judgment, in order to assess the "claimant's share in the responsibility for the damage" which he has suffered as a result of the defendants' established negligence, the judge must ask himself to what extent, if at all, the plaintiff has also been part author of his own damage. This obviously requires careful evaluation of the plaintiff's conduct in the light of all the circumstances of the accident, and those circumstances, of course, include the conduct of all the defendants who have been found guilty of causative negligence. Circumstances will, naturally, differ infinitely. In the instant case the plaintiff's conduct set in motion the chain of events that led to the accident. If the plaintiff had not ignored or failed to observe that the lights were against him and in favour of the traffic when he decided to cross the pelican crossing, then the accident would never have happened. It was the negligent response of each of the defendants to the dangerous situation thus created by the plaintiff which established their joint and several liability.

In other situations it might be the defendants who, for example, through their negligent driving, or negligent operation of a factory or building site, create the initial danger and it is then the response of the plaintiff to that dangerous situation that has to be assessed. What accounted for the reduction in the damages awarded to the plaintiff was his degree of culpability in setting the scene for the collision. In different circumstances, where the initial danger of injury is created by the negligence of the defendants, then it is the plaintiff's response to that situation which has to be assessed. In neither event does the exercise of assessing the plaintiff's share in the responsibility for the damage which he has sustained necessitate the determination of the extent of the individual culpability of each of the defendants, once the judge is satisfied that the defendants each caused or materially contributed to the plaintiff's damage. While the plaintiff's conduct has to be contrasted with that of the defendants in order to decide to what extent it is just and equitable to reduce the damages which would be awarded to him if the defendants were solely liable, it does not involve an assessment of the extent to which the fault of each of the defendants contributed to that damage. What is being contrasted is the plaintiff's conduct on the one hand with the totality of the tortious conduct of the defendants on the other. As previously stated, the determination of the extent of each of the defendants' responsibility for the damage is not made in the main action but in the contribution proceedings between the defendants, *inter se*, and this does not concern the plaintiff.'

Comment

Contribution between tortfeasors is governed principally by the Civil Liability (Contribution) Act 1978. Under s 1(1) a defendant is entitled to recover contribution from 'any other person liable in respect of the same damage', even where the defendant making the claim has settled before judgment, provided that 'he would have been liable assuming that the factual basis of the claim against him could be established' (s 1(4)). The basis for determining the amount of contribution is the same as for contributory negligence, see p 323, i.e. such amount 'as may be found by the court to be just and equitable having regard to the extent of that person's responsibility for the damage in question'.

Owners of Dredger Liesbosch v Owners of Steamship Edison [1933] AC 449 House of Lords

The respondents, having lost their dredger due to the appellants' negligence, were obliged to hire another dredger in order to meet their contractual obligations in relation to some construction work. They did not have sufficient funds available to buy a similar dredger outright, and the dredger they hired was more expensive to run, so the question for the court concerned the exact extent of the compensatable losses. The House of Lords concluded that all costs were recoverable except those special losses which arose specifically from the respondents' financial state.

Lord Wright: '... The substantial issue is what in such a case as the present is the true measure of damage. It is not questioned that when a vessel is lost by collision due to the sole negligence of the wrongdoing vessel the owners of the former vessel are entitled to what is called *restitutio in integrum*, which means that they should recover such a sum as will replace them, so far as can be done by compensation in money, in the same position as if the loss had not been inflicted on them, subject to the rules of law as to remoteness of damage ... The law cannot take account of everything that follows a wrongful act; it regards some subsequent matters as outside the scope of its selection, because "it were infinite for the law to judge the cause of causes", or consequences of consequences. Thus the loss of a ship by collision due to the other vessel's sole fault, may force the shipowner into bankruptcy and that again may involve his family in suffering, loss of education or opportunities in life, but no such loss could be recovered from the wrongdoer. In the varied web of affairs, the law must abstract some consequences as relevant, not perhaps on grounds of pure logic but simply for practical reasons.'

Overseas Tankship (UK) Ltd v Morts Dock & Engineering Co Ltd, The Wagon Mound
[1961] 1 All ER 404 Privy Council

The facts are as set out on p 248. The plaintiffs in this case had suffered damage to their dock by fouling as well as from the fire. The Privy Council held that there was no liability for the fire damage which was too remote to be recoverable.

Viscount Simonds: '... There can be no doubt that the decision of the Court of Appeal in *Polemis* plainly asserts that, if the defendant is guilty of negligence, he is responsible for all the consequences, whether reasonably foreseeable or not ...

Enough has been said to show that the authority of *Polemis* has been severely shaken, though lip-service has from time to time been paid to it. In their Lordships' opinion, it should no longer be regarded as good law. It is not probable that many cases will for that reason have a different result, though it is hoped that the law will be thereby simplified, and that, in some cases at least, palpable injustice will be avoided. For it does not seem consonant with current ideas of justice or morality that, for an act of negligence, however slight or venial, which results in some trivial foreseeable damage, the actor should be liable for all consequences, however unforeseeable and however grave, so long as they can be said to be "direct". It is a principle of civil liability, subject only to qualifications which have no present relevance, that a man must be considered to be responsible for the probable consequences of his act. To demand more of him is too harsh a rule, to demand less is to ignore that civilised order requires the observance of a minimum standard of behaviour. This concept, applied to the slowly developing law of negligence, has led to a great variety of expressions which can, as it appears to their Lordships, be harmonised with little difficulty with the single exception of the so-called rule in *Polemis*. For, if it is asked why a man should be responsible for the natural or necessary or probable consequences of his act (or any other similar description of them), the answer is that it is not because they are natural or necessary or probable, but because, since they have this quality, it is judged, by the standard of the reasonable man, that he ought to have foreseen them. Thus it is that, over and over again, it has happened that, in different judgments in the same case and sometimes in a single judgment, liability for a consequence has been imposed on the ground that it was reasonably foreseeable, or alternatively on the ground that it was natural or necessary or probable. The two grounds have been treated as conterminous, and so they largely are. But, where they are not, the question arises to which the wrong answer was given in *Polemis*. For, if some limitation must be imposed on the consequences for which the negligent actor is to be held responsible – and all are agreed that some limitation there must be – why should that test (reasonable foreseeability) be rejected which, since he is judged by what the reasonable man ought to foresee, corresponds with the common conscience of mankind, and a test (the "direct" consequence) be substituted which leads to nowhere but the never-ending and insoluble problems of causation. "The lawyer", said Sir Frederick Pollock, "cannot afford to adventure himself with philosophers in the logical and metaphysical controversies that beset the idea of cause." Yet this is just what he has most unfortunately done and must continue to do if the rule in *Polemis* is to prevail. A conspicuous example occurs when the actor seeks to escape liability on the ground that the "chain of causation" is broken by a *nova causa* or *novus actus interveniens*... .

Applying the rule in *Polemis* and holding, therefore, that the unforeseeability of the damage by fire afforded no defence, [the court at first instance] went on to consider the remaining question. Was it a "direct" consequence? On this, Manning J said:

> "Notwithstanding that, if regard is had separately to each individual occur-
> rence in the chain of events that led to this fire, each occurrence was
> improbable and, in one sense, improbability was heaped upon improbability, I
> cannot escape from the conclusion that if the ordinary man in the street had
> been asked, as a matter of common sense, without any detailed analysis of
> the circumstances, to state the cause of the fire at Morts Dock, he would
> unhesitatingly have assigned such cause to spillage of oil by the appellants'
> employees."

Perhaps he would, and probably he would have added "I never should have thought it possible". But, with great respect to the full court, this is surely irrelevant, or, if it is relevant, only serves to show that the *Polemis* rule works in a very strange way. After the event even a fool is wise. Yet it is not the hindsight of a fool, but it is the foresight of the reasonable man which alone can determine responsibility. The *Polemis* rule, by substituting "direct" for "reasonably foreseeable" consequence, leads to a conclusion equally illogical and unjust ...

It is, no doubt, proper when considering tortious liability for negligence to analyse its elements and to say that the plaintiff must prove a duty owed to him by the defendant, a breach of that duty by the defendant, and consequent damage. But there can be no liability until the damage has been done. It is not the act but the consequences on which tortious liability is founded. Just as (as it has been said) there is no such thing as negligence in the air, so there is no such thing as liability in the air. Suppose an action brought by A for damage caused by the carelessness (a neutral word) of B, for example a fire caused by the careless spillage of oil. It may, of course, become relevant to know what duty B owed to A, but the only liability that is in question is the liability for damage by fire. It is vain to isolate the liability from its context and to say that B is or is not liable, and then to ask for what damage he is liable. For his liability is in respect of that damage and no other. If, as admittedly it is, B's liability (culpability) depends on the reasonable foreseeability of the consequent damage, how is that to be determined except by the foreseeability of the damage which in fact happened – the damage in suit? And, if that damage is unforeseeable so as to displace liability at large, how can the liability be restored so as to make compensation payable? But, it is said, a different position arises if B's careless act has been shown to be negligent and has caused some foreseeable damage to A. Their Lordships have already observed that to hold B liable for consequences, however unforeseeable, of a careless act, if, but only if, he is at the same time liable for some other damage, however trivial, appears to be neither logical nor just. This becomes more clear if it is supposed that similar unforeseeable damage is suffered by A and C, but other foreseeable damage, for which B is liable, by A only. A system of law which would hold B liable to A but not to C for the similar damage suffered by each of them could not easily be defended. Fortunately, the attempt is not necessary. For the same fallacy is at the root of the proposition. It is irrelevant to the question whether B is liable for unforeseeable damage that he is liable for foreseeable damage, as irrelevant as would the fact that he had trespassed on Whiteacre be to the question whether he had trespassed on Blackacre. Again, suppose a claim for A for damage for fire by the careless act of B. Of what relevance is it to that claim that he has another claim arising out of the same careless act? It would surely not prejudice his claim if that other claim failed; it cannot assist it if it succeeds. Each of them rests on its own bottom and will fail if it can be established that the damage could not reasonably be foreseen. We have come back to the plain common sense stated by Lord Russell of Killowen in *Hay (or Bourhill) v Young*. As Denning LJ said in *King v Phillips* "… there can be no doubt since *Hay (or Bourhill) v Young* that the test of *liability for shock is* foreseeability of *injury by* shock". Their Lordships substitute the word "fire" for "shock" and endorse this statement of the law.

Their Lordships conclude this part of the case with some general observations. They have been concerned primarily to displace the proposition that unforeseeability is irrelevant if damage is "direct". In doing so, they have inevitably insisted that the essential factor in determining liability is whether the damage is of such a kind as the reasonable man should have foreseen. This accords with the general view thus stated by Lord Atkin in *M'Alister (or Donoghue) v Stevenson*: "The liability for negligence, whether you style it such or treat it as in other systems as a species of 'culpa', is no doubt based upon a general public sentiment of moral wrongdoing for which the offender must pay." It is a departure from this sovereign principle if liability is made to depend solely on the damage being the "direct" or "natural" consequence of the precedent act. Who knows or can be assumed to know all the processes of nature? But if it would be wrong that a man should be held liable for damage unpredictable by a reasonable man because it was "direct" or "natural", equally it would be wrong that he should escape liability, however "indirect" the damage, if he foresaw or could reasonably foresee the intervening events which led to its being done; cf. *Woods v Duncan*. Thus foreseeability becomes the effective test. In reasserting this principle, their Lordships conceive that they do not depart from, but follow and develop, the law of negligence as laid down by Alderson B in *Blyth v Birmingham Waterworks Co.*'

Comment

(1)   In *Re Polemis* stevedores employed by the defendants were unloading a ship when they negligently caused some planking to fall into the hold. Quite unexpectedly this made a spark which ignited some petrol vapour, starting a fire which completely destroyed the ship. The Court of Appeal held the defendants liable. Scrutton LJ said:

> ' ... it was negligence ... to knock down the planks ... for they might easily cause some damage either to workmen, or cargo, or the ship. The fact that they did directly produce an unexpected result ... does not relieve the person who was negligent from the damage which his negligent act directly caused.'

The test in *Polemis*, in which according to Bankes LJ 'the anticipations of the person whose negligent act has produced the damage [are] irrelevant', was wholly inconsistent with the general approach in negligence which is firmly based on the notion of what is reasonably to be expected of the reasonable man.

(2)   Having established that the modern test is one based on reasonable foreseeability, one must then ask precisely what must the defendant have foreseen, for example in terms of the nature and scope of the damage and how it was inflicted.

According to Lord Denning MR, in *Stewart v West African Terminals*:

> 'It is not necessary that the precise concatenation of circumstances should be envisaged. If the consequence was one which was within the general range which any reasonable person might foresee (and was not of an entirely different kind which no one would anticipate) then it is within the rule that a person who has been guilty of negligence is liable for the consequences.'

Hughes v Lord Advocate
[1963] I All ER 705 House of Lords

Workmen had opened a manhole which they left protected during a tea-break by a small tent surrounded by red lamps. The eight-year-old appellant, with a ten-year-old companion, took a ladder and one of the lamps and entered the tent to explore. The appellant then tripped over the lamp which fell into the hole, igniting the paraffin vapour. There was a large explosion and the appellant was thrown into the hole and suffered severe burns. The House of Lords held the respondents liable on the basis that some sort of burn injury was foreseeable.

Lord Pearce:'... The defenders are ... liable for all the foreseeable consequences of their neglect. When an accident is of a different type and kind from anything that a defender could have foreseen he is not liable for it (see *The Wagon Mound*). But to demand too great precision in the test of foreseeability would be unfair to the pursuer since the facets of misadventure are innumerable. In the case of an allurement to children it is particularly hard to foresee with precision the exact shape of the disaster that will arise. The allurement in this case was the combination of a red paraffin lamp, a ladder, a partially closed tent, and a cavernous hole within it, a setting well fitted to inspire some juvenile adventure that might end in calamity. The obvious risks were burning and conflagration and a fall. All these in fact occurred, but unexpectedly the mishandled lamp instead of causing an ordinary conflagration produced a violent explosion. Did the explosion create an accident and damage of a different type from the misadventure and damage that could be foreseen? In my judgment it did not. The accident was but a variant of the foreseeable. It was, to quote the words of Denning LJ in *Roe v Ministry of Health*, "within the risk created by the negligence". No unforeseeable extraneous, initial occurrence fired the train. The children's entry into the tent with the ladder, the descent into the hole, the mishandling of the lamp, were all foreseeable. The greater part of the path to injury had thus been trodden, and the mishandled lamp was quite likely at that stage to spill and cause a conflagration. Instead, by some curious chance of combustion, it exploded and no conflagration occurred, it would seem, until after the explosion. There was thus an unexpected manifestation of the apprehended physical dangers. But it would be, I think, too narrow a view to hold that those who created the risk of fire are excused from the liability for the damage by fire, because it came by way of explosive combustion. The resulting damage, though severe, was not greater than or different in kind from that which might have been produced had the lamp spilled and produced a more normal conflagration in the hole.'

Comment

(1)   The range of damage that might properly be foreseen in cases involving children was questioned in *Jolley v Sutton London Borough Council*. In that

case, for some two years, the defendant local authority had permitted to remain on their land an abandoned and derelict boat. K, the 14-year-old claimant, and a friend decided to repair the boat and used a car jack to raise it off the ground. While the claimant was working underneath the boat it fell on him, causing him severe spinal injuries. The trial judge found for the claimant on the basis that the boat constituted an allurement and a trap, and it was foreseeable that children might be injured playing with it. The Court of Appeal, while agreeing that the boat posed a significant risk, held that the accident differed in type and kind from that which was foreseeable and allowed the appeal. In particular, Judge LJ cautioned against assuming that, in cases involving children, a defendant should be liable for any consequences however unpredictable:

' ... As Lord Pearce commented in *Hughes v Lord Advocate*:

"In the case of an allurement to children it is particularly hard to foresee with precision the exact shape of the disaster that will arise."

There is, however, a tendency to proceed from the proposition that once meddling by children is foreseeable then, whatever form it may take, none of its manifestations can be regarded as unexpected. This approach is flawed. ... In my judgment this accident was of a different type and kind from anything which the defendants could reasonably have foreseen when they carelessly permitted the boat to remain where it was. Accordingly although they might have been held liable for other accidents involving children injured playing with or near the boat (if there had been any), it has not been established that they should be held liable for this particular accident.'

On appeal to the House of Lords, the decision of the trial judge was restored. Lord Steyn said:

'Very little needs to be said about the law. The decision in this case has turned on the detailed findings of fact at first instance on the particular circumstances of this case. Two general observations are, however, appropriate. First, in this corner of the law the results of decided cases are inevitably very fact sensitive. Both counsel nevertheless at times invited your Lordships to compare the facts of the present case with the facts of other decided cases. That is a sterile exercise. Precedent is a valuable stabilising influence in our legal system. But, comparing the facts of and outcomes of cases in this branch of the law is a misuse of the only proper use of precedent, namely to identify the relevant rule to apply to the facts as found.

Secondly, Lord Woolf MR made an observation casting doubt on part of Lord Reid's speech in *Hughes v Lord Advocate*. ... In the present case Lord Woolf MR cited the following parts of the speech of Lord Reid:

"So we have (first) a duty owned by the workmen, (secondly) the fact that if they had done as they ought to have done there would have been no accident, and (thirdly) the fact that the injuries suffered by the appellant, though perhaps different in degree, did not differ in kind from injuries which might have resulted from an accident of a foreseeable nature. *The ground on which this case has been decided against the appellant is that the accident was of an unforeseeable type. Of course the pursuer has to prove that the defender's fault caused the accident and there could be a case where the intrusion of a new and unexpected factor could be regarded as the cause of the accident rather than the fault of the defender. But that is not this case. The cause of this accident was a known source of danger, the lamp, but it behaved in an unpredictable way.* This accident was caused by a known source of danger, but caused in a way which could not have been foreseen, and in my judgment that affords no defence." [Lord Woolf MR's emphasis.]

Lord Woolf MR observed that he had difficulty in reconciling these remarks with the approach in The *Wagon Mound* (*No 1*). It is true that in *The Wagon Mound* (*No 1*) Viscount Simonds at one stage observed:

"If, as admittedly it is, B's liability (culpability) depends on the reasonable foreseeability of the consequent damage, how is that to be determined416 except by the foreseeability of the damage which in fact happened – the damage in suit?"

But this is to take one sentence in the judgment in *The Wagon Mound* (*No 1*) out of context. Viscount Simonds was in no way suggesting that the precise manner of which the injury occurred nor its extent had to be foreseeable. And Lord Reid was saying no more. The speech of Lord Reid in *Hughes*'s case is in harmony with the other judgments. It is not in conflict with *The Wagon Mound* (*No 1*). The scope of the two modifiers – the precise manner in which the injury came about and its extent – is not definitively answered by either *The Wagon Mound* (*No 1*) or *Hughes*'s case. It requires determination in the context of an intense focus on the circumstances of each case: see Fleming *The Law of Torts* (9th edn, 1998) pp 240–243.'

(2)   The House of Lords approved the trial judge's pragmatic approach to the foreseeable activities of children, and in particular to his acknowledgement that children in play will very often mimic what they perceive to be the behaviour of adults in like circumstances.

(3)   For allurements and traps in the context of occupiers' liability see p 390.

Doughty v Turner Manufacturing Co Ltd
[1964] I All ER 98 Court of Appeal

The plaintiff was standing beside a large vat of chemicals used in a heat-treatment process when another workman inadvertently knocked an asbestos cement cover into the vat. The composition of the cover had always been supposed to be safe for this use but after a short while the hot liquid in the vat erupted, due to a violent chemical reaction, and the plaintiff was injured. The Court of Appeal held that the employers were not liable because the risk of such an injury occurring in this manner was not reasonably foreseeable.

Diplock LJ: '... There is no room today for mystique in the law of negligence. It is the application of common morality and common sense to the activities of the common man. He must take reasonable care to avoid acts or omissions which he can reasonably foresee would be likely to injure his neighbours; but he need do no more than this. If the act which he does is not one which he could, if he thought about it, reasonably foresee would injure his neighbour it matters not whether he does it intentionally or inadvertently. The learned judge's finding, uncontested on appeal, that in the state of knowledge as it was at the time of the accident the defendants could not reasonably have foreseen that the immersion of the asbestos cement cover in the liquid would be likely to injure anyone, must lead to the conclusion that they would have been under no liability to the plaintiff if they had intentionally immersed the cover in the liquid. The fact that it was done inadvertently cannot create any liability, for the immersion of the cover was not an act which they were under any duty to take any care to avoid.

It was, however, argued by counsel for the plaintiff that, even though the risk of explosion on immersion of the cover was not one which the defendants could reasonably foresee, the plaintiff can, nevertheless, recover because one of the defendants' servants inadvertently either knocked the cover into the liquid or allowed it to slip in, thus giving rise to a foreseeable risk of splashing the hot liquid on to the plaintiff and injuring him by burning. The actual damage sustained by the plaintiff was damage of the same kind, that is by burning, as could be foreseen as likely to result from knocking the cover into the liquid or allowing it to slip in, and his counsel contended that this was sufficient to impose a duty on the defendants owed to the plaintiff to take reasonable care to avoid knocking the cover into the liquid, or allowing it to slip in, and that the plaintiff's damage flowed from their breach of this duty. Such a proposition might, before *The Wagon Mound*, have been supported by *Re Polemis*, but that decision of the Court of Appeal is no longer law; and counsel for the plaintiff relied principally on *Hughes v Lord Advocate*, a case in which the House of Lords treated *The Wagon Mound* as correctly stating the law, but distinguished it on the facts. I do not think that this authority assists him. In *Hughes v Lord Advocate* the breach of duty by the defendant on which reliance was placed was his omission to guard a dangerous allurement to children, which was liable to cause them injury (*inter alia*) by burning. The infant plaintiff, to whom the duty was owed, was allured and was injured by burning, although the particular concatenation of circumstances which resulted in his burns being more serious than they would have been expected to be could not reasonably have been foreseen. They were, nevertheless, the direct consequence of the defendant's breach of duty and the injury was of the same kind as could reasonably have been foreseen, although of unforeseen gravity. But in the present case the defendants' duty owed to the plaintiff in relation to the only foreseeable risk, that is of splashing, was to take reasonable care to avoid knocking the cover into the liquid or allowing it to slip in such a way as to cause a splash which would injure the plaintiff. Failure to avoid knocking it into the liquid, or allowing it to slip in, was of itself no breach of duty to the plaintiff. It is not clear on the evidence whether the dropping of the cover on to the liquid caused any splash at all. The judge made no finding on this. The reasoning in his judgment is not sufficiently explicit to make it clear whether the point argued by counsel for the plaintiff, with which I am now dealing, formed part of his *ratio decidendi*, though some of his observations in the course of the hearing suggest that it was not. However that may be, it is incontrovertible that, even if there was some slight splash when the cover fell on to the liquid, the plaintiff was untouched by it and it caused him no injury. There was thus, in the circumstances of this case, no breach of duty to the plaintiff involved in inadvertently knocking the cover into the liquid or inadvertently allowing it to slip in.'

Comment

(1)   Although it seems hard to reconcile this case with *Hughes* if one looks at the type of injury – i.e. burning by eruption is as much a variant of burning by splash as burning by explosion is of burning by fire – it is not inconsistent when viewed as a question of duty. In *Hughes* there was a duty to the foreseeable plaintiff not to injure him by fire, in *Doughty* a duty not to injure such a plaintiff by splashing. On the facts of *Doughty* there was no evidence of a splash nor, since the plaintiff was out of range of a splash, was he a foreseeable plaintiff.

(2)   In many cases the issue of the type of harm is inextricably linked with the manner in which it was suffered. In *Tremain v Pike* the plaintiff was a herdsman on the defendant's farm on which there were a great number of rats. He contracted Weil's disease from contact with the rats' urine but was unable to claim damages. Payne J held that the disease was 'entirely different in kind from the effect of a rat bite, or food poisoning by the consumption of food or drink contaminated by rats. I do not accept that all illness or infection arising from an infestation of rats should be regarded as of the same kind'. Even if he is right, and despite the fact that Weil's disease is still relatively rare, it must surely now be regarded as a foreseeable consequence of contact with rats.

(3) Generally, where the damage was of the kind foreseen but of a greater extent the defendants will be liable. See, e.g., *Vacwell Engineering Co Ltd v BDH Chemicals Ltd* and *Bradford v Robinson Rentals Ltd.* In *Bradford* the plaintiff, a van driver, succeeded in a claim for damages after suffering frostbite when his employers negligently exposed him to extreme cold.

(4) Distinguishing between different *kinds* of damage and different *degrees* of damage is not altogether straightforward. In *Margereson v J W Roberts Ltd* the plaintiff's husband had died of an asbestos-related condition, mesothelioma, which had not been identified as a potential risk until about 1933. It was shown that the victim's exposure to asbestos dust had been in his childhood, prior to 1933, which the defendants argued meant that there was no culpable lack of foresight on their part. The Court of Appeal, however, upheld the judge's view that the relevant *kind* of harm was some sort of damage to the lungs, a risk which had been known since well before the victim's birth. Mesothelioma, although unrecognised as a specific risk at the time, was damage of the same kind.

Smith v Leech Brain & Co Ltd
[1961] 3 All ER 1159 Queen's Bench Division

The plaintiff, S, was employed to dip objects into a tank of molten metal and flux. A splash from the tank burned his lip which later became ulcerated and developed into cancer from which the plaintiff died some three years later. The court rejected an argument that the decision in *The Wagon Mound* prevented the operation of the 'eggshell skull' rule and held the defendants liable despite the fact that the plaintiff's lip was already in a pre-malignant condition at the time of the injury which triggered his final illness.

Lord Parker CJ: '... For my part, I am quite satisfied that the Judicial Committee in *The Wagon Mound* did not have what I may call, loosely, the "thin skull" cases in mind. It has always been the law of this country that a tortfeasor takes his victim as he finds him. It is unnecessary to do more than refer to the short passage in the decision of Kennedy J in *Dulieu v White & Sons* where he said: "If a man is negligently run over or otherwise negligently injured in his body, it is no answer to the sufferer's claim for damages that he would have suffered less injury, or no injury at all, if he had not had an unusually thin skull or an unusually weak heart." ...

There is not a day that goes by where some trial judge does not adopt that principle, that the tortfeasor takes his victim as he finds him. If the Judicial Committee had any intention of making an inroad into that doctrine, I am quite satisfied that they would have said so ... The Judicial Committee were, I think, disagreeing with the decision in *Re Polemis* that a man is no longer liable for the type of damage which he could not reasonably anticipate. The Judicial Committee were not, I think, saying that a man is only liable for the extent of damage which he could anticipate, always assuming the type of injury could have been anticipated. That view is really supported by the way in which cases of this sort have been dealt with in Scotland. Scotland has never, as far as I know, adopted the principle laid down in *Re Polemis*, and yet I am quite satisfied that they have throughout proceeded on the basis that the tortfeasor takes the victim as he finds him.

In those circumstances, it seems to me that this is plainly a case which comes within the old principle. The test is not whether these defendants could reasonably have foreseen that a burn would cause cancer and that S would die. The question is whether these defendants could reasonably foresee the type of injury which he suffered, namely, the burn. What, in the particular case, is the amount of damage which he suffers as a result of that burn, depends on the characteristics and constitution of the victim. Accordingly, I find that the damages which the plaintiff claims are damages for which these defendants are liable.'

Comment

(1)   *Smith* was applied by the Court of Appeal in *Robinson v The Post Office and another* in which the plaintiff slipped and grazed his leg as a result of his employers' negligence. He later consulted his GP who gave him an anti-tetanus injection. Several days after the injection the plaintiff suffered encephalitis, a reaction to the serum, and was left with permanent brain damage. On the issue of remoteness Orr LJ said:

'In the present case the judge held that it was plainly foreseeable (1) that if oil was negligently allowed to escape on to a ladder a workman was likely to slip and sustain the type of wound in question; and (2) that such injury might well require medical treatment; and on this basis alone he was prepared to hold the defendants liable for encephalitis, but he held in addition that, having regard to the nature of the plaintiff's work and the area in which he was working, it was also foreseeable that some form of anti-tetanus prophylactic would be deemed necessary. In the result he concluded that every relevant matter was foreseeable except the terrible extent of the injury which was due to the plaintiff's allergy to a second dose of ATS, in which respect the Post Office must take their victim as they found him.

On this appeal counsel for the Post Office did not challenge the correctness of Lord Parker CJ's reasoning and conclusion in the *Leech Brain* case ... but he claimed that an essential link which was missing in the present case was that it was not foreseeable that administration of a form of anti-tetanus prophylaxis would itself give rise to a rare serious illness. In our judgment, however, there was no missing link and the case is governed by the principle that the Post Office had to take their victim as they found him, in this case with an allergy to a second dose of ATS ... In our judgment the principle that a defendant must take the plaintiff as he finds him involves that if a wrongdoer ought reasonably to foresee that as a result of his wrongful act the victim may require medical treatment he is, subject to the principle *of novus actus interveniens,* liable for the consequences of the treatment applied although he could not reasonably foresee those consequences or that they could be serious.'

(2) See also *Bloor v Liverpool Derricking & Carrying Co Ltd* (pre-existing heart condition), *Oman v McIntyre* (broncho-pneumonia following leg injury) and *Bidwell v Briant* (haemophiliac).

Meah v McCreamer and others (No 2)
[1986] I All ER 943 Queen's Bench Division

The plaintiff had suffered serious head injuries and brain damage as a result of a car crash caused by the defendant's negligence. The resulting change of personality gave him a propensity to make violent sexual attacks on women. Two of his victims succeeded in claiming damages from him and the plaintiff sought to recover the money from the original defendant. The judge held that these losses were too remote.

Woolf J: '... So far as the main question is concerned, the issue appears to me to be this. Are the damages that the plaintiff has to pay to his victims so remote that, although they are a consequence of the accident, they are not recoverable at law? In approaching the matter that way, I start with the foreseeability test, which is now generally accepted to govern issues of this nature. That was the test propounded in *Overseas Tankship (UK) Ltd v Morts Dock and Engineering Co Ltd, The Wagon Mound (No 1)* ...

With regard to that general statement certain glosses have been recognised and established. The first of these, so far as the circumstances of this case are concerned, is the fact that a defendant must take the plaintiff as he finds him. In relation to that principle, it is relevant to draw attention to the fact that in my previous judgment in *Meah v McCreamer (No 1)* I stated that both Dr G and Dr N regarded the plaintiff, to use Dr G's words, as "the worst possible person to sustain an injury of this kind", and I added, "because he had inherent tendencies which could be triggered off". To use the expression which was used in argument by counsel, he had an "egg-shell personality".

The second gloss which must be borne in mind with regard to the general principle is that, as long as the damage suffered is of the type which is foreseeable, it will be recoverable, although it is not necessarily foreseeable that damage of that precise nature would be suffered. Here I rely on a passage in *Winfield and Jolowitz on Tort* (12th edn., 1984), which reads as follows:

"Even in cases where liability is based upon negligence, foreseeability as a test of remoteness is heavily qualified by the fact that neither the precise extent of the damage nor the precise manner of its infliction need be foreseeable ..."

The third gloss which I would make on the general principle is that causation, that is to say foreseeability of damage, can be broken by an intervening act, and the intervening act which is relevant is of the plaintiff himself. In this connection it is relevant to refer to *Pigney v Pointer's Transport Services Ltd.* In that case a husband sustained head injuries as a result of an accident in the course of his employment. After he had commenced proceedings against his employers, but before his action had come to trial, he committed suicide as a result of a neurosis caused by his injuries, although he was not at that time insane under the M'Naughton Rules. His widow continued the action and also brought a second action under the Law Reform (Miscellaneous Provisions) Act 1934 and the Fatal Accidents Acts 1846 and 1908, and in the consolidated trial the judge, after finding the defendants guilty of negligence, held that the damage which the widow had sustained was directly traceable to the negligent act of the defendants, and was not due to the operation of independent causes. It was further held, as the headnote states:

"That although it was against public policy to allow the personal representative of a suicide to succeed in a derivative claim (for to do so would permit
a felon, by his crime, to benefit his own estate), it was not against public
policy to allow a widow of a suicide to prosecute a statutory cause of action
under the Fatal Accidents Acts, 1846–1908, since no benefit accrued thereby
to the estate of the deceased husband."

That case was decided before the foreseeability test had been laid down in *The Wagon Mound*. However, it is of some relevance here, but it should be noted that in that case the wife was recovering damages due to her husband's death. Here, the plaintiff is seeking to recover, not in respect of his own injuries or his own damage, but in respect of the damage he caused to third parties, namely the victims of his assaults.

Under the foreseeability rule it is left to the court to decide whether or not a particular head of damages is foreseeable. There must always be cases where there can be loss caused as a result of an accident of this sort, but the loss is not foreseeable. In considering this matter it is relevant to have regard to questions of policy, because policy must play a part in deciding whether or not a particular loss should be recoverable as a matter of law. So far as the question of foreseeability is concerned, it is important to bear in mind what was said by the House of Lords in *McLoughlin v O'Brian*. That case dealt with the question of foreseeability in relation to establishing a duty of care and not the question of foreseeability in relation to the issue whether or not a particular head of damages is recoverable. However, it seems to me that everything that their Lordships said with regard to the circumstances there under consideration are equally applicable here ...

As I understand [certain] passages from that decision, they make it clear that the question what is or is not foreseeable should not in the normal way be dealt with as a pure matter of policy, but there is a proper role for the court to play and a proper role for the legislature and in the appropriate circumstances the courts can decide that a particular category of damage is not recoverable from a defendant.

Before proceeding further, I should also deal with the decision of the Court of Appeal in *Jones v Jones*. That was also a case where a person suffered brain damage. In that case it was a husband who suffered brain damage and as a result of that his marriage broke up and his wife divorced him. In proceedings as a result of an accident caused by the defendant's admitted negligence the husband recovered a sum which he had to pay to his wife in respect of the matrimonial home. The judgment of the court was given by Dunn LJ, and he was not prepared to reject that claim on the basis of the "floodgates" argument. However, when the case is considered, it is apparent that there are distinctions between that case and this, because it was one consequence of the plaintiff's own injuries that he was required to set up a separate home, and it was foreseeable that additional expense would be caused to him as a result of having to live apart from his former wife. In my view, *Jones v Jones* is not authority which assists the plaintiff in his claim against the driver or that driver's insurers, but it is valuable support for the correctness of the decision which was taken on behalf of the first defendant not to argue that the consequences of the plaintiff's imprisonment, in respect of which I awarded him damages, were too remote.

In his argument on the particular loss with which I am concerned here, counsel for the plaintiff contends that, if the plaintiff is entitled to recover damages in respect of his imprisonment in consequence of his attacking the victims, then he must also be entitled to recover the damages which he has to pay to those victims. He submits that there cannot be any distinction in logic or in policy drawn between the two situations. In deciding whether that is right, it is helpful to ask whether the victims themselves could have brought proceedings, not against the plaintiff, but against the driver of the vehicle which caused him to sustain the injuries which resulted in him developing the features of his personality which led to him attacking them. I say that because the test of whether a duty is owed is almost identical to the test that is applied whether damages are too remote. However, I recognise that although the tests are almost identical, the answer to one question does not necessarily provide the final answer to the other question, and here I refer to what Lane J said in *Malcolm v Broadhurst*:

> "Since both the cause of action and the recoverability of damages depend on foreseeability, the answer logically should be the same in each case. Logic however is not always an infallible guide in problems of remoteness of damage. The 'eggshell skull' principle itself, for example, is hard to reconcile logically with the foreseeability test."

So, clearly, if an action had been brought by the two victims against the driver, in respect of the sexual attacks which were inflicted on them by the plaintiff, the courts would have held that that damage was remote, and that no duty was owed by the driver to the victims of the plaintiff's sexual assaults. So far as the plaintiff's personality changes are concerned, on the other hand, they were clearly foreseeable. It may be that it was not foreseeable as to the precise type of personality change that would occur, but, in today's state of medical knowledge, it is well known that the head injuries which can be caused in traffic accidents often give rise to personality changes which are significant and a real head of damage to the person who has sustained the injuries. The real difference here is that the plaintiff is now not seeking to recover in respect of his own injuries or in respect of his direct financial loss, but the indirect loss he suffers as a result of having to pay damages to a third party.

In approaching the matter in what has been suggested is the right approach of the court in these circumstances, namely in a "robust" manner, as was suggested by Watkins LJ in *Lamb v Camden London Borough*, I have no hesitation in saying that I regard the present claims as being too remote ... Both my intellectual and instinctive response to approaching the matter in that way is that, as I have already indicated, the loss is not recoverable by the plaintiff either from the driver of the car or that driver's insurers. I consider that this approach is supported by the following considerations. First of all, if a victim of these attacks had had a child, would the defendant, that is the driver, and his insurers be responsible for maintaining that child? The person who raped the mother certainly should be so responsible, but, in my view, it would be contrary to common sense to suggest that a careless driver should have to saddle himself with that sort of long-term expense.

Again, one of the victims who sought damages yesterday before me alleged that the consequence of the attack on her was the break-up of her marriage. I did not accept that that was indeed the consequence. But, if I had come to a different conclusion, are the driver and his insurers to be taken to have foreseen that this would be the result of his negligent driving? I answer the question, No.

Furthermore, I bear in mind that where a person sustains the sort of personal injuries that this plaintiff sustained, many years later he could attack a further victim. He is detained at the present time and is regarded as a category A prisoner for this very reason. Is the court to be required to give a declaration to the plaintiff that he is entitled to be, in effect, indemnified in respect of any claim which is brought against him in respect of any further attack of that nature?

That brings me to a separate argument which was advanced on behalf of the defendants. It was argued that it would be contrary to public policy that the plaintiff should be indemnified for the consequences of his crime. I am bound to say that to allow the plaintiff to succeed would certainly be distasteful ... In my view, if I am wrong in my judgment in regard to the question of foreseeability, then this in fact would be a further ground for holding that the plaintiff is not entitled to be indemnified for his criminal attacks on the two ladies concerned.'

Comment

(1)   The same judge, in *Meah v McCreamer (No 1)*, had awarded the plaintiff damages in respect of the criminal consequences of his attacks, namely his loss of liberty while in prison. At first sight it would seem hard logically to reconcile the judge's approach to compensating the civil law consequences of the plaintiff's mental condition with his approach to compensating the criminal consequences. Each consequence would appear to be equally foreseeable and equally direct. Woolf J makes it clear, however, that this is a case in which pure logic gives way to the robust common-sense approach. Although he expresses the public policy consideration as an alternative basis for his decision, it seems likely that it is also reflected in the common-sense approach.

(2)   In *Clunis v Camden and Islington Health Authority* the plaintiff alleged that the health authority had been negligent in failing to ensure that he received appropriate psychiatric treatment which would, he argued, have deprived him of the opportunity to commit manslaughter, the crime for which he had been convicted. He cited *Meah v McCreamer (No 1)* in support of his claim for damages in relation to his resulting loss of liberty. The Court of Appeal noted the different outcomes in the two *Meah* cases, preferring the second, with the observation that, 'Whilst any decision of Lord Woolf must be given the greatest weight, we do not consider that, in the absence of any argument on the issue of public policy, his decision in *Meah v McCreamer (No 1)* can be regarded as authoritative on this issue.' The public policy issue in *Clunis* was identified as the principle *ex turpi causa non oritur actio*. For a fuller account of how the principle was applied, see p 360.

(3)   In *Wilson v Coulson* the claimant, who was already a Class A drugs user, took to heroin in order to ease headaches following an injury negligently caused by the defendant. He became addicted and eventually took an overdose causing further brain damage. The judge held that the defendant bore no responsibility for the latter damage, both because the claimant's voluntary and wholly unreasonable act amounted to a *novus actus*, and by application of the same policy principle as in *Clunis*.

(4)   For policy considerations in relation to matrimonial proceedings where it is alleged that the victim's injury resulted in a divorce, see *Pritchard v Cobden, Jones v Jones*.

CHAPTER 6

Defences to negligence

A number of general defences may be available to the defendant in a negligence action, as well as being equally applicable to most other forms of tort. Some, such as consent and necessity, are strictly only of relevance to specific torts and are dealt with in the appropriate chapter. Those covered here are: contributory negligence, *volenti non fit injuria* and illegality or *ex turpi causa*.

Contributory negligence is a partial defence in that the claimant's damages may be reduced by such a degree as is just and equitable in circumstances where the damage was caused in part by the claimant's own lack of care.

The maxim *volenti non fit injuria*, which operates as a complete defence, is sometimes described in terms of consent. This is appropriate in relation to trespass, for example (see p 493), but in negligence it is perhaps less confusing to think of it as a voluntary assumption of risk by the claimant. In *Nettleship v Weston*, Lord Denning MR considered that the courts' application of the defence in recent times had been severely limited. He said:

> 'Knowledge of the risk of injury is not enough. Nor is a willingness to take the risk of injury. Nothing will suffice short of an agreement to waive any claim for negligence. The plaintiff must agree, expressly or impliedly, to waive any claim for any injury that may befall him due to the lack of reasonable care by the defendant: or more accurately, due to the failure of the defendant to measure up to the standard of care that the law requires of him.'

The maxim *ex turpi causa non oritur actio*, which is not strictly a defence but more properly a bar to a claim, is based on considerations of public policy. It relies on the illegality of the conduct in which the claimant participated and from which the claimant's injury flowed. The exact scope of the principle has not yet been fully resolved by the courts, and is the subject of Law Commission Consultation Paper No 160 (published in 2002) entitled 'The Illegality Defence in Tort'.

Law Reform (Contributory Negligence) Act 1945

1 Apportionment of liability in case of contributory negligence

(1) Where any person suffers damage as the result partly of his own fault and partly of the fault of any other person or persons, a claim in respect of that damage shall not be defeated by reason of the fault of the person suffering the damage, but the damages recoverable in respect thereof shall be reduced to such extent as the court thinks just and equitable having regard to the claimant's share in the responsibility for the damage ...

4 Interpretation

The following expressions have the meanings hereby respectively assigned to them, that is to say—

...

'damage' includes loss of life and personal injury;

'fault' means negligence, breach of statutory duty or other act or omission which gives rise to liability in tort or would, apart from this Act, give rise to the defence of contributory negligence.

Jones v Livox Quarries Ltd
[1952] 2 QB 608 Court of Appeal

Despite instructions to the contrary, the plaintiff, who worked at a quarry, took a ride on the back of a vehicle known as a traxcavator. He was seriously injured when this vehicle collided with a dumper truck which, due to its driver's negligence, ran into the back of the traxcavator. The Court of Appeal held that the plaintiff's injuries were 'partly the result of his own fault' and reduced his damages accordingly.

Denning LJ: '... Although contributory negligence does not depend on a duty of care, it does depend on foreseeability. Just as actionable negligence requires the foreseeability of harm to others, so contributory negligence requires the foreseeability of harm to oneself. A person is guilty of contributory negligence if he ought reasonably to have foreseen that, if he did not act as a reasonable, prudent man, he might be hurt himself; and in his reckonings he must take into account the possibility of others being careless.

Once negligence is proved, then no matter whether it is actionable negligence or contributory negligence, the person who is guilty of it must bear his proper share of responsibility for the consequences. The consequences do not depend on foreseeability but on causation. The question in every case is: What faults were there which caused the damage? Was his fault one of them? The necessity of causation is shown by the word "result" in s 1(1) of the Act of 1945, and it was accepted by this court in *Davies v Swan Motor Co (Swansea) Ltd.*

There is no clear guidance to be found in the books about causation. All that can be said is that causes are different from the circumstances in which, or on which, they operate. The line between the two depends on the facts of each case. It is a matter of common sense more than anything else. In the present case, as the argument of [counsel] proceeded, it seemed to me that he sought to make foreseeability the decisive test of causation. He relied on the trial judge's statement that a man who rode on the towbar of the traxcavator "ran the risk of being thrown off and no other risk". That is, I think, equivalent to saying that such a man could reasonably foresee that he might be thrown off the traxcavator, but not that he might be crushed between it and another vehicle.

In my opinion, however, foreseeability is not the decisive test of causation. It is often a relevant factor, but it is not decisive. Even though the plaintiff did not foresee the possibility of being crushed, nevertheless in the ordinary plain common sense of this business the injury suffered by the plaintiff was due in part to the fact that he chose to ride on the towbar to lunch instead of walking down on his feet. If he had been thrown off in the collision, [counsel] admits that his injury would be partly due to his own negligence in riding on the towbar; but he says that because he was crushed, and not thrown off, his injury is in no way due to it. That is too fine a distinction for me. I cannot believe that that purely fortuitous circumstance can make all the difference to the case. As Scrutton LJ said in *Re Polemis and another and Furness, Withy & Co Ltd*: "Once the act is negligent, the fact that its exact operation was not foreseen is immaterial."

In order to illustrate this question of causation, I may say that if the plaintiff, whilst he was riding on the towbar, had been hit in the eye by a shot from a negligent sportsman, I should have thought that the plaintiff's negligence would in no way be a cause of his injury. It would only be the circumstance in which the cause operated. It would only be part of the history. But I cannot say that in the present case. The man's negligence here was so much mixed up with his injury that it cannot be dismissed as mere history. His dangerous position on the vehicle was one of the causes of his damage just as it was in *Davies v Swan Motor Co (Swansea) Ltd.*

The present case is a good illustration of the practical effect of the Act of 1945. In the course of the argument my Lord suggested that before the Act of 1945 he would have regarded this case as one where the plaintiff should recover in full. That would be because the negligence of the dumper driver would then have been regarded as the predominant cause. Now, since the Act, we have regard to all the causes, and one of them undoubtedly was the plaintiff's negligence in riding on the towbar of the traxcavator. His share in the responsibility was not great – the trial judge assessed it at one-fifth – but, nevertheless, it was his share, and he must bear it himself.'

Comment

(1)   In *Davies v Swan Motor Co* the plaintiff's husband was killed while riding on the back of a dustcart which collided with a bus due to the negligence of both drivers. The Court of Appeal had to consider the application of the Law Reform (Contributory Negligence) Act 1945 to the case. Denning LJ explained how the Act had changed the law:

'The legal effect of the Act of 1945 is simple enough. If the plaintiff's negligence was one of the causes of his damage, he is no longer defeated altogether. He gets reduced damages. The practical effect of the Act is, however, wider than its legal effect. Previously, to mitigate the harshness of the doctrine of contributory negligence, the courts in practice sought to select, from a number of competing causes, which was the cause – the effective or predominant cause – of the damage and to reject the rest. Now the courts have regard to all the causes and apportion the damages accordingly. This is not a change in the law as to what constitutes contributory negligence – the search, in theory, was always for all the causes – but it is a change in the practical application of it.'

(2)   In the *Davies* case Denning LJ also reviewed, and rejected, the notion that contributory negligence is based upon duty, and he said:

'It has sometimes been suggested that an injured plaintiff is not guilty of contributory negligence unless he is under a duty of care towards the defendant ... In my opinion, it is not a correct approach. When a man steps into the road he owes a duty to himself to take care for his own safety, but he does not owe to a motorist who is going at an excessive speed any duty to avoid being run down. Nevertheless, if he does not keep a good lookout, he is guilty of contributory negligence. The real question is not whether the plaintiff was neglecting some legal duty, but whether he was acting as a responsible man and with reasonable care ...'

See also *Froom v Butcher* below.

(3)　Although the wording of the Act clearly requires the plaintiff's conduct to have caused the damage in some degree, this is to be distinguished from the type of conduct whose nature is such as to break the chain of causation and relieve the defendant of liability entirely, see p 296.

Froom and others v Butcher
[1975] 3 All ER 520 Court of Appeal

The plaintiff suffered head and chest injuries when the car he was driving collided with another car driven by the defendant. The plaintiff bore no responsibility for the accident but the Court of Appeal held that his own failure to wear a seat belt had contributed to the severity of his injuries.

Lord Denning MR: '... Negligence depends on a breach of duty, whereas contributory negligence does not. Negligence is a man's carelessness in breach of duty to *others*. Contributory negligence is a man's carelessness in looking after *his own* safety. He is guilty of *contributory* negligence if he ought reasonably to have foreseen that, if he did not act as a reasonable prudent man, he might be hurt himself: see *Jones v Livox Quarries Ltd.* Before 1945 a plaintiff who was guilty of contributory negligence was disentitled from recovering anything if his own negligence was one of the substantial causes of the injury: see *Swadling v Cooper.* Since 1945 he is no longer defeated altogether. He gets reduced damages: see *Davies v Swan Motor Co (Swansea) Ltd.* The present law is contained in s 1(1) of the Law Reform (Contributory Negligence) Act 1945 ... [and] Section 4. [He quoted the provisions of the Act and continued.] ... Those provisions must be borne in mind as we take our consideration further.

THE CAUSE OF THE DAMAGE

In these seat belt cases, the injured plaintiff is in no way to blame for the accident itself. Sometimes he is an innocent passenger sitting beside a negligent driver who goes off the road. At other times he is an innocent driver of one car which is run into by the bad driving of another car which pulls out on to its wrong side of the road. It may well be asked: why should the injured plaintiff have his damages reduced? The accident was solely caused by the negligent driving by the defendant. Sometimes outrageously bad driving. It should not lie in his mouth to say: "You ought to have been wearing a seat belt." That point of view was strongly expressed in *Smith v Blackburn* by O'Connor J. He said: "... The idea that the insurers of a grossly negligent driver should be relieved in any degree from paying what is proper compensation for injuries is an idea that offends ordinary decency. Until I am forced to do so by higher authority, I will not so rule." I do not think that is the correct approach. The question is not what was the cause of the accident. It is rather what was the cause of the damage. In most accidents on the road the bad driving, which causes the accident, also causes the ensuing damage. But in seat belt cases the cause of the accident is one thing. The cause of the damage is another. The *accident* is caused by the bad driving. The *damage* is caused in part by the bad driving of the defendant, and in part by the failure of the plaintiff to wear a seat belt. If the plaintiff was to blame in not wearing a seat belt, the damage is in part the result of his own fault. He must bear some share in the responsibility for the damage and his damages fall to be reduced to such extent as the court thinks just and equitable. In Admiralty the courts used to look to the causes of the *damage:* see *The Margaret.* In a leading case in this court, under the 1945 Act, we looked to the cause of the *damage:* see *Davies v Swan Motor Co.* In the crash helmet cases this court also looked at the causes of the damage: see *O'Connell v Jackson.* So also we should in seat belt cases ...

THE SHARE OF RESPONSIBILITY

Whenever there is an accident, the negligent driver must bear by far the greater share of responsibility. It was his negligence which caused the accident. It was also a prime cause of the whole of the damage. But in so far as the damage might have been avoided or lessened by wearing a seat belt, the injured person must bear some share. But how much should this be? Is it proper to enquire whether the driver was grossly negligent or only slightly negligent? Or whether the failure to wear a seat belt was entirely inexcusable or almost forgivable? If such an enquiry could easily be undertaken, it might be as well to do it. In *Davies v Swan Motor Co* we said that consideration should be given not only to the causative potency of a particular factor, but also to its blameworthiness. But we live in a practical world. In most of these cases the liability of the driver is admitted; the failure to wear a seat belt is admitted; the only question is: what damages should be payable? This question should not be prolonged by an expensive enquiry into the degree of blameworthiness on either side, which would be hotly disputed. Suffice it to assess a share of responsibility which will be just and equitable in the great majority of cases.

Sometimes the evidence will show that the failure made no difference. The damage would have been the same, even if a seat belt had been worn. In such cases the damages should not be reduced at all. At other times the evidence will show that the failure made all the difference. The damage would have been prevented altogether if a seat belt had been worn. In such cases I would suggest that the damages should be reduced by 25 per cent. But often enough the evidence will only show that the failure made a considerable difference. Some injuries to the head, for instance, would have been a good deal less severe if a seat belt had been worn, but there would still have been some injury to the head. In such case I would suggest that the damages attributable to the failure to wear a seat belt should be reduced by 15 per cent.'

Comment

(1) At the time, Lord Denning based his view on the fact that 'everyone knows, or ought to know, that when he goes out in a car he should fasten the seat belt'. Now, of course, it is unlawful to fail to wear a seat belt (subject to a few exceptions) but it is the failure to behave in a reasonably prudent manner which underlies a claim of contributory negligence, not the unlawfulness.

(2) Note that, at least for seat belt cases, the balancing of responsibility for the accident and responsibility for the damage never results, according to Lord Denning's scheme, in the defendant's share being reduced below 75 per cent. This may seem odd in cases where the damage would not have occurred at all if a seat belt had been worn. It might be argued that there is a public benefit since drivers will be encouraged to ensure that their passengers are properly protected but the result seems unduly harsh when the imprudent passenger is travelling in another vehicle beyond the defendant's control.

(3) In *Pitts v Hunt* it was held that the plaintiff's contributory negligence could never amount to 100 per cent. Beldam LJ reasoned as follows:

> 'Section 1 [of the Law Reform (Contributory Negligence) Act 1945] begins with the premise that the person suffers damage as a result partly of his own fault and partly of the fault of any other person or persons. Thus before the section comes into operation, the court must be satisfied that there is fault on the part of both parties which has caused damage. It is then expressly provided that the claim shall not be defeated by reason of the fault of the person suffering the damage. To hold that he is himself entirely responsible for the damage effectively defeats his claim. It is then provided that the damages recoverable in respect thereof ... shall be reduced. It therefore presupposes that the person suffering the damage will recover some damage. Finally reduction is to be to such extent as the court thinks just and equitable, having regard to the claimant's share in the responsibility for the damage. To hold that the claimant is 100 per cent responsible is not to hold that he shared in the responsibility for the damage.'

This reasoning was accepted by the majority of the Court of Appeal in *Reeves v Commissioner of Police for the Metropolis* on the basis that 100 per cent contributory negligence would amount to 'the same ... in law as a *novus actus*' and that cases such as *Jayes v IMI (Kynoch) Ltd*, in which a workman had been held to be 100 per cent responsible for his own injury, 'are properly to be understood as based on causation'.

In the House of Lords' decision in *Reeves* Lord Hoffmann referred to the trial judge and Morritt LJ having considered that the deceased was 100 per cent contributorily negligent, but made no comment as to the permissibility of such a finding (see p 296).

Owens v Brimmell
[1976] 3 All ER 765 Queen's Bench Division

The plaintiff and the defendant went out together in the defendant's car for an evening's drinking. In the course of the evening both drank a considerable amount of beer, much of it just before they set off for home. The plaintiff, who was not wearing a seat belt, suffered severe injuries when the car collided with a lamp-post. Although there was no evidence as to whether his injuries were increased by the failure to wear a seat belt, the court held that his damages should be reduced by 20 per cent for his contributory negligence in travelling with a driver whom he knew to be drunk.

Watkins J: '... [T]here is widespread and weighty authority abroad for the proposition that a passenger may be guilty of contributory negligence if he rides with the driver of a car whom he knows has consumed alcohol in such quantity as is likely to impair to a dangerous degree that driver's capacity to drive properly and safely. So, also, may a passenger be guilty of contributory negligence if he, knowing that he is going to be driven in a car by his companion later, accompanies him on a bout of drinking which has the effect, eventually, of robbing the passenger of clear thought and perception and diminishes the driver's capacity to drive properly and carefully. Whether this principle can be relied on successfully is a question of fact and degree to be determined in the circumstances out of which the issue is said to arise.

In the instant case, the plaintiff and the defendant drank a fairly considerable amount of beer, much of it within a relatively short period before the beginning of the fateful journey. They were both reasonably intelligent young men and the plaintiff, in particular, must have appreciated at some part of the evening, in my view, that to continue the bout of drinking would be to expose himself to the risk of being driven later by someone who would be so much under the influence of drink as to be incapable of driving safely. I think it more than likely, however, that the two of them were bent on making what is known as a pub crawl and gave little, if any, thought to the possible consequences of it, or were recklessly indifferent to them.

In these circumstances I refer once more to what Lord Denning MR said in *Froom v Butcher*. The plaintiff told me that he appreciated there was a risk in driving with someone who had taken drink, but I must beware of accepting a statement of that kind from him at its face value, having regard to the damage done to his intellect, to which I shall be referring in more detail in a moment. On the plaintiff's behalf it is argued that the drink taken was consumed over a fairly long period of time. That may have been so, but it does not in my opinion in any appreciable way diminish the force of the facts I have found and the inferences arising properly, in my judgment, from them.

It is said, further, that the defendant, although he had taken drink, was ever mindful and anxious to avoid damage to his car because, as I have said earlier, it had recently been resprayed or repaired or both, and, in addition, that he had never given the plaintiff any cause for alarm when they had previously been out drinking together and had driven away from wherever it was they had taken drink. This argument might have been of use to the plaintiff had the drink taken on the night in question been less, so as to allow the benefit of doubt as to the existence of risk of injury to him, but I do not so regard it.

I think this is a clear case on the facts of contributory negligence, either on the basis that the minds of the plaintiff and the defendant, behaving recklessly, were equally befuddled by drink so as to rid them of clear thought and perception, or, as seems less likely, the plaintiff remained able to, and should have, if he actually did not, foresee the risk of being hurt by riding with the defendant as passenger. In such a case as this the degree of blameworthiness is not, in my opinion, equal. The driver, who alone controls the car and has it in him, therefore, to do whilst in drink great damage, must bear by far the greater responsibility. I, therefore, adjudge the plaintiff's contribution to be 20 per cent.'

Comment

(1) It had been argued for the plaintiff that the defence of contributory negligence could only apply to his decision to travel with an intoxicated driver if he was himself sufficiently sober for the decision to be intentional. The judge, while not rejecting this argument in principle, followed the approach in *Insurance Commissioner v Joyce* in which Latham LJ said that:

'If ... the plaintiff was sober enough to know and understand the danger of driving with [the defendant] in a drunken condition, he was guilty of contributory negligence ... But if he was not sober enough to know and understand such a danger ... if he drank himself into a state of stupidity or worse, he thereby disabled himself from avoiding the consequences of negligent driving by [the defendant], and his action fails on the ground of contributory negligence.'

(2) Intoxication is only one factor which may affect the degree of prudence which is reasonably to be expected of a plaintiff. For example, the Court of Appeal in *Gough v Thorne* showed its unwillingness to recognise contributory negligence in the conduct of children. In that case, the 13-year-old plaintiff was waiting to cross the road when she was waved across by the driver of a lorry which stopped for her. She set off across the road but was hit and injured by a car which was negligently driven by the defendant. The trial judge had assessed the plaintiff's degree of responsibility at one-third. Allowing the appeal, Lord Denning MR said:

'I cannot agree with the judge. A very young child cannot be guilty of contributory negligence. An older child may be; but it depends on the circumstances. A judge should only find a child guilty of contributory negligence if he or she is of such an age as reasonably to be expected to take precautions for his or her own safety: and then he or she is only to be found guilty if blame should be attached to him or her.'

By contrast, in *C v Imperial Design Ltd* the 13-year-old claimant was seriously injured in an explosion caused when he set fire to some solvent he had found in an abandoned container left on open land. The Court of Appeal concluded that the claimant, while too young and inexperienced to assume full responsibility for the consequences, was well aware that what he was doing was both wrong and dangerous, and assessed his contributory negligence at 50 per cent.

(3) The plaintiff's ability to act prudently may be affected by the need, in an emergency, to decide on a course of action without time for full consideration. In *Jones v Boyce* the plaintiff was travelling outside on a coach which went out of control due to the defendant's negligence. Believing (erroneously, as it proved) that the coach was about to overturn, he attempted to jump to safety but seriously injured his leg in the fall. The court, in awarding him damages, held that:

'To enable the plaintiff to sustain an action ... it is sufficient if he was placed by the misconduct of the defendant in such a situation as obliged him to adopt the alternative of a dangerous leap, or to remain at certain peril ... The question is, whether he was placed in such a situation as to render what he did a prudent precaution, for the purpose of self-preservation.'

Even in an emergency, the plaintiff is expected to act reasonably prudently in all the circumstances: see *Holmis v Dubuc*. The circumstances may include the degree of skill which is to be expected of such a plaintiff: see *Harrison v BRB* (below).

Harrison v British Railways Board and others
[1981] 3 All ER 679 Queen's Bench Division

The plaintiff was a guard on a passenger train when the defendant H tried to board the train as it moved out of the station. In compliance with regulations, the plaintiff attempted to signal to the driver to stop but inadvertently gave the wrong signal. He then tried to take hold of the defendant to help him on to the train but the continued acceleration caused them both to fall from the train. The court held that the defendant owed a duty of care to the plaintiff but that damages should be reduced for his contributory negligence in failing to reduce the risk to himself.

Boreham J: '... I turn now to the case against the second defendant. [T]he facts ... leave me in no doubt that the second defendant was negligent to the extent that he acted with a reckless disregard for his own safety. As a very experienced railwayman, and in particular as an ex-train guard, he was well aware of the rule against attempting to board a moving train, and he was well aware of the reasons for making that rule. With all his experience he knew that by grasping a handrail in order to board a moving train, particularly an electric train which has rapid acceleration, he was likely to find himself in grave danger. Had he expected the train to stop, he would not have been so determined to grab at the handrail. He hoped to board the train whilst it was in motion and he knew that the only hope of doing so was to aim for the guard's door. It was the only door that was open and it was the only door which opened inwards. It would have been hopeless to attempt to board via an outward-opening passenger door. Moreover, he knew that the guard, the plaintiff, had seen him and he ought to have anticipated, indeed I think he probably expected, that if he got into trouble the guard would do his best to help him. He ought to have foreseen that by intervening in such circumstances the guard would probably endanger himself.

One might perhaps be forgiven for thinking that in those circumstances H, the second defendant, must be liable to the plaintiff. Counsel for H says ... H is not liable because he, being the person rescued, owed no duty to the plaintiff ...

The question that has to be considered is this: is a man who, through lack of care for his own safety, puts himself into a situation of danger, and who ought, as a reasonable person, to have foreseen that another might endanger himself by attempting to rescue him, liable to his rescuer for injuries sustained in the course of the rescue, or attempted rescue? In the absence of authority I should have answered Yes. It has long been established that a duty of care arises whenever a reasonable person would foresee that if he did not take care he would put another in danger. That duty is owed to all who are within the sphere of the danger thus created. It is also owed to a rescuer, provided that the defendant ought, as a reasonable man, to have foreseen that someone would, or might, come to the rescue of the person imperilled by the defendant's negligence: see *Haynes v Harwood*. For some time there appeared to be room for the argument that the duty owed to the rescuer was what was called a derivative, or secondary, duty, namely a duty which arose only when the defendant owed a duty to the person being rescued: see *Dupuis v New Regina Trading*. There was, however, another school of thought; see, for instance, *Baker v Hopkins* per Barry J.

So far as this court is concerned, the principle has now been established that a duty will be owed to the rescuer if his intervention is reasonably foreseeable, albeit that the defendant owes no duty to the person being rescued: see *Videan v British Transport Commission*. The remaining question, namely whether or not a duty is owed to the rescuer when the person being rescued is he who created the dangerous situation, has, so far as I am aware, not previously been decided in this country. If however, as was decided in *Videan v British Transport Commission*, the duty may be owed to the rescuer, although no duty is owed to the person in danger, I see no reason in principle why it should not be owed to the rescuer when the person being rescued is the person who created the peril. Why should the defendant, who, by lack of reasonable care for his own safety, creates a dangerous situation which invites rescue, be in a better position than he who creates a similar situation by lack of reasonable care for another's safety? I can think of no reason, nor has any been suggested to me. In each case, of course, liability will attach only if the defendant ought, as a reasonable man, to have foreseen the likelihood of intervention by a rescuer. I am comforted by the thought that this approach is in line with the most recent decision of the Supreme Court of Canada in *Horsley v MacLaren, The Ogopogo.* Laskin J had this to say:

"Moreover, the liability to the rescuer, although founded on the concept of duty, is now seen as stemming from an independent and not a derivative duty of the negligent person. As *Fleming on Torts* (3rd edn.) has put it, the cause of action of the rescuer, in arising out of the defendant's negligence, is based ' ... not in its tendency to imperil the person rescued but in its tendency to induce the rescuer to encounter the danger. Thus viewed, the duty to the rescuer is clearly independent ...' This explanation of principle was put forward as early as 1924 by Professor Bohlen (*Studies in the Law of Torts*) in recognition of the difficulty of straining the notion of foreseeability to embrace the rescuer of a person imperilled by another's negligence. Under this explanation of the basis of liability, it is immaterial that the imperilled person does not in fact suffer any injury, or that, as it turns out, the negligent person was under no liability to him either because the injury was not caused by the negligence or the damage was outside the foreseeable risk of harm to him: cf. *Videan v British Transport Commission.* It is a further consequence of the recognition of independent duty that a person who imperils himself by his carelessness may be as fully liable to a rescuer as a third person would be who imperils another. In my opinion, therefore, *Dupuis v New Regina Trading Company Ltd* ought no longer to be taken as a statement of the common law in Canada in so far as it denies recovery because the rescuer was injured in going to the aid of a person who imperilled himself."

This seems to me to follow almost inevitably the decision in *Videan v British Transport Commission.* It is the law of Canada. It is, in my judgment, the law of England.

Thus, two questions arise: had the second defendant, H, by a lack of reasonable care for his own safety, created a situation of danger? I have no doubt that he had. The second question: ought he, as a reasonable man, to have foreseen that the plaintiff might very well come to his aid? I have said enough already to indicate that in my view he should have foreseen, and he probably did foresee, the probability of the plaintiff's intervention. In these circumstances I hold that the second defendant is liable in negligence to the plaintiff ... Finally, so far as liability is concerned, the second defendant contends that the plaintiff was guilty of contributory negligence.

Counsel for the second defendant argues that the plaintiff failed to observe the rules by failing to apply the emergency brake. The plaintiff's case is that he considered applying the brake but refrained from doing so because he was afraid that the sudden deceleration of the train would make matters worse for the second defendant ... in that it would almost inevitably have made him lose his grip and fall between the train and the platform. The difficulty I have in accepting this explanation is that I am satisfied that H was not hanging on to the train when the plaintiff went into the guard's van to try and bring the train to a stop. Had H by then grabbed the rail I am sure the plaintiff would have tried to help him aboard. On the other hand, H's intentions must have been clear to the plaintiff and I am prepared to accept that he assumed at the time he was in the van that H had, or might well have, grasped and hung on to some part of the train. But the fact remains that if he had wished to stop the train (and I accept that he did) the only proper means of doing so was by the emergency brake. I accept the evidence ... that the brake may be applied slowly and thus a too-sudden deceleration would be avoided. Indeed, that is the proper way to apply it. It was the plaintiff's duty, according to the rules, to apply the brake in an emergency; he knew it and I think he was negligent in not doing so. Had he done so, the speed of the train would have been reduced. He should have known it was his duty, and I believe he did know it. As it was, he gave (no doubt in the heat of the moment) a meaningless signal and the train continued to accelerate. In these circumstances, I have come to the conclusion that had he acted as he should have done it is probable, though not certain, that both the chance of his being injured at all and the severity of his injuries would have been reduced. He should, therefore, bear some of the blame for those injuries.

One has a feeling of distaste about finding a rescuer guilty of contributory negligence. It can rarely be appropriate to do so, in my judgment. Here, however, the contributory negligence which is alleged does not relate to anything done in the course of the actual rescue. What is alleged is the failure by the man in authority to reduce the danger by doing what he was duty-bound to do. The major responsibility must, of course, be borne by the second defendant. I assess the plaintiff's share at 20 per cent.'

Condon v Basi
[1985] 2 All ER 453 Court of Appeal

The plaintiff suffered a broken leg as the result of a 'reckless and dangerous' tackle by the defendant in a game of football. The Court of Appeal rejected the argument that participation in a sport amounted to such an acceptance of risk as to relieve players of any duty of care towards one another.

Sir John Donaldson MR: '... It is said that there is no authority as to what is the standard of care which governs the conduct of players in competitive sports generally and, above all, in a competitive sport whose rules and general background contemplate that there will be physical contact between the players, but that appears to be the position. This is somewhat surprising, but appears to be correct. For my part I would completely accept the decision of the High Court of Australia in *Rootes v Shelton*. I think it suffices, in order to see the law which has to be applied, to quote briefly from the judgment of Barwick CJ and from the judgment of Kitto J. Barwick CJ said:

"By engaging in a sport or pastime the participants may be held to have accepted risks which are inherent in that sport or pastime: the tribunal of fact can make its own assessment of what the accepted risks are: but this does not eliminate all duty of care of the one participant to the other. Whether or not such a duty arises, and, if it does, its extent, must necessarily depend in each case upon its own circumstances. In this connexion, the rules of the sport or game may constitute one of those circumstances: but, in my opinion, they are neither definitive of the existence nor of the extent of the duty; nor does their breach or non-observance necessarily constitute a breach of any duty found to exist."

Kitto J said:

"... in a case such as the present, it must always be a question of fact, what exoneration from a duty of care otherwise incumbent upon the defendant was implied by the act of the plaintiff joining in the activity. Unless the activity partakes of the nature of a war or of something else in which all is notoriously fair, the conclusion to be reached must necessarily depend, according to the concepts of the common law, upon the reasonableness, in relation to the special circumstances, of the conduct which caused the plaintiff's injury. That does not necessarily mean the compliance of that conduct with the rules, conventions or customs (if there are any) by which the correctness of conduct for the purposes of the carrying on of the activity as an organised affair is judged; for the tribunal of fact may think that in the situation in which the plaintiff's injury was caused a participant might do what the defendant did and still not be acting unreasonably, even though he infringed the 'rules of the game'. Non-compliance with such rules, conventions or customs (where they exist) is necessarily one consideration to be attended to upon the question of reasonableness; but it is only one, and it may be of much or little or even no weight in the circumstances."

I have cited from those two judgments because they show two different approaches which, as I see it, produce precisely the same result. One is to take a more generalised duty of care and to modify it on the basis that the participants in the sport or pastime impliedly consent to taking risks which otherwise would be a breach of the duty of care. That seems to be the approach of Barwick CJ. The other is exemplified by the judgment of Kitto J, where he is saying, in effect, that there is a general standard of care, namely the Lord Atkin approach that you are under a duty to take all reasonable care taking account of the circumstances in which you are placed (see *Donoghue (or M'Alister) v Stevenson*); which, in a game of football, are quite different from those which affect you when you are going for a walk in the countryside.

For my part I would prefer the approach of Kitto J, but I do not think it makes the slightest difference in the end if it is found by the tribunal of fact that the defendant failed to exercise that degree of care which was appropriate in all the circumstances, or that he acted in a way to which the plaintiff cannot be expected to have consented. In either event, there is liability ... It was submitted by the counsel on behalf of the defendant that the standard of care was subjective to the defendant and not objective, and if he was a wholly incompetent football player, he could do things without risk of liability which a competent football player could not do. For my part I reject that submission. The standard is objective, but objective in a different set of circumstances. Thus there will of course be a higher degree of care required of a player in a First Division football match than of a player in a local league football match.'

Comment

As to the degree of care to be expected, this last remark may be hard to reconcile with the approach to learner-drivers in *Nettleship v Weston*.

Wooldridge v Sumner and another
[1962] 2 All ER 978 Court of Appeal

The plaintiff, a professional photographer, was filming at the National Horse Show when a competitor galloped round the corner of the arena and the plaintiff was knocked down and injured. The Court of Appeal, *inter alia*, considered the application of the maxim *volenti non fit injuria* to sporting events.

Diplock LJ: '... The matter has to be looked at from the point of view of the reasonable spectator as well as the reasonable participant; not because of the maxim *volenti non fit injuria*, but because what a reasonable spectator would expect a participant to do without regarding it as blameworthy is as relevant to what is reasonable care as what a reasonable participant would think was blameworthy conduct in himself. The same idea was expressed by Scrutton LJ in *Hall v Brooklands Auto-Racing Club*:

"What is reasonable care would depend on the perils which might be reasonably expected to occur, and the extent to which the ordinary spectator might be expected to appreciate and take the risk of such perils."

A reasonable spectator attending voluntarily to witness any game or competition knows, and presumably desires, that a reasonable participant will concentrate his attention on winning, and if the game or competition is a fast-moving one will have to exercise his judgment and attempt to exert his skill in what, in the analogous context of contributory negligence, is sometimes called "the agony of the moment". If the participant does so concentrate his attention and consequently does exercise his judgment and attempt to exert his skill in circumstances of this kind which are inherent in the game or competition in which he is taking part, the question whether any mistake he makes amounts to a breach of duty to take reasonable care must take account of those circumstances.

The law of negligence has always recognised that the standard of care which a reasonable man will exercise depends on the conditions under which the decision to avoid the act or omission relied on as negligence has to be taken. The case of the workman engaged on repetitive work in the noise and bustle of the factory is a familiar example. More apposite for present purposes are the collision cases where a decision has to be made on the spur of the moment.

> "... A's negligence makes collision so threatening that, though by the appropriate measure B could avoid it, B has not really time to think and by mistake takes the wrong measure. B is not held to be guilty of any negligence and A wholly fails." (*Admiralty Comrs v SS Volute*)

A fails not because of his own negligence; there never has been any contributory negligence rule in Admiralty. He fails because B has exercised such care as is reasonable in circumstances in which he has not really time to think. No doubt, if he has got into those circumstances as a result of a breach of duty of care which he owes to A, A can succeed on this antecedent negligence; but a participant in a game or competition gets into the circumstances in which he has no time or very little time to think by his decision to take part in the game or competition at all. It cannot be suggested that the participant, at any rate if he has some modicum of skill, is by the mere act of participating in breach of his duty of care to a spectator who is present for the very purpose of watching him do so. If, therefore, in the course of the game or competition at a moment when he really has not time to think, a participant by mistake takes a wrong measure, he is not, in my view, to be held guilty of any negligence.

Furthermore, the duty which he owes is a duty of care, not a duty of skill. Save where a consensual relationship exists between a plaintiff and a defendant by which the defendant impliedly warrants his skill, a man owes no duty to his neighbour to exercise any special skill beyond that which an ordinary reasonable man would acquire before indulging in the activity in which he is engaged at the relevant time. It may well be that a participant in a game or competition would be guilty of negligence to a spectator if he took part in it when he knew or ought to have known that his lack of skill was such that, even if he exerted it to the utmost, he was likely to cause injury to a spectator watching him. No question of this arises in the present case. It was common ground that H was an exceptionally skilful and experienced horseman.

The practical result of this analysis of the application of the common law of negligence to participant and spectator would, I think, be expressed by the common man in some such terms as these: "A person attending a game or competition takes the risk of any damage caused to him by any act of a participant done in the course of and for the purposes of the game or competition, notwithstanding that such act may involve an error of judgment or a lapse of skill, unless the participant's conduct is such as to evince a reckless disregard of the spectator's safety." The spectator takes the risk because such an act involves no breach of the duty of care owed by the participant to him. He does not take the risk by virtue of the doctrine expressed or obscured by the maxim *volenti non fit injuria*. That maxim states a principle of estoppel applicable originally to a Roman citizen who consented to being sold as a slave. Although pleaded and argued below, it was only faintly relied on by counsel for the first defendant in this court. In my view, the maxim, in the absence of express contract, has no application to negligence *simpliciter* where the duty of care is based solely on proximity or "neighbourship" in the Atkinian sense. The maxim in English law pre-supposes a tortious act by the defendant. The consent that is relevant is not consent to the risk of injury but consent to the lack of reasonable care that may produce that risk ... and requires on the part of the plaintiff at the time at which he gives his consent full knowledge of the nature and extent of the risk that he ran ... In *Dann v Hamilton*, Asquith J expressed doubts whether the maxim ever could apply to license in advance a subsequent act of negligence, for, if the consent precedes the act of negligence, the plaintiff cannot at that time have full knowledge of the extent as well as the nature of the risk which he will run. Asquith J, however, suggested that the maxim might, nevertheless, be applicable to cases where a dangerous physical condition had been brought about by the negligence of the defendant, and the plaintiff with full knowledge of the existing danger elected to run the risk thereof. With the development of the law of negligence in the last 20 years, a more consistent explanation of this type of case is that the test of liability on the part of the person creating the dangerous physical condition is whether it was reasonably foreseeable by him that the defendant would so act in relation to it as to endanger himself. This is the principle which has been applied in the rescue cases (see *Cutler v United Dairies (London) Ltd*, and contrast *Haynes v Harwood*), and that part of Asquith J's judgment in *Dann v Hamilton* dealing with the possible application of the maxim to the law of negligence was not approved by the court in [*Baker v T E Hopkins & Son Ltd*]. In the type of case envisaged by Asquith J, if I may adapt the words of Morris LJ in [*Baker v Hopkins*], the plaintiff could not have agreed to run the risk that the defendant might be negligent for the plaintiff would only play his part after the defendant had been negligent.

Since the maxim has, in my view, no application to this or any other case of negligence *simplicter*, the fact that the plaintiff, owing to his ignorance of horses, did not fully appreciate the nature and extent of the risk he ran did not impose on H any higher duty of care towards him than that which he owed to any ordinary reasonable spectator with such knowledge of horses and vigilance for his own safety as might be reasonably expected to be possessed by a person who chooses to watch a heavyweight hunter class in the actual arena where the class is being judged. He cannot rely on his personal ignorance of the risk any more than the plaintiff in *Murray v Harringay Arena Ltd* could rely on his ignorance of the risk involved in ice-hockey, excusable though such ignorance may have been in a six-year-old child.'

Comment

According to this approach, the question of *volenti*, or voluntary assumption of risk, is irrelevant because there can be no breach of duty provided that the competitor acts without 'a reckless disregard of the spectator's safety'. Logically, however, this view is not without its difficulties since it relies on the fact that spectators are a special category of the general public, namely those 'who might be expected to appreciate and take the risk of such perils'. This was expressed in another way by Sellers LJ:

' ... There would, I think, be a difference, for instance, in assessing blame which is actionable between an injury caused by a tennis ball hit or a racket accidentally thrown in the course of play into the spectators at Wimbledon and a ball hit or a racket thrown into the stands in temper or annoyance when play was not in progress. The relationship of spectator and competitor or player is a special one, as I see it, as the standard of conduct of the participant, as accepted and expected by the spectator, is that which the sport permits or involves.'

Dann v Hamilton
[1939] I All ER 59 King's Bench Division

The plaintiff was injured when the car in which she was a passenger left the road and crashed due to the negligence of the driver, who was killed. The plaintiff knew that the driver had been drinking and the quality of his driving prior to the accident was such as to confirm the fact that he was drunk. The court rejected an argument that this knowledge was such as to support the defence of *volenti*.

Asquith J: '... How stands the matter with regard to the tort of negligence, as we may now venture to call it? Does the maxim [*volenti non fit injuria*] apply to negligence at all? *Cleghorn v Oldham* seems to decide that in relation to negligence the maxim does not apply at all. This case, however, was decided in relation to a particular game – namely, golf – and it would be improper to stretch general propositions laid down in it beyond the subject-matter immediately concerned.

Some textbook writers of authority, notably *Beven on Negligence* (4th ed.), roundly deny that the maxim applies to cases of negligence at all. This is a hard saying, and must be read, I think, subject to some implied limitation. Where a dangerous physical condition has been brought about by the negligence of the defendant, and, after it has arisen, the plaintiff, fully appreciating its dangerous character, elects to assume the risk thereof, the maxim has often been held to apply, and to protect the defendant. Instances are *Torrance v Ilford Urban District Council* and the more recent *Cutler v United Dairies (London) Ltd*. Where, however, the act of the plaintiff relied on as a consent precedes, and is claimed to license in advance, a possible subsequent act of negligence by the defendant (and this, I think, must be the case Beven had in mind), the case may well be different. Here, *Smith v Baker & Sons* does not help as much as might be expected. In any case, it turned on contract, which is not in question here.

With some qualifications, *Pollock on Torts* (13th edn.) supports Beven's *dictum*, declaring: "The whole law of negligence assumes the principle of *volenti non fit injuria* not to be applicable." He points out, quoting the observations of Lord Halsbury LC, in *Smith v Baker & Sons*, that anyone crossing a London street knows that a substantial percentage of drivers are negligent. If a man crosses deliberately, with this knowledge, and is negligently run down, he is certainly not *volens*, and is not, therefore, precluded from a remedy. Sir Frederick Pollock adds: "A man is not bound at his peril to fly from a risk from which it is another's duty to protect him, merely because the risk is known."

In *Woodley v Metropolitan District Ry Co*, Mellish LJ carries this illustration a step further. He says:

"Suppose this case: a man is employed by a contractor for cleansing the street, to scrape a particular street, and for the space of a fortnight he has the opportunity of observing that a particular hansom cabman drives his cab with extremely little regard for the safety of the men who scrape the streets. At the end of a fortnight the man who scrapes the streets is negligently run over by the cabman. An action is brought in the county court, and the cabman says in his defence: 'You know my style of driving, you had seen me drive for a fortnight, I was only driving in my usual style'."

The judgment of Mellish LJ in this particular case was a minority judgment, but seems to have been preferred to that of the majority [by] the House of Lords in the later case of *Membery v Great Western Ry Co*.

Cannot a yet further step be safely taken? I find it difficult to believe, although I know of no authority directly in point, that a person who voluntarily travels as a passenger in a vehicle driven by a driver who is known by the passenger to have driven negligently in the past is *volens* as to future negligent acts of such driver, even though he could have chosen some other form of transport if he had wished. Then, to take the last step, suppose that such a driver is likely to drive negligently on the material occasion, not because he is known to the plaintiff to have driven negligently in the past, but because he is known to the plaintiff to be under the influence of drink. That is the present case. Ought the result to be any different? After much debate, I have come to the conclusion that it should not, and that the plaintiff, by embarking in the car, or re-entering it, with knowledge that through drink the driver had materially reduced his capacity for driving safely, did not impliedly consent to, or absolve the driver from liability for, any subsequent negligence on his part whereby the plaintiff might suffer harm.

There may be cases in which the drunkenness of the driver at the material time is so extreme and so glaring that to accept a lift from him is like engaging in an intrinsically and obviously dangerous occupation, inter-meddling with an unexploded bomb or walking on the edge of an unfenced cliff. It is not necessary to decide whether in such a case the maxim *volenti non fit injuria* would apply, for in the present case I find as a fact that the driver's degree of intoxication fell short of this degree. I therefore conclude that the defence fails, and the claim succeeds. I arrive at this conclusion with the less reluctance in that it would be unjust that the deceased man's estate should be protected from suit by the mere fact that he got drunk before committing the final act of negligence, whereas, if he had committed the same act when sober, his estate would have been liable.'

Comment

Now, under the Road Traffic Act 1988, s 149(3), the defence of *volenti* cannot affect liability 'in circumstances such that ... there is required to be in force ... such a policy of insurance or such a security in respect of third party risks as complies with [the Act]': see *Pitts v Hunt*. The same bar applies to exclusion notices. For the effect of exclusion notices generally see p 398.

Morris v Murray and another
[1990] 3 All ER 801 Court of Appeal

The plaintiff and the deceased, M, met in a pub after having several drinks. After several more they decided, at the deceased's invitation, to take a ride in his light aircraft. They drove to the aerodrome where, despite such poor weather conditions that other flying had been suspended, they took off downwind and uphill. The plane crashed almost immediately, killing the pilot and seriously injuring the plaintiff. The Court of Appeal held that any claim in negligence was defeated by the defence of *volenti*.

Fox LJ: '... In my opinion, on the evidence the plaintiff knew that he was going on a flight, he knew that he was going to be piloted by M and he knew that M had been drinking heavily that afternoon. The plaintiff's actions that afternoon, from leaving the Blue Boar to the take-off suggest that he was capable of understanding what he was doing. There is no clear evidence to the contrary. I think that he knew what he was doing and was capable of appreciating the risks. I do not overlook that the plaintiff's evidence was that, if he had been sober, he would not have gone on the flight. That is no doubt so but it does not establish that he was in fact incapable of understanding what he was doing that afternoon.

If he was capable of understanding what he was doing, then the fact is that he knowingly and willingly embarked on a flight with a drunken pilot. The flight served no useful purpose at all; there was no need or compulsion to join it. It was just entertainment. The plaintiff co-operated fully in the joint activity and did what he could to assist it. He agreed in evidence that he was anxious to start the engine and to fly. A clearer source of great danger could hardly be imagined. The sort of errors of judgment which an intoxicated pilot may make are likely to have a disastrous result. The high probability was that M was simply not fit to fly an aircraft. Nothing that happened on the flight itself suggests otherwise, from the take-off downwind to the violence of the manoeuvres of the plane in flight.

The situation seems to me to come exactly within Asquith J's example of the case where: "the drunkenness of the driver at the material time is so extreme and so glaring that to accept a lift from him is like engaging in an intrinsically and obviously dangerous occupation ..." (see *Dann v Hamilton*).

I think that in embarking on the flight the plaintiff had implicitly waived his rights in the event of injury consequent on M's failure to fly with reasonable care.

The facts go far beyond *Dann v Hamilton*, *Nettleship v Weston* and *Slater v Clay Cross Co Ltd*. It is much nearer to the dangerous experimenting with the detonators in *Imperial Chemical Industries Ltd v Shatwell*. I would conclude, therefore, that the plaintiff accepted the risks and implicitly discharged M from liability from injury in relation to the flying of the plane.

The result, in my view, is that the maxim *volenti non fit injuria* does apply in this case ... Considerations of policy do not lead me to any different conclusion. *Volenti* as a defence has, perhaps, been in retreat during this century, certainly in relation to master and servant cases. It might be said that the merits could be adequately dealt with by the application of the contributory negligence rules. The judge held that the plaintiff was only 20 per cent to blame (which seems to me to be too low) but if that were increased to 50 per cent, so that the plaintiff's damages were reduced by half, both sides would be substantially penalised for their conduct. It seems to me, however, that the wild irresponsibility of the venture is such that the law should not intervene to award damages and should leave the loss where it falls. Flying is intrinsically dangerous and flying with a drunken pilot is great folly. The situation is very different from what has arisen in motoring cases.'

Comment

(1)   The starting point for this judgment was Lord Herschell's explanation of the maxim in *Smith v Baker & Sons*. He said: '[It] is founded on good sense and justice. One who has invited or assented to an act being done towards him cannot, when he suffers from it, complain of it as a wrong.'

(2)   Fox LJ's remark that the journey 'served no useful purpose' suggests that the result might perhaps have been different if, for example, the flight involved a rescue. In such a case, however, it may be that the usefulness of the objective to be achieved would so modify the standard of care as to defeat any claim, see *Watt v Herts CC*. For the application of *volenti* to rescuers generally, see *Baker and another v T E Hopkins & Son Ltd* (p 345).

(3)   Changes in the application of the maxim to the master–servant relationship may be seen in *Smith v Baker & Sons* (below). See also the Animals Act 1971, s 6(5).

(4)   In *Imperial Chemical Industries Ltd v Shatwell* two shotfirers were injured when they decided to ignore safety regulations and test a detonator using a cable which was too short for them to be able to shelter from the blast. The question for the House of Lords was whether the defendants were to be held vicariously liable for the negligence of one worker towards another. On the defence of *volenti*, Lord Reid said:

'... I think that most people would say ... that there is a world of difference between two fellow servants collaborating carelessly, so that the acts of both contribute to cause injury to one of them, and two fellow servants combining to disobey an order deliberately, though they know the risk involved. It seems reasonable that the injured man should recover some compensation in the former case, but not in the latter ... In the second [case] *volenti non fit injuria* is a complete defence ...'

(5)   See also *Ashton v Turner*, *Pitts v Hunt*, p 352.

Smith v Baker & Sons
[1891] AC 325 House of Lords

The plaintiff was employed in a quarry to drill stones in a cutting over which large stones were passed in the sling of a crane. He had previously reported his view that this practice was dangerous and when, due to the negligence of the defendants, he was injured by a falling stone it was argued by them that his continuing in the job demonstrated his voluntary acceptance of the risk. The House of Lords disagreed.

Lord Halsbury LC: '... The objection raised, and the only objection raised, to the plaintiff's right to recover was that he had voluntarily undertaken the risk ... The question of law that seems to be in debate is whether upon these facts, and on an occasion when the very form of his employment prevented him looking out for himself, he consented to undergo this particular risk, and so disentitled himself to recover when a stone was negligently slung over his head or negligently permitted to fall on him and do him injury.

My Lords, I am of opinion that the application of the maxim *volenti non fit injuria* is not warranted by these facts. I do not think the plaintiff did consent at all. His attention was fixed upon a drill, and while, therefore, he was unable to take precautions himself, a stone was negligently slung over his head without due precautions against its being permitted to fall ... For my own part, I think that a person who relies on the maxim must shew a consent to the particular thing done. Of course, I do not mean to deny that a consent to the particular thing may be inferred from the course of conduct, as well as proved by express consent; but if I were to apply my proposition to the particular facts of this case, I do not believe that the plaintiff ever did or would have consented to the particular act done under the particular circumstances. He would have said, "I cannot look out for myself at present. You are employing me in a form of employment in which I have not the ordinary means of looking out for myself; I must attend to my drill. If you will not give me warning when the stone is going to be slung, at all events let me look out for myself, and do not place me under a crane which is lifting heavy stones over my head when you keep my attention fixed upon an operation which prevents me looking out for myself."

It appears to me that the proposition upon which the defendants must rely must be a far wider one than is involved in the maxim, *volenti non fit injuria*. I think they must go to the extent of saying that whenever a person knows there is a risk of injury to himself, he debars himself from any right of complaint if an injury should happen to him in doing anything which involves that risk. For this purpose, and in order to test this proposition, we have nothing to do with the relation of employer and employed. The maxim in its application in the law is not so limited; but where it applies, it applies equally to a stranger as to any one else; and if applicable to the extent that is now insisted on, no person ever ought to have been awarded damages for being run over in London streets; for no one (at all events some years ago, before the admirable police regulations of later years) could have crossed London streets without knowing that there was a risk of being run over.

It is, of course, impossible to maintain a proposition so wide as is involved in the example I have just given; and in both *Thomas v Quartermaine* and *Yarmouth v France* it has been taken for granted that mere knowledge of the risk does not necessarily involve consent to the risk. Bowen LJ carefully points out in ... [*Thomas v Quartermaine*] that the maxim is not *scienti non fit injuria*, but *volenti non fit injuria*. And Lindley LJ, in quoting Bowen LJ's distinction with approval, adds:

> "The question in each case must be, not simply whether the plaintiff knew of the risk, but whether the circumstances are such as necessarily to lead to the conclusion that the whole risk was voluntarily incurred by the plaintiff."

… I am of opinion myself, that in order to defeat a plaintiff's right by the application of the maxim relied on, who would otherwise be entitled to recover, the jury ought to be able to affirm that he consented to the particular thing being done which would involve the risk, and consented to take the risk upon himself. It is manifest that if the proposition which I have just enunciated be applied to this case, the maxim could here have no application. So far from consenting, the plaintiff did not even know of the particular operation that was being performed over his head until the injury happened to him, and consent, therefore, was out of the question.

As I have intimated before, I do not deny that a particular consent may be inferred from a general course of conduct. Every sailor who mounts the rigging of a ship knows and appreciates the risk he is encountering. The act is his own, and he cannot be said not to consent to the thing which he himself is doing. And examples might be indefinitely multiplied where the essential cause of the risk is the act of the complaining plaintiff himself, and where, therefore, the application of the maxim, *volenti non fit injuria*, is completely justified.'

Comment

In the same case, Lord Herschell's view was that the reality of a master–servant relationship was such that a failure to 'straightway refuse to continue his service' ought not to be seen as a voluntary acceptance of risk, but he did accept an argument that 'the employed might, on account of special risk in his employment, receive higher wages, and that it would be unjust that in such a case he should seek to make the employer liable for the result of the accident'.

Baker and another v T E Hopkins & Son Ltd
[1959] 3 All ER 225 Court of Appeal

The defendants were engaged to carry out work on a well. H, a director of the company, noticed that a petrol-driven pump which had been lowered into the well in order to clear out the water had produced noxious fumes. He instructed his workmen to go to the well but on no account to enter it until he arrived. Both workmen went down the well and were overcome by fumes, whereupon B, a doctor who had been called to the scene, had himself lowered to them by rope. He was also overcome but efforts to pull him out were frustrated when the rope jammed, and he died. The Court of Appeal, in awarding damages, considered the defence of *volenti* in relation to rescuers.

Willmer LJ: '… Dr B's case falls to be determined on the basis that H's own negligence was at least a substantial cause of the peril in which the two men, Ward and Wileman, found themselves, and which led to their death. The case, therefore, raises once more the not unfamiliar problems, much discussed in the so-called "rescue cases", which arise where A's wrongful act puts B in a situation of peril, and C, a stranger, suffers injury in the course of attempting to rescue B.

It seems to me that in this case, as in any case where a plaintiff is injured in going to the rescue of a third party put in peril by the defendants' wrongdoing, the questions which have to be answered are fourfold. (1) Did the wrongdoer owe any duty to the rescuer in the circumstances of the particular case? (2) If so, did the rescuer's injury result from a breach of that duty, or did his act in going to the rescue amount to a *novus actus*? (3) Did the rescuer, knowing the danger, voluntarily accept the risk of injury, so as to be defeated by the maxim *volenti non fit injuria*? (4) Was the rescuer's injury caused or contributed to by his own failure to take reasonable care for his own safety? All these questions are raised by the circumstances of this case, and have been much canvassed in argument before us. I will endeavour to deal with each in turn.

(1)   The question whether the wrongdoer owed any duty to the rescuer must be determined, in my judgment, by reference to Lord Atkin's familiar statement of the law in *M'Alister (or Donoghue) v Stevenson* when he said: "You must take reasonable care to avoid acts or omissions which you can reasonably foresee would be likely to injure your neighbour." In the circumstances of the particular case, is the rescuer in law the "neighbour" of the wrongdoer, in the sense that he is so closely and directly affected by the wrongdoer's act that the latter ought reasonably to have him in contemplation as being so affected? Where the act of the wrongdoer has been such as to be likely to put someone in peril, reasonable foresight will normally contemplate the probability of an attempted rescue, in the course of which the rescuer may receive injury. In the American case of *Wagner v International Ry Co* Cardozo J, as it seems to me, foreshadowed in a remarkable way Lord Atkin's statement of principle, and applied it to a typical rescue case. He said:

> "Danger invites rescue. The cry of distress is the summons to relief. The law does not ignore these reactions of the mind in tracing conduct to its consequences. It recognises them as normal. It places their effects within the range of the natural and probable. The wrong that imperils life is a wrong to the imperilled victim; it is a wrong also to his rescuer."

Then a little later he went on:

> "The risk of rescue, if only it be not wanton, is born of the occasion. The emergency begets the man. The wrongdoer may not have foreseen the coming of a deliverer. He is accountable as if he had."

The judgment of Cardozo J, was referred to with approval by Lord Wright in *Hay (or Bourhill) v Young* and Lord Wright went on to say:

> "This again shows how the ambit of the persons affected by negligence or misconduct may extend beyond persons who are actually subject to physical impact. There, indeed, may be no one injured in a particular case by actual

impact; but still a wrong may be committed to anyone who suffers nervous shock or is injured in an act of rescue."

I should also refer to *Lord v Pacific Steam Navigation Co Ltd, The Oropesa* where Lord Wright said, quoting from the speech of Lord Haldane in *Canadian Pacific Ry Co v Kelvin Shipping Co Ltd, The Metagama:* "Reasonable human conduct is part of the ordinary course of things ...". Assuming the rescuer not to have acted unreasonably, therefore, it seems to me that he must normally belong to the class of persons who ought to be within the contemplation of the wrongdoer as being closely and directly affected by the latter's act. In the present case the fact that Dr B was a doctor is of itself significant. Having regard to the nature of the peril created by the wrongful act of H, it was only too likely that a doctor would be summoned ... and, if summoned, would attempt to do all he could for the victim, even at the risk of his own safety. In such circumstances I am satisfied that Dr B was one of the class who ought to have been within the contemplation of H when he brought about the dangerous situation in this well. I do not think, therefore, that it is open to the defendant company to contend that no duty was owed by H to Dr B.

(2) The question whether the act of the rescuer amounts to a *novus actus* answers itself, in my judgment, as soon as it is determined that it is the kind of act which ought to have been within the contemplation of the wrongdoer, so as to bring the rescuer within the class of persons to whom a duty was owed. I cannot do better than quote the words used by Greer LJ in *Haynes v Harwood* – a case in which a police officer was injured while attempting to stop two runaway horses drawing a van, which had been left unattended through the negligence of the defendants' servant. Dealing with the contention that the plaintiff's act amounted to a *novus actus*, Greer LJ said:

"If what is relied upon as *novus actus interveniens* is the very kind of thing which is likely to happen if the want of care which is alleged takes place, the principle embodied in the maxim is no defence. The whole question is whether or not ... the accident can be said to be 'the natural and probable result' of the breach of duty. If it is the very thing which ought to be anticipated by a man leaving his horses, or one of the things likely to arise as a consequence of his wrongful act, it is no defence; it is only a step in the way of proving that the damage is the result of the wrongful act."

In *Hyett v Great Western Ry Co*, these words of Greer LJ were expressly approved and followed by Tucker LJ, with whose judgment the other two members of the court concurred. They must, therefore, be regarded as authoritative so far as this court is concerned. In my judgment, it was a natural and probable result of the wrongdoing of H that, in the likely event of someone being overcome by the carbon monoxide poisoning, a doctor would be called in, and that such doctor, having regard to the traditions of his profession, would, even at the risk of his own safety, descend the well for the purpose of attempting a rescue. Unless it can be shown, therefore, that Dr B displayed such an unreasonable disregard for his own safety as to amount to negligence on his own part – with which suggestion I will presently deal – I do not think that it can be said that his act constituted a *novus actus interveniens*.

(3)   The next question is whether the plaintiffs in Dr B's case are defeated by the maxim *volenti non fit injuria*. Our attention was directed to a passage in the judgment of Asquith J in *Dann v Hamilton*, where he said:

> "Where a dangerous physical condition has been brought about by the negligence of the defendant, and, after it has arisen, the plaintiff, fully appreciating its dangerous character, elects to assume the risk thereof, the maxim has often been held to apply, and to protect the defendant."

These words were clearly *obiter*, for the actual question in issue in that case was whether the plaintiff took the risk of future negligence on the part of the defendant by accepting a lift in his motor car when she knew that he was the worse for drink. If the learned judge meant that, in all cases where the dangerous physical condition has already come into existence before the plaintiff's intervention, the plaintiff is liable to be defeated by a plea of *volenti*, I think that he went too far. So applied the maxim would defeat the plaintiff's claim in any rescue case, save possibly a case in which the rescuer had acted so instinctively, or so much on the impulse of the moment, that his conduct cannot be regarded as a conscious act of volition. But, as was said by Greer LJ in *Haynes v Harwood*: "It would be absurd to say that if a man deliberately incurs a risk he is entitled to less protection than if he acts on a sudden impulse without thinking whether he should do so or not."

It seems to me that, when one is determined that the act of the rescuer was the natural and probable consequence of the defendant's wrongdoing, there is no longer any room for the application of the maxim *volenti non fit injuria*. It would certainly be a strange result if the law were held to penalise the courage of the rescuer by depriving him of any remedy. Greer LJ in *Haynes v Harwood* was clearly of the view that the maxim cannot be applied to defeat the plaintiff's claim in a rescue case. He quotes from an article by Professor Goodhart in the *Cambridge Law Journal* (vol. V) as follows:

> "The American rule is that the doctrine of the assumption of risk does not apply where the plaintiff has, under an exigency caused by the defendants' wrongful misconduct, consciously and deliberately faced a risk, even of death, to rescue another from imminent danger of personal injury or death, whether the person endangered is one to whom he owes a duty of protection, as a member of his family, or is a mere stranger to whom he owes no such special duty."

Greer LJ goes on: "In my judgment, that passage not only represents the law of the United States but also the law of this country." It is by no means clear that the other two members of the court were prepared to go so far as Greer LJ, in stating the principle, and they appear to have based their judgments to a great extent on the fact that in the particular case the plaintiff was a police officer. But for my part I am content to accept Greer LJ's statement of the law, and to hold that the maxim *volenti non fit injuria* cannot be invoked in this case to defeat the second plaintiff's claim. In my judgment, the real question to be determined in a case such as the present is, not whether the rescuer voluntarily accepted the risk of injury, but whether his injury was caused or contributed to by any failure on his part to take reasonable care for his own safety …

(4)   I pass, therefore, to the fourth and last question, which is raised by the defendant company's plea that the death of Dr B was caused or contributed to by his own negligence. The burden of proof with regard to this allegation is on the defendant company, and in order to succeed I think they would have to show that the conduct of Dr B was so foolhardy as to amount to a wholly unreasonable disregard for his own safety. Bearing in mind that danger invites rescue, the court should not be astute to accept criticism of the rescuer's conduct from the wrongdoer who created the danger. Moreover, I think it should be remembered that it is fatally easy to be wise after the event. It is not enough that, when all the evidence has been sifted and all the facts ascertained in the calm and deliberate atmosphere of a court of law, the rescuer's conduct can be shown ex post facto to have been misguided or foolhardy. He is entitled to be judged in the light of the situation as it appeared to him at the time, i.e. in a context of immediate and pressing emergency. Here Dr B was faced with a situation in which two men were in danger of speedy death in the well, unless something were done very quickly. He was a doctor, and he had been specially summoned to help. Any man of courage in his position would have felt impelled to act, even at the risk of his own safety. Time was pressing; immediate action was necessary if the men in danger were to be helped; there was virtually no opportunity for reflection, or for estimating the risks involved in an act of rescue. If Dr B in such circumstances had instinctively gone straight down the well, without stopping to take any precautions at all, it would, I think, have been difficult enough to criticise him; but in point of fact he did take the very wise precaution of securing himself with a rope, whereby those on the surface could pull him up if he himself were overcome. The immediate cause of his death was the sheer mischance of the rope becoming caught on some obstruction, so as to make it impossible for those on the surface to pull him to safety. I do not think that, having regard to the emergency in which he was acting, he is to be blamed for not foreseeing and guarding against the possibility of such a mischance. On the contrary, I entirely agree with the view expressed by the learned judge that the defendant company, whose negligence brought about the danger, must accept the risk of mischances of this kind. In all the circumstances, I find it impossible to accept the contention that Dr B was guilty of any negligence either causing or contributing to his death.'

Kirkham v Chief Constable of the Greater Manchester Police
[1990] 3 All ER 246 Court of Appeal

The plaintiff's husband committed suicide while in a remand centre. The plaintiff had told the police at the time of his arrest of his suicidal tendencies but they had negligently failed to pass this information to the remand authorities. The Court of Appeal rejected arguments for the defence both that the claim was defeated by the defence of *volenti* and that the claim was barred by the maxim *ex turpi causa non oritur actio*.

Lloyd LJ:'... I come now to the two defences which lie at the heart of this appeal. They are expressed, for convenience, in two Latin maxims, *volenti non fit injuria* and *ex turpi causa non oritur actio*.

I deal first with *volenti non fit injuria*. Where a man of sound mind injures himself in an unsuccessful suicide attempt, it is difficult to see why he should not be met by a plea of *volenti non fit injuria*. He has not only courted the risk of injury by another; he has inflicted the injury himself. In *Hyde v Tameside Area Health Authority* the plaintiff, who had made an unsuccessful suicide attempt, brought an action for damages against the health authority alleging negligence on the part of the hospital staff. Lord Denning MR doubted whether a defence of *volenti non fit injuria* would be available in such a case, "seeing that [the plaintiff] did not willingly injure himself. He wanted to die". I find that reasoning hard to follow. Any observation of Lord Denning MR is, of course, entitled to great weight; but the observation was *obiter*, since the court held that the hospital staff had not been negligent. Moreover we were told by counsel for the plaintiff, who happened to have appeared for the plaintiff in that case, as well, that the point was never argued.

So I would be inclined to hold that where a man of sound mind commits suicide, his estate would be unable to maintain an action against the hospital or prison authorities, as the case might be. *Volenti non fit injuria* would provide them with a complete defence. There should be no distinction between a successful attempt and an unsuccessful attempt at suicide. Nor should there be any distinction between an action for the benefit of the estate under the Law Reform Act and an action for the benefit of dependants under the Fatal Accidents Act. In so far as Pilcher J drew a distinction between the two types of action in *Pigney v Pointers Transport Services Ltd*, I would respectfully disagree.

But in the present case K was not of sound mind. True, he was sane in the legal sense. His suicide was a deliberate and conscious act. But Dr S, whose evidence the judge accepted, said that K was suffering from clinical depression. His judgment was impaired. If it had been a case of murder, he would have had a defence of diminished responsibility due to disease of the mind.

I have had some doubt on this aspect of the case in the light of Dr S's further evidence that, though his judgment was impaired, K knew what he was doing. But in the end I have been persuaded by counsel for the plaintiff that, even so, he was not truly *volens*. Having regard to his mental state, he cannot, by his act be said to have waived or abandoned any claim arising out of his suicide. So I would reject the defence of *volenti non fit injuria*.

I turn last to *ex turpi causa non oritur actio*. This is the most difficult part of the case. Prior to 1961 suicide was a crime. Although there appears to be no reported case directly in point, I do not doubt that a claim based on the failure of the authorities to prevent a suicide would have failed. The courts would have declined to lend their aid to enforce such a claim. But by s 1 of the Suicide Act 1961 the rule of law whereby it was a crime for a person to commit suicide was abrogated. The question is whether that Act, by abrogating the criminal nature of suicide, has taken away the defence of *ex turpi causa*. The judge took the straightforward line that the defence depends on some causally related criminal activity. He referred to *Hardy v Motor Insurers' Bureau* and *Murphy v Culhane* and considered that, since suicide is no longer a crime, the defence *ex turpi causa* is no longer available.

Unfortunately, the judge was not referred to three recent cases in which the scope of the defence has been considered: *Thackwell v Barclays Bank plc*, *Saunders v Edwards* and *Euro-Diam Ltd v Bathurst*. The last two cases contain an elaborate analysis of the relevant principles by Kerr LJ. It would be superfluous to summarise the principles here. It is sufficient to quote two sentences from Kerr LJ's judgment in the *Euro-Diam* case:

> "The *ex turpi causa* defence ultimately rests on a principle of public policy that the courts will not assist a plaintiff who has been guilty of illegal (or immoral) conduct of which the courts should take notice. It applies if, in all the circumstances, it would be an affront to the public conscience to grant the plaintiff the relief which he seeks because the court would thereby appear to assist or encourage the plaintiff in his illegal conduct or to encourage others in similar acts ..."

It is apparent from these authorities that the *ex turpi causa* defence is not confined to criminal conduct. So we cannot adopt the simple approach favoured by the judge. We have to ask ourselves the much more difficult question whether to afford relief in such a case as this, arising, as it does, directly out of a man's suicide, would affront the public conscience, or, as I would prefer to say, shock the ordinary citizen. I have come to the conclusion that the answer should be No. I would give two reasons.

In the first place the Suicide Act 1961 does more than abolish the crime of suicide. It is symptomatic of a change in the public attitude to suicide generally. It is no longer regarded with the same abhorrence as it once was. It is, of course, impossible for us to say how far the change in the public attitude has gone. But that there has been a change is beyond doubt. The fact that aiding and abetting suicide remains a crime under s 2 of the 1961 Act does not diminish the force of the argument.

The second reason is that in at least two decided cases courts have awarded damages following a suicide or attempted suicide. In *Selfe v Ilford and District Hospital Management Committee* Hinchcliffe J awarded the plaintiff damages against a hospital for failing to take proper precautions when they knew that the plaintiff was a suicide risk. In *Pigney v Pointers Transport Services Ltd* to which I have already referred, Pilcher J awarded damages to the dependants of a suicide under the Fatal Accidents Act 1846. Moreover, in *Hyde v Tameside Area Health Authority*, another hospital case, the judge awarded £200,000 damages in respect of an unsuccessful suicide attempt. The Court of Appeal allowed the defendant's appeal on the ground that there had been no negligence on the part of the hospital, but not on the ground that the plaintiff's case of action arose *ex turpi causa*; the appeal was allowed. *Selfe's* case and *Pigney's* case are not binding on us. But they are important for this reason. They show, or appear to show, that the public conscience was not affronted. It did not occur to anyone to argue in either case that the granting of a remedy would shock the ordinary citizen; nor did it occur to the court.

For the above reason I would hold that the defence of *ex turpi causa* is not available in these cases, at any rate where, as here, there is medical evidence that the suicide is not in full possession of his mind. To entertain the plaintiff's claim in such a case as the present would not, in my view, affront the public conscience, or shock the ordinary citizen. I thus reach the same conclusion as the judge on this aspect of the case, but for somewhat different reasons.'

Comment

(1)   Farquharson LJ agreed, adding, on the issue of *volenti*, a second ground:

'... that the defence is inappropriate where the act of the deceased relied on is the very act which the duty cast on the defendant required him to prevent. If in such circumstances the defendant could raise this defence, as counsel for the plaintiff submits, no action would ever lie in respect of a suicide or attempted suicide where a duty of care could be proved.'

(2)   The House of Lords had to consider broadly similar facts in *Reeves v Commissioner of Police for the Metropolis*. For their analysis of the issues of *volenti* and contributory negligence see p 296. The issue of *ex turpi causa* in relation to suicides was not pursued in the House of Lords, having been soundly rejected in the Court of Appeal. Morritt LJ had observed that it would not be 'appropriate for a court to brand as contrary to public policy or offensive to the public conscience an act which Parliament has so recently legalised'.

Pitts v Hunt and another
[1990] 3 All ER 344 Court of Appeal

After spending the evening drinking at a disco, the plaintiff and a friend set off for home on a motor cycle, the friend driving with the plaintiff riding on the pillion. The plaintiff was aware that the driver was neither licensed nor insured. The journey was both reckless and dangerous with the driver, encouraged by the plaintiff, trying to frighten members of the public. The plaintiff was injured and the driver killed when the motor-cycle collided with an oncoming car. The Court of Appeal, having regard to the plaintiff's active participation in the illegal enterprise which led to his injuries, held that his claim was barred by the maxim *ex turpi causa non oritur actio*.

Beldam LJ: '... In defence to a claim in tort based on negligence ... public policy based on the rule *ex turpi causa non oritur actio* has not often been raised. It was raised in *National Coal Board v England*. A mineworker who was injured in an explosion of a detonator in a colliery at Aberdare claimed damages for breach of statutory duty by the shotfirer who fired the shot, without first ascertaining that all persons in the vicinity had taken shelter. The plaintiff had aided and abetted the shotfirer by coupling up the charges when he was not supposed to do so. It was contended that he could not recover because of his own illegal acts. Although the House of Lords had little difficulty in rejecting this contention, Lord Asquith said:

> "Cases where an action in tort has been defeated by the maxim are exceedingly rare. Possibly a party to an illegal prize fight who is damaged in the conflict cannot sue for assault ... But it seems to me in principle that the plaintiff cannot be precluded from suing simply because the wrongful act is committed after the illegal agreement is made and during the period involved in its execution. The act must, I should have supposed, at least be a step in the execution of the common illegal purpose. If two burglars, A and B, agree to open a safe by means of explosives, and A so negligently handles the explosive charge as to injure B, B might find some difficulty in maintaining an action for negligence against A. But if A and B are proceeding to the premises which they intend burglariously to enter, and before they enter them B picks A's pocket and steals his watch, I cannot prevail on myself to believe that A could not sue in tort (provided he had first prosecuted B for larceny). The theft is totally unconnected with the burglary. There is, however, a surprising dearth of authority on this point."

The case in which this question arose directly was *Ashton v Turner*. The plaintiff was one of three young men who, after an evening's drinking, used a motor car belonging to one of them on a joint enterprise of burglary. Having stolen some radios and set off the alarm, they tried to make their escape in the car which, due to the negligent driving of the defendant, crashed and the plaintiff sustained injury. He sought to recover damages from the driver. Ewbank J dismissed the plaintiff's claim holding that as a matter of public policy the law would not recognise a duty of care owed by one participant in a crime to another. He held in the alternative that, even if a duty of care was owed, the plaintiff had willingly accepted as his the risk of negligence and injury resulting from it.

In arriving at this conclusion Ewbank J was much influenced by two decisions in the courts of Australia: *Godbolt v Fittock* and *Smith v Jenkins*. In the latter case the High

Court of Australia held that no action would lie by the passenger in a motor vehicle to recover damages for injuries sustained by the careless driving of the vehicle when the passenger and driver were at the time of the accident participating jointly in the offence of unlawfully using the motor vehicle. Although all the judges were agreed that the plaintiff could not recover, there was a difference of opinion about the legal basis for the decision. Kitto and Walsh JJ considered that in the circumstances public policy would not recognise a right of action. Barwick CJ, Windeyer and Owen JJ considered that the basis for dismissing the claim should be that the law would not hold that a duty of care arose out of the relationship of joint participants in an illegal enterprise.

The question again came before the High Court of Australia in 1977 in *Jackson v Harrison*. The respondent was injured when he was travelling as a passenger in a motor car driven by a driver he knew to be disqualified. The two of them were jointly participating in an offence under the Motor Vehicles Act 1959. The majority distinguished *Smith v Jenkins* and held that the passenger was not disabled from recovering damages on the ground that the illegality did not bear on the standard of care reasonably to be expected of the driver. Barwick CJ dissented and in the course of his judgment he said:

"It seems to me that where there is a joint venture to do an act punishable by fine or imprisonment, no narrow or pedantic view should be taken of the nature and scope of the arrangement between the parties when applying the principle of *Smith v Jenkins* and that the consequence to one of the participants of any act done in furtherance of the arrangement or in obtaining the benefit of having carried it out should not give rise to a cause of action. The relationship of those participants should not be regarded as giving rise to relevant rights or duties. The public policy which the denial of a cause of action in such circumstances is designed to serve is not satisfied if the miscreant is not denied rights against his co-participant in the commission of the offence in respect of acts related to that commission."

Mason J said:

"If a joint participant in an illegal enterprise is to be denied relief against a coparticipant for injury sustained in that enterprise, the denial of relief should be related not to the illegal character of the activity but rather to the character and incidents of the enterprise and to the hazards which are necessarily inherent in its execution. A more secure foundation for denying relief, though more limited in its application – and for that reason fairer in its operation – is to say that the plaintiff must fail when the character of the enterprise in which the parties are engaged is such that it is impossible for the court to determine the standard of care which is appropriate to be observed."

Jacobs J based his conclusion on the fact that the type of offence in which they were jointly engaged did not bear at all on the standard of care which was to be expected of the driver in the circumstances.

In another jurisdiction nearer home in *Winnik v Dick*, the Second Division of the Inner House also considered the question whether public policy would preclude an action for damages by a passenger in a motor car which was being driven by a driver with whom he had been drinking all day and knew that he was drunk. Lord Hunter said:

> "... either because in law one joint participant would not in such circumstances be held to owe a duty of care to the other joint participant or because on grounds of public policy, the court would not countenance nor adjudicate on a claim by one such joint participant against another. I see no reason why a Scottish court should not, on the basis of one or other or both of these principles, arrive in appropriate circumstances at a result the same as that reached in several cases in other jurisdictions, to which we were referred. See, e.g. *Smith v Jenkins; Ashton v Turner*."

The Lord Justice Clerk (Wheatley), however, felt that such a defence would have far-reaching effects and could give rise to delicate decisions on what is embraced in "crime" in this context and he felt that in the circumstances of that case, since the pleadings did not raise the issue with clarity, the point should not be decided.

In opening his appeal on behalf of the plaintiff, counsel drew attention to *Saunders v Edwards*. This court, he said, had approved a test for determining whether in the circumstances the court would decline to allow the plaintiff to recover in cases of illegality. It was based on a helpful review of cases by Hutchison J in *Thackwell v Barclays Bank plc*. The plaintiff in that case was a party to a fraudulent scheme under which a cheque had been made payable to him. The plaintiff's signature indorsing the cheque to a third party was forged and in reliance on the forgery the bank credited the third party. The plaintiff sued the bank for conversion. In defence the bank relied on the maxim ex *turpi causa*. The test applied by Hutchison J in that case and approved by the court in *Saunders v Edwards*:

> "involved the court looking at the quality of the illegality relied on by the defendant and all the surrounding circumstances, without fine distinctions, and seeking to answer two questions: first, whether there had been illegality of which the court should take notice and, second, whether in all the circumstances it would be an affront to the public conscience if by affording him the relief sought the court was seen to be indirectly assisting or encouraging the plaintiff in his criminal act."

Counsel for the plaintiff relied particularly on the passage in the judgment of Bingham LJ where he said:

> "Where issues of illegality are raised, the courts have (as it seems to me) to steer a middle course between two unacceptable positions. On the one hand it is unacceptable that any court of law should aid or lend its authority to a party seeking to pursue or enforce an object or agreement which the law prohibits. On the other hand, it is unacceptable that the court should, on the

first indication of unlawfulness affecting any aspect of a transaction, draw up its skirts and refuse all assistance to the plaintiff, no matter how serious his loss or how disproportionate his loss to the unlawfulness of his conduct."

Bingham LJ went on to point out that the cases which had been referred to in the judgments of Kerr and Nicholls LJJ were valuable both for the statements of principle which they contained and for the illustrations which they give of the courses which courts had in fact steered in different factual situations. It was his view that, on the whole, the courts had tended to adopt a pragmatic approach to these problems, seeking where possible to see that genuine wrongs were righted so long as the court did not thereby promote or countenance a nefarious object or bargain which it was bound to condemn. So counsel argued for the plaintiff that the court should take a pragmatic approach and, in deciding whether the public conscience would be shocked by allowing the plaintiff to recover damages in the circumstances of this case, the court should have regard to the serious injuries which he had suffered and from which he would suffer for the rest of his life and should regard the public conscience as being as greatly shocked by the idea that he would recover no compensation for those injuries as it would be by the thought of allowing him to recover by basing his claim on the unlawful escapade in which he suffered the injuries.

The particular sphere of social behaviour and activity arising from the use of motor vehicles in modern conditions is one in which Parliament has been continuously active during this century ... Thus it seems to me that the primary source of public policy in this sphere must be the Acts of Parliament themselves. That policy is properly supplemented by taking into account the reasons given by the courts of this country for refusing to enforce rights based on conduct which has been regarded as sufficiently antisocial and contrary to the policy of the Acts. I would regard decisions in other jurisdictions which may have different social attitudes as of but secondary guidance, though of course entitled to respect and consideration. Although it is part of that policy that passengers carried on or in vehicles who sustain injury should be compensated ... Parliament did ... provide that, of the various offences specifically relating to the use of motor vehicles, causing death by reckless driving, reckless driving itself and driving when under the influence of drink and drugs were to be regarded as among the most serious of offences and were to be punishable by imprisonment ...

The policy underlying the provisions for compulsory insurance for passengers ... injured in road accidents is clearly one intended for their benefit; it does not follow that if an offence is committed jointly by the driver and passenger of a kind not regarded as so serious as to disentitle the driver from claiming indemnity for the benefit of an innocent passenger, the passenger who is a joint offender can, subject to questions of contributory negligence, recover compensation from the driver. If, however, the offence, or series of offences, is so serious that it would preclude the driver on grounds of public policy from claiming indemnity under a policy required to be effected under the Act for the benefit of a passenger, that public policy would in my judgment also preclude the passenger jointly guilty of that offence from claiming compensation.

On the facts found by the judge in this case the plaintiff was playing a full and active part in encouraging the young rider to commit offences which, if a death other than that of the young rider himself had occurred, would have amounted to manslaughter. And not just manslaughter by gross negligence on the judge's findings. It would have been manslaughter by the commission of a dangerous act either done with the intention of frightening other road users or when both the plaintiff and the young rider were aware or but for self-induced intoxication would have been aware that it was likely to do so and nevertheless they went on and did the act regardless of the consequences. Thus on the findings made by the judge in this case I would hold that the plaintiff is precluded on grounds of public policy from recovering compensation for the injuries which he sustained in the course of the very serious offences in which he was participating. On a question on which, as Bingham LJ said, the courts have tended to adopt a pragmatic approach, I do not believe that it is desirable to go further in an attempt to categorise the degree of seriousness involved in offences which will not preclude recovery of compensation. I would, however, add that the public attitude to driving a motor vehicle on a road when under the influence of drink has, I believe, changed markedly with the increasing number of serious accidents and the dreadful injuries which are the consequence of such driving. The public conscience is ever-increasingly being focused not only on those who commit the offence but, in the words of recent publicity, those who ask the driver to drink and drive ...

As to the defence raised that the plaintiff voluntarily undertook to run the risk of injury by taking part in such a foolhardy, risky and illegal activity, I would have been prepared to say that it was obvious from the description of the plaintiff's behaviour whilst he was participating that he had done so. However the judge accepted that the effect of s 148(3) of the Road Traffic Act 1972 was that any agreement or understanding that risk of injury would be the plaintiff's was of no effect ... I think ... that the words of s 148(3) clearly mean that it is no longer open to the driver of a motor vehicle to say that the fact of his passenger travelling in a vehicle in circumstances in which for one reason or another it could be said that he had willingly accepted a risk of negligence on the driver's part relieves him of liability for such negligence.'

Balcombe LJ: '... In a case of this kind I find the ritual incantation of the maxim ex *turpi causa non oritur actio* more likely to confuse than to illuminate. I prefer to adopt the approach of the majority of the High Court of Australia in the most recent of the several Australian cases to which we were referred, *Jackson v Harrison*. That is to consider what would have been the cause of action had there been no joint illegal enterprise, that is the tort of negligence based on the breach of a duty of care owed by the deceased to the plaintiff, and then to consider whether the circumstances of the particular case are such as to preclude the existence of that cause of action. I find myself in complete agreement with the following passage from the judgment of Mason J in *Jackson v Harrison*:

> "If a joint participant in an illegal enterprise is to be denied relief against a coparticipant for injury sustained in that enterprise, the denial of relief should be related not to the illegal character of the activity but rather to the character and incidents of the enterprise and to the hazards which are necessarily inherent in its execution. A more secure foundation for denying relief, though more limited in its application – and for that reason fairer in its operation – is to say that the plaintiff must fail when the character of the enterprise in which the parties are engaged is such that it is impossible for the court to determine the standard of care which is appropriate to be observed ... It matters not whether this in itself provides a complete answer to the plaintiff's claim or whether it leads in theory to the conclusion that the defendant owes no duty of care to the plaintiff because no standard of care can be determined in the particular case."

... I prefer to found my judgment on the simple basis that the circumstances of this particular case were such as to preclude the court from finding that the deceased owed a duty of care to the plaintiff.'

Dillon LJ: '... I find a test that depends on what would or would not be an affront to the public conscience very difficult to apply, since the public conscience may well be affected by factors of an emotional nature, e.g. that these boys by their reckless and criminal behaviour happened to do no harm to anyone but themselves ... Beyond that, appeal to the public conscience would be likely to lead to a graph of illegalities according to moral turpitude, and I am impressed by the Comments of Mason J in *Jackson v Harrison*, where he said:

> "... there arises the difficulty, which I regard as insoluble, of formulating a criterion which would separate cases of serious illegality from those which are not serious. Past distinctions drawn between felonies and misdemeanours, *malum in se* and *malum prohibitum*, offences punishable by imprisonment and those which are not, non-statutory and statutory offences offer no acceptable discrimen."

Bingham LJ's dichotomy between cases where the plaintiff's action in truth arises directly *ex turpi causa* and cases where the plaintiff has suffered a genuine wrong to which allegedly unlawful conduct is incidental avoids this difficulty, in that it does not involve grading illegalities according to moral turpitude ... That a defence of illegality can be pleaded to a case founded in tort is, in my judgment, clear, whether or not the defence is correctly called *ex turpi causa*. *Thackwell v Barclays Bank plc* is one instance. Another is *Murphy v Culhane*. There the plaintiff as the widow and administratrix of the estate of her deceased husband claimed damages from the defendant on the ground that the defendant had unlawfully assaulted the deceased by beating him about the head with a plank by which assault he was killed. The plaintiff did not have to plead any illegality as part of her case, but on a preliminary issue the defendant was allowed by this court to plead that the assault alleged occurred during and as part of a criminal affray initiated by the deceased and others with the joint criminal purpose of assaulting and beating the defendant. Lord Denning MR considered that a man who took part in a criminal affray might well be said to have been guilty of such a wicked act as to deprive himself of a cause of action; alternatively, even if the plaintiff were entitled to damages, they might fall to be reduced under the Law Reform (Contributory Negligence) Act 1945 ... [He reviewed the Australian cases and continued.] I feel unable to draw any valid distinction between the reckless riding of the motor cycle in the present case by the deceased boy and the plaintiff under the influence of drink, and the reckless driving of the cars, albeit stolen, in *Smith v Jenkins* and *Bondarenko v Sommers*. The words of Barwick CJ in *Smith v Jenkins*:

"The driving of the car by the appellant, the manner of which is the basis of the respondent's complaint, was in the circumstances as much a use of the car by the respondent as it was a use by the appellant. That use was their joint enterprise of the moment."

apply with equal force to the riding of the motor cycle in the present case. This is a case in which, in Bingham LJ's words, the plaintiff's action in truth arises directly *ex turpi causa*.'

Comment

(1)   Beldam LJ was not entirely happy with the view that a duty of care might not exist between the driver and the plaintiff. He said:

'I am not convinced of the wisdom of a policy which might encourage a belief that the duty to behave responsibly in driving motor vehicles is diminished even to the limited extent that they may in some circumstances not owe a duty to each other, particularly when those circumstances involve conduct which is highly dangerous to others.'

(2)   In *Revill v Newbery* the plaintiff was shot while attempting to enter the defendant's shed in order to steal some valuable property which was stored there. The Court of Appeal rejected the defendant's claim that he was relieved of all liability on the basis of *ex turpi causa*, not least because its application would thwart the apparent intention of Parliament to provide a duty of care owed to trespassers under the Occupiers' Liability Act 1984. Evans LJ drew a distinction between the 'criminal enterprise' cases such as *Pitts v Hunt* and the present case: however, he said:

'This does not mean that the rule cannot apply, because the underlying principle is that there is a public interest which requires that the wrong-doer should not benefit from his crime or other offence. But it would mean, if it does apply in circumstances such as these, that the trespasser who was also a criminal was effectively an outlaw, who was debarred by the law from recovering compensation for any injury which he might sustain. This same consideration also prompts the thought that it is one thing to deny a plaintiff any fruits from his illegal conduct, but different and far more far-reaching to deprive him even of compensation for injury which he suffers and which otherwise he is entitled to recover at law.'

Having rejected the *ex turpi causa* argument, the court's preferred solution was a two-thirds reduction in damages for contributory negligence.

(3) In *Clunis v Camden and Islington HA* (for facts see p 321) the Court of Appeal considered the application of *ex turpi causa* to a situation where the defendant was not a joint participant in the crime. Beldam LJ, after noting the general proposition that anyone found guilty of committing a crime could not recover damages from any other who had participated in its commission, went on to say: 'The argument is even more pertinent if the claim to damages is against someone who has not participated in the crime.' A particular complica-tion in *Clunis's* case arose from the fact that the crime in question was manslaughter on the grounds of diminished responsibility. Counsel for the claimant sought to argue that the nature of C's crime was not such as to justify the application of the principle. Beldam LJ said:

'[Counsel's] next submission [was] that not all criminal or illegal acts will prevent the court from entertaining a plaintiff's claim. Pertinently he said that there are today many summary offences which are not sufficiently serious to warrant the invocation of the maxim; the offence of man-slaughter is an offence which varies greatly in its moral blameworthiness, especially if the manslaughter is by reason of diminished responsibility. He urged the court to say that, where the degree of responsibility was diminished by reason of mental disorder, the court should not apply the maxim. He prayed in aid in this regard a test which this court has adopted in other cases between 1986 and 1994, namely whether the result in a particular case would be acceptable to "the public conscience".

In *Tinsley v Milligan* Lord Goff, Lord Keith and Lord Browne-Wilkinson regarded such a test as unsatisfactory. Lord Goff preferred to accept the reason for the rule stated by Ralph Gibson LJ in the Court of Appeal in that case that, in so far as the maxim is directed at deterrence, the force of the deterrent effect is in the existence of the known rule and its stern application. Lord Goff said:

"But, bearing in mind the passage from the judgment of Ralph Gibson LJ which I have just quoted, I have to say that it is by no means self-evident that the public conscience test is preferable to the present strict rules. Certainly, I do not feel able to say that it would be appropriate for your Lordships House, in the face of a long line of unbroken authority stretching back over two hundred years, now by judicial decision to replace the principles established in those authorities by a wholly different discretionary system."

Lord Browne-Wilkinson said:

"My Lords, I agree with the speech of my noble and learned friend Lord Goff of Chieveley that the consequences of being a party to an illegal transaction cannot depend, as the majority of the Court of Appeal held, on such an imponderable factor as the extent to which the public conscience would be affronted by recognising rights created by legal transactions."

In the present case the plaintiff has been convicted of a serious criminal offence. In such a case public policy would in our judgment preclude the court from entertaining the plaintiff's claim unless it could be said that he did not know the nature and quality of his act or that what he was doing was wrong. The offence of murder was reduced to one of manslaughter by reason of the plaintiff's mental disorder but his mental state did not justify a verdict of not guilty by reason of insanity. Consequently, though his responsibility for killing Z is diminished, he must be taken to have known what he was doing and that it was wrong. A plea of diminished responsibility accepts that the accused's mental responsibility is substantially impaired but it does not remove liability for his criminal act. We do not consider that in such a case a court can or should go behind the conviction and, even if it could, we do not see in the medical report attached to the statement of claim any statement which would justify the court taking the view that this plaintiff had no responsibility for the serious crime to which he pleaded guilty. The plaintiff in this case, though his responsibility is in law reduced, must in Best CJ's words be presumed to have known that he was doing an unlawful act.'

Vellino v Chief Constable of Greater Manchester
[2002] 3 All ER 78 Court of Appeal

The claimant, who lived in a second-floor flat, had been in the habit (well-known to the police) of attempting to evade arrest by jumping from the window to the ground below. On the occasion in question, he was severely injured. He claimed that the police officers, who he alleged had stood idly by as he was making his escape, had acted negligently in failing to prevent his (foreseeable) attempted escape. The judge dismissed the claim, holding that the police had not owed the claimant a duty of care. The Court of Appeal had to consider whether the principle *ex turpi causa non oritur actio* operated, and, if so, whether that precluded the existence of the duty of care in these circumstances. The majority (Sedley LJ dissenting) held that escaping from custody was a sufficiently serious criminal offence to attract the operation of the *ex turpi causa* principle, and in those circumstances the police did not owe an arrested person a duty to take care that he was not injured in a foreseeable attempt to escape police custody.

Schieman LJ: '...

[7]   The judge said this in relation to the legal issues:

> "Analytically there are two different questions, was there a duty of care and, if so, is the defendant prevented from recovering damages by the application of the principle *ex turpi causa non oritur actio*. In fact, however, in my judgment the two questions interrelate, but I will begin by considering them independently. There is no doubt that the police owe a duty of care to an arrested person. They must take reasonable care to ensure that he does not suffer physical injury as a consequence of their own acts, such as if they are driving carelessly or the acts of a third party, but the question here is whether they owed any duty to protect him from himself, in circumstances where the conduct of the claimant involves the commission of a criminal offence at common law, i e whether they must take reasonable care to ensure he does not injure himself, as a consequence of his own deliberate decision to escape from custody."

[8]   After considering *Caparo Industries plc v Dickman*, *Stovin v Wise*, and *Reeves v Metropolitan Police Comr*, the judge concluded that the mere fact that the claimant suffered injury as a result of his own deliberate act did not automatically inhibit the imposition of a duty of care on the police. He concluded that the considerations which determine whether it is fair just and reasonable to impose a duty of care were essentially the same as those which determine whether the *ex turpi causa* defence is applicable.

[9]   He then considered *Clunis v Camden and Islington Health Authority*, *Kirkham v Chief Constable of the Greater Manchester*, and *Sacco v Chief Constable of South Wales Constabulary* and came to the conclusion that the existing authorities strongly support the view that escaping from custody was a sufficiently serious criminal offence to attract the operation of the ex turpi causa principle and that in those circumstances the police owed to an arrested person no duty to take care that he was not injured in a foreseeable attempt by him to escape from police custody. He accepted that the police were under a public law duty not negligently to permit a person to escape from custody but held that this was not a duty owed to the escaper. ...

[13]   It is common ground that under our law two persons can stand aside and watch a third jump to his death: there is no legal duty to rescue. Not all legal

systems adopt that as their approach but for better or for worse that is the established position in English law. It is common ground that, prior to uttering the words "I arrest you", the police owed him no duty to prevent him hurting himself while trying to escape.

[14] How then is the position of the police in the present case to be distinguished from that of the ordinary citizen? The submission is that by arresting the claimant they notionally took him into their care and owed him a duty of care. The claimant relies on *Reeves's* case. There the claimant committed suicide whilst in a cell in a police station. It was accepted in the House of Lords that the police were in breach of their duty of care to the prisoner, a known suicide risk.

[15] For my part I am content to assume, without so deciding, that when a police officer arrests a citizen the police officer puts himself in a relationship with that prisoner which can involve the police officer in having some duties for the breach of which the prisoner can sue. But in every case one has to identify the particular duty which it is that has allegedly been broken.

[16] For instance if the officer detains the citizen then I would accept that he must take reasonable care that the citizen is not injured by lack of water. The officer might, if the roof showed signs of collapsing, be under a duty to take or let the citizen out of the flat where he was arrested. The fact that the citizen would never have been detained had he not previously committed a crime would not prevent an action from succeeding. The reasoning behind that approach is that by the fact of detention the man is prevented from getting his own water or escaping danger. It is not the arrest which gives rise to the duty of care to the man. It is his detention. That is also why there is a duty to try and prevent known suicide risks in prison from committing suicide.

[17] However, where a man breaks away from the arresting officer the position is manifestly different. By so doing the man commits a crime and he is no longer in the immediate power of the officer.

[18] [Counsel] for the claimant had a difficult case and had some difficulty in formulating his propositions as to the nature of the duty of care which was allegedly broken.

[19] To suggest that the police owe a criminal the duty to prevent the criminal from escaping, and that the criminal who hurts himself while escaping can sue the police for the breach of that duty, seems to me self-evidently absurd. No policy reason has been suggested for the law adopting such a course. [Counsel] expressly disavowed this way of putting his case.

[20] I understood him to submit that the police are under a duty owed to the claimant to prevent him from sustaining foreseeable injury whilst foreseeably attempting to escape from custody. This with respect seems to me equally untenable: it would require the police to hold him in the loosest of grasps so that

there was no danger of him wrenching his shoulder as he struggled to break free. Again no policy reason has been suggested for declaring this to be the law.

[21]   Moreover, even this formulation does not cover the present case. The claimant injured himself after he had escaped from custody, if by that one means containment by the police in some physical sense rather some jurisprudential concept.

[22]   The difficulties which [Counsel] had in formulating the duty of care would only be intensified if his concepts were expressed in terms of the criminal's rights. In contexts such as this the police duties to the criminal give rise to correlative rights in the criminal. It would be difficult without making oneself sound foolish to formulate a right in the criminal against the police not to be exposed to danger whilst escaping which is perhaps why [he] did not try.

[23]   Similarly in the context of prisoners there is in my judgment no right in a prisoner who hurts himself while leaping from a high boundary wall to be compensated on the basis that it is foreseeable that prisoners will try and escape and that if they leap off high walls they may well hurt themselves.

[24]   *National Coal Board v England* shows that there can be circumstances where a claimant who is committing a criminal act none the less has a remedy against a defendant who is also committing a criminal act. ... However in my judgment it is of no present assistance. No statutory provision to the effect that an escaping criminal who hurts himself in the very attempt of escape has a remedy against the police who negligently let him escape has been drawn to our attention.

[25]   The judge cited a passage from a judgment of mine in *Sacco's* case with which Thorpe LJ agreed which still represents my opinion:

"There is, we are told, no case in which it has been established that a person in this situation is entitled to recover damages from the police. We are being asked to create a precedent to that effect. I see no reason why we should do so, but there is a number of reasons for my reluctance to give this plaintiff any relief. First, he seems to me to be guilty of his own misfortune. He did something which he knew or must be taken to have known was dangerous. In so far as his appreciation of the dangers involved was lessened by his intake of alcohol that was also his own fault. Second, he was engaged in a criminal act, namely attempting to escape from lawful custody. As a matter of legal policy, I see no reason to permit a man to recover damages against the police if he hurts himself as part of that illegal enterprise. The basis of such recovery must be either an allegation of a breach of duty owed to him not to let him escape, or of a duty owed to him to take care that he does not hurt himself if he tries to escape. I see no reason to create such a duty owed to him. It is common ground the policy of the law is not to permit one criminal to recover damages from a fellow criminal who fails to take care of him whilst they are both engaged in a criminal enterprise. The reason for that rule is not the law's tenderness towards the criminal defendant, but the law's unwilling-ness to afford a criminal plaintiff a remedy in such circumstances. I see no reason why that unwillingness should be any less because a defendant is a policeman and not engaged in any crime."

[26] I am prepared to assume for the purposes of the present case that the police negligence in letting the claimant leap out of the window was such as to amount to a crime although, in fairness to the officers, I must make clear that I am making no finding to that effect and, so far as I know, no court has. That assumption however does not in my judgment have the effect of strengthening the claimant's case. If the police were not at the moment of arrest under a duty owed to the claimant to take care that he did not hurt himself whilst escaping then I fail to see how it can be said that the police had such a duty thrust on them at the moment he broke free.

[27] Finally, I point out that, if we were to accept the submissions of [Counsel], it would lead to the oddest results. Suppose that with the claimant there had been another man who thought that the police were after him for some crime. The police come in and arrest the claimant first. The other man rightly thinks he is about to be arrested. It is foreseeable, as it often must be, that those who think they are about to be arrested will make a run for it. Both the claimant and the other man leap out the window. The police just stand by and gaze instead of blocking the physical progress of either and without going on to arrest the other man. The claimant and the other man suffer injuries. Mr Stockdale accepts that the other man would have no remedy but asserts that the claimant has. That result would surely be indefensible.

[28] At the conclusion of the argument I was of the view that the appeal must fail essentially for the reasons given by the judge. He pointed out that there is an overlap between the considerations which go to the question "is there a duty?" and those which attend the defence of *ex turpi causa*. I agree. He based his decision on absence of duty rather than on that defence. So would I.

[29] Nevertheless, we reserved judgment because of the imminent publication of the Law Commission's consultation paper on The Illegality Defence in Tort (2001) (Law Com no 160). It draws attention to some cases to which no reference was made in argument and to various unsatisfactory features of some of the reasoning in relation to the *ex turpi causa* defence in some of the cases although it expressly states that it considers the outcome in the cases was correct – para 4.87.

[30] There is nothing in the paper to suggest that in a case such as the present the law as it currently stands in this court entitles the claimant to succeed or that this court can or that the House of Lords or Parliament should, reform the law so as to enable someone in the present claimant's position to succeed ...

[35]   In the present circumstances I do not find it unjust to deny the claimant a right to damages. As I observed in *Sacco's* case in a passage cited by the Law Commission at para 2.45:

> "Whether one expresses the refusal of a remedy as being based on absence of causation, absence of duty in these circumstances, absence of a breach of a wider duty, or as being based upon the application of a wider principle that a plaintiff as a matter of policy is denied recovery on tort when his own wrongdoing is so much part of the claim that it can not be overlooked, or because the plaintiff had voluntarily assumed the risk of it, is perhaps a matter of jurisprudential predilection on the part of the judge."

[36]   Like Elias J I would find that in the present case that the officers did not owe the claimant any duty to bar his progress through the window.'

Comment

(1)   Sedley LJ, in his dissenting judgment, was critical of the consequences of aggregating the duty issue with the *ex turpi causa* principle. He said:

> '[59]   ... If one is driven, as Elias J considered he was, to dismiss the claim, it does not matter whether it is because there is no duty of care or no cause of action or no jurisdiction. This corresponds, I think, with Schiemann LJ's reasoning both in *Sacco's* case and in the present case. But once turpitude is understood, as I believe the modern common law understands it, not as an indiscriminate barrier to unworthy claimants but as a large-mesh filter for criminality in claims, the difference becomes critical. Once through it, as I consider this claim is entitled to go, the next and discrete questions are whether there was a duty of care; if there was, what standard of care it imported in the situation facing the court; whether in the light of the standard the duty was broken; and whether, if it was, the claimant is nevertheless partly or wholly responsible for his own loss. The judge's and my own answers to these, set out above, entitle the claimant to an appropriate fraction of his damages.

> [60]   The House of Lords in *Tinsley v Milligan* rejected the "public conscience" test articulated by Hutchison J in *Thackwell v Barclays Bank plc* as a filter on claims with a criminal dimension. We are not now required, in other words, to look over our shoulders at what we fear the press will make of our decisions in this already difficult field. The public conscience, an elusive thing, as often as not turns out to be an echo chamber inhabited by journalists and public moralists. To allow judicial policy to be dictated by it would be as inappropriate as to let judges dictate editorial policy. ... The "fair, just and reasonable" test is now the established judicial control on ground-breaking in tort. If the law were

ever to revert to an exogenous test, it should be one which gauges the response of people who actually know what the court's reasoning is; and no court which has confidence in its own reasoning should be worried about that.'

(2) Sir Murray Stuart-Smith, agreeing with Schieman LJ, summarised the correct approach:

'[70] From these authorities I derive the following propositions. (1) The operation of the principle arises where the claimant's claim is founded upon his own criminal or immoral act. The facts which give rise to the claim must be inextricably linked with the criminal activity. It is not sufficient if the criminal activity merely gives occasion for tortious conduct of the defendant. (2) The principle is one of public policy; it is not for the benefit of the defendant. Since if the principle applies, the cause of action does not arise, the defendant's conduct is irrelevant. There is no question of proportionality between the conduct of the claimant and defendant. (3) In the case of criminal conduct this has to be sufficiently serious to merit the application of the principle. Generally speaking a crime punishable with imprisonment could be expected to qualify. If the offence is criminal, but relatively trivial, it is in any event difficult to see how it could be integral to the claim. (4) The 1945 Act is not applicable where the claimant's action amounts to a common law crime which does not give rise to liability in tort.

[71] Applying these principles it is common ground that the claimant has to rely on his criminal conduct in escaping lawful custody to found his claim. It is integral to the claim. The crime of escape is a serious one; it is a common law offence for which the penalty is large. It is almost invariably punished by a sentence of imprisonment, although the length of the sentence is usually measured in months rather than years. In my judgment it is plainly a sufficiently serious offence for the purpose of the application of the maxim.'

(3) In *Hewison v Meridian Shipping and others*, the claimant suffered an accident at work due to the negligence of his employers. The defendants invoked *ex turpi causa* on the basis that the claimant had obtained pecuniary advantage by deception in that he had failed to disclose the fact that he was epileptic. Ward LJ considered that Sir Murray Stuart-Smith's propositions provided 'valuable guidance', though his application of them placed his conclusion in the minority. Tuckey LJ, on the other hand, thought that Ward LJ's approach was 'over structured'. He cited with approval a passage from McLachlin J in *Hall v Hebert* (a Canadian case), '... the law must aspire to be a unified institution, the parts of which – contract, tort, the criminal law – must be in essential harmony. For the courts to punish conduct with the one hand while rewarding it with the other would be to create an intolerable fissure in the

law's conceptually seamless web', and added, 'A broad test enables this objective to be achieved; a more structured one might not'. The majority view was that the conditions for *ex turpi causa* were satisfied in that the claimant was obliged to rely on his own unlawful act, since his projected lost earnings depended on his continued employment, which in turn depended on his maintaining the deceit.

CHAPTER 7

Occupiers' liability

The specific common law duty owed by an occupier to visitors relied on a number of distinctions between classes of visitor (invitees or licensees). Such distinctions were made redundant by the Occupiers' Liability Act 1957, under which the common law was effectively codified. The 1957 Act substitutes a simple distinction, that between visitors and non-visitors. To speak of 'lawful' visitors is to fail to make the correct distinction, since there are non-visitors who may be lawfully on premises but who will be outside the scope of the 1957 Act (albeit within the scope of the Occupiers' Liability Act 1984). Today a 'common' duty of care is owed to all visitors, and the word 'common' indicates that the same duty is owed to all visitors, irrespective of the purpose of the visit.

The duty owed to persons who cannot be classed as visitors, e.g. trespassers, having first been brought within the scope of possible recovery of compensation by the decision in *British Railways Board v Herrington*, is now governed by the Occupiers' Liability Act 1984.

As the balancing test carried out by the House of Lords in *Tomlinson v Congleton Borough Council*, see p 403, shows, the standard of care owed to a visitor under the 1957 Act is identical to the standard of care for common law negligence. Indeed, there are many cases where the latter will be pleaded rather than the former – see, for example, *Ogwo v Taylor*, where the suit by fire-fighters injured tackling a blaze in a confined space was decided applying ordinary principles of negligence without reference to the Act. Another comparison with basic negligence is that liability under each of the Acts arises out of the relationship of the occupier with a person who comes on to the land, either as a visitor or as a non-visitor. In negligence the duty is fixed by reference to general principles of neighbourhood.

Occupiers' Liability Act 1957

1   Preliminary

(1)   The rules enacted by the two next following sections shall have effect, in place of the rules of the common law, to regulate the duty which an occupier of premises owes to his visitors in respect of dangers due to the state of the premises or to things done or omitted to be done on them.

(2)   The rules so enacted shall regulate the nature of the duty imposed by law in consequence of a person's occupation or control of premises and of any invitation or permission he gives (or is to be treated as giving) to another to enter or use the premises, but they shall not alter the rules of the common law as to the persons on whom a duty is so imposed or to whom it is owed; and accordingly for the purpose of the rules so enacted the persons who are to be treated as an occupier and as his visitors are the same (subject to subsection 4 of this section) as the persons who would at common law be treated as an occupier and as his invitees or licensees.

(3)   The rules so enacted in relation to an occupier of premises and his visitors shall also apply, in like manner and to like extent as the principles applicable at common law to an occupier of premises and his invitees or licensees would apply, to regulate—

(a)   the obligations of a person occupying or having control over any fixed or moveable structure, including any vessel, vehicle or aircraft; and

(b)   the obligations of a person occupying or having control over any premises or structure in respect of damage to property, including the property of persons who are not themselves his visitors.

(4)   A person entering any premises in exercise of rights conferred by virtue of—

(a)   section 2(1) of the Countryside and Rights of Way Act 2000, or

(b)   an access agreement or order under the National Parks and Access to the Countryside Act 1949,

is not, for the purposes of this Act, a visitor of the occupier of the premises.

2   Extent of occupier's ordinary duty

(1)   An occupier of premises owes the same duty, the common duty of care, to all his visitors, except in so far as he is free to and does extend, restrict, modify or exclude his duty to any visitor or visitors by agreement or otherwise.

(2)   The common duty of care is a duty to take such care as in all the circumstances of the case is reasonable to see that the visitor will be reasonably safe in using the premises for the purposes for which he is invited or permitted by the occupier to be there.

(3)   The circumstances relevant for the present purpose include the degree of care, and of want of care, which would ordinarily be looked for in such a visitor, so that (for example) in proper cases–

(a)   an occupier must be prepared for children to be less careful than adults; and

(b)   an occupier may expect that a person, in the exercise of his calling, will appreciate and guard against any special risks ordinarily incident to it, so far as the occupier leaves him free to do so.

(4)   In determining whether the occupier of premises has discharged the common duty of care to a visitor, regard is to be had to all the circumstances, so that (for example)–

(a)   where damage is caused to a visitor by a danger of which he had been warned by the occupier, the warning is not to be treated without more as absolving the occupier from liability, unless in all the circumstances it was enough to enable the visitor to be reasonably safe; and

(b)   where damage is caused to a visitor by a danger due to the faulty execution of any work of construction, maintenance or repair by an independent contractor employed by the occupier, the occupier is not to be treated without more as answerable for the danger if in all the circumstances he had acted reasonably in entrusting the work to an independent contractor and had taken such steps (if any) as he reasonably ought in order to satisfy himself that the contractor was competent and that the work had been properly done.

(5)   The common duty of care does not impose on an occupier any obligation to a visitor in respect of risks willingly accepted as his by the visitor (the question whether a risk was so accepted to be decided on the same principles as in other cases in which one person owes a duty of care to another).

(6)   For the purposes of this section, persons who enter premises for any purpose in the exercise of a right conferred by law are to be treated as permitted by the occupier to be there for that purpose, whether they in fact have his permission or not.

3   Effect of contract on occupier's liability to third party

(1)   Where an occupier of premises is bound by contract to permit persons who are strangers to the contract to enter or use the premises, the duty of care which he owes to them as his visitors cannot be restricted or excluded by that contract, but (subject to any provision of the contract to the contrary) shall include the duty to perform his obligations under the contract, whether undertaken for their protection or not, in so far as those obligations go beyond the obligations otherwise involved in that duty.

(2)   A contract shall not by virtue of this section have the effect, unless it expressly so provides, of making an occupier who has taken all reasonable care

answerable to strangers to the contract for dangers due to the faulty execution of any work of construction, maintenance or repair or other like operation by persons other than himself, his servants and persons acting under his direction and control.

(3)   In this section 'stranger to the contract' means a person not for the time being entitled to the benefit of the contract as a party to it or as the successor by assignment or otherwise of a party to it, and accordingly includes a party to the contract who has ceased to be so entitled.

(4)   Where by the terms or conditions governing any tenancy ... either the landlord or the tenant is bound, though not by contract, to permit persons to enter or use premises of which he is the occupier, this section shall apply as if the tenancy were a contract between the landlord and the tenant.

(5)   This section, so far as it prevents the common duty of care from being restricted or excluded, applies to contracts entered into and tenancies created before the commencement of this Act, as well as to those entered into or created after its commencement; but, in so far as it enlarges the duty owed by an occupier beyond the common duty of care, it shall have effect only in relation to obligations which are undertaken after the commencement or which are renewed by agreement (whether express or implied) after that commencement.

...

5   Implied terms in contracts

(1)   Where persons enter or use, or bring or send goods to, any premises in exercise of a right conferred by contract with a person occupying or having control of the premises, the duty he owes them in respect of dangers due to the state of the premises or to things done or omitted to be done on them, in so far as the duty depends on a term to be implied in the contract by reason of its conferring that right, shall be the common duty of care.

(2)   The foregoing subsection shall apply to fixed and moveable structures as it applies to premises.

Comment

(1)   'Premises' in the Occupiers' Liability Act 1957 extends to land, buildings and moveable structures such as taxis, buses, railway carriages, gangways and scaffolding. The important thing is that the defendant should have retained control over them, as opposed to the position in negligence at common law where the defendant may be liable for harm done by dangerous chattels over which he has ceased to have control, e.g. the ladder loaned to an independent contractor in *Wheeler v Copas*.

(2) The duty arises in respect of dangers due to the state of the premises or to things done or omitted to be done on the premises. This terminology is repeated in the Occupiers' Liability Act 1984 and what amounts to a danger due to the state of the premises was explored by the House of Lords in *Tomlinson v Congleton BC*, see p 403, where the reasoning on this point was the *ratio* of the decision.

(3) As to exclusion of liability see p 398.

(4) In *AMF v Magnet* it was said that there might be recovery of financial loss flowing from damage to property as well as compensation for the physical injury to the property itself.

McGeown v Northern Ireland Housing Executive
[1994] 3 All ER 53 House of Lords

The appellant plaintiff lived in a house with her husband who was tenant; the landlord was the defendant housing executive. The house was on an estate laid out by the defendants and was part of a terrace on one side of a cul-de-sac. Much of the area between that terrace and the one opposite had been adopted by the Department of the Environment as highway authority, but the remainder, entirely surrounded by adopted land, was owned by the defendants. A footpath, over which the public had acquired a right of way, ran across this retained land. As the plaintiff was walking along the footpath, she tripped in a hole and fell, breaking a leg. The hole was there owing to a failure to keep the surface of the pathway in good repair, and it constituted a danger to persons using the pathway.

The House of Lords held, first, that the owner of land over which a public right of way ran was under no liability, to members of the public using it, for negligent non-feasance; and, second, that a person using a public right of way was neither the licensee nor invitee of the owner of the soil, over which the public right of way ran and was not owed a duty of care under the Occupiers' Liability (Northern Ireland) Act 1957.

Lord Keith: '... The appeal raises two principal issues. The first concerns the soundness of what has come to be known as the rule in *Gautret v Egerton*, to the effect that the owner of land over which a public right of way passes is under no liability for negligent nonfeasance towards members of the public using it. The second issue is whether certain persons using the right of way may in appropriate circumstances fall to be treated not simply as members of the public but as visitors of the landowner so that a duty is owed towards them under s 2 of the Occupiers' Liability Act (Northern Ireland) 1957.

[Lord Keith briefly examined *Gautret v Egerton*, *Greenhalgh v British Railways Board* and *Holden v White* and continued:]

These authorities ... are sufficient to show that the rule in *Gautret v Egerton* is deeply entrenched in the law. Further, the rule is in my opinion undoubtedly a sound and reasonable one. Rights of way pass over many different types of terrain, and it would place an impossible burden upon landowners if they not only had to submit to the passage over them of anyone who might choose to exercise them but also were under a duty to maintain them in a safe condition. Persons using rights of way do so not with the permission of the owner of the solum but in the exercise of a right. There is no room for the view that such persons might have been licensees or invitees of the landowner under the old law or that they are his visitors under the British and Northern Irish Acts of 1957. There may indeed be a question whether the owner of the solum is occupier of the right of way for the purposes of these Acts. Doubts about that were expressed in *Holden v White* but it is unnecessary for present purposes to decide it.

It is, however, necessary to consider next whether the common duty of care under the 1957 Act was owed by the defendants to the plaintiff by reason that the pathway where she sustained her injuries formed part of a means of access to and from her husband's dwelling house. In *Fairman v Perpetual Investment Building Society*, the defendants owned a block of flats which they let to various tenants, retaining possession and control of the common staircase leading to the flats. The plaintiff, who lodged with one of the tenants, while descending the staircase, caught her heel in a depression in one of the steps and fell, sustaining injuries. The House of Lords held that the plaintiff was a licensee of the defendants and that they owed her a duty of care accordingly, but decided by a majority that there had been no breach of the duty ...

If the pathway on which the plaintiff fell in the present case had not become subject to a public right of way it seems clear that the defendants would have owed her the common duty of care under the 1957 Act and would have been liable accordingly. The question is whether the licence to use the pathway which the defendants would have been held to have granted the plaintiff before it became subject to the public right of way is to be held to have become merged in that right of way and so been extinguished, or whether it can be treated as having a continued existence.

[Lord Keith examined briefly *Brackley v Midland Railway* and *Greenhalgh v British Railways Board* and continued:]

The concept of licensee or visitor involves that the person in question has at least the permission of the relevant occupier to be in a particular place. Once a public right of way has been established, there is no question of permission being granted by the owner of the *solum* to those who choose to use it. They do so as of right and not by virtue of any licence or invitation. In the present case the pathway upon which the plaintiff fell had not been adopted by the highway authority, and it was therefore not responsible for the maintenance of it. Adjoining areas had been so adopted, in particular the strip of ground immediately adjoining the terrace where the plaintiff and her husband lived, and which she had to cross in order to get to or from his house. If the plaintiff was the licensee of the defendants upon the pathway where she fell she was equally their licensee upon that strip of ground. The circumstance that the highway authority was responsible under public law for its maintenance cannot logically make any difference to the position. The defendants would still owe a personal duty to the plaintiff to maintain the pathway in a reasonably safe condition, and be liable to her if she suffered injury owing to the area not being in such condition. That unreasonable result can be avoided if it is held that dedication as a public highway puts an end to any duty which might otherwise be owed by the housing executive ...'

Comment

(1) The user of a private right of way is owed a duty of care under the Occupiers' Liability Act 1984, see p 400, but the user of a highway (a public right of way) is not, see Occupiers' Liability Act 1984, s 1(7).

(2) Lord Browne-Wilkinson noted that there was a wide range of land over which the public might be invited to pass and repass, and that dedication of the land as a public highway might lessen the protection afforded to the public:

'To my mind it would be unfortunate if, as a result of the decision in this case, the owner of a railway bridge or shopping centre could, by expressly dedicating the land as a public highway or submitting to long public useage, free himself from all liability to users whose presence he had encouraged. Who, other than the occupier, is to maintain these artificial structures and protect from injury those encouraged to use them by the occupier for the occupier's own business reasons?

For these reasons, I am very reluctant to reach a conclusion which will leave unprotected those who, for purposes linked to the business of the owners of the soil, are encouraged, expressly or impliedly, to use facilities which the owner has provided.

In the present case, I can see no escape from the logic of Lord Keith's conclusion that, after the presumed dedication of the pathway as a public right of way, the housing executive ceased to owe any duty of care to the plaintiff. The plaintiff would, at best, be the licensee of the housing executive ... But it does not necessarily follow that the existence of a public right of way is incompatible with the owner of the soil owing a duty of care to an invitee, as opposed to a licensee. In the case of an invitee there is no logical inconsistency between the plaintiff's right to be on the premises in exercise of the right of way and his actual presence there in response to the express or implied invitation of the occupier. It is the invitation which gives rise to the occupier's duty of care to an invitee. I do not understand your Lordships to be deciding that it is impossible to be an invitee (and therefore a visitor) on land over which there is a public right of way. I wish expressly to reserve my view on that point.'

(3) Their remaining Lordships agreed with Lord Keith. If the impact of Lord Browne-Wilkinson's reservation is to resurrect the distinction between the two classes of visitor then the law will become more, not less, complex and the aim of the Occupiers' Liability Act 1957 will be defeated, albeit in a relatively minor class of case. Invitees are classed as such not because of invitation *simpliciter* but because of a common interest with the occupier: 'a person who (without any contract) entered on business of interest both to himself and the occupier (e.g. a customer coming into a shop to view the wares)', *Winfield & Jolowicz* (14th edn, 1994).

Fairchild v Glenhaven
[2002] I WLR 1052 Court of Appeal

F first worked for an employer who carried out subcontract work for the L City Council in the early 1960s; in this work he used asbestos. F then worked for a builder renovating a factory for W plc, and he cut asbestos sheeting. F inhaled dust containing asbestos fibre which caused him to suffer a mesothelioma from which he died in 1996. Each occupier had carelessly exposed F to the inhalation of asbestos fibres. The Court of Appeal held that F was unable to demonstrate which exposure had led to the disease being contracted and thus his action failed. The House of Lords overturned the Court of Appeal on the point relating to causation of damage, see p 268. The Court of Appeal had made comments on the issue of the Occupiers' Liability Act 1957 which were not before the House of Lords. In particular it had considered the scope of the 1957 Act.

Delivering the judgment of the Court of Appeal, Brooke LJ said:

'114. The distinction is sometimes made between "occupancy duties" and "activity duties", and sometimes between duties relating to "the static condition of the premises" and "current operations"…

118. That an occupier's occupancy duties arise from unusual dangers in the static condition of his premises is clear from the helpful lists of what had been held, respectively, to be unusual and not unusual dangers in the 3rd Edition of *Charlesworth on Negligence* (1956) at pp 195–197.

119. The emerging distinction between occupancy duties and activity duties can be seen in *Glasgow Corporation v Muir* … Lord Thankerton made it clear … that that case was not concerned with an unusual danger in the structural condition of the shop premises. If it had been, the issue would have been whether the invitor knew or ought to have known that the invitees were being exposed to that unusual danger. Instead, the question was whether in granting permission for the two men

to carry the urn through the shop, the manageress of the shop did not use reasonable foresight to guard the children from unusual danger arising from the use of the premises. In other words, the ordinary common law principles of the law of negligence were applied in deciding whether she was careless in the steps she took to guard the children from harm. The House of Lords held that she was not ...

[Brooke LJ cited the Occupiers' Liability Act 1957, ss 1(1), (2) and 2(2), (3), (4) and examined the speeches in *Ferguson v Welsh*:]

129. While we must not assume that in using the language adopted in section 2(2) of the 1957 Act Parliament necessarily decided to adopt the emerging distinction between "occupancy liability" and "activity liability", the selection of the phrase "care ... to see that the visitor will be reasonably safe in using the premises for the [invited or permitted] purposes" is a fairly strong indication that Parliament intended the Act to be concerned with what used to be described as "occupancy liability". Section 1(1) refers to dangers due to the state of the premises or to things done or omitted to be done on them, and Lord Keith [in *Ferguson v Welsh*] explained the need for the final words when he posited that a visitor might be struck by falling masonry which was only a danger because an obviously incompetent contractor had failed to secure it properly.

130. We have had the benefit of much fuller argument than was available to the House of Lords in *Ferguson v Welsh*, and we can see nothing in the speeches of the other members of the House which casts any doubt on the correctness of Lord Goff's interpretation of section 2(2). Lord Oliver clearly tended to make the same distinction between occupancy liability and activity liability [see p 380].

131. In ... *Makepeace v Evans Brothers (Reading)* Mantell LJ said ... that the question whether the common law duty of care is subsumed in the common duty of care created by the 1957 Act or survived as an independent basis of claim in respect of activities carried out on premises was of no practical importance save possibly as a pleading point, and that it was unnecessary to attempt to resolve the question on that appeal. The present appeals show how it may be essential sometimes to make this distinction ... The Act does not provide an answer ... when a question arises whether an occupier, without more, is liable to a visitor for an injury he suffers as a result of an activity conducted by a third party on his premises. For that purpose one has to go to the common law to see if a duty of care exists, and if so, what is its scope, or to some other statutory provision ...

149. ... The statutory duty of care created by [the 1957] Act imposed a duty on those occupiers to see that F was reasonably safe in using the premises for the purposes for which he entered them, and he encountered no dangers in his use of the premises, as he would have done if he had fallen through an unguarded hole in the floor. It was what was going on in those premises which caused him harm.'

Comment

(1)   The case makes the point that there are concurrent duties. One of these duties is in respect of the occupancy, the other in respect of the activities. The first is the subject of the Occupiers' Liability Act 1957, the latter is the subject of the common law.

(2)   The problems associated with duties owed to independent contractors' employees seems to be relevant in particular for the activity duty, and it was this that concerned the House of Lords in *Ferguson v Welsh*, see p 380.

Wheat v E Lacon & Co Ltd
[1966] I All ER 582 House of Lords

R1 and R2 ran a pub as manager for L Co, the respondents. The pub's ground floor was given over to drinks and so on, but R1 and R2 lived upstairs and carried on a business as a boarding house. W was a lodger. There were two sets of stairs, one frequently used by lodgers, one rarely used by anyone and not needed to be used by lodgers. W was using the latter stairs when an accident occurred and he was killed; the stairs had a short handrail, were very steep with narrow treads and a light bulb was missing.

The agreement between R1 and R2 and L Co did not distinguish between the two floors and effectively left L Co in occupation of both (together with R1 and R2). R1 and R2 and L Co were found to have exercised due care and on appeal to the House of Lords against the decision concerning L Co, the House of Lords found that there had been no failure to take care.

Lord Denning: '... The case raises this point of law: did the respondents owe any duty to W to see that the handrail was safe to use or to see that the stairs were properly lighted? That depends on whether the respondents were "an occupier" of the private portion of the "Golfer's Arms", and W was their "visitor" within the Occupiers' Liability Act 1957: for, if so, the respondents owed him the "common duty of care".

In order to determine this question we must have resort to the law before the Occupiers' Liability Act 1957 ... At the outset, I would say that no guidance is to be obtained from the use of the word "occupier" in other branches of law: for its meaning varies according to the subject-matter. In the Occupiers' Liability Act 1957, the word "occupier" is used in the same sense as it was used in the common law cases on occupiers' liability for dangerous premises. It was simply a convenient word to denote a person who had a sufficient degree of control over premises to put him under a duty of care towards those who came lawfully on to the premises. Those persons were divided into two categories, invitees and licensees: and a higher duty was owed to invitees than to licensees ... The Act of 1957 ... did away, once and for all, with invitees and licensees and classed them all as "visitors"; and it put on the occupier the same duty to all of them, namely, the common duty of care. This duty is simply a particular instance of the general duty of care, which each man owes to his "neighbour"...

Translating this general principle into its particular application to dangerous premises, it becomes simply this: wherever a person has a sufficient degree of control over premises that he ought to realise that any failure on his part to use care may result in injury to a person coming lawfully there, then he is an "occupier" and the person coming lawfully there is his "visitor"; and the "occupier" is under a duty to his "visitor" to use reasonable care. In order to be an "occupier" it is not necessary for a person to have entire control over the premises. He need not have exclusive occupation. Suffice it that he has some degree of control. He may share the control with others. Two or more may be "occupiers", and whenever this happens, each is under a duty to use care towards persons coming lawfully on to the premises, dependent on his degree of control. If each fails in his duty, each is liable to a visitor who is injured in consequence of his failure, but each may have a claim to contribution from the other.

In *Salmond on Torts* (14th edn., 1965), it is said that an "occupier" is "he who has the immediate supervision and control and the power of permitting or prohibiting the entry of other persons". This definition was adopted by Roxburgh J in *Hartwell v Grayson Rollo and Clover Docks Ltd* and by Diplock LJ in the present case. There is no doubt that a person who fulfils that test is an "occupier". He is the person who says "come in"; but I think that that test is too narrow by far. There are other people who are "occupiers", even though they do not say "come in". If a person has any degree of control over the state of the premises it is enough ...

I ask myself whether the respondents had a sufficient degree of control over the premises to put them under a duty to a visitor. Obviously they had complete control over the ground floor and were "occupiers" of it. But I think that they had also sufficient control over the private portion. They had not let it out to R1 by a demise. They had only granted him a licence to occupy it, having a right themselves to do repairs. That left them with a residuary degree of control ... They were in my opinion "an occupier" within the Act of 1957. R1, who had a licence to occupy, had also a considerable degree of control. So had R2, who catered for summer guests. All three of them were, in my opinion, "occupiers" of the private portion of the "Golfer's Arms". There is no difficulty in having more than one occupier at one and the same time, each of whom is under a duty of care to visitors ...'

Comment

(1) In *Harris v Birkenhead* it was held that a local authority was the occupier of a house acquired by compulsory purchase from the moment the previous occupant left until the authority entered the property.

(2)   In *AMF International v Magnet*, M contracted with T to build a complex building. A installed delicate timber work which was ruined by T's failure to secure the building. It was held, *inter alia*, that both M and T were occupiers and were liable.

(3)   In *Collier v Anglia Water Authority*, P was injured when walking along a sea wall and promenade created by D1 (the water authority) on land owned by D2 (the local government authority). There was an unevenness in the surface which consisted of large slabs of concrete laid side by side. Each of D1 and D2 had different responsibilities, e.g. D2 cleaned it, and D1 repaired it. It was held that both D1 and D2 were in occupation but, as with the other cases, the nature of the occupation dictated the precise content of the duty. The injury related to the state of repair and was therefore the responsibility of D1.

(4)   This concept of dual occupation was applied to a case under the Occupiers' Liability Act 1984 in respect of a right of way vested in a highway authority but which ran over the defendant's land as the servient tenement, even though the claimant herself also had occupational control over the right of way; see *Vodden v Gayton & Gayton*.

(5)   A person may be a visitor as far as one occupier is concerned yet a non-visitor as far as another is concerned, see Lord Goff's comment to this effect in *Ferguson v Welsh*.

Ferguson v Welsh and others
[1987] 3 All ER 777 House of Lords

A council invited tenders for the demolition of a building on the site of a housing scheme. S, a contractor, put in a tender which was accepted. There was an express condition that the work was not to be subcontracted without the council's authority but S arranged for the W brothers to carry out the actual demolition. W brothers offered F, the appellant, a job. In the course of the demolition work, the W brothers employed an unsafe system of work which caused a wall to collapse, with the result that the F was seriously injured. He sued W brothers, S and the council. F's damages were agreed at £150,000 but neither the W brothers nor S had public liability insurance. The judge held that the W brothers were liable to F, but that S and the council were not. The judge held that the council and S were occupiers of the premises but that since the council had neither invited F onto the premises nor delegated to S the right to invite him, F was not a visitor of the council. F appealed, seeking a new trial against S and the council. The Court of Appeal ordered a new trial against S but not against the council. F appealed to the House of Lords seeking a new trial against the council.

The House of Lords held that normally it would not be reasonable to expect an occupier to supervise a contractor to ensure that a safe system of work was being used. In exceptional circumstances such a duty might arise if the occupier knew or reasonably suspected that an unsafe system was being used. Therefore, in the absence of special features in this case the occupier, the council, would not owe a duty of care to an employee of the contractor injured because of the unsafe system adopted by the contractor. The injury to F arose out of the unsafe system and not from use of premises within the scope of the duty in the Occupiers' Liability Act 1957.

Lord Keith: '... The principal argument for F was related to the application of the Occupiers' Liability Act 1957. It was accepted on behalf of the council that, for the purposes of the Act, they were occupiers of the building along with S ... [T]he first matter for consideration is whether in relation to the council F was their visitor ... In my opinion, there is evidence capable of establishing that S had ostensible authority from the council to invite the W brothers and their employees onto the site. S was placed in control of the site for demolition purposes, and to one who had no knowledge of the council's policy of prohibiting sub-contracts this would indicate that he was entitled to invite whomsoever he pleased onto the site for the purpose of carrying out demolition.

The next question is whether the council were in breach of the common duty of care owed to visitors under the 1957 Act [s 2(2)] ... The safety referred to is safety not only from dangers due to the state of the premises but also known dangers due to things done or omitted to be done on them.

A problem at once arises as to the purposes for which the council are to be taken as having invited F to be on the premises, and whether in taking part in the demolition of the building he was using the premises for these purposes. I consider that the council, having put S into occupation of the premises and thus put him into a position to invite the W brothers and their employees onto them for the purpose of demolishing the building, must be taken to have invited F in for that purpose. It is more difficult to hold that F was, within the meaning of the subsection, using the premises for the purpose of demolishing the building, but, assuming that he was, the question remains whether the absence of reasonable safety which resulted in the accident arose out of his use of the premises. The absence of safety arose directly out of the system of work adopted by the W brothers, and the nature of the instructions given by them to F as to how he should go about performing his work for them. It would be going a very long way to hold that an occupier of premises is liable to the employee of an independent contractor engaged to do work on the premises in respect of dangers arising not from the physical state of the premises but from an unsafe system of work adopted by the contractor. In this connection, however, it is necessary to consider s 2(4)(b) of the 1957 Act ...

The enactment is designed to afford some protection from liability to an occupier who has engaged an independent contractor who has executed the work in a faulty manner. It is to be observed that it does not specifically refer to demolition, but a broad and purposive interpretation may properly lead to the conclusion that demolition is embraced by the word "construction". Further the pluperfect tense employed in the last words of the paragraph, "the work had been properly done", might suggest that there is in contemplation only the situation where the work has been completed, but has been done in such a way that there exists a danger related to the state of the premises. That would, however, in my opinion, be an unduly strict construction, and there is no good reason for narrowing the protection afforded so as not to cover liability from dangers created by a negligent act or omission by the contractor in the course of his work on the premises. It cannot have been intended not to cover, for example, dangers to visitors from falling masonry or other objects brought about by the negligence of the contractor. It may therefore be inferred that an occupier might, in certain circumstances, be liable for something done or omitted to be done on his premises by an independent contractor if he did not take reasonable steps to satisfy himself that the contractor was competent and that the work was being properly done.

It would not ordinarily be reasonable to expect an occupier of premises having engaged a contractor whom he has reasonable grounds for regarding as competent, to supervise the contractor's activities in order to ensure that he was discharging his duty to his employees to observe a safe system of work. In special circumstances, on the other hand, where the occupier knows or has reason to suspect that the contractor is using an unsafe system of work, it might well be reasonable for the occupier to take steps to see that the system was made safe.

[Lord Keith considered that there were no grounds for allowing the re-trial based on the issue of whether or not there was evidence that the council were aware that S had been in the habit of sub-contracting the work, and dismissed the appeal.]'

Lord Goff: '... The principal submission advanced on behalf of F was that such a new trial should be ordered, on the basis that the council might be held liable under the Occupiers' Liability Act 1957. Like my noble and learned friend Lord Keith, I am unable to accept this submission, though I have reached that conclusion by a rather different route.

I, for myself, can see no difficulty in law in reaching a conclusion that F may have been a lawful visitor in relation to S but a trespasser in relation to the council. Once it is accepted that two persons may be in occupation of the same land, it seems to me inevitable that on certain facts such a conclusion may have to be reached. If it be the case that one only of such occupiers authorises a third person to come onto the land, then plainly the third person is, vis-à-vis that occupier, a lawful visitor. But he may not be a lawful visitor vis-à-vis the other occupier. Whether he is so or not must, in my opinion, depend on the question whether the occupier who authorised him to enter had authority, actual (express or implied) or ostensible, from the other occupier to allow the third party onto the land. If he had, then the third party will be, vis-à-vis that other occupier, a lawful visitor; if he had not, then the third party will be, *vis-à-vis* that other occupier, a trespasser. No doubt, in the ordinary circumstances of life, the occupier who allows the third party to come onto the land will frequently have implied or ostensible authority so to do on behalf of the other occupier, as will, I think, usually be the case when the first occupier is a builder, in occupation of a building site with the authority of the building owner, who authorises a servant or independent contractor to come onto the site. But this may not always be so, as for example where the third party is aware that the building owner has expressly forbidden the builder to allow him on the site. These problems have, as I see it, to be solved by the application of the ordinary principles of agency law.

I am content to assume, for the purposes of the present appeal, that there is evidence capable of establishing that S did have the ostensible authority of the council to allow the W brothers (and, through them, F) onto the land. Even so, in my judgment F's action against the council must fail because I cannot see how the council could be held liable to him, in particular under the 1957 Act.

On the assumption that F was the lawful visitor of the council on the land, the council owed to him the common duty of care ... I [emphasise] the words "in using the premises" because it seems to me that the key to the problem in the present case lies in those words. I can see no basis ... for holding that F's injury arose from any breach by the council of that duty. There can, no doubt, be cases in which an independent contractor does work on premises which result in such premises becoming unsafe for a lawful visitor coming on them, as when a brick falls from a building under repair onto the head of a postman delivering the mail. In such circumstances the occupier may be held liable to the postman, though in considering whether he is in breach of the common duty of care there would have to be considered, *inter alia*, the circumstances specified in s 2(4)(b) of the 1957 Act. But if I ask myself, in relation to the facts of the present case, whether it can be said that F's injury arose from a failure by the council to take reasonable care to see that persons in his position would be reasonably safe in using the premises for the relevant purposes, the answer must, I think, be No. There is no question as, I see it, of F's injury arising from any such failure for it arose not from his use of the premises but from the manner in which he carried out his work on the premises. For this simple reason, I do not consider that the 1957 Act has anything to do with the present case.

I wish to add that I do not, with all respect, subscribe to the opinion that the mere fact that an occupier may know or have reason to suspect that the contractor carrying out work on his building may be using an unsafe system of work can of itself be enough to impose on him a liability under the 1957 Act, or, indeed, in negligence at common law, to an employee of the contractor who is thereby injured, even if the effect of using that unsafe system is to render the premises unsafe and thereby to cause the injury to the employee. I have only to think of the ordinary householder who calls in an electrician; and the electrician sends in a man who, using an unsafe system established by his employer creates a danger in the premises which results in his suffering injury from burns. I cannot see that, in ordinary circumstances, the householder should be held liable under the 1957 Act, or even in negligence, for failing to tell the man how he should be doing his work. I recognise that there may be special circumstances which may render another person liable to the injured man together with his employer, as when they are, for some reason, joint tortfeasors; but such a situation appears to me to be quite different.

On the evidence in the present case, I can see no special circumstances by reason of which the council, as occupier, might be held liable to F under the 1957 Act. Nor can I see any other basis on which the council might be held liable to him. In these circumstances, though I feel great sympathy for F, I agree that his appeal must be dismissed.'

Comment

(1) There seem to be two issues in relation to independent contractors. The first is that the Occupiers' Liability Act 1957, s 2(4)(b) is not concerned with creating vicarious liability but with the circumstances relevant to the discharge of the duty of care under the Act. Defendant occupiers may well be able to discharge their duty under the Act by employing independent contractors and bringing themselves within the conditions of s 2(4)(b). In *Woodward v Hastings*, not a case under the Act, the cleaning of steps was thought to be only a simple task, and there will be no escaping liability in such instances even if an appropriate independent contractor is used. However, even though the job might not be such as to warrant the intervention of an expert, it must still be shown that there was a failure to achieve the correct standard. On the other hand, in *AMF International v Magnet*, M contracted with T to build a complex building. A installed delicate timber work which was ruined by T's failure to secure the building. It was held, *inter alia*, that both M and T were occupiers and were liable. M had failed to instruct a qualified person to check the premises and to install anti-flooding precautions before A had been allowed to enter and install their timber. M could not benefit from s 2(4)(b) since, although it had been proper for M to have used T, M had not appointed an independent contractor to check the work, and even if the architect involved had been an independent contractor (which he was not), he had not been instructed on that particular point. T was in occupation of the building as a whole and had not been excluded from any part of it and failure to provide anti-flood protection was a breach of duty.

(2) The second issue is whether or not the occupier owes a duty under the Act to an employee of an independent contractor. The Occupiers' Liability Act 1957 will impose the common duty of care where the risk arises from the

state of the premises. The common law may impose a duty of care under normal negligence principles where the activities of the occupier are under consideration. This common law duty of care has been considered in *Makepeace v Evans* which concerned a painter employed by subcontractors engaged on a construction site. He was injured when the tower scaffold on which he was working fell over. The scaffold belonged to the main contractors and had been loaned to the claimant to enable him to paint the outside of the premises. The Court of Appeal held that this was not a case where the main contractor would owe a duty of care to the employee of a subcontractor because the scaffold was an ordinary piece of equipment not inherently dangerous and commonly used by painters and decorators. The case was distinguished by the Court of Appeal in *McGarvey v EVE NCI Ltd* where the claimant, an employee of the subcontractor, had been instructed by the defendant main contractor to use a particular ladder which was entirely inappropriate for the task, and the claimant was not an experienced or trained worker.

(3) In *Bottomley v Todmorden Cricket Club and others* the defendant cricket club engaged the second and third defendants, a two-man stunt team, to conduct a pyrotechnic display. The second and third defendants invited the claimant to help them in the show. The claimant was severely burned when a mortar tube exploded in his face. The claimant was untrained and had no experience of such events. The Club knew that the proposed stunt was particularly dangerous. The safety equipment provided to the claimant was inadequate and the second and third defendants had operated an amateurish organisation in a field which required the highest degree of professionalism if danger was to be avoided. The judge concluded that the Club had failed to take reasonable care in its selection of a suitable contractor, and had owed the claimant a duty of care in making that selection, and that all the defendants were liable. The first defendant appealed. Lord Justice Brooke recalled that *Fairchild v Glenhaven* as decided in the Court of Appeal was binding on the court and that this was not a case to which the Occupiers' Liability Act 1957 applied because it was an activity and not an occupational duty. The Court of Appeal held that in the circumstances of this case a duty of care in the selection of a contractor was owed at common law by the occupier to an employee or agent of the contractors because of the extra-hazardous nature of the activities being undertaken.

(4) Is there a duty owed by an occupier to a visitor to ensure that any independent contractor is appropriately insured? In *Gwilliam v West Hertfordshire Hospital NHS Trust* the first defendant, the Trust, had organised a charity event and had agreed with the second defendant (whose name they had found in the Yellow Pages) that he would bring along his 'splat-wall' as one of the entertainments. A member of the public would put on a 'velcro' suit then bounce on a trampoline and onto a wall where they would stick. The trust

enquired orally as to the existence of insurance and was told that it was in place. The 63-year-old claimant was badly injured when her foot caught in the poorly assembled trampette in front of the splat wall. She had not been warned that she should not use the equipment because of her age, nor had she been instructed as to how to use the equipment. It transpired that the second defendant's insurance had expired shortly before the event.

The majority in the Court of Appeal concluded that the first defendant owed a duty of care to the claimant but that there had been no breach of that duty. The reasoning of the majority differed. Lord Woolf CJ concluded that the Occupiers' Liability Act 1957 provided the duty of care and, by analogy with s 2(4)(b), the duty involved checking that the independent contractor was reasonably chosen and competent. An enquiry into insurance with a positive response was a suitable indicator that the independent contractor was in fact competent. Lord Justice Waller preferred to found his decision on the basis of the common law duty of care and concluded that it was fair, just and reasonable to impose a duty of care on the first defendant to choose an independent contractor who can properly meet any potential liability. There was a very persuasive dissenting judgment by Lord Justice Sedley.

The issue of insurance was explored further in *Naylor v Payling*. The Court of Appeal emphasised that the duty on an employer of an independent contractor was to take reasonable care in the selection of that contractor. There was no duty to check the insurance position of the independent contractor. The case concerned the use of a door attendant at a night-club and the court distinguished the hazardous activities being undertaken in both *Gwilliam* and *Bottomley*.

Wheat v Lacon
[1966] I All ER 582 House of Lords

For facts see p 378. On the application of the standard of care:

Lord Denning: '... What did the common duty of care demand of each of these occupiers towards their visitors? Each was under a duty to take such care as "in all the circumstances of the case" was reasonable to see that the visitor would be reasonably safe. So far as the respondents were concerned, the circumstances demanded that on the ground floor they should, by their servants, take care not only of the structure of the building, but also the furniture, the state of the floors and lighting, and so forth, at all hours of day or night when the premises were open. In regard to the private portion, however, the circumstances did not demand so much of L Co. They ought to have seen that the structure was reasonably safe, including the handrail, and that the system of lighting was efficient; but I doubt whether they were bound to see that the lights were properly switched on or the rugs laid safely on the floor. L Co were entitled to leave those day to day matters to R1 and R2. They, too, were occupiers. The circumstances of the case demanded that R1 and R2 should take care of those matters in the private portion of the house. And of the other matters, too. If they had realised that the handrail was dangerous, they should have reported it to L Co.

We are not concerned here with R1 and R2. The judge has absolved them from any negligence and there is no appeal. We are only concerned with L Co. They were, in my opinion, occupiers and under a duty of care. In this respect I agree with Sellers LJ and Winn J, but I come to a different conclusion on the facts. I can see no evidence of any breach of duty by L Co. So far as the handrail was concerned, the evidence was overwhelming that no one had any reason before this accident to suppose that it was in the least dangerous. So far as the light was concerned, the proper inference was that it was removed by some stranger shortly before W went down the staircase. Neither L Co nor R1 and R2 could be blamed for the act of a stranger.'

Viscount Dilhorne: '... Did L Co fail to take such care as in all the circumstances was reasonable to see that W was reasonably safe in using the premises?

They had built the staircase in 1938. Between then and 1958 no accident had happened on it. Winn J held that the steepness of the stairs was not such as of itself to make the stairs dangerous. The only unusual feature was the ending of the handrail before the bottom of the stairs so that the last two stairs had no handrail beside them.

L Co had provided a light at the top of the stairs, operated at the top and bottom of the staircase. The fact that the bulb was missing at the time of the accident was no fault of theirs. Winn J held that its removal, by whomever it was effected, was a *novus actus* and that there was no ground on which to find that R2 knew that the bulb was missing in time to see that it was replaced.

Ought, then, L Co reasonably to have foreseen that a visitor would use the staircase when it was dark or insufficiently lit? And, if so, ought they to have made some further provision with regard to it? I think that L Co ought to have foreseen that a visitor might use the staircase when unlit. A visitor might not discover the switch to operate the light. I do not myself consider, however, that this staircase, if unlit, was a dangerous staircase for someone to use who was taking proper care for his own safety. Though steep it was not dangerously steep and it was straight. Anyone who chose to go down it in the dark and who took care to see that the foot he put forward was resting on something solid before he put his weight on it, could have gone down it perfectly safely.

I do not think that L Co could be reasonably expected to have foreseen that W when he reached the end of the handrail would "step out with the confidence that his foot was about to come upon the floor level", if he could not see the floor. As Diplock LJ said: "My neighbour does not enlarge my duty to care for his safety by neglecting it himself." Whether the accident happened in the way which Winn J thought probable or in some other way, in my opinion, there was no breach of the duty on the part of the respondents to take such care as in all the circumstances was reasonable to see that visitors were reasonably safe in using the premises ...'

Comment

(1)   There is a tendency to elevate questions of fact to the status of law. The law in the Occupiers' Liability Act 1957 is quite simple, but the application to the facts may be more difficult. Lord Pearce remarked that: 'Once the duty of care is imposed, the question whether a defendant failed in that duty becomes a question of fact in all the circumstances.' The court will consider relevant matters such as the obvious nature of the danger, any warnings, lighting, fencing, the age and infirmity of the visitor, the purpose of the visit, the conduct of the visitor and the knowledge of the occupier.

There are many instances of accidents involving poor lighting. In *Campbell v Shelbourne*, P, a guest at a hotel, walked along a passageway to find a toilet; the passage and steps were unlit and as a consequence P fell down the steps. D was held liable. In *Rae v Mars* an experienced chartered surveyor went to D's factory premises. He entered a room which was in darkness and fell into an inspection pit immediately adjacent to the door. D failed to warn him of this particular danger although D's servant was showing P around and said there was a light switch on the other side of the room. But P did not exercise reasonable care for his own safety and was contributorily negligent (33 per cent), e.g. he could have turned on his torch or looked more carefully. As an additional point, the judge held that even if P had been warned D ought to have maintained either a barrier or a notice at the scene so as properly to discharge his duty, and in such an event (i.e. if a warning had been given) then P would have been 66 per cent to blame.

(2)   It is a duty to take reasonable care that the visitor will be reasonably safe, not that the premises will be reasonably safe for the purposes for which the visitor entered. The circumstances are amplified but not defined in s 2(3). Performance of the duty may be by way of a warning, e.g. an adequate notice.

(3)   In most instances liability under the Occupiers' Liability Act 1957 may be indistinguishable from liability on ordinary principles of negligence, see e.g. *Ward v Tesco*, p 249, where the Act was not mentioned although it might have been an appropriate case for it to have been applied.

(4)   It should also be remembered that liability in respect of premises can flow from other relationships. Thus a local education authority might be liable to pupils at a school by virtue of the relationship which exists between a pupil and a schoolmaster. In *Ward v Hertfordshire CC* there was no liability under the Act for a child's injuries sustained where he ran across a playground, tripped and

cut his head on a flint wall. The supervision was adequate. There may also be statutory provisions as to the construction or maintenance of a building, and thus the possibility of a claim for breach of statutory duty, see p 449.

(5) The correct identification of the duty and the breach can be very important, see *Ferguson v Welsh* per Lord Goff.

Glasgow Corporation v Taylor
[1922] 1 AC 44 House of Lords

T, aged seven, went into G's recreation park to play. G had grown, on a piece of land immediately adjacent to the park and fenced off but easily accessible from it, shrubs including Deadly Nightshade Atropa belladona – very tempting in appearance to young children and also very poisonous. The piece of land was open to the public, the shrub was not isolated nor was any warning appended to or near it. T picked and ate some berries and died. It was held that G were liable since they knew that children of tender years, in a place where they were entitled to be (the park), would by G's own actions be brought into contact with an allurement – i.e. something harmless in appearance, attractive but dangerous in reality – and had not taken reasonable steps to prevent harm.

Lord Shaw: '... There is no trespass in the case. The child, having a right to be in these gardens, was, in my opinion, entitled, as were also his parents, to rely upon the gardens being left in a reasonably safe condition: or in the language of the Lord Justice-Clerk: "The playground for the children must be taken as being provided as a place reasonably suitable and safe for children, and I think the parents were entitled so to regard it."

To this would I venture to add that it matters not that the gardens were, or were called, Botanic Gardens. They admittedly were a public place of recreation for the citizens of Glasgow. In ground open to the public as of right the duty resting upon the proprietors, or statutory guardians like a municipality, of making them reasonably safe does not include an obligation of protection against dangers which are themselves obvious. Dangers, however, which are not seen and obvious, should be made the subject either of effectively restricted access or of such express and actual warning of prohibition as reaches the mind of the persons prohibited ...

When the danger is familiar and obvious no special responsibility attaches to the municipality or owner in respect of an accident having occurred to children of tender years. The reason of that appears to me to be this – that the municipality or owner is entitled to take into account that reasonable parents will not permit their children to be sent into the midst of familiar and obvious dangers except under protection or guardianship. The parent or guardian of the child must act reasonably; the municipality or guardian of the park must act reasonably. This duty rests upon both and each, but each is entitled to assume it of the other. Where the dangers are not familiar and obvious, and where in particular they are or ought to be known to the municipality or owner, special considerations arise. In the case of objects, whether artificial and, so to speak, dangerous in themselves, such as loaded guns or explosives, or natural objects, such as trees bearing poisonous fruits which are attractive in appearance, it cannot be considered a reasonably safe procedure for a municipality or owner to permit the exhibition of these things with their dangerous possibilities in a place of recreation, and without any special and particular watch and warning. There can be no fault on the part of a parent in trusting that such obligations of safety would be duly performed by the municipality or owner, and in allowing his child accordingly to pass into the grounds unattended the parent commits no negligent act. As for the child itself, while it may do things and incur dangers by inquisitively meddling with things which it should not touch, it is plain that, when the occurred danger, against which no protection or sufficient warning was directed to anybody, produces its unfortunate evil effect, the municipality or owner is answerable for these, and there is no defence of contributory negligence ...

I do not find myself able to draw a distinction in law between natural objects, such as shrubs whose attractive fruitage may be injuriously or fatally poisonous, and artificial objects, such as machines left in a public place unattended and liable to produce danger if tampered with. The act of tampering might be contributory negligence on the part of a grown-up person, but would not be so reckoned on the part of a child ...'

Comment

(1)   According to the court, the park was the sort of place to which children could be expected to go, and to go there unsupervised. Also the parents were not at fault in permitting the children to be there. To a child of tender years these bushes were not obviously a source of danger, but to an adult they would have been. Lord Sumner said: 'The child had no right to pluck the berries, but the corporation had no right to tempt the child to its death or to expose it to temptation regardless of consequences.'

(2)   The concept of an allurement was usefully deployed to deal with difficult cases where there would have otherwise been no remedy for a child's injuries. The common law developed two legal devices to try to alleviate the plight of children: allurements and traps. The first is in the nature of a temptation which leads into danger, the latter is in the nature of a hidden danger. The editors of *Salmond and Heuston* observe that:

'It is better not to use "allurement" to signify the circumstances under which a child enters premises; it remains a trespasser, however natural it may have been for it to enter. But once it has entered with permission it may find on the premises some attractive object which tempts it to meddle when it ought to abstain. This is an "allurement": a trap is something defective in the state of premises themselves.'

The learned authors' reference to the circumstances in which children enter premises reflects another device adopted by the common law to lessen the harshness of the rule that no duty was owed to trespassers. In an exceptional case the acquiescence of an occupier in entry by trespassers could be regarded as an implied invitation. The device thus converted an apparent trespasser into a visitor towards whom a duty was owed. This device was deprecated by the House of Lords in *British Railways Board v Herrington* which in any event lessened the harshness of the rule towards trespassers.

Care has to be taken when considering traps and allurements. The categorisation of something as one or the other is not the basis of liability. The basis of liability of an occupier is the breach of the duty of care; this is evidenced by, for example, leaving on the premises something which will entice a child and yet be dangerous to it. And, even if something cannot be said to be a trap or allurement, then liability might still flow, e.g. there might be something on the land which is equally dangerous to a child and an adult.

Phipps v Rochester Corporation
[1955] I All ER 129 Queen's Bench Division

A local authority owned a large open space and had dug a deep trench 100 yards long, two feet wide, nine feet deep. Children living locally used the space and the authority knew this but took no steps to object. P, aged five, and S, aged seven, went on to the land. P fell into the trench and broke his leg. It was held that the local authority were not liable.

Devlin J: '... There are limits to [a licensor's] duty which exist quite independently of the behaviour of the licensee in any particular case. His duty is to consider with reasonable care whether there are on his premises, so far as he knows their condition, any dangers that would not be obvious to the persons whom he has permitted to use them; and if there are, to give warning of them or to remove them. If he rightly determines a danger to be obvious, he will not be liable because some individual licensee, albeit without negligence in the special circumstances of his case, fails to perceive it. He must be taken to know generally the "habits, capacities and propensities" of those whom he himself has licensed, but not their individual peculiarities. In the light of that general knowledge and on the assumption that they will behave reasonably, he must determine what step he will take. If he makes that determination carefully, he cannot be made liable, whatever may subsequently happen.

I think it would be an unjustifiable restriction of the principle if one were to say that, although the licensor may in determining the extent of his duty have regard to the fact that it is the habit, and also the duty, of prudent people to look after themselves, he may not in that determination have a similar regard to the fact that it is the habit, and also the duty, of prudent people to look after their little children. If he is entitled, in the absence of evidence to the contrary, to assume that parents will not normally allow their little children to go out unaccompanied, he can decide what he should do and consider what warnings are necessary on that basis. He cannot then be made liable for the exceptional child that strays nor will he be required to prove that any particular parent has been negligent. It is, I think, preferable that this result should be achieved by allowing the general principle to expand in a natural way rather than by restricting its influence and then having to give it artificial aids in order to make it work at all in the case of little children.

The principle I am seeking to express is that contained in the passage which I have quoted from the speech of Lord Shaw ... in *Glasgow Corporation v Taylor*, where he says that the municipality is entitled to take into account that reasonable parents will not permit their children to be sent into danger without protection; that the guardians of the child and of the park must each act reasonably; and that each is entitled to assume of the other that he will. That passage was not spoken in reference to the English law of licence, but nevertheless it seems to me to express perfectly the way in which the English law can reasonably be applied. A licensor who tacitly permits the public to use his land without discriminating between its members must assume that the public may include little children. But as a general rule he will have discharged his duty towards them if the dangers which they may encounter are only those which are obvious to a guardian or of which he has given a warning comprehensible by a guardian. To every general rule there are, of course, exceptions. A licensor cannot divest himself of the obligation of finding out something about the sort of people who are availing themselves of his permission and the sort of use they are making of it. He may have to take into account the social habits of the neighbourhood. No doubt, there are places where little children go to play unaccompanied. If the licensor knows or ought to anticipate that, he may have to take steps accordingly. But the responsibility for the safety of little children must rest primarily on the parents; it is their duty to see that such children are not allowed to wander about by themselves, or, at the least, to satisfy themselves that the places to which they do allow their children to go unaccompanied are safe for them to go to. It would not be socially desirable if parents were, as a matter of course, able to shift the burden of looking after their children from their own shoulders to those of persons who happen to have accessible bits of land. Different considerations may well apply to public parks or to recognised playing grounds where parents allow their children to go unaccompanied in the reasonable belief that they are safe ...

If this be the true principle to apply, then I have to consider whether the defendants ought in this case to have anticipated the presence of the infant plaintiff unaccompanied. I say "unaccompanied" because the sister, while doubtless able to take care of herself as is shown by her own avoidance of the trench, was not old enough to take care of her little brother as well. There is no evidence in this case to show that little children frequently went unaccompanied on the open space in a way which ought to have brought home to the defendant that that was the use that was being made of their licence. Apart from evidence of that sort, I do not think that the defendants ought to have anticipated that it was a place in which children aged five years would be sent out to play by themselves. It is not an overcrowded neighbourhood; it is not as if it were the only green place in the centre of the city. The houses had gardens in which small children could play; if it be material, I believe that at the relevant time the plaintiff's garden was in fact fenced. The parents of children who might be expected to play there all live near and could have made themselves familiar with the space. They must have known that building operations were going on nearby and ought to have realised that that might involve the digging of trenches and holes. Even if it be prudent, which I do not think it is, for a parent to allow two small children out in this way on an October evening, the parents might at least have satisfied themselves that the place to which they allowed these little children to go held no dangers for them. Any parent who looked could have seen the trench and taken steps to prevent his child going there while it was still open. In my judgment, the defendants are entitled to assume that parents would behave in this naturally prudent way, and are not obliged to take it on themselves, in effect, to discharge parental duties. I conclude, therefore, that the infant plaintiff was on the land as a licensee, but that there was no breach of the defendants' duty towards him ...'

Comment

(1) The principle in *Phipps v Rochester* may well create problems for parents. In the absence of a trap, if a reasonably prudent parent would consider the premises safe for the young child to go unaccompanied, then what else can an occupier do? And, if a reasonably prudent parent would not consider the premises safe for an unaccompanied child, then the burden is on the parent not to let the child go there.

(2) The problem is that simply stating that there is a common duty of care might obscure the fact that there may well be a range of visitors with a very wide range of experience or inexperience. The Act recognises this and highlights two particular types: children and experts (for experts, see below). There may well be others, e.g. the blind person, see *Haley v London Electricity Board*, p 74.

(3) For an example of the operation of the principle, see *Maloney v Lambeth LBC* where the plaintiff child was injured when he fell through a gap in a staircase which would have presented no danger to an adult. The problem with children is their inability to leave well alone.

Roles v Nathan
[1963] 2 All ER 908 Court of Appeal

Two chimney-sweeps were employed to clean the flues of a chimney. On two occasions they were told of the risks of working in certain conditions. They were warned again that when the sweep-hole in the flue was sealed they should quickly leave. The flue was lit but the sweeps took some time to reseal the hole. They returned in the evening, but in the morning were found dead, having been overcome by fumes. It was held that the warnings were sufficient and the duty of care had been discharged, and that the danger was a special risk ordinarily incident to the expert's calling.

Lord Denning MR: '... [The Occupiers' Liability Act 1957, s 2(2)] is comprehensive. All the circumstances have to be considered. But the Act goes on to give examples of the circumstances that are relevant. The particular one in question here is in s 2(3) ... That subsection shows that *Christmas v General Cleaning Contractors Ltd* is still good law under this new Act. There a window-cleaner ... was sent to clean the windows of a club. One of the windows was defective; it had not been inspected and repaired as it should have been. In consequence, when the window-cleaner was cleaning it, it ran down quickly and trapped his hand, thus causing him to fall. It was held that he had no cause of action against the club. If it had been a guest who had his fingers trapped by the defective window, the guest could have recovered damages from the club. But the window-cleaner could not do so. The reason is this: The householder is concerned to see that the windows are safe for his guests to open and close, but he is not concerned to see that they are safe for a window-cleaner to hold on to. The risk of a defective window is a special risk, but it is ordinarily incidental to the calling of a window-cleaner, and so he must take care for himself, and not expect the householder to do so. Likewise, in the case of a chimney-sweep who comes to sweep the chimneys or to seal up a sweep-hole. The householder can reasonably expect the sweep to take care of himself so far as any dangers from the flues are concerned. These chimney-sweeps ought to have known that there might be dangerous fumes about and ought to have taken steps to guard against them. They ought to have known that they should not attempt to seal up the sweep-hole whilst the fire was still alight. They ought to have had the fire withdrawn before they attempted to seal it up, or at any rate they ought not to have stayed in the alcove too long when there might be dangerous fumes about. All this was known to these two sweeps; they were repeatedly warned about it, and it was for them to guard against the danger. It was not for the occupier to do it, even though he was present and heard the warnings. When a householder calls in a specialist to deal with a defective installation on his premises, he can reasonably expect the specialist to appreciate and guard against the dangers arising from the defect. The householder is not bound to watch over him to see that he comes to no harm. I would hold, therefore, that the occupier here was under no duty of care to these sweeps, at any rate in regard to the dangers which caused their deaths. If it had been a different danger, as for instance if the stairs leading to the cellar gave way, the occupier might no doubt be responsible, but not for these dangers which were special risks ordinarily incidental to their calling ...

The question arises whether the duty was discharged by the warning that was given to them. This brings us to s 2(4) ... It was inserted so as to clear up the unsatisfactory state of the law as it had been left by the decision of the House of Lords in *London Graving Dock Co Ltd v Horton*. That case was commonly supposed to have decided that, when a person comes on to premises as an invitee, and is injured by the defective or dangerous condition of the premises (due to the default of the occupier), it is, nevertheless, a complete defence for the occupier to prove that the invitee knew of the danger, or had been warned of it. Supposing, for instance, that there was only one way of getting into and out of premises and it was by a footbridge over a stream which was rotten and dangerous. According to *Horton's* case the occupier could escape all liability to any visitor by putting up a notice: "This bridge is dangerous", even though there was no other way by which the visitor could get in or out, and he had no option but to go over the bridge. In such a case, s 2(4)(a) makes it clear that the occupier would nowadays be liable. But if there were two footbridges one of which was rotten, and the other safe a hundred yards away, the occupier could still escape liability, even today by putting up a notice: "Do not use this footbridge. It is dangerous. There is a safe one further upstream." Such a warning is sufficient because it does enable the visitor to be reasonably safe.

I think that the law would probably have developed on these lines in any case ... but the subsection has now made it clear. A warning does not absolve the occupier unless it is enough to enable the visitor to be reasonably safe. Apply s 2(4) to this case. I am quite clear that the warnings which were given to the sweeps were enough to enable them to be reasonably safe. The sweeps would have been quite safe if they had heeded these warnings. They should not have come back that evening and attempted to seal up the sweep-hole while the fire was still alight. They ought to have waited till next morning, and then they should have seen that the fire was out before they attempted to seal up the sweep-hole. In any case they should not have stayed too long in the sweep-hole. In short, it was entirely their own fault. The judge held that it was contributory negligence. I would go further and say that, under the Act, the occupier has, by the warnings, discharged his duty ...'

Comment

(1) Lord Denning MR and Harman LJ thought that the risks were ordinarily incidental to the exercise of the sweeps' calling, but Pearson LJ thought not. The point is not one of law but of fact. The problem here is the converse of the child problem described above. These individuals have an abundance of experience and expertise and are therefore, self-evidently, to be treated 'differently' from any other group.

(2)   There is a difference between (a) carrying out a duty or attempting to do so by giving a warning of the existence of a danger, and (b) attempting to exclude liability. The Occupiers' Liability Act 1957 permits performance of the duty by warning or exclusion or modification of the duty insofar as permitted. It is not necessary for the warning to be written, an oral warning can be enough. The common law seemed to have decided in *London Graving Dock v Horton* that a warning which ensured that P knew of the danger was sufficient performance of his duty irrespective of whether P freely and voluntarily undertook the risk, or not. See the example of two bridges given by Lord Denning MR above. Now, a warning is only one factor to be considered.

(3)   A notice may also be relevant to a defence of *volens*, see Occupiers' Liability Act 1957, s 2(5); knowledge is not of itself sufficient to satisfy this defence.

(4)   The Court of Appeal in *Ratcliff v McConnell* and the House of Lords in *Tomlinson v Congleton BC*, see p 403, accept that there is no general duty to warn of a danger which was obvious. Although these were cases on the Occupiers' Liability Act 1984, this is the same position as under the Occupiers' Liability Act 1957, see p 370.

White v Blackmore
[1972] 3 All ER 158 Court of Appeal

W was an expert jalopy racer. In the morning he entered for a race to be held at a site run by B and others. In the afternoon he returned to the site before the race with his family, and he did not pay an entrance fee for himself since he was a competitor. A notice at the entrance purported to exclude liability to spectators and ticket-holders. W raced and then stood with his family as a spectator. He did not enter the enclosure where they were, but rather stood on one side of a rope barrier with his family on the other side. An announcement required spectators to keep behind that rope. A car crashed and caused the rope to catapult W into the air and he was killed. It was held (Lord Denning dissenting) that: (1) *volenti* did not apply because he did not have full knowledge of the risk; (2) he had entered as a spectator on the second occasion; and (3) entry was subject to the notice which had effectively excluded liability.

Buckley LJ: '... When the deceased returned with his family in the afternoon, the notice ... was prominently displayed near the entrance to the ground. The learned judge found as a fact that the deceased saw that notice and appreciated that it was a notice governing the conditions under which people were to be admitted to watch the racing ...

In my opinion, when the deceased came on to the field in the afternoon, he did so as a gratuitous licensee. I have already said that, in my view, no contract was made in the morning. The deceased made no payment for entry in the afternoon. Nothing that occurred in the morning could afford consideration for any contract entered into in the afternoon. In my judgment, no contract between the promoters and the deceased was made in the afternoon. The deceased remained willing to take part in the races and the promoters remained willing to allow him to do so. On the evidence, he was not, in my judgment, either bound or entitled contractually to take part in the races. In this state of affairs he was allowed on to the field free of charge.

I think that when the deceased came on to the field in the afternoon he did so in a dual capacity, as a prospective competitor and as a spectator. He was not intending to take part in all the races run on that afternoon, and I can feel no doubt that part of his object in attending the meeting was to enjoy watching those races in which he was not a competitor as well as to compete in those races in which he proposed to compete. There was considerable discussion in the course of the argument whether this notice was applicable to the deceased ... Since ... the deceased had no legal right to insist on taking part in the races, there is no reason to regard any licence granted to him in the morning as irrevocable until he had completed those races in which he proposed to take part. In the circumstances of this case I think any licence granted to the deceased in the morning was revocable summarily subject only to his right to recover his jalopy. If it was revocable, it was to a like extent variable.

What then was the effect of the situation which arose when the deceased returned to the field in the afternoon? It is clear that the occupier of land, who permits someone else to enter on that land as his licensee, can by imposing suitable conditions limit his own liability to the licensee in respect of any risks which may arise while the licensee is on the land (*Ashdown v Samuel Williams & Sons Ltd*). The Occupiers' Liability Act 1957, which in s 2(1) refers to an occupier excluding his duty of care to any visitor "by agreement or otherwise", has not altered the law in this respect. Counsel for the plaintiff concedes that in the present case the notice displayed at the entrance to the ground was sufficient to exclude liability on the part of the organisers of the meeting to all spectators properly so called, but he contends that a distinction is to be drawn between competitors and spectators for this purpose. It is common ground that the deceased was not a ticket-holder within the meaning of the notice, but, in my judgment, he was a spectator. The learned judge so held, and I think that he was right in doing so. The notice was, in my opinion, sufficiently explicit in its application to the deceased. I feel unable to accept the suggestion that the heading "Warning to the Public" should be read in a restrictive sense excluding competitors. Reading the document as a whole, I think there can be no doubt that it was addressed to all persons answering the descriptions of spectators or ticket-holders ... I think that he came on to the field in the afternoon on the terms contained in the notice displayed at the entrance to the ground.

The liability of the organisers of the meeting to visitors attending it for the purpose of taking part in some races and watching others was in my opinion limited in two respects. Such a visitor, in my judgment, as a competitor and when engaged in the role of a competitor, accepted all the risks inherent in the sport of jalopy racing. The organisers owed no duty to him to protect him against those risks. The express warning to the effect that competitors took part in the races at their own risk, which may have been attached to the signing-on sheet, is consequently, in my view, of little importance. As a spectator, such a visitor was, I think, subject to the condition set out in the warning notice. At the time when the accident occurred the deceased was, in my opinion, a spectator. The limitation on the liability of the organisers in these circumstances is to be found in the notice. The condition set out in the notice was that they were to be absolved from all liabilities arising out of accidents causing damage or personal injury howsoever caused. The use of the words "howsoever caused" makes clear that the absolution was intended to be of a general character. The effect of the condition must, in my judgment, amount to the exclusion of liability for accidents arising from the organisers' own negligence ...'

Comment

(1)   As to the extent to which it can be said that someone is truly a volunteer, see also *Burnett v BWB*, a case not directly on the 1957 Act, where it was suggested that such a term will not be applicable where P had no real choice but to enter the premises. There P was employed on a barge and had no real choice whether to enter D's dock where he was injured by a defective rope.

(2)   In *Ashdown v Samuel Williams*, decided on the common law, P was injured by the shunting of railway trucks. Notices purported to exclude liability; the Court of Appeal held that the notices were effective. The original position of the common law was that adopted in *London Graving Dock v Horton* and *Ashdown v Samuel Williams* to the effect that visitors may enter at their own risk even though unaware of the notice imposing the exclusion of liability. The question is, did the occupier take reasonable steps to tell visitors of the risk?

(2)   The Unfair Contract Terms Act 1977 was not in operation when the facts in *White v Blackmore* occurred. This Act provides that:

'1(1)   ... "negligence" means the breach ... (c) of the common duty of care imposed by the Occupiers' Liability Act 1957 ...

(3)   ... sections 2 to 7 apply ... only to business liability, that is liability for breach of obligations or duties arising ... (b) from the occupation of premises used for the business purposes of the occupier; and references to liability are to be read accordingly [but liability of an occupier of premises for breach of an obligation or duty towards a person obtaining access to

the premises for recreational or educational purposes, being liability for loss or damage suffered by reason of the dangerous state of the premises, is not a business liability of the occupier unless granting that person such access for the purposes concerned falls within the business purposes of the occupier].

...

2(1) A person cannot by reference to any contract term or to a notice given to persons generally or to particular persons exclude or restrict his liability for death or personal injury resulting from negligence.

(2) In the case of other loss or damage, a person cannot so exclude or restrict his liability for negligence except in so far as the term or notice satisfies the requirement of reasonableness.

(3) Where a contract term or notice purports to exclude or restrict liability for negligence a person's agreement to or awareness of it is not of itself to be taken as indicating his voluntary acceptance of any risk.

...

14 In this part of this Act–

"business" includes a profession and the activities of any government department or local or public authority; ...

"negligence" has the meaning given by section 1(1);

"notice" includes an announcement, whether or not in writing, and any other communication or pretended communication; and

"personal injury" includes any disease and any impairment of physical or mental condition.'

Section 11 amplifies the requirement of reasonableness.

The ability to restrict liability is widely restricted by the Act, which applies only business liability defined in s 1(3). Note that the test of business liability is the purpose for which the occupier uses the property and not the purpose of the visitor in visiting it.

The part of s 1(3) above in square brackets added by the Occupiers' Liability Act 1984 is aimed at the grant of access to premises for recreational/educational purposes where the granting of access is not part of the business purpose of the occupier. Therefore, a local authority granting access to a sports centre cannot exclude liability – access is part of their business which is recreational or educational. A farmer who grants access to a field for educational purposes would not incur business liability and may exclude liability. But, if the farmer charges, he or she may not. Where there is no business liability the common law rules apply to the scheme of the Occupiers' Liability Act 1957.

Note that s 2 does not extend to the duty owed to trespassers under the Occupiers' Liability Act 1984.

Occupiers' Liability Act 1984

1   Duty of occupier to persons other than his visitors

(1)   The rules enacted by this section shall have effect, in place of the rules of the common law, to determine–
(a)   whether any duty is owed by a person as occupier of premises to persons other than his visitors in respect of any risk of their suffering injury on the premises by reason of any danger due to the state of the premises or to things done or omitted to be done on them; and
(b)   if so, what that duty is.

(2)   For the purposes of this section, the persons who are to be treated respectively as an occupier of any premises (which, for those purposes, include any fixed or moveable structure) and as his visitors are–
(a)   any person who owes in relation to the premises the duty referred to in section 2 of the Occupiers' Liability Act 1957 (the common duty of care); and
(b)   those who are his visitors for the purposes of that duty.

(3)   An occupier of premises owes a duty to another (not being his visitor) in respect of any such risk is as referred to in subsection (1) above if–
(a)   he is aware of the danger or has reasonable grounds to believe that it exists;
(b)   he knows or has reasonable grounds to believe that the other is in the vicinity of the danger concerned or that he may come into the vicinity of the danger (in either case, whether the other has lawful authority for being in that vicinity or not); and
(c)   the risk is one against which, in all the circumstances of the case, he may reasonably be expected to offer the other some protection.

(4)   Where, by virtue of this section, an occupier of premises owes a duty to another in respect of such a risk the duty is to take such care as is reasonable in all the circumstances of the case to see that he does not suffer injury on the premises by reason of the danger concerned.

(5)   Any duty owed by virtue of this section in respect of a risk may, in an appropriate case, be discharged by taking such steps as are reasonable in all the circumstances of the case to give warning of the danger concerned or to discourage persons from incurring the risk.

(6)   No duty is owed by virtue of this section to any person in respect of risks willingly accepted as his by that person (the question whether a risk was so accepted to be decided on the same principles as in other cases in which one person owes a duty of care to another).

(6A)   At any time when the right conferred by section 2(1) of the Countryside and Rights of Way Act 2000 is exercisable in relation to land which is access land for the purposes of Part I of that Act, an occupier of the land owes (subject to subsection (6C) below) no duty by virtue of this section to any person in respect of–
(a)   a risk resulting from the existence of any natural feature of the landscape, or any river, stream, ditch or pond whether or not a natural feature, or
(b)   a risk of that person suffering injury when passing over, under or through any wall, fence or gate, except by proper use of the gate or of a stile.

(6B)   For the purposes of subsection (6A) above, any plant, shrub or tree, of whatever origin, is to be regarded as a natural feature of the landscape.

(6C)   Subsection (6A) does not prevent an occupier from owing a duty by virtue of this section in respect of any risk where the danger concerned is due to anything done by the occupier–
(a)   with the intention of creating that risk, or
(b)   being reckless as to whether that risk is created.

(7)   No duty is owed by virtue of this section to persons using the highway, and this section does not affect any duty owed to such persons.

(8)   Where a person owes a duty by virtue of this section, he does not, by reason of any breach of the duty, incur any liability in respect of any loss of or damage to property.

(9)   In this section–

'highway' means any part of a highway other than a ferry or waterway;

'injury' means anything resulting in death or personal injury, including any disease and any impairment of physical or mental condition; and

'movable structure' includes any vessel, vehicle or aircraft.

1A   Special considerations relating to access land

In determining whether any, and if so what, duty is owed by virtue of section 1 by an occupier of land at any time when the right conferred by section 2(1) of the Countryside and Rights of Way Act 2000 is exercisable in relation to the land, regard is to be had, in particular, to–
(a)   the fact that the existence of that right ought not to place an undue burden (whether financial or otherwise) on the occupier,

(b)   the importance of maintaining the character of the countryside, including features of historic, traditional or archaeological interest, and

(c)   any relevant guidance given under section 20 of that Act.

Comment

(1)   The common law duty to take such steps as common sense or common humanity would dictate, see *British Railways Board v Herrington*, has been replaced by the Occupiers' Liability Act 1984. The commonest form of non-visitor will be trespassers, but the Act also operates in respect of non-trespassers who were not visitors within the Occupiers' Liability Act 1957, such as those persons who enter land in circumstances outlined in s 1(4) of the 1957 Act, as amended, see p 370.

Where entry is under the Countryside and Rights of Way Act 2000, no duty will be owed under s 1 of the 1984 Act 'to any person in respect of a risk resulting from the existence of any natural feature of the landscape or any river, stream, ditch or pond whether or not a natural feature'. This seems to be the position in any event under the 1984 Act *vis-à-vis* non-visitors or visitors under the 1957 Act, see the approach to the 'state' of natural features in *Darby v National Trust, Cotton v Derbyshire Dales, Tomlinson v Congleton* and *Donoghue v Folkestone Properties*. However, a duty may be owed in respect of dangers presented by such non-natural features as buildings, machinery, wells or mine shafts, provided that the test for the existence of a duty in s 1 of the 1984 Act is satisfied. At what stage artificial features become natural features is open to speculation, e.g. ancient ridge and furrow farming techniques, mining, quarrying and damming have left indelible imprints on the landscape which, after the long passage of time, we might hesitate to call non-natural. As regards the references to water, there is ample scope for differentiating between those categories specified in the Act and canals, estuaries, mill-races and lakes. Was the lake in *Tomlinson* (see p 403) a natural feature? It was more than a pond. In any event, s 1A qualifies the judicial considerations for deciding whether a duty is owed and, if so, the content of the duty.

The exclusion of a duty in respect of natural features does not apply to persons entering land under an access agreement or order under the National Parks and Access to the Countryside Act 1949.

(2)   For the distinction between 'activity duty' and 'occupational duty' see p 376 and *Revill v Newbery*. Here, a defendant fired a shotgun in defence of his property and injured a burglar. Neill J in the Court of Appeal referred to the uncertainty surrounding both the 1957 Act and the 1984 Act and observed that:

'... the better view is that the duty imposed by s 1 of the 1984 Act is a duty imposed on an occupier as occupier. Section 1 is concerned with the safety of the premises and with dangers due to things done or omitted to be done on the premises. In considering whether [the occupier] is liable ... the fact that he was an occupier is irrelevant.'

Evans LJ thought that it was unnecessary to decide the point and expressed no concluded view.

(3)   Only injury to the person is covered by the 1984 Act; loss of or damage to property is not covered by the 1984 Act. On the other hand, the 1957 Act provides that both fall within the duty in that Act.

(4)   The occupier may perform the duty by taking reasonable steps to warn, s 1(5) of the 1984 Act. Thus, a warning notice may be sufficient to discharge the duty. Section 1(5) includes reasonable steps to discourage, e.g. fencing, barbed wire. A warning will often be insufficient *vis-à-vis* children but an obstacle may be more effective.

(5)   The 1984 Act does not contain a provision similar to that in the 1957 Act for the exclusion of liability by a disclaimer notice. Opinion varies as to whether such a notice would be effective; if it were possible to exclude liability under the Act, the Unfair Contract Terms Act 1977 would not apply to the notice since that Act refers only to common law duties to take reasonable care and the statutory duty under the 1957 Act.

An anomaly would arise if it were possible to exclude liability under the 1957 Act but not under the 1984 Act, in that a visitor might be in a worse position than a trespasser. Of course, difficulties would still remain over the entry to the premises of lawful non-visitors. Another way the problem might arise is if A is permitted to enter a particular part of B's property subject to a valid exclusion term, but then goes into a different part of B's premises and is injured there. The role of exclusion notices may become important where rights of access under the Countryside and Rights of Way Act 2000 are granted.

(6)   The defence of *volenti non fit injuria* is preserved by s 1(6) of the 1984 Act. It may be enough to demonstrate knowledge of risk coupled with trespassory entry, but contrast lawful non-visitors where entry would not signify *volens*.

(7)   The aspects of the test in s 1(3)(a) and (b)of the 1984 Act are largely subjective but s 1(3)(c) is objectively assessed. The content of the duty is described in s 1(4), it is objective and does not depend on the skill or resources of the occupier but depends on all the circumstances.

Tomlinson v Congleton Borough Council and another
[2003] 3 All ER 1022 House of Lords

The defendant council was the occupier of a country park in which there was a disused sand quarry which had been converted into a lake and around which there were beaches for the public to use. People would paddle in the water and the public were allowed access to the lake for canoeing and windsurfing. Swimming was prohibited and signs were erected to this effect; park wardens often had to deal with youngsters who were swimming. Over a period of years the council became concerned at the limited effect that the notices were having and the number of swimming-related incidents. The council concluded that measures to reduce the temptation to swim would have to be put in place, e.g. the creation of reed beds to hinder access to the water. A decision was taken to implement the deterrent scheme but there were budgetary considerations and the work was delayed. During the delay the claimant was injured. For many years the claimant had been in the habit of going to the lake with friends and diving and swimming as part of this. On this occasion, he ran into the water up to his knees and then dived forwards. His head hit the bottom and he was rendered tetraplegic.

The House of Lords held that for the purposes of the Occupiers' Liability Act 1984, s 1(1)(a) there was no risk of injury to non-visitors by reason of danger due to the state of the premises or to things done or omitted to be done on the premises. The House of Lords then went on to ask whether, had there been such a risk of danger, there would have been a duty of care under s 1(3). On this point, *obiter*, the House of Lords concluded that despite the reasonably foreseeable risk of injury, other factors had to be brought into balance. Of these the most important were (a) the free will of the claimant in deciding to engage in hazardous activities and (b) the social value of the activities which steps to eradicate swimming would have involved. By comparison with the Occupiers' Liability Act 1957, since there would have been no duty under that Act to warn of obvious dangers, so too under the Occupiers' Liability Act 1984 it would not be reasonable to expect the occupier to offer protection to a non-visitor.

Lord Hoffmann:

'11.   The case has therefore proceeded upon a concession that the relevant duty, if any, is that to a trespasser under section 1(4) of the 1984 Act and not to a lawful visitor under section 2(2) of the 1957 Act. On one analysis, this is a rather odd hypothesis. Mr Tomlinson's complaint is that he should have been prevented or discouraged from going into the water, that is to say, from turning himself into a trespasser. Logically, it can be said, that duty must have been owed to him (if at all) while he was still a lawful visitor. Once he had become a trespasser, it could not have meaningful effect. In the Court of Appeal, Longmore LJ was puzzled by this paradox ...

12.   In the later case of *Donoghue v Folkestone Properties Ltd* Lord Phillips of Worth Matravers MR said that he shared these reservations about the concession ...

13.   As a matter of logic, I see the force of these observations. But I have nevertheless come to the conclusion that the concession was rightly made. The

duty under the 1984 Act was intended to be a lesser duty, as to both incidence and scope, than the duty to a lawful visitor under the 1957 Act. That was because Parliament recognised that it would often be unduly burdensome to require landowners to take steps to protect the safety of people who came upon their land without invitation or permission. They should not ordinarily be able to force duties upon unwilling hosts. In the application of that principle, I can see no difference between a person who comes upon land without permission and one who, having come with permission, does something which he has not been given permission to do. In both cases, the entrant would be imposing upon the landowner a duty of care which he has not expressly or impliedly accepted. The 1984 Act provides that even in such cases a duty may exist, based simply upon occupation of land and knowledge or foresight that unauthorised persons may come upon the land or authorised persons may use it for unauthorised purposes. But that duty is rarer and different in quality from the duty which arises from express or implied invitation or permission to come upon the land and use it.

14. In addition, I think that the concession is supported by the high authority of Lord Atkin in *Hillen v ICI (Alkali) Ltd*. There too, it could be said that the stevedores' complaint was that they should have been warned not to go upon the hatch cover and that logically this duty was owed to them, if at all, when they were lawfully on the barge.

15. I would certainly agree with Longmore LJ that the incidence and content of the duty should not depend on the precise moment at which Mr Tomlinson crossed the line between the status of lawful visitor and that of trespasser. But there is no dispute that the act in respect of which Mr Tomlinson says that he was owed a duty, namely, diving into the water, was to his knowledge prohibited by the terms upon which he had been admitted to the Park. It is, I think, for this reason that the Council owed him no duty under the 1957 Act and that the incidence and content of any duty they may have owed was governed by the 1984 Act. But I shall later return to the question of whether it would have made any difference if swimming had not been prohibited and the 1957 Act had applied ...

[Lord Hoffmann examined the history of the lake and continued:]

25. The conditions in section 1(3) of the 1984 Act determine whether or not a duty is owed to "another" in respect of "any such risk as is referred to in subsection (1)". Two conclusions follow from this language. First, the risks in respect of which the Act imposes a duty are limited to those mentioned in subsection (1)(a) – risks of injury "by reason of any danger due to the state of the premises or to things done or omitted to be done on them." The Act is not concerned with risks due to anything else. Secondly, the conditions have to be satisfied in respect of the claimant as "another"; that is to say, in respect of a class of persons which includes him and a description of risk which includes that which caused his injury.

A DANGER "DUE TO THE STATE OF THE PREMISES"

26.   The first question, therefore, is whether there was a risk within the scope of the statute; a danger "due to the state of the premises or to things done or omitted to be done on them". The judge found that there was "nothing about the mere at Brereton Heath which made it any more dangerous than any other ordinary stretch of open water in England". There was nothing special about its configuration; there were no hidden dangers. It was shallow in some places and deep in others, but that is the nature of lakes. Nor was the Council doing or permitting anything to be done which created a danger to persons who came to the lake. No power boats or jet skis threatened the safety of either lawful windsurfers or unlawful swimmers. So the Council submits that there was no danger attributable to the state of premises or things done or omitted on them. In *Donoghue v Folkestone Properties Ltd* Lord Phillips of Worth Matravers MR expressed the same opinion. He said that he had been unable to identify the "state of the premises" which carried with it the risk of the injury suffered by Mr Tomlinson:

"It seems to me that Mr Tomlinson suffered his injury because he chose to indulge in an activity which had inherent dangers, not because the premises were in a dangerous state."

27.   In making this comment, the Master of the Rolls was identifying a point which is in my opinion central to this appeal. It is relevant at a number of points in the analysis of the duties under the 1957 and 1984 Acts. Mr Tomlinson was a person of full capacity who voluntarily and without any pressure or inducement engaged in an activity which had inherent risk. The risk was that he might not execute his dive properly and so sustain injury. Likewise, a person who goes mountaineering incurs the risk that he might stumble or misjudge where to put his weight. In neither case can the risk be attributed to the state of the premises. Otherwise any premises can be said to be dangerous to someone who chooses to use them for some dangerous activity. In the present case, Mr Tomlinson knew the lake well and even if he had not, the judge's finding was that it contained no dangers which one would not have expected. So the only risk arose out of what he chose to do and not out of the state of the premises.

28.   Mr Braithwaite was inclined to accept the difficulty of establishing that the risk was due to the state of the premises. He therefore contended that it was due to "things done or omitted to be done" on the premises. When asked what these might be, he said that they consisted in the attraction of the lake and the Council's inadequate attempts to keep people out of the water. The Council, he said, were "luring people into a deathtrap". Ward LJ said that the water was "a siren call strong enough to turn stout men's minds". In my opinion this is gross hyperbole. The trouble with the island of the Sirens was not the state of the premises. It was that the Sirens held mariners spellbound until they died of hunger. The beach, give or take a fringe of human bones, was an ordinary Mediterranean beach. If Odysseus had gone ashore and accidentally drowned himself having a swim, Penelope would

have had no action against the Sirens for luring him there with their songs. Likewise in this case, the water was perfectly safe for all normal activities. In my opinion "things done or omitted to be done" means activities or the lack of precautions which cause risk, like allowing speedboats among the swimmers. It is a mere circularity to say that a failure to stop people getting into the water was an omission which gave rise to a duty to take steps to stop people from getting into the water.

29. It follows that in my opinion, there was no risk to Mr Tomlinson due to the state of the premises or anything done or omitted upon the premises. That means that there was no risk of a kind which gave rise to a duty under the 1957 or 1984 Acts. I shall nevertheless go on to consider the matter on the assumption that there was.

THE CONDITIONS FOR THE EXISTENCE OF A DUTY

(i) Knowledge or foresight of the danger

30. Section 1(3) has three conditions which must be satisfied. First, under paragraph (a), the occupier must be aware of the danger or have reasonable grounds to believe that it exists. For this purpose, it is necessary to say what the relevant danger was. The judge thought it was the risk of suffering an injury through diving and said that the Council was aware of this danger because two men had suffered minor head injuries from diving in May 1992. In the Court of Appeal, Ward LJ described the relevant risk much more broadly. He regarded all the swimming incidents as indicative of the Council's knowledge that a danger existed. I am inclined to think that this is too wide a description. The risk of injury from diving off the beach was in my opinion different from the risk of drowning in the deep water. For example, the Council might have fenced off the deep water or marked it with buoys and left people to paddle in the shallows. That would have reduced the risk of drowning but would not have prevented the injury to Mr Tomlinson ...I accept that the Council must have known that there was a possibility that some boisterous teenager would injure himself by horseplay in the shallows and I would not disturb the concurrent findings that this was sufficient to satisfy paragraph (a). But the chances of such an accident were small. I shall return later, in connection with condition (c), to the relevance of where the risk comes on the scale of probability.

(ii) Knowledge or foresight of the presence of the trespasser

31. Once it is found that the risk of a swimmer injuring himself by diving was something of which the Council knew or which they had reasonable grounds to believe to exist, paragraph (b) presents no difficulty. The Council plainly knew that swimmers came to the lake and Mr Tomlinson fell within that class.

(iii) Reasonable to expect protection

32.   That leaves paragraph (c). Was the risk one against which the Council might reasonably be expected to offer the claimant some protection? ... [Lord Hoffmann outlined the decision of the Judge and of the Court of Appeal on this point, and continued]

THE BALANCE OF RISK, GRAVITY OF INJURY, COST AND SOCIAL VALUE

34.   My Lords, the majority of the Court of Appeal appear to have proceeded on the basis that if there was a foreseeable risk of serious injury, the Council was under a duty to do what was necessary to prevent it. But this in my opinion is an oversimplification. Even in the case of the duty owed to a lawful visitor under section 2(2) of the 1957 Act and even if the risk had been attributable to the state of the premises rather than the acts of Mr Tomlinson, the question of what amounts to "such care as in all the circumstances of the case is reasonable" depends upon assessing, as in the case of common law negligence, not only the likelihood that someone may be injured and the seriousness of the injury which may occur, but also the social value of the activity which gives rise to the risk and the cost of preventative measures. These factors have to be balanced against each other.

35.   For example, in *Overseas Tankship (UK) Ltd v Miller Steamship Pty Ltd (The Wagon Mound (No. 2))* there was no social value or cost saving in the defendant's activity. Lord Reid said:

"In the present case there was no justification whatever for discharging the oil into Sydney Harbour. Not only was it an offence to do so, but it involved considerable loss financially. If the ship's engineer had thought about the matter, there could have been no question of balancing the advantages and disadvantages. From every point of view it was both his duty and his interest to stop the discharge immediately."

36.   So the defendants were held liable for damage which was only a very remote possibility. Similarly in *Jolley v Sutton London B.C.* there was no social value or cost saving to the Council in creating a risk by leaving a derelict boat lying about. It was something which they ought to have removed whether it created a risk of injury or not. So they were held liable for an injury which, though foreseeable, was not particularly likely. On the other hand, in *The Wagon Mound (No. 2)* Lord Reid drew a contrast with *Bolton v Stone* in which the House of Lords held that it was not negligent for a cricket club to do nothing about the risk of someone being injured by a cricket ball hit out of the ground. The difference was that the cricket club were carrying on a lawful and socially useful activity and would have had to stop playing cricket at that ground.

37.   This is the kind of balance which has to be struck even in a situation in which it is clearly fair, just and reasonable that there should in principle be a duty of care

or in which Parliament, as in the 1957 Act, has decreed that there should be. And it may lead to the conclusion that even though injury is foreseeable, as it was in Bolton v Stone, it is still in all the circumstances reasonable to do nothing about it.

THE 1957 AND 1984 ACTS CONTRASTED

38.   In the case of the 1984 Act, there is the additional consideration that unless in all the circumstances it is reasonable to expect the occupier to do something, that is to say, to "offer the other some protection", there is no duty at all. One may ask what difference there is between the case in which the claimant is a lawful visitor and there is in principle a duty under the 1957 Act but on the particular facts no duty to do anything, and the case in which he is a trespasser and there is on the particular facts no duty under the 1984 Act. Of course in such a case the result is the same. But Parliament has made it clear that in the case of a lawful visitor, one starts from the assumption that there is a duty whereas in the case of a trespasser one starts from the assumption that there is none.

THE BALANCE UNDER THE 1957 ACT

39.   My Lords, it will in the circumstances be convenient to consider first the question of what the position would have been if Mr Tomlinson had been a lawful visitor owed a duty under section 2(2) of the 1957 Act. Assume, therefore, that there had been no prohibition on swimming. What was the risk of serious injury? To some extent this depends upon what one regards as the relevant risk. As I have mentioned, the judge thought it was the risk of injury through diving while the Court of Appeal thought it was any kind of injury which could happen to people in the water. Although, as I have said, I am inclined to agree with the judge, I do not want to put the basis of my decision too narrowly. So I accept that we are concerned with the steps, if any, which should have been taken to prevent any kind of water accident. According to the Royal Society for the Prevention of Accidents, about 450 people drown while swimming in the United Kingdom every year (see *Darby v National Trust*). About 25–35 break their necks diving and no doubt others sustain less serious injuries. So there is obviously some degree of risk in swimming and diving, as there is in climbing, cycling, fell walking and many other such activities.

40.   I turn then to the cost of taking preventative measures. Ward LJ described it (£5,000) as "not excessive". Perhaps it was not, although the outlay has to be seen in the context of the other items (rated "essential" and "highly desirable") in the Borough Council budget which had taken precedence over the destruction of the beaches for the previous two years.

41.   I do not however regard the financial cost as a significant item in the balancing exercise which the court has to undertake. There are two other related considerations which are far more important. The first is the social value of the activities which would have to be prohibited in order to reduce or eliminate the risk from

swimming. And the second is the question of whether the Council should be entitled to allow people of full capacity to decide for themselves whether to take the risk.

42.   The Court of Appeal made no reference at all to the social value of the activities which were to be prohibited. The majority of people who went to the beaches to sunbathe, paddle and play with their children were enjoying themselves in a way which gave them pleasure and caused no risk to themselves or anyone else. This must be something to be taken into account in deciding whether it was reasonable to expect the Council to destroy the beaches.

43.   I have the impression that the Court of Appeal felt able to brush these matters aside because the Council had already decided to do the work. But they were held liable for having failed to do so before Mr Tomlinson's accident and the question is therefore whether they were under a legal duty to do so. Ward LJ placed much emphasis upon the fact that the Council had decided to destroy the beaches and that its officers thought that this was necessary to avoid being held liable for an accident to a swimmer. But the fact that the Council's safety officers thought that the work was necessary does not show that there was a legal duty to do it. In *Darby v National Trust* the claimant's husband was tragically drowned while swimming in a pond on the National Trust estate at Hardwick Hall. Miss Rebecca Kirkwood, the Water and Leisure Safety Consultant to the Royal Society for the Prevention of Accidents, gave uncontradicted evidence, which the judge accepted, that the pond was unsuitable for swimming because it was deep in the middle and the edges were uneven. The National Trust should have made it clear that swimming in the pond was not allowed and taken steps to enforce the prohibition. But May LJ said robustly that it was for the court, not Miss Kirkwood, to decide whether the Trust was under a legal duty to take such steps. There was no duty because the risks from swimming in the pond were perfectly obvious.

FREE WILL

44.   The second consideration, namely the question of whether people should accept responsibility for the risks they choose to run, is the point made by Lord Phillips of Worth Matravers MR in *Donoghue v Folkestone Properties Ltd* and which I said was central to this appeal. Mr Tomlinson was freely and voluntarily undertaking an activity which inherently involved some risk. By contrast, Miss Bessie Stone, to whom the House of Lords held that no duty was owed, was innocently standing on the pavement outside her garden gate at 10 Beckenham Road, Cheetham when she was struck by a ball hit for 6 out of the Cheetham Cricket Club ground. She was certainly not engaging in any activity which involved an inherent risk of such injury. So compared with *Bolton v Stone*, this is an *a fortiori* case.

45.   I think it will be extremely rare for an occupier of land to be under a duty to prevent people from taking risks which are inherent in the activities they freely

choose to undertake upon the land. If people want to climb mountains, go hang gliding or swim or dive in ponds or lakes, that is their affair. Of course the landowner may for his own reasons wish to prohibit such activities. He may think that they are a danger or inconvenience to himself or others. Or he may take a paternalist view and prefer people not to undertake risky activities on his land. He is entitled to impose such conditions, as the Council did by prohibiting swimming. But the law does not require him to do so.

46. My Lords, as will be clear from what I have just said, I think that there is an important question of freedom at stake. It is unjust that the harmless recreation of responsible parents and children with buckets and spades on the beaches should be prohibited in order to comply with what is thought to be a legal duty to safeguard irresponsible visitors against dangers which are perfectly obvious. The fact that such people take no notice of warnings cannot create a duty to take other steps to protect them. I find it difficult to express with appropriate moderation my disagreement with the proposition of Sedley LJ (at para. 45) that it is "only where the risk is so obvious that the occupier can safely assume that nobody will take it that there will be no liability". A duty to protect against obvious risks or self-inflicted harm exists only in cases in which there is no genuine and informed choice, or in the case of employees, or some lack of capacity, such as the inability of children to recognise danger (*British Railways Board v Herrington*) or the despair of prisoners which may lead them to inflict injury on themselves (*Reeves v Commissioner of Police*).

47. It is of course understandable that organisations like the Royal Society for the Prevention of Accidents should favour policies which require people to be prevented from taking risks. Their function is to prevent accidents and that is one way of doing so. But they do not have to consider the cost, not only in money but also in deprivation of liberty, which such restrictions entail. The courts will naturally respect the technical expertise of such organisations in drawing attention to what can be done to prevent accidents. But the balance between risk on the one hand and individual autonomy on the other is not a matter of expert opinion. It is a judgment which the courts must make and which in England reflects the individualist values of the common law.

48. As for the Council officers, they were obviously motivated by the view that it was necessary to take defensive measures to prevent the Council from being held liable to pay compensation. The Borough Leisure Officer said that he regretted the need to destroy the beaches but saw no alternative if the Council was not to be held liable for an accident to a swimmer. So this appeal gives your Lordships the opportunity to say clearly that local authorities and other occupiers of land are ordinarily under no duty to incur such social and financial costs to protect a minority (or even a majority) against obvious dangers. On the other hand, if the decision of the Court of Appeal were left standing, every such occupier would feel obliged to take similar defensive measures. Sedley LJ was able to say that if the logic

of the Court of Appeal's decision was that other public lakes and ponds required similar precautions, "so be it". But I cannot view this prospect with the same equanimity. In my opinion it would damage the quality of many people's lives.

49.   In the particular case of diving injuries, there is little evidence that such defensive measures have had much effect. Dr Penny, the Council's expert, said that over the past decade there had been little change in the rate of serious diving accidents. Each year, as I have mentioned, there are about 25–35 fracture-dislocations of the neck. Almost all those affected are males and their average age is consistently around 25 years. In spite of greatly increased safety measures, particularly in swimming pools, the numbers (when Dr Penny gave evidence) had remained the same for a decade:

> "This is probably because of the sudden, unpredictable nature of these dangerous dives, undertaken mostly by boisterous young men ... hence the common description the 'Macho Male Diving Syndrome'."

50.   My Lords, for these reasons I consider that even if swimming had not been prohibited and the Council had owed a duty under section 2(2) of the 1957 Act, that duty would not have required them to take any steps to prevent Mr Tomlinson from diving or warning him against dangers which were perfectly obvious. If that is the case, then plainly there can have been no duty under the 1984 Act. The risk was not one against which he was entitled under section 1(3)(c) to protection.'

Comment

(1)   The House of Lords clearly felt that it was creating an antidote to a popular culture of litigation in instances where something bad happens. Lord Hobhouse observed:

> '81.   ... it is not, and should never be, the policy of the law to require the protection of the foolhardy or reckless few to deprive, or interfere with, the enjoyment by the remainder of society of the liberties and amenities to which they are rightly entitled. Does the law require that all trees be cut down because some youths may climb them and fall? Does the law require the coast line and other beauty spots to be lined with warning notices? Does the law require that attractive water side picnic spots be destroyed because of a few foolhardy individuals who choose to ignore warning notices and indulge in activities dangerous only to themselves? The answer to all these questions is, of course, no. But this is the road down which your Lordships, like other courts before, have been invited to travel and which the councils in the present case found so inviting. In truth, the arguments for the claimant have involved an attack upon the liberties of the citizen which should not be countenanced. They attack the liberty of the individual to engage in dangerous, but otherwise harmless, pastimes at

his own risk and the liberty of citizens as a whole fully to enjoy the variety and quality of the landscape of this country. The pursuit of an unrestrained culture of blame and compensation has many evil consequences and one is certainly the interference with the liberty of the citizen.'

(2) There was some disagreement about whether the concession that the Occupiers' Liability Act 1984 applied was correctly made. Lord Scott thought that it was the Occupiers' Liability Act 1957 which applied, since whatever the claimant had done could not amount to swimming. However, all their Lordships agreed that whether the 1984 Act or the 1957 Act applied made no difference to the outcome of the case.

(3) Lord Hutton thought that there was a risk due to the state of the premises, in this case the murky water which obscured the bottom. But he too considered strongly that the risk of the claimant striking his head when diving was not one against which the defendants might reasonably have been expected to offer some protection. As to state of the premises see also *Donoghue v Folkestone Properties*, p 416.

(4) The correct identification of the risk also arose in *Ratcliff v McConnell*, the first major exploration of the application of the Occupiers' Liability Act 1984. Late one night, and contrary to the rules of the college, the plaintiff, a 19-year-old college student, and two friends entered the defendant college's swimming pool as trespassers by climbing over a high gate. The plaintiff knew that he was not permitted to be there and that diving into swimming pools could be dangerous, and he did not know the depth of water in that particular pool. He intended to execute a running dive but probably dived more sharply than intended. He struck his head on the bottom of the pool and was seriously injured. The Court of Appeal held that (1) the particular risk or danger in the case was that someone diving into the pool where there was insufficient depth of water could suffer injury but (2) such danger was obvious to adults and to children who were old enough to learn to dive, therefore there was no duty to warn of that particular risk or danger, and (3) in any event, the plaintiff had been aware of the risk and had voluntarily accepted it, therefore no duty of care arose. Stuart-Smith LJ also observed that had the relevant risk been that children would come into close proximity to the pool then, by fencing off the pool, the defendants had offered protection against that.

In the light of both *Tomlinson v Congleton* and *Ratcliff v McConnell* the legal obstacles which beset the path of the adult claimant under the 1984 Act will prove very difficult to overcome, and clambering over, through or round any barrier will be tantamount to *volenti non fit injuria*. Further, use of a suitable warning sign will almost certainly lead to a finding that any duty has been discharged and that *volenti* will be made out. Of course, where there are obvious dangers then it would not be appropriate for a duty to arise, see cases at comment (8) below.

(5)   In *White v St Albans City Council*, in the dark the plaintiff took a short cut through a council's premises and suffered injury when he fell while crossing a narrow concrete 'bridge' (which was fenced off) into an adjoining car-park. The bridge and the gap it spanned were regarded as the 'danger' and the court held that the council were aware of it. The issue was whether the judge had been correct in his finding that the defendant council had not had reasonable grounds to believe that anyone would use that route as a short cut and so come into the vicinity of the danger. The council had provided allegedly ineffective barriers around their site. The plaintiff said that once it was established that precautions had been taken to guard against trespassers entering the land, then the inference should be drawn that the council must have had reasonable grounds to believe that someone was likely to come into the vicinity of the danger. This approach was rejected by the Court of Appeal which observed that the circumstances of a private site with a wooden fence at the front, a wire fence at the rear and a barrier at the front, did not permit a court to infer knowledge of trespassers. There was no evidence that anyone had previously used the site as a short cut to the knowledge of the occupier, nor was there any evidence from which the occupier ought to have known that such short cuts were occurring.

(6)   In *Ward v Norweb plc*, the plaintiff, aged 15, gained access to a substation which was surrounded by an eight-foot-high chain wire fence and two gates with high-security padlocks. There were also prominent notices as to the danger. The judge formed the view that the plaintiff had entered with a view to theft, and although he was illiterate he knew that electricity was dangerous and that he ought not to have been there. The Court of Appeal proceeded on the basis that a duty of care existed and that all aspects of the Occupiers' Liability Act 1984, s 1(3) were satisfied. In considering breach of duty, the Court of Appeal thought that the judge had required too high a standard of care.

In assessing the care which ought to have been taken the judge had regard to: (1) the proximity of the gypsy camp from which the plaintiff had come; (2) the enormity of the danger posed by the high voltage; (3) the valuable items on the site, i.e. copper wire; (4) the high incidence of burglary in the area; and (5) the recent history of the substation which showed break-ins at the adjoining compound and damage to the locks on the transformer compound. He thought that there ought to have been better locks and that the gates should have had alarms fitted. Accordingly there was a breach of duty. The Court of Appeal regarded the judge as having set too high a standard and that he had effectively sought to guarantee safety rather than ensure reasonable protection as demanded by the Act.

For cases involving trespassers and pylons and liability under the Electricity Supply Regulations 1988, see *Swift v Yorkshire Electricity Group plc* where the judge found the defendant not liable under the Occupiers' Liability Act 1984 but liable for breach of the Regulations (then in their 1937 form), and *Adams v Southern Electricity Board*.

(7) One issue left in doubt after *White v St Albans City Council* was whether the test in s 1(3)(b) of the 1984 Act was objective or whether it was to be satisfied on the basis of the actual knowledge and understanding of the occupier or on the constructive knowledge of the occupier, i.e. that the occupier ought to have been aware of the presence or likely presence of the non-visitor. In *White v St Albans City Council* the Court of Appeal divided two-to-one on the point, although even applying the different tests the same result negativing any duty was reached.

In *Swain v Puri* the Court of Appeal regarded the matter as requiring either actual knowledge of the fact of trespassers coming into the vicinity of the danger or knowledge of facts from which a reasonable person would deduce that trespassers were or would be likely to come into the vicinity of the danger. This approach was adopted, bearing in mind the similar approach of Lord Diplock when considering the duty enunciated in *British Railways Board v Herrington*. The court rejected the suggestion that the 1984 Act meant that a relevant duty would be owed if an occupier ought to know that trespassers would be likely to come into the vicinity of the danger. The Court of Appeal commented that occupiers who deliberately shut their eyes to facts, by wilful disregard rather than lack of care, should be regarded as having actual knowledge of such facts, either as would support actual knowledge that trespassers were coming into the vicinity of the danger or from which a reasonable person would realise that this was so.

(8) Several cases under the Occupiers' Liability Act 1957 have addressed the issue of obvious dangers. *Darby v National Trust* concerned a non-trespassing adult swimmer where the court held that the risk of swimming in a pond was so obvious as not to require a notice, and this was so whether the risk was from the state of the bottom of the pond or from the coldness of the water. Compare *Rhind v Astbury Water Park Ltd* where the claimant had run into water and dived forwards to recover his football. Even though swimming was prohibited he was treated as a visitor, but the risk of injury through diving was obvious and there was no duty to warn. As regards the finding that he was a visitor, a court may be unlikely to take this view following the approach in *Tomlinson v Congleton*, but this is unlikely to have any impact on the outcome.

In *Staples v West Dorset District Council* the plaintiff was walking at Lyme Regis on the Cobb (a massive stone breakwater popular with tourists and holidaymakers) when he slipped on the wet stone surface of the Cobb. The Court of Appeal held that the danger was obvious and that there was no duty under the 1957 Act to warn of a danger which was obvious. Kennedy LJ made it clear that the defendant owes a duty to the particular plaintiff as an individual 'so that it can only be said that there was a duty to warn if without a warning the visitor in question would have been unaware of the nature and extent of the risk'. Also, later he asks 'whether there was any relevant danger of which ... this plaintiff needed to be warned'. Significantly in that case the plaintiff was described as an experienced visitor and on his own evidence had been able to evaluate the dangers posed by the wet and algae-covered sloping surface of the Cobb.

In *Cotton v Derbyshire Dales DC* the plaintiff strayed from a path and was injured when he fell off a steep cliff. The Court of Appeal had held that the plaintiff's claim failed because there was no general duty on an occupier to warn visitors of obvious dangers, in this case the danger posed by a steep slope leading to a cliff edge.

(9)   In *Ratcliff v McConnell* Stuart-Smith LJ made the point that:

'The duty, if any, is owed to the individual trespasser, though he may be a member of a class that the occupier knows or has reasonable grounds to believe is in the vicinity of the danger.'

This point can be seen clearly in *Donoghue v Folkestone Properties Ltd*. There, the claimant dived from a slipway into a harbour, struck his head on a submerged pile, broke his neck and was rendered tetraplegic. Approving *White v St Alban's City Council*, the Court of Appeal emphasised that for the purposes of s 1(3)(b) of the 1984 Act it would have to be shown that the defendant had or ought reasonably to have foreseen the presence of the trespassing claimant in proximity to the danger under the circumstances which applied at the time the accident had in fact happened. This could be defined with a certain degree of particularity. The defendant here could not reasonably have foreseen that the claimant would have gone swimming from a slipway in Folkestone harbour in the depths of winter in the middle of the night, even though he had been one of a group the defendant would have had in mind at other times of the year. The council accepted that it owed a duty of care to those who, as it was well aware, swam and dived in the vicinity of the slipway in the summer. In the light of *Tomlinson*, liability might not follow even if such a duty were to be owed, but the piling grid (submerged when the tide was in) might, on the facts, have been something of which a warning might have been expected.

As to the meaning of 'the state of the premises' Lord Phillips MR said:

'[35]   There are some features of land that are not inherently dangerous but which may tempt a person on the land to indulge in an activity which carries a risk of injury. Such activities include cliff climbing, mountaineering, skiing, and hang-gliding by way of example. It does not seem to me that a person carrying on such an activity can ascribe to the "state of the premises" an injury sustained as a result of a mishap in the course of carrying on the activity – provided of course that the mishap is not caused by an unusual or latent feature of the landscape. I do not consider that the 1984 Act imposes any duty on an occupier to protect a trespasser from making use of a particular feature of the premises in order to carry on an activity simply because that activity carries with it an inherent risk of injury.

[36]   This brings me to swimming and diving. An expanse of water, be it a lake, pond, river or the sea, does not normally pose any danger to a person on land. If a trespasser deliberately enters the water to swim, then the trespasser chooses to indulge in an activity which carries a degree of inherent risk. If the trespasser gets cramp or becomes exhausted and drowns, it cannot properly be said that this tragedy is attributable to the "state of the premises". Where a trespasser suffers injury as a result of diving onto the bottom, or onto an obstruction that stands proud of the bottom, the position is less simple.

[37]   If a trespasser jumps down a bank and injures himself by contact with the ground, his injury cannot properly be said to be attributable to the "state of the premises". If the bank is on the edge of a lake, and the ground is beneath the water, I still have difficulty in seeing how his injury can be said to be attributable to the "state of the premises". If, however, there is a concealed obstruction beneath what appears to be deep water, it then becomes arguable that an injury suffered by a trespasser who dives upon it is attributable, in part, to the "state of the premises". It will not, of course, necessarily follow that the occupier will be liable under the 1984 Act. This will depend upon the application of the other criteria laid down by the Act.'

(10)   In the *Donoghue* case Brooke LJ observed that in answering the question whether the risk is one against which, in all the circumstances of the case, an occupier might reasonably be expected to offer a trespasser some protection, courts should refer to paragraph 28 of the 1976 Law Commission Report. This made it clear that a clear distinction will be drawn between a visitor and a trespasser, and between an adult and a child trespasser.

(11)   Once it is decided that a duty of care can arise, then the next step will be to decide on the content of the duty. The Law Commission Report, paragraph 29 suggested that: 'In the range of circumstances to which the courts will have regard in deciding whether the occupier has acted reasonably, the application of the duty towards trespassers may again be expected to differ markedly from the common duty of care.' It might also be added that it will vary according to the age of the non-visitor.

CHAPTER 8

Product liability

This topic is of importance not the least because of the difficulties encountered by those who have tried to bring actions in negligence against multinational companies for significant injuries allegedly caused by defective products. The position prior to 1932 was in some doubt, but it appears likely that there was no scope for recovery outside a strict contractual relationship. The classic statement of the duty owed by a manufacturer is that of Lord Atkin in *Donoghue v Stevenson*:

> '... a manufacturer of products, which he sells in such a form as to show that he intends them to reach the ultimate consumer in the form in which they left him with no reasonable possibility of intermediate examination, and with the knowledge that the absence of reasonable care in the preparation or putting up of the product will result in an injury to the consumer's life or property, owes a duty to the consumer to take that reasonable care.'

It is also worthwhile noting the words of Lord Thankerton:

> 'The present case is that of a manufacturer and a consumer, with whom he has no contractual relation, of an article which the manufacturer did not know to be dangerous, and, unless the consumer can establish a special relationship with the manufacturer, it is clear, in my opinion, that neither the law of Scotland nor the law of England will hold that the manufacturer has any duty towards the consumer to exercise diligence ...

> The special circumstances from which the appellant claims that such a relationship of duty should be inferred may, I think, be stated thus – namely, that the respondent, in placing his manufactured article of drink upon the market, has intentionally so excluded interference with, or examination of, the article by any intermediate handler of the goods between himself and the consumer that he has, of his own accord,

brought himself into direct relationship with the consumer, with the result that the consumer is entitled to rely upon the exercise of diligence by the manufacturer to secure that the article shall not be harmful to the consumer.'

In tort, where harm is caused by a defective product, the focus is not the fact of the defect but the reason for the defect and the harm caused by it. *Donoghue v Stevenson* side-stepped privity of contract and provided a new remedy, but one dependent on fault. This may occasionally lead to odd results; see *Daniels & Daniels v White*, p 423. The difficulties in establishing breach of duty were sometimes overstated; nonetheless Parliament provided an easier route to a remedy in the form of the Consumer Protection Act 1987. The impetus for this legislative activity was a Directive from the European Community. The Act may assist in resolving some difficulties, but since the greatest burden was proof of causation, which remains, it is still to be seen how effective a remedy it will provide. Equally, the Act does not protect business consumers and the principles in *Donoghue v Stevenson* continue to have widespread relevance.

Grant v Australian Knitting Mills Ltd
[1935] All ER Rep 209 Privy Council

The plaintiff purchased two pairs of woollen long-johns manufactured by the defendant. Chemicals used in the manufacturing process were subject to further processes to remove them. As a result of excess of sulphite in the ankle ends of the underwear he suffered a severe attack of dermatitis which involved lengthy periods of confinement to bed and hospitalisation. There was a threat to his life. Lord Wright observed of the evidence of a test sample which also showed excess of sulphite, that 'the significance of this experiment seems to be that, however well designed the manufacturers' proved system may be to eliminate deleterious substances, it may not invariably work according to plan. Some employee may blunder.' The plaintiff also sued the retailer in contract. He succeeded against both the retailer (in contract) and the manufacturer (in tort). The Privy Council applied the principle in *Donoghue v Stevenson*.

Lord Wright: '... The facts ... show in their Lordships' judgment negligence in manufacture. According to the evidence, the method of manufacture was correct; the danger of excess sulphites being left was recognised and was guarded against; the process was intended to be foolproof. If excess sulphites were left in the garment, that could only be because someone was at fault. The appellant is not required to lay his finger on the exact person in all the chain who was responsible or to specify what he did wrong. Negligence is found as a matter of inference from the existence of the defects taken in connection with all the known circumstances; even if the manufacturers could by apt evidence have rebutted that inference they have not done so.

On this basis, the damage suffered by the appellant was caused in fact (because the interposition of the retailers may for this purpose in the circumstances of the case be disregarded) by the negligent or improper way in which the manufacturers made the garments. But this mere sequence of cause and effect is not enough in law to constitute a cause of action in negligence, which is a complex concept, involving a duty as between the parties to take care, as well as a breach of that duty and resulting damage. It might be said that here was no relationship between the parties at all; the manufacturers, it might be said, parted once and for all with the garments when they sold them to the retailers and were, therefore, not concerned with their future history, except in so far as under their contract with the retailers they might come under some liability; at no time, it might be said, had they any knowledge of the existence of the appellant; the only peg on which it might be sought to support a relationship of duty was the fact that the appellant had actually worn the garments, but he had done so because he had acquired them by a purchase from the retailers, who were at that time the owners of the goods, by a sale which had vested the property in the retailers and divested both property and control from the manufacturers. It was said there could be no legal relationship in the matter save those under the two contracts between the respective parties to those contracts, the one between the manufacturers and the retailers and the other between the retailers and the appellant. These contractual relationships (it might be said) covered the whole field and excluded any question of tort liability; there was no duty other than the contractual duties.

This argument was based on the contention that the present case fell outside the decision of the House of Lords in *Donoghue v Stevenson*. Their Lordships, like the judges in the courts in Australia, will follow that decision, and the only question here can be what that authority decides and whether this case comes within its principles ... In order to ascertain whether the principle applies to the present case, it is necessary to define what the decision involves and consider the points of distinction relied upon before their Lordships.

It is clear that the decision treats negligence, where there is a duty to take care, as a specific tort in itself, and not simply as an element in some more complex relationship or in some specialised breach of duty, and still less as having any dependence on contract. All that is necessary as a step to establish the tort of actionable negligence is to define the precise relationship from which the duty to take care is to be deduced. It is, however, essential in English law that the duty should be established; the mere fact that a man is injured by another's act gives in itself no cause of action; if the act is deliberate, the party injured will have no claim in law even though the injury is intentional, so long as the other party is merely exercising a legal right; if the act involves lack of due care, again no case of actionable negligence will arise unless the duty to be careful exists. In *Donoghue's* case, the duty was deduced simply from the facts relied on, namely, that the injured party was one of a class for whose use, in the contemplation and intention of the makers, the article was issued to the world, and the article was used by that party in the state in which it was prepared and issued without it being changed in any way and without there being any warning of, or means of detecting, the hidden danger; there was, it is true, no personal intercourse between the maker and the user; but though the duty is personal, because it is *inter partes*, it needs no interchange of words, spoken or written, or signs of offer or assent; it is thus different in character from any contractual relationship; no question of consideration between the parties is relevant; for these reasons the use of the word "privity" in this connection is apt to mislead because of the suggestion of some overt relationship like that in contract, and the word "proximity" is open to the same objection; if the term proximity is to be applied at all, it can only be in the sense that the want of care and the injury are in essence directly and intimately connected; though there may be intervening transactions of sale and purchase and intervening handling between these two events, the events are themselves unaffected by what happened between them: proximity can only properly be used to exclude any element of remoteness, or of some interfering complication between the want of care and the injury, and, like "privity", may mislead by introducing alien ideas. Equally also may the word "control" embarrass, though it is conveniently used in the opinions in *Donoghue's* case to emphasise the essential factor that the consumer must use the article exactly as it left the maker, that is in all material features, and use it as it was intended to be used. In that sense the maker may be said to control the thing until it is used. But that again is an artificial use, because, in the natural sense of the word, the makers parted with all control when they sold the article and divested themselves of possession and property. An argument used in the present case based on the world "control" will be noticed later.

It is obvious that the principles thus laid down involve a duty based on the simple facts detailed above, a duty quite unaffected by any contracts dealing with the thing, for instance, of sale by maker to retailer, and again by retailer to consumer or to the consumer's friend.

It may be said that the duty is difficult to define, because when the act of negligence in manufacture occurs there was no specific person towards whom the duty could be said to exist: the thing might never be used: it might be destroyed by accident or it might be scrapped, or in many ways fail to come into use in the normal way: in other words, the duty cannot at the time of manufacture be other than potential or contingent, and only can become vested by the fact of actual use by a particular person. But the same theoretical difficulty has been disregarded in cases like *Heaven v Pender*, or in the case of things dangerous *per se* or known to be dangerous, where third parties have been held entitled to recover on the principles explained in *Dominion Natural Gas Co Ltd v Collins*. In *Donoghue's* case, the thing was dangerous in fact, though the danger was hidden, and the thing was dangerous only because of want of care in making it; as Lord Atkin points out in *Donoghue's* case, the distinction between things inherently dangerous and things only dangerous because of negligent manufacture cannot be regarded as significant for the purpose of the questions here involved.

One further point may be noted. The principle of *Donoghue's* case can only be applied where the defect is hidden and unknown to the consumer, otherwise the directness of cause and effect is absent: the man who consumes or uses a thing which he knows to be noxious cannot complain in respect of whatever mischief follows because it follows from his own conscious volition in choosing to incur the risk or certainty of mischance.

If the foregoing are the essential features of *Donoghue's* case they are also to be found, in their Lordships' judgment, in the present case. The presence of the deleterious chemical in the pants, due to negligence in manufacture, was a hidden and latent defect, just as much as were the remains of the snail in the opaque bottle: it could not be detected by any examination that could reasonably be made. Nothing happened between the making of the garments and their being worn to change their condition. The garments were made by the manufacturers for the purpose of being worn exactly as they were worn in fact by the appellant: it was not contemplated that they should be first washed. It is immaterial that the appellant has a claim in contract against the retailers, because that is a quite independent cause of action, based on different considerations, even though the damage may be the same. Equally irrelevant is any question of liability between the retailers and the manufacturers on the contract of sale between them. The tort liability is independent of any question of contract.

It was argued, but not perhaps very strongly, that *Donoghue's* case was a case of food or drink to be consumed internally, whereas the pants here were to be worn externally. No distinction, however, can be logically drawn for this purpose between a noxious thing taken internally and a noxious thing applied externally: the garments were made to be worn next the skin: indeed Lord Atkin specifically puts as examples of what is covered by the principle he is enunciating things operating externally, such as "an ointment, a soap, a cleaning fluid, or cleaning powder".

Counsel for the respondents, however, sought to distinguish *Donoghue's* case from the present on the ground that in the former the makers of the ginger beer had retained "control" over it in the sense that they had placed it in stoppered and sealed bottles, so that it would not be tampered with until it was opened to be drunk, whereas the garments in question were merely put into paper packets, each containing six sets, which in ordinary course would be taken down by the shopkeeper and opened and the contents handled and disposed of separately so that they would be exposed to the air. He contended that, though there was no reason to think that the garments, when sold to the appellant were in any other condition, least of all regards sulphur contents, than when sold to the retailers by the manufacturers, still the mere possibility and not the fact of their condition having been changed was sufficient to distinguish *Donoghue's* case: there was no "control" because nothing was done by the manufacturers to exclude the possibility of any tampering while the goods were on their way to the user. Their Lordships do not accept that contention. The decision in *Donoghue's* case did not depend on the bottle being stoppered and sealed; the essential point in this regard was that the article should reach the consumer or user subject to the same defect as it had when it left the manufacturer. That this was true of the garment is in their Lordships' opinion beyond question. At most there might in other cases be a greater difficulty of proof of the fact ...

In their Lordships' opinion it is enough for them to decide this case on its actual facts. No doubt, many difficult problems will arise before the precise limits of the principle are defined: many qualifying conditions and many complications of fact may in the future come before the Courts for decision. It is enough now to say that their Lordships hold the present case to come within the principle of *Donoghue's* case ...'

Comment

(1) In *Daniels & Daniels v White*, the first plaintiff had purchased from T, the second defendant, a bottle of lemonade manufactured by W, the *first* defendant. The plaintiff had shared this with his wife, the second plaintiff. The bottle contained a strong acid solution which injured both plaintiffs. The first plaintiff succeeded in contract against T but both plaintiffs failed in their action in negligence against W. Lewis J observed:

'I have to remember that the duty owed ... by the manufacturer is not to ensure that his goods are perfect. All he has to do is to take reasonable care to see that no injury is done ... In other words, his duty is to take reasonable care to see that there exists no defect that is likely to cause such injury.'

The judge was satisfied not only that the system was foolproof but that there was adequate supervision of the workers within the system. The case may be contrasted with the decision in *Grant v Australian Knitting Mills*, and it is unlikely to be followed. Perhaps the answer is for all parties who are likely to use a product to join in the contract.

Doubts about the extent to which a manufacturer might be able to rely upon proof of a foolproof system and preference for the approach of the Privy Council in *Grant v Australian Knitting Mills* were raised in *Hill v James Crowe (Cases) Ltd*. This matter has now been resolved by the Court of Appeal in *Carroll and others v Fearon and others*. Here tyre manufacturers were held liable under the principle in *Donoghue v Stevenson* in respect of a tyre fitted to a car driven by one person and owned by another which crashed into another vehicle when the tyre failed. One person was killed and many others were severely injured as a result of the crash. The evidence was that the tyre had been manufactured defectively even though it was impossible to demonstrate either the precise acts or omissions, or the specific individuals, responsible for the defect. The manufacturers were unable to produce evidence suggesting that it was not their negligence which had been the cause of the defect.

The court approved the *dictum* of Lord Wright in *Grant v Australian Knitting Mills* that the plaintiff was

> 'not required to lay his finger on the exact person in all the chain who was responsible for what he did wrong. Negligence is found as a matter of inference from the existence of defects taken in connection with all the known circumstances; even if the manufacturers could by apt evidence have rebutted that inference they have not done so.'

The *Carroll* case arose in respect of the supply of goods prior to the passing of the Consumer Protection Act 1987 (see p 427), s 50(2) of which states that:

> 'Nothing in this Act ... shall make any person liable by virtue of Part I of this Act for any damage caused wholly or partly by a defect in a product which was supplied to any person by its producer before the coming into force of Part I of this Act.'

Part I of the Act came into force on 1 March 1987.

(2)   Other cases impose the standard of care at a high level and tend to suggest a higher standard amounting almost to strict liability, e.g. in *Winward v TVR* a car manufactured by TVR incorporated an engine manufactured by F whose design incorporated a carburettor designed and manufactured by W, a specialist manufacturer. The carburettor was defective in design. Eight years after the manufacture the plaintiff's car caught fire. It was held that TVR had been negligent in failing to examine or test the product of W and in failing to warn owners of the existence of the danger. Sir Roualeyn Cumming Bruce LJ thought that:

> 'the judge ... was right to hold that the defendant as a manufacturer was under an obligation to address his mind to the safety of the components that he was proposing to purchase and incorporate and was not entitled blindly to purchase and incorporate such materials and gadgets as F or other manufacturers such as W were putting on the market. It was his duty to apply such engineering skill and knowledge as is appropriate to the manufacturer and marketer of a motor car ...'

(3)   In *Watson v Buckley, Osborne, Garrett & Co Ltd* the plaintiff's hair had been dyed by the first defendant with a product manufactured by the third defendants and distributed by the second defendants. The product had to be diluted by the first defendant before use. The second defendants advertised the product as requiring no preliminary testing, and they had been assured by the third defendants that the product would be 4 per cent solution and undertook no testing. It turned out to be 10 per cent solution and the plaintiff contracted dermatitis. The third defendants had gone into liquidation and the plaintiff

sued the hairdresser and the distributor, the second defendant. The hairdresser was found liable in contract and the second defendant was found liable in negligence. Stable J said:

'... It is extremely difficult to arrive at a legal decision without some guidance as to the sort of test one applies as to whether or not there is a duty. I think I am thrown back on the words of Lord Thankerton in *Donoghue v Stevenson* [see p 418]. I do not think that it matters whether the man is a manufacturer or whether he is a distributor. It seems to me to be the same in the case of a person through whose hands there has passed a commodity which ultimately reaches a consumer to his detriment. Where that person has intentionally so excluded interference with, or examination of, the article by the consumer, then he has, of his own accord, brought himself into direct relationship with that consumer so as to be responsible to the consumer for any injury the consumer may sustain as a result of the distributor's negligence. The duty is there ... The negligent act of the manufacturer was putting in the acid in too strong a solution. The negligent acts of the distributor were the various acts and omissions and representations which intervened between the manufacture of the article and its reaching [the plaintiff].'

(4) In *Kubach v Holland*, the plaintiff schoolgirl had been injured when a chemistry experiment at school had gone wrong. The teacher had added to a mixture that he thought was one particular chemical but which turned out to be another. The plaintiff sued the school (the first defendant) in negligence and contract but did not succeed. She successfully sued in negligence the second defendant, the distributor, who had put a label on to the product mis-describing it. The second defendant failed in the proceedings to obtain an indemnity from the third party, the manufacturer, since the manufacturer had no notice of the specific use to which the chemical would be put, that there were many possible uses and he had appended a notice to his product when he put it into circulation and made it clear that an intermediate examination of the product should be made.

(5) In *Muirhead v Industrial Tank Specialities Ltd* (see p 132), the judge was satisfied that the defendant pump manufacturer knew that the pumps would be used to oxygenate a tank for lobsters. The pumps failed and caused the death of the lobsters, and consequential economic loss. The manufacturer was held liable.

(6) The cases illustrate the importance of the intermediate examination. For the manufacturer to be liable there will have to be no intermediate examination such as would reveal the defect. The mere possibility of examination will not operate so as to save the manufacturer – the absence of reasonable probability of intermediate examination means that the defect will continue to be the

responsibility of the manufacturer and that, subject to any instructions the manufacturer might give, it would be its intention that the product should be used in that condition.

If the manufacturer can demonstrate that it was intended that there should be examination or that it was probable or that it did occur, then the manufacturer will be able to escape liability since the duty will not arise.

In *Aswan Engineering Establishment Co v Lupdine Ltd* the Court of Appeal said that the absence of a reasonable possibility of intermediate examination is not an independent requirement which the plaintiff must satisfy in order to be successful, but is a factor which has to be assessed by the courts in deciding whether or not the damage was reasonably foreseeable. If there were a reasonable possibility of intermediate examination then it would be unlikely that there would be reasonable foreseeability of loss. If there were no reasonable possibility, then it would be the case that the loss or damage would be reasonably foreseeable.

(7)   In *Aswan Engineering Establishment Co v Lupdine Ltd* the plaintiff, a construction company, sued the second defendant who had manufactured plastic pails which the first defendant had used as containers for the sale of its own product, a water-proofing compound. While in transit in Kuwait, the pails had been stacked in containers which in turn were left in the direct sun. Under the intense heat they collapsed and the entire load was lost. The first defendant went into liquidation and the plaintiff sued the second defendant for the loss of the compound. The Court of Appeal rejected the plaintiff's claim. Lloyd and Fox LJJ held that the compound was property of the plaintiff distinct from its container:

'One can think of other cases by way of illustration ... If I buy a defective tyre for my car and it bursts, I can sue the manufacturer of the tyre for damage to the car as well as injury to my person. But what if the tyre was part of the original equipment? Presumably the car is *other* property of the plaintiff, even though the tyre was a component part of the car, and property in the tyre and property in the car passed simultaneously. Another example ... would be if I buy a bottle of wine and find that the wine is undrinkable owing to a defect in the cork. Is the wine other property, so as to enable me to bring an action against the manufacturer or the cork in tort? ... My provisional view is that in all these cases there is damage to other property of the plaintiff, so that the threshold of liability is crossed ...'

Whether this aspect of the judgment remains sound after *Murphy v Brentwood*, p 139, is open to question. Lloyd and Fox LJJ went on to hold that the duty of the defendant as manufacturer did not extend beyond consequences of a type which were reasonably foreseeable:

'But the type of damage which occurred and the conditions in which it occurred were altogether outside the range of what was reasonably foreseeable, and therefore outside the scope of their duty of care. To hold otherwise on the facts of the present case would be to impose on the manufacturers a liability not far short of that of an insurer.'

Nicholls LJ took a different route to rejection of the plaintiff's claim. He held that:

'The pails were as fit for the purposes for which goods of the appropriate kind are commonly bought as it was reasonable to expect, having regard to all the relevant circumstances. The relevant circumstances here included no special or unusual circumstance. Nor were [the manufacturers] aware that their customer intended to stack the pails five and six high for some days at temperatures over 50 degrees centigrade ... it seems to me that this claim, that the manufacturer was in breach of a duty to take "reasonable" care, is hopeless.'

He went on to say that to apply the principle in *Donoghue v Stevenson* to containers of the sort in question would be to extend it:

'If a customer buys a light and fragile piece of jewellery in a jeweller's shop, and the assistant hands the jewellery to the customer inside an elegant carrier bag, is the carrier bag manufacturer liable to the customer, if through carelessness in manufacture, the bag tears open outside the shop and the expensive piece of jewellery falls out and is broken?'

It might be asked whether the issue identified by Nicholls LJ goes to the existence of a duty or to remoteness of damage. For example, would it really be so outrageous if the carrier-bag manufacturer knew that the bag would be used to carry fragile jewellery?

Consumer Protection Act 1987, Part I

PART I PRODUCT LIABILITY

1 Purpose and construction of Part I

(1) This part shall have effect for the purpose of making such provision as is necessary in order to comply with the product liability Directive and shall be construed accordingly.

(2) In this Part, except in so far as the context otherwise requires—

...

'producer', in relation to a product, means—

(a)   the person who manufactured it;

(b)   in the case of a substance which has not been manufactured but has been won or abstracted, the person who won or abstracted it;

(c)   in the case of a product which has not been manufactured, won or abstracted but essential characteristics of which are attributable to an industrial or other process having been carried out (for example, in relation to agricultural produce), the person who carried out that process;

'product' means any goods or electricity and (subject to subsection (3) below) includes a product which is comprised in another product, whether by virtue of being a component part or raw material or otherwise; ...

(3) ... a person who supplies any product in which products are comprised, whether by virtue of being component parts or raw materials or otherwise, shall not be treated by reason only of his supply of that product as supplying any of the products so comprised.

2   Liability for defective products

(1)   Subject to the following provisions ... where any damage is caused wholly or partly by a defect in a product, every person to whom subsection (2) below applies shall be liable for the damage.

(2)   This subsection applies to—

(a)   the producer of the product;

(b)   any person who, by putting his name on the product or using a trade mark or other distinguishing mark in relation to the product, has held himself out to be the producer of the product;

(c)   any person who has imported the product into a member State from a place outside the member States in order, in the course of any business of his, to supply it to another.

(3)   Subject as aforesaid, where any damage is caused wholly or partly by a defect in a product, any person who supplied the product (whether to the person who suffered the damage, to the producer of any product in which the product in question is comprised or to any other person) shall be liable for the damage if—

(a)   the person who suffered the damage requests the supplier to identify one or more of the persons (whether still in existence or not) to whom subsection (2) above applies in relation to the product;

(b)   that request is made within a reasonable period after the damage occurs and at a time when it is not reasonably practicable for the person making the request to identify all those persons; and

(c)   the supplier fails, within a reasonable period after receiving the request, either to comply with the request or to identify the person who supplied the product to him.

...

(5)   Where two or more persons are liable ... for the same damage, their liability shall be joint and several.

(6)   This section shall be without prejudice to any liability arising otherwise than by virtue of this part.

3   Meaning of 'defect'

(1)   ... there is a defect in a product ... if the safety of the product is not such as persons generally are entitled to expect; and ... 'safety' ... shall include safety with respect to products comprised in that product and safety in the context of risks of damage to property, as well as in the context of risks of death or personal injury.

(2)   In determining ... what persons generally are entitled to expect in relation to a product all the circumstances shall be taken into account, including–
(a)   the manner in which, and purposes for which, the product has been marketed, its get-up, the use of any mark in relation to the product and any instructions for, or warnings with respect to, doing or refraining from doing anything with or in relation to the product;
(b)   what might reasonably be expected to be done with or in relation to the product; and
(c)   the time when the product was supplied by its producer to another;

and nothing ... shall require a defect to be inferred from the fact alone that the safety of a product which is supplied after that time is greater than the safety of the product in question.

4   Defences

(1)   ... it shall be a defence ... to show– ...
(b)   that the person proceeded against did not at any time supply the product to another; or
(c)   that the following conditions are satisfied ...
   (i)   that the only supply of the product to another by the person proceeded against was otherwise than in the course of a business of that person's; and
   (ii) that section 2(2) above does not apply to that person or applies to him by virtue only of things done otherwise than with a view to profit; or
(d)   that the defect did not exist in the product at the relevant time; or
(e)   that the state of scientific and technical knowledge at the relevant time was not such that a producer of products of the same description as the product in question might be expected to have discovered the defect if it had existed in his products while they were under his control; or
(f)   that the defect–

(i)   constituted a defect in a product (the subsequent product) in which the product in question had been comprised; and

(ii)   was wholly attributable to the design of the subsequent product or to compliance by the producer of the product in question with instructions given by the producer of the subsequent product.

(2) ... 'the relevant time' ... means—

(a)   if the person proceeded against is a person to whom subsection (2) of section 2above applies in relation to the product, the time when he supplied the product to another;

(b)   if that subsection does not apply to that person in relation to the product, the time when the product was last supplied by a person to whom that subsection does apply in relation to the product.

5   Damage giving rise to liability

(1) ... 'damage' means death or personal injury or any loss of or damage to any property (including land).

(2)   A person shall not be liable under section 2 above in respect of any defect in a product for the loss of or any damage to the product itself or for the loss of or any damage to the whole or any part of any product which has been supplied with the product in question comprised in it.

(3)   A person shall not be liable under section 2 above for any loss of or damage to any property which, at the time it is lost or damaged, is not—

(a)   of a description of property ordinarily intended for private use, occupation or consumption; and

(b)   intended by the person suffering the loss or damage mainly for his own private use, occupation or consumption.

(4)   No damages shall be awarded to any person ... in respect of any loss of or damage to any property if the amount which would fall to be awarded to that person apart from this subsection and any liability for interest does not exceed £275.

...

6   Application of certain enactments

...

(4)   Where any damage is caused partly by a defect in a product and partly by the fault of the person suffering the damage, the Law Reform (Contributory Negligence) Act 1945 and section 5 of the Fatal Accidents Act 1976 (contributory negligence) shall have effect as if the defect were the fault of every person liable by virtue of this Part for the damage caused by the defect.

(5) In subsection (4) above 'fault' has the same meaning as in the said Act of 1945.

...

7 Prohibition on exclusions from liability

The liability of a person by virtue of this Part to a person who has suffered damage caused wholly or partly by a defect in a product, or to a dependant or relative of such a person, shall not be limited or excluded by any contract term, by any notice or by any other provision.

Comment

(1) The Consumer Protection Act 1987 is intended to satisfy the European Community Directive on product liability (85/374/EEC) and the Act states that it should be so construed. Consumer protection is the real focus of the reform (rather than business efficiency or 'laissez-faire') and from this perspective the manufacturer is in a better position to insure against its risks, to build that cost into the product price and to take all necessary precautions to avoid risks. The object of the EC Directive is to bring about approximation of the laws of the member states concerning liability for defective products, to avoid divergences which according to the preamble to the Directive may 'distort competition and affect the movement of goods within the common market and entail a differing degree of protection of the consumer against damage caused by a defective product to his health or property'.

(2) The Commission indicated in its Consumer Policy Action Plan for 1999–2001 that it would examine the safety regime in respect of services; an earlier Commission proposal had been withdrawn because of lack of support in the Council and the Parliament. The Commission launched a Green Paper in 2000 and the responses to the Green Paper formed the basis for the Report from the Commission on the Application of Directive 85/374 on Liability for Defective Products. Several options to develop the law are open – e.g. to make a presumption of causation if the damage and defect are demonstrated, to alter the burden of proof and to remove the lower limit of property damage. Generally, the EU is concerned with the safety of products and there are several specific directives as well as a general directive on product safety.

(3) Failure to implement the Directive in other jurisdictions has been examined in C-154/00 and C-52/00. There were also references to the ECJ in C-203/99 and in C-183/00.

(4) The rationale underpinning the Directive is explored further in *A v National Blood Authority*, see p 436, and the 'state of the art' defence was

considered by the Advocate-General (G Tesauro) in *European Commission v United Kingdom* where he drew heavily on academic sources in Italy and the United States:

'16.   The producer's liability for marketing defective products has been in the forefront of topics considered in learned writings concerned with civil liability, above all in the most recent decades. The chief reason for this is that it has constituted a test bench at the systematic level for moving from a system of imposing liability for unlawful acts and omissions solely on the basis of negligence to a system of strict liability, which is more consonant with the requirements of protecting injured parties, as part of a recasting of the rules of civil liability in terms no longer only of sanctions but also, if not chiefly, in terms of compensation.

The tendency which I have just described has been stimulated moreover by the growth of industrial activity. With the ever increasing complexity of manufacturing processes, the risks associated with product defects multiplied and became difficult to avoid and it became clear that the system of liability founded on the producer's negligence was inappropriate to secure adequate protection for the consumer. Albeit injured by a defective product, consumers were in fact – and too often – deprived of an effective remedy, since it proved very difficult procedurally to prove negligence on the part of the producer, that is to say, that he had failed to take all appropriate steps to avoid the defect arising. Seen from this perspective it can be readily appreciated why it was in the United States, owing to the scale of industrial growth in that country, that the theoretical premises of a system of producer liability uncoupled from any requirement for negligence were first worked out, starting in the 1960s. Those premises may be summarised as follows: (a) the producer's greater contractual and economic power compared with the consumer and the more effective deterrent function performed by the system of strict liability as against liability for negligence; (b) the principle of the distribution of risks within a particular social organisation through recourse to insurance: in other words, internalisation of the costs arising out of harmful acts or omissions on the part of the producer; (c) reduction of so-called secondary and tertiary administrative costs and achievement of major social benefits as a result of the introduction of a system of strict liability on the part of the producer.

17.   ... The Commission's proposal, drawing its inspiration from the US model, provided for a system of no-fault liability on the part of the producer, which, on the one hand, was regarded as the most suitable means of securing adequate protection for the consumer (fourth recital) and, on the other, was justified by the fact that the producer is the ideal centre to which to impute the damage, since he may "include the

expenditure which he incurs to cover this liability in his production costs when calculating the price and therefore divide it among all consumers of products which are of the same type but free from defects" (fifth recital).

18. The type of liability outlined in the Commission's proposal, however, went beyond the system of strict liability as described earlier, being one of absolute liability in that the producer could put forward no evidence in rebuttal ... This precluded the producer from raising the "state of the art" defence ... In other words, the producer was made to shoulder also "development risks", that is to say, risks present in production sectors in which an advance in technological and scientific knowledge may make a product appear defective ex post, whereas it was not regarded as such at the time when it was manufactured.

19. In contrast, the directive as it was adopted by the EC Council opted for a system of strict liability which was no longer absolute, but limited, in deference to a principle of the fair apportionment of risk between the injured person and the producer, the latter having to bear only quantifiable risks, but not development risks which are, by their nature, unquantifiable. Under the directive, therefore, in order for the producer to be held liable for defects in the product, the injured party is required to prove the damage, the defect in the product and the causal relationship between defect and damage, but not negligence on the part of the producer.

The producer, however, may exonerate himself from liability by proving that the "state of the art" at the time when he put the product into circulation was not such as to cause the product to be regarded as defective. This is what art 7(e) of the directive provides.'

(5) Liability under *Donoghue v Stevenson* remains relevant for several reasons. The Act has no application to damage caused by the defective product to property which is not the sort of property ordinarily intended for private use, occupation or consumption and it is not intended (by the person suffering the loss or damage) for his or her own private use, occupation or consumption. Thus if a defect in a product damages an individual, the individual will be able to recover. But if it damages property, then the nature of the property damaged will be relevant to the issue of recovery: if the property is not 'domestic' property then recovery will not be permitted under the Act and recourse to ordinary negligence will be necessary; if the property is 'domestic' then recovery will be permitted. The Act would have no relevance to cases such as *Aswan Engineering Establishment Co v Lupdine Ltd* and *Muirhead v Industrial Tank Specialities Ltd.*

Another reason for the continued relevance of the ordinary law of tort is that where the damage to property (but not injury to the person) is less than £275 then there will be no liability under the Act. Additionally, the Act has no application to harm caused by defects which were present in goods supplied to any person by the producer of the goods before the coming into force of the Act (s 50(2)) on 1 March 1987, see *Carroll and others v Fearon and others*, p 423. Finally, the limitation periods are different as between the common law of negligence and liability under the Act, and it is possible to envisage circumstances where the complex limitation period under the Act may lead to a statutory tort being time-barred when the period for negligence might be capable of extension with leave of the court.

(6)   Liability is imposed in respect of damage caused to a consumer (who may well be anyone who suffers injury). That is what the man in the street, or as s 3 states 'persons generally', might regard as 'reasonable' and it was certainly the focus of the Royal Commission on Civil Liability and Compensation for Personal Injury.

(7)   Liability attaches to manufacturers and those who hold themselves out as manufacturers, and an 'own brander' will have to show that an item was made 'for it' and not by it. An own brander will probably hold itself out as the producer – after all, the item will have been manufactured to its specifications. Liability attaches to the person who imports the product into a member state of the EC: s 2(2)(c). But there may be liability on what may be called substituted defendants. These will be those who supply products. Ordinarily these will not be made liable but may make themselves liable if s 2(3) applies. Section 2(3) is an attempt to create a mechanism whereby the chain of supply will lead back to a 'producer'. If a supplier fails to answer the points raised in s 2(3) then it will have broken the chain and will be substituted as defendant for the actual producer.

(8)   In addition to the cause of action under Part I of the Act, under s 41 a plaintiff may be able to maintain an action for breach of statutory duty in respect of breaches of the safety provisions contained in Part II of the Act or relevant Regulations, the particular emphasis of which is their enforcement by criminal sanction. The formula in s 41 is similar to provisions employed in other legislation and does not permit exclusion of liability.

(9)   Section 46 defines 'supply' as including (whether as agent or principal) selling, hiring out, lending, exchanging goods for consideration other than money, providing goods pursuant to a statutory function, giving the goods as a prize or 'otherwise making a gift of the goods'. Section 46 contains further explanation in various contexts ranging from finance agreements to building contracts.

(10)   Among the definitions in s 45 are:

> '"goods" includes substances, growing crops and things comprised in land by virtue of being attached to it and any ship, aircraft or vehicle;

"personal injury" includes any disease and any other impairment of a person's physical or mental condition.'

(11) The Directive permits a number of defences enabling the producer to avoid liability on the basis of what the ECJ described as 'a fair apportionment of risk between the injured person and the producer implies that the producer should be able to free himself from liability if he furnishes proof as to the existence of certain exonerating circumstances'.

One area of concern was that the development risks defence in s 4(1)(e) went further than permitted by the directive. In *European Commission v United Kingdom* (Case C-300/95), the Commission sought a declaration that the UK had failed to implement the Directive correctly. The Court of Justice held that the Commission had failed to demonstrate that the UK courts would not interpret s 4(1)(e) in such a way as to achieve conformity with the requirements of the Directive.

The Court of Justice addressed article 7(e) (see p 437) and said:

'26. First, as the Advocate General rightly observes in para 20 of his opinion ... since that provision refers to "scientific and technical knowledge at the time when [the producer] put the product into circulation", art 7(e) is not specifically directed at the practices and safety standards in use in the industrial sector in which the producer is operating, but, unreservedly, at the state of scientific and technical knowledge, including the most advanced level of such knowledge, at the time when the product in question was put into circulation.

27. Second, the clause providing for the defence in question does not contemplate the state of knowledge of which the producer in question actually or subjectively was or could have been apprised, but the objective state of scientific and technical knowledge of which the producer is presumed to have been informed.

28. However, it is implicit in the wording of art 7(e) that the relevant scientific and technical knowledge must have been accessible at the time when the product in question was put into circulation.

29. It follows that, in order to have a defence under art 7(e) of the directive, the producer of a defective product must prove that the objective state of scientific and technical knowledge, including the most advanced level of such knowledge, at the time when the product in question was put into circulation was not such as to enable the existence of the defect to be discovered. Further, in order for the relevant scientific and technical knowledge to be successfully pleaded against the producer, that knowledge must have been accessible at the time when the product in question was put into circulation. On this last point, contrary to what the

Commission seems to consider, art 7(e) of the directive raises difficulties of interpretation which, in the event of litigation, the national courts will have to resolve having recourse, if necessary, to art 177 of the EC Treaty.'

The ECJ then looked at s 4(1) and concluded that there was nothing in the wording to suggest that there had been a failure to transpose the Directive and that there had been no suggestion that a national court would fail to interpret the Act consistently with the Directive. *A v National Blood Authority* makes it clear that an English court will interpret the Act in such a way as to apply the Directive; indeed in that case the court went to the wording of the Directive, rather than the Act, in order to reach its decision.

(12)   The ECJ acknowledged that there may be difficult factual issues; for example when can it be said that scientific speculation or theorising amounts to *knowledge* for current purposes, and when is it 'the most advanced'? In respect of these matters the opinion of the Advocate-General (G Tesauro) contains views which were relied on by the English Court in *A v National Blood Authority*. In addition to the passages relied on there the Advocate-General also said:

'21.   ... The progress of scientific culture does not develop linearly, in so far as new studies and new discoveries may initially be criticised and regarded as unreliable by most of the scientific community, yet subsequently after the passage of time undergo an opposite process of "beatification" whereby they are virtually unanimously endorsed. It is therefore quite possible that at the time when a given product is marketed, there will be isolated opinions to the effect that it is defective, whilst most academics do not take that view. The problem at this juncture is to determine whether in such a situation, that is to say, where there is a risk that is not certain and will be agreed to exist by all only ex post, the producer may still rely on the defence provided for in art 7(e) of the directive.

In my view, the answer to this question must be in the negative. In other words, the state of scientific knowledge cannot be identified with the views expressed by the majority of learned opinion, but with the most advanced level of research which has been carried out at a given time.'

A and others v National Blood Authority and another
[2001] 3 All ER 289 QBD

The claimants sought damages arising out of their infection with Hepatitis C from blood and blood products through blood transfusions from 1 March 1988, the date when the Consumer Protection Act 1987 was brought into force. The blood was 'infected' because, exceptionally, the donor's blood was already infected by Hepatitis C. They sued the defendants who were the authorities responsible for the production of blood and blood products. The Hepatitis C virus had not been discovered at the date the claims commenced. During the period when the claimants were infected, the risk of such infection through blood transfusions was known to the medical profession but was impossible to avoid, either because the virus itself had not yet been discovered or because after it had been discovered there was no way of testing for its presence in donated blood. No screening test to discover the presence of such virus in a donor's blood was known about until a scientific account publicised in spring/summer 1989. It was not alleged that the UK blood authorities were negligent in not introducing the screening tests until 1 April 1991.

In particular, articles 6 and 7(e) of the Directive fell for extensive consideration.

Article 6 provides that:

'1. A product is defective when it does not provide the safety which a person is entitled to expect, taking all circumstances into account, including: (a) the presentation of the product; (b) the use to which it could reasonably be expected that the product would be put; (c) the time when the product was put into circulation.

2. A product shall not be considered defective for the sole reason that a better product is subsequently put into circulation.'

Article 7 provides that:

'The producer shall not be liable as a result of this Directive if he proves ... (e) that the state of scientific and technical knowledge at the time when he put the product into circulation was not such as to enable the existence of the defect to be discovered.'

Burton J had to consider what circumstances had to be taken into account in deciding whether or not there was a defect in a product (article 6) and the extent of the application of the development risk defence (article 7). In particular, was avoidability of risk relevant to article 6, and, if not, ought the court to include it within article 7(e) as a relevant factor in considering the development risk defence.

The extracts below deal only with these two issues and not with the other issues which fell to be decided in the case such as the findings of fact in each of the six leading cases and the extent of damages.

Burton J: '...

[49] Such common ground is as follows. (i) The state of scientific and technical knowledge referred to is the most advanced available (to anyone, not simply to the producer in question), but it must be "accessible". In response to a more extreme position being taken by the Commission, the Advocate General answered as

follows, in his opinion in *European Commission v UK* Case (paras 22–24), which, although not expressly approved in the judgment of the Court of Justice, is taken to be the state of the law:

> "22.   ... Where in the whole gamut of scientific opinion at a particular time there is also one isolated opinion (which, as the history of science shows, might become with the passage of time *opinio communis*) as to the potentially defective and/or hazardous nature of the product, the manufacturer is no longer faced with an unforeseeable risk, since, as such, it is outside the scope of the rules imposed by the directive.
>
> 23.   The aspect which I have just been discussing is closely linked with the question of the availability of scientific and technical knowledge in the sense of the accessibility of the sum of knowledge at a given time to interested persons. It is undeniable that the circulation of information is affected by objective factors, such as, for example, its place of origin, the language in which it is given and the circulation of the journals in which it is published.
>
> To be plain, there exist quite major differences in point of the speed in which it gets into circulation and the scale of its dissemination between a study of a researcher in a university in the United States published in an international English-language journal and, to take an example given by the Commission, similar research carried out by an academic in Manchuria published in a local scientific journal in Chinese, which does not go outside the boundaries of the region.
>
> 24.   In such a situation, it would be unrealistic and, I would say, unreasonable to take the view that the study published in Chinese has the same chances as the other of being known to a European product manufacturer. So, I do not consider that in such a case a producer could be held liable on the ground that at the time at which he put the product into circulation the brilliant Asian researcher had discovered the defect in it. More generally, the 'state of knowledge' must be construed so as to include all data in the information circuit of the scientific community as a whole, bearing in mind, however, on the basis of a reasonableness test the actual opportunities for the information to circulate."

... (ii)   The article is not concerned with the conduct or knowledge of individual producers. As the court made clear [in para 29]:

> "... the producer of a defective product must prove that the objective state of scientific and technical knowledge, including the most advanced level of such knowledge, at the time when the product in question was put into circulation was not such as to enable the existence of the defect to be discovered."

It is clear from ... para 36 of the court's judgment that "the availability of the defence [does not depend] on the subjective knowledge of a producer taking reasonable care in the light of the standard precautions taken in the industrial sector in question". (iii) The relevant time to assess the state of such scientific and technical knowledge is the time when the product was put into circulation. (iv) Whether or not the defect for the purposes of art 6 should be defined as "unscreenedness" as discussed in para 46(i) above, there is no dispute that the defect for the purposes of art 7(e) is its infection by Hepatitis C (and of course the claimants rely on this, when this dispute becomes relevant, as a further argument, based on consistency in the construction of the directive, why the defendants' such definition of defect in art 6 is wrong).

The issues between the parties

[50]   ... The crux of the dispute therefore is as follows. (i) The claimants say that once the defect in blood is known about, as it was, it is a known risk. A known but unavoidable risk does not qualify for art 7(e). It may qualify for art 6, not because it was unavoidable ... but if it could be shown that, because the risk is known, it was accepted, and lowered public expectations – like poison and alcohol. But otherwise once it is known, then the product cannot be supplied, or is supplied at the producer's risk and has no protection from art 7(e). Hence an art 7(e) defence is, as was intended, a development risks defence; for if it is not known that a particular product, perhaps a pioneering such product (such as a scrid), [*ed, a scrid is a hypothetical product envisioned by the judge and legal representatives*] has or can have a harmful characteristic, whether by virtue of its inherent nature, its raw materials, its design or its method of manufacture, and then the defect materialises, or is published about, for the first time, it has prior to that time been a true development risk, and protection is available under art 7(e). However, once the risk is known, then if the product is supplied, and if the defect recurs, by then it is a known risk, and, even if undiscoverable in a particular example of the product, there is no escape. There is only one stage of consideration, and if there be "non-Manchurianly accessible" knowledge about the product's susceptibility to a defect, be it a manufacturing or design defect, there is no availability of art 7(e). As it is common ground in this case that there was such knowledge, the defendants cannot avail themselves of art 7(e). (ii) The defendants say that if a risk is unavoidable, it falls within art 6 ... but, if not, then it can still qualify for protection under art 7(e), if non-Manchurianly accessible information cannot enable a producer to discover the defect in the particular product. There may be no "stage one" – i.e. knowledge of the risk – but, even if there is, there is a "stage two" – namely consideration as to whether any accessible knowledge could have availed the producer to take any steps which he did not take. The defendants say there were none such here ...

[The court examined in detail the arguments for each interpretation and the Travaux préparatoires in respect of the Directive, the legal authorities from around the world and the academic arguments on the point, and continued:]

CONCLUSIONS ON ARTICLE 6

[55]   I do not consider it to be arguable that the consumer had an actual expectation that blood being supplied to him was not 100% clean, nor do I conclude that he had knowledge that it was, or was likely to be, infected with Hepatitis C. It is not seriously argued by the defendants, notwithstanding some few newspaper cuttings which were referred to, that there was any public understanding or acceptance of the infection of transfused blood by Hepatitis C.

Doctors and surgeons knew, but did not tell their patients unless asked, and were very rarely asked. It was certainly, in my judgment, not known and accepted by society that there was such a risk ... Thus blood was not, in my judgment, the kind of product referred to in the ... question and answer in the European Parliament i.e. "a product which by its very nature carries a risk and which has been presented as such (instructions for use, labelling, publicity, etc.)", "risks which are ... inherent in [a] product and generally known": nor.. as being risks which "consumers can be taken to have chosen to expose themselves to in order to benefit from the product".

[56]   I do not consider that the legitimate expectation of the public at large is that legitimately expectable tests will have been carried out or precautions adopted. Their legitimate expectation is as to the safeness of the product (or not). The court will act as ... called the appointed representative of the public at large, but in my judgment it is impossible to inject into the consumer's legitimate expectation matters which would not by any stretch of the imagination be in his actual expectation. He will assume perhaps that there are tests, but his expectations will be as to the safeness of the blood. In my judgment it is as inappropriate to propose that the public should not "expect the unattainable" — in the sense of tests or precautions which are impossible — at least unless it is informed as to what is unattainable or impossible, as it is to reformulate the expectation as one that the producer will not have been negligent or will have taken all reasonable steps.

[57]   In this context I turn to consider what is intended to be included within "all circumstances" in art 6. I am satisfied that this means all relevant circumstances. It is quite plain to me that ... the directive was intended to eliminate proof of fault or negligence. I am satisfied that this was not simply a legal consequence, but that it was also intended to make it easier for claimants to prove their case, such that not only would a consumer not have to prove that the producer did not take reasonable steps, or all reasonable steps, to comply with his duty of care, but also that the producer did not take all legitimately expectable steps either. In this regard I note para 16 of the Advocate General's opinion in *European Commission v UK* where, in setting out the background to the directive, he pointed out that:

> "Albeit injured by a defective product, consumers were in fact and too often deprived of an effective remedy, since it proved very difficult procedurally to prove negligence on the part of the producer, that is to say, that he failed to take all appropriate steps to avoid the defect arising."

[58]   The Court of Justice in its judgment perhaps refers implicitly to this when it states [in para 24]: "In order for a producer to incur liability for defective products under art 4 of the directive, the victim must prove the damage, the defect and the causal relationship between defect and damage, but not that the producer was at fault." It seems to me clear that, even without the full panoply of allegations of negligence, the adoption of tests of avoidability or of legitimately expectable safety precautions must inevitably involve a substantial investigation.

What safety precautions or tests were available or reasonably available? Were they tests that would have been excessively expensive? Tests which would have been more expensive than justified the extra safety achieved? Are economic or political circumstances or restrictions to be taken into account in legitimate expectability? Once it is asserted that it is legitimately expectable that a certain safety precaution should have been taken, then the producer must surely be able to explain why such was not possible or why he did not do it; in which case it will then be explored as to whether such tests would or could have been carried out, or were or would have been too expensive or impracticable to carry out. If risk and benefit should be considered, then it might be said that, the more beneficial the product, the lower the tolerable level of safety; but this could not be arrived at without consideration as to whether, beneficial or not, there would have nevertheless been a safer way of setting about production or design ...

[59]   Mr Underhill submitted that he accepted that liability was irrespective of fault and that investigation of negligence was inappropriate, and that that was not the exercise he submitted the court was involved in. No criticisms were being made of the defendants on the basis that they were negligent. The investigation that was being carried out was not, as it would have been in a negligence action, as to what steps actually taken by these defendants were negligent, so that their individual acts and omissions were not being investigated. However, many of Mr Underhill's submissions were indistinguishable from those that he would have made had a breach of a duty of care – albeit one with a high standard of care, so that breach of it might not carry any stigma or criticism – been alleged against him ...

[63]   I conclude therefore that avoidability is not one of the circumstances to be taken into account within art 6. I am satisfied that it is not a relevant circumstance, because it is outwith the purpose of the directive, and indeed that, had it been intended that it would be included as a derogation from, or at any rate a palliation of, its purpose, then it would certainly have been mentioned; for it would have been an important circumstance, and I am clear that, irrespective of the absence of any word such as "notamment" in the English-language version of the directive, it was intended that the most significant circumstances were those listed.

[64]   This brings me to a consideration of art 7(e) in the context of consideration of art 6. Article 7(e) provides a very restricted escape route, and producers are, as emphasised in *European Commission v UK*, unable to take advantage of it, unless they

come within its very restricted conditions ... The significance seems to be as follows. Article 7(e) is the escape route (if available at all) for the producer who has done all he could reasonably be expected to do (and more); and yet that route is emphatically very restricted, because of the purpose and effect of the directive ... This must suggest a similarly restricted view of art 6, indeed one that is even more restricted, given the availability of the (restricted) art 7(e) escape route. If that were not the case, then if the art 7(e) defence were excluded, an option permitted (and indeed taken up, in the case of Luxembourg and Finland) for those member states who wish to delete this "exonerating circumstance" as "unduly restricting the protection of the consumer" (Recital 16 and art 15), then, on the defendants' case, an even less restrictive "exonerating circumstance", and one available even in the case of risks known to the producer, would remain in art 6; and indeed one where the onus does not even rest on the defendant, but firmly on the claimant.

[65] Further, in my judgment, the infected bags of blood were non-standard products. I have already recorded that it does not seem to me to matter whether they would be categorised in US tort law as manufacturing or design defects. They were in any event different from the norm which the producer intended for use by the public. (i) I do not accept that all the blood products were equally defective because all of them carried the risk. That is a very philosophical approach. It is one which would ... be equally apt to a situation in which one tyre in one million was defective because of an inherent occasional blip in the strength of the rubber's raw material. The answer is that the test relates to the use of the blood bag. For, and as a result of, the intended use, 99 out of 100 bags would cause no injury and would not be infected, unlike the 100th. (ii) Even in the case of standard products such as drugs, side-effects are to my mind only capable of being "socially acceptable" if they are made known. ... I am satisfied ... that the problem was not known to the consumer. However, in any event, I do not accept that the consumer expected, or was entitled to expect, that his bag of blood was defective even if (which I have concluded was not the case) he had any knowledge of any problem. I do not consider ... that he was expecting or entitled to expect a form of Russian roulette. That would only arise if, contrary to my conclusion, the public took that as socially acceptable ... For such knowledge and acceptance there would need to be at the very least publicity and probably express warnings, and even that might not, in the light of the no-waiver provision in art 12 set out above, be sufficient.

[66] Accordingly I am quite clear that the infected blood products in this case were non-standard products (whether on the basis of being manufacturing or design defects does not appear to me to matter). Where, as here, there is a harmful characteristic in a non-standard product, a decision that it is defective is likely to be straightforward, and I can make my decision accordingly. However, the consequence of my conclusion is that "avoidability" is also not in the basket of circumstances, even in respect of a harmful characteristic in a standard product. So I shall set out what I consider to be the structure for consideration under art 6. It must be emphasised that safety and intended, or foreseeable, use are the linchpins: and,

leading on from these, what legitimate expectations there are of safety in relation to foreseeable use. (i) I see no difficulty, on that basis, in an analysis which is akin to contract or warranty. Recital 6 ("the defectiveness of the product should be determined by reference not to its fitness for use but to the lack of the safety which the public at large are entitled to expect") does not in my judgment counter-indicate an approach analogous to contract, but is concerned to emphasise that it is safety which is paramount. (ii) In the circumstances, there may in a simple case be a straightforward answer to the art 6 question, and the facts may be sufficiently clear. But an expert may be needed (and they were instructed in *Richardson's* case, the "*Cosytoes* case" and the "*German Bottle* case"). For art 6 purposes, the function of such expert would be, in my judgment, to describe the composition or construction of the product and its effect and consequence in use: not to consider what could or should have been done, whether in respect of its design or manufacture, to avoid the problem (that may be relevant in relation to art 7(e), if that arises). (iii) In the following analysis I ignore questions that may obviously arise, either by way of "exoneration" in respect of other heads of art 7 or in respect of misuse or contributory negligence (art 8, set out in [16] above).

[67]   The first step must be to identify the harmful characteristic which caused the injury (art 4). In order to establish that there is a defect in art 6, the next step will be to conclude whether the product is standard or non-standard. This will be done (in the absence of admission by the producer) most easily by comparing the offending product with other products of the same type or series produced by that producer. If the respect in which it differs from the series includes the harmful characteristic, then it is, for the purpose of art 6, non-standard. If it does not differ, or if the respect in which it differs does not include the harmful characteristic, but all the other products, albeit different, share the harmful characteristic, then it is to be treated as a standard product.

Non-standard products

[68]   The circumstances specified in art 6 may obviously be relevant – the product may be a second – as well as the circumstances of the supply. But it seems to me that the primary issue in relation to a non-standard product may be whether the public at large accepted the non-standard nature of the product – i.e. they accept that a proportion of the products is defective (as I have concluded they do not in this case). That, as discussed, is not of course the end of it, because the question is of legitimate expectation, and the court may conclude that the expectation of the public is too high or too low. But manifestly questions such as warnings and presentations will be in the forefront. However, I conclude that the following are not relevant: (i) avoidability of the harmful characteristic – i.e. impossibility or unavoidability in relation to precautionary measures; (ii) the impracticality, cost or difficulty of taking such measures; and (iii) the benefit to society or utility of the product (except in the context of whether – with full information and proper knowledge – the public does and ought to accept the risk).

[69] ... This is obviously a tough decision for any common lawyer to make. But I am entirely clear that this was the purpose of the directive, and that without the exclusion of such matters (subject only to the limited defence of art 7(e)) it would not only be toothless but pointless ...

Standard products

[71] If a standard product is unsafe, it is likely to be so as a result of alleged error in design, or at any rate as a result of an allegedly flawed system. The harmful characteristic must be identified, if necessary with the assistance of experts. The question of presentation / time / circumstances of supply / social acceptability etc will arise as above. The sole question will be safety for the foreseeable use. If there are any comparable products on the market, then it will obviously be relevant to compare the offending product with those other products, so as to identify, compare and contrast the relevant features. There will obviously need to be a full understanding of how the product works – particularly if it is a new product, such as a scrid, so as to assess its safety for such use. Price is obviously a significant factor in legitimate expectation, and may well be material in the comparative process. But again it seems to me there is no room in the basket for: (i) what the producer could have done differently; and (ii) whether the producer could or could not have done the same as the others did.

[72] Once again there are areas of anomaly ... The second area arises out of art 6(2): "A product shall not be considered defective for the sole reason that a better product is subsequently put into circulation." In the comparative process, the claimant may point to a product which is safer, but which the producer shows to be produced five years later. Particularly if no other contemporary product had these features, this is likely to be capable of being established, and insofar as such product has improved safety features which have only evolved later in time, they should be ignored, as a result of art 6(2). The claimant might, however, want to allege that the later safety features could have been developed earlier by the producer. That would obviously amount to the claimant running the evidence of "should have done", to which the producer would no doubt respond "could not have done". This would, however, once again go to the issue of avoidability, which I have concluded to be outside the ambit of art 6, and so once again if the claimant really wanted to do so he could run the point, but only in negligence.

[73] I can accept that resolution of the problem of the defective standard product will be more complex than in the case of a non-standard product. This trial has been in respect of what I am satisfied to be a non-standard product, and I see, after a three-month hearing, no difficulty in eliminating evidence of avoidability from art 6. It may be that, if I am right in my analysis, and if it is followed in other cases, problems may arise in the consideration of a standard product on such basis, but I do not consider any such problems will be insurmountable if safety, use and the

identified circumstances are kept in the forefront of consideration. Negligence, fault and the conduct of the producer or designer can be left to the (limited) ambit of art 7(e), to which I now turn.

CONCLUSIONS ON ARTICLE 7(E)

[74] As to construction: (i) I note (without resolving the question) the force of the argument that the defect in art 7(b) falls to be construed as the defect in the particular product; but I do not consider that to be determinative of the construction of art 7(e), and indeed I am firmly of the view that such is not the case in art 7(e); (ii) the analysis of art 7(e), with the guidance of *European Commission v UK*, seems to me to be entirely clear. If there is a known risk, ie the existence of the defect is known or should have been known in the light of non-Manchurianly accessible information, then the producer continues to produce and supply at his own risk. It would, in my judgment, be inconsistent with the purpose of the directive if a producer, in the case of a known risk, continues to supply products simply because, and despite the fact that, he is unable to identify in which if any of his products that defect will occur or recur, or, more relevantly in a case such as this, where the producer is obliged to supply, continues to supply without accepting the responsibility for any injuries resulting, by insurance or otherwise; and (iii) the existence of the defect is in my judgment clearly generic. Once the existence of the defect is known, then there is then the risk of that defect materialising in any particular product.

[75] The purpose of the directive, from which art 7(e) should obviously not derogate more than is necessary (see Recital 16) is to prevent injury, and facilitate compensation for injury. The defendants submit that this means that art 7(e) must be construed so as to give the opportunity to the producer to do all he can in order to avoid injury: thus concentrating on what can be done in relation to the particular product. The claimants submit that this will rather be achieved by imposing obligation in respect of a known risk irrespective of the chances of finding the defect in the particular product, and I agree.

[76] The purpose of art 7(e) was plainly not to discourage innovation, and to exclude development risks from the directive, and it succeeds in its objective, subject to the very considerable restrictions that are clarified by *European Commission v UK*: namely that the risk ceases to be a development risk and becomes a known risk not if and when the producer in question (or, as the CPA inappropriately sought to enact in s 4(1)(e) "a producer of products of the same description as the product in question") had the requisite knowledge, but if and when such knowledge were accessible anywhere in the world outside Manchuria. Hence it protects the producer in respect of the unknown (*inconnu*). But the consequence of acceptance of the defendants' submissions would be that protection would also be given in respect of the known.

[77]   The effect is ... that non-standard products are incapable of coming within art 7(e). Non-standard products may qualify *once* – ie if the problem which leads to an occasional defective product is (unlike the present case) not known: this may perhaps be more unusual than in relation to a problem with a standard product, but does not seem to me to be an impossible scenario. However, once the problem is known by virtue of accessible information, then the non-standard product can no longer qualify for protection under art 7(e).

THE RESULT IN LAW ON ISSUE I

[78]   Unknown risks are unlikely to qualify by way of defence within art 6. They may, however, qualify for art 7(e). Known risks do not qualify within art 7(e), even if unavoidable in the particular product. They may qualify within art 6 if fully known and socially acceptable.

[79]   The blood products in this case were non-standard products, and were unsafe by virtue of the harmful characteristics which they had and which the standard products did not have.

[80]   They were not *ipso facto* defective (an expression used from time to time by the claimants) but were defective because I am satisfied that the public at large was entitled to expect that the blood transfused to them would be free from infection. There were no warnings and no material publicity, certainly none officially initiated by or for the benefit of the defendants, and the knowledge of the medical profession, not materially or at all shared with the consumer, is of no relevance. It is not material to consider whether any steps or any further steps could have been taken to avoid or palliate the risk that the blood would be infected ...

The consequence

[82]   In those circumstances the claimants recover against the defendants because their claim succeeds within art 4, the blood bags being concluded to be defective within art 6, and art 7(e) does not avail.'

Comments

(1)   Burton J considered that because the Consumer Protection Act 1987 was to be read consistently with the Directive it was appropriate to direct his mind to the content of the Directive rather than the Act (thereby allowing him to deal more readily with the range of Community sources to which he was referred).

(2)   Burton J distinguished standard from non-standard products:

'a standard product is one which is and performs as the producer intends. A non-standard product is one which is different, obviously because it is deficient or inferior in terms of safety, from the standard product: and where it is the harmful characteristic or characteristics present in the non-standard product, but not in the standard product, which has or have caused the material injury or damage.'

In the *Cosytoes* case (*Abouzaid v Mothercare (UK) Ltd*) there was a standard product which was defective. The strap on the product operated as the manufacturer intended and when it sprang back and hit the claimant in the eye this was an undesired, but foreseeable, incident in the case of all such products. It was not a rogue piece of elastic or a rogue fixing.

(3) When it came to what the public was entitled to expect by way of safety, Burton J held that the judge was an informed member of the public who had to take into account all relevant circumstances. Burton J held that the avoidability of harm was not relevant to article 6 because this raised issues similar to negligence, which the Directive had been framed to eliminate. Equally, relevant circumstances did not include the impracticability, cost or difficulty of precautionary measures, nor did they include the benefit to society or the utility of the particular product. The bags of defective blood in this case were non-standard products because they were different from the norm intended by the producer and they were defective because the public was entitled to expect that the blood would be free from infection. The purpose of the Directive was to promote the safety of consumers and to make it easier for those damaged by products to achieve compensation. Thus, once the defect and subsequent risk were known then article 7(e) did not apply even if the risk was unavoidable and even if, as in this case, the defendant was obliged by law to provide the product examples of which might contain the defect.

The *German Bottle* case concerned an exploding bottle of mineral water which injured the plaintiff. The defect was a very fine hairline crack which was not discovered despite an examination process involving seven inspections and the very latest technology. The German court held that this was a defect and a consumer was entitled to expect such bottles to be free of defects likely to cause them to explode. The technical impossibility of detecting such cracks did not alter the consumer's expectations. Additionally, it seems that the court in that case also concluded that the risks associated with reusing bottles were known and that the unavoidability of the defect was irrelevant to the development risks defence.

(4) The criminal law and the civil law are closely allied here. Burton J commented:

'In the criminal field, the United Kingdom courts have responded stringently to manufacturing errors: this appears clearly from the House of

Lords decision in *Smedleys Ltd v Breed*, where, notwithstanding non-negligent quality control, there was strict liability at criminal law where a caterpillar identical in colour, size, density and weight to the peas in a tin survived the process in one out of three million tins: but that too would be a non-standard product.'

CHAPTER 9

Breach of statutory duty

The law may in some circumstances, by a process of implication, provide a remedy for breach of a duty imposed by statute. This is a distinct common law remedy perceived by the judges as necessary to ensure that parliamentary intention is effective. Although of ancient origin, it came to its modern shape as a result of the increase in legislation which coincided with the expansion of government activity in the late nineteenth century. The nature of the remedy was described in *London Passenger Transport Board v Upson*:

> '... a claim for damages for breach of statutory duty intended to protect a person in the position of the particular plaintiff is a specific common law right which is not to be confused in essence with a claim in negligence. The statutory right has its origins in the statute, but the particular remedy of an action for damages is given by the common law in order to make effective, for the benefit of the injured plaintiff, his right to the performance by the defendant of the defendant's statutory duty. It is an effective sanction. It is not a claim in negligence in the strict or ordinary sense ... whatever the resemblances, it is essential to keep in mind the fundamental differences of the two classes of claim.'

The remedy is susceptible to criticism in particular because it involves the use of a legal fiction: the intention of Parliament. The search for this has been likened to trying to discover 'the will-o'-the-wisp of a non-existing legislative intention'. The remedy has been described as 'a barefaced fiction because ... the legislature's silence on the question ... rather points to the conclusion that it either did not have it in mind or deliberately omitted to provide for it'. But *Winfield and Jolowicz* adopt Lord Du Parcq's comments in *Cutler v Wandsworth Stadium*: 'silence ... is a deliberate invitation to the courts to decide the question for themselves'.

The courts have been reluctant to approach the matter in any way other than to use presumptions adopted in the early part of the nineteenth century: see *Doe (deceased) Bishop of Rochester v Bridges, Lonrho Ltd v Shell Petroleum*, below; *Cutler v Wandsworth Stadium*, p 455; *Atkinson v Newcastle Waterworks*, p 456. But above all, what matters is the proper construction of a particular statutory provision (whether primary or secondary legislation): see *Cutler v Wandsworth Stadium*.

The conclusion has been that whether or not there is a remedy is difficult to forecast with any degree of precision. In *Ex p Island Records* Lord Denning thought that: 'The dividing line between the pro-cases and the contra-cases is so blurred and ill-defined that you might as well toss a coin to decide it.'

Once the precise duty has been established (and the standard expected may vary from absolute to reasonable care), it must be shown that the claimant falls within the scope of the duty, that there has been a breach and that the breach caused the damage. In these latter respects the tort is similar to negligence.

The claims in negligence and breach of statutory duty are different and there is no reason in principle why they may not co-exist: *West Wiltshire DC v Garland*, *X and others v Bedfordshire CC*. The relationship between the torts of negligence and breach of statutory duty, and between these torts and principles governing judicial review and governmental decision-making, have been addressed most recently by the House of Lords in *X and others v Bedfordshire CC*. The difficulty in establishing a cause of action for breach of statutory duty is demonstrated by that case, see p 461.

Lonrho Ltd and others v Shell Petroleum Co Ltd and others [1981] 2 All ER 456 House of Lords

The plaintiffs alleged that they had suffered damage as a result of the breach of a statutory Order in Council made under the Southern Rhodesia Act 1965 relating to trade with the breakaway regime of Ian Smith in the then Southern Rhodesia. The Order in Council specifically provided a criminal sanction for breach. The House of Lords concluded that there was no civil remedy for breach of the Order in Council.

Lord Diplock:'... it is well settled by authority of this House in *Cutler v Wandsworth Stadium* Ltd that the question whether legislation which makes the doing or omitting to do a particular act a criminal offence renders the person guilty of such offence liable also in a civil action for damages at the suit of any person who thereby suffers loss or damage is a question of construction of the legislation ...

The sanctions order thus creates a statutory prohibition on the doing of certain classes of acts and provides the means of enforcing the prohibition by prosecution for a criminal offence which is subject to heavy penalties including imprisonment. So one starts with the presumption laid down originally by Lord Tenterden CJ in *Doe d. Bishop of Rochester v Bridges* ... where he spoke of the "general rule" that:

"where an Act creates an obligation, and enforces the performance in a specified manner ... that performance cannot be enforced in any other manner", a statement that has frequently been cited with approval ever since, including on several occasions in speeches in this House. Where the only manner of enforcing performance for which the Act provides is prosecution for the criminal offence of failure to perform the statutory obligation or for contravening the statutory prohibition which the Act creates there are two classes of exception to this general rule.

The first is where on the true construction of the Act it is apparent that the obligation or prohibition was imposed for the benefit or protection of a particular class of individuals, as in the case of the Factories Acts and similar legislation. As Lord Kinnear put it in *Black v Fife Coal Co Ltd*, in the case of such a statute:

> "There is no reasonable ground for maintaining that a proceeding by way of penalty is the only remedy allowed by the statute ... We are to consider the scope and purpose of the statute and in particular for whose benefit it is intended. Now the object of the present statute is plain. It was intended to compel mine owners to make due provision for the safety of the men working in their mines, and the persons for whose benefit all these rules are to be enforced are the persons exposed to danger. But when a duty of this kind is imposed for the benefit of particular persons there arises at common law a correlative right in those persons who may be injured by its contravention."

The second exception is where the statute creates a public right (i.e. a right to be enjoyed by all those of Her Majesty's subjects who wish to avail themselves of it) and a particular member of the public suffers what Brett J in *Benjamin v Storr* described as "particular, direct and substantial" damage "other and different from that which was common to all the rest of the public". Most of the authorities about this second exception deal not with the public rights created by statute but with public rights existing at common law, particularly in respect of use of highways. *Boyce v Paddington Borough Council* is one of the comparatively few cases about a right conferred on the general public by statute. It is in relation to that class of statute only that Buckley J's oft-cited statement as to the two cases in which a plaintiff, without joining the Attorney-General, could himself sue in private law for interference with that public right must be understood. The two cases he said were:

> "first, where the interference with the public right is such as that some private right of his is at the same time interfered with ... and, secondly, where no private right is interfered with, but the plaintiff, in respect of his public right, suffers special damage peculiar to himself from the interference with the public right."

The first case would not appear to depend on the existence of a public right in addition to the private one; while to come within the second case at all it has first to be shown that the statute, having regard to its scope and language, does fall within that class of statutes which create a legal right to be enjoyed by all of Her Majesty's subjects who wish to avail themselves of it. A mere prohibition on members of the public generally from doing what it would otherwise be lawful for them to do is not enough ...

Clearly [the Orders] were not within the first category of exception. They were not imposed for the *benefit* or *protection* of a particular class of individuals who were engaged in supplying or delivering crude oil or petroleum products to Southern Rhodesia. They were intended to put an end to such transactions. Equally plainly they did not create any public right to be enjoyed by all those of Her Majesty's subjects who wished to avail themselves of it. On the contrary, what they did was to withdraw a previously existing right of citizens of, and companies incorporated in, the United Kingdom to trade with Southern Rhodesia in crude oil and petroleum products. Their purpose was, perhaps, most aptly stated by Fox LJ. He said:

> "I cannot think that they were concerned with conferring rights either on individuals or the public at large. Their purpose was the destruction, by economic pressure, of the UDI regime in Southern Rhodesia; they were instruments of state policy in an international matter."

... I can see no ground on which contraventions by Shell and BP of the sanctions orders, though not amounting to any breach of their contract with Lonrho, nevertheless constituted a tort for which Lonrho could recover in a civil suit any loss caused to them by such contraventions.

Briefly parting from this part of the case, however, I should mention briefly two cases, one in the Court of Appeal of England, *Ex parte Island Records Ltd* and one in the High Court of Australia, *Beaudesert Shire Council v Smith* which counsel for Lonrho, as a last resort, relied on as showing that some broader principle has of recent years replaced those long-established principles that I have just stated for determining whether a contravention of a particular statutory prohibition by one private individual makes him liable in tort to another private individual who can prove that he has suffered damage as a result of the contravention.

Ex parte Island Records Ltd was an unopposed application for an Anton Piller order against a defendant who, without the consent of the performers, had made records of musical performances for the purposes of trade. This was an offence, punishable by a relatively small penalty under the Dramatic and Musical Performers' Protection Act 1958. The application for the Anton Piller order was made by performers whose performances had been "bootlegged" by the defendant without their consent and also by record companies with whom the performers had entered into exclusive contracts. So far as the application by performers was concerned, it could have been granted for entirely orthodox reasons. The Act was passed for the protection of a particular class of individuals, dramatic and musical performers;

even the short title said so. Whether the record companies would have been entitled to obtain the order in a civil action to which the performers whose performances had been bootlegged were not parties is a matter which for present purposes it is not necessary to decide. Lord Denning MR, however, with whom Waller LJ agreed (Shaw LJ dissenting) appears to enunciate a wider general rule, which does not depend on the scope and language of the statute by which a criminal offence is committed, that whenever a lawful business carried on by one individual in fact suffers damage as the consequence of a contravention by another individual of any statutory prohibition the former has a civil right of action against the latter for such damage.

My Lords, with respect, I am unable to accept that this is the law; and I observe that in his judgment rejecting a similar argument by the appellants in the instant appeal Lord Denning MR accepts that the question whether a breach of sanctions orders gives rise to a civil action depends on the object and intent of those orders, and refers to *Ex parte Island Records Ltd* as an example of a statute passed for the protection of private rights and interests, viz. those of the performers.

Beaudesert Shire Council v Smith is a decision of the High Court of Australia. It appeared to recognise the existence of a novel innominate tort of the nature of an "action for damages upon the case" available to "a person who suffers harm or loss as the inevitable consequence of the unlawful, intentional and positive acts of another". The decision, although now 15 years old, has never been followed in any Australian or other common law jurisdiction. In subsequent Australian cases it has invariably been distinguished, most recently by the Privy Council in *Dunlop v Woollahra Municipal Council* on appeal from the Supreme Court of New South Wales. It is clear now from a later decision of the Australian High Court in *Kitano v Commonwealth of Australia* that the adjective "unlawful" in the definition of acts which give rise to this new action from damages on the case does not include *every* breach of statutory duty which in fact causes damage to the plaintiff. It remains uncertain whether it was intended to include acts done in contravention of a wider range of statutory obligations or prohibitions than those which under the principles that I have discussed above would give rise to a civil action at common law in England if they are contravened. If the tort described in *Beaudesert* was really intended to extend that range, I would invite your Lordships to declare that it forms no part of the law of England …'

Comment

(1)   Lord Diplock states and applies traditional principles. Although there are examples within the first exception, e.g. *Groves v Lord Wimborne*, p 458, examples in the second exception are less easy to identify, save in the context of special damage permitting recovery for a private right of action arising from a public nuisance, see p 684.

(2)   If the Act provides a criminal sanction, the starting point is that that will be the only remedy: *Atkinson v Newcastle Waterworks*, p 456, and *Cutler v Wandsworth Stadium*, p 455. But see also *Groves v Lord Wimborne*, p 458.

(3)   The concept of an alternative means of enforcement or remedy is flexibly applied. In *Reffel v Surrey CC*, the plaintiff was injured by a defective door in a school. The plaintiff had a statutory right to complain to the Secretary of State but this was not regarded as an alternative remedy such as to deprive the plaintiff of an action for breach of statutory duty. In *Wyatt v Hillingdon* representations to the Secretary of State in connection with the refusal of a home help were regarded as a suitable alternative remedy and no action for breach of statutory duty was available. In *McCall v Abelesz* the alternative remedy of breach of covenant was cited as one reason for not recognising an action for breach of statutory duty for tenants suffering harassment.

In *Wentworth v Wiltshire CC*, an alternative remedy by way of application to the Crown Court to enforce a highway authority's duty of repair was held to preclude the enforcement of the duty by way of common law action except in relation to injury or damage to road users, not economic loss for loss of profit while a road was unusable.

(4)   In *Re HIV Haemophiliac Litigation*, an action alleging, *inter alia*, breach of statutory duty in respect of the running of the health service and involving the supply of faulty blood products to haemophiliacs, a cause of action in negligence was regarded as existing and thus was an alternative remedy suggesting the absence of an action for breach of statutory duty. It might be observed that an alternative remedy provided by the statute in question is one thing – Parliament may legitimately be said to have been alerted to its existence – but a remedy outside the Act is entirely different, especially in the light of the lottery of deciding whether a duty of care arises: see also *R v Knowsley, BC ex p Maguire, West Wilts DC v Pugh* and *West Wiltshire DC v Garland*.

In *West Wiltshire DC v Garland*, an application to strike out a case as disclosing no cause of action, the Court of Appeal held that it was arguable that a district council could maintain an action against district auditors for breach of statutory duty and also for negligence for errors in the audit. The Chancery Division had already held that the auditors could not be liable for breach of statutory duty at the suit of senior employees of the council since the statutory provisions were intended to protect only the council and not the employees. There had been no appeal against that decision.

The Court of Appeal went on to hold that it would not be fair, just and reasonable to impose a duty of care in negligence on the auditors in respect of the senior employees whom the auditors might seek to criticise in the context of their report. The emphasis here was on the statutory powers under which the auditors were acting. The existence of statutory powers was sufficient to distinguish the case from the decision in *Spring v Guardian Assurance plc*.

(5)   Note the irony that a public duty is less important than a private one. This is judicially recognised: see, e.g., the comment in *Phillips v Britannia Hygienic Laundry*:

'... it would be strange if a less important duty, which is owed to a section of the public, may be enforced by action, which a more important duty owed to the public at large cannot'.

(6)   Attempts to suggest that Lord Diplock had freed the courts from their strict rules have been rejected: see *Hague v Deputy Governor of Parkhurst Prison*, p 460 and *Pickering v Liverpool Daily Post & Echo Newspaper plc*, p 461. Lord Diplock very effectively placed a significant limitation upon the development of the tort. The move by Lord Denning to which Lord Diplock referred had not received judicial support. *Ex p Island Records* had not been followed and had been rejected as incorrect to that extent in *RCA v Pollard*.

(7)   There is now the possibility of an action based upon breach of legislation stemming from European Community jurisprudence. The initial acceptance of this in *Garden Cottage Foods Ltd v Milk Marketing Board* was followed by rejection in *Bourgoin SA v Ministry of Agriculture Fisheries and Food*. It has now been accepted that *Bourgoin* was in error: see *Kirklees MBC v Wickes*. Further, the scope for direct action against national governments for failure to implement directives has been acknowledged in *Francovich v Italy* and subsequent cases.

(8)   In *Cutler v Wandsworth Stadium*, there was an obligation in the Betting and Lotteries Act 1934 to 'take such steps as are necessary to secure that ... there is available for bookmakers space on the track where they can conveniently carry on bookmaking', and there was a criminal offence in respect of failure so to do. The House of Lords held that the obligation was for the benefit of the public, not bookmakers, and that breach was not a private wrong remediable by action at the instance of the bookmaker. The criminal sanction was an indicator away from a remedy at common law, and there was nothing in the Act to take the court away from that conclusion. Lord Simonds:

'I do not propose to try to formulate any rules by reference to which such a question can infallibly be answered. The only rule which in all circumstances is valid is that the answer must depend on a consideration of the whole Act and the circumstances, including the pre-existing law, in which it was enacted. But that there are indications which point with more or less force to the one answer or the other is clear from authorities which ... have great weight with the House. For instance, if a statutory duty is prescribed, but no remedy by way of penalty or otherwise for its breach is imposed, it can be assumed that a right of civil action accrues to the person who is damnified by the breach. For if it were not so, the statute would be but a pious aspiration ... The sanction of criminal proceedings emphasises that this statutory obligation, like many others ... is imposed for the public benefit and that the breach of it is a public, not a private, wrong.'

Lord Du Parcq commented that:

'To a person unversed in the science, or art, of legislation it may well seem strange that Parliament has not by now made it a rule to state explicitly what its intention is in a matter which is often of no little importance, instead of leaving it to the courts to discover, by a careful examination and analysis of what is expressly said, what that intention may be supposed probably to be. There are, no doubt, reasons which inhibit the legislature from revealing its intention in plain words. I do not know, and must not speculate, what those reasons may be. I trust, however, that it will not be thought impertinent, in any sense of that word, to suggest respectfully that those who are responsible for framing legislation might consider whether the traditional practice which obscures, if it does not conceal, the intention which Parliament has, or must be presumed to have, might not safely be abandoned.'

Atkinson v Newcastle Waterworks Co
[1874–80] All ER Rep 757 Court of Appeal

The defendant company had powers and duties under an Act of Parliament which related to the supply of water to the city of Newcastle. One obligation was to provide water at a specific pressure to fire-plugs for the purpose of fire-fighting. The plaintiff's premises caught fire and the pressure in the plugs was insufficient to allow the fire to be fought. The plaintiff's action alleging breach of statutory duty failed.

Lord Cairns LC: '... The statutory duty ... arises under s 42 of the Waterworks Clauses Act 1847. The scheme of these clauses seems to be this: The undertakers apply to Parliament for powers to take land and construct works for the supply of water, and in consideration of the powers which they obtain they come under certain obligations. As to fire-plugs they are under an obligation to fix them at intervals along the streets, and, if requested, to fix them near premises used as manufactories, and to keep them charged up to the prescribed pressure, unless prevented by frost, drought, or other unavoidable cause or accident, and to allow all persons to take and use water for the purpose of extinguishing fire, without making compensation. They are willing to accept the Parliamentary obligation to keep the mains charged. That this creates a statutory duty no one can dispute; but does it give a right of action to any individual who can aver, as the plaintiff does here, that his premises were near the pipes, that a fire broke out, that there was no water to extinguish it, and that his premises were burnt? He does not say that he was not allowed to take the water, but he complains of a failure in the duty to keep the mains charged.

The proposition *a priori* appears to be somewhat startling that a company supplying a town with water – although they are willing to be put under obligation to keep up the pressure, and to be subject to penalties if they fail to do so – should further be willing to assume, or that Parliament should think it necessary to subject them to, liability to individual actions by any householder who could make out a case. In the one case they are merely under liability to penalties if they neglect to perform their duty, in the other case they are practically insurers, so far as water can produce safety from damage by fire. It is necessary to look at the provisions of s 43. Four cases are there specified, which cover all the duty imposed by the former sections, and for neglect of any one of these duties, there is a penalty of £10. For neglect of two of them, viz., to furnish to the town commissioners a sufficient supply of water for public purposes, and to furnish a supply of water to the owner or occupier, there is a further penalty of 40s. a day, payable to every person who has paid or tendered the rate, for as long as such neglect or refusal continues after notice in writing has been given of the want of supply. It is not material to say, but it is possible that it might be held that neglect or refusal to fix fire-plugs would also subject the company to the 40s. penalty. If so that penalty would be applicable in three cases out of the four. We have to consider why in some cases the penalty should go into the pocket of the individuals injured, and not in others. In the case of the obligation to keep the pipes charged, and allow all persons to use the water for the purpose of extinguishing fires, the provision is for the benefit of the public, and not of any individual specially, and the guarantee for the performance of the obligation is the liability to the public penalty of £10.

Apart from authority, I should be of opinion that the scheme of the Act and its true construction was not to create a duty which should be the subject of an action by any individual who might be injured, not to give a right to an individual to bring an action, but to lay down a series of duties, and provide a guarantee for their performance by s 43, which imposes penalties in case of neglect or refusal. Where it is convenient that it should be so, the penalty goes into the pocket of the injured party; otherwise they are public penalties, imposed by way of security that all the public duty will be performed. The contrary intention is that we ought to say that where the penalty goes into the pocket of an individual no action will lie, but that otherwise a right of action exists, that in the other cases an individual would have no right of action, but that any one of the public could bring an action if there was no water in the main, and he suffered damage in consequence. I think it is impossible to adopt this view. The scheme must be judged by ss 42 and 43, taken as a whole. Where we find that in most cases a penalty is imposed which would stop the right of action, it seems to me that the same result would follow in the other case provided for by s 43. That is my opinion, unless there is some authority to the contrary.

The authority which is said to lead to a different conclusion is *Couch v Steel*. That was a case of some peculiarity. The plaintiff, who was a seaman, and had served on board the defendant's vessel, sued the defendant for not providing a proper supply of medicines for the voyage, which he was bound to do by [statute], in consequence of which the plaintiff suffered from illness. In the declaration no claim was made on the Act of Parliament, but it was produced in the argument, and relied on in support of the plaintiff's case. With regard to the case and that Act of Parliament, if the decision were before us for review, I should desire further time for consideration; but that is not the case here, for the Act we have to deal with is widely different from the Act on which that case was decided. I must venture ... to express a doubt whether the authorities referred to by Lord Campbell in giving judgment justified the broad expressions which were used. It is not necessary to go through all the authorities which are there referred to ... but it appears to me to be questionable whether they justify the broad general statement that wherever there is a statutory duty imposed, and any person is injured by the non-performance of that duty, an action can be maintained. It must depend on the particular statute, and where it is like a private legislative bargain, into which the undertakers of the works have entered, it differs from the case where a general public duty is imposed ...'

Comment

(1)   *Atkinson v Newcastle Waterworks Co* is said to be the authority which imposed a restrictive approach to breach of statutory duty. Certainly *Couch v Steel*, dismissed by the Court of Appeal, was broader in its approach.

(2)   For another case on water legislation see *Read v Croydon Corporation* where breach of a provision in the same Act, but related to the purity of water, was held to confer a right to sue on a ratepayer in respect of medical expenses for a daughter who contracted typhoid but not on the daughter in respect of the illness.

Groves v Lord Wimborne
[1895–99] All ER Rep 147 Court of Appeal

The plaintiff sued the employers for damages for personal injury suffered as a result of breach of the defendant's statutory duty under the Factory and Workshop Act 1878, s 5 to fence securely all dangerous parts of machinery. The Court of Appeal held that despite the imposition of a criminal penalty, there was a remedy by way of action.

A L Smith LJ: '... It is a public Act passed to compel the occupiers of factories to take certain precautions on behalf of their workmen. It is not ... in the nature of a private legislative bargain between masters and men, but a legislative enactment in compulsion of the masters ... Assuming that the matter depended on s 5 alone, and that ss 81, 82 and 86 had formed no part of the Act, could it be doubted that a person injured as the plaintiff has been could sue for the damage caused to him by the breach of the statutory duty imposed on the defendant? Clearly not. Therefore, unless it can be found from the whole purview of the Act that the legislature intended that the only remedy for a breach of the duty created by the Act should be the infliction of a fine upon the master, it seems clear to me that upon proof of such a breach of duty and of an injury done to the workman, a cause of action is given to the workman against the master.

That brings me to the question whether the cause of action which would *prima facie* be given by the Act has been taken away by any of the provisions enacted in the statute. Reliance has been placed upon ss 81, 82, and 86, and it has been argued that, under these sections, the only remedy provided in a case where a workman has been injured by a breach of a duty imposed upon the master by the Act is an application to a court of summary jurisdiction for the infliction of a fine. In considering this question, I ask myself in whose favour was the Act passed? As was pointed out by Kelly CB in *Gorris v Scott* the purposes which the legislature had in view in passing the Act are very material. I feel no doubt that the Act was passed for the benefit of workmen in factories by compelling the masters to do certain things for their protection. I do not think that ss 81, 82, and 86 can be interpreted so as to take away from an injured workman the remedy which otherwise he would have under the statute against his master. Not one penny of a fine imposed under these sections need ever go into the pocket of the person injured. It is only when a Secretary of State so determines that any part of the fine is to be applied for the benefit of the injured workman. I cannot think that such an enactment was intended to deprive the workman of his right of action. Moreover, upon what grounds are the magistrates to whom application has been made under these sections to estimate the amount of the fine to be imposed? Suppose that a workman has been killed in consequence of a breach of the master's statutory duty to fence his machinery, should the fine be of the same amount whether the breach of duty was a flagrant one or not? It is contended that the magistrates ought to take into consideration the nature of the injury which the workman has suffered, but I do not feel at all clear that that is what the legislature intended by these sections. I am inclined to think that the object of these provisions is the infliction of punishment on the master who has neglected his duty, and that the fine should be in proportion to his offence. The consideration of these points leads me to the conclusion that it was not the intention of the legislature to take away by means of these sections the right which the workmen would otherwise have to be properly compensated for any injury caused to him by his master's neglect of duty.

There is also another ground which I should have mentioned which supports me in arriving at that conclusion. It is this. There is no necessity that the fine inflicted under these sections should be payable by the master, who would presumably be a man of some means. Under ss 86 and 87 the fine may be imposed upon the actual offender ...

... The actual offender may be a workman earning weekly wages, and yet it is said that the infliction of a fine on him is to be the only remedy that the injured person is to have. I cannot read this statute in the way in which the defendant seeks to read it. In my opinion, s 5 gives to a workman a right of action upon the statute, when he has been injured through a breach of the duties created by the statute, and his rights of compensation are not limited by the provisions of the Act with regard to a fine that may be imposed by a court of summary jurisdiction.'

Comment

(1) Rigby LJ, who also concluded that there was an action for breach of statutory duty approached the case by examining the maximum penalty and comparing it to the huge range of possible contraventions and their consequences which might obtain.

(2) In instances of factory safety legislation the hurdle of proving a relevant statutory intention is easily overcome. There remain the important issues of causation (e.g. see *Ginty v Belmont Building Supplies*, p 464) and showing that the injury was caused in a way anticipated by the legislation, e.g. see *Close v Steel Co of South Wales* where the machinery came into contact with the plaintiff (a piece broke off and hit the plaintiff) rather than the plaintiff coming into contact with the machinery, or *Chipchase v British Titan Products* where the legislation did not apply because the plaintiff was working on a plank six inches below the height to which the statutory safety provision would have applied.

(3) In *Gorris v Scott* statute provided for the carriage of animals in pens of a particular style and dimensions. The purpose of the Act was the prevention of the spread of disease. The plaintiff's sheep were not penned as the Act required and were swept overboard. There was no liability for breach of statutory duty since the plaintiff was outside the scope of the Act. Compare *Knapp v Railway Executive* where it was held that level crossing regulations had been intended to protect road users or train passengers and not train drivers.

(4) In *Hague v Deputy Governor of Parkhurst Prison and others, Weldon v Home Office* the House of Lords adopted the traditional approach when considering a breach of the Prison Rules. For the facts see p 536. This aspect of the case concerns the plea that rule 43 of the Prison Rules, made under the Prison Act 1952, provided for the segregation of prisoners and that since the rule was strictly limited in operation there was implicit a recognition of a remedy for breach of statutory duty. The plaintiff argued that a breach of

statutory duty unaccompanied by a statutory remedy or penalty affords a right of action to a person injured thereby where the plaintiff belongs to a class which the statutory provision was intended to protect, and where the breach caused the plaintiff damage of a kind against which the provision was intended to protect him. This was rejected by the House of Lords. The fact that a particular provision was intended to protect certain individuals is not of itself sufficient to confer private law rights of action upon them, something more is required to show that the legislature intended to confer a right of action. The matter was one where the court had to ascertain the intention of Parliament. In this case the rule was to allow the segregation of a prisoner who was likely to disturb the good order of a prison and could not have been intended to confer a right to sue on a prisoner who was so segregated. In that case it was pointed out that prisoners had a range of other remedies such as complaint to the Governor, judicial review of the actions of both Governor and Secretary of State, and private law remedies such as damages for misfeasance in public office, assault or negligence.

(5)   In *Pickering v Liverpool Daily Post & Echo Newspapers plc* the plaintiff made an application to a Mental Health Review Tribunal. In the light of previous publicity he sought an injunction to restrain reporting of his application. The House of Lords held that the application would be protected by rule 21 of the Mental Health Tribunal Rules 1983, which required details of certain information not to be reported. However, that provision did not confer on the plaintiff a cause of action for breach of statutory duty where there had been unauthorised disclosure of information presented to the tribunal.

X and others v Bedfordshire County Council, and other appeals
[1995] 3 All ER 353 House of Lords

In a number of cases arising from local authorities' duties under education and child-care legislation, the House of Lords had to consider, *inter alia*, whether or not the children might sue for breach of statutory duty. The House of Lords in each case held that there was no cause of action for breach of statutory duty.

Lord Browne-Wilkinson: ' ... Although the question is one of statutory construction and therefore each case turns on the provisions in the relevant statute, it is significant that your Lordships were not referred to any case where it had been held that statutory provisions establishing a regulatory system or a scheme of social welfare for the benefit of the public at large had been held to give rise to a private right of action for damages for breach of statutory duty. Although regulatory or welfare legislation affecting a particular area of activity does in fact provide protection to those individuals particularly affected by that activity, the legislation is not to be treated as being passed for the benefit of those individuals but for the benefit of society in general. Thus legislation regulating the conduct of betting or prisons did not give rise to a statutory right of action vested in those adversely affected by the breach of the statutory provisions, i.e. bookmakers and prisoners: see *Cutler v Wandsworth Stadium Ltd* and *Hague v Deputy Governor of Parkhurst Prison.* The cases where a private right of action for breach of statutory duty have been held to arise are all cases in which the statutory duty has been very limited and specific as opposed to general administrative functions imposed on public bodies and involving the exercise of administrative discretions.

[After extensive review of other causes of action, the facts and the relevant statutory framework, Lord Browne-Wilkinson continued in respect of the child abuse cases:]

My starting point is that the Acts in question are all concerned to establish an administrative system designed to promote the social welfare of the community. The welfare sector involved is one of peculiar sensitivity, involving very difficult decisions how to strike the balance between protecting the child from immediate feared harm and disrupting the relationship between the child and its parents. Decisions often have to be taken on the basis of inadequate and disputed facts. In my judgment in such a context it would require exceptionally clear statutory language to show a parliamentary intention that those responsible for carrying out these difficult functions should be liable in damages if, on subsequent investigation with the benefit of hindsight, it was shown that they had reached an erroneous conclusion and therefore failed to discharge their statutory duties.

It is true that the legislation was introduced primarily for the protection of a limited class, namely children at risk, and that until April 1991 the legislation itself contained only limited machinery for enforcing the statutory duties imposed. But in my view those are the only pointers in favour of imputing to Parliament an intention to create a private law cause of action. When one turns to the actual words used in the primary legislation to create the statutory duties relied upon in my judgment they are inconsistent with any intention to create a private law cause of action.

Thus, the duty imposed by s 2(2) of the 1969 Act to bring care proceedings is made conditional upon the subjective judgment of the local authority that there are grounds for so doing. Similarly, the duty to receive a child into care under s 2(1) of the 1980 Act only arises "where it appears to a local authority" that the parents are prevented from providing properly for the child and that its intervention is necessary in the interest of the child. So far as the 1989 Act is concerned, the duty relied on in s 17 is described as "a general duty" which has two parts: (a) to safeguard the children and (b) "so far as is consistent" with (a) to promote the upbringing of the children by their families. Thus not only is the duty not a specific one but the section itself points out the basic tension which lies at the root of so much child protection work: the decision whether to split the family in order to protect the child. I find it impossible to construe such a statutory provision as demonstrating an intention that even where there is no carelessness by the authority it should be liable in damages if a court subsequently decided with hindsight that the removal, or failure to remove, the child from the family either was or was not "consistent with" the duty to safeguard the child.

All the duties imported by Sch 2 to the 1989 Act are to "take reasonable steps" to do certain things. The duty to make inquiries under s 47 is limited to "such inquiries as they consider necessary". Thus all the statutory provisions relied upon in the Bedfordshire case are, as one would expect, made dependent upon the subjective judgment of the local authority. To treat such duties as being more than public law duties is impossible.

The decision in *Thornton v Kirklees Metropolitan BC* was relied upon as showing that a statute can create a private law cause of action for damages for breach of a statutory duty even if the duty is dependent upon the defendant having first formed a subjective belief. That decision is in some respects a puzzling one and may need to be reconsidered at some future date: see *Cocks v Thanet DC*. It is sufficient to say that it has no application to the present case since in that case it was conceded by the defendants that the condition precedent to the creation of the statutory duty (i.e. the formation of the belief) had been satisfied and that a legal duty was owed to the plaintiff as an individual ...'

Comment

(1) *X v Bedfordshire* was applied in *Phelps v Hillingdon LBC* where no action for breach of statutory duty was discovered. Lord Slynn said:

> 'In the present case, although the duties were intended to benefit a particular group, mainly children with special educational needs, the Act is essentially providing a general structure for all local education authorities in respect of all children who fall within its provision. The general nature of the duties imposed on local authorities in the context of a national system of education and the remedies available by way of appeal and judicial review indicate that Parliament did not intend to create a statutory remedy by way of damages. Much of the Act is concerned with conferring discretionary powers or administrative duties in an area of social welfare where normally damages have not been awarded when there has been a failure to perform a statutory duty. The situation is quite different from that concerning the maintenance of factory premises as in *Groves v Lord Wimborne*.'

There seems to be now little scope for developing an action based on breach of statutory duty in respect of the comprehensive regulatory schemes commonly deployed by government and which operate either at a national or a local level.

(2)   Both *X v Bedfordhire* and *Phelps v Hillingdon* are significant cases in the identification of a duty of care in negligence, and in vicarious liability for the careless acts of professionals in the educational sphere, see p 64.

(3)   In the Court of Appeal in *X and others v Bedfordshire CC* Staughton LJ, commenting on the *dictum* of Lord Du Parcq in *Cutler v Wandsworth Stadium*, see p 455, observed that:

> 'One can, I think, legitimately infer that it might have been politically embarrassing to insert in the Children Act 1989 a section reading "No local authority shall be liable to a child for negligence in performing its duties under this Act, or in failing to do so". Some members might have hesitated to vote for so explicit a disclaimer. Would there have been embarrassment and hesitation if instead the section had said that the local authority was to be liable? One cannot tell, as Lord du Parcq implied, and must not speculate.'

Ginty v Belmont Building Supplies Ltd and another
[1959] I All ER 414 Queen's Bench Division

P was employed by D, a roofing contractor, and knew that he was supposed to use boards when working on asbestos roofs and that there was a statutory provision to this effect. P went to E's factory to replace the asbestos roof, but despite being told where there was an ample supply of boards, he failed to use them and fell through the roof. It was held that P had been supplied with boards. Another regulation obliged the employer, D, to use the boards, i.e. vicariously through P. The same regulation obliged P to use the boards. Although both P and D were therefore in breach of their respective duties under the regulations, the fault lay with the plaintiff and he could not recover damages.

Pearson J: '… This accident was caused manifestly by the plaintiff working on an asbestos roof, which was a fragile roof, without using boards. The special feature of this case is that that wrongful act of his constitutes a breach by him of his instructions and of the regulations as they apply to him; but it also constitutes, technically at any rate, a breach by his employer under his obligation under reg 31(3)(a) to use the boards. The actual wrongful act was the plaintiff's wrongful act, but in one aspect it constitutes a breach by himself and in another aspect it constitutes a breach by his employer. So what is the position?

There has been a number of cases, to which I shall refer in a moment, in which it has been considered whether or not the employer delegated to the employee the performance of the statutory duty. In my view, the law which is applicable here is clear and comprehensible if one does not confuse it by seeking to investigate this very difficult and complicated question whether or not there was a delegation. In my view, the important and fundamental question in a case like this is not whether there was a delegation, but simply the usual question: Whose fault was it? I shall refer to some of the decided cases to demonstrate what I have said. If the answer to that question is that in substance and reality the accident was solely due to the fault of the plaintiff, so that he was the sole author of his own wrong, he is disentitled to recover. But that has to be applied to the particular case and it is not necessarily conclusive for the employer to show that it was a wrongful act of the employee plaintiff which caused the accident. It might also appear from the evidence that something was done or omitted by the employer which caused or contributed to the accident; there may have been a lack of proper supervision or lack of proper instructions; the employer may have employed for this purpose some insufficiently experienced men, or he may in the past have acquiesced in some wrong behaviour on the part of the men. Therefore, if one finds that the immediate and direct cause of the accident was some wrongful act of the man, that is not decisive. One has to inquire whether that fault of the employer under the statutory regulations consists of, and is co-extensive with, the wrongful act of the employee. If there is some fault on the part of the employer which goes beyond or is independent of the wrongful act of the employee, and was a cause of the accident, the employer has some liability. I have stated what, in my view, the proper rule is. For this rule several explanations can be given and several bases can be provided, and I will mention three. First, there is the common law principle that a person cannot derive any advantage from his own wrong. As applied to this case, that means that a person cannot by his own wrongful act impose on his employers the liability to pay damages to him. On that, I will refer to a recent case, *Goulandris Bros Ltd v B Goldman & Sons Ltd*, in which that principle of the common law was considered in relation to a different subject-matter.

Secondly ... let us consider the effect of the plaintiff's own negligence at common law, that is, before the passing of the Law Reform (Contributory Negligence) Act 1945. If the accident was caused wholly or in part by the plaintiff's own negligence, he was barred from recovering anything, and his action failed. The Law Reform (Contributory Negligence) Act 1945, s 1(1), modified that position ... That applies only in a case where the accident is caused partly by the fault of the plaintiff and partly by the fault of somebody else; but the peculiarity of a situation such as we have here is that the accident is caused wholly by one wrongful act, and that act constitutes in one aspect a breach of obligation by the plaintiff and in another aspect a breach of obligation by his employer. Therefore, although one could say that the accident was wholly caused by the fault of the plaintiff, one could also say that the accident was wholly caused by the fault of the first defendant. In my view, that takes a case of this kind outside the scope of the Law Reform (Contributory Negligence) Act 1945, and one has to revert to common law principles to see what the position is. If one does that, the common law principle is still valid to this extent, that, if the accident is wholly caused by the plaintiff's own fault, he is disentitled to recover.

Then there is a third explanation, or basis, which can be provided; that is the need for avoiding circuity of action. Circuity of action would arise in this way. Suppose that the plaintiff said that his employer committed a breach of statutory obligation whereby damage was caused to him, and he was entitled to recover damages from his employer. The employer would reply that by the contract of employment the employee owed a duty to his employer, who, therefore, was entitled to recover damages against the employee, and that the amount of damages which the employer was entitled to recover was equal to the amount of the damages which the employee was supposedly entitled to recover against the employer. If that were the position, the litigation would go round in a circle, and for that reason there is, in my view, a valid plea of circuity of action ... Those are three explanations of the rule, which, in my view, is a valid one ...

That being the position, we have here the case in which the fault of the employer – and it is a fault under the definition of "fault" contained in the definition section, s 4, of the Law Reform (Contributory Negligence) Act 1945 – was a breach of statutory obligation by the employer because, through the employee, the employer did not use the boards; but that fault of the employer consisted of, and was co-extensive with, that of the plaintiff, and in substance this unfortunate accident was due to the fault of the plaintiff in breach of, and in defiance of, his instructions and of regulations which were well known to him. He decided to do the work on this roof without the use of boards. It would not be right, however, to take too severe a view; he was not in any direct sense going to gain anything for himself; he was taking the risk for himself with a view to getting the work done. Yet it is quite impossible to impose a liability on his employer, because the plaintiff himself decided to take the risk and not to use the boards, and in those circumstances the plaintiff must fail.'

Comment

Causation is a problem within very many areas of tort (see Chapter 5). It raises its head in a potentially absurd fashion in breach of statutory duty. The common-sense result achieved in *Ginty v Belmont Building Supplies Ltd* was confirmed by the House of Lords in *Boyle v Kodak Ltd*. B, the appellant, was employed by K, the respondent, as a painter. He was told to paint a large oil storage tank. Statutory regulations provided that ladders should so far as practicable be secured at the top and the bottom; this was an absolute duty on both the employer and the employee. There was a staircase leading to the top of the tank, but instead of using that B climbed the ladder with a view to lashing it to the tank and fell off as he was undertaking the climb. It was held that B would be entitled to recover damages since the employer had not done all he could reasonably have done to ensure that his employees complied with the regulations.

Lord Reid said:

'... The doctrine of absolute liability, which was invented by the courts, can lead to absurd results when coupled with the employer's vicarious liability. It would be absurd if, notwithstanding the employer having done all he could reasonably be expected to do to ensure compliance, a workman, who deliberately disobeyed his employer's orders and thereby put the employer in breach of a regulation, could claim damages for injury caused to him solely by his own wrongdoing. So the courts have quite properly introduced a qualification of the employer's absolute liability. A principle of law has been established that, although in general the employer is under absolute liability in respect of such a breach, the employer may have a defence to an action against him by an employee who is also in breach ...

... once the plaintiff has established that there was a breach of an enactment which made the employer absolutely liable, and that that breach caused the accident, he need do no more. But it is then open to the employer to set up a defence that in fact he was not in any way in fault but that the plaintiff employee was alone to blame. That does not mean that the employer must lead evidence, he may be able to prove this from the evidence for the plaintiff, but I do not think that I went too far in [*Ross v Associated Portland Cement Manufacturers Ltd*] in saying that he "cannot complain if in those circumstances the most favourable inferences are drawn from the appellant's evidence of which it is reasonably capable".

In the present case the appellant was a skilled and experienced painter, accustomed to working from ladders. The trial judge, dealing with his common law claim, which failed, rejected the contention that he required instruction or supervision with regard to practical matters. But the appellant's case is not that he ought to have been instructed about the technique of his craft. He thought that what he was doing was the normal procedure and he had seen the other man who gave evidence doing the same thing. He knew that there were regulations but either he had not studied them or he failed to understand their application to the circumstances in which he was working. His fault was not deliberate. Counsel for the respondents very properly did not argue that his fault was anything more than a misapprehension of his statutory duty.

The respondents led no evidence. So the crucial question is whether they have proved by the evidence of the appellant's witnesses that they did everything which they could reasonably be expected to do to prevent this breach. In fact they did nothing. Their case is that they were entitled to assume that a skilled and experienced man would know his duty under the regulations and comply with it. In a case where the regulations require no more to be done than any skilled man would know from his practical experience to be necessary, it may well be that the employer is under no duty to instruct the man as to his duty. But in the present case both the witnesses thought that the manner in which the work was being done was the correct manner, and there is nothing to suggest that any skilled man, going by his practical experience, would have thought otherwise.

It may be that neither the respondents nor their foreman knew that the work was being done in this way. But ought they to have realised, if they had given thought to the matter, that there was a substantial risk that a skilled workman would not be sufficiently familiar with the regulations to know that this method involved breach of the regulations? If they ought to have realised that, then it was plainly their duty to instruct the man as to what he ought to do in order to avoid a breach. They would be quite entitled to trust him to do what he had been told to do.

Employers are bound to know their statutory duty and take all reasonable steps to prevent their men from committing breaches. If an employer does not do that he cannot take advantage of his defence. On the respondents' admission there is a difference under this regulation between cases where there is another practicable means of access to the top of the ladder, and cases where there is none or where there is nothing to which the ladder can be lashed. In the former case the man must use the alternative means of access, here the stairway, to get to the top to lash the ladder, and then return that way before ascending the ladder; in the latter case he is permitted to ascend the ladder without lashing it. I think the evidence shows that a skilled practical man might easily fail to appreciate this and that the respondents ought to have realised that and instructed their men accordingly. So they have not proved that they did all they could reasonably be expected to do to ensure compliance and they cannot rely on this defence so as to avoid their absolute vicarious liability under the regulation ...

It therefore becomes necessary to determine apportionment of liability. Neither party was gravely to blame and I think that equal apportionment is the fairest course ...'

CHAPTER 10

Liability for animals

Ordinary rules of tortious liability often deal satisfactorily with cases of damage done by animals to persons or property. In trespass, for example, if a dog owner deliberately sets his or her dog on a peaceable citizen, the owner is liable for assault and battery in the ordinary way. And there may be liability in trespass to land, e.g. where hounds strayed on to land which a hunt had been prohibited from entering, see *League Against Cruel Sports v Scott*. Examples of liability in nuisance abound. In negligence, 'there is the ordinary duty of a person to take care that his animal or his chattel is not put to such a use as is likely to injure his neighbour', per Lord Atkin in *Fardon v Harcourt-Rivington*.

In *Draper v Hodder* the defendant was held liable in negligence for the terrible injuries which his pack of young Jack Russell Terriers inflicted on the three-year-old plaintiff. The defendant kept the puppies locked up in a barn, and it was held that it was reasonably foreseeable that if he did not take care to control them it was likely that when on the loose in a pack they would attack, this being a manifestation of their natural hunting instinct. The defendant was found to have been negligent in failing to take care to see that they were securely locked in the barn.

In addition, the common law developed a number of actions imposing 'strict liability' for harm done by animals – 'cattle trespass' and the '*scienter* action'. The common law also imposed certain restrictions on the application of the ordinary principles of liability in negligence in the case of animals straying on to a highway – the rule in *Searle v Wallbank*, straying on to other land, and by statute (Dogs Act 1906) special rules relating to harm done by dogs to livestock were created.

The common law was based on a distinction between animals *ferae naturae* (colloquially but inaccurately 'wild animals') and animals *mansuetae naturae* (colloquially but inaccurately 'tame animals'). In regard to the former, knowledge on the part of the keeper of their dangerous propensities was conclusively presumed and liability flowed (subject to available defences). In regard to the latter, liability was based upon the demonstration of actual knowledge of a propensity to do harm, i.e. '*scienter*', see Devlin J in *Behrens v Bertram Mills*.

The history of the reshaping of the law in this area is outlined in the important House of Lords decisions in *Mirvahedy v Henley*, p 484, but the Act 'adopts the pattern of the common law and seems to have been designed to restate many existing principles with incidental improvements rather than to introduce any radically new shape to the law' (*Clerk & Lindsell*). As often as not, a case will be pleaded under both the Animals Act and negligence (or nuisance or trespass, as appropriate). The complexity of the operative section for liability for non-dangerous species can be seen in *Curtis v Betts*, *Cummings v Grainger* and *Mirvahedy v Henley*.

The Act also deals with liability for straying animals as well as providing a defence for shooting a dog which is worrying livestock, and a power to detain straying animals causing damage.

Reference may also be made to the Dangerous Wild Animals Act 1976, the Guard Dogs Act 1975, the Dangerous Dogs Acts and other legislation. These have no direct impact upon the provisions of the Act, although there may be some other implications, e.g. keeping an animal unmuzzled and unleashed in breach of the modern legislation may well be strong evidence of negligence.

Animals Act 1971

1   New provisions as to strict liability for damage done by animals

(1)   The provisions of sections 2 to 5 of this Act replace–

(a)   the rules of the common law imposing a strict liability in tort for damage done by an animal on the ground that the animal is regarded as ferae naturae or that its vicious or mischievous propensities are known or presumed to be known; ...

(c)   the rules of the common law imposing a liability for cattle trespass ...

2   Liability for damage done by dangerous animals

(1)   Where any damage is caused by an animal which belongs to a dangerous species, any person who is a keeper of the animal is liable for the damage, except as otherwise provided by this Act.

(2)   Where damage is caused by an animal which does not belong to a dangerous species, a keeper of the animal is liable for the damage, except as otherwise provided by this Act, if–

(a) the damage is of a kind which the animal, unless restrained, was likely to cause or which, if caused by the animal, was likely to be severe; and

(b) the likelihood of the damage or of its being severe was due to characteristics of the animal which are not normally found in animals of the same species or are not normally so found except at particular times or in particular circumstances; and

(c) those characteristics were known to that keeper or were at any time known to a person who at that time had charge of the animal as that keeper's servant or, where that keeper is the head of a household, were known to another keeper of the animal who is a member of that household and under the age of sixteen.

3   Liability for injury done by dogs to livestock

Where a dog causes damage by killing or injuring livestock, any person who is a keeper of the dog is liable for the damage, except as otherwise provided by this Act.

4   Liability for damage and expenses due to trespassing livestock

(1) Where livestock belonging to any person strays on to land in the ownership or occupation of another and—

(a) damage is done by the livestock to the land or to any property on it which is in the ownership or possession of the other person; or

(b) any expenses are reasonably incurred by that other person in keeping the livestock while it cannot be restored to the person to whom it belongs or while it is detained in pursuance of section 7 of this Act, or in ascertaining to whom it belongs;

the person to whom the livestock belongs is liable for the damage or expenses, except as otherwise provided by this Act.

(2) For the purposes of this section any livestock belongs to the person in whose possession it is.

5   Exceptions from liability under sections 2 to 4

(1) A person is not liable under sections 2 to 4 of this Act for any damage which is due wholly to the fault of the person suffering it.

(2) A person is not liable under section 2 of this Act for any damage suffered by a person who has voluntarily accepted the risk thereof.

(3) A person is not liable under section 2 of this Act for any damage caused by an animal kept on premises or structure to a person trespassing there, if it is proved either—

(a)   that the animal was not kept there for the protection of persons or property; or

(b)   (if the animal was kept there for the protection of persons or property) that keeping it there for that purpose was not unreasonable.

(4)   A person is not liable under section 3 of this Act if the livestock was killed or injured on land on to which it had strayed and either the dog belonged to the occupier or its presence on land was authorised by the occupier.

(5)   A person is not liable under section 4 of this Act where the livestock strayed from a highway and its presence there was a lawful use of the highway.

(6)   In determining whether any liability for damage under section 4 of this Act is excluded by subsection (1) of this section the damage shall not be treated as due to the fault of the person suffering it by reason only that he could have prevented it by fencing; but a person is not liable under that section where it is proved that the straying of the livestock on to the land would not have occurred but for a breach by any other person, being a person having an interest in the land, of a duty to fence.

6   Interpretation of certain expressions used in sections 2 to 5

(1)   The following provisions apply to the interpretation of sections 2 to 5 of this Act.

(2)   A dangerous species is a species—
(a)   which is not commonly domesticated in the British Islands; and
(b)   whose fully grown animals normally have such characteristics that they are likely, unless restrained, to cause severe damage or that any damage they may cause is likely to be severe.

(3)   Subject to subsection (4) of this section, a person is a keeper of an animal if—
(a)   he owns the animal or has it in his possession; or
(b)   he is the head of a household of which a member under the age of sixteen owns the animal or has it in his possession;

and if at any time an animal ceases to be owned by or to be in the possession of a person, any person who immediately before that time was a keeper thereof by virtue of the preceding provisions of this subsection continues to be a keeper of the animal until another person becomes a keeper thereof by virtue of those provisions.

(4)   Where an animal is taken into and kept in possession for the purpose of preventing it from causing damage or of restoring it to its owner, a person is not a keeper of it by virtue only of that possession.

(5)   Where a person employed as a servant by a keeper of an animal incurs a risk incidental to his employment he shall not be treated as accepting it voluntarily.

7 Detention and sale of trespassing livestock

[Section 7 creates the right of an occupier of land to seize and detain livestock straying on to the land and provides complex rules for disposal of the livestock.]

8 Duty to take care to prevent damage from animals straying on to the highway

(1) So much of the rules of the common law relating to liability for negligence as excludes or restricts the duty which a person might owe to others to take such care as is reasonable to see that damage is not caused by animals straying on to a highway is hereby abolished.

(2) Where damage is caused by animals straying from unfenced land to a highway a person who placed them on the land shall not be regarded as having committed a breach of the duty to take care by reason only of placing them there if–
(a) the land is common land, or is land situated in an area where fencing is not customary, or is a town or village green; and
(b) he had a right to place the animals on that land.

9 Killing of or injury to dogs worrying livestock

[Section 9 provides a defence where someone kills or injures a dog in order to protect livestock.]

10 Application of certain enactments to liability under sections 2 to 4

For the purposes of the Fatal Accidents Act 1976, the Law Reform (Contributory Negligence) Act 1945 and the Limitation Act 1980 any damage for which a person is liable under sections 2 to 4 of this Act shall be treated as due to his fault.

11 General interpretation

In this Act–

'common land', and 'town or village green' have the same meanings as in the Commons Registration Act 1965;

'damage' includes the death of, or injury to, any person (including any disease and any impairment of physical or mental condition);

'fault' has the same meaning as in the Law Reform (Contributory Negligence) Act 1945;

'fencing' includes the construction of any obstacle designed to prevent animals from straying;

'livestock' means cattle, horses, asses, mules, hinnies, sheep, pigs, goats and poultry, and also deer not in the wild state and, in sections 3 and 9, also, while in captivity, pheasants, partridges and grouse;

'poultry' means the domestic varieties of the following, that is to say, fowls, turkeys, geese, ducks, guinea-fowls, pigeons, peacocks and quails; and

'species' includes sub-species and variety.

12   Application to Crown

[Section 12 deals with the liability of the Crown.]

Comment

(1)   Reported cases on dangerous species are rare. In *Tutin v Chipperfield Promotions Ltd* the plaintiff, a well-known actress, had agreed to take part in a celebrity camel race at the Horse of the Year Show. She saw camel races in progress and could not have failed to notice the extremely awkward gait with which such animals moved; despite this she continued with her decision to participate. As the race started she was thrown off the camel by its violent, awkward movements. The court concluded that there had been negligence in the organising of the race and the releasing of the camels, and found for the plaintiff. The plaintiff did not succeed under the Animals Act 1971. Although the animal belonged to a dangerous species and it had caused the damage, the plaintiff had voluntarily accepted the risk within the meaning of s 5(2).

(2)   In *Behrens v Bertram Mills*, a case under the common law, P1 and P2 ran a booth in a fun-fair operated on the defendants' site where the defendants ran a circus. The booth was adjacent to a corridor down which the defendants' Burmese elephants passed on the way to the ring. A small dog owned by W, who leased the booth to P1 and P2, ran out of the booth and frightened the elephant known as Bullu, which knocked down the booth containing the plaintiffs who were injured.

The defendants were held liable. Elephants had earlier been held to be *ferae naturae* and the court was unable to depart from that decision on a matter of law even though Bullu was a different sub-species: a Burmese elephant.

Among the reasons given by the court was that there need only be a causal link between the injury and the animal; the injury did not have to be the sort of injury you would expect from an elephant, e.g. crushing. The court gave the example of waking up to find a tiger on your bed; damages would be recoverable for any heart attack which followed. Another example would be tripping over an obstacle in an attempt to escape from the animal. In this respect the Animals Act 1971 and the common law are similar. The court also discounted *volenti non fit injuria* as a defence, and it remains of interest in that respect.

(3)   Head of household is a curious concept to employ in this day and age.

Curtis v Betts
[1990] 1 All ER 769 Court of Appeal

The plaintiff, L, aged 11 at the time of the incident, sued for personal injuries sustained in an attack upon him by the defendants' dog Max, a bull mastiff weighing nearly 10 stone. The families were well known to each other. The defendants used to load Max into a Land Rover for the purposes of conveying him to the park for a walk. On the day of the incident, L, on his cycle, approached the Land Rover into which Max was about to be loaded, and called his name. When L was near to the vehicle Max, who was held by the son of the defendants, leapt at L and bit him on the face. Evidence showed that one characteristic of the bull mastiff breed is the defence of territory, and that Max regarded the Land Rover as its own territory.

No blame was attached to L and the defences in s 5 did not apply, nor was there any contributory negligence. Although negligence was alleged, the judge held that there had been the exercise of proper control but that the action based on the Animals Act 1971, s 2(2) succeeded. L succeeded in the Court of Appeal. The majority preferred to rewrite the wording of the Act in order to reflect the view that what mattered for the purpose of s 2(2)(b) was that there had to be a causal link between the characteristics of the animal and the damage suffered.

Slade LJ: '... Lord Denning MR in *Cummings v Granger* described s 2(2) as "very cumbrously worded" and giving rise to "several difficulties". I agree. Particularly in view of the somewhat tortuous wording of the subsection, I think it desirable to consider each of the three requirements separately and in turn.

REQUIREMENT (A)

The kind of damage in the present case was personal injury. The judge, rightly, did not find that this damage was "of a kind which [Max] unless restrained was likely to cause". Indeed, he made it plain that in general Max was a docile and lazy dog. However, he found that Max's action "in jumping up and biting a child on the side of the face was likely to cause severe damage". By this route he found that the personal injury caused to L was of a kind "which, if caused by the animal, was likely to be severe", so that the second head of requirement (a) was satisfied.

Counsel for the defendants submitted that the judge's approach to requirement (a) was erroneous. In this context he referred us to and relied on a passage in North, *The Modern Law of Animals* (1972), p. 56 where it is said:

"This second type of damage envisaged by s 2(2)(a) is one that must prove to be rare in practice. For there to be liability on this basis, an animal must have caused damage in circumstances where it was unlikely that an animal of that species would cause the kind of damage in question but the animal had such abnormal characteristics that it was likely that, if it did cause damage, the damage would be severe."

He pointed out that there was no evidence or finding that Max had *abnormal* characteristics (that is to say abnormal in the case of bull mastiffs as a breed) such as rendered it likely that, if he did damage, the damage would be severe.

I agree with the latter point, but, with respect to Professor North, am unable to agree with the approach to the construction of requirement (a) suggested by him, for two reasons. First, while I accept that requirements (b) and (c) have to be read in conjunction with the preceding requirement (a), I see no necessity or justification for reading words into requirement (a) itself through a process of implication effected by reference to the succeeding requirements. The broad purpose of requirement (a), as I read it, is to subject the keeper of a non-dangerous animal to liability for the damage caused by it in any circumstances where the damage is of a kind which the particular animal in question, unless restrained, was likely to cause or which, if caused by that animal, was likely to be severe, provided that the plaintiff can also satisfy the additional requirements (b) and (c). While conceivably the reference to the likelihood of severity of damage may give rise to questions of degree on particular facts, I would not, for my part, ordinarily anticipate difficulty in applying requirement (a) in practice.

Second, Professor North's work (including p. 56) was drawn to the attention of this court in argument in *Cummings v Granger*. Nevertheless, Lord Denning MR, with whose judgment Bridge LJ expressly agreed, himself adopted the simple approach to the construction of the second limb of requirement (a) which, with respect, seems to me the right one. In the context of requirement (a) he did not find it necessary to consider whether the dog in question had characteristics not normal to Alsatians. He said: "Section 2(2)(a): this animal was a dog of the Alsatian breed. If it did bite anyone, the damage was 'likely to be severe'." So too in the present case. Max was a dog of the bull mastiff breed. If he did bite anyone, the damage was likely to be severe. For this simple reason the judge was, in my judgment, right to hold that requirement (a) was satisfied.

REQUIREMENT (B)

The construction and application of requirement (b) give rise to rather greater difficulties. In particular, on a first reading I was puzzled by the legislature's use of the phrase "the likelihood of the damage or of its being severe", instead of the simple phrase "the damage", especially since the subsequent phrase "due to" at first sight appeared to me to bear the simple meaning "caused by". However, another, broader, meaning is also given to the word "due" by the Shorter *Oxford Dictionary* (3rd edn), namely "To be ascribed or attributed". If one reads the phrase "due to" as bearing the broader sense of "attributable to" I think that this particular difficulty disappears.

Just as in my view requirement (a) in any given case falls to be considered having regard to the particular facts of that case, so too in my view, in the consideration of requirement (b) the existence or non-existence of the relevant likelihood has to be determined having regard to the particular facts. If, therefore, the plaintiff is relying on the second limb of requirement (b) he will have to show that *on the particular facts* the likelihood of the damage or of its being severe was attributable to characteristics of the animal not normally found except at particular times or in particular circumstances corresponding with the particular facts of the case.

The broad purpose of requirement (b), as I read it, is to ensure that even in a case falling within requirement (a) the defendant, subject to one exception, will still escape liability if, on the particular facts, the likelihood of damage was attributable to potentially dangerous characteristics of the animal which are normally found in animals of the same species. The one exception is this. The mere fact that a particular animal shared its potentially dangerous characteristics with other animals of the same species will not preclude the satisfaction of requirement (b) if on the particular facts the likelihood of damage was attributable to characteristics normally found in animals of the same species at times or in circumstances corresponding with those in which the damage actually occurred. In *Cummings v Granger* Ormrod LJ gave the examples of "a bitch with pups or an Alsatian dog running loose in a yard which it regards as its territory when a stranger enters into it". If, in his example, the damage is caused by a bitch accompanying her pups or an Alsatian dog defending its territory requirement (b) will be satisfied.

It was, I think, common ground before us that, in concluding that requirement (b) was satisfied, the judge based his conclusion exclusively on the second limb of that requirement, i.e. he found that the likelihood of the severe damage being caused by Max was: "due to characteristics of the animal which are not normally found in animals of the same species ... except at particular times or in particular circumstances". This conclusion gives rise to two questions: (1) what were the relevant characteristics of Max? and (2) in the particular circumstances, was the likelihood of the damage due (i.e. attributable) to those characteristics?

As to question (1), the judge concluded that bull mastiffs have a tendency to react fiercely at particular times and in particular circumstances, namely when defending the boundaries of what they regard as their own territory ... On the basis of all th[e] evidence, the judge was ... entitled to find that Max had characteristics which are not normally found in bull mastiffs, except at particular times or in particular circumstances, namely the tendency to react fiercely when defending what they regarded as their own territory.

However, to establish requirement (b) the plaintiff still had to establish that the likelihood of damage was, on the particular facts, due to these characteristics. The judge concluded that this had been established, but, with respect, his reasons for this conclusion might perhaps have been stated with greater clarity ... In my judgment, in the light of all the evidence and of his own common knowledge and experience, it was open to the judge, albeit without expert evidence to support his conclusion, to infer that Max regarded his territory as including the rear of the Land Rover ...

It follows that, in my judgment, there are no sufficient grounds for interfering with the judge's conclusion that the likelihood of the damage being severe was on the facts due to the relevant characteristics of the dog. Requirement (b) is thus satisfied. But were those characteristics known to the defendants?

REQUIREMENT (C)

... In this court counsel for the defendants accepted that, in the light of the judge's findings, this court must proceed on the basis that ... the defendants knew at least that [the dog] had the habit of jumping up at the school gate in the playground and growling and snarling at passers-by. This concession was, in my opinion, a realistic one, having regard to all the evidence. In my judgment, it follows that the defendants must be taken to have known of Max's relevant characteristics, namely his tendency to react fiercely when defending what he regarded as his own territory. In my judgment, therefore, the remaining requirement, requirement (c), is satisfied and liability on the part of the defendants is established.

CONCLUSION

I have sympathy, not only with [the plaintiff] who suffered this wretched accident (from which I am glad to know he has now made a very good recovery), but also with the defendants. They were the keepers of a dog whose disposition was obviously in general an amiable one and they have been acquitted of any personal negligence in regard to the accident. However, in enacting s 2(2) of the 1971 Act the legislature has expressed its intention that, if certain conditions are satisfied, the keepers of an animal, albeit not of a dangerous species, will incur liability for any damage caused by it, even if there has been no personal negligence on their part. The judge was, in my judgment, justified in finding that those conditions were satisfied in the present case. I would therefore dismiss this appeal.'

Stuart-Smith LJ: '... At the time of this incident Max was a big dog: he weighed about 10 stone and he had big teeth and a large mouth. I agree with the judge that if he did bite anyone the damage was likely to be severe.

Paragraph (b) presents more difficulty. Here again there are two limbs to the subsection. The first deals with what may for convenience be called permanent characteristics, the second, temporary characteristics. Dogs are not normally fierce or prone to attack humans; a dog which has a propensity to do this at all times and in all places and without discrimination as to persons would clearly fall within the first limb. One that is only aggressive in particular circumstances, for example when guarding its territory or, if a bitch, when it has a litter of pups, will come within the second limb. In the present case the judge concluded that Max fell within the second limb ...

To my mind the difficulty in the subsection arises from the first three words, "the likelihood of". Without these words, it would be plain that para (b) was concerned with the causation of damage. The plaintiff would have to prove that the damage of one of the types in para (a) was caused by either a permanent or temporary characteristic specified in para (b). This makes good sense. But the first three words seem to connote a concept of foreseeability and not causation. This would have remarkable consequences. If all that is necessary is that it be likely that a bitch with a litter of pups may have a propensity to be fierce and provided she is large enough to cause severe damage, the owner of such a bitch would be liable (if para (c) is satisfied) if the bitch causes severe damage at any time, whether or not she has pups or is with them. I cannot think that this was the intention of Parliament. Although I find difficulty in giving content to the words "the likelihood of", I am satisfied that there must be a causal link between the characteristic in question and the damage suffered. In particular where the case falls under the second limb, the temporary characteristic, the time or circumstances in which the damage is caused must be those during which the particular characteristics are or were prone to be exhibited. In my judgment, the judge correctly directed himself on this aspect of the matter ...'

Comment

(1) *Curtis v Betts* remains important for the analysis of the relationship between the Animals Act 1971, s 2(2)(a) and s 2(2)(b), and for the analysis of the opening words of s 2(2)(b). Nourse LJ thought that '[it] may be that the draftsman reproduced the wrong part of sub-s (2)(a), that is to say he reproduced the formula "the likelihood of the damage or of its being severe" when all that was meant was "the damage" ... I agree that effect must be given to sub-s (2)(b) as if it read: "*the damage* was due to characteristics of the animal which" '.

(2) Despite the judicial rewriting of s 2, there has been no legislative improvement to what has been regarded almost universally as an obviously ill-drafted provision; one exception to this view is Lord Hobhouse in *Mirvahedy v Henly* who, unlike the other members of the House of Lords, saw it as a having a plain and clear meaning.

(3) *Gloster v Chief Constable of Greater Manchester Police* presents an interesting point as to liability for a trained dog.

Cummings v Granger
[1977] I All ER 104 Court of Appeal

D ran a breaker's yard where he kept at night for security purposes an unchained Alsatian. H, who had a right of access, and P who did not, entered the site at night, and both knew about the dog. P was attacked and injured. The Animals Act 1971, s 2(2)(a) was satisfied – although Alsatians are not normally vicious (and thus the first part of s 2(2)(a) could not be satisfied), the damage was likely to be severe. Section 2(2)(b) was satisfied – the dog was running around and barking (characteristics) and guarding its territory (particular circumstances). The defence in s 5(1) did not apply since the damage was not due wholly to the fault of the person suffering it. But s 5(3) applied: P was a trespasser and it was not unreasonable to keep the dog there. And s 5(2) applied, as she knew all about the dog. The dog was regarded on the evidence as a normal Alsatian guarding territory and thus likely to defend its territory.

Lord Denning MR:' ... Now it seems to me that this is a case where the keeper of the dog is strictly liable unless he can bring himself within one of the exceptions. I say this because the three requirements for strict liability are satisfied. [Section 2] is very cumbrously worded and will give rise to several difficulties in future. But in this case the judge held that the three requirements were satisfied and I agree with him for the following reasons. Section 2(2)(a): this animal was a dog of the Alsatian breed; if it did bite anyone, the damage was "likely to be severe". Section 2(2)(b): this animal was a guard dog kept so as to scare intruders and frighten them off. On the defendant's own evidence, it used to bark and run round in circles, especially when coloured people approached. Those characteristics – barking and running around to guard its territory – are not normally found in Alsatian dogs except in circumstances where they are used as guard dogs. Those circumstances are "particular circumstances" within s 2(2)(b). It was due to those circumstances that the damage was likely to be severe if an intruder did enter on its territory. Section 2(2)(c): those characteristics were known to the defendant. It follows that the defendant is strictly liable unless he can bring himself within one of the exceptions in s 5. Obviously s 5(1) does not avail. The bite was not *wholly* due to the fault of the lady, but only *partly* so.

Section 5(3) may, however, avail the keeper ... The judge held that the defendant was unreasonable in keeping it in this yard ... I take a different view. This was a yard in the East End of London where persons of the roughest type come and go. It was a scrap-yard, true, but scrap-yards, like building sites, often contain much valuable property. It was deserted at night and at weekends. If there was no protection, thieves would drive up in a lorry and remove the scrap with no one to see them or to stop them. The only reasonable way of protecting the place was to have a guard dog. True it was a fierce dog. But why not? A gentle dog would be no good. The thieves would soon make friends with him. It seems to me that it was very reasonable – or, at any rate, not unreasonable – for the defendant to keep this dog there ...

Alternatively there is another defence provided by s 5(2) ...

[Lord Denning referred to the case of *Ilott v Wilkes* (1820) – a case about a spring gun which went off and injured a trespasser, and continued:]

That reasoning [of that case] applies here. The plaintiff certainly knew the animal was there. She worked next door. She knew all about it. She must have seen this huge notice on the door: "Beware of the Dog". Nevertheless she went in, following her man friend. In the circumstances she must be taken voluntarily to have incurred this risk. So with any burglar or thief who goes on to premises knowing that there is a guard dog there. If he is bitten or injured, he cannot recover. He voluntarily takes the risk of it. Even if he does not know a guard dog is there, he might be defeated by the plea *ex turpi causa nonoritur actio.*

There is only one further point I would mention. This accident took place in November 1971 very shortly after the Animals Act 1971 was passed. In 1975 the Guard Dogs Act 1975 was passed. It does not apply to this case. But it makes it quite clear that in future a person is not allowed to have a guard dog to roam about on his premises unless the dog is under the control of a handler. If he has no handler, the dog must be chained up so that it is not at liberty to roam around. If a person contravenes the Act, he can be brought before a magistrate and fined ... But it is only criminal liability. It does not confer a right of action in any civil proceedings. It may however have the effect in civil proceedings of making it unreasonable for the defendant to let a dog free in the yard at night (as this defendant did) and it may thus deprive the defendant of a defence under s 5(3)(b). But he might still be able to rely on the defence under s 5(2) of *volenti non fit injuria.*

Coming back to the present case, I think the defendant is not under any strict liability to the plaintiff because she was a trespasser and also because she voluntarily took the risk. I would therefore allow the appeal and enter judgment for the defendant.'

Comment

(1)   Ormrod LJ said of the definition of species in the Animals Act 1971, s 11 that:

'Those words have very much the ring of biological terms of art, and no doubt they should be given that meaning. In other words, it would be wrong to treat, say, a guard dog as being a variety of a species or sub-species for the purposes of the section. What we have to deal with here is a sub-species of dog or variety of dog called "Alsatian".'

Hunt v Wallis concerned a border collie which knocked over the plaintiff. The main issue was which species was to be the comparator species. Pill J said:

'The comparison for the purpose of para (b) is, in my judgment, between [the dog] and the characteristic border collie. Where there is an identifiable breed of longstanding with acknowledged and identifiable characteristics, at least where it is a breed whose qualities are recognised as beneficial to man, the comparison should be with that breed or sub-species. Border collies are not normally dangerous. A comparison can sensibly be made between the dog and the generality of his breed ... On the evidence I am not able to hold that the dog had any characteristics of a kind not normally found in Border Collies.'

It is not immediately apparent why Pill J mentions qualities 'recognised as beneficial to man'.

(2)   Ormrod LJ also said of s 2(2)(b) that it had 'remarkably opaque language'; compare the comments in *Curtis v Betts*. See also Comyn J in *Bearfield v Culmer* who called it 'a very difficult section to read intelligibly and intelligently'. The judicial rewriting of s 2(2)(b) reflects these comments.

(3)   Ormrod LJ further commented on the defence in s 5(2):

'I would like to read those words in their ordinary English meaning and not to complicate the question too much with the old, long history of the doctrine of *volenti*. That doctrine was developed in quite different conditions. It has nothing to do with strict liability; and I would not, for my part, like to see that defence whittled down by too fine distinctions as to what "voluntarily accepted the risk" means. They are, to my mind, fairly simple English words and should in this context be treated as such. In this case I do not think it is open to any doubt whatever on the plaintiff's evidence that, assuming she did go into this yard, she accepted the risk. No doubt she knew about the dog, she said that she was frightened of the dog. For whatever reason she went in I would myself come to the conclusion that she accepted the risk ...'

Dhesi v Chief Constable of West Midlands Police involved a suspect failing to come out of hiding and surrender when called upon to do so by a police officer assisted by a dog. In the Court of Appeal, Stuart-Smith LJ said that: '... a suspect who ignores clear warnings to come out or a dog will be sent to find him has only himself to blame if he suffers injury as a result.'

(4)   The basic proposition is that, unlike s 2(1), liability attaches only where the damage is due to the particular abnormal characteristics of the animal or the

species. For example, being 'accidentally' trodden on by a horse renowned for biting will not result in liability under the Act. See further *Jaundrill v Gillett* and *Mirvahedy v Henley*.

(5) Lord Denning also thought that the principle *ex turpi causa* might apply to a burglar (e.g. if the keeping of a guard dog was unreasonable). At first glance s 2(2) appears to exclude all other defences save those in s 5, e.g. the defence of act of third party would not be available. One answer may be that *ex turpi causa* acts as a bar to an action and not as a defence, see p 322.

(6) It should be noted that the defence in s 5 applies to animals kept to protect persons or property, rather than simply dogs kept for that purpose. Other animals may be used; thus a farmer who places a llama in a field to protect lambs against the predations of foxes would be able to rely on the defence against someone injured by it, as would owners of a factory who keep geese to sound the alarm against trespassers in the grounds. Lord Denning referred to the Guard Dogs Act 1975. As well as matters of control, this Act requires a person using a guard dog on premises to exhibit a warning notice at each entrance to the premises. The Act applies to land, but not to agricultural land.

(7) In *Kite v Napp* the plaintiff succeeded under the Animals Act 1971 in the case of an attack by a dog which was demonstrated to have had the tendency to rush out and attack passers-by who were carrying bags. The judge said:

'... I am quite satisfied that the damage ... was of a kind which the dog ... was likely to cause unless restrained and that it was indeed likely if caused to be severe. Further that the likelihood of that damage was due to characteristics of that dog which were not normally found in animals of the same species except at particular times or in particular circumstances. This is a case of particular circumstances when somebody was carrying a shopping bag, as I find.'

Did the judge get it wrong? Surely the likelihood of damage was due to characteristics not normally found in animals of the same species at any time, i.e. this is a case of unusual characteristics not particular circumstances. Compare *Flack v Hudson*, p 491. There was also a successful plea based on negligence in the light of the defendant's knowledge and failure to restrain the dog.

In *Smith v Prendergast* the plaintiff had been attacked by an Alsatian. The dog had, of its own volition, established residence in a scrap-yard and had been fed by the owner of the scrap-yard who let it wander about the yard. There was no liability under the Animals Act 1971, given the lack of knowledge of the propensity of the dog, but the Court of Appeal upheld the finding that the failure to observe the dog, to keep it without proper training, supervision or restraint was sufficient to sustain a plea of negligence.

In *Smith v Ainger* (Court of Appeal), A was walking his large mongrel dog, an Alsatian cross, towards S and his dog. Just as the parties crossed, A's dog flew at S's dog, and in so doing knocked S to the ground, and broke his leg. There was evidence that the dog had a propensity to attack other dogs and that on such other occasions the owners had intervened and had been slightly injured. In the Court of Appeal Neill LJ considered that 'likely' in s 2 included an event that 'might happen', 'such as might well happen' or 'where there is a material risk that it will happen', as well as events more probable than not. In other words the court gives a very broad meaning to the word 'likely'. Neill LJ continued:

> 'It seems to me, however, that in the light of the findings of the judge that this dog either had a general and abnormal propensity to attack other dogs, or had a propensity to attack another dog if it offended him or when he was under the control of someone who did not have complete command over him, the injuries caused to S did constitute damage of a kind which, in the circumstances existing at the time, [the dog] unless restrained, was likely to cause.
>
> On the second limb of (a) the judge came to the conclusion that it could not be said that it was likely that any injury caused by the dog would be severe ... In the light of [*Cummings v Granger* and *Curtis v Betts*] ... it seems that damage caused by a large dog such as an Alsatian is likely to be "severe" within the meaning of s 2(2) ...'

Mirvahedy v Henley and another
[2003] 2 All ER 401 House of Lords

The defendants kept horses in a field. Something frightened the horses and they stampeded out of the field, fled 300 yards up a track and then for almost a mile along a minor road. They then reached a major road. The claimant was driving on the road and a collision occurred between his car and one of the horses. The claimant suffered serious personal injuries. At all times the horses were behaving in a way which was usual in the circumstances of horses alarmed by a threat. The claimant sued relying on the Animals Act 1971, s 2(2). His claim in negligence failed at first instance and he did not appeal against that decision. The Court of Appeal upheld his appeal against the judge's decision rejecting his claim under the Animals Act. The House of Lords, by a majority of three to two (Lords Slynn and Scott dissenting) dismissed the defendant's appeal and held that s 2(2)(b) of the 1971 Act applied to behaviour which, although abnormal to the species for the most part, was nevertheless normal for that species in the particular circumstances which had occurred. As to causation, the House of Lords held that the damage was caused by the characteristics which founded liability under s 2(2), i.e. a propensity to bolt when frightened and to flee in a way which ignored all obstacles.

Lord Walker: '...

[133] My Lords ... it may be worth reflecting on why s 2(2) has given rise to so many difficulties.

[134] It is not necessary to go far into the old common law rules which imposed strict liability for wild animals (animals ferae naturae) or for tame or domesticated animals with a known vicious propensity (the scienter basis of liability). The old rules were both questionable in their foundations and uncertain in their limits ... The Goddard Committee (which reported in 1953) proposed to abolish strict liability for damage caused by animals, but the Law Commission in its report Civil Liability for Animals (Law Com no 13) (published in 1967 as one of the Law Commission's earliest reports) took a different view. The Law Commission recommended that the principle of strict liability should not be abolished, but should be modified and simplified. It is clear that in enacting the 1971 Act, Parliament was (in the most general terms) following the Law Commission's recommendations to retain the principle in a modified form. It is unfortunately far from clear that Parliament achieved the objective of simplification.

[135] Part of the problem is that s 2 of the 1971 Act is expressed in very general terms. It is notable that the Law Commission inquired into the prevalence of particular types of damage caused by animals. Its report contains some detailed statistics about road accidents in which animals were involved. But in s 2 Parliament has not chosen to identify or make specific provision for the varying circumstances in which animals do most commonly cause damage. In practice s 2(1) has a very narrow scope, being almost entirely limited to incidents in (or following escapes from) zoos or circuses. Section 2(2) has to cover the whole range of incidents involving animals of species classified as non-dangerous (which I will call domesti- cated animals, although that is not an entirely accurate term). That range includes: (i) physical injury to humans by biting (especially by dogs) or kicking or knocking down (especially by horses); (ii) injuries caused to livestock (such as a dog worrying a neighbour's sheep, or a cat killing a neighbour's chickens); (iii) road traffic accidents, especially those caused by animals straying onto the highway; (iv) damage caused by livestock getting out onto neighbouring land and destroying crops or gardens; and (v) injury or damage caused by the spread of animal infection or by the smell or noise of animals (a class which shades off into cases normally classified as nuisance). So s 2(2) has a lot of work to do. It is expressed in general, abstract terms and it has to be applied to a wide range of disparate incidents.

[136] Other sections of the 1971 Act do contain more specific provisions ... But the only special provision made for animals straying on the highway is the abolition by s 8 (subject to qualifications in s 8(2)) of the old common law rule which gave immunity (see *Searle v Wallbank*). It has not been contended in your Lordships' House (although it was contended at first instance) that s 8 has the effect of excluding possible liability under s 2(2).

[137]   Section 2(2) must therefore be treated as capable of applying (one way or another) to cases of horses straying onto a highway and causing an accident, as well as to cases ... where humans have been injured by being bitten by large dogs. Many of the epithets used in the cases relating to dog bites (such as fierce, ferocious and vicious) are not apposite to describe a horse sent into a state of panic by some unknown cause. But it cannot be doubted that for a riderless horse to be on the highway in such a state is a danger to other road users, even though it is (in its state of panic) acting in an entirely natural way. If the Court of Appeal was right the 1971 Act has in this respect extended the possible scope of strict liability for domesticated animals (while narrowing the class of dangerous species by the definition in s 6(2)).

[138]   After these general comments I come to the particular linguistic difficulties presented by s 2(2). One is the meaning of the important term "characteristics" used in paras (b) and (c) of s 2(2), but not defined in the 1971 Act. The context makes clear that the expression cannot mean something buried in an animal's psyche ... It must refer to character or disposition as evinced by overt behaviour – for instance, a dog which had the habit of attacking people who were carrying bags (see *Kite v Napp*). The distinction between "permanent" and "temporary" characteristics drawn by Stuart-Smith LJ in *Curtis'* case, is useful but must be treated with some caution: all dangerous characteristics are likely to be more or less permanent but they may show themselves either frequently and randomly (as with the unreliable horse in *Wallace v Newton*), or under a stimulus peculiar to the particular animal (such as bag-carrying in *Kite's* case), or under some internal or external stimulus (such as the animal's hormones or a perceived challenge to its territory) which can be expected to produce similar behaviour in most animals of its species.

[139]   That is the point to which the words "at particular times or in particular circumstances" are directed, but there is force in the observation made by the trial judge, in his careful judgment, that one can always find particularity attaching to any time or to any circumstance. I consider that Mr Sharp QC (for the respondent) must be right in suggesting that predictability (of how animals of the same species react to a particular stimulus or situation) is one of the indicia of characteristic behaviour which falls within the second limb of s 2(2)(b).

[140]   That leads to the central problem on this appeal. It is agreed that s 2(2)(b) contains two limbs, linked by the word "or". The second limb contains what is akin to a double negative ("not ... except") and this (coupled with the cumbersome words at the beginning of para (b), the feature which has so far attracted most of the adverse judicial comment) makes it difficult to see what para (b) as a whole is getting at. The cumbersome words at the beginning appear to me to reflect the simple proposition (familiar from the law of negligence: see for instance *Paris v Stepney BC*) that risk is a product of two factors, the likelihood of injury and the severity of the possible injury. So the subsection could be set out in a simplified form (using the abbreviation "risk" and some other simplifications) as follows:

"The [risk] was due to characteristics of the [horse] which are not normally found in [horses] or are not normally ... found [in horses] except [on particular occasions]."

[141] If para (b) is simplified in this way, it is easier to see that there are two possible interpretations of the second limb. Each is permissible (although not necessarily equally acceptable) as a matter of language. Which is to be preferred depends on the legislative context and purpose, and in particular, on what appears to be the essential purpose of the second limb as a whole. This can be illustrated by the example (based on *Barnes v Lucille Ltd* and discussed both by the Law Commission and in later authorities) of the bitch which acts fiercely and bites in defence of her pups. Suppose that a Labrador bitch (which is not nursing pups and is not subjected to any other provocation) bites a pedestrian in the park. That would on the face of things be abnormal behaviour for a Labrador, and the first limb of para (b) would apply. The only function of the second limb (one argument goes) is to forestall the owner's excuse, "but all Labrador bitches have a propensity to bite sometimes" in a case where that excuse cannot, on the facts, make any difference.

[142] The competing explanation of the second limb is that it adds a further possible head of liability where the particular circumstances are actually present (in the example, where the bitch is nursing pups). In such a case the animal's normal behaviour in abnormal circumstances is equated with a more vicious dog's abnormal behaviour in normal circumstances. Either is to be treated as introducing the element of abnormal, dangerous behaviour which goes towards the establishment of strict liability, if the other elements (in paras (a) and (c) of s 2(2)) are also present.

[Lord Walker examined the competing authorities of *Cummings v Granger* and *Curtis v Betts*, on the one hand, and *Breeden v Lampard*, on the other. He then continued:]

[155] In my view the crux of the matter is this. Both sides agree that Parliament intended to impose strict liability only for animals which are (in some sense) dangerous. Subsections (1) and (2) of s 2 mark the first subdivision which Parliament has made in identifying one (very limited) class of dangerous animals. This rather crude subdivision has contributed to the difficulties which have arisen, since it implies (but does not clearly spell out) that entirely normal behaviour of an animal of a non-dangerous species can never give rise to strict liability (this is the basis of the first anomaly relied on by the appellants). Domesticated animals are to be the subject of strict liability only if their behavioural characteristics are (in some sense) abnormal (and so dangerous). Did Parliament contemplate that the generality of animals in a domesticated species might in some circumstances show dangerous behavioural characteristics so as to be liable to be treated, in those circumstances, as dangerous? Or is there a presumption underlying the 1971 Act (and providing guidance as to the correct construction of s 2) that an animal of a

domesticated species behaving in a way that is (in particular circumstances) normal and natural for its species cannot be treated as dangerous?

[156]   In my view the scheme and language of the 1971 Act do not yield any such underlying presumption. I consider that the respondent's proposed construction of the second limb of s 2(2)(b) is more natural as a matter of language, and that it is not inconsistent with Parliament's general intention to impose strict liability only for animals known to present special dangers. The suggested anomalies, although far from insignificant, could be matched by comparable anomalies arising from the alternative construction. Moreover the respondent's proposed construction is in my view closer to what [counsel for the defendant] (echoing the Law Commission) referred to as the common experience of everyday life.

[157]   It is common knowledge (and was known to the appellants in this case) that horses, if exposed to a very frightening stimulus, will panic and stampede, knocking down obstacles in their path (in this case an electric fence, a post and barbed wire fence behind that, and then high undergrowth) and may continue their flight for a considerable distance. Horses loose in that state, either by day or by night, are an obvious danger on a road carrying fast-moving traffic. The appellants knew these facts; they could decide whether to run the unavoidable risks involved in keeping horses; they could decide whether or not to insure against those risks. Although I feel sympathy for the appellants, who were held not to have been negligent in the fencing of the field, I see nothing unjust or unreasonable in the appellants having to bear the loss resulting from their horses' escape rather than the respondent (who suffered very serious and painful injuries in the accident, although he was wearing a seatbelt and slowed down as soon as he saw the first horse in his headlights).

[158]   The Law Commission report provides useful background material to the 1971 Act but is to my mind of little or no assistance on the crucial issue of construction. Two paragraphs of the report (para 18(i) and the summary at para 91(iv)) appear to favour the respondent but the draft Bill prepared by the Law Commission did not cover the point one way or the other (it referred to "characteristics" without indicating whether they had to be normal or abnormal) ...

[161]   On the other principal issue in the appeal, the issue of causation, I see some force in the submission of [counsel for the defendant] that it was illogical for Hale LJ to deal with this issue first, before she had dealt with the main issue of construction. However the essential point is that in order to recover the claimant had to show that the damage which he had suffered was caused, not merely by the horses escaping and being on the main road, but by the characteristics which are capable of founding strict liability under s 2(2) – in short, a frightened horse's propensity to bolt, to continue to flee, and to ignore obstacles in its path.

[162]   The trial judge (following the Court of Appeal in *Jaundrill v Gillett*) thought that the damage was caused by the presence of the horses on the highway, rather

than by any relevant characteristic. Hale LJ and the other members of the Court of Appeal took a different view. Hale LJ said:

"In this case, however, it is indeed difficult to conclude that it was anything other than the particular characteristics of these horses once they had been terrified which led to their escape and to this accident taking place. They were still not behaving in the ordinary way in which they would behave when taken on the road. One witness referred to them bolting; another to them trotting across the road in front of the vehicles; they crashed into the vehicles rather than the other way about. It is precisely because they were behaving in the unusual way caused by their panic that the accident took place."

[163] I consider that that was the correct approach. I think that the Court of Appeal reached the right conclusion on both issues. I would therefore dismiss this appeal.'

Comment

(1) The competing explanations as to how the Animals Act 1971, s 2(2)(b) was to apply to normal behaviour for animals in particular circumstances were extensively examined by all their Lordships. The example given by Stuart-Smith LJ in the Court of Appeal in *Curtis v Betts* makes the distinction clear:

'Dogs are not normally fierce or prone to attack humans; a dog which has a propensity to do this at all times and in all places and without discrimination as to persons would clearly fall within the first limb. One that is only aggressive in particular circumstances, for example when guarding its territory or, if a bitch, when it has a litter of pups, will come within the second limb.'

Dicta in *Breeden*'s case took the opposite approach. A mounted hunt follower was kicked by the horse of another member of the hunt. Her leg was broken. The horses in the hunt had just changed direction and several were in close proximity to one another. The offending horse was wearing a red patch on its tail but the trial judge found that it was not a horse which was prone to kicking and dismissed the claim. Lloyd LJ summarised his view:

'If liability is based on the possession of some abnormal characteristic known to the owner, then I cannot see any sense in imposing liability when the animal is behaving in a perfectly normal way for all animals of that species in those circumstances, even though it would not be normal for those animals to behave in that way in other circumstances, for example, a bitch with pups or a horse kicking out when approached too suddenly, or too closely, from behind.'

(2)   An alternative approach to the Goddard Committee's proposal to abolish strict liability and to allow negligence to fill the gaps would be to invoke strict liability for damage caused by any animal irrespective of normal/abnormal characteristics.

(3)   The dissentients (Lord Scott and Lord Slynn) preferred the '*Breeden*' argument as representing the correct interpretation. In short, the view of the dissentients was expressed by Lord Slynn:

'[58]   If Parliament had intended that the keeper of a non-dangerous animal should be liable where the damage is caused by characteristics or behaviour which are normal at particular times, but not generally, (so that in effect the animal is to be treated as dangerous) it would have been sufficient to state quite simply that there should be liability if the likelihood of there being damage or if its being severe was due to characteristics of the animal which are not normally found in animals of the same species. The addition of the second part of (b) "are not normally so found except at particular times or in particular circumstances" should be read as meaning that if the characteristics are normally found in animals of the same species at particular times or in particular circum-stances then there is no liability. It is only if the characteristics are abnormal at such times that liability attaches subject to paras (a) and (c) being satisfied.

[59]   To summarise, the intendment of para (b) is that if the animal does what is normal for the species (a) usually or (b) only in special circum-stances or at special times then it should not be treated as dangerous and there should be no strict liability, it being always remembered that liability in negligence is preserved.'

(4)   Lord Scott, dissenting, expressed himself in wide terms. In particular he did not fully accept that the first limb of s 2(2)(a) had been made out, but because the point was not pursued in the House of Lords he could only express reservations about the judge's conclusion:

'[96]   The word "likely" should, in my opinion, be accorded the same meaning in s 2(2)(a) as it has in s 6(2)(b). If a commonly domesticated animal causes damage, the first two questions, if strict liability is to be imposed, are whether the damage is of a kind that the animal, unless restrained, was likely to cause or whether the damage is of a kind which, if caused by the animal, was likely to be severe. The answer to these questions cannot be answered by simply referring to the seriousness of the damage actually caused in the case in question. To do so would be to ignore the inclusion in the statutory language of the word "likely". If a large domesticated animal, say a horse or a bullock, finds itself loose and unrestrained in a public place it may cause personal injury or injury to property. But is it likely to do so? If it does cause personal injury or injury to property is injury of that kind likely to be severe? Neither of these questions can be answered simply by saying that the animal has in fact caused severe personal injury to the complainant or has in fact caused severe damage to his property. If that were the right approach para (a) could simply have read "or which, if caused by the animal, was severe".'

(5) Lord Scott also spoke of domestication, which has received little comment in the reported cases:

'[87] The verb "domesticate" has a number of possible meanings. One of these, according to the Shorter Oxford English Dictionary (3rd edn, 1973) p 593, and that which I think best accords with the context of s 6, is "to tame or bring under control". So species of animals which are commonly tamed and brought under control in this country cannot belong to a "dangerous species". Animals which would, under the old law, have been *mansuetae naturae* in this country are excluded. But an animal not commonly domesticated (in this country), for example, an animal *ferae naturae* under the old law, does not necessarily belong to a "dangerous species". The animal must belong to a species which satisfies para (b) of s 6(2). Thus, for example, a deer, kept in captivity, would not, in my opinion, satisfy the s 6(2)(b) requirement and would not belong to a "dangerous species" for s 2 purposes.'

He then went on to speculate about how the law would apply to a deer which might have escaped from a farm.

(6) It is also possible to borrow two questions posed by Lord Scott:

'a. Suppose there is in a field with a public footpath running through it a normal, docile horse. Suppose a mischievous individual using the footpath hits the horse with a projectile causing the horse to bolt and knock an innocent passer-by. Assuming knowledge on the part of the owner that any horse shot in such a way would be likely to bolt, what would be the result?

b. Suppose a police horse and rider are controlling a demonstration but a demonstrator jabs the horse's rump with a sharp instrument. Police horses are very well trained, in general do not kick at those in their vicinity, and are accustomed to crowds and loud noises. But all horses will kick out when stabbed in such a way. If the kick connects with the wrongdoer, he would be barred by s 5(1). But if the kick connects an innocent demonstrator, would the injured person have a strict liability claim against the police?'

(7) *Flack v Hudson* concerned a horse which had previously bolted at the sight of a tractor. On another occasion it did so and injured the defendant's

husband. It was arranged that F would ride and exercise the horse. As F was riding it down a country lane, a tractor approached; the horse was frightened by the agricultural machinery and bolted. F was thrown and died from her injuries. At first instance it was found that both F and the defendant had been keepers of the horse, but that the horse's propensity to bolt at agricultural machinery was a characteristic known only to the defendant. The Court of Appeal confirmed that the Animals Act 1971 would allow one keeper of an animal to sue another keeper and that the horse had a characteristic within s 2(2)(b) (the propensity to bolt at agricultural machinery) which was abnormal in horses and not common to all horses. In the absence of knowledge there could have been no voluntary assumption of risk.

CHAPTER 11

Trespass to the person

Trespass to the person is concerned with intentional and direct interferences with the individual, usually, but not necessarily, involving the deliberate touching or threat of touching; actual harm is not a requirement. Despite its ancient origins and relatively fixed boundaries, it is a variety of tort which even now is being questioned and developed; see, for example, *Murray v Ministry of Defence*, p 533, *F v West Berkshire Health Authority*, p 540 and *Hague v Deputy Governor of Parkhurst Prison*, p 536. There remain some areas of doubt, albeit on matters of classification, e.g. see *Letang v Cooper*, p 497 and *Stubbings v Webb*, below. Even where the activities of the defendant fall outside the narrow boundaries of trespass, the common law may still provide a remedy under the principle in *Wilkinson v Downton*, although the development of that principle has received a serious set-back from the House of Lords in *Wainwright v Home Office*, p 512.

The development of trespass is important in the context of medical treatment where human frailty and emotions, medical ethics and legal reasoning are being worked out on a case-by-case basis; sometimes with conspicuous success, e.g. *Airedale NHS Trust v Bland*, p 549; always attended by conspicuous controversy, e.g. *Airedale NHS Trust v Bland* and the case of the conjoined twins, *Re A (Children) (Conjoined Twins: Medical Treatment) (No 1)*. It is in the field of medicine that the boundaries of consent are being mapped out.

Trespass has often been the medium through which basic liberties have been declared, whether indirectly, e.g. see *Collins v Wilcock*, p 499, or directly, e.g. see *Murray v Ministry of Defence*, p 533. Since the law cannot distinguish easily between degrees of touching, it prohibits all deliberate touching but then attempts to reconcile this extreme with the vagaries of commonplace social interaction.

Of course, the power of the state ensures that there are ample powers which will override the basic common law premise and will provide the defence of lawful authority; the Police and Criminal Evidence Act 1984 (PACE) is only one example. More insidious are the powers which relate to the mentally incapacitated, see for example *R v Bournewood, ex p L*, p 525 and *St George's Healthcare NHS Trust v S*, p 555. In all of these instances the courts, apparently, espouse the traditional value of the sanctity of the person, see for example *Lindley v Rutter*, Donaldson LJ:

> 'It is the duty of the courts to be ever zealous to protect personal freedom, privacy and dignity of all who live in these islands. Any claim to be entitled to take action which infringes these rights is to be examined with very great care.'

Stubbings v Webb
[1993] I All ER 322 House of Lords

The respondent claimed that as a child aged between two and fourteen, she had been abused by the appellants, her stepfather and stepbrother. She commenced her action at the age of 30. The appellants sought to strike out her action on the basis that it was outside the limitation period in the Limitation Act 1980. That Act extended the period of limitation in the case of children so that it would expire either six or three years after the child reached majority, depending on the type of cause of action. On that basis the claim would still have been out of time, but the respondent contended that the period of limitation in the case of actions subject to a three-year limitation might be extended under the Act where she could show that the writ was issued within three years of knowledge of the injury, and that she did not acquire such knowledge until September 1984 when she realised that there might be a link between her psychiatric problems in adult life and the abuse, and that she had commenced her writ within three years of that date.

The House of Lords held that the allegations related to battery and that the period of limitation in trespass was six years and not three years. But, even though the six-year period did not commence until she reached her majority, the 1980 Act contained no provision allowing the period of limitation to be extended. Thus she was out of time.

Lord Griffiths: '... In *Letang v Cooper an* attempt was made to escape from [the] new three-year limitation period. The plaintiff had been sunbathing on the grass in the car park of an hotel when the defendant drove his car over her legs. The accident happened on 10 July 1957 but the plaintiff did not issue her writ claiming damages for personal injuries until 2 February 1961, which was outside the three-year limitation period provided by the 1954 Act. This accident was obviously one to which the three-year limitation period was intended to apply but in an attempt to escape the consequences of failing to issue a writ within the three-year time limit the plaintiff's legal advisers claimed in both negligence and trespass to the person. This manoeuvre succeeded before the trial judge, who held that the defendant had been negligent but went on to hold that the phrase "negligence, nuisance or breach of duty" in s 2(1) of the 1954 Act did not include an action for trespass to the person so that the plaintiff had six years in which to bring her claim. If this decision was correct it would have nullified the effect of s 2(1) of the 1954 Act for all claims for personal injuries could henceforth be framed in trespass and thus be subject to a six-year limitation period. It is not therefore surprising that the Court of Appeal reversed the decision of the judge and held that s 2(1) applied to the plaintiff's claim which was thereby statute-barred.

Lord Denning MR solved the problem by holding that the only cause of action lay in negligence and was thus statute-barred ... However he also went on to hold that if he was wrong and the plaintiff had a cause of action for trespass to the person he would hold that the phrase "breach of duty" covered a breach of any duty under the law of tort. Danckwerts LJ agreed with both Lord Denning MR's reasons for allowing the appeal. Diplock LJ held that on the facts pleaded the cause of action was one in negligence within the meaning of s 2 and that the period of limitation was therefore three years. But he also held that the words "breach of duty" should be construed as applying to any cause of action which gives rise to a claim for damages for personal injury. Leave to appeal to the House of Lords was refused and there the matter has rested until the present case ...

I accept that *Letang v Cooper was* correctly decided in so far as it held that negligent driving is a cause of action falling within s 2(1) of the 1954 Act. But I cannot agree that the words "breach of duty" have the effect of including within the scope of the section all actions in which damages for personal injuries are claimed which is the other ground upon which the Court of Appeal decided *Letang v Cooper.* If that had been the intention of the draftsman it would have been easy enough to say so in the section. On the contrary the draftsman has used words of limitation; he has limited the section to actions for negligence, nuisance and breach of duty and the reason he did so was to give effect to the recommendation of the Tucker Committee that the three-year period should not apply to a number of causes of action in which damages for personal injury might be claimed, namely damages for trespass to the person, false imprisonment, malicious prosecution or defamation. There can be no doubt that rape and indecent assault fell within the category of trespass to the person.

Lord Denning MR in *Letang v Cooper* was not prepared to assume that Parliament did intend to give effect to the Tucker Committee's recommendations, but we can now look at Hansard and can see that it was the express intention of Parliament to do so ... Even without reference to Hansard I should not myself have construed "breach of duty" as including a deliberate assault. The phrase lying in juxtaposition with "negligence" and "nuisance" carries with it the implication of a breach of duty of care not to cause personal injury, rather than an obligation not to infringe any legal right of another person. If I invite a lady to my house one would naturally think of a duty to take care that the house is safe but would one really be thinking of a duty not to rape her. But, however this may be, the terms in which this Bill was introduced to my mind make it clear beyond peradventure that the intention was to give effect to the Tucker recommendation that the limitation period in respect of trespass to the person was not to be reduced to three years but should remain at six years. The language of s 2(1) of the 1954 Act is in my view apt to give effect to that intention, and cases of deliberate assault such as we are concerned with in this case are not actions for breach of duty within the meaning of s 11(1) of the 1980 Act.

The language of s 2(1) of the 1954 Act was carried without alteration into the 1975 Act and then into s 11(1) of the 1980 Act where it must bear the same meaning as it had in the 1954 Act.

It thus follows that the respondent's causes of action against both appellants were subject to a six-year limitation period. This period was suspended during her infancy but commenced to run when she attained her majority: see s 28 of the 1980 Act. This period expired many years before she issued her writ in these proceedings. There are no provisions for extending this period and her actions are therefore statute-barred and cannot proceed ...'

Comment

(1)   In *Stubbings and others v UK* the European Court of Human Rights held that there had been no violation of the plaintiff's right to a fair trial (article 6) or of her right to respect for her private life (article 8) or of her right not to be discriminated against. Time-limits are placed upon rights of action in pursuance of a legitimate aim in the interests of the good administration of justice. The court acknowledged that it was likely that member states of the Council of Europe might soon have to take steps to incorporate special provisions for child sexual abuse victims in the light of the increasing volume of research on and understanding of the particular psychological problems associated with victims of abuse. The Human Rights Act 1998 makes it increasingly likely that the European Convention on Human Rights will achieve greater prominence in the resolution of tort disputes.

(2)   The decision in *Stubbings v Webb* was extensively considered in *KR and others v Bryn Alyn Community (Holdings) Ltd (in liquidation) and another*, a case arising from the catalogue of abuse at a children's home in Wales.

(3)   A case demonstrating an imaginative and more practically sympathetic approach to difficulties facing a victim of incest is *K M v H M*, a decision of the Supreme Court of Canada. The plaintiff had been the victim of sexual abuse as a child and exhibited typical psychological problems associated with such abuse. In the view of the court, adopting the general approach of the literature

on the topic, the victim would have been unable to realise that a cause of action existed until she was much older. At the age of 28 she commenced an action. In the context of a differently worded Limitation Act, the court was able to allow the claim to proceed since it had been commenced when the cause of action was reasonably discoverable. Furthermore, the court concluded that the activities of the abuser amounted to the concealment of the cause of action by fraud: 'it is the very nature of an incestuous assault that tends to conceal its wrongness from the victim'. The court was able also to conclude that incestuous assaults amounted to breach of a fiduciary duty and thus were not debarred by the limitation provisions.

(4) Ironically, where the abused person is pursuing a claim in negligence, for example, perhaps against a local authority or non-abusing parent, then that claim will benefit from the shorter, but extendable, limitation period, see *S v W* (*child abuse: damages*), although establishing an actionable duty of care may prove difficult, see for example the cases dealt with at pp 52–72. In the *Bryn Alyn* case this anomalous position was noted and Lord Justice Auld remarked:

'[*S v W* (*child abuse: damages*)] though concerned with different conduct by two defendants giving rise to the same personal injury, is a logical application of that reasoning. There, the plaintiff issued proceedings against her father and mother, alleging physical and sexual abuse against her father and want of parental care against her mother. The Court of Appeal ruled that the claim against the father, described by Russell LJ as "plainly a claim alleging trespass to the person", was governed by the six years period of limitation and out of time, but that the claim against the mother, as a claim in negligence, was within section 11 and thus capable of disapplication under section 33. Two members of the Court, Millett LJ and Sir Ralph Gibson, referred to the anomaly of there being different periods of limitation as between a perpetrator of abuse and someone negligent in not preventing it and of the potential extension of the limitation period for the latter instead of, as the Tucker Committee had intended, a reduction of the period in such cases. They invited the Law Commission to consider the anomaly. It has done so, recommending that claims for personal injuries, including those of child abuse, whether in trespass to the person or in negligence, should be subject to the same core regime of an extendable three years limitation period with discretion to disapply ... For what it is worth, we warmly commend such a proposal. Early statutory implementation of it would obviate much arid and highly wasteful litigation turning on a distinction of no apparent principle or other merit.'

(5) In *Letang v Cooper* Lord Denning MR said that:

'... Instead of dividing actions for personal injuries into *trespass* (direct damage) or *case* (consequential damage), we divide the causes of action now according as the defendant did the injury intentionally or unintentionally. If one man intentionally applies force directly to another, the plaintiff has a cause of action in assault and battery, or, if you so please to describe it, in trespass to the person ... If he does not inflict injury intentionally, but only unintentionally, the plaintiff has no cause of action today in trespass. His only cause of action is in negligence, and then only on proof of want of reasonable care. If the plaintiff cannot prove want of reasonable care, he may have no cause of action at all. Thus, it is not enough nowadays for the plaintiff to plead that "the defendant shot the plaintiff". He must also allege that he did it intentionally or negligently. If intentional, it is the tort of assault and battery. If negligent and causing damage, it is the tort of negligence.

The modern law on this subject was well expounded by my brother Diplock J in *Fowler v Lanning* with which I fully agree. But I would go this one step further: when the injury is not inflicted intentionally, but negligently, I would say that the only cause of action is negligence and not trespass. If it were trespass, it would be actionable without proof of damage; and that is not the law today ...'

In *Stanley v Powell* it was decided that there had to be established either intention or negligence for there to be a trespass. *Fowler v Lanning* decided that the burden of proof was on the plaintiff and the defendant need not prove the absence of negligence. It is still not clear whether or not trespass can be committed negligently as well as intentionally (see the conflicting comments of Lord Denning and Diplock LJ in *Letang v Cooper*). The matter is largely academic in the light of the burden of proof on the plaintiff and the requirement that damage must be shown for negligence (*Fowler v Lanning*). In *Wilson v Pringle*, p 504, the Court of Appeal was of the opinion that the view of Lord Denning was correct.

(6)   Subject to what was said in *Stubbings v Webb* about the other aspects of the decision in that case, the following comment by Diplock LJ remains a valuable account:

'A cause of action is simply a factual situation the existence of which entitles one person to obtain from the court a remedy against another person. Historically the means by which the remedy was obtained varied with the nature of the factual situation and causes of action were divided into categories according to the "form of action" by which the remedy was obtained in the particular kind of factual situation which constituted the cause of action; but that is legal history, not current law. If A, by failing to exercise reasonable care, inflicts direct personal injury on B, those facts constitute a cause of action on the part of B against A for damages in respect of such personal injuries. The remedy for this cause of action could, before 1873, have been obtained by alternative forms of action, namely, originally either trespass *vi et armis* or trespass on the case, later either trespass to the person or negligence ... Certain procedural consequences, the importance of which diminished considerably after the Common Law Procedure Act 1852, flowed from the plaintiff's pleader's choice of the form of action used. The Supreme Court of Judicature Act 1873 abolished forms of action. It did not affect causes of action; so it was convenient for lawyers and legislators to continue to use, to describe the various categories of factual situations which entitled one person to obtain from the court a remedy against another, the names of the various "forms of action" by which formerly the remedy appropriate to the particular category of factual situations was obtained. But it is essential to realise that when, since 1873, the name of a form of action is used to identify a cause of action, it is used as a convenient and succinct description of a particular category of factual situation which entitles one person to obtain from the court a remedy against another person. To forget this will indeed encourage the old forms of action to rule us from their graves.'

(7) In the case of a surgeon who operates without consent or without any lawful justification such as necessity (see p 540), the operation will amount to a battery and it must be presumed that this will be subject to the longer period of limitation. Where the operation is carried out with consent or other justification, but carelessly, then the shorter, but extendable, limitation period will apply.

Collins v Wilcock
[1984] 3 All ER 374 Divisional Court

In order to record the defendant's name and address and administer a caution in connection with her soliciting for the purposes of prostitution, a police officer had detained the defendant by holding her by the elbow. The defendant had scratched the police officer and was charged with assaulting a constable in the execution of her duty. In order for the charge to be made out, it had to be shown that at the time of the detention the police officer was acting in the execution of her duty, and in order to demonstrate this it had to be shown that she was acting lawfully. The Divisional Court held that the detention amounted to a battery and that this took the police officer outside the execution of her duty.

Robert Goff LJ: '... We are here concerned primarily with battery. The fundamental principle, plain and incontestable, is that every person's body is inviolate. It has long been established that any touching of another person, however slight, may amount to a battery. So Holt CJ held in 1704 that "the least touching of another in anger is a battery": see *Cole v Turner*. The breadth of the principle reflects the fundamental nature of the interest so protected; as Blackstone wrote in his Commentaries, "the law cannot draw the line between different degrees of violence, and therefore totally prohibits the first and lowest stage of it; every man's person being sacred, and no other having a right to meddle with it, in any the slightest manner"... The effect is that everybody is protected not only against physical injury but against any form of physical molestation.

But so widely drawn a principle must inevitably be subject to exceptions. For example, children may be subjected to reasonable punishment; people may be subjected to the lawful exercise of the power of arrest; and reasonable force may be used in self-defence or for the prevention of crime. But, apart from these special instances where the control or constraint is lawful, a broader exception has been created to allow for the exigencies of everyday life. Generally speaking, consent is a defence to battery; and most of the physical contacts of ordinary life are not actionable because they are impliedly consented to by all who move in society and so expose themselves to the risk of bodily contact. So nobody can complain of the jostling which is inevitable from his presence in, for example, a supermarket, an underground station or a busy street; nor can a person who attends a party complain if his hand is seized in friendship, or even if his back is (within reason) slapped (see *Tuberville v Savage*). Although such cases are regarded as examples of implied consent, it is more common nowadays to treat them as falling within a general exception embracing all physical contact which is generally acceptable in the ordinary conduct of daily life. We observe that, although in the past it has sometimes been stated that a battery is only committed where the action is "angry, or revengeful, or rude, or insolent" ... we think that nowadays it is more realistic, and indeed more accurate, to state the broad underlying principle, subject to the broad exception.

Among such forms of conduct, long held to be acceptable, is touching a person for the purpose of engaging his attention, though of course using no greater degree of physical contact than is reasonably necessary in the circumstances for that purpose. So, for example, it was held by the Court of Common Pleas in 1807 that a touch by a constable's staff on the shoulder of a man who had climbed on a gentleman's railing to gain a better view of a mad ox, the touch being only to engage the man's attention, did not amount to a battery (see *Wiffin v Kincard*; for another example, see *Coward v Baddeley*). But a distinction is drawn between a touch to draw a man's attention, which is generally acceptable, and a physical restraint, which is not. So we find Parke B observing in *Rawlings v Till*, with reference to *Wiffin v Kincard*, that: "There the touch was merely to engage a man's attention, not to put a restraint on his person." Furthermore, persistent touching to gain attention in the face of obvious disregard may transcend the norms of acceptable behaviour, and so be outside the exception. We do not say that more than one touch is never permitted; for example, the lost or distressed may surely be permitted a second touch, or possibly even more, on a reluctant or impervious sleeve or shoulder, as may a person who is acting reasonably in the exercise of a duty. In each case, the test must be whether the physical contact so persisted in has in the circumstances gone beyond generally acceptable standards of conduct; and the answer to that question will depend on the facts of the particular case.

The distinction drawn by Parke B in *Rawlings v Till* is of importance in the case of police officers. Of course, a police officer may subject another to restraint when he lawfully exercises his power of arrest; and he has other statutory powers ... with which we are not concerned. But, putting such cases aside, police officers have for present purposes no greater rights than ordinary citizens. It follows that, subject to such cases, physical contact by a police officer with another person may be unlawful as a battery, just as it might be if he was an ordinary member of the public. But a police officer has his rights as a citizen, as well as his duties as a policeman. A police officer may wish to engage a man's attention, for example if he wishes to question him. If he lays his hand on the man's sleeve or taps his shoulder for that purpose, he commits no wrong. He may even do so more than once; for he is under a duty to prevent and investigate crime, and so his seeking further, in the exercise of that duty, to engage a man's attention in order to speak to him may in the circumstances be regarded as acceptable ... But if, taking into account the nature of his duty, his use of physical contact in the face of non-co-operation persists beyond generally acceptable standards of conduct, his action will become unlawful; and if a police officer restrains a man, for example by gripping his arm or his shoulder, then his action will also be unlawful, unless he is lawfully exercising his power of arrest. A police officer has no power to require a man to answer him, though he has the advantage of authority, enhanced as it is by the uniform which the state provides and requires him to wear, in seeking a response to his enquiry. What is not permitted, however, is the unlawful use of force or the unlawful threat (actual or implicit) to use force; and, excepting the lawful exercise of his power of arrest, the lawfulness of a police officer's conduct is judged by the same criteria as are applied to the conduct of any ordinary citizen of this country.

We have been referred by counsel to certain cases directly concerned with charges of assaulting a police officer in the execution of his duty, the crucial question in each case being whether the police officer, by using physical force on the accused in response to which the accused assaulted the police officer, was acting unlawfully and so not acting in the execution of his duty ... [The court then cited *Kenlin v Gardner, Ludlow v Burgess, Bentley v Brudzinski* and *Donnelly v Jackman*.]

We now return to the facts of the present case ... counsel for the respondent submitted that the purpose of the police officer was simply to carry out the cautioning procedure and that, having regard to her purpose, her action could not be regarded as unlawful. Again, we cannot accept that submission. If the physical contact went beyond what is allowed by law, the mere fact that the police officer has the laudable intention of carrying out the cautioning procedure in accordance with the established practice cannot, we think, have the effect of rendering her action lawful ... The fact is that the respondent took hold of the appellant by the left arm to restrain her. In so acting, she was not proceeding to arrest the appellant; and since her action went beyond the generally acceptable conduct of touching a person to engage his or her attention, it must follow, in our judgment, that her action constituted a battery on the appellant, and was therefore unlawful ...'

Comment

(1)   Goff LJ indicates the distinctions in trespass to the person:

'The law draws a distinction, in terms more easily understood by philologists than by ordinary citizens, between an assault and a battery. An assault is an act which causes another person to apprehend the infliction of immediate, unlawful, force on his person; a battery is the actual infliction of unlawful force on another person. Both assault and battery are forms of trespass to the person. Another form of trespass to the person is false imprisonment, which is the unlawful imposition of constraint on another's freedom of movement from a particular place. The requisite mental element is of no relevance in the present case.'

The distinctions are important. See also *Tuberville v Savage*, cited in *Wilson v Pringle*, p 504. In *Thomas v NUM*, p 689, the inability of the working miners to maintain assault prevented the grant of an injunction, Scott J said:

'Assault is defined in *Clerk and Lindsell on Torts* (15th edn, 1982) as "an overt act indicating an immediate intention to commit a battery, coupled with the capacity to carry that intention into effect". The tort of assault is not, in my view, committed. Since the working miners are in vehicles and the pickets are held back from the vehicles, I do not understand how even the most violent of threats or gestures could be said to constitute an assault.'

(2)   Goff LJ also commented upon the ambiguity of the word 'detain':

'... the word "detaining" can be used in more than once sense. For example, it is a commonplace of ordinary life that one person may request another to stop and speak to him; if the latter complies with the request, he may be said to do so willingly or unwillingly, and in either event the first person may be said to be "stopping and detaining" the latter. There is nothing unlawful in such an act. If a police officer so "stops and detains" another person, he in our opinion commits no unlawful act, despite the fact that his uniform may give his request a certain authority and so render it more likely to be complied with. But if a police officer, not exercising his power of arrest, nevertheless reinforces his request with the actual use of force, or with the threat (actual or implicit) to use force if the other person does not comply, then his act in thereby detaining the other person will be unlawful. In the former event, his action will constitute a battery; in the latter event, detention of the other person will amount to false imprisonment. Whether the action of a police officer in any particular case is to be regarded as lawful or unlawful must be a question to be decided on the facts of the case.'

(3)   Goff LJ refused to construe statute as impliedly authorising the detention:

'The fact that [the Street Offences Act 1959] recognises the practice of cautioning by providing a review procedure does not ... carry with it an implication that police officers have the power to stop and detain women for the purpose of implementing the system of cautioning. If it had been intended to confer any such power on police officers that power could and should ... have been expressly conferred by the statute.'

(4)   It has been observed that an omission cannot found an action for trespass. What amounts to an omission may be difficult to state with clarity. In *Fagan v Metropolitan Police Commissioner* the defendant had parked his car, unknowingly, on the foot of a police officer and had refused to move it for a short time. He was charged with assaulting a constable acting in the execution of his duty. James J:

'... some intentional act must have been performed; a mere omission to act cannot amount to an assault. Without going into the question whether words alone can constitute an assault, it is clear that the words spoken by the appellant could not alone amount to an assault; they only shed a light on the appellant's action. For our part, we think that the crucial question is whether ... the act of the appellant can be said to be complete and spent at the moment of time when the car wheel came to rest on the foot, or whether his act is to be regarded as a continuing act operating until the wheel was removed ... On the facts found, the action of the appellant may have been initially unintentional, but the time came when, knowing that the wheel was on the officer's foot, the appellant (i) remained seated in the car so that his body through the medium of the car was in contact with the officer, (ii) switched off the ignition of the car, (iii) maintained the wheel of the car on the foot, and (iv) used words indicating the intention of keeping the wheel in that position ... We cannot regard such conduct as mere omission or inactivity. There was an act constituting a battery ...'

Bridge J (dissenting):

'... what was it that the appellant did which constituted the act of assault? However the question is approached, the answer which I feel obliged to give is: precisely nothing ...'

Wilson v Pringle
[1986] 2 All ER 440 Court of Appeal

The defendant schoolboy admitted that he had pulled a bag which the plaintiff schoolboy was carrying over his shoulder. This caused the plaintiff to fall to the ground and he was injured. The plaintiff alleged that he had been jumped on by the defendant. The plaintiff applied for summary judgment on the basis that the defendant's admission amounted to an admission of a trespass. The application was allowed on appeal by a judge and the defendant appealed to the Court of Appeal which held that the judge had erred in deciding what amounted to a trespass to the person and that a number of issues remained for investigation in evidence.

Croom-Johnson LJ: '... Another ingredient in the tort of trespass to the person is that of hostility. The references to anger sufficing to turn a touch into a *battery* (*Cole v Turner*) and the lack of an intention to assault which prevents a gesture from being an assault are instances of this. If there is hostile intent, that will by itself be cogent evidence of hostility. But the hostility may be demonstrated in other ways.

The defendant in the present case has sought to add to the list of necessary ingredients. He has submitted that before trespass to the person will lie it is not only the touching that must be deliberate but the infliction of injury. The plaintiff's counsel, on the other hand, contends that it is not the injury to the person which must be intentional, but the act of touching or battery which precedes it: as he puts it, what must be intentional is the application of force and not the injury ...

It is the act and not the injury which must be intentional. An intention to injure is not essential to an action for trespass to the person. It is the mere trespass by itself which is the offence.

That does not answer the question, what does entitle an injured plaintiff to sue for the tort of trespass to the person? Reference must be made to one further case: *Williams v Humphrey*, decided by Talbot J. There the defendant, a boy just under 16, pushed the plaintiff into a swimming pool and caused him physical injury. The judge found the defendant acted negligently and awarded damages. But there was another claim in trespass. Talbot J rejected the submission that the action would not lie unless there was an intent to injure. He held that it was sufficient, if the act was intentional, that there was no justification for it. In the present Ord 14 proceedings the judge relied on that decision.

The reasoning in *Williams v Humphrey* is all right as far as it goes, but it does not go far enough. It did not give effect to the reasoning of the older authorities, such as *Tuberville v Savage*, *Cole v Turner*, and *Williams v Jones* that for there to be either an assault or a battery there must be something in the nature of hostility. It may be envinced by anger, by words or gesture. Sometimes the very act of battery will speak for itself, as where somebody uses a weapon on another.

What, then, turns a friendly touching (which is not actionable) into an unfriendly one (which is)?

We have been referred to two criminal cases. *R v Sutton* was decided in the Court of Appeal, Criminal Division. It was a case concerning alleged indecent assaults on boys who consented in fact although in law they were too young to do so. They were asked to pose for photographs. The only touching of the boys by the appellant was to get them to stand in poses. It was touching on the hands, arms, legs or torso but only for the purpose of indicating how he wanted them to pose. It was not hostile or threatening. The court, which was presided over by Lord Widgery CJ, held these were therefore not assaults.

[After extensive citation from *Collins v Wilcock*, he continued:]

This rationalisation by Robert Goff LJ draws the so-called "defences" to an action for trespass to the person (of which consent, self-defence, ejecting a trespasser, exercising parental authority, and statutory authority are some examples) under one umbrella of "a general exception embracing all physical contact which is generally acceptable in the ordinary conduct of daily life". It provides a solution to the old problem of what legal rule allows a casualty surgeon to perform an urgent operation on an unconscious patient who is brought into hospital. The patient cannot consent, and there may be no next of kin available to do it for him. Hitherto it has been customary to say in such cases that consent is to be implied for what would otherwise be a battery on the unconscious body. It is better simply to say that the surgeon's action is acceptable in the ordinary conduct of everyday life, and not a battery. It will doubtless be convenient to continue to tie the labels of the "defences' to the facts of any case where they are appropriate. But the rationalisation explains and utilises the expressions of judicial opinion which appear in the authorities. It also prevents the approach to the facts, which, with respect to the judge in the present case, causes his judgment to read like a ruling on a demurrer in the days of special pleading.

Nevertheless, it still remains to indicate what is to be proved by a plaintiff who brings an action for battery. Robert Goff LJ's judgment is illustrative of the considerations which underlie such an action, but it is not practicable to define a battery as "physical contact which is not generally acceptable in the ordinary conduct of daily life".

In our view, the authorities lead one to the conclusion that in a battery there must be an intentional touching or contact in one form or another of the plaintiff by the defendant. That touching must be proved to be a hostile touching. That still leaves unanswered the question, when is a touching to be called hostile? Hostility cannot be equated with ill-will or malevolence. It cannot be governed by the obvious intention shown in acts like punching, stabbing or shooting. It cannot be solely governed by an expressed intention, although that may be strong evidence. But the element of hostility, in the sense in which it is now to be considered, must be a question of fact for the tribunal of fact. It may be imported from the circumstances. Take the example of the police officer in *Collins v Wilcock*. She touched the woman deliberately, but without an intention to do more than restrain her temporarily. Nevertheless, she was acting unlawfully and in that way was acting with hostility. She was acting contrary to the woman's legal right not to be physically restrained. We see no more difficulty in establishing what she intended by means of question and answer, or by inference from the surrounding circumstances, than there is in establishing whether an apparently playful blow was struck in anger. The rules of law governing the legality of arrest may require strict application to the facts of appropriate cases, but in the ordinary give and take of everyday life the tribunal of fact should find no difficulty in answering the question, "was this, or was it not, a battery?" Where the immediate act of touching does not itself demonstrate hostility, the plaintiff should plead the facts which are said to do so.

Although we are all entitled to protection from physical molestation, we live in a crowded world in which people must be considered as taking on themselves some risk of injury (where it occurs) from the acts of others which are not in themselves unlawful. If negligence cannot be proved, it may be that an injured plaintiff who is also unable to prove a battery, will be without redress.

Defences like self-defence, and exercising the right of arrest, are relevant here. Similarly, it may be that allowances must be made, where appropriate, for the idiosyncrasies of individuals or ... the irresponsibility of childhood and the degree of care and awareness which is to be expected of children.

In our judgment the judge who tried the RSC Ord 14 proceedings took too narrow a view of what has to be proved in order to make out a case of trespass to the person. It will be apparent that there are a number of questions which must be investigated in evidence.'

Comment

(1)   *Collins v Wilcock* provides a more consistent and logical account than *Wilson v Pringle*. The latter is an interesting attempt to find what, in law, distinguishes one touching from another, but it does so by introducing a vague concept: 'hostility'. The only attempt to say what it is, rather than what it is not, is to seek to apply it to *Collins v Wilcock*. That application is flawed and circular. If hostility is an essential element in battery, then there seems no sound reason why it should not also be an ingredient in both assault and false imprisonment, as the reference to *Tuberville v Savage* implicitly recognises. It might be asked what would be the result of applying the principle in *Collins v Wilcock* to the facts of *Wilson v Pringle*: in the particular milieu, is that sort of behaviour 'physical contact which is generally acceptable in the ordinary conduct of daily life'?

(2)   The explanation in *Collins v Wilcock* does not serve the purpose declared by Croom-Johnson LJ in *Wilson v Pringle*. For example, Goff LJ did not seek to rationalise the invasive treatment by a doctor on the basis of commonplace touchings, see *F v West Berkshire HA*, p 540.

(3)   *Wilson v Pringle* has fared badly when compared with *Collins v Wilcock* which has been approved in *T v T* (a medical treatment case) and, *obiter*, in *F v West Berkshire Health Authority* (albeit by Lord Goff), see p 540. Given both the rejection in those cases and the lack of any apparent meaning to the word 'hostility', the authority of *Wilson v Pringle* is seriously undermined. On the other hand, there was limited support for *Wilson v Pringle* in *R v Brown*, a criminal case, although little was added. Lord Slynn described hostility in terms of something done, 'intentionally and against the will of the person to whom it is done'. Lord Jauncey adopted the circular argument of Croom-Johnson LJ: 'If the appellants' activities in relation to the receivers were unlawful they were also hostile and a necessary ingredient of assault was present.'

R v Ireland
R v Burstow
[1997] 4 All ER 225 House of Lords

In *Burstow* the appellant had pleaded guilty to maliciously inflicting grievous bodily harm contrary to the Offences against the Person Act 1861, s 20. In *Ireland* the appellant had pleaded guilty to assault occasioning actual bodily harm contrary to s 47 of the Act. In respect of both appellants the issue for the House of Lords was whether or not the psychiatric harm suffered by the victims fell within the statutory offences; the House of Lords held that it did.

In *Ireland* the further point involved was whether or not the conduct was capable in law of amounting to an assault. The facts were that during a period of three months in 1994 the appellant harassed three women by making repeated telephone calls, mostly at night, during which he remained silent. Sometimes he resorted to heavy breathing. It was accepted by the judge and the Court of Appeal that he caused the victims to suffer psychiatric illness.

The House of Lords upheld the dismissal of the appeal by the Court of Appeal, and held that such behaviour was capable in law of constituting an assault. Given that the defendant had pleaded guilty, the factual and causative details of the case did not require examination.

Lord Steyn:'… My Lords, It is easy to understand the terrifying effect of a campaign of telephone calls at night by a silent caller to a woman living on her own. It would be natural for the victim to regard the calls as menacing. What may heighten her fear is that she will not know what the caller may do next. The spectre of the caller arriving at her doorstep bent on inflicting personal violence on her may come to dominate her thinking. After all, as a matter of common sense, what else would she be terrified about? The victim may suffer psychiatric illness such as anxiety neurosis or acute depression. Harassment of women by repeated silent telephone calls, accompanied on occasions by heavy breathing, is apparently a significant social problem. That the criminal law should be able to deal with this problem, and so far as is practicable, afford effective protection to victims is self evident ...

It is now necessary to consider whether the making of silent telephone calls causing psychiatric injury is capable of constituting an assault under section 47... Having carefully considered the literature and counsel's arguments, I have come to the conclusion that the appeal ought to be dismissed.

The starting point must be that an assault is an ingredient of the offence under s 47. It is necessary to consider the two forms which an assault may take. The first is battery, which involves the unlawful application of force by the defendant upon the victim. Usually, s 47 is used to prosecute in cases of this kind. The second form of assault is an act causing the victim to apprehend an imminent application of force upon her (see *Fagan v Metropolitan Police Commissioner*).

One point can be disposed of, quite briefly. The Court of Appeal was not asked to consider whether silent telephone calls resulting in psychiatric injury is capable of constituting a battery. But encouraged by some academic comment it was raised before your Lordships' House ... In my view it is not feasible to enlarge the generally accepted legal meaning of what is a battery to include the circumstances of a silent caller who causes psychiatric injury.

It is to assault in the form of an act causing the victim to fear an immediate application of force to her that I must turn. Counsel argued that as a matter of law an assault can never be committed by words alone and therefore it cannot be committed by silence. The premise depends on the slenderest authority, namely, an observation by Holroyd J to a jury that "no words or singing are equivalent to an assault" (see *Meade's and Belt's Case*). The proposition that a gesture may amount to an assault, but that words can never suffice, is unrealistic and indefensible. A thing said is also a thing done. There is no reason why something said should be incapable of causing an apprehension of immediate personal violence, e.g. a man accosting a woman in a dark alley saying "come with me or I will stab you". I would, therefore, reject the proposition that an assault can never be committed by words.

That brings me to the critical question whether a silent caller may be guilty of an assault. The answer to this question seems to me to be "yes, depending on the facts". It involves questions of fact within the province of the jury. After all, there is no reason why a telephone caller who says to a woman in a menacing way "I will be at your door in a minute or two" may not be guilty of an assault if he causes his victim to apprehend immediate personal violence. Take now the case of the silent caller. He intends by his silence to cause fear and he is so understood. The victim is assailed by uncertainty about his intentions. Fear may dominate her emotions, and it may be the fear that the caller's arrival at her door may be imminent. She may fear the *possibility* of immediate personal violence. As a matter of law the caller may be guilty of an assault: whether he is or not will depend on the circumstance and in particular on the impact of the caller's potentially menacing call or calls on the victim. Such a prosecution case under s 47 may be fit to leave to the jury. And a trial judge may, depending on the circumstances, put a common sense consideration before jury, namely what, if not the possibility of imminent personal violence, was the victim terrified about? I conclude that an assault may be committed in the particular factual circumstances which I have envisaged. For this reason I reject the submission that as a matter of law a silent telephone caller cannot ever be guilty of an offence under s 47 ...'

Comment

(1)   If silent telephone calls may constitute an assault, then so in an appropriate case may telephonic threats. In Australia in *Barton v Armstrong*, an assault was alleged to have been committed by telephone calls involving threats rather than mere silence. The decision that this was an assault was approved by the Court of Appeal in *R v Ireland* and is consistent with the decision of the House of Lords.

(2)   Because of the guilty plea and the appeal on a narrow point of law, the questions whether there was a fear of immediate violence and how the concept of immediacy is to be applied in such a case did not arise for decision.

(3)   Although the case is a criminal case and one where the House of Lords had to deal with the ability of the criminal law to respond to the type of behaviour involved, the same questions need to be asked in the law of tort, which also concerns itself with the protection which may be afforded to a victim.

(4)   In *R v Lynsey* the Court of Appeal decided that in the Criminal Justice Act 1988, s 40 the words 'common assault' included 'battery' even though s 39 of the same Act referred to common assault and battery as if they were distinct offences. The court discussed the historical and terminological difficulties surrounding the use of the word 'assault' so as to include both forms of trespass. See also *R v Williams.*

(5)   In *R v Burstow* the appellant was charged with unlawfully and maliciously inflicting grievous bodily harm, contrary to the Offences against the Person Act 1861, s 20. The House of Lords indicated that the statutory offence was sufficiently broad to include infliction of psychiatric harm by a means not involving the direct or indirect application of force, i.e. where in the civil law there would be no battery.

In the case of the civil law, the intentional infliction of psychiatric harm in such a way as not to involve either battery or assault will be tortious either under general principles of negligence or simply as an application of the principle in *Wilkinson v Downton.* In the same way, the intentional infliction of physical harm without the presence of an assault or battery will be actionable. For example, if use of a bright light does not amount to a battery (but see *Kaye v Robertson,* p 579) then, in the event of harm, either *Wilkinson v Downton* will apply or general principles of negligence. The law of tort would have no difficulty in concluding that lacing a hair-dryer with acid, which was then used by an unsuspecting victim, would be tortious even though not a battery. The criminal law struggles with this as a species of infliction of harm, see *DPP v X.*

For cases on liability for careless acts resulting in psychiatric harm, see Chapter 2.

(6)   The Offences against the Person Act 1861, ss 44 and 45 mean that a victim may not be able to succeed in a civil suit commenced after the determination of criminal prosecutions brought by or on the victim's behalf, whether it ends in conviction or acquittal. These curious provisions are redolent of an earlier age when policing was less effective and there was more common recourse by way of private prosecution. The rationale for continuing with this provision is less than clear, although the criminal courts now have powers to award compensation. The scope of the bar was examined in *Wong v Parkside NHS Trust* where the claimant sought to use an assault in respect of which the claimant brought a successful private prosecution resulting in a compensation award and costs (both of which were paid) to demonstrate the imputed intention to cause harm needed to succeed under the principle in *Wilkinson v Downton* (but now see *Wainwright v Home Office* on the scope of this principle). Hale LJ said:

> '[16]   ... the victim of an assault has a choice. If the authorities choose to prosecute, there is no problem. But if they do not, she must choose between bringing a private prosecution or a civil action. The former will destroy her right to bring the latter, irrespective of the outcome. The alleged perpetrator is not to be put in double jeopardy for the same cause. This may be an anomalous approach in today's world, given the differences in the burden of proof and sometimes in the level of compensation awarded by criminal and civil courts. But for as long as s 45 of the 1861 Act is on the statute book, the effect in a case such as this is clear: the claimant cannot rely upon the assault in any other proceedings. The recorder was therefore right to exclude it from his consideration.'

(7)   Lord Steyn commented on the relative difficulties of applying other statutory offences to harassing behaviour and concluded that measures such as the Telecommunications Act 1984, s 43(1) (which makes it an offence persistently to make use of a public telecommunications system for the purpose of causing annoyance, inconvenience or needless anxiety to another) and the

Protection from Harassment Act 1997, ss 1, 2 and 4 might be ineffective either by virtue of their potential penalty or limited *actus reus.*

(8)   In *R v Johnson* the Court of Appeal, applying the principles in *Attorney-General v PYA Quarries*, p 679, held that the defendant had committed the criminal offence of public nuisance by using a telephone system to make a very large number of obscene telephone calls to several women, and had thereby placed at risk a wider range of women who might be harassed and caused annoyance, alarm and distress. In the private civil action which may arise out of a public nuisance, see p 684, the courts have awarded damages for personal injury but this possibility may now have been overtaken by the decision in *Hunter v Canary Wharf*, see p 604.

Wilkinson v Downton
[1895–99] All ER Rep 267 Queen's Bench Division

As a practical joke, the defendant told the plaintiff that her husband had been badly injured in an accident and that she should take a cab and collect him. The plaintiff suffered a violent shock to her nervous system producing serious physical consequences. Her claim for travel expenses incurred in reliance on the statement was within the scope of fraud. The court also allowed recovery for the nervous shock.

Wright J:'... The real question is as to the £100, the greatest part of which is given as compensation for the female plaintiff's illness and suffering ... The defendant has, as I assume for the moment, wilfully done an act calculated to cause physical harm to the female plaintiff, i.e. to infringe her legal right to personal safety, and has thereby in fact caused physical harm to her. That proposition, without more, appears to me to state a good cause of action, there being no justification alleged for the act. This wilful *injuria* is in law malicious, although no malicious purpose to cause the harm which was caused, nor any motive of spite, is imputed to the defendant.

It remains to consider whether the assumptions involved in the proposition are made out. One question is whether the defendant's act was so plainly calculated to produce some effect of the kind which was produced, that an intention to produce it ought to be imputed to the defendant regard being had to the fact that the effect was produced on a person proved to be in an ordinary state of health and mind. I think that it was. It is difficult to imagine that such a statement, made suddenly and with apparent seriousness, could fail to produce grave effects under the circumstances upon any but an exceptionally indifferent person, and therefore an intention to produce such an effect must be imputed, and it is no answer in law to say that more harm was done than was anticipated, for that is commonly the case with all wrongs. The other question is whether the effect was, to use the ordinary phrase, too remote to be in law regarded as a consequence for which the defendant is answerable. Apart from authority I should give the same answer, and on the same grounds, as to the last question, and say that it was not too remote. Whether ... the criterion is in asking what would be the natural effect on reasonable persons, or whether ... the possible infirmities of human nature ought to be recognised, it seems to me that the connection between the cause and the effect is sufficiently close and complete ...'

Comment

Although the principle in *Wilkinson v Downton* has been applied in a number of common law jurisdictions, it did not have a great impact on English jurisprudence. Its history is explored and its role firmly restricted in *Wainwright v Home Office*.

Wainwright and another v Home Office
[2003] 4 All ER 969 House of Lords

Mrs Wainwright and her son, Alan, visited a prisoner in prison. They underwent full strip searches which were undertaken in a way which was not provided for by the prison rules and which involved a battery on Alan and humiliation to each. As a result Alan suffered a psychiatric injury (post-traumatic stress disorder) and Mrs Wainwright was emotionally upset. Before the House of Lords the question was whether the searches or the manner in which they were conducted gave the claimants a cause of action. The House of Lords concluded that there was no common law tort of invasion of privacy. It held further that in the absence of specific intention to cause physical or psychiatric injury there would be no recovery under the principle in *Wilkinson v Downton*. The House of Lords left open the question whether or not an intention to cause emotional distress falling short of psychiatric damage would be actionable in tort.

Lord Hoffmann: '...

15.   My Lords, let us first consider the proposed tort of invasion of privacy. Since the famous article by Warren and Brandeis ("The Right to Privacy" (1890) 4 Harvard LR 193) the question of whether such a tort exists, or should exist, has been much debated in common law jurisdictions. Warren and Brandeis suggested that one could generalise certain cases on defamation, breach of copyright in unpublished letters, trade secrets and breach of confidence as all based upon the protection of a common value which they called privacy or, following Judge Cooley (*Cooley on Torts*, 2nd ed (1888), p 29) "the right to be let alone". They said that identifying this common element should enable the courts to declare the existence of a general principle which protected a person's appearance, sayings, acts and personal relations from being exposed in public.

16.   Courts in the United States were receptive to this proposal and a jurisprudence of privacy began to develop. It became apparent, however, that the developments could not be contained within a single principle; not, at any rate, one with greater explanatory power than the proposition that it was based upon the protection of a value which could be described as privacy. Dean Prosser, in his work on *The Law of Torts*, 4th ed (1971), p 804, said that:

> "What has emerged is no very simple matter … it is not one tort, but a complex of four. To date the law of privacy comprises four distinct kinds of invasion of four different interests of the plaintiff, which are tied together by the common name, but otherwise have almost nothing in common except that each represents an interference with the right of the plaintiff 'to be let alone'."

17.   Dean Prosser's taxonomy divided the subject into (1) intrusion upon the plaintiff's physical solitude or seclusion (including unlawful searches, telephone tapping, long-distance photography and telephone harassment) (2) public disclosure of private facts and (3) publicity putting the plaintiff in a false light and (4) appropriation, for the defendant's advantage, of the plaintiff's name or likeness. These, he said, at p 814, had different elements and were subject to different defences.

18.   The need in the United States to break down the concept of "invasion of privacy" into a number of loosely-linked torts must cast doubt upon the value of any high-level generalisation which can perform a useful function in enabling one to deduce the rule to be applied in a concrete case. English law has so far been unwilling, perhaps unable, to formulate any such high-level principle. There are a number of common law and statutory remedies of which it may be said that one at least of the underlying values they protect is a right of privacy. Sir Brian Neill's well known article "Privacy: a challenge for the next century" in *Protecting Privacy* (ed B Markesinis, 1999) contains a survey. Common law torts include trespass, nuisance, defamation and malicious falsehood; there is the equitable action for breach of confidence and statutory remedies under the Protection from Harassment Act 1997 and the Data Protection Act 1998. There are also extra-legal remedies under Codes of Practice applicable to broadcasters and newspapers. But there are gaps; cases in which the courts have considered that an invasion of privacy deserves a remedy which the existing law does not offer. Sometimes the perceived gap can be filled by judicious development of an existing principle. The law of breach of confidence has in recent years undergone such a process: see in particular the judgment of Lord Phillips of Worth Matravers MR in *Campbell v MGN Ltd*. On the other hand, an attempt to create a tort of telephone harassment by a radical change in the basis of the action for private nuisance in *Khorasandjian v Bush* was held by the House of Lords in *Hunter v Canary Wharf Ltd* to be a step too far. The gap was filled by the 1997 Act.

19.   What the courts have so far refused to do is to formulate a general principle of "invasion of privacy" (I use the quotation marks to signify doubt about what in

such a context the expression would mean) from which the conditions of liability in the particular case can be deduced. The reasons were discussed by Sir Robert Megarry V-C in *Malone v Metropolitan Police Comr.* I shall be sparing in citation but the whole of Sir Robert's treatment of the subject deserves careful reading. The question was whether the plaintiff had a cause of action for having his telephone tapped by the police without any trespass upon his land. This was, as the European Court of Justice subsequently held in *Malone v United Kingdom*, an infringement by a public authority of his right to privacy under article 8 of the Convention, but because there had been no trespass, it gave rise to no identifiable cause of action in English law. Sir Robert was invited to declare that invasion of privacy, at any rate in respect of telephone conversations, was in itself a cause of action. He said ... :

"I am not unduly troubled by the absence of English authority: there has to be a first time for everything, and if the principles of English law, and not least analogies from the existing rules, together with the requirements of justice and common sense, pointed firmly to such a right existing, then I think the court should not be deterred from recognising the right. On the other hand, it is no function of the courts to legislate in a new field. The extension of the existing laws and principles is one thing, the creation of an altogether new right is another."

[After further citation from that case and after reference to *R v Khan (Sultan)* Lord Hoffmann continued:]

23.   The absence of any general cause of action for invasion of privacy was again acknowledged by the Court of Appeal in *Kaye v Robertson*, in which a newspaper reporter and photographer invaded the plaintiff's hospital bedroom, purported to interview him and took photographs. The law of trespass provided no remedy because the plaintiff was not owner or occupier of the room and his body had not been touched. Publication of the interview was restrained by interlocutory injunction on the ground that it was arguably a malicious falsehood to represent that the plaintiff had consented to it. But no other remedy was available. At the time of the judgment (16 March 1990) a Committee under the chairmanship of Sir David Calcutt QC was considering whether individual privacy required statutory protection against intrusion by the press. Glidewell LJ said ...:

"The facts of the present case are a graphic illustration of the desirability of Parliament considering whether and in what circumstances statutory provision can be made to protect the privacy of individuals."

24.   Bingham LJ likewise said ...: "The problems of defining and limiting a tort of privacy are formidable but the present case strengthens my hope that the review now in progress may prove fruitful."

25.   Leggatt LJ ... referred to Dean Prosser's analysis of the development of the law of privacy in the United States and said that similar rights could be created in

England only by statute: "it is to be hoped that the making good of this signal shortcoming in our law will not be long delayed."

26. All three judgments are flat against a judicial power to declare the existence of a high-level right to privacy and I do not think that they suggest that the courts should do so. The members of the Court of Appeal certainly thought that it would be desirable if there was legislation to confer a right to protect the privacy of a person in the position of Mr Kaye against the kind of intrusion which he suffered, but they did not advocate any wider principle. And when the Calcutt Committee reported in June 1990, they did indeed recommend that "entering private property, without the consent of the lawful occupant, with intent to obtain personal information with a view to its publication" should be made a criminal offence: see Report of the Committee on Privacy and Related Matters (1990) Cm 1102, para 6.33. The Committee also recommended that certain other forms of intrusion, like the use of surveillance devices on private property and long-distance photography and sound recording, should be made offences.

27. But the Calcutt Committee did not recommend, even within their terms of reference (which were confined to press intrusion) the creation of a generalised tort of infringement of privacy: paragraph 12.5. This was not because they thought that the definitional problems were insuperable. They said that if one confined the tort to "publication of personal information to the world at large" (paragraph 12.12) it should be possible to produce an adequate definition and they made some suggestions about how such a statutory tort might be defined and what the defences should be. But they considered that the problem could be tackled more effectively by a combination of the more sharply-focused remedies which they recommended: paragraph 12.32. As for a "general wrong of infringement of privacy", they accepted, at paragraph 12.12, that it would, even in statutory form, give rise to "an unacceptable degree of uncertainty". There is nothing in the opinions of the judges in *Kaye v Robertson* which suggests that the members of the court would have held any view, one way or the other, about a general tort of privacy.

28. The claimants placed particular reliance upon the judgment of Sedley LJ in *Douglas v Hello! Ltd.* Sedley LJ drew attention to the way in which the development of the law of confidence had attenuated the need for a relationship of confidence between the recipient of the confidential information and the person from whom it was obtained – a development which enabled the UK Government to persuade the European Human Rights Commission in *Earl Spencer v United Kingdom* that English law of confidence provided an adequate remedy to restrain the publication of private information about the applicants' marriage and medical condition and photographs taken with a telephoto lens. These developments showed that the basic value protected by the law in such cases was privacy. Sedley LJ said ... at para 126:

"What a concept of privacy does, however, is accord recognition to the fact that the law has to protect not only those people whose trust has been abused but those who simply find themselves subjected to an unwanted intrusion into their personal lives. The law no longer needs to construct an artificial relationship of confidentiality between intruder and victim: it can recognise privacy itself as a legal principle drawn from the fundamental value of personal autonomy."

29.   I read these remarks as suggesting that, in relation to the publication of personal information obtained by intrusion, the common law of breach of confidence has reached the point at which a confidential relationship has become unnecessary. As the underlying value protected is privacy, the action might as well be renamed invasion of privacy. "To say this" said Sedley LJ at para 125, "is in my belief to say little, save by way of a label, that our courts have not said already over the years."

30.   I do not understand Sedley LJ to have been advocating the creation of a high-level principle of invasion of privacy. His observations are in my opinion no more (although certainly no less) than a plea for the extension and possibly renaming of the old action for breach of confidence. As Buxton LJ pointed out in this case in the Court of Appeal at paras 96–99, such an extension would go further than any English court has yet gone and would be contrary to some cases (such as *Kaye v Robertson*) in which it positively declined to do so. The question must wait for another day. But Sedley LJ's dictum does not support a principle of privacy so abstract as to include the circumstances of the present case.

31.   There seems to me a great difference between identifying privacy as a value which underlies the existence of a rule of law (and may point the direction in which the law should develop) and privacy as a principle of law in itself. The English common law is familiar with the notion of underlying values – principles only in the broadest sense – which direct its development. A famous example is *Derbyshire County Council v Times Newspapers Ltd*, in which freedom of speech was the underlying value which supported the decision to lay down the specific rule that a local authority could not sue for libel. But no one has suggested that freedom of speech is in itself a legal principle which is capable of sufficient definition to enable one to deduce specific rules to be applied in concrete cases. That is not the way the common law works.

32.   Nor is there anything in the jurisprudence of the European Court of Human Rights which suggests that the adoption of some high level principle of privacy is necessary to comply with article 8 of the Convention. The European Court is concerned only with whether English law provides an adequate remedy in a specific case in which it considers that there has been an invasion of privacy contrary to article 8(1) and not justifiable under article 8(2). So in *Earl Spencer v United Kingdom* it was satisfied that the action for breach of confidence provided an adequate remedy for the Spencers' complaint and looked no further into the rest of the

armoury of remedies available to the victims of other invasions of privacy. Likewise, in *Peck v United Kingdom* the court expressed some impatience, at paragraph 103, at being given a tour d'horizon of the remedies provided and to be provided by English law to deal with every imaginable kind of invasion of privacy. It was concerned with whether Mr Peck (who had been filmed in embarrassing circumstances by a CCTV camera) had an adequate remedy when the film was widely published by the media. It came to the conclusion that he did not.

33.   Counsel for the Wainwrights relied upon *Peck's* case as demonstrating the need for a general tort of invasion of privacy. But in my opinion it shows no more than the need, in English law, for a system of control of the use of film from CCTV cameras which shows greater sensitivity to the feelings of people who happen to have been caught by the lens. For the reasons so cogently explained by Sir Robert Megarry in *Malone v Metropolitan Police Comr*, this is an area which requires a detailed approach which can be achieved only by legislation rather than the broad brush of common law principle.

34.   Furthermore, the coming into force of the Human Rights Act 1998 weakens the argument for saying that a general tort of invasion of privacy is needed to fill gaps in the existing remedies. Sections 6 and 7 of the Act are in themselves substantial gap fillers; if it is indeed the case that a person's rights under article 8 have been infringed by a public authority, he will have a statutory remedy. The creation of a general tort will, as Buxton LJ pointed out in the Court of Appeal, at para 92, pre-empt the controversial question of the extent, if any, to which the Convention requires the state to provide remedies for invasions of privacy by persons who are not public authorities.

35.   For these reasons I would reject the invitation to declare that since at the latest 1950 there has been a previously unknown tort of invasion of privacy.

36.   I turn next to the alternative argument based upon *Wilkinson v Downton*. This is a case which has been far more often discussed than applied ... The jury awarded [the plaintiff] £100 for nervous shock and the question for the judge on further consideration was whether she had a cause of action.

37.   The difficulty in the judge's way was the decision of the Privy Council in *Victorian Railway Comrs v Coultas*, in which it had been said that nervous shock was too remote a consequence of a negligent act (in that case, putting the plaintiff in imminent fear of being run down by a train) to be a recoverable head of damages. RS Wright J distinguished the case on the ground that Downton was not merely negligent but had intended to cause injury. Quite what the judge meant by this is not altogether clear; Downton obviously did not intend to cause any kind of injury but merely to give Mrs Wilkinson a fright. The judge said ... that as what he said could not fail to produce grave effects "upon any but an exceptionally indifferent person", an intention to cause such effects should be "imputed" to him.

38.   The outcome of the case was approved and the reasoning commented upon by the Court of Appeal in *Janvier v Sweeney*. During the First World War Mlle Janvier lived as a paid companion in a house in Mayfair and corresponded with her German lover who was interned as an enemy alien on the Isle of Man. Sweeney was a private detective who wanted secretly to obtain some of her employer's documents and sent his assistant to induce her to co-operate by pretending to be from Scotland Yard and saying that the authorities wanted her because she was corresponding with a German spy. Mlle Janvier suffered severe nervous shock from which she took a long time to recover. The jury awarded her £250.

39.   By this time, no one was troubled by *Victorian Railway Comrs v Coultas*. In *Dulieu v White & Sons* the Divisional Court had declined to follow it; Phillimore J said ... that in principle "terror wrongfully induced and inducing physical mischief gives a cause of action". So on that basis Mlle Janvier was entitled to succeed whether the detectives intended to cause her injury or were merely negligent as to the consequences of their threats. Duke LJ observed ... that the case was stronger than *Wilkinson v Downton* because Downton had intended merely to play a practical joke and not to commit a wrongful act. The detectives, on the other hand, intended to blackmail the plaintiff to attain an unlawful object.

40.   By the time of *Janvier v Sweeney*, therefore, the law was able comfortably to accommodate the facts of *Wilkinson v Downton* in the law of nervous shock caused by negligence. It was unnecessary to fashion a tort of intention or to discuss what the requisite intention, actual or imputed, should be. Indeed, the remark of Duke LJ to which I have referred suggests that he did not take seriously the idea that Downton had in any sense intended to cause injury.

41.   Commentators and counsel have nevertheless been unwilling to allow *Wilkinson v Downton* to disappear beneath the surface of the law of negligence. Although, in cases of actual psychiatric injury, there is no point in arguing about whether the injury was in some sense intentional if negligence will do just as well, it has been suggested (as the claimants submit in this case) that damages for distress falling short of psychiatric injury can be recovered if there was an intention to cause it. This submission was squarely put to the Court of Appeal in *Wong v Parkside Health NHS Trust* and rejected ... Hale LJ said that before the passing of the Protection from Harassment Act 1997 there was no tort of intentional harassment which gave a remedy for anything less than physical or psychiatric injury. That leaves *Wilkinson v Downton* with no leading role in the modern law.

42.   In *Khorasandjian v Bush* the Court of Appeal, faced with the absence of a tort of causing distress by harassment, tried to press into service the action for private nuisance. In *Hunter v Canary Wharf Ltd* ... the House of Lords regarded this as illegitimate and, in view of the passing of the 1997 Act, unnecessary. I did however observe ... that: "The law of harassment has now been put on a statutory basis ... and it is unnecessary to consider how the common law might have developed. But as at present advised, I see no reason why a tort of intention should be subject

to the rule which excludes compensation for mere distress, inconvenience or discomfort in actions based on negligence ... The policy considerations are quite different." ...

44.   I do not resile from the proposition that the policy considerations which limit the heads of recoverable damage in negligence do not apply equally to torts of intention. If someone actually intends to cause harm by a wrongful act and does so, there is ordinarily no reason why he should not have to pay compensation. But I think that if you adopt such a principle, you have to be very careful about what you mean by intend. In *Wilkinson v Downton* RS Wright J wanted to water down the concept of intention as much as possible. He clearly thought, as the Court of Appeal did afterwards in *Janvier v Sweeney*, that the plaintiff should succeed whether the conduct of the defendant was intentional or negligent. But the *Victorian Railway Comrs* case prevented him from saying so. So he devised a concept of imputed intention which sailed as close to negligence as he felt he could go.

45.   If, on the other hand, one is going to draw a principled distinction which justifies abandoning the rule that damages for mere distress are not recoverable, imputed intention will not do. The defendant must actually have acted in a way which he knew to be unjustifiable and intended to cause harm or at least acted without caring whether he caused harm or not. Lord Woolf CJ [in the Court of Appeal] might have been inclined to accept such a principle. But the facts did not support a claim on this basis. The judge made no finding that the prison officers intended to cause distress or realized that they were acting without justification in asking the Wainwrights to strip ...

46.   Even on the basis of a genuine intention to cause distress, I would wish, as in *Hunter's* case, to reserve my opinion on whether compensation should be recoverable. In institutions and workplaces all over the country, people constantly do and say things with the intention of causing distress and humiliation to others. This shows lack of consideration and appalling manners but I am not sure that the right way to deal with it is always by litigation. ... The requirement [in the Protection from Harassment Act 1997] of a course of conduct shows that Parliament was conscious that it might not be in the public interest to allow the law to be set in motion for one boorish incident. It may be that any development of the common law should show similar caution.

47.   In my opinion, therefore, the claimants can build nothing on *Wilkinson v Downton*. It does not provide a remedy for distress which does not amount to recognized psychiatric injury and so far as there may a tort of intention under which such damage is recoverable, the necessary intention was not established. I am also in complete agreement with Buxton LJ [in the Court of Appeal] that *Wilkinson v Downton* has nothing to do with trespass to the person.

48.   Counsel for the Wainwrights submit that unless the law is extended to create a tort which covers the facts of the present case, it is inevitable that the European

Court of Human Rights will find that the United Kingdom was in breach of its Convention obligation to provide a remedy for infringements of Convention rights. In addition to a breach of article 8, they say that the prison officers infringed their Convention right under article 3 not to be subjected to degrading treatment.

49.   I have no doubt that there was no infringement of article 3. The conduct of the searches came nowhere near the degree of humiliation which has been held by the European Court of Human Rights to be degrading treatment in the cases on prison searches to which we were referred ...

51.   Article 8 is more difficult. Buxton LJ thought ... that the Wainwrights would have had a strong case for relief under section 7 if the 1998 Act had been in force. Speaking for myself, I am not so sure. Although article 8 guarantees a right of privacy, I do not think that it treats that right as having been invaded and requiring a remedy in damages, irrespective of whether the defendant acted intentionally, negligently or accidentally. ... Article 8 may justify a monetary remedy for an intentional invasion of privacy by a public authority, even if no damage is suffered other than distress for which damages are not ordinarily recoverable. It does not follow that a merely negligent act should, contrary to general principle, give rise to a claim for damages for distress because it affects privacy rather than some other interest like bodily safety ...

52.   Be that as it may, a finding that there was a breach of article 8 will only demonstrate that there was a gap in the English remedies for invasion of privacy which has since been filled by sections 6 and 7 of the 1998 Act. It does not require that the courts should provide an alternative remedy which distorts the principles of the common law.

53.   I would therefore dismiss the appeal.'

Comment

(1)   The utility of the principle in *Wilkinson v Downton* (which is not a trespassory tort) has been considerably curtailed. *Wilkinson v Downton* has been applied in many common law jurisdictions to a wide range of fact situations; see, for example, *Stevenson v Basham* – threat by the defendant to burn down a house, overheard by the plaintiff's wife who suffered a miscarriage. It has been applied to acts as well as to words, and see also the bizarre facts in *Bradley v Wingnut Films Ltd*. The principle was applied in *Khorasandjian v Bush* to conduct which could not 'strictly be classified as threats' and which was shown to be a serious risk to the plaintiff's health. An interlocutory injunction was granted to compel the defendant to stop pestering the plaintiff with telephone calls after a relationship broke down. Dillon LJ observed that:

'The law expects the ordinary person to bear the mishaps of life with fortitude and ... customary phlegm; but it does not expect ordinary young women to bear indefinitely such a campaign of persecution as that to which the defendant has subjected the plaintiff.'

(2) In some respects the scope of the protection afforded by the principle in *Wilkinson v Downton* may be wider than under the law of nuisance or negligence, but this will depend to the extent that intentional distress is permitted to fall within the principle. Although the new statutory tort of harassment is welcome, it should not be forgotten that the reported cases on the principle in *Wilkinson v Downton* – such as *Janvier v Sweeney*, *Stephenson v Basham* and *Bielitski v Obadiak* – concern behaviour that would have fallen outside the scope of the new Act as not being part of a course of conduct, which, according to s 7(3), must involve conduct on at least two occasions.

(3) The absence of adequate protection for privacy *per se* and the judicial dislike for intrusive press reporting may be discerned in the context of defamation in *Charleston v News Group Newspapers Ltd*, p 742. As far as trespass to land is concerned, see p 571.

Protection from Harassment Act 1997

1 Prohibition of harassment

(1) A person must not pursue a course of conduct–
(a) which amounts to harassment of another, and
(b) which he knows or ought to know amounts to harassment of the other.

(2) For the purposes of this section, the person whose course of conduct is in question ought to know that it amounts to harassment of another if a reasonable person in possession of the same information would think the course of conduct amounted to harassment of the other.

(3) Subsection (1) does not apply to a course of conduct if the person who pursued it shows–
(a) that it was pursued for the purpose of preventing or detecting crime,
(b) that it was pursued under any enactment or rule of law or to comply with any condition or requirement imposed by any person under any enactment, or
(c) that in the particular circumstances the pursuit of the course of conduct was reasonable.

...

3   Civil remedy

(1)   An actual or apprehended breach of section I may be the subject of a claim in civil proceedings by the person who is or may be the victim of the course of conduct in question.

(2)   On such a claim, damages may be awarded for (among other things) any anxiety caused by the harassment and any financial loss resulting from the harassment.

(3)   Where–
(a)   in such proceedings the High Court or a county court grants an injunction for the purpose of restraining the defendant from pursuing any conduct which amounts to harassment, and
(b)   the plaintiff considers that the defendant has done anything which he is prohibited from doing by the injunction,

the plaintiff may apply for the issue of a warrant for the arrest of the defendant.

[Subsections (4) to (9) deal with procedure and punishment for breach of the order.]

...

7   Interpretation of this group of sections

(1)   This section applies for the interpretation of sections I to 5.

(2)   References to harassing a person include alarming the person or causing the person distress.

(3)   A 'course of conduct' must involve conduct on at least two occasions.

(3A)   A person's conduct on any occasion shall be taken, if aided, abetted, counselled or procured by another—
(a)   to be conduct on that occasion of the other (as well as conduct of the person whose conduct it is); and
(b)   to be conduct in relation to which the other's knowledge and purpose, and what he ought to have known, are the same as they were in relation to what was contemplated or reasonably foreseeable at the time of the aiding, abetting, counselling or procuring.

(4)   'Conduct' includes speech.

Comment

(1)   The history of the attempts at common law to create a tort of harassment is dealt with by the Court of Appeal in *Wong v Parkside NHS Trust*; see also the response of private nuisance, p 604.

(2)   Other than in s 7(2), the Protection from Harassment Act 1997 does not attempt to define 'harassment'; since this is an ordinary word of the English language and is incapable of further definition it ought to be given its ordinary meaning. Whether behaviour amounts to harassment (or alarm and distress) will be a question of fact. The widening of harassment by s 7(2) may be compared with the offence in the Public Order Act 1986, s 5, which prohibits certain types of behaviour which are likely to cause a person harassment, alarm or distress.

(3)   In *Huntingdon Life Sciences Ltd v Curtin*, in interlocutory proceedings based on s 1, the Court of Appeal suggested that the word 'person' in s 1(1) would include a body corporate and that an injunction might extend to prevent harassment by such a body. The point arose again in several cases where it was suggested that the victim could not be a body corporate and that neither should the perpetrator. In *Daiichi UK Ltd v Stop Huntingdon Animal Cruelty and others* the Queen's Bench Division considered the matter and concluded that for the purposes of s 1 the word 'person' did not include a body corporate, and accordingly a body corporate could be neither the perpetrator (as in that case) nor the victim. As the court pointed out, it would be possible for the body corporate to be vicariously liable for the actions of its employees, e.g. as might be argued in the case of *Thomas v Newsgroup Newspapers Ltd*.

(4)   The Act creates two criminal offences: harassment contrary to s 2; and putting a person in fear of violence contrary to s 4. Under s 5, a court sentencing or otherwise dealing with a person convicted of either offence may make an order prohibiting that person from doing anything described in the order for the purpose of protecting the victim, or any other person mentioned in the order, from further conduct which either amounts to harassment or will cause fear of violence. Breach of such an order is itself a criminal offence. Breach of an injunction granted under the civil law aspect of the Act will be a criminal offence and the plaintiff may apply for a warrant for the arrest of the defendant.

Robinson v Balmain New Ferry Co Ltd
[1910] AC 295 Privy Council

A ferry company had only one point of payment: passengers disembarking had to pay there for their journey, passengers wishing to travel in the opposite direction paid on entry to the terminal. The plaintiff entered upon payment of one penny then decided not to travel; he was asked to pay another penny in order to leave. He refused and his way was obstructed for some time before he was able to squeeze past the turnstile; he sued for false imprisonment. The defendants succeeded.

Lord Loreburn LC: '... in the circumstances admitted it is clear to their Lordships that there was no false imprisonment at all. The plaintiff was merely called upon to leave the wharf in the way in which he contracted to leave it. There is no law requiring the defendants to make the exit from their premises gratuitous to people who come there upon a definite contract which involves their leaving the wharf by another way; and the defendants were entitled to resist a forcible passage through their turnstile. The question whether the notice which was affixed to these premises was brought home to the knowledge of the plaintiff is immaterial, because the notice itself is immaterial. When the plaintiff entered the defendants' premises there was nothing agreed as to the terms on which he might go back, because neither party contemplated his going back. When he desired to do so the defendants were entitled to impose a reasonable condition before allowing him to pass through their turnstile from a place to which he had gone of his own free will. The payment of a penny was a quite fair condition, and if he did not choose to comply with it the defendants were not bound to let him through. He could proceed on the journey he had contracted for ...'

Herd v Weardale Steel Coal & Coke Co Ltd
[1915] AC 67 House of Lords

A miner who had gone down a pit at the beginning of a shift complained of the working conditions and wished to be taken to the surface. There was some delay in giving him permission to use a cage and he sued for false imprisonment.

Viscount Haldane LC said that: '... by the law of this country no man can be restrained of his liberty without authority in law. That is a proposition the maintenance of which is of great importance; but at the same time it is a proposition which must be read in relation to other propositions which are equally important. If a man chooses to go into a dangerous place at the bottom of a quarry or the bottom of a mine, from which by the nature of physical circumstances he cannot escape, it does not follow from the proposition I have enunciated about liberty that he can compel the owner to bring him up out of it. The owner may or may not be under a duty arising from circumstances, on broad grounds the neglect of which may possibly involve him in a criminal charge or a civil liability. It is unnecessary to discuss the conditions and circumstances which might bring about such a result, because they have, in the view I take, nothing to do with false imprisonment.

My Lords, there is another proposition which has to be borne in mind, and that is the application of the maxim *volenti non fit injuria*. If a man gets into an express train and the doors are locked pending its arrival at its destination, he is not entitled, merely because the train has been stopped by signal, to call for the doors to be opened to let him out. He has entered the train on the terms that he is to be conveyed to a certain station without the opportunity of getting out before that, and he must abide by the terms on which he has entered the train. So when a man goes down a mine, from which access to the surface does not exist in the absence of special facilities given on the part of the owner of the mine, he is only entitled to the use of these facilities (subject possibly to the exceptional circumstances to which I have alluded) on the terms on which he has entered. I think it results from what was laid down by the Judicial Committee of the Privy Council in *Robinson v Balmain New Ferry Co* that that is so ... It was held that [there] was not false imprisonment; *volenti non fit injuria*. The man had gone in upon the pier knowing that those were the terms and conditions as to exit, and it was not false imprisonment to hold him to conditions which he had accepted. So ... it is not false imprisonment to hold a man to the conditions he has accepted when he goes down a mine ... There was no refusal to bring him up at the ordinary time which was in his bargain; but there was a refusal – and I am quite ready to assume that the motive of it was to punish him, I will assume it for the sake of argument, for having refused to go on with his work – by refusing to bring him up at the moment when he claimed to come. Did that amount to false imprisonment? In my opinion it did not. No statutory right under the Coal Mines Regulation Act 1887, avails him ... Nor had he any right in contract. His right in contract was to come up at the end of his shift. Was he then falsely imprisoned? There were facilities, but they were facilities which, in accordance with the conditions that he had accepted by going down, were not available to him until the end of his shift, at any rate as of right.

My Lords, under these circumstances I find it wholly impossible to come to the conclusion that the principle to which I have alluded, and on which the doctrine of false imprisonment is based, has any application to the case. *Volenti non fit injuria*. The man chose to go to the bottom of the mine under these conditions – conditions which he accepted. He had no right to call upon the employers to make use of special machinery put there at their cost, and involving cost in its working, to bring him to the surface just when he pleased ...'

Comment

The picture presented by these two cases is less than clear. Is Viscount Haldane's explanation of *Robinson v Balmain New Ferry* consistent with what Lord Loreburn said? Why should an owner of land be able to impose only reasonable conditions? In any event how is reasonableness to be assessed? When does the price of freedom become too high to be reasonable?

R v Bournewood Community and Mental Health NHS Trust, ex p L [1998] 3 All ER 289 House of Lords

L was severely mentally handicapped and was incapable of consenting to medical treatment. He had been discharged into the community and looked after by carers, Mr and Mrs E, since 1994. While at a day centre L became seriously agitated and because Mr and Mrs E could not be contacted he was taken by ambulance to accident and emergency at Bournewood hospital where a sedative was administered. When he later became agitated the hospital psychiatrist recommended inpatient treatment and he was transferred to the behavioural unit in the hospital. His consultant, Dr M, decided that it was in his best interests that he should be re-admitted but decided that since he was compliant there was no need to employ the provisions of the Mental Health Act 1983. Proceedings were commenced against the hospital in the name of L in respect of false imprisonment. The Court of Appeal held that L had been detained without authority and awarded the sum of £1 by way of damages. The hospital then regularised the position of L using the Mental Health Act 1983 and he was later discharged back into the care of Mr and Mrs E.

The majority in the House of Lords held that L had not been detained and that in the absence of detention there could be no false imprisonment. The minority held that there had been a detention but that the defence of necessity had not been removed by the Mental Health Act 1983 and that it provided a defence to false imprisonment.

Lord Goff:'... I turn to consider the question whether, as the Court of Appeal held, there has been any unlawful detention of Mr L in this case. I should record at once my understanding that the question is whether the tort of false imprisonment has been committed against Mr L; and I do not wish the use of the word "detention" in this context to distract attention from the true nature of the question.

In the course of their judgment, the Court of Appeal stated that: "... a person is detained in law if those who have control over the premises in which he is have the intention that he shall not be permitted to leave those premises and have the ability to prevent him from leaving." I observe however that no mention is here made of the requirement that, for the tort of false imprisonment to be committed, there must in fact be a complete deprivation of, or restraint upon, the plaintiff's liberty. On this the law is clear. As Atkin LJ said in *Meering v Grahame-White Aviation Co Ltd*, "any restraint within defined bounds which is a restraint in fact may be an imprisonment". Furthermore, it is well settled that the deprivation of liberty must be actual, rather than potential. Thus in *Syed Mahamad Yusuf-ud-Din v Secretary of State* for India, Lord Macnaghten said that: "Nothing short of actual detention and complete loss of freedom would support an action for false imprisonment." And in *Meering* Atkin LJ was careful to draw a distinction between restraint upon the plaintiff's liberty which is conditional upon his seeking to exercise his freedom (which would not amount to false imprisonment), and an actual restraint upon his liberty, as where the defendant decided to restrain the plaintiff within a room and placed a policeman outside the door to stop him leaving (which would amount to false imprisonment). In cases such as the present it is, I consider, important that the courts should have regard to the ingredients of the tort as laid down in the decided cases, and consider whether those ingredients are in fact found to exist on the particular facts of the case in question. With that in mind, I turn to consider the facts of the present case ...

In the light of this account, the following conclusions may be drawn. The first is that, as I have already recorded, although Mr L had been discharged from hospital into the community on a trial basis, and on that basis had gone to live with Mr and Mrs E as his paid carers, nevertheless he had not been finally discharged. It followed that the appellant trust remained responsible for his treatment, and that it was in discharge of that responsibility that the steps described by Dr M were taken. The second is that when, on 22 July, Mr L became agitated and acted violently, an emergency in any event arose which called for intervention, as a matter of necessity, in his best interests and, at least in the initial stages, to avoid danger to others. Plainly it was most appropriate that the appellant trust, and Dr M in particular, should intervene in these circumstances; certainly Mr and Mrs E, as Mr L's carers, could not assert any superior position. Third, I have no doubt that all the steps in fact taken, as described by Dr M, were in fact taken in the best interests of Mr L and, in so far as they might otherwise have constituted an invasion of his civil rights, were justified on the basis of the common law doctrine of necessity.

I wish to add that the latter statement is as true of any restriction upon his freedom of movement as then occurred, as it is of any touching of his person. There were times during the episode when it might be said that Mr L was "detained" in the sense that, in the absence of justification, the tort of false imprisonment would have been committed. I have particularly in mind the journey by ambulance from the Day Centre to the Accident and Emergency Unit. But that journey was plainly justified by necessity, as must frequently be so in the case of removal to hospital by ambulance of unfortunate people who have been taken ill or suffered injury and as a result are incapacitated from expressing consent. I wish further to add that I cannot see that Dr M's statements to the effect that she would if necessary have taken steps compulsorily to detain Mr L under the Act of 1983 have any impact on the above conclusions. Those concerned with the treatment and care of mentally disordered persons must always have this possibility in mind although, like Dr M, they will know that this power is only to be exercised in the last resort and they may hope, as in the present case, that it would prove to be unnecessary to exercise it. Such power, if exercised in accordance with the statute, is of course lawful. In the present case all the steps in fact taken by Dr M were, in my opinion, lawful because justified under the common law doctrine of necessity, and this conclusion is unaffected by her realisation that she might have to invoke the statutory power of detention. Finally, the readmission of Mr L to hospital as an informal patient under s 131(1) of the Act of 1983 could not, in my opinion, constitute the tort of false imprisonment. His readmission, as such, did not constitute a deprivation of his liberty. As Dr M stated in paragraph 9 of her affidavit, he was not kept in a locked ward after he was admitted and the fact that she, like any other doctor in a situation such as this, had it in her mind that she might thereafter take steps to detain him compulsorily under the Act, did not give rise to his detention in fact at any earlier date.

Furthermore his treatment while in hospital was plainly justified on the basis of the common law doctrine of necessity. It follows that none of these actions constituted any wrong against Mr L.

For these reasons, I would allow the appeal ...'

Lord Steyn (dissenting on the question whether or not there had been a detention of L): '... If the judgment of the Court of Appeal is upheld it would mean that in practice compliant incapacitated patients, such as L, could only be admitted to hospitals and mental nursing homes under the Act of 1983. On that basis the statutory safeguards would apply to them ...

If the decision of the Court of Appeal is reversed almost all the basic protections under the Act of 1983 will be inapplicable to compliant incapacitated patients: see s 57(2) for an exception. The result would be an indefensible gap in our mental health law. In oral argument counsel for the Secretary of State for Health did not seek to justify such differential treatment on the grounds of resource implications. That is understandable. After all, how we address the intractable problems of mental health care for all classes of mentally incapacitated patients must be a touchstone of our maturity as a civilised society. Counsel for the Secretary of State did not seek to justify such differential treatment on the grounds of the views and wishes of health care professionals. That is also understandable. If protection is necessary to guard against misjudgment and professional lapses, the confident contrary views of professionals ought not to prevail. Professions are seldom enthusiastic about protective measures to guard against lapses by their members. And health care professionals are probably no different. But the law would be defective if it failed to afford adequate protective remedies to a vulnerable group of incapacitated mental patients.

For these reasons I would have wished to uphold the judgment of the Court of Appeal if that were possible. But as the issues were intensively probed in oral argument it became clear to me that, on a contextual interpretation of the Act of 1983, this course was not open to the House. Given the importance of the matter, I will explain my reasons. Two issues arose: (1) Was L detained? (2) If he was detained, was his detention lawful?

The first is a question of fact and the second is a matter of pure law.

THE APPROACH TO BE ADOPTED

... In my view, the two issues should be considered separately, and that the issue of detention must be considered and determined before one can turn to the issue of justification ... To start with an enquiry into the lawfulness of conduct, or to conflate the two issues, is contrary to legal principle and authority. And such an approach tends to erode legal principles fashioned for the protection of the liberty of the individual.

DETENTION

It is unnecessary to attempt a comprehensive definition of detention. In my view, this case falls on the wrong side of any reasonable line that can be drawn between what is or what is not imprisonment or detention. The critical facts are as follows: (1) When on 22 July 1997 at the Day Centre L became agitated and started injuring himself, he was sedated and then physically supported and taken to the hospital. Even before sedation he was unable to express dissent to his removal to hospital. (2) Health care professionals exercised effective power over him. If L had physically resisted, the psychiatrist would immediately have taken steps to ensure his compulsory admission. (3) In hospital, staff regularly sedated him. That ensured that he remained tractable. This contrasts with the position when he was with carers: they seldom resorted to medication and then only in minimal doses. (4) The psychiatrist vetoed visits by the carers to L. She did so, as she explained to the carers, in order to ensure that L did not try to leave with them. The psychiatrist told the carers that L would be released only when she, and other health care professionals, deemed it appropriate. (5) While L was not in a locked ward, nurses closely monitored his reactions. Nurses were instructed to keep him under continuous observation and did so.

Counsel for the Trust and the Secretary of State argued that L was in truth always free not to go to the hospital and subsequently to leave the hospital. This argument stretches credulity to breaking point. The truth is that for entirely bona fide reasons, conceived in the best interests of L, any possible resistance by him was overcome by sedation, by taking him to hospital, and by close supervision of him in hospital. And, if L had shown any sign of wanting to leave, he would have been firmly discouraged by staff and, if necessary, physically prevented from doing so. The suggestion that L was free to go is a fairy tale.

At one stage counsel for the Trust suggested that L was not detained because he lacked the necessary will, or more precisely the capacity to grant or refuse consent. That argument was misconceived. After all, an unconscious or drugged person can be detained: see *Meering v Grahame-White Aviation Co Ltd*, dictum approved in *Murray v Ministry of Defence*. In my view L was detained because the health care professionals intentionally assumed control over him to such a degree as to amount to complete deprivation of his liberty ...'

Comment

(1) The issue of detention was before the Court of Appeal in *Meering v Grahame-White Aviation*, where by a majority of two to one the Court held that

the plaintiff had been detained. For Warrington LJ, detention arose when the plaintiff first came under the influence of the two factory security guards sent to fetch him to the factory; for Atkin LJ the detention occurred when the guards were placed outside the waiting-room with instructions not to let him leave until the police arrived. In any event, the matter was one for the jury as a matter of fact. Disagreeing on that point, Duke LJ felt that there was no evidence of detention which might properly be left to the jury and from which it could conclude that there was a detention in fact. For the issue of knowledge of the fact of detention, see pp 533–536.

(2)   The totality of the reduction in liberty is emphasised in *Bird v Jones*. The plaintiff complained that he had been prevented from crossing a bridge but would have been allowed to go back the way he had come. He complained about his subsequent arrest and detention and the legality of the refusal to permit him to cross became an issue, the plaintiff suggesting that it had amounted to false imprisonment. Coleridge J in the majority said that:

'To call it [imprisonment] appears to me to confound partial obstruc-tion ... with total obstruction or detention. A prison may have its boundary ... but a boundary it must have; and that boundary the party imprisoned must be prevented from passing; he must be prevented from leaving that place ... Some confusion seems to me to arise from confound-ing imprisonment of the body with mere loss of freedom; it is one part of the definition of freedom to go whithersoever one pleases; but imprison-ment is something more than mere loss of this power, it includes the notion of restraint within some limits defined by a will or power exterior to our own ...'

This view was not in accord with the dissent of Lord Denman who said that:

'... this liberty to do something else does not appear to me to affect the question of imprisonment. As long as I am prevented from doing what I have a right to do, of what importance is it that I am permitted to do something else? How does the imposition of an unlawful condition show that I am not restrained? If I am locked in a room, am I not imprisoned because I might effect my escape through a window, or because I might find an exit dangerous or inconvenient to myself, as by wading through water or by taking a route so circuitous that my necessary affairs would suffer by delay. It appears to me that this is a total deprivation of liberty with reference to the purpose for which he lawfully wished to employ his liberty ...'

(3)   In the unusual case of *Pritchard v Ministry of Defence* it was decided by the Queen's Bench Division that requiring a soldier to serve in the armed forces beyond the period for which he had enlisted was capable of amounting to a false imprisonment:

'... Throughout the time that a man is committed to service in ... the army he is obliged under compulsion of military law to comply with all lawful requirements as to where he shall be and what he shall do. He is not free to leave barracks for his own purposes unless expressly authorised to do so. He may be permitted to absent himself on leave but ... he has to return to barracks at the expiration of his leave ... Whilst it is true that limited liberty is granted to the individual whilst on army service, for example, freedom to move about within or even outside barracks when not on duty, nevertheless the soldier is at all other times subject to restriction as to where he may be and what he may do which restriction will be enforced ... by military law. The power of compulsion is sufficient to constitute "imprisonment", whether or not the compulsion has been exercised. The availability of the power of compulsion is sufficient coercion to constitute "imprisonment".'

(4) Some observations of the Court of Appeal as to the nature of false imprisonment are worthy of note. In *Weldon v Home Office*, Ralph Gibson J observed that:

'... The law protects the right of the individual to be free of any unjustified interference with his personal security and personal liberty ... It is clear that the policy of the law is jealously to protect personal liberty. Thus, it appears that, if a man is without justification confined in a room, it would be no defence to show that, if he had not been locked in, he would not in fact have had occasion to leave the room during the period of time over which he was so confined, although, again, that would be relevant to damages. The wrong done is the infringement of the right to the ability to leave and go elsewhere. Further, it would appear to follow that, if a man should be under some restraint not to leave a particular place for a period of time, for example because he does not have the means to leave, or because he has contracted to stay there to guard the place, or because, as a soldier or policeman, he has been ordered to remain there, he could, nevertheless, claim damages for false imprisonment if, without justification, he should be imprisoned within that place. The immediate and wholly unrestricted freedom and ability to go somewhere else are not, therefore, a precondition for asserting a claim in false imprisonment ... The intention necessary for commission of the tort is intentionally to do the act which causes the imprisonment. Added malice towards the imprisoned plaintiff is not necessary ... It is not necessary for present purposes to consider whether negligence would suffice.'

(5) In *R v Governor of Brockhill Prison, ex p Evans (No 2)* all members of the House of Lords were consistent in their statements that false imprisonment was a tort of strict liability not dependent on the fault of the tortfeasor; in that case a prison Governor who had innocently miscalculated the period of detention.

The court was concerned to indicate that the Governor had acted without malice and without carelessness; but there was a continued application of the detention and thus the intention to detain was not an issue.

(6)   In certain circumstances, a person who instigates arrest or prosecution may be liable in either false imprisonment or malicious prosecution. In *Davidson v Chief Constable of North Wales* the police arrested the plaintiff following receipt of information from a store detective whose powers of arrest were more limited than those of the police, see the Police and Criminal Evidence Act 1984, s 24. The police were held not liable for false imprisonment and the case proceeded against the defendants, the employers of the store detective. The suggestion was that the police officers had merely acted as agents, and that the arrest was for and on behalf of the store detective. The Court of Appeal concluded that the law distinguished between, on the one hand, the giving of information for the police to make up their own minds in the exercise of their discretion, and, on the other, directing or requiring or procuring or requesting or encouraging the police to effect an arrest. Liability will not flow in respect of the former but will in respect of the latter. On the facts, the store detective had simply presented the information and had left it to the police to decide how to proceed, and no tort had been committed.

In *Grinham v Willey* Pollock CB said: 'A person ought not to be held responsible in trespass, unless he directly and immediately causes the imprisonment.' And, Bramwell B drew a distinction between 'the defendant being the cause of the arrest in the sense that he had given the information which induced the officer to make it, and causing it in the sense that he directed the officer to make it.'

Martin v Watson was an action for malicious prosecution where the defendant had supplied information to the police as a result of which a warrant for the arrest of the plaintiff had been issued by a magistrate. False imprisonment was not an issue since judicial discretion is a *novus actus interveniens*. In deciding whether or not the plaintiff was prosecuted by the defendant, i.e. that the law was set in motion against him by the defendant, Lord Keith stated that:

'Where an individual falsely and maliciously gives a police officer information indicating that some person is guilty of a criminal offence and states that he is willing to give evidence in court of the matters in question, it is properly to be inferred that he desires and intends that the person he names should be prosecuted. Where the circumstances are such that the facts relating to the alleged offence can be within the knowledge only of the complainant, as was the position here, then it becomes virtually impossible for the police officer to exercise any independent discretion or judgment, and if a prosecution is instituted by the police officer the proper view of the matter is that the prosecution has been procured by the complainant.'

For malicious prosecution generally now see *Gregory v Portsmouth City Council* which demonstrates the reluctance of the House of Lords to extend the scope of the tort.

Murray v Ministry of Defence
[1988] 2 All ER 521 House of Lords

In Northern Ireland, police and army personnel arrived at the plaintiff's house to arrest her for questioning in connection with terrorist matters. She was aware that that was the reason for the search and entry although words of arrest were not spoken until half an hour after entry and at the time when the plaintiff was about to leave the premises with the soldiers and police. On the issue of the manner of the arrest the House of Lords held that the delay in specifying the fact and grounds of arrest for half an hour was reasonable and did not invalidate the arrest. On the issue of knowledge of the fact of detention, the House of Lords held that this was not a necessary ingredient of the tort of false imprisonment.

Lord Griffiths: '... Although on the facts of this case I am sure that the plaintiff was aware of the restraint on her liberty from 7.00 a.m., I cannot agree with the Court of Appeal that it is an essential element of the tort of false imprisonment that the victim should be aware of the fact of denial of liberty. The Court of Appeal relied on *Herring v Boyle* for this proposition which they preferred to the view of Atkin LJ to the opposite effect in *Meering v Grahame-White Aviation Co Ltd. Herring v Boyle* is an extraordinary decision of the Court of Exchequer: a mother went to fetch her 10-year-old son from school on 24 December 1833 to take him home for the Christmas holidays. The headmaster refused to allow her to take her son home because she had not paid the last term's fees, and he kept the boy at school over the holidays. An action for false imprisonment brought on behalf of the boy failed. In giving judgment Bolland B said:

> "... as far as we know, the boy may have been willing to stay; he does not appear to have been cognizant of any restraint, and there was no evidence of any act whatsoever done by the defendant in his presence. I think that we cannot construe the refusal to the mother in the boy's absence, and without his being cognizant of any restraint, to be an imprisonment of him against his will ..."

I suppose it is possible that there are schoolboys who prefer to stay at school rather than go home for the holidays but it is not an inference that I would draw, and I cannot believe that on the same facts the case would be similarly decided today. In *Meering v Grahame-White Aviation Co Ltd* the plaintiff's employers, who suspected him of theft, sent two of the works' police to bring him in for questioning at the company's offices. He was taken to a waiting-room where he said that if he was not told why he was there he would leave. He was told he was wanted for the purpose of making inquiries about things that had been stolen and he was wanted to give evidence; he then agreed to stay. Unknown to the plaintiff, the works' police had been instructed not to let him leave the waiting-room until the Metropolitan Police arrived. The works' police therefore remained outside the waiting-room and would not have allowed the plaintiff to leave until he was handed over to the Metropolitan Police, who subsequently arrested him. The question for the Court of Appeal was whether on this evidence the plaintiff was falsely imprisoned during the hour he was in the waiting-room, or whether there could be no "imprisonment" sufficient to found a civil action unless the plaintiff was aware of the restraint on his liberty. Atkin LJ said:

"… it appears to me that a person could be imprisoned without his knowing it. I think a person can be imprisoned while he is asleep, while he is in a state of drunkenness, while he is unconscious, and while he is a lunatic. Those are cases where it seems to me that the person might properly complain if he were imprisoned, though the imprisonment began and ceased while he was in that state. Of course, the damages might be diminished and would be affected by the question whether he was conscious or of it or not. So a man might in fact, to my mind, be imprisoned by having the key of a door turned against him so that he is imprisoned in a room in fact although he does not know that the key has been turned. It may be that he is being detained in that room by persons who are anxious to make him believe that he is not in fact being imprisoned, and at the same time his captors outside that room may be boasting to persons that he is imprisoned, and it seems to me that if we were to take this case as an instance supposing it could be proved that [the works' police officer] had said while the plaintiff was waiting: 'I have got him detained there waiting for the detective to come in and take him to prison' – it appears to me that that would be evidence of imprisonment. It is quite unnecessary to go on to show that in fact the man knew that he was imprisoned. If a man can be imprisoned by having the key turned upon him without his knowledge, so he can be imprisoned if, instead of a lock and key or bolts and bars, he is prevented from, in fact, exercising his liberty by guards and warders or policemen. They serve the same purpose. Therefore it appears to me to be a question of fact. It is true that in all cases of imprisonment so far as the law of civil liberty is concerned that 'stone walls do not a prison make', in the sense that they are not the only form of imprisonment, but any restraint within defined bounds which is a restraint in fact may be an imprisonment."

I agree with this passage. In the first place it is not difficult to envisage cases in which harm may result from unlawful imprisonment even though the victim is unaware of it. Dean William L Prosser gave two examples in "False Imprisonment: Consciousness of Confinement" (1955) 55 Col LR 847, in which he attacked … the American Law Institute's *Restatement of the Law of Torts*, which at that time stated the rule that "there is no liability for intentionally confining another unless the person physically restrained knows of the confinement". Dean Prosser wrote:

> "Let us consider several illustrations. A locks B, a child two days old, in the vault of a bank. B is, of course, unconscious of the confinement, but the bank vault cannot be opened for two days. In the meantime, B suffers from hunger and thirst, and his health is seriously impaired; or it may be that he even dies. Is this no tort? Or suppose that A abducts B, a wealthy lunatic, and holds him for ransom for a week. B is unaware of his confinement, but vaguely understands that he is in unfamiliar surroundings, and that something is wrong. He undergoes mental suffering affecting his health. At the end of the week, he is discovered by the police and released without ever having known that he has been imprisoned. Has he no action against B? ... If a child of two is kidnapped, confined, and deprived of the care of its mother for a month, is the kidnapping and the confinement in itself so minor a matter as to call for no redress in tort at all?"

The *Restatement of the Law of Torts* has now been changed and requires that the person confined "is conscious of the confinement or is harmed by it" (see *Restatement of the Law*, Second, Torts 2d (1965)) ...

If a person is unaware that he has been falsely imprisoned and has suffered no harm, he can normally expect to recover no more than nominal damages, and it is tempting to redefine the tort in the terms of the present rule in the American Law Institute's *Restatement of the Law of Torts*. On reflection, however, I would not do so. The law attaches supreme importance to the liberty of the individual and if he suffers a wrongful interference with that liberty it should remain actionable even without proof of special damage ...'

Comment

(1)   There may be some sympathy for the view that the statement in *Herring v Boyle* was the *ratio* of the case, that the statement in *Meering v Grahame-White* was *per incuriam*, *Herring v Boyle* not having been before the court, and that the statement in *Murray v Ministry of Defence* was *obiter* since the plaintiff knew that she was no longer free. Nonetheless, the principle which emerges from *Murray v Ministry of Defence* is consistent with other varieties of trespass.

(2)   Although the principle adopted by the House of Lords in *Murray v Ministry of Defence* accords primacy to the liberty of the individual it is interesting that the Court of Appeal in Northern Ireland were quite content to permit the opposite conclusion to apply.

(3)   In the absence of any authorities examining the state of mind of the defendant there is some doubt whether intention is required or whether negligence will suffice, e.g. there is a distinction between locking a room

knowing that someone is inside and locking the door without checking. A variation on this point is the locking of a door carelessly, e.g. by letting it slam. See the differences between *Street on Torts* and *Winfield and Jolowicz on Tort* on this issue.

A claimant who is aware of the fact of detention is falsely imprisoned even though unaware of the illegality of the detention, see *Roberts v Chief Constable of Cheshire.*

(4)   If a person deliberately sets a trap to be operated by the victim's own act then there is no reason why this should not be false imprisonment, although the issue of directness may arise. A person who enters a vehicle left by police as a lure to thieves which seals itself (e.g. when the ignition is tampered with) is imprisoned, and the imprisonment requires justification by reference to the police powers of arrest, see *Dawes v DPP.*

Hague v Deputy Governor of Parkhurst Prison
Weldon v Home Office
[1991] 3 All ER 733 House of Lords

The appeals raised the question whether convicted prisoners treated contrary to the Prison Rules had a cause of action in private law against the prison governor or the Home Office on the ground either of a breach of statutory duty or of the tort of false imprisonment.

W was serving a four-year prison sentence and claimed in an action for false imprisonment, assault and battery, that he had been seized by prison officers, dragged downstairs and placed in a cell in the punishment block where his clothes were removed. He alleged that he remained there overnight. The issue was whether or not the action for false imprisonment should be struck out as disclosing no reasonable cause of action. The Court of Appeal refused to strike out the action and held that the prisoner retained a residual liberty which could be protected by the tort of false imprisonment and that this would be available to the prisoner if he could show actions by the prison staff outside the scope of their power provided that he could show that the actions were in bad faith. False imprisonment might also be based on the imposition on the prisoner of intolerable conditions.

H was serving a 15-year prison sentence. He was removed from association with other prisoners under rule 43 of the Prison Rules. The Court of Appeal held that a prisoner *wrongly* segregated under rule 43 would not have a remedy in false imprisonment. Detention in intolerable conditions would be capable of amounting to false imprisonment but, contrary to *Weldon*'s case, bad faith was not an element in that tort.

The House of Lords decided that a prisoner had no residual liberty *vis-à-vis* the prison Governor which could be protected by action for false imprisonment. Prison authorities could raise the Prison Act 1952, s 12 as a defence to such an action, but other prisoners could not. The House of Lords also held that there was no tort of false imprisonment by virtue of the imposition of intolerable conditions.

For the decision on breach of statutory duty, see p 460.

Lord Jauncey: '... False imprisonment is defined in *Clerk and Lindsell on Torts* (16th edn, 1989) as "complete deprivation of liberty for any time, however short, without lawful cause". *Clerk and Lindsell* then quotes Termes de la Ley:

> "Imprisonment is no other thing but the restraint of a man's liberty, whether it be in the open field, or in the stocks, or in the cage in the streets or in a man's own house, as well as in the common gaols; and in all places the party so restrained is said to be a prisoner so long as he hath not his liberty freely to go at all times to all places whither he will without bail or mainprise or otherwise."

The latter definition of imprisonment was cited with approval by Duke and Atkin LJJ in *Meering v Grahame-White Aviation Co Ltd*. The reference to liberty to go "at all times to all places" must, of course, be read in the context of the normal restrictions imposed by general law or contract on the ability of individuals to go where and when they please.

RESIDUAL LIBERTY

In the Court of Appeal in *Weldon's* case Ralph Gibson LJ ... said: "It is apparent ... from consideration of [the Prison Rules] that the legislative intention is that a prisoner should, subject to any lawful order given to him and to any rules laid down in the prison, enjoy such liberty, his residual liberty, within prison as is left to him."
...

[I]n each case what was said to constitute false imprisonment was not the confinement in the particular prison but rather the treatment therein, or, as Goddard LJ put it in *Arbon v Anderson*, the conditions and not the nature of the imprisonment. The alteration in the conditions infringed the residual liberty possessed by the two men and thus constituted false imprisonment.

This proposition presupposes that a prisoner lawfully confined in prison has, vis-à-vis the governor, residual liberty which can be protected by private law remedies. That a prisoner has a right to sue in respect of torts committed against him in prison is beyond doubt (see *Raymond v Honey*). If he is assaulted by a prison officer he may sue for damages, and if he is negligently cared for whereby he sustains injury to his health he may likewise sue. But does he have such residual liberty, vis-à-vis the governor, as amounts to a right protectable in law? I do not consider that he does.

He is lawfully committed to a prison and while there is subject to the Prison Act 1952 and the Prison Rules 1964. His whole life is regulated by the regime. He has no freedom to do what he wants, when he wants. His liberty to do anything is governed by the prison regime. Placing Weldon in a strip cell and segregating Hague altered the conditions under which they were detained but did not deprive them of any liberty which they had not already lost when initially confined.

INTOLERABLE CONDITIONS

In the Court of Appeal in *Weldon's* case Ralph Gibson LJ concluded that the plaintiff's allegation included "an assertion of fact capable of constituting such 'intolerable conditions of detention' as to render the detention unlawful within the principle stated by Ackner LJ in the *Middleweek* case". In ... *Middleweek v Chief Constable of the Merseyside Police*, Ackner LJ after referring to an unreported decision of the Divisional Court in *R v Comr of Police of the Metropolis, ex p Nahar* said:

> "We agree with the views expressed by the Divisional Court that it must be possible to conceive of hypothetical cases in which the conditions of detention are so intolerable as to render the detention unlawful and thereby provide a remedy to the prisoner in damages for false imprisonment. A person lawfully detained in a prison cell would, in our judgment, cease to be so lawfully detained if the conditions in that cell were such as to be seriously prejudicial to his health if he continued to occupy it, e.g. because it became and remained seriously flooded, or contained a fractured gas pipe allowing gas to escape into the cell. We do not therefore accept as an absolute proposition that, if detention is initially lawful, it can never become unlawful by reason of changes in the conditions of imprisonment."

My Lords, there is no doubt that in the conditions predicated by Ackner LJ the prisoner would have a public law remedy and, if he sustained injury to health, a private law remedy as well, but the latter remedy would lie in negligence other than in false imprisonment. To say that detention becomes unlawful when the conditions thereof become intolerable is to confuse conditions of confinement with the nature of confinement and to add a qualification to s 12(1). If, as I believe to be the case, a prisoner at any time has no liberty to be in any place other than where the regime permits, he has no liberty capable of deprivation by the regime so as to constitute the tort of false imprisonment. An alteration of conditions therefore deprives him of no liberty because he has none already. I am therefore of the opinion that the above quoted *dictum* of Ackner LJ in *Middleweek's* case is an incorrect statement of the law.

GENERAL

There are certain further matters which are relevant to both of the arguments on residual liberty and intolerable conditions. [Counsel] argued that a substantial breach of a justiciable prison rule affected the legality of the detention and could give rise to false imprisonment. This argument is unsound for two reasons. In the first place it turns the tort of false imprisonment into one of degree dependent upon whether or not the breach in question is substantial. Such a concept is at odds with the definition of the tort and particularly at odds with the *dictum* of Atkin LJ in *Meering v Grahame-White Aviation Co Ltd* …If a man can be falsely imprisoned when he is unaware of the fact it is difficult to see what relevance comfort or discomfort has to the constitution of the tort. In my view, imprisonment is either lawful or false and questions of degree do not arise. In the second place, the argument seeks to obtain by the back door the remedy which is not available by the front, namely that based on breach of statutory duty.

If deprivation of residual liberty or subjection to intolerable conditions could constitute false imprisonment it would mean adding to s 12(1) some such words as "so long as the conditions of his confinement are tolerable and the provisions of this Act and of any rules made hereunder are observed in relation to him in all material aspects". I see no justification for so qualifying s 12(1). In my view that subsection provides a complete answer to any claim of false imprisonment against the governor or anyone acting on his authority.

It was suggested during argument that if no action of false imprisonment could lie against the governor, a prisoner would have no remedy against a fellow prisoner who locked him in some confined space. While a prisoner has no residual liberty vis-à-vis the governor, it does not necessarily follow that vis-à-vis fellow prisoners he does not have such measure of liberty as is permitted to him by the prison regime.

Furthermore, s 12 would provide no defence to a fellow prisoner. As the matter is not necessary to the determination of these appeals and was not fully argued I say no more. It was further suggested that as a matter of general principle someone who had already suffered some deprivation of liberty could not thereafter suffer false imprisonment. This appears to misunderstand the definition of the tort which is total deprivation of liberty, that is to say of all such liberty as the individual presently enjoys and not deprivation of total liberty, namely liberty which is otherwise wholly unrestricted. I see no reason why an individual enjoying restricted liberty such as an undergraduate "gated" within his college should not be falsely imprisoned if the result thereof is to deprive him totally of such liberty as he presently enjoys …'

Comment

(1) In *Hague's* case, in the Court of Appeal Taylor LJ observed that:

'... the action contemplated by Ralph Gibson LJ (in *Weldon*) involved adding to the ordinary definition of false imprisonment not only detention under intolerable conditions but knowledge on the part of the defendant that the conditions were intolerable, i.e. bad faith. Again I observe that bad faith has never been a necessary ingredient in the tort of false imprisonment. Moreover if the plaintiff can show bad faith his proper cause of action would probably be for misfeasance in a public office, assuming that he could bring his case within the criteria laid down in *Bourgoin SA v Ministry of Agriculture, Fisheries and Food* ... I am not convinced that any added ingredient can be grafted on to the established definition of false imprisonment so as to make a claim possible in a prison context ... To require proof of bad faith would be to alter the tort of false imprisonment and in effect to create a new tort special to prisons and prisoners ...'

The rejection of the attempt to widen trespass, the boundaries of which were long ago fixed, is seen by some as a missed opportunity to develop trespass in the modern context to protect individuals whose position is precarious. Such individuals do have a private law remedy if they suffer harm (negligence), and possibly misfeasance in a public office (see *Bourgoin SA v Ministry of Agriculture, Fisheries and Food* and *Jones v Swansea CC*), but not in trespass or breach of statutory duty, see p 460. Any other remedy is a matter of public law, and perhaps under the Human Rights Act 1998.

(2) In *R v The Governor HM Prison Brockhill, ex p Evans* (*No 2*) detention of a prisoner beyond the time limit permitted on a proper calculation of the sentence amounted to false imprisonment, even though, in calculating the sentence, the Governor of the prison had been faced with conflicting judicial decisions as to the correct method of calculating the release date. In *Roberts v Chief Constable of Cheshire*, continued detention of a prisoner in breach of the review provisions in the Police and Criminal Evidence Act 1984 was unlawful and amounted to a false imprisonment. On the other hand, in *Olotu v Home Office* the detention of a prisoner in gaol beyond the statutory time limits was nonetheless lawful because the governor was justified in relying on the warrant of detention issued by a judge.

F v West Berkshire Health Authority
[1989] 2 All ER 545 House of Lords

F, aged 36, was under a serious mental disability and had the mental capacity of a child aged four. She had for 22 years been a voluntary in-patient at the hospital run by the defendants. She formed a sexual relationship with another patient and the medical evidence was that pregnancy would be disastrous for her. Contraception was out of the question and sterilisation was proposed. The

Mental Health Act 1983 permitted certain kinds of treatment for the patient's mental disorder but did not make provision for treatment for any conditions other than mental disorder. The House of Lords held that there was no jurisdiction in a court to give consent or approval to such an operation but that there was jurisdiction to grant a declaration as to the lawfulness of the proposed operation. The House of Lords then held that, despite the inability of the plaintiff to consent, the principles of necessity would apply and the procedure would be lawful provided it was considered by the doctors to be in the best interests of the patient.

Lord Goff: '... if the operation on F is to be justified, it can only be justified on the applicable principles of common law. The argument of counsel revealed the startling fact that there is no English authority on the question whether as a matter of common law (and if so in what circumstances) medical treatment can lawfully be given to a person who is disabled by mental incapacity from consenting to it. Indeed, the matter goes further, for a comparable problem can arise in relation to persons of sound mind who are, for example, rendered unconscious in an accident or rendered speechless by a catastrophic stroke. All such persons may require medical treatment and, in some cases, surgical operations. All may require nursing care. In the case of mentally disordered persons, they may require care of a more basic kind, dressing, feeding and so on, to assist them in their daily life, as well as routine treatment by doctors and dentists. It follows that, in my opinion, it is not possible to consider in isolation the lawfulness of the proposed operation of sterilisation in the present case. It is necessary first to ascertain the applicable common law principles and then to consider the question of sterilisation against the background of those principles.

Counsel for the Official Solicitor advanced the extreme argument that, in the absence of a *parens patriae* or statutory jurisdiction, no such treatment or care of the kind I have described can lawfully be given to a mentally disordered person who is unable to consent to it. This is indeed a startling proposition, which must also exclude treatment or care to persons rendered unconscious or unable to speak by accident or illness. For centuries, treatment and care must have been given to such persons, without any suggestion that it was unlawful to do so. I find it very difficult to believe that the common law is so deficient as to be incapable of providing for so obvious a need. Even so, it is necessary to examine the point as a matter of principle.

I start with the fundamental principle, now long established, that every person's body is inviolate. As to this, I do not wish to depart from what I myself said in the judgment of the Divisional Court in *Collins v Wilcock*, and in particular from the statement that the effect of this principle is that everybody is protected not only against physical injury but against any form of physical molestation.

Of course, as a general rule physical interference with another person's body is lawful if he consents to it; though in certain limited circumstances the public interest may require that his consent is not capable of rendering the act lawful. There are also specific cases where physical interference without consent may not be unlawful: chastisement of children, lawful arrest, self-defence, the prevention of crime and so on. As I pointed out in *Collins v Wilcock*, a broader exception has been created to allow for the exigencies of everyday life: jostling in a street or some other crowded place, social contact at parties and such like. This exception has been said to be founded on implied consent, since those who go about in public places, or go to parties, may be taken to have impliedly consented to bodily contact of this kind. Today this rationalisation can be regarded as artificial; and, in particular, it is difficult to impute consent to those who, by reason of their youth or mental disorder, are unable to give their consent. For this reason, I consider it more appropriate to regard such cases as falling within a general exception embracing all physical contact which is generally acceptable in the ordinary conduct of everyday life.

In the old days it used to be said that, for a touching of another's person to amount to a battery, it had to be a touch "in anger" (see *Cole v Turner*); and it has recently been said that the touching must be "hostile" to have that effect (see *Wilson v Pringle*). I respectfully doubt whether that is correct. A prank that gets out of hand, an over-friendly slap on the back, surgical treatment by a surgeon who mistakenly thinks that the patient has consented to it, all these things may transcend the bounds of lawfulness, without being characterised as hostile. Indeed, the suggested qualification is difficult to reconcile with the principle that any touching of another's body is, in the absence of lawful excuse, capable of amounting to a battery and a trespass. Furthermore, in the case of medical treatment, we have to bear well in mind the libertarian principle of self-determination which, to adopt the words of Cardozo J (in *Schloendorff v Society of New York Hospital*), recognises that: "Every human being of adult years and sound mind has a right to determine what shall be done with his own body; and a surgeon who performs an operation without his patient's consent, commits an assault ..."

... It is against this background that I turn to consider the question whether, and if so when, medical treatment or care of a mentally disordered person who is, by reason of his incapacity, incapable of giving his consent can be regarded as lawful. As is recognised in Cardozo J's statement of principle, and elsewhere (see, e.g. *Sidaway v Bethlem Royal Hospital Governors*), some relaxation of the law is required to accommodate persons of unsound mind. In *Wilson v Pringle* the Court of Appeal considered that treatment or care of such persons may be regarded as lawful, as falling within the exception relating to physical contact which is generally acceptable in the ordinary conduct of everyday life. Again, I am with respect unable to agree. That exception is concerned with the ordinary events of everyday life, jostling in public places and such like, and affects all persons, whether or not they are capable of giving their consent. Medical treatment, even treatment for minor ailments, does not fall within that category of events. The general rule is that consent is necessary to render such treatment lawful. If such treatment administered without consent is not to be unlawful, it has to be justified on some other principle.

On what principle can medical treatment be justified when given without consent? We are searching for a principle on which, in limited circumstances, recognition may be given to a need, in the interests of the patient, that treatment should be given to him in circumstances where he is (temporarily or permanently) disabled from consenting to it. It is this criterion of a need which points to the principle of necessity as providing justification.

That there exists in the common law a principle of necessity which may justify action which would otherwise be unlawful is not in doubt. But historically the principle has been seen to be restricted to two groups of cases, which have been called cases of public necessity and cases of private necessity. The former occurred when a man interfered with another man's property in the public interest, for example (in the days before we could dial 999 for the fire brigade) the destruction of another man's house to prevent the spread of a catastrophic fire, as indeed occurred in the Great Fire of London in 1666. The latter cases occurred when a man interfered with another's property to save his own person or property from imminent danger, for example when he entered on his neighbour's land without his consent in order to prevent the spread of fire on to his own land.

There is, however, a third group of cases, which is also properly described as founded on the principle of necessity and which is more pertinent to the resolution of the problem in the present case. These cases are concerned with action taken as a matter of necessity to assist another person without his consent. To give a simple example, a man who seizes another and forcibly drags him from the path of an oncoming vehicle, thereby saving him from injury or even death, commits no wrong. But there are many emanations of this principle, to be found scattered through the books. These are concerned not only with the preservation of the life or health of the assisted person, but also with the preservation of his property (sometimes an animal, sometimes an ordinary chattel) and even to certain conduct on his behalf in the administration of his affairs. Where there is a pre-existing relationship between the parties, the intervener is usually said to act as an agent of necessity on behalf of the principal in whose interests he acts, and his action can often, with not too much artificiality, be referred to the pre-existing relationship between them. Whether the intervener may be entitled either to reimbursement or to remuneration raises separate questions which are not relevant to the present case.

We are concerned here with action taken to preserve the life, health or well-being of another who is unable to consent to it. Such action is sometimes said to be justified as arising from an emergency; in *Prosser and Keeton Torts* (5th edn, 1984) the action is said to be privileged by the emergency. Doubtless, in the case of a person of sound mind, there will ordinarily have to be an emergency before such action taken without consent can be lawful; for otherwise there would be an opportunity to communicate with the assisted person and to seek his consent. But this is not always so; and indeed the historical origins of the principle of necessity do not point to emergency as such as providing the criterion of lawful intervention without consent ... But, when a person is rendered incapable of communication either permanently or over a considerable period of time (through illness or accident or mental disorder), it would be an unusual use of language to describe the case as one of "permanent emergency", if indeed such a state of affairs can properly be said to exist. In truth, the relevance of an emergency is that it may give rise to a necessity to act in the interests of the assisted person without first obtaining his consent. Emergency is however not the criterion or even a prerequisite; it is simply a frequent origin of the necessity which impels intervention. The principle is one of necessity, not of emergency ...

[Lord Goff referred to statements of principles of necessity from mercantile law.]

In a sense, these statements overlap. But from them can be derived the basic requirements, applicable in these cases of necessity, that, to fall within the principle, not only (1) must there be a necessity to act when it is not practicable to communicate with the assisted person, but also (2) the action taken must be such as a reasonable person would in all the circumstances take, acting in the best interest of the assisted person.

On this statement of principle, I wish to observe that officious intervention cannot be justified by the principle of necessity. So intervention cannot be justified when another more appropriate person is available and willing to act; nor can it be justified when it is contrary to the known wishes of the assisted person, to the extent that he is capable of rationally forming such a wish. On the second limb of the principle, the introduction of the standard of a reasonable man should not in the present context be regarded as materially different from that of Sir Montague Smith's "wise and prudent man", because a reasonable man would, in the time available to him, proceed with wisdom and prudence before taking action in relation to another man's person or property without his consent. I shall have more to say on this point later. Subject to that, I hesitate at present to indulge in any greater refinement of the principle, being well aware of many problems which may arise in its application, problems which it is not necessary, for present purposes, to examine. But as a general rule, if the above criteria are fulfilled, interference with the assisted person's person or property (as the case may be) will not be unlawful. Take the example of a railway accident, in which injured passengers are trapped in the wreckage. It is this principle which may render lawful the actions of other citizens, railway staff, passengers or outsiders, who rush to give aid and comfort to the victims; the surgeon who amputates the limb of an unconscious passenger to free him from the wreckage; the ambulance man who conveys him to hospital; the doctors and nurses who treat him and care for him while he is still unconscious. Take the example of an elderly person who suffers a stroke which renders him incapable of speech or movement. It is by virtue of this principle that the doctor who treats him, the nurse who cares for him, even the relative or friend or neighbour who comes in to look after him will commit no wrong when he or she touches his body.

The two examples I have given illustrate, in the one case, an emergency and, in the other, a permanent or semi-permanent state of affairs. Another example of the latter kind is that of a mentally disordered person who is disabled from giving consent. I can see no good reason why the principle of necessity should not be applicable in his case as it is in the case of the victim of a stroke. Furthermore, in the case of a mentally disordered person, as in the case of a stroke victim, the permanent state of affairs calls for a wider range of care than may be requisite in an emergency which arises from accidental injury. When the state of affairs is permanent, or semi-permanent, action properly taken to preserve the life, health or well-being of the assisted person may well transcend such measures as surgical operation or substantial medical treatment and may extend to include such humdrum matters as routine medical or dental treatment, even simple care such as dressing and undressing and putting to bed.

The distinction I have drawn between cases of emergency and cases where the state of affairs is (more or less) permanent is relevant in another respect. We are here concerned with medical treatment, and I limit myself to cases of that kind. Where, for example, a surgeon performs an operation without his consent on a patient temporarily rendered unconscious in an accident, he should do no more than is reasonably required, in the best interests of the patient, before he recovers consciousness. I can see no practical difficulty arising from this requirement, which derives from the fact that the patient is expected before long to regain conscious-ness and can then be consulted about longer term measures. The point has however arisen in a more acute form where a surgeon, in the course of an operation, discovers some other condition which, in his opinion, requires operative treatment for which he has not received the patient's consent. In what circum-stances he should operate forthwith, and in what circumstances he should postpone the further treatment until he has received the patient's consent, is a difficult matter which has troubled the Canadian courts (see *Marshall v Curry* and *Murray v McMurchy*), but which it is not necessary for your Lordships to consider in the present case.

But where the state of affairs is permanent or semi-permanent, as may be so in the case of a mentally disordered person, there is no point in waiting to obtain the patient's consent. The need to care for him is obvious; and the doctor must then act in the best interests of his patient, just as if he had received his patient's consent so to do. Were this not so, much useful treatment and care could, in theory at least, be denied to the unfortunate. It follows that, on this point, I am unable to accept the view expressed by Neill LJ in the Court of Appeal, that the treatment must be shown to have been necessary. Moreover, in such a case, as my noble and learned friend Lord Brandon has pointed out, a doctor who has assumed responsibility for the care of a patient may not only be treated as having the patient's consent to act, but also be under a duty so to act. I find myself to be respectfully in agreement with Lord Donaldson MR when he said:

> "I see nothing incongruous in doctors and others who have a caring responsibility being required, when acting in relation to an adult who is incompetent, to exercise a right of choice in exactly the same way as would the court or reasonable parents in relation to a child, making due allowance, of course, for the fact that the patient is not a child, and I am satisfied that that is what the law does in fact require."

In these circumstances, it is natural to treat the deemed authority and the duty as interrelated. But I feel bound to express my opinion that, in principle, the lawfulness of the doctor's action is, at least in its origin, to be found in the principle of necessity. This can perhaps be seen most clearly in cases where there is no continuing relationship between doctor and patient. The "doctor in the house" who volunteers to assist a lady in the audience who, overcome by the drama or by the heat in the theatre, has fainted away is impelled to act by no greater duty than that imposed by his own Hippocratic oath. Furthermore, intervention can be justified in the case of a non-professional, as well as a professional, man or woman who has no pre-existing relationship with the assisted person, as in the case of a stranger who rushes to assist an injured man after an accident. In my opinion, it is the necessity itself which provides the justification for the intervention.

I have said that the doctor has to act in the best interests of the assisted person. In the case of routine treatment of mentally disordered persons, there should be little difficulty in applying this principle. In the case of more serious treatment, I recognise that its application may create problems for the medical profession; however, in making decisions about treatment, the doctor must act in accordance with a responsible and competent body of relevant profession opinion, on the principles set down in *Bolam v Friern Hospital Management Committee*. No doubt, in practice, a decision may involve others besides the doctor. It must surely be good practice to consult relatives and others who are concerned with the care of the patient.

Sometimes, of course, consultation with a specialist or specialists will be required; and in others, especially where the decision involves more than a purely medical opinion, an inter-disciplinary team will in practice participate in the decision. It is very difficult, and would be unwise, for a court to do more than to stress that, for those who are involved in these important and sometimes difficult decisions, the overriding consideration is that they should act in the best interests of the person who suffers from the misfortune of being prevented by incapacity from deciding for himself what should be done to his own body in his own best interests.'

Comment

(1) Lord Goff's observations about the nature of battery must be related to the analysis in *Collins v Wilcock* and *Wilson v Pringle*, pp 499 and 504.

(2) The relationship between the criminal law, the law of tort and medical law has been explored in various cases. Most conspicuous of these was *Re A (children) (conjoined twins: surgical separation)*. Here the essence of the case was that for one of the conjoined twins (Mary) separation meant instant death because her heart and lungs would be incapable by themselves of sustaining life. But the other twin (Jodie) was capable on separation of a separate and viable existence. If left joined then both would both die within a few months because Jodie's heart would fail. In the absence of a consent by the parents, the hospital sought a declaration that separation would be lawful. In the extraordinary circumstances of the case, the Court of Appeal confirmed that causing the death of Mary in order to preserve Jodie would not be murder, and granted the declaration.

(3) The *Bolam* test emerged from *Bolam v Friern Hospital Management Committee*, see p 206. It is: 'that a doctor will not be negligent if he establishes that he acted in accordance with a practice accepted at the time by a responsible body of medical opinion skilled in the particular form of treatment in question.'

(4) Necessity as a defence is available in a wide range of torts; for other cases on necessity see p 585. See also the comments in *Rigby v Chief Constable of Northamptonshire* for comment on the availability of necessity in the context of *Rylands v Fletcher*, p 709.

(5) The majority in the House of Lords in *F v West Berkshire* thought that treatment would be lawful despite the absence of a declaration by the court. The Court of Appeal and Lord Griffiths in the House of Lords would have had it otherwise; the latter on the basis of a new development in the common law to protect those incompetent through mental incapacity or youth.

(6) The power of the court to grant declarations and the ability of interested parties to invoke the jurisdiction of the court are vital if the impact of judicial control and influence is to be felt. The procedural complexities of the cases are difficult to extricate from the substantive legal points. The relevant authorities are reviewed by the Court of Appeal in *Re S (hospital patient: court's jurisdiction)* and the comments of Zamir and Woolf, *The Declaratory Judgment* (2nd edn, 1993) were approved: 'Collectively, these cases appear to constitute the development of a new advisory jurisdiction.'

In *Re S* a wealthy, elderly Norwegian domiciled in England had been taken seriously ill and was unable to take decisions for himself. There was a 'tug of love' between his family (the defendants) and Mrs A (the plaintiff) with whom he had been living for many years and who had been actively involved in assuming a duty of caring for S after he became ill. The procedural issue for the court was whether or not Mrs A had sufficient standing to invoke the jurisdiction of the English courts to make various declarations, including one to the effect that it would be unlawful to remove S from England to Norway. The Court of Appeal applied a test of whether or not the plaintiff had been able to establish a serious justiciable issue and that she had a genuine and legitimate interest such as to make her more than a mere busybody.

The substantive law relating to S's legal rights was not before the Court of Appeal, but it would seem that the same principles as were expounded in cases such as *F v West Berkshire HA* and *Airedale NHS Trust v Bland* would be invoked. As Hale J put it at first instance in the Family Division: 'The legal rights at issue are just the same, whatever it is proposed to do with a person's body without his agreement.' At a later hearing in the Family Division, *Re S (hospital patient: foreign curator)*, Hale J concluded that it was in S's best interests to enable the Norwegian guardian appointed under Norwegian law to arrange for the return of S to Norway for care.

(7)   The potential breadth of the principle in *F v West Berkshire HA* may be seen from *Re Y (mental patient: bone marrow donation)* which falls into the broad category identified by Lord Goff as 'action properly taken to preserve the life, health or well being of the assisted person'. Here the 25-year-old severely mentally incapacitated defendant lived in a community home, but close links had been retained between her sisters, her mother and the plaintiff. Unfortunately the defendant's sister, the plaintiff, developed a pre-leukaemic bone marrow disorder. The best hope for a suitable donor was the defendant, who was both unaware of the plaintiff's illness and unable to consent to the relevant procedures. The plaintiff sought a declaration that preliminary blood tests and a conventional bone marrow harvesting operation under general anaesthetic could be performed lawfully without the consent of the defendant. The basis for the application was that the two matters were in the best interests of the defendant and outweighed any possible detriment. It was also relevant that the health of the defendant's mother was deteriorating and that it was in the defendant's interests that the family unit should not be further reduced.

Connell J distinguished *F v West Berkshire Health Authority* because a significant benefit would flow to another person. But, he was satisfied that the procedures would benefit the defendant and that benefits flowing to the plaintiff were relevant in that they had 'a positive effect upon the best interests of the defendant'. He compared the decision of the Supreme Court of Illinois in *Curran v Bosze* where the best interests test had been applied to permit bone marrow harvesting from twins for the benefit of their brother.

(8)   Where consent is possible then said Lord Brandon:

' ... At common law a doctor cannot lawfully operate on adult patients of sound mind, or give them any other treatment involving the application of physical force however small ... without their consent. If a doctor were to operate on such patients, or give them other treatment, without their consent, he would commit the actionable tort of trespass to the person.'

Note that in *F v West Berkshire Health Authority* what was meant by consent was not before the court, nor was the position of minors.

Airedale NHS Trust v Bland
[1993] I All ER 821 House of Lords

B was in a persistent vegetative state, unlikely ever to improve, even marginally; his brain-stem was still alive and functioning, accordingly he was alive and was so regarded as a matter of law. The question for the court was whether or not it would be lawful to discontinue both artificial support for his life and the administering of life-prolonging drugs. The House of Lords considered that the test should be what was in the best interests of the patient, and that doctors should as a matter of practice seek the guidance of the court in such cases in the form of a declaration.

Lord Goff: ' ... the principle of self-determination requires that respect must be given to the wishes of the patient, so that, if an adult patient of sound mind refuses, however unreasonably, to consent to treatment or care by which his life would or might be prolonged, the doctors responsible for his care must give effect to his wishes, even though they do not consider it to be in his best interests to do so ... To this extent, the principle of the sanctity of human life must yield to the principle of self-determination and, for present purposes perhaps more important, the doctor's duty to act in the best interests of his patient must likewise be qualified. On this basis, it has been held that a patient of sound mind may, if properly informed, require that life support should be discontinued: see *Nancy B v Hotel-Dieu de Quebec*. Moreover the same principle applies where the patient's refusal to give his consent has been expressed at an earlier date, before he became unconscious or otherwise incapable of communicating it; though in such circumstances especial care may be necessary to ensure that the prior refusal of consent is still properly to be regarded as applicable in the circumstances which have subsequently occurred (see e.g. *Re T (adult: refusal of medical treatment)*) ...

I must however stress ... that the law draws a crucial distinction between cases in which a doctor decides not to provide, or to continue to provide, for his patient treatment or care which could or might prolong his life and those in which he decides, for example by administering a lethal drug, actively to bring his patient's life to an end. As I have already indicated, the former may be lawful, either because the doctor is giving effect to his patient's wishes by withholding the treatment or care, or even in certain circumstances in which (on principles which I shall describe) the patient is incapacitated from stating whether or not he gives his consent. But it is not lawful for a doctor to administer a drug to his patient to bring about his death, even though that course is prompted by a humanitarian desire to end his suffering, however great that suffering may be ...

[I]f the justification for treating a patient who lacks the capacity to consent lies in the fact that the treatment is provided in his best interests, it must follow that the treatment may, and indeed ultimately should be, discontinued where it is no longer in his best interests to provide it. The question which lies at the heart of the present case is, as I see it, whether on that principle the doctors responsible for the treatment and care of [B] can justifiably discontinue the process of artificial feeding upon which the prolongation of his life depends.

It is crucial ... that the question itself should be correctly formulated ... The question is whether the doctor should or should not continue to provide his patient with medical treatment or care which, if continued, will prolong his patient's life ... the question is not whether it is in the best interests of the patient that he should die. The question is whether it is in the best interests of the patient that his life should be prolonged by the continuance of this form of medical treatment or care.

The correct formulation of the question is of particular importance in a case such as the present, where the patient is totally unconscious and where there is no hope whatsoever of any amelioration of his condition. In circumstances such as these, it may be difficult to say that it is in his best interests that the treatment should be ended. But, if the question is asked, as in my opinion it should be, whether it is in his best interests that treatment which has the effect of artificially prolonging his life should be continued, that question can sensibly be answered to the effect that it is not in his best interests to do so.

Even so, a distinction may be drawn between (1) cases in which, having regard to all the circumstances (including, for example, the intrusive nature of the treatment, the hazards involved in it and the very poor quality of the life which may be prolonged for the patient if the treatment is successful), it may be judged not to be in the best interests of the patient to initiate or continue life-prolonging treatment and (2) cases such as the present in which, so far as the living patient is concerned, the treatment is of no benefit to him because he is totally unconscious and there is no prospect of any improvement in his condition. In both classes of case the decision whether or not to withhold treatment must be made in the best interests of the patient. In the first class, however, the decision has to be made by weighing the relevant considerations ...

With this class of case, however, your Lordships are not directly concerned in the present case; and, though I do not wish to be understood to be casting any doubt upon any of the reported cases on the subject, nevertheless I must record that argument was not directed specifically towards these cases and for that reason I do not intend to express any opinion about the precise principles applicable in relation to them.

By contrast, in the latter class of case, of which the present case provides an example, there is in reality no weighing operation to be performed. Here the condition of the patient, who is totally unconscious and in whose condition there is no prospect *of* any improvement, is such that life-prolonging treatment is properly regarded as being, in medical terms, useless ...

In *F v West Berkshire Health Authority* it was stated that, where a doctor provides treatment for a person who is incapacitated from saying whether or not he consents to it, the doctor must ... act in accordance with a responsible and competent body of relevant medical opinion ... In my opinion, this principle must equally be applicable to decisions to initiate, or to discontinue life support, as it is to other forms of treatment ...'

Comment

Airedale NHS Trust v Bland concerned the discontinuance of life-preserving treatment; other cases may involve the withholding of it. One such is *Frenchay Healthcare NHS Trust v S*, where the defendant patient was in a persistent vegetative state and was fed through a tube which been introduced surgically into the stomach; the tube had been pulled out as a result of the patient's own movements. The Court of Appeal considered the evidence in order to answer the question, 'What is in the best interests of the patient?' and concluded that the plaintiff hospital could lawfully refrain from renewing life-sustaining treatment. Commenting on the need for the judges to test the evidence carefully, Sir Thomas Bingham MR said that:

'It is, I think, important that there should not be a belief that what the doctor says is the patient's best interest *is* the patient's best interest. For my part I would certainly reserve to the court the ultimate power and duty to review the doctor's decision in the light of all the facts.'

In both *Airedale NHS Trust v Bland* and *Frenchay NHS Trust v S* the patients exhibited no cognitive functions, there were no 'glimmerings of awareness' (Lord Mustill's phrase), although the evidence in the later case was not as conclusive as that in the earlier case. The distinguishing feature of the later case was that there was an emergency and that there was a less than full investigation of the sort usually required by the procedures in place to deal with such cases.

Secretary of State for the Home Department v Robb [1995] 1 All ER 677 Family Division

The Secretary of State sought declarations concerning the defendant prisoner, R, who suffered from a personality disorder. R went on hunger strike and was determined to see it to an end. Psychiatrists agreed that he was of sound mind and understanding, the personality disorder notwithstanding. Eventually, agreement was reached that declarations should be made: first, that the plaintiff (1) may lawfully observe and abide by the refusal of the defendant to receive nutrition and (2) may lawfully abstain from providing hydration and nutrition, whether by artificial means or otherwise, for so long as the defendant retains the capacity to refuse the same. Given the absence of any modern authority as to the duty of the Home Office in relation to a prisoner on hunger strike, the judge was asked to deliver a judgment.

Thorpe J: '... The first principle is that every person's body is inviolate and proof against any form of physical molestation ... Secondly, the principle of self-determination requires that respect must be given to the wishes of the patient ...

The next proposition ... is that a patient who is entitled to consent to treatment which might or would have the effect of prolonging his life and who refuses so to consent, and by reason of the refusal subsequently dies, does not commit suicide. A doctor who, in accordance with his duty, complied with the patient's wishes in such circumstances does not aid or abet a suicide.

As to capacity to make a decision to refuse medical treatment, the analysis of Lord Donaldson MR in *Re T* establishes the circumstances in which the presumption of capacity may be rebutted by long-term mental incapacity or other circumstances. Then the definition of capacity as now formulated by expert forensic psychiatry is the threefold test adopted in *Re C* (*adult: refusal of medical treatment*).

Against that background, it seems to me that the definition of the duty of the Home Office in relation to prisoners on hunger strike is relatively straightforward. There is a surprising dearth of authority in this jurisdiction and that dearth has led the plaintiff to seek this declaration and judgment. The only seemingly relevant case is *Leigh v Gladstone*, in which Lord Alverstone CJ directed the jury that it was the duty of prison officials to preserve the health of prisoners in their custody and that that duty extended to force feeding. For many reasons it seems to me that that authority is of no surviving application and can be consigned to the archives of legal history. It was a case in which a suffragette who had been force fed in prison sought damages against the then Home Secretary. It was decided at a time when there was no question in the mind of government that the Home Secretary had both the power and the duty to force feed hunger-striking prisoners. It was decided at a time when suicide was a criminal act, as was the aiding and abetting of that act. It was a decision taken in the climate of dramatic conflict between the suffragette movement and the government of the day. The point does not seem to have been fully argued and the charge to the jury of Lord Alverstone CJ is of little relevance or weight in modern times in determining the current law.

The only reference to the duty of the Home Office in modern authority is the briefest passage in the speech of Lord Keith of Kinkel in *Airedale NHS Trust v Bland*, in which he said:

"... the principle of the sanctity of life ... is not an absolute one. It does not compel a medical practitioner on pain of criminal sanctions to treat a patient, who will die if he does not, contrary to the express wishes of the patient. It does not authorise forcible feeding of prisoners on hunger strike. It does not compel the temporary keeping alive of patients who are terminally ill where to do so would merely prolong their suffering."

There have been much fuller developments in other common law jurisdictions, particularly in the United States, and all counsel have drawn attention to and relied upon a number of decisions, all of which consider the right of the individual to refuse nutrition in differing circumstances. I will refer only to a recent decision in the United States that is directly concerned with adult prisoners on hunger strike. The most recent, and for me the most helpful, is the decision of the Supreme Court of California, *Thor v Superior Court.* That authority upheld a decision at first instance that the prison authorities failed in their application for an order authorising force feeding of a quadriplegic prison inmate who had determined to refuse food and medical treatment necessary to maintain his life. The conclusion of the court was that the right of self-determination prevailed but the court recognised that the right of self-determination was not absolute and that there were four specific state interests that might countervail. They were specifically (i) preserving life, (ii) preventing suicide, (iii) maintaining the integrity of the medical profession, and (iv) protecting innocent third parties.

The other United States case which is relevant to these arguments is the case of *Re Caulk.* There, the Supreme Court of New Hampshire identified a very similar balancing exercise but found that the balance tipped against the right of self-determination. It seems that that decision was not specifically considered in the judgments given in the later case of *Thor*, and I have to say that I find more persuasive the dissenting judgment of Douglas J than the judgment of the majority given by Bachelder J.

These decisions are obviously relevant and helpful in reaching a decision as to how the law stands in this jurisdiction. I consider specifically the four countervailing state interests that were set against the individual's right of self-determination.

The first, namely the interest that the state holds in preserving life, seems to me to be but part and parcel of the balance that must be struck in determining and declaring the right of self-determination. The principle of the sanctity of human life in this jurisdiction is seen to yield to the principle of self-determination. It is within that balance that the consideration of the preservation of life is reflected.

The second countervailing state interest, preventing suicide, is recognisable but seems to me to be of no application in cases such as this where the refusal of nutrition and medical treatment in the exercise of the right of self-determination does not constitute an act of suicide.

The third consideration of maintaining the integrity of the medical profession is one that I find hard to recognise as a distinct consideration. Medical ethical decisions can be acutely difficult and it is when they are at their most acute that applications for declaratory relief are made to the High Court. I cannot myself see that this is a distinct consideration that requires to be set against the right of self-determination of the individual.

The fourth consideration of protecting innocent third parties is one that is undoubtedly recognised in this jurisdiction, as is evidenced by the decision of Sir Stephen Brown P in *Re S (adult: refusal of medical treatment)*. Also recognised within this jurisdiction is a consideration that was given weight in the decision of *Re Caulk*, namely the need to preserve the internal order, discipline and security within the confines of the jail.

But neither of these considerations arise in the present case.

It seems to me that within this jurisdiction there is perhaps a stronger emphasis on the right of the individual's self-determination when balance comes to be struck between that right and any countervailing interests of the state. So this decision is not a borderline one: this is a plain case for declaratory relief. The right of the defendant to determine his future is plain. That right is not diminished by his status as a detained prisoner. The rights of the prisoner ... are plainly stated in *Leech v Parkhurst Prison Deputy Governor*. Against the specific right of self-determination held by the defendant throughout his sentence there seems to me in this case to be no countervailing state interest to be set in the balance. I have no hesitation in making the declarations in the form ultimately agreed between counsel.'

Comment

(1) The case does not decide that force feeding can never be justified. In the case of anorexics, force feeding may be justified under statute, see *B v Croydon Health Authority*. There the patient had been detained compulsorily under the Mental Health Act 1983, s 3 which permitted detention only where treatment was proposed which would be likely to alleviate or prevent a deterioration in the condition of the patient. B accepted food only under threat of the insertion of a naso-gastric tube. It was held that the threatened force feeding could be justified by the Mental Health Act, s 63 as an ancillary part of medical treatment for the mental disorder.

(2) Prisoners are in a relatively vulnerable position. In *Freeman v Home Office* it was held that a prisoner in a prison hospital was legally competent to give consent, but that care should be taken to see that it was real consent. Compare the comments of Lord Donaldson MR in *Re T (adult: refusal of medical treatment)*, p 564.

(3) In *Re C* Thorpe J was prepared to grant an injunction to restrain a hospital and surgeon, both for the present and the future, from amputating the plaintiff's legs without the written consent of the plaintiff. The court was satisfied that, despite an exceptionally low IQ and chronic paranoid schizophrenia, C understood the nature, purpose and effect of the treatment he was refusing and the considerable risk of death associated with refusal. Thorpe J adopted the test for capacity:

'I consider helpful Dr E's analysis of the decision making process into three stages; first, comprehending and retaining treatment information, second, believing it and, third, weighing it in the balance to arrive at a choice. The Law Commission has proposed a similar approach in para 2.20 of its consultation paper 129, *Mentally Handicapped Adults and Decision-Making* ... I am completely satisfied that the presumption that C has the right of self-determination has not been displaced.'

Thorpe J considered that the capacity to decide extended to not only a present refusal but also an anticipatory refusal of future treatment whatever changes might occur.

St George's Healthcare NHS Trust v S
R v Collins and others, ex p S
[1998] 3 All ER 673 Court of Appeal

The plaintiff, S, was pregnant and pre-eclampsia was diagnosed. She was advised that she needed urgent attention with admission to hospital for an induced delivery. Without this treatment the health and life of S and her baby were in real danger. S fully understood the risks but rejected the advice. An application was made under the Mental Health Act 1983, s 2 by a social worker for S's admission to Springfield Hospital 'for assessment'. Two doctors signed the necessary written recommendations and S was admitted to Springfield Hospital against her will. Shortly before midnight, again against her will, she was transferred to St George's Hospital. The NHS Trust obtained a declaration from Hogg J dispensing with S's consent to treatment and S was delivered of a baby girl by caesarean section. On 30 April S was returned to Springfield Hospital and on 2 May her detention under s 2 of the Act was terminated. Against medical advice, S discharged herself from hospital. At no time was S treated for mental disorder or mental illness.

S appealed against the grant of the declaration and also sought judicial review of the decisions (i) to admit her to Springfield Hospital under s 2; (ii) to transfer, detain and treat her at St George's Hospital; (iii) to apply to Hogg J for a declaration; (iv) to apply the medical procedures which culminated in the birth; and (v) to return her to and treat her at Springfield Hospital.

The Court of Appeal held that S was an adult of sound mind and was therefore entitled to refuse medical treatment even when the refusal put at risk her own or her unborn child's life. Accordingly the declaration was set aside. Further, the Mental Health Act could be employed only to allow for treatment for a mental disorder and not simply because the decision of S was apparently irrational or contrary to the view of the majority of the community. The treatment permitted under the Act extended only to treatment for the mental disorder and a patient could not be forced to undergo unconnected medical treatment. The judicial review application succeeded.

Judge LJ: '... Even when his or her own life depends on receiving medical treatment, an adult of sound mind is entitled to refuse it. This reflects the autonomy of each individual and the right of self-determination. Lest reiteration may diminish the impact of this principle, it is valuable to recognise the force of the language used when the right of self-determination was most recently considered in the House of Lords in *Airedale NHS Trust v Bland*.

[After citing briefly from the speeches in *Bland* Judge LJ continued:]

The speeches in *Airedale NHS Trust v Bland* did not establish the law, but rather underlined the principle found in a series of authoritative decisions. With the exception of one short passage from the observations of Lord Reid in *S v S, W v Official Solicitor*, no further citation is necessary.

In that case the House of Lords considered whether it was right to order blood tests on two infants to help establish whether or not they were legitimate. Lord Reid examined the legal position and said:

> "There is no doubt that a person of full age and capacity cannot be ordered to undergo a blood test against his will ... The real reason is that English law goes to great lengths to protect a person of full age and capacity from interference with his personal liberty. We have too often seen freedom disappear in other countries not only by *coups d'état* but by gradual erosion; and often it is the first step that counts. So it would be unwise to make even minor concessions."

The importance of this salutary warning remains undiminished.

There are occasions when an individual lacks the capacity to make decisions about whether or not to consent to treatment. This may arise when he is unconscious or suffering from mental disability. This question will have to be examined more closely in due course, but dealing with it generally for the moment, where the adult patient is disabled from giving consent the medical practitioners must act in his best interests and if appropriate, may carry out major invasive surgery without express consent.

THE STATUS OF THE FOETUS

Ignoring those occasions when consent may be implied or dispensed with on the ground of incapacity, each woman is entitled to refuse treatment for herself. It does not follow without any further analysis that this entitles her to put at risk the healthy viable foetus which she is carrying. Concern for the sanctity of human life led Lord Donaldson MR in *Re T (adult: refusal of medical treatment)* to express a degree of hesitation against making any such assumption:

> "An adult patient who ... suffers from no mental incapacity has an absolute right to choose ... one rather than another of the treatments being offered. The only possible qualification is a case in which the choice may lead to the death of a viable foetus. That is not this case and, if and when it arises, the courts will be faced with a novel problem of considerable legal and ethical complexity."

... Whatever else it may be, a 36-week foetus is not nothing; if viable, it is not lifeless and it is certainly human. In *A-G's Reference (No 3 of 1994)* the House of Lords considered the status of the foetus before birth in the context of an allegation of murder arising when a pregnant woman was stabbed and, following premature labour, gave birth to a child who survived for 121 days before dying as a result of the stabbing. The conclusion of the Court of Appeal was that the foetus should be treated as an integral part of the mother in the same way as any other part of her body, such as her foot or her arm. This view was rejected in the House of Lords.

[Judge LJ quoted briefly from the speeches in the House and continued:]

... Accordingly, the interests of the foetus cannot be disregarded on the basis that in refusing treatment which would benefit the foetus, a mother is simply refusing treatment for herself.

In the present case there was no conflict between the interests of the mother and the foetus; no one was faced with the awful dilemma of deciding on one form of treatment which risked one of their lives in order to save the other. Medically, the procedures to be adopted to preserve the mother and her unborn child did not involve a preference for one rather than the other. The crucial issue can be identified by expressing the problem in different ways. If human life is sacred why is a mother entitled to refuse to undergo treatment if this would preserve the life of the foetus without damaging her own? In the United States, where such treatment has on occasions been forced on an unwilling mother, this question has been described as "the unborn child's right to live" and "the State's compelling interest in preserving the life of the foetus" (*Jefferson v Griffin Spalding County Hospital Authority*) or "the potentiality of human life" (in *Re Madyyun*). In *Winnipeg Child and Family Services (Northwest Area) v G*, ... in his dissenting judgment Major J commented: "Where the harm is so great and the temporary remedy so slight, the law is compelled to act ... Someone must speak for those who cannot speak for themselves." That said however, how can a forced invasion of a competent adult's body against her will even for the most laudable of motives (the preservation of life) be ordered without irremediably damaging the principle of self-determination? When human life is at stake the pressure to provide an affirmative answer authorising unwanted medical intervention is very powerful. Nevertheless, the autonomy of each individual requires continuing protection even, perhaps particularly, when the motive for interfering with it is readily understandable, and indeed to many would appear commendable; hence the importance of remembering Lord Reid's warning against making "even minor concessions". If it has not already done so, medical science will no doubt one day advance to the stage when a very minor procedure undergone by an adult would save the life of his or her child, or perhaps the life of a child of a complete stranger. The refusal would rightly be described as unreasonable, the benefit to another human life would be beyond value, and the motives of the doctors admirable. If however the adult were compelled to agree, or rendered helpless to resist, the principle of autonomy would be extinguished.

In *McFall v Shimp* Flaherty J used more dramatic language when sustaining the entitlement of a defendant to refuse to submit to treatment which would save the life of the plaintiff who suffered from a rare bone marrow disease and desperately required a bone marrow transplant from a compatible donor. It was not therefore a case involving a pregnant woman and her foetus. Nevertheless he highlighted the potential tensions:

> "Our society, contrary to many others, has as its first principle, the respect for the individual, and that society and government exist to protect the individual from being invaded and hurt by another. Many societies adopt a contrary view which has the individual existing to serve the society as a whole. In preserving such a society as we have it is bound to happen that great moral conflicts will arise and will appear harsh in a given instance ... Morally this decision rests with the defendant, and in the view of the court, the refusal of the defendant is morally indefensible. For our law to *compel* the defendant to submit to an intrusion of his body would change every concept and principle upon which our society is founded. To do so would defeat the sanctity of the individual ..." (Flaherty J's emphasis.)

In the particular context of the mother's right to self-determination and the interests of her foetus, this tension was considered in *Re MB (an adult: medical treatment)*. In this most difficult area of the law, practical decisions affecting the rights of a mother and her unborn child and the position of those responsible for their care, frequently require urgent resolution without the luxury of time to analyse the complex ethical problems which invariably arise. Accordingly, with the advantage of detailed skeleton arguments, the relevant statutory provisions and authorities were closely studied.

Giving the judgment of the court, Butler-Sloss LJ said:

" ... a competent woman who has the capacity to decide may, for religious reasons, other reasons, or no reasons at all, choose not to have medical intervention even though ... the consequence may be the death or serious handicap of the child she bears or her own death. She may refuse to consent to the anaesthesia injection in the full knowledge that her decision may significantly reduce the chance of her unborn child being born alive. The foetus up to the moment of birth does not have any separate interests capable of being taken into account when a court has to consider an application for a declaration in respect of a caesarean section operation. The court does not have the jurisdiction to declare that such medical intervention is lawful to protect the interests of the unborn child even at the point of birth."

As the mother in *Re MB* was found not to have been competent, strictly speaking this question did not arise for decision and, as Butler-Sloss LJ herself recognised, the observation was *obiter*.

[After considering *Winnipeg Child and Family Services (Northwest Area) v G* Judge LJ continued:]

In our judgment while pregnancy increases the personal responsibilities of a woman it does not diminish her entitlement to decide whether or not to undergo medical treatment. Although human, and protected by the law in a number of different ways set out in the judgment in *Re MB*, an unborn child is not a separate person from its mother. Its need for medical assistance does not prevail over her rights. She is entitled not to be forced to submit to an invasion of her body against her will, whether her own life or that of her unborn child depends on it. Her right is not reduced or diminished merely because her decision to exercise it may appear morally repugnant. The declaration in this case involved the removal of the baby from within the body of her mother under physical compulsion. Unless lawfully justified, this constituted an infringement of the mother's autonomy. Of themselves, the perceived needs of the foetus did not provide the necessary justification ...'

Comment

(1) The decision effectively overrules the decision in *Re S (adult: refusal of medical treatment)* where Sir Stephen Brown P granted a declaration that, notwithstanding a pregnant woman's refusal of consent, on religious grounds, a caesarean section could be performed on her to save both her life and that of her unborn child. The judge did not have the luxury of time or detailed argument given the urgency of the application in that case.

In *Norfolk and Norwich Healthcare (NHS) Trust v W* and *Rochdale Healthcare (NHS) Trust v C*, women in labour refused their consent to caesarean sections.

It was found that they were incompetent to give or refuse consent, thereby introducing the possibility of necessitous intervention. On rather stronger evidence, in *Re M B* the court found that the pregnant woman in that case lacked the capacity to consent to a caesarean section. Her phobia of needles caused her to panic in the operating theatre and there thus was a temporary impairment of her mental functioning. Accordingly, the principle of necessity operated to render the procedure lawful. *Re L (patient: non-consensual treatment)* is a similar case.

(2)   In the *St George's* case the Court of Appeal deprecated the use of the Mental Health Act 1983 to achieve detention of the plaintiff against her will. The coercive powers in the Act cannot be used simply because the thinking process of the individual is unusual or seemingly bizarre and irrational to the majority of the community, and because there is a natural desire to safeguard the interests of the child. The prescribed conditions for detention must be used. Furthermore, even if detention under the Act is justified, treatment itself must be within the Act, i.e. it must be to treat the relevant mental disorder identified. Finally, said Judge LJ:

'In the final analysis, a woman detained under the Act for mental disorder cannot be forced into medical procedures unconnected with her mental condition unless her capacity to consent to such treatment is diminished. When she retains her capacity her consent remains an essential prerequisite and whether she does, or not, must be decided on the basis of the evidence in each individual case ...'

Accordingly, the correctness of *Tameside and Glossop Acute Service Trust v CH* must be doubted in the light of the decision in the *St George's* case. In the *Tameside* case the court was prepared to accept a caesarean section as being justified by the Mental Health Act 1983. The *St George's* case is a rejection of the broad approach in the *Tameside* case which culminated in the view that the performance of a caesarean section was medical treatment for the patient's mental disorder. The actual decision in the *Tameside* case is justifiable because the patient failed the three-fold test as to capacity to consent set down in *Re C*.

Chatterton v Gerson
[1981] I All ER 257 Queen's Bench Division

The plaintiff sued the defendant specialist in trespass and negligence. She complained that although she had received the treatment described to her she had not been warned of the possible side-effects – risk of numbness and loss of muscle power. The court rejected the notion of informed consent and found for the defendant on the issue of trespass, and also on the related matter of negligence.

Bristow J: '... It is clear law that in any context in which consent of the injured party is a defence to what would otherwise be a crime or a civil wrong, the consent must be real. Where, for example, a woman's consent to sexual intercourse is obtained by fraud, her apparent consent is no defence to a charge of rape. It is not difficult to state the principle or to appreciate its good sense. As so often the problem lies in its application.

No English authority was cited before me of the application of the principle in the context of consent to the interference with bodily integrity by medical or surgical treatment ... In my judgment what the court has to do in each case is to look at all the circumstances and say, "Was there a real consent?" I think justice requires that in order to vitiate the reality of the consent there must be a greater failure of communication between doctor and patient than that involved in a breach of duty if the claim is based on negligence. When the claim is based on negligence the plaintiff must prove not only the breach of duty to inform but that had the duty not been broken she would not have chosen to have the operation. Where the claim is based on trespass to the person, once it is shown that the consent is unreal, then what the plaintiff would have decided if she had been given the information which would have prevented vitiation of the reality of her consent is irrelevant.

In my judgment once the patient is informed in broad terms of the nature of the procedure which is intended, and gives her consent, that consent is real, and the cause of action on which to base a claim for failure to go into risks and implications is negligence, not trespass. Of course, if information is withheld in bad faith, the consent will be vitiated by fraud ...'

Comment

(1) At first instance in *Freeman v Home Office*, informed consent was described as being that ' ... the plaintiff must have been told (a) what he was suffering from, (b) what was the precise nature of the treatment being proposed and (c) what, if any, were the adverse effects and risks involved in the treatment'.

At first instance and in the Court of Appeal, that doctrine was rejected as having no place in the law of battery. The decision had already been overtaken by the decision of the Court of Appeal in *Sidaway v Bethlem Royal Hospital Governors*, which rejected informed consent in the context of trespass to the person. For the role of informed consent in negligence see *Sidaway v Bethlem Royal Hospital Governors*, p 209.

(2) *Volenti non fit injuria* and consent are distinct. Sir John Donaldson MR in *Freeman v Home Office* observed that *volenti:*

'... provides a bar to enforcing a cause of action. It does not negative the cause of action itself. This is a wholly different concept from consent which, in this context, deprives the act of its tortious character. *Volenti* would be a defence in the unlikely scenario of a patient being held not to have in fact consented to treatment, but having by his conduct caused the doctor to believe he had consented.'

If consent is a defence, it is something to be established by the defendant; if its absence is an aspect of the definition of the tort, then it is something to be established by the plaintiff. This difficult issue of principle, but not practice, was alluded to in *Freeman v Home Office* at first instance where the judge held that the burden of proving absence of consent was on the plaintiff. Not all textbook writers would agree.

In *R v Brown*, a criminal case, Lord Jauncey, *obiter*, regarded consent as a defence, and its absence not a necessary ingredient in an assault.

(3)   In *Hegarty v Shine*, the plaintiff lived with a man who, unknown to her, suffered from a venereal disease; she sued in trespass in respect of the communication to her of that disease. The Court of Appeal upheld the defendant's appeal for a new trial on the basis of a misdirection by the judge. The plaintiff was aware of the nature of the act leading to the particular consequences although not, of course, the consequences themselves. The criminal law context of this type of situation, although no this case itself, was considered by the Court of Appeal in *R v Dica* which reviewed earlier criminal law cases.

In *Latter v Braddell*, the employers of a housemaid requested a doctor to examine her. She denied that she had consented to the examination and sued her employers and the doctor. The Court of Appeal rejected the plaintiff's appeal against the withdrawal from the jury of the case against the employers and the finding of the jury in favour of the doctor. The majority of the Court of Appeal felt that there was no evidence other than reluctant obedience to the employers' orders, possibly in the light of a mistake of law. The dissent of Lopes J is more sympathetic to modern ears, and he would have allowed the case to go to the jury.

(4)   Many of the cases on consent are criminal law cases and the law on this point may not be consistent as between the two disciplines. It seems that fraud or misrepresentations as to the nature of the behaviour will vitiate consent in each discipline. For example, in *R v Williams*, a criminal case, a music teacher who misrepresented to a pupil that the act of sexual intercourse was in fact a method of voice improvement was properly convicted of rape; the consent had been given for a specific purpose and not that which occurred.

On the other hand, fraud or misrepresentation as to ancillary matters or consequences will not vitiate the consent in criminal law, see *R v Linekar* and *R v Richardson*. In the first case, the services of a prostitute were engaged upon a promise by the defendant to pay. Afterwards the defendant refused to pay and left. Upon a charge of rape the jury found that he had never intended to pay. In assessing the criminal cases, the court focused on the issue of consent and asked whether the victim had consented to the act of intercourse with that particular person. Since the answer was in the affirmative, there could be no question of the fraud negativing the consent and the defendant was entitled to be acquitted. In *R v Richardson*, the court concluded that what mattered was not the reason for a particular mistaken consent, whether it be fraudulently induced or self-induced, but the nature of the mistake. Thus, the victim in that case had consented to dental treatment by the defendant who, unknown to her, had been suspended from practice. Although she would not have consented had she known that the dentist was not entitled to practice, the mistake was not such as to invalidate her consent and the defendant was acquitted.

It is unclear whether or not the civil law would follow the criminal law lead. *Hegarty v Shine* may be seen as a case concerning the nature of the act but it might, to modern eyes, be seen also as a case where the consequences affect the nature of the act. And there are suggestions from commentators suggesting even more difficult distinctions, e.g. in a bigamous marriage is sexual intercourse of a different nature to that to which the innocent party consented? There is Commonwealth authority that in such a case the consent of the innocent spouse would be a defence to a charge of rape.

(5)   There may, in criminal law, be acts to which consent may not, as a matter of law, be given. Thus, in *R v Brown* a group indulged in sado-masochistic practices involving acts of violence to which the parties agreed. The House of Lords held that there was no defence to charges of wounding contrary to the Offences Against the Person Act 1861, s 47. In such a case public policy played a significant role and the law of tort, which has distinct objectives, may take a different view.

(6)   In addition for the law of tort, the plea of *ex turpi causa* may be invoked as a bar to an action, see *Lane v Holloway* and *Murphy v Culhane*, p 358. In the Court of Appeal in *Cross v Kirkby* the claimant was an anti-hunt protestor who had been ejected from land. As he saw his partner being ejected he picked up a baseball bat, banged it on the ground with sufficient force to split it, and attacked the defendant as the latter tried to walk away. The defendant warded off some blows, wrested the bat from the claimant and struck him one blow on the head, fracturing his skull. The judge rejected the defendant's claim of self-defence on the basis that the force was disproportionate and stated that as a consequence the defendant was not permitted to plead *ex turpi causa*. The Court of Appeal rejected the judge's findings on lack of proportion and held that he had weighed the conduct too finely.

Further, as regards *ex turpi causa*, the Court of Appeal held that, properly understood, the plea required the court to ask whether or not the *claimant* was precluded from recovering because of his illegal and criminal conduct. Since the judge had asked whether the *defendant* was precluded from relying on the plea because of his behaviour, the judge had fallen into error. For the plea to succeed the claimant's claim has to be inseparable from the illegal nature of his behaviour. See further p 352.

The Criminal Justice Act 2003, s 329 provides that where (i) a claimant seeks to sue a defendant in trespass and (ii) the claimant has been convicted of an imprisonable offence committed on the same occasion as the act of trespass, then the claimant may sue only with the permission of the court. The discretion of the court to give permission is circumscribed by the conditions set out in the section. This provision is reasonably clear in its intent, but it is arguable that it simply puts into statutory form a version of *ex turpi causa* defence. Consider the case of *Revill v Newberry* in the context of this section.

Re T (adult: refusal of medical treatment)
[1992] 4 All ER 649 Court of Appeal

The plaintiff had been seriously injured and required a caesarean section when she went into premature labour. After representations that blood transfusions after caesarean section were not often needed and that there were other methods of blood expansion available (both statements were erroneous), she signed a form refusing a blood transfusion. Her condition deteriorated and a transfusion became necessary. A judge at a second hearing held that the plaintiff had neither consented nor refused consent. The Court of Appeal held that on the facts the doctors had been entitled to treat the case as an emergency and disregard the signed form on the basis that there had been undue influence by the mother which had deprived the plaintiff of the power to decide.

Lord Donaldson MR: '... This appeal is not ... about the "right to die" ... This appeal is about the "right to choose how to live". This is quite different, even if the choice, when made, may make an early death more likely. It is also about whether Miss T really did choose and, if so, what choice she made ... An adult patient who, like Miss T, suffers from no mental incapacity has an absolute right to choose whether to consent to medical treatment, to refuse it or to choose one rather than another of the treatments being offered. The only possible qualification is a case in which the choice may lead to the death of a viable foetus. That is not this case and, if and when it arises, the courts will be faced with a novel problem of considerable legal and ethical complexity. This right of choice is not limited to decisions which others might regard as sensible. It exists notwithstanding that the reasons for making the choice are rational, irrational, unknown or even non-existent (see *Sidaway v Bethlem Royal Hospital Governors*).

But just because adults have the right to choose, it does not follow that they have in fact exercised that right. Determining whether or not they have done so is a quite different and sometimes difficult matter. And if it is clear that they have exercised their right of choice, problems can still arise in determining what precisely they have chosen. This appeal illustrates both these problems.

THE ROLE OF CONSENT

The law requires that an adult patient who is mentally and physically capable of exercising a choice must consent if medical treatment of him is to be lawful, although the consent need not be in writing and may sometimes be inferred from the patient's conduct in the context of the surrounding circumstances. Treating him without his consent or despite a refusal of consent will constitute the civil wrong of trespass to the person and may constitute a crime. If, however, the patient has made no choice and, when the need for treatment arises, is in no position to make one ... the practitioner can lawfully treat the patient in accordance with his clinical judgment of what is in the patient's best interest ...

[Lord Donaldson considered the facts and continued.]

The fact that, "emergency cases" apart, no medical treatment of an adult patient of full capacity can be undertaken without his consent creates a situation in which the absence of consent has much the same effect as a refusal. That does not necessarily create any problem for doctors or hospitals. On some occasions it may not be of great importance to the patient's health whether he is treated at that time or perhaps at all. Or it may be a question of choices. The doctor may advise that treatment A is preferable, or much preferable, to treatment B, but that he is prepared to undertake either. The patient may elect for and consent to treatment B and thereby impliedly decline to consent to treatment A. Again there will be no problem. Where the problem arises is in the comparatively rare situation in which an adult patient declines to consent to treatment which in the clinical judgment of those attending him is necessary if irreparable damage is not to be done to his health or, in some cases, if his life is to be saved. It is only in that context that this appeal may afford guidance to the doctors and hospitals.

If there is a distinction between a failure to consent and a refusal of consent, it is because a refusal can take the form of a declaration of intention never to consent in the future or never to consent in some future circumstances.

THE CONFLICT OF PRINCIPLE

This situation gives rise to a conflict between two interests, that of the patient and that of the society in which he lives. The patient's interest consists of his right to self-determination – his right to live his own life how he wishes, even if it will damage his health or lead to his premature death. Society's interest is in upholding the concept that all human life is sacred and that it should be preserved if at all possible. It is well established that in the ultimate the right of the individual is paramount. But this merely shifts the problem where the conflict occurs and calls for a very careful examination of whether, and if so the way in which, the individual is exercising that right. In case of doubt, that doubt falls to be resolved in favour of the preservation of life, for if the individual is to override the public interest he must do so in clear terms.

CAPACITY TO DECIDE

The right to decide one's own fate presupposes a capacity to do so. Every adult is presumed to have that capacity, but it is a presumption which can be rebutted. This is not a question of the degree of intelligence or education of the adult concerned. However a small minority of the population lack the necessary mental capacity due to mental illness or retarded development (see, for example, *F v West Berkshire Health Authority*). This is a permanent or at least a long-term state. Others who would normally have that capacity may be deprived of it or have it reduced by reason of temporary factors, such as unconsciousness or confusion or other effects of shock, severe fatigue, pain or drugs being used in their treatment.

Doctors faced with a refusal of consent have to give very careful and detailed consideration to the patient's capacity to decide at the time when the decision was made. It may not be the simple case of the patient having no capacity because, for example, at that time he had hallucinations. It may be the more difficult case of a temporarily reduced capacity at the time when his decision was made. What matters is that the doctors should consider whether at that time he had a capacity which was commensurate with the gravity of the decision which he purported to make. The more serious the decision, the greater the capacity required. If the patient had the requisite capacity, they are bound by his decision. If not, they are free to treat him in what they believe to be his best interests.

This problem is more likely to arise at a time when the patient is unconscious and cannot be consulted. If he can be consulted, this should be done, but again full account has to be taken of his then capacity to make up his own mind.

As I pointed out at the beginning of this judgment, the patient's right of choice exists whether the reasons for making that choice are rational, irrational, unknown or even non-existent. That his choice is contrary to what is to be expected of the vast majority of adults is only relevant if there are other reasons for doubting his capacity to decide. The nature of his choice or the terms in which it is expressed may then tip the balance.

THE VITIATING EFFECT OF OUTSIDE INFLUENCE

A special problem may arise if at the time the decision is made the patient has been subjected to the influence of some third party. This is by no means to say that the patient is not entitled to receive and indeed invite advice and assistance from others in reaching a decision, particularly from members of the family. But the doctors have to consider whether the decision is really that of the patient. It is wholly acceptable that the patient should have been persuaded by others of the merits of such a decision and have decided accordingly. It matters not how strong the persuasion was, so long as it did not overbear the independence of the patient's decision. The real question in each such case is: does the patient really mean what he says or is he merely saying it for a quiet life, to satisfy someone else or because the advice and persuasion to which he has been subjected is such that he can no longer think and decide for himself? In other words, is it a decision expressed in form only, not in reality?

When considering the effect of outside influences, two aspects can be of crucial importance. First, the strength of the will of the patient. One who is very tired, in pain or depressed will be much less able to resist having his will overborne than one who is rested, free from pain and cheerful. Second, the relationship of the "persuader' to the patient may be of crucial importance. The influence of parents on their children or of one spouse on the other can be, but is by no means necessarily, much stronger that would be the case in other relationships. Persuasion based upon religious belief can also be much more compelling and the fact that arguments based upon religious beliefs are being deployed by someone in a very close relationship with the patient will give them added force and should alert the doctors to the possibility – no more – that the patient's capacity or will to decide has been overborne. In other words the patient may not mean what he says.

THE SCOPE AND BASIS OF THE PATIENT'S DECISION

If the doctors consider that the patient had the capacity to decide and has exercised his right to do so, they still have to consider what was the true scope and basis of that decision. If at the time the issue arises the patient still has capacity to decide, they can not only explore the scope of his decision with the patient, but can seek to persuade him to alter that decision. However this problem will usually arise at that time when this *cannot* be done. In such circumstances what the doctors cannot do is to conclude that if the patient still had had the necessary capacity in the changed situation he would have reversed his decision. This would be simply to deny his right of decision. What they *can* do is to consider whether at the time the decision was made it was intended by the patient to apply in the changed situation. It may well have been so intended, as it was in the Canadian case of *Malette v Shulman* where the Jehovah's Witness carried a card stating in unequivocal terms that she did not wish blood to be administered to her in any circumstances. But it may not have been so intended. It may have been of more limited scope, e.g. "I refuse to have a blood transfusion, so long as there is an effective alternative". Or again it may have been based upon an assumption, e.g., "As there is an effective alternative, I refuse to have a blood transfusion". If the factual situation falls outside the scope of the refusal or if the assumption upon which it is based is falsified, the refusal ceases to be effective. The doctors are then faced with a situation in which the patient has made no decision and, he by then being unable to decide for himself, they have both the right and the duty to treat him in accordance with what in the exercise of their clinical judgment they consider to be his best interests ...'

Comment

(1)   Lord Donaldson MR commented upon two matters. The first was that the next of kin cannot consent upon behalf of the patient, although consultation may provide evidence of what may be in the best interests of the patient, e.g. if it reveals that the patient is a Jehovah's Witness then this may point to the doctor delaying or choosing a different method of treatment. Second, he observed that failure to explain the nature and effect of a relevant procedure would not vitiate consent or refusal, but would be a matter for negligence. Misinformation about the procedure would vitiate the consent (in which case trespass might lie) or refusal (in which case negligence might lie).

(2)   In *Malette v Shulman*, a doctor administered a blood transfusion to the unconscious and seriously injured plaintiff despite the fact that she carried a card stating that she was a Jehovah's Witness and that no blood transfusion was to be given. The doctor was held liable in trespass. In *Re T* Butler-Sloss LJ observed:

'I agree with the reasoning ... in *Malette v Shulman* ... [where] Robins JA said:

"At issue here is the freedom of the patient as an individual to exercise her right to refuse treatment and accept the consequences of her own decision. Competent adults, as I have sought to demonstrate, are generally at liberty to refuse medical treatment even at the risk of death. The right to determine what shall be done with one's own body is a fundamental right in our society. The concepts inherent in this right are the bedrock upon which the principles of self-determination and individual autonomy are based. Free individual choice in matters affecting this right should, in my opinion, be accorded very high priority."

He excluded from consideration the interest of the state in protecting innocent third parties and preventing suicide. I agree with the principles set out above although I do not believe an English court would give damages in those particular circumstances. Doctors therefore who treat such a patient against his known wishes do so at their peril ...'

(3)   Where children are involved then matters may become more complex in that the child itself, parents, courts, local authorities and others may, from time to time, have responsibility for decision-making. A broad view of the position was given in *Re W (a minor) (wardship: medical treatment) (1992)* where W, a

16-year-old girl, had refused treatment for an eating disorder other than at the specialist adolescent residential unit run by a consultant psychiatrist to which she had been admitted some time previously. The local authority having care of W wished to place her in a hospital specialising in eating disorders. The Court of Appeal held that its inherent jurisdiction over minors gave it power to override the wishes of W to the contrary. Lord Donaldson MR summarised the position:

'... Thus far I have ... been looking at the problem in the context of a conflict between parents and the minor, either the minor consenting and the parents refusing consent or the minor refusing consent and the parents giving it. Although that is not this case, I have done so both because we were told that it would be helpful to all those concerned with the treatment of minors and also perhaps the minors themselves and because it seems to be a logical base from which to proceed to consider the powers of the court and how they should be exercised [after considering the facts he continued] ... There is ample authority for the proposition that the inherent powers of the court under its *parens patriae* jurisdiction are theoretically limitless and that they certainly extend beyond the powers of a natural parent, see, e.g., *Re R (a minor) (wardship: medical treatment)* ... There can therefore be no doubt that it has power to override the refusal of a minor, whether over the age of 16 or under that age but "*Gillick* competent". It does not do so by ordering the doctors to treat, which, even if within the court's powers, would be an abuse of them, or by ordering the minor to accept treatment, but by authorising the doctors to treat the minor in accordance with their clinical judgment, subject to any restrictions which the court may impose ...

1. No question of a minor consenting to or refusing medical treatment arises unless and until a medical or dental practitioner advises such treatment and is willing to undertake it.

2. Regardless of whether the minor or anyone else with authority to do so consents to the treatment, that practitioner will be liable to the minor in negligence if he fails to advise with reasonable skill and care and to have due regard to the best interests of his patient.

3. This appeal has been concerned with the treatment of *anorexia nervosa.* It is a peculiarity of this disease that the disease itself creates a wish not to be cured or only to be cured if and when the patient decides to cure himself or herself, which may well be too late. Treatment has to be directed at this state of mind as much as to restoring body weight.

4. Section 8 of the Family Law Reform Act 1969 gives minors who have attained the age of 16 a right to consent to surgical, medical or dental treatment. Such a consent cannot be overridden by those with parental

responsibility for the minor. It can, however, be overridden by the court. This statutory right does not extend to consent to the donation of blood or organs.

5.   A minor of any age who is *"Gillick* competent" in the context of particular treatment has a right to consent to that treatment, which again cannot be overridden by those with parental responsibility, but can be overridden by the court. Unlike the statutory right this common law right extends to the donation of blood or organs.

6.   No minor of whatever age has power by refusing consent to treatment to override a consent to treatment by someone who has parental responsibility for the minor and *a fortiori* a consent by the court. Nevertheless such a refusal is a very important consideration in making clinical judgments and for parents and the court in deciding whether themselves to give consent. Its importance increases with the age and maturity of the minor.

7.   The effect of consent to treatment by the minor or someone else with authority to give it is limited to protecting the medical or dental practitioner from claims for damages for trespass to the person.'

The '*Gillick* competent' child refers to a child of sufficient intelligence and understanding who can consent to treatment, notwithstanding the absence of the parents' consent and even an express prohibition by the parents (see *Gillick v West Norfolk and Wisbech Area Health Authority*). Later cases have confirmed that a parent or court might, in some instances, override a refusal to treatment given by an otherwise competent child. Lord Donaldson MR later said in *Re W*:

'On reflection I regret my use in *Re R* (*a minor*) (*wardship: medical treatment*)... of the keyholder analogy, because keys can lock as well as unlock. I now prefer the analogy of the legal "flak jacket" which protects the doctor from claims by the litigious whether he acquires it from his patient, who may be a minor over the age of 16 or a "*Gillick* competent" child under that age, or from another person having parental responsibilities which include a right to consent to treatment of the minor. Anyone who gives him a flak jacket (i.e. consent) may take it back, but the doctor only needs one and so long as he continues to have one he has the legal right to proceed ...'

R v M graphically illustrates the difficulties in this field. Here the High Court made an order in respect of a young woman aged 15-and-a-half, that she might undergo a heart transplant and subsequent medication (which was likely to last a lifetime) despite the refusal of consent by the young woman herself.

CHAPTER 12

Trespass to land

The courts are keen to protect the inviolability of land: the maxim 'an Englishman's home is his castle' is as true today as it always has been, even if there are rather more legal keys to unlock the castle gates. What a claimant needs is sufficient possession to maintain an action, e.g. a guest in a hotel bedroom will not (usually) be entitled to maintain an action in trespass. Compare this with the requirement in private nuisance that the claimant should have a proprietary interest in land: see *Hunter v Canary Wharf*, p 604.

The merest entry will be trespass; an unwanted arm through an open door will be trespass, *Franklin v Jeffries*. An intentional and direct entry on to land will be trespass, even if the entry is as a result of mistake, e.g. believing that the property belonged to another. Thus, 'trespasser' will encompass a wide range of persons from a straying child to an adult burglar. The interest protected extends above the surface of the soil to the column of air above it – although not as far as the heavens, see *Bernstein v Skyviews*, p 573 and the *Anchor Brewhouse* case, p 576.

Placing or throwing an object on to land will usually amount to a continuing trespass. Where, in an action based on a continuing trespass, judgment is given, if the item remains on the land then a new cause of action arises, and so on: *Holmes v Wilson*. In many instances an action in trespass to land is a convenient way of settling a boundary or other dispute, see *Patel v W H Smith (Eziot) Ltd*, the leading modern authority on interlocutory injunctive relief in this context. Where the relief sought is an injunction, the observations in *Jaggard v Sawyer*, p 594, are important.

Whether an act is direct may provoke problems, e.g. the discharge of oil on to the surface of the sea in such a way that it drifted on to the shoreline, was thought by some to be direct and others to be indirect. If direct, it is trespass; if indirect, then nuisance: see *Esso Petroleum v Southport Corporation*, cited in *Rigby v Chief Constable of Northants*, p 586.

Consent, as with trespass to the person, will be available either as a defence or to remove the cause of action. There is a range of defences as with other intentional torts, see e.g. necessity, p 585. The range of powers to enter and search available to authorities as diverse as Customs and Excise, police, local authorities and the security services is beyond the scope of this book.

Morris v Beardmore
[1980] 2 All ER 753 House of Lords

The House of Lords considered whether or not a statutory provision should be construed so as to imply a power of entry.

Lord Scarman: '... Had Parliament intended to empower a policeman to enter or remain on the private premises of a suspect against his will ... Parliament could ... have included in the relevant legislation an express power or right of entry. But in s 8 ... Parliament has not done so; and it is not the task of the judges, exercising their ingenuity in the field of implication, to go further in the invasion of fundamental private rights and liberties than Parliament has expressly authorised ... When one compares, as one must, the silence of Parliament in this section with the elaborate provisions and safeguards enacted for the search of private premises and seizure of evidence ... it becomes inconceivable that Parliament in its breathalyser legislation could have authorised, by implication, the entry into a suspect's private house, against his will and ... at a time when, according to the cherished principle of English criminal law, the suspect was entitled to be presumed innocent ... I have deliberately used an adjective which has an unfamiliar ring in the ears of common lawyers. I have described the right of privacy as "fundamental". I do so for two reasons. First, it is apt to describe the importance attached by the common law to the privacy of the home. It is still true, as was said by Lord Camden CJ in *Entick v Carrington*: "No man can set his foot upon my ground without my licence, but he is liable to an action, though the damage be nothing ... if he admits the fact, he is bound to shew by way of justification, that some positive law has empowered or excused him." Second, the right enjoys the protection of the European Convention for the Protection of Human Rights and Fundamental Freedoms ...'

Comment

There are many other cases where the courts have emphasised that they should be slow to grant powers of entry, e.g. see *McLorie v Oxford*, or to imply such powers, as *Morris v Beardmore* illustrates. The recourse of Lord Scarman to the European Convention on Human Rights may be contrasted with Lord Diplock who thought that the absence of a power owed nothing to that source. The Human Rights Act 1998 will now be relevant in analysis of powers to enter land. Although the topic is more fitted to constitutional and administrative law texts, the context in which trespass to land may occur is often of vital importance, as *Entick v Carrington* reminds us.

Bernstein of Leigh v Skyviews & General Ltd
[1977] 2 All ER 902 Divisional Court

The defendant took photographs of the plaintiff's country residence from an over-flying aeroplane. The plaintiff alleged that the defendant had trespassed in his airspace. The court held that there had been no trespass.

Griffiths J: '... The plaintiff claims that as owner of the land he is also owner of the air space above the land, or at least has the right to exclude any entry into the air space above his land. He relies upon the old Latin maxim, *cujus est solum ejus est usque ad coelum et ad inferos*, a colourful phrase often upon the lips of lawyers since it was first coined by Accursius in Bologna in the thirteenth century. There are a number of cases in which the maxim has been used by English judges, but an examination of those cases shows that they have all been concerned with structures attached to the adjoining land, such as overhanging buildings, signs or telegraph wires, and for their solution it has not been necessary for the judge to cast his eyes towards the heavens; he has been concerned with the rights of the owner in the air space immediately adjacent to the surface of the land.

That an owner has certain rights in the air space above his land is well established by authority. He has the right to lop the branches of trees that may overhang his boundary, although this right seems to be founded in nuisance rather than trespass: see *Lemmon v Webb*. In *Wandsworth Board of Works v United Telephone Co Ltd* the Court of Appeal did not doubt [*obiter*] that the owner of land would have the right to cut a wire placed over his land ...

In *Gifford v Dent*, Romer J held that it was a trespass to erect a sign that projected 4 ft. 8 in. over the plaintiff's forecourt and ordered it to be removed. He invoked the old maxim in his judgment; the report reads: "... the plaintiffs were tenants of the forecourt and were accordingly tenants of the space above the forecourt *usque ad coelum*, it seemed to him that the projection was clearly a trespass upon the property of the plaintiffs." That decision was followed by McNair J in *Kelsen v Imperial Tobacco Co (of Great Britain and Ireland) Ltd*, in which he granted a mandatory injunction ordering the defendants to remove a sign which projected only 8 in. over the plaintiff's property. The plaintiff relies strongly upon this case, and in particular upon the following passage ...:

"[*Gifford v Dent*] has been recognised by the textbook writers ... as stating the true law. It is not without significance that the legislature in the Air

Navigation Act 1920, s 9 (replaced by s 40 (1) of the Civil Aviation Act 1949), found it necessary expressly to negative the action of trespass or nuisance arising from the mere fact of an aeroplane passing through the air above the land. It seems to me clearly to indicate that the legislature at least were not taking the same view of the matter as Lord Ellenborough in *Pickering v Rudd*, but rather taking the view accepted in the later cases, such as the *Wandsworth District* case, subsequently followed by Romer J in *Gifford v Dent*. Accordingly, I reach the conclusion that a trespass and not a mere nuisance was created by the invasion of the plaintiff's air-space by the sign."

I very much doubt if in that passage McNair J was intending to hold that the plaintiff's rights in the air space continued to an unlimited height or *ad coelum* as [counsel for the plaintiff] submits. The point that the judge was considering was whether the sign was a trespass or a nuisance at the very low level at which it projected. This to my mind is clearly indicated by his reference to *Winfield on Tort* (6th ed. 1954), in which the text reads: "it is submitted that trespass will be committed by [aircraft] to the air space if they fly so low as to come within the area of ordinary user". The author in that passage is careful to limit the trespass to the height at which it is contemplated an owner might be expected to make use of the air space as a natural incident of the user of his land. If, however, the judge was by his reference to the Civil Aviation Act 1949 and his disapproval of the views of Lord Ellenborough in *Pickering v Rudd*, indicating the opinion that the flight of an aircraft at whatever height constituted a trespass at common law, I must respectfully disagree.

I do not wish to cast any doubts upon the correctness of the decision upon its own particular facts. It may be a sound and practical rule to regard any incursion into the air space at a height which may interfere with the ordinary user of the land as a trespass rather than a nuisance. Adjoining owners then know where they stand; they have no right to erect structures overhanging or passing over their neighbours' land and there is no room for argument whether they are thereby causing damage or annoyance to their neighbours about which there may be much room for argument and uncertainty. But wholly different considerations arise when considering the passage of aircraft at a height which in no way affects the user of the land.

There is no direct authority on this question, but as long ago as 1815 Lord Ellenborough in *Pickering v Rudd* expressed the view that it would not be a trespass to pass over a man's land in a balloon; and in *Saunders v Smith*, Shadwell V-C said:

"Thus, upon the maxim of law, '*Cujus est solum ejus est usque ad coelum*', an injunction might be granted for cutting timber and severing crops; but, suppose a person should apply to restrain an aerial wrong, as by sailing over a person's freehold in a balloon; this surely would be too contemptible to be taken notice of."

In *Commissioner for Railways v Valuer-General*, Lord Wilberforce had this to say of the maxim:

> "... its use, whether with reference to mineral rights, or trespass in the air space by projections, animals or wires, is imprecise and it is mainly serviceable as dispensing with analysis: cf. *Pickering v Rudd* and *Ellis v Loftus Iron Co.* In none of these cases is there an authoritative pronouncement that 'land' means the whole of the space from the centre of the earth to the heavens: so sweeping, unscientific and unpractical a doctrine is unlikely to appeal to the common law mind."

I can find no support in authority for the view that a landowner's rights in the air space above his property extend to an unlimited height. In *Wandsworth Board of Works v United Telephone Co Ltd*, Bowen LJ described the maxim, *usque ad coelum*, as a fanciful phrase, to which I would add that if applied literally it is a fanciful notion leading to the absurdity of a trespass at common law being committed by a satellite every time it passes over a suburban garden. The academic writers speak with one voice in rejecting the uncritical and literal application of the maxim ... I accept their collective approach as correct. The problem is to balance the rights of an owner to enjoy the use of his land against the rights of the general public to take advantage of all that science now offers in the use of air space. This balance is in my judgment best struck in our present society by restricting the rights of an owner in the air space above his land to such height as is necessary for the ordinary use and enjoyment of his land and the structures upon it, and declaring that above that height he has no greater rights in the air space than any other member of the public.

Applying this test to the facts of this case, I find that the defendants' aircraft did not infringe any rights in the plaintiff's air space, and thus no trespass was committed. It was on any view of the evidence flying many hundreds of feet above the ground and it is not suggested that by its mere presence in the air space it caused any interference with any use to which the plaintiff put or might wish to put his land. The plaintiff's complaint is not that the aircraft interfered with the use of his land but that a photograph was taken from it. There is, however, no law against taking a photograph, and the mere taking of a photograph cannot turn an act which is not a trespass into the plaintiff's air space into one that is a trespass.

I was told by [counsel] that Lord Bernstein was particularly anxious that his house should not be photographed from the air lest the photograph should fall into criminal hands as it might prove a valuable aid to a terrorist. This anxiety is readily understandable and must attract sympathy, although I should add that it is not suggested that this was a likely consequence as a result of the defendants' activities. [Counsel] ... conceded that he was unable to cite any principle of law or authority that would entitle Lord Bernstein to prevent someone taking a photograph of his property for an innocent purpose, provided they did not commit some other tort such as trespass or nuisance in doing so. It is therefore interesting to reflect what a sterile remedy Lord Bernstein would obtain if he was able to establish that mere infringement of the air space over his land was a trespass. He could prevent the defendants flying over his land to take another photograph, but he could not prevent the defendants taking the virtually identical photograph from the adjoining land provided they took care not to cross his boundary, and were taking it for an innocent as opposed to a criminal purpose ...

It is, however, to be observed that the protection given [by Civil Aviation Act 1949 s 40(1)] is limited by the words "by reason only of the flight", so although an owner can found no action in trespass or nuisance if he relies solely upon the flight of the aircraft above his property as founding his cause of action, the section will not preclude him from bringing an action if he can point to some activity carried on by or from the aircraft that can properly be considered a trespass or nuisance, or some other tort. For example, the section would give no protection against the deliberate emission of vast quantities of smoke that polluted the atmosphere and seriously interfered with the plaintiff's use and enjoyment of his property; such behaviour remains an actionable nuisance. Nor would I wish this judgment to be understood as deciding that in no circumstances could a successful action be brought against an aerial photographer to restrain his activities. The present action is not founded in nuisance for no court would regard the taking of a single photograph as an actionable nuisance. But if the circumstances were such that a plaintiff was subjected to the harassment of constant surveillance of his house from the air, accompanied by the photographing of his every activity, I am far from saying that the court would not regard such a monstrous invasion of his privacy as an actionable nuisance for which they would give relief. However, that question does not fall for decision in this case and will be decided if and when it arises.

On the facts of this case even if contrary to my view the defendants' aircraft committed a trespass at common law in flying over the plaintiff's land, the plaintiff is prevented from bringing any action in respect of that trespass by the terms of s 40(1) of the Civil Aviation Act 1949.'

Anchor Brewhouse Developments Ltd and others v Berkley House (Docklands Developments) Ltd
(1987) 38 BLR 82 Chancery Division

A site was being developed with the assistance of very tall cranes. These cranes were left untethered when not in use to prevent them being blown over. The cranes would then overswing the plaintiff's adjoining property over which no right to do so had been negotiated. The plaintiffs sought and obtained an interlocutory injunction to prevent such overswinging. It was held that the overswinging was capable of amounting to a trespass into airspace.

Scott J: '... The first question with which I must deal is whether the oversailing cranes are committing trespass or whether the invasion of air space by tower cranes sounds only in nuisance ... The conclusion of McNair J [in *Kelsen v Imperial Tobacco Co Ltd*] corresponds with the concession made by counsel before Stamp J in *Woollerton and Wilson Ltd v Richard Costain Ltd*, that the oversailing boom of a tower crane represented trespass ... So the question whether the oversailing represented trespass was not the subject of decision by Stamp J. It was, however, the subject of decision in an Australian case, *Graham v K D Morris & Sons Pty Ltd*. This case too involved the oversailing boom of a tower crane. It was argued that the oversailing and the invasion of the air space was nuisance at most and not trespass, but Campbell J held that it was trespass. He said this:

> "In my opinion the invasion of the plaintiff's air space by the crane jib is a trespass by the defendant and not a mere nuisance. I am not prepared to take a different view of this issue which differs from that expressed by McNair J in *Kelsen v Imperial Tobacco Co.*"

... Griffiths J (as he then was) in *Bernstein v Skyviews & General Ltd* ... was not prepared to hold that the invasion of air space by an overflying aircraft represented trespass. [After extensive citation, Scott J continued.] [Counsel for the defendant] fastened on [Griffiths J's] reference to balancing the rights of an owner against the rights of the public and contended that it justified a whole new appraisal of ownership in so far as it extended to all space above the property owned.

In my view, it would be an incorrect use of authority to extract Griffiths J's approach to the difficult question of overflying aircraft and to seek to apply that approach to the invasion of air space in general. Griffths J was dealing with an argument that the incursion by an aircraft into the air space above the plaintiff's land represented trespass. He was not prepared to accept that that was necessarily so. But he accepted ... that adjoining owners had no right to erect structures projecting over their neighbours' land. His *dictum* about balancing the owners' rights against the rights of the general public was not, in my opinion, intended to limit the complaints of trespass that might in that event be made by neighbours. [Counsel for the defendant] argued that, in view of the *Bernstein* case, the critical question was whether the invasion of air space interfered with the ordinary use and enjoyment of the land. The owner of the land is entitled to complain of trespass if the invasion is at a level above the land that does so interfere. Otherwise the invasion should, said [counsel], be rejected as trespass. I am not satisfied that represents a permissible application of Griffiths J's approach in the *Bernstein* case nor that it would be workable in practice.

What is complained of in the present case is infringement of air space by a structure positioned upon a neighbour's land. The defendant has erected tower cranes on its land. Attached to each tower crane is a boom which swings over the plaintiffs' land. The booms invade the air space over the plaintiffs' land. Each boom is part of the structure on the defendant's land. The tort of trespass represents an interference with possession or with the right to possession. A landowner is entitled, as an attribute of his ownership of the land, to place structures on his land

and thereby to reduce into actual possession the air space above his land. If an adjoining owner places a structure on his (the adjoining owner's) land that overhangs his neighbour's land, he thereby takes into his possession air space to which his neighbour is entitled. That, in my judgment, is trespass. It does not depend upon any balancing of rights.

The difficulties posed by overflying aircraft or balloons, bullets or missiles, seem to me to be wholly separate from the problem which arises where there is invasion of air space by a structure placed or standing upon the land of a neighbour. One of the characteristics of the common law of trespass is, or ought to be, certainty. The extent of proprietary rights enjoyed by landowners ought to be clear. It may be that, where aircraft or overflying missiles are concerned, certainty cannot be achieved. I do not wish to dissent at all from Griffith J's approach to that problem in the *Bernstein* case. But certainty is capable of being achieved where invasion of air space by tower cranes, advertising signs and other structures are concerned. In my judgment, if somebody erects on his own land a structure, part of which invades the air space above the land of another, the invasion is trespass. That conclusion is consistent with the judgment of McNair J in *Kelsen*, with the concession made in *Woollerton and Wilson v Costain*, with the decision of Campbell J in the Australian case, and also with the *dictum* of Griffiths in the *Bernstein* case. If that is right, then the cranes oversailing the plaintiffs' land commit trespass.

In my view, the defendant is committing trespass by its use of its oversailing cranes ...'

Comment

(1)   The means by which the invasion occurs seems to be at the heart of the resolution of the problem. The two cases are not inconsistent provided that this is borne in mind. In *Hunter v Canary Wharf*, see p 604, reference was made to the limitations placed by planning law on the rights of an occupier of land to enjoy their rights *usque ad coelum*. Nonetheless, in that case the ability to reduce air space into actual occupation by a tall building was an essential element of a finding that the use of land had been reasonable in the law of nuisance.

(2)   Parliament has conferred rights on adjacent occupiers in certain circumstances to enter for the purposes of repair and maintenance, see the Access to Neighbouring Land Act 1992. Parliament has also greatly extended the rights of the public to gain access to certain types of land in private ownership, see the Countryside and Rights of Way Act 2000.

(3)   Lord Bernstein was really complaining about the photography. There is no general right to privacy sounding in the law of tort, see the discussion in *Wainwright v Home Office*, p 512. The range of the protection in trespass to land is haphazard: photography from inside a boundary wall is trespass but

from outside is not. Also, the remedy may not be appropriate, e.g. damages may be inadequate when you want the photograph kept out of circulation, see *Kaye v Robertson*.

'Unauthorised photography may be actionable as a breach of confidence or as a breach of contract in an appropriate case, see *Pollard v Photographic Co*. But, the general principle stated in *Sports and General Press Agency v Our Dogs Publishing Co Ltd* by Horridge J remains true subject to the proposition that the law now recognises a greater scope to confidentiality: "In my judgment no one possesses a right of preventing another person photographing him any more than he has a right of preventing another person giving a description of him, provided the description is not libellous or otherwise wrongful." '

An example of borrowing by description of events taking place on the plaintiff's land occurred in *Victoria Park Racing & Recreation Grounds Co Ltd v Taylor* where the defendants broadcast a commentary on races being held on the plaintiff's racecourse, thereby causing the plaintiff economic loss. By a majority of three to two the High Court of Australia held that the conduct was not actionable.

(4) The law on confidentiality is rapidly becoming the chief weapon in the armoury of the law in support of the principle of privacy. An early example is derived from the *dictum* of Laws J in *Hellewell v Chief Constable of Derbyshire* which concerned the photographing of the plaintiff by the police at the police station where the plaintiff had no choice but to be photographed, and the subsequent release of the photographs to shopkeepers. The plaintiff sought an injunction and declaratory relief but failed in the light of the public interest in the dissemination to local shopkeepers of relevant information about suspected trouble-makers, and the police had acted in good faith. The photograph was confidential information because of the surrounding circumstances, and the police were under an obligation to use the information reasonably. In a passage going wider than strictly required by the case, but subsequently approved as correct, Laws J observed that:

'If someone with a telephoto lens were to take from a distance and with no authority a picture of another engaged in some private act, his subsequent disclosure of the photograph would, in my judgment, as surely amount to a breach of confidence as if he had found or stolen a letter or diary in which the act was recounted and proceeded to publish it. In such a case, the law would protect what might reasonably *be* called a right of privacy, although the name accorded to that cause of action would be breach of confidence. It is, of course, elementary that, in all such cases, a defence based on the public interest would be available.'

In *Douglas v Hello!* this was described as '*obiter*, but it has been understandably influential in the thinking of lawyers and commentators since it was said'.

Bernstein v Skyviews was not cited to the court, nor was confidentiality before the court in that case. *Kaye v Robertson* was relied on by counsel in skeleton argument but was not cited by the court.

The development of the law on confidentiality and in particular the improper taking and publication of photographs has been brought to the attention of a wider audience by virtue of *Douglas v Hello!* and *Campbell v MGN Ltd* where it was said by Lord Hoffmann that 'privacy is in a general sense one of the values, and sometimes the most important value, which underlies a number of more specific causes of action ...'. The impact of the Human Rights Act 1998 is also being felt in this area. See also the decision of the European Court of Human Rights in *Peck v UK*.

(5)   There may not always be an invasion of a right recognised and protected by law and thereby remediable by way of trespass. For example, in *Malone v Metropolitan Police Commissioner (No 2)*, the plaintiff's phone was tapped at the telephone exchange, and there was no invasion of property. This meant that the tapping did not have to be justified by reference to the principle in *Entick v Carrington*. In *Perera v Vandiyar*, the cutting by a landlord of power to a flat was not a trespass, and the law did not provide a remedy for breach of statutory duty, see also *McCall v Abelesz*, p 454.

(6)   There may be trespass to the highway. This is axiomatic, the right to use the highway is not absolute. Abuse of the right will amount to trespass: see *Hickman v Maisey, Harrison v Duke of Rutland*. The law relating to trespass on the highway was considered extensively by the House of Lords in *DPP v Jones*. An assembly of more than 20 objectors, including the defendants, gathered on the verge of the highway adjacent to Stonehenge to protest at the imposition of restrictions on access to Stonehenge. An order prohibiting trespassory assemblies had been made under the Public Order Act 1986, s 14A. The Act provides that '"limited" in relation to a right of access by the public to land, means that their use of it is restricted to use for a particular purpose (as in the case of a highway or road) ...'. For an assembly to be trespassory, those assembled would have to have committed trespass either by entering land to which they had no right of access or by exceeding a limited right of access to land. The defendants were convicted of taking part in a trespassory assembly, but the court found that there had been no obstruction of the highway nor any abusive, threatening or insulting behaviour, nor any breaches of the peace. The House of Lords, by a majority of three to two, found that there had been no trespass and therefore no breach of the order under s 14A. Although the majority view was not entirely consistent, the speech of Lord Irvine represents the clearest assertion of wide public rights in connection with the highway. Lord Irvine said:

' ... A highway may be created either by way of the common law doctrine of dedication and acceptance, or by some statutory provision. Dedication presupposes an intention by the owner of the soil to dedicate the right of passage to the public. Whilst the intention may be expressed, it is more often to be inferred; but the requirement of an inference of an intention to dedicate does not, in my judgment, advance the question of the extent of the public's right of user of the highway. The dedication is for the public's use of the land as a highway and the question remains: what is the proper extent of the public's use of the highway? Given that intention to dedicate is usually inferred, it would be a legal fiction to assert that actual intention was confined to the right to pass and repass and activities incidental or ancillary to that right. There is no room in the judgment of Collins LJ in *Hickman v Maisey* for the fiction of an immutable, subjective original intention. Neither highway users nor the courts are in any position to ascertain what the landowner's original intentions may have been, years or even centuries after the event. In many cases, where the intention to dedicate is merely inferred from the fact of user as of right, there will not even have been a subjective intention. Nor would it be sensible to hold that the extent of the public's right of user should differ from highway to highway, as necessarily it would if actual subjective intention were the test. It is time to recognise that the so-called intention of the landowner is no more than a legal fiction imputed to the landowner by the court. It would have been possible for the common law to have imposed tight constraints on the public's right of user of the highway in one of two ways. First, it could have held that the right was no wider than the bare minimum required for the use of the highway as such: a test of necessity. Or, secondly, it could have been held that the right was static, so that a user, which could not have been in contemplation as reasonable and usual at the time of dedication, could never become a lawful user in changing social circumstances. I have already demonstrated that the former has been rejected. Nor could the latter be sustained. I doubt whether, when a highway was first dedicated in, say, the early nineteenth century, a landowner would have contemplated the traversal at very high speed of the land dedicated by vehicles powered by internal combustion engines. The fact is that the common law permits vehicles to be driven at high speed on the highway because that is a reasonable user in modern conditions: it would be a fiction to attribute that to an actual intention at the time of dedication.

I conclude therefore the law to be that the public highway is a public place which the public may enjoy for any reasonable purpose, provided the activity in question does not amount to a public or private nuisance and does not obstruct the highway by unreasonably impeding the primary right of the public to pass and repass: within these qualifications there is a public right of peaceful assembly on the highway.

Since the law confers this public right, I deprecate any attempt artificially to restrict its scope. It must be for the magistrates in every case to decide whether the user of the highway under consideration is both reasonable in the sense defined and not inconsistent with the primary right of the public to pass and repass. In particular, there can be no principled basis for limiting the scope of the right by reference to the subjective intentions of the persons assembling. Once the right to assemble within the limitations I have defined is accepted, it is self-evident that it cannot be excluded by an intention to exercise it. Provided an assembly is reasonable and non-obstructive, taking into account its size, duration and the nature of the highway on which it takes place, it is irrelevant whether it is premeditated or spontaneous: what matters is its objective nature. To draw a distinction on the basis of anterior intention is in substance to reintroduce an incidentality requirement. For the reasons I have given, that requirement, properly applied, would make unlawful commonplace activities which are well accepted. Equally, to stipulate in the abstract any maximum size or duration for a lawful assembly would be an unwarranted restriction on the right defined. These judgments are ever ones of fact and degree for the court of trial. Further, there can be no basis for distinguishing highways on publicly owned land and privately owned land. The nature of the public's right of use of the highway cannot depend upon whether the owner of the sub-soil is a private landowner or a public authority. Any fear, however, that the rights of private landowners might be prejudiced by the right as defined are unfounded. The law of trespass will continue to protect private landowners against unreasonably large, unreasonably prolonged or unreasonably obstructive assemblies upon these highways.'

(7)   What of private spaces? The point was made in *CIN Properties v Rawlins* that in the absence of any dedication of property as a public right of way the owner of land had an absolute right to terminate licences which particular members of the public had to enter land; in this case a shopping centre where the defendants were holding a demonstration. The court held that there was no concept in English law of a quasi-public right to enter and remain on such premises. This was confirmed by the Court of Appeal in *Porter v Commissioner of Police of the Metropolis*; in this case the land was an electricity board show-room. The European Convention on Human Rights context of this was explored in *Appleby v UK* and the European Court of Human Rights concluded that the restriction placed by the owners of a shopping centre on demonstrators was not a breach of the Convention, article 10 (freedom of expression) and that the Government had not failed in any positive obligation to protect the applicants' freedom of expression. For the occupiers' liability aspects of the highway see the rule in *Gautret v Egerton*, p 373.

Robson v Hallett
[1967] 2 All ER 407 Divisional Court

Two police constables (P and J) and a sergeant (M) approached a house in order to make enquiries of T, the son of the owner. M was invited into the house by T but P and J remained in the garden. When inside, M's permission to be there was withdrawn by the father and he attempted to leave. Before he could do so he was attacked by T, and constable J intervened. A mêlée developed and D, another son, joined in. D and T were accused of assaulting P, J and M in the execution of their duty. It was held that the defendants were guilty since: (a) the sergeant had not been a trespasser at the time of the attack: a person whose licence had been revoked was entitled to a reasonable time to leave the premises; and (b) the constables were in the garden under implied licence which had not been revoked; even if they had been outside the garden, at the time of the attack they were entitled to enter to deal with breaches of the peace.

Diplock LJ: '... These appeals raise three simple points on the law of trespass on land which affect all members of the public as well as the police officers with whom this appeal is concerned. The points are so simple that the combined researches of counsel have not revealed any authority on them. There is no authority because no one has thought it plausible up till now to question them. The first is this, that when a householder lives in a dwelling-house to which there is a garden in front and does not lock the gate of the garden, it gives an implied licence to any member of the public who has lawful reason for doing so to proceed from the gate to the front door or back door, and to inquire whether he may be admitted and to conduct his lawful business. Such implied licence can be rebutted by express refusal of it, as in this case the Robsons could no doubt have rebutted the implied licence to the police officers by putting up a notice on their front gate: "No admittance to police officers"; but that was not done in this case. The second proposition is this, that when, having knocked at the front door of the dwelling-house, someone who is inside the dwelling-house invites the person who has knocked to come in, there is an implied authority in that person which can be rebutted on behalf of the occupier of the dwelling-house to invite him to come in, and so license him to come into the dwelling-house itself. In the present case it was the son ... and not the father who was the occupier, who invited M to come in. In those circumstances M, whilst in the dwelling-house on the invitation of the son, was no trespasser. The licence, however, could be withdrawn by the father, who was the person entitled to give it. He withdrew it and, on its being withdrawn, M had a reasonable time to leave the premises by the most appropriate route for doing so, namely, out of the front door, down the steps and out of the gate, and, provided that he did so with reasonable expedition, he would not be a trespasser while he was so doing. That is sufficient to give the reasons for allowing the appeal of the prosecution in the case of the attack upon M.

As regards [the police constables], it does not seem to me to matter whether, when they were denied entrance at the front door, they were trespassers in remaining in the garden, if they did remain in the garden after that, because there are two ways in which a person who enters land of another person may fail to be a trespasser. One is leave and licence of the person entitled to possession, to which I have already referred; the other is in the exercise of an independent right to proceed on the land. In the case of the [police constables], once a breach of the peace was taking place under their eyes, they had not only an independent right but a duty to go and stop it, and it matters not from that moment onwards whether they started off on their journey to stop it from outside the premises or from inside the premises. They were entitled, once the breach of the peace occurred, to be on the premises for the purpose of preventing it or stopping it ...'

Comment

(1)   See also *Davis v Lisle* where a police officer who had entered garage repair premises under an implied licence failed to leave when told to do so and attempted to show that he was in fact a police officer. This was taken by the court to be an assertion of a right to remain and therefore he became a trespasser as from that moment and could be ejected using reasonable force by way of self-help.

(2)   In *Halliday v Nevill* the High Court of Australia said:

'Nor ... will the implied licence ordinarily be restricted to presence on the open driveway or path for the purpose of going to the entrance of the house. A passer-by is not a trespasser if, on passing an open driveway with no indication that entry is forbidden or unauthorised, he or she steps upon it either unintentionally or to avoid an obstruction such as a vehicle parked across the footpath. Nor will such a passer-by be a trespasser if, for example, he or she goes upon the driveway to recover some item of his or her property which has fallen or blown upon it or to lead away an errant child. To adapt the words of Lord Parker CJ in *Robson v Hallett*, the law is not such an ass that the implied or tacit licence in such a case is restricted to stepping over the item of property or around the child for the purpose of going to the entrance and asking the householder whether the item of property can be reclaimed or the child led away. The path or driveway is, in such circumstances, held out by the occupier as the bridge between the public thoroughfare and his or her private dwelling upon which a passer-by may go for a legitimate purpose that in itself involves no interference with the occupier's possession nor injury to the occupier, his or her guests or his, her or their property.'

(3)   The occupier who wishes to keep out everyone or specific groups must display a prominent notice to that effect – see Diplock LJ's reference to a notice excluding police officers. Where there is another occupier, then the question of actual or ostensible authority to invite a stranger on to the land may become an

issue of some importance. In *Chrystal v Rickard Miller Ltd* the Queen's Bench Division considered whether a child had ostensible authority to grant a licence to adults to enter his parent's house. The defendants were in dispute with the claimant, their employee, about an employment matter. They had been admitted by the claimant's 13-year-old son to the claimant's house and had taken away a computer and some disks. The court concluded that the question of ostensible authority was a question of fact, depending on the age of the child and the nature of the visitor seeking permission to come in. In this case the visitor was a stranger who was in dispute with the claimant and the child was 13, accordingly there was no such authority and the defendant had trespassed and had converted the goods.

(4) For the requirements of revocation of express or implied licence, see *Snook v Mannion* and *Gilham v Breidenbach* where the mere use of foul and abusive language was held, on the facts, to be insufficient to indicate an unequivocal statement that the police officers should leave.

(5) If permission to enter for a specific purpose is abused then the visitor may become a trespasser from the moment of abuse. Where there is entry under power of law then abuse of that power by a positive act will generally (see *Elias v Pasmore*) render the entrant a trespasser *ab initio*, i.e. from the moment of entry, see *The Six Carpenters'* case. In that latter case there was a failure to pay for food and drink. It was held that this was an omission and that the principle did not apply: 'It was resolved *per totam curiam* that not doing cannot make the party who has authority or licence by the law a trespasser *ab initio*, because not doing is no trespass.' For adverse criticism of the principle see Lord Denning in *Chic Fashions v Jones*, but see *Cinnamond v British Airports Authority* where the same judge commented on its potential usefulness.

Rigby v Chief Constable of Northamptonshire
[1985] 2 All ER 985 Queen's Bench Division

During a strike by the fire service, there was a siege of a gun shop in which a wanted man was hiding. The police fired a tear-gas canister into the shop, this ignited powder which caused a serious fire. The police had obtained the assistance of a fire-fighting vehicle which had had to leave the scene prior to the tear-gas being used in order to attend another incident. The plaintiff shop owners claimed in trespass to land and negligence. The defendant Chief Constable pleaded necessity. This was upheld in respect of the plea of trespass. The claim in negligence based on the selection of the particular type of tear-gas supplied to the force was rejected, but the negligence claim based on the failure to provide fire-fighting cover succeeded.

Taylor J: '... There is a surprising dearth of authority as to the nature and limits of necessity as a defence in tort. Counsel for the defendant referred me to three cases. *Cope v Sharpe (No 2)* was a case of alleged trespass where the defendant had sought to prevent a heather fire from spreading. *Cresswell v Sirl* was a case of alleged trespass to a dog which the defendant had shot to prevent it worrying sheep. In each case the defence prevailed. *Esso Petroleum Co Ltd v Southport Corp* is the leading case on the topic and both counsel referred to it in detail. It concerned an oil tanker stranded in a river estuary. Her master jettisoned 400 tons of oil cargo to prevent the tanker breaking her back. The tide carried the oil slick on to a foreshore causing damage. The foreshore owners sued the shipowners in trespass, nuisance and negligence. However, the only negligence alleged on the pleadings was faulty navigation by the master for which it was said the owners were vicariously liable. The owners' case was that the stranding was due to faulty steering gear caused by a crack in the stern frame. The defence of necessity was raised *inter alia* and Devlin J upheld it. The Court of Appeal reversed Devlin J's judgment but it was restored by the House of Lords. Earl Jowitt said:

> "Devlin J decided that the fact that it was necessary to discharge the oil in the interest of the safety of the crew afforded a sufficient answer to the claim based on trespass or nuisance. I agree with him ..."

The case is therefore clear authority for the application of necessity as a defence to trespass especially where human life is at stake.

However, counsel for the plaintiffs relies on *dicta* in their Lordships' speeches to support the proposition that the defence is not available if the necessity is brought about by the defendant's own negligence, and that the burden of negativing negligence lies on the defendant once the issue has been raised. The Court of Appeal took the view that the defendants had failed to discharge the burden of showing that the cracked frame causing a defect in the steering gear was not due to their negligence. Counsel for the plaintiffs says the House of Lords restored Devlin J's judgment solely on pleading grounds. There had been no allegation of negligence against the ship-owners except in relation to the master's handling of the vessel.

The two propositions of counsel for the plaintiffs are clearly right. Necessity is not a good defence if the need to act is brought about by negligence on the part of the defendant. Once that issue is raised the defendant must show on the whole of the evidence that the necessity arose without negligence on his part. The more difficult question is what is meant by "negligence" in this context. Counsel for the plaintiffs relies on passages from the speeches of Lord Normand and Lord Radcliffe in the *Esso Petroleum* case. Lord Normand said:

> "The majority of the Court of Appeal, however, held that the *onus* lay on the owners to show that the accident which caused the damage was inevitable, and to do this it would have been necessary to show that no care which they might have taken would have avoided the damage. As the appellants had made no attempt to lead evidence to discharge this *onus*, the majority of the Court of Appeal found them liable in damages."

Lord Radcliffe said:

> "But, assuming that the event was itself *prima facie* evidence of negligence, and that the respondents had so framed their case, I do not doubt that the majority of the Court of Appeal were right in saying that the appellants would not have displaced that evidence by merely showing that their failure in navigation was due to a failure in the steering apparatus of the ship. They would have had to go further and show that they had not omitted any reasonable precaution to ensure that failures did not occur in that steering apparatus or in their control of the steering."

From these passages, counsel for the plaintiffs argues that in the present case, where the issue *has* been raised, unless the defendant can show that to have equipped himself with the Ferret would not have been a reasonable precaution, he fails to discharge the onus of proof. Necessity would therefore not avail him. I have already indicated that in my judgment the defendant was not negligent in exercising his discretion not to purchase the Ferret. However, counsel for the plaintiffs argues that notwithstanding that, if the purchase of the Ferret would have been a reasonable or not unreasonable precaution then the necessity to use the CS canister would have been brought about by fault on the part of the defendant.

I cannot accept this argument. The passages cited above were both in the context of a defence of inevitable accident as raised in *The Merchant Prince* on which, as Lord Radcliffe said, much of the argument in the *Esso Petroleum* case turned. I do not think that the observations of Lord Normand and Lord Radcliffe, which were *obiter* in any event, were intended to lay down a higher duty than the duty in the tort of negligence as a condition precedent to the application of the defence of necessity. It would be most unfair to do so. Whether or not the defendant has been negligent prior to the occurrence of the alleged necessity must surely be viewed as at the time of the alleged negligence. If by ordinary criteria of negligence the defendant can show that at that time he was not at fault, it cannot be just when the necessity arises to impose retrospectively a higher duty on the defendant. Nor do I think the *Esso Petroleum* case is authority for that proposition. I am reinforced in this view by statements in two of the leading textbooks on the law of tort. In *Winfield and Jolowicz on Tort* (12th edn, 1984), the matter is put thus: "Necessity negatives liability in tort provided, of course, that the occasion of necessity does not arise from the defendants' own negligence, though the authority on it is scanty." In *Salmond and Heuston on the Law of Torts* (18th edn, 1981), the authors say: "In any case, the defence [of necessity] is hardly available if the predicament in which the defendant found himself was brought about by his own negligence." In each passage the authority cited is the *Esso Petroleum* case.

I therefore hold that a defence of necessity is available in the absence of negligence on the part of the defendant creating or contributing to the necessity. In this case there was a dangerous armed psychopath whom it was urgently necessary to arrest. I have already found that it was not negligent of the defendant to be without the Ferret. It is conceded that the only alternative was to fire in a CS gas canister, which was done. I therefore find that the defence of necessity prevails and that the cause of action in trespass fails ...'

Comment

(1) The problem in necessity, as opposed to self-defence, is that someone who is innocent has to lose. If I break down your door to reach a child reasonably believed to be in danger of burning, then your door is broken down nonetheless, but you will bear the cost of it. The same may not be true if I break your door down to rescue a picture of importance to the nation believed to be in danger. In *Esso v Southport Corporation*, the defendant discharged oil from a stricken ship in order to save not just the ship but also the crew. At first instance Devlin J made the point that:

'The safety of human lives belongs to a different scale of values from the safety of property. The two are beyond comparison and the necessity for saving life has at all times been considered a proper ground for inflicting such damage as may be necessary upon another's property.'

(2) In *Cope v Sharpe (No 2)*, the defendant leased shooting rights over the plaintiff's land. The defendant's gamekeeper reasonably believed that the plaintiff's efforts to extinguish a fire were ineffectual and would not be successful. Accordingly, he went on to the land and burned strips of heather in order to prevent the spread of the fire to the nesting birds under his care. It was held that necessity was not to be judged with the benefit of hindsight and the fact that the plaintiff succeeded in extinguishing the fire before it could spread was to be disregarded. Intervention had been necessary in the sense that there was a real and imminent danger and what was done was reasonable relative to that danger. In the view of Kennedy LJ, reasonableness would include a weighing of comparative values of the property destroyed and that which was preserved.

London Borough of Southwark v Williams
[1971] 2 All ER 175 Court of Appeal

The defendants entered empty council property as squatters. The local authority sought a possession order and the defendants' defence was that the council was in breach of its duty under relevant legislation and that they were entitled to occupy the property as a matter of necessity. The Court of Appeal held that the enforcement procedures under the legislation were the only method available to the defendants to enforce the council's statutory duty, furthermore the defence of necessity had to be kept within narrow bounds and had no application to the facts.

Lord Denning MR: '... There is authority for saying that in case of great and imminent danger, in order to preserve life, the law will permit of an encroachment on private property. That is shown by *Mouse's* case, where the ferryman at Gravesend took 47 passengers into his barge to carry them to London. A great tempest arose and all were in danger. Mr Mouse was one of the passengers. He threw a casket belonging to the plaintiff overboard so as to lighten the ship. Other passengers threw other things. It was proved that, if they had not done so, the passengers would have been drowned. It was held by the whole court that "in any case of necessity, for the safety of the lives of the passengers" it was lawful for Mr Mouse to cast the casket out of the barge. The court said it was like the pulling down of a house, in time of fire, to stop it spreading; which has always been held justified *pro bono publico.*

The doctrine so enunciated must, however, be carefully circumscribed. Else necessity would open the door to many an excuse ... So here. If homelessness were once admitted as a defence to trespass, no one's house could be safe. Necessity would open a door which no man could shut. It would not only be those in extreme need who would enter. There would be others who would imagine that they were in need, or would invent a need, so as to gain entry. Each man would say his need was greater than the next man's. The plea would be an excuse for all sorts of wrongdoing. So the courts must, for the sake of law and order, take a firm stand. They must refuse to admit the plea of necessity to the hungry and the homeless; and trust that their distress will be relieved by the charitable and the good. Applying these principles, it seems to me the circumstances of these squatters are not such as to afford any justification or excuse in law for their entry into these houses. We can sympathise with the plight in which they find themselves. We can recognise the orderly way in which they made their entry. But we can go no further. They must make their appeal for help to others, not to us. They must appeal to the council, who will, I am sure, do all it can. They can go to the minister, if need be. But, so far as these courts are concerned, we must, in the interest of law and order itself, uphold the title to these properties. We cannot allow any individuals, however great their despair, to take the law into their own hands and enter these premises. The court must exercise its summary jurisdiction and order the defendants to go out.'

Comment

(1) See also the treatment of necessity in connection with trespass to the person.

(2) Where there is a clash between public and private interests the courts may have regard to the role of the local authority in the democratic process, see for example the comments in *Page Motors v Epsom Borough Council*, p 670, and also the observations as to the grant of planning permissions in nuisance cases, see p 632. In *London Borough of Southwark v Williams*, Megaw LJ said:

'But in the end it is a matter of policy, and I have no doubt that the squatting association are firmly convinced that the policy which they urge and which they would wish to see adopted is indeed the one which is best not only for the members of their association, but for the community as a whole. I have no doubt that the borough council also are convinced that the policy which they have adopted is that which is best for their borough as a whole. It is a matter of policy in the widest sense of the word – a political matter. The borough council are an elected body in a democratic society. If their policy – the policy which they prefer in a matter in which policy-making was for them – is not that which is accepted by the community as a whole, then the community has its remedy in a democratic society. But what is suggested here is that individuals have the right in law to take steps to go upon the property of the borough council in such a way and with the intention and necessary result of defeating the policy which that elected body has decided to be the appropriate policy. In my judgment the doctrine of necessity in this country does not go so far, or anything like so far, as to say that those who take such a step in such circumstances are not committing an offence against the law, or that when they go upon property of another they are not trespassing.'

(3)   The principles described in *London Borough of Southwark v Williams* fell for consideration in *Monsanto v Tilly and others* where the Court of Appeal considered matters of considerable contemporary importance. In a well-advertised protest, of which the press had advance notice, protestors entered fields and pulled up genetically modified crops as part of their campaign against the development of such products. By way of symbolic action, the protestors pulled up only a few plants on each occasion and did not attempt to destroy the entire crop. The claimants did not own the fields but they did own the exclusive rights to the crops under agreement with the farmers concerned. The claimants sought an injunction against the protestors who claimed that they were acting in order to protect not only the public at large but also local organic farmers. The question for the court was whether or not there was an arguable defence of necessity or otherwise in the public interest.

The Court of Appeal held: (1) applying *Back v Daniels* and *Wellaway v Courtier* that the claimants had sufficient interest in the land or in the crops to maintain an action in trespass to land or goods; and (2) that the respondents did not have an arguable defence that their actions were justified as being necessary to protect third parties or in the public interest. Stuart-Smith LJ said:

'28... [counsel for the protestors] relied on the speech of Lord Goff of Chieveley in *F v West Berkshire Health Authority* [see p 540] ... The case is a long way from the present, since Monsanto are able to give or withhold consent to trespass and it is inconceivable that they would consider it in their best interests to consent ...

30... I would make a number of observations ... First, I doubt whether the reference to the right to destroy neighbouring houses in event of serious fire can be regarded as any longer correct. In *Burmah Oil Co Ltd v Lord Advocate* Lord Upjohn, after referring to the supposed right and the cases where commanders of ships had scuttled them to avoid them falling into enemy hands, said:

> "No doubt in earlier times the individual had some such rights of self-help or destruction in immediate emergency, whether caused by enemy action or by fire, and the legal answer was that he could not in such circumstances be sued for trespass on or destruction of his neighbour's property. Those rights of the individual are now at least obsolescent. No man now, without risking some action against him in the courts, could pull down his neighbour's house to prevent the fire spreading to his own; he would be told that he ought to have dialled 999 and summoned the local fire brigade. No man now could conceivably erect a bulwark to prevent enemy invasion."

That case was concerned with whether the Crown in the exercise of the royal prerogative could confiscate and destroy property in the dire emergency of war to prevent it falling into enemy hands without paying compensation. It was held that they could not. If that is correct, it strongly suggests that the individual has no right to destroy the property of another in the public interest in the sense of protecting others from danger, save in very restricted circumstances; still less that he may do so to attract publicity to what is alleged to be a good cause or to persuade government to legislate against a perceived danger.

31. The third and fourth paragraphs of the passage cited from Lord Goff"'s speech are concerned with action which is for the benefit of the person who for one reason or another is incapable of giving consent. That is what the case was concerned with. It is to be noted that Lord Goff says that in the case of a person of sound mind there will ordinarily have to be an emergency, since otherwise there is an opportunity to communicate with him.

32. [Counsel for the protestors] also referred the court to two cases involving shooting dogs worrying sheep. In *Cresswell v Sirl* it was held that in order to justify shooting the dog it must be shown that the sheep were in real or imminent danger and any reasonable man would, in the circumstances of the case, have concluded that there was no alternative to shooting the dog if the sheep were to be preserved. In that case the sheep were owned by the defendant's father.

Workman v Cooper was a criminal case, the defendant being charged with malicious damage. He shot a stray fox-hound which had run wild and presented a danger to lambs in the vicinity. It was held that the same test as that laid down in *Cresswell*'s case applied when considering whether the defendant had a lawful excuse in protecting the property of others.

33.   Those cases show that the danger must be immediate and obvious and that a reasonable person would conclude that there was no alternative to the act of trespass. A case which further illustrates the extremely circumscribed extent of the defence of justification by necessity is *Southwark Borough Council v Williams* ...

34.   Megaw LJ's judgment is of particular interest because he refers to the conflicting principles of the Council and the Squatters' Association. This is particularly pertinent here where the object of the respondent's campaign is to change government policy. In a democratic society that must be effected by lawful and not unlawful means. Those who suffer infringement of their lawful rights are entitled to the protection of the law; if others deliberately infringe those rights in order to attract publicity to their cause, however sincerely they believe in its correctness, they must bear the consequences of their lawbreaking. This is fundamental to the rule of law in a civilised and democratic society.

35.   ... if the respondents wish to challenge the legality of the licences granted by the DETR, they must do so, if at all through judicial review. I must not be taken to encourage such a course because the respondents would have to discharge the very considerable burden of showing that the grant of the licences was perverse in the *Wednesbury* sense.'

Burton v Winters
[1993] 3 All ER 847 Court of Appeal

The plaintiff sought a mandatory injunction to compel the removal of a garage wall which trespassed four-and-a-half inches into her land. The wall had been built by the defendants' predecessors in title some 11 years before the plaintiff commenced her action. In the light of the minimal encroachment, the mandatory injunction was refused but a declaration as to the boundary was made. Her appeal against the refusal of the injunction was dismissed. The plaintiff then embarked on a course of conduct involving trespass to the defendants' land and damage to the garage. In proceedings arising out of the original action the court granted an injunction against her. She disobeyed the injunction frequently and her eventual committal to prison for two years for contempt of court was upheld by the Court of Appeal. The court commented upon a suggestion that the plaintiff might have been exercising her right of self-help or abatement and that there would be no contempt.

Lloyd LJ: 'There is a common law right of self-redress for trespass by encroachment, which was always regarded as an ancient remedy in the time of Bracton. It is similar to the common law right of abatement in the case of nuisance. But at an early stage of our history the right of abatement was supplemented by the assize of nuisance ... The action lay to have the nuisance abated by the defendants and to recover damages (see *Baten's* case). If the plaintiff abated the nuisance himself, he lost his right to recover damages. With the coming of equity, the common law action for abatement was supplanted by the mandatory injunction. But the remedy by way of self-help was still available ... It was argued [in *Lane v Capsey*] that there could be no right of abatement since the plaintiffs had already failed to obtain a mandatory injunction. Chitty J left the point open ... [It] falls to us to determine the point on facts which are virtually identical. Fortunately the answer is not difficult.

Ever since the assize of nuisance became available, the courts have confined the remedy by way of self-redress to simple cases such as an overhanging branch, or an encroaching root, which would not justify the expense of legal proceedings, and urgent cases which require an immediate remedy. Thus, it was Bracton's view that where there is resort to self-redress, the remedy should be taken without delay. In [*Blackstone's Commentaries*] we find:

"And the reason why the law allows this private and summary method of doing one's self justice, is because injuries of this kind, which obstruct or annoy such things as are of daily convenience and use, require an immediate remedy; and cannot wait for the slow progress of the ordinary forms of justice."

... In Prosser and Keeton we find:

"Consequently, the privilege [of abatement] must be exercised within a reasonable time after knowledge of the nuisance is acquired or should have been acquired by the person entitled to abate; if there has been sufficient delay to allow a resort to legal process, the reason for the privilege fails, and the privilege with it."

... [I]t is obvious that it is now far too late for the plaintiff to have her remedy by way of abatement. The garage wall was built in 1975. Not only was there ample time for the plaintiff to "wait for the slow progress of the ordinary forms of justice"; she actually did so.

But it is not only a question of delay. There is modern House of Lords authority for the proposition that the law does not favour the remedy of abatement (see *Lagan Navigation Co v Lambeg Bleaching Dyeing and Finishing Co Ltd*). In my opinion, this never was an appropriate case for self-redress, even if the plaintiff had acted promptly. There was no emergency. There were difficult questions of law and fact to be considered and the remedy by way of self-redress, if it had resulted in the demolition of the garage wall, would have been out of all proportion to the damage suffered by the plaintiff. But even if there had ever been a right of self-redress, it ceased when Judge Main refused to grant a mandatory injunction ... Self-redress is a summary remedy, which is justified only in clear and simple cases, or in an emergency. Where a plaintiff has applied for a mandatory injunction and failed, the sole justification for a summary remedy has gone. The court has decided the very point in issue. This is so whether the complaint lies in trespass or nuisance. In the present case, the court has decided that the plaintiff is not entitled to have the wall on her side of the boundary removed. It follows that she has no right to remove it herself ...'

Comment

(1)   See also *Lemmon v Webb*. The law dislikes the remedy of self-help, which should be invoked with care, especially where there is risk of a breach of the peace; see, for example, *R v Chief Constable for Devon & Cornwall, ex p CEGB*. In *London Borough of Southwark v Williams*, p 588, Edmund Davies LJ observed:

'... one thing emerges with clarity from the decisions, and that is that the law regards with the deepest suspicion any remedies of self-help, and permits those remedies to be resorted to only in very special circumstances. The reason for such circumspection is clear – necessity can very easily become simply a mask for anarchy. As far as my reading goes, it appears that all the cases where a plea of necessity has succeeded are cases which deal with an urgent situation of imminent peril ...'

(2)   It seems strange to talk of the plaintiff being made subject to an injunction and imprisoned in the way that happened in this case, but not once it is realised that the contempt proceedings arose out of the original case.

(3)   The plaintiff was left to her remedy in damages which both the Court of Appeal and the court at first instance said related to the diminution in the value of her property. But there is authority which suggests that in awarding damages the court could have regard to the profit or benefit to the defendant, see below.

Jaggard v Sawyer
[1995] 2 All ER 189 Court of Appeal

Purchasers of houses entered into covenants which forbade the use of any part of the land being unbuilt upon to be used other than as a garden, and required the upkeep of the private road fronting the properties. Purchasers bought not only the plot on which the house was built but also the roadway immediately in front of that plot, up to the centre of the roadway. The local authority had stated that the road was a public highway but later accepted that it was a private road.

The defendants bought a house (no 5) and, later, part of an adjoining garden on which they began to build a house (no 5A), intending to use part of their original garden as access to and from the road. The plaintiff, who owned a house on the road, objected to the plans and threatened to bring proceedings but did not commence these until the building work was at an advanced stage. The only access to the site was over the road.

Instead of an injunction the trial judge awarded the plaintiff damages, holding that the defendants should have been prepared to pay each resident £694.44 for release of the covenants and grant of a right of way, and he awarded the plaintiff that sum. The plaintiff appealed. The Court of Appeal upheld the decision of the judge to refuse an injunction and to award damages in lieu. The damages could be awarded 'once and for all' in respect of future trespasses since the damages were awarded in substitution for the grant of an injunction.

Sir Thomas Bingham: '... In considering the legal issues in this case, I should acknowledge at the outset my debt to an illuminating article by Professor Jolowicz "Damages in Equity – A Study of Lord Cairns' Act" [1975] CLJ 224.

Historically, the remedy given by courts of common law was damages. These afforded retrospective compensation for past wrongs. If the wrongs were repeated or continued, a fresh action was needed. Courts of equity, in contrast, were able to give prospective relief by way of injunction or specific performance. A mandatory injunction would require the defendant to observe a legal obligation or undo the effects of a past breach of legal obligation. A negative injunction would restrain a defendant from committing breaches of legal obligation in future. But these courts could not award damages. This anomaly was mitigated by the Common Law Procedure Act 1854, which gave courts of common law a limited power to grant equitable relief as well as damages. It was further mitigated by the Chancery Amendment Act 1858 (Lord Cairns' Act), which gave the Court of Chancery the power to award damages.

Section 2 of Lord Cairns' Act provided:

"In all cases in which the Court of Chancery has jurisdiction to entertain an application for an injunction against a breach of any covenant, contract, or agreement, or against the commission or continuance of any wrongful act, or for the specific performance of any covenant, contract, or agreement, it shall be lawful for the same Court, if it shall think fit, to award damages to the party injured, either in addition to or in substitution for such injunction or specific performance; and such damages may be assessed in such manner as the Court shall direct."

This enabled the Chancery Court on appropriate facts to award damages for unlawful conduct in the past as well as an injunction to restrain unlawful conduct in the future. It also enabled the Chancery Court to award damages instead of granting an injunction to restrain unlawful conduct in the future. Such damages can only have been intended to compensate the plaintiff for future unlawful conduct, the commission of which, in the absence of any injunction, the court must have contemplated as likely to occur. Despite the repeal of Lord Cairns' Act, it has never been doubted that the jurisdiction thereby conferred on the Court of Chancery is exercisable by the High Court and by county courts. The authorities show that there were, not surprisingly, differing approaches to the exercise of this new jurisdiction. In the leading case of *Shelfer v City of London Electric Lighting Co* the operations of the defendant electricity company caused structural damage to a house and nuisance to its occupier. The owner and occupier sought relief by way of injunction. The trial judge refused injunctive relief and awarded damages. His decision was reversed by the Court of Appeal, which roundly rejected the view that wrongs should be permitted to continue simply because the wrongdoer was able and willing to pay damages. But the authority is chiefly notable for the guidance given by A L Smith LJ on the circumstances in which damages may properly be awarded in lieu of an injunction. The following passage in his judgment has been cited very frequently, but must be cited again:

"Many Judges have stated, and I emphatically agree with them, that a person by committing a wrongful act (whether it be a public company for public purposes or a private individual) is not thereby entitled to ask the Court to sanction his doing so by purchasing his neighbour's rights, by assessing damages in that behalf, leaving his neighbour with the nuisance, or his lights dimmed, as the case may be. In such cases the well-known rule is not to accede to the application, but to grant the injunction sought, for the plaintiff's legal right has been invaded, and he is *prima facie* entitled to an injunction. There are, however, cases in which this rule may be relaxed, and in which damages may be awarded in substitution for an injunction as authorised by this section. In any instance in which a case for an injunction has been made out, if the plaintiff by his acts or laches has disentitled himself to an injunction the Court may award damages in its place. So again, whether the case be for a mandatory injunction or to restrain a continuing nuisance, the appropriate remedy may be damages in lieu of an injunction, assuming a case for an injunction to be made out. In my opinion, it may be stated as a good working rule that – (1.) If the injury to the plaintiff's legal rights is small, (2.) And is one which is capable of being estimated in money, (3.) And is one which can be adequately compensated by a small money payment, (4.) And the case is one in which it would be oppressive to the defendant to grant an injunction: – then damages in substitution for an injunction may be given. There may also be cases in which, though the four above-mentioned requirements exist, the defendant by his conduct, as, for instance, hurrying up his buildings so as if possible to avoid an injunction, or otherwise acting with reckless disregard to the plaintiff's rights, has disentitled himself from asking that damages may be assessed in substitution for an injunction. It is impossible to lay down any rule as to what, under the differing circumstances of each case, constitutes either a small injury, or one that can be estimated in money, or what is a small money payment, or an adequate compensation, or what would be oppressive to the defendant. This must be left to the good sense of the tribunal which deals with each case as it comes up for adjudication. For instance, an injury to the plaintiff's legal right to light to a window in a cottage represented by £15 might well be held to be not small but considerable; whereas a similar injury to a warehouse or other large building represented by ten times that amount might be held to be inconsiderable. Each case must be decided upon its own facts; but to escape the rule it must be brought within the exception. In the present case it appears to me that the injury to the Plaintiff is certainly not small, nor is it in my judgment capable of being estimated in money, or of being adequately compensated by a small money payment."

Many later cases have turned on the application of this good working rule to the particular facts of the case before the court. This case may be said to do the same.

In *Leeds Industrial Co-op Society Ltd v Slack* doubts about the scope of Lord Cairns' Act were dispelled. Viscount Finlay said:

"The power given is to award damages to the party injured, either in addition to or in substitution for an injunction. If the damages are given in addition to the injunction they are to compensate for the injury which has been done and the injunction will prevent its continuance or repetition. But if damages are given in substitution for an injunction they must necessarily cover not only injury already sustained but also injury that would be inflicted in the future by the commission of the act threatened. If no injury has yet been sustained the damages will be solely in respect of the damage to be sustained in the future by injuries which the injunction, if granted, would have prevented."

The claim for an injunction in *Kelsen v Imperial Tobacco Co (of GB and Ireland) Ltd* arose out of the infringement by the defendants of the plaintiff's air space by erection and maintenance of an advertising sign above the plaintiff's shop. McNair J did not doubt his discretion to award damages in lieu of an injunction if he saw fit. He regarded the injury to the plaintiff's rights as small and the damages, if capable of being estimated at all, as nominal. He did not regard the grant of an injunction as oppressive to the defendants. He granted an injunction. He proceeded on the express assumption that, if he did not grant an injunction and the defendants' tortious conduct continued, it would be open to the plaintiff to seek further damages in a later action. It does not appear to have been contemplated that the measure of damage could be based on the reasonable fee which the plaintiff could require to permit exhibition of the sign, although the judge was very much alive to the commercial considerations underlying the dispute. *Woollerton & Wilson Ltd v Richard Costain Ltd* involved a trespass into the plaintiff's air space by the jib of the defendant's crane. No damage was done. But Stamp J regarded the absence of damage as a reason for, not against, the grant of an injunction and held that A L Smith LJ's working rule did not apply in cases of trespass founding a claim for nominal damages only. On the facts, however, he thought it right to suspend the operation of the injunction for a period which would enable the defendants to finish the job for which the crane was required. This decision cannot in my view be supported. The working rule formulated by A L Smith LJ cannot be limited in the way suggested, and the fact that a plaintiff has suffered only nominal damage cannot in common sense be a reason for confining his remedy to an injunction if the court is then, by suspending the injunction, to deny him any remedy at all.

In *Wrotham Park Estate Co v Parkside Homes Ltd* a developer built a number of houses in breach of a covenant restraining him from building save in accordance with a layout plan submitted and approved by the plaintiffs. The plaintiffs issued proceedings claiming an injunction shortly after the building work began but did not seek interlocutory relief and all the houses were complete by the date of trial. The plaintiffs then sought a mandatory injunction requiring demolition of the houses built in breach of covenant. Brightman J refused to grant such an injunction. He said:

> "Counsel for the plaintiffs submitted, and I accept, that it is no answer to a claim for a mandatory injunction that the plaintiffs, having issued proceedings, deliberately held their hand and did not seek the assistance of the court for the purpose of preserving the status quo. On the other hand, it is, in my view, equally true that a plaintiff is not entitled 'as of course' to have everything pulled down that was built after the issue of the writ. The erection of the houses, whether one likes it or not, is a *fait accompli* and the houses are now the homes of people. I accept that this particular *fait accompli* is reversible and could be undone. But I cannot close my eyes to the fact that the houses now exist. It would, in my opinion, be an unpardonable waste of much needed houses to direct that they now be pulled down and I have never had a moment's doubt during the hearing of this case that such an order ought to be refused. No damage of a financial nature has been done to the plaintiffs by the breach of the layout stipulation. The plaintiffs' use of the Wrotham Park estate has not been and will not be impeded. It is totally unnecessary to demolish the houses in order to preserve the integrity of the restrictive covenants imposed on the rest of area 14. Without hesitation I decline to grant a mandatory injunction. But the fact that these houses will remain does not spell out a charter entitling others to despoil adjacent areas of land in breach of valid restrictions imposed by the conveyances. A developer who tries that course may be in for a rude awakening."

Brightman J did not confine the plaintiffs to nominal damages. He concluded that a just substitute for a mandatory injunction would be such a sum of money as might reasonably have been demanded by the plaintiffs from the developer as a *quid pro quo* for relaxing the covenant.

Facts almost indistinguishable from the present came before the court in *Bracewell v Appleby*. In that case, as in this, the plaintiffs voiced their objection before building work began but did not issue proceedings until after. Application was made for an interlocutory injunction, but not until after the new house had been finished and then it was refused. At trial the plaintiffs sought an injunction which Graham J was unwilling to grant. He acknowledged that an injunction would not require the new house to be pulled down, but it would make it uninhabitable. Instead, he awarded damages in lieu, holding (in accordance with the approach of Brightman J in *Wrotham Park*) that the defendant should be liable to pay an amount of damages which, in so far as it could be estimated, would be equivalent to a fair and proper price payable for the acquisition of the right of way in question.

In *John Trenberth Ltd v National Westminster Bank Ltd* Walton J echoed doubts already expressed in *Charrington v Simons & Co Ltd* about the correctness of Stamp J's suspension of the injunction granted in *Woollerton & Wilson*, but asserted with emphasis that the absence of damage, far from being a reason why an injunction should not be granted, was the very reason why it should.

It was the unlawful parking of vehicles in their yard which founded the plaintiffs' claim for relief in *Patel v WH Smith (Eziot) Ltd*. The Court of Appeal held that *prima facie* a landowner whose title is not in issue is entitled to an injunction to restrain trespass on his land whether or not the trespass harms him. But the court accepted that there would be exceptional circumstances in which the court would not think it appropriate to grant an injunction.

Trespass to the plaintiffs' air space by crane jibs was again the ground of complaint in *Anchor Brewhouse Developments Ltd v Berkley House (Docklands Developments) Ltd*. Founding himself on *Woollerton & Wilson*, *John Trenberth* and *Patel*, Scott J held that *prima facie*, and in the absence of special circumstances, the plaintiffs were entitled to an injunction. He held that there were no such circumstances and so held that the plaintiffs were entitled "as of course" to injunctions to restrain continuing trespass. He described *Bracewell v Appleby* as "an odd case" and said:

> "I find some difficulty with *Bracewell v Appleby* mainly because, as it seems to me, the learned judge regarded the damages he was awarding as a once and for all payment. But it was, as I see it, not within the power of the judge to produce that result. Whether or not an injunction were granted, the defendant's use of the right of way would, after the judgment as well as before, represent trespass unless and until he were granted a right of way. The judge could not by an award of damages put the defendant in the position of a person entitled to an easement of way. So assuming, which is not clear from the case, that there had not been some agreement by the plaintiffs to treat the damages as entitling the defendant to a right of way, the defendant's subsequent use of the private road would have constituted a continuing trespass. A succession of further actions for damages could have been brought. In those circumstances it seems to me very difficult to justify the withholding of the injunction. By withholding the injunction the court was

allowing a legal wrong to continue unabated. Nonetheless [counsel for the defendants] is entitled to refer to the case as one in which an injunction was refused."

I, for my part, find some difficulty in these observations of Scott J. It is of course true that the court cannot, on an application of this kind, revoke a covenant or grant the defendant a right of way. But if the court, in exercise of its jurisdiction derived from Lord Cairns' Act, instead of granting the plaintiff an injunction to restrain the defendant's apprehended future unlawful conduct, awards the plaintiff damages to compensate him for that conduct, it seems to me that a succession of future actions based on that conduct would, if brought, be dismissed or struck out, since a plaintiff could not complain of that for which he had already been compensated.

[Sir Thomas Bingham considered *Surrey County Council v Bredero Homes Ltd*, and continued:]

I cannot, however, accept that Brightman J's assessment of damages in *Wrotham Park* was based on other than compensatory principles. The defendants had committed a breach of covenant, the effects of which continued. The judge was not willing to order the defendants to undo the continuing effects of that breach. He had therefore to assess the damages necessary to compensate the plaintiffs for this continuing invasion of their right. He paid attention to the profits earned by the defendants, as it seems to me, not in order to strip the defendants of their unjust gains, but because of the obvious relationship between the profits earned by the defendants and the sum which the defendants would reasonably have been willing to pay to secure release from the covenant. I am reassured to find that this is the view taken of *Wrotham Park* by Megarry V-C in *Tito v Waddell (No 2)* …

I can see no reason why a judge should not assess damages on the *Wrotham Park* basis when he declines to prevent commission of a future wrong.

THE PRESENT CASE

The judge recognised that a plaintiff who can show that his legal right will be violated by the defendant's conduct is *prima facie* entitled to the grant of an injunction. He accepted that the court will only rarely and reluctantly permit such violation to occur or continue. But he held that this case fulfilled the four tests laid down by A L Smith LJ in *Shelfer v City of London Electric Lighting Co* to bring this case within the exception. The real question in this appeal is whether that judgment is sustainable.

(1) He regarded the injury to the plaintiff's right as small. This is in my view so. It is not suggested that the increase in traffic attributable to the existence of No 5A will be other than minimal, or that the cost of keeping up the road will be significantly increased. The defendants have, in any event, offered throughout to

contribute to the cost of upkeep and are willing, if a draft is tendered to them, to execute a deed binding themselves by the same covenants as other residents of the [road]. It is not suggested that the driveway to No 5A impairs the visual amenity of the plaintiff's house or affects its value. There is of course a violation of the plaintiff's strict legal right, but that will be so in any case of this kind.

(2) The judge considered the value of the injury to the plaintiff's right as capable of being estimated in money. He based himself on the *Wrotham Park* approach. In my view he was justified. He valued the right at what a reasonable seller would sell it for. In situations of this kind a plaintiff should not be treated as eager to sell, which he very probably is not. But the court will not value the right at the ransom price which a very reluctant plaintiff might put on it. I see no error in the judge's approach to this aspect.

(3) The judge held that the injury to the plaintiff's legal right was one which could be adequately compensated by a small money payment. I agree, and I do not think this conclusion can be faulted.

(4) The judge concluded that in all the circumstances it would be oppressive to the defendants to grant the injunctions sought. Most of the argument turned on this condition, and in particular on the significance which the judge attached to the plaintiff's failure to seek interlocutory relief.

It is important to bear in mind that the test is one of oppression, and the court should not slide into application of a general balance of convenience test. But oppression must be judged as at the date the court is asked to grant an injunction, and (as Brightman J recognised in *Wrotham Park*) the court cannot ignore the reality with which it is then confronted. It is relevant that the plaintiff could at an early stage have sought interlocutory relief, which she would seem very likely to have obtained; but it is also relevant that the defendants could have sought a declaration of right. These considerations are not decisive. It would weigh against a finding of oppression if the defendants had acted in blatant and calculated disregard of the plaintiff's rights, of which they were aware, but the judge held that this was not so, and the plaintiff's solicitors may be thought to have indicated that damages would be an acceptable remedy. It was suggested that an injunction restraining trespass on the plaintiff's roadway would not be oppressive since the occupiers of No 5A could use the other half of the roadway outside the plaintiff's house, but this would seem to me unworkable in practice, a recipe for endless dispute and a remedy which would yield nothing of value to the plaintiff. It was suggested that the occupiers of No 5A could be restrained from using the driveway over the land formerly part of No 5 for vehicular access, while access on foot would be permitted. But this, as it seems to me, would impose inconvenience and loss on the occupier and owner of No 5A without upholding the plaintiff's right or yielding any practical benefit to her. As s 84 of the Law of Property Act 1925 makes clear, restrictive covenants cannot be regarded as absolute and inviolable for all time. The judge was, in my view, entitled to hold on all the facts before the court at trial that the grant of an injunction would be oppressive to the defendants, and I share that view.

The only argument pressed on damages was that the only damages properly awardable on compensatory principles would have been nominal and that therefore an injunction should have been granted. As already indicated, I think that the *Wrotham Park* approach was appropriate even on pure compensatory principles and the judge followed it correctly ... I am of the clear opinion that the appeal must be dismissed.'

Comment

(1) The grant of equitable relief is entirely a matter for the court applying well-established principles indicated in *Shelfer*; as Millett LJ put it:

'Reported cases are merely illustrations of circumstances in which particular judges have exercised their discretion, in some cases by granting an injunction, and in others by awarding damages instead. Since they are all cases on the exercise of a discretion, none of them is a binding authority on how the discretion should be exercised. The most that any of them can demonstrate is that in similar circumstances it would not be wrong to exercise the discretion in the same way. But it does not follow that it would be wrong to exercise it differently.'

(2) Where a plaintiff seeks a mandatory injunction to pull down a building, the court is faced with a *fait accompli* and, in the ordinary course of events, a court will be very reluctant to grant an injunction. In cases of trespass to the plaintiff's airspace, the court will generally not be faced with a *fait accompli*. The grant of an injunction restores the parties to the same position they were in before the trespass began. It may be otherwise where the trespass to airspace is in a more or less permanent form, such as a building, but, even in such a case, it is possible to find instances of the grant of a mandatory injunction to remove the offending structure.

(3) In *Anchor Brewhouse* Scott J granted an injunction to prohibit the oversailing jibs but lamented the possibility that an owner of land might behave like 'a dog in a manger' and obtain an injunction simply to thwart the plans of someone developing adjacent land. He said:

'It would in many respects be convenient if the court had power, in order to enable property developments to be expeditiously and economically completed, to allow, on proper commercial terms, some use to be made by the developers of the land of neighbours. But the court has no such power and ought not, in my view, to claim it indirectly by the withholding of injunctions in cases like the present.'

CHAPTER 13

Private nuisance

Not everything that might ordinarily be regarded as annoying or a nuisance necessarily amounts to an actionable nuisance. The matter is further complicated by there being three forms of nuisance: (a) public nuisance (essentially a crime at common law); (b) a private action arising out of a public nuisance; and (c) private nuisance. It is necessary also to consider the principle in *Rylands v Fletcher*, which derives from private nuisance and serves a similar purpose. The torts are not mutually exclusive and often are pleaded together; nor does the fact that a form of conduct is an actionable nuisance prevent it from also being actionable as negligence.

In private nuisance the gist of the action is the 'interference with a person's use or enjoyment of land or some right over or in connection with it' (*Winfield & Jolowicz*). Its basic function is to assist in the regulation of relationships between neighbours, but it may well also relate to the conduct of those who are not neighbours and whose conduct upsets an occupier's enjoyment of land, e.g. a ship discharging oil into the sea which then pollutes the shoreline (cf *Esso v Southport Corporation*).

Private nuisance is concerned with the protection of interests in and the enjoyment of land, and is readily distinguishable from public nuisance which is not so limited. The continued application of this fundamental principle has been reaffirmed by the House of Lords in *Hunter v Canary Wharf*, despite attempts to argue to the contrary by the Court of Appeal in that case.

In public nuisance it used to be suggested that the behaviour of the defendant would be independently unlawful, but this view has not been followed in *Gillingham BC v Medway (Chatham) Dock Co Ltd*, p 632. In private nuisance the behaviour of the defendant will generally be lawful and rendered an actionable nuisance only where unreasonable. Public nuisance may provide a means for compensating personal injury, but the House of Lords in *Hunter v*

Canary Wharf has confirmed that damages for personal injury are not available in private nuisance, and by analogy this may well be true of *Rylands v Fletcher*, despite *dicta* to the contrary, see p 708. Unlike trespass, in nuisance there is a need to establish damage, although in some instances this will be assumed. In trespass the harm must be caused directly, as opposed to indirectly in the case of nuisance, e.g. contrast the overhanging shed roof and the straying branch of a shrub.

Nuisances are said to arise from a state of affairs. However, an isolated incident may give rise to an action if it stems from a 'continuing underlying state of affairs' from which the actual harm was foreseeably likely to occur. See *Bolton v Stone* in which there was no liability but it was said: 'The gist of such an action in nuisance is the causing or permitting of a state of affairs from which the damage is likely to result.' There still appears to be some confusion over this matter, see *British Celanese v Hunt*: 'Most nuisances do arise from a long continuing condition, and many isolated happenings do not constitute a nuisance. It is, however, clear from the authorities that an isolated happening by itself can create an actionable nuisance.' And *SCM v Whittall*: 'While there is no doubt that a single isolated escape may cause the damage that entitles a plaintiff to sue for nuisance, yet it must be proved that the nuisance arose from the condition of the defendant's land or premises or property or activities thereon that constituted a nuisance.'

The role of reasonableness in nuisance is distinct from that in negligence. Although negligence in the sense of failure to take reasonable care does have some part to play in nuisance, this is so only in certain limited respects. The closer assimilation of nuisance and negligence was remarked upon in *Transco plc v Stockport Metropolitan Borough Council* (a case on the principle in *Rylands v Fletcher*) e.g. as regards the element of reasonable foresight in causation, see p 255, and the notion of a duty as between adjacent occupiers where there is a 'natural' nuisance, see p 651.

Hunter and others v Canary Wharf Ltd
Hunter and others v London Docklands Corporation
[1997] 2 All ER 426 House of Lords

In the first action, the plaintiffs sought damages in respect of interference with television reception at their homes caused, they claimed, by the construction of the Canary Wharf Tower, which was built on land developed by the defendants. The plaintiffs claimed that, because of its considerable size and the extensive use of stainless steel cladding and metallised windows, the building interfered with television signals. The plaintiffs lived in an area affected by the interference, 'the shadow area', and claimed that the interference began in 1989, during the construction of the tower. A relay transmitter built to overcome the problem of interference came into operation in April 1991. The claim was framed in nuisance and in negligence, though the latter claim was abandoned.

In the second action, the plaintiffs sought damages in respect of damage caused, they claimed, by excessive amounts of dust created during the construction of a link road by the defendants. The plaintiffs claimed in negligence and nuisance, but abandoned a claim based on the rule in *Rylands v Fletcher.*

The House of Lords (Lord Cooke dissenting) held that in order to maintain an action in nuisance the plaintiff must have a right to exclusive possession of land and that a mere licensee or occupier had no right to sue. As to the second point (for extracts see p 637), the House of Lords held unanimously that interference with television reception caused by the mere presence of a building on land was incapable of constituting an actionable nuisance.

Lord Goff: '... I turn next to the question of the right to sue in private nuisance ... The basic position is, in my opinion, most clearly expressed in Professor Newark's classic article on "The Boundaries of Nuisance" in (1949) 65 LQR 480, when he stated that the essence of nuisance was that "it was a tort to land. Or to be more accurate it was a tort directed against the plaintiff's enjoyment of rights over land."
...

[It] has for many years been regarded as settled law that a person who has no right in the land cannot sue in private nuisance. For this proposition, it is usual to cite the decision of the Court of Appeal in *Malone v Laskey.* In that case, the manager of a company resided in a house as a licensee of the company which employed him. The plaintiff was the manager's wife who lived with her husband in the house. She was injured when a bracket fell from a wall in the house. She claimed damages from the defendants in nuisance and negligence, her claim in nuisance being founded upon an allegation, accepted by the jury, that the fall of the bracket had been caused by vibrations from an engine operating on the defendants' adjoining premises. The Court of Appeal held that she was unable to succeed in her claim in nuisance ...

I should add that an alternative claim by the plaintiff in negligence also failed, though that claim would have succeeded today: (see *A C Billings & Sons Ltd v Riden*).

The decision in *Malone v Laskey* on nuisance has since been followed in many cases, of which notable examples are *Cunard v Antifyre Ltd* and *Oldham v Lawson (No 1)*. Recently, however, the Court of Appeal departed from this line of authority in *Khorasandjian v Bush* ...

[Lord Goff considered the decision which relied heavily on the decision of a Canadian court in *Motherwell v Motherwell* that a wife with no interest in the matrimonial home was able to sue in private nuisance:]

This conclusion [in *Motherwell v Motherwell*] was very largely based on the decision of the Court of Appeal in *Foster v Warblington UDC*, which Clement JA understood to establish a distinction between "one who is 'merely present'" and "occupancy of a substantial nature", and that in the latter case the occupier was entitled to sue in private nuisance. However Foster does not in my opinion provide authority for the proposition that a person in the position of a mere licensee, such as a wife or husband in her or his spouse's house, is entitled to sue in that action. This misunderstanding must, I fear, undermine the authority of *Motherwell* on this point; and in so far as the decision of the Court of Appeal in *Khorasandjian v Bush* is founded upon *Motherwell* it is likewise undermined.

But I must go further. If a plaintiff, such as the daughter of the householder in *Khorasandjian v Bush*, is harassed by abusive telephone calls, the gravamen of the complaint lies in the harassment which is just as much an abuse, or indeed an invasion of her privacy, whether she is pestered in this way in her mother's or her husband's house, or she is staying with a friend, or is at her place of work, or even in her car with a mobile phone. In truth, what the Court of Appeal appears to have been doing was to exploit the law of private nuisance in order to create by the back door a tort of harassment which was only partially effective in that it was artificially limited to harassment which takes place in her home. I myself do not consider that this is a satisfactory manner in which to develop the law, especially when, as in the case in question, the step so taken was inconsistent with another decision of the Court of Appeal, viz. *Malone v Laskey*, by which the court was bound. In any event, a tort of harassment has now received statutory recognition: see the Protection from Harassment Act 1997. We are therefore no longer troubled with the question whether the common law should be developed to provide such a remedy. For these reasons, I do not consider that any assistance can be derived from *Khorasandjian v Bush* by the plaintiffs in the present appeals.

It follows that, on the authorities as they stand, an action in private nuisance will only lie at the suit of a person who has a right to the land affected. Ordinarily, such a person can only sue if he has the right to exclusive possession of the land, such as a freeholder or tenant in possession, or even a licensee with exclusive possession. Exceptionally however, as *Foster* shows, this category may include a person in actual possession who has no right to be there; and in any event a reversioner can sue in so far as his reversionary interest is affected. But a mere licensee on the land has no right to sue.

The question therefore arises whether your Lordships should be persuaded to depart from established principle, and recognise such a right in others who are no more than mere licensees on the land. At the heart of this question lies a more fundamental question, which relates to the scope of the law of private nuisance. Here I wish to draw attention to the fact that although, in the past, damages for personal injury have been recovered at least in actions of public nuisance, there is now developing a school of thought that the appropriate remedy for such claims as these should lie in our now fully developed law of negligence, and that personal injury claims should be altogether excluded from the domain of nuisance. The most forthright proponent of this approach has been Professor Newark, in his article in

(1949) 65 LQR 480 ... Furthermore, it is now being suggested that claims in respect of physical damage to the land should also be excluded from private nuisance (see, e.g., the article by Mr Conor Gearty on "The Place of Private Nuisance in a Modern Law of Torts" in [1989] CLJ 214). In any event, it is right for present purposes to regard the typical cases of private nuisance as being those concerned with interference with the enjoyment of land and, as such, generally actionable only by a person with a right in the land. Characteristic examples of cases of this kind are those concerned with noise, vibrations, noxious smells and the like. The two appeals with which your Lordships are here concerned arise from actions of this character.

For private nuisances of this kind, the primary remedy is in most cases an injunction, which is sought to bring the nuisance to an end, and in most cases should swiftly achieve that objective. The right to bring such proceedings is, as the law stands, ordinarily vested in the person who has exclusive possession of the land. He or she is the person who will sue, if it is necessary to do so. Moreover he or she can, if thought appropriate, reach an agreement with the person creating the nuisance, either that it may continue for a certain period of time, possibly on the payment of a sum of money, or that it shall cease, again perhaps on certain terms including the time within which the cessation will take place. The former may well occur when an agreement is reached between neighbours about the circumstances in which one of them may carry out major repairs to his house which may affect the other's enjoyment of his property. An agreement of this kind was expressly contemplated by Fletcher Moulton LJ in his judgment in *Malone v Laskey*. But the efficacy of arrangements such as these depends upon the existence of an identifiable person with whom the creator of the nuisance can deal for this purpose. If anybody who lived in the relevant property as a home had the right to sue, sensible arrangements such as these might in some cases no longer be practicable.

Moreover, any such departure from the established law on this subject, such as that adopted by the Court of Appeal in the present case, faces the problem of defining the category of persons who would have the right to sue. The Court of Appeal adopted the not easily identifiable category of those who have a "substantial link" with the land, regarding a person who occupied the premises "as a home" as having a sufficient link for this purpose. But who is to be included in this category? It was plainly intended to include husbands and wives, or partners, and their children, and even other relatives living with them. But is the category also to include the lodger upstairs, or the au pair girl or resident nurse caring for an invalid who makes her home in the house while she works there? If the latter, it seems strange that the category should not extend to include places where people work as well as places where they live, where nuisances such as noise can be just as unpleasant or distracting. In any event, the extension of the tort in this way would transform it from a tort to land into a tort to the person, in which damages could be recovered in respect of something less serious than personal injury and the criteria for liability were founded not upon negligence but upon striking a balance between the interests of neighbours in the use of their land. This is, in my opinion, not an acceptable way in which to develop the law.

It was suggested in the course of argument that at least the spouse of a husband or wife who, for example as freeholder or tenant, had exclusive possession of the matrimonial home should be entitled to sue in private nuisance. For the purposes of this submission, your Lordships were referred to the relevant legislation, notably the Matrimonial Homes Act 1983 and the Family Law Act 1996. I do not, however, consider it necessary to go through the statutory provisions. As I understand the position, it is as follows. If under the relevant legislation a spouse becomes entitled to possession of the matrimonial home or part of it, there is no reason why he or she should not be able to sue in private nuisance in the ordinary way. But I do not see how a spouse who has no interest in the matrimonial home has, simply by virtue of his or her cohabiting in the matrimonial home with his or her wife or husband whose freehold or leasehold property it is, a right to sue. No distinction can sensibly be drawn between such spouses and other co-habitees in the home, such as children, or grandparents. Nor do I see any great disadvantage flowing from this state of affairs. If a nuisance should occur, then the spouse who has an interest in the property can bring the necessary proceedings to bring the nuisance to an end, and can recover any damages in respect of the discomfort or inconvenience caused by the nuisance. Even if he or she is away from home, nowadays the necessary authority to commence proceedings for an injunction can usually be obtained by telephone. Moreover, if the other spouse suffers personal injury, including injury to health, he or she may, like anybody else, be able to recover damages in negligence. The only disadvantage is that the other spouse cannot bring an independent action in private nuisance for damages for discomfort or inconvenience ...

For all these reasons, I can see no good reason to depart from the law on this topic as established in the authorities. I would therefore hold that *Khorasandjian v Bush* must be overruled in so far as it holds that a mere licensee can sue in private nuisance, and I would allow the appeal or cross-appeal of the defendants in both actions and restore the order of Judge Havery on this issue.'

Lord Lloyd: '... Private nuisances are of three kinds. They are (1) nuisance by encroachment on a neighbour's land; (2) nuisance by direct physical injury to a neighbour's land; and (3) nuisance by interference with a neighbour's quiet enjoyment of his land. In cases (1) and (2) it is the owner, or the occupier with the right to exclusive possession, who is entitled to sue. It has never, so far as I know, been suggested that anyone else can sue, for example, a visitor or a lodger; and the reason is not far to seek. For the basis of the cause of action in cases (1) and (2) is damage to the land itself, whether by encroachment or by direct physical injury.

In the case of encroachment the plaintiff may have a remedy by way of abatement. In other cases he may be entitled to an injunction. But where he claims damages, the measure of damages in cases (1) and (2) will be the diminution in the value of the land. This will usually (though not always) be equal to the cost of reinstatement. The loss resulting from diminution in the value of the land is a loss suffered by the owner or occupier with the exclusive right to possession (as the case may be) or both, since it is they alone who have a proprietary interest, or stake, in the land. So it is they alone who can bring an action to recover the loss ...

It has been said that an actionable nuisance is incapable of exact definition. But the essence of private nuisance is easy enough to identify, and it is the same in all three classes of private nuisance, namely, interference with land or the enjoyment of land. In the case of nuisances within class (1) or (2) the measure of damages is, as I have said, the diminution in the value of the land. Exactly the same should be true of nuisances within class (3). There is no difference of principle. The effect of smoke from a neighbouring factory is to reduce the value of the land. There may be no diminution in the market value. But there will certainly be loss of amenity value so long as the nuisance lasts. If that be the right approach, then the reduction in amenity value is the same whether the land is occupied by the family man or the bachelor.

If the occupier of land suffers personal injury as a result of inhaling the smoke, he may have a cause of action in negligence. But he does not have a cause of action in nuisance for his *personal* injury, nor for interference with his *personal* enjoyment. It follows that the quantum of damages in private nuisance does not depend on the number of those enjoying the land in question. It also follows that the only persons entitled to sue for loss in amenity value of the land are the owner or the occupier with the right to exclusive possession ...

Each member of a family does not have a separate cause of action. There is no more than one potential cause of action for each home ... It follows that the proceedings in the instant case were never properly constituted. Instead of the 690 plaintiffs named in the Schedule to the Statement of Claim, there should have been only one plaintiff for each address.'

Comment

(1) In *Khorasandjian v Bush*, the plaintiff was a young girl who complained of the harassment of her by a former friend. The harassment included persistent telephone calls to the home where she lived with her parents. The Court of Appeal preferred the approach in *Motherwell v Motherwell* and decided not to follow *Malone v Laskey* even though the plaintiff had no legal or equitable interest in the house. In *Motherwell v Motherwell* the court held that a woman who was the subject of unwanted telephone harassment by her daughter was entitled an injunction even though she had no interest in the home where she lived with her husband.

For further analysis of *Khorasandjian v Bush*, see p 518 and the Protection from Harassment Act 1997, see p 521. The history of the attempt at common law to create a tort of harassment is dealt with the Court of Appeal in *Wong v Parkside NHS Trust*.

(2)   In *Foster v Warblington UDC* the defendant council discharged sewage into oyster beds which had been occupied for many years by the plaintiff. The beds had been constructed on the foreshore, which belonged to the Lord of the Manor. The plaintiff excluded everybody from the oyster beds, and nobody interfered with his occupation of them. The Court of Appeal held that, since *jus tertii* is not a defence to an action in nuisance, a person in exclusive possession of land may sue even though he cannot prove title to it and that the plaintiff could sue the defendant in nuisance, even though he could not prove his title.

Lord Hoffmann observed that *Metropolitan Properties v Jones* was wrongly decided and that a tenant *de facto* in exclusive possession would be able to sue in respect of nuisance created by the landlord's noisy motor in adjoining premises.

In *Butcher Robinson & Staples Ltd and others v London Regional Transport and another* the claimants occupied premises and were companies in a complicated grouping of holding, service, subsidiary and sub-subsidiary companies. The nature of these arrangements meant that actual possession and occupation of the premises constantly shifted between different companies in the grouping. Chapter Group plc owned both the premises and the claimant companies, but was not itself a claimant. In the High Court (Technology and Construction Court), Judge Bowsher QC held as a preliminary issue that none of the claimant companies had sufficient proprietary interest to sue in private nuisance. There was no right to exclusive possession amounting either to a tenancy or a licence.

In *Pemberton v Southwark London Borough Council* the Court of Appeal held that a 'tolerated trespasser' (a peculiar category in landlord and tenant law, see *Burrows v Brent London BC*) was entitled to maintain a claim in nuisance against the defendant local authority which had been her former landlord. The Court of Appeal observed that a tolerated trespasser retained the right to exclusive possession of the property and that the local authority landlord would require a court order to obtain possession. The original tenancy could be revived on application to the court upon fulfilment of appropriate conditions. Although the mutual obligations in the previous tenancy disappeared, the local authority was obliged to conduct itself in such a way that it did not create a nuisance, in this case by allowing an infestation of cockroaches in the common parts of a block of flats. One factor persuading the court that the tolerated trespasser retained sufficient interest to sue was the protection afforded by article 8 of the European Convention on Human Rights.

(3) Insofar as non-owning spouses are concerned, Lord Hoffmann made comments similar to those of Lord Goff and observed that 'so far as it is thought desirable that the wife should be able to sue for injury to a proprietary or possessory interest in the home, the answer lies in the law of property, not the law of tort'.

(4) The case effectively settles the question whether or not damages for personal injuries are available in an action for private nuisance. Lord Hoffmann observed that inconvenience, annoyance and even illness suffered by persons on the land were not damage consequent upon the injury to the land but were evidence of injury to the amenity of the land. He went on:

'So far as the claim is for personal injury, it seems to me that the only appropriate cause of action is negligence. It would be anomalous if the rules for recovery of damages under this head were different according as to whether, for example, the plaintiff was at home or at work. It is true, as I have said, that the law of negligence gives no remedy for discomfort or distress which does not result in bodily or psychiatric illness. But this is a matter of general policy and I can see no logic in making an exception for cases in which the discomfort or distress was suffered at home rather than somewhere else.'

It may be presumed that, in the light of the close relationship between nuisance and the principle in *Rylands v Fletcher*, damages for personal injury will not be available under that principle, see now the *Transco* case, p 715. It is also doubtful whether personal injury damages will now be available under the heading of public nuisance.

(5) In *Hussain v Lancaster City Council* the Court of Appeal considered the overlap between nuisance and negligence in the case of physical damage. Hirst LJ said:

'Lord Wright [in *Sedleigh-Denfield v O'Callaghan*] stated:

"The forms which nuisance may take are protean. Certain classifications are possible, but many reported cases are no more than illustrations of particular matters of fact which have been held to be nuisances. But where, as here, a plaintiff is damaged by his land being flooded, the facts bring it well within the sphere of nuisance. Such a case has a certain similarity with those to which the rule of *Rylands v Fletcher* applies, but there are obvious differences in substance. There are indeed well-marked differences between the two juristic concepts. This case has, therefore, properly been treated as a case of nuisance. It has affinity also with a claim for negligence, because the trouble arose from the negligent fitting of the grid. The gist of the present action, however, is the unreasonable and unjustified interference by the defendants in the user of their land with the plaintiff's right to enjoy his property. Negligence, moreover, is not a necessary condition of a claim for nuisance. What is done may be done deliberately, and in good faith, and in a genuine belief that it is justified. Negligence here is not an independent cause of action, but is ancillary to the actual cause of action, which is nuisance ..."

Professor Newark's article (65 LQR 480 at 489) which was approved expressly by Lord Goff in *Hunter v Canary Wharf Ltd* as the first of the theses which he was "prepared ... to nail ... to the doors of the Law Courts and to defend against all comers", "The term 'nuisance' is properly applied only to such actionable user of land as interferes with the enjoyment by the plaintiff of rights in land."

Professor Gearty's article, which was referred to by Lord Goff in the same case, stated ([1989] CLJ 214 at 242):

"D owes P a duty to take reasonable care to avoid causing damage to his property. The duty is not one to manage a business well, or to operate an efficient factory; it is to avoid damage to land. There are only a few very particular situations where no such duty attaches to the conduct of D. The cases usually treat the matter as one of negligence though nuisance is often referred to and may sometimes be the preferred head of liability ... This duty of care should properly belong to the tort of negligence. The label 'nuisance' should play no part in its formulation or application. That it has is a reflection of the difficulty the courts have had in moving the principles of *Donoghue v Stevenson* sideways into the law on neighbours. Private nuisance should be restricted to the protection of property from non-physical damage, i.e. noxious fumes and noise and the like. With its independence assured, and freed from negligence's debilitating concern with the yardstick of the reasonable defendant, there is no reason why nuisance (and consequently environmental protection) should not thrive once again. It is submitted that the cases have now reached the point where this move is possible. It is also desirable because it accords with principle and greatly simplifies the law."

[After referring extensively to relevant authorities Hirst LJ concluded.]

Having regard to *Smith v Littlewoods Organisation Ltd*, and to Lord Goff's references to Professor Gearty's article in *Hunter v Canary Wharf Ltd*, it seems to me clear that the law is now moving strongly in the direction favoured by Professor Gearty, viz. to assimilate the law of nuisance into that of negligence in cases involving physical damage; but in view of my conclusion on nuisance in the present case, it is not necessary to decide whether Professor Gearty's goal has yet been reached.'

(6) In *Thomas v NUM* the court developed a novel form of nuisance involving interference with the lawful use of the highway by striking miners picketing a pit. Scott J said:

' ... Nuisance is strictly concerned with, and may be regarded as confined to, activity which unduly interferes with the use or enjoyment of land or of easements. But there is no reason why the law should not protect on a similar basis the enjoyment of other rights. All citizens have the right to use the public highway. Suppose an individual were persistently to follow another on a public highway, making rude gestures or remarks in order to annoy or vex. If continuance of such conduct were threatened no one can doubt but that a civil court would, at the suit of the victim, restrain by an injunction the continuance of the conduct. The tort might be described as a species of private nuisance, namely unreasonable interference with the victim's rights to use the highway, but the label for the tort does not, in my view, matter.

In the present case, the working miners have the right to use the highway for the purpose of going to work. They are, in my judgment, entitled under the general law to exercise that right without unreasonable harassment by others. Unreasonable harassment of them in their exercise of that right would, in my judgment, be tortious.'

This attempt has not met with universal approval, see e.g. comments in *News Group v SOGAT*, but the Court of Appeal in *Khorasandjian v Bush* was not prepared to examine the correctness of the decision in *Thomas v NUM*.

(7) The defendant need not have an interest in the land, see, for example, *Esso v Southport Corpn* and *Halsey v Esso* where the nuisances, or some of them, did not emanate from land in the occupation of the defendant. The defendant may even be a trespasser, per Devlin J, *obiter*, in *Southport Corpn v Esso Petroleum*: 'I can see no reason why if the defendant as a licensee or trespasser mis-uses someone else's land, he should not be liable in nuisance in the same way as an adjoining occupier would be.' That a defendant trespassing on the plaintiff's land may commit a nuisance has been decided in New Zealand, see *Paxhaven Holdings Ltd v Attorney-General, Clearite Holdings Ltd v Auckland City Corpn.*

Delaware Mansions Ltd and another v Westminster City Council
[2001] 4 All ER 737 House of Lords

The Church Commissioners were the original owners and developers of a property comprising several blocks of flats. The individual tenants occupied under long leases from the Church Commissioners. In April 1990 the Church Commissioners agreed to sell the freehold reversion to Flecksun (the second plaintiff); this sale was completed in June 1990. Flecksun was a wholly-owned subsidiary company of Delaware Mansions Ltd (the first plaintiff) which was a management company owned by the tenants of Delaware Mansions. Only Flecksun was concerned in the appeals to the Court of Appeal and House of Lords.

The local authority owned a tree growing in the footpath four metres from the front boundary of the property. During 1989 cracks began to appear in the structure. In March 1990 engineers reported that the cracking had been caused by the roots of the tree and recommended removal of the tree or, if that were not possible, the underpinning of the property. The authority was sent a copy of the report in August 1990. No action resulted. A more detailed survey in January 1991 revealed that the worst cracking had resulted from foundation damage and that urgent underpinning was necessary. In January 1991, the authority agreed to carry out root-pruning, but Flecksun indicated that underpinning works would have to proceed. The work was completed in July 1992 at a cost of almost £571,000. If the tree had been removed in 1990, underpinning would not have been necessary, and the cost of repair to the property would only have been £14,000. Flecksun sued to recover the sum spent on the remedial work.

The House of Lords found for the plaintiff and, relying on concepts of reasonableness as between neighbours, concluded that where there was a continuing nuisance of which the defendant knew or ought to have known, reasonable remedial expenditure could be recovered by the owner who had had to incur it.

Lord Cooke: '...

[3]   My Lords, this case raises an issue, on which there is surprisingly little authority in English law, about the recoverability of remedial expenditure incurred after encroachment by tree roots ...

[28]   It seems to me therefore that any decision which your Lordships may give in this case must to some extent break new ground in English law. One point at least is clear. Double recovery could not be permitted. But there is no question of that in the present case ... The Church Commissioners here had not incurred the remedial expenditure; and ... they could apparently not have recovered depreciation in the market value of their property resulting from apprehension of future damage.

[29]   Beyond that I think that the answer to the issue falls to be found by applying the concepts of reasonableness between neighbours (real or figurative) and reasonable foreseeability which underlie much modern tort law and, more particularly, the law of nuisance. The great cases in nuisance decided in our time have these concepts at their heart.

[Lord Cooke referred to *Sedleigh-Denfield v O'Callaghan* and *Overseas Tankship (UK) Ltd v The Miller Steamship Co Pty, The Wagon Mound (No 2)* and continued:]

[30] ... in *Goldman v Hargrave*, the Privy Council per Lord Wilberforce, as to an occupier's duty to take reasonable steps to prevent the spreading of a fire caused by lightning striking a tree, said, and likewise not discriminating between nuisance and negligence:

"So far it has been possible to consider the existence of a duty, in general terms; but the matter cannot be left there without some definition of the scope of his duty. How far does it go? What is the standard of the effort required? What is the position as regards expenditure? It is not enough to say merely that these must be 'reasonable' since what is reasonable to one man may be very unreasonable, and indeed ruinous, to another: the law must take account of the fact that the occupier on whom the duty is cast has, *ex hypothesi*, had this hazard thrust upon him through no seeking or fault of his own. His interest, and his resources, whether physical or material, may be of a very modest character either in relation to the magnitude of the hazard, or as compared with those of his threatened neighbour. A rule which required of him in such unsought circumstances in his neighbour's interest a physical effort of which he is not capable, or an excessive expenditure of money, would be unenforceable or unjust. One may say in general terms that the existence of a duty must be based upon knowledge of the hazard, ability to foresee the consequences of not checking or removing it, and the ability to abate it. Moreover in many cases, as for example in Scrutton LJ's hypothetical case of stamping out a fire [see *Job Edwards Ltd v Birmingham Navigations Co*], or the present case, where the hazard could have been removed with little effort and no expenditure, no problem arises; but other cases may not be so simple. In such situations the standard ought to be to require of the occupier what it is reasonable to expect of him in his individual circumstances. Thus, less must be expected of the infirm than of the able-bodied: the owner of small property where a hazard arises which threatens a neighbour with substantial interests should not have to do so much as one with larger interests of his own at stake and greater resources to protect them: if the small owner does what he can and promptly calls on his neighbour to provide additional resources, he may be held to have done his duty: he should not be liable unless it is clearly proved that he could, and reasonably in his individual circumstance should, have done more. This approach to a difficult matter is in fact that which the courts in their more recent decisions have taken."

[31] In both *The Wagon Mound (No 2)* and *Goldman's* case the judgments, which repay full rereading, are directed to what a reasonable person in the shoes of the defendant would have done. The label nuisance or negligence is treated as of no real significance. In this field, I think, the concern of the common law lies in working out the fair and just content and incidents of a neighbour's duty rather than affixing a label and inferring the extent of the duty from it.

[32] Even in the field of *Rylands v Fletcher* strict liability the House of Lords in *Cambridge Water Co v Eastern Counties Leather plc* has stressed the principles of reasonable user and reasonable foreseeability ... It was the absence of reasonable foreseeability of harm of the relevant type that excluded liability in that case.

[33] Approaching the present case in the light of those governing concepts and the judge's findings, I think that there was a continuing nuisance during Flecksun's ownership until at least the completion of the underpinning and the piling in July 1992. It matters not that further cracking of the superstructure may not have occurred after March 1990. The encroachment of the roots was causing continuing damage to the land by dehydrating the soil and inhibiting rehydration. Damage consisting of impairment of the load-bearing qualities of residential land is, in my view, itself a nuisance ... Cracking in the building was consequential. Having regard to the proximity of the plane tree to Delaware Mansions, a real risk of damage to the land and the foundations was foreseeable on the part of Westminster, as in effect the judge found. It is arguable that the cost of repairs to the cracking could have been recovered as soon as it became manifest. That point need not be decided, although I am disposed to think that a reasonable landowner would notify the controlling local authority or neighbour as soon as tree root damage was suspected. It is agreed that if the plane tree had been removed, the need to underpin would have been avoided and the total cost of repair to the building would have been only £14,000. On the other hand the judge has found that, once the council declined to remove the tree, the underpinning and piling costs were reasonably incurred, despite the council's trench.

[34] ... If reasonableness between neighbours is the key to the solution of problems in this field, it cannot be right to visit the authority or owner responsible for a tree with a large bill for underpinning without giving them notice of the damage and the opportunity of avoiding further damage by removal of the tree. Should they elect to preserve the tree for environmental reasons, they may fairly be expected to bear the cost of underpinning or other reasonably necessary remedial works; and the party on whom the cost has fallen may recover it, even though there may be elements of hitherto unsatisfied pre-proprietorship damage or protection for the future. But, as a general proposition, I think that the defendant is entitled to notice and a reasonable opportunity of abatement before liability for remedial expenditure can arise. In this case Westminster had ample notice and time before the underpinning and piling, and is in my opinion liable.

[Lord Cooke considered developments elsewhere in the world and concluded:]

[38] In the end, in my opinion, the law can be summed up in the proposition that, where there is a continuing nuisance of which the defendant knew or ought to have known, reasonable remedial expenditure may be recovered by the owner who has had to incur it. In the present case this was Flecksun ...'

Halsey v Esso Petroleum Co Ltd
[1961] 2 All ER 145 Queen's Bench Division

The defendant's depot received deliveries of oil by barge and heated the oil to allow it to be pumped more easily. The chimneys disgorged acid smuts and oily drops which damaged the plaintiff's clothes hung out to dry and car parked on the road. There was noise and vibration at night from the boiler and pumps, and also a pungent and nauseating smell. The plaintiff and others in the street were also adversely affected by the noise of tankers collecting oil as they entered and left the depot, and noises associated with the loading of tankers.

Veale J: '... As long ago as 1865, in *St Helen's Smelting Co v Tipping* Lord Westbury LC said:

> "... in matters of this description it appears to me that it is a very desirable thing to mark the difference between an action brought for a nuisance upon the ground that the alleged nuisance produces material injury to the property, and an action brought for a nuisance on the ground that the thing alleged to be a nuisance is productive of sensible personal discomfort. With regard to the latter, namely, the personal inconvenience and interference with one's enjoyment, one's quiet, one's personal freedom, anything that discomposes or injuriously affects the senses or the nerves, whether that may or may not be denominated a nuisance, must undoubtedly depend greatly on the circumstances of the place where the thing complained of actually occurs. If a man lives in a town, it is necessary that he should subject himself to the consequences of those operations of trade which may be carried on in his immediate locality, which are actually necessary for trade and commerce, and also for the enjoyment of property, and for the benefit of the inhabitants of the town and of the public at large. If a man lives in a street where there are numerous shops, and a shop is opened next door to him, which is carried on in a fair and reasonable way, he has no ground for complaint, because to himself individually there may arise much discomfort from the trade carried on in that shop. But when an occupation is carried on by one person in the neighbourhood of another, and the result of that trade, or occupation, or business, is a material injury to property, then there unquestionably arises a very different consideration. I think, my Lords, that in a case of that description, the submission which is required from persons living in society to that amount of discomfort which may be necessary for the legitimate and free exercise of the trade of their neighbours, would not apply to circumstances the immediate result of which is sensible injury to the value of the property."

In this case smell and noise come into one category, actual deposits in the way of harmful smuts and oily drops come into the other. I bear in mind the observations of Lord Loreburn LC, in *Polsue & Alfieri Ltd v Rushmer* ...:

"The law of nuisance undoubtedly is elastic, as was stated by Lord Halsbury in the case of *Colls v Home & Colonial Stores Ltd*. He said: 'What may be called the uncertainty of the test may also be described as its elasticity. A dweller in towns cannot expect to have as pure air, as free from smoke, smell, and noise as if he lived in the country, and distant from other dwellings, and yet an excess of smoke, smell, and noise may give a cause of action, but in each of such cases it becomes a question of degree, and the question is in each case whether it amounts to a nuisance which will give a right of action.' This is a question of fact."

… One useful approach to the considerations to be taken into account in a case of alleged nuisance by noise is to be found in the judgment of Luxmoore J in *Vanderpant v Mayfair Hotel Co Ltd* …:

"Apart from any right which may have been acquired against him by contract, grant or prescription, every person is entitled as against his neighbour to the comfortable and healthy enjoyment of the premises occupied by him, and in deciding whether, in any particular case, his right has been interfered with and a nuisance thereby caused, it is necessary to determine whether the act complained of is an inconvenience materially interfering with the ordinary physical comfort of human existence, not merely according to elegant or dainty modes and habits of living, but according to plain and sober and simple notions obtaining among English people: see *Walter v Selfe* and the remarks of Knight-Bruce V-C. It is also necessary to take into account the circumstances and character of the locality in which the complainant is living. The making or causing of such a noise as materially interferes with the comfort of a neighbour, when judged by the standard to which I have just referred, constitutes an actionable nuisance, and it is no answer to say that the best known means have been taken to reduce or prevent the noise complained of, or that the cause of the nuisance is the exercise of a business or trade in a reasonable and proper manner. Again, the question of the existence of a nuisance is one of degree and depends on the circumstances of the case."

So far as the present case is concerned, liability for nuisance by harmful deposits could be established by proving damage by the deposits to the property in question, provided, of course, that the injury was not merely trivial. Negligence is not an ingredient of the cause of action, and the character of the neighbourhood is not a matter to be taken into consideration. On the other hand nuisance by smell or noise is something to which no absolute standard can be applied. It is always a question of degree whether the interference with comfort or convenience is sufficiently serious to constitute a nuisance. The character of the neighbourhood is very relevant and all the relevant circumstances have to be taken into account. What might be a nuisance in one area is by no means necessarily so in another. In an urban area, everyone must put up with a certain amount of discomfort and annoyance from the activities of neighbours, and the law must strike a fair and reasonable balance between the right of the plaintiff on the one hand to the undisturbed enjoyment of his property, and the right of the defendant on the other hand to use his property for his own lawful enjoyment. That is how I approach this case.

It may be possible in some cases to prove that noise or smell have in fact diminished the value of the plaintiff's property in the market. That consideration does not arise in this case, and no evidence has been called in regard to it. The standard in respect of discomfort and inconvenience from noise and smell that I have to apply is that of the ordinary reasonable and responsible person who lives in this particular area of Fulham. This is not necessarily the same as the standard which the plaintiff chooses to set up for himself. It is the standard of the ordinary man, and the ordinary man, who may well like peace and quiet, will not complain for instance of the noise of traffic if he chooses to live on a main street in an urban centre, nor of the reasonable noises of industry, if he chooses to live alongside a factory.

Nuisance is commonly regarded as a tort in respect of land ... In this connexion the allegation of damage to the plaintiff's motor calls for special consideration, since the allegation is that when the offending smuts from the defendants' chimney alighted on it, the motor car was not actually on land in the plaintiff's occupation, but was on the public highway outside his door. Whether or not a claim in respect of private nuisance lies for damage to the motor car in these circumstances, in my judgment such damage is covered by the doctrine in *Rylands v Fletcher*. If it be the fact that harmful sulphuric acid or harmful sulphate escaped from the defendants' premises and damaged the motor car in the public highway, I am bound by the decision of the Court of Appeal in *Charing Cross Electricity Supply Co v Hydraulic Power Co*, and *Miles v Forest Rock Granite Co (Leicestershire) Ltd*, in neither of which cases was the plaintiff in occupation of land. This doctrine of *Rylands v Fletcher* ... applies to the sulphuric acid or sulphate in smuts or oily drops wherever they alight: on washing hung out to dry, as well as on to a motor car in the street. In my judgment the plaintiff is also right in saying that if the motor car was damaged in this way while on the public highway, it is a public nuisance in respect of which he has suffered special damage ... I have no evidence as to the period during which the plaintiff's motor car was outside his door; but even if the plaintiff was using the road as a place to garage his motor car, and he was not entitled to do so, I do not regard those facts as disentitling him to claim damages in respect of injury to the motor car ...

I have no doubt at all that the defendants had been the cause of the emission into the atmosphere of noxious smuts which had caused damage to the plaintiff's washing and to his motor car. The smuts are noxious acid smuts, and it does not matter whether they contain sulphate or sulphuric acid. For this damage the defendants in my judgment are liable, both as for a nuisance and under *Rylands v Fletcher*. It is not necessary for the plaintiff to prove or for me to decide precisely why this has happened. It is necessary for the plaintiff to prove the fact of it happening, and this I am satisfied that he has done ...

This nuisance to the plaintiff may, partly at all events, be due to the shortcomings of one of the chimney stacks. I do not know and I do not have to decide. The fact is that noxious smuts have come from the defendants' depot and have done damage.

[Veale J examined the facts concerning the smell and noise from the depot and concluded that they constituted a nuisance; he then examined the facts concerning the noise connected with the use of the highway, and continued:]

It is said by the defendants that since the public highway is for the use of everyone, the plaintiff cannot complain if all that the defendants do is to make use of their right to use the public highway. I agree, if that is all that the defendants have done. If a person makes an unreasonable use of the public highway, for instance, by parking stationary vehicles on it, a member of the public who suffers special damage has a cause of action against him for public nuisance. Similarly, in my view, if a person makes an unreasonable use of the public highway by concentrating in one small area of the highway vehicles in motion and a member of the public suffers special damage, he is equally entitled to complain, although in most cases concentration of moving as opposed to stationary vehicles will be more likely to be reasonable. This is a question of reasonable user ...

In the particular circumstances of this case I do not think that it matters very much whether one regards the alleged nuisance by vehicular noise as a private or a public nuisance ... [in private nuisance] the ground of responsibility is the possession and control of the land from which the nuisance proceeds, though Lord Wright [in *Sedleigh-Denfield v O'Callaghan*] refers to "possibly certain anomalous exceptions". Public nuisance, on the other hand, can, as Denning LJ said in the Court of Appeal in *Southport Corporation v Esso Petroleum Co Ltd* cover a multitude of sins, great and small ...

Denning LJ, on the facts of that particular case, thought that there was no private nuisance because the offending oil had come from a ship at sea, and with that Lord Radcliffe in the House of Lords agreed.

In the present case the offending noise is partly in the depot before and as the vehicles emerge into the highway, and as they re-enter, and partly in the short stretch of highway immediately outside the entrance and exit to the depot, which is also immediately outside the plaintiff's house. There is no element of obstruction of or danger on and to the highway as such. The noise is an interference with the enjoyment by the plaintiff of his house. It is not an interference with the rights of the plaintiff or his visitors as members of the public to use the highway. The fact is that the defendants concentrate at their premises a number of particularly heavy and noisy vehicles. They send them out at night, making a very loud noise as they go, and they direct them to return, and the vehicles make a further very loud noise as they come back.

The noise outside and inside the plaintiff's house is, in my judgment, attributable to the defendants' mode of operation of their depot, and the principles of law to be applied seem to me to be the same as those in respect of alleged nuisance by noise of the plant itself. Applying those principles which involve consideration of the whole of the relevant circumstances, I hold that the defendants are also guilty of nuisance in this respect, but only during the night shift. I do not think that any proper comparison can be made with noisy undertakings like railways, which are carried on under statutory authority, nor, in my judgment, can Rainville Road, Fulham, properly be compared with the Great North Road. It is said that a decision in the plaintiff's favour on this point involves making new law. I do not think so. I do not regard motor vehicles, even the defendants' tankers, as dangerous within *Rylands v Fletcher*; but I do not really think that there is anything new in the circumstances of this case, if the defendants are held liable for nuisance in respect of this particular noise. Part of the offending noise, indeed, comes from inside the depot itself, as the vehicles enter or leave. The rest of it is directly related to the operation of the depot. In *Bartlett v Marshall* the nuisance of noise, as in the present case, was committed at all events largely on the public highway. In *Vanderpant v Mayfair Hotel Co Ltd* Luxmoore J granted an injunction in respect of nuisance by noise committed by the staff of the defendants' hotel as they arrived at and left the hotel, and by the delivery of goods from the street to the hotel premises ...

If these cases are more properly to be regarded as instances of public nuisance, I do not think, as already indicated, that the result is any different. If I treat this part of the case as public nuisance, as counsel for the plaintiff argued in the alternative, I ask myself: Is it reasonable to concentrate outside the plaintiff's house during the night, not on odd occasions, but every night, and not once a night, but at irregular intervals during the night and early hours of the morning, particularly noisy vehicles, sometimes in convoy ...? I bear in mind the importance of the defendants' business. I also, I hope, bear in mind all the circumstances, including the circumstance that a man is entitled to sleep during the night in his own house. I have no hesitation in saying that the plaintiff has satisfied me that the defendants' user of their tankers in all the circumstances is unreasonable. On this view they are liable as for a public nuisance, since it is conceded that noise can be special damage if it affects the plaintiff more than the ordinary member of the public. On this alternative view also the defendants are liable, since I find that the plaintiff has indeed suffered a special damage which is substantial and not transient or fleeting.

The joint effect of the noise of the tankers and of the plant has been, in my judgment, to create a very serious interference with the enjoyment by the plaintiff of [his home]. Some noise has in the past been made by the activities of the drivers as distinct from the noise of the vehicles themselves. The defendants have been at great pains to keep this noise to the minimum, and in my judgment, it is the vehicles rather than the drivers themselves which are the trouble. I think a noise made by drivers and workmen might easily of itself become a nuisance if they are not continually kept under strict control. I emphasise that the plaintiff lives almost opposite to the entrance to the depot. By saying that in my view the degree of noise of the tankers constitutes in his case a nuisance, I do not want it to be thought that I should necessarily come to the same conclusion in so far as residents in other streets are concerned. But there is more than one household where the occupants have to sleep in a room at the back instead of in the front, and also have to keep their windows shut at night in order to escape so far as possible from the noise ...'

Comment

(1)   For public nuisance see p 679; for *Rylands v Fletcher* see p 691. In *Gillingham BC v Medway (Chatham) Dock Co Ltd* the court refused to regard *Halsey v Esso Petroleum* as wrongly decided insofar as nuisance from the highway was concerned.

(2)   It is the reasonableness of the conduct that is decisive. It is this, measured in objective terms, that renders the defendant's conduct unlawful on the basis of the test of Knight-Bruce V-C in *Walter v Selfe*. This involves the consideration of a number of factors, e.g. the suitability of the locality, nature and intensity of the interference, duration, repetition and malice. Veale J commented:

> 'Applying and adapting the well-known words of Knight-Bruce V-C in *Walter v Selfe*, this inconvenience is ... more than fanciful, more than one of mere delicacy or fastidiousness. It is an inconvenience materially interfering with the ordinary comfort physically of human existence, not merely according to the elegant or dainty modes of living, but according to plain and sober and simple notions among ordinary people living in this part of Fulham.'

(3)   Where the nature of the invasion of another's interest is 'sensible material injury to property' this can never be justified as being reasonable by reference to the locality, see *St Helen's Smelting v Tipping* where the plaintiff complained that the noxious substances emitted by the defendant's copper smelting works had damaged the trees on his estate. Lord Hoffmann in *Hunter v Canary Wharf* described *St Helen's Smelting Co v Tipping* as a landmark case which 'drew the line beyond which rural and landed England did not have to accept external costs imposed upon it by industrial pollution'.

(4)   In *Halsey v Esso Petroleum* Veale J reaches the conclusion that there is a nuisance whether or not the noise from the road may be classified as a private or a public nuisance. In the context of the case this is correct since it was the arrangements for the use of the premises which constituted the state of affairs amounting to a nuisance. In the same way in *Attorney-General v Corke* (gypsies) and *Thompson Schwab v Costaki* (prostitutes), it was the underlying use of the premises which gave rise to the nuisance. This point is explored further in

Lippiatt v South Gloucestershire Council, which also makes the point that offensive behaviour may occur on the land of the claimant even though the state of affairs giving rise to this relates to the defendant's use of the defendant's own property. See also *Hussain v Lancaster City Council* and *Page Motors v Epsom*, p 670.

(5)   In *Harrison v Southwark* it was said that:

'a man who pulls down his house for the purpose of building a new one no doubt causes considerable inconvenience to his next door neighbours during the process of demolition; but he is not responsible as for a nuisance if he uses all reasonable skill and care to avoid annoyance to his neighbour by the works of demolition. Nor is he liable to an action even though the noise and dust and the consequent annoyance be such as would constitute a nuisance if the same, instead of being created for the purpose of demolition of the house, had been created in sheer wantonness, or in the execution of works for a purpose involving a permanent continuance of the noise and dust. For the law, in adjudging what constitutes a nuisance, does take into consideration both the object and the duration of that which is said to constitute the nuisance.'

See also *Matania v National Provincial, Grosvenor Hotel v Hamilton, Andreae v Selfridge* and *Vanderpant v Mayfair Hotel*. One must put up with trivial interferences, but sometimes the effect of a small amount of noise may be considerable, e.g. one night's sleep as in *Andreae v Selfridge*. But usually to be material the interference will have to be continuous or at least regular.

Southwark London Borough Council v Mills
Baxter v Camden London Borough Council
[1999] 4 All ER 449 House of Lords

The appellants, T and B, were tenants of the respondent councils, one lived in a block of flats and the other in the first-floor flat in a converted Victorian house. They both complained of being able to hear all the normal day-to-day sounds made by their neighbours but did not allege that the neighbours were acting unreasonably. The flats had no sound insulation. The consequent lack of privacy caused tension and distress. The tenants alleged that there was a breach of a covenant of quiet enjoyment, and in addition B alleged that the council was liable in nuisance.

The House of Lords held that: (1) neither expressly nor by implication of law did the tenancy agreement contain a warranty by the landlord that the flat had sound insulation or was fit to live in; the covenant for quiet enjoyment had not been breached since the tenants had taken the properties as they stood; (2) the neighbours were not committing a nuisance since the noise was caused by the ordinary enjoyment of the property, therefore the councils could not be liable for authorising them to commit a nuisance.

The extract which follows concerns only the issue of nuisance.

Lord Millett: '... The law of nuisance is concerned with balancing the conflicting interests of adjoining owners. It is often said to be encapsulated in the Latin maxim *sic utere tuo ut alienum non laedas*. This suggests a strict liability, but in practice the law seeks to protect the competing interests of both parties so far as it can. For this purpose it employs the control mechanism described by Lord Goff of Chieveley in *Cambridge Water Co v Eastern Counties Leather plc* as "the principle of reasonable user – the principle of give and take".

The use of the word "reasonable" in this context is apt to be misunderstood. It is no answer to an action for nuisance to say that the defendant is only making reasonable use of his land ... What is reasonable from the point of view of one party may be completely unreasonable from the point of view of the other. It is not enough for a landowner to act reasonably in his own interest. He must also be considerate of the interest of his neighbour. The governing principle is good neighbourliness, and this involves reciprocity. A landowner must show the same consideration for his neighbour as he would expect his neighbour to show for him. The principle which limits the liability of a landowner who causes a sensible interference with his neighbour's enjoyment of his property is that stated by Bramwell B in *Bamford v Turnley*:

> "There must be, then, some principle on which such cases must be excepted. It seems to me that that principle may be deduced from the character of these cases, and is this, viz. that those acts necessary for the common and ordinary use and occupation of land and houses may be done, if conveniently done, without subjecting those who do them to an action ... There is an obvious necessity for such a principle as I have mentioned. It is as much for the advantage of one owner as of another; for the very nuisance the one complains of, as the result of the ordinary use of his neighbour's land, he himself will create in the ordinary use of his own, and the reciprocal nuisances are of a comparatively trifling character. The convenience of such a rule may be indicated by calling it a rule of give and take, live and let live."

It is true that Bramwell B appears to justify his conclusion by the fact that the resulting nuisances are normally of a comparatively trifling character, and that is not the present case. But he cannot have intended the defence to be confined to such cases. Trifling nuisances have never been actionable, and Bramwell B was searching for the principle which exempts from liability activities which would otherwise be actionable. His conclusion was that two conditions must be satisfied: the acts complained of must (i) "be necessary for the common and ordinary use and occupation of land and houses" and (ii) must be "conveniently done", that is to say done with proper consideration for the interests of neighbouring occupiers. Where these two conditions are satisfied, no action will lie for that substantial interference with the use and enjoyment of his neighbour's land that would otherwise have been an actionable nuisance.

In *Ball v Ray* the occupier of a house in a street in Mayfair had many years previously converted the ground floor into a stable. A new occupier altered the location of the stable so that the noise of the horses became an annoyance to the next-door neighbour and prevented him from letting his house as lodgings. Lord Selborne LC said:

> "In making out a case of nuisance of this character, there are always two things to be considered, the right of the plaintiff and the right of the defendant. If the houses adjoining each other are so built that from the commencement of their existence it is manifest that each adjoining inhabitant was intended to enjoy his own property for the ordinary purposes for which it and all the different parts of it were constructed, then so long as the house is so used there is nothing that can be regarded in law as a nuisance which the other party has a right to prevent. But, on the other hand, if either party turns his house, or any portion of it, to unusual purposes in such a manner as to produce a substantial injury to his neighbour, it appears to me that that is not according to principle or authority a reasonable use of his own property; and his neighbour, shewing substantial injury, is entitled to protection. I do not regard it as a reasonable or as a usual manner of using the front portion of a dwelling house in such a street as Green Street, that it should be turned into stables for horses; and, if it is so used, then the proprietor is bound to take care that it is so used as not to be a substantial annoyance, detrimental to the comfort and to the value of the neighbours' property."

The stabling of horses may have been necessary for the common and ordinary use and occupation of a dwelling house in 1873, but the layout of the premises was so altered that it was no longer "conveniently done".

In my opinion Tuckey LJ [in the Court of Appeal] was correct in stating that the ordinary use of residential premises without more is not capable of amounting to a nuisance. As he rightly explained, this is why adjoining owner-occupiers are not liable to one another if the party wall between their flats is not an adequate sound barrier so that the sounds of everyday activities in one flat substantially interfere with the use and enjoyment of the other.

Counsel for B is prepared to argue if necessary that the tenants of the other flats could be held liable to her in nuisance. In this he would be wrong; their activities are not merely reasonable, they are the necessary and inevitable incidents of the ordinary occupation of residential property. They are unavoidable if those tenants are to continue in occupation of their flats. But his primary submission is that the Council is liable in nuisance as the common landlord. In this he is, in my opinion, plainly wrong.

Once the activities complained of have been found to constitute an actionable nuisance, more than one party may be held legally responsible. The person or persons directly responsible for the activities in question are liable; but so too is anyone who authorised them. Landlords have been held liable for nuisances committed by their tenants on this basis. It is not enough for them to be aware of the nuisance and take no steps to prevent it. They must either participate directly in the commission of the nuisance, or they must be taken to have authorised it by letting the property: see *Malzy v Eichholz*. But they cannot be held liable in tort for having authorised the commission of an actionable nuisance unless what they have authorised is an actionable nuisance. The logic of the proposition is obvious. A landlord cannot be liable to an action for authorising his tenant to do something that would not be actionable if he did it himself.

Counsel for B relies on the fact that the Council not only let the adjoining flats for residential occupation but did so without first installing adequate sound insulation. It thereby authorised the use of the flats for residential occupation in circumstances which, the argument runs, inevitably caused a nuisance. But in my opinion this takes the matter no further. What B must show, but cannot show, is that they inevitably caused an actionable nuisance. The Council has no obligation to soundproof her property to keep noise out, whether it emanates from her neighbours or from traffic or aircraft. It is under no positive duty to her to soundproof the adjoining flats in order to keep the noise in; such a duty could only arise by statute or contract. It is under no duty to bring the nuisance to an end, whether by regaining possession of the flats or by soundproofing the premises, unless it is an actionable nuisance.

My Lords, I would not wish to be thought indifferent to B's plight. I have the greatest sympathy for her. But the fact remains that she took a flat on the first floor of a house, knowing that the ground and second floors were also occupied as residential flats, and expecting their occupants to live normal lives. That is all that they are doing. She has no cause to complain of their activities, which mirror her own; or of the Council for having permitted them by letting the adjoining flats. Her real complaint is, and always has been, of the absence of adequate sound insulation. Her complaint, however well founded, cannot be redressed by the law of tort; any remedy must lie in statute or contract ...'

Comment

The case provides a useful reminder of what it is that comprises an actionable nuisance and demonstrates that tort cannot be viewed in isolation from other possible remedies. The case also highlights the limited scope of the judicial function. According to the speech of Lord Millett, the cost to Southwark London Borough Council of remedying the specific insulation problem would be £37 million (£1.271 billion to bring the housing stock up to modern standards in general). Lord Millett said:

'These cases raise issues of priority in the allocation of resources. Such issues must be resolved by the democratic process, national and local. The judges are not equipped to resolve them. All that we can do is to say that there is nothing in the relevant tenancy agreements or current legislation, or in the common law, which would enable the tenants to obtain redress through the courts.'

The need for there to be a multi-agency approach to social problems, and to look elsewhere than the law of tort, was also the subject of comment in the case of *Hussain v Lancaster City Council*, p 631.

Lippiatt and another v South Gloucestershire Council [1999] 4 All ER 149 Court of Appeal

The plaintiffs were tenant farmers of land which, they alleged, was seriously affected by the activities of a large group of travellers who had occupied the defendant council's nearby land as trespassers between October 1991 and June 1994, when they were evicted. The council tolerated this 'unauthorised encampment' and provided toilet, water and other facilities. It was alleged that the travellers frequently trespassed on the plaintiffs' land and committed many serious acts of vandalism and harassment. At first instance the judge held that there could not be a nuisance because the activities of the travellers had not involved the use of the council's land. The Court of Appeal held that the facts alleged revealed a tort of nuisance despite the fact that the activities took place on the plaintiffs' land and not on the council's land.

Evans LJ: ' ... The allegation ... is of activities by the travellers which took place off the council's land and in all respects save one on the land of the plaintiffs themselves ... Apart from that one exception, [counsel for the council] submits that no actionable nuisance is alleged, because the activities relied upon were those of independent third parties, the travellers, and they took place outside the council's land ...

A-G v Corke and the later case of *Smith v Scott*, where the liability of a landlord was also in issue, can be considered together. In *A-G v Corke* Bennett J granted an injunction restraining the owner of a disused brick field from allowing the occupiers of caravans, whom he had permitted to use his land, from committing acts, which included trespass, in the neighbourhood of the property. He did so on the express basis that the acts complained of gave rise to a public nuisance in respect of which the Attorney General and the local authority could sue. His judgment includes:

"The acts which, I think, give rise to a danger to the health of the neighbourhood, are acts done, not on the defendant's land, but off it by people who live on it" and he continued:

> "The plaintiffs have, however, failed to prove that anything done on the
> defendant's land gives rise to a complaint by the neighbours ... All the acts
> which do interfere with the comfort and convenience of the neighbourhood,
> and which threaten the health of the neighbourhood, are acts done not on
> the defendant's land, but off it, by people whom the defendant brings on to it
> for his profit."

He then addressed the argument for the defendant, reported as "The defendant
cannot be made responsible for acts done by the caravan-dwellers off the
defendant's property". [Counsel] submitted in reply: "The wrongful act of the
defendant is the placing of caravans on the land." The judge held that liability was
established under the principle in *Rylands v Fletcher*, which he said:

> " ... affords in my judgment a basis upon which the defendant can be made
> responsible in law for the nuisance which undoubtedly exists, on the facts, in
> the vicinity of this camp, and which nuisance is caused by some of the people
> whom he brings there for his own profit."

[Counsel for the plaintiffs] therefore is entitled to submit that the point raised by
the council in the present case was decided there against the defendant in an
action for nuisance; but equally, [counsel for the council] is right to say that the
claim was brought in respect of a public nuisance, and he could have added that the
decision was subsequently the subject matter of academic discussion (see e.g. *Clerk
and Lindsell* para 19–07). But the law is clarified by the judgment of Pennycuick V-C
in *Smith v Scott*. The plaintiffs alleged that a nuisance was created by tenants of the
defendant's property. The nuisance included damage caused to the plaintiffs'
property as well as noise disturbance near it ("near no 27"). Pennycuick V-C said
that he was "satisfied beyond doubt, indeed it is not challenged, that the conduct of
the Scott family as a whole was altogether intolerable both in respect of physical
damage and of noise". He referred to *A-G v Corke* and doubted whether the rule in
Rylands v Fletcher did apply in that case, but he expressed no doubt as to the
correctness of the decision:

> "I should respectfully have thought that *Attorney-General v Corke* could at least
> equally well have been decided on the basis that the landowner there was in
> possession of the property and was himself liable in nuisance for the acts of
> his licensees: see *White v Jameson*."

This judgment therefore provides clear authority for [counsel for the plaintiffs']
submission that *A-G v Corke* was correctly decided and, more generally, that there is
no rule of law which prevents the owner-occupier of land from being held liable for
the tort of nuisance by reason of the activities of his licensees which take place off
his land.

The submission is further supported by the judgments in *Thompson-Schwab v Costaki*. The plaintiff lived at 13 Chesterfield Street. The defendants used the next-door property, No 12, for the purposes of –

> "carrying on their practices as prostitutes; they were … walking for the purposes of solicitation towards Curzon Street, returning to the house with the men whom they had solicited, and then the men would leave the house and the women would leave after them."

Wynn-Parry J granted an interlocutory injunction against "using the premises for the purposes of prostitution" and this was upheld by the Court of Appeal. The submission was that "no case has come before the courts in which this kind of activity has been held to constitute a common law nuisance". The primary argument was that, whilst the susceptibilities of ordinary people might be shocked, there was no material (physical) interference with the plaintiffs' land or their use of it. Lord Evershed MR described the basis of the defendants' (alleged) liability as follows:

> "The perambulations of the prostitutes and of their customers is something which is obvious, which is blatant, and which as I think the first plaintiff has shown *prima facie* to constitute not a mere hurt of his sensibilities as a fastidious man, but so as to constitute a sensible interference with the comfortable and convenient enjoyment of his residence …"

This he described as "the alleged nuisance". Romer LJ made it clear that the plaintiff alleged a private nuisance and Parker LJ agreed with both judgments. In *Hunter v Canary Wharf Ltd, Hunter v London Docklands Development Corp* in a quite different context the House of Lords considered the legal nature of a private nuisance in some detail. In the leading speech, Lord Goff stated the general principle and referred to *Thompson-Schwab's* case with qualified approval:

> "Indeed, for an action in private nuisance to lie in respect of interference with the plaintiff's enjoyment of his land, it will generally arise from something emanating from the defendant's land. Such an emanation may take many forms – noise, dirt, fumes, a noxious smell, vibration and suchlike. Occasionally, activities on the defendant's land are in themselves so offensive to neighbours as to constitute an actionable nuisance, as in *Thompson-Schwab v Costaki*, where the sight of prostitutes and their clients entering and leaving neighbouring premises were held to fall in that category. Such cases must, however, be relatively rare."

It has not been suggested, therefore, in any reported case since the unsuccessful argument in *A-G v Corke* that the defendant occupier of land cannot be held liable in nuisance when the activities complained of were those of his licensees and they took place off his land. I would hold, before coming to consider *Page Motors Ltd v Epsom and Ewell BC* and *Hussain v Lancaster City Council*, that there is no such rule of law. The judgments in *Thompson-Schwab's* case and *Smith v Scott* are clear authority against it, although it can be said that in neither case was the particular issue raised. Since it had been raised and rejected in *A-G v Corke*, that suggests to my mind that the reason for not raising it in the later cases was not that it was overlooked. *Thompson-Schwab's* case might be distinguished on the ground that the activities of the prostitutes and their customers, whilst taking place off the defendant's land, did so on the highway rather than on the plaintiff's land itself. But that would mean that that there was no nuisance if the prostitutes solicited from the doorway of the plaintiff's home. That in my view would be an absurd distinction to make.

The principle, as stated by Lord Goff with whom Lord Lloyd agreed, is that as a general rule some form of "emanation" from the defendant's land is required. On analysis, what "emanated" in the present case was the travellers themselves. I do not find this form of emanation difficult to accept. If it was somehow excluded from the definition of a nuisance, then any number of examples come to mind where the distinction would be artificial in the extreme. Keeping fierce dogs and allowing them to roam would be a nuisance; taking them onto the neighbour's land and releasing them there would not. [Counsel for the council] submits that the defendant cannot be held liable in nuisance for the deliberate act of a third party. But that is not generally true, because there clearly can be liability for a nuisance created deliberately by a third party, even a trespasser, on the defendants' land. If there was an exception limited to deliberate acts off the defendant's land, then that merely restates the general submission which, for the reasons given, I would reject.

So I come finally to the *Page Motors* case and to *Hussain's* case. The former is noteworthy, in my judgment, only because no attention was paid to the question whether the acts complained of took place on or off the defendant's land. For the most part they were the former, and the alleged nuisance was of the conventional and usual kind. (The principal issue decided by the court was whether the defendant could be held liable as occupier for the activities of trespassers on his land.) ... In *Hussain's* case the defendant was held not liable in its capacity as the local housing authority for what the plaintiffs alleged was a nuisance created by its tenants on the local housing estate. The plaintiffs were shopowners and they claimed to have suffered severe harassment from tenants which included threats, racial abuse, the throwing of missiles and attempts to burn down their premises. They alleged that "the harassment comes from a number of identifiable people both men, including teenagers and boys, and women". Some individuals had been prosecuted, and a total number of 106 was involved.

The first question considered by the court was whether, on these alleged facts, the plaintiffs could establish a claim against the defendants in nuisance. Applying "Professor Newark's statement of general principle that its essence is that the defendant's use of the defendant's land interferes with the plaintiff's enjoyment of the plaintiff's land", which was "amply vindicated" by Lord Goff's approval in *Hunter v Canary Wharf Ltd, Hunter v London Docklands Development Corp*, the court held that the acts complained of "did not involve the tenants' use of the tenants' land and therefore fell outside the scope of the tort". In a later passage, Hirst LJ distinguished the *Page Motors* case where the conduct of gypsies "involved use (or rather misuse) of the council's land".

In my judgment, the facts alleged in *Hussain's* case were materially different from those in the present case. The disturbance complained of in *Hussain's* case was a public nuisance for which the individual perpetrators could be held liable, and they were identified as individuals who lived in council property; but their conduct was not in any sense linked to, nor did it emanate from, the homes where they lived. Here, the allegation is that the travellers were allowed to congregate on the council's land and that they used it as a base for the unlawful activities of which the plaintiffs, as neighbours, complain. It is at least arguable that this can give rise to liability in nuisance, and so the claim should not be struck out; and it seems to me that upon proof of the alleged facts, and subject to any defences, e.g. the statutory responsibilities of the council, such liability could be established.

The view taken in *Hussain's* case was that the alleged nuisance was "originally perpetrated by the culprits". It may be that the correct analysis, where it is alleged that the owner/occupier of the land is liable for the activities of his licensees, is that he is liable, if at all, for a nuisance which he himself has created by allowing the troublemakers to occupy his land and to use it as a base for causing unlawful disturbance to his neighbours. Counsel so submitted in 1932 [in *A-G v Corke*]. If that is correct, then strictly the question whether the owner/occupier has "adopted" a nuisance created by the travellers ... may not arise. For that reason, I express no other view than that, on the facts alleged in the present case, the council's objection that the claim in nuisance cannot succeed, as a matter of law, must be rejected, and the appeal should be allowed.'

Comment

(1) It was not alleged that there was either a tenancy or an adoption of the nuisance and so the principles raised in *Smith v Scott* and *Sedleigh-Denfield v O'Callaghan* did not arise.

(2) In *Hussain's* case Thorpe LJ referred to the nature of the problem facing the parties and said:

' ... I was particularly impressed by two considerations: first that the plaintiffs have been the victims of racial harassment much of which measures high on the scale of criminality. In the multi-disciplinary response the police would seem to be the agency with primary responsibility. Second, the perpetrators of these crimes are legion and in some instances clearly not in legal relationship with the city council ... Although these considerations may be said to be more relevant to trial than to a strike-out application, they fortify the conclusion that the wrongs which the plaintiffs have suffered must be fought by multi-disciplinary co-operation and not by civil suit against one of the relevant agencies.'

Gillingham Borough Council v Medway (Chatham) Dock Co Ltd and others
[1992] 3 All ER 923 Queen's Bench Division

Gillingham Borough Council brought an action under their statutory powers in the Local Government Act 1972, s 222 'to promote or protect the interests of the inhabitants in its area'. The council alleged that there was a public nuisance caused by the company which operated former naval dockyards as a commercial port. The allegations centred upon the use of residential roads at night by a large number of heavy goods vehicles. Planning permission for the use of the premises as a port had been given despite the evidence that there would be extensive use of one particular entrance both day and night. The issue for the court was whether or not the considerable disturbance which occurred was reasonable having regard to the locality. The court held that the locality had to be assessed by reference to the grant of planning permission, rather than the prior state of affairs.

Buckley J: '... I have not been referred to any case which has directly considered the interplay between planning permission and the law of nuisance. Many cases, of course, have considered statutory authority as a defence to nuisance ... [In] *Tate & Lyle Industries Ltd v Greater London Council* ... Lord Templeman said:

"The defence of statutory authority to an action for nuisance was summarised in the speech of Lord Wilberforce in *Allen v Gulf Oil Refining Ltd* as follows:'It is now well settled that where Parliament by express direction or by necessary implication has authorised the construction and use of an undertaking or works, that carries with it an authority to do what is authorised with immunity from any action based on nuisance. The right of action is taken away ... To this there is made the qualification, or condition, that the statutory powers are exercised without 'negligence', that word here being used in a special sense so as to require the undertaker, as a condition of obtaining immunity from action, to carry out the work and conduct the operation with all reasonable regard and care for the interests of other persons ..."

Doubtless one of the reasons for this approach is that Parliament is presumed to have considered the interests of those who will be affected by the undertaking or works and decided that benefits from them should outweigh any necessary adverse side effects. I believe that principle should be utilised in respect of planning permission. Parliament has set up a statutory framework and delegated the task of balancing the interests of the community against those of individuals and of holding the scales between individuals to the local planning authority. There is the right to object to any proposed grant, provision for appeals and inquiries, and ultimately the minister decides. There is the added safeguard of judicial review. If a planning authority grants permission for a particular construction or use in its area it is almost certain that some local inhabitants will be prejudiced in the quiet enjoyment of their properties. Can they defeat the scheme simply by bringing an action in nuisance? If not, why not? It has been said, no doubt correctly, that planning permission is not a licence to commit nuisance and that a planning authority has no jurisdiction to authorise nuisance. However, a planning authority can, through its development plans and decisions, alter the character of a neighbourhood. That may have the effect of rendering innocent activities which, prior to the change, would have been an actionable nuisance ...

The point arises in this case. Prior to January 1984 [the] roads had been relatively quiet residential roads ... It seems to me that I must judge the present claim in nuisance by reference to the present character of the neighbourhood pursuant to the planning permission for use of the dockyard as a commercial port. Thus, these roads are now in the neighbourhood of and lead immediately to a commercial port which operates 24 hours per day. In those circumstances I hold that the undoubted disturbance to the residents is not actionable. [Counsel] urged that even adopting this approach, I should find that the operation of the port was unreasonable and without proper regard for the interests of the residents ... This argument has its attractions, and I note by way of analogy with the statutory authority cases that it is only a nuisance inevitably resulting from the authorised works on which immunity is conferred. However, the planning permission here was to operate a commercial port in a precisely delineated area. It was not merely permissive as in the sense of the general power conferred by the Metropolitan Port Act 1867, considered in *Metropolitan Asylum District Managers v Hill* ...

The dock company could not operate a commercial port at the dockyard without disturbing nearby residents. The aim of any commercial undertaking is to operate to the best advantage or in other words to do as much trade as it can. It would be quite unrealistic to attempt to draw a line in the dock company's operation to limit the amount of trade it can permit at the port. It would be a task for which a court would be ill-equipped, involving as it would the need to consider the interests of the locality as a whole and the plaintiff's and county council's plans in respect of it. In some cases even the national interest would have to be considered. These are matters to be decided by the planning authority and, if necessary, the minister and should be subject only to judicial review. I do not find that the dock company has operated or operates the port other than as a normal commercial undertaking. The plaintiff can now impose conditions upon or even revoke the permission it has granted. It can (with the consent of the Kent County Council) make traffic regulations controlling the use of these and other roads in the immediate vicinity of the port ... [The] plaintiff had brought these proceedings instead, in order to avoid paying compensation under the Town and Country Planning Act 1990 if it altered or withdrew the consent. Further, the county council has not yet given its consent to the imposition of any traffic regulations.

These matters confirm me in the view already expressed that the disturbance complained of in this case is not actionable. Alternatively, they are matters together with those specifically mentioned below which would influence me against granting an injunction.

I do not believe that my views are inconsistent with cases such as *Halsey's* case or the *PYA Quarries* case. There may well have been planning permission for the activities in question in those cases. Certainly there was in the *PYA Quarries* case, but the complaints there related to unreasonable uses. The depot and the quarry in those cases could have been operated commercially in accordance with the planning permission without causing the damage or disturbance complained of.

In short, where planning consent is given for a development or change of use, the question of nuisance will thereafter fall to be decided by reference to a neighbourhood with that development or use and not as it was previously ...'

Comment

(1)   Although the context was an application by the local authority under statutory powers to protect the inhabitants of the borough, it was necessary for the court to decide whether there was conduct capable of amounting to a nuisance. For other extracts from the judgment relating to public nuisance see p 683.

(2)   The case comes perilously close to regarding the issues as decided by the grant of planning permission. This may be beneficial in the light of the democratic functions of local authorities. Difficult issues of fact may still arise as to whether the activity has been carried on reasonably within the revised view of the locality. In *Wheeler v J J Saunders Ltd* the Court of Appeal sought to limit the decision to its narrow facts, i.e. the extensive nature of the permission granted and its impact on the locality.

Wheeler and another v J J Saunders Ltd and others
[1995] 2 All ER 697 Court of Appeal

Dr and Mrs W, the plaintiffs, bought a farmhouse on land next to farmland. They obtained planning permission to convert the outbuildings into holiday homes, and there was a condition in the conveyance that that should be the only use for the outbuildings. The farmland was sold to K Ltd, in which JJS Ltd had 85 per cent of the shares and Dr W had 15 per cent of the shares, and of which Dr W was managing director. It was intended that K Ltd should breed pigs.

Dr W fell out with JJS Ltd and was dismissed as managing director of K Ltd. JJS Ltd obtained planning permissions to build two pig housing units ('Trowbridge houses') very close to the plaintiffs' holiday cottages. The plaintiffs successfully sued JJS Ltd and K Ltd in respect of nuisance in the form of smell from the pig housing units. The defendants appealed on the basis that they had obtained planning permission for the pig housing units and the smell could not amount to an actionable nuisance.

The Court of Appeal held that a planning authority had no jurisdiction to authorise a nuisance except insofar as the grant of planning permission changed the character of a neighbourhood and that the nuisance inevitably resulted from the authorised use. In this case, the nuisance did flow from the authorised use but the planning permission was not such as would change the character of the neighbourhood.

Peter Gibson LJ: '... [Counsel] for the defendants submitted that the judge should have held, consistently with [*Gillingham BC v Medway (Chatham) Dock Co Ltd*], that as planning permission had been given for the Trowbridge houses, the question of nuisance fell to be decided by reference to the neighbourhood with that development or use and not as it was previously, and as the use made was authorised by the planning permission the plaintiffs could not succeed in nuisance. If the defendants are right, the grant of planning permission has the effect of depriving those adversely affected by the use of buildings or works authorised by the planning permission of their common law rights without compensation. It will readily be seen that the issue raised is one of general importance ...

[Peter Gibson LJ referred to the defence of statutory authority and *Allen v Gulf Oil Refining Ltd* and continued:]

The defence of statutory authority is allowed on the basis of the true construction of the scope and effect of the statute. Parliament is presumed to have considered the competing interests in the particular circumstances which are the subject of the statute and to have determined which is to prevail in the public interest in authorising the particular development and use of land and whether or not compensation is to be paid to those whose common law rights are adversely affected by the authorised development and use. But in the case of planning permission granted pursuant to the statutory scheme contained in the town and country planning legislation it is far from obvious to me that Parliament must be presumed to have intended that in every case it should have the same effect on private rights as direct statutory authority, regardless of the circumstances that were in fact taken into account. True it is that Parliament by that legislation has provided a mechanism for regulating the development and use of land in the public interest and that it has delegated to the local planning authority the function of making planning decisions; but Parliament will also have been aware of the range of such decisions and the variety of possible circumstances in which they may be taken. It would also have been aware of the limited scope open to an objector to challenge a grant of planning permission.

Prior to *Gillingham BC v Medway (Chatham) Dock Co Ltd* the general assumption appears to have been that private rights to claim in nuisance were unaffected by the permissive grant of planning permission, the developer going ahead with the development at his own risk if his activities were to cause a nuisance. The *Gillingham* case, if rightly decided, calls that assumption into question, at any rate in cases, like *Gillingham* itself, of a major development altering the character of a neighbourhood with wide consequential effects such as required a balancing of competing public and private interests before permission was granted. I can well see that in such a case the public interest must be allowed to prevail and that it would be inappropriate to grant an injunction (though whether that should preclude any award of damages in lieu is a question which may need further consideration). But I am not prepared to accept that the principle applied in the *Gillingham* case must be taken to apply to every planning decision. The court should be slow to acquiesce in the extinction of private rights without compensation as a result of administrative decisions which cannot be appealed and are difficult to challenge.

If the test of the application of the principle applied in the *Gillingham* case requires that there be a change in the character of the neighbourhood, that is not satisfied in the present case. The defendants' land remains a pig farm with merely an intensified use of part of it. The planning decisions taken did not involve considerations of community or public interest, but merely whether the private interests of the applicants for planning permission should prevail over the private interests of the plaintiff objectors. Moreover, it appears from the evidence of one of the plaintiffs' experts ... that no consultation took place between the planning department of the council and its environmental health department, even though the plaintiffs' objections should have alerted officers to the problems of the site and of the nuisance likely to be caused by the use of the Trowbridge houses ... It is hard to believe that there was a proper balancing by the council of the interests of the defendants and the environmental effects on the plaintiffs. If the justification for the principle applied in the *Gillingham* case is that the local planning authority would already have balanced the relevant competing interests, that justification would not appear to apply in the present case.

[Counsel's] submission that in the light of the *Gillingham* case the plaintiffs can have no claim in nuisance resulting from the use of the Trowbridge houses for which there was planning permission goes too far, in my opinion, in any event. From the evidence it is apparent that feeding whey to the pigs causes a greater malodour than other feeds. Accordingly, the nuisance to that extent is not inevitable. But I accept that a nuisance resulting from the use of the Trowbridge houses in the position in which they stand was inevitable. In my judgment, for the reasons which

I have given, the judge was entitled to conclude that the planning consents did not prevent the plaintiffs from succeeding in their claim in nuisance. I regret that this means that the defendants, having constructed the Trowbridge houses in accordance with planning permission, cannot now use them, but they are not wholly blameless in that the information which they submitted in the planning applications was not as accurate or as complete as it might have been ...'

Comment

(1) It is clear that the principle enunciated in the *Gillingham* case will be restricted to planning permissions involving 'a strategic planning decision affected by considerations of public interest' or 'a major development altering the character of a neighbourhood with wide consequential effects such as required a balancing of competing public and private interests before permission was granted'.

(2) Another example of the interplay of nuisance and planning permission is *Hunter v Canary Wharf Ltd*, in which Lord Cooke and Lord Goff made several important observations about the role of planning permission, see p 640 and p 638 respectively.

(3) The cases highlight the problem of resolving conflict between competing private interests, and between private interests and the broader public interests. The state of the law remains uncertain, but it seems that the courts are currently favouring the resolution of problems in favour of the individual interests in property.

(4) *Wheeler v J J Saunders* also indicates the overlap with public law remedies. One feature of the decisions is that they highlight the inadequacy of planning permission procedures, whether in general or the 'fast-track' procedures employed in cases like the Docklands redevelopment as described in *Hunter v Canary Wharf*, p 604. This inadequacy may call into doubt the justification implicit in the *Gillingham* case, viz that the democratic processes should decide where the impact of a nuisance should fall. The absence of appeals in the planning process leaves the claimants only with a choice as to action in tort or application for judicial review (a course of action doubted in *Wheeler v J J Saunders*). In the *Wheeler* case the Local Government Commissioner (the 'Ombudsman') was involved but his decisions are not legally enforceable and lie against the local authority not against the recipient of the planning permission.

Hunter and others v Canary Wharf Ltd
[1997] 2 All ER 426 House of Lords

For the facts see p 604. The House of Lords considered whether or not the interference with television reception by the mere presence of the building was capable of constituting a nuisance. All their Lordships agreed on this point.

Lord Goff: 'I turn ... to consider the question whether interference with television signals may give rise to an action in private nuisance. This question was first considered over thirty years ago by Buckley J in *Bridlington Relay Ltd v Yorkshire Electricity Board*. That case was concerned not with interference caused by the presence of a building, but with electrical interference caused by the activities of the defendant Electricity Board. Buckley J held that such interference did not constitute a legal nuisance, because it was interference with a purely recreational facility, as opposed to interference with the health or physical comfort or well-being of the plaintiffs. He did not however rule out the possibility that ability to receive television signals free from interference might one day be recognised as "so important a part of an ordinary householder's enjoyment of his property that such interference should be regarded as a legal nuisance". Certainly the average weekly hours for television viewing in this country, which your Lordships were told were 24 hours per week, show that many people devote much of their leisure time to watching television, even allowing for the fact that it is not clear whether the relevant statistic is based more on the time when television sets are turned on, rather than being actually watched. Certainly it can be asserted with force that for many people television transcends the function of mere entertainment, and in particular that for the aged, the lonely and the bedridden it must provide a great distraction and relief from the circumscribed nature of their lives. That interference with such an amenity might in appropriate circumstances be protected by the law of nuisance has been recognised in Canada in *Nor-Video Services Ltd v Ontario Hydro*.

However, as I see the present case, there is a more formidable obstacle to this claim. This is that the complaint rests simply upon the presence of the defendants' building on land in the neighbourhood as causing the relevant interference. The gravamen of the plaintiffs' case is that the defendants, by building the Canary Wharf Tower, interfered with the television signals and so caused interference with the reception on the plaintiffs' television sets; though it should not be overlooked that such interference might be caused by a smaller building and moreover that, since it is no defence that the plaintiff came to the nuisance, the same complaint could result from the simple fact of the presence of the building which caused the interference. In this respect the present case is to be distinguished from the *Bridlington Relay* case, in which the problem was caused not just by the presence of a neighbouring building but by electrical interference resulting from the defendant Electricity Board's activities.

As a general rule, a man is entitled to build on his own land, though nowadays this right is inevitably subject to our system of planning controls. Moreover, as a general rule, a man's right to build on his land is not restricted by the fact that the presence of the building may of itself interfere with his neighbour's enjoyment of his land. The building may spoil his neighbour's view (see *Attorney-General v Doughty, and Fishmongers' Co v East India Co*); in the absence of an easement, it may restrict the flow of air on to his neighbour's land (see *Bland v Mosely* cited in *Aldred's Case*, and *Chastey v Ackland*); and, again in the absence of an easement, it may take away light from his neighbour's windows (*Dalton v Angus* …): nevertheless his neighbour generally cannot complain of the presence of the building, though this may seriously detract from the enjoyment of his land. As Lindley LJ said in *Chastey v Ackland* (a case concerned with interference with the flow of air):

> "… speaking generally, apart from long enjoyment, or some grant or agreement, no one has a right to prevent his neighbour from building on his own land, although the consequence may be to diminish or alter the flow of air over it on to land adjoining. So to diminish a flow of air is not actionable as a nuisance."

From this it follows that, in the absence of an easement, more is required than the mere presence of a neighbouring building to give rise to an actionable private nuisance. Indeed, for an action in private nuisance to lie in respect of interference with the plaintiff's enjoyment of his land, it will generally arise from something emanating from the defendant's land. Such an emanation may take many forms – noise, dirt, fumes, a noxious smell, vibrations, and suchlike. Occasionally activities on the defendant's land are in themselves so offensive to neighbours as to constitute an actionable nuisance, as in *Thompson-Schwab v Costaki*, where the sight of prostitutes and their clients entering and leaving neighbouring premises were held to fall into that category. Such cases must, however, be relatively rare. In one New Zealand case, *Bank of New Zealand v Greenwood*, the glass roof of a verandah which deflected the sun's rays so that a dazzling glare was thrown on to neighbouring buildings was held, *prima facie*, to create a nuisance; but it seems that the effect was not merely to reflect the sunlight but to deflect it at such an angle and in such a manner as to cause the dazzling glare, too bright for the human eye to bear, to shine straight into the neighbouring building. One expert witness explained that the verandah glass diffused the light, as if from a multitude of mirrors, into what he described as a high intensity dazzle, which was extremely difficult to look at. On that basis, such a case can be distinguished from one concerned with the mere presence of a building on neighbouring land. At all events the mere fact that a building on the defendant's land gets in the way and so prevents something from reaching the plaintiff's land is generally speaking not enough for this purpose.

It is of some interest that the same conclusion has been reached in German law. I refer in particular to the decision of the *Bundesgerichtshof in G v City of Hamburg*. The facts of the case were very similar to the present case. The plaintiffs were the owners of their family home. The local municipality erected a nine storey hospital on a neighbouring site, and as a result there was significant interference with television reception in the plaintiffs' house, making it impossible for them to receive certain programmes. The plaintiffs' claim for damages against the municipality failed. Nothing was emitted from the defendants' land, and the so-called "negative Immissionen" (negative effects) which resulted in interference with the plaintiffs' television reception gave rise to no cause of action. It was stated that the court, by the adoption of the settled jurisprudence of the Reichsgericht, had repeatedly affirmed that the so-called "negative adverse effects" caused by interference with access to natural amenities like light and air are not "impermissible" within the meaning of the relevant provisions of the German Civil Code. Within the boundaries of his land the owner may in principle deal with his property as he wishes.

That decision demonstrates that English law is not alone in reaching this conclusion. The German principle appears to arise from the fact that the appropriate remedy falls within the law of property, in which competing property rights have to be reconciled with each other. In English law liability falls, for historical reasons, within the law of torts, though the underlying policy considerations appear to be similar.

In the result I find myself to be in agreement on this point with Pill LJ, who delivered the judgment of the Court of Appeal, when he expressed the opinion that no action lay in private nuisance for interference with television caused by the mere presence of a building. That a building may have such an effect has to be accepted. If a large building is proposed in a neighbouring area, it will usually be open to local people to raise the possibility of television interference with the local planning authority at the stage of the application for planning permission. It has, however, to be recognised that the problem may well not be appreciated until after the building is built, when it will be too late for any such representations to be made. Moreover in the present case, in which the Secretary of State had designated the relevant area as an Enterprise Zone with the effect that planning permission was deemed to have been granted for any form of development, no application for permission had to be made. But in any event, with the rapid spread of the availability of cable television in urban areas, interference of this kind is likely to become less and less important; and it should not be forgotten that satellite television is also available. In the present case, the problem was solved in the end by the introduction by the BBC of a new relay station, though not until after a substantial lapse of time.

For these reasons I would dismiss the appeal of the plaintiffs in the first action on this issue.'

Lord Cooke (concurring as to this point): ' ... Television has become a significant and, to many, almost an indispensable amenity of domestic life. For the reasons given more fully by Robins J in *Nor-Video Services Ltd v Ontario Hydro* and my noble and learned friend Lord Goff, I agree that, in appropriate cases, television and radio reception can and should be protected by the law of nuisance, although no doubt rights to reception cannot be acquired by prescription. Inhabitants of the Isle of Dogs and many another concentrated urban areas might react with incredulity, and justifiably so, to the suggestion that the amenity of television and radio reception is fairly comparable to a view of the surroundings of their homes. Neither in nature nor in value is that so. It may be suspected that only a lawyer would think of such a suggestion.

What in my opinion must defeat an action for interference with television reception by the construction of a building, not only in this but in most cases, is the principle of reasonable user, of give and take.

[Lord Cooke referred to a decision of the German Federal Supreme Court, and decisions from the United States and continued:]

... Control of building height is such a common feature of modern town planning regimes that it would be inadequate to say that at the present day owners of the soil generally enjoy their rights *usque ad coelum et ad inferos*. Although the primary responsibility for enforcement falls on the administering authorities, I see no reason why neighbours prejudicially affected should not be able to sue in nuisance if a building does exceed height, bulk or location restrictions. For then the developer is not making either a lawful or a reasonable use of landowning rights. This is to treat planning measures not as creating rights of action for breach of statutory duty but as denoting a standard of what is acceptable in the community.

In the light of the versatility of human malevolence and ingenuity, it is as well to add a second qualification. The malicious erection of a structure for the purpose of interfering with television reception should be actionable in nuisance on the principle of such well-known cases as *Christie v Davey* and *Hollywood Silver Fox Farm Ltd v Emmett*. Obviously this has no bearing on the present case or on the vast majority of cases ...

Even putting malice aside, compliance with planning controls is not itself a defence to a nuisance action, as is brought out by the pighouse case, *Wheeler v J J Saunders Ltd*, an instance of an injudicious grant of planning consent, procured apparently by the supply of inaccurate and incomplete information. But it must be of major importance that the Canary Wharf Tower, although said to be the highest building in Great Britain and certainly an exceptional feature of the London skyline, was built in an enterprise zone in an urban development area and authorised under the special procedure designed to encourage regeneration.

The Canary Wharf project, in general, and the tower at One Canada Square, in particular, were obviously of a scale totally transforming the environment. There was an original planning condition that building heights were not to exceed 120ft except by agreement with the enterprise zone authority. Agreements were obtained and it is not suggested that they were insufficient for what was done. Under the fast-track procedure the rights of residents were limited to the making of representations regarding the project. It may be that what seems plain with hindsight, that there would be a dramatic effect on television reception, was not at first sufficiently realised. After a year or so, however, the problem was rectified by the establishment of a relay station and adjustment of the aerials of affected properties (apparently without cost to the owners). Although this was presumably the result, not of representations under the statutory procedure, but of subsequent complaints, it does show that the right to make representations is not necessarily without real value. The tower is clad in stainless steel and the windows are metallised but it would seem hopeless to contend that the use of these materials and the design of the tower constituted any unreasonable or unexpected mode of constructing a building of this height. In these circumstances, to adopt the words of Staughton LJ in *Wheeler*, the tower falls fairly within the scope of "a strategic planning decision affected by considerations of public interest".

Staughton LJ used those words in distinguishing the decision of Buckley J in *Gillingham Borough Council v Medway (Chatham) Dock Co Ltd*, a case somewhat similar to the present case, in that it concerned the development of a new commercial port on the site of a disused naval dockyard. Heavy vehicle traffic at night undoubtedly had a seriously deleterious effect on the comfort of local residents, but the judge held that, although a planning consent could not authorise a nuisance, it could change the character of the neighbourhood by which the standard of reasonable user fell to be judged. This principle appears to me to be sound and to apply to the present case as far at least as television reception is concerned. Although it did interfere with television reception the Canary Wharf Tower must, I think, be accepted as a reasonable development in all the circumstances. The effect of the tower on television reception was extensive enough to bring the concept of public nuisance into play, but I see no material difference on this point between public and private nuisance.

For these reasons, while not satisfied that a categorical universally applicable answer can be given to the issue about television reception, I agree that in this case the claim of nuisance consisting of interference with such reception cannot succeed ...'

Comment

(1)   As to the effect of malice as part of the balancing process see *Hollywood Silver Fox Farm v Emmett*, p 648, and see especially *Mayor of Bradford v Pickles*, p 649. In *Hunter v Canary Wharf* both Lord Cooke and Lord Hope refer to the absence of any allegation of malice in the erection of the building.

(2)   As well as consideration of the protection of television reception, in *Bridlington Relay v Yorkshire Electricity Board* Buckley J also considered that the plaintiff in that case was seeking greater protection than an ordinary householder and was thereby putting his land to a hypersensitive use, see p 644. This was a view discounted by the court in the *Nor-Video Services* case, see p 647. But the point may be superfluous now, see the comments in *Morris (t/A Soundstar Studio) v Network Rail Infrastructure Ltd*, p 647.

(3)   Several of their Lordships expressed the view that any other conclusion on the TV reception point would lead to a huge burden of potential liability to a

large number of potential plaintiffs being placed on developers. This is a version of the floodgates argument, from time to time advanced or rejected in the context of negligence.

(4) All their Lordships, either expressly or by implication, left open the question whether in an appropriate case there could be an actionable nuisance in the case of interference with television reception, e.g. in the case of malicious erection of a building or other structure, or some activity interfering with reception or the emanation of something from the defendant's land. See Lord Goff's distinction between the facts of *Hunter v Canary Wharf* and those in the *Bridlington Relay* case. Lord Hoffmann observed that in the *Bridlington Relay* case:

> 'The learned judge was plainly not laying down a general rule that interference with television can never be an actionable nuisance. In principle I do not see why in an appropriate case it should not. *Bridlington Relay* was a case of alleged interference by electro-magnetic radiation from high tension electric cables. The Court of Appeal left open the question of whether interference of such a kind could be actionable and so would I.'

Lord Lloyd agreed that there was an analogy between a building which interferes with a view and a building which interferes with the reception of television signals, and went on to say:

> 'Another argument which Lord Irvine put forward, but did not press, is that the interference with television reception was not due to any activity on the part of the defendants on their land. It was due solely to the existence of the building itself. However, as Hardie Boys J pointed out in *Bank of New Zealand v Greenwood*, nuisance does not depend in every case on an activity, although it usually does. It may arise from a mere state of affairs on a man's land which he allows to continue. *Leakey v National Trust* is a good example. So I would not decide the case on the ground that interference with the plaintiffs' television reception did not involve any activity on the defendants' part.
>
> If further precision is needed in answering the question why the plaintiffs have no legal redress in nuisance, it could be, as my noble and learned friend Lord Goff has suggested, because there is nothing emanating from the defendants' land in the present case. The eminently sensible conclusion reached in *Bank of New Zealand v Greenwood* might not be easy to reconcile with this approach. So that case may go to the limit of the law of nuisance. But the facts were most unusual, as Hardie Boys J pointed out, and every case depends on its own particular facts. This is especially true in the field of nuisance.'

(5)   In *Anglian Water Services Ltd v Crawshaw Robbins & Co Ltd* Stanley Burnton J in the Queen's Bench Division considered whether there would be an actionable nuisance in respect of the interruption of a gas supply to houses where the damage causing the interruption occurred outside the premises and where the interference was with the use of ordinary domestic appliances. A civil engineering company, employed by the claimant, damaged a water main and a gas main. The claimant sued the contractor in contract in respect of payments made by householders. The judgment explores in detail *British Celanese Ltd v A H Hunt (Capacitators) Ltd* and *SCM (United Kingdom) v W J Wittal*. The judge concluded that the negligent interruption of a supply of gas by a third party is not actionable as a private nuisance because it does not involve an invasion of the claimant's land nor was it one of the exceptional cases of liability in nuisance without such an invasion (such as). A home owner or tenant does not have a property right in the supply of gas (or electricity). To this extent the case adopts the orthodoxy of *Hunter v Canary Wharf*.

Bridlington Relay Ltd v Yorkshire Electricity Board
[1965] I All ER 264 Chancery Division

It was alleged that the defendant electricity company's overhead lines would interfere with the transmission of broadcasts from the plaintiff's relay system. On one occasion some slight interference from the line during an agreed test period had been encountered. The court refused to grant an injunction *quia timet* since the defendants were willing to ensure that interference would be suppressed. The court also thought, *obiter*, that interference with a mere recreational enjoyment of the property could not be an actionable nuisance. Finally, the court held that the use by the plaintiff was exceptionally sensitive.

Buckley J: '... This is sufficient to dispose of the case, but lest I should be held to be wrong in anything I have so far said, I should, I think, proceed to state my view on another aspect of the matter which has been fully canvassed before me: that is, whether, if the tendency of the power line to cause interference at the plaintiffs' aerials is ineradicable, or if, contrary to the view which I have expressed, the fact that it may be remediable is irrelevant, the plaintiffs could successfully maintain a claim in nuisance.

If interference of the kind experienced by the plaintiffs on I June were to recur at all frequently, it is very probable that the plaintiffs' business would be damaged. If such damage were established, and it were shown that it would be likely to continue or recur, would the plaintiffs have a cause of action in nuisance? For the plaintiffs it is contended that to receive television is now an ordinary use of land and that causing radiation which results in preventing, or interfering with, the satisfactory reception of television transmissions is something which unwarrantably interferes with the legitimate and reasonable enjoyment of neighbouring property by its owners. It is said that, if that interference is of a sufficiently grave character, it may amount to an actionable nuisance on either or both of two grounds: viz. that it interferes with the beneficial use of the neighbouring property and that it affects the value of that property. On the other hand, the defendants contend that the plaintiffs are using the aerial mast for a purpose requiring exceptional immunity from electrical interference; that not only are the aerials exceptionally sensitive to such interference, but also the plaintiffs' business is one of a kind requiring a higher standard of interference-free reception than an ordinary viewer using a domestic aerial would demand ...

In taking judicial notice of the widespread reception of television in domestic circles, I do so on the footing that in those circles television is enjoyed almost entirely for what I think must be regarded as recreational purposes, notwithstanding that the broadcast programmes include material which may have some educational content, some political content and, it may be, some other content not strictly or exclusively recreational in character. Those programmes, the purposes of which are strictly educational, are not, I presume, intended for domestic consumption or very much looked at in private homes. I mention these matters because, in my judgment, the plaintiffs could not succeed in a claim for damages for nuisance if what I may call an ordinary receiver of television by means of an aerial mounted on his own house could not do so. It is, I think, established by authority that an act which does not, or would not, interfere with the ordinary enjoyment of their property by neighbours in the ordinary modes of using such property cannot constitute a legal nuisance. I quote:

> "A man cannot increase the liabilities of his neighbour by applying his own property to special uses, whether for business or pleasure." (*Eastern and South African Telegraph Co Ltd v Cape Town Tramways Co Ltd.*)

In *Robinson v Kilvert*, Cotton LJ stated the principle thus:

> "If a person does what in itself is noxious, or which interferes with the ordinary use and enjoyment of a neighbour's property, it is a nuisance. But no case has been cited where the doing of something not in itself noxious has been held a nuisance, unless it interferes with the ordinary enjoyment of life, or the ordinary use of property for the purposes of residence or business."

The dissemination of electrical interference is not, in my judgment, "noxious" in the sense in which, I think, the learned Lord Justice is there using the term. Could such interference as is here in question be held to cause an interference with the ordinary enjoyment of life or the ordinary use of the plaintiffs' property for the purposes of residence or business of such a kind as to amount to an actionable nuisance?

There are, of course, many reported cases in which something adversely affecting the beneficial enjoyment of property has been held to constitute a legal nuisance; but I have been referred to no case in which interference with a purely recreational facility has been held to do so. Considerations of health and physical comfort and well being appear to me to be on a somewhat different level from recreational considerations. I do not wish to be taken as laying down that in no circumstances can something which interferes merely with recreational facilities or activities amount to an actionable nuisance. It may be that in some other case the court may be satisfied that some such interference should be regarded, according to such "plain and sober and simple notions" as Knight Bruce V-C referred to in a well-known passage in his judgment in *Walter v Selfe*, as detracting from the beneficial use and enjoyment by neighbouring owners of their properties to such an extent as to warrant their protection by the law. For myself, however, I do not think that it can at present be said that the ability to receive television free from occasional, even if recurrent and severe, electrical interference is so important a part of an ordinary householder's enjoyment of his property that such interference should be regarded as a legal nuisance, particularly, perhaps, if such interference affects only one of the available alternative programmes.

Accordingly, I do not think that even if the conditions which existed on the evening of I June would have produced the same effect on the screen of a householder using an aerial mounted on his own house at the site of the plaintiffs' mast, this would have constituted an actionable nuisance. In fact, no evidence was adduced that anyone in Bridlington on that evening receiving television by means of an ordinary domestic aerial, experienced any such interference as was experienced by the plaintiffs ... The evidence did not establish that the signal received by the user of an ordinary domestic aerial mounted in the ordinary way on his house would have been the same or similar to the signal received by the plaintiffs by means of their large directional aerial mounted at the head of their aerial mast; but even if this be assumed in the plaintiffs' favour, I am of opinion for the reasons which I have already stated, that such a user of an ordinary domestic aerial for domestic enjoyment could not succeed on a claim for nuisance.

The plaintiffs' complaint is concerned not with interference with domestic amenities; their complaint is that their business will be damaged. But their business is such that to prosper it requires an exceptional degree of immunity from interference. To prosper it must be able to offer its subscribers a better service than they could obtain through aerials of their own. It was not established to my satisfaction that the aerial used by the plaintiffs for receiving BBC transmissions from Holme Moss was proportionately more sensitive to interference than domestic aerials are in the same area, but it was established that the business of the plaintiffs was exceptionally sensitive in the sense which I have just indicated. The use of their aerial for this particular kind of business was, in my judgment, use of a special kind unusually vulnerable to interference, just as the business carried on by the plaintiff in *Robinson v Kilvert* was exceptionally vulnerable to the effects of heat.

For these reasons as well as the other reasons given earlier in this judgment I am of opinion that the plaintiffs cannot succeed in this action ...'

Comment

(1) Compare the dismissive view of private television reception with the more populist approach in *Nor-Video v Ontario Hydro*, where the court regarded the interference with television viewing as undoubtedly detracting from the beneficial use and ownership of property. In the *Nor-Video* case Robins J observed that:

> 'In this day and age [TV reception] is simply one of the benefits and pleasures commonly derived from domestic occupancy of property; its social value and utility to a community, perhaps even more so to a remote community such as the one in this case, cannot be doubted. The category of interests covered by the tort of nuisance ought not to be and need not be closed, in my opinion, to new or changing developments associated from time to time with normal usage and enjoyment of land.'

(2) In *Robinson v Kilvert* the appellant complained that the brown paper which he stored in his premises suffered damage from heat in the basement below, and it was held by the Court of Appeal that no actionable wrong had been committed by the defendant since the heating was not of such a character as would interfere with the ordinary use of the rest of the house. The storage of brown paper was especially susceptible to variations in heat and humidity.

Where it is demonstrated that there is interference with the ordinary use of land then interference with especially susceptible property or use will be remediable.

The future of the distinction between ordinary enjoyment of land and hypersensitive use is in some doubt following the decision of the Court of Appeal in *Morris (t/a Soundstar Studio) v Network Rail Infrastructure Ltd (formerly Railtrack plc)*. Here the claimant alleged that there was electromagnetic interference with sensitive electric guitars being used in its sound-recording studio. Although the Court of Appeal was divided as to whether or not this was an extra-sensitive use of the land, the claimant failed on the basis that the harm suffered was unforeseeable. In a passage which may prove to be influential Lord Justice Buxton said:

> '35. ... it is difficult to see any further life in some particular rules of the law of nuisance, such as for instance the concept of "abnormal sensitiveness" drawn from *Robinson v Kilvert*. That rule was developed at a time when liability in nuisance, for damaging a neighbour by use of one's own land, was thought to be strict ... The unreasonable results that could flow from that approach were mitigated by a number of rules of thumb; for instance, as shown by the passages from *Robinson v Kilvert* ... that an activity that could only injure an exceptionally delicate trade could not be a nuisance at all ...It is very difficult not to think that such particular rules are now subsumed under the general view of the law of nuisance expressed in *Delaware Mansions*: not dissimilarly to the way in which the

generalisation of the law of negligence initiated by *Donoghue v Stevenson* has rendered obsolete the previous categories of dangerous chattels; duties of occupiers of land; duties attaching to specific trades; and the like.'

(3)   In *Hollywood Silver Fox Farm Ltd v Emmett*, the plaintiff ran a fur farm adjacent to the defendant's land. The defendant thought that the attractiveness of his site as a development of private housing would be adversely affected by the farm. He instructed his son to shoot his rifle in the vicinity of the foxes, which were particularly susceptible to loud noises during the mating season, and this action would encourage the vixens to eat their young. The court held that even if there would have been no nuisance apart from the malice of the defendant, that malice was sufficient to make the conduct unreasonable. Macnaghten J commented:

'... It is a perfectly lawful thing to keep a silver fox farm and I think the fact that the shooting took place intentionally for the purpose of injuring the plaintiffs made it actionable. The authority for the view that in cases of alleged nuisance by noise, the intention of the person making the noise is not to be disregarded is to be found in the case of *Gaunt v Fynney*. Lord Selborne LC ... said this: "A nuisance by noise (supposing malice to be out of the question) is emphatically a question of degree." It has been observed by high authority that Lord Selborne was always extremely careful in the use of language and that parenthetical statement "supposing malice to be out of the question" clearly indicates what his Lordship thought in the case of alleged nuisance by noise, where the noise was made maliciously. Different considerations would apply to cases where that ingredient was absent.'

(4)   In *Christie v Davey*, the plaintiff and the defendant lived side-by-side in semi-detached houses in Brixton. The plaintiff was a teacher of music and he had a musical family. The result was that music was heard in the defendant's house and in retaliation he took to making noises himself by beating trays and rapping on the wall. North J granted an injunction restraining the defendant from permitting any sounds or noises in his house so as to annoy the plaintiff or the occupiers of his house:

'... the noises which were made in the defendant's house were not of a legitimate kind. They were what, to use the language of Lord Selborne in *Gaunt v Fynney* "ought to be regarded as excessive and unreasonable". I am satisfied that they were made deliberately and maliciously for the purpose of annoying the plaintiffs. If what has taken place had occurred between two sets of persons, both perfectly innocent, I should have taken an entirely different view of the case. But I am persuaded that what was done by the defendant was done only for the purpose of annoyance, and in my opinion it was not a legitimate use of the defendant's house to use it for the purpose of vexing and annoying his neighbours.'

In *Ibbotson v Peat*, I's land adjoined a grouse moor belonging to R. I, for the purpose of inducing the grouse to come on to his own land, put out corn. The defendant P was employed by R. To prevent I from gaining any advantage, P let off fireworks, rockets and bombs, as near as he could get to I's land, in order to frighten off the grouse. P's defence was that he was justified in letting off the rockets and bombs, because of the improper conduct of I. The court said that nuisance by noise intentionally made for the purpose of injuring the plaintiff was a good cause of action.

(5) If an incidental consequence of a defendant's conduct is to injure the claimant it might not be unlawful, but if the sole aim is to injure or annoy, the defendant will almost certainly be liable. This is one of the rare instances in tort where malice affects the lawfulness of the defendant's conduct. The privilege to make a noise is defeated by the malice. The right to make a noise or to enjoy peace and quiet is not absolute but is to be balanced against the countervailing rights of others. Where absolute rights are involved then different principles apply, see *The Mayor of Bradford v Pickles*, below.

The Mayor, Aldermen and Burgesses of the Borough of Bradford v Pickles
[1895–99] All ER Rep 984 House of Lords

The plaintiffs supplied Bradford with water drawn from beneath their own land. The water percolated in undefined channels underneath the defendant's land before reaching the plaintiffs' land. In order to gain access to the mineral deposits under his land, the defendant began to drain the water-bearing strata. This reduced the volume of water reaching the plaintiffs' land and, from time to time, had the effect of discolouring the water abstracted by them. The plaintiffs alleged that the true reason for the defendant's activity was to compel them either to purchase his land or the water supply. The plaintiffs sought an injunction to restrain the defendant from drawing off water or doing anything which would lead to the water being polluted or injuriously affected. The House of Lords held that the defendant was entitled to abstract water flowing under his land in undefined channels whatever his motive might have been and that the plaintiffs had no rights in the water until such time as it might reach their own land.

Lord Halsbury:' ... The only remaining point is the question of fact alleged by the plaintiffs, that the acts done by the defendant are done, not with any view which deals with the use of his own land or the percolating water through it, but is done, in the language of the pleader, "maliciously". I am not certain that I can understand or give any intelligible construction to the word so used. Upon the supposition ... that the defendant did maliciously something that he had a right to do ...

This is not a case in which the state of mind of the person doing the act can affect the right to do it. If it was a lawful act, however ill the motive might be, he had a right to do it. If it was an unlawful act, however good his motive might be, he would have no right to do it. Motives and intentions in such a question as is now before your Lordships seem to me to be absolutely irrelevant. But I am not prepared to adopt Lindley LJ's view of the moral obliquity of the person insisting on his right when that right is challenged ...

[If] the owner of the adjoining land is in a situation in which an act of his, lawfully done on his own land, may divert the water which would otherwise go into the possession of this trading company, I can see no reason why he should not insist on their purchasing his interest from which this trading company desires to make a profit.'

Lord Watson: '... No use of property, which would be legal if due to a proper motive, can become illegal because it is prompted by a motive which is improper or even malicious.'

Lord Ashbourne: '... The plaintiffs have no case unless they can shew that they are entitled to the flow of water in question, and that the defendant has no right to do what he is doing ... [The defendant] has acted within his legal rights throughout; and is he to forfeit those legal rights and be punished for their legal exercise because certain motives are imputed to him? If his motives were the most generous and philanthropic in the world, they would not avail him when his actions were illegal. If his motives are selfish and mercenary, that is no reason why his rights should be confiscated when his actions are legal.'

Lord Macnaghten: '... Why should [the defendant], he may think, without fee or reward, keep his land as a store-room for a commodity which the corporation dispense, probably not gratuitously, to the inhabitants of Bradford? He prefers his own interests to the public good. He may be churlish, selfish, and grasping. His conduct may seem shocking to a moral philosopher. But where is the malice? [The defendant] has no spite against the people of Bradford. He bears no ill-will to the corporation. They are welcome to the water, and to his land too, if they will pay the price for it ... But the real answer to the claim of the corporation is that in such a case motives are immaterial. It is the act, not the motive for the act, that must be regarded. If the act, apart from motive, gives rise merely to damage without legal injury, the motive, however reprehensible it may be, will not supply that element.'

Comment

(1) Are the comments of Lord Cooke in *Hunter v Canary Wharf* consistent with those in the *Bradford* case? If, as with abstraction of water, the erection of

a building on one's own land is an absolute right (but the manner of building it may be a matter of balance, e.g. as to dust and noise), how can motive be relevant where the mere presence of the building interferes with something to which the prospective recipient has no right (compare the non-receipt of water with the non-receipt of air, light or TV signals). Lord Cooke did not cite the *Bradford* case, although he did observe that he did 'not think that the view that malice is irrelevant in nuisance would have wide acceptance today'. The Canadian courts have declined to follow the principle in the *Bradford* case, see *Pugliese v National Capital* and *T H Critelli v Lincoln Trust & Savings Co.*

(2) In England the complex law on water rights was examined in *Home Brewery Co Ltd v William Davis & Co (Loughborough) Ltd* where the court held that a landowner is entitled to stop water encroaching on to his or her land even if this is repelled on to land of another. The lower owner cannot be compelled to accept percolating water but must act reasonably in repelling it; malice would by implication be an element in the balancing process. See also *Ryecroft Homes Ltd and another v Sevenoaks District Council.*

(3) Where there is physical harm to the claimant's land then the matter may be different. Where a tall building causes wind turbulence leading to damage to adjoining property then it is possible that a court would find an actionable nuisance in the same way as it might were the building to cause rain-water to be projected off its roof on to the adjoining land (compare the reflection of the sunshine in *Bank of New Zealand v Greenwood*). In the same way, the deposit of huge volumes of snow on an adjoining building caused by the erection of a tall building adjacent to a lower building may be actionable, see *T H Critelli v Lincoln Trust & Savings Co*, or the lowering of a water table caused by the construction of a sewer and leading to injury to the plaintiff's land, see *Pugliese v National Capital etc.* However, in England it has been held that no tort is committed where the defendant abstracts water percolating under his or her land in such quantities as to cause physical damage to adjoining property, see *Stephens v Anglian Water.*

Leakey v National Trust for Places of Historic Interest or Natural Beauty
[1980] I All ER 17 Court of Appeal

The plaintiffs' homes were threatened by the defendant's hill which was in danger of slipping. The threat of slippage stemmed from the actions of rain, sun, wind etc, on the type of clay. The Court of Appeal held that there was a duty imposed upon occupiers of land in relation to hazards which arose from the operation of nature provided the danger was known, or reasonably ought to have been known. It was a duty to do what was reasonable in all the circumstances to prevent or minimise the risk of damage.

Megaw LJ: '... The decision in the *Sedleigh-Denfield* case was in a case where, on the facts, something which might be described as "not natural" had been introduced on to the defendant's land in the building of the culvert, but not by the defendant. It had been done by a trespasser without the defendant's knowledge or consent. It was not a case in which the potential damage to the neighbour's land had been brought about by natural causes. Therefore it may be said that the *Sedleigh-Denfield* case did not decide, so as to bind lower courts in England, that an owner or occupier of land was under a duty to exercise reasonable care where natural causes, as distinct from the act of a trespasser, brought about the dangerous condition of the land, of which he, the owner or occupier, knew or which he should have realised. If I had taken the view that the *Sedleigh-Denfield* case does not bear on the question raised by the present appeal (and therefore also ought not to have influenced the decision in *Goldman v Hargrave*), I should have reached a different conclusion on this appeal. I do not, however, accept the suggested distinction.

My first comment is that the whole tenor of the speeches in the *Sedleigh-Denfield* case suggests that the view of their Lordships, if not their decision, was that the same duty arose. The approval of the passage in *Salmond on the Law of Torts*, to which I have previously referred, so suggests. A passage in Lord Wright's speech gives, I believe, a fair reflection of the attitude of their Lordships:

> "The liability for a nuisance is not, at least in modern law, a strict or absolute liability. If the defendant, by himself or those for whom he is responsible, has created what constitutes a nuisance, and if it causes damage, the difficulty now being considered does not arise; but he may have taken over the nuisance, ready made as it were, when he acquired the property, or the nuisance may be due to a latent defect or to the act of a trespasser or stranger. Then he is not liable unless he continued or adopted the nuisance, or, more accurately, did not without undue delay remedy it when he became aware of it, or with ordinary and reasonable care should have become aware of it. This rule seems to be in accord with good sense and convenience."

I am confident that Lord Wright's words "latent defect" were intended to include a defect in the land itself. Lord Wright was making the same point, the lack of any valid distinction, in this context, between a trespasser's act and an act of nature, as he had made when he was Wright J, in *Noble v Harrison*. There, after referring to *Barker v Herbert*, he said:

> "The nuisance in that case was caused by the act of a trespasser, but I think the same principle applies to a nuisance (in this case the latent crack in the branch with the resulting risk that some day it would fall) caused by a secret and unobservable operation of nature."

So long as the defect remains "latent" there is no duty on the occupier, whether the defect has been caused by a trespasser or by nature. Equally, once the latent becomes patent, a duty will arise, whether the causative agent of the defect is man or nature. But the mere fact that there is a duty does not necessarily mean that inaction constitutes a breach of the duty.

My second comment on the suggested distinction is that it involves a fallacy. I cite a passage from the judgment in *Goldman v Hargrave* which ... makes this clear beyond dispute:

"It was suggested as a logical basis for the distinction that in the case of a hazard originating in an act of man, an occupier who fails to deal with it can be said to be using his land in a manner detrimental to his neighbour and so to be within the classical field of responsibility in nuisance, whereas this cannot be said when the hazard originates without human action so long at least as the occupier merely abstains. The fallacy of this argument is that, as already explained, the basis of the occupier's liability lies not in the use of his land: in the absence of 'adoption' there is no such use; but in the neglect of action in the face of something which may damage his neighbour. To this, the suggested distinction is irrelevant."

[Megaw LJ then examined *Rylands v Fletcher* and concluded that it was irrelevant.]

... Suppose that we are not bound by *Rylands v Fletcher* or any other authority to hold in favour of the defendants where the nuisance arises solely from natural forces; but suppose also that we are not bound by the decision in *Sedleigh-Denfield* or other binding authority to hold that there is a duty on the defendants in a case such as the present. Ought we as a matter of policy to develop the law by holding that there is a duty in a case such as the present?

If, as a result of the working of the forces of nature, there is, poised above my land, or above my house, a boulder or a rotten tree, which is liable to fall at any moment of the day or night, perhaps destroying my house, and perhaps killing or injuring me or members of my family, am I without remedy? (Of course the standard of care required may be much higher where there is risk to life or limb as contrasted with mere risk to property, but can it be said that the duty exists in the one case and not in the other?) Must I, in such a case, if my protests to my neighbour go unheeded, sit and wait and hope that the worst will not befall? If it is said that I have in such circumstances a remedy of going on my neighbour's land to abate the nuisance, that would, or might, be an unsatisfactory remedy. But in any event, if there were such a right of abatement, it would, as counsel for the plaintiffs rightly contended, be because my neighbour owed me a duty. There is, I think, ample authority that, if I have a right to abatement, I have also a remedy in damages if the nuisance remains unabated and causes me damage or personal injury. That is what Scrutton LJ said in the *Job Edwards* case with particular reference to *Attorney-General v Tod Heatley*. It is dealt with also in the speech of Viscount Maugham in the *Sedleigh-Denfield* case, and in the speech of Lord Atkin.

In the example which I have given above, I believe that few people would regard it as anything other than a grievous blot on the law if the law recognises the existence of no duty on the part of the owner or occupier. But take another example, at the other end of the scale, where it might be thought that there is, potentially, an equally serious injustice the other way. If a stream flows through A's land, A being a small farmer, and there is a known danger that in times of heavy rainfall, because of the configuration of A's land and the nature of the stream's course and flow, there may be an overflow, which will pass beyond A's land and damage the property of A's neighbours: perhaps much wealthier neighbours. It may require expensive works, far beyond A's means, to prevent or even diminish the risk of such flooding. Is A to be liable for all the loss that occurs when the flood comes, if he has not done the impossible and carried out these works at his own expense?

In my judgment, there is, in the scope of the duty as explained in *Goldman v Hargrave*, a removal, or at least a powerful amelioration, of the injustice which might otherwise be caused in such a case by the recognition of the duty of care. Because of that limitation on the scope of the duty, I would say that, as a matter of policy, the law ought to recognise such a duty of care.

This leads on to the question of the scope of the duty. This is discussed, and the nature and extent of the duty is explained, in the judgment in *Goldman v Hargrave*. The duty is a duty to do that which is reasonable in all the circumstances, and no more than what, if anything, is reasonable, to prevent or minimise the known risk of damage or injury to one's neighbour or to his property. The considerations with which the law is familiar are all to be taken into account in deciding whether there has been a breach of duty, and, if so, what that breach is, and whether it is causative of the damage in respect of which the claim is made. Thus, there will fall to be considered the extent of the risk. What, so far as reasonably can be foreseen, are the chances that anything untoward will happen or that any damage will be caused? What is to be foreseen as to the possible extent of the damage if the risk becomes a reality? Is it practicable to prevent, or to minimise, the happening of any damage? If it is practicable, how simple or how difficult are the measures which could be taken, how much and how lengthy work do they involve, and what is the probable cost of such works? Was there sufficient time for preventive action to have been taken, by persons acting reasonably in relation to the known risk, between the time when it became known to, or should have been realised by, the defendant, and the time when the damage occurred? Factors such as these, so far as they apply in a particular case, fall to be weighed in deciding whether the defendant's duty of care requires, or required, him to do anything, and, if so, what.

There is a passage in this part of the judgment in *Goldman v Hargrave* defining the scope of the duty, which, on the one hand, is said to be likely, if accepted, to give rise to insuperable difficulties in its practical working, and, on the other hand, is said to provide a sensible and just limitation on the scope of the duty, avoiding the danger of substantial injustice being caused, even in exceptional cases, by the existence of the duty. The passage in question reads as follows:

"... the owner of a small property where a hazard arises which threatens a neighbour with substantial interest should not have to do so much as one with larger interests of his own at stake and greater resources to protect them: if the small owner does what he can and promptly calls on his neighbour to provide additional resources, he may be held to have done his duty: he should not be liable unless it is clearly proved that he could, and reasonably in his individual circumstances should, have done more."

... The defendant's duty is to do that which it is reasonable for him to do. The criteria of reasonableness include, in respect of a duty of this nature, the factor of what the particular man, not the average man, can be expected to do, having regard, amongst other things, where a serious expenditure of money is required to eliminate or reduce the danger, to his means. Just as, where physical effort is required to avert an immediate danger, the defendant's age and physical condition may be relevant in deciding what is reasonable, so also logic and good sense require that, where the expenditure of money is required, the defendant's capacity to find the money is relevant. But this can only be in the way of a broad, and not a detailed, assessment; and, in arriving at a judgment on reasonableness, a similar broad assessment may be relevant in some cases as to the neighbour's capacity to protect himself from damage, whether by way of some form of barrier on his own land or by way of providing funds for expenditure on agreed works on the land of the defendant.

Take, by way of example, the hypothetical instance which I gave earlier: the landowner through whose land a stream flows. In rainy weather, it is known, the stream may flood and the flood may spread to the land of neighbours. If the risk is one which can readily be overcome or lessened, for example by reasonable steps on the part of the landowner to keep the stream free from blockage by flotsam or silt carried down, he will be in breach of duty if he does nothing or does too little. But if the only remedy is substantial and expensive works, then it might well be that the landowner would have discharged his duty by saying to his neighbours, who also know of the risk and who have asked him to do something about it, "You have my permission to come on to my land and to do agreed works at your expense", or, it may be, "on the basis of a fair sharing of expense". In deciding whether the landowner had discharged his duty of care, if the question were thereafter to come before the courts, I do not think that, except perhaps in a most unusual case, there would be any question of discovery as to the means of the plaintiff or the defendant, or evidence as to their respective resources. The question of reasonableness of what had been done or offered would fall to be decided on a broad basis, in which, on some occasions, there might be included an element of obvious discrepancy of financial resources. It may be that in some cases the introduction of this factor may give rise to difficulties to litigants and to their advisers and to the courts. But I believe that the difficulties are likely to turn out to be more theoretical than practical ... If and when problems do arise, they will have to be solved. I do not think that the existence of such potential difficulties justifies a refusal to accept as a part of the law of England the duty as laid down in *Goldman v Hargrave*, including the whole of the exposition as to the scope of the duty. As I have said, no difficulty now arises in this present appeal as regards the application of the *Goldman v Hargrave* scope of the duty, once it is held that the duty exists ...'

Comment

(1) This complex case identifies the close link between nuisance and negligence. The existence of a duty in nuisance, in particular circumstances, is made clear. The specific duty will depend upon the precise facts of each case. Megaw LJ was not drawing an exhaustive catalogue of the factors to be considered, see *Page Motors Ltd v Epsom and Ewell BC*, p 670.

(2) In *Sedleigh-Denfield v O'Callaghan*, some three years before the events complained of, a trespassing local authority had entered the defendant's land and had created a culvert. The grille at the entrance had been sited carelessly and allowed a build-up of material at the mouth of the culvert. This build-up prevented the free flow of water and there was a flood of the plaintiff's property. The House of Lords held that the defendant knew or ought to have known of the state of affairs amounting to the nuisance, and had come under a common law duty to remedy the defect. The House of Lords approved the dissenting judgment of Scrutton LJ in *Job Edwards Ltd v Birmingham Navigations* when he had said:

'... the landowner in possession is liable for a nuisance created by a trespasser, which causes damage to others, if he could, after he knows or ought to have known of it, prevent by reasonable care its spreading.'

Viscount Maugham said:

'My Lords, in the present case, I am of opinion that the respondents both continued and adopted the nuisance. After the lapse of nearly 3 years, they must be taken to have suffered the nuisance to continue, for they neglected to take the very simple step of placing a grid in the proper place, which would have removed the danger to their neighbour's land. They adopted the nuisance, for they continued during all that time to use the artificial contrivance of the conduit for the purpose of getting rid of water from their property without taking the proper means for rendering it safe.'

(3) In *Goldman v Hargrave* a redgum tree on the defendant's land was struck by lightning and caught fire. The defendant cleared the land around the tree, cut down the tree and sawed it into sections. He then left the tree and failed to adopt the common practice of dousing the tree with water. This he could have done without substantial trouble or cost. It was foreseeable that the weather would become hotter and windier, and this is what happened. The core of the

tree was still very hot and caused the tree to burst into flames. The fire spread across the defendant's land to the neighbouring plaintiff's land. According to the Privy Council the question of law was whether or not an occupier who, when faced with a hazard accidentally arising on his land, fails to act with reasonable prudence so as to remove the hazard, can be liable in negligence. It was pointed out in *Leakey* that the essence of the legal cause of action is breach of duty and that the precise name (nuisance or negligence) is largely irrelevant.

Lord Wilberforce:

'On principle therefore, their lordships find in the opinions of the House of Lords in *Sedleigh-Denfield v O'Callaghan* and in the statements of the law by Scrutton LJ and Salmond, of which they approve, support for the existence of a general duty on occupiers in relation to hazards occurring on their land, whether natural or man-made ...

[Lord Wilberforce cited Australian and New Zealand authority and continued:]

The cumulative result of these is to establish the occupier's duty of care towards his neighbour to a similar extent as the English and New Zealand cases ...

Thirdly their lordships have considered the modern text books of authority on the law of torts ... All of these endorse the development, which their lordships find in the decisions, towards a measured duty of care by occupiers to remove or reduce hazards to their neighbours.

So far it has been possible to consider the existence of a duty, in general terms; but the matter cannot be left there without some definition of the scope of his duty. How far does it go? What is the standard of the effort required? What is the position as regards expenditure? It is not enough to say merely that these must be "reasonable" since what is reasonable to one man may be very unreasonable, and indeed ruinous, to another: the law must take account of the fact that the occupier on whom the duty is cast, has, *ex hypothesi*, had this hazard thrust on him through no seeking or fault of his own. His interest, and his resources whether physical or material, may be of a very modest character either in relation to the magnitude of the hazard, or as compared with those of his threatened neighbour. A rule which required of him in such unsought circumstances in his neighbour's interest a physical effort of which he is not capable, or an excessive expenditure of money, would be unenforceable or unjust. One may say in general terms that the existence of a duty must be based on knowledge of the hazard, ability to foresee the consequences of not checking or removing it, and the ability to abate it. Moreover in many cases, as for example in Scrutton LJ's ... hypothetical case of stamping out a fire, or the present case, where the hazard could have been removed with little effort and no expenditure, no problem arises; but other cases may not be so simple. In such situations the standard ought to be to require of the occupier what it is reasonable to expect of him in his individual circumstances. Thus, less must be expected of the infirm than of the able bodied: the owner of small property where a hazard arises which threatens a neighbour with substantial interests should not have to do so much as one with larger interests of his own at stake and greater resources to protect them: if the small owner does what he can and promptly calls on his neighbour to provide additional resources, he may be held to have done his duty: he should not be liable unless it is clearly proved that he could, and reasonably in his individual circumstance should, have done more. This approach to a difficult matter is in fact that which the courts in their more recent decisions have taken. It is in accordance with the actual decision in the *Job Edwards* case where to remove the hazard would have cost the occupier some £1,000 – on this basis the decision itself seems obviously right. It is in accordance with *Pontardawe Rural Council v Moore-Gwyn* where to maintain the rocks in a state of safety would have cost the occupier some £300; and if some of the situations such as those in *Giles v Walker* (thistledown) and *Sparke v Osborne* (prickly pears) were to recur to-day, it is probable that they would not be decided without a balanced consideration of what could be expected of the particular occupier as compared with the consequences of inaction ... In the present case it has not been argued that the action necessary to put the fire out ... was not well within the capacity and resources of the appellant. Their lordships therefore reach the conclusion that the respondents' claim for damages, on the basis of negligence, was fully made out.'

(4)   Megaw LJ rejected suggestions that the subjective nature of the duty, involving as it does a comparison between the resources of the parties, would lead to 'unpredictability of the outcome of litigation, delay in reaching decisions ... as to protective measures to prevent damage, and the increased complexity, length and expense of litigation'.

(5)   In *Holbeck Hall Hotel Ltd v Scarborough County Council* a geological fault extended under both the claimants' and the council's land. Following land-slips on the site in 1982 and 1985, the council became aware that there was a fault under the land and undertook some remedial work. This was ineffective because the fault was vastly more serious than their geological survey suggested (in a parallel action it was held that the surveyors had been negligent but that the negligence had not been the cause of Scarborough's liability to the claimants). In 1993 there was a catastrophic land-slip as a result of which the claimants' hotel had to be demolished. The issue of liability fell to be decided applying principles in *Leakey v National Trust*. The Court of Appeal upheld the defendant's appeal against liability.

First, the court found that the principles in *Leakey* applied not only to danger due to escape or encroachment but also to danger due to lack of support.

Second, the court held that the 'measured duty of care' required either actual or presumed knowledge of the danger on the part of the defendant; as Stuart-Smith LJ said: 'It is the existence of the defect coupled with the danger that constitutes the nuisance; it is knowledge or presumed knowledge of the nuisance that involves liability for continuing it when it could reasonably be abated.'

Third, as to the scope of the duty, Stuart-Smith LJ said that: 'In considering the scope of the measured duty of care, the courts are still in relatively uncharted waters ...'. Where, as in this case, the danger was latent the defendant was not to be held liable simply because upon further investigation the defect would have been identified. In a case where the defect is patent then the duty will exist where the landowner observed or should have observed it. In this case the council did not foresee the scale of the danger which occurred and could not have done so without further expert survey. Distinguishing the case from the position in negligence where a defendant will be under a duty of care and will be liable for all damage of the type which was foreseeable, whether the actual extent of the damage is foreseeable or not, Stuart-Smith LJ observed that in nuisances of this sort the duty of care was 'a measured duty of care'. Accordingly it would not be appropriate to impose on the defendant a duty of care in respect of damage which was vastly more extensive than that which was foreseen or could have been foreseen without extensive further geological investigation. This was so in particular where the defect existed just as much on the claimant's land as on the defendant's.

Stuart-Smith LJ also sought to align the principles closely to the development of tests for a duty of care in negligence. Echoing the language of *Caparo v Dickman* and *Marc Rich & Co v Bishop Rock Marine Co Ltd*, he thought that it would not be fair, just and reasonable 'to impose liability for damage which is greater in extent than anything that was foreseen or foreseeable' (without further geological investigation), especially where the defect and danger existed as much on the claimant's land as the defendant's.

Finally, Stuart-Smith LJ indicated, *obiter*, that in a case such as the present, where the defect existed in both parties' land, it was at least arguable that the measured duty of care might only require the defendant to alert the claimant to the nature of the problem as understood by the defendant at the time.

(6) Ordinarily (and subject to any obligations arising from land law) the common law will not require an owner of land to repair their property, but if it is or threatens to be a nuisance then this may well be an occasion for the common law to impose a duty (for example *Leakey* itself). *Abbahall Ltd v Smee* in the Court of Appeal concerned the allocation of the share of responsibility

for repairing a roof to protect two properties. The upper two floors of a property, including a second floor which was a living space created in the roof space, were residential premises occupied by the defendant, Miss Smee, the freehold owner who had obtained her title through adverse possession. The ground floor comprised commercial premises let by a tenant of the claimant, Abbahall Ltd, the freehold owner of the ground floor. The flat owned and occupied by Miss Smee was thus a 'flying freehold'.

Miss Smee had allowed the roof to fall into disrepair and as a result water leaked into the ground floor and there was a danger of masonry falling onto visitors to the ground floor. Abbahall obtained an injunction enabling it to enter the flat to carry out work and then sought to recover the cost of the necessary work. The Judge held that Miss Smee was under a duty to contribute one-quarter of the costs of the past and future repairs. Abbahall appealed.

The Court of Appeal held that, in the case of a flying freehold, where the roof protected the claimant's and the defendant's premises, common sense, common justice and reasonableness as between neighbours required that those who took the benefit of the works should also take the burden of paying for them; and if the parties would derive equal benefit from the works, they should share the cost equally. The court also made comments about the extent to which the relative wealth of the parties should be taken into account.

Munby J:

'[57] [Counsel for Abbahall] submits, and I agree, that the nature of the duties governing neighbours in a case such as this simply cannot depend on such transient matters as their means. Such a rule would, in my judgment, be wrong in principle. It would be neither fair nor just nor reasonable. It would not serve the interests of good neighbourliness. Quite the contrary. It would in my judgment be unjust to the point of absurdity.

[58] Moreover, and as [counsel] also points out, the approach for which [counsel for Miss Smee] contends is not merely wrong in principle: it is highly inconvenient in practice, for the respective liabilities to contribute would be unpredictable, difficult to assess and liable to change every time any owner either left or suffered some marked change in his economic fortunes.

[59] The fact is that in a case such as this the obligation to contribute to the common task of maintaining the roof is simply an ordinary incident of the ownership of property, albeit that for largely historical and technical reasons the liability is regulated not by the law of property but by the law of tort.

[60] In my judgment it is simply not reasonable as between neighbours for Miss Smee to say that because of her poverty her only obligation is to

allow Abbahall entry to her property to carry out the repairs at its sole expense. Reasonableness between neighbours who choose to live together in the same building, sharing the same roof, requires that all share – and share equally – the cost of repairing and maintaining the roof. The reality, assuming that Miss Smee really does not have the money to pay her appropriate share of the cost, is that she is choosing to live in a property she cannot afford. In this context there is ... force in [the] comment that Miss Smee is being asked to do no more than any ordinary householder would ordinarily do without compulsion. If she cannot afford to do so, then I can see no reason why her poverty should throw the burden, or an increased burden, on her neighbour. If she cannot afford to maintain the flat she should move to a property which she can afford. If she chooses not to move she should not be enabled in effect to offload her liability onto her more solvent neighbour. In the final analysis, in my judgment, it is simply not reasonable as between neighbours for Miss Smee to go on living in a leaking property which is damaging her neighbour's property, all the time doing nothing to contribute to the cost of remedying things because she chooses to live in a property she cannot afford to maintain.

[61]   I should add that there is nothing in any way inconsistent here with what Lord Wilberforce [in *Goldman*] and Megaw LJ [in *Leakey*] were saying. The types of case they were considering were far removed from a case such as this. And neither went so far as to assert that the defendant's financial resources are always relevant, let alone determinative. In many cases, no doubt, they will be relevant – as, indeed, in the types of case they were considering. But not in every case. And not in a case such as this.'

Marcic v Thames Water Utilities Ltd
[2003] UKHL 66 House of Lords

Thames Water, a statutory undertaker, was responsible under a statutory scheme governed by the Water Industry Act 1991 for the surface and foul water sewers where Mr Marcic lived. Originally, the sewers were sufficient to serve the area but there had been a substantial rise in the number of houses and each householder was entitled as a matter of right to drain into the sewers. Thames Water had not failed to clean or maintain the sewers. As a consequence of this inadequacy of the system to cope, the area suffered from serious periodic flooding. Mr Marcic did not seek to use the statutory enforcement procedures but installed at a cost of £16,000 a flood defence scheme. He sought to recover damages for nuisance and also alleged that the flooding was in breach of article 8 and protocol 1 of the European Convention on Human Rights as guaranteed under the Human Rights Act 1998.

The Court of Appeal decided that the law of nuisance had been altered by cases such as *Goldman v Hargrave* and that, despite the line of cases to the contrary, a public authority's failure to construct new sewers would be actionable as a nuisance. The House of Lords concluded that the previous line of cases summarised by Lord Justice Denning in *Pride of Derby* remained good law: the failure of a local authority to enlarge and improve sewer facilities was not actionable as a nuisance when additional housing linking into the sewers as a matter of right caused the system to overflow. The claim for damages under the Human Rights Act 1998 also failed.

Lord Hoffmann: '...

61.   ... If the *Sedleigh-Denfield* case lays down a general principle that an owner of land has a duty to take reasonable steps to prevent a nuisance arising from a known source of hazard, even though he did not himself create it, why should that not require him to construct new sewers if the court thinks it would have been reasonable to do so?

62.   The difference in my opinion is that the *Sedleigh-Denfield*, *Goldman* and *Leakey* cases were dealing with disputes between neighbouring landowners simply in their capacity as individual landowners. In such cases it is fair and efficient to impose reciprocal duties upon each landowner to take whatever steps are reasonable to prevent his land becoming a source of injury to his neighbour. Even then, the question of what measures should reasonably have been taken may not be uncomplicated. As Lord Wilberforce said in *Goldman's* case, the court must (unusually) have regard to the individual circumstances of the defendant. In *Leakey's* case Megaw LJ recoiled from the prospect of a detailed examination of the defendant's financial resources and said it should be done "on a broad basis".

63.   Nevertheless, whatever the difficulties, the court in such cases is performing its usual function of deciding what is reasonable as between the two parties to the action. But the exercise becomes very different when one is dealing with the capital expenditure of a statutory undertaking providing public utilities on a large scale. The matter is no longer confined to the parties to the action. If one customer is given a certain level of services, everyone in the same circumstances should receive the same level of services. So the effect of a decision about what it would be reasonable to expect a sewerage undertaker to do for the plaintiff is extrapolated across the country. This in turn raises questions of public interest. Capital expenditure on new sewers has to be financed; interest must be paid on borrowings and privatised undertakers must earn a reasonable return. This expenditure can be met only be charges paid by consumers. Is it in the public interest that they should have to pay more? And does expenditure on the particular improvements with which the plaintiff is concerned represent the best order of priorities?

64.   These are decisions which courts are not equipped to make in ordinary litigation. It is therefore not surprising that for more than a century the question of whether more or better sewers should be constructed has been entrusted by Parliament to administrators rather than judges. ...

65. The enforcement procedure under the 1991 Act is much more elaborate [than its statutory precursors]. The Director has a duty under section 30(4) to consider a complaint and take such steps as he considers appropriate. He has a prima facie duty under section 18(1) to make an enforcement order if he satisfied that the company is contravening its statutory duty. But that duty is qualified by section 19(1), which provides that he is not required to make an order if satisfied, among other things, that the company is willing to give suitable undertakings or that the duties imposed upon him by Part I of the Act preclude the making of such an order. His duties under Part I require him to exercise his powers in the manner best calculated to achieve certain objectives. The overriding objectives (section 2(2)) are to secure that the functions of a sewerage undertaker are properly carried out and that the undertakers are able "(in particular, by securing reasonable returns on their capital)" to finance the proper carrying out of their functions. More particular objectives are to protect the interests of customers liable to pay charges and promote economy and efficiency on the part of the company.

66. Pursuant to these duties, the Director has to address himself to the question of flooding and formulated policies which the statutory undertakers should follow. Undertakers are required to submit a quinquennial strategic business plan which includes a statement of the capital expenditure required to achieve a reasonable level of alleviation of flooding. If the Director accepts such expenditure as reasonable, it is taken into account in assessing the charges which will give the undertaker a reasonable return on capital. Otherwise it is not. During the three quinquennia starting in 1990, the Director was willing to allow expenditure on work in relation to properties classified as at risk of internal flooding. But no allowance was made for properties, like that of Mr Marcic, which were only at risk of external flooding.

67. After the widespread floods of October 2000, the Director commissioned further studies of the flooding problem. In March 2002 he issued a consultation paper proposing a policy revision for the 2005–2010 quinquennium by which remedial work for properties only at risk of external flooding should also be included. He also made an interim agreement with Thames by which he approved additional investment before 2005 to free 250 properties (including that of Mr Marcic) from risk of external flooding. Your Lordships were told that this work has been done.

68. It is plain that the Court of Appeal, in deciding that better sewers should have been laid to serve Mr Marcic's property, was in no position to take into account the wider issues which Parliament requires the Director to consider. The judge, who heard fairly detailed evidence about what the cost of such improvements would be, confessed himself unable to decide whether the priorities laid down by the Director were fair or not.

[70] ... The 1991 Act makes it even clearer than the earlier legislation that Parliament did not intend the fairness of priorities to be decided by a judge. It

intended the decision to rest with the Director, subject only to judicial review. It would subvert the scheme of the 1991 Act if the courts were to impose upon the sewerage undertakers, on a case by case basis, a system of priorities which is different from that which the Director considers appropriate.'

Lord Nicholls: '…

THE CLAIM UNDER THE HUMAN RIGHTS ACT 1998

37.   I turn to Mr Marcic's claim under the Human Rights Act 1998. His claim is that as a public authority within the meaning of section 6 of the Human Rights Act 1998 Thames Water has acted unlawfully. Thames Water has conducted itself in a way which is incompatible with Mr Marcic's Convention rights under article 8 of the Convention and article 1 of the First Protocol to the Convention. His submission was to the following effect. The flooding of Mr Marcic's property falls within the first paragraph of article 8 and also within article 1 of the First Protocol. That was common ground between the parties. Direct and serious interference of this nature with a person's home is prima facie a violation of a person's right to respect for his private and family life (article 8) and of his entitlement to the peaceful enjoyment of his possessions (article 1 of the First Protocol). The burden of justifying this interference rests on Thames Water. At the trial of the preliminary issues Thames Water failed to discharge this burden. The trial judge found that the system of priorities used by Thames Water in deciding whether to carry out flood alleviation works might be entirely fair. The judge also said that on the limited evidence before him it was not possible to decide this issue, or to decide whether for all its apparent faults the system fell within the wide margin of discretion open to Thames Water and the Director.

38.   To my mind the fatal weakness in this submission is the same as that afflicting Mr Marcic's claim in nuisance: it does not take sufficient account of the statutory scheme under which Thames Water is operating the offending sewers. The need to adopt some system of priorities for building more sewers is self-evident. So is the need for the system to be fair. A fair system of priorities necessarily involves balancing many intangible factors. Whether the system adopted by a sewerage undertaker is fair is a matter inherently more suited for decision by the industry regulator than by a court. And the statutory scheme so provides. Moreover, the statutory scheme provides a remedy where a system of priorities is not fair. An unfair system of priorities means that a sewerage undertaker is not properly discharging its statutory drainage obligation so far as those who are being treated unfairly are concerned. The statute provides what should happen in these circumstances. The Director is charged with deciding whether to make an enforcement order in respect of a sewerage undertaker's failure to drain property properly. Parliament entrusted this decision to the Director, not the courts.

39.   What happens in practice accords with this statutory scheme. When people affected by sewer flooding complain to the Director he considers whether he

should require the sewerage undertaker to take remedial action. Before doing so he considers, among other matters, the severity and history of the problem in the context of that undertaker's sewer flooding relief programme, as allowed for in its current price limits. In many cases the company agrees to take action, but sometimes he accepts that a solution is not possible in the short term.

40. So the claim based on the Human Rights Act 1998 raises a broader issue: is the statutory scheme as a whole, of which this enforcement procedure is part, Convention-compliant? Stated more specifically and at the risk of over-simplification, is the statutory scheme unreasonable in its impact on Mr Marcic and other householders whose properties are periodically subjected to sewer flooding?

41. The recent decision of the European Court of Human Rights, sitting as a Grand Chamber, in *Hatton v United Kingdom* confirms how courts should approach questions such as these. In *Hatton's* case the applicants lived near Heathrow airport. They claimed that the government's policy on night flights at Heathrow violated their rights under article 8. The court emphasised "the fundamentally subsidiary nature" of the Convention. National authorities have "direct democratic legitimation" and are in principle better placed than an international court to evaluate local needs and conditions. In matters of general policy, on which opinions within a democratic society may reasonably differ widely, 'the role of the domestic policy maker should be given special weight": see para 97. A fair balance must be struck between the interests of the individual and of the community as a whole.

42. In the present case the interests Parliament had to balance included, on the one hand, the interests of customers of a company whose properties are prone to sewer flooding and, on the other hand, all the other customers of the company whose properties are drained through the company's sewers. The interests of the first group conflict with the interests of the company's customers as a whole in that only a minority of customers suffer sewer flooding but the company's customers as a whole meet the cost of building more sewers. As already noted, the balance struck by the statutory scheme is to impose a general drainage obligation on a sewerage undertaker but to entrust enforcement of this obligation to an independent regulator who has regard to all the different interests involved. Decisions of the Director are of course subject to an appropriately penetrating degree of judicial review by the courts.

43. In principle this scheme seems to me to strike a reasonable balance. Parliament acted well within its bounds as policy maker. In Mr Marcic's case matters plainly went awry. It cannot be acceptable that in 2001, several years after Thames Water knew of Mr Marcic's serious problems, there was still no prospect of the necessary work being carried out for the foreseeable future. At times Thames Water handled Mr Marcic's complaint in a tardy and insensitive fashion. But the malfunctioning of the statutory scheme on this occasion does not cast doubt on its overall fairness as a scheme. A complaint by an individual about his particular case

can, and should, be pursued with the Director pursuant to the statutory scheme, with the long stop availability of judicial review. That remedial avenue was not taken in this case.

44.   I must add that one aspect of the statutory scheme as presently administered does cause concern. This is the uncertain position regarding payment of compensation to those who suffer flooding while waiting for flood alleviation works to be carried out. A modest statutory compensation scheme exists regarding internal flooding ... There seems to be no statutory provision regarding external sewer flooding. Some sewerage undertakers make payments, others do not. They all provide a free clean up and disinfecting service, including removal of residual effluent.

45.   It seems to me that, in principle, if it is not practicable for reasons of expense to carry out remedial works for the time being, those who enjoy the benefit of effective drainage should bear the cost of paying some compensation to those whose properties are situate lower down in the catchment area and, in consequence, have to endure intolerable sewer flooding, whether internal or external. As the Court of Appeal noted, the flooding is the consequence of the benefit provided to those making use of the system. The minority who suffer damage and disturbance as a consequence of the inadequacy of the sewerage system ought not to be required to bear an unreasonable burden. This is a matter the Director and others should reconsider in the light of the facts in the present case.

46.   For these reasons I consider the claim under the Human Rights Act 1998 is ill-founded. The scheme set up by the 1991 Act is Convention-compliant. The scheme provides a remedy for persons in Mr Marcic's unhappy position, but Mr Marcic chose not to avail himself of this remedy.'

Tetley and others v Chitty and others
[1986] I All ER 663 Queen's Bench Division

The defendant council had leased to another defendant a site for the purpose of running a go-kart club. The council were aware from several sources including their own advisers of the likely consequences of granting permission. On the issue of liability the court decided that there was a nuisance for which the council could be liable since they were aware of the noise as either an ordinary and necessary consequence or natural and necessary consequence of the use of go-karts. The court granted an injunction.

McNeill J: '... [Counsel for the plaintiff's] argument was that a landlord ... or licensor prior to the granting of the lease, is liable if he authorises a nuisance on his land or grants a lease of his land with a nuisance on it or knowing that a nuisance is going to be caused on it, or for any operation which inevitably will cause a nuisance. Counsel for the council did not dissent from this as a formulation of the appropriate test.

In so far as this case turns on the grant of the lease, this ... did not occur until 16 January 1981 and it could not be and really was not argued that by that date the council did not know perfectly well the facts which constituted the nuisance and knew of the complaints that had been made, even though it may not have appreciated what the legal consequences were. There can be no answer to the claim as far as the last few days during which the nuisance continued on this point, that is to say from 16 until 27 January. [Counsel] accepted that the council was not relieved of liability otherwise on it by clauses in the lease or in the antecedent agreement for a lease or licence under which it obliged the club not to do or permit or suffer to be done in or on the land anything which would become a nuisance or annoyance to owners and occupiers of neighbouring premises and limited the hours of operation, or took an indemnity from the club.

What then is the effect of the authorities? In *White v Jameson* the short head-note reads:

> "Where the occupier of lands grants a licence to another to do certain acts on the land, and the licensee in doing them commits a nuisance, the occupier may be made a Defendant to a suit to restrain the nuisance."

That was a case in which the landlord had authorised another to burn in his yard, into bricks, clay found in the yard; but the landlord had taken no active part either in erecting the kiln or in burning the bricks. Jessel MR, having decided that the burning of the bricks was a nuisance to the plaintiff, held the landlord liable to be sued for the acts complained of. He said: "The land on which they were committed was his; and, independently of his having an interest in the profits, the Defendant Proffitt did these acts by his licence ...". It will be noted that in that case it would not seem as if the man Proffitt had any exclusive right in the land and it may be in the light of later authorities that that case, perhaps, goes further than the law as it now stands. In that case the occupier had merely a revocable licence.

Counsel for the second defendants relied on a more recent decision, that of Pennycuick V-C in *Smith v Scott* and on the older decision of *Harris v James*. Counsel contended that liability could only be established if the nuisance were committed with the landlord's express or implied authority. It is, he said, insufficient to show merely a likely consequence: a plaintiff to succeed must show a necessary consequence. Here the necessary consequence that nuisance would be caused to each of the plaintiffs has not, he said, been established.

In *Harris v James* Blackburn J pointed out:

> "There can be no doubt that where a person authorises and requires another to commit a nuisance he is liable for that nuisance, and if the authority be given in the shape of a lease he is not the less liable ... I do not think when a person demises property he is to be taken to authorise all that the occupier may do ... In the present case, as I understand the averments, the field was let for the very purpose and object of being worked as a lime

quarry and for the erecting [of] lime kilns and burning lime. When, then, it is stated as a fact that the injury complained of arose from the natural and necessary consequence of carrying out this object, and as the result of lime getting and lime burning, then I think we must say that the landlord authorised the lime burning and the nuisance arising from it as being the necessary consequence of letting the field in the manner and with the objects described."

... In *Smith v Scott* Pennycuick V-C had to deal with a somewhat unusual factual situation. The plaintiff was the owner of a dwelling-house in a street other houses in which were being acquired by the local authority for housing homeless families. The local authority put into the house next to the plaintiff's house a family known by the corporation to be likely to cause a nuisance though on terms expressly prohibiting the committing of a nuisance. Well, it will be no surprise to see that after the tenants went in they so damaged the plaintiff's premises and caused such a noise that he had to leave and go and live elsewhere. The case was framed in three ways: in nuisance, in the rule in *Rylands v Fletcher* and in negligence. I do not deal with Pennycuick V-C's ruling on the second and third of those, as they have no relevance to the present case. But he did hold, dismissing the action, that the corporation were not liable, as landlords, for a nuisance committed by their tenants for they had neither expressly nor impliedly authorised the nuisance. It was on those last words that counsel for the second defendant founded his submission. Pennycuick V-C said:

"I must then consider the law applicable to the foregoing conclusions of fact. Apart from the allegation of improper motive, counsel for Mr Smith based his case on three propositions of law, namely, (1) the corporation in placing the Scotts in No 25 with knowledge that they were likely to cause a nuisance to their neighbours themselves committed the wrongful act of nuisance ... I will consider those propositions in the same order. (2) It is established beyond question that the person to be sued in nuisance is the occupier of the property from which the nuisance emanates. In general, a landlord is not liable for nuisance committed by his tenant, but to this rule there is, so far as now in point, one recognised exception, namely, that the landlord is liable if he has authorised his tenant to commit the nuisance: see *Harris v James*. But this exception has, in the reported cases, been rigidly confined to circumstances in which the nuisance has either been expressly authorised or is certain to result from the purposes for which the property is let ..."

Pennycuick V-C then referred to *Rich v Basterfield*, *Ayers v Hanson Stanley & Prince* and passages in *Clerk and Lindsell on Torts* (13th edn, 1969), *Salmond on Torts* (15th edn, 1969) and *Winfield and Jolowicz on Tort* (9th edn, 1971). He continued:

"I have used the word 'certain', but 'certainty' is obviously a very difficult matter to establish. It may be that, as one of the textbooks suggests, the proper test in this connection is 'virtual certainty' which is another way of saying a very high degree of probability, but the authorities are not, I venture to think, altogether satisfactory in this respect. Whatever the precise test may be, it would, I think, be impossible to apply the exception to the present case. The exception is squarely based in the reported cases on express or implied authority – see in particular the judgment of Blackburn J in *Harris v James*. The exception is not based on cause and probable result, apart from express or implied authority. In the present case, the corporation let no 25 to the Scotts as a dwelling-house on conditions of tenancy which expressly prohibited the committing of a nuisance, and, notwithstanding that the corporation knew the Scotts were likely to cause a nuisance, I do not think it is legitimate to say that the corporation impliedly authorised the nuisance."

In the circumstances, the claim on that head, as, indeed, on the other heads, failed ... Counsel for the plaintiff contended, in my view rightly, that the law did not require it to be shown that the nuisance was a necessary consequence of the use of the land; the cases did not go so far, and the judgments cited did not require him to go so far in this case ... Authority elsewhere points to objective foreseeability as the proper test: what was the foreseeable result of the decision to permit go-karting? He referred to *The Wagon Mound (No 2), Overseas Tankship (UK) Ltd v Miller Steamship Co Pty Ltd.*

If I were obliged to do so I should accept this as correct but I am not. In this case the nuisance from noise generated by go-kart racing and practising was, in my view on the facts, an ordinary and necessary consequence of the operation in Lush J's words, or a natural and necessary consequence of the operation in Blackburn J's words, both in *Harris v James*. There was, in my view, adapting Pennycuick V-C's test, express or at the least implied consent to do that which on the facts here inevitably would amount to a nuisance ...

Each plaintiff is entitled to damages. Each claims, in addition, a permanent injunction ...

To my mind damages would be a wholly insufficient remedy here, and the plaintiffs are entitled to an injunction. This case is unlike the *Kennaway* case in that the plaintiffs were already there and had for some time been there when the nuisance began, and I have come to the conclusion that as things stand at present there should be a permanent injunction. There is no question here of such an injunction being unworkable ... and, second, it is not, I think, for this court to work out for defendants at fault the way in which they can continue an operation which, as if it has been continued, was an offending operation. It is not merely that the council ... accept that they would have little, if any, control of what actually went on at the track, but it is also clear from [the] evidence the council has not applied itself to any sound barriers or other measures which would reduce the volume and pitch of noise created by the operation, or taken professional advice ...'

Comment

(1) In *Page Motors Ltd v Epsom & Ewell BC*, a distinction was sought to be drawn between the state of premises and the activities of trespassers. This was rejected by the Court of Appeal, Fox LJ: 'I see no difference in principle between allowing a trespasser to alter the condition of your land so that it floods your neighbour's land and allowing a trespasser so to use your land that he prevents or inhibits lawful access to your neighbour's land.' In that case a large number of gypsies occupied a site belonging to the defendant local authority and adjacent to the property of the plaintiff. The objectionable activities of the gypsies had a seriously detrimental effect on the business of the plaintiffs and their ability to recruit and keep staff. The local authority had for some years been trying to evict the trespassing gypsies. It had obtained several possession orders but had failed to enforce them, often after intervention by a government department. Eventually the council created an alternative site for the gypsies and they moved off the land.

The Court of Appeal agreed with the judge that the council had adopted and continued the nuisance within the principle in *Sedleigh-Denfield v O'Callaghan*. In applying *Leakey v National Trust*, and assessing the factors comprising the specific duty of the council, the Court of Appeal did not restrict the judgment of Megaw LJ to physical and financial resources. Reasonableness was to include reference to the legitimate process of consultation with interested parties prior to the creation of an alternative site.

(2) The liability of landlords has been considered in *Lippiatt v South Gloucestershire County Council* and *Hussain v Lancaster City Council*, see p 627, and *Southwark London Borough Council v Mills*, see p 623.

Sturges v Bridgman
(1879) 11 ChD 852 Court of Appeal

The plaintiff, a doctor, ran a practice from his house. Eight years after moving into the house, he built a consulting-room at the end of his garden. The premises of the defendant, a confectioner, abutted the plaintiff's garden adjacent to the consulting-room and they shared a party-wall. The defendant had two large pestle and mortars used for his business for at least the previous 26 years. The plaintiff complained that the noise and vibration seriously interfered with his practice and in particular listening to patients' chests and otherwise concentrating. On the issue of the defence of prescription, the Court of Appeal held that the right to make the noise and vibration commenced only 20 years after they first became a nuisance and that they did not become a nuisance until the plaintiff built his consulting-room.

Thesiger LJ: '... a man cannot, as a general rule, be said to consent to or acquiesce in the acquisition by his neighbour of an easement through an enjoyment of which he has no knowledge, actual or constructive, or which he contests and endeavours to interrupt, or which he temporarily licenses. It is a mere extension of the same notion ... to hold, that an enjoyment which a man cannot prevent raises no presumption of consent or acquiescence ... [u]ntil the noise became an actionable nuisance, which it did not at any time before the consulting-room was built, the basis of the presumption of the consent, viz. the power of prevention physically or by action, was never present.

It is said that if this principle is applied in cases like the present, and were carried out to its logical consequences, it would result in the most serious practical inconveniences, for a man might go – say into the midst of the tanneries of Bermondsey, or into any other locality devoted to a particular trade or manufacture of a noisy or unsavoury character – and, by building a private residence upon a vacant *piece* of land, put a stop to such trade or manufacture altogether. The case also is put of a blacksmith's forge built away from all habitations, but to which, in course of time, habitations approach. We do not think that either of these hypothetical cases presents any real difficulty. As regards the first, it may be answered that whether anything is a nuisance or not is a question to be determined, not merely by an abstract consideration of the thing itself, but in reference to its circumstances; what would be a nuisance in Belgrave Square would not necessarily be so in Bermondsey; and where a locality is devoted to a particular trade or manufacture carried on by the traders or manufacturers in a particular and established manner not constituting a public nuisance, Judges and juries would be justified in finding, and may be trusted to find, that the trade or manufacture so carried on in that locality is not a private or actionable wrong. As regards the blacksmith's forge, that is really an *idem per idem* case with the present. It would be on the one hand in a very high degree unreasonable and undesirable that there should be a right of action for acts which are not in the present condition of the adjoining land, and possibly never will be any annoyance or inconvenience to either its owner or occupier; and it would be on the other hand in an equally degree unjust, and, from a public point of view, inexpedient that the use and value of the adjoining land should, for all time and under all circumstances, be restricted and diminished by reason of the continuance of acts incapable of physical interruption, and which the law gives no power to prevent. The smith in the case supposed might protect himself by taking a sufficient curtilage to ensure what he does from being at any time an annoyance to his neighbour, but the neighbour himself would be powerless in the matter. Individual cases of hardship may occur in the strict carrying out of the principle upon which we found our judgment, but the negation of the principle would lead even more to individual hardship, and would at the same time produce a prejudicial effect upon the development of land for residential purposes ...'

Comment

(1) There is no defence of coming to the nuisance. Mere knowledge of the activity will not be sufficient, see, for example, the facts of *Kennaway v Thompson*, p 675. As to the desirability of this aspect of the decision in *Sturges v Bridgman* see the comments of Lord Denning in *Miller v Jackson*, below.

(2) In *Bliss v Hall*, the defendant had set up a tallow-chandlery which emitted 'divers noisome, noxious and offensive vapours, fumes smells and stenches' to the discomfort of the plaintiff, who had taken a house near it. It was held to be no defence that the business had been in existence for three years before the plaintiff's arrival. Tindal CJ held that he 'came to the house with all the rights which the common law affords, and one of them is the right to wholesome air'.

Miller v Jackson
[1977] 3 All ER 338 Court of Appeal

For many years the defendant cricket club had played cricket on a small ground. Adjoining land was developed. Houses were built and were so sited that, despite there being a boundary fence, some balls were bound to be hit into the houses or their gardens. The plaintiffs sued in nuisance and negligence in respect of cricket balls being hit into their garden. A majority of the Court of Appeal (Lord Denning dissenting) held that there was both negligence and nuisance. As to the remedy, a different majority of the Court of Appeal (Geoffrey Lane LJ dissenting) held that there should be no injunction.

Geoffrey Lane LJ (after concluding that there was negligence, he considered whether there was nuisance): 'There is, however, one obviously strong point in the defendants' favour. They or their predecessors have been playing cricket on this ground (and no doubt hitting sixes out of it) for 70 years or so. Can someone, by building a house on the edge of the field in circumstances where it must have been obvious that balls might be hit over the fence, effectively stop cricket being played? Precedent apart, justice would seem to demand that the plaintiffs should be left to make the most of the site they have elected to occupy with all its obvious advantages and all its equally obvious disadvantages. It is pleasant to have an open space over which to look from your bedroom and sitting room windows, so far as it is possible to see over the concrete wall. Why should you complain of the obvious disadvantages which arise from the particular purpose to which the open space is being put? Put briefly, can the defendants take advantage of the fact that the plaintiffs have put themselves in such a position by coming to occupy a house on the edge of a small cricket field, with the result that what was not a nuisance in the past now becomes a nuisance? If the matter were *res integra*, I confess I should be inclined to find for the defendants. It does not seem just that a long-established activity – in itself innocuous – should be brought to an end because someone chooses to build a house nearby and so turn an innocent pastime into an actionable nuisance. Unfortunately, however, the question is not open. In *Sturges v Bridgman*, this very problem arose ... That decision involved the assumption, which so far as one can discover has never been questioned, that it is no answer to a claim in nuisance for the defendant to show that the plaintiff brought the trouble on his own head by building or coming to live in a house so close to the defendant's premises that he would inevitably be affected by the defendant's activities, where no one had been affected previously: see also *Bliss v Hall*. It may be that this rule works injustice, it may be that one would decide the matter differently in the absence of authority. But we are bound by the decision in *Sturges v Bridgman*; it is not for this court as I see it to alter a rule which stood for so long ...'

Lord Denning MR (dissenting): '... In support of the case, the plaintiffs rely on the *dictum* of Lord Reid in *Bolton v Stone*: "If cricket cannot be played on a ground without creating a substantial risk, then it should not be played there at all." I would agree with that saying if the houses or road was there first, and the cricket ground came there second. We would not allow the garden of Lincoln's Inn to be turned into a cricket ground. It would be too dangerous for windows and people. But I would not agree with Lord Reid's *dictum* when the cricket ground has been there for 70 years and the houses are newly built at the very edge of it. I recognise that the cricket club are under a duty to use all reasonable care consistently with the playing of the game of cricket, but I do not think the cricket club can be expected to give up the game of cricket altogether. After all they have their rights in their cricket ground. They have spent money, labour and love in the making of it: and they have the right to play upon it as they have done for 70 years. Is this all to be rendered useless to them by the thoughtless and selfish act of an estate developer in building right up to the edge of it? Can the developer or a purchaser of the house say to the cricket club: "Stop playing. Clear out." I do not think so. And I will give my reasons ...

It has been often said in nuisance cases that the rule is *sic utere tuo ut alienum non laedas*. But that is a most misleading maxim. Lord Wright put it in its proper place in *Sedleigh-Denfield v O'Callaghan*:

> "[It] is not only lacking in definiteness but is also inaccurate. An occupier may make in many ways a use of his land which causes damage to the neighbouring landowners and yet be free from liability ... a useful test is perhaps what is reasonable according to the ordinary usages of mankind living in society, or more correctly in a particular society."

I would, therefore, adopt this test. Is the use by the cricket club of this ground for playing cricket a reasonable use of it? To my mind it is a most reasonable use. Just consider the circumstances. For over 70 years the game of cricket has been played on this ground to the great benefit of the community as a whole, and to the injury of none. No one could suggest that it was a nuisance to the neighbouring owners simply because an enthusiastic batsman occasionally hit a ball out of the ground for six to the approval of the admiring onlookers. Then I would ask: does it suddenly become a nuisance because one of the neighbours chooses to build a house on the very edge of the ground – in such a position that it may well be struck by the ball on the rare occasion when there is a hit for six? To my mind the answer is plainly No. The building of the house does not convert the playing of cricket into a nuisance when it was not so before. If and in so far as any damage is caused to the house or anyone in it, it is because of the position in which it was built. Suppose that the house had not been built by a developer, but by a private owner. He would be in much the same position as the farmer who previously put his cows in the field. He could not complain if a batsman hit a six out of the ground, and by a million to one chance it struck a cow or even the farmer himself. He would be in no better position than a spectator at Lord's or the Oval or at a motor rally. At any rate, even if he could claim damages for the loss of the cow or the injury, he could not get an injunction to stop the cricket. If the private owner could not get an injunction, neither should a developer or a purchaser from him.

It was said, however, that the case of the physician's consulting-room was to the contrary: *Sturges v Bridgman*. But that turned on the old law about easements and prescriptions, and so forth. It was in the days when rights of property were in the ascendant and not subject to any limitations except those provided by the law of easements. But nowadays it is a matter of balancing the conflicting interests of the two neighbours. That was made clear by Lord Wright in *Sedleigh-Denfield v O'Callaghan*, when he said: "A balance has to be maintained between the right of the occupier to do what he likes with his own, and the right of his neighbour not to be interfered with."

In this case it is our task to balance the right of the cricket club to continue playing cricket on their cricket ground – as against the right of the householder not to be interfered with. On taking the balance, I would give priority to the right of the cricket club to continue playing cricket on the ground, as they have done for the last 70 years. It takes precedence over the right of the newcomer to sit in his garden undisturbed. After all, he bought the house four years ago in mid-summer when the cricket season was at its height. He might have guessed that there was a risk that a hit for six might possibly land on his property. If he finds that he does not like it, he ought, when cricket is played, to sit on the other side of the house or in the front garden, or go out: or take advantage of the offers the club have made to him of fitting unbreakable glass, and so forth. Or, if he does not like that, he ought to sell his house and move elsewhere. I expect there are many who would gladly buy it in order to be near the cricket field and open space. At any rate he ought not be allowed to stop cricket being played on this ground ...'

Comment

(1) The utility of the defendant's conduct may be implicit in the test of reasonableness and is to be contrasted with the interest of the plaintiff which is

to be protected, see *Bridlington Relay Ltd v Yorkshire Electricity Ltd.* However, the principle has arisen more recently in the form of a conflict between public and private interests and the suggestion by Lord Denning in *Miller v Jackson* that in such cases the public interest should prevail. This was rejected as a universal principle by the Court of Appeal in *Kennaway v Thompson* (below) where, after denying that the public interest must always prevail, the Court of Appeal was able to grant an injunction which struck a reasonable balance between the competing interests of the parties.

(2) In certain aspects of the balancing process the court may take into account the usefulness of the purpose to be achieved, e.g. by the claimant. Would the court decide that a church service had social utility and that it ought to be protected against interferences, but that watching TV might not? On the other hand, as to the defendant's conduct, would the court regard building work as deserving more flexible treatment than a cricket match? Is this all that the court was doing in *Christie v Davey*?

(3) A striking example of public interest being relegated to a secondary role is *Dennis v Ministry of Defence.* The court noted that in most modern industrial or similar developments such as railways, canals and roads, there had been statutory intervention providing a means of balancing competing public and private interests. This was not true in the case of the armed forces and the training of jet fighter pilots. Here the court was prepared to conclude, having regard to the balance properly to be struck, that the extent of overflight of the claimant's land by jet fighters of the RAF amounted to a nuisance despite the very obvious public interest in training RAF pilots. However in this case the public interest in training pilots was to be given full effect when identifying the appropriate remedy. Here the appropriate remedy lay in damages for diminution of the value of the property rather than injunction. See also in this context *Hatton v United Kingdom* in the European Court of Human Rights.

Kennaway v Thompson
[1980] 3 All ER 329 Court of Appeal

The plaintiff lived in a house next to a lake on which there were watersports. The club had begun racing on the lake some ten years before the plaintiff built and occupied her house adjoining the lake. She had always lived in the vicinity and had inherited the lake from her father. Over the years immediately prior to and after this, the use of the lake and the noise level increased considerably. In the Court of Appeal the defendants, a motor-boat racing club, accepted that some of their activities caused a nuisance. The judge had awarded damages but refused an injunction. The Court of Appeal granted an injunction and applied the principle in *Shelfer v City of London Electric Lighting Co.*

Lawton LJ: ' ... Counsel for the plaintiff has submitted that the judge misdirected himself. What he did, it was said, was to allow the club to buy itself the right to cause a substantial and intolerable nuisance. It was no justification to say that this was for the benefit of that section of the public which was interested in motor boat racing. Once the plaintiff had proved that the club caused a nuisance which interfered in a substantial and intolerable way with the use and enjoyment of her house she was entitled to have it stopped by injunction.

Counsel for the defendant submitted that this court should not interfere with the exercise of the judge's discretion. He was entitled to take into account the effect which an injunction would have on the club and on those members of the public who enjoyed watching or taking part in motor boat racing.

Counsel for the plaintiff based his submissions primarily on the decision of this court in *Shelfer v City of London Electric Lighting Co.* The opening paragraph of the headnote, which correctly summarises the judgment, is as follows:

> "*Lord Cairns' Act* (21 and 22 Vict. c. 27), in conferring upon Courts of Equity a jurisdiction to award damages instead of an injunction, has not altered the settled principles upon which those Courts interfered by way of injunction; and in cases of continuing actionable nuisance the jurisdiction so conferred ought only to be exercised under very exceptional circumstances."

... in a much-quoted passage, Lindley LJ said:

> "... ever since *Lord Cairns' Act* was passed the Court of Chancery has repudiated the notion that the Legislature intended to turn that Court into a tribunal for legalising wrongful acts; or in other words, the Court has always protested against the notion that it ought to allow a wrong to continue simply because the wrongdoer is able and willing to pay for the injury he may inflict. Neither has the circumstance that the wrongdoer is in some sense a public benefactor (e.g., a gas or water company or a sewer authority) ever been considered a sufficient reason for refusing to protect by injunction an individual whose rights are being persistently infringed."

A L Smith LJ, in his judgment, set out what he called a good working rule for the award of damages in substitution for an injunction. His working rule does not apply in this case. The injury to the plaintiff's legal rights is not small; it is not capable of being estimated in terms of money save in the way the judge tried to make an estimate, namely by fixing a figure for the diminution of the value of the plaintiff's house because of the prospect of a continuing nuisance; and the figure he fixed could not be described as small. The principles enunciated in *Shelfer's* case, which is binding on us, have been applied time and time again during the past 85 years. The only case which raises a doubt about the application of the *Shelfer* principles to all cases is *Miller v Jackson*, a decision of this court ... We are of the opinion that there is nothing in *Miller v Jackson*, binding on us, which qualifies what was decided in *Shelfer*. Any decisions before *Shelfer's* case (and there were some at first instance as counsel for the defendants pointed out) which give support for the proposition that the public interest should prevail over the private interest must be read subject to the decision in *Shelfer's* case.

It follows that the plaintiff was entitled to an injunction and that the judge misdirected himself in law in adjudging that the appropriate remedy for her was an award of damages under Lord Cairns' Act. But she was only entitled to an injunction restraining the club from activities which caused a nuisance, and not all of their activities did. As the judge pointed out, and counsel for the plaintiff accepted in this court, an injunction in general terms would be unworkable.

Our task has been to decide on a form of order which will protect the plaintiff from the noise which the judge found to be intolerable but which will not stop the club from organising activities about which she cannot reasonably complain.

When she decided to build a house alongside Mallam Water she knew that some motor boat racing and water skiing was done on the club's water and she thought that the noise which such activities created was tolerable. She cannot now complain about that kind of noise provided it does not increase in volume by reason of any increase in activities. The intolerable noise is mostly caused by the large boats; it is these which attract the public interest.

Now nearly all of us living in these islands have to put up with a certain amount of annoyance from our neighbours. Those living in towns may be irritated by their neighbours' noisy radios or incompetent playing of musical instruments; and they in turn may be inconvenienced by the noise caused by our guests slamming car doors and chattering after a late party. Even in the country the lowing of a sick cow or the early morning crowing of a farmyard cock may interfere with sleep and comfort. Intervention by injunction is only justified when the irritating noise causes inconvenience beyond what other occupiers in the neighbourhood can be expected to bear. The question is whether the neighbour is using his property reasonably, having regard to the fact that he has a neighbour. The neighbour who is complaining must remember, too, that the other man can use his property in a reasonable way and there must be a measure of "give and take, live and let live".

Understandably the plaintiff finds intolerable the kind of noise which she has had to suffer for such long periods in the past; but if she knew that she would only have to put up with such noise on a few occasions between the end of March and the beginning of November each year, and she also knew when those occasions were likely to occur, she could make arrangements to be out of her house at the material times. We can see no reason, however, why she should have to absent herself from her house for many days so as to enable the club members and others to make noises which are a nuisance. We consider it probable that those who are interested in motor boat racing are attracted by the international and national events, which tend to have the larger and noisier boats. Justice will be done, we think, if the club is allowed to have, each racing season, one international event extending over three days, the first day being given over to practice and the second and third to racing. In addition there can be two national events, each of two days but separated from the international event and from each other by at least four weeks. Finally there can be three club events, each of one day, separated from the international and national events and each other by three weeks. Any international or national event not held can be replaced by a club event of one day. No boats creating a noise of more than 75 decibels are to be used on the club's water at any time other than when there are events as specified in this judgment. If events are held at weekends, as they probably will be, six weekends, covering a total of ten days, will be available for motor boat racing on the club's water. Water-skiing, if too many boats are used, can cause a nuisance by noise. The club is not to allow more than six motor boats to be used for water-skiing at any one time. An injunction will be granted to restrain motor boat racing, water-skiing and the use of boats creating a noise of more than 75 decibels on the club's water save to the extent and in the circumstances indicated.'

Comment

Compare the ability of the court to arrange a suitable compromise by way of injunction in cases of nuisance with their inability to do so in trespass to land, see p 594. See also *Dennis v Ministry of Defence*.

CHAPTER 14

Public nuisance

Attorney-General (on the relation of Glamorgan County Council & Pontardawe Rural District Council) v PYA Quarries Ltd [1957] 1 All ER 894 Court of Appeal

Houses neighbouring a quarry were adversely affected by dust and vibrations from the quarrying operations. The action against the defendant quarry owners was brought by the Attorney-General on the relation of the county council and the rural district council. The defendant appealed against the grant of an injunction on the basis that the nuisance was insufficiently widespread to be a public nuisance. The Court of Appeal held that there was a sufficiently wide impact for the nuisance to be a public nuisance and that the injunctions had been properly granted.

Romer LJ: ' ... Before considering these contentions in any detail it would, I think, be convenient to consider the nature of a public nuisance as distinct from nuisances which are customarily described as "private" ... In *Stephen's Digest of the Criminal Law* (9th ed.) it is stated that:

"A common nuisance is an act not warranted by law or an omission to discharge a legal duty, which act or omission obstructs or causes inconvenience or damage to the public in the exercise of rights common to all His Majesty's subjects."

The following definition of nuisance appears in 3 *Blackstone's Commentaries*:

"Nuisance ... signifies any thing that works hurt, inconvenience, or damage. And nuisances are of two kinds; *public* and *common* nuisances, which affect the public, and are an annoyance to *all* the king's subjects; for which reason we must refer them to the class of public wrongs, or crimes and misdemeanours; and *private* nuisances ..."

... It is difficult to ascertain with any precision from these citations how widely spread the effect of a nuisance must be for it to qualify as a public nuisance and to become the subject of a criminal prosecution or of a relator action by the

Attorney-General. It is obvious ... that it is not a prerequisite of a public nuisance that all of Her Majesty's subjects should be affected by it; for otherwise no public nuisance could ever be established at all.

In *Soltau v De Held* Kindersley V-C said:

"I conceive that, to constitute a public nuisance, the thing must be such as, in its nature or its consequences, is a nuisance – an injury or a damage, to all persons who come within the sphere of its operation, though it may be so in a greater degree to some than it is to others."...

In *R v Lloyd* an indictment for a nuisance by noise was preferred by the Society of Clifford's Inn. It appeared in evidence that the noise complained of affected only three houses in the Inn. Lord Ellenborough said that on that evidence the indictment could not be sustained; and that it was, if anything, a private nuisance. It was confined to the inhabitants of three numbers of Clifford's Inn only; it did not extend to the rest of the society and could be avoided by shutting the windows; it was therefore not sufficiently general to support an indictment ...

In *A-G v Keymer Brick & Tile Co Ltd* Joyce J said:

"The only question I have to decide is purely one of fact, namely, whether or not what the defendants have done has created or occasioned a public nuisance within the neighbourhood of their brickfields. Now, in law, a public nuisance need not be injurious to health. It is not necessary to show that people have been made ill by what has been done. It is sufficient to show that there has been what is called injury to their comfort, a material interference with the comfort and convenience of life of the persons residing in or coming within the sphere of the influence of that which has been done by the defendants on their works ... The conclusion I have arrived at is that ... a serious and disgusting public nuisance has been occasioned by the defendants in the neighbourhood of their brickworks ... "

... The expression "the neighbourhood" has been regarded as sufficiently defining the area affected by a public nuisance in other cases also (see, for example, *A-G v Stone*; *A-G v Cole & Son*; and *A-G v Corke*).

I do not propose to attempt a more precise definition of a public nuisance than those which emerge from the text-books and authorities to which I have referred. It is, however, clear, in my opinion, that any nuisance is "public" which materially affects the reasonable comfort and convenience of life of a class of Her Majesty's subjects. The sphere of the nuisance may be described generally as "the neighbourhood"; but the question whether the local community within that sphere comprises a sufficient number of persons to constitute a class of the public is a question of fact in every case. It is not necessary, in my judgment, to prove that every member of the class has been injuriously affected; it is sufficient to show that a representative cross-section of the class has been so affected for an injunction to issue ...'

Denning LJ: 'I entirely agree with the judgment of Romer LJ, and have little to add. Counsel for the defendants raised at the outset this question: What is the difference between a public nuisance and a private nuisance? He is right to raise it because it affects his clients greatly. The order against them restrains them from committing a public nuisance, not a private one. The classic statement of the difference is that a public nuisance affects Her Majesty's subjects generally, whereas a private nuisance only affects particular individuals. But this does not help much. The question: when do a number of individuals become Her Majesty's subjects generally? is as difficult to answer as the question: when does a group of people become a crowd? Everyone has his own views. Even the answer "Two's company, three's a crowd" will not command the assent of those present unless they first agree on "which two". So here I decline to answer the question how many people are necessary to make up Her Majesty's subjects generally. I prefer to look to the reason of the thing and to say that a public nuisance is a nuisance which is so widespread in its range or so indiscriminate in its effect that it would not be reasonable to expect one person to take proceedings on his own responsibility to put a stop to it, but that it should be taken on the responsibility of the community at large. Take the blocking up of a public highway or the non-repair of it: it may be a footpath very little used except by one or two householders; nevertheless the obstruction affects everyone indiscriminately who may wish to walk along it. Take next a landowner who collects pestilential rubbish near a village or permits gypsies with filthy habits to encamp on the edge of a residential neighbourhood. The householders nearest to it suffer the most, but everyone in the neighbourhood suffers too. In such cases the Attorney-General can take proceedings for an injunction to restrain the nuisance: and when he does so he acts in defence of the public right, not for any sectional interest ... When, however, the nuisance is so concentrated that only two or three property owners are affected by it, such as the three attorneys in Clifford's Inn, then they ought to take proceedings on their own account to stop it and not expect the community to do it for them ... Applying this test, I am clearly of opinion that the nuisance by stones, vibration and dust in this case was at the date of the writ so widespread in its range and so indiscriminate in its effect that it was a public nuisance.

The defendants, however, have now taken such good remedial measures that objectionable incidents take place only rarely and then by accident. So far as stones are concerned, the injunction is absolute: but so far as dust and vibration are concerned it is dependent on it being a nuisance "to Her Majesty's subjects", that is, a public nuisance. The question then arises whether every rare incident is a public nuisance. Suppose six months went by without any excessive vibration and then there was by some mischance a violent explosion on an isolated occasion terrifying many people. Would that be a public nuisance? Would it subject the defendants to proceedings for contempt? I should have thought that it might, but the punishment would be measured according to the degree to which the defendants were at fault. I quite agree that a private nuisance always involves some degree of repetition or continuance. An isolated act, which is over and done with, once and for all, may give rise to an action for negligence or an action under the rule in *Rylands v Fletcher*, but not an action for nuisance. A good example is an explosion in a factory which breaks windows for miles around. It gives rise to an action under *Rylands v Fletcher*, but no other action if there was no negligence: see *Read v J Lyons & Co Ltd*. But an isolated act may amount to a public nuisance if it is done in such circumstances that the public right to condemn it should be vindicated. I referred to some authorities on this point in *Southport Corporation v Esso Petroleum Co Ltd*. In the present case, in view of the long history of stones, vibrations and dust, I should think it incumbent on the defendants to see that nothing of the kind happens again such as to be injurious to the neighbourhood at large, even on an isolated occasion.'

Comment

(1)   In *R v Shorrock* Rattee J, in the Court of Appeal, observed that 'public nuisance is defined by reference to private nuisance and as differing from private nuisance only in the range of its effect'. This was true insofar as the event in that case was concerned (an 'acid house party') but may not necessarily be so.

(2)   The confusion over public nuisance arises out of its historical development. It is a means of vindicating public rather than private rights. At common law, public nuisance is a crime of great versatility, but a class of persons affected by it have the right to sue for an injunction (the action being a relator action brought by the Attorney-General on behalf of the class). Local authorities have power to seek an injunction on behalf of the community, see Local Government Act 1972, s 222. A private right of action is available for those who suffer special damage, see e.g. *Halsey v Esso Petroleum*, p 617. It is important not to overstate the importance of public nuisance as a tort. Its usefulness lies in the range of conduct which it prohibits but it is far removed from the context of private nuisance which concerns itself with the protection of interests in property, see, for example, the use of public nuisance as a crime to control contagious diseases, *R v Vantandillo*, referred to in *R v Shorrock*.

(3)   Much of the judgment of Romer LJ is given over to a discussion of the evidence, which showed that there was scope for further abatement of the nuisance at the time of trial, and he observed that:

'Some public nuisances (for example the pollution of rivers) can often be established without the necessity of calling a number of individual complainants as witnesses. In general, however, a public nuisance is proved by the cumulative effect which it is shown to have had on the people living within its sphere of influence. In other words, a normal and legitimate way of proving a public nuisance is to prove a sufficiently large collection of private nuisances.'

(4)   A typical example of public nuisance would be obstruction of the highway. Unusual illustrations might include the exhibit of certain items in a window which attract a large crowd thereby blocking the highway, e.g. *R v Carlile* (an anti-clerical protest involving the display of effigies of bishops) and adopting an unreasonable method of running a shop adjacent to the highway, e.g. see *Fabri v Morris.* Note the use of public nuisance as a means of obtaining an injunction against pickets and demonstrators, e.g. see *Hubbard v Pitt* (also a case on private nuisance), *News Group v SOGAT.* In *Railtrack v Wandsworth London Borough Council* there was a public nuisance where the railway company failed to take steps to clear a bridge of pigeon infestation. The pigeons caused fouling of the pavement and road below which led to inconvenience and annoyance to pedestrians.

(5)   In *Gillingham Borough Council v Medway (Chatham) Dock Co Ltd*, the court considered the view that public nuisance involves an otherwise unlawful activity. Buckley J said:

'The first submission by [counsel for the defendant] was that a public nuisance cannot arise out of a lawful act, whatever its consequences, and as what is complained of here, namely HGVs being driven along [the] Roads, is a lawful act, no public nuisance can arise. He relied upon the definition of public nuisance in *Stephen's Digest of Criminal Law* (9th edn, 1950): "... an act not warranted by law or omission to discharge a legal duty which obstructs or causes inconvenience or damage to the public in the exercise of rights common to all the Queen's subjects." This is adopted in 34 *Halsbury's Laws* (4th edn) and *Clerk and Lindsell on Torts* (6th edn, 1989). [Counsel] cited numerous cases in which the acts complained of were in themselves unlawful and in which there are many references to unlawful acts in the context of public nuisance. The sheer weight of *dicta* amassed was intimidating, but [counsel] conceded that he could find no authority actually binding on me. It is not surprising that in many or most of the cases, particularly the more modern ones, the act itself is unlawful. That is because a large number of cases on public nuisance arise out of some misuse of the highway (inherently unlawful) and due to the growth of statutory offences touching such matters as health and environment. However, I have always assumed that public nuisance was primarily concerned with the effect of the act complained of as opposed to its inherent lawfulness or unlawfulness. There are cases in which prosecutions failed because the nuisance did not interfere with a sufficient number of the public. That suggests that there was no other unlawful act involved. I am greatly indebted to J R Spencer for a most interesting article entitled "Public nuisance – a critical examination" (1989) 48 CLJ 55, where it is stated: "In the days before there was much legislation on public health matters, public nuisance was the only offence for which it was possible to prosecute those who stank out the neighbourhood with fumes from glassworks, tanneries and smelters, or who kept pigs in the streets, or kept explosives in dangerous places ...". Later in the article three specific cases are mentioned in which the conduct complained of was not, at the time, an offence, other than public nuisance: *R v Wheeler, R v Madden* and *R v Holme.*

Finally, there is the type of public nuisance arising out of private nuisance which affects a sufficiently large number of people that it would not be reasonable to expect one person to take proceedings on his own responsibility (see *A-G (ex rel Glamorgan CC and Pontardawe RDC) v PYA Quarries Ltd*). The main judgment given by Romer LJ lends no support to [counsel's] contention. Private nuisance need not be based on an unlawful act. I therefore reject the submission that a public nuisance requires an unlawful act. If it is correct, in general, that a public nuisance cannot arise out of the lawful use of a highway, as [counsel] submitted, it is not, in my judgment, because there is no unlawful act. It is because a consideration of the neighbourhood in the vicinity of the highway will lead to the conclusion that the noise or fumes are not an actionable wrong in all the circumstances of the case. In other words, those who live close by public highways must accept the inevitable disturbance for the greater good of the public. Certainly this principle applies in private nuisance (see *Sturges v Bridgman*) and I can see no reason for a different approach in public nuisance, at least of the kind alleged in this case. Also many types of road which might otherwise give rise to noise nuisance will have been constructed pursuant to statutory powers after all relevant planning procedures have been complied with and compensation paid where appropriate. Actions in nuisance, if successful, would make a nonsense of the whole scheme. The private right must usually yield to the greater public interest.

It is not necessary for me to hold that otherwise lawful use of a highway can never amount to a public nuisance, whatever the circumstances and however excessive the use. Extreme circumstances may arise when it could be right so to hold (see *Halsey v Esso Petroleum Co Ltd*).'

(6)   For actions involving land occupied by groups regarded by some as undesirables (Lord Denning's 'gypsies with filthy habits') see *Page Motors v Epsom, A-G v Corke*, invoking *Rylands v Fletcher*, and *Smith v Scott.* Consider the use of public nuisance as a means of dealing with unwelcome nearby concerts, 'acid house parties' or new-age travellers.

(7)   For the criminal context see *R v Shorrock*, where the defendant let his field for a weekend to three individuals who held an 'acid house party' which caused great disturbance over a wide area. Although he denied specific knowledge of the purposes of the licensees, he was convicted. On the question of the judge's direction on *mens rea*, Rattee J in the Court of Appeal held that:

'... the appellant was guilty of the offence ... if either he knew or ought to have known, in the sense that the means of knowledge were available to him, that there was a real risk that the consequences of the licence granted by him in respect of his field would be to create the sort of nuisance that in fact occurred ...'

The conviction was upheld. The Court of Appeal applied *Sedleigh-Denfield v O'Callaghan* in reaching its decision on the relevant *mens rea* and concluded that the basis of liability in both criminal and civil jurisdictions was the same.

(8)   An award of punitive damages is not available in public nuisance, see *A B v Southwest Water Services Ltd.*

Tate & Lyle Industries Ltd v Greater London Council and another [1983] I All ER I159 House of Lords

The plaintiff company, TL, operated a sugar refinery on the north bank of the Thames. They built a jetty from which refined sugar could be loaded on to boats. From one of the defendants (the Port of London Authority – PLA) they obtained a statutory licence to dredge a deeper channel and to build a new jetty for the off-loading of raw sugar. Shortly before the licence was granted another defendant, the Greater London Council (GLC), with the statutory approval of the PLA, built two ferry terminals. Shortly after they were built the work on the raw sugar jetty was completed. The effect of the terminals was to cause siltation which seriously affected the raw sugar and refined sugar jetties. The plaintiff company had to expend several hundreds of thousands of pounds to dredge the access to the jetties until the PLA altered the shipping channel of the Thames which had the effect of preventing further silting. The plaintiff sued the GLC for causing the silting and the PLA for approving the plans responsible for the siltation. The action in negligence failed because the plaintiffs did not possess any private rights which would enable them to insist on any particular depth of water in connection with the operation of the licensed jetties; for the same reason the case in private nuisance failed. The case based on public nuisance succeeded (Lord Diplock dissenting) against the GLC but failed against the PLA.

Lord Templeman: ' ... An action in private nuisance must also fail if TL have no private rights in connection with the depth of the River Thames. The siltation caused by the GLC did not interfere with TL's use and occupation of the jetties but with TL's use of the River Thames. TL rely on the decision in *Booth v Ratte*. In that case the plaintiff was a riparian owner who constructed a floating wharf and warehouse moored to his bank of the river. The defendant operated a saw mill upstream of the plaintiff's land and polluted the river with sawdust, bark and other refuse which were deposited in front of the plaintiff's wharf and warehouse ... The only defence was that the plaintiff had no title to the wharf and boathouse. It was held that the plaintiff either was the owner of part of the river bed on which the wharf and boathouse were placed or was a licensee. Either title sufficed to enable the plaintiff to maintain an action based on damage or threatened damage to the wharf and to recover damages in private nuisance or public nuisance for damage to his business carried on upon his land, wharf and warehouse caused by smell and impurity of water. In *Booth v Ratte* the plaintiff was claiming to be left undisturbed in the use and occupation of the wharf and boathouse which he occupied. He was not claiming any rights over the river. In the present case nothing has happened to disturb the possession by TL of their jetties. TL complain of interference with their use of the bed of the River Thames. They must prove some private right over the bed of the River Thames before they can complain that the siltation of the bed and consequent decrease of the depth of the water constitute an actionable infringement of their private rights whether in negligence or in nuisance.

PUBLIC NUISANCE

The Thames is a navigable river over which the public have the right of navigation, that is to say a right to pass and re-pass over the whole width and depth of water in the River Thames and the incidental right of loading and unloading. The public right of navigation was expressly preserved by s 210 of the Port of London (Consolidation) Act 1920 ... The construction of the ferry terminals interfered with the public right of navigation over the Thames between the main shipping channel and TL's jetties by causing siltation on the bed and foreshore of the river and siltation in the channel and berth dredged by TL. This interference with the public right of navigation caused particular damage to TL because vessels of the requisite dimensions were unable to pass and re-pass over the bed and foreshore between the main channel and the refined sugar jetty and ... over the channel dredged by TL between the main shipping channel and the raw sugar jetty and could not be accommodated in the berth dredged by TL adjacent to the raw sugar jetty.

An individual who suffers damage resulting from a public nuisance is, as a general rule, entitled to maintain an action. In the present case the GLC and the PLA assert that in constructing the ferry terminals the GLC were acting in pursuance of statutory authority contained in the London County Council (Improvements) Act 1962 and the Port of London (Consolidation) Act 1920, and the combined effect of those two Acts was to authorise the interference with the public right of navigation which was in fact caused by the construction of the ferry terminals. There was therefore no public nuisance and TL have no cause of action in respect of any public nuisance.

In the alternative, it is argued, TL's damages based on public nuisance must be limited to damages suffered in connection with the refined sugar jetty. The plans of the GLC for the ferry terminals were approved in 1964. The licences to TL granted by the PLA to construct the raw sugar jetty and to dredge the channel and berth required for the raw sugar jetty were not granted until 1965. TL, it is submitted, have no right of action in respect of the raw sugar jetty which was constructed after the plans for the ferry terminals were approved and contemporaneously with the construction of the ferry terminals.

STATUTORY AUTHORITY

The GLC plead that if they were guilty of creating a public nuisance they are nevertheless excused because they were authorised by the London County Council (Improvements) Act 1962 to carry out the operations of which complaint is made. They were authorised by statute to construct the terminals in accordance with a design approved by the PLA and not otherwise.

The defence of statutory authority to an action for nuisance was summarised in the speech of Lord Wilberforce in *Allen v Gulf Oil Refining Ltd* as follows:

"It is now well settled that where Parliament by express direction or by necessary implication has authorised the construction and use of an undertaking or works, that carries with it an authority to do what is authorised with immunity from any action based on nuisance. The right of action is taken away ... To this there is made the qualification, or condition, that the statutory powers are exercised without 'negligence', that word here being used in a special sense so as to require the undertaker, as a condition of obtaining immunity from action, to carry out the work and conduct the operation with all reasonable regard and care for the interests of other persons ..."

In the present case Parliament authorised the terminals and thereby granted immunity from the consequences of the terminals provided that the GLC paid "all reasonable regard and care for the interests" of public navigation and for the interests of TL liable to suffer particular damage from any interference with the right of public navigation ...

THE PLA

The action ... against the PLA can only succeed if the PLA by their negligence bear some responsibility for the faulty design of the terminals ... Your Lordships were not ... referred to any fact or circumstances which should have alerted the PLA to the possibility that the terminals might unnecessarily cause the unforeseen and disastrous amount of siltation which took place ... The judge thought the PLA were 30 per cent to blame, but in my view, they are not liable to TL ... [I]t was submitted that the PLA had "continued" the nuisance created by the terminals ... In the present case the approval of the plans of the terminals by the PLA did not in my opinion continue or adopt or otherwise make liable the PLA for any nuisance created by the terminals ...

THE RAW SUGAR JETTY

The channel and the berth dredged for the purposes of the raw sugar jetty were authorised works in the Thames which by statute the PLA were entitled to sanction. The public right of navigation extended over the channel and berth once they were dredged. The interference caused by the terminals, on the other hand, was an interference with the public right of navigation which was not justified by the statute under which the GLC erected the terminals. TL suffered particular damage because vessels were prevented from plying between the main shipping channel and the raw sugar jetty. TL are entitled to damages for the particular damage suffered by them as a result of the interference with the public right of navigation unnecessarily caused by the terminals.

The PLA approved the plans of the terminals before they granted the raw sugar jetty licences. But the terminals, so far as they caused more siltation than was necessary, created a public nuisance. The GLC cannot escape the consequences of a public nuisance merely because it was created before TL suffered damage.'

Comment

(1)   Lord Diplock dissented on the basis, *inter alia*, that:

' ... In all the cases to which your Lordships were referred in which particular damage sustained in consequence of a public nuisance has been recognised as giving rise to a cause of action in civil law the particular damage has been caused by injury to proprietary rights of the plaintiff in corporeal or incorporeal hereditaments that are in proximity to the public nuisance; and I would accept that in principle where the injury is to proprietary rights it is no defence to say that the plaintiff either created or increased the particular damage that he sustained by the use to which he chose to put his property after the public nuisance had come into existence, so long as such use was a lawful one. But in the instant case your Lordships have held that *no* proprietary rights of TL have been injured by the accumulation of additional silt at the jetty heads. When the licence to erect the raw sugar jetty was granted by the PLA to TL the construction of the ferry terminals to [this] design had been already authorised. Assuming that during its construction and after its completion it created a public nuisance by its interference with the public right of navigation in the area in which TL chose subsequently to obtain a licence for the erection of the raw sugar jetty head, it was that choice which was the cause of their sustaining particular damage of a kind not suffered by other members of the public who wished to exercise their public right of navigation over that area. I do not think that particular damage arising from the choice of a person as to how he uses his public as distinguished from his proprietary rights can, in principle, give rise to a civil cause of action in damages against the creator of the public nuisance.'

(2)   A case giving rise to similar issues is *Jan de Nul (UK) Ltd v AXA Royale Belge SA (formerly NV Royale Belge)*.

(3)   An individual may bring a private action for damages in respect of harm suffered as a result of a public nuisance. The basis for such an action was explained by Brett J in *Benjamin v Storr*:

'By the common law of England, a person guilty of public nuisance might be indicted; but if injury resulted to a private individual, other and greater than that which was common to all the Queen's subjects, the person injured has his remedy by action ... in order to entitle a person to maintain an action for damage caused by that which is a public nuisance, the damage must be particular, direct and substantial.'

In that case the defendant's horse-drawn vans were constantly standing in the street outside the plaintiff's coffee-house. They intercepted the light to his windows so that he had to burn gas nearly all day; they obstructed access by his customers; and the stench from the horses was highly objectionable; all of which seriously affected the plaintiff's business.

In *Campbell v Paddington Corpn* the defendants erected stands in the highway on the occasion of Edward VII's funeral, causing an obstruction. The stands also blocked the view from the plaintiff's house thereby preventing her from letting the rooms to spectators as she normally did on state occasions.

(4)   See also *Rose v Miles*, also a case of obstructing a navigable waterway. In *Thomas v NUM* the absence of special damage prevented the working miners from maintaining an action based upon obstruction of the highway. Scott J said:

' ... Counsel for the plaintiffs argued that ... the large numbers of pickets present at the colliery gates were almost bound to be obstructing some part of the highway, even if only the pavements. That may be so, but it does not follow that the obstruction would represent a tort actionable at the suit of the working miners. The present state of affairs ... is that the working miners' entry into and egress from the colliery is not being physically prevented by the pickets. If the pickets are obstructing the highway, the obstruction is not causing any special damage to the working miners. On principle, therefore, the plaintiffs cannot ... have a cause of action in tort for obstruction of the highway.

Counsel submitted that *Hubbard v Pitt* provided authority to the contrary effect. I do not agree. It is true that, at first instance, Forbes J granted an interlocutory injunction to restrain the picketing of premises of a firm of estate agents who were, in the view of the pickets, acting for undesirable property developers ... and without any express reference to whether special damage was being caused to the plaintiffs by the obstruction. But, in the Court of Appeal Lord Denning MR, who dissented, would have discharged the injunction on the ground, *inter alia,* that the picketing was not an obstruction, and the majority, Stamp and Orr LJJ, decided the case on quite different grounds from those of Forbes J. Further, Stamp LJ said: "Let me say at once that much of what was said by the judge in his judgment in the court below was not directed to the question whether the defendants' acts constituted the common law tort consisting of private nuisance, and that much of the argument in this court, and so it would appear in the court below, was concerned with the extent of the right of the public to use a highway. In the result I cannot regard the judge's conclusions of law as a satisfactory application of the law to the facts which he found."

Accordingly, this case cannot be regarded as any authority for the startling proposition that the plaintiffs can, without special damage, sue in tort for obstruction to the highway.'

(5)   *Allen v Gulf Oil Refining Ltd* is the leading case on the defence of statutory authority, see also the discussion of that point in the *Gillingham BC* case, p 632 and *Wheeler v J J Saunders Ltd*, p 634.

(6)   For the interrelationship of public nuisance, private nuisance and *Rylands v Fletcher*, see especially *Halsey v Esso Petroleum*, p 617.

(7)   Since no special qualifications are required to be a plaintiff in public nuisance other than being a member of the class affected, while in private nuisance it may be necessary for the plaintiff to have some kind of interest in the land affected, public nuisance continues to have relevance for the provision of a remedy, albeit anomalous. Public nuisance might also be appropriate where personal injury is suffered. The possibility that public nuisance may permit the recovery of damages for personal injury may now be in some doubt following the decision of the House of Lords in *Hunter v Canary Wharf*, see p 604.

CHAPTER 15

Rylands v Fletcher

Although related to nuisance, the rule in *Rylands v Fletcher* differs from nuisance in that liability is strict: the claimant can succeed without having to prove either negligence or intention on the part of the defendant, although defences are available. But it has now been decided that, as with the case of nuisance, it must be demonstrated that the harm was reasonably foreseeable. This will have the effect of drawing the principle in *Rylands v Fletcher* even closer to the law of nuisance from which it emerged and thus ever closer to principles of negligence: see *Cambridge Water Co v Eastern Counties Leather plc.*

The classic statement of the rule is in the judgment of Blackburn J which was subsequently approved with minor, and possibly inadvertent, modification by the House of Lords. That modification, and the consequent restricted approach to non-natural use (see *Rickards v Lothian* and *Read v Lyons*), have proved a significant restraint on the development of the rule. Other jurisdictions have not been so reticent in allowing full rein to *Rylands v Fletcher* or even in rejecting it outright in favour of a negligence-based approach as in Scotland and Australia, see *Transco plc v Stockport MBC*, p 715. Although there was some indication that English courts might rethink their view of the rule (see *Cambridge Water Co v Eastern Counties Leather plc*), the continued availability and appropriateness of the principle has been clearly asserted by the House of Lords in *Transco plc v Stockport MBC*, p 715. Where hazardous activities are planned, then the role of protecting individuals or property has now been allocated to planning or statutory safety procedures, supported in appropriate cases by strict or absolute statutory liability.

Rylands v Fletcher
[1861–73] All ER Rep I House of Lords

Using reputable engineers, the defendants constructed a reservoir to supply water to power their mill. The plaintiff owned a coal mine nearby. The engineers came across old shafts but did not seal them effectively. The defendants and their engineers had no way of knowing that these shafts connected to the plaintiff's shafts. The water in the reservoir poured down the shafts and into the plaintiff's pit. It was found that the defendants had not been negligent but that the engineers had not taken reasonable care in dealing with the disused shafts. The plaintiff succeeded both in the Court of Exchequer Chamber and in the House of Lords.

EXCHEQUER CHAMBER

Blackburn J: '... The question of law, therefore, arises: What is the liability which the law casts upon a person who, like the defendants, lawfully brings on his land something which, though harmless while it remains there, will naturally do mischief if it escape out of his land? It is agreed on all hands that he must take care to keep in that which he has brought on the land, and keep it there in order that it may not escape and damage his neighbour's, but the question arises whether the duty which the law casts upon him under such circumstances is an absolute duty to keep it in at his peril, or is ...– merely a duty to take all reasonable and prudent precautions in order to keep it in, but no more. If the first be the law, the person who has brought on his land and kept there something dangerous, and failed to keep it in, is responsible for all the natural consequences of its escape. If the second be the limit of his duty, he would not be answerable except on proof of negligence, and consequently would not be answerable for escape arising from any latent defect which ordinary prudence and skill could not detect ...

We think that the true rule of law is that the person who, for his own purposes, brings on his land, and collects and keeps there anything likely to do mischief if it escapes, must keep it in at his peril, and if he does not do so, he is *prima* facie answerable for all the damage which is the natural consequence of its escape. He can excuse himself by showing that the escape was owing to the plaintiff's default, or, perhaps, that the escape was the consequence of *vis major*, or the act of God; but, as nothing of the sort exists here, it is unnecessary to enquire what excuse would be sufficient. The general rule, as above stated, seems on principle just. The person whose grass or corn is eaten down by the escaped cattle of his neighbour, or whose mine is flooded by the water from his neighbour's reservoir, or whose cellar is invaded by the filth of his neighbour's privy, or whose habitation is made unhealthy by the fumes and noisome vapours of his neighbour's alkali works, is damnified without any fault of his own; and it seems but reasonable and just that the neighbour who has brought something on his own property which was not naturally there, harmless to others so long as it is confined to his own property, but which he knows will be mischievous if it gets on his neighbour's, should be obliged to make good the damage which ensues if he does not succeed in confining it to his own property. But for his act in bringing it there no mischief could have accrued, and it seems but just that he should at his peril keep it there, so that no mischief may accrue, or answer for the natural and anticipated consequences. On authority this, we think, is established to be the law, whether the thing so brought be beasts or water, or filth or stenches ...'

HOUSE OF LORDS

Lord Cairns LC: '... The principles on which this case must be determined appear to me to be extremely simple. The defendants ... might lawfully have used that close for any purpose for which it might, in the ordinary course of the enjoyment of land, be used, and if, in what I may term the natural user of that land, there had been any accumulation of water, either on the surface or underground, and if by the operation of the laws of nature that accumulation of water had passed off into the close occupied by the plaintiff, the plaintiff could not have complained that that result had taken place. If he had desired to guard himself against it, it would have lain on him to have done so by leaving or by interposing some barrier between his close and the close of the defendants in order to have prevented that operation of the laws of nature.

[Lord Cairns referred to *Smith v Kenrick* and continued:]

On the other hand, if the defendants, not stopping at the natural use of their close, had desired to use it for any purpose which I may term a non-natural use, for the purpose of introducing into the close that which, in its natural condition, was not in or upon it – for the purpose of introducing water, either above or below ground, in quantities and in a manner not the result of any work or operation on or under the land, and if in consequence of their doing so, or in consequence of any imperfection in the mode of their doing so, the water came to escape and to pass off into the close of the plaintiff, then it appears to me that that which the defendants were doing they were doing at their own peril; and if in the course of their doing it the evil arose to which I have referred – the evil, namely, of the escape of the water, and its passing away to the close of the plaintiff and injuring the plaintiff – then for the consequence of that, in my opinion, the defendants would be liable ... The same result is arrived at on the principles referred to by Blackburn J ... In that opinion ... I entirely concur ...'

Comment

(1)   Lord Carnworth regarded the rule of law as correctly stated by Blackburn J.

(2) At the time there would have been no liability for the independent contractor, nor in nuisance by virtue of the isolated escape, nor in trespass since the damage was not direct.

Read v J Lyons & Co Ltd
[1946] 2 All ER 471 House of Lords

The plaintiff worked in an armaments factory during war time. She was injured when a shell exploded. It was held by the House of Lords that the principle in *Rylands v Fletcher* did not apply since there had been no escape and no non-natural user of the land. It was also doubted whether or not the principle extended to permit recovery for personal injury in the absence of negligence.

Viscount Simon:'... It has not always been sufficiently observed that in the House of Lords, when the appeal from *Fletcher v Rylands* was dismissed and Blackburn J's pronouncement was expressly approved, Lord Cairns LC emphasised another condition which must be satisfied before liability attaches without proof of negligence. This is that the use to which the defendant is putting his land is a "non-natural" use. Blackburn J had made a parenthetic reference to this sort of test ... I confess to finding this test of "non-natural" user (or of bringing on the land what was not "naturally there", which is not the same test) difficult to apply. Blackburn J ... treats cattle-trespass as an example of his generalisation. The pasturing of cattle must be one of the most ordinary uses of land, and strict liability for damage done by cattle enclosed on one man's land if they escape thence into the land of another is one of the most ancient propositions of our law. It is, in fact, a case of pure trespass to property, and thus constitutes a wrong without any question of negligence ... The circumstances in *Fletcher v Rylands* did not constitute a case of trespass because the damage was consequential, not direct. It is to be noted that all the counts in the declaration in that case set out allegations of negligence, but in the House of Lords Lord Cairns LC begins his opinion by explaining that ultimately the case was treated as determining the rights of the parties independently of any question of negligence.

The classic judgment of Blackburn J besides deciding the issue before the court and laying down the principle of duty between neighbouring occupiers of land on which the decision was based, sought to group under a single and wider proposition other instances in which liability is independent of negligence ... There are instances, no doubt, in our law in which liability for damage may be established apart from proof of negligence, but it appears to me logically unnecessary and historically incorrect to refer to all these instances as deduced from one common principle. The conditions under which such a liability arises are not necessarily the same in each class of case. Lindley LJ issued a valuable warning in *Green v Chelsea Waterworks Co*, when he said of *Rylands v Fletcher* that that decision:"... is not to be extended beyond the legitimate principle on which the House of Lords decided it.

If it were extended as far as strict logic might require, it would be a very oppressive decision." It seems better, therefore, when a plaintiff relies on *Rylands v Fletcher* to take the conditions declared by this House to be essential for liability in that case and to ascertain whether these conditions exist in the actual case.

Now, the strict liability recognised by this House to exist in *Rylands v Fletcher* is conditioned by two elements which I may call the condition of "escape" from the land of something likely to do mischief if it escapes, and the condition of "non-natural use" of the land. This second condition has in some later cases, which did not reach this House, been otherwise expressed, e.g., as "exceptional" user, when such user is not regarded as "natural" and at the same time is likely to produce mischief if there is an "escape" … It is not necessary to analyse this second condition on the present occasion, for in the case now before us the first essential condition of "escape" does not seem to me to be present at all. "Escape", for the purpose of applying the proposition in *Rylands v Fletcher* means escape from a place which the defendant has occupation of, or control over, to a place which is outside his occupation or control. Blackburn J several times refers to the defendant's duty as being the duty of "keeping a thing in" at the defendant's peril and by "keeping in" he means, not preventing an explosive substance from exploding, but preventing a thing which may inflict mischief from escaping from the area which the defendant occupies or controls …

In *Howard v Furness Houlder Argentine Lines Ltd* Lewis J had before him a case of injury caused by an escape of steam on board a ship where the plaintiff was working. The judge was, I think, right in refusing to apply the doctrine of *Rylands v Fletcher* on the ground that the injuries were caused on the premises of the defendants. Apart altogether from the judge's doubt (which I share) whether the owners of the steamship by generating steam therein are making a non-natural use of their steamship, the other condition on which the proposition in *Rylands v Fletcher* depends was not present, any more than it is in the case with which we have now to deal. Here there is no escape of relevant kind at all and the appellant's action fails on that ground.

In these circumstances it becomes unnecessary to consider other objections that have been raised, such as the question whether the doctrine of *Rylands v Fletcher* applies where the claim is for damages for personal injury as distinguished from damages to property. It may be noted, in passing, that Blackburn J himself when referring to the doctrine of *Rylands v Fletcher* in the later case of *Cattle v Stockton Waterworks* leaves this undealt with. He treats damages under the *Rylands v Fletcher* principle as covering damages to property, such as workmen's clothes or tools, but says nothing about liability for personal injuries …'

Comment

(1)   Viscount Simon also referred, *obiter*, to non-natural use of land and approved the analysis by Lord Moulton in *Rickards v Lothian*. But he also suggested that:

'if the question had hereafter to be decided whether the making of munitions in a factory at the government's request in time of war for the purpose of helping to defeat the enemy is a "non-natural" use of land, adopted by the occupier "for his own purposes", it would not seem to me that the House would be bound by [*Rainham Chemical Works Ltd v Belvedere Fish Guano Co*] to say that it was.'

Later cases such as *Transco plc v Stockport MBC*, p 715, doubt this suggestion.

(2)   Absence of escape was also the reason Lord Scott gave for excluding liability in *Transco plc v Stockport MBC*, p 715.

(3)   *Rylands v Fletcher* was successfully argued in *Halsey v Esso Petroleum*, see p 617.

(4)   In *British Celanese Ltd v A H Hunt (Capacitors) Ltd*, as a preliminary issue the court was asked whether the defendants might be liable where they collected metal strips as part of their business, these were blown about by the wind and some landed on an electricity sub-station and caused a power failure to the plaintiff's factory. The defendants were aware from previous experience that this was likely to happen. The plaintiffs claimed in negligence, private and public nuisance and under the principle in *Rylands v Fletcher*. Lawton J held that the claim in *Rylands v Fletcher* would fail but that the other claims would be allowed to continue. Lawton J:

'... Textbook writers have said that the opinions expressed in the House of Lords in *Read v J Lyons & Co Ltd* indicate a tendency to place a more restricted interpretation on "non-natural use" and that some of the earlier cases may require reconsideration ... The defendants are alleged to occupy premises on a trading estate. Such estates are planned and laid out for the purpose of accommodating manufacturers. The defendants are manufacturers. It follows that they are using this site for the very purpose for which sites were made available on the estate. The use of the site for manufacturing would be an ordinary one; the use of the site for any other purpose would be unusual. Does the particular kind of manufacturing which is done in the defendants' factory constitute, in Lord Moulton's words, "some special use bringing with it increased danger to others"? The manufacturing of electrical and electronic components in the year 1964, which is the material date, cannot be adjudged to be a special use nor can the bringing and storing on the premises of metal foil be a special use in itself. The way the metal foil was stored may have been a negligent one; but the use of the premises for storing such foil did not by itself create special risks. The metal foil was there for use in the manufacture of goods of a common type which at all material times were needed for the general benefit of the community. It follows that the defendants' first answer disposes of the plaintiffs' contentions under this head.

... There is nothing in the dictum of Blackburn J which says that the escape must be on to a plaintiff's land and do mischief there. A defendant is liable, prima facie, if he brings on his land and collects and keeps there anything likely to do mischief if it escapes; he must keep it in at his peril; and if he does not do so he is answerable for all the danger which is the natural consequence of its escape. In *Read v J Lyons & Co Ltd* Lord Simon said: "Escape ... means escape from a place which the defendant has occupation of, or control over, to a place which is outside his occupation or control." Once there has been an escape in this sense, those damnified may claim. They need not be the occupiers of adjoining land or indeed of any land. In *Charing Cross Electricity Supply Co Ltd v Hydraulic Power Co* the successful plaintiffs only had a licence to lay cables under certain public streets; they had no right of property in the soil. In *Halsey v Esso Petroleum Co Ltd* the successful plaintiff suffered damage to his motor car which was standing in the highway ...'

Cambridge Water Co v Eastern Counties Leather plc [1994] 1 All ER 53 House of Lords

Eastern Counties Leather plc (ECL) had for many years operated a tannery in an industrial 'village'. The Cambridge Water Company (CWC) drew water from a nearby bore-hole, fed by an aquifer which ran under the land of ECL. This was found to have been contaminated by chemicals shown to have come from ECL's processes; an alternative source of water had to be developed by CWC; the development cost represented the loss sustained by CWC.

The processes used by ECL involved a highly volatile solvent (PCE), and between 1960 and 1976 at least 1,000 gallons had been spilled. The judge at first instance held that a reasonable supervisor at ECL would not have foreseen that repeated spillages of small quantities of PCE would lead to any environmental hazard, i.e. would not have foreseen either that the PCE would enter an aquifer or, if it did, that detectable quantities would have been found downstream.

Lord Goff, delivering the judgment of the House of Lords, held that reasonable foreseeability of harm of the type complained about was an essential element of the rule in *Rylands v Fletcher*, and, *obiter*, observed that the use of land for storing substantial quantities of chemicals should be regarded as a non-natural use of land.

Lord Goff: '... the strict position now is that CWC, having abandoned its claim in nuisance, can only uphold the decision of the Court of Appeal on the basis of the rule in *Rylands v Fletcher*. However, one important submission advanced by ECL before the Appellate Committee was that strict liability for an escape only arises under that rule where the defendant knows or reasonably ought to have foreseen, when collecting the relevant things on his land, that those things might, if they escaped, cause damage of the relevant kind. Since there is a close relationship between nuisance and the rule in *Rylands v Fletcher*, I myself find it very difficult to form an opinion as to the validity of that submission without first considering whether foreseeability of such damage is an essential element in the law of nuisance. For that reason, therefore, I do not feel able altogether to ignore the latter question simply because it was no longer pursued by CWC before the Court of Appeal.

In order to consider the question in the present case in its proper legal context, it is desirable to look at the nature of liability in a case such as the present in relation both to the law of nuisance and the rule in *Rylands v Fletcher*, and for that purpose to consider the relationship between the two heads of liability.

I begin with the law of nuisance. Our modern understanding of the nature and scope of the law of nuisance was much enhanced by Professor Newark's seminal article "The Boundaries of Nuisance" (1949) 65 LQR 480. The article is avowedly an historical analysis, in that it traces the nature of the tort of nuisance to its origins, and demonstrates how the original view of nuisance as a tort to land (or more accurately, to accommodate interference with servitudes, a tort directed against the plaintiff's enjoyment of rights over land) became distorted as the tort was extended to embrace claims for personal injuries, even where the plaintiff's injury did not occur while using land in his occupation. In Professor Newark's opinion, this development produced adverse effects, viz. that liability which should have risen only under the law of negligence was allowed under the law of nuisance which historically was a tort of strict liability; and that there was a tendency for "cross-infection to take place, and notions of negligence began to make an appearance in the realm of nuisance proper". But, in addition, Professor Newark considered it contributed to a misappreciation of the decision in *Rylands v Fletcher*.

> "This case is generally regarded as an important landmark, indeed a turning point – in the law of tort; but an examination of the judgments shows that those who decided it were quite unconscious of any revolutionary or reactionary principles implicit in the decision. They thought of it as calling for no more than a restatement of settled principles, and Lord Cairns went so far as to describe those principles as 'extremely simple'. And in fact the main principle involved was extremely simple, being no more than the principle that negligence is not an element in the tort of nuisance. It is true that Blackburn J in his great judgment in the Exchequer Chamber never once used the word 'nuisance', but three times he cited the case of fumes escaping from an alkali works – a clear case of nuisance – as an instance of liability under the rule which he was laying down. Equally it is true that in 1866 there were a number of cases in the reports suggesting that persons who controlled dangerous things were under a strict duty to take care, but as none of these cases had anything to do with nuisance Blackburn J did not refer to them. But the profession as a whole, whose conceptions of the

boundaries of nuisance were now becoming fogged, failed to see in *Rylands v Fletcher* a simple case of nuisance. They regarded it as an exceptional case – and the rule in *Rylands v Fletcher* as a generalisation of exceptional cases, where liability was to be strict on account of 'the magnitude of danger, coupled with the difficulty of proving negligence' [*Pollock on Torts*, 14th edn, p 386] rather than on account of the nature of the plaintiff's interest which was invaded. They therefore jumped rashly to two conclusions: firstly, that the rule in *Rylands v Fletcher* could be extended beyond the case of neighbouring occupiers: and, secondly, that the rule could be used to afford a remedy in cases of personal injury. Both these conclusions were stoutly denied by Lord Macmillan in *Read v Lyons*, but it remains to be seen whether the House of Lords will support his opinion when the precise point comes up for decision."

We are not concerned in the present case with the problem of personal injuries, but we are concerned with the scope of liability in nuisance and in *Rylands v Fletcher*. In my opinion it is right to take as our starting point the fact that, as Professor Newark considered, *Rylands v Fletcher* was indeed not regarded by Blackburn J as a revolutionary decision; see e.g. his observations in *Ross v Fedden*. He believed himself not to be creating new law, but to be stating existing law, on the basis of existing authority; and, as is apparent from his judgment, he was concerned in particular with the situation where the defendant collects things upon his land which are likely to do mischief if they escape, in which event the defendant will be strictly liable for damage resulting from any such escape. It follows that the essential basis of liability was the collection by the defendant of such things upon his land; and the consequence was a strict liability in the event of damage caused by their escape, even if the escape was an isolated event. Seen in its context, there is no reason to suppose that Blackburn J intended to create a liability any more strict than that created by the law of nuisance; but even so he must have intended that, in the circumstances specified by him, there should be liability for damage resulting from an isolated escape.

Of course, although liability for nuisance has generally been regarded as strict, at least in the case of a defendant who has been responsible for the creation of a nuisance, even so that liability has been kept under control by the principle of reasonable user – the principle of give and take as between neighbouring occupiers of land, under which "... those acts necessary for the common and ordinary use and occupation of land and houses may be done, if conveniently done, without subjecting those who do them to an action": see *Bamford v Turnley*. The effect is that, if the user is reasonable, the defendant will not be liable for consequent harm to his neighbour's enjoyment of his land; but if the user is not reasonable, the defendant will be liable, even though he may have exercised reasonable care and skill to avoid it. Strikingly, a comparable principle has developed which limits liability under the rule in *Rylands v Fletcher*. This is the principle of natural use of the land. I shall have to consider the principle at a later stage in this judgment. The most authoritative statement of the principle is now to be found in the advice of the Privy Council delivered by Lord Moulton in *Rickards v Lothian* when he said of the rule in *Rylands v Fletcher*:

> "It is not every use to which land is put that brings into play that principle. It must be some special use bringing with it increased danger to others, and must not merely be the ordinary use of the land or such a use as is proper for the general benefit of the community".

It is not necessary for me to identify precise differences which may be drawn between this principle, and the principle of reasonable user as applied in the law of nuisance. It is enough for present purposes that I should draw attention to a similarity of function. The effect of this principle is that, where it applies, there will be no liability under the rule in *Rylands v Fletcher*; but that where it does not apply, i.e. where there is a non-natural use, the defendant will be liable for harm caused to the plaintiff by the escape, notwithstanding that he has exercised all reasonable care and skills to prevent the escape from occurring.

FORESEEABILITY OF DAMAGE IN NUISANCE

It is against this background that it is necessary to consider the question whether foreseeability of harm of the relevant type is an essential element of liability either in nuisance or under the rule in *Rylands v Fletcher*. I shall take first the case of nuisance. In the present case, as I have said, this is not strictly speaking a live issue. Even so, I propose briefly to address it, as part of the analysis of the background to the present case.

It is, of course, axiomatic that in this field we must be on our guard, when considering liability for damages in nuisance, not to draw inapposite conclusions from cases concerned only with a claim for an injunction. This is because, where an injunction is claimed, its purpose is to restrain further action by the defendant which may interfere with the plaintiff's enjoyment of his land, and *ex hypothesi* the defendant must be aware, if and when an injunction is granted, that such interference may be caused by the act which he is restrained from committing. It follows that these cases provide no guidance on the question whether foreseeability of harm of the relevant type is a prerequisite of the recovery of damages for causing such harm to the plaintiff. In the present case, we are not concerned with liability in damages in respect of a nuisance which has arisen through natural causes, or by the act of a person for whose actions the defendant is not responsible, in which cases the applicable principles in nuisance have become closely associated with those applicable in negligence: see *Sedleigh-Denfield v O'Callaghan* and *Goldman v Hargrave*. We are concerned with the liability of a person where a nuisance has been created by one for whose actions he is responsible. Here, as I have said, it is still the law that the fact that the defendant has taken all reasonable care will not of itself exonerate him from liability, the relevant control mechanism being found within the principle of reasonable user. But it by no means follows that the defendant should be held liable for damage of a type which he could not reasonably foresee; and the development of the law of negligence in the past sixty years points strongly towards a requirement that such foreseeability should be a prerequisite of liability in damages for nuisance, as it is of liability in negligence. For if a plaintiff is in ordinary circumstances only able to claim damages in respect of personal injuries where he can prove such foreseeability on the part of the defendant, it is difficult to see why, in common justice, he should be in a stronger position to claim damages for interference with the enjoyment of his land where the defendant was unable to foresee such damage. Moreover, this appears to have been the conclusion of the Privy Council in *Overseas Tankship (UK) Ltd v Miller Steamship Co Pty (The Wagon Mound (No 2))* ...

Lord Reid [said]:

> "It could not be right to discriminate between different cases of nuisance so as to make foreseeability a necessary element in determining damages in those cases where it is a necessary element in determining liability, but not in others. So the choice is between it being a necessary element in all cases of nuisance or in none. In their Lordships' judgment the similarities between nuisance and other forms of tort to which *The Wagon Mound (No. 1)* applies far outweigh any differences, and they must therefore hold that the judgment appealed from is wrong on this branch of the case. It is not sufficient that the injury suffered by the respondents' vessels was the direct result of the nuisance if that injury was in the relevant sense unforeseeable."

It is widely accepted that this conclusion, although not essential to the decision of the particular case, has nevertheless settled the law to the effect that foreseeability of harm is indeed a prerequisite of the recovery of damages in private nuisance, as in the case of public nuisance ...– It is unnecessary in the present case to consider the precise nature of this principle: but it appears from Lord Reid's statement of the law that he regarded it essentially as one relating to remoteness of damage.

FORESEEABILITY OF DAMAGE UNDER THE RULE IN *RYLANDS V FLETCHER*

It is against this background that I turn to the submission advanced by ECL before your Lordships that there is a similar prerequisite of recovery of damages under the rule in *Rylands v Fletcher* ... Blackburn J spoke of "anything *likely to* do mischief if it escapes": and later he spoke of something "which he *knows* to be mischievous if it gets on to his neighbour's [property]", and the liability to "answer for the natural *and anticipated consequences*". Furthermore, time and again he spoke of the strict liability imposed upon the defendant as being that he must keep the thing in at his peril; and, when referring to liability in actions for damage occasioned by animals, he referred to the established principle "that it is quite immaterial whether the escape is by negligence or not". The general tenor of his statement of principle is therefore that knowledge, or at least foreseeability of the risk, is a prerequisite of the recovery of damages under the principle; but that the principle is one of strict liability in the sense that the defendant may be held liable notwithstanding that he has exercised all due care to prevent the escape from occurring.

There are, however, early authorities in which foreseeability of damage does not appear to have been regarded as necessary ... Moreover, it was submitted by [Counsel] for CWC that the requirement of foreseeability of damage was negatived in ... the decision of the Court of Appeal in *West v Bristol Tramways Co* and the decision of this House in *Rainham Chemical Works Ltd v Belvedere Fish Guano Co Ltd* ...

I feel bound to say that these two cases provide a very fragile base for any firm conclusion that foreseeability of damage has been authoritatively rejected as a prerequisite of the recovery of damages under the rule in *Rylands v Fletcher*. Certainly, the point was not considered by this House in the *Rainham Chemicals* case. In my opinion, the matter is open for consideration by your Lordships in the present case, and, despite recent *dicta* to the contrary (see, e.g. *Leakey v National Trust for Places of Historic Interest or Natural Beauty*), should be considered as a matter of principle. Little guidance can be derived from either of the two cases in question, save that it seems to have been assumed that the strict liability arising under the rule precluded reliance by the plaintiff on lack of knowledge or the means of knowledge of the relevant danger.

The point is one on which academic opinion appears to be divided: cf. *Salmond and Heuston on Torts* (20th edn), which favours the prerequisite of foreseeability, and *Clerk and Lindsell on Torts* (16th edn), which takes a different view. However, quite apart from the indications to be derived from the judgment of Blackburn J ... to which I have already referred, the historical connection with the law of nuisance must now be regarded as pointing towards the conclusion that foreseeability of damage is a prerequisite of the recovery of damages under the rule. I have already referred to the fact that Blackburn J himself did not regard his statement of principle as having broken new ground; furthermore, Professor Newark has convincingly shown that the rule in *Rylands v Fletcher* was essentially concerned with an extension of the law of nuisance to cases of isolated escape. Accordingly since, following the observations of Lord Reid when delivering the advice of the Privy Council in *The Wagon Mound (No 2)*, the recovery of damages in private nuisance depends on foreseeability by the defendant of the relevant type of damage, it would appear logical to extend the same requirement to liability under the rule in *Rylands v Fletcher*.

Even so, the question cannot be considered solely as a matter of history. It can be argued that the rule in *Rylands v Fletcher* should not be regarded simply as an extension of the law of nuisance, but should rather be treated as a developing principle of strict liability from which can be derived a general rule of strict liability for damage caused by ultra-hazardous operations, on the basis of which persons conducting such operations may properly be held strictly liable for the extraordinary risk to others involved in such operations. As is pointed out in *Fleming on Torts*, 8th edn, this would lead to the practical result that the cost of damage resulting from such operations would have to be absorbed as part of the overheads of the relevant business rather than be borne (where there is no negligence) by the injured person or his insurers, or even by the community at large. Such a development appears to have been taking place in the United States, as can be seen from paragraph 519 of the *Restatement of Torts* (2d) vol 3 (1977). The extent to which it has done so is not altogether clear; and I infer from paragraph 519, and the Comment on that paragraph, that the abnormally dangerous activities there referred to are such that their ability to cause harm would be obvious to any reasonable person who carried them on.

I have to say, however, that there are serious obstacles in the way of the development of the rule in *Rylands v Fletcher* in this way. First of all, if it was so to develop it should logically apply to liability to all persons suffering injury by reason of the ultra-hazardous operations; but the decision of this House in *Read v J Lyons & Co Ltd*, which establishes that there can be no liability under the rule except in circumstances where the injury has been caused by an escape from land under control of the defendant, has effectively precluded any such development. Professor Fleming has observed that "the most damaging effect of the decision in *Read v Lyons* is that it prematurely stunted the development of a general theory of strict liability for ultra-hazardous activities" (see *Fleming on Torts* (8th edn)). Even so, there is much to be said for the view that the courts should not be proceeding down the path of developing such a general theory. In this connection, I refer in particular to the Report of the Law Commission on *Civil Liability for Dangerous Things and Activities* (Law Com No 32), 1970. In paragraphs 14–16 of the Report, the Law Commission expressed serious misgivings about the adoption of any test for the application of strict liability involving a general concept of "especially dangerous" or "ultrahazardous" activity, having regard to the uncertainties and practical difficulties of its application. If the Law Commission is unwilling to consider statutory reform on this basis, it must follow that judges should if anything be even more reluctant to proceed down that path.

Like the judge in the present case, I incline to the opinion that, as a general rule, it is more appropriate for strict liability in respect of operations of high risk to be imposed by Parliament, than by the courts. If such liability is imposed by statute, the relevant activities can be identified, and those concerned can know where they stand. Furthermore, statute can where appropriate lay down precise criteria establishing the incidence and scope of such liability.

It is of particular relevance that the present case is concerned with environmental pollution. The protection and preservation of the environment is now perceived as being of crucial importance to the future of mankind; and public bodies, both national and international, are taking significant steps towards the establishment of legislation which will promote the protection of the environment, and make the polluter pay for damage to the environment for which he is responsible – as can be seen from the WHO, EEC and national regulations to which I have previously referred. But it does not follow from these developments that a common law principle, such as the rule in *Rylands v Fletcher*, should be developed or rendered more strict to provide for liability in respect of such pollution. On the contrary, given that so much well-informed and carefully structured legislation is now being put in place for this purpose, there is less need for the courts to develop a common law principle to achieve the same end, and indeed it may well be undesirable that they should do so.

Having regard to these considerations, and in particular to the step which this House has already taken in *Read v Lyons* to contain the scope of liability under the rule in *Rylands v Fletcher*, it appears to me to be appropriate now to take the view that foreseeability of damage of the relevant type should be regarded as a prerequisite of liability in damages under the rule. Such a conclusion can, as I have already stated, be derived from Blackburn J's original statement of the law; and I can see no good reason why this prerequisite should not be recognised under the rule, as it has been in the case of private nuisance ... It would moreover lead to a more coherent body of common law principles if the rule were to be regarded essentially as an extension of the law of nuisance to cases of isolated escapes from land, even though the rule as established is not limited to escapes which are in fact isolated. I wish to point out, however, that in truth the escape of the PCE from ECL's land, in the form of trace elements carried in percolating water, has not been an isolated escape, but a continuing escape resulting from a state of affairs which has come into existence at the base of the chalk aquifer underneath ECL's premises. Classically, this would have been regarded as a case of nuisance; and it would seem strange if, by characterising the case as one falling under the rule in *Rylands v Fletcher*, the liability should thereby be rendered more strict in the circumstances of the present case.

THE FACTS OF THE PRESENT CASE

Turning to the facts of the present case, it is plain that, at the time when the PCE was brought on to ECL's land, and indeed when it was used in the tanning process there, nobody at ECL could reasonably have foreseen the resultant damage which occurred at CWC's borehole at Sawston.

However, there remains for consideration a point adumbrated in the course of argument, which is relevant to liability in nuisance as well as under the rule in *Rylands v Fletcher*. It appears that, in the present case, pools of neat PCE are still in existence at the base of the chalk aquifer beneath ECL's premises, and the escape of dissolved phase PCE from ECL's land is continuing to the present day. On this basis it can be argued that, since it has become known that PCE, if it escapes, is capable of causing damage by rendering water available at boreholes unsaleable for domestic purposes, ECL could be held liable, in nuisance or under the rule in *Rylands v Fletcher*, in respect of damage caused by the continuing escape of PCE from its land occurring at any time after such damage had become foreseeable by ECL.

For my part, I do not consider that such an argument is well founded. Here we are faced with a situation where the substance in question, PCE, has so travelled down through the drift and the chalk aquifer beneath ECL's premises that it has passed beyond the control of ECL. To impose strict liability on ECL in these circumstances, either as the creator of a nuisance or under the rule in *Rylands v Fletcher*, on the ground that it has subsequently become reasonably foreseeable that the PCE may, if it escapes, cause damage, appears to me to go beyond the scope of the regimes imposed under either of these two related heads of liability. This is because when ECL created the conditions which have ultimately led to the present state of affairs – whether by bringing the PCE in question on to its land, or by retaining it there, or by using it in its tanning process – it could not possibly have foreseen that damage of the type now complained of might be caused thereby. Indeed, long before the relevant legislation came into force, the PCE had become irretrievably lost in the ground below. In such circumstances, I do not consider that ECL should be under any greater liability than that imposed for negligence. At best, if the case is regarded as one of nuisance, it should be treated no differently from, for example, the case of the landslip in *Leakey v National Trust for Places of Historic Interest or National Beauty*.

I wish to add that the present case may be regarded as one of what is nowadays called historic pollution, in the sense that the relevant occurrence (the seepage of PCE through the floor of ECL's premises) took place before the relevant legislation came into force; and it appears that, under the current philosophy, it is not envisaged that statutory liability should be imposed for historic pollution (see, e.g., the Council of Europe's Draft Convention on Civil Liability for Damages Resulting from Activities Dangerous to the Environment (Strasbourg 29 January 1993) art 5.1, and paragraph 48 of the Explanatory Report). If so, it would be strange if liability for such pollution were to arise under a principle of common law.

In the result, since those responsible at ECL could not at the relevant time reasonably have foreseen that the damage in question might occur, the claim of CWC for damages under the rule in *Rylands v Fletcher* must fail.

NATURAL USE OF LAND

I turn to the question whether the use by ECL of its land in the present case constituted a natural use, with the result that ECL cannot be held liable under the rule in *Rylands v Fletcher*. In view of my conclusion on the issue of foreseeability, I can deal with this point shortly ...

It is a commonplace that this particular exception to liability under the rule has developed and changed over the years. It seems clear that Blackburn J's statement of the law was limited to things which are brought by the defendant on to his land, and so did not apply to things that were naturally upon the land. Furthermore, it is doubtful whether in the House of Lords in the same case Lord Cairns, to whom we owe the expression "non-natural use" of the land, was intending to expand the concept of natural use beyond that envisaged by Blackburn J. Even so, the law has long since departed from any such simple idea, redolent of a different age; and, at least since ... *Rickards v Lothian* natural use has been extended to embrace the ordinary use of land ...

Rickards v Lothian itself was concerned with a use of a domestic kind, viz. the overflow of water from a basin whose runaway had become blocked. But over the years the concept of natural use, in the sense of ordinary use, has been extended to embrace a wide variety of uses, including not only domestic uses but also recreational uses and even some industrial uses.

It is obvious that the expression "ordinary use of the land" in Lord Moulton's statement of the law is one which is lacking in precision. There are some writers who welcome the flexibility which has thus been introduced into this branch of the law, on the ground that it enables judges to mould and adapt the principle of strict liability to the changing needs of society; whereas others regret the perceived absence of principle in so vague a concept, and fear that the whole idea of strict liability may as a result be undermined. A particular doubt is introduced by Lord Moulton's alternative criterion "or such a use as is proper for the general benefit of the community". If these words are understood to refer to a local community, they can be given some content as intended to refer to such matters as, for example, the provision of services; indeed the same idea can, without too much difficulty, be extended to, for example, the provision of services to industrial premises, as in a business park or an industrial estate. But if the words are extended to embrace the wider interests of the local community or the general benefit of the community at large, it is difficult to see how the exception can be kept within reasonable bounds. A notable extension was considered in your Lordships' House in *Read v J Lyons & Co Ltd*, where it was suggested that, in time of war, the manufacture of explosives might be held to constitute a natural use of land, apparently on the basis that, in a country in which the greater part of the population was involved in the war effort, many otherwise exceptional uses might become "ordinary" for the duration of the war. It is however unnecessary to consider so wide an extension as that in a case such as the present. Even so, we can see the introduction of another extension in the present case, when the judge invoked the creation of employment as clearly for the benefit of the local community, viz. "the industrial village" at Sawston. I myself, however, do not feel able to accept that the creation of employment as such, even in a small industrial complex, is sufficient of itself to establish a particular use as constituting a natural or ordinary use of land.

Fortunately, I do not think it is necessary for the purposes of the present case to attempt any redefinition of the concept of natural or ordinary use. This is because

I am satisfied that the storage of chemicals in substantial quantities, and their use in the manner employed at ECL's premises, cannot fall within the exception. For the purpose of testing the point, let it be assumed that ECL was well aware of the possibility that PCE, if it escaped, could indeed cause damage, for example by contaminating any water with which it became mixed so as to render that water undrinkable by human beings. I cannot think that it would be right in such circumstances to exempt ECL from liability under the rule in *Rylands v Fletcher* on the ground that the use was natural or ordinary. The mere fact that the use is common in the tanning industry cannot, in my opinion, be enough to bring the use within the exception, nor the fact that Sawston contains a small industrial community which is worthy of encouragement or support. Indeed I feel bound to say that the storage of substantial quantities of chemicals on industrial premises should be regarded as an almost classic case of non-natural use; and I find it very difficult to think that it should be thought objectionable to impose strict liability for damage caused in the event of their escape. It may well be that, now that it is recognised that foreseeability of harm of the relevant type is a prerequisite of liability in damages under the rule, the courts may feel less pressure to extend the concept of natural use to circumstances such as those in the present case; and in due course it may become easier to control this exception, and to ensure that it has a more recognisable basis of principle. For these reasons, I would not hold that ECL should be exempt from liability on the basis of the exception of natural use ...'

Comment

(1) Lord Porter in *Read v J Lyons & Co Ltd*, when considering what can be 'dangerous' and what is a non-natural use, makes the point that:

'... there is a considerable body of case law dealing with these questions and a series of findings or assumptions as to what is sufficient to establish their existence. Among dangerous objects have been held to be included gas, explosive substances, electricity, oil, fumes, rusty wire, poisonous vegetation, vibrations, a flag-pole, and even dwellers in caravans ... If these questions ever come directly before this House it may become necessary to lay down principles for their determination. For the present I need only say that each seems to be a question of fact subject to a ruling of the judge whether the particular object can be dangerous or the particular use can be non-natural, and in deciding this question I think that all the circumstances of the time and place and practice of mankind must be taken into consideration so that what might be regarded as dangerous or non-natural may vary according to those circumstances ...'

For planted yew trees, see *Crowhurst v Amersham*; for 'chair-o-plane', see *Hale v Jennings*; for flag-pole, see *Schiffman v Order of St John*; for caravan dwellers, see *A-G v Corke*. The continuing validity of these is in doubt following *Transco plc v Stockport MBC*, p 715.

(2)   Lord Macmillan in *Read v J Lyons & Co Ltd* observed that:

'... The doctrine of *Rylands v Fletcher* ... derives from a conception of the mutual duties of adjoining or neighbouring landowners and its congeners are trespass and nuisance. If its foundation is to be found in the injunction *sic utere tuo ut alienum non laedas*, then it is manifest that it has nothing to do with personal injuries. The duty is to refrain from injuring not *alium* but *alienum*.'

Further, the decision in *Hunter v Canary Wharf*, that nuisance is a tort concerned with injury to interests in land and not with personal injury, leads inevitably to the view that the same conclusion will flow in respect of the principle in *Rylands v Fletcher*, and this was the approach favoured, *obiter*, by the House of Lords in the *Transco* case, see Lord Hoffmann. Comments in other cases to the contrary allowing recovery of personal injury damages must now be treated as of doubtful authority, e.g. see *Hale v Jennings, Schiffman v Order of St John, Howard v Furness Houlder Argentine Lines Ltd* and *Perry v Kendrick's Transport Ltd*.

(3)   There is scope for argument over whether or not the need for reasonable foreseeability is as much of a handicap as has been suggested. It certainly is a hurdle to be overcome by the plaintiff, but in most instances it is unlikely to be unduly difficult, particularly in the light of the likely pleadings of negligence which will often accompany a claim. For the meaning and application of reasonable foreseeability in this context see p 697.

(4)   The issue of what is or is not a natural use of land remains open, and, although Lord Goff in the *Cambridge Water* case eschewed any definition, the general conclusion tends to accord with a reduction in the severity of the test. One complicating feature in Lord Goff's speech is the reference to the storage of chemicals coupled with their use in the manner adopted by the company. The ambiguity leading to confusion is that the 'use' referred to may be, on the one hand, the sloppy handling of the chemical, or, on the other hand, the industrial process as a whole. The latter is to be preferred, and is likely to be what Lord Goff meant since he goes on to assume that liability would have flowed had there been foreseeability of harm in the event of an assumed escape.

(5)   Although it is case on nuisance, given that *Rylands v Fletcher* is a derivative of nuisance *Hunter v Canary Wharf* also suggests that a restrictive approach should be taken as to those plaintiffs who would be able to maintain an action under the principle in *Rylands v Fletcher*. Consistent with *Transco plc v Stockport MBC, Hunter v Canary Wharf* and *Read v Lyons* would be the conclusion that only those who have an interest in the land may sue. Thus, comments to the contrary in cases such as *Halsey v Esso Petroleum* may fall to be reconsidered insofar as that case applied to damage to cars parked on the road outside the property.

(6) In *Rigby v Chief Constable of Northants*, see p 585, the police deliberately fired a tear-gas canister into a building in order to flush out an armed man. Taylor J could not see that the fact that the discharge was from the highway was relevant to the principle in *Rylands v Fletcher*; in his view the issue was control of the thing rather than ownership or occupation of property from which the thing escapes. Secondly, he inclined to the view that *Rylands v Fletcher* does not apply to an intentional or voluntary release of a dangerous thing. In any event, the judge concluded that if (which he doubted) *Rylands v Fletcher* applied to the facts of the case then necessity would provide a good defence.

In the light of the judicial reluctance to develop *Rylands v Fletcher* further, these *dicta* need to be approached with caution. This cautious approach was evident in *Crown River Cruises Ltd v Kimbolton Fireworks Ltd*, a case involving liability in negligence and private nuisance arising from a fireworks display based on a barge on the River Thames. Debris from the display fell upon a vessel moored nearby and caused a fire. Although not finding liability under *Rylands v Fletcher*, the Queen's Bench Division held, *obiter*, that the principle applied equally to deliberate release as to escape, and that it would apply to accumulations on a vessel on a navigable river as it would to an accumulation on any other highway. The entitlement to sue in nuisance that case was based on a licence to occupy the site.

(7) The case reveals the relatively conservative nature of the common law. The reluctance of the court to follow the lead given by statute *vis-à-vis* liability for historic pollution means that the law of tort is less effective as a method of environmental protection and the field is now occupied only by the relevant statutory provisions.

(8) There are still vital distinctions between nuisance and *Rylands v Fletcher* on the one hand, and negligence on the other. In particular, the taking of all reasonable steps will avoid liability in negligence but not in nuisance or *Rylands v Fletcher.*

(9) There must be an escape as a result of the activity connected with the thing, and although usually it will be the thing itself which will escape this may not always be the case. In *Miles v Forest Rock* the plaintiff was injured by rocks blasted out of the defendant's property; they had been there naturally (and therefore were not within the rule) but the thing was the explosives. See also the comments in *Mason v Levy Auto Parts*, p 714.

(10) In *Smeaton v Ilford Corporation*, in times of heavy rain the plaintiff's house suffered flooding from the defendant local authority's sewer. The plaintiff alleged nuisance but failed because it could not be shown that the defendant had adopted or continued the nuisance. The corporation was statutorily bound to permit others to discharge into the sewer, and it was this overload which constituted the nuisance (on this point now see p 661). The court held that the

legal personality of the defendant (in this case a local authority) was irrelevant and that even though the defendant acted for the general benefit of the community there was no exception to the rule in *Rylands v Fletcher*. Further, the collection of sewage in large volumes in pipes was a non-natural use. Accordingly, the defendant might still be liable under the principle in *Rylands v Fletcher*. But, the defendants were entitled to rely as a defence on the Public Health Act 1936, s 31 as statutory authority.

After the comments of Lord Goff in the House of Lords in the *Cambridge Water* case, it seems that there is unlikely to be any scope for arguing that the use is for the benefit of the local community, even though jobs are supported in an industrial village.

Rickards v Lothian
[1913] AC 263 Privy Council

The plaintiff's stock was damaged by an escape of water from the defendant's water supply to a lavatory. The taps to a sink had been turned on and the overflow and waste-pipe deliberately obstructed. The defendant was held not liable in negligence on the basis of causation, as the damage was caused by the act of a third party. On liability under the principle in *Rylands v Fletcher*, the Privy Council held that the use of the premises was not non-natural and that liability did not extend to the unforeseen acts of a third party.

Lord Moulton: '... It will be seen that Blackburn J, with characteristic carefulness, indicates that exceptions to the general rule may arise where the escape is in consequence of *vis major*, or the act of God, but declines to deal further with that question because it was unnecessary for the decision of the case then before him ... The judgment of the Court of Appeal [in *Nicholls v Marsland*] ... was read by Mellish LJ ...:

> " ... the present case is distinguished from that of *Rylands v Fletcher* in this, that it is not the act of the defendant in keeping this reservoir, an act in itself lawful, which alone leads to the escape of the water, and so renders wrongful that which but for such escape would have been lawful. It is the supervening vis major of the water caused by the flood, which, superadded to the water in the reservoir (which of itself would have been innocuous), causes the disaster. A defendant cannot, in our opinion, be properly said to have caused or allowed the water to escape, if the act of God or the Queen's enemies was the real cause of its escaping without any fault on the part of the defendant. If a reservoir was destroyed by an earthquake, or the Queen's enemies destroyed it in conducting some warlike operation, it would be contrary to all reason and justice to hold the owner of the reservoir liable for any damage which might be done by the escape of the water. We are of

opinion, therefore, that the defendant was entitled to excuse herself by proving that the water escaped through the act of God."

Their Lordships are of opinion that all that is there laid down as to a case where the escape is due to *vis major* or the King's enemies applies equally to a case where it is due to the malicious act of a third person, if, indeed, that case is not actually included in the above phrase. To follow the language of the judgment just recited – a defendant cannot in their Lordships' opinion be properly said to have caused or allowed the water to escape if the malicious act of a third person was the real cause of its escaping without any fault on the part of the defendant. It is remarkable that the very point involved in the present case was expressly dealt with by Bramwell B ... in the same case. He says:

"What has the defendant done wrong? What right of the plaintiff has she infringed? She has done nothing wrong, she has infringed no right. It is not the defendant who let loose the water and sent it to destroy the bridges. She did indeed store it, and store it in such quantities that if it was let loose it would do as it did, mischief. But suppose that a stranger let it loose, would the defendant be liable? If so, then if a mischievous boy bored a hole in a cistern in any London house, and the water did mischief to a neighbour, the occupier of the house would be liable. That cannot be. Then why is the defendant liable if some agent over which she has no control lets the water out? ... I admit that it is not a question of negligence. A man may use all care to keep the water in ... but would be liable if through any defect, though latent, the water escaped ... But here the act is that of an agent he cannot control."

Following the language of this judgment their Lordships are of opinion that no better example could be given of an agent which the defendant cannot control than that of a third party surreptitiously and by a malicious act causing the overflow.

The same principle is affirmed in *Box v Jubb*. In that case the defendants had a reservoir on their land which was connected both for supply and discharge with a water course or main drain. Through the sudden emptying of another reservoir into the drain at a higher level than their reservoir and by the blocking of the main drain below, the defendants' reservoir was made to overflow and damage was done to the lands of the plaintiff. The defendants were guilty of no negligence either in the construction or maintenance of the reservoir, and the acts which led to its overflow were done by persons over whom they had no control. In giving judgment, Kelly CB says:

"The question is, what was the cause of this overflow? Was it anything for which the defendants are responsible – did it proceed from their act or default, or from that of a stranger over which they had no control? The case is abundantly clear on this, proving beyond a doubt that the defendants had no control over the causes of the overflow, and no knowledge of the existence of the obstruction. The matters complained of took place through no default or breach of duty of the defendants, but were caused by a stranger over whom and at a spot where they had no control. It seems to me to be immaterial whether this is called *vis major* or the unlawful act of a stranger; it is sufficient to say that the defendants had no means of preventing the occurrence. I think the defendants could not possibly have been expected to anticipate that which happened here, and the law does not require them to construct their reservoir and sluices and gates leading to it to meet any amount of pressure which the wrongful act of a third person may impose."

Their Lordships agree with the law as laid down in the judgments above cited, and are of opinion that a defendant is not liable on the principle of *Rylands v Fletcher* for damage caused by the wrongful acts of third persons.

But there is another ground upon which their Lordships are of opinion that the present case does not come within the principle laid down in *Rylands v Fletcher*. It is not every use to which land is put that brings into play that principle. It must be some special use bringing with it increased danger to others and must not merely be the ordinary use of the land or such a use as is proper for the general benefit of the community. To use the language of Lord Robertson in *Eastern and South African Telegraph Co v Cape Town Tramways Co*, the principle of *Rylands v Fletcher* "subjects to a high liability the owner who uses his property for purposes other than those which are natural".

This is more fully expressed by Wright J, in his judgment in *Blake v Woolf*. In that case the plaintiff was the occupier of the lower floors of the defendant's house, the upper floors being occupied by the defendant himself. A leak occurred in the cistern at the top of the house which, without any negligence on the part of the defendant, caused the plaintiff's premises to be flooded. In giving judgment for the defendant, Wright J says:

> " ... The bringing of water on to such premises as these and the maintaining a cistern in the usual way seems to me to be an ordinary and reasonable user of such premises as these were; and, therefore, if the water escapes without any negligence or default on the part of the person bringing the water in and owning the cistern, I do not think that he is liable for any damage that may ensue."

This is entirely in agreement with the judgment of Blackburn J in *Ross v Fedden*. In that case the defendants were the occupiers of the upper floor of a house of which the plaintiff occupied the lower floor. The supply and overflow pipes of a water-closet which was situated in the defendants' premises and was for his use and convenience got out of order, and caused the plaintiff's premises to be flooded. Negligence was negatived. In giving judgment in favour of the defendant, Blackburn J says:

> " ... I do not think that the maxim *sic utere tuo ut alienum non laedas* applies. Negligence is negatived; and probably, if the defendants had got notice of the

state of the valve and pipe and had done nothing, there might have been ground for the argument that they were liable for the consequences; but I do not think that the law casts on the defendants any such obligation as the plaintiff contends for."

Their Lordships are in entire sympathy with these views. The provision of a proper supply of water to the various parts of the house is not only reasonable, but has become, in accordance with modern sanitary views, an almost necessary feature of town life. It is recognised as being so desirable in the interests of the community that in some form or other it is usually made obligatory in civilised countries. Such a supply cannot be installed without causing some concurrent danger of leakage or overflow. It would be unreasonable for the law to regard those who install or maintain such a system of supply as doing so at their own peril, with an absolute liability for any damage resulting from its presence even when there has been no negligence. It would be still more unreasonable if, as the respondent contends, such liability were to be held to extend to the consequences of malicious acts on the part of third persons. In such matters as the domestic supply of water or gas, it is essential that the mode of supply should be such as to permit ready access for the purpose of use, and hence it is impossible to guard against wilful mischief. Taps may be turned on, ball cocks fastened open, supply pipes cut, and waste pipes blocked. Against such acts no precaution can prevail. It would be wholly unreasonable to hold an occupier responsible for the consequences of such acts which he is powerless to prevent, when the provision of the supply is not only a reasonable act on his part but probably a duty. Such a doctrine would, for example, make a householder liable for the consequences of an explosion caused by a burglar breaking into his house during the night and leaving a gas tap open. There is, in their Lordships' opinion, no support either in reason or authority for any such view of the liability of a landlord or occupier. In having on his premises such means of supply he is only using those premises in an ordinary and proper manner, and, although he is bound to exercise all reasonable care, he is not responsible for damage not due to his own default, whether that damage be caused by inevitable accident or the wrongful acts of third persons ...'

Comment

(1) Natural use is one factor limiting the scope of the rule. It includes the ideas of 'abnormal use', 'for his own benefit' and 'added hazards'. See in particular the *obiter* remarks of Lord Goff in the *Cambridge Water* case and *British Celanese Ltd v Hunt*, p 696.

(2) See also *Perry v Kendricks Transport Ltd*, p 714. For cases in negligence in respect of the acts of malicious third parties, see p 285. For liability in nuisance for the acts of third parties see *Sedleigh-Denfield v O'Callaghan, Page Motors v Epsom & Ewell BC* and *Smith v Scott*. For liability for attracting third parties of an undesirable nature, see *A-G v Corke*. Bennet J said:

' ... It is, of course, not unlawful for a person to grant licences to caravan dwellers to place their caravans on his land. But it seems to me that, in bringing on to his land, for his own profit, a number of people who dwell in caravans, the defendant has put his land to an abnormal use. Persons whose homes are in caravans, moving about from place to place, have habits of life many of which are offensive to those who have fixed homes, and when collected together in large numbers, on a comparatively small parcel of land, such persons would be expected by reasonable people to do the kind of things which have been complained of in this action ... On that view of the matter the principle which underlies the decision in *Rylands v Fletcher* affords ... a basis upon which the defendant can be made responsible in law for the nuisance which undoubtedly exists ... and which is caused by some of the people whom he brings there for his own profit ...'

(3)   A significant emphasis to non-natural use was given in *Mason v Levy Auto Parts Ltd* where the defendant had stored large quantities of flammable material in a way which made fire-fighting difficult and which amounted to negligence. MacKenna J identified the case as one to which the principle *sic utere tuo ut alienum non laedas* applied, i.e. the principle which it is said is the basis of *Rylands v Fletcher*. He asked if there was a natural use of the land:

'... I feel the difficulty which any judge must feel in deciding what is a non-natural user of the land, and have prepared myself for answering the question by reading what is said about it in *Salmond on Torts* and in *Winfield on the Law of Torts* ... Thus conditioned, I would say that the defendants' use of their land in the way described earlier in this judgment was non-natural. In saying this I have regard (i) to the quantities of combustible material which the defendants brought on their land, (ii) to the way in which they stored them, and (iii) to the character of the neighbourhood. It may be that these considerations would also justify a finding of negligence. If that is so, the end would be the same as I have reached by a more laborious and perhaps more questionable route.'

Various aspects of the law relating to liability for fires were extensively examined in *Johnson v BJW Property Developments Ltd*.

(4)   In *Perry v Kendricks Transport Ltd* the Court of Appeal was prepared to accept that a motor coach left on land with an empty petrol tank was something of a kind likely to do mischief if it or something from it escaped, and that an action for damages for personal injuries would lie in such a case. The cap on the tank was removed and a match thrown in by one of two other children present. The plaintiff child suffered burns when the vapour in the tank exploded. It was held that the actions leading to the explosion were the acts of a stranger over whom the defendant had no control, and which were unforesee-able, and that there was no liability in *Rylands v Fletcher*. Jenkins LJ said:

' ... in the circumstances of a particular case, it may be that children doing some mischievous act whereby the dangerous thing escapes are not strangers. I cannot, however, regard that as aiding a plaintiff in an action such as this, unless it can be shown that in the circumstances of the case the dangerous thing was left by the defendants in such a condition that it was a reasonable and probable consequence of their action, which they ought to have foreseen, that children might meddle with the dangerous thing and cause it to escape. If facts such as those were made out in any particular case, then in my view, the defendants could not claim to rely on the act of the mischievous child as constituting the act of a stranger. It would be an act brought about by the defendants' own negligence in dealing with the dangerous thing, and the foreseeable consequence of a negligent act. If that were made out, however, one reaches the point where the claim based on *Rylands v Fletcher* merges into the claim in negligence: for if such a state of affairs could be made out, then it would no longer be necessary for the plaintiff to rely on *Rylands v Fletcher* at all. He could rely simply on the defendants' negligence ...'

Transco plc v Stockport Metropolitan Borough Council
[2004] I All ER 589 House of Lords

In 1966 the North Western Gas Board, under an agreement with the British Railways Board, laid a 16-inch high-pressure steel gas main beneath the surface of a railway and the Board acquired an easement to maintain its pipe in the soil of the railway bed. The pipe then passed to Transco. Stockport MBC's predecessor built a housing estate bordering the railway line which became disused; the council then bought the line and surfaced it for use by walkers and cyclists.

In the summer of 1992 a leak developed in a high-pressure pipe belonging to the council which supplied water to Hollow End Towers, an 11-storey tower block on the estate. The pipe had a capacity 16 times greater than the normal pipe in common domestic use because it supplied the large tanks in the basement of Hollow End Towers. The water was then pumped to tanks on the roof which supplied the flats in the block. The pipe probably fractured because of subsidence in a landfill site under the tower.

The leak was discovered and repaired in September 1992 and the well of the lift shaft at Hollow End Towers was found to be flooded. Two days after the leak had been found, water was seen bubbling up near the old railway below the tower. The landfill site below the tower had been soaking up water and had become saturated. The water ran along the railway bed but where the railway bed was carried on an embankment the water spilled down the sides. This caused a section of the embankment to give way and a section of Transco's gas pipe line was left unsupported and exposed. Transco repaired the damage at a cost of £93,681 and sued to recover the cost of repair. It did not allege carelessness and Transco's main claim was that the council was liable without proof of negligence under the rule in *Rylands v Fletcher.*

The House of Lords held that the rule in *Rylands v Fletcher* remained good law in England and Wales and should not be abrogated. There had been no non-natural user of the land. Lord Scott also held that there had been no escape from land owned by the council to any other property.

Lord Bingham: '...

[3.] Few cases in the law of tort or perhaps any other field are more familiar, or have attracted more academic and judicial discussion, than *Rylands v Fletcher.* This relieves me of the need both to summarise the well-known facts of the case and to rehearse yet again the passages ... in which Blackburn J and Lord Cairns LC expressed the *ratio* of their decisions. I content myself with three points, none of them controversial:

(1) The plaintiff framed his claim as one of negligence ... It was only when a majority of the Court of Exchequer (Pollock CB and Martin B, Bramwell B dissenting) held against him, ruling that no claim would lie in the absence of negligence, that the plaintiff changed tack and contended that defendants were liable even if negligence could not be established against them.

(2) Blackburn J did not conceive himself to be laying down any new principle of law. When, in *Ross v Fedden,* it was later suggested to him by counsel that the question in *Rylands v Fletcher* had never been decided until the adjudication of that case, he rejected the suggestion in robust terms. The Lord Chancellor regarded the principles on which the case was to be determined as "extremely simple". Had the House regarded the case as raising issues of great moment, steps might no doubt have been taken to assemble a stronger quorum to hear the appeal: see Heuston, "Who was the Third Lord in *Rylands v Fletcher?*" (1970) 86 LQR 160–165. It seems likely, as persuasively contended by Professor Newark ("The Boundaries of Nuisance" (1949) 65 LQR 480, 487–488), that those who decided the case regarded it as one of nuisance, novel only to the extent that it sanctioned recovery where the interference by one occupier of land with the right or enjoyment of another was isolated and not persistent.

(3) Those involved in *Rylands v Fletcher,* as counsel or judges, must have been very much alive to the catastrophic results which may ensue when reservoir dams burst. Professor Brian Simpson has drawn attention ("Legal Liability for Bursting Reservoirs: The Historical Context of *Rylands v Fletcher*" (1984) 13 Journal of Legal Studies 209) to two such catastrophes, one in 1852, some eight years before the inundation of Mr Fletcher's colliery, the second in 1864, after *Fletcher's* case had been heard at first instance but before the hearing in the three appellate courts. In the Court of Exchequer Chamber, Blackburn J expressly referred to the case of

damage done by the bursting of waterworks companies' reservoirs. Lord Cairns, as Sir Hugh Cairns QC, had advised on the payment of compensation when the second disaster occurred. No matter how broadly the principle was expressed when judgment was given, the risk of escape of water from an artificially constructed reservoir was one which the judges must have had vividly in mind. The damage suffered by Fletcher was not the result of a dam failure, but nor was Rylands' reservoir a mere pond: inspecting it before writing his article, Simpson found it still in use, with a capacity of over 4 million gallons and covering 1½ acres when full.

THE FUTURE DEVELOPMENT OF *RYLANDS V FLETCHER*

4.   In the course of his excellent argument for the council, Mr Mark Turner QC canvassed various ways in which the rule in *Rylands v Fletcher* might be applied and developed in future, without however judging it necessary to press the House to accept any one of them. The boldest of these courses was to follow the trail blazed by a majority of the High Court of Australia in *Burnie Port Authority v General Jones Property Ltd* by treating the rule in *Rylands v Fletcher* as absorbed by the principles of ordinary negligence. In reaching this decision the majority were influenced by the difficulties of interpretation and application to which the rule has undoubtedly given rise, by the progressive weakening of the rule by judicial decision, by recognition that the law of negligence has been very greatly developed and expanded since *Rylands v Fletcher* was decided and by a belief that most claimants entitled to succeed under the rule would succeed in a claim for negligence anyway.

5.   Coming from such a quarter these comments of course command respect, and they are matched by expressions of opinion here. Megaw LJ observed in *Leakey v National Trust for Places of Historic Interest or Natural Beauty* that application of the decision and of the *dicta* in *Rylands v Fletcher* had given rise to continual trouble in the law of England. In its report on Civil Liability for Dangerous Things and Activities (1970) (Law Com No 32), p 12, para 20(a) the Law Commission described the relevant law as "complex, uncertain and inconsistent in principle". There is a theoretical attraction in bringing this somewhat anomalous ground of liability within the broad and familiar rules governing liability in negligence. This would have the incidental advantage of bringing the law of England and Wales more closely into line with what I understand to be the law of Scotland (see *RHM Bakeries (Scotland) Ltd v Strathclyde Regional Council*, where Lord Fraser of Tullybelton described the suggestion that the decision in *Rylands v Fletcher* had any place in Scots law as "a heresy which ought to be extirpated"). Consideration of the reported English case law over the past 60 years suggests that few if any claimants have succeeded in reliance on the rule in *Rylands v Fletcher* alone.

6.   I would be willing to suppress an instinctive resistance to treating a nuisance-based tort as if it were governed by the law of negligence if I were persuaded that it would serve the interests of justice to discard the rule in *Rylands v Fletcher* and

treat the cases in which it might have been relied on as governed by the ordinary rules of negligence. But I hesitate to adopt that solution for four main reasons. First, there is in my opinion a category of case, however small it may be, in which it seems just to impose liability even in the absence of fault. In the context of then recent catastrophes *Rylands v Fletcher* itself was understandably seen as such a case. With memories of the tragedy at Aberfan still green, the same view might now be taken of *Attorney General v Cory Brothers and Co Ltd* even if the claimants had failed to prove negligence, as on the facts they were able to do. I would regard *Rainham Chemical Works Ltd v Belvedere Fish Guano Co Ltd*, and *Cambridge Water Co v Eastern Counties Leather Plc* (had there been foreseeability of damage), as similarly falling within that category. Second, it must be remembered that common law rules do not exist in a vacuum, least of all rules which have stood for over a century during which there has been detailed statutory regulation of matters to which they might potentially relate. With reference to water, section 209 of the Water Industry Act 1991 imposes strict liability (subject to certain exemptions) on water undertakers and Schedule 2 to the Reservoirs Act 1975 appears to assume that on facts such as those of *Rylands v Fletcher* strict liability would attach. If the law were changed so as to require proof of negligence by those previously thought to be entitled to recover under the rule in *Rylands v Fletcher* without proving negligence, the effect might be (one does not know) to falsify the assumption on which Parliament has legislated, by significantly modifying rights which Parliament may have assumed would continue to exist. Third, although in *Cambridge Water*, the possibility was ventilated that the House might depart from *Rylands v Fletcher* in its entirety, it is plain that this suggestion was not accepted. Instead, the House looked forward to a more principled and better controlled application of the existing rule. While this is not a conclusive bar to acceptance of the detailed argument presented to the House on this occasion, "stop-go" is in general as bad an approach to legal development as to economic management. Fourth, while replacement of strict *Rylands v Fletcher* liability by a fault-based rule would tend to assimilate the law of England and Wales with that of Scotland, it would tend to increase the disparity between it and the laws of France and Germany. Having reviewed comparable provisions of French and German law, van Gerven, Lever and Larouche (*Cases, Materials and Text on National, Supranational and International Tort Law* (2000), p 205) observe:

> "Even if the contours of the respective regimes may differ, all systems studied here therefore afford a form of strict liability protection in disputes between neighbouring landowners."

The authors indeed suggest (p 205) that the English rule as laid down in *Rylands v Fletcher* is "the most developed of these regimes".

7. Should, then, the rule be generously applied and the scope of strict liability extended? There are certainly respected commentators who favour such a course and regret judicial restrictions on the operation of the rule: see Fleming, *The Law of*

Torts, 9th ed (1998), p 377; Markesinis and Deakin, *Tort Law*, 5th ed (2003), p 544. But there is to my mind a compelling objection to such a course, articulated by Lord Goff of Chieveley in *Cambridge Water*:

> "Like the judge in the present case, I incline to the opinion that, as a general rule, it is more appropriate for strict liability in respect of operations of high risk to be imposed by Parliament, than by the courts. If such liability is imposed by statute, the relevant activities can be identified, and those concerned can know where they stand. Furthermore, statute can where appropriate lay down precise criteria establishing the incidence and scope of such liability."

It may be added that statutory regulation, particularly when informed by the work of the Law Commission, may take such account as is judged appropriate of the comparative law considerations on which I have briefly touched.

8. There remains a third option, which I would myself favour: to retain the rule, while insisting upon its essential nature and purpose; and to restate it so as to achieve as much certainty and clarity as is attainable, recognising that new factual situations are bound to arise posing difficult questions on the boundary of the rule, wherever that is drawn.

9. The rule in *Rylands v Fletcher* is a sub-species of nuisance, which is itself a tort based on the interference by one occupier of land with the right in or enjoyment of land by another occupier of land as such. From this simple proposition two consequences at once flow. First, as very clearly decided by the House in *Read v J Lyons & Co Ltd*, no claim in nuisance or under the rule can arise if the events complained of take place wholly on the land of a single occupier. There must, in other words, be an escape from one tenement to another. Second, the claim cannot include a claim for death or personal injury, since such a claim does not relate to any right in or enjoyment of land. This proposition has not been authoritatively affirmed by any decision at the highest level. It was left open by Parker LJ in *Perry v Kendricks Transport Ltd*, and is inconsistent with decisions such as *Shiffman v Order of St John of Jerusalem* and *Miles v Forest Rock Granite Co (Leicestershire) Ltd*. It is however clear from Lord Macmillan's opinion in *Read ...* that he regarded a personal injury claim as outside the scope of the rule, and his approach is in my opinion strongly fortified by the decisions of the House in *Cambridge Water* and *Hunter v Canary Wharf Ltd*, in each of which nuisance was identified as a tort directed, and directed only, to the protection of interests in land.

10. It has from the beginning been a necessary condition of liability under the rule in *Rylands v Fletcher* that the thing which the defendant has brought on his land should be "something which ... will naturally do mischief if it escape out of his land" (per Blackburn J in *Rylands v Fletcher*), "something dangerous" (ibid), "anything likely to do mischief if it escapes" (ibid), "something ... harmless to others so long as it is confined to his own property, but which he knows to be mischievous if it

gets on his neighbour's ..." (ibid), "... anything which, if it should escape, may cause damage to his neighbour ..." (per Lord Cranworth). The practical problem is of course to decide whether in any given case the thing which has escaped satisfies this mischief or danger test, a problem exacerbated by the fact that many things not ordinarily regarded as sources of mischief or danger may nonetheless be capable of proving to be such if they escape. I do not think this condition can be viewed in complete isolation from the non-natural user condition to which I shall shortly turn, but I think the cases decided by the House give a valuable pointer. In *Rylands v Fletcher* itself the courts were dealing with what Lord Cranworth called "a large accumulated mass of water" stored up in a reservoir, and I have touched on the historical context of the decision in paragraph 3(3) above. *Rainham Chemical Works*, involved the storage of chemicals, for the purpose of making munitions, which "exploded with terrific violence". In *Attorney General v Cory Brothers and Co Ltd*, the landslide in question was of what counsel described as an "enormous mass of rubbish", some 500,000 tons of mineral waste tipped on a steep hillside. In *Cambridge Water* the industrial solvents being used by the tannery were bound to cause mischief in the event, unforeseen on the facts, that they percolated down to the water table. These cases are in sharp contrast with those arising out of escape from a domestic water supply (such as *Carstairs v Taylor*, *Ross v Fedden* or *Anderson v Oppenheimer*) which, although decided on other grounds, would seem to me to fail the mischief or danger test. Bearing in mind the historical origin of the rule, and also that its effect is to impose liability in the absence of negligence for an isolated occurrence, I do not think the mischief or danger test should be at all easily satisfied. It must be shown that the defendant has done something which he recognised, or judged by the standards appropriate at the relevant place and time, he ought reasonably to have recognised, as giving rise to an exceptionally high risk of danger or mischief if there should be an escape, however unlikely an escape may have been thought to be.

11.   No ingredient of *Rylands v Fletcher* liability has provoked more discussion than the requirement of Blackburn J that the thing brought on to the defendant's land should be something "not naturally there", an expression elaborated by Lord Cairns when he referred to the putting of land to a "non-natural use" ... Read literally, the expressions used by Blackburn J and Lord Cairns might be thought to exclude nothing which has reached the land otherwise than through operation of the laws of nature. But such an interpretation has been fairly described as "redolent of a different age" (*Cambridge Water*), and in *Read v J Lyons & Co Ltd* and *Cambridge Water* the House gave its imprimatur to Lord Moulton's statement, giving the advice of the Privy Council in *Rickards v Lothian*:

> "It is not every use to which land is put that brings into play that principle. It must be some special use bringing with it increased danger to others, and must not merely be the ordinary use of the land or such a use as is proper for the general benefit of the community."

I think it clear that ordinary user is a preferable test to natural user, making it clear that the rule in *Rylands v Fletcher* is engaged only where the defendant's use is shown to be extraordinary and unusual. This is not a test to be inflexibly applied: a use may be extraordinary and unusual at one time or in one place but not so at another time or in another place (although I would question whether, even in wartime, the manufacture of explosives could ever be regarded as an ordinary user of land, as contemplated by ... in *Read v J Lyons & Co Ltd*). I also doubt whether a test of reasonable user is helpful, since a user may well be quite out of the ordinary but not unreasonable, as was that of *Rylands*, *Rainham Chemical Works* or the tannery in *Cambridge Water*. Again, as it seems to me, the question is whether the defendant has done something which he recognises, or ought to recognise, as being quite out of the ordinary in the place and at the time when he does it. In answering that question, I respectfully think that little help is gained (and unnecessary confusion perhaps caused) by considering whether the use is proper for the general benefit of the community. In *Rickards v Lothian* itself, the claim arose because the outflow from a wash-basin on the top floor of premises was maliciously blocked and the tap left running, with the result that damage was caused to stock on a floor below: not surprisingly, the provision of a domestic water supply to the premises was held to be a wholly ordinary use of the land. An occupier of land who can show that another occupier of land has brought or kept on his land an exceptionally dangerous or mischievous thing in extraordinary or unusual circumstances is in my opinion entitled to recover compensation from that occupier for any damage caused to his property interest by the escape of that thing, subject to defences of Act of God or of a stranger, without the need to prove negligence.

THE PRESENT APPEAL

12.   By the end of the hearing before the House, the dispute between the parties had narrowed down to two questions: had the council brought on to its land at Hollow End Towers something likely to cause danger or mischief if it escaped? and was that an ordinary user of its land? Applying the principles I have tried to outline, I think it quite clear that the first question must be answered negatively and the second affirmatively, as the Court of Appeal did.

13.   It is of course true that water in quantity is almost always capable of causing damage if it escapes. But the piping of a water supply from the mains to the storage tanks in the block was a routine function which would not have struck anyone as raising any special hazard. In truth, the council did not accumulate any water, it merely arranged a supply adequate to meet the residents' needs. The situation cannot stand comparison with the making by Mr Rylands of a substantial reservoir. Nor can the use by the council of its land be seen as in any way extraordinary or unusual. It was entirely normal and routine ... I am satisfied that the conditions to be met before strict liability could be imposed on the council were far from being met on the facts here.'

Comment

(1)   Lord Hoffmann commented on the social background to the rule:

'28.   Although the judgment of Blackburn J is constructed in the traditional common law style of deducing principle from precedent, without reference to questions of social policy, Professor Brian Simpson has demonstrated in his article "Legal Liability for Bursting Reservoirs: The Historical Context of *Rylands v Fletcher*" (1984) 13 J Leg Stud 209 that the background to the case was public anxiety about the safety of reservoirs, caused in particular by the bursting of the Bradfield Reservoir near Sheffield on 12 March 1864, with the loss of about 250 lives. The judicial response was to impose strict liability upon the proprietors of reservoirs. But, since the common law deals in principles rather than *ad hoc* solutions, the rule had to be more widely formulated.

29.   It is tempting to see, beneath the surface of the rule, a policy of requiring the costs of a commercial enterprise to be internalised; to require the entrepreneur to provide, by insurance or otherwise, for the risks to others which his enterprise creates. That was certainly the opinion of Bramwell B, who was in favour of liability when the case was before the Court of Exchequer. He had a clear and consistent view on the matter: see *Bamford v Turnley* and *Hammersmith and City Railway Co v Brand*. But others thought differently. They considered that the public interest in promoting economic development made it unreasonable to hold an entrepreneur liable when he had not been negligent: see *Wildtree Hotels Ltd v Harrow London Borough Council* for a discussion of this debate in the context of compensation for disturbance caused by the construction and operation of works authorised by statutory powers. On the whole, it was the latter view – no liability without fault – which gained the ascendancy. With hindsight, *Rylands v Fletcher* can be seen as an isolated victory for the internalisers. The following century saw a steady refusal to treat it as laying down any broad principle of liability.'

(2)   In identifying the background against which rationalisation of the principle ought to occur, Lord Hoffmann said:

'45.   Two features of contemporary society seem to me to be relevant. First, the extension of statutory regulation to a number of activities, such as discharge of water (section 209 of the Water Industry Act 1991) pollution by the escape of waste (section 73(6) of the Environmental Protection Act 1990) and radio-active matter (section 7 of the Nuclear Installations Act 1965). It may have to be considered whether these and similar provisions create an exhaustive code of liability for a particular form of escape which excludes the rule in *Rylands v Fletcher*.

46. Secondly, so far as the rule does have a residuary role to play, it must be borne in mind that it is concerned only with damage to property and that insurance against various forms of damage to property is extremely common. A useful guide in deciding whether the risk has been created by a "non-natural" user of land is therefore to ask whether the damage which eventuated was something against which the occupier could reasonably be expected to have insured himself. Property insurance is relatively cheap and accessible; in my opinion people should be encouraged to insure their own property rather than seek to transfer the risk to others by means of litigation, with the heavy transactional costs which that involves. The present substantial litigation over £100,000 should be a warning to anyone seeking to rely on an esoteric cause of action to shift a commonplace insured risk.'

Lord Hobhouse also commented on the role of insurance:

'60. ... it is argued that the risk of property damage is "insurable", just as is public liability. It is then said that, since insurers are likely to be the real parties behind any litigation, the rule has become unnecessary. This is an unsound argument for a number of reasons. It is historically unsound: in the second half of the 19th century there already existed in England, as the common law judges were well aware, a developed insurance market. The existence of an insurance market does not mean that such insurance is available free of charge: premiums have to be paid. Some risks may only be insurable at prohibitive rates or at rates which for the proposer are not commercially viable and so make the risk, for him, commercially uninsurable. (Indeed, in recent times it has been the experience that some insurers will not cover certain risks at all, e.g. loss or damage caused by flooding.) The rationale, he who creates the risk must bear the risk, is not altered at all by the existence of an insurance market. It is an application of the same concept, an acknowledgement of risk. The economic burden of insuring against the risk must be borne by he who creates it and has the control of it. Further, the magnitude of the burden will depend upon who ultimately has to bear the loss: the rule provides the answer to this. The argument that insurance makes the rule unnecessary is no more valid than saying that, because some people can afford to and sensibly do take out comprehensive car insurance, no driver should be civilly liable for his negligent driving. It is unprincipled to abrogate for all citizens a legal rule merely because it may be unnecessary as between major corporations.'

CHAPTER 16

Defamation

Defamation is concerned with reputations, and in this and other ways it may be distinguished from malicious falsehood, see *Joyce v Sengupta*, p 733. Although in some respects defamation protects privacy, a wealthy claimant may be able to coerce newspapers, writers and others into abstaining from criticism which in a free society ought to be made. A gagging writ is a powerful weapon, especially with the ever-present threat of immense damages and costs should the defendant lose. It then resembles an engine of oppression rather than a mechanism for protection of the individual, and the impact on a defendant can be far-reaching. In some instances, the courts are evidently seeking to promote freedom of expression, and the link between civil liberties and defamation may well be made clearer in the near future: see, for example, *Derbyshire CC v Times Newspapers*, p 726 and *Reynolds v Times Newspapers*, p 774. The utility of the law for the ordinary individual – as opposed to the well-heeled businessperson, pop star or politician – is weakened both by the absence of any provision for legal aid and the deterrent effect of huge costs, although the Defamation Act 1996 may have gone some way to alleviating some of the burdens on litigants.

All too often, reported cases are concerned with detailed pleading points and niceties which have little place in a modern legal system, and which make the cases inaccessible to students. It is now accepted that the law is so horrendously tangled that there is little hope of a common law, judge-led revision; the calls for extensive legislative changes have gone unanswered. Diplock LJ in *Slim v Daily Telegraph* observed that 'the law of defamation is a fit topic for the attention of the Law Commission. It has passed beyond redemption by the courts'. The limited statutory interventions are piecemeal attempts to deal with specific, limited issues. These have not been collected here, and are adequately dealt with in the standard texts. The Defamation Act 1996 has brought about far-reaching changes to trial procedures, matters relating to damages, limitation of actions and, in particular, some of the available defences; in other respects the law remains unchanged.

Whether the defamation is libel or slander depends on the medium of publication. Libel is a defamatory statement published in a permanent form, writing, printing or even a wax effigy as in *Monson v Mme Tussauds*. Defamatory statements in motion pictures are libels: *Youssoupoff v MGM*; as are radio and TV broadcasts (Defamation Act 1952) and the public performance of a play. Slander could consist of exactly the same statement but published in a transient form such as the spoken word or gestures.

In order to be actionable it must be proved that the statement was defamatory, that it referred to the claimant and that it was published by the defendant. The most widely-accepted definition of defamation is in the words of Lord Atkin in *Sim v Stretch*, p 733, but a wide range of definitions was explored in *Berkoff v Burchill*, p 729. The claimant must state what he or she understands by the words, including any innuendo alleged, and prove the existence of facts to support the innuendo. The meaning of words will be a matter upon which, in the absence of an innuendo, no evidence may be tendered; and the publication in which the alleged defamatory material appears must be read as a whole: *Slim v Daily Telegraph Ltd, Charleston v News Group*.

It must be shown as a matter of law that words are capable of referring to the claimant and as a matter of fact that words lead reasonable people, who know the appellant, to the conclusion that they do refer to the claimant. There is little scope for class defamation: see *Browne v D C Thompson* and *Knupffer v London Express Newspapers*.

It is possible to defame a trading or non-trading corporation where the corporate reputation is injured, but there is no scope for defamation in the context of the reputation of a local authority: see *Derbyshire CC v Times Newspapers*, p 726, generally regarded as one of the more significant cases where the freedom of the press has received a boost.

'Publication' is interpreted in a wide sense and means 'communication of the words to at least one person other than the plaintiff'. The range of possibilities is unlimited and the cases are full of examples, see e.g. *Byrne v Deane*, p 747. The 'multiple publication rule' in English Law – whereby each publication and republication of a statement is actionable (and each has its own limitation period) – has been confirmed by the Court of Appeal in *Loutchansky v Times Newspapers (No 2)*, p 782. This has serious implications for those who maintain Internet sites or newspaper archives. The test for causation and remoteness of damage where there was foreseeable republication of statements by third parties was explored in *McManus v Beckham*, p 740.

Finally, even if the claimant can establish that the words are defamatory, the defendant may raise one or more defence – e.g. justification, absolute privilege, qualified privilege and fair comment. The scope of the defence of qualified privilege has been explored at great length in several newspaper cases: see *Reynolds v Times Newspapers*, p 774; *Loutchansky v Times Newspapers (No 2)*, p 782; *Kearns v General Council of the Bar*, p 767; and *McCartan v Turkington*, p 771.

Derbyshire County Council v Times Newspaper Ltd and others [1993] I All ER 1011 House of Lords

It was alleged by the plaintiff local authority that the defendant newspaper had made defamatory remarks about the authority's control and investment of its superannuation fund. The House of Lords held that local authorities had no right to sue for defamation.

Lord Keith of Kinkel: '... this appeal raises ... the question whether a local authority is entitled to maintain an action in libel for words which reflect on it in its governmental and administrative functions. That is the way the preliminary point of law was expressed in the order of the master, but it has opened out into an investigation of whether a local authority can sue for libel at all ...

[Lord Keith considered earlier authorities and continued:]

The authorities cited above clearly establish that a trading corporation is entitled to sue in respect of defamatory matters which can be seen as having a tendency to damage it in the way of its business. Examples are those that go to credit such as might deter banks from lending to it, or to the conditions experienced by its employees, which might impede the recruitment of the best qualified workers, or make people reluctant to deal with it. [*South Hetton Coal Co Ltd v North-Eastern News Association Ltd*] would appear to be an instance of the latter kind, and not, as suggested by Browne J [in *Bognor Regis UDC v Campion*] an authority for the view that a trading corporation can sue for something that does not affect it adversely in the way of its business. The trade union cases are understandable upon the view that defamatory matter may adversely affect the union's ability to keep its members or attract new ones or to maintain a convincing attitude towards employers. Likewise in the case of a charitable organisation the effect may be to discourage subscribers or otherwise impair its ability to carry on its charitable objects. Similar considerations can no doubt be advanced in connection with the position of a local authority. Defamatory statements might make it more difficult to borrow or to attract suitable staff and thus affect adversely the efficient carrying out of its functions.

There are, however, features of a local authority which may be regarded as distinguishing it from other types of corporation, whether trading or non-trading.

The most important of these features is that it is a governmental body. Further, it is a democratically elected body, the electoral process nowadays being conducted almost exclusively on party political lines. It is of the highest public importance that a democratically elected governmental body, or indeed any governmental body, should be open to uninhibited public criticism. The threat of a civil action for defamation must inevitably have an inhibiting effect on freedom of speech.

In *City of Chicago v Tribune Co* the Supreme Court of Illinois held that the city could not maintain an action of damages for libel. Thompson CJ said:

> "The fundamental right of freedom of speech is involved in this litigation and not merely the right of liberty of the press. If this action can be maintained against a newspaper it can be maintained against every private citizen who ventures to criticise the ministers who are temporarily conducting the affairs of his government. Where any person by speech or writing seeks to persuade others to violate existing law or to overthrow by force or other unlawful means the existing government he may be punished ... but all other utterances or publications against the government must be considered absolutely privileged. While in the early history of the struggle for freedom of speech the restrictions were enforced by criminal prosecutions, it is clear that a civil action is as great, if not a greater, restriction than a criminal prosecution. If the right to criticise the government is a privilege which, with the exceptions above enumerated, cannot be restricted, then all civil as well as criminal actions are forbidden. A despotic or corrupt government can more easily stifle opposition by a series of civil actions than by criminal prosecutions ..."

After giving a number of reasons for this, he said:

> "It follows, therefore, that every citizen has a right to criticise an inefficient or corrupt government without fear of civil as well as criminal prosecution. This absolute privilege is founded on the principle that it is advantageous for the public interest that the citizen should not be in any way fettered in his statements, and where the public service or due administration of justice is involved he shall have the right to speak his mind freely."

These propositions were endorsed by the Supreme Court of the United States in *New York Times Co v Sullivan*. While these decisions were related most directly to the provisions of the American Constitution concerned with securing freedom of speech, the public interest considerations which underlaid them are no less valid in this country. What has been described as "the chilling effect" induced by the threat of civil actions for libel is very important. Quite often the facts which would justify a defamatory publication are known to be true, but admissible evidence capable of proving those facts is not available. This may prevent the publication of matters which it is very desirable to make public ...

It is of some significance to observe that a number of departments of central government in the United Kingdom are statutorily created corporations, including the Secretaries of State for Defence, Education and Science, Energy, Environment and Social Services. If a local authority can sue for libel there would appear to be no reason in logic for holding that any of these departments (apart from two which are made corporations only for the purpose of holding land) were not also entitled to sue. But as is shown by the decision in *A-G v Guardian Newspapers Ltd (No 2)*, a case concerned with confidentiality, there are rights available to private citizens which institutions of central government are not in a position to exercise unless they can show that it is in the public interest to do so. The same applies, in my opinion, to local authorities. In both cases I regard it as right for this House to lay down that not only is there no public interest favouring the right of organs of government, whether central or local, to sue for libel, but that it is contrary to the public interest that they should have it. It is contrary to the public interest because to admit such actions would place an undesirable fetter on freedom of speech ...

In the case of a local authority temporarily under the control of one political party or another it is difficult to say that the local authority as such has any reputation of its own. Reputation in the eyes of the public is more likely to attach itself to the controlling political party, and with a change in that party the reputation itself will change. A publication attacking the activities of the authority will necessarily be an attack on a body of councillors which represents the controlling party, or on the executives who carry on the day-to-day management of its affairs. If the individual reputation of any of these is wrongly impaired by the publication any of these can himself bring proceedings for defamation. Further, it is open to the controlling body to defend itself by public utterances and in debate in the council chamber.

The conclusion must be, in my opinion, that under the common law of England a local authority does not have the right to maintain an action of damages for defamation. That was the conclusion reached by the Court of Appeal, which did so principally by reference to art 10 of the European Convention on Human Rights ...

I have reached my conclusion upon the common law of England without finding any need to rely upon the European Convention. Lord Goff of Chieveley in *A-G v Guardian Newspaper Ltd (No 2)* expressed the opinion that in the field of freedom of speech there was no difference in principle between English law on the subject and art 10 of the Convention. I agree, and can only add that I find it satisfactory to be able to conclude that the common law of England is consistent with the obligations assumed by the Crown under the treaty in this particular field.

For these reasons I would dismiss the appeal. It follows that *Bognor Regis UDC v Campion* was wrongly decided and should be overruled.'

Comment

(1) The argued account of the relationship between the requirements of the ECHR and English law, in the Court of Appeal, is to be preferred to the

assumptions made in the House of Lords. Reference to *A-G v Guardian Newspapers (No 2)* cannot hide the fact that *A-G v Guardian Newspapers (No 1)* significantly impinged upon freedom of speech. Nonetheless, the *Derbyshire CC* case does make it clear that matters of the wider public interest may be addressed by the courts when developing the law of defamation: see also *Rantzen v Mirror Group Newspapers (1986) Ltd* and *Reynolds v Times Newspapers*, p 774.

(2) The guiding principle in the *Derbyshire* case was applied in *Goldsmith v Bhoyrul* where the plaintiff was a political party. It took the legal form of a company limited by guarantee but had been formed only for the purposes of acting as a political party. Buckley J held that it could not maintain an action in defamation. This decision does not affect the general principle that companies, trades unions and charities may sue in defamation. Equally, individual politicians, candidates and party officials may sue in defamation. A pressure group which fields candidates from time to time in elections may be in a different position from the party in the *Goldsmith* case.

Berkoff v Burchill and another
[1996] 4 All ER 1008 Court of Appeal

The plaintiff, Steven Berkoff, the well-known actor, director and writer, sued the first defendant, Julie Burchill, cinema critic for the second defendants, Times Newspapers Ltd. In her review of the film *The Age of Innocence* Ms Burchill said: '... film directors, from Hitchcock to Berkoff, are notoriously hideous-looking people ...'. Eight months later her review of *Frankenstein* described a character thus:

'The Creature is made as a vessel for Waldman's brain, and rejected in disgust when it comes out scarred and primeval. It's a very new look for the Creature – no bolts in the neck or flat-top hairdo – and I think it works; it's a lot like Stephen Berkoff, only marginally better-looking.'

The plaintiff sued, alleging that the passages meant and were understood to mean that he was hideously ugly. The court was asked whether as a question of law: '... the meaning pleaded ... is capable of being defamatory ...'.

The judge dismissed the defendants' application to strike out the plaintiff's action, but the Court of Appeal, Millett J dissenting, held that the words were capable of being defamatory as exposing the plaintiff to ridicule.

Phillips LJ:'... In almost every case in the books, words which have been held to be defamatory have been words which have denigrated the character or personality of the plaintiff, not the corporeal envelope housing that personality. The law of defamation protects reputation, and reputation is not generally dependent upon physical appearance. Exceptionally there has been a handful of cases where words have been held defamatory, notwithstanding that they do not attack character or personality.

In *Boyd v Mirror Newspapers Ltd* as Hunt J observed:

"At common law, in general, an imputation, to be defamatory of the plaintiff, must be disparaging of him ... I say that this is 'in general' the position, as the common law also recognises as defamatory an imputation which, although not disparaging, tends to make other persons 'shun or avoid' the plaintiff, for example, by attributing to him that he is insane: *Morgan v Lingen;* or by attributing to her that she has been raped ... as well as an imputation that displays the plaintiff in a ridiculous light, notwithstanding the absence of any moral blame on his part ..."

"SHUN OR AVOID"

It is not easy to find the touchstone by which to judge whether words are defamatory which tend to make other persons shun or avoid the plaintiff, but it is axiomatic that the words must relate to an attribute of the plaintiff in respect of which hearsay alone is enough to provoke this reaction. That was once true of a statement that a woman had been raped and would still be true of a statement that a person has a serious infectious or contagious disease, or is physically unwholesome or is mentally deranged. There is precedent for holding all such statements defamatory. There is, however, with one possible exception, no precedent for holding it defamatory to describe a person as ugly. In my judgment, such a statement differs in principle from those statements about a person's physical condition which have been held to be defamatory. Those statements have, in every case, been allegations of fact – illness, madness, filthiness or defilement. Hearsay factual statements about a person's physical condition can clearly be capable of causing those who hear or read them to avoid the subject of them. In contrast, a statement that a person is ugly, or hideously ugly, is a statement of subjective appreciation of that individual's features. To a degree both beauty and ugliness are in the eye of the beholder. It is, perhaps, just possible to think of a right minded person shunning one of his fellow men because of a subjective distaste for his features. What I find impossible to accept is that a right minded person would shun another merely because a third party had expressed distaste for that other person's features.

It is perhaps for this reason that statements disparaging, however strongly, a person's features – and many such statements must have been published – have never been the subject of a successful claim for defamation.

My conclusion is that a statement that a person is hideously ugly does not fall into that category of statements that are defamatory because they tend to make people shun or avoid the plaintiff.

RIDICULE

The class of cases where it has been held defamatory, or potentially defamatory, to damage a plaintiff's reputation by exposing him to ridicule is too elusive to encapsulate in any definition ... The preliminary point which is the subject of this appeal does not require us to decide whether the publications complained of are capable of constituting defamation of the plaintiff. The question which we are asked to answer is whether "the meaning pleaded in para 6 of the statement of claim is capable of being defamatory". The defendants' skeleton argument opened with the following proposition:

> "The question of law for decision is whether a statement that an individual is ugly is capable of being defamatory. If this statement is defamatory in one case, it must be in all cases (in the absence of any distinguishing features of a particular case), so that there is no distinction to be drawn between the technical issue of law, whether it is capable of being defamatory, and the technical issue of fact, whether it is defamatory."

I cannot accept this proposition. Where the issue is whether words have damaged a plaintiff's reputation by exposing him to ridicule, that question cannot be answered simply by considering whether the natural and ordinary meaning of the words used is defamatory *per se*. The question has to be considered in the light of the actual words used and the circumstance in which they are used. There are many ways of indicating that a person is hideously ugly, ranging from a simple statement of opinion to that effect, which I feel could never be defamatory, to words plainly intended to convey that message by way of ridicule. The words used in this case fall into the latter category. Whether they have exposed the plaintiff to ridicule to the extent that his reputation has been damaged must be answered by the jury ...'

Comment

(1) In a short dissenting judgment, Millett J observed that:

> 'Defamation has never been satisfactorily defined. All attempted defini-
> tions are illustrative. None of them is exhaustive. All can be misleading if
> they cause one to forget that defamation is an attack on reputation, that is
> on a man's standing in the world ... A decision that it is an actionable
> wrong to describe a man as "hideously ugly" would be an unwarranted
> restriction on free speech. And if a bald statement to this effect would not
> be capable of being defamatory, I do not see how a humorously exagger-
> ated observation to the like effect could be.'

(2) Neill LJ, in a lengthy judgment, reviewed the many judicial and extra-judicial definitions of 'defamatory' but said that he knew of none which was

entirely satisfactory. He also reviewed a large number of cases which provided guidance on the specific issue before the court. Of these, the most commonly cited is *Youssoupoff v Metro-Goldwyn-Mayer Pictures Ltd.* Neill LJ said:

' … the plaintiff complained that she could be identified with the character Princess Natasha in the film "Rasputin, the Mad Monk". The princess claimed damages on the basis that the film suggested that, by reason of her identification with "Princess Natasha", she had been seduced by Rasputin. The princess was awarded £25,000 damages. In the Court of Appeal it was contended that if the film indicated any relations between Rasputin and "Natasha" it indicated a rape of Natasha and not a seduction. Slesser LJ considered the defamatory nature of the film:

"I, for myself, cannot see that from the plaintiff's point of view it matters in the least whether this libel suggests that she has been seduced or ravished. The question whether she is or is not the more or the less moral seems to me immaterial in considering this question whether she has been defamed, and for this reason, that, as has been frequently pointed out in libel, not only is the matter defamatory if it brings the plaintiff into hatred, ridicule, or contempt by reason of some moral discredit on her part, but also if it tends to make the plaintiff be shunned and avoided and that without any moral discredit on her part. It is for that reason that persons who have been alleged to have been insane, or to be suffering from certain diseases, and other cases where no direct moral responsibility could be placed upon them, have been held to be entitled to bring an action to protect their reputation and their honour."

Slesser LJ had added, in relation to the facts in that case:

"One may, I think, take judicial notice of the fact that a lady of whom it has been said that she has been ravished, albeit against her will, has suffered in social reputation and in opportunities of receiving respectable consideration from the world." '

(3)   *Berkoff v Burchill* was considered in *Norman v Future Publishing*. In an in-depth article on a renowned opera singer, it was suggested in jest that the singer had become trapped in swing doors and, when told to free herself by turning sideways, had replied 'Honey I ain't got no sideways'. The court rejected the over-elaborate analysis of words and concluded that there was nothing about the words (in the context of the article as a whole) to suggest to an ordinary reasonable reader that the words portrayed the claimant as an American-African stereotype or caricature. The whole of the article, which was generally exceptionally complimentary of her, had to be looked at. It was not intended to (nor did it) expose her to ridicule.

(4) *Joyce v Sengupta* demonstrates the differences between defamation and malicious falsehood (the potential importance of which may also be seen from *Kaye v Robertson*, p 579). The defendant had published certain allegations (which were in fact false) about the plaintiff to the effect that she had stolen letters belonging to her employer. The plaintiff sued for malicious falsehood. The defendant failed in an attempt to have the plaintiff's action struck out as an abuse of the process of the court. Proof of malicious falsehood places burdens on the plaintiff including proof of actual financial loss, falseness of the statement and malice. The plaintiff did not have to show that the statement was defamatory, although it might well be that it was. Legal aid was then available for malicious falsehood but not defamation. Malicious falsehood did not carry a right to trial by jury but defamation did. The Court of Appeal confirmed that a plaintiff might chose to sue in either cause of action, or in both, despite the difficulties in her way and despite depriving the defendant of a right to jury trial.

Sim v Stretch
[1936] 2 All ER 1237 House of Lords

The plaintiff was the former employer of E, a maid, who returned to work for the defendant on 12 April. The defendant sent a telegram to the plaintiff asking her to '... send [E's] possessions and the money you borrowed also her wages ...'. The reference to borrowing related to an arrangement between E and the plaintiff by which E had suggested that while the plaintiff was on holiday for a week at the end of March, E would pay any bills due out of a sum left by the plaintiff and if the bills were more than the sum left then E would pay the amount and would be repaid by the plaintiff on her return. In fact the small payment made by E was paid shortly after E returned to work for the defendant. The House of Lords considered whether, on their ordinary meaning, the words might be defamatory.

Lord Atkin: '... The question, then, is whether the words in their ordinary signification are capable of being defamatory. Judges and textbook writers alike have found difficulty in defining with precision the word "defamatory". The conventional phrase exposing the plaintiff to hatred, ridicule and contempt is probably too narrow. The question is complicated by having to consider the person or class of persons whose reaction to the publication is the test of the wrongful character of the words used. I do not intend to ask your Lordships to lay down a formal definition, but after collating the opinions of many authorities I propose in the present case the test: would the words tend to lower the plaintiff in the estimation of right-thinking members of society generally? Assuming such to be the test of whether words are defamatory or not there is no dispute as to the relative functions of judge and jury, of law and fact. It is well settled that the judge must decide whether the words are capable of a defamatory meaning. That is a question of law: is there evidence of a tort? If they are capable, then the jury is to decide whether they are in fact defamatory. Now, in the present case it is material to notice that there is no evidence that the words were published to anyone who had any knowledge at all of any of the facts that I have narrated above. There is no direct evidence that they were published to anyone who had ever heard of the plaintiff. The post office officials at Maidenhead would not be presumed to know him, and we are left without any information as to the officials at Cookham Dean. The plaintiff and his wife dealt at the shop at which was the sub-post office, but there is no evidence that the shopkeeper was the telegraph clerk; the probability is that he was not. It might, however, be inferred that the publication of the telegram at Cookham Dean was to someone who knew the plaintiff. What would he or she learn by reading the telegram? That E had been in the plaintiff's employment; that she had that day entered the defendant's employment; and that the former employer was requested to send on to the new place of employment the servant's possessions together with the money due to her for money borrowed and for wages. How could perusal of that communication tend to lower the plaintiff in the estimation of the right-thinking peruser who knows nothing of the circumstances but what he or she derives from the telegram itself? The defamatory imputation is said to be in the words "the money you borrowed", coupled with the request for the return of it sent in a telegram. It was said by the learned judge at the trial and accepted by the two members of the Court of Appeal who affirmed the judgment that the words were capable of conveying to anybody that the plaintiff had acted in a mean way borrowing money from his own maid and not paying her as he was required to and required to by telegram and also withholding her wages. With the greatest respect, that is imputing to the words a suggestion of meanness both in borrowing and in not repaying which I find it impossible to extract from their ordinary meaning. The sting is said to be in the borrowing. It happens that the phrase is substantially true ... But I am at a loss to understand why a person's character should be lowered in anyone's estimation if he or she has borrowed from a domestic servant. I should have thought it such a usual domestic occurrence for small sums to be advanced in such circumstances as the present, and with the assent of everyone concerned to be left outstanding for some days that the mere fact of borrowing from a servant bears not the slightest tinge of "meanness". Of course there may be special circumstances, and so large an amount may be borrowed or left so long unpaid that the facts when known would reflect on the character of the master. But to make an imputation which is based upon the existence of facts unknown and not to be inferred from the words attacked is surely exactly to come under the ban of [Brett LJ cited in *Nevill v Fine Art & General Insurance Co*]:

> "It seems to me unreasonable that, when there are a number of good interpretations, the only bad one should be seized upon to give a defamatory sense to the document."

It is not a case where there is only the choice between two reasonable meanings, one harmless and one defamatory. It is a case where there is only one reasonable meaning which is harmless, and where the defamatory meaning can only be given by inventing a state of facts which are not disclosed, and are in fact non-existent ...'

Comment

(1) Pity litigants when experienced judges disagree on whether words are capable of being defamatory. In *Sim v Stretch*, three judges had already held the words capable of being defamatory and the jury held they were in fact defamatory.

(2) This case also concerns innuendo, see also *Lewis v Daily Telegraph* and *Cassidy v Daily Mirror*. Legal innuendo is concerned with apparently innocent statements which are to be damned by virtue of the knowledge of third parties and the conclusion which they might reasonably draw. In *Slim v Daily Telegraph* Salmon LJ said that:

'... Words may be defamatory in their ordinary and natural meaning. They may also, or in the alternative, bear a defamatory innuendo. A "true" or "legal" innuendo is a meaning which is different from the ordinary and natural meaning of the words, and defamatory because of special facts and circumstances known to those to whom the words are published. The ordinary meaning and the innuendo give rise to different causes of action, and, accordingly, must be separately pleaded – *Sim v Stretch* ...'

In *Tolley v J S Fry & Sons Ltd*, at a time when the distinction between amateur and professional status was vital, a photograph of the plaintiff, a prominent amateur golfer, was incorporated in an advertisement for a bar of chocolate. He alleged an innuendo that:

'the defendants meant, and were understood to mean, that the plaintiff had agreed or permitted his portrait to be exhibited for the purpose of the advertisement of the defendants' chocolate; that he had done so for gain and reward; that he had prostituted his reputation as an amateur golf player for advertising purposes; that he was seeking notoriety and gain ...; and that he had been unworthy of his status as an amateur golfer'.

The House of Lords held that the advertisement was capable of bearing the meaning alleged in the innuendo. A jury had already found the words to be defamatory in fact. Viscount Dunedin said:

'... It has been stated again and again and is not in dispute that the question for the judge is whether the writing or publication complained of is capable of a libellous meaning. It is for the jury, if the judge so rules, to say whether it has that meaning ... I find that the caricature of the plaintiff, innocent itself as a caricature, is so to speak imbedded in an advertisement. It is held out as part of an advertisement, so that its presence there gives rise to speculation as to how it got there, or in other words provokes in the mind of the public an inference as to how and why the plaintiff's picture, caricatured as it was, became associated with a commercial advertisement. The inference that is suggested is that his consent was given either gratuitously or for a consideration to its appearance. Then it is said, and evidence on that point was given, and not cross-examined to, that if that were so the status of the plaintiff as an amateur golfer would be called in question. It seems to me that all this is within the province of a jury to determine. The idea of the inference in the circumstances is not so extravagant as to compel a judge to say it was so beside the mark that no jury ought to be allowed to consider it.

My Lords, I come to this conclusion on a consideration of the advertisement alone, explained with the evidence of the golf players and the golf secretary. There are here two separate propositions: (1) Would the caricature associated with the advertisement admit of a reasonable inference that the plaintiff had assented to be so depicted? That depends on the view taken of the picture, of its surroundings, and of its use. (2) If that inference were drawn would it be deleterious to the plaintiff's position as an amateur golfer, and do him harm? That depends on the evidence of the golfers ...'

Lewis v Daily Telegraph
Lewis v Associated Newspapers Ltd
[1963] 2 All ER 151 House of Lords

Two newspapers published articles stating that the Fraud Squad was inquiring into L's company. L and his company brought actions contending that the words meant that they had been guilty of, or were suspected by the police of being guilty of, fraud or dishonesty. The defendants accepted that it was defamatory to state that the police were inquiring into a particular matter but pleaded justification, alleging that it was true that the Fraud Squad was inquiring into the company's affairs at the date of the article.

The issue was whether the words were capable of meaning that the plaintiff was actually guilty of fraud. It was held by the House of Lords (Lord Morris dissenting) that they were not, and that the most serious meaning of which they were capable was that the plaintiff was reasonably suspected of being guilty of fraud.

Lord Devlin: '... In the first place [counsel] relies on what are called the "rumour cases". I agree, of course, that one cannot escape liability for defamation by putting the libel behind a prefix such as "I have been told that ..." or "It is rumoured that ...", and then asserting that it was true that one had been told or that it was in fact being rumoured. "You have", as Horridge J said, in a passage that was quoted with approval by Greer LJ in *Cookson v Harewood*, "to prove that the subject-matter of the rumour was true." But this is not a case of repetition or rumour ... Anyway, even if this is to be treated as a rumour case, it is still necessary to find out what the rumour is. A rumour that a man is suspected of fraud is different from one that he is guilty of it. For the purpose of the law of libel a hearsay statement is the same as a direct statement, and that is all there is to it ...

It is not therefore correct to say as a matter of law that a statement of suspicion imputes guilt. It can be said as a matter of practice that it very often does so, because although suspicion of guilt is something different from proof of guilt, it is the broad impression conveyed by the libel that has to be considered and not the meaning of each word under analysis. A man who wants to talk at large about smoke may have to pick his words very carefully, if he wants to exclude the suggestion that there is also a fire; but it can be done. One always gets back to the fundamental question: what is the meaning that the words convey to the ordinary man; a rule cannot be made about that. They can convey a meaning of suspicion short of guilt; but loose talk about suspicion can very easily convey the impression that it is a suspicion that is well founded.

In the libel which the House has to consider there is, however, no mention of suspicion at all. What is said is simply that the plaintiff's affairs are being inquired into. That is defamatory, as is admitted, because a man's reputation may in fact be injured by such a statement even though it is quite consistent with innocence ... But a statement that an inquiry is on foot may go further and may positively convey the impression that there are grounds for the inquiry, i.e. that there is something to suspect. Just as a bare statement of suspicion may convey the impression that there are grounds for belief in guilt, so a bare statement of the fact of an inquiry may convey the impression that there are grounds for suspicion. I do not say that in this case it does; but I think that the words in their context and in the circumstances of publication are capable of conveying that impression. But can they convey an impression of guilt? Let it be supposed, first, that a statement that there is an inquiry conveys an impression of suspicion; and, secondly, that a statement of suspicion conveys an impression of guilt. It does not follow from these two suppositions that a statement that there is an inquiry conveys an impression of guilt. For that, two fences have to be taken instead of one. While ... I am prepared to accept that the jury could take the first I do not think that in a case like the present, where there is only the bare statement that a police inquiry is being made, it could take the second in the same stride. If the ordinary sensible man was capable of thinking that wherever there was a police inquiry there was guilt, it would be almost impossible to give accurate information about anything; but in my opinion he is not.'

Lord Reid: '... There is no doubt that in actions for libel the question is what the words would convey to the ordinary man: it is not one of construction in the legal sense. The ordinary man does not live in an ivory tower and he is not inhibited by a knowledge of the rules of construction. So he can and does read between the lines in the light of his general knowledge and experience of worldly affairs ...

What the ordinary man would infer without special knowledge has generally been called the natural and ordinary meaning of the words. But that expression is rather misleading in that it conceals the fact that there are two elements in it. Sometimes it is not necessary to go beyond the words themselves, as where the plaintiff has been called a thief, or a murderer. But more often the sting is not so much in the words themselves as in what the ordinary man will infer from them, and that is also regarded as part of their natural and ordinary meaning. Here there would be nothing libellous in saying that an inquiry into the appellant's affairs was proceeding: the inquiry might be by a statistician or other expert. The sting is in inferences drawn from the fact that it is the fraud squad which is making the inquiry. What those inferences should be is ultimately a question for the jury but the trial judge has an important duty to perform.

Generally the controversy is whether the words are capable of having a libellous meaning at all, and undoubtedly it is the judge's duty to rule on that. I shall have to deal later with the test which he must apply. Here the controversy is in a different form. The respondents admit that their words were libellous, although I am still in some doubt as to what is the admitted libellous meaning. But they sought and seek a ruling that these words are not capable of having the particular meaning which the appellants attribute to them. I think that they are entitled to such a ruling and that the test must be the same as that applied in deciding whether the words are capable of having any libellous meaning ...

In this case it is, I think, sufficient to put the test in this way. Ordinary men and women have different temperaments and outlooks. Some are unusually suspicious and some are unusually naive. One must try to envisage people between these two extremes and see what is the most damaging meaning that they would put on the words in question. So let me suppose a number of ordinary people discussing one of these paragraphs which they had read in the newspaper. No doubt one of them might say, "Oh, if the fraud squad are after these people you can take it they are guilty." But I would expect the others to turn on him, and if he did say that, with such remarks as "Be fair. This is not a police state. No doubt their affairs are in a mess or the police would not be interested. But that could be because Lewis or the cashier has been very stupid or careless. We really must not jump to conclusions. The police are fair and know their job and we shall know soon enough if there is anything in it. Wait till we see if they charge him. I wouldn't trust him until this is cleared up, but it is another thing to condemn him unheard."

What the ordinary man, not avid for scandal, would read into the words complained of must be a matter of impression ...

Before leaving this part of the case I must notice an argument to the effect that you can only justify a libel that the plaintiffs have so conducted their affairs as to give rise to suspicion of fraud, or as to give rise to an inquiry whether there has been fraud, by proving that they have acted fraudulently. Then it is said that, if that is so, there can be no difference between an allegation of suspicious conduct and an allegation of guilt. To my mind there is a great difference between saying that a man has behaved in a suspicious manner and saying that he is guilty of an offence and I am not convinced that you can only justify the former statement by proving guilt. I can well understand that if you say there is a rumour that X is guilty you can only justify by proving that he is guilty because repeating someone else's libellous statement is just as bad as making the statement directly. But I do not think that it is necessary to reach a decision on this matter of justification in order to decide that these paragraphs can mean suspicion but cannot be held to infer guilt.'

Comment

(1)   The principles referred to in the House of Lords have been applied on many occasions; see, for example, the Court of Appeal in *Mapp v News Group*.

(2)   Their Lordships make reference to rumour and the principle that a repetition of a defamatory statement is itself a republication of the libel. Lord Hodson said:

'Rumour and suspicion do, however, essentially differ from one another. To say that something is rumoured to be the fact is, if the words are defamatory, a republication of the libel. One cannot defend an action for libel by saying that one has been told the libel by someone else, for this might be only to make the libel worse ... It is wholly different with suspicion. It may be defamatory to say that someone is suspected of an offence, but it does not carry with it that that person has committed the offence, for this must surely offend against the ideas of justice, which reasonable persons are supposed to entertain. If one repeats a rumour one adds one's own authority to it, and implies that it is well founded, that is to say, that it is true. It is otherwise when one says or implies that a person is under suspicion of guilt. This does not imply that he is in fact guilty, but only that there are reasonable grounds for suspicion, which is a different matter.'

This principle was explored in the case of *Stern v Piper* in which the defendant sought to justify its remarks, which comprised quotations drawn from an affirmation filed in the High Court in the course of other proceedings by the person who was the plaintiff in those other proceedings. The Court of Appeal regarded the quotations as hearsay and therefore within the rule against repetition. The defences of absolute and qualified privilege were not available to the newspaper since the affirmations had not been made or given in open court, and the reports were neither fair and accurate contemporaneous reports of proceedings in open court (absolute privilege) nor fair and accurate reports of proceedings in open court (qualified privilege). The affirmation itself was protected by absolute privilege as a document brought into being for legal proceedings and used as such.

McManus and others v Beckham
[2002] 4 All ER 497 Court of Appeal

In their shop the claimants sold memorabilia autographed by famous personalities. They alleged that the defendant, Victoria Beckham, had come into their shop and had told customers in a loud and unreasonable way that the autograph on a photograph of her husband was a fake. The claimants also said that she had announced that the claimants habitually sold memorabilia with fake autographs, and that customers should not buy such items. This incident received extensive press coverage and the claimants said that their business suffered a loss as a result of that coverage. The question arose whether the claimants were entitled to rely upon the press coverage in establishing the extent of their alleged loss. The newspapers were not sued.

Laws LJ: '...

[37]   ... The case on the claimants' pleadings, reduced to its essentials, involves these propositions. (1) The defendant utters, to a very limited audience, words which slander the claimants in the way of their business. (2) Shortly thereafter the gist or sting (but not the exact words) of the slander is repeated in the national and local press (I will call their reports the "second publications"); alternatively part only of the sting is so repeated. (3) After the second publications, the claimants suffer a grave downturn in the turnover of their business. (4) The claimants sue the defendant in slander and claim the whole of their business loss as damages. They accept that but for the second publications they cannot establish that the slander uttered by the defendant has caused the loss, or by far the greater part of the loss, which they seek to recover.

[38]   The case thus presents a particular feature which is by no means confined to the law of defamation. It is that the claimant C seeks to hold the defendant D responsible for damage occasioned (or at least, directly occasioned) by the agency of a third party X. The law of negligence is replete with instances of this feature. The law's stock response has been to consider whether it can truly be said that D's act or omission is a substantial or effective cause of the damage, or whether rather

the chain of causation is broken by the act or omission of X; if it has been, then X's act or omission is called a *novus actus interveniens*, and C cannot claim against D the loss occasioned by it. However, reasoning of that kind raised the false hope of a decisive objective test of causation. It was as if the court was saying, if only we look hard enough and long enough, we shall be able to discern from the evidence whether this really is a case where D's wrongdoing caused the damage, or it is one of *novus actus interveniens*. But that was always a search for a pot of gold at the end of the rainbow. The courts have never articulated such a decisive test; for the good reason that there is none to articulate ...

[40] The problem of a second cause or *novus actus interveniens* should have no more absolutist or metaphysical overtones for the law of defamation than it does for the law of negligence. Of course the conception of a duty of care has no analogue in defamation. But that, if anything, serves to simplify the approach to be taken in defamation cases to the task of ascertaining in any given case the extent of any liable defendant's responsibility for the loss and damage which the claimant has suffered where a potential *novus actus* is involved.

[41] The defamation cases have over time been girt about with unhelpful complexities ...

[42] The law needs to be simplified. The root question is whether D, who has slandered C, should justly be held responsible for damage which has been occasioned, or directly occasioned, by a further publication by X. I think it plain that there will be cases where that will be entirely just ...

[43] It will not however in my judgment be enough to show that D's slander is a cause of X's further publication: for such a cause might exist although D could have no reason to know of it; and then to hold D responsible would not be just. This is why the old formula, 'natural and probable cause', is inapt even as a figurative description of the relationship that needs to be shown between D's slander and the further publication if D is to be held liable for the latter. It must rather be demonstrated that D foresaw that the further publication would probably take place, or that D (or a reasonable person in D's position) should have so foreseen and that in consequence increased damage to C would ensue.'

Comment

(1) Lord Justice Waller delivered a lengthy judgment in which he explored a full range of decisions in great depth, but in summary his view is expressed in the following passage:

'[34] What the law is striving to achieve in this area is a just and reasonable result by reference to the position of a reasonable person in the position of the defendant. If a defendant is actually aware (1) that what she says or does is likely to be reported, and (2) that if she slanders someone that slander is likely to be repeated in whole or in part, there is no injustice in her being held responsible for the damage that the slander causes via that publication. I would suggest further that if a jury were to conclude that a reasonable person in the position of the defendant should have appreciated that there was a significant risk that what she said would be repeated in whole or in part in the press and that that would increase the damage caused by the slander, it is not unjust that the defendant should be liable for it. Thus I would suggest a direction along the above lines rather than by reference to "foreseeability".'

(2)   The case is concerned with causation rather than liability for republication *per se*. Generally, a person who makes a defamatory statement is not liable where it is re-published by another, and a person who re-publishes the defamatory statement cannot escape liability by simply saying that they are repeating what was told to them. The voluntary publication of what has been said already will usually be a *novus actus* but *McManus v Beckham* explores the test for deciding the point. The person defamed will therefore have the choice of suing the original maker of the claim and seeking to show that the damage includes that caused by the republication, or suing the re-publisher in a separate head of claim. If the original maker of the statement repeats it then there will be a separate cause of action, see *Loutchansky v Times Newspapers* (*No 2*), p 782.

Charleston and another v News Group Newspapers Ltd
[1995] 2 All ER 313 House of Lords

The plaintiff actors played a husband and wife in a popular television serial. The defendant publishers of a mass circulation Sunday newspaper printed an article which included two photographs to which the plaintiffs objected. In the first, the heads of the plaintiffs were superimposed on the bodies of two persons apparently engaged in sexual activity. In the second, the female plaintiff's head was superimposed on that of a woman dressed in a sexually provocative outfit. The banner headline read: 'Strewth! What's Harold up to with our Madge?'. Below the photographs was a smaller headline: 'Porn Shocker for Neighbours Stars'. The article made it clear that the photographs were taken from a pornographic computer game in which the plaintiffs' faces had been used without their knowledge or consent, and the article described the plaintiffs as victims.

The plaintiffs alleged that the photographs and headlines were defamatory because their ordinary and natural meaning was that the plaintiffs had posed for pornographic photographs. The Court of Appeal upheld the decision of the judge that the publications were not capable of bearing the meanings alleged. The House of Lords held that the entire article had to be read together in order to establish the meaning which would be conveyed to the ordinary, reasonable, fair-minded reader.

Lord Bridge of Harwich: '... The single question of law to which the appeal gives rise is whether the plaintiffs have any remedy in the tort of defamation on the basis of their pleaded claim, and this in turn narrows down to the question whether a claim in defamation in respect of a publication which, it is conceded, is not defamatory if considered as a whole, may nevertheless succeed on the ground that some readers will have read part only of the published matter and that this part, considered in isolation, is capable of bearing a defamatory meaning.

The plaintiffs' statement of claim alleges that the publication conveyed to the reader a number of defamatory meanings. The basis on which all these alleged meanings rest is that the reader would have drawn the inference that the plaintiffs had been willing participants in the production of the photographs, either by posing for them personally or by agreeing that their faces should be superimposed on the bodies of others. But it is conceded on the plaintiffs' behalf, and is indeed obvious, that no reader could possibly have drawn any such inference if he had read beyond the first paragraph of the text. Thus the essential basis on which [counsel's] argument in support of the appeal rests is that, in appropriate circumstances, it is possible and legitimate to identify a particular group of readers who read only part of a publication which conveys to them a meaning injurious to the reputation of a plaintiff and that in principle the plaintiff should be entitled to damages for the consequent injury he suffers in the estimation of this group.

It is well settled ... that, save in the case of a legal innuendo dependent on extrinsic facts known to certain readers, no evidence is admissible as to the sense in which readers understood an allegedly defamatory publication. No legal innuendo is here alleged. But here, so [counsel's] argument runs, it goes without saying and no evidence is required to establish that, out of the many millions constituting the readership of a mass circulation newspaper like the *News of the World*, a significant proportion, when they saw the page of which the plaintiffs complain, would have done no more than to have read the headlines and looked at the photographs. It will be convenient to refer to this group as the "limited readers". The argument before your Lordships was substantially confined to the effect of the publication on the minds of the limited readers. They would, [counsel] submits, have drawn an inference defamatory of the plaintiffs as actors willing to participate in pornographic films and it should be left to a jury to estimate the size of the group constituted by the limited readers and to award damages accordingly for the injury which the plaintiffs' reputation must have suffered in the estimation of this group.

The first formidable obstacle which [counsel's] argument encounters is a long and unbroken line of authority the effect of which is accurately summarised in *Duncan and Neill on Defamation* (2nd edn, 1983) as follows:

> "In order to determine the natural and ordinary meaning of the words of which the plaintiff complains it is necessary to take into account the context in which the words were used and the mode of publication. Thus a plaintiff

cannot select an isolated passage in an article and complain of that alone if other parts of the article throw a different light on that passage."

The *locus classicus* is a passage from the judgment of Alderson B in *Chalmers v Payne*, where he said:

"But the question here is, whether the matter be slanderous or not, which is a question for the jury; who are to take the whole together, and say whether the result of the whole is calculated to injure the plaintiff's character. In one part of this publication, something disreputable to the plaintiff is stated, but that is removed by the conclusion; the bane and antidote must be taken together."

This passage has been so often quoted that it has become almost conventional jargon among libel lawyers to speak of the bane and the antidote. It is often a debatable question which the jury must resolve whether the antidote is effective to neutralise the bane and in determining this question the jury may certainly consider the mode of publication and the relative prominence given to different parts of it. I can well envisage also that questions might arise in some circumstances as to whether different items of published material relating to the same subject matter were sufficiently closely connected as to be regarded as a single publication. But no such questions arise in the instant case. There is no dispute that the headlines, photographs and article relating to these plaintiffs constituted a single publication nor that the antidote in the article was sufficient to neutralise any bane in the headlines and photographs. Thus it is essential to the success of [counsel's] argument that he establish the legitimacy in the law of libel of severance to permit a plaintiff to rely on a defamatory meaning conveyed only to the category of limited readers.

Your Lordships were very properly referred to the many authorities in which the principle of *Chalmers v Payne* has been affirmed and applied. But it is unnecessary to go through them, since [counsel] accepts that these authorities, so far as they go, are unanimously against his proposition and that he is unable to rely on any other authority in support of the principle of severance which he now advances.

The theme of [counsel's] argument runs on the following lines. All the earlier authorities, he submits, are explicable on the basis that the allegedly defamatory matter with which they were concerned was located somewhere in a document in which there was no likelihood that it would be read in isolation. In such a situation it is natural and proper to look for the meaning conveyed to the reader by considering the publication as a whole. The techniques of modern tabloid journalism, however, confront the courts with a novel situation with which the law has not hitherto had to grapple. It is plain that the eye-catching headline and the eye-catching photograph will first attract the reader's attention, precisely as they were intended to do, and equally plain that a significant number of readers will not trouble to read any further. This phenomenon must be well known to newspaper editors and publishers, who cannot, therefore, complain if they are held liable in damages for any libel thus published to the category of limited readers.

At first blush this argument has considerable attractions, but I believe that it falls foul of two principles which are basic to the law of libel. The first is that, where no legal innuendo is alleged to arise from extrinsic circumstances known to some readers, the "natural and ordinary meaning" to be ascribed to the words of an allegedly defamatory publication is the meaning, including any inferential meaning, which the words would convey to the mind of the ordinary, reasonable, fair-minded reader. This proposition is too well established to require citation of authority. The second principle, which is perhaps a corollary of the first, is that, although a combination of words may in fact convey different meanings to the minds of different readers, the jury in a libel action, applying the criterion which the first principle dictates, is required to determine the single meaning which the publication conveyed to the notional reasonable reader and to base its verdict and any award of damages on the assumption that this was the one sense in which all readers would have understood it. The origins and the implications of this second principle are the subject of a characteristically penetrating analysis in the judgment of Diplock LJ in *Slim v Daily Telegraph Ltd* from which it will, I think, be sufficient to cite the following passages:

> "Everyone outside a court of law recognises that words are imprecise instruments for communicating the thoughts of one man to another. The same words may be understood by one man in a different meaning from that in which they are understood by another and both meanings may be different from that which the author of the words intended to convey; but the notion that the same words should bear different meanings to different men, and that more than one meaning should be 'right', conflicts with the whole training of a lawyer. Words are the tools of his trade. He uses them to define legal rights and duties. They do not achieve that purpose unless there can be attributed to them a single meaning as the 'right' meaning. And so the argument between lawyers as to the meaning of words starts with the unexpressed major premise that any particular combination of words has one meaning, which is not necessarily the same as that intended by him who published them or understood by any of those who read them, but is capable of ascertainment as being the 'right' meaning by the adjudicator to whom the law confides the responsibility of determining it ... Where, as in the present case, words are published to the millions of readers of a popular newspaper, the chances are that if the words are reasonably capable of being understood as bearing more than one meaning, some readers will have understood them as bearing one of those meanings and some will have understood them as bearing others of those meanings. But none of this matters. What does matter is what the adjudicator at the trial thinks is the one and only meaning that the readers as reasonable men should have collectively understood the words to bear. That is 'the natural and ordinary meaning' of words in an

action for libel ... Juries, in theory, must be unanimous on every issue on which they have to adjudicate; and, since the damages that they award must depend on the defamatory meaning that they attribute to the words, they must all agree on a single meaning as being the 'right' meaning. So the unexpressed major premise that any particular combination of words can bear but a single 'natural and ordinary meaning' which is 'right', survived the transfer from judge to jury of the function of adjudicating on the meaning of words in civil actions for libel."

It is precisely the application of the principle so clearly expounded in these passages which, in a libel action where no legal innuendo is alleged, prevents either side from calling witnesses to say what they understood the allegedly defamatory publication to mean. But it would surely be even more destructive of the principle that a publication has "the one and only meaning which the readers as reasonable men should have collectively understood the words to bear" to allow the plaintiff, without evidence, to invite the jury to infer that different groups of readers read different parts of the entire publication and for that reason understood it to mean different things, some defamatory, some not.

Whether the text of a newspaper article will, in any particular case, be sufficient to neutralise the defamatory implication of a prominent headline will sometimes be a nicely balanced question for the jury to decide and will depend not only on the nature of the libel which the headline conveys and the language of the text which is relied on to neutralise it but also on the manner in which the whole of the relevant material is set out and presented. But the proposition that the prominent headline, or as here the headlines plus photographs, may found a claim in libel in isolation from its related text, because some readers only read headlines, is to my mind quite unacceptable in the light of the principles discussed above.

I have no doubt that [counsel] is right in his assertion that many *News of the World* readers who saw the offending publication would have looked at the headlines and photographs and nothing more. But if these readers, without taking the trouble to discover what the article was all about, carried away the impression that two well-known actors in legitimate television were also involved in making pornographic films, they could hardly be described as ordinary, reasonable, fair-minded readers ...'

Comment

(1)   After citing the facts Lord Bridge observes that:

'The remainder of the article castigates the makers of the "sordid computer game" in a tone of self-righteous indignation which contrasts oddly with the prominence given to the main photograph. The plaintiffs must have found this publication deeply offensive and insulting. Many people will not only deplore this kind of gutter journalism but will think that the law ought to give some redress to the plaintiffs against the publication of such degrading faked photographs irrespective of what the accompanying text may have said. I have considerable sympathy with this point of view. However, your Lordships are not concerned to pronounce on any question of journalistic ethics nor to consider whether the publication of the photographs by itself constituted some novel tort.'

(2)   A one-line, remedial assertion tucked away at the end of an article is likely to be insufficient antidote, as Lord Nicholls said:

'This is not to say that words in the text of an article will always be efficacious to cure a defamatory headline. It all depends on the context, one element in which is the lay-out of the article. Those who print defamatory headlines are playing with fire. The ordinary reader might not be expected to notice curative words tucked away further down in the article. The more so, if the words are on a continuation page to which a reader is directed. The standard of the ordinary reader gives a jury adequate scope to return a verdict meeting the justice of the case.'

(3)   *Charleston v Newsgroup* was applied in *Norman v Future Publishing Ltd.*

Byrne v Deane
[1937] 2 All ER 204 Court of Appeal

The defendants were directors and proprietors of a golf club where some illegal gambling machines had been installed. As a result of a complaint made to the police the machines were removed. A lampoon was placed on the club-house wall which included the lines:

'But he who gave the game away
May he byrne in hell and rue the day.'

The defendants failed to remove it. The plaintiff alleged that the notice referred to him and that it meant that he had been disloyal to the members of the club and thereby deserved censure and was a person unfit to be a member of the club. The Court of Appeal held that there had been publication but (Greer LJ dissenting) the only meaning which could be attached was that the plaintiff had informed the police and that could not be defamatory.

Greene LJ: '... With regard to the question whether these words are defamatory, the point raised is one of importance and of difficulty. The alleged meaning of the words is set out in the innuendo which is pleaded. With regard to that innuendo, it is to be observed that the learned judge in his judgment did not in terms as I read it, accept that innuendo as it is drawn. Looking at his judgment, I find that the meaning which he attributes to the words is this: that the plaintiff was the one who had informed the police, and thereby lost for the members of the club the fun of the "diddler' machines, and then he says again: "I cannot help thinking that this did aim at Mr Byrne the accusation that he had given information to the police." That is the only part of the innuendo which the judge in terms accepts. I should have thought, with great deference to those who think otherwise, that that is the meaning, in the circumstances, of the language used. It is to be observed that the complaint in the lampoon is that the plaintiff gave the game away, and, reading that in connection with the first four lines of the lampoon, I should myself read it as meaning that he gave the game away with the result that the members were deprived of their sport. When the innuendo is looked at, this is said: "That he was guilty of underhand disloyalty to the defendants and his fellow members of the said club ..."

I read that myself in this sense: that he was guilty of disloyalty by reporting the matter to the police. If that be the true meaning of it, and if that be the meaning of the words, it does not appear to me that by adding the reference to disloyalty the matter is carried any further. If the allegation that he reported the matter to the police is not defamatory, in my judgment the allegation that in reporting the matter to the police he was guilty of disloyalty cannot be defamatory. If that be right, the matter resolves itself into this: are words capable of a defamatory meaning which say of the plaintiff that he reported to the police that, on the premises of the club of which he was a member, a criminal offence was being habitually committed? Now, it is said that the ordinary sense of society would say of a man who had done that, in the case of this particular criminal offence, that he had behaved in a disloyal and underhand fashion. It is said that this particular offence is one which can be looked at with an indulgent eye, and that there is something dishonourable in setting in motion the constitutional machinery provided in this country for the suppression of crime. I myself find it embarrassing to take into consideration questions of the way in which members of clubs might regard such an action. It seems to me that no distinction can be drawn in a court of law between various categories of crime ... It seems to me that, if the argument is to be accepted, it would involve the court in this position, that it would have to differentiate between different kinds of crime, and put in one category crimes which are of so bad a character as to call for universal reprobation, even among the more easy-minded, and in another category crimes which many people think are stupid, and ought never to have been made crimes at all.

It seems to me that, whatever may be the view of individuals on matters of that kind, this court cannot draw a distinction of that description. In point of fact, it may very well be that the legislature, in its wisdom, has made into a crime something which the public conscience of many persons in this country does not consider involves any sort of moral reprobation; but this court cannot be concerned with considerations of that kind, and to say of a man that he has put in motion the proper machinery for suppressing crime is a thing which, in my judgment, cannot, on the face of it, be defamatory ... In my opinion, therefore, the words in question are words that are not capable of a defamatory meaning, and on that ground I consider that the appeal should be allowed.'

Comment

(1)   It was held that there had been publication, Greene LJ:

'... publication ... is a question of fact, and it must depend on the circumstances in each case whether or not publication has taken place. It is said that, as a general proposition, where the act of the person alleged to have published a libel has not been any positive act, but has been merely the refraining from doing some act, he cannot be guilty of publication. I am quite unable to accept any such general proposition. It may very well be that, in some circumstances, a person, by refraining from removing or obliterating the defamatory matter, is not committing any publication at all. In other circumstances, he may be doing so. The test, it appears to me, is this: having regard to all the facts of the case, is the proper inference that, by not removing the defamatory matter, the defendant really made himself responsible for its continued presence in the place where it had been put?.:. You have a case such as the present, where the removal of this particular notice was a perfectly simple and easy thing to do, involving no trouble whatsoever. The defendants, having the power of removing it, and the right to remove it, and being able to do it without any difficulty at all, and knowing that members of the club, when they came into the room, would see it, I think must be taken to have elected deliberately to leave it there. The proper inference, therefore, in those circumstances, it seems to me, is that they were consenting parties to its continued presence on the spot where it had been put up.'

(2)   Greer LJ thought that the meaning of the innuendo went beyond that accepted by the majority. He thought that while it would not be defamatory to say of someone that he or she had reported a matter to the police, the statement went beyond that and independently asserted disloyalty. That would be defamatory:

'We have to consider only what the words would convey to an ordinary reasonable member of the club, and, in my judgment, they would convey, either in their natural meaning, or as stated in the innuendo that the plaintiff had been guilty of underhand disloyalty to the defendants and to his fellow members of the club, and that, therefore, the judge was justified in finding, not only that the words were capable of a defamatory meaning, but also that they were defamatory of the plaintiff.'

He concluded by saying that:

> 'It is similar to a case in which there had been a statement that the police had been informed by the plaintiff, and, therefore, the plaintiff was a blackguard. It would obviously be no answer, in such a case as that, to prove that informing the police did not make him a blackguard. It would still be defamatory of him to say that he was a blackguard, though the foundation for the statement was quite insufficient to prove that he was a blackguard.'

(3)   For other cases on publication see *Theaker v Richardson*, in which a letter referred to the plaintiff as a 'lying, low down, brothel keeping whore and thief'. It was placed in an envelope, addressed to the plaintiff and delivered to the plaintiff's house. The plaintiff's husband opened it thinking it was an election address. It was held to be a publication. See also *Huth v Huth*, non-publication of a letter addressed to P and posted to P and opened by the butler.

(4)   For innocent publication and mechanical distributors (e.g. newsagents, libraries) see *Vizetelly v Mudie's Select Library Ltd*. The new statutory defence under the Defamation Act 1996, s 1(1) effectively supersedes the common law defence of innocent dissemination. Note also the new defence of offer and amends under s 2(1).

Newstead v London Express Newspaper Ltd
[1939] 4 All ER 319 Court of Appeal

The defendants published an account that one Harold Newstead, a 30-year-old Camberwell man, had been convicted of bigamy. The plaintiff was Harold Newstead, about 30 years of age and a hairdresser from Camberwell. His action for defamation succeeded and the Court of Appeal agreed that there was evidence from which the jury could conclude that reasonable persons would have understood the description to refer to the plaintiff.

Sir Wilfrid Greene MR: '... If the words used, when read in the light of the relevant circumstances, are understood by reasonable persons to refer to the plaintiff, then refer to him they do for all relevant purposes. Their meaning cannot be affected by the recklessness or honesty of the writer.

I do not propose to refer to the authorities which establish this proposition, except to quote the words of Lord Loreburn LC, in *Hulton & Co v Jones*:

> "What does the tort consist in? It consists in using language which others knowing the circumstances would reasonably think to be defamatory of the person complaining of and injured by it."

In the case of libel, once it is held that the words are capable of referring to the plaintiff, it is, of course, for the jury to say whether or not they do so refer. Subject to this, the principle is in truth an illustration of the rule that the author of a written document is to be taken as having intended his words to have the meaning which they convey when understood in the light of the relevant surrounding circumstances. In the case of libel, the same words may reasonably convey a different meaning to each of a number of different persons or groups of persons, and so be held to be defamatory of more persons than one.

After giving careful consideration to the matter, I am unable to hold that the fact that defamatory words are true of A makes it a matter of law impossible for them to be defamatory of B which was in substance the main argument on behalf of the appellants. At first sight, this looks as though it would lead to great hardship, but the hardships are in practice not so serious as might appear, at any rate in the case of statements which are *ex facie* defamatory. Persons who make statements of this character may not unreasonably be expected, when describing the person of whom they are made, to identify that person so closely as to make it very unlikely that a judge would hold them to be reasonably capable of referring to someone else, or that a jury would hold that they did so refer. This is particularly so in the case of statements which purport to deal with actual facts. If there is a risk of coincidence, it ought, I think, in reason to be borne, not by the innocent party to whom the words are held to refer, but by the party who puts them into circulation. In matters of fiction, there is no doubt more room for hardship. Even in the case of matters of fact it is no doubt possible to construct imaginary facts which would lead to hardship. There may also be hardship if words, not on their faces defamatory, are true of A but are reasonably understood by some as referring to B, and, as applied to B, are defamatory. Such cases, however, must be rare. The law as I understand it is well settled, and can be altered only by legislation. The appeal must be dismissed with costs.'

Du Parq LJ: '... There was evidence ... which would justify a jury in finding ... that the description "Harold Newstead, 30-year-old Camberwell man" substantially fits the plaintiff. The plaintiff is known as a hairdressers' assistant to a comparatively wide circle of customers and other acquaintances in Camberwell, where he has acquired a modest fame. A reasonable man who had some acquaintance with him might have been prudent enough, on reading the alleged libel, to say "This may refer to some other Harold Newstead", but I am not satisfied that every reasonable man would necessarily have been so cautious. The man who believes no ill of his neighbour until the accusation is proved beyond doubt against him is without question a reasonable man, but it would be fallacious to argue that every reasonable man attains to that high standard of judicial fairness. Evidence proving the existence of another person to whom the words might have been taken to refer is only relevant to this first question because it proves the words to have been capable of more than one meaning, and of at least one meaning which would not be defamatory of the plaintiff. It cannot now be argued ... that, in the words of Scrutton LJ in *Cassidy v Daily Mirror Newspapers*: "if words are capable of several meanings, some defamatory and some innocent, they should not be left to the jury". The correct view is that, if the words are reasonably capable of two or more meanings, of which one is defamatory, it must be left to the jury to determine in which sense a reasonable man would understand them.

... In my opinion, it is now settled law that, in the words of Russell LJ in *Cassidy v Daily Mirror Newspapers*: "Liability for libel does not depend on the intention of the defamer; but on the fact of defamation". I quote these words of Russell LJ as conveniently summarising the effect of his own judgment, and of that of Scrutton LJ in *Cassidy's* case, and as clearly stating the principle established by *Hulton & Co v Jones*. It seems to me to be impossible, consistently with this principle, to make the defendant's liability depend on the accuracy of his words in relation to some person other than the plaintiff at whom he says he meant to strike. Nor do I think ... that any doctrine which would make the defendant's liability depend upon his state of mind, or the degree of care which he exercised, is reconcilable with this principle. In the present case, and in any similar case in which a defendant says that he was only speaking the truth of another person, and not meaning to attack the plaintiff, it may well be right to direct the jury that a reasonable man must be aware of the possibility (it is for them to say in each case whether it amounts to a possibility) that in any district there may be more than one person of the same name, and that, in considering how a reasonable man would understand the words, they must assume that he will read them with such care as may fairly be expected of him, not ignoring any parts of the description which are inapplicable to the plaintiff. If a defendant has been careful and precise, he may by his care avoid the risk of a successful action, but he cannot, in my opinion, escape liability merely by showing that he was careful and that his intentions were good ...'

Comment

(1)   In *Cassidy v Daily Mirror Newspapers*, the defendant newspaper published a photograph of Mr C, who was married to Mrs C, the plaintiff. The photograph was taken at a race meeting and showed Mr C in the company of a lady, named as X. The caption commented that the photograph showed Mr C and Miss X, whose engagement has been announced. Female acquaintances of the plaintiff gave evidence that they had read the newspaper and had formed the view that the plaintiff was not married to Mr C and had no legal right to take his name. The plaintiff sued and pleaded an innuendo that the words meant that she was an immoral woman who had cohabited with Mr C without being married to him. The Court of Appeal held that the defendants could be liable even though they did not know the facts which enabled others to draw an inference defamatory of the plaintiff. Scrutton LJ said that:

'If newspapers, who have no more rights than private persons, publish statements which may be defamatory of other people, without inquiry as to their truth, in order to make their newspaper attractive, they must take the consequences if, on subsequent enquiry, their statements are found to be untrue or capable of defamatory and unjustifiable inferences ...'

Lord Reid observed in *Morgan v Odhams Press Ltd*:

'It does not matter whether the publisher intended to refer to the plaintiff or not. It does not even matter if he knew of the plaintiff's existence. And it does not matter that he did not know or could not have known the facts which caused the readers with special knowledge to connect the statement with the plaintiff.'

(2) In *Hulton v Jones* a newspaper published a fictional account of a trip to Dieppe by one Artemus Jones, a churchwarden from Peckham, in which he was accused of having an affair with 'a woman who is not his wife, who must be – you know – the other thing'. The plaintiff was an Artemus Jones, a barrister, not a churchwarden, unmarried and who did not live in Peckham but who had contributed in the past to the defendant's newspapers. There was evidence that the plaintiff was well-known where the paper had been circulated and that some people had believed it to refer to him. The writer of the article claimed never to have heard of the plaintiff and that he had made up the name. The House of Lords held that it was not necessary to show that the defendant should have intended the defamatory statement to refer to the plaintiff. The issue is whether those to whom it was published knowing the circumstances would reasonably think the plaintiff was the person to whom it referred.

(3) Any terror which might flow from these decisions is lessened by the likelihood that an unmeritorious claim will be met by a rebuff from the jury, at least in damages, as was the result of *Newstead v London Express Newspapers* itself. Equally, the Defamation Act 1996, s 2(1) provides for settlement of a claim by way of publication of a correction and an apology and payment of agreed damages.

(4) As to the situation where there is no one named, see *Morgan v Odhams Press Ltd* – extrinsic evidence may be introduced to show that the plaintiff was referred to.

(5) Defamation of a class is difficult to maintain: see *Knuppfer v London Express Newspapers Ltd*; Lord Atkin:

'The only relevant rule is that in order to be actionable the defamatory words must be understood to be published of and concerning the plaintiff. It is irrelevant that the words are published of two or more persons if they are proved to be published of him, and it is irrelevant that the two or more persons are called by some generic or class name. There can be no law that a defamatory statement made of a firm ... is not actionable, if the words would reasonably be understood as published of each member of the firm ... The reason why a libel published of a large or

indeterminate number of persons described by some general name generally fails to be actionable is the difficulty of establishing that the plaintiff
was, in fact, included in the defamatory statement, for the habit of
making unfounded generalisations is ingrained in ill-educated or vulgar
minds, or the words are occasionally intended to be a factious exaggera-
tion. Even in such cases words may be used which enable the plaintiff to
prove that the words complained of were intended to be published of
each member of the group, or, at any rate, of himself ... It will be as well
for the future for lawyers to concentrate on the question whether the
words were published of the plaintiff rather than on the question whether
they were spoken of a class ...'

London Artists Ltd v Littler
[1969] 2 All ER 193 Court of Appeal

The defendant was convinced that there was a plot to stop a play being staged
by him and thereby allow another play to be moved into the theatre from
another theatre. Four actors gave notice through the defendant, their agent, at
the same time and the likely effect was the termination of the play. He
implicated other plaintiffs in the alleged plot including the company which
owned or controlled the theatres in question. The defendant's plea of fair
comment was rejected by the Court of Appeal because the allegation of a plot
was a statement of fact and not comment.

Lord Denning MR:'... Three points arise on the defence of fair comment. First, was
the comment made on a matter of public interest? The judge ruled that it was not.
I cannot agree with him. There is no definition in the books as to what is a matter
of public interest. All we are given is a list of examples, coupled with the statement
that it is for the judge and not for the jury. I would not myself confine it within
narrow limits. Whenever a matter is such as to affect people at large, so that they
may be legitimately interested in, or concerned at, what is going on; or what may
happen to them or to others; then it is a matter of public interest on which
everyone is entitled to make fair comment. A good example is *South Hetton
Coal Co Ltd v North-Eastern News Association Ltd.* A colliery company owned most of
the cottages in the village. It was held that the sanitary conditions of those cottages
– or rather their insanitary condition – was a matter of public interest.
Lord Esher MR said that it was "a matter of public interest that the conduct of the
employers should be criticised". There the public were legitimately *concerned*. Here
the public are legitimately *interested*. Many people are interested in what happens in
the theatre. The stars welcome publicity. They want to be put at the top of the bill.
Producers wish it too. They like the house to be full. The comings and goings of the
performers are noticed everywhere. When three top stars and a satellite all give
notice to leave at the same time – thus putting a successful play in peril – it is to my
mind a matter of public interest on which everyone, press and all, are entitled to
comment freely.

The second point is whether the allegation of a "plot" was a fact which the defendant had to prove to be true, or was it only comment? In order to be fair, the commentator must get his basic facts right. The basic facts are those which go to the pith and substance of the matter ... They are the facts on which the comments are based or from which the inferences are drawn – as distinct from the comments or inferences themselves. The commentator need not set out in his original article all the basic facts, see *Kemsley v Foot*; but he must get them right and be ready to prove them to be true. He must indeed afterwards in legal proceedings, when asked, give particulars of the basic facts ... but he need not give particulars of the comments or the inferences to be drawn from those facts. If in his original article he sets out basic facts which are themselves defamatory of the plaintiff, then he must prove them to be true: and this is the case just as much after s 6 of the Defamation Act 1952, as it was before ... It is indeed the whole difference between a plea of fair comment and a plea of justification. In fair comment he need only prove the basic facts to be true. In justification he must prove also that the comments and inferences are true also ...

But for the three reasons which I have given, I do not think the statement of a "plot" was reasonably capable of being considered as comment. It was a statement of fact which was itself defamatory of the plaintiffs. The defendant, in order to succeed, had to prove it to be true. He failed to do so, and along with it went the defence of fair comment.

In case, however, I am wrong about this and it could be regarded as comment, then I turn to the third point, which is this: Were there any facts on which a fair-minded man might honestly make such a comment? I take it to be settled law that, in order for the defence of fair comment to be left to the jury, there must at least be a sufficient basis of fact to warrant the comment, in this sense, that a fair-minded man might on those facts honestly hold that opinion. There is no need for the defendant to prove that his opinion was correct or one with which the jury agree. He is entitled to the defence of fair comment unless it can be said: "No fair-minded man could honestly hold that opinion." ... In this case I am sure that the defendant acted honestly and in good faith. He honestly thought that there was a plot to bring to a stop the run of "The Right Honourable Gentleman". He was himself so convinced of it that he took the extreme step of telling it to the world. But I fear that he went beyond the bounds of a fair-minded man. He jumped too hastily to his conclusion. He ought not to have been so precipitate. He ought to have made enquiries of the artistes. He ought to have made enquiries of his brother ... By jumping so quickly to a conclusion the defendant came at odds with the law. He made a public condemnation not only of the artistes themselves but of the plaintiffs, Associated Television, and the agents, London Artists, Mr Lew Grade and the Grade Organisation. The judge held that in alleging that all those were parties to a plot he was making an imputation without any basis of fact to support it. I think the judge was quite right in so holding and in not leaving it to the jury.

In the upshot it comes to this: the fate of 'The Right Honourable Gentleman" was a matter of public interest. The defendant was fully entitled to comment on it as long as his comment was fair and honest. He was entitled to give his views to the public through the press. But I think he went beyond the bounds of fair comment. He was carried away by his feelings at the moment. He did not wait long enough to check the facts and to get them right ...'

Comment

(1)   In general, a person's private life will be beyond comment unless that private life impinges upon the ability to hold public office, e.g. *Seymour v Butterworth* in which the private conduct of the plaintiff, a QC, Member of Parliament and judge, 'was open to criticism if it tended to show that he was destitute and devoid of such qualities as integrity, honesty, and honour which were essential for a man in his public office'.

(2)   As to facts underpinning a comment see *Kemsley v Foot*, below, and *Telnikoff v Matusevitch*, p 759.

(3)   As to malice, see *Horrocks v Lowe*, p 773, and *Telnikoff v Matusevitch*, p 759.

(4)   Where the defendant alleges dishonesty then the fairness of a comment will depend upon the defendant being able to show a reasonable basis of fact for the statement: see *Campbell v Spottiswoode.*

Kemsley v Foot and others
[1952] 1 All ER 501 House of Lords

The writer of an article and the owners of the newspaper where it was published were sued by the plaintiff, a well-known newspaper proprietor. He complained of the article which was captioned 'Lower than Kemsley' and which proceeded to attack another newspaper. The plaintiff alleged that the words reflected badly on him. The defendants' plea of fair comment succeeded.

Lord Porter: '... It is not, as I understand, contended that the words contained in that article are fact and not comment. Rather it is alleged that they are comment with no facts to support it. The question for your Lordships' decision is, therefore, whether a plea of fair comment is only permissible where the comment is accompanied by a statement of facts on which the comment is made, and to determine the particularity with which the facts must be stated.

Before one comes to consider the general question it is, I think, desirable to determine what the language of the alleged libel can be held to assert. It may, in my opinion, be construed as containing an inference that the Kemsley Press is of a low and undesirable quality and that Lord Kemsley is responsible for its tone. Indeed, as I understand the defence and such particulars as have been delivered, an imputation no less severe has been accepted by the respondents as being a true interpretation of the words used. Although the article complained of uses the phrase "Lower than Kemsley", that language is accompanied by an attack on Lord Beaverbrook's papers, and it is at least arguable that the attack is on the Kemsley Press and not on Lord Kemsley's personal character save in so far as it is exhibited in the Press for which he is responsible. Nevertheless, libel must reflect on a person and Lord Kemsley is held up as worthy of attack on the ground that he is a newspaper proprietor who prostitutes his position by conducting his newspapers or permitting them to be conducted in an undesirable way. In this sense the criticism does not differ from that which takes place when what is called literary criticism comes in question. In such case the attack is not on the personal character of the person libelled, it is on him as responsible for certain productions, e.g. an article in the Press, a book, a musical composition, or an artistic work. Later I shall have to come back to the truth and accuracy of this analogy, but I have thought it right to set out the basis of literary criticism at this point, because a distinction is sought to be drawn and, indeed, in some of the decided cases has been drawn, between literary criticism and a personal attack on the character of an individual.

If an author writes a play or a book or a composer composes a musical work, he is submitting that work to the public and, thereby, inviting comment. Not all the public will see or read or hear it, but the work is public in the same sense as a case in the law courts is said to be heard in public. Obviously not all those who wish to attend a trial can do so, but in so far as there is room for them in the court all are entitled to do so, and the subject-matter on which comment can be made is indicated to the world at large. The same observation is true of a newspaper. Whether the criticism is confined to a particular issue or deals with the way in which it is, in general, conducted, the subject-matter on which criticism has been made has been submitted to the public, though by no means all those to whom the alleged libel has been published will have seen or are likely to see the various issues. Accordingly, its contents and conduct are open to comment on the ground that the public have at least the opportunity of ascertaining for themselves the subject-matter on which the comment is founded. I am assuming that the reference is to a known journal. For the present purpose it is not necessary to consider how far criticism without facts on which to base it is subject to the same observation in the case of an obscure publication. A further ground for the distinction sought to be drawn between an attack on an individual and criticism of a literary work appears to suggest that comment on the literary production must be confined to criticism of it as literature. This is not so. A literary work can be criticised for its treatment of life and morals as freely as it can for bad writing, e.g. it can be criticised as having an immoral tendency. The fairness of the criticism does not depend on the fact that it is confined to form or literary content.

The question, therefore, in all cases is whether there is a sufficient substratum of fact stated or indicated in the words which are the subject-matter of the action, and I find my view well expressed in the remarks contained in *Odgers on Libel and Slander* (5th edn, 1911):

> "Sometimes, however, it is difficult to distinguish an allegation of fact from an expression of opinion. It often depends on what is stated in the rest of the article. If the defendant accurately states what some public man has really done, and then asserts that 'such conduct is disgraceful', this is merely the expression of his opinion, his comment on the plaintiff's conduct. So, if without setting it out, he identifies the conduct on which he comments by a clear reference. In either case, the defendant enables his readers to judge for themselves how far his opinion is well founded; and, therefore, what would otherwise have been an allegation of fact becomes merely a comment. But if he asserts that the plaintiff has been guilty of disgraceful conduct, and does not state what that conduct was, this is an allegation of fact for which there is no defence but privilege or truth. The same considerations apply where a defendant has drawn from certain facts an inference derogatory to the plaintiff. If he states the bare inference without the facts on which it is based, such inference will be treated as an allegation of fact. But if he sets out the facts correctly, and then gives his inference, stating it as his inference from those facts, such inference will, as a rule, be deemed a comment. But even in this case the writer must be careful to state the inference as an inference, and not to assert it as a new and independent fact; otherwise, his inference will become something more than a comment, and he may be driven to justify it as an allegation of fact."

But the question whether an inference is a bare inference in this sense must depend on all the circumstances. Indeed, it was ultimately admitted on behalf of the appellant that the facts necessary to justify comment might be implied from the terms of the impugned article, and, therefore, the inquiry ceases to be: Can the defendant point to definite assertions of fact in the alleged libel on which the comment is made? and becomes: Is there subject-matter indicated with sufficient clarity to justify comment being made? and whether the comment actually made is such as an honest though prejudiced man might make.

Is there, then, in this case sufficient subject-matter on which to make comment? In an article which is concerned with what has been described as "the Beaverbrook Press" and which is violently critical of Lord Beaverbrook's newspapers, it is, I think, a reasonable construction of the words "Lower than Kemsley" that the allegation which is made is that the conduct of the Kemsley Press was similar to, but not quite so bad as, that of the Press controlled by Lord Beaverbrook, i.e. it is possibly dishonest, but in any case low. The exact meaning, however, is not, in my opinion, for your Lordships, but for the jury. All I desire to say is that there is subject-matter and it is at least arguable that the words of known newspapers and that the conduct of those newspapers is in question. Had the contention that all the facts justifying the comment must appear in the article been maintainable, the appeal must have succeeded. But the appellant's representatives did not feel able to, and, I think, could not, support so wide a contention. The facts, they admitted, might be implied and the respondents' answer to their contention is: "We have pointed to your Press. It is widely read. Your readers will, and the public generally can, know at what our criticism is directed. It is not bare comment. It is comment on a well-known matter, much better known, indeed, than a newly printed book or a once performed play" ...'

Comment

(1) What material a jury can look at to ascertain what is fact was considered in *Telnikoff v Matusevitch*. The plaintiff, a Russian emigré, wrote an article for a national newspaper in which he criticised the BBC's Russian Service. The defendant, another emigré, wrote a letter in response, published in the newspaper, in which he alleged that the article was racialist and anti-Semitic. The plaintiff sued and the defendant raised the defence of fair comment. The House of Lords held that whether or not the letter was capable of being a statement of facts rather than comment had to be decided by reference to the letter on its own and not in conjunction with the original article to which it was a response; but, if the jury decided that it was comment, then they could look at the article to see if the comment amounted to 'fair comment'. The House of Lords also held that the defendant did not have to demonstrate an honest belief in the views expressed. The onus was on the plaintiff to establish that the views were actuated by malice. The plaintiff had failed to adduce any evidence of express malice and had also failed to demonstrate that the defendant did not honestly hold the views expressed. As to the test for fairness, Lord Keith said:

'... Drake J also refused to leave to the jury the question whether, assuming that paras (6) and (7) were pure comment, they constituted fair comment on a matter of public interest, and the Court of Appeal upheld his decision on this matter also. Both took the view that on an application of the normal objective test of fair comment any reasonable jury would be bound to hold that it was satisfied. Lloyd LJ correctly stated the test as being whether any man, however prejudiced and obstinate, could honestly hold the view expressed by the defendant in his letter. I agree with Drake J and the Court of Appeal as to the only reasonable outcome of a proper application of that test, and find it unnecessary to elaborate the matter. It was, however, argued by counsel for the plaintiff ... that in addition to satisfying the objective test a defendant pleading fair comment must prove affirmatively that the comment represented his own honest opinion, which the present defendant failed to do, since the case was withdrawn from the jury before any evidence had been given by him. Lloyd LJ, after an extensive review of the authorities, concluded that this argument was unsound. These authorities included *Cherneskey v Armadale Publishers Ltd* in the Supreme Court of Canada. The defendants were the editor and the owner and publisher of a newspaper which had published a letter to the editor in which the writers accused the plaintiff of holding racist views. The writers of the letter did not give evidence, but the defendants in their evidence made it clear that the letter complained of did not represent the honest expression of their own views. The trial judge refused to leave the defence of fair comment to the jury, and the Supreme Court, by a majority of six to three, held that he had acted rightly. Lloyd LJ expressed himself as preferring the judgment of the minority to that of the majority, and as regarding the former as being fully supported by the English authorities cited in his extensive review. I find myself in respectful agreement with him and feel that to repeat his review would be a work of supererogation. The law is correctly stated in *Gatley on Libel and Slander* (8th edn, 1981) as follows:

> "*Onus of proof of malice: fair comment.* In the same way, the defendant who relies on a plea of fair comment does not have to show that the comment is an honest expression of his views. In alleging any unfairness the plaintiff takes on him or herself the onus, also taken by an allegation of malice, to prove that the criticism is unfair either from the language used or from some extraneous circumstance." '

(2)   *Telnikoff v Matusevich* has settled that in fair comment there is a two-stage approach. The first is that the defendant must show that the view expressed is such as any man, however prejudiced and obstinate, could honestly hold. The second is that the claimant must, if the defence is to be defeated, show that the defendant was actuated by malice. A claimant able to show that the defendant did not hold the views expressed would usually be well placed to demonstrate malice. But, as the facts of *Cherneskey v Armadale Publishers Ltd* demonstrate, a newspaper would be in an intolerable position if English law were to follow the majority rather than the minority in that case.

(3)   Although Lord Ackner in *Telnikoff* dissented in part, he made the following comments concerning the importance of fair comment as a defence:

> '... There have been many judicial pronouncements on how vital to the functioning of a democratic society is the freedom to comment on matters of public interest. I content myself with citations from two cases. In *Lyon v Daily Telegraph Ltd* ... Scott LJ said: "The reason why, once a plea of fair comment is established, there is no libel, is that it is in the public interest to have free discussion of matters of public interest." Towards the end of his judgment Scott LJ added: "[The right of fair comment] is one of the fundamental rights of free speech and writing

which are so dear to the British nation, and it is of vital importance to the rule of law upon which we depend for our personal freedom, that the courts should preserve the right of 'fair comment' undiminished and unimpaired."

In *Slim v Daily Telegraph Ltd* Lord Denning MR said: "... the right of fair comment is one of the essential elements which go to make up our freedom of speech. We must ever maintain this right intact. It must not be whittled down by legal refinements."

In the *Report of the Committee on Defamation* (Cmnd 5909 (1975)) under the chairmanship of the late Faulks J it is stated (at para 151): "The very wide breadth of the main criterion for the defence of fair comment (could an honest albeit prejudiced person have expressed such an opinion?) has stood for over a century. It is generally regarded as a bulwark of free speech." '

(4)   The law attempts to balance competing interests. Fair comment protects criticism but not defamatory statements of fact, and is available to all, not just newspapers. Birkett LJ in *Kemsley v Foot* (affirmed by the House of Lords) commented that:

'The defence of fair comment is now recognised to be one of the most valuable parts of the law of libel and slander. It is an essential part of the greater right of free speech. It is the right of every man to comment freely, fairly and honestly on any matter of public interest, and this is not a privilege which belongs to particular persons in particular circumstances. It matters not whether the comments are made to the few or to the many, whether they are made by a powerful newspaper or by an individual, whether they are written or spoken: the defence that the words are fair comment on a matter of public interest is open to all.'

Slim v Daily Telegraph Ltd
[1968] 1 All ER 497 Court of Appeal

S, the plaintiff, a solicitor, had been Town Clerk of Hammersmith and on his retirement became legal adviser to V Ltd. A dispute arose as to whether or not V Ltd had a right of way for vehicles over a path in respect of which S, when Town Clerk, had erected a notice forbidding cycling. H, a nearby resident, wrote a letter published in the *Daily Telegraph* which the plaintiff alleged meant that he had acted in an improper and dishonourable fashion and that the second and third plaintiffs, V Ltd and its chairman, had acted in a hypocritical and insincere fashion in stating on other occasions that they wished to improve riverside walks. The Court of Appeal held that even if the words had been defamatory, they were fair comment on a matter of public interest.

Lord Denning MR: '... I think that the correct approach is simply this: were these letters fair comment on a matter of public interest? The company, V Ltd, claimed that they had a right of way for vehicles along Upper Mall. That was a matter of public interest. So also was the conduct of their officers in regard thereto. That is conceded. The defendants were, therefore, entitled to make any fair comment on it. The letters contained a recital of facts which were virtually undisputed. At any rate, no serious complaint was made about the facts. The complaints which counsel for the plaintiffs made were about the comments. In particular, he complained about the comments "Double Think" and "cynical" in the letter of 30 March 1964; and of the comments "protestations of injured innocence" and "How can Mr. Graves pretend to associate himself" in the letter of 23 April 1964. These comments are capable of various meanings. They may strike some readers in one way and others in another way. One person may read into them imputations of dishonesty, insincerity and hypocrisy (as the judge did). Another person may only read into them imputations of inconsistency and want of candour (as I would). In considering a plea of fair comment, it is not correct to canvass all the various imputations which different readers may put on the words. The important thing is to determine whether or not the writer was actuated by malice. If he was an honest man expressing his genuine opinion on a subject of public interest, then no matter that his words conveyed derogatory imputations: no matter that his opinion was wrong or exaggerated or prejudiced; and no matter that it was badly expressed so that other people read all sorts of innuendoes into it; nevertheless, he has a good defence of fair comment. His honesty is the cardinal test. He must honestly express his real view. So long as he does this, he has nothing to fear, even though other people may read more into it, see *Turner (otherwise Robertson) v Metro-Goldwyn-Mayer Pictures Ltd*, per Lord Porter and *Silkin v Beaverbrook Newspapers Ltd*, per Diplock J. I stress this because the right of fair comment is one of the essential elements which go to make up our freedom of speech. We must ever maintain this right intact. It must not be whittled down by legal refinements. When a citizen is troubled by things going wrong, he should be free to "write to the newspaper": and the newspaper should be free to publish his letter. It is often the only way to get things put right. The matter must, of course, be one of public interest. The writer must get his facts right: and he must honestly state his real opinion. But that being done, both he and the newspaper should be clear of any liability. They should not be deterred by fear of libel actions. When I said to counsel for the plaintiffs that I thought that the real defence here was fair comment, he suggested that it was not based on true facts and it was actuated by malice. But he did not obtain any such finding from the judge: and in the absence of it, I am not prepared to accept the suggestion. Looking at the published correspondence, it seems to me that these were hard-hitting comments by both protagonists, of which neither can complain in a court of law. On the face of these letters, I think that the comments made by H and the *Daily Telegraph* were fair comments on a matter of public interest. They honestly said what they thought. Even if the words did impute dishonesty, insincerity and hypocrisy (which I do not think that they did), nevertheless the writers were expressing their honest opinion; and that is enough to clear them of any liability ...'

Comment

(1)   Lord Diplock said:

'... It would be an evil day for free speech in this country if this kind of controversy on a matter of public though local interest were discouraged by the fear that every word written to be read in haste should be subjected to minute linguistic analysis in a court of law of the kind to which these letters have been subjected on this appeal. As the law of libel now stands, it is not easy to avoid it ...'

(2)   Diplock J in *Silkin v Beaverbrook Newspapers* had said that:

'People are entitled to hold and to express freely on matters of public interest strong views, views which some of you, or indeed all of you, may think are exaggerated, obstinate, or prejudiced, provided – and this is the important thing – that they are views which they honestly hold. The basis of our public life is that the crank, the enthusiast, may say what he honestly thinks just as much as the reasonable man or woman who sits on a jury, and it would be a sad day for freedom of speech in this country if a jury were to apply the test of whether it agrees with the comment instead of applying the true test: was this an opinion, however exaggerated, obstinate or prejudiced, which was honestly held by the writer?'

Watt v Longsdon
[1929] All ER Rep 292 Court of Appeal

A company had in Casablanca a manager, B, and a managing director, W. The chairman, S, was in England and held most of the shares in the company. L was a director and had spent some time in Casablanca on business and had been friendly with W and B, and was a friend of Mrs W. The company went into voluntary liquidation in 1927, and L was appointed liquidator. In April 1928, Mrs W was in England, and her husband in Casablanca. L, in England, received a letter at the beginning of May from B in Casablanca stating that W had left for Lisbon to look for a job, that he had left a bill for £88 for whisky unpaid, and that he had been for two months in immoral relations with his housemaid, who was now publicly raising claims against him for money matters. The woman was described as an old woman, stone deaf, almost blind and with dyed hair. The letter also suggested that W had been planning to seduce Mrs B.

L, without making inquiries, sent B's letter to S. L wrote to B saying that he had long suspected W's immorality, but had no proof, that he thought it cruel that Mrs W should be in the dark, and that B should obtain a sworn statement from the woman. Shortly thereafter, L sent the letter to Mrs W. Mr and Mrs W separated, and Mrs W instituted divorce proceedings.

Mr W sued L for libel in respect of (i) the publication of B's letter to S; (ii) L's letter to B; (iii) the publication of that letter to Mrs W.

The defendant did not plead justification, but did plead qualified privilege. The Court of Appeal held that (i) and (ii) were protected by qualified privilege but not (iii).

Scrutton LJ: '... By the law of England there are occasions on which a person may make defamatory statements about another which are untrue without incurring any legal liability for his statements. These occasions are called privileged occasions. A reason frequently given for this privilege is that the allegation that the speaker has "unlawfully and maliciously published" is displaced by proof that the speaker had either a duty or an interest to publish, such duty or interest conferring the privilege. But communications made on these occasions may lose their privilege. (i) They may exceed the privilege of the occasion by going beyond the limit of the duty or interest, or (ii) they may be published with express malice, so that the occasion is not being legitimately used, but abused. A very careful discussion of the way in which these two grounds of loss of privilege should be considered will be found in Lord Dunedin's judgment in *Adam v Ward*. The classical definition of "privileged occasions" is that of Parke B, in *Toogood v Spyring* ...

> "In general, an action lies for the malicious publication of statements which are false in fact, and injurious to the character of another ... and the law considers such publication as malicious, unless it is fairly made by a person in the discharge of some public or private duty, whether legal or moral, or in the conduct of his own affairs, in matters where his interest is concerned. In such cases, the occasion prevents the inference of malice, which the law draws from unauthorised communications, and affords a qualified defence depending upon the absence of actual malice. If fairly warranted by any reasonable occasion or exigency, and honestly made, such communications are protected for the common convenience and welfare of society; and the law has not restricted the right to make them within any narrow limits."

It will be seen that the learned judge requires: (i) A public or private duty to communicate, whether legal or moral; (ii) "fairly warranted by any reasonable occasion or exigency"; (iii) a statement in the conduct of his own affairs where his interest is concerned. Parke B had given several other definitions in slightly varying terms. For instance, in *Cockayne v Hodgkisson* he had directed the jury:

"Where the writer is acting on any duty, legal or moral, towards the person to whom he writes, or where he has, by his situation, to protect the interests of another, that which he writes under such circumstances is a privileged communication."

This adds to the protection of his own interest spoken of in *Toogood v Spyring*, the protection of the interests of another where his situation requires him to do so. This, I think, involves that his "situation" imposes on him a legal or moral duty. The question whether the occasion was privileged is for the judge, and so far as "duty" is concerned, the question is: Was there a duty, legal, moral or social, to communicate? As to legal duty, the judge should have no difficulty; the judge should know the law. But as to moral or social duties of imperfect obligation, the task is far more troublesome. The judge had no evidence as to the view which the community takes of moral or social duties. All the help the Court of Appeal can give him is contained in Lindley LJ's judgment in *Stuart v Bell*:

"The question of moral or social duty being for the judge, each judge must decide it as best he can for himself. I take moral or social duty to mean a duty recognised by English people of ordinary intelligence and moral principle, but at the same time not a duty enforceable by legal proceedings whether civil or criminal. My own conviction is that all, or at all events, the great mass of right-minded men in the position of the defendant would have considered it their duty, under the circumstances, to inform Stanley of the suspicion which had fallen on the plaintiff."

Is the judge merely to give his own view of moral and social duty, though he thinks a considerable portion of the community hold a different opinion, or is he to endeavour to ascertain what view "the great mass of right-minded men" would take? It is not surprising that with such a standard both judges and text writers treat the matter as one of great difficulty in which no definite line can be drawn ...

In 1855 in *Harrison v Bush* Lord Campbell, giving the judgment of the Court of Queen's Bench, accepted a principle stated thus:

"A communication made bona fide upon any subject-matter in which the party communicating has an interest, or in reference to which he has a duty, is privileged, if made to a person having a corresponding interest or duty, although it contains criminatory matter which, without this privilege, would be slanderous and actionable."

This is the first of a series of statements that both parties, the writer and the recipient, must have a corresponding interest or duty ... Lord Atkinson in *Adam v Ward*, expresses it thus:

"It was not disputed, in this case on either side, that a privileged occasion is, in reference to qualified privilege, an occasion where the person who makes a communication has an interest or a duty, legal, social, or moral, to make it to the person to whom it is made, and the person to whom it is so made has a corresponding interest or duty to receive it. This reciprocity is essential."

With slight modifications in particular circumstances, this appears to me to be well established law ... Except in the case of common interest justifying intercommunication, the correspondence must be between duty and interest; there may, in the common interest cases, be also a common or reciprocal duty. It is not every interest which will create a duty in a stranger or volunteer ... but I think it should be expanded into "either (i) a duty to communicate information believed to be true to a person who has a material interest in receiving the information, or (ii) an interest in the speaker to be protected by communicating information, if true, relevant to that interest, to a person honestly believed to have a duty to protect that interest, or (iii) a common interest and reciprocal duty in the subject-matter of the communication between speaker and recipient." ...

[I]n *Stuart v Bell* ... Stanley, the explorer, and his valet Stuart, were staying with the mayor of Newcastle, Bell. The Edinburgh police made a very carefully worded communication to the Newcastle police that there had been a robbery in Edinburgh at an hotel where Stuart was staying, and it might be well to make very careful and cautious inquiry into the matter. The Newcastle police showed the letter to the mayor, who, after consideration, showed it to Stanley, who dismissed Stuart. Stuart sued the mayor. Lindley LJ and Kay LJ held that the mayor had a moral duty to communicate, and Stanley a material interest to receive; Lopes LJ held that, in the circumstances, there was no moral duty to communicate, though, in some circumstances, there might be such a duty in a host towards a guest. I myself should have agreed with the majority, but the difference of opinion between such experienced judges shows the difficulty of the question ...

[I]t is necessary to consider, in the present case, whether there was, as to each communication, a duty to communicate, and an interest in the recipient. First, as to the communication between L and S, I think the case must proceed on the admission that at all material times W, L, and B were in the employment of the same company, and the evidence of the answer to the interrogatory put in by the plaintiff that L honestly believed the statements in B's letter. In my view, on these facts, there was a duty, moral and business, on L to communicate the letter to S, the chairman of his company, who, apart from questions of present employment, might be asked by W for a testimonial to a future employer. Equally, I think L receiving the letter from B, might discuss the matter with him, and ask for further information, on the ground of a common interest in the affairs of the company, and to obtain further information for his chairman. I should, therefore, agree with the view of Horridge J that these two occasions were privileged though for different reasons ...

The communication to Mrs W stands on a different footing. I have no intention of writing an exhaustive treatise on the circumstances when a stranger or a friend should communicate to husband or wife information he receives as to the conduct of the other party to the marriage. I am clear that it is impossible to say that he is always under a moral or social duty to do so; it is equally impossible to say that he is never under such a duty. It must depend on the circumstances of each case, the nature of the information, and the relation of speaker and recipient. It cannot, on the one hand, be the duty even of a friend to communicate all the gossip the friend hears at men's clubs or women's bridge parties to one of the spouses affected. On the other hand, most men would hold that it was the moral duty of a doctor who attended his sister-in-law, and believed her to be suffering from a miscarriage, for which an absent husband could not be responsible, to communicate that fact to his wife and the husband ... [T]he decision must turn on the circumstances of each case, the judge being much influenced by the consideration that, as a general rule, it is not desirable for anyone, even a mother-in-law, to interfere in the affairs of man and wife. Using the best judgment I can in the difficult matter, I have come to the conclusion that there was not a moral or social duty in L to make this communication to Mrs W such as to make the occasion privileged, and that there must be a new trial so far as it relates to the claim for publication of a libel to Mrs W. The communications to S and B being made on a privileged occasion, there must be a new trial of the issue as to malice defeating the privilege. There must also be a new trial of the complaint as to publication to Mrs W, the occasion being held not to be privileged ...'

Kearns and others v General Council of the Bar
[2003] 2 All ER 534 Court of Appeal

A barrister sought guidance from the Bar Council. In response S (the head of the Bar Council's Professional Standards and Legal Services Department) sent a circular letter to all heads of chambers, senior clerks and practice managers. In this circular S stated that the claimants were not solicitors and that it would be improper for a barrister to accept work from them unless certain specified conditions were satisfied. This was an error of fact and two days later, S sent a letter of apology in which he corrected the mistake and attributed it to administrative error. The claimants sued in defamation and the Bar Council relied on qualified privilege. The claimants did not allege malice.

Relying on the approach of Lord Nicholls in *Reynolds v Times Newspapers Ltd* (below) the claimants stated that the Bar Council had not investigated thoroughly and thus were in breach of the privilege. The Court of Appeal held that in communications between those in an established relationship, the adequacy of investigation and verification went to the issue of malice, not to the issue of whether or not the occasion of the communication had been privileged. Such instances were to be distinguished from those where no such relationship had been established and the communication was between strangers (or had been volunteered otherwise than by reference to their relationship). In this case the

Bar Council had written its circular to those with whom it was in an established relationship requiring the flow of free and frank communications. Accordingly the letter attracted qualified privilege.

Simon Brown LJ: '...

[30] The argument, as it seems to me, has been much bedevilled by the use of the terms "common interest" and "duty-interest" for all the world as if these are clear-cut categories and any particular case is instantly recognisable as falling within one or other of them. It also seems to me surprising and unsatisfactory that privilege should be thought to attach more readily to communications made in the service of one's own interests than in the discharge of a duty – as at first blush this distinction would suggest. To my mind an altogether more helpful categorisation is to be found by distinguishing between on the one hand cases where the communicator and the communicatee are in an existing and established relationship (irrespective of whether within that relationship the communications between them relate to reciprocal interests or reciprocal duties or a mixture of both) and on the other hand cases where no such relationship has been established and the communication is between strangers (or at any rate is volunteered otherwise than by reference to their relationship). This distinction I can readily understand and it seems to me no less supportable on the authorities than that for which [counsel for the Bar Council] contends. Once the distinction is made in this way, moreover, it becomes to my mind understandable that the law should attach privilege more readily to communications within an existing relationship than to those between strangers. The latter present particular problems. I find it unsurprising that many of the cases where the court has been divided or where the defence has been held to fail have been cases of communications by strangers. *Coxhead v Richards* was just such a case. As Coltman J, one of those who held that privilege did not attach, observed:

> "The duty of not slandering your neighbour on insufficient grounds, is so clear, that a violation of that duty ought not to be sanctioned *in the case of voluntary communications*, except under circumstances of great urgency and gravity." (my emphasis.)

[31] *Stuart v Bell* was another case where the court was divided. There, of course, Mr Bell was to be regarded as a stranger for the purposes of the communication sued upon since he no longer had any interest in the matter; his was a voluntary communication. *Watt v Longsdon* involved communications of both sorts ...

[32] One searches the authorities in vain for comparable statements in the context of communications made between those in an established relationship which, by its very nature, involves reciprocal interests and/or duties ...

[35] I must come at this stage to a particular authority upon which [counsel for the claimant] places very considerable reliance, *De Buse v McCarty*, an authority not cited to the judge below. The facts there were that the defendant town clerk had

sent out a notice convening a meeting of the borough council to consider a committee report about the loss of petrol from one of the council's depots. The report was attached to the notice which was posted at the town hall and in public libraries. The plaintiffs complained that the report was defamatory of them. The defendants pleaded that the publication was made on a privileged occasion on the ground that there was a common interest between the council and the ratepayers in the subject matter of the words complained of. The Court of Appeal, reversing the decision of the judge, held that the defence failed, because –

> "there could be no common interest, as far as I can see, between the council and the ratepayers to have what, in the circumstances, was only a preliminary stage in the investigation communicated to the ratepayers in the form in which it was communicated".

[36] Earlier in his judgment Lord Greene MR had cited Lord Atkinson's speech in *Adam v Ward* and continued:

> "I prefer that language – referring to an interest or duty to make a communication – to language, sometimes found, which refers to an interest in the subject-matter of the communication. The latter phrase appears to me to be vague and leave uncertain what degree of relevance to a particular subject-matter the communication has to bear. Adopting the language of Lord Atkinson, we have to consider, first, what interest or duty the council had to communicate to the ratepayers the report of a committee which the council was proposing to consider ... I cannot see that it can possibly be said that the council was under any duty to make that communication to the ratepayers."

So too here, submits [counsel for the claimant] S's circular letter to the Bar was likewise premature because in this case, as in *De Buse v McCarty*, there had been no investigation or verification of the complaint.

[37] The argument based on *De Buse v McCarty* is to my mind fallacious. What S was here communicating was indeed the Bar Council's conclusion upon the request for guidance it had received. Whether it had been adequately investigated is another matter. That, however, as Lord Diplock explained in *Horrocks v Lowe*, in the context of an established relationship goes to malice rather than whether the occasion of the communication is privileged. The parallel with *De Buse v McCarty* would be if the Bar Council had circularised the barrister's request for guidance (and the implicit charge against the appellants) before ruling upon it. That they were entitled, indeed bound, to give a ruling, cannot be in doubt. Nor, in my judgment, can it be doubted that they did so in the context of an established relationship between the Bar Council and the Bar which, with regard to relevant communications between them, must necessarily attract qualified privilege.

[38] In his judgment below, Eady J referred to the facts of *Stuart v Bell* and continued:

"[33] ... This again was a case which turned upon duty rather than an established personal or business relationship. This, submits [counsel for the Bar Council] in my judgment correctly, is why the court was concerned to evaluate the quality of the information. It was relevant to go into the specific information, rather than confining the inquiry to the broad subject matter of the conversation, in order to decide whether a specific duty had arisen. [Counsel for the claimant] asks rhetorically why should one evaluate the quality of information for a social or moral duty case, as in *Reynolds v Times Newspapers Ltd* or *Stuart v Bell* for example, but not in cases of a common and corresponding interest? The answer to that question is, it seems to me, that it has long been the policy of the law to protect persons in certain kinds of relationship with one another, and indeed to encourage in such cases free and frank communications in what is perceived to be the general interest of society. In those cases, one does not need to assess the interest of society afresh in each case. We all need to know where we stand. In this area the law was thought to be settled, on the basis that the balance would fairly be struck if liability in such situations was confined to those cases where the occasion of communication was abused — in the sense that malice could be established. Nothing short of malice would undermine the law's protection."

[39] Subject only to the point I have already made about preferring for my part a distinction between cases depending on whether they do or do not involve an existing relationship rather than a distinction between common interest cases and those involving duty-interest, I agree with the approach taken in that paragraph. It matters not at all whether S and the Bar Council are properly to be regarded as owing a duty to the Bar to rule on questions of professional conduct such as arose here, or as sharing with the Bar a common interest in maintaining professional standards. What matters is that the relationship between them is an established one which plainly requires the flow of free and frank communications in both directions on all questions relevant to the discharge of the Bar Council's functions

...

[42] I would not wish to part from this appeal without expressing some considerable sympathy for these appellants. Were this to have been a media publication and *Reynolds v Times Newspapers Ltd* therefore to apply, there could be no question of qualified privilege attaching. And the *Reynolds* approach, one reflects, attaches on occasion to publications circulating no more widely and hardly more generally than in the present case ... The law with regard to non-media publications, however, is different. Here, as Lord Diplock observed in *Horrocks v Lowe*, a man's right to "vindicate his reputation against calumny" gives way to "the competing public interest in permitting men to communicate frankly and freely with one another ... if they have acted in good faith in compliance with a legal or moral duty or in protection of a legitimate interest" and in these cases "the law demands no more" than that the defendant shall have honestly believed what he said ...

[43] I would dismiss this appeal.'

Comment

(1) Qualified privilege may be accorded either by statute or common law. As to the former see e.g. the Parliamentary Papers Act 1840 and the Defamation Act 1996, s 15 and Sch 1. The Defamation Act 1996 extends the application of absolute privilege both in respect of the relevant courts and the media through which the reports are published (s 14). Section 15 and Schs 1 and 2 also extend the benefit of qualified privilege in regards both to the bodies, reports of whose proceedings are protected, and the media through which those reports are published. In respect of parliamentary matters the restrictive rules developed by the common law in cases such as *Prebble v Television New Zealand* have been reversed by s 13 of the 1996 Act.

In *McCartan Turkington Breen (a firm) v Times Newspapers Ltd* the House of Lords had occasion to examine the scope of the qualified privilege attaching to newspaper reports of public meetings. In 1990 Private Clegg was manning an army checkpoint in Belfast when he fired at a car which drove through the checkpoint. His shots killed two people in the car. He was convicted of murder and appeals against conviction were dismissed. The conviction was a matter of great controversy and the 'Clegg Committee' was formed to campaign for his release and acquittal. The Committee used the media to enlist public support for its campaign. In January 1995 the Clegg Committee organised a large press conference at the home of one of the committee members and notices of the press conference were sent to the Press Association and to individual news-papers, television and radio organisations throughout Britain. Around 50 to 80 people attended the press conference, including reporters from most national newspapers, some local papers and television and radio journalists. There were a few members of the public present and access to the meeting was not restricted in any way. At the meeting a press release was distributed, statements were made and questions were answered. Defamatory statements were made concerning the solicitors' defence of Private Clegg and the next day *The Times* reported those statements.

The newspaper relied on the defence of qualified privilege on the basis that there had been a fair and accurate report by a newspaper of the proceedings at a public meeting in the United Kingdom. The relevant law was contained in s 7 and para 9 of the Defamation Act (Northern Ireland) 1955 (but is identical to the law in England & Wales). The House of Lords distinguished the role of the press in investigative reporting, which might be protected by qualified privilege under *Reynolds v Times Newspapers*, and its role in reporting events. The proper interpretation of the statute had to be, said Lord Steyn, 'in the light of the legal norms of the contemporary legal system. And freedom of expression is a basic norm of our constitution'.

The House of Lords held that (1) the newspaper report was privileged because, in the light of modern reporting, the press conference was a public meeting within the Act and members of the press were to be regarded as either members of the public or the eyes and ears of the public; (2) the press release had been part of the material communicated at a public meeting to those attending and could be reported as part of the proceedings even if not read out; but (3) anything said by the organisers to individual members of the press after the press conference would not be part of the public meeting unless they in effect repeated what had been said at the meeting.

Lord Bingham explored the matter in some detail. He emphasised the critical role of the press and observed that:

'The proper functioning of a modern participatory democracy requires that the media be free, active, professional and enquiring. For this reason the courts, here and elsewhere, have recognised the cardinal importance of press freedom and the need for any restriction on that freedom to be proportionate and no more than is necessary to promote the legitimate object of the restriction.'

He concluded by saying that:

'Everything points towards the public character of the press conference in issue here. The object was to stimulate public pressure to rectify what the committee as promoters of the conference saw as a grave miscarriage of justice, and publicity was the essence of the exercise. A general invitation to attend was issued to the press. While the attendance of other members of the public was not solicited, nor was admission denied to anyone, journalist or non journalist. Both journalists and other members of the public in fact attended in significant numbers. A public meeting need not involve participation, or the opportunity for participation, by those attending it, but here the opportunity to ask questions and make state-ments was extended to those attending. Save that the meeting was held at Lord St. Oswald's home, there was nothing whatever private about it ...'

Lord Steyn observed pithily:

'In my view the test must be the objective of the organisers of a meeting. It is sufficient to say that when they organise a general press conference to which the media, or an interested sector of the media, are invited in order to publicise to the public at large what the organisers regard as ideas of public concern the requirement of para 9 that the meeting must be public as opposed to a private one is satisfied. On the facts pertaining to the highly organised press conference in the present case this test is amply satisfied.'

(2) The overlap between qualified privilege and negligence was extensively reviewed in *Spring v Guardian Assurance plc*, see p 25. As a result of that case it is now clear that the defence of qualified privilege in respect of references still

remains, albeit that there is the potential for the giver of a reference to be liable in negligence. In *Spring v Guardian Assurance plc* the plaintiff would not have succeeded in defamation; he would not have been able to defeat the claim of qualified privilege. He had failed to establish the malice of the defendant as part of his action in malicious falsehood. It is the jury's function to decide if there has been actual malice.

(3)   Privilege attaches to the occasion and not to the statement. For a case where two parties joined in a statement but only one was protected by qualified privilege, see *Watts v Times Newspapers.*

(4)   Qualified privilege may be defeated by malice; that is what concerned the House of Lords in *Horrocks v Lowe*. The plaintiff, a councillor, claimed that he had been defamed by the defendant, another councillor, at a council meeting. It was held that the occasion was protected by qualified privilege and that the defendant had not been motivated by malice. As to malice Lord Diplock said:

'But indifference to the truth of what he publishes is not to be equated with carelessness, impulsiveness or irrationality in arriving at a positive belief that it is true. The freedom of speech protected by the law of qualified privilege may be availed of by all sorts and conditions of men. In affording to them immunity from suit if they have acted in good faith in compliance with a legal or moral duty or in protection of a legitimate interest the law must take them as it finds them. In ordinary life it is rare indeed for people to form their beliefs by a process of logical deduction from facts ascertained by a rigorous search for all available evidence and a judicious assessment of its probative value. In greater or in less degree according to their temperaments, their training, their intelligence, they are swayed by prejudice, rely on intuition instead of reasoning, leap to conclusions on inadequate evidence and fail to recognise the cogency of material which might cast doubt on the validity of the conclusions they reach. But despite the imperfection of the mental process by which the belief is arrived at it may still be "honest", ie a positive belief that the conclusions they have reached are true. The law demands no more.

Even a positive belief in the truth of what is published on a privileged occasion – which is presumed unless the contrary is proved – may not be sufficient to negative express malice if it can be proved that the defendant misused the occasion for some purpose other than that for which the privilege is accorded by the law. The commonest case is where the dominant motive which actuates the defendant is not a desire to perform the relevant duty or to protect the relevant interest, but to give vent to his personal spite or ill-will towards the person he defames. If this be proved, then even positive belief in the truth of what is published will not enable the defamer to avail himself of the protection of the privilege to which he would otherwise have been entitled. There may be instances of improper motives which destroy the privilege apart from personal spite. A defendant's dominant motive may have been to obtain some private advantage unconnected with the duty or the interest which constitutes the reason for the privilege. If so, he loses the benefit of the privilege despite his positive belief that what he said or wrote was true.

Judges and juries should, however, be very slow to draw the inference that a defendant was so far actuated by improper motives as to deprive them of the protection of the privilege unless they are satisfied that he did not believe that what he said or wrote was true or that he was indifferent to its truth or falsity.'

Reynolds v Times Newspapers Ltd and others
[1999] 4 All ER 609 House of Lords

In November 1994 there was a political crisis in Dublin and Mr Reynolds resigned as Taoiseach (prime minister) of Ireland and leader of the Fianna Fáil party. His reasons for resignation were of public significance and interest in the United Kingdom because he was one of the chief architects of the Northern Ireland peace process. Mr Reynolds announced his resignation in the Dáil (the House of Representatives) of the Irish Parliament on Thursday, 17 November 1994. On the following Sunday, 20 November, *The Sunday Times* published in its British mainland edition a one-page article entitled 'Goodbye gombeen man' and sub-headed 'Why a fib too far proved fatal for the political career of Ireland's peacemaker and Mr Fixit'.

Mr Reynolds objected to the article and sued in libel. He pleaded that the sting of the article was that he had deliberately and dishonestly misled the Dáil on Tuesday, 15 November 1994 by suppressing vital information. Further, that he had deliberately and dishonestly misled his coalition cabinet colleagues, especially Mr Spring, the Tanaiste (deputy prime minister) and minister for foreign affairs, by withholding this information and had lied to them about when the information had come into his possession.

The jury decided that the defamatory allegation of which Mr Reynolds complained was not true and the defence of justification failed. The jury decided that neither the author nor the editor were acting maliciously in writing and publishing the words complained of. So, if the occasion was privileged – and that was a question for the judge – the defence of qualified privilege would succeed. Despite their rejection of the defence of justification, the jury awarded Mr Reynolds no damages. The judge substituted an award of one penny. In the light of this award, costs were the only remaining issue. On this matter the defence of qualified privilege was still a live question. If this defence were to be available to the defendants, they would have a complete defence to the action, and the judge would have ordered Mr Reynolds to pay the defendants' costs of the action. The judge then heard submissions on the question of qualified privilege. The defendants unsuccessfully argued for a wide qualified privilege at common law for 'political speech'. The judge ruled that publication of the article was not privileged.

Mr Reynolds appealed, contending that the judge had generally misdirected the jury. The defendants cross-appealed only on the qualified privilege point. The Court of Appeal concluded that the misdirections denied Mr Reynolds a fair trial and ordered a new trial. The Court of Appeal also held that the defendants would not be permitted to rely on qualified privilege at the retrial.

The issues before the House of Lords were: (1) Was there a generic qualified privilege extending to publication by a newspaper to the public at large of information including assertions of fact concerning government and political matters which affect the people of the United Kingdom? (2) If not, then was the Court of Appeal correct to develop 'a circumstantial test'? (3) If not, then what is the applicable law regarding qualified privilege in respect of political speech containing a defamatory and factually false statement which was honestly believed to be true?

The House of Lords held that there was no generic privilege nor a circumstantial test, but the appropriate test for the existence of qualified privilege was the two-fold test of duty and interest taking into account all the circumstances. By a majority of three to two, on the facts of the case, the appeal was dismissed but there would be a re-trial. Since the Court of Appeal had directed itself correctly its discretion could not be interfered with and at the retrial qualified privilege could not be raised by the newspaper.

Lord Steyn:'... Important issues regarding the reconciliation of the colliding right of free speech and the right to reputation need to be considered in the light of the new legal landscape. In what was at the time regarded as a classic direction on fair comment to the jury Diplock J in *Silkin v Beaverbrook Newspapers Ltd* observed:

> "In the first place, every man, whether he is in public life or not, is entitled not to have lies told about him; and by that is meant that one is not entitled to make statements of fact about a person which are untrue and which redound to his discredit, that is to say, tend to lower him in the estimation of right-thinking men."

The present case involves a defamatory and factually false statement which the newspaper honestly believed to be true. If the observation of Diplock J is taken not only as the starting point but as reflecting an absolute rule, there would be no room for any qualified privilege in respect of political speech. But the law has not stood still.

[Lord Steyn considered *A-G v Guardian Newspapers Ltd (No 2)* and *Derbyshire County Council v Times Newspaper Ltd* which decided that English Law was entirely consistent with the requirements of article 10 of the ECHR. He referred to the commencement date of the Human Rights Act 1998, and continued:]

The new landscape is of great importance inasmuch as it provides the taxonomy against which the question before the House must be considered. The starting point is now the right of freedom of expression, a right based on a constitutional or higher legal order foundation. Exceptions to freedom of expression must be justified as being necessary in a democracy. In other words, freedom of expression is the rule and regulation of speech is the exception requiring justification. The existence and width of any exception can only be justified if it is underpinned by a pressing social need. These are fundamental principles governing the balance to be struck between freedom of expression and defamation ...

ISSUE (1): GENERIC QUALIFIED PRIVILEGE AND POLITICAL SPEECH

Counsel for the newspaper did not invite your Lordships to develop English law in line with the landmark case of *New York Times Co v Sullivan*. The United States Supreme Court unanimously held that a public official could not succeed in an action for libel without proving that the defendant was actuated by actual malice, that is, at least with a reckless disregard of the truth. The question was whether a particular advertisement forfeited constitutional protection by reason of the falsity of some of the factual statements and the alleged defamation of a public official. The Supreme Court declared the relevant state law unconstitutional ...

Counsel submitted that the House should recognise a qualified privilege extending to the publication by a newspaper to the public at large of factual information, opinions and arguments concerning government and political matters that affect the people of the United Kingdom. For convenience, I will call this a generic qualified privilege of political speech. A distinctive feature of political speech published by a newspaper is that it is communicated to a large audience. And this characteristic must be kept in mind in weighing the arguments in the present case. It is further essential not to lose sight of the factual framework in which the question arises, namely a defamatory and factually incorrect statement which the newspaper believed to be true.

It is now necessary to explain what is meant by a generic qualified privilege. It is to be contrasted with each case being considered in the light of its own particular circumstances, that is, in an ad hoc manner, in the light of the concrete facts of the case, and balancing in each case the gravity of the damage to the plaintiff's reputation against the value of publication on the particular occasion. A generic privilege, on the other hand, uses the technique of applying the privilege to a category or categories of cases. An example is the rule in the *Sullivan* case, which requires proof of malice in all defamation actions by public officials and public figures. In the present case counsel for the newspaper argues for a generic test not applicable to a category of victim (such as public figures) but dependent on the subject matter (political speech).

This is a branch of law in which common law courts have arrived at sharply divergent solutions. In the *Sullivan* case the United States Supreme Court upheld a public figure defence. In *Lange v Australian Broadcasting Corporation* the Australian High Court allowed a qualified privilege of political speech subject to a requirement of due care. In impressive and valuable judgments Elias J (now Chief Justice) and the Court of Appeal of New Zealand allowed a generic defence of free speech, the rationale of the decisions being policy considerations applicable to New Zealand: *Lange v Atkinson*. And in *Reynolds v Times Newspaper Ltd* the Court of Appeal enunciated a circumstantial test depending substantially on the source of the information. There are at stake powerful competing arguments of policy. They pull in different directions. It is a hard case in which it is unrealistic to say that there is only one right answer. And in considering the decisions in other jurisdictions it is right to take into account that cultural differences have played an important role.

Counsel for Mr Reynolds submitted that a generic qualified privilege of political speech, defeasible only by proof of malice or reckless disregard of the truth, would make the prospect of suing a newspaper which published defamatory and false allegations about a politician without checking the facts unduly difficult. On the other hand, counsel for the newspaper argued that in the case of an unchecked publication alleging grave misconduct the newspaper would be at significant risk of an adverse jury verdict on the ground of recklessness. He submitted that in the absence of a generic qualified privilege investigative journalism into political matters is inadequately protected. He argued that the generic test will result in more predictable decisions. And he emphasised that it would be consistent with the spirit of the new legal landscape to develop the law in this way ...

On balance two particular factors have persuaded me to reject the generic test. First, the rule and practice in England is not to compel a newspaper to reveal its sources: see s 10 of the Contempt of Court Act 1981; RSC, Ord 82, r 6; and *Goodwin v United Kingdom*. By contrast a plaintiff in the United States is entitled to a pre-trial enquiry into the sources of the story and editorial decision-making: *Herbert v Lando*. Without such information a plaintiff suing for defamation in England will be substantially handicapped. Counsel for the newspaper observed that the House could recommend a reform of the procedural rule. This is an unsatisfactory basis to embark on a radical development of the law. Given the procedural restrictions in England I regard the recognition of a generic qualified privilege of political speech as likely to make it unacceptably difficult for a victim of defamatory and false allegations of fact to prove reckless disregard of the truth. Secondly, a test expressed in terms of a category of cases, such as political speech, is at variance with the jurisprudence of the European Court of Human Rights which in cases of competing rights and interests requires a balancing exercise in the light of the concrete facts of each case. While there is as yet no decision directly in point, it seems to me that Professor John Fleming is right in saying that the basic approach of the European Court of Human Rights has been close to the German approach by insisting on individual evaluation of each case rather than categories:

"Libel and Constitutional Free Speech" in *Essays for Patrick Atiyah* (ed) Cane and Stapleton (1991) p. 333 at pp. 337 and 345. Our inclination ought to be towards the approach that prevails in the jurisprudence on the Convention. In combination these two factors make me sceptical of the value of introducing a rule dependent on general categorisation, with the attendant sacrifice of individual justice in particular cases.

I would answer question (1) by saying that there is no generic qualified privilege of political speech in England.

ISSUE (2): SOUNDNESS OF THE CIRCUMSTANTIAL TEST

My Lords, it is important to appreciate that the judgment of the Court of Appeal marked a development of English law in favour of freedom of expression. In the context of political speech the judgment recognised a qualified privilege, dependent on the particular circumstance of the case, provided that three requirements are fulfilled. The first and second are the familiar requirements of duty and interest. The Court of Appeal then stated a third and separate requirement. The passage in the judgment reads as follows:

> "Were the nature, status and source of the material, and the circumstances of the publication, such that the publication should in the public interest be protected in the absence of proof of express malice? (We call this the circumstantial test.)..."

... In my view such a development would involve a radical re-writing of our law of defamation. Contrary to the submissions of counsel I also do not think it is a satisfactory way of redressing the imbalance between freedom of speech and defamation in England. I would reject this argument ...

ISSUE (3): THE ALTERNATIVE TESTS OF DUTY AND INTEREST

If both the generic test and the circumstantial test are rejected, as I have done, the only sensible course is to go back to the traditional twofold test of duty and interest. These tests are flexible enough to embrace, depending on the occasion and the particular circumstances, a qualified privilege in respect of political speech published at large.

The critical question is then to decide what requirements should be imposed in respect of qualified privilege in the context of political speech. In my view the passages in the Court of Appeal judgment which I have cited should not be elevated to legal requirements. Those passages, with a distinction drawn between official and "unofficial sources", and between "a government press release" and "the statement by a political opponent", could create the impression that if information is not obtained from a *prima facie* authoritative source, a privileged occasion does not arise. A rule, principle or approach that in considering a plea of qualified privilege of political speech greater weight should be given to what is said on behalf of the government than what is said on behalf of the opposition, other political parties or pressure groups is unacceptable in our democracy. And I am confident that the Court of Appeal did not intend to make such a ruling.

Counsel for Mr Reynolds did not invite your Lordships to endorse the observations of the Court of Appeal. Instead he submitted that in the context of political speech qualified privilege must always fulfil as part of the duty test three legal requirements: (1) that the occasion must be one in respect of which it can fairly be said that it is in the public interest that the information should be published; and (2) that a report which "failed to report the other side" would always fail the test; (3) that there is a burden on a publisher of a report to prove that there is a cogent reason why it should be excused in the particular circumstances from justifying the truth of the assertion.

My Lords, the first proposition involves nothing radical or extravagant. It builds on the web of existing law. I am content to accept that it should be the governing principle. The second proposition put forward by counsel as an independent legal requirement is implausible. A failure to report the other side will often be evidence tending to show that the occasion ought not to be protected by qualified privilege. But it would not necessarily always be so, e.g. when the victim's explanation is unintelligible or plain nonsense. This was recognised in the Australian *Lange* case. The suggested strict requirement runs counter both to the pragmatic approach of the common law and a test dependent on particular circumstances. The third proposition overlaps with the first requirement. But as expressed it would emasculate the qualified privilege of political speech. I would reject it.

Returning now to the requirement that the occasion must be one in respect of which it can fairly be said to be in the public interest that the information about political matters should be published, I would accept that it may be objected that this requirement is imprecise. But this is a corner of the law which could do with the minimum of legal rules. And what is in the public interest is a well-known and serviceable concept. It will, of course, have to be given practical content. Inevitably the question will arise in concrete cases whether the newspaper was entitled to rely on the information it had obtained before publishing. This issue can be accommodated within the test of an occasion in the public interest warranting publication. In my view such an approach complies with the requirement of legal certainty. And in practice the issue will have to be determined on the whole of the evidence. If a newspaper stands on the rule protecting its sources, it may run the risk of what the judge and jury will make of the gap in the evidence.

The context in which the qualified privilege of free speech should be applied is all important. It was said by counsel for the newspaper that the English courts have not yet recognised that the press has a general duty to inform the public of political matters and that the public has a right to be so informed. If there is any doubt on the point, this is the occasion for the House to settle the matter. It is an open space in the law which can be filled by the courts. It is true that in our system the media have no specially privileged position not shared by individual citizens. On the other hand, it is necessary to recognise the "vital public watchdog role of the press" as a practical matter: see *Goodwin v The United Kingdom*. The role of the press, and its duty, was well described by the European Court of Human Rights in *Castells v Spain* in the following terms:

> " ... the pre-eminent role of the press in a state governed by the rule of law must not be forgotten. Although it must not overstep various bounds set, *inter alia*, for the prevention of disorder and the protection of the reputation of others, it is nevertheless incumbent on it to impart information and ideas on political questions and on other matters of public interest.
>
> Freedom of the press affords the public one of the best means of discovering and forming an opinion of the ideas and attitudes of their political leaders. In particular, it gives politicians the opportunity to reflect and comment on the preoccupations of public opinion; it thus enables everyone to participate in the free political debate which is at the very core of the concept of a democratic society."

In *De Haes Gijsels v Belgium* the European Court of Human Rights again emphasised that the press plays an essential role in a democratic society. The court trenchantly observed:

> "It is incumbent on the press to impart information and ideas of public interest. Not only does the press have the task of imparting such information and ideas: the public also has a right to receive them."

This principle must be the foundation of our law on qualified privilege of political speech.

The correct approach to the line between permissible and impermissible political speech was indicated by the European Court of Human Rights in *Lingens v Austria:*

> "The limits of acceptable criticism are accordingly wider as regards a politician as such than as regards a private individual. Unlike the latter, the former inevitably and knowingly lays himself open to close scrutiny of his every word and deed by both journalists and the public at large, and he must consequently display a greater degree of tolerance. No doubt art 10(2) enables the reputation of others – that is to say, of all individuals – to be protected, and this protection extends to politicians too, even when they are not acting in their private capacity; but in such cases the requirements of such protection have to be weighed in relation to the interests of open discussion of political issues."

Implicit in that *dictum* is the distinction that speech about political matters has a higher value than speech about private lives of politicians ... Moreover, it will always be necessary to take into account the dynamics of the role of the press and that "news is a perishable commodity and to delay its publication, even for a short period, may well deprive it of all its value and interest": *The Sunday Times v United Kingdom (No 2)*. If the matter is approached in this liberal way the balance in our law between freedom of information and the right to reputation should fulfil the Convention requirement of being necessary in a democracy.

In the result I would uphold qualified privilege of political speech, based on a weighing of the particular circumstances of the case.'

Comment

(1) Although Lord Steyn dissented as to the application of the law to the particular case, and in particular as to the way in which the Court of Appeal had directed itself, his assessment of the relevant principles is consistent with the majority of the House of Lords.

(2) In a summary which is proving influential in shaping the development of the law, Lord Nicholls concluded his elaborate discussion of the law by saying:

'My conclusion is that the established common law approach to misstatements of fact remains essentially sound. The common law should not develop "political information" as a new "subject-matter" category of qualified privilege, whereby the publication of all such information would attract qualified privilege, whatever the circumstances. That would not provide adequate protection for reputation. Moreover, it would be unsound in principle to distinguish political discussion from discussion of other matters of serious public concern. The elasticity of the common law principle enables interference with freedom of speech to be confined to what is necessary in the circumstances of the case. This elasticity enables the court to give appropriate weight, in today's conditions, to the importance of freedom of expression by the media on all matters of public concern.

Depending on the circumstances, the matters to be taken into account include the following. The comments are illustrative only.

1. The seriousness of the allegation. The more serious the charge, the more the public is misinformed and the individual harmed, if the allegation is not true. 2. The nature of the information, and the extent to which the subject-matter is a matter of public concern. 3. The source of the information. Some informants have no direct knowledge of the events. Some have their own axes to grind, or are being paid for their stories. 4. The steps taken to verify the information. 5. The status of the information. The allegation may have already been the subject of an investigation which commands respect. 6. The urgency of the matter. News is often a

perishable commodity. 7. Whether comment was sought from the plaintiff. He may have information others do not possess or have not disclosed. An approach to the plaintiff will not always be necessary. 8. Whether the article contained the gist of the plaintiff's side of the story. 9. The tone of the article. A newspaper can raise queries or call for an investigation. It need not adopt allegations as statements of fact. 10. The circumstances of the publication, including the timing.

This list is not exhaustive. The weight to be given to these and any other relevant factors will vary from case to case. Any disputes of primary fact will be a matter for the jury, if there is one. The decision on whether, having regard to the admitted or proved facts, the publication was subject to qualified privilege is a matter for the judge. This is the established practice and seems sound. A balancing operation is better carried out by a judge in a reasoned judgment than by a jury. Over time, a valuable corpus of case law will be built up.

In general, a newspaper's unwillingness to disclose the identity of its sources should not weigh against it. Further, it should always be remembered that journalists act without the benefit of the clear light of hindsight. Matters which are obvious in retrospect may have been far from clear in the heat of the moment. Above all, the court should have particular regard to the importance of freedom of expression. The press discharges vital functions as a bloodhound as well as a watchdog. The court should be slow to conclude that a publication was not in the public interest and, therefore, the public had no right to know, especially when the information is in the field of political discussion. Any lingering doubts should be resolved in favour of publication.'

Loutchansky v Times Newspapers Ltd and others (No 2) [2002] 1 All ER 652 Court of Appeal

In 1999, the defendant published two articles alleging that the claimant ran a major Russian criminal organisation and was involved in both money-laundering and the smuggling of nuclear weapons. Both articles were later posted on the newspaper's website. In December 1999 the claimant commenced proceedings for libel against the newspaper's publishers, its editor and two of its journalists. In December 2000 the claimant brought a second action for libel against the defendants in respect of the continued Internet publication of the two articles on the newspaper's website after February 2000, the date of the defence in the first action. The Internet archive site did not attempt to qualify the original stories in any way, e.g. by suggesting that the contents were subject to dispute. The defendants relied on the defence of qualified privilege and the claim that the limitation period should run only from the date of the original publication.

The Court of Appeal
both the original newspa~
accessible on the Internet, a~ scope of qualified privilege in respect of
and republication amounted to a~ the archived copies of the newspaper
ate restriction on the freedom of exp~ not the rule that each publication
Act 1998. ~se of action was a disproportion-
~ranteed by the Human Rights

Lord Phillips: '...

[35] ... Once *Reynolds* privilege is recognised, as it
jurisprudential creature from the traditional form of privileg~ be, as a different
the particular nature of the "interest" and "duty" which under~ which it sprang,
be understood. ~n more easily

[36] The interest is that of the public in a modern democracy in free ex~ ssion
and, more particularly, in the promotion of a free and vigorous press to keep ~~
public informed. The vital importance of this interest has been identified and
emphasised time and again in recent cases and needs no restatement here. The
corresponding duty on the journalist (and equally his editor) is to play his proper
role in discharging that function. His task is to behave as a responsible journalist.
He can have no duty to publish unless he is acting responsibly any more than the
public has an interest in reading whatever may be published irresponsibly. That is
why in this class of case the question whether the publisher has behaved
responsibly is necessarily and intimately bound up with the question whether the
defence of qualified privilege arises. Unless the publisher is acting responsibly
privilege cannot arise. That is not the case with regard to the more conventional
situations in which qualified privilege arises. A person giving a reference or
reporting a crime need not act responsibly: his communication will be privileged
subject only to relevance and malice.

[37] Consider what Lord Diplock said in *Horrocks v Lowe* [see p 773]:

[38] *Reynolds* privilege could not arise in such circumstances: "carelessness,
impulsiveness or irrationality" would cost a journalist dear in the evaluation of his
claim to privilege under several of the *Reynolds* factors, perhaps most notably
factors 3, 4, 6, 7 and 8. As Lord Nicholls said:

"[It] is for the court to have regard to all the circumstances when deciding
whether the publication of particular material was privileged because of its
value to the public. Its value to the public depends upon its quality as well as
its subject matter. This solution has the merit of elasticity ... It can be applied
appropriately to all information published by a newspaper, whatever its
source or origin."

[39] This court in *Al-Fagih*'s case adopted the approach suggested by Lord Hobhouse of Woodborough in *Reynolds'* case, namely to ask: " ... what it is in the public

interest that the public should kno... the publisher could properly
consider that he was under a publi... the public".
[40] ... In the final analysis it... the court, not the journalist, to decide
whether he was acting resp... appears clearly from several passages in
Reynolds' case: in rejecting t...per's commended "reliance upon the ethics of
professional journalism"...icholls referred to "the sad reality ... that the
overall handling of th...ers by the national press, with its own commercial
interests to serve, ...ot always command general confidence". Lord Cooke
suggested that "...ice of libel litigation is apt to generate a suspicion that" the
restriction of f...tation...m of speech thought necessary to give reasonable protection
to personal...n tends rather to chill the publication of untruths than of
material...n may be true but cannot be proved to be true. Lord Hope of
Craigh...too spoke of situations in which the "chilling" effect of the law "is a
nec...ary protection for the individual". Perhaps one need look no further than
..rd Nicholls' dictum in Reynolds' case:

> "The common law does not seek to set a higher standard than that of responsible journalism, a standard the media themselves espouse. An incursion into press freedom which goes no further than this would not seem to be excessive or disproportionate."

[41]   In deciding in any given case whether the standard of responsible journalism has been satisfied, the following considerations are likely to feature prominently in the court's thinking. (i) If the publication is held privileged, that, to all intents and purposes, will provide the publishers with a complete defence. In this class of case, as already observed, a finding of privilege will effectively pre-empt a finding of malice. Lord Nicholls described malice as "notoriously difficult to prove", Lord Cooke as "a dubious safeguard", and Lord Hope as "very difficult, if not impossible, [to prove] if the sources of the information cannot be identified". Accordingly, if the defence is established, that, as Gray J pointed out [at first instance] has "the effect of denying any remedy, whether by way of compensation or other vindication, to a person who has been libelled". The damaging consequences of that, not merely for the aggrieved individual but for society at large, are highlighted by Lord Nicholls in Reynolds' case:

> "Reputation is an integral and important part of the dignity of the individual. It also forms the basis of many decisions in a democratic society which are fundamental to its well-being: whom to employ or work for, whom to promote, whom to do business with or to vote for. Once besmirched by an unfounded allegation in a national newspaper, a reputation can be damaged for ever, especially if there is no opportunity to vindicate one's reputation. When this happens, society as well as the individual is the loser. For it should not be supposed that protection of reputation is a matter of importance only to the affected individual and his family. Protection of reputation is conducive to the public good. It is in the public interest that the reputation of public figures should not be debased falsely."

(ii) Setting the standard of journalistic responsibility too low would inevitably encourage too great a readiness to publish defamatory matter. Journalists should be rigorous, not lax, in their approach. It is in the interests of the public as well as the defamed individual that, wherever possible, truths and not untruths should be told. This is in the interests of the media too: once untruths can be published with impunity, the public will cease to believe any communications, true or false. (iii) Setting the standard too high, however, would be no less damaging to society. This would deter newspapers from discharging their proper function of keeping the public informed. When determining in respect of any given article whether or not it should attract qualified privilege, the court must bear in mind the likely impact of its ruling not only upon the case in hand but also upon the media's practices generally. Qualified privilege ordinarily falls to be judged as a preliminary issue and before, therefore, the truth or falsity of the communication is established. The question to be posed is accordingly whether it was in the public interest to publish the article, true or false, rather than whether it was in the public interest to publish an untruth. Even, moreover, when the untruth of the article is established (or when, as here, it is not formally disputed), it is important to remember that the defence of qualified privilege tolerates factual inaccuracy for two purposes: first so as not to deter the publication sued upon (which might have been true); and secondly so as not to deter future publications of truthful information.

[42] [Lord Phillips analysed sections of Gray J's judgment, and concluded that the judge had applied the wrong test.]

THE INTERNET SINGLE PUBLICATION APPEAL

[57] It is a well-established principle of the English law of defamation that each individual publication of a libel gives rise to a separate cause of action, subject to its own limitation period. *Duke of Brunswick and Luneberg v Harmer* provides a striking illustration of this principle. On 19 September 1830 an article was published in the *Weekly Dispatch*. The limitation period for libel was then six years. The article defamed the Duke of Brunswick. Seventeen years after its publication an agent of the Duke purchased a back number containing the article from the *Weekly Dispatch's* office. Another copy was obtained from the British Museum. The Duke sued on those two publications. The defendant contended that the cause of action was time barred, relying on the original publication date. The Court of Queen's Bench held that the delivery of a copy of the newspaper to the plaintiff's agent constituted a separate publication in respect of which suit could be brought.

[58] In *Godfrey v Demon Internet Ltd* the respondent brought an action in defamation against the appellants who were Internet service providers. They had received and stored on their news server an article, defamatory of the respondent, which had been posted by an unknown person using another service provider. The issue was whether the appellants had a defence under s 1(1) of the Defamation Act 1996. The judge held that they did not. He observed:

"In my judgment the defendant, whenever it transmits and whenever there is transmitted from the storage of its news server a defamatory posting, publishes that posting to any subscriber to its [Internet service provider] who accesses the newsgroup containing that posting. Thus every time one of the defendant's customers accesses 'soc.culture.thai' and sees that posting defamatory of the plaintiff there is a publication to that customer."

[Lord Phillips referred to *Berezovsky v Michaels, Glouchkov v Michaels* where on a jurisdictional matter there were comments by members of the House of Lords supporting the continuation of the multiple publication rule in English Law.]

[73]   ... In our judgment the crucial question in relation to this part of the appeal is whether the appellants have made good their assertion that the rule in the *Duke of Brunswick's* case is in conflict with art 10 of the Convention because it has a chilling effect upon the freedom of expression that goes beyond what is necessary and proportionate in a democratic society for the protection of the reputation of others.

[74]   We do not accept that the rule in the *Duke of Brunswick's* case imposes a restriction on the readiness to maintain and provide access to archives that amounts to a disproportionate restriction on freedom of expression. We accept that the maintenance of archives, whether in hard copy or on the Internet, has a social utility, but consider that the maintenance of archives is a comparatively insignificant aspect of freedom of expression. Archive material is stale news and its publication cannot rank in importance with the dissemination of contemporary material. Nor do we believe that the law of defamation need inhibit the responsible maintenance of archives. Where it is known that archive material is or may be defamatory, the attachment of an appropriate notice warning against treating it as the truth will normally remove any sting from the material. ...

THE INTERNET QUALIFIED PRIVILEGE APPEAL

[77]   The judge struck out the defence of qualified privilege in the second action on the ground that he would be bound to hold that the privilege was not available ...

[79]   ... The judge considered that the republication of back numbers of *The Times* on the Internet was made in materially different circumstances from those obtaining at the time of the publication of the original hardcopy versions in September and October 1999. We agree. The failure to attach any qualifications to the articles published over the period of a year on *The Times*' website could not possibly be described as responsible journalism. We do not believe that it can be convincingly argued that the appellants had a *Reynolds* duty to publish those articles in that way without qualification. It follows that we consider that the judge was right to strike out the qualified privilege defence in the second action although not

for the primary reason that he gave for so doing. For these reasons the Internet single publication appeal is also dismissed.'

Comment

(1)   The Court of Appeal held that in deciding whether there had been a duty to publish defamatory words to the world at large, the standard to be applied was that of responsible journalism, and the Court of Appeal gave guidance as to the factors that a court should take into account in assessing this standard.

(2)   The court, in favouring the multiple publication rule, rejected the opportunity to adopt the single publication rule favoured in the United States, i.e. that the publication of defamatory matter in, for example, a newspaper gives rise to only one cause of action for libel and that the period of limitation runs from the date of publication and later sales or deliveries do not create a new cause of action.

(3)   The Court of Appeal acknowledged that once the *Reynolds* privilege attaches then it will be almost impossible for a claimant to demonstrate malice. Actual malice consists either of recklessness, i.e. not believing the statement to be true or being indifferent as to its truth, or a dominant motive of injuring the claimant. Any judge applying Lord Nicholls' ten-points factors and finding in favour of qualified privilege will have discounted the suggestion of recklessness or intention to harm (compare the comments of the courts in *GKR Karate (UK) Ltd v Yorkshire Post Newspapers Ltd* and *Al-Fagih v HH Saudi Research Marketing (UK) Ltd*).

CHAPTER 17

Vicarious liability

For policy reasons the law has decided that there may be circumstances where one person may be held responsible for the acts of another. Vicarious liability applies most commonly within the employer–employee relationship, although there are a number of other situations in which liability may arise from the acts of a person other than the tortfeasor. For examples see liability for an independent contractor in limited circumstances, p 814; liability of a Chief Officer for the acts of police officers, p 815; and *Morgans v Launchbury*, p 812. The House of Lords has recently explored vicarious liability for torts within the partnership context, see *Dubai Aluminium Co Ltd v Salaam and others*, p 802.

Generally, the question of whether an individual is an employee or an independent contractor is beyond the scope of this book. As to the circumstances when the employer will be liable, these may be judged in terms of 'time and space' and by reference to the nature of the activity. In relation to the latter, the test described in *Salmond on Torts* continues to exert its influence subject to the important critical examination of it in *Lister v Hesley Hall*, p 793.

Smith v Stages and another
[1989] 1 All ER 833 House of Lords

The plaintiff's husband, M, and a colleague, S, who were employed as peripatetic laggers, were taken from the job on which they were working in the Midlands and sent to carry out some urgent work at a power-station in Wales. They were paid a day's wages in relation to each journey (there and back) in addition to an allowance for rail fares, although there was no stipulation as to the mode of transport to be used. There was also an allowance of one day's pay for sleeping time at the end of the job. By working almost continuously for several days the two men managed to finish the work early on the morning of August Bank Holiday Monday and they set off for home in S's car. As a result of S's negligent driving the car was involved in an accident and both men were seriously injured. The House of Lords upheld the Court of Appeal's decision that S was acting in the course of his employment and that the employers were vicariously liable.

Lord Goff of Chieveley: '... I now turn to the applicable principles of law. The fundamental principle is that an employee is acting in the course of his employment when he is doing what he is employed to do, to which it is sufficient for present purposes to add, or anything which is reasonably incidental to his employment. In *Canadian Pacific Rly Co v Lockhart* (a case concerned with vicarious liability) Lord Thankerton said: "In these cases the first consideration is the ascertainment of what the servant was employed to do." This statement reflects a statement of principle by Lord Atkinson in an earlier case, *St Helens Colliery Co Ltd v Hewitson* (a workmen's compensation case), in which he said:

> "I myself have been rash enough to suggest a test – namely, that a workman is acting in the course of his employment when he is engaged 'in doing something he was employed to do'. Or what is, in other and I think better words, in effect the same thing – namely, when he is doing something in discharge of a duty to his employer, directly or indirectly, imposed upon him by his contract of service. The true ground upon which the test should be based is a duty to the employer arising out of the contract of employment, but it is to be borne in mind that the word 'employment' as here used covers and includes things belonging to or arising out of it."

As usual, it is comparatively easy to state the principle; but it is more difficult to apply it to the facts of individual cases. Even so, it is important always to keep the principle in mind.

As I have already observed, we are here concerned with a case which may be seen as one of those cases concerned with travelling to or from work. I have used guarded language in so describing it, because (as will appear) I do not consider the present case to fall strictly within that category of case. Even so, it is helpful to use the cases in that category as a starting point. We can begin with the simple proposition that, in ordinary circumstances, when a man is travelling to or from his place of work, he is not acting in the course of his employment. So a bank clerk who commutes to the City of London every day from Sevenoaks is not acting in the course of his employment when he walks across London Bridge from the station to his bank in the City. This is because he is not employed to travel from his home to the bank: he is employed to work at the bank, his place of work, and so his duty is to arrive there in time for his working day. Nice points can arise about the precise time, or place, at which he may be held to have arrived at work; but these do not trouble us in the present case. Likewise, of course, he is not acting in the course of his employment when he is travelling home after his day's work is over. If, however, a man is obliged by his employer to travel to work by means of transport provided by his employer, he may be held to be acting in the course of his employment when so doing.

These are the normal cases. There are, however, circumstances in which, when a man is travelling to (or from) a place where he is doing a job for his employer, he will be held to be acting in the course of his employment. Some of these are listed by Lord Atkin in *Blee v London and North Eastern Rly Co.* So, if a man is employed to do jobs for his employer at various places during the day, such as a man who goes from door to door canvassing for business, or who distributes goods to customers, or who services equipment like washing machines or dishwashers, he will ordinarily be held to be acting in the course of his employment when travelling from one destination to another, and may also be held to do so when travelling from his home to his first destination and home again after his last. Again, it has been held that, in certain circumstances, a man who is called out from his home at night to deal with an emergency may be acting in the course of his employment when travelling from his home to his place of work to deal with the emergency …

But how do we distinguish the cases in this category in which a man is acting in the course of his employment from those in which he is not? The answer is, I fear, that everything depends on the circumstances. As Sir John Donaldson MR said in *Nancollas v Insurance Officer,* the authorities:

"approve an approach which requires the court to have regard to and to weigh in the balance every factor which can be said in any way to point towards or away from a finding that the claimant was in the course of his employment. In the context of the present appeals, there are a number of such factors to which we must have regard, but none is of itself decisive."

For example, the fact that a man is being paid by his employer in respect of the relevant period of time is often important, but cannot of itself be decisive. A man is usually paid nowadays during his holidays; and it often happens that an employer may allow a man to take the afternoon off, or even a whole day off, without affecting his wages. In such circumstances, he will ordinarily not be acting in the course of his employment despite that fact that he is being paid. Indeed, any rule that payment at the relevant time is decisive would be very difficult to apply in the case of a salaried man. Let me, however, give an example concerned with travelling to work. Suppose that a man is applying for a job, and it turns out that he would have a pretty arduous journey between his home and his new place of work, lasting about an hour each way, which is deterring him from taking the job. His prospective employer may want to employ him, and may entice him by offering him an extra hour's pay at each end of the day, say ten hours' pay a day instead of eight. In those circumstances he would not, I think, be acting in the course of his employment when travelling to or from work. This is because he would not be employed to make the journey: the extra pay would simply be given to him in recognition of the fact that his journey to and from work was an arduous one.

That example serves, I think, to point up the two alternative solutions under consideration in the present case. For to me, the question is this. Was S employed to travel to and from Pembroke? Or was the pay given to him simply in recognition of the fact that he had lost two days' work …? If we can solve that problem, we can answer the question whether S was acting in the course of his employment when, worn out, he crashed his car …

[This is] a case where an employee, who has for a short time to work for his employers at a different place of work some distance away from his usual place of work, has to move from his ordinary base to a temporary base … from which he will travel to work at the temporary place of work each day. For the purpose of moving base, a normal working day was set aside for S's journey, for which he was paid as for an eight-hour day. In addition to his day's pay he was given a travel allowance for his journey, and an allowance for his lodgings at his temporary base in Pembroke. In my opinion, in all the circumstances of the case, S was required by the employers to make this journey, so as to make himself available to do his work at the Pembroke power station, and it would be proper to describe him as having been employed to do so. The fact that he was not required by his employer to make the journey by any particular means, nor even required to make it on the particular working day made available to him, does not detract from the proposition that he was employed to make the journey. Had S wished, he could have driven down on the afternoon of Sunday, 21 August, and have devoted the Monday to (for example) visiting friends near Pembroke. In such circumstances it could, I suppose, be said that S was not travelling "in his employers' time". But this would not matter; for the fact remains that the Monday, a normal working day, was made available for the journey, with full pay for that day to perform a task which he was required by the employers to perform.

I have it very much in mind that M and S were described by counsel for the employers as peripatetic laggers working at such sites as were available. This may well be an accurate description of their work … However, the present case can in any event be differentiated on the basis that it was a departure from the norm in that it was concerned with a move to a temporary base to deal with an emergency, on the terms I have described.

I turn to S's journey back. Another ordinary working day, Tuesday, 30 August, was made available for the journey, with the same pay, to enable him to return to his base in the Midlands to be ready to travel to work on the Wednesday morning. In my opinion, he was employed to make the journey back, just as he was employed to make the journey out to Pembroke. If he had chosen to go to sleep on the Monday morning and afternoon for eight hours or so, and then to drive home on the Monday evening so that he could have Tuesday free (as indeed [the employer] expected him to do), that would not have detracted from the proposition that his journey was in the course of his employment. For this purpose, it was irrelevant that Monday was a bank holiday. Of course, it was wrong for him to succumb to the temptation of driving home on the Monday morning, just after he had completed so long a spell of work; but once again that cannot alter the fact that his journey was made in the course of his employment.'

Comment

(1)   Lord Goff commented several times on the inconvenience of having to reach a conclusion without being able to refer to S's contract of employment, which he referred to as a 'highly material document' in such cases.

(2)   In *Staton v NCB* an employee who had finished work was cycling across his employers' premises in order to fetch his wages from the office. On the way, he negligently knocked down and killed another employee. It was argued for the defendants that they could not be vicariously liable because the course of the employee's employment ended when he finished work. The court concluded, however, that collecting wages at the end of a shift without having left the employers' premises was within the course of employment.

The extent of course of employment at the start of the day fell to be considered in *Compton v McClure*. In that case the employee, who was late for work and anxious to clock-in on time, drove too fast across the employer's premises and negligently injured the plaintiff. May J considered cases in which there had been no vicarious liability for damage caused by employees before they had arrived at work, and concluded that a logical place to draw the line would be at the boundary of the employer's premises. On the facts of the case before him, therefore, the employee was within the course of his employment, despite having ignored a speed limit imposed by the employer.

(3)   Another question arises when the employee commits a tort in the course of the working day but, for example, during a detour or a lunch- or tea-break. As always, the connection between the tortious act and the employment is to be determined from all the circumstances. In *Whatman v Pearson*, an employee who was not supposed to take a detour to go home for lunch or to leave his horse and cart unattended, did both. While unattended the horse bolted, causing some property damage. The employers were vicariously liable because the court held that the employee was employed to look after the horse and cart, wherever it was at the time. For other lunch-break cases see *Harvey v O'Dell Ltd, Crook v Derbyshire Stone, Hilton v Thomas Burton (Rhodes) Ltd.*

In *Storey v Ashton*, the employee was employed to deliver wine and to carry the empties back to his employers' shop. On the return journey he took a detour in order to pick up and deliver a cask for the private purposes of the clerk who was accompanying him. When, during the detour, he negligently ran down and injured the plaintiff, the employers were held not to be vicariously liable.

Lister and others v Hesley Hall Ltd
[2001] 2 All ER 769 House of Lords

The defendant company ran a school for boys with emotional and behavioural difficulties. G, an employee, was the warden of a residential boarding annex. The claimants were residents in the annex and G systematically sexually abused them over a long period of time. He was convicted of multiple offences involving sexual abuse. The claimants claimed that the defendant was vicariously liable for the torts committed by its employee. Both the judge and the Court of Appeal were bound by a decision of the Court of Appeal in *Trotman v North Yorkshire CC* that the defendants in such cases could not be vicariously liable for an employee's torts since sexual abuse was outside the course of employment and could not be regarded as an improper mode of carrying out an authorised act. The House of Lords examined the common law in the context of developments in Canada and held that when determining whether an employer was vicariously liable for an employee's tort, it was necessary to concentrate on the relative closeness of the connection between the nature of the employment and the particular tort, taking a broad approach to the nature of the employment by asking what was the job on which the employee was engaged for his employer. Applying this, the question was not whether the acts of sexual abuse were modes of doing authorised acts. The defendants had undertaken to care for boys and G had been employed for this purpose. There was a very close connection between his employment and his torts insofar as they had been committed at the defendant's premises at a time when G was busy caring for the boys whilst carrying out his duties. G's torts were so closely connected with his employment that it would be fair and just to hold the defendants vicariously liable.

Lord Millett: '...

[64] The case ... raises in a particularly stark form the question in what circumstances an employer may be vicariously liable for the deliberate and criminal wrongdoing of his employee, wrongdoing in which the employee indulged for his own purposes and which the employer must be taken to have expressly or at least impliedly prohibited.

[65] Vicarious liability is a species of strict liability. It is not premised on any culpable act or omission on the part of the employer; an employer who is not personally at fault is made legally answerable for the fault of his employee. It is best understood as a loss-distribution device: see Cane's edition of *Atiyah's Accidents, Compensation and the Law* (6th edn, 1999) p 85 and the articles cited by Atiyah in his monograph on *Vicarious Liability in the Law of Torts* (1967) p 24. The theoretical underpinning of the doctrine is unclear. Glanville Williams wrote ("Vicarious Liability and the Master's Indemnity" (1957) 20 MLR 220 at 231):

"Vicarious liability is the creation of many judges who have had different ideas of its justification or social policy, or no idea at all. Some judges may have extended the rule more widely, or confined it more narrowly than its true rationale would allow; yet the rationale, if we can discover it, will remain valid so far as it extends."

Fleming observed (*The Law of Torts* (9th edn, 1998) p 410) that the doctrine cannot parade as a deduction from legalistic premises. He indicated that it should be frankly recognised as having its basis in a combination of policy considerations, and continued:

> "Most important of these is the belief that a person who employs others to advance his own economic interest should in fairness be placed under a corresponding liability for losses incurred in the course of the enterprise ..."

Atiyah *Vicarious Liability in the Law of Torts* wrote to the same effect. He suggested (at p 171): "The master ought to be liable for all those torts which can fairly be regarded as reasonably incidental risks to the type of business he carries on." These passages are not to be read as confining the doctrine to cases where the employer is carrying on business for profit. They are based on the more general idea that a person who employs another for his own ends inevitably creates a risk that the employee will commit a legal wrong. If the employer's objectives cannot be achieved without a serious risk of the employee committing the kind of wrong which he has in fact committed, the employer ought to be liable. The fact that his employment gave the employee the opportunity to commit the wrong is not enough to make the employer liable. He is liable only if the risk is one which experience shows is inherent in the nature of the business.

[66]   While this proposition has never, so far as I am aware, been adopted in so many words as a test of vicarious liability in any of the decided cases, it does I think form the unspoken rationale of the principle that the employer's liability is confined to torts committed by an employee in the course of his employment. The problem is that, as Townshend-Smith has observed ((2000) 8 Tort Law Review 108 at 111), none of the various tests which have been proposed to determine this essentially factual question is either intellectually satisfying or effective to enable the outcome of a particular case to be predicted. The danger is that in borderline situations, and especially in cases of intentional wrongdoing, recourse to a rigid and possibly inappropriate formula as a test of liability may lead the court to abandon the search for legal principle.

[67]   In the very first edition of his book on *Torts* (1907) p 83 Sir John Salmond wrote:

> "1. A master is not responsible for a wrongful act done by his servant unless it is done in the course of his employment. It is deemed to be so done if it is either (a) a wrongful act authorised by the master, or (b) a wrongful and unauthorised *mode* of doing some act authorised by the master." (Author's emphasis.)

This passage has stood the test of time. It has survived unchanged for 21 editions, and has probably been cited more often than any other single passage in a legal textbook. Yet it is not without blemish. As has often been observed, the first of the two alternatives is not an example of vicarious liability at all. Its presence (and the word "deemed") may be an echo of the discredited theory of implied authority. More pertinently, the second is not happily expressed if it is to serve as a test of vicarious liability for intentional wrongdoing. ...

[68] In the present case the warden was employed to look after the boys in his care and secure their welfare. It is stretching language to breaking-point to describe the series of deliberate sexual assaults on them on which he embarked as merely a wrongful and unauthorised mode of performing that duty. In *Trotman v North Yorkshire CC* the employee in question was the deputy headmaster of a special school run by the local council. He was charged with the responsibility of caring for a handicapped teenager on a foreign holiday, and he sexually assaulted the boy. Butler-Sloss LJ asked rhetorically whether that was in principle an improper mode of carrying out an authorised act on behalf of his employer or an independent act outside the course of his employment. She held that it fell into the latter category, because:

> "His position of caring for the plaintiff by sharing a bedroom with him gave him the opportunity to carry out the sexual assaults. But availing himself of that opportunity seems to me to be far removed from an unauthorised mode of carrying out a teacher's duties on behalf of his employer. Rather it is a negation of the duty of the council to look after the children for whom it was responsible".

In the same case Chadwick LJ agreed that the traditional test was not satisfied. He said:

> "I find it impossible to hold that the commission of acts of indecent assault can be regarded as a mode – albeit, an improper and unauthorised mode – of doing what, on the case advanced, the deputy headmaster was employed by the council to do. In the circumstances alleged, [MS] was employed to supervise the plaintiff's welfare while on the holiday in Spain. The commission by him of acts of indecent assault on a pupil in his charge cannot be regarded as a way of doing that. *Rather, it must be regarded as an independent act of self-indulgence or self-gratification.*" (My emphasis.)

This antithesis lies at the heart of the present appeal.

[69] In a passage which is unfortunately less often cited, however, Sir John Salmond (*Salmond on Torts* (1st edn, 1907)) continued his exposition as follows (at pp 83–84):

> "But a master, as opposed to the employer of an independent contractor, is liable even for acts which he has not authorised, provided they are so

connected with acts which he has authorised, that they may rightly be regarded as modes – although improper modes – of doing them."

This could, I think, usefully be elided to impose vicarious liability where the unauthorised acts of the employee are so connected with acts which the employer has authorised that they may properly be regarded as being within the scope of his employment. Such a formulation would have the advantage of dispensing with the awkward reference to "improper modes" of carrying out the employee's duties; and by focussing attention on the connection between the employee's duties and his wrongdoing it would accord with the underlying rationale of the doctrine and be applicable without straining the language to accommodate cases of intentional wrongdoing.

[70]   But the precise terminology is not critical. The *Salmond* test, in either formulation, is not a statutory definition of the circumstances which give rise to liability, but a guide to the principled application of the law to diverse factual situations. What is critical is that attention should be directed to the closeness of the connection between the employee's duties and his wrongdoing and not to verbal formulae. This is the principle on which the Supreme Court of Canada recently decided the important cases of *Bazley v Curry* and *Jacobi v Griffiths* which provide many helpful insights into this branch of the law and from which I have derived much assistance.

[71]   Cases of intentional wrongdoing have always proved troublesome. At one time it was thought that the employer could not be held vicariously liable for his employee's deliberate wrongdoing. This view was not maintained, but even as late as the beginning of the twentieth century it was regarded as axiomatic that an employer could not be vicariously liable for his employee's dishonest acts unless they were committed for the benefit of his employer: see *Cheshire v Bailey* where the defendant was held not responsible for the theft of his customer's goods by his employee because the theft was outside the scope of his employment. As Salmon LJ explained in *Morris v C W Martin & Sons*, this view derived from a misunderstanding of what Willes J had said in *Barwick v English Joint Stock Bank*. Observing that no sensible distinction could be drawn between the case of fraud and any other wrong, he had stated that the general rule was that—

"the master is answerable for every such wrong of the servant or agent as is committed in the course of the service *and for the master's benefit*, though no express command or privity of the master be proved." (My emphasis.)

But this was very different, as Lord Macnaghten pointed out in *Lloyd v Grace, Smith & Co*, from saying that a master cannot be liable for the fraud of his servant unless carried out for his benefit or with his privity. This may be a sufficient condition of liability, but it is not a necessary one.

[72]   The heresy was not exposed until *Lloyd's* case, and despite this has proved remarkably resilient. It took another 50 years until *Morris'* case for it to be

recognised that *Cheshire*'s case was no longer good law; and regrettable traces of it appear in *Trotman*'s case. If the employer is to be absolved from liability in that case (or this) it cannot be because the acts complained of were "independent acts of self-indulgence or self-gratification".

[73]   In *Lloyd*'s case a solicitor's managing clerk defrauded a client of the firm by obtaining her instructions to realise her property. He induced her to hand over the title deeds and to execute conveyances in his favour which he did not read over or explain to her. They enabled him to sell the property and pocket the proceeds. The firm was held liable for the fraud even though it was committed for the clerk's own benefit. In the course of argument before your Lordships in the present case it was accepted that the firm would not have been liable if the clerk had stolen the contents of his client's handbag. That is true, for the clerk would merely have been taking advantage of an opportunity which his employment gave him. But there was a much closer connection between the clerk's duties and his wrongdoing than that. The firm's liability arose from the fact that throughout the transaction the fraudulent clerk acted as the representative of the firm, and he received the custody of the documents of title with the consent of the client given because he was acting in that capacity.

[74]   In the same year Laski (in "The Basis of Vicarious Liability" (1916) 26 Yale Law Journal 105 at 130) had observed that there was no valid *a priori* reason why the doctrine of vicarious liability should cease to operate at that border where tort becomes crime. In England this had already been established: see *Dyer v Munday*. Once this limitation on the operation of the doctrine is rejected, it is impossible to maintain the fiction that it is based on any kind of implied authority. An excessively literal application of the *Salmond* test must also be discarded. Stealing a client's property cannot sensibly be described as an unauthorised mode of dealing with it on her behalf. It is, as Butler-Sloss LJ put it in *Trotman v North Yorkshire CC*, the negation of the employer's duty. Yet the employer may be liable none the less.

[75]   In *Morris*' case a firm of cleaners was held vicariously liable to a customer whose fur was stolen by one of its employees. The firm was a sub-bailee for reward, but the decision was not based on the firm's own failure to take care of the fur and deliver it upon termination of the bailment. It was held vicariously liable for the conversion of the fur by its employee. Diplock LJ said, that he based his decision—

> "on the ground that the fur was stolen *by the very servant* whom the defendants as bailees for reward had employed to take care of it and to clean it." (my emphasis.)

Salmon LJ too, was anxious to make it plain that the conclusion which he had reached depended on the fact that the thief was "the servant through whom the defendants chose to discharge their duty to take reasonable care of the plaintiff's fur". He added that—

> "A bailee for reward is not answerable for a theft by any of his servants, but only for a theft by such of them as are deputed by him to discharge some part of his duty of taking reasonable care. A theft by any servant who is not employed to do anything in relation to the goods bailed is entirely outside the scope of his employment and cannot make the master liable."

The employee's position gave him the opportunity to steal the fur, but as Diplock LJ was at pains to make clear, this was not enough to make his employer liable. What brought the theft within the scope of his employment and made the firm liable was that in the course of its business the firm had entrusted him with the care of the fur, and he stole it while it was in his custody as an employee of the firm.

[76]   As my noble and learned friend Lord Steyn has observed, *Morris'* case has consistently been held to be an authority on vicarious liability generally and not confined to cases of bailment. The case was expressly approved by the Privy Council in *Port Swettenham Authority v T W Wu & Co (M) Sdn Bhd*, not altogether surprisingly as the opinion of the board was delivered by Lord Salmon. That was another case of bailment. But in *Photo Production Ltd v Securicor Transport Ltd*, where a patrolman employed by a security firm deliberately set fire to the premises he was employed to protect, neither Lord Wilberforce nor Lord Salmon saw any difficulty in holding the employer vicariously liable on the principle stated in *Morris'* case. That was not a case of bailment. Yet the patrolman was said (per Lord Salmon) to be "indubitably acting in the course of his employment".

[77]   Just as an employer may be vicariously liable for deliberate and criminal conduct on the part of his employee, so he may be vicariously liable for acts of the employee which he has expressly forbidden him to do. In *Ilkiw v Samuels* a lorry driver was under strict instructions from his employers not to allow anyone else to drive the lorry. He allowed a third party, who was incompetent, to drive it without making any inquiry into his competence to do so. The employers were held vicariously liable for the resulting accident. Diplock LJ explained that some prohibitions limited the sphere of employment and others only dealt with conduct within the sphere of employment. In order to determine into which category a particular prohibition fell it was necessary to determine what would have been the sphere, scope, or course (nouns which he considered to amount to the same thing) if the prohibition had not been imposed. In a passage which is of some importance in the present case, he added:

> "As each of these nouns implies, the matter must be looked at broadly, not dissecting the servant's task into its component activities – such as driving, loading, sheeting and the like – by asking: What was the job on which he was engaged for his employer? and answering that question as a jury would."

He reasoned that the job which the driver was engaged to perform was to collect a load of sugar and transport it to its destination, using for that purpose his employers' lorry, of which he was put in charge. He was expressly forbidden to permit anyone else to drive the lorry in the course of performing this job. That was not a prohibition which limited the scope of his employment, but one which dealt with his conduct within the sphere of his employment.

[78] The case was followed in *Rose v Plenty* where despite strict instructions not to do so a milk roundsman employed a boy to help him deliver milk and let him accompany him on his float. The employer was held liable for injuries sustained by the boy when he fell off the float as a result of the roundsman's negligent driving. Scarman LJ agreed that the roundsman was certainly not employed to give the boy a lift, and that if one confined one's analysis of the facts to the incident which caused injury to the boy, then it could be said that carrying the boy on the float was not in the course of his employment. But quoting with approval the passage cited above from the judgment of Diplock LJ in *Ilkiw v Samuels* he adopted a broad approach to the nature of the roundsman's employment. His job was to deliver milk, collect empties, and obtain payment. Disregarding his instructions he enlisted the boy's assistance in carrying out his job. If one asked: why was the boy on the float the answer was that it was because he was assisting the roundsman to do his job.

[79] So it is no answer to say that the employee was guilty of intentional wrongdoing, or that his act was not merely tortious but criminal, or that he was acting exclusively for his own benefit, or that he was acting contrary to express instructions, or that his conduct was the very negation of his employer's duty. The cases show that where an employer undertakes the care of a client's property and entrusts the task to an employee who steals the property, the employer is vicariously liable. This is not only in accordance with principle but with the underlying rationale if Atiyah has correctly identified it. Experience shows that the risk of theft by an employee is inherent in a business which involves entrusting the custody of a customer's property to employees. But the theft must be committed by the very employee to whom the custody of the property is entrusted. He does more than make the most of an opportunity presented by the fact of his employment. He takes advantage of the position in which the employer has placed him to enable the purposes of the employer's business to be achieved. If the boys in the present case had been sacks of potatoes and the defendant, having been engaged to take care of them, had entrusted their care to one of its employees, it would have been vicariously liable for any criminal damage done to them by the employee in question, though not by any other employee. Given that the employer's liability does not arise from the law of bailment, it is not immediately apparent that it should make any difference that the victims were boys, that the wrongdoing took the form of sexual abuse, and that it was committed for the personal gratification of the employee.

[80] Employers have long been held vicariously liable in appropriate circumstances for assaults committed by their employees. Clearly an employer is liable where he has placed the employee in a situation where he may be expected on

occasions to have to resort to personal violence: see *Dyer v Munday*, where the employer was held vicariously liable for a criminal assault committed by his employee while attempting to repossess his employer's property. Equally clearly the employer is not liable for an assault by his employee on a customer merely because it was the result of a quarrel arising out of his employment: see *Warren v Henlys Ltd*, where a petrol pump attendant assaulted a customer as a result of a dispute over payment. The case was decided partly on the ground that the customer had paid for the petrol and was driving away when he was assaulted, and partly on the ground that he was assaulted because he had threatened to report the attendant to his employer. The reasoning has been criticised, and the better view may be that the employer was not liable because it was no part of the duties of the pump attendant to keep order. Attention must be concentrated on the closeness of the connection between the act of the employee and the duties he is engaged to perform broadly defined.

[81]   In *Deatons Pty Ltd v Flew* the owner of a hotel was held not to be vicariously liable for an unprovoked assault by a barmaid who threw a glass of beer into a customer's face. The ground of decision was that the barmaid was not in charge of the bar – the publican was close at hand – and she did not throw the glass in the course of maintaining discipline or restoring order. In the words of Dixon J ... it was–

> "an act of passion and resentment done neither in furtherance of the master's interests nor under his express or implied authority *nor as an incident to or in consequence of anything the barmaid was employed to do*. It was a spontaneous act of retributive justice. The occasion for administering it and the form it took may have arisen from the fact that she was a barmaid but retribution was not within the course of her employment as a barmaid." (My emphasis.)

In other words, the barmaid's employment gave her the opportunity to wreak some personal vengeance of her own, but that was all; and it was not enough to make her employer liable. Had she been in charge of the bar and authorised to maintain order, the result might well have been different. It would not, in my opinion, have been enough in itself to exclude the employer's liability that she had been paying off a private score of her own. If so, then there is no *a priori* reason why an employer should not be vicariously liable for a sexual assault committed by his employee, though naturally such conduct will not normally be within the scope of his employment.

[82]   In the present case the warden's duties provided him with the opportunity to commit indecent assaults on the boys for his own sexual gratification, but that in itself is not enough to make the school liable. The same would be true of the groundsman or the school porter. But there was far more to it than that. The school was responsible for the care and welfare of the boys. It entrusted that

responsibility to the warden. He was employed to discharge the school's responsibility to the boys. For this purpose the school entrusted them to his care. He did not merely take advantage of the opportunity which employment at a residential school gave him. He abused the special position in which the school had placed him to enable it to discharge its own responsibilities, with the result that the assaults were committed by the very employee to whom the school had entrusted the care of the boys. It is not necessary to conduct the detailed dissection of the warden's duties of the kind on which the Supreme Court of Canada embarked in *Bazley's* case and *Jacobi's* case. I would hold the school liable.

[83] I would regard this as in accordance not only with ordinary principle deducible from the authorities but with the underlying rationale of vicarious liability. Experience shows that in the case of boarding schools, prisons, nursing homes, old people's homes, geriatric wards, and other residential homes for the young or vulnerable, there is an inherent risk that indecent assaults on the residents will be committed by those placed in authority over them, particularly if they are in close proximity to them and occupying a position of trust.

[84] I would hold the school vicariously liable for the warden's intentional assaults, not (as was suggested in argument) for his failure to perform his duty to take care of the boys. That is an artificial approach based on a misreading of *Morris'* case. The cleaners were vicariously liable for their employee's conversion of the fur, not for his negligence in failing to look after it. Similarly in the *Photo Production* case the security firm was vicariously liable for the patrolman's arson, not for his negligence. The law is mature enough to hold an employer vicariously liable for deliberate, criminal wrongdoing on the part of an employee without indulging in sophistry of this kind. I would also not base liability on the warden's failure to report his own wrongdoing to his employer, an approach which I regard as both artificial and unrealistic. Even if such a duty did exist, on which I prefer to express no opinion, I am inclined to think that it would be a duty owed exclusively to the employer and not a duty for breach of which the employer could be vicariously liable. The same reasoning would not, of course, necessarily apply to the duty to report the wrongdoing of fellow employees, but it is not necessary to decide this.

[85] I would overrule *Trotman's* case and allow the appeal.'

Comment

(1) For *Rose v Plenty* see p 808. That was a case concerned with negligence and the analysis of Scarman LJ is entirely consistent with the general tenor of Lord Millett's speech.

(2) In *Balfron Trustees v Peterson*, a case involving fraud by an employee solicitor, the court emphasised that the focus of the enquiry should be the nature of the relationship between the employer and the victim of the fraud. In

the light of this, the court should evaluate whether or not the employer ought to be held vicariously liable. The risk here is that the test will conflate primary with vicarious liability. Compare the approach in *Phelps v Hillingdon LBC*, p 64.

(3)   In *Dubai Aluminium Co Ltd v Salaam and others*, there was an elaborate fraud on the plaintiff and the fraudsters received $40 million under a bogus consultancy agreement. A firm of solicitors ('the Amhurst firm') prepared the necessary paperwork and the fraudsters were dealt with by Mr Amhurst, the senior partner, who did not benefit from the fraud, apart from the fees paid to the firm in respect of the legal work he had carried out. The plaintiff sued both Mr Amhurst and the Amhurst firm, alleging that the firm was vicariously liable for Mr Amhurst's activities which it claimed were fraudulent. Mr Amhurst denied any wrongdoing and there had been no trial on that matter.

The defendant fraudsters settled with the plaintiff, and the claims against Mr Amhurst and the Amhurst firm were settled on payment by the Amhurst firm of $10m to the plaintiff. The judge ordered that the Amhurst firm should receive a contribution amounting to a full indemnity from the fraudsters. The fraudsters appealed on the basis that there was no vicarious liability for the torts of a partner and accordingly that there was no basis on which the other partners could obtain contribution from the fraudsters in respect of the settlement.

The House of Lords confirmed that there might be vicarious liability between partners in respect of the torts of partners where the partner was acting in the ordinary course of the firm's business, and that the test for this would be the principle in *Lister v Hesley Hall*. On the facts, it would have been open to the judge to have reached the conclusion that there was vicarious liability and the judge's order as to contribution would stand. Lord Millett referred to the vicarious liability of partners for equitable wrongdoing and then observed in connection with vicarious liability for torts arising from dishonest conduct:

'[122]   The vicarious liability of an employer does not depend upon the employee's authority to do the particular act which constitutes the wrong. It is sufficient if the employee is authorised to do acts of the kind in question ... This is equally true of partners, though it is perhaps less obvious in their case, since the relation between partners is essentially one of agency. An employer may authorise his employee to drive, but he does not authorise him to drive negligently. A firm of solicitors may authorise a partner to draft agreements for a client, but it does not authorise him to draft sham agreements ...

[123]   In *Lister*'s case several of your Lordships observed that the traditional *Salmond* test ... for determining whether an employee's act was in the course of his employment is not happily expressed when

applied to the case of intentional or fraudulent wrongdoing ...To say that a solicitor drafted an agreement negligently is to describe the way in which he drafted it; it is to accuse him of having done an authorised act in a wrongful and unauthorised way. But to say that he drafted an agreement dishonestly, or that he drafted a sham agreement, does not describe either the way in which he drafted it or the nature of the document. Rather it describes the purpose for which he intended it to be used.

[124] But these differences are immaterial. If regard is paid to the closeness of the connection between the employee's wrongdoing and the class of acts which he was employed to perform, or to the underlying rationale of vicarious liability, there is no relevant distinction to be made between performing an act in an improper manner and performing it for an improper purpose or by an improper means ...'

(4)   In *Morris v Martin* Scarman LJ, as well as confirming that the tort of the tortfeasor need not be for the benefit of the employer, said:

'I am anxious ... to make it plain that the conclusion which I have reached depends on M being the servant through whom the defendants chose to discharge their duty to take reasonable care of the plaintiff's fur. The words of Willes J in *Barwick*'s case are entirely applicable to these facts. The defendants "put [their] agent [M] in [the defendants'] place as to such a class of acts, and ... must be answerable for the manner in which the agent conducts himself in doing the business which is the business of the master." A bailee for reward is not answerable for a theft by any of his servants, but only for a theft by such of them as are deputed by him to discharge some part of his duty of taking reasonable care. A theft by any servant who is not employed to do anything in relation to the goods bailed is entirely outside the scope of his employment and cannot make the master liable. So in this case, if someone employed by the defendants in another depot had broken in and stolen the fur, the defendants would not have been liable. Similarly in my view if a clerk employed in the same depot had seized the opportunity of entering the room where the fur was kept and had stolen it, the defendants would not have been liable. The mere fact that the master, by employing a rogue, gives him the opportunity to steal or defraud does not make the master liable for his depredations ... It might be otherwise if the master knew or ought to have known that his servant was dishonest, because then the master could be liable in negligence for employing him.'

(5)   Consider how *Harrison v Michelin Tyre Co* would be decided applying the *Lister* test. L, the plaintiff employee of the defendant, was standing on a duck-board operating a machine. Another employee was pushing a truck between the rows of machines and, as a joke, pushed the truck towards the plaintiff. This caught the duck-board, the plaintiff fell and was injured. The defendant was held vicariously liable.

804 Cases and Commentary on Tort

What would be the result in *Aldred v Nacanco*? In that case the defendant had deliberately pushed an insecure wash-basin in the direction of the plaintiff who twisted to avoid it and was injured. The Court of Appeal held that there was no vicarious liability.

(6)　In *General Engineering Services Ltd v Kingston and St Andrew Corporation* some fire-fighters who were engaged in an industrial dispute were operating a 'go slow' policy. As a result, they took five times as long as normal to reach a fire at the plaintiff's premises which were completely destroyed. The Privy Council rejected an argument that driving so slowly was merely an unauthorised mode of doing an authorised act, in favour of the view that this was not a performance of the act at all.

(7)　In *Century Insurance Co Ltd v Northern Ireland Road Transport Board* an employee of the respondents was in the process of delivering bulk petrol from a tanker lorry when he lit a cigarette and threw down the lighted match. The resulting fire and explosion caused considerable damage to property. The appellants, who had insured the respondents against third-party liability, argued that there was no vicarious liability on the part of the employer since the employee, although admittedly negligent, was outside the course of his employment. The House of Lords held that the driver's primary activity at the time of the incident was the delivery of petrol which was within the course of his employment. Lord Wright observed that:

'... On the other question, namely, whether D's negligence was in the course of his employment, all the decisions below have been against the appellants. I agree with them and need add little.

The act of a workman in lighting his pipe or cigarette is an act done for his own comfort and convenience and at least, generally speaking, not for his employer's benefit. That last condition, however, is no longer essential to fix liability on the employer (*Lloyd v Grace Smith & Co*). Nor is such an act *prima facie* negligent. It is in itself both innocent and harmless. The negligence is to be found by considering the time when and the circumstances in which the match is struck and thrown down. The duty of the workman to his employer is so to conduct himself in doing his work as not negligently to cause damage either to the employer himself or his property or to third persons or their property, and thus to impose the same liability on the employer as if he had been doing the work himself and committed the negligent act. This may seem too obvious as a matter of common sense to require either argument or authority. I think that what plausibility the contrary argument might seem to possess results from treating the act of lighting the cigarette in abstraction from the circumstances as a separate act.'

Lord Wright agreed with the approach taken by the Court of Appeal in *Jefferson v Derbyshire Farmers Ltd*, a similar case in which a farm-boy had lit a cigarette while filling tins with petrol from a drum, and where Warrington LJ said:

'Horridge J [at first instance] decided ... that what the boy did in lighting and throwing away the match was not in the scope of his employment. In one sense it was not; he was not employed to light the match and throw it away; but that is not the way in which to approach the question. It was in the scope of his employment to fill the tin with motor spirit from the drum. That work required special precautions. The act which caused the damage was an act done while he was engaged in this dangerous operation, and it was an improper act in the circumstances. That is to say, the boy was doing the work of his employers in an improper way and without taking reasonable precautions; and in that case the employers are liable.'

(8)   It is clear that merely providing an opportunity for the employee's criminal act will not suffice for vicarious liability. In *Heasmans v Clarity Cleaning Co Ltd* an employee took advantage of a night-time cleaning job to make almost £1500 worth of telephone calls. The Court of Appeal rejected an argument that the employee had been entrusted with the building and its contents and concluded that the use of the telephone was outside the scope of the cleaner's employment. Purchas LJ said:

'... before the master can be held to be vicariously liable ... there must be established some nexus other than mere opportunity between the tortious or criminal act of the servant and the circumstances of his employment. In the present case, apart from the obligation to dust and once a week to disinfect the telephone, there is nothing more than the provision of the opportunity to commit the tort or crime.'

This was not a case of property being entrusted to the errant employee, as had been the case in *Morris v Martin*.

Keppel Bus Co Ltd v Sa'ad bin Ahmad
[1974] 2 All ER 700 Privy Council

The respondent was a passenger on a bus owned by the appellants. During the journey, the conductor, an employee of the appellants, was rude to an elderly female passenger and was rebuked by the respondent. The conductor made as if to attack the respondent but was prevented by other passengers; however, some time later, after the woman had left the bus and some new passengers had got on, the conductor verbally abused the respondent and then hit him in the face with a ticket punch, causing the loss of his eye. The Privy Council held that the conductor's acts fell outside the scope of his authorised duties and that there was no vicarious liability.

Lord Kilbrandon: '... The course of the employment is not limited to the obligations which lie on an employee in virtue of his contract of service. It extends to acts done on the implied authority of the master. In *Poland v John Parr & Sons* a carter, who had handed over his wagon and was going home to his dinner, struck a boy whom he suspected, wrongly but on reasonable grounds, of stealing his master's property. The master was held liable for the consequences, since a servant has implied authority, at least in an emergency, to protect his master's property.

> "Maybe his action was mistaken and maybe the force he used was excessive; he might have pushed the boy instead of striking him. But that was merely acting in excess of what was necessary in doing an act which he was authorised to do. The excess was not sufficient to take the act out of the class of authorised acts ..." (per Scrutton LJ)

There is no dispute about the law. The Court of Appeal relied on the well-known passage from *Salmond on Torts* ...

The Court of Appeal rightly point out that the question in every case is whether on the facts the act done, albeit unauthorised and unlawful, is done in the course of the employment; that question is itself a question of fact ...

It is necessary, accordingly, in the present appeal to examine the grounds on which the learned judge held that, on the facts, this assault was committed in the course of carrying out, by a wrong mode, work which the conductor was expressly or impliedly authorised and therefore employed to do, and to see whether there is any evidence to support them. If there be no evidence, it is a matter of law that his conclusions could not stand. The passage in which those grounds are stated is as follows:

> "I find that the conductor when he hit the [respondent] was acting in the course of his duties. He was then maintaining order amongst the passengers in the bus. He was in effect telling the [respondent] by his act not to interfere with him in his due performance of his duties. He may have acted in a very high handed manner but nonetheless I am of the opinion that he was acting in the due performance of his duties then."

On the facts as found by the learned judge, and after examining, with the assistance of learned counsel, the testimony of those witnesses whom the judge accepted as credible, their Lordships are unable to find any evidence which, if it had been under the consideration of a jury, could have supported a verdict for the respondent. It may be accepted that the keeping of order among the passengers is part of the duties of a conductor. But there was no evidence of disorder among the passengers at the time of the assault. The only sign of disorder was that the conductor had gratuitously insulted the respondent, and the respondent had asked him in an orderly manner not to do it again. Their Lordships do not consider the question whether the events of that morning are to be regarded as one incident, or as two incidents separated by a gap, to be of much importance. Certainly the end result can be related back to the treatment of the Malay lady; on the other hand she had by now left the bus, normalcy had been restored, except, apparently, for some simmering resentment in the conductor which caused him to misbehave himself. But to describe what he did in these circumstances as an act of quelling disorder seems to their Lordships to be impossible on the evidence; on the story as a whole, if anyone was keeping order on the bus it was the passengers. The evidence falls far short of establishing an implied authority to take violent action where none was called for. In *Bank of New South Wales v Owston*, where the question was whether a bank manager was within his authority in bringing a criminal charge, Sir Montague Smith observed in relation to evidence that such an action might be taken in an emergency:

> "An authority to be exercised only in cases of emergency, and derived from the exigency of the occasion, is evidently a limited one, and before it can arise a state of facts must exist which shows that such exigency is present, or from which it might reasonably be supposed to be present."

Their Lordships are of opinion that no facts have been proved from which it could be properly inferred that there was present in that bus an emergency situation, calling for forcible action, justifiable on any express or implied authority, with which the appellants could be said on the evidence to have clothed the conductor.

A similar criticism can be levelled at the second ground on which the learned judge found that the conductor was acting under authority. There is no evidence that the respondent was interfering with the conductor in his due performance of his duty. His interference, if so it could be described, was a protest against the conductor's insulting language. Insults to passengers are not part of the due performance of a conductor's duty, as the learned judge seems to recognise in the paragraph of his judgment which follows.

The function of a bus conductor, from which could be deduced the scope of the authority committed to him, was attractively put by counsel for the respondent as "managing the bus"; it was said that what he did arose out of that power and duty of management. But this concept, it seems, if pushed to its extreme, could serve to bring anything which the conductor did during his employment within the class of things done in the course of it. There must be room for some distinction between the acts of a manager, however foreign to his authority, and acts of management, properly so called. Probably this way of putting the case is fundamentally no different from that which the learned trial judge adopted and their Lordships reject, because there is no evidence of circumstances which would suggest that what the manager actually did was, although wrongful, within the scope of his authority, express or implied, and thus an act of management.'

Comment

(1)   It is likely that even with the application of the test in *Lister v Hesley Hall* the result would have been the same. See also *Fennelly v Connex South*

Eastern Ltd (which pre-dated *Lister v Hesley Hall*) where the alleged battery of the claimant by a ticket-inspector was held to have been in the course of the latter's employment. Here the altercation between the ticket-inspector and the claimant had started at a time when the ticket-inspector was entitled to challenge the claimant to produce a ticket even though the actual battery had occurred some time later. Even though each case is fact-sensitive, it is likely that the result would have flowed from an application of the *Lister v Hesley Hall* test. On the other hand, in *Mattis v Pollock*, a serious assault was committed by a door-man at a night-club. The court applied the principles to emerge from *Lister v Hesley Hall* and concluded that there was an insufficient connection between the act of the door-man and the employer, accordingly it would not be fair, just and reasonable to impose vicarious liability. The door-man had been motivated by a desire for revenge and had injured the claimant in a vicious attack a long time after an incident at the club that same night.

(2) These cases illustrate a particular difficulty which arises where an employee uses excessive violence in carrying out a duty either to keep order or to protect the employer's property. It can be seen that very detailed analysis is required in order to distinguish between the unauthorised mode of doing what has been authorised, and the wholly independent act. *Poland v Parr* (referred to in the judgment above) should be contrasted with *Warren v Henlys Ltd* in which the employee was a garage attendant who accused the plaintiff, in loud abusive terms, of trying to leave without paying for his petrol. The plaintiff paid, then called the police and threatened to report the attendant to his employer. The attendant then struck the plaintiff and the court held that this act had no connection with his employment since his duty to his employer had been satisfied when the plaintiff paid. The subsequent assault must therefore have been an independent act. In *Lister v Hesley Hall* Lord Millett in connection with these cases urged that: 'Attention must be concentrated on the closeness of the connection between the act of the employee and the duties he is engaged to perform broadly defined.'

Rose v Plenty and another
[1976] I All ER 97 Court of Appeal

The employee, a milk-roundsman, despite an express prohibition, employed the plaintiff, a 13-year-old boy, to help him with his duties, and let him ride around on his milk float. While doing this, the plaintiff was injured as a result of the milkman's negligent driving. The Court of Appeal held the employers vicariously liable because, despite the prohibition, the milkman's activities were for the purpose of the employers' business.

Scarman LJ: '... as I understand it, the employer is made vicariously liable for the tort of his employee not because the plaintiff is an invitee, nor because of the authority possessed by the servant, but because it is a case in which the employer, having put matters into motion, should be liable if the motion that he has originated leads to damage to another. What is the approach which the cases identify as the correct approach in order to determine this question of public policy? First, as Lord Denning MR has already said, one looks to see whether the servant has committed a tort on the plaintiff. In the present case it is clear that the first defendant, the servant of the dairy company, who are the second defendants, by the negligent driving of the milk float, caused injury to the plaintiff, ... who was on the float at his invitation. There was therefore a tort committed by the servant. The next question, as Lord Denning MR has said, is whether the employer should shoulder the liability for compensating the person injured by the tort. With all respect to the points developed by Lawton LJ, it does appear to me to be clear, since the decision of *Limpus v London General Omnibus Co*, that that question has to be answered by directing attention to what the first defendant was employed to do when he committed the tort that has caused damage to the plaintiff. The first defendant was, of course, employed at the time of the accident to do a whole number of operations. He was certainly not employed to give the plaintiff a lift, and if one confines one's analysis of the facts to the incident of injury to the plaintiff, then no doubt one would say that carrying the plaintiff on the float – giving him a lift – was not in the course of the first defendant's employment. But in *Ilkiw v Samuels* Diplock LJ indicated that the proper approach to the nature of the servant's employment is a broad one. He said:

> "As each of these nouns implies [he is referring to the nouns used to describe course of employment, sphere, scope and so forth] the matter must be looked at broadly, not dissecting the servant's task into its component activities – such as driving, loading, sheeting and the like – by asking: What was the job on which he was engaged for his employer? and answering that question as a jury would."

Applying those words to the employment of the first defendant, I think it is clear from the evidence that he was employed as a roundsman to drive his float round his round and to deliver milk, to collect empties and to obtain payment. That was his job. He was under an express prohibition – a matter to which I shall refer later – not to enlist the help of anyone doing that work. And he was also under an express prohibition not to give lifts on the float to anyone. How did he choose to carry out the task which I have analysed? He chose to disregard the prohibition and to enlist the assistance of the plaintiff. As a matter of common sense, that does seem to me to be a mode, albeit a prohibited mode, of doing the job with which he was entrusted. Why was the plaintiff being carried on the float when the accident occurred? Because it was necessary to take him from point to point so that he could assist in delivering milk, collecting empties and, on occasions, obtaining payment. The plaintiff was there because it was necessary that he should be there in order that he could assist, albeit in a way prohibited by the employers, in the job entrusted to the first defendant by his employers.

We have taken a brief look at the historical origins of the doctrine of vicarious liability. One finds in the analysis of the facts which I have just given an echo of words used by Sir John Holt as long ago as 1700. In *Hern v Nichols* he was enunciating, with I think a good deal of prophetic wisdom, the principle of vicarious liability as he saw it. He said, and one notes the factor of public policy in his thinking: "... seeing somebody must be a loser by this deceit, it is more reason that he that employs and puts a trust and confidence in the deceiver should be a loser, than a stranger"...

It does seem to me that the principle that I have been attempting to describe is to be found in the case law, notably in *Limpus v London General Omnibus Co*, *Hilton v Thomas Burton (Rhodes) Ltd* and *Ilkiw v Samuels*. Yet it is said that the flow of this current of authority must be dammed and the stream of the law diverted because of the two decisions to which Lawton LJ has referred: *Twine v Bean's Express Ltd* and *Conway v George Wimpey & Co Ltd*. Both of those decisions seem to me distinguishable on their facts. In *Twine's* case, at the very end of the judgment, Lord Greene MR said: "The other thing that he [i.e. the servant] was doing simultaneously was something totally outside the scope of his employment, namely, giving a lift to a person who had no right whatsoever to be there." In that case the conclusion of fact was that the express prohibition on giving lifts was not only a prohibition but was also a limiting factor on the scope of the employment; and, of course, once a prohibition is properly to be treated as a defining or limiting factor on the scope of employment certain results follow. In *Twine's* case the driver was engaged to drive his employers' van, his employers having a contract with the Post Office. When so doing, he gave Mr Twine a lift from A to B. True A and B happened to be, both of them, offices of the Post Office. Yet I can well understand why the court reached the conclusion that in the circumstances of that case it was not possible to say that the driver in giving Mr Twine a lift was acting within the scope of his employment or doing improperly that which he was employed to do. Similarly when one looks at *Conway's* case, one again sees that on the facts of that case the court considered it right so to define the scope of employment that what was done, namely giving somebody a lift, was outside it and was not a mode of doing that which the servant was employed to do. That also was a case of a lift: the person lifted was not in any way engaged, in the course of the lift or indeed otherwise, in doing the master's business or in assisting the servant to do the master's business; and no doubt it was for that reason that Asquith LJ was able to say that what was done – that is giving somebody else's employee a lift from the airport home – was not a mode of performing an act which the driver was employed to do, but was the performance of an act which he was not employed to perform. In the present case the first defendant, the servant, was employed to deliver milk, to collect empties, to obtain payment from customers. The plaintiff was there on the float in order to assist the first defendant to do those jobs. I would have thought therefore that whereas *Conway v George Wimpey & Co Ltd* was absolutely correctly decided on its facts, the facts of the present case lead to a very different conclusion. The dividing factor between, for instance, the present case and the decisions in *Twine v Bean's Express Ltd* and *Conway v George Wimpey & Co Ltd* is the category into which the court, on the study of the facts of the case, puts the express prohibition issued by the employers to their servants. In *Ilkiw v Samuels* Diplock LJ, in a judgment to which I have already referred, dealt with this problem of the prohibition, and quoted a *dictum* of Lord Dunedin in *Plumb v Cobden Flour Mills Co Ltd*, which itself has been approved in the Privy Council case of *Canadian Pacific Railway Co v Lockhart*. Lord Dunedin said: "there are prohibitions which limit the sphere of employment, and prohibitions which only deal with conduct within the sphere of employment." Now those words are in fact an echo of what has long been the law. Much the same thing but in a different social context was said by Lord Blackburn in *Limpus v London General Omnibus Co* and I will quote just one sentence:

> "A footman might think it for the interest of his master to drive the coach, but no one could say that it was within the scope of the footman's employment, and that the master would be liable for damage resulting from the wilful act of the footman in taking charge of the horses."

And, coming right down to today, one finds the same idea being followed and developed by this court in *Iqbal v London Transport Executive*. In that case the Court of Appeal had to consider whether London Transport Executive was liable for the action of a bus conductor in driving, contrary to his express instructions, a motor bus a short distance in a garage. Of course, the court had no difficulty at all in distinguishing between the spheres of employment of a driver and a conductor in London Transport. Accordingly, it treated the prohibition on conductors acting as drivers of motor buses as a prohibition which defined his sphere of employment. Now there was nothing of that sort in the prohibition in this case. The prohibition is twofold: (1) that the first defendant was not to give lifts on his float; and (2) that he was not to employ others to help him in delivering the milk and so forth. There was nothing in those prohibitions which defined or limited the sphere of his employment. The sphere of his employment remained precisely the same after as before the prohibitions were brought to his notice. The sphere was as a roundsman to go round the rounds delivering milk, collecting empties and obtaining payment. Contrary to instructions, this roundsman chose to do what he was employed to do in an improper way. But the sphere of his employment was in no way affected by his express instructions.

Finally, I think one can see how careful one must be not to introduce into a study of this sort of problem ideas of trespass and agency. It is perfectly possible, on the principle that I am now considering, that an employer may authorise his servant, if the servant chooses to do it – "permit" is perhaps a better word – to give lifts. But the effect of that permission does not make the employer liable if in the course of recreational or off duty but permitted activity the servant drives the vehicle negligently and injures the passenger. *Hilton v Thomas Burton (Rhodes) Ltd* is a case in which the plaintiff failed although the journey was a permitted journey, because he was not able to show that the journey on which he was being carried was a journey which occurred in the course of the servant's employment. Conversely one has the classic case of *Limpus v London General Omnibus Co* when what the servant was doing was a defiance and disregard of the bus company's instructions. Nevertheless the plaintiff who was injured by the defiant and disobedient acts was entitled to recover against the employer.'

Comment

Clearly, so far as prohibitions are concerned, the determination whether an employee is in the course of his or her employment or not is easy to make when, for example, a conductor is prohibited from driving a bus. The question becomes more difficult when the prohibited act is incidental to the chief duty of the employee. It can be hard logically to reconcile *Rose v Plenty* with *Twine's* case, although one interpretation is that in *Rose* the employers' business benefited from the employment of the boy whereas in *Twine* there was no benefit to the employer. Two points arise from this analysis: (a) that the result in *Twine* might have been different if the passenger had been picked up to give the driver directions; and (b) the decision in *Rose* seems unfair on the employers who made it quite plain that they did not want their business to benefit from the employment of children.

Morgans v Launchbury
[1972] 2 All ER 606 House of Lords

The plaintiffs were passengers in a car registered in the name of the defendant and driven by C, a friend of H, the defendant's husband, who was also in the car. The plaintiffs were injured in a crash caused by the negligence of C and in which C and H were killed. At first instance the defendant was sued in her personal capacity and as administratrix for H on the basis that both were vicariously liable for C. Judgment was given against the defendant in both respects and she appealed against the finding that she was personally liable vicariously for the actions of C.

The car was regarded as a family car and used freely by each, although used by H for going to and from work. There was an understanding that if H were ever to have had too much to drink then he would not drive but would either telephone the defendant or ask someone else to drive. One evening he telephoned his wife to say that he was going out with friends for the evening. During the evening he realised he would not be fit to drive and asked C to drive. After visiting several pubs, H fell asleep in the car and C suggested to his passengers that they should go for a meal. It was during that journey that the accident occurred.

Lord Wilberforce: '... Who could [the plaintiffs] sue? In the first place, there was the estate of C as the negligent driver; in the second, the estate of H who requested C to drive, this resting on the normal principle of the law of agency. But [the plaintiffs] seek to go further and to place vicarious liability on the [defendant]. As to this, apart from the special circumstances of the "understanding" there would seem, on accepted principle, to be insuperable difficulties in their way. The car cannot by any fair process of analysis be considered to have been used for the [defendant's] purposes at the time of the accident. During the whole of the evening's progress it was as clearly used for the husband's purposes as any car should be ...

It is said ... that there are authorities which warrant a wider and vaguer test of vicarious liability for the negligence of another; a test of "interest or concern" ... On the general law, no authority was cited to us which would test vicarious liability on so vague a test, but it was said that special principles applied to motor cars. I should be surprised if this were so, and I should wish to be convinced of the reason for a special rule. But in fact there is no authority for it ... I regard it as clear that in order to fix vicarious liability on the owner of a car in such a case as the present, it must be shown that the driver was using it for the owner's purposes, under delegation of a task or duty. The substitution for this clear conception of a vague test based on "interest" or "concern" has nothing in reason or authority to commend it. Every man who gives permission for the use of his chattel may be said to have an interest or concern in its being carefully used, and, in most cases if it is a car, to have an interest or concern in the safety of the driver, but it has never been held that mere permission is enough to establish vicarious liability. And the appearance of the words in certain judgments ... in a negative context (no interest or concern, therefore no agency) is no warrant whatever for transferring them into a positive test. I accept entirely that "agency" in contexts such as these is merely a concept, the meaning and purpose of which is to say "is vicariously liable" and that either expression reflects a judgment of value – *respondeat superior* is the law saying that the owner ought to pay. It is this imperative which the common law has endeavoured to work out through the cases. The owner ought to pay, it says, because he has authorised the act, or requested it, or because the actor is carrying out a task or duty delegated, or because he is in control of the actor's conduct. He ought not to pay (on accepted rules) if he has no control over the actor, has not authorised or requested the act, or if the actor is acting wholly for his own purposes. These rules have stood the test of time remarkably well. They provide, if there is nothing more, a complete answer to the [plaintiffs'] claim against the [defendant] ...'

Comment

(1)   Lord Wilberforce went on to reject the submission that the understanding that H would not drive was sufficient to turn C into the defendant's agent.

(2)   Lord Wilberforce refused to countenance the development in that case of a new rule fixing liability on the owner of a car and based upon the concept, suggested in the Court of Appeal by Lord Denning, of a matrimonial car used for the purposes of both partners. He based his refusal on:

(a)   the range of possible means by which the owner could be fixed with liability and the inability of the court to pin-point the principle upon which a choice could be made in a matter of social policy;

(b)   'Liability and insurance are so intermixed that judicially to alter the basis of liability without adequate knowledge (which we have not the means to obtain) as to the impact this might make on the insurance system would be dangerous, and in my opinion, irresponsible';

(c)   the likely hardship resulting from upsetting established legal relationships retrospectively. Such a policy change is a matter for Parliament.

(3)   In *Ormrod v Crossville Motor Services* M arranged with O that O would drive M's car to Monte Carlo while M took part in the Monte Carlo rally in a different car. O collided with the plaintiff's bus. It was held that M was vicariously liable for the driving of O who was acting as M's agent and on his business.

(4)   In certain limited circumstances a person who employs an independent contractor may be liable for the acts or omissions of the independent contractor. It is perhaps not accurate to describe this as vicarious liability since the cases emphasise the personal and non-delegable nature of the obligation; it is thus primary and not vicarious liability.

In *Honeywill & Stein v Larkin Bros* the plaintiffs were employed to do some work in a cinema and the owners of the cinema, at the request of the plaintiffs, permitted the work to be photographed by the defendants. The technique for flash photography carried with it a high risk of fire and as a result of carelessness by the defendants some curtains were damaged. The plaintiffs compensated the owners of the cinema and claimed an indemnity from the defendants who maintained that since they were independent contractors the plaintiffs had not been obliged to compensate the owners. Slesser LJ said:

'The plaintiffs, in procuring this work to be performed by their contractors ... assumed an obligation to the cinema company which was, as we think, absolute, but which was at least an obligation to use reasonable precautions to see that no damage resulted to the cinema company from those dangerous operations. That obligation they could not delegate by employing the defendants as independent contractors, but they were liable in this regard for the defendants' acts.'

Slesser LJ thought that the trial judge had ignored the special rules relating to extra hazardous or dangerous operations. He said:

'As instances of such operations may be given those of removing support from adjoining houses, doing dangerous work on the highway, or creating fire or explosion ... But the rule of liability for independent contractors attaches to those operations, because they are inherently dangerous, and hence are done at the principal employer's peril.'

See further, *Matania v National Provincial Bank Ltd*, *Salsbury v Woodland*, *Tarry v Ashton*, and also the Occupiers' Liability Act 1957, s 2(4), where the point has received considerable analysis, see p 371. *Honeywill v Stein* remains good law; see *Gwilliam v West Hertfordshire Hospital NHS Trust* and other cases at p 385 above.

(5)   According to the Police Act 1996, s 88(1):

'The chief officer of police for a police area shall be liable in respect of torts committed by constables under his direction and control in the performance or purported performance of their functions in like manner as a master is liable in respect of torts committed by his servants in the course of their employment, and accordingly shall in respect of any such tort be treated for all purposes as a joint tortfeasor.'

The Act remedied the lacuna identified in *Fisher v Oldham Corporation* which was that constables were office-holders and were not in a master–servant relationship with a local authority, accordingly vicarious liability would not follow. Under s 88(2) a police authority must indemnify chief officers in respect of costs and damages; under s 88(4) a police authority has a discretion whether to indemnify particular police officers in respect of costs and damages. Police officers who act outside the execution of their duty (i.e. unlawfully) for the purposes of the Police Act 1996, s 89 may nonetheless be acting in the performance or purported performance of their functions. Were this not so, the Act would have no meaning. For a case involving a police officer not in the purported performance of his functions, see *Makanjuola v Metropolitan Police Commissioner*.

There are several examples of statutory forms of vicarious liability. See, for example, *Bracebridge Engineering Ltd v Darby*, a case on sex discrimination; and *Jones v Tower Boot Co Ltd*, a case of racial discrimination. In the latter case, Waite LJ held that there was no requirement that the statutory provisions should be construed in accordance with the common law cases, since to do so would 'seriously undermine the statutory scheme of the Discrimination Acts and flout the purposes which they were passed to achieve'.

Index